THE OXFO

MUSIC AND DISABILITY STUDIES

THE OXFORD HANDBOOK OF

MUSIC AND DISABILITY STUDIES

Edited by

BLAKE HOWE,

STEPHANIE JENSEN-MOULTON,

NEIL LERNER,

and

JOSEPH STRAUS

Oxford University Press is a department of the University of Oxford. It furthers the University's objective of excellence in research, scholarship, and education by publishing worldwide.

Oxford New York
Auckland Cape Town Dar es Salaam Hong Kong Karachi
Kuala Lumpur Madrid Melbourne Mexico City Nairobi
New Delhi Shanghai Taipei Toronto

With offices in
Argentina Austria Brazil Chile Czech Republic France Greece
Guatemala Hungary Italy Japan Poland Portugal Singapore
South Korea Switzerland Thailand Turkey Ukraine Vietnam

Oxford is a registered trademark of Oxford University Press in the UK and certain other countries.

Published in the United States of America by
Oxford University Press
198 Madison Avenue, New York, NY 10016

First issued as an Oxford University Press paperback, 2016

Library of Congress Cataloging-in-Publication Data
The Oxford handbook of music and disability studies /
edited by Blake Howe, Stephanie Jensen-Moulton, Neil Lerner, and Joseph Straus.
pages cm
Includes bibliographical references and index.
ISBN 978-0-19-933144-4 (hardcover : alk. paper); 978-0-19-065060-5 (paperback : alk. paper)
1. People with disabilities in music.
2. Disability studies. 3. Musicians with disabilities. I. Howe, Blake.
II. Jensen-Moulton, Stephanie. III. Lerner, Neil William, 1966- IV. Straus, Joseph Nathan.
ML3916.O96 2016
780.87—dc23
2015013132

Contents

PART 2 PERFORMING DISABILITY

PART 3 RACE, GENDER, SEXUALITY

PART 4 WAR AND TRAUMA

PART 5 PREMODERN CONCEPTIONS

PART 6 THE CLASSICAL TRADITION

PART 7 MODERNISM AND AFTER

PART 8 FILM AND MUSICAL THEATRE

Acknowledgments

This book was Suzanne Ryan's idea. She recognized that the emerging subfield of music and disability had begun to attract widespread attention and had reached sufficient maturity to merit an Oxford Handbook, and she committed the resources of Oxford University Press to the enterprise. After we assembled our dream team of contributors, scholars from every corner of our discipline and at every career stage, we convened an author's conference at the City University of New York Graduate Center in May 2013, generously underwritten by City University of New York administrators William Ebenstein and Christopher Rosa. At this conference, we exchanged early drafts and engaged in intense discussion and critique, forging an intellectual community and laying the groundwork for what has been a profoundly collaborative enterprise: every essay in this book is the product of communal effort. As the book neared completion, we benefited from the assistance of many people, including Inés Thiebault and Tom Johnson (who prepared some of the musical examples) and an outstanding editorial team at Oxford University Press. Above all, we are grateful to the authors in this collection whose intellectual and emotional commitment to our shared issues and ideals has been an inspiration to us.

Blake Howe
Stephanie Jensen-Moulton
Neil Lerner
Joseph Straus

Contributors

Michael Accinno is a PhD candidate in musicology at the University of California, Davis. His research interests include nineteenth-century American music and Disability Studies. His dissertation explores musical training at schools for the blind in the United States.

Michael B. Bakan is Professor of ethnomusicology and head of world music ensembles program at Florida State University. He is the author of the books *Music of Death and New Creation* and *World Music: Traditions and Transformations* and of more than forty other publications. His research on the ethnomusicology of autism has been funded by the National Endowment for the Arts.

Samantha Bassler is Adjunct Professor of music at Rutgers University at Newark, William Paterson University, and Westminster Choir College of Rider University. In addition to published work on music and disability, she researches the reception history of early music, issues in early music analysis, and popular music.

Michael Beckerman is the Carroll and Milton Petrie Professor of Music at New York University and Distinguished Professor of History at Lancaster University. He is author of *New Worlds of Dvořák*, *Janáček as Theorist*, and *Janáček and His World*, as well as articles on Mozart, film music, "Gypsy" music, music in the concentration camps, Schubert, and Gilbert and Sullivan. He is currently writing a book about Gideon Klein's final Terezin composition.

Devin Burke is Assistant Professor of musicology at the University of Louisville. He has given talks on topics including disability in Civil War era popular culture and the impact of nineteenth-century views of deafness on the mythology of Beethoven. In 2012, he chaired the Society of Ethnomusicology's first conference panel on music and disability studies. His current research traces the musical history of living statues in early modern French spectacle.

Licia Carlson is Associate Professor of philosophy at Providence College in Rhode Island. She has published widely in the area of philosophy and intellectual disability, including works on feminist philosophy, biomedical ethics, phenomenology, and aesthetics. She is the author of *The Faces of Intellectual Disability: Philosophical Reflections* and coeditor of *Cognitive Disability and Its Challenge to Moral Philosophy*.

Michael Scott Cuthbert is Associate Professor of music at the Massachusetts Institute of Technology. He works on fourteenth- and fifteenth-century music, minimalism, and other musical styles of the last fifty years, and is the creator of the music21 toolkit, a software package enabling computational approaches to the study and teaching of music history and music theory. He is a fellow of the American Academy in Rome, Villa I Tatti, and the Radcliffe Institute.

James Deaville is Professor in the music program of the School for Studies in Art and Culture at Carleton University, Ottawa, Canada. He has written about invisible disability in *Music Theory Online* and has spoken about music and madness at the Pittsburgh meeting of the American Musicological Society (2013) and the City University of New York Graduate Center (2013). He has occupied the disability portfolio on the Equity Issues Steering Committee of the Canadian Federation for the Humanities and Social Sciences, producing blogs about invisible disability in academia.

Ann M. Fox is Professor of English at Davidson College and specializes in modern and contemporary dramatic literature and Disability Studies. Her scholarship on disability and theater has been published widely, and she has cocurated three disability-related art exhibitions. She has served on the executive board of the Society for Disability Studies and the Executive Committee of the Division on Disability Studies of the Modern Language Association, and her current book project traces the representation of disability on the twentieth-century commercial stage.

Will Fulton is Assistant Professor at LaGuardia Community College. His research focuses on American popular music and recording technology. He has contributed articles to *American Music Review* and the *Grove Dictionary of American Music, 2nd Edition*. He is currently a PhD candidate in musicology at the Graduate Center of the City University of New York.

Allen Gimbel is Professor Emeritus at Lawrence University's Conservatory of Music, Appleton, Wisconsin. He holds degrees in composition from Eastman and Juilliard, and has published articles in *19th-Century Music*, *Journal of Schenkerian Studies*, and *Music Theory Online* as well as reviews for *Notes* and *American Record Guide*.

Floyd Grave is Professor of music at Rutgers University. Coauthor (with Margaret Grupp Grave) of *In Praise of Harmony: The Teachings of Abbé Georg Joseph Vogler* and *The String Quartets of Joseph Haydn*, he has written extensively on issues of style and compositional technique in instrumental music of the late eighteenth century.

Brian Hogan holds a PhD in ethnomusicology from the University of California, Los Angeles. His research focuses on African music, African American music, new media, percussion, Disability Studies, and medical ethnomusicology. His publications critique the relationship between music and categories of difference in cross-cultural perspective, including studies of Muslim West African women who collectivize and contest structured inequalities through song and blind West African musicians who resist the spiritual terms of African ableism.

Stefan Sunandan Honisch is a doctoral candidate in the Center for Cross Faculty Inquiry in Education at the University of British Columbia. His research interests include the educative possibilities and limitations of musical performance, focusing in particular on the ways in which performances by disabled musicians may teach performer and audience alike to question normative definitions of selfhood.

Blake Howe is Assistant Professor of musicology at Louisiana State University. His articles have appeared in the *Journal of the American Musicological Society, Music Theory Spectrum, The Journal of Musicology*, and *The Musical Quarterly*. He is currently writing a book on musical representations of disability.

Jennifer Iverson is Assistant Professor of music theory at the University of Iowa. Her research areas include Ligeti, the Darmstadt School, electronic music, and Disability Studies.

Stephanie Jensen-Moulton is Associate Professor of musicology at Brooklyn College, City University of New York. Her edition of Miriam Gideon's 1958 Opera *Fortunato* was published with A-R's Recent Researches in American Music Series, and she has published articles on American music topics including "Blind Tom" Wiggins, Pauline Oliveros, and women in hip-hop. Her article "Intellectual Disability in Carlisle Floyd's *Of Mice and Men*" appears in *American Music*, and comes from her most recent book project, which centers on American opera and disability.

Shersten Johnson is Associate Professor of music theory and composition at the University of St. Thomas in St. Paul, Minnesota. Her research interests include twentieth-century opera and art song, Disability Studies, and the intersections between cognitive-linguistic theories and music. Her writings have appeared in *Music Theory Spectrum, Music and Letters*, and *Music Theory Online*, among other venues.

Jeannette DiBernardo Jones is a PhD candidate in historical musicology at Boston University. She has continuing research interests in music in Deaf culture, and her dissertation is on the environment of polyphony in fifteenth-century Francophone Europe.

Beth Keyes is currently pursuing a PhD in musicology at the Graduate Center of the City University of New York. Her forthcoming dissertation focuses on the multiple intersections between historically defined forms of madness and music of the nineteenth and twentieth centuries.

Marianne Kielian-Gilbert is Professor of music in The Jacobs School of Music at Indiana University, Bloomington. Recent publications concern music, philosophy and feminist theory, and music and analysis in different experiential, cultural, material/media, and philosophical orientations. Her essay "Beyond Abnormality—Dis/ability and Music's Metamorphic Subjectivities," appeared in *Sounding Off: Theorizing Disability in Music*, edited by Neil Lerner and Joseph Straus.

Raymond Knapp, Professor and chair of musicology at UCLA, has authored four books and coedited two others, including *The American Musical and the Formation of National*

Identity (winner of the George Jean Nathan Award for Dramatic Criticism), *The American Musical and the Performance of Personal Identity*, and *The Oxford Handbook of the American Musical*. He is currently working on a book that considers Haydn and American popular music in the context of German Idealism.

Hedy Law is Assistant Professor of musicology at the University of British Columbia. She has written for *Cambridge Opera Journal, Musique et Geste en France, Oxford Handbook of Music Censorship, CENTER: Architecture and Design in America*, and *Noise, Audition, Aurality: Histories of the Sonic Worlds in Europe: 1500–1918*.

Sherry D. Lee, an associate professor of music history and culture at the University of Toronto, pursues research interests in the areas of music and culture in *fin-de-siècle* Vienna, opera and modernism, music and technology, and the musical thought of Theodor W. Adorno. Her book *Adorno at the Opera* is forthcoming.

Kendra Preston Leonard is a musicologist whose work focuses on women and music in the twentieth and twenty-first centuries, music and screen history, and music and disability. She is the Director of the Silent Film Sound and Music Archive.

Neil Lerner is the E. Craig Wall, Jr. Distinguished Teaching Professor in the Humanities and Professor of Music at Davidson College, where he chairs the Humanities Program and teaches in the Film and Media Studies Program. He coedited *Sounding Off: Theorizing Disability in Music* with Joseph Straus and edits the Routledge Music and Screen Media Series. He edited the journal *American Music* and coedited *Music in Video Games: Studying Play*.

Anabel Maler is a doctoral student in music theory and history at the University of Chicago. Her research interests include music and gesture, Deaf culture, music of the late twentieth century, the music of Arvo Pärt, the history of theory, and feminist music theory. Her work on sign language songs has also appeared in *Music Theory Online*.

Fred Everett Maus is Associate Professor of critical and comparative studies in the Department of Music at the University of Virginia. He has written on theory and analysis, gender and sexuality, popular music, aesthetics, and dramatic and narrative aspects of instrumental music.

George McKay is Professor of media studies at the University of East Anglia, UK. His research has focused on cultural and media studies and cultural politics, and his most recent books are *Radical Gardening: Politics, Idealism and Rebellion in the Garden, Shakin' All Over: Popular Music and Disability*, and, as editor, *The Pop Festival: History, Music, Media, Culture*.

Sean Murray is a doctoral student in musicology at the City University of New York Graduate Center. He has presented conference papers on race, gender, and disability in American music and published on the relationship between the nineteenth-century piano industry and the African ivory and slave trades. His dissertation examines the relationship between blackness and disability in American music.

Bruce Quaglia teaches music theory at the University of Minnesota. His research interests include twelve-tone theory and analysis, the aesthetics of serialism, and also matters of form and narrative in eighteenth- and nineteenth-century music.

Daniella Santoro is a doctoral student in medical anthropology at Tulane University. Her doctoral research is based in New Orleans, Louisiana, and examines the experiences of disability and rehabilitation after spinal cord injuries due to gun violence. Her other interests include collaborative ethnography, disability advocacy, and the social history of vernacular dance forms of southern Louisiana and southern Spain.

Jessica A. Schwartz is Assistant Professor of musicology at the University of California, Los Angeles. Her research interests include Marshallese music, sonic ecologies of the nuclear era, and punk/rock. Her work on Marshallese musical responses to US nuclear weapons testing has appeared in the journals *Music and Politics* and *Women and Music*.

Julie Singer is Associate Professor of French at Washington University in St. Louis. Her research focuses on medieval literature and medicine, the cultural history of science and technology, and Disability Studies. She is the author of *Blindness and Therapy in Late Medieval French and Italian Poetry*.

Elaine Sisman is the Anne Parsons Bender Professor of Music at Columbia University. Her numerous publications on Haydn, Mozart, and Beethoven include the recent "Haydn's Solar Poetics: The *Tageszeiten* Symphonies and Enlightenment Knowledge" in the *Journal of the American Musicological Society*. A member of the Joseph Haydn-Institut (Cologne) and the Mozart-Akademie (Salzburg), she has been elected to Honorary Membership in the American Musicological Society (2011) and to the American Academy of Arts and Sciences (2014).

Jessica Sternfeld is Associate Professor of music history/musicology at the Hall-Musco Conservatory of Music at Chapman University. Her research interests include the cultural reception of musicals, especially megamusicals of the 1980s, television musicals, and student productions. She is the author of *The Megamusical*, which explores the history and societal impact of popular and often maligned hits.

Laurie Stras is Professor of music at the University of Southampton. She is editor of *She's So Fine: Reflections on Whiteness, Femininity, Adolescence and Class in 1960s Music*, co-editor of *Eroticism in Early Modern Music*, and the author of numerous articles and chapters on the music of sixteenth-century Italy and twentieth-century America. She is currently completing a monograph on female musicians at the court and in the convents of sixteenth-century Ferrara; she is codirector of the early music ensemble Musica Secreta and the female-voice choir Celestial Sirens.

Joseph Straus is Distinguished Professor of music at the Graduate Center of the City University of New York. He has published widely on topics in modernist music and at the intersection of music and Disability Studies, including *Extraordinary Measures: Music and Disability*.

Ingrid Sykes is a research fellow at La Trobe University, Melbourne, Australia. She has published widely on eighteenth- and nineteenth-century French cultural history, history of medicine, and science. She has a particular interest in the history of sound and has a forthcoming book *Society, Culture and the Auditory Imagination in Modern France: The Humanity of Hearing.*

About the Companion Website

www.oup.com/us/ohmds

Oxford has created a website to accompany this *Handbook of Music and Disability Studies*. There you will find video and audio illustrations for seventeen of the essays in the book. Examples available online are indicated in the text with Oxford's symbol .

THE OXFORD HANDBOOK OF

MUSIC AND DISABILITY STUDIES

INTRODUCTION

Disability Studies in Music, Music in Disability Studies

BLAKE HOWE, STEPHANIE JENSEN-MOULTON,
NEIL LERNER, AND JOSEPH STRAUS

Cultural Disability Studies

In recent years, disability has emerged as a category of cultural analysis in the humanities, tracking the earlier trajectories of gender, sexuality, and race/ethnicity. Emerging with the disability rights movement of the late 1980s (which led to the passage of the Americans with Disabilities Act of 1990), the new, interdisciplinary field of Disability Studies has offered a sociopolitical analysis of disability, focusing on its social construction and shifting attention from biology to culture.[1] The medical sciences consider disability a deficit with respect to normal standards of good health and seek diagnosis and cure. In contrast, Disability Studies explores the social, cultural, and political meanings of disability with the goal of understanding human variety and difference. At the core of this field is the contention that, although it may have a concrete, somatic basis, disability is endowed with meaning by elaborate interpretive networks that emerge within particular societies and cultures. Disability is simultaneously real, tangible, and physical and also an imaginative construct whose purpose is to make sense of the diversity of human morphology, capability, and behavior. While we may relegate the study of biological impairments to the medical establishment, this cultural study of disability has been energetically undertaken by humanists from a variety of disciplines.

The word *disability* forges a binary between what one can do (ability) and what one cannot do (dis-ability). Indeed, disability throughout history has often emerged as an antithesis to some other desirable standard. Before the nineteenth century, this standard was often imagined as an idealized body: the body of God, Adam before the Fall, the King, the cosmos, or some other perfection, from which all human bodies were poorly fractioned and morally compromised. This is the moral or religious model of disability, in which bodily differences are stigmatized as deviant from some elusive ideal. Beginning in the nineteenth century, this "ideal body" was usurped by the "normal body." Normalcy, a concept popularized by the rise of statistics, imagines human morphology on a bell-shaped curve: most people are of average height, while some are too tall, and others are too short. This is the medical model of disability, in which disabled people are cast as outliers, requiring either rehabilitation by medical science or elimination by eugenics (Davis 1995).

More recently, the social model of disability, advocated in politics by the disability rights movement and in scholarship by Disability Studies, has argued for the value of bodily difference. Under this model, disability is not a fixed, medical condition; rather, it emerges from a society that chooses to accommodate some bodies and exclude others. As Davis 2002 explains, "An impairment involves a loss or diminution of sight, hearing, mobility, mental ability, and so on. But an impairment only becomes a disability when the ambient society creates environments with barriers" (41). Indeed, Straus 2006 defines disability as "any culturally stigmatized bodily difference" (119): bodies themselves are neutrally defined, accruing their stigma only through cultural reception. A wheelchair user is disabled by curbs, but not by sloped curbs. A deaf person is disabled by oral language, but not by sign language. Noting the ubiquity of accommodation that all bodies (disabled or nondisabled) receive, some scholars have recently sought to reconceive bodily difference without hierarchy. For example, Davis 2013 seeks "a new category [of identity] based on the partial, incomplete subject, whose realization is not autonomy and independence, but dependency and interdependence" (275).

As claimed in Sandahl and Auslander 2005, the social model casts disability not as a fixed physical or mental state, but as a process: "To think of disability not as a physical condition but as a way of interacting with a world that is frequently inhospitable is to think of disability in performative terms—as something one *does* rather than something one *is*" (10). This argument, linking disability with performance, is long-standing, as Davidson 2008 explains: "From nineteenth-century freak shows and carnival acts, through the photographic displays of eugenics textbooks to Jerry Lewis telethons, disability has been synonymous with the theatrical display of 'different' bodies" (18–19).[2] Much scholarship within Disability Studies has examined these and other "theatrical displays," drawing parallels between the social performance of disability and its similar performances on stage—whether within the dehumanizing frame of the freak show (Garland-Thomson 1996; Adams 2001), or in newly liberatory scripts associated with dance (Albright 1997) and performance art and theatre (Sandahl and Auslander 2005).

Marked against prevailing social norms, the disabled body has often served a rhetorical function within narrative. As Garland-Thomson 1997 argues, "A disability functions only as visual difference that signals meaning. Consequently, literary texts necessarily make disabled characters into freaks, stripped of normalizing contexts and engulfed by a single stigmatic trait" (10–11)—from Captain Ahab to Captain Hook. Many narratives, requiring tension before release, requiring a problem before its resolution, appropriate disability as their obstacle of choice. Mitchell and Snyder (2000) have termed this appropriation of disability "narrative prosthesis." The narrative prosthesis (usually a disabled character within a story) has two main functions: it gives the story a problem to solve; and it defines by counterexample the desirability of the subsequent resolution.

Disability scholars have identified some familiar scenarios that narratives use when confronted with the apparent problem of disability. Most commonly, the disability may be rehabilitated, or the disabled character may be expelled. This is what one disability scholar terms the "cure or kill" paradigm, drawn from a "cultural logic of euthanasia" that "draws a sharp distinction between disabled bodies imagined as redeemable and others considered disposable. One approach would rehabilitate disabled bodies; the other would eliminate them" (Garland-Thomson 2004, 779). (Thus, Captain Ahab is swallowed by a whale and Captain Hook is swallowed by a crocodile.) Other common scenarios involve a disabled figure overcoming disability by acquiring superpowers that render his or her disability moot, or passing as able-bodied so that the disability is nearly undetectable; the film *Avatar* (2009) traffics in both tropes.

None of these narrative strategies appreciates disability as a valid and stable mode of embodiment; it is a disruptive abnormality, one that requires a compensatory solution (curing, killing, overcoming, or passing). In contrast, at the ethical core of Disability Studies is an argument for placing a positive value on formerly stigmatized bodily differences. When assessing disabled bodies and the activities of people with disabilities, Disability Studies is interested in what the disability has enabled and in what has been achieved not in spite of disability, or as an overcoming of disability, but rather by, through, and because of disability.

Brief History of Disability Studies in Relation to Music

Musicology (including ethnomusicology and music theory) has been a relatively recent arrival within Disability Studies, and has witnessed an impressive burst of scholarly activity since around 2005.[3] In the process, while musical scholars have found many different ways of applying the insights of Disability Studies to the study of music, they have also made a significant contribution from their musical vantage point to the study of disability.

Musical scholars began to take note of disability issues in 2004 with a panel discussion at a meeting of the American Musicological Society. Several of the participants in that panel later contributed to a published collection of essays coedited by Neil Lerner and Joseph Straus (2006), who return as two of the four coeditors of the present volume. That was the first published collection of essays to bring music and disability into a productive relationship. Several of its contributors (Stephanie Jensen-Moulton, Jennifer Iverson, Laurie Stras, and Marianne Kielian-Gilbert) have contributed to the present collection—Jensen-Moulton as its third coeditor, and all four as authors. In the ensuing years, musical scholars, including many of the contributors to this Handbook, have shaped this new subfield and brought it to an early maturity.

The central theoretical categories of cultural Disability Studies have proven extraordinarily fruitful in the study of music. First, disability has been shown to be a core feature of the musical identity of music makers (especially composers and performers), often an identity that is affirmatively *claimed* in the face of widespread stigma (Linton 1998). For example, Blake Howe (the fourth of our four coeditors) has explored the ways that Paul Wittgenstein claimed the identity of a one-handed pianist through a series of prominent commissions, and saw the critical reception of his performances refracted through the lens of disability (Howe 2010b). Similarly, Honisch 2009 seeks to understand how physical disability can be "re-narrated" through musical performance, providing an aural medium for the self-expression of disability identity. Although disability has typically been interpreted as a defect or abnormality, these and other studies have sought to understand disability as an important and valuable component of identity, akin to gender, sexuality, and race; notably, this negotiation of identity can occur in the cultural domains of music.

Second, disability has inflected reception of the lives and work of composers and performers. If the composer or performer is identified as having a disability, the language that accretes around them tends to incorporate a rich (if predictable and stereotypical) network of disability-related metaphors. Thus Beethoven is understood as a Heroic Overcomer—someone whose music and life represents a triumph over deafness; Evelyn Glennie and Thomas Quasthoff are understood as Saintly Sages—their disabilities are understood to confer on them a higher, transcendent wisdom; Glenn Gould and Robert Schumann are Mad Geniuses—their work is both marred and ennobled by disability.[4]

In their reception these composers and performers are (to return to the terminology of Garland-Thomson 1997, cited earlier) "engulfed by a single stigmatic trait." Although Disability Studies argues for the cultural significance of disability, the process of "engulfment" results in its overdetermination: because of its marked status, disability is often treated as the most important (and perhaps only) governing feature of a person's life and career. As Lerner 2006 argues, "To claim the title *pianist*, one must have two functioning hands. With only one functioning hand, someone who wishes to play the piano becomes not a pianist but a one-handed pianist" (75). Against the norms of music composition and performance, "disabled music" composed by or for "disabled musicians" is almost always branded as such.

Third, although music is a famously nonrepresentational art form, scholars have shown that musical works represent disability in various ways. Through harmonic imbalance, melodic disfluency, or formal deformations, musical texts may be said to embody various disabled states; indeed, according to Straus 2006 and 2011, many theoretical traditions (including organicism, energetics, embodiment, the *Formenlehre*) commonly apply metaphors of disability to describe various states of musical dysfunction. These tools have helped some scholars seek to locate signs of a disabled composer's identity within his or her musical language: for example, expressions of madness in Alkan's music (Burstein 2006), expressions of autism in "Blind Tom" Wiggins's music (Jensen-Moulton 2006), and expressions of aging in the "late styles" of Bartók, Schoenberg, and Copland (Straus 2008). Complementary texts, such as song lyrics, symphonic programs, opera librettos, and film, can further specify the presence of a disability within a musical work. These representations of disability tend to follow familiar cultural scripts and archetypes—for instance, the associations between disfigurement and derangement (*Rigoletto*), between stuttering and feeblemindedness (Vašek in *The Bartered Bride*), and between blindness and prophecy (Tiresias in *Oedipus Rex*). Of course, there is no medical basis for these associations; they are entirely cultural.

Beyond the direct representation of disability, music has also been shown to embody certain narrative trajectories that engage disability, most commonly through the "cure or kill" paradigm. For example, in *Lucia Di Lammermoor*, Lucia's madness presents Act III with an extreme problem, one that disrupts the normal social order: her subsequent death rehabilitates this chaos. In opera, we might think of the many mad characters in opera who regain their reason just before curtain call (Handel's Orlando or Paisiello's Nina). We might also think of the many mad characters who do not last that long (Wozzeck or Peter Grimes). The mechanism of the "cure" need not be strictly medical. For example, Grave 2008 examines narratives of recuperation, transformation, and transcendence in the string quartets of Haydn. Roughly contemporaneous with the rise of the medical model of disability, these and other musical narratives in the late eighteenth and early nineteenth centuries introduce rhythmic or tonal disruptions subsequently remediated over the course of the work (see also Straus 2011). These are enduring tropes: Singer 2010 identifies compensatory narratives about blindness in the songs and writings of Machaut and Landini.

Finally, and perhaps most important, music has proven a fertile ground for exploring the contention within Disability Studies that disability (like gender) can be understood as a performance: something you do rather than something you are. In particular, musical performers with disabilities have the dual task of performing their music and their disabilities, and these two sorts of performances are intertwined (Straus 2011). Recent studies of Glenn Gould (Maloney 2006), Paul Wittgenstein (Howe 2010b), and Thomas Quasthoff (Straus 2011) have developed this theme, examining how the reception of disabled musicians so often accounts for both performances—musical and social. In a related vein, Stras 2006 offers a compelling example of the cultural malleability of disability within a musical context: vocal trauma (such as hoarseness) is profoundly disabling for performers of opera, but not for performers of many popular genres like the blues, where such scratchy timbres are culturally valuable.[5] This is a provocative and important example of the cultural model of disability: impairments can be stigmatizing and enabling in different cultural contexts. What is interesting (and, for many disability scholars, ethical) about this model of disability is that it assigns stigma not to the imperfect person or to the abnormal person, but rather to the exclusionary societies that fail to accommodate bodily differences.

This Handbook

This Handbook is tangible evidence of a field that is mature enough to have spawned an impressive array of scholarship that shares a common point of departure, grounded within cultural Disability Studies, yet still young enough that a spirit of pioneering energy is felt in every essay, where virtually every topic represents a first encounter. The diversity of these essays is as impressive as their originality. The chronology of the subject matter ranges from the biblical (Howe), the medieval (Singer, Cuthbert), and the Elizabethan (Bassler, Leonard), through the canonical classics of the eighteenth and nineteenth centuries (Graves, Sisman, Quaglia, Deaville), up to modernist styles (Straus, Gimbel, Lee) and contemporary musical theatre and popular genres (Iverson, Maler, Jones, McKay, Fox, Knapp), with stops along the way in post–Civil War America (Accinno, Burke), Ghana and the South Pacific (Hogan, Schwarz), and many other interesting times and places. Disability is a broad, heterogeneous, and porous identity, and that diversity is reflected in the variety of bodily conditions under discussion here, including autism and intellectual disability (Bakan, Carlson, Straus), deafness (Maler, Jones), blindness (Fulton, Hogan, Sykes, Johnson, Honisch, Cuthbert, Lerner), and mobility impairment often coupled with bodily deformity (Accinno, Burke, Law, Lee, Leonard, Murray, Straus).

Cultural Disability Studies has, from its inception, been oriented toward physical and sensory disabilities, and has generally been less effective in dealing with cognitive and intellectual impairments and with the sorts of emotions and behaviors that in our era are often medicalized as "mental illness." In that context, it is notable that so many of these essays are centrally concerned with madness, that broad and ever-shifting cultural category (Bassler, Beckerman, Deaville, Howe, Jensen-Moulton, Keyes, Schwarz, Singer, Sisman). This is one of the areas in which musical scholars have their opportunity to make a significant contribution to Disability Studies—our nonverbal art form may make it easier for us to discuss the representation of affective states, without the distractions of narrative or dramatic language. There is also a perhaps surprising diversity of subject matter—it turns out that disability is everywhere when you start looking for it—including YouTube videos (Maler), Ghanaian drumming (Hogan), Cirque du Soleil (Jensen-Moulton), piano competitions (Honisch), castrati (Law), Hollywood films (Lerner), medieval smoking songs (Singer), and popular musicals (Knapp, Fox, Sternfeld).

Amid this diversity of time, place, style, medium, and topic, these essays share two core commitments. First, they are united in their theoretical and methodological connection to Disability Studies, especially its central idea that disability is a social and cultural construction. Disability both shapes and is shaped by culture, including musical culture. Second, these essays individually and collectively make the case that disability is not something at the periphery of culture and music, but something central to our art and to our humanity.

Beyond those central commitments, we note seven general themes that animate these essays:

1. **Normalcy.** Many of these essays probe the boundary between the *normal* and *disabled,* terms that have been defined historically in relation to each other (Iverson, Kielian-Gilbert). Traditionally, that process of definition unfolds within the prevailing medical model, with its orientation toward diagnosis and cure of perceived deficits. Medical models themselves, however, are historically contingent, and many of these essays explore and challenge medical explanations ranging from humors to modern psychiatry and neurology (Singer, Cuthbert, Sisman, Jensen-Moulton, Deaville, Straus). Disability and normality are both cultural constructions. They emerge in parallel, intertwined, mutually influential ways, and music plays a central role both in embodying and shaping them.
2. **Otherness.** In music, as in art, literature, and film, disability is often inflected by and intertwined with race/ethnicity, gender, and sexuality. It is not essential to agree with Mitchell and Snyder (2000) that "disability is the master trope of human disqualification" (2–3) to recognize that the stigmatizing and othering of personal identity takes similar forms in each of these domains. Some of these essays take race/ethnicity, gender, or sexuality as their principal topic (Maus, Kielian-Gilbert, Murray); many others weave these concerns into their narratives.
3. **Enfreakment.** In artistic representations, as in life, people with disabilities are often depicted in negative ways, confined to narrow and stigmatized roles. In film and in literature, these roles include Obsessive Avengers, Charity Cripples, and Mad Geniuses (Kriegel 1987; Norden 1996). Such stereotypes have the effect of othering these "starees," causing us to look down at them in pity for their deficits, or across a vast distance at them in amazement or horror at their exoticism or freakishness, or up at them in awe of their apparently superhuman difference.[6] Indeed, many of these essays invoke the tradition of the "freak show" as a paradigm for the stigmatizing perception of extraordinary bodies (Jensen-Moulton, Stras, Sternfeld, Accinno). In the process, many of these essays interrogate the most punishing complex of metaphors that have accreted around disability, metaphors that take disability as a sign of irreducible otherness, including moral evil (Bassler, Howe, Leonard, Hogan, Lee, Sternfeld). The explicit or implicit goal of virtually all of the essays is not to ignore disability or to pretend that it is irrelevant, but instead to find a realistic mode of looking at and thinking about disability.
4. **Commotion.** Many of these essays acknowledge the subversive potential of disability to undermine and disrupt normal, conventional ways of doing things, both in art and in life. When disability comes onto the scene, it creates a commotion (Sandahl and Auslander 2005). Within musical narratives, disability often enters as a disruptive problem, which the music may expel, overcome, accommodate, or perhaps embrace. In such works, disability functions as a narrative prosthesis, enacting a drama that simultaneously calls attention to and attempts to efface disability (Howe, Grave, Quaglia).

5. **Self-Representation.** One of the slogans of the disability rights movement is "nothing about us without us." In most times and places, people with disabilities have had their economic, social, and cultural lives significantly circumscribed by ambient political and cultural structures. Many of these essays chart and celebrate a countervailing trend toward disability communities formed, in part, around music making, which becomes an important mode of self-expression and self-representation (Santoro, Honisch, Bakan, Carlson, Jones, Maler, Sykes, Hogan, Johnson, Accinno, Schwarz).
6. **Performance.** Many of these essays deal directly with the onstage musical performances of performers with disabilities (Bakan, Jones, Hogan, Sykes, Maler, Howe, Honisch, Fulton, Law, Murray, Accinno, Knapp, Stras, Jensen-Moulton, Straus). Virtually all of them deal with disability as a performed identity. Onstage and off, people with disabilities construct their identity by making their disability visible (audible) in particular ways.
7. **Myths of Autonomy.** Many able-bodied people ("normates" in Garland-Thomson's [1997] useful formulation that calls attention to the constructed nature of the concept of normality), cling to an ideology of autonomy: every person is (or should be) independent and self-supporting. People with disabilities generally know better than that, and understand the networks of mutual dependence, care, and assistance that bind us all together. A critique of the ideology of autonomy and a related interest in subverting the boundary between normal ability and disability is a theme in many of these essays (Iverson, Fulton, Stras, Howe, Lerner).

Developing these and other themes, the essays in this volume examine familiar musical topics—and uncover new ones—from the fresh perspective of Disability Studies. They also address an important lacuna within a Disability Studies that has mostly overlooked (or underheard) the musical arts as a medium through which disability has been and continues to be constructed. Indeed, as much as a cultural understanding of disability can teach us about music, music also has much to teach us about the culture of disability.

Notes

1. Among the principal publications in Disability Studies in the humanities, sometimes referred to as "cultural disability studies," all from the past fifteen years, see Albrecht et al. 2001; Bauman 2008; Corker and French 1999; Corker and Shakespeare 2002; Couser 1997; Davidson 2008; Davis 1995, 2002, 2008, and 2013; Garland-Thomson, 1997 and 2009; Kuppers 2001; Linton 1998; Longmore 2003; Longmore and Umansky 2001; McRuer 2006; Mitchell and Snyder 1997 and 2000; Poore 2009; Sandahl and Auslander 2005; Scully 2008; Shakespeare 2006; Siebers 2008 and 2010; Smith and Hutchison 2004; and Wendell 1996.
2. The freak show is a common point of reference for cultural disability studies. See Adams 2001 and Garland-Thomson 1996.

3. The book-length literature on music and Disability Studies prior to the current volume includes Howe 2010a, Lerner and Straus 2006, Lubet 2011, McKay 2013, Rowden 2009, and Straus 2011. See also special issues of two journals: *Music Theory Online* 15 (3–4) (2009) and *Popular Music* 28 (3) (2009). For a complete bibliography of publications in this area, see http://musicdisabilitystudies.wordpress.com/reading-list-for-disability-and-music/.
4. For typologies of disability representations, see Kriegel 1987 and Norden 1996. This issue is explored in a musical context in Straus 2011.
5. For additional consideration of vocal disfluency as a contextually defined disability, see Goldmark 2006 and Oster 2006.
6. "Staree" is a coinage of Rosemarie Garland-Thomson (2009), as are the modes of staring described in the rest of this paragraph.

References

Adams, Rachel. 2001. *Sideshow U.S.A.: Freaks and the American Cultural Imagination*. Chicago: University of Chicago Press.

Albrecht, Gary, Katherine Seelman, and Michael Bury, eds. 2001. *Handbook of Disability Studies*. Thousand Oaks, CA: Sage.

Albright, Ann Cooper. 1997. *Choreographing Difference: The Body and Identity in Contemporary Dance*. Middletown, CT: Wesleyan University Press.

Bassler, Samantha. 2012. " 'That suck'd the honey of his music vows': Disability Studies in Early Modern Musicological Research." *Postmedieval* 3: 182–194.

Bauman, H-Dirksen, ed. 2008. *Open Your Eyes: Deaf Studies Talking*. Minneapolis: University of Minnesota Press.

Burstein, L. Poundie. 2006. "*Les chansons des fous*: On the Edge of Madness with Alkan." In *Sounding Off: Theorizing Disability in Music*, edited by Neil Lerner and Joseph N. Straus, 187–198. New York: Routledge.

Corker, Mairian, and Sally French, eds. 1999. *Disability Discourse*. Buckingham and Philadelphia, PA: Open University Press.

Corker, Mairian, and Tom Shakespeare, eds. 2002. *Disability/Postmodernity: Embodying Disability Theory*. London and New York: Continuum.

Couser, Thomas G. 1997. *Recovering Bodies: Illness, Disability and Life Writing*. Madison: University of Wisconsin Press.

Davidson, Michael. 2008. *Concerto for the Left Hand: Disability and the Defamiliar Body*. Ann Arbor: University of Michigan Press.

Davis, Lennard. 1995. *Enforcing Normalcy: Disability, Deafness, and the Body*. London and New York: Verso.

Davis, Lennard. 2002. *Bending Over Backwards: Disability, Dismodernism, and Other Difficult Positions*. New York: New York University Press.

Davis, Lennard. 2008. *Obsession: A History*. Chicago: University of Chicago Press.

Davis, Lennard, ed. 2013. *The Disability Studies Reader*. 4th ed. New York: Routledge.

Garland-Thomson, Rosemarie, ed. 1996. *Freakery: Cultural Spectacles of the Extraordinary Body*. New York: New York University Press.

Garland-Thomson, Rosemarie. 1997. *Extraordinary Bodies: Figuring Physical Disability in American Culture and Literature*. New York: Columbia University Press.

Garland-Thomson, Rosemarie. 2009. *Staring: How We Look*. New York: Oxford University Press.

Goldmark, Daniel. 2006. "Stuttering in American Popular Song, 1890–1930." In *Sounding Off: Theorizing Disability in Music*, edited by Neil Lerner and Joseph N. Straus, 75–90. New York: Routledge.

Grave, Floyd. 2008. "Recuperation, Transformation, and the Transcendence of Major over Minor in the Finale of Haydn's String Quartet, Op. 76, No. 1." *Eighteenth-Century Music* 5 (1): 27–50.

Honisch, Stefan Sunandan. 2009. "'Re-narrating Disability' through Musical Performance." *Music Theory Online* 15 (3–4). http://www.mtosmt.org/.

Howe, Blake. 2010a. "Music and the Embodiment of Disability." PhD diss., City University of New York.

Howe, Blake. 2010b. "Paul Wittgenstein and the Performance of Disability." *Journal of Musicology* 27 (2): 135–180.

Jensen-Moulton, Stephanie. 2006. "Finding Autism in the Composition of a 19th-Century Prodigy." In *Sounding Off: Theorizing Disability in Music*, edited by Neil Lerner and Joseph N. Straus, 199–216. New York: Routledge.

Kriegel, Leonard. 1987. "The Cripple in Literature." In *Images of Disability, Disabling Images*, edited by A. Gartner and T. Joe, 31–46. New York: Praeger.

Kuppers, Petra. 2001. *Disability and Contemporary Performance: Bodies on Edge*. London: Routledge.

Leonard, Kendra. 2009. *Shakespeare, Madness, and Music: Scoring Insanity in Cinematic Adaptations*. Lanham, MD: Scarecrow.

Lerner, Neil, and Joseph N. Straus, eds. 2006. *Sounding Off: Theorizing Disability in Music*. New York: Routledge.

Linton, Simi. 1998. *Claiming Disability: Knowledge and Identity*. New York: New York University Press.

Longmore, Paul. 2003. *Why I Burned My Book and Other Essays on Disability*. Philadelphia, PA: Temple University Press.

Longmore, Paul, and Lauri Umansky, eds. 2001. *The New Disability History: American Perspectives*. New York: New York University Press.

Lubet, Alex. 2011. *Music, Disability, and Society*. Philadelphia, PA: Temple University Press.

Maloney, S. Timothy. 2006. "Glenn Gould, Autistic Savant." In *Sounding Off: Theorizing Disability in Music*, edited by Neil Lerner and Joseph N. Straus, 121–135. New York: Routledge.

McKay, George. 2013. *Shakin' All Over: Popular Music and Disability*. Ann Arbor: University of Michigan Press.

McRuer, Robert. 2006. *Crip Theory: Cultural Signs of Queerness and Disability*. New York: New York University Press.

Mitchell, David, and Sharon Snyder, eds. 1997. *The Body and Physical Difference: Discourses of Disability*. Ann Arbor: University of Michigan Press.

Mitchell, David, and Sharon Snyder. 2000. *Narrative Prosthesis: Disability and the Dependencies of Discourse*. Ann Arbor: University of Michigan Press.

Norden, Martin. 1996. *The Cinema of Isolation: A History of Physical Disability in the Movies*. New Brunswick, NJ: Rutgers University Press.

Oster, Andrew. 2006. "Melisma as Malady: Cavalli's *Il Giasone* (1649) and Opera's Earliest Stuttering Role." In *Sounding Off: Theorizing Disability in Music*, edited by Neil Lerner and Joseph N. Straus, 157–172. New York: Routledge.

Poore, Carol. 2009. *Disability in Twentieth-Century German Culture*. Ann Arbor: University of Michigan Press.

Rowden, Terry. 2009. *The Songs of Blind Folk: African-American Musicians and the Cultures of Blindness*. Ann Arbor: University of Michigan Press.

Sandahl, Carrie, and Philip Auslander, eds. 2005. *Bodies in Commotion: Disability and Performance*. Ann Arbor: University of Michigan Press.

Scully, Jackie Leach. 2008. *Disability Bioethics: Moral Bodies, Moral Difference*. Lanham, MD: Rowman & Littlefield.

Shakespeare, Tom. 2006. *Disability Rights and Wrongs*. London: Routledge.

Siebers, Tobin. 2008. *Disability Theory*. Ann Arbor: University of Michigan Press.

Siebers, Tobin. 2010. *Disability Aesthetics*. Ann Arbor: University of Michigan Press.

Singer, Julie. 2010. "Playing by Ear: Compensation, Reclamation, and Prosthesis in Fourteenth-Century Song." In *Disability in the Middle Ages: Reconsiderations and Reverberations*, edited by Joshua R. Eyler, 39–52. Aldershot, UK: Ashgate.

Smith, Bonnie G., and Beth Hutchison, eds. 2004. *Gendering Disability*. New Brunswick, NJ, and London: Rutgers University Press.

Stras, Laurie. 2006. "The Organ of the Soul: Voice, Damage, and Affect." In *Sounding Off: Theorizing Disability in Music*, edited by Neil Lerner and Joseph N. Straus, 173–184. New York: Routledge.

Straus, Joseph N. 2006. "Normalizing the Abnormal: Disability in Music and Music Theory." *Journal of the American Musicological Society* 59 (1): 113–184.

Straus, Joseph N. 2008. "Disability and Late Style in Music." *Journal of Musicology* 25 (1): 3–45.

Straus, Joseph N. 2011. *Extraordinary Measures: Disability in Music*. New York: Oxford University Press.

Wendell, Susan. 1996. *The Rejected Body: Feminist Philosophical Reflections on the Disabled Body*. New York: Routledge.

PART 1

DISABILITY COMMUNITIES

CHAPTER 1

TOWARD AN ETHNOGRAPHIC MODEL OF DISABILITY IN THE ETHNOMUSICOLOGY OF AUTISM

MICHAEL B. BAKAN

Who says autism is a bad thing?... Autism isn't cholera; it isn't some disease you can just cure.... And there is no cure. There really isn't. It's just there, wound into your personality.

—Mara Chasar

THE Centers for Disease Control and Prevention (CDC) estimates that approximately one out of every sixty-eight children in the United States is affected by an ASD, or autism spectrum disorder. The rate of prevalence is much higher among boys than girls, and the overall rate of ASD (aka ASC, or autism spectrum condition, a preferable though less widely used designation) has risen sharply in recent decades. For example, as recently as the year 2000 the CDC estimate of rate of incidence was just one in 150 (CDC 2015).

Medical sources describe autism as a neurodevelopmental disorder with an early childhood onset and a pervasive lifelong course; its scope of impact is both biological and social. Key criteria for the diagnosis of autism include "delays and atypicalities in reciprocal social interaction; impaired development of language and communication skills; and highly circumscribed, stereotypic behaviors and interests" (Sirota 2010, 94; see also American Psychiatric Association 2000, 2013).

Autism is conceptualized as "a spectrum disorder that includes a broad range of manifestations," and people diagnosed with autism disorder or with related spectrum conditions such as Asperger syndrome and PDD-NOS (pervasive developmental disorder—not otherwise specified)[1] "span a wide continuum and may demonstrate functional capacities that range from profoundly limited to extraordinarily gifted" (Sirota 2010, 94).[2]

Yet in spite of this heterogeneity, writes anthropologist Karen Sirota (2010, 94), people across the entire spectrum of autism "have often been portrayed in the professional literature and the popular media as asocial creatures bereft of words and subjective worldviews." In turn, they have been cast as suffering from "an inability to co-create culture" (Vinden and Astington 2000, 515). With the medicalization of their personhood framed against a triadic backdrop of "inability, lack, and loss" (Titchkosky 2007, 8), individuals diagnosed with ASD are customarily mapped onto a larger topography of disability that has become virtually inextricable from pervasive tropes of absence, negation, and abnormality. The "concept of disability," writes Rosemarie Garland-Thomson (1997, 24), "unites a highly marked, heterogeneous group whose only commonality is being considered abnormal." This leads to recognition of a "negating sort" for the disabled-labeled individual, to what Judith Butler has described as "a form of qualified recognition that does not lead to a viable life" and that is founded on an often unarticulated premise that certain individuals and classes of individuals are categorically recognized as less human than others (Butler 2004, 2; see also Titchkosky 2007, 8).

"Our Autism is called a 'tragedy' or even, by some parent groups, 'the enemy' to be fought at all costs," writes autistic self-advocate Penni Winter in the landmark 2012 volume *Loud Hands: Autistic People, Speaking*.[3] "We're said to 'ruin' our parents' lives and break up marriages, and we get discussed in terms of the 'burden' we are on our families, the 'difficulty' we cause others. What we might feel or think or want is hardly even asked—because, oh yeah, that's right, we don't *have* feelings or needs" (Winter 2012, 119).

But as Julia Bascom, in her Foreword to *Loud Hands*, asserts, this need not—and should not—be the status quo. "Autistic brains are different from non-autistic brains—not better or worse, just different," she explains. "Autistic voices, similarly, can take different forms or styles or express different things through different means than non-autistic voices. These facts are simple and neutral, but regularly obscured and overridden by cultural scripts and fallacies demanding broken, voiceless not-people stranded by huge chasms from the rest of the world in place of everyday autistics" (Bascom 2012a: 8, 10).

The better way forward, states Bascom, "starts with the basic, foundational idea that *there is nothing wrong with us*. We are fine. We are complete, complex, human beings leading rich and meaningful existences and deserving dignity, respect, human rights, and the primary voice in the conversation about us" (Bascom 2012a, 10). There is a pressing need to move toward the achievement of social and cultural environments wherein, to quote the anthropologist Elizabeth Fein, the "interaction between autistic individuals and their social surroundings is a bi-directional process of influence, in which social practices influence autistic individuals while the characteristic needs, behaviors, and communicative styles of those individuals also shape the communicative practice of their surroundings" (Fein 2012, 31).[4]

The Artism Ensemble, a neurodiverse group that features children on the autism spectrum performing original music together with their parents and professional musicians, is committed to such goals.[5] The ensemble and the larger Artism Music Project of which it is a part have been central to my activities as a musician and ethnomusicologist for the past several years. Anthropologists Olga Solomon and Nancy Bagatell have called for "movement away from dominant biomedical discourses that focus largely on symptoms to a more phenomenological and ethnographic stance that addresses experiences of living with autism" (Solomon and Bagatell 2010, 1). Artism may be regarded as a musical and ethnomusicological response to that call. It belongs to a large and ever growing movement of advocacy and epistemological reconfiguration that encompasses intersecting streams flowing through the autistic self-advocacy movement, Disability Studies, the disability rights movement, the philosophy of disability, linguistic anthropology, cultural anthropology, comparative human development, and certain sectors and cohorts within music disciplines including historical musicology, music theory, music education, and music therapy.[6] Artism draws on and cuts across much of this broadly interdisciplinary landscape while remaining primarily ethnomusicological in its foundations and orientation. To pinpoint its identity even more precisely, Artism is an applied ethnomusicology endeavor, in the sense that Jeff Todd Titon has defined *applied ethnomusicology* as "the process of putting ethnomusicological research to practical use" (Titon 2011).[7]

In this essay, I explore Artism ethnomusicologically and use that exploration as a springboard for larger discussions relating to issues of autistic self-advocacy, Disability Studies and rights, the anthropology of autism, and epistemological and pragmatic debates and consequences of competing autism discourses and philosophies. I propose an ethnographic model of disability as a potential alternative and complement to the existing social and medical models, and I endeavor to create a polyvocal narrative that weaves together my own words and ideas with those of child members of the Artism Ensemble, autistic self-advocates, and scholars from a range of disciplines, most especially Disability Studies and the anthropology of autism.

My core argument is that musical projects like Artism hold the capacity to contribute productively and meaningfully to the causes of autistic self-advocacy and quality of life, modeling new horizons of possibility for the cultivation of neurodiverse environments of cultural co-creation and self-determination while transforming public perceptions of autism from the customary tropes of deficit, disorder, despair, hopelessness, and stigma to alternate visions of wholeness, ability, diversity, possibility, and acceptance. In this sense, such projects might be described as having a therapeutic potential, not by virtue of their capacity to correct or reduce the so-called symptoms of autism or other forms of neurodiversity, but conversely on account of their power to modulate public perceptions away from assumptions and paradigms of pathology while at the same time creating productive spaces in which neurodivergent people have freedom and agency to be themselves on their own terms.

I will additionally engage Artism from a more critical perspective. The need to do so is based on my realization that despite its mission to challenge and move beyond the limiting constraints and typologies of conventional autism-related discourse and practice it critiques, the project, at least as currently configured, remains entrapped in some of the very negating constructs it ostensibly defies, sometimes in ways that are remediable, other times in ways that are intractable.

The Artism Music Project: A Different Way of Doing Things

Twelve-year-old Mara moves back and forth between her preferred black "spinny chair" and the two filing cabinets against my office wall. As she paces, she talks about her own compositions and those of her three fellow ASD-diagnosed child members of the Artism Ensemble:

> You know, I like to make my songs funny. And NICKstr likes to make his songs really precise. E.S. liked to make her songs quiet. And Coffeebot likes to make his songs precise and sort of loud, and he really likes the steel drum. Me, I really like all their songs. They're always so great. . . . And honestly, it's really cool seeing all these kids come up with different songs and different styles of songs.
>
> And of course the Autism Ensemble [*sic*] is not a cure. I don't treat it like a cure, because it isn't, and if you call it a cure I will disagree with you. It's simply the kind of way you can calm down and, you know, help with the bad parts of autism without restricting the good parts. . . . What I [mean by that] is that Artism kind of helps with my anger issues without restricting my creativity. . . .
>
> It's the fact that I'm allowed to bang on drums for a while—and any instrument I want (as long as I don't break it or it's not meant to be banged)—without anybody telling me I'm supposed to do it this way, or I'm supposed to do it that way, or I'm supposed to put *this* there or that THERE, or I'm doing it wrong. . . . Because I'm told that every day. I want a break from it! . . . It's just nice being there with other people without them telling me what to do, or just jabbering about all the things they can do that I can't. . . .
>
> We're all just kids in the end. I mean, that's the whole point. We're all just kids in the end. Who friggin' cares whether we're autistic or not? Why does it matter?

ARTISM is an acronym for "Autism: Responding Together In Sound and Movement." The Artism Ensemble is a neurodiverse, intergenerational, and intercultural creative music performance collective that features four to five children with autism spectrum conditions,[8] their co-participating parents, and professional musicians of diverse musicultural background performing improvisation-driven music together on an E-WoMP, or Exploratory World Music Playground. The E-WoMP comprises a large array of percussion instruments that both the child and adult players are free to explore, as they wish to and on their own terms, individually or collectively; thus the "playground" identifier in the name. Most of the E-WoMP's instruments were manufactured by the Remo percussion instrument company and are modeled after traditional drums and other percussion instruments originating in West Africa, Latin America, Native America, and other world regions. They include *djembes*, congas, bongos, ocean drums, thunder tubes, *cuicas*, a Native American–type gathering drum, tom-toms, egg shakers, and steelpans (steel drums), among many others. All instruments selected for the E-WoMP must meet two basic requirements: high yield for low input (i.e., easy to produce pleasing/satisfying sounds without need of specialized training) and safety for use by the children in the program. Flexible rubber swimming pool dive sticks are the main types of mallets, and other mallets and sticks with padded or rubber ends are used to ensure optimal safety as well. The use of rubber and padded beaters also helps to prevent the production of excessively loud sounds and harsh timbres, which is important given that people on the autism spectrum often have sensory challenges including a high level of sensitivity to loud and abrasive sounds.

Artism's staff musicians play both the E-WoMP percussion instruments and their own instruments, including guitar, bass, steelpan, flute, and clarinet. In previous years, other instruments, such as the *zheng* Chinese zither and the Aboriginal Australian *didgeridoo*, were also featured. The diverse backgrounds of the musicians on staff, which has included master musicians/ethnomusicologists from Peru, Trinidad, Bolivia, and China as well as Canada and different regions of the United States, contributes to the profusely intercultural palette of musical resources from which Artism's music springs. Compositions, arrangements, and directed improvisations by the children reflect this musicultural diversity, as elements of festejo, rumba, flamenco, calypso, raga, and gamelan combine with those of jazz, blues, funk, hip-hop, rock, classical, and other genres—as well as with ideas and concepts that are uniquely the children's own and bear no recognizable resemblance to any preexisting musical genre or tradition—to forge the distinctive sound and approach that define Artism's music. (Six brief videos of Artism performances are available on the Companion Website for this book.)

The Artism Ensemble was founded in Tallahassee, Florida, in January 2011. It represents an extension and outgrowth of its predecessor program, the Music-Play Project (Bakan et al. 2008a, 2008b; Bakan 2009; Koen et al. 2008), and has likewise been a product of collaboration between researchers, musicians, and clinicians associated with the College of Music, Center for Autism and Related Disabilities, Autism Institute, and College of Medicine at Florida State University. Since its creation, Artism has been jointly sponsored by the National Endowment for the Arts, the Florida Department of State's Division of Cultural Affairs, Remo Inc., and other supporting institutions.

Toward an Ethnographic Model of Disability

In its on-the-ground and philosophical commitments to relying on the creative and agentive priorities of its child members for its musical identity and social life, the Artism Ensemble privileges autistic ability over disability, supportively responding to the creative initiatives and impulses of children with autism rather than trying to restrain, retrain, or redirect them. Moreover, the ensemble, through its concerts and other public events, serves as a social model in its own right: a model of inclusive sociality, music making, and cultural coproduction that promotes public recognition of and appreciation for the abilities of people on the autism spectrum; that displays a productive and creative domain of musical praxis built on the elimination of conventional boundaries and barriers of identity and ability construction; and that in turn challenges conventional assumptions about musical expertise, musical value, and the ostensibly self-evident social hierarchies that exist within group music-making environments. Artism aspires through its musicultural practice and performances to contribute to the enablement and empowerment of people who have historically been disenabled, build culture and community in environments where "conventional logic" would seem to deny the very possibility, and publicly perform autistic ability and sociocultural inclusivity as public challenges and alternatives to autistic disability and exclusion.[9]

Key to such aspirations is an epistemological stance that differs fundamentally from what is often described in Disability Studies discourses as the medical model of disability. In this medical model, the site of disability is the allegedly disabled individual him- or herself, who is affected by some form of physical, mental, or cognitive defect or flaw (disorder, disease, pathological condition, illness, impairment) in ways that create forms of difference demanding medical intervention—diagnosis, therapy, rehabilitation, and ideally cure (Straus 2013, 462).

Given such an epistemological position, it follows that proponents of the medical model, whether acting as researchers, physicians, or therapists, as teachers, aides, or even parents, operate from a fundamental position that there is a need to *change* the autistic or otherwise disabled person. They are effectively agents of change in search of solutions. Music therapists are a case in point, as we learn in the 2012 online article "Music Therapy as a Treatment Modality for Autism Spectrum Disorders," published by the American Music Therapy Association (AMTA) on its website:

> Music Therapy is the clinical and evidence-based use of music interventions to accomplish individualized goals within a therapeutic relationship by a credentialed professional who has completed an approved music therapy program. . . . Music therapy provides a unique variety of music experiences in an intentional and developmentally appropriate manner to effect changes in behavior and facilitate development of skills. . . . Music therapy can stimulate individuals [with ASD] to reduce negative and/or self-stimulatory responses and increase participation in more appropriate and socially acceptable ways. . . . Because music is processed in both hemispheres of the brain, it can stimulate cognitive functioning and may be used for remediation of some speech/language skills [in persons with ASD]. (American Music Therapy Association 2012)[10]

As an ethnomusicologist of autism, I operate from a different premise than most of my counterparts in the music therapy profession. I am not interested in changing the people whose lives and music I endeavor to understand. My goals are basically ethnographic, not therapeutic; and to the extent that a therapeutic aim may be said to exist at all, it is to cultivate a space in which the children in Artism get to be themselves as they wish to be, a space devoid of the kinds of externally imposed pressures, expectations, assessments, and objectives that customarily go hand in hand with programs and activities rooted in symptomatological epistemologies of autism and autistic experience.

In contradistinction not only to the medical model of disability but also, to a lesser degree, to the social model of disability (which "opposes the medical model by defining disability relative to the social and built environment, arguing that disabling environments produce disability in bodies and require interventions at the level of social justice"—see Siebers 2008, 25),[11] the guiding model for an ethnomusicology of autism might be described as an ethnographic model of disability. Consistent with our ethnographic and musicianly leanings, ethnomusicologists are interested in understanding the subjects of our investigations—in the present case of my own work, children with autism—principally according to their terms and from their perspectives: learning from them, sharing experiences with them (including but not limited to musical ones), comprehending their conceptions and values of community, personhood, social experience, humor, work and play, pleasure and pain, joy and suffering, and of course music. To borrow an oft-quoted turn of phrase from Clifford Geertz, I am "seeking, in the widened sense of the term in which it encompasses very much more than talk, to converse with them, a matter a great deal more difficult, and not only with strangers, than is commonly recognized" (Geertz 1973, 13).

I am interested as an ethnomusicologist in the music, thoughts, lives, and musical communities of the autistic children with whom I currently work and play music in much the same way that I was interested in the music, thoughts, lives, and musical communities of Balinese musicians with whom I worked and played music in Indonesia in the 1980s and 1990s (Bakan 1999). I did not endeavor to remediate the performance practices of my Balinese fellow musicians, nor to cure them of their preference for paired tunings over equal tempered ones. I assumed that these Balinese musicians were competent practitioners of the Balinese musical arts with which they were associated, and that their distinctive clusters of behaviors, abilities, and attitudes in musical and social practice reflected individual manifestations of a broader Balinese worldview and ontology. I welcomed opportunities to learn from them through musical and social interactions, through performances and conversations that yielded ethnomusicological insights into Balinese ways of being and of being musical.

I assume similar things and welcome similar experiences and insights in my musical collaborations with the child members of the Artism Ensemble. Entering the E-WoMP, the principal site of Artism musical production, I approach matters much as I did when entering the *bale banjar*, the principal site of Balinese gamelan music production: as a learning musician, a curious and committed ethnographer, and a co-participant in the making of music and cultural community.[12] Here, though, the culture bearers are not musicians in Bali who play on a gamelan but American children on the autism spectrum who play on an E-WoMP. It is these children who direct Artism's musical proceedings, guiding the course of group improvisations, coming up with themes and variations that blossom into full-grown compositions, selecting preexisting materials—a melody from Liszt's *Hungarian Rhapsody No. 2*, a Bo Diddley beat under an extemporized rendition of Dr. Seuss's *Green Eggs and Ham*—from which to create inspired arrangements that cleverly combine precomposed and improvised passages.

As for the adult members of the ensemble, the professional musicians and "nonmusician" parents alike, we are not there to teach or direct the children; rather, we are there to learn from and respond to them. We apply whatever skills and attributes we bring to the E-WoMP, individually and collectively, to nurture the children's creativity, agency, individual and social aspirations (musical and otherwise), and reciprocity. There are no preestablished repertoires, right or wrong notes, specific musical goals or demands, or defined expectations of any kind beyond ensuring that all participants contribute to maintaining a safe environment emphasizing mutual respect and support for one another.

Typically, rehearsals and concerts move in round-robin fashion from one piece to another, with each child taking charge of the composition/arrangement and ensemble direction duties for one or more of their own pieces per program. This protocol was not created or imposed by me or any of the other adult ensemble members. Rather, it was an organic and gradually forming outgrowth of the children's own desires for how Artism's musical process should work, one that was worked out collectively among them in rehearsals. The development of this protocol seemed to emerge as a direct response to the children's learning at the outset of the project in 2011 that the ensemble was not going to function exclusively in a "play lab" environment, as it had in the Music-Play Project, but would additionally be getting out in public and performing concerts. Once they realized that they were going to have an audience, they almost immediately became committed to the idea of fashioning a "high quality" musical product warranting public consumption, and in tandem with their specifically musical goals they became quite deeply invested in delivering the goods with showmanship and style, that is, with showmanship and style defined on *their* terms, which have often been deliciously and provocatively at odds with "conventional" musical tastes and sensibilities. It was fascinating to witness this strategic and aesthetic shift from a participatory to a presentational mode of performance (Turino 2008) and to both observe and be a participant in the making of the distinctive sound, look, feel, and identity that have come to define Artism's unique musicultural brand over time.

It is also important to mention that in both their broad outlines and specific characteristics, the generative processes of musical production and social engagement that define the Artism Ensemble's approach contrast in key regards with "best practices" positions regarding clinical, therapeutic, and educational approaches to working with people with autism:

> Individuals on the autism spectrum tend to gravitate toward preordered systems in which the relationship between parts can be predicted based on rules, and struggle to function within open-ended systems requiring flexibility, improvisation, and intuition. They thus gravitate toward and function best under a "stable symbolic and social order," under conditions where social expectations and givens are consistent, explicit, systematic, and shared between interlocutors. (Fein 2012, 69–70)

Artism's open-ended approach, reliant as it is on flexibility, improvisation, and intuition, may be seen to push back against such logic to a considerable degree, even if other key features of the project—the regular weekly meeting time and location, its stable membership, the relatively predictable structure of the round-robin protocol described above—do offer frameworks of consistency and reliability within which the more fluid and improvisatory elements may unfold. There is no doubt that children in the group (and adults as well) often *do* struggle with the overall unpredictability and open-endedness of the process, and that in many respects their individual and collective decisions to create quasi-structured musical works and to take charge of the ensemble in a directorial way, rather than to maintain a more free-flowing improvisational environment, are commensurate with their desires for a certain measure of systematicity, control, and consistency. But there is likewise no doubt that over time they have come to revel in the open-ended possibilities for spontaneous invention and co-creation that the E-WoMP environment affords. Each in their way, they have come to find both the challenges and triumphs of contending with the inherent fluidity of Artism's musicultural process to be empowering and rewarding.

On the basis of what I have observed relative to my work on the ethnomusicology of autism over the past decade, and also as a member of a family affected by autism for roughly the same period, I believe that people with autism are not necessarily any less spontaneous, intuitive, flexible, or improvisatory than other people are; rather, they appear to be that way because they are almost invariably forced to contend with life situations and settings in which their particular attributes and preferences for expressing spontaneity, intuition, flexibility, and improvisational ability are demeaned, or are patronized, or go unacknowledged or unrecognized altogether by their interlocutors. The evidence coming from the autism self-advocacy movement, as well as from Artism and similar types of projects (see, for example, Fein 2012, Bagatell 2010, Bascom 2012b), suggests that in situations where autistic people are given opportunities to have their talents enabled rather than disenabled, nurtured rather than quashed, and embraced for what they are rather than being subjected to therapeutic interventions aimed at their transformation or remediation, they can and will thrive in ways that people without autism would never think possible unless they witnessed it firsthand. A primary purpose of Artism is therefore to provide neurotypical people with precisely that opportunity: to witness, enjoy, appreciate, and celebrate autistic ability rather than identify, symptomatize, marginalize, and take pity on autistic disability.

The child stars of the Artism Ensemble, together with their supporting cast of parents and professional musicians, make good and innovative music, make good culture and community, and make change. They do this through their compositions and arrangements, their improvisatory explorations, their concert performances, and their public presentations of individual and collective selfhood. Change is achieved internally among the group's members through our joint musicultural ventures and all that they reveal. It is achieved externally as we reach out to audiences through concerts in which Artism's players, the children foremost of all, are *applied* to the cause of transforming public perceptions of autism from disability-centered to ability-centered ones, from recognition of a negating sort to recognition of the more affirming and celebratory kind.

Critiquing Artism

Whatever its merits may be, it must be acknowledged that Artism, as a program that has received funding and sponsorship specifically because of its connection to autism, and that presents public performances in which the autistic identities of key players are either explicitly or implicitly acknowledged, highlights and benefits from the staging of autism and the performance of disability. In so doing it simultaneously and paradoxically resists and is co-opted by hegemonic stances that have long dominated both medical-scientific and mainstream public/media discourses in their positing of "autistic" in contradistinction to "normal."

Artism may thus be justifiably criticized for propagating the very constructs of exclusion and hierarchy it aims to overturn, at least in some measure. Such criticisms were raised by panelists on a June 28, 2013, session I attended at the twenty-sixth annual conference of the Society for Disability Studies in Orlando, Florida (see Grace et al. 2013). Several autistic members of the panel had attended the Artism concert performed at the meeting's Opening General Session two days prior. The concert seemed to have gone extremely well, an unqualified success in all respects as far as I could determine in its immediate aftermath, but the comments offered up by these panelists revealed significant issues in need of address and remediation.

The autistic scholar, author, and advocate Zach Richter served as the primary spokesperson. He and his colleagues provided constructive criticism and suggestions on how the approach of Artism could be revised to put the group in better compliance with the priorities of autistic people and the autistic rights movement (at least to the extent that the positions of organizations like the Autistic Self Advocacy Network and Autism Network International may be regarded as representative of the broader views of the autistic community). Key to their critique was the point that Artism featured autistic children performing together with their nonautistic parents and with professional musicians who likewise were not autistic. Thus, all of the children were autistic, while none of the adults were. It was strongly recommended that adult autistic musicians be recruited to either join the ensemble or serve as professional consultants. This is a suggestion we are now in the process of implementing, and one that will without doubt enrich the ensemble both musically and socially, as well as in terms of its capacity to work on behalf of effectively promoting autistic ability, self-determination, and acceptance.

The future addition of neurotypical children to the ensemble would seem to be another logical extension of the neurodiversity ideal principle. The feedback received from members of the autistic community—within and outside of the ensemble's membership—has increasingly convinced me that maintaining separate demographic profiles within age-set classes in the ensemble (autistic children, neurotypical adults) is counterproductive to our mission.

Richter and his fellow panelists offered other useful recommendations that we are in the process of incorporating as well. These include the following:

- Strive to decrease the loudness of the performance in accordance with the aforementioned sensory challenges of many autistic people, this for the benefit of both members of the ensemble and their audiences.
- Instruct audiences to show their appreciation not by clapping, which is disturbing to many sound-sensitive autistics, but rather by employing the customary forms of silent applause used at autistic community gatherings (e.g., "jazz hands"-style silent applause).
- Completely avoid reference to the phrase *autism awareness*, which we had unfortunately included on a concert evaluation questionnaire distributed to the audience; this phrase, closely associated with Autism Speaks and other organizations that are not run by autistic people, is considered to be offensive within the autistic self-advocacy movement, which instead promotes the principle of *autism acceptance*.

The tempered outlining of criticisms and suggestions above fails to capture the impassioned mode in which they were presented to me at the conference. Richter, in particular, found several elements of Artism's performance to be, in his words, "offensive" and "disturbing," and while these words stung at the time, I was and remain deeply grateful to him and his colleagues for helping me and my Artism collaborators to rethink our approaches and priorities and move toward a better way of doing what we do.

Like most manifestations of disability practice and discourse, Artism exists in a complexly contested space wherein empowerment and appropriation are dialectically intertwined. Abundant opportunities exist to make things worse rather than better, regardless of our intentions or our efforts to do otherwise, whether through the kinds of unwitting insensitivities that brought offense to Richter and others in the autistic cohort at the Society for Disability Studies meeting or by inadvertently contributing to regressive essentialisms about autism that we are endeavoring to combat (e.g., an audience member walking away from an Artism concert saying, "Oh, isn't that special; isn't it nice that those disabled kids get to do something fun with music since they surely couldn't play in a *real* band or orchestra"). It is all a rather risky venture, but ultimately a worthwhile one, for in promoting autistic personhood as "something different from undesired difference" (Titchkosky 2007, 9), Artism holds the capacity to use music to make a real and positive difference.

Mara Spins

Mara has been spinning round and round in my black office chair for some time now.

"Spinning chairs! Spinning chairs make *everyone* happy!" she sings. Then, in a mock serious tone, "I get distracted easily," and after that, throwing back her hair and laughing wildly, "*especially by things like this that are SPINNY CHAIRS!!*"

"You know," I say to Mara, laughing along with her as she continues to spin away, "the scientists and the doctors and therapists and people like that who specialize in autism . . . would say that what you're doing now—spinning and spinning and spinning while we have this conversation—is an example of *stimming*, that it's a 'symptom' of your Asperger's or your autism or whatever."

"Stim-*what*?" Mara asks, seemingly confused. "What *is* that?"

"Stimming," I repeat. "It's a word that they use to describe so-called 'self-stimulating behaviors' that autistic people do when they're, I don't know, feeling stressed or uncomfortable or whatever, or maybe the scientists don't know why they do those things but they know they do them and they say that's one of the things that makes them autistic."

Mara's laughter now escalates to a fever pitch.

"That's just *ridiculous*!" she states incredulously. "I mean, I bet that the president has a spinny chair and sometimes *he* spins around. . . . [He] probably [doesn't] laugh like I do because the president doesn't laugh, or at least lots of people think that, but that's just another stereotype—but still. Spinny chairs. I *like* spinny chairs."

Zolabean Stims

Self-stimulatory behavior, or "stimming," is identified as a classic symptom of "autistic stereotypy" (Bagatell 2010, 39). Common "stims" include hand flapping, covering of the ears, spinning and twirling, and rocking back and forth or from side to side. Autism researchers offer competing theories regarding the causality of stimming. Some suggest that sensory overstimulation (hypersensitivity) is the main causal factor; others contend that sensory understimulation (hyposensitivity) is the key issue. Either way, there is agreement that stimming is practiced by autistics due "to some dysfunctional system in the brain or periphery" (Edelson n.d.), and training people with ASD to control or eliminate their stimming behaviors is a goal of many therapeutic interventions, including some music therapy interventions which, as noted earlier, may be employed to "stimulate individuals to reduce negative and/or self-stimulatory responses and increase participation in more appropriate and socially acceptable ways" (American Music Therapy Association 2012).

For Mara and a great many other people on the autism spectrum, though, there is nothing "dysfunctional" about stimming at all. In her ethnographic study of an autistic self-advocacy group to which she ascribes the pseudonym AACT (Autistic Adults Coming Together), Nancy Bagatell observes that

> actions viewed as "self-stimulatory" by the biomedical community, such as rocking and hand flapping, are reframed as a valued activity[,] not a meaningless action that should be "extinguished." Many members told me that they enjoyed these activities tremendously and felt a sense of relief being in a place where they could, in fact, be themselves. (Bagatell 2010, 39)

Zolabean, a former member of the Artism Ensemble who played in the group for its first two seasons in 2011 and 2012, is a stimmer. Two years prior to joining, she had participated in Artism's predecessor program, the Music-Play Project. At that time, she was an adorable, petite eight-year-old with straight blonde hair, a charmingly wry pixie grin, and a diagnostic label of Asperger's syndrome. She was reserved yet articulate, highly intelligent, and possessed of considerable creative talents as a musical improviser from the start. When there was no music being played, she tended to be rather passive, even flat, in affect, but as soon as the music started up she became an engaged and intense participant. She almost never stimmed, and on the rare occasions that she did (usually for a fleeting moment of hand-flapping) she would quickly check herself and stop.

It was thus both surprising and disturbing for me to see Zolabean stimming profusely and barely participating at all musically during our opening session of the Artism Ensemble program in January 2011. She spent most of the gathering flapping her hands, incessantly straightening and bending her legs, and twisting her fingers together awkwardly. What had happened?

Several months later, in the aftermath of Artism's inaugural season, I finally got an answer to that question. In the interim, Zolabean had seemingly "come around" as a member of the group, taking on an active role as both a composer and performer from about the third session onward. But throughout the season, she had continued to stim frequently as well, often moving between periods of instrumental playing and intensive stimming with a kind of fluidity that acquired a logic and aesthetic all its own. During a conversation with her and her mother, Suzanne, she explained how this had all come to pass:

MICHAEL (M): So, let's talk about Artism for a minute.
ZOLABEAN (Z): OK.
M: 'Cause you like that.
Z: Yes.
M: [During] the first couple of weeks, you . . . were participating in your way . . . but you weren't playing, you weren't playing instruments very much at all—sometimes I think you didn't play them at all. Do you remember in [the] Music-Play Project [in 2009]? There you used to play quite a bit, I seem to recall.
Z: Well, there was a reason why I played a lot in that. I was afraid that someone was going to tell me I had to play if I didn't. . . . There were people with video cameras. It was just a lot of pressure and I felt like I had to play the instruments, like [that] was why I was there. [But] during the Artism project [Zolabean trails off mid-sentence, pauses thoughtfully, then shifts gears and resumes]—I have characters in my head. I think about them a *ton*, like probably more than I think about my own life. That's fine with me because they kind of relate to me. A lot of them have similar diagnosises [*sic*] . . . And what's happening was, they were all musicians, the people in my head, and so I was imagining them playing the instruments, like I had one on the *zheng* and one on the *djembe*, and everything. . . .
M: [So] because you've got these characters in your head and then they were playing the instruments [you didn't feel the need to play yourself]?

Z (smiling glowingly): Yes!
M: But then, at a certain point, that changed, and then you became [involved] very actively [in] playing and composing and directing the band. [Why?]
Z: At the beginning I was a little nervous that I'd have to play like in the last one [MPP 2009]. But after a while I realized it was cool if I could just express myself in any way. And in the end I felt comfortable enough and my characters kind of merged with it. That's when I started playing more.
M: So the main thing, then, it sounds like, there were two things: the characters sort of merging [Z cuts M off midsentence to interject]
Z: And it was also just me getting more comfortable with it.

"OK," I say to Zolabean. "So when you say the characters merged, did they become you?"

She pauses, considers the question thoughtfully, ponders it as she looks out the window. Then she turns back toward Suzanne and me, but as she answers my question, she looks not at me but deeply and intently into her mother's eyes."Yes!" she exclaims, an affirming smile curling the corners of her lips upward as a look of resolute clarity spreads across her face.

A pregnant pause hangs in the air until Suzanne breaks through it."Cool!" she exclaims in a moment of quiet fascination, and in that same moment Zolabean, poised and composed up to now, starts stimming intensely. She shakes her foot nervously, twirls her hair around her fingers momentarily, then chews on her t-shirt as she looks back and forth furtively between Suzanne and me, as though seeking reassurance that it's OK for her to have characters in her head, that it's OK for them to merge and become her, that it's OK for her to be who she is where she is and how she is. And while there is a touch of apprehension, even a tinge of anxiety, in her current state, there is a far stronger sense of excitement and hope. Zolabean has made the connection. Suzanne and I "get it" now.

The "seemingly natural conflation" of Zolabean's particular brand of disability, the one labeled Asperger's syndrome, with "undesired vulnerability and ineptitude" (Titchkosky 2007, 10) has been not only disrupted, but fully overturned in this moment of revelation and discovery. Zolabean has shown that her decision to not play instruments early on in Artism, to instead stim or listen silently while jamming with the "band of brothers" in her head, was just that: a decision. It was not an action of retreat or regression determined by her autism, but rather a choice determined by her preference; not a symptom of isolationism and social impairment, but an expression of creative exploration and inventiveness. And when, later on, she did choose to connect in a more conventionally "musical" manner (at least some of the time)—playing instruments, interacting with the rest of us in readily tangible ways, leading the ensemble in some pieces and following her fellow players in others—this did not constitute a positive outcome of a successful therapeutic intervention. It merely made manifest a fluid progression between two different modes of productive musical engagement, one centered on stimming-based movement and adventurous flights of imagination, the other on performance and explicit social connection with the other music makers in the room. While a symptomatic reading would show the latter of these modes to be "normative" and the former to be "autistic," neither is in actuality any more normal or autistic than the other. They are just different—and they are, moreover, relational, dialectical, and organically in tandem with one another. They are alternate ways of being musical and being tuned in, which is a far cry from the contrasting view that they are oppositional ways of being musical versus being tuned out.

Conclusion: Toward Living and Imagining a Little Differently

My adult Artism Ensemble colleagues and I have had the pleasure of seeing Zolabean, Mara, and the other three children who are or have been members of the group—E.S., Coffebot, and NICKstr—grow as people and musicians, engage in meaningful relationships and form friendships, work through musical and behavioral challenges with strength and resolve, and become increasingly confident, agentive, and willing and able to connect and negotiate with each other and with us. But all such prospective indicators of the practical utility of the Artism Music Project are misunderstood if they are interpreted as measures of progress *away* from autism or as remediations of autistic symptoms. That is not the point. The adult participants—the parents and the professional musicians alike—have demonstrated similar albeit distinct patterns of growth and development in their musical and social abilities, as well as in agency, reciprocity, and self-confidence, through their participation in the project. To grow and learn in such ways within the type of musical environment that Artism cultivates is not an autistic thing; it's a human thing, and as such it is prone to the myriad shortcomings, limitations, missteps, and misunderstandings that define human endeavors generally. It is all worth the effort, though. We carry on. We do our best. We are all in this together.

Notes

1. In DSM-5 (American Psychiatric Association 2013), the various separate "disorders" of the autism spectrum have been collapsed into a single diagnostic category: ASD, or autism spectrum disorder. This encompasses the conditions that were formerly categorized (in DSM–IV) as autism, Asperger syndrome, and PDD-NOS. Two conditions that were previously (in DSM–IV) encompassed within the ASD rubric, childhood disintegrative disorder and Rett's syndrome, have been eliminated from the ASD category in DSM–5 (Kaufmann 2012).
2. The classificatory scheme of "low-functioning" versus "high-functioning" forms of autism/ASD is often used as a baseline for marking gradations along this identified continuum. This is a fraught area marked by contentious debate in contemporary ASD discourse and research, and it is one with which I have consciously chosen not to engage in this essay beyond the present note. There are several reasons for this decision, but rather

than detailing them I will defer to the expressed views of the autistic author and advocate Amy Sequenzia:

> I am autistic, non-speaking. I am also labeled "low-functioning." This label is a pre-judgment based on what I cannot do. It makes people look at me with pity instead of trying to get to know me, to listen to my ideas. . . . All the labels given to us only help to make myths seem like the reality. By classifying a non-speaking autistic as low-functioning, one is lowering expectations for the autistic individual. He or she is not given a chance to express him/herself and maybe show hidden abilities. We, autistic, have tried hard and accepted the neurotypical way of doing things to make it easier for non-autistic people to understand us, interact with us. Despite some progress there is still very little reciprocity. (Sequenzia 2012, 159 and 161)

Suffice it to say that among the more than thirty children who have participated in the Artism Music Project and/or the Music-Play Project since 2005, a very large portion of the autism spectrum, as accounted for within the established "low-functioning" to "high-functioning" continuum, has been represented, although the majority representation has consistently leaned toward the "high-functioning" end.

3. Additional published works addressing issues of autism and living with ASD that have been authored or coauthored by autistic people include the following: Williams 1992, Lawson 2000, Shore 2003 (of additional interest on account of Shore's professional status as a musician and music educator), Miller 2003, Prince-Hughes 2004, Biklen 2005, Ariel and Naseef 2006, Tammet 2007, Robison 2007, Prince 2010, Mukhopadhyay 2011. Numerous documentary films, blogs, websites, and other media also contribute to the increasingly present and essential autistic voice of ASD discourses.
4. Fein's work is representative of a burgeoning literature on the anthropology of autism that aligns in many key respects with both the Disability Studies and ethnomusicological sensibilities foregrounded in this article. See also Ochs et al. 2001, 2004, and 2005; Kremer-Sadlik 2004; Solomon 2010a and 2010b; Sterponi and Fasulo 2010; Grinker 2010; and Brezis 2012.
5. The intersectionality of autistic and child identities that largely defines the demographic of the Artism Ensemble is not addressed explicitly in this essay on account of both space limitations and my endeavor to maintain a manageable scope of inquiry. Exploring such intersectionality is of potentially great significance, however. Ethnomusicologically oriented, ethnography-informed approaches to the study of children's music making, as exemplified, for example, in publications by Campbell (2010), Marsh (2008), and Gaunt (2006), offer valuable models and possibilities relative to future projects and studies on the musical lives of autistic children.
6. Selected literature from these many areas and disciplines is cited and discussed throughout this chapter. Notable is the emergence of a body of relatively recent books, dedicated exclusively to autism, which approach their subject from positions that run contrary to the mainstream medical-scientific paradigm. Beyond the aforementioned *Loud Hands* volume (Bascom 2012a), these include Biklen 2005, Nadesan 2005, Grinker 2007, Murray 2008, and Osteen 2008.
7. For additional perspectives on applied ethnomusicology, see also Titon 1992; Sheehy 1992; Alviso 2003; Harrison, Pettan, and Mackinlay 2010; and Harrison 2012.
8. Participants were recruited through the client registry of the Center for Autism and Related Disabilities (CARD) at Florida State University. At all phases, the project has been

reviewed and approved by the Human Subjects Committee of the Institutional Review Board at Florida State University.

9. Of related interest are a variety of sources that approach the subject of music and autism from a Disability Studies perspective. These include Straus 2011, Marrero 2012, Lubet 2011, and the chapters contributed by Headlam (2006), Jensen-Moulton (2006), and Maloney (2006) to the edited volume *Sounding Off: Theorizing Disability in Music* (Lerner and Straus 2006).
10. Music therapy is a highly diverse field. The positions set forth in this AMTA publication should not be seen as representative of the field as a whole, let alone of its individual practitioners. That said, I would maintain that the basic distinction between the therapeutic goals of music therapists and the ethnographic goals of ethnomusicologists constitutes a fundamental epistemological difference that impacts theories, practices, and values at a most fundamental level: therapists generally endeavor to effect changes in their clients, whereas ethnographers generally do not endeavor to effect changes in the subjects of their investigations. For a range of approaches in music therapy, see Nordoff and Robbins 1977, Bruscia 1987, Edgerton 1994, Clarkson 1998, Ruud 1998, Aigen 2002, Stige 2002, Kern 2004, Pavlicevic and Ansdell 2004, Whipple 2004, Walworth 2007, Gold 2011, Reschke-Hernández 2011, and Simpson and Keen 2011. For perspectives on music in special education relating to autism, see Hammel and Hourigan 2013.
11. *The Disability Studies Reader* (4th ed.), edited by Lennard J. Davis (2013a), explores social versus medical models of disability from multiple perspectives. In particular in that volume, see Davis 2013b and 2013c, Shakespeare 2013, Siebers 2013, Garland-Thomson 2013, and Straus 2013. For perspectives from the philosophy of disability, see Silvers 2010 and Carlson 2009.
12. I am aware that this comparative analogy can only be taken so far. Whereas the gamelan-based musical activities of the *bale banjar* long predated my arrival in Bali as an ethnomusicologist, the E-WoMP is a built environment that was created as a musicultural space for the creative musical activities of autistic children and their nonautistic adult interlocutors by myself and other neurotypical adults. Therefore, I may rightly be accused of having essentially created the ethnographic field site that I now visit and research. While recognizing that there is some irony in this situation ethnographically speaking, I hold to the conviction that a large measure of "ownership" of the E-WoMP space and of Artism's musical and social processes and priorities overall have been claimed and maintained by the children in the group.

References

Aigen, Kenneth. 2002. *Playin' in the Band: A Qualitative Study of Popular Music Styles as Clinical Improvisation*. New York: Nordoff-Robbins Center for Music Therapy.

Alviso, J. Ricardo. 2003. "Applied Ethnomusicology and the Impulse to Make a Difference." *Folklore Forum* 34 (1/2): 89–96.

American Music Therapy Association (AMTA). 2012. "Music Therapy as a Treatment Modality for Autism Spectrum Disorders." Accessed August 19, 2013. http://www.musictherapy.org/assets/1/7/MT_Autism_2012.pdf.

American Psychiatric Association. 2000. *Diagnostic and Statistical Manual of Mental Disorders*. 4th ed., text revision (DSM–IV–TR). Washington, DC: American Psychiatric Association.

American Psychiatric Association. 2013. *Diagnostic and Statistical Manual of Mental Disorders.* 5th ed, (DSM–5). Arlington, VA: American Psychiatric Publishing.

Ariel, Cindy N., and Robert A. Naseef, eds. 2006. *Voices from the Spectrum: Parents, Grandparents, Siblings, People with Autism, and Professionals Share Their Wisdom.* London and Philadelphia, PA: Jessica Kingsley.

Bagatell, Nancy. 2010. "From Cure to Community: Transforming Notions of Autism." *Ethos* 38 (1): 33–55.

Bakan, Michael B. 1999. *Music of Death and New Creation: Experiences in the World of Balinese Gamelan Beleganjur.* Chicago: University of Chicago Press.

Bakan, Michael B. 2009. "Measuring Happiness in the 21st Century: Ethnomusicology, Evidence-Based Research, and the New Science of Autism." *Ethnomusicology* 53 (3): 510–518.

Bakan, Michael B., Benjamin D. Koen, Fred Kobylarz, Lindee Morgan, Rachel Goff, Sally Kahn, and Megan Bakan. 2008a. "Following Frank: Response-Ability and the Co-Creation of Culture in a Medical Ethnomusicology Program for Children on the Autism Spectrum." *Ethnomusicology* 52 (2): 163–202.

Bakan, Michael B., Benjamin D. Koen, Fred Kobylarz, Lindee Morgan, Rachel Goff, Sally Kahn, and Megan Bakan. 2008b. "Saying Something Else: Improvisation and Facilitative Music-Play in a Medical Ethnomusicology Program for Children on the Autism Spectrum." *College Music Symposium* 48: 1–30.

Bascom, Julia. 2012a. "Foreword." In *Loud Hands: Autistic People, Speaking,* edited by Julia Bascom, 6–11. Washington, DC: The Autistic Press/The Autistic Self Advocacy Network.

Bascom, Julia, ed. 2012b. *Loud Hands: Autistic People, Speaking.* Washington, DC: The Autistic Press/The Autistic Self Advocacy Network.

Biklen, Douglas. 2005. *Autism and the Myth of the Person Alone.* New York: New York University Press.

Brezis, R. 2012. "Autism as a Case for Neuroanthropology: Delineating the Role of Theory of Mind in Religious Experience." In *The Encultured Brain: An Introduction to Neuroanthropology,* edited by Daniel H. Lende and Greg Downey, 291–314. Boston: MIT Press.

Bruscia, Kenneth E. 1987. *Improvisational Models of Music Therapy.* Springfield, IL: Charles C. Thomas.

Butler, Judith. 2004. *Undoing Gender.* New York: Routledge.

Campbell, Patricia Shehan. 2010. *Songs in Their Heads: Music and Its Meaning in Children's Lives.* New York: Oxford University Press.

Carlson, Licia. 2009. *The Faces of Intellectual Disability: Philosophical Reflections.* Bloomington: Indiana University Press.

Centers for Disease Control and Prevention (CDC). 2015. "CDC Home: Autism Spectrum Disorders (ASDs)." Accessed May 19 , 2015. http://www.cdc.gov/ncbddd/autism/data.html.

Clarkson, Ginger. 1998. *I Dreamed I Was Normal: A Music Therapist's Journey into the Realms of Autism.* St. Louis, MO: MMB Music.

Davis, Lennard J. 2013a. *The Disability Studies Reader.* 4th ed. New York: Routledge.

Davis, Lennard J. 2013b. "The End of Disability Politics: On Disability as an Unstable Category." In *The Disability Studies Reader,* 4th ed., edited by Lennard J. Davis, 263–277. New York: Routledge.

Davis, Lennard J. 2013c. "Introduction: Disability, Normality, and Power." In *The Disability Studies Reader,* 4th ed., edited by Lennard J. Davis, 1–14. New York: Routledge.

Edelson, Stephen M. n.d. "Self-Stimulatory Behavior." Autism Research Institute. Accessed August 27, 2013. http://www.autism.com/index.php/symptoms_self-stim.

Edgerton, Cindy Lu. 1994. "The Effect of Improvisational Music Therapy on Communicative Behaviors of Autistic Children." *Journal of Music Therapy* 31 (1): 31–62.

Fein, Elizabeth. 2012. "The Machine Within: An Ethnography of Asperger's Syndrome, Biomedicine, and the Paradoxes of Identity and Technology in the Late Modern United States." PhD diss., University of Chicago.

Garland-Thomson, Rosemarie. 1997. *Extraordinary Bodies: Figuring Physical Disability in American Culture and Literature*. New York: Columbia University Press.

Garland-Thomson, Rosemarie. 2013. "Integrating Disability, Transforming Feminist Theory." In *The Disability Studies Reader*, 4th ed., edited by Lennard J. Davis, 333–353. New York: Routledge.

Gaunt, Kyra D. 2006. *The Games Black Girls Play: Learning the Ropes from Double-Dutch to Hip-Hop*. New York: New York University Press.

Geertz, Clifford. 1973. *The Interpretation of Cultures*. New York: Basic Books.

Gold, Christian. 2011. "Special Section: Music Therapy for People with Autistic Spectrum Disorder." *Nordic Journal of Music Therapy* 20 (2): 105–107.

Grace, Elizabeth J., Aiyana Bailin, Zach Richter, Allegra Stout, and Alyssa Z. 2013. "Intersectionalities in Autistic Culture(s): A Discussion Instigated by This Posse of Autistics and Friends." Program abstract, Society for Disability Studies 26th Annual Conference, 42.

Grinker, Roy Richard. 2007. *Unstrange Minds: Remapping the World of Autism*. New York: Basic Books.

Grinker, Roy Richard. 2010. "Commentary: On Being Autistic, and Social." *Ethos* 38 (1): 172–178.

Hammel, Alice M., and Ryan M. Hourigan. 2013. *Teaching Music to Students with Autism*. New York: Oxford University Press.

Harrison, Klisala, Svanibor Pettan, and Elizabeth Mackinlay, eds. 2010. *Applied Ethnomusicology: Historical and Contemporary Approaches*. Newcastle Upon Tyne, UK: Cambridge Scholars.

Harrison, Klisala. 2012. "Epistemologies of Applied Ethnomusicology." *Ethnomusicology* 56 (3): 505–529.

Headlam, Dave. 2006. "Learning to Hear Autistically." In *Sounding Off: Theorizing Disability in Music*, edited by Neil Lerner and Joseph N. Straus, 109–120. New York: Routledge.

Jensen-Moulton, Stephanie. 2006. "Finding Autism in the Compositions of a 19th-Century Prodigy: Reconsidering 'Blind Tom' Wiggins." In *Sounding Off: Theorizing Disability in Music*, edited by Neil Lerner and Joseph N. Straus, 199–215. New York: Routledge.

Kaufmann, Walter E. 2012. "DSM-5: The New Diagnostic Criteria for Autism Spectrum Disorders." Slides for a presentation at the Research Symposium of the Autism Consortium, October 24. http://www.autismconsortium.org/symposium-files/WalterKaufmannAC2012Symposium.pdf.

Kern, Petra. 2004. "Making Friends in Music: Including Children with Autism in an Interactive Play Setting." *Music Therapy Today* 5 (4): 1–43.

Koen, Benjamin D., Michael B. Bakan, Fred Kobylarz, Lindee Morgan, Rachel Goff, Sally Kahn, and Megan Bakan. 2008. "Personhood Consciousness: A Child-Ability-Centered Approach to Socio-Musical Healing and Autism Spectrum 'Disorders.'" In *The Oxford Handbook of Medical Ethnomusicology: Music, Medicine, and Culture*, edited by Benjamin D. Koen, 461–481. New York: Oxford University Press.

Kremer-Sadlik, T. 2004. "How Children with Autism and Asperger Syndrome Respond to Questions: A 'Naturalistic' Theory of Mind Task." *Discourse Studies* 6 (2): 185–206.

Lawson, Wendy. 2000. *Life Behind Glass: A Personal Account of Autism Spectrum Disorder*. London and Philadelphia, PA: Jessica Kingsley.

Lerner, Neil, and Joseph N. Straus, eds. 2006. *Sounding Off: Theorizing Disability in Music*. New York: Routledge.

Lubet, Alex. 2011. *Music, Disability, and Society*. Philadelphia, PA: Temple University Press.

Maloney, S. Timothy. 2006. "Glenn Gould, Autistic Savant." In *Sounding Off: Theorizing Disability in Music*, edited by Neil Lerner and Joseph N. Straus, 121–135. New York: Routledge.

Marrero, Elyse. 2012. Performing Neurodiversity: Musical Accommodation by and for an Adolescent with Autism. MA thesis, Florida State University.

Marsh, Kathryn. 2008. *The Musical Playground: Global Tradition and Change in Children's Songs and Games*. New York: Oxford University Press.

Miller, Jean Kerns. 2003. *Women from Another Planet? Our Lives in the Universe of Autism*. Bloomington, IN: First Books.

Mukhopadhyay, Tito Rajarshi. 2011. *How Can I Talk if My Lips Don't Move? Inside My Autistic Mind*. New York: Arcade. First published 2008.

Murray, Stuart. 2008. *Representing Autism: Culture, Narrative, Fascination*. Liverpool: Liverpool University Press.

Nadesan, Majia Holmer. 2005. *Constructing Autism: Unraveling the "Truth" and Understanding the Social*. New York: Routledge.

Nordoff, Paul, and Clive Robbins. 1977. *Creative Music Therapy: Individualized Treatment for the Handicapped Child*. New York: John Day.

Ochs, Elinor, Tamar Kremer-Sadlik, Olga Solomon, and Karen Gainer Sirota. 2001. "Inclusion as Social Practice: Views of Children with Autism." *Social Development* 10 (3): 399–419.

Ochs, Elinor, Tamar Kremer-Sadlik, Karen Gainer Sirota, and Olga Solomon. 2004. "Autism and the Social World: An Anthropological Perspective." *Discourse Studies* 6 (2): 147–183.

Ochs, Elinor, Olga Solomon, and Laura Sterponi. 2005. "Limitations and Transformations of Habitus in Child-Directed Communication." *Discourse Studies* 7 (4–5): 547–583.

Osteen, Mark, ed. 2008. *Autism and Representation*. New York: Routledge.

Pavlicevic, Mercédès, and Gary Ansdell, eds. 2004. *Community Music Therapy*. London: Jessica Kingsley.

Prince, Dawn Eddings. 2010. "An Exceptional Path: An Ethnographic Narrative Reflecting on Autistic Parenthood from Evolutionary, Cultural, and Spiritual Perspectives." *Ethos* 38 (1): 56–68.

Prince-Hughes, Dawn. 2004. *Songs of the Gorilla Nation: My Journey through Autism*. New York: Harmony.

Reschke-Hernández, Alaine E. 2011. "History of Music Therapy Treatment Interventions for Children with Autism." *Journal of Music Therapy* 48 (2): 169–207.

Robison, John Elder. 2007. *Look Me in the Eye: My Life with Asperger's*. New York: Crown.

Ruud, Even. 1998. *Music Therapy: Improvisation, Communication, and Culture*. Gilsum, NH: Barcelona.

Sequenzia, Amy. 2012. "Non-Speaking, 'Low-Functioning.'" In *Loud Hands: Autistic People, Speaking*, edited by Julia Bascom, 159–161. Washington, DC: The Autistic Press/The Autistic Self Advocacy Network.

Shakespeare, Tom. 2013. "The Social Model of Disability." In *The Disability Studies Reader*, 4th ed., edited by Lennard J. Davis, 214–221. New York: Routledge.

Sheehy, Daniel E. 1992. "A Few Notions about Philosophy and Strategy in Applied Ethnomusicology." *Ethnomusicology* 36 (3): 323–336.

Shore, Stephen. 2003. *Beyond the Wall: Personal Experiences with Autism and Asperger Syndrome.* 2nd ed. Shawnee Mission, KS: Autism Asperger.

Silvers, Anita. 2010. "An Essay on Modeling: The Social Model of Disability." In *Philosophical Reflections on Disability*, edited by D. Christopher Ralston and Justin Ho, 19–36. Dordrecht, Heidelberg, London, and New York: Springer.

Siebers, Tobin. 2008. *Disability Theory*. Ann Arbor: University of Michigan Press.

Siebers, Tobin. 2013. "Disability and the Theory of Complex Embodiment—For Identity Politics in a New Register." In *The Disability Studies Reader*, 4th ed., edited by Lennard J. Davis, 278–297. New York: Routledge.

Simpson, Kate, and Deb Keen. 2011. "Music Interventions for Children with Autism: Narrative Review of the Literature." *Journal of Autism and Developmental Disorders* 41: 1507–1514.

Sirota, Karen Gainer. 2010. "Narratives of Distinction: Personal Life Narrative as a Technology of the Self in the Everyday Lives and Relational Worlds of Children with Autism." *Ethos* 38 (1): 93–115.

Solomon, Olga. 2010a. "Sense and the Senses: Anthropology and the Study of Autism." *Annual Review of Anthropology* 39: 241–259.

Solomon, Olga. 2010b. "What a Dog Can Do: Children with Autism and Therapy Dogs in Social Interaction." *Ethos* 38 (1): 143–166.

Solomon, Olga, and Nancy Bagatell. 2010. "Introduction—Autism: Rethinking the Possibilities." *Ethos* 38 (1): 1–7.

Sterponi, Laura. 2004. "Construction of Rules, Accountability and Moral Identity by High-Functioning Children with Autism." *Discourse Studies* 6 (2): 207–228.

Sterponi, Laura, and Allesandra Fasulo. 2010. "'How to Go On': Intersubjectivity and Progressivity in the Communication of a Child with Autism." *Ethos* 38 (1): 116–142.

Stige, Brynjulf. 2002. *Culture-Centered Music Therapy.* Gilsum, NH: Barcelona.

Straus, Joseph N. 2011. *Extraordinary Measures: Disability in Music.* New York: Oxford University Press.

Straus, Joseph N. 2013. "Autism as Culture." In *The Disability Studies Reader*, 4th ed., edited by Lennard J. Davis, 460–484. New York: Routledge.

Tammet, Daniel. 2007. *Born on a Blue Day: A Memoir (Inside the Extraordinary Mind of an Autistic Savant).* New York: Free Press.

Titchkosky, Tanya. 2007. *Reading and Writing Disability Differently: The Textured Life of Embodiment.* Toronto: University of Toronto Press.

Titon, Jeff Todd. 2011. "The Curry Lecture: Applied Ethnomusicology." *Sustainable Music: A Research Blog on the Subject of Sustainability and Music*, April 24. http://sustainablemusic.blogspot.com/2011/04/curry-lecture-applied-ethnomusicology.html.

Titon, Jeff Todd. 1992. "Music, the Public Interest, and the Practice of Ethnomusicology." *Ethnomusicology* 36 (3): 315–322.

Turino, Thomas. 2008. *Music as Social Life: The Politics of Participation*. Chicago: University of Chicago Press.

Vinden, Penelope G., and Janet W. Astington. 2000. "Culture and Understanding Other Minds." In *Understanding Other Minds: Perspectives from Developmental Cognitive Neuroscience*, 2nd ed., edited by Simon Baron-Cohen, Helen Tager-Flusberg, and Donald J. Cohen, 503–520. New York: Oxford University Press.

Walworth, Darcy DeLoach. 2007. "The Use of Music Therapy within the SCERTS Model for Children with Autism Spectrum Disorder." *Journal of Music Therapy* 44 (1): 2–22.

Whipple, Jennifer. 2004. "Music in Intervention for Children and Adolescents with Autism: A Meta-Analysis." *Journal of Music Therapy* 41 (2): 90–106.

Williams, Donna. 1992. *Nobody, Nowhere: The Extraordinary Autobiography of an Autistic*. New York: Harper Collins.

Winter, Penni. 2012. "Loud Hands & Loud Voices." In *Loud Hands: Autistic People, Speaking*, edited by Julia Bascom, 115–128. Washington, DC: The Autistic Press/The Autistic Self Advocacy Network.

CHAPTER 2

MUSIC, INTELLECTUAL DISABILITY, AND HUMAN FLOURISHING

LICIA CARLSON

PEOPLE with intellectual disabilities[1] have suffered multiple forms of marginalization: they have been housed on the margins of society in institutional settings, they have experienced isolation and exclusion from participation in community life because they have not conformed to society's blueprint of normalcy, and they have been relegated to the margins of personhood and defined as profoundly "other" by scholars working in a broad range of disciplines (Carlson 2010). Until recently, intellectual disability has also figured less prominently than other forms of disability in the field of Disability Studies. This is rapidly changing, as there is a burgeoning body of work that addresses this lacuna and problematizes the very meaning and nature of intellectual disability. This critical scholarship explores the experiences and perspectives of people who are labeled with a broad range of conditions that fall under the umbrella of "intellectual disability," exposes forms of oppression, and traces the powerful advocacy and self-advocacy movements that have been so central in articulating and celebrating a positive identity for people with intellectual disabilities. One question that lies at the heart of much of this work is, What does it mean for people with intellectual disabilities to flourish as human beings in a world with others? The significance of this question cannot be underestimated, as it resonates with some of the most important themes and challenges raised in Disability Studies: the concept of quality of life, the importance of acknowledging and valuing both independence and dependency, and the demand that individual, familial, social, and political conditions be met so that individuals can realize their full potential.

In this essay I explore the connections between musical experience and human flourishing. In doing so, I am interested in moving beyond a medical and therapeutic model of disability and music, beyond what Joseph Straus has termed the two "ghettos" wherein discussions of disability are typically found: abnormal psychology and music therapy (Straus 2011, 158). My interest here is not in music as a means of *curing* or *normalizing* disability; rather, it is in the ethical significance that musical experience holds for people with intellectual disabilities and those around them. In this regard, this project is also a departure from certain standard approaches to the philosophy of music. In *The Music of Our Lives*, Kathleen Higgins writes that the tendency of Western aesthetics "to treat music as an autonomous structural object and to minimize concern with the holistic character of musical experience . . . has obscured the experiential bases for recognizing music's . . . roles with respect to ethical living" (Higgins 2011, 114). Adopting a more holistic approach to musical experience, as Higgins advocates, means broadening the scope of analysis and considering various sites and forms of engagement with music. I find Christopher Small's definition of *musicking* to be particularly useful here: "To musick is to take part, in any capacity, in a musical performance, whether by performing, by listening, by rehearsing or practicing, by providing material for performance (what is called composing), or by dancing" (Small 1998, 9). In addition to recognizing that musicking can take place anywhere and can be done by anyone, Small argues, "The fundamental nature and meaning of music lie not in objects, not in musical works at all, but in action, in what people do. It is only by understanding what people do as they take part in a musical act that we can hope to understand its nature and the function it fulfills in human life" (Small 1998, 8).

In this chapter, I explore *musicking* by people with intellectual disabilities, thereby challenging a number of problematic assumptions often made about "the intellectually disabled." Specifically, I explore the significance of music in the lives of people with intellectual disabilities in two ways. The first part focuses on the value that music has for the individual; the second part traces the ways that musical experience can establish and reshape relationships. I then conclude with a brief consideration of how the intersections between music and intellectual disability can contribute to the field of Disability Studies more broadly. This critical project of bringing philosophical questions to bear on music and intellectual disability is greatly indebted to the emerging scholarship on disability and music (Straus 2011; Lerner and Straus 2006; Lubet 2011) and disability aesthetics (Siebers 2010). I share with these authors and my fellow contributors to this volume the conviction that the fields of Disability Studies, aesthetics, and I would add philosophy, stand to gain from these new alliances. These disciplines will be mutually enriched by inviting the "figure of disability" into the concert hall, the academy, the conservatory, and into everyday spaces where music is shared (Siebers 2010; Carlson 2013).

Musical Lives

Associations between intellectual disability and music can be found in many disciplinary contexts. In neuroscience, for example, researchers are examining a wide range of questions regarding music, intellectual disability, and the brain. People with various forms of intellectual disability (autism, Williams syndrome, Down syndrome) have provided the occasion to pursue a number of questions: What is the relationship between music and language? What parts of the brain are responsible for various dimensions of musical experience and performance? How does damage to one part of the brain (e.g., the left hemisphere) enhance potential or capacities in other parts of the brain? The field of music therapy has also been central in defining a new therapeutic space within which music can serve many functions for people with intellectual disabilities, including the development of motor skills, social skills, communication, cognitive skills, self-confidence, and a fuller sense of identity. Finally, "musical savants" continue to receive popular attention as, arguably, the prototypical case of music and intellectual disability, "enshrining them as a species of 'super-crip,' people whose unusual ability in one narrow area has enabled them to transcend their general disability" (Straus 2014).

Yet these approaches to music and intellectual disability, in addition to perpetuating a model of disability that considers "the intellectually disabled" as abnormal and/or as an exceptional curiosity, do not explicitly address ethical questions regarding how music shapes the lives of people with intellectual disability and how it may contribute to their flourishing and to the very possibility of a *good life*. As a philosopher, I am particularly interested in exploring these questions because the assumption that people with intellectual disabilities are incapable of living even "minimally satisfying lives" is so widespread in philosophical discourse (Carlson, 2010). Thus, by considering the ways that music "facilitates a sense of selfhood" and enables expression and the capacity for "musical joy" (Higgins 2011, 120), I hope to provide an antidote to these attenuated philosophical portraits of intellectual disability. Kathleen Higgins says that while music is often connected to the idea of self-*transcendence* (i.e., it allows us to transcend ourselves, to escape or move beyond ourselves), little attention has been paid to the relationship between music and self-*awareness*. In response to this, she identifies three aspects of selfhood that emerge through music: it reveals my existence as a temporal, embodied, and vital being (Higgins 2011, 120–121). If we consider the emergence of musical selfhood in the context of intellectual disability, a picture emerges that challenges assumptions that have been made about people with intellectual disabilities: that they do not have a meaningful sense of self, that intellectual disability is a static condition, and that having an intellectual disability necessarily means a diminished quality of life.

Crip Time, Musical Time

There are a number of ways that the experience of disability can affect one's temporal existence. Philosopher Susan Wendell has argued that, in addition to all of the other ways that our society is structured around the nondisabled "normal" body, time is structured according to norms as well. For example, many people with disabilities may not be able to complete tasks in what is considered an appropriate time, and this can impact their ability to work and partake in activities in ways that are expected (Wendell 1996).[2] Moreover, living with a disability may affect the experience of one's life course, of the broader trajectory on which one maps out the future. Depending on the nature of the disability, the experience of time may be radically transformed by the treatments one may have to undergo, and the concept of "life expectancy" may be affected in distinct ways. Finally, the ways in which intellectual disability has been defined are temporally articulated according to developmental norms. The very term *mental retardation* suggests that the process of normal development has been slowed, and the practice of classifying people with intellectual disability according to "mental age" as opposed to chronological age is another example of how temporal norms intersect with definitions of disability.

An interesting example of the juxtaposition between normative, chronological time and musical time can be found in researchers' descriptions of the musicality and "rhythmicity" of people with Williams syndrome. Levitin and Bellugi observe that people with this relatively rare congenital condition "appear to be more engaged than normal subjects" and demonstrate a high degree of rhythmic engagement and musicality (Levitin and Bellugi 1998, 375). People with Williams syndrome exceed not only the expectations that researchers have of them given their cognitive "deficiencies" (often expressed in terms of their "mental age"), but they outperform the "normal" subjects. While I say more about the musical lives of people with Williams syndrome later, I introduce this particular study here because it provides a good example of how the "normal listener" (or in this case "normal participant") is constructed in the process of researching musical cognition (Straus 2011). This discourse, informed by the medical model, highlights the dissonance between normal/nondisabled and abnormal/disabled subject, and also between mental age/cognitive ability and musical ability.

While the experience of disability may be defined in negative terms when people fail to live according to what is considered to be *normal time*, the temporal dimensions of living with a disability can have powerful positive consequences as well. In her book *Feminist, Queer, Crip*, Alison Kafer asks, "What would it mean to explore disability in time or to articulate 'crip time'?", and devotes a chapter to mapping out a broad range of intersections between disability and temporality (Kafer 2013). What might happen if we transpose "crip time" into a musical key? If people with disabilities experience their lives temporally in distinct ways, how might this be relevant to Higgins's recognition that, "As a listener [of music] I am a temporal being?" (Higgins 2011, 120).

In some instances, terms that have a negative connotation in relation to disability may take on a new meaning in a musical context. Consider the term *retardation*. In analyzing Heinrich Schenker's discussion of the musical work through the lens of disability, Straus highlights the important roles that blockages and obstacles can play within the musical work. Here he quotes Schenker: "'In the art of music, as in life, motion toward the goal encounters obstacles, reverses, disappointments, and involves great distances, detours, expansions, interpolations, and, in short, retardations of all kinds'" (Straus 2011, 118). In recasting musical terms in the context of disability, and by repositioning terms often associated with disability in a musical setting, new linguistic and metaphorical possibilities may emerge that may provide a kind of "reverse discourse," a new musical lexicon for Disability Studies.

If we move from the discursive to the phenomenological, there are important ways in which music can also transform the *experience* of time. In his discussion of the phenomenology of music in "Musical Presence: Towards a New Philosophy of Music," Charles Ford explains what makes music distinctive, temporally, in comparison with the other arts:

> Music is the only art that forms time through sound, and then so much so that listeners' intentional time *becomes* that of music. In Hegel's words, music thereby "penetrates the self, grips it in its simplest being."... But, this "gripping," rather than being inner and individual and "expressing feelings," frees us from the fragile limits of the individual ego, delivering us over to the collective anonymity of musical style, whilst perhaps also resounding the collective anonymity of the nonconceptual world. (Ford 2010)

In the act of listening, one marks the passage of musical time, taking up a new rhythm of existence and experiencing time in a way that is distinct from the temporal demands and markers that dictate daily activities and functions. This can be liberating for people with disabilities whose bodies and abilities may not conform to dominant temporal expectations.

Consider the example of Sesha, a woman with profound disabilities whose "mental age" does not correspond with her chronological age (she is now in her 40s). In speaking about his experience of listening to music by Beethoven with his daughter, Jeffrey Kittay writes: "To make a special occasion with Sesha is to put on one of her favorites and sit next to her to listen. She is rejoicing to the music, we are visibly rejoicing at her pleasure and our redoubled appreciation of the music as we listen to it through her, and she is elated as she sees her musical pleasure shared and validated by those closest to her, so that she is not alone in these feelings both deeply held and finely wrought." (Kittay 2008; Carlson 2013). This description resonates with my own musical introduction to intellectual disability. As an undergraduate in Poughkeepsie, New York, I volunteered in a classroom for children labeled "multiply handicapped," and we spent much of our time listening to music together. We not only were moved by the music but also moved with it in a shared temporal landscape, achieving a synchrony in our embodied responses that brought us together in ways that verbal communication could not. This was not a therapeutic endeavor with a set goal; rather than being directed at teaching, normalizing, or cultivating particular skills, this musical experience unfolded organically and was valuable and valued for its own sake.

Partaking in musical time together happens in musical performance as well. In playing in an ensemble, the individual's experience of marking time becomes a part of the rhythm and tempo of the piece, enveloping each participant into a greater temporal whole. In some cases it may be less rigid, allowing individual players to mark their own rhythmic time and move to a distinct, improvised musical beat. For individuals who may otherwise be assumed to lack such capabilities, or for whom normative demands don't allow them to realize these creative modes of expression, this experience can be transformative. In his chapter in this volume, Michael Bakan describes the ways that musical performance through the ARTISM project enables performers with autism to move beyond normative expectations: "I believe that people with autism are not necessarily any less spontaneous, intuitive, flexible, or improvisatory than other people are; rather, they appear to be that way because they are almost invariably forced to contend with life situations and settings in which their particular attributes and preferences for expressing spontaneity, intuition, flexibility, and improvisational ability are demeaned, or are patronized, or go unacknowledged or unrecognized altogether by their interlocutors." Thus, in the act of performing music together, people can inhabit a *shared* temporal landscape. This may offer forms of connection and expression for individuals who, according to other normative measures, would not "share time" in this way.

"Music is my favorite way of thinking"

The capacity for engaging with music also raises questions about the adequacy of current models that measure cognitive ability. Rather than assuming that the experience of music by people with intellectual disability is a purely affective, emotional response, such experiences may, in fact, involve certain cognitive capacities that were otherwise assumed to be lacking in these individuals. As I indicated earlier, there has been considerable attention paid to individuals with Williams syndrome, as they seem to possess a striking collection of musical abilities and an appreciation for music. Williams syndrome is a congenital genetic condition that affects about 1 in 10,000 individuals. Though these individuals often exhibit significant intellectual disabilities (and relatively low IQ scores), they also have sophisticated linguistic and musical abilities that have become the focus of a number of researchers interested in music and the brain (Levitin and Bellugi 1998; Lenhoff et al. 1997; Sacks 2007). In their study of individuals with Williams syndrome, Levitin and Bellugi argue that the existence of musicality, rhythmic ability, perfect pitch, and other musical traits indicates that they possess a form of "musical intelligence," one of the eight kinds of intelligence proposed by psychologist Howard Gardner in his theory of multiple intelligences: "The profile of abilities we found in subjects with Williams syndrome supports Gardner's theory that musical ability constitutes a separate faculty and is to a large degree uncorrelated with other aspects of cognitive functioning" (Levitin and Bellugi 1998, 380–381; the reference is to Gardner 1999). Howard Lenhoff, a retired biologist whose study of music and Williams syndrome was inspired by his daughter Gloria, a talented singer who has received national attention, echoes this conviction that people with Williams syndrome possess cognitive abilities that would otherwise be obscured or untapped without the experience of music: "I don't call them retarded. I call them mentally asymmetric. Williams people have a real musical intelligence, often surpassing that of normal individuals. Many other mentally handicapped populations might have untapped potentials waiting to be discovered, if only researchers, and society, would take the time and trouble to look for and cultivate them" (Sforza 2006, 255).

From the vantage point of Disability Studies, there are a number of critical questions that this research raises. First, the very notion of testing and measuring "intelligence" as a reified concept is problematic and has been critiqued by Disability Studies scholars (Carlson 2010).[3] Second, some of the attention that has been given to individuals like Gloria is consistent with the super-crip and savant narratives that run the risk of further *othering* people with disabilities and contributing to their "enfreakment" (Straus 2014; Sforza 2006).[4]

Yet in recognizing the significance of musical experience for people with Williams syndrome, one need not fall prey to either tendency (i.e., to reify yet another form of intelligence or to perpetuate the problematic figure of the "idiot savant"). To view music in the narrowest terms as simply a new kind of litmus test for a particular form of intelligence, exceptionality, or abnormality is to miss the greater sense in which musical experience is a form of flourishing for people with Williams syndrome. It is not only extremely talented individuals with Williams syndrome who possess a high degree of musicality; the fact that music is a source of joy, community, and engagement for so many is confirmed not just by scientists but also by family members, friends, and by the individuals themselves. In the words of one of the participants of "Music & Minds" summer music program, which has become the Berkshire Hills Music Academy, a post-secondary program devoted to cultivating music through an integrated curriculum for people with intellectual disability in Lenox, Massachusetts: "Music is my favorite way of thinking" (Levitin and Bellugi 1998).[5]

The language of music also affords people with intellectual disabilities new modes of expression though performance and composition. In speaking about his son, composer Hikari Oe, who was born with significant disabilities, Nobel prize–winning author Kenzaburo Oe writes,

> If Hikari had not composed, he would surely never have been able at any time in his life to convey the rich, profound, crystalline and radiant message contained in this music. For our part, had Hikari not composed, we would have never realized, nor would we have been able even to imagine, that he possessed this sensibility. The scope of what we might have gained from this world and understood of it would have been significantly narrowed. I feel we would have missed gaining an insight into some of the most important and humble aspects of the meaning of human life. (Oe 1994; see also Carlson 2013)

Hikari Oe is considered a musical savant by many, and so one might attribute his forms of musical expression to his talent. Yet there are many individuals with intellectual disabilities, who would not qualify as "savants," for whom music is a mode of communication and expression. In the documentary *Praying with Lior* (Trachtman 2007), Lior Liebling, a boy with Down syndrome who is preparing for his Bar Mitzvah, expresses himself through singing and davening, a form of Jewish prayer. The power of the sung word is not only the basis for his deep connection with God but also a way of maintaining a connection with his beloved mother, who died when he was young. Through music, Lior's capacities for self-expression, memory, and spirituality flourish. Kevin Finn, whose daughter Meghan attended the camp in Lenox, Massachusetts, puts it this way: "It's like music is their language—the sound of music is their way of thinking and feeling" (Sforza 2006, 255). In Meghan's own words: "Music is a huge part of my life. To me music is like soup: music comes down your throat and feels so warm. So music is like soup. It tastes good" (Sforza 2006, 193).

Dynamism and Musical Joy

Music affords the possibility of recognizing oneself and others as temporal, embodied, creative, and expressive beings. And as Meghan's description earlier illustrates, musical experience confirms our own vitality as human beings: "Music, simultaneously engaging our physical, emotional, and intellectual receptivities, makes us feel fully alive. The dynamism of music, moreover, reminds us of our own dynamism" (Higgins 2011, 121). The animating power of music is reflected in a broad range of musical experiences that people with and without intellectual disabilities have. And this dynamism challenges certain assumptions and stereotypes about disability. Historically, a static portrait of intellectual disability has been perpetuated in multiple ways (including a broad range of scientific, psychological, and pedagogical incarnations.) This persistent view of people with intellectual disabilities as in a state of arrested development, of extreme passivity and incapacity, has contributed to their dehumanization and has justified many of the cruel and violent forms of treatment to which they have been subjected (Trent 1994; Carlson 2010).[6] Through musical experience, people with a broad range of intellectual disabilities have the opportunity, whether through listening or performing, to actively engage, to enact and simultaneously reveal dynamic modes of being. Describing the summer residential program Music & Minds for children with Williams syndrome, Reis et al., explain, "The majority of parents indicated that their son or daughter displayed an unusual affinity with and love for music and interpreted this joy in music as an important factor in the personal happiness that would be achieved in life. 'For my son, life without music is life without heart and joy,' one parent explained. Parents of eight other participants used language that echoed this sentiment." In the words of Charles, one of the participants, "Music is my life" (Reis et al. 2000).

Attending to the significance of music for people with intellectual disabilities, then, can reveal a number of important dimensions of their lives: music can "call forth the self" (Sacks 2007, 346) in ways that might otherwise have been left obscure or unnoticed and can foster the cultivation of particular capacities and forms of joy that may contribute to the individual's flourishing (Carlson 2013). This is evident in the profiles of band members of groups like interPLAY, Flame, and Heavy Load, all of which include musicians with intellectual disabilities. Their performances embody the power that music has to harness freedom and creativity and are imbued with energy, engagement, and vitality.[7] As Roberta B. Hochberg, an interPLAY board member, says, "You cannot help but be profoundly affected by watching the joy on the faces of the band members when they play and then receive positive feedback from the audience" (Weeks 2010).

In demonstrating the ways they are able to connect with their fellow band members and audiences, these musicians highlight the social nature of musicking. This points to an equally important dimension of their musical lives: the fact that they are experienced in the presence of others. Higgins writes,

> Music's appeal to our physical nature gives us a very immediate sense of enjoyably sharing our world with others. This sense of sharing is ethically beneficial in that it makes it difficult to consider others' experience alien to our own. In fact, we feel that others' living experience is in this case actually our own. . . . We rejoice beyond ourselves in musical experience. I cannot think of a better basis for ethical concern" (Higgins 2011, 128)

It is to the nature of these relationships forged through music that I now turn.

Transposing Relationships between Selves and Others

Philosopher of disability Anita Silvers opens her article "From the Crooked Timber of Humanity, Beautiful Things Can be Made" with two images: in the foreground she sees her friend who was born with certain physical, visible disabilities; behind her friend, Picasso's painting of a face. She provides a lengthy description of the similarities between the cubist portrait and her friend's disfigured appearance, confessing: "I am drawn to dwell on the face in the painting, yet my eyes avert from the real face, even though it is closer to me. . . . By looking away rather than seeing my friend, I make her invisible. While doing so, I condemn myself for joining in a visual practice that sustains the stigma our culture imposes on impaired bodies" (Silvers 2000, 197).

The question that motivates her subsequent reflections is this: "Why do we see the corporeal anomalies configured into Picasso's rendition of the human face as being beautiful but perceive my friend's facial anomalies as an unfortunate disability?" (Silvers 2000, 205). Put another way, "Why does the normal hold so much less sway in art than in life? We see a painted face in cubist style as beautiful, but see a similarly configured fleshly face as deviant" (Silvers 2000, 216). In developing her answer to these questions, she argues for the transformative and ethical power of art: "Art has a positive transfigurative—almost a redemptive—effect on configurations we otherwise would apprehend as being ugly. . . . Art can make impairment powerful." Thus she considers the possibility that enlarging "our aesthetic responsiveness to real people . . . would enlarge our moral capacities" (Silvers 2000, 206, 215).

Silvers's discussion prompts a number of responses. First, it is not certain that everyone *does* experience Picasso's paintings as beautiful, and art may not make impairment powerful, or beautiful for that matter, for all who experience it. Second, the question of how impairment functions in a work of art, as opposed to in a live exchange between two individuals, is worthy of further consideration and raises questions about disability, impairment, and forms of representation. Finally, there may well be numerous *dis*analogies between Silvers's discussion of beauty, impairment, and art and the connections I am drawing between music and intellectual disability. However, I think her questions can be applied in a musical context: How can musical experience "reform exclusionary practices" that currently contribute to the devaluation of intellectually disabled people? And how might music serve to expand the moral imagination and transform the relationship between self and other? I will first consider the relationship between people with intellectual disabilities and nondisabled others and then move beyond this binary to consider how music establishes certain kinds of relationships more generally.[8]

There are many musical relationships between individuals with and without disabilities, and music can function in distinct ways in each of these. One might think most immediately of the ways that music functions in a therapeutic context and serves as a basis for the interaction between client and therapist. Yet it can also play a part in other capacities that are not explicitly therapeutic but that are meant to enhance both the individual's quality of life and the relationships they have with others. For example, in the activity of caregiving, Jeffrey Kittay speaks about how music might serve as a means of structuring certain forms of care and shape the auditory environment in ways that are beneficial to individuals with profound disabilities (Kittay 2008; Carlson 2013).

Higgins argues that music also "trains our capacity for empathy." While empathy is clearly important in caregiving, Higgins considers it in a broader sense. First, she says it teaches us to adopt a nondefensive and noncompetitive stance toward others. Thus, the "enjoyment of music involves the experience of taking satisfaction in a state of mind in which one does not oppose oneself to other human beings" (Higgins 2011, 129). In the context of disability, this might mean the transgression of expected roles and boundaries, particularly in cases where an individual with a disability has been considered to be only the passive recipient of care rather than an active agent. In speaking about the transformative power of art, philosopher Amy Mullin explains, "Art can start an encounter with another, and it can destabilize our terms of reference governing that encounter. To this extent it may enhance the possibilities that we will emerge from that encounter with changed beliefs and attitudes—but we cannot predict where those changes will take us" (Mullin 2000, 132). Though Mullin is speaking about the visual arts, her point applies to music as well. Musical encounters can be transformative insofar as they can move beyond perceptions of alterity and establish the ground for a shared world wherein a new model of the relationship between self and other emerges: one that is reciprocal rather than one-sided. In the case of disabled performers and composers, the nondisabled listener becomes the recipient of their gifts; in the case of listening together, the experience of hearing a piece may be transformed by listening to it *with* another; and in the case of playing and singing together, disabled and nondisabled individuals are equal participants in the creation of music (Carlson 2013).

Higgins says that music also "affords a ground for empathy with particular others" because it "creates intimacy" (Higgins 2011, 130). This idea is particularly intriguing in cases where barriers prevent individuals with disabilities from connecting with others. These barriers might include the perception of an individual with an intellectual disability as radically "other," various obstacles to communication (for example in persons who are nonverbal), and social and structural barriers that prevent such relationships from being forged. Musical relationships can be transformative in that they overcome such obstacles and provide the possibility of finding new grounds of commonality. Higgins states, "One listens to music, not as lover, lawyer, or mother, but as a human being, and one relates to other listeners as human beings like oneself. This kinship is not grounded on the relatively contingent fact of occupying roles that are similar to or linked with those of other individuals. Instead it is built on sharing the freedom of imagination that enables one to feel empathy with the movement of tones, the simultaneous bodily response to stimuli that one receives without inhibition" (Higgins 2011, 132). The notion that certain roles and identities fall away in musical experience is an intriguing one, particularly in cases where music provides the basis for participation in a shared activity between individuals who might lack other means of establishing a connection.

Yet I do not agree that we must necessarily check all dimensions of ourselves at the door when engaging in a musical encounter. In fact, part of the power of exploring music in the context of disability is to recognize ways in which music and disability are performed together by uniquely embodied individuals. Just as music can call forth the self as a dynamic, temporal being, musical experience can *enable* and enact disability in unique, interesting, and positive ways. This may be in the form of "disablist hearing," like autistic, blind, or deaf hearing (Straus 2011), or through the many examples of musically performing disability contained within the chapters of this volume. Musicking is fully a part of our embodied existence.

Musical experience and relationships can also provide the occasion to cultivate certain virtues like appreciation and reverence. While these can be directed at the performers, composer, or the music itself, Higgins recognizes that in the process of valuing and gaining joy from musical experience, the possibility of a deeper appreciation for *others* in general can be developed. She characterizes this reverence for music as a "contagious and expansive emotion" that has ethical value because of what it can generate: "One values another person more for being sensitive to aesthetic experience. One becomes momentarily attuned to the other person's inner life. One realizes that . . . he or she remains vulnerable to being moved. Such vulnerability is precious for its contribution to the person's own life, but it is also a precondition for openness toward others" (Higgins 2011, 135). The idea of an individual *vulnerable to being moved* radically shifts the conception of vulnerability that is so often associated with people with intellectual disabilities. Vulnerability has been typically linked to dependency, to a lack of autonomy and self-possession, and to the features of a more infantile and hence precarious existence.

Yet to say one is vulnerable to being moved is to recognize a responsive power, an active capacity within a person whose subjectivity is brought out in the act of being moved by a piece of music.

In his book *Receiving the Gift of Friendship*, theologian Hans Reinders argues that it is not enough to ensure that the rights of people with intellectual disabilities are recognized. In order for them to lead full lives, to flourish as human beings, they are in need of the "gift of friendship." He writes,

> Rights certainly create new opportunities by opening up institutional space, and they are extremely important in that capacity; in creating new opportunities, they affect our lives as citizens. But disabled people, just like other people, are human beings before they are citizens: to live a human life, properly so called, they must not merely be included in our institutions and have access to our public spaces; they must also be included in other people's lives, not only by natural familial necessity but by choice. . . . Friendship is special because it is freely chosen. Our friends want us as friends for our own sake. No other relationships, either professional or kinship, can give what friendship gives. (Reinders 2008, 5)

Is it possible to draw connections between the nature of friendship and the kinds of relationships that are established through musicking? And might these hold promise for people with intellectual disabilities?

Sharing music is one way to partake in community, to establish and engage in a particular form of *being-with*, and to enrich our human lives. This is especially significant for people with intellectual disabilities who have been excluded or marginalized within ableist society. Insofar as music provides a basis for connecting with others, it may have what Higgins has called a "humanizing" effect, a phenomenon worthy of attention in view of the multiple forms of dehumanization that people with intellectual disabilities have endured. This musical attunement to the "other" can come in a variety of forms: in the act of listening together, through joint participation in a musical performance, and in the relationship between audience and performer. What is significant about these moments is that they can disrupt the expected *asymmetry* in a relationship between the "nondisabled" and "disabled"; there is a shared experience that is centered on a third term, one in which the traditional binaries and imbalances may be erased.

Yet there is also value in moving beyond the designations of disabled/nondisabled altogether when considering music and intellectual disability. Almost all of the ensembles that I have referenced here are collaborative projects that include individuals with and without disabilities; thus it is equally important to explore the nature of their experience *as musicians* rather than remaining ensconced in the able/disabled binary. In theorizing about relationships between individuals, in reflecting on the power of *being-with* in a musical context, new roles and identities may emerge as rich models for Disability Studies scholarship. These might include the virtues of generosity, openness, respect, and tolerance that underlie the relationship between audience and performer; the distinct forms of knowledge necessary for musical improvisation and collaboration among musicians; and the examples of nonverbal expression and communication that take place among cocreators of a musical performance.

Finally, in thinking about musical relationships in the context of disability, there is a parallel between what Reinders says about friendship and what I am arguing about musical experience. The examples I have examined speak to the value of music *in itself*, rather than as a means to some other end. When music is chosen freely and for its own sake, as Reinders says friends are chosen, it contributes to the depth and value of shared human experience, and allows both musical encounters and musical lives to flourish. This is why it is so important that people with intellectual disabilities be given a broad range of musical opportunities *beyond* the clinic and the research lab. And it is here that discussions of flourishing and art intersect with ethical questions of justice and access (Carlson 2013; Wong 2010).

Conclusion: Music, Intellectual Disability, and Disability Studies

The forms of marginalization that many people with intellectual disabilities experience are not limited to the social sphere; there are also ways in which these patterns of exclusion are repeated within Disability Studies itself. While there has been increasing attention paid to various forms of intellectual disabilities within the purview of Disability Studies, there is still room for this interdisciplinary field to continue to expand and make itself more inclusive. In this vein, inquiring further into the varied and complex intersections between music and intellectual disabilities may prove instructive and fruitful.

Taking music or the aesthetic as a starting point in addressing intellectual disabilities may generate new ways of talking about the experience of disability. For example, new metaphors, analogies, and models may be found in the complexities and mysteries of the musical work, and in the nature and range of musical relationships (e.g., the relation between performers and between performer and audience). Speaking differently about intellectual disability may in turn allow it to be reimagined in the way that Silvers says art can expand the moral imagination. Recognizing the significance of music can also point out the limitations of theoretical models currently in use. In the context of moral philosophy, Higgins writes, "Music's value to philosophical ethics is to remind it of aspects of our ethical experience that are forgotten in other models" (Higgins 2011, 163). This might be articulated in terms of Disability Studies as well, as one considers how the musical lives of people with intellectual disabilities may challenge, expand, and enrich the current models of disability.

Many of the issues I have explored in this chapter also introduce certain questions and tensions that disability scholars must address. First, when considering musical intelligence and explanations of musical cognition and perception, what place should studies on music and the brain have in Disability Studies? On the one hand, there are very good reasons to resist the medical model of disability and approaches to music and disability that simply reify intelligence and perpetuate essentialist definitions of disability and problematic categories of the "normal" and "abnormal." However, there may be important ways in which scientific research on musical perception can also challenge existing assumptions about intellectual disability, replace older problematic definitions of intelligence with more capacious and varied models, and open up new and fruitful paths of inquiry. Second, there is a tension between eschewing the very categories of disabled/nondisabled in the process of recognizing the nature and value of shared musical experience and preserving these designations so that "disablist" forms of musical expression and listening may be defined, explored, and celebrated. Given the heterogeneity of the very category of "intellectual disability" (Carlson 2010), there is also the question of whether any generalizations specific to particular kinds of intellectual disability (e.g., autism, Williams syndrome, Down syndrome) can or should be made when making claims about music. What *does* seem certain is that there is far more work to be done to foster the development of musical lives, to learn from and celebrate these forms of musical experience, and to critically analyze the barriers that prevent them from being recognized and realized.

Finally, paying attention to musicking, to the varied ways and places in which music is performed, composed, and experienced, is a reminder that the lived experience of music is distinct from theorizing and philosophizing about it. The French existentialist philosopher Gabriel Marcel, in speaking about the significance that music had for him, said, "In conditions that can only remain mysterious, music has always been for me, in the course of this hectic philosophical quest I have pursued, a permanent guarantee of that reality that I was attempting to reach by the arid paths of pure reflection" (Marcel 2005, 17). There is always the danger that the fullness and complexity of lived musical lives will be diminished in the process of trying to give voice to them in theoretical works. This concern is particularly salient for people with intellectual disabilities, who have so often been *spoken about* and *spoken for* rather than being given the opportunity to speak for themselves. Just as the totality of the musical work cannot be reduced to the score or to any single performance of it (Ingarden 1989), the lived, embodied experience of people with disabilities cannot be contained within labels and categories. Attempts to explain, analyze, and define both music *and* disability often call attention to the limits of language and the inadequacy of conceptual models. Perhaps in bringing music and disability together, new dimensions of this challenge will be taken up by critical disability scholars, philosophers, and music theorists alike, and more inclusive musical spaces may be created.

Musical communities can be temporary or permanent, large and small, improvised or well defined, professional or casual, with permeable, dynamic, or fixed boundaries. The vast range of musical encounters and relationships that can be established may serve as a basis for rethinking the very nature of community and the meaning of access and inclusion. In speaking about the group interPLAY, the Scottish tympanist Evelyn Glennie, who is deaf, said that a band for people with cognitive disabilities is about inclusion not exclusion: "Society cannot continue to disable themselves through their need to categorize people or make assumptions as to another individual's abilities. . . . The human body and mind are tremendous forces that are continually amazing scientists and society. Therefore, we have no choice but to keep an open mind as to what the human being can achieve" (Weeks 2010). For people with intellectual disabilities who have experienced stigmatized and isolated identities, the possibility of sharing their musical lives with others, in whatever form, may prove to be fertile ground in which friendships and social connections can grow and flourish. In this way, attention to music might "reform exclusionary practices" both within and beyond the field of Disability Studies, and generate new modes of solidarity, community, and flourishing.

Acknowledgments

I thank all of the contributors to this volume, whose careful and thoughtful suggestions were invaluable. I am especially grateful to Joseph Straus, Stephanie Jensen-Moulton, and Blake Howe for organizing the wonderful authors' conference and for their insights and editorial wisdom in bringing this project to fruition.

Notes

1. The category "intellectual disability" is, of course, a varied and complex one and by no means straightforward. In invoking it here, my focus is primarily on those individuals who have been diagnosed as having some form of cognitive and/or developmental impairment. However, I do not view the terms and categories that accompany a diagnosis of "intellectual disability" as essential, nor do I wish to reify "intelligence" in any way. I also want to acknowledge that, though I include examples of autism, many individuals with autism are not classified as "intellectually disabled."
2. Disability scholar Tanya Titchkosky examines this phenomenon in the context of university life in Titchkosky 2010.
3. It is worth noting that Gardner himself rejects any kind of essentialist account of intelligence (Gardner 1999).
4. Even the description on the front and back book jacket on *The Strangest Song*, a wonderfully rich book about Gloria, Williams syndrome, and music more broadly, states: "Since she can't read music, each note is stored in her brain, which is only 80 percent as large as yours or mine. . . . Williams syndrome . . . exacts an enormous toll on body, brain and personality. The result is an atypical body, a profoundly asymmetrical mind, and often an amazing talent for music" (Sforza 2006).
5. See http://www.berkshirehills.org/student-life/student-stories.html.
6. I cannot help but think of the images of institutions like Willowbrook, where inmates were deprived all forms of human contact and modes of expression or enjoyment that might have enabled forms of expression that would directly contradict and challenge the diagnoses they had been given.

7. See http://www.friendshipcircle.org/blog/2013/03/08/5-amazing-bands-who-look-beyond-their-disabilities/.
8. Two notes about my use of the "disabled"/"nondisabled" categories. First, I do not mean to attribute any essentialist meaning to them. Second, I have deliberately referred to the "nondisabled" individual as *other* here to reverse the more common designation of "the disabled as other."

References

Carlson, Licia. 2010. *The Faces of Intellectual Disability: Philosophical Reflections*. Bloomington: Indiana University Press.

Carlson, Licia. 2013. "Musical Becoming: Intellectual Disability and the Transformative Power of Music." In *Foundations of Disability Studies*, edited by Matthew Wappett and Katrina Arndt. New York: Palgrave Macmillan.

Ford, Charles. 2010. "Musical Presence: Towards a New Philosophy of Music." *Contemporary Aesthetics* 8. http://www.contempaesthetics.org/newvolume/pages/article.php?articleID=582.

Gardner, Howard. 1999. *Intelligence Reframed: Multiple Intelligences for the 21st Century*. New York: Basic Books.

Higgins, Kathleen Marie. 2011. *The Music of Our Lives*. Lanham, MD: Lexington Books.

Ingarden, Roman. 1989. *Ontology of the Work of Art*. Athens: University of Ohio Press.

Kafer, Alison. 2013. *Feminist, Queer, Crip*. Bloomington: Indiana University Press.

Kittay, Jeffrey. 2008. "The Sound Surround: Exploring How One Might Design the Everyday Soundscape for the Truly Captive Audience." *Nordic Journal of Music Therapy* 17 (1): 41–54.

Lenhoff, Howard, P. P. Wang, F. Greenberg, and U. Bellugi. 1997. "Williams Syndrome and the Brain." *Scientific American* 277: 68–73.

Lerner, Neil, and Joseph N. Straus, eds. 2006. *Sounding Off: Theorizing Disability in Music*. New York: Routledge.

Levitin, Daniel, and Ursula Bellugi. 1998. "Musical Abilities in Individuals with Williams Syndrome." *Music Perception* 15 (4): 357–389.

Lubet, Alex. 2011. *Music, Disability, and Society*. Philadelphia: Temple University Press.

Marcel, Gabriel. 2005. *Music and Philosophy*. Translated by Stephen Maddux and Robert E. Wood. Milwaukee, WI: Marquette University Press.

Mullin, Amy. 2000. "Art, Understanding, and Political Change." *Hypatia* 15 (3): 113–139.

Oe, Hikari. 1994. *The Music of Hikari Oe*. Vol. 1. Denon CO-78952, compact disc.

Reinders, Hans. 2008. *Receiving the Gift of Friendship: Profound Disability, Theological Anthropology, and Ethics*. Grand Rapids, MI: Eerdmans.

Reis, Sally M., Robin Schader, Laurie Shute, Audrey Don, Harry Milne, Robert Stevens, and Greg Williams. 2000. "Williams Syndrome: A Study of Unique Musical Talents in Persons with Disabilities." *National Research Center on the Gifted and Talented Newsletter*. Accessed December 30, 2013. http://www.gifted.uconn.edu/general/faculty/reis/Williams_Syndrome.html.

Sacks, Oliver. 2007. *Musicophilia: Tales of Music and the Brain*. New York: Vintage.

Sforza, Teri, with Howard Lenhoff and Sylvia Lenhoff. 2006. *The (Strangest) Song: One Father's Quest to Help His Daughter Find Her Voice*. Amherst, NY: Prometheus Books.

Siebers, Tobin. 2010. *Disability Aesthetics*. Ann Arbor: University of Michigan Press.

Silvers, Anita. 2000. "From the Crooked Timber of Humanity, Beautiful Things Can be Made." In *Beauty Matters*, edited by Peg Zeglin Brand, 197–222. Bloomington: Indiana University Press.

Small, Christopher. 1998. *Musicking: The Meanings of Performing and Listening*. Middletown, CT: Wesleyan University Press.

Straus, Joseph. 2011. *Extraordinary Measures: Disability in Music*. New York: Oxford University Press.

Straus, Joseph. 2014. "Idiots Savants, Retarded Savants, Talented Aments, Mono-Savants, Autistic Savants, Just Plain Savants, People with Savant Syndrome, and Autistic People Who Are Good at Things: A View from Disability Studies." *Disability Studies Quarterly* 34 (3).

Titchkosky, Tanya. 2010. "The Not-Yet-Time of Disability in the Bureaucratization of University Life." *Disability Studies Quarterly* 30 (3/4). http://dsq-sds.org/article/view/1295/1331.

Trachtman, Ilana (director). (2007) 2009. *Praying with Lior*. First Run Features, DVD.

Trent, James. 1994. *Inventing the Feeble Mind: A History of Mental Retardation in the United States*. Berkeley: University of California Press.

Weeks, Linton. 2010. "Enabling the Disabled to Play Sweet Music." NPR, November 26. http://www.npr.org/2010/11/18/131413172/enabling-the-disabled-to-play-sweet-music.

Wendell, Susan. 1996. *The Rejected Body: Feminist Philosophical Reflections on Disability*. New York: Routledge.

Wong, Sophia. 2010. "Duties of Justice to Citizens with Cognitive Disabilities." In *Cognitive Disability and Its Challenge to Moral Philosophy*, edited by Eva Kittay and Licia Carlson, 127–146. Malden, MA: Wiley-Blackwell.

CHAPTER 3

IMAGINED HEARING

Music-Making in Deaf Culture

JEANNETTE DIBERNARDO JONES

HEARING is something many musicians take for granted. Few hearing musicians stop to consider what it might mean to hear deafly. As hearing musicians increasingly become aware of the physiological experience of deaf bodies, hearing deafly is something that all types of bodies can do. Yet musicians and listeners can also participate in hearing Deafly, with a capital D that signals the cultural minority of those with hearing loss, as we become more aware of the political implications of the history and language of Deaf culture.[1]

"DEAF PEOPLE CAN DO ANYTHING, EXCEPT HEAR"

In the spring of 1988, students, faculty, and alumni gathered on the lawn of Gallaudet University, the only Deaf liberal arts university in the United States, to protest the election of a hearing candidate to the university presidency. Beyond the campus, the Deaf community across the country rallied against not only the hearing president-elect but also hearing members of the Board of Trustees. With forceful cheers in American Sign Language, "Deaf President Now!" (DPN), the protest—sometimes referred to as the "Gallaudet Revolution"—was highly visible and achieved all of its demands. In what became a pivotal moment in Deaf history, protesters borrowed a banner from the civil rights movement: "We still have a dream!" (Barnartt and Scotch 2001, 199–201; Garey and Hott 2007). Jack R. Gannon (1989), who had observed the protest, writes, "The world deaf community looks to Gallaudet for leadership, for innovation, for hope, and inspiration. If there could not be a deaf president here, at Gallaudet, at this time, then where, and when? There was no turning back. As I listened and watched, I finally understood what the world would come to understand—the Gallaudet students could not lose" (10).

Today the 1988 Gallaudet protest is a highlight in Deaf historical consciousness. For the Deaf community, the DPN movement came to symbolize its rejection of nearly two hundred years of paternalism perpetuated by hearing medical and educational professionals (Jankowski 1997, 132–135).[2] Most culturally Deaf people are familiar with the words of I. King Jordan, who became the first Deaf president of Gallaudet University in the aftermath of the protest: "Deaf people can do anything, except hear." The phrase has been a mantra of empowerment since the Gallaudet protest. Deaf Pride draws its rhetoric from the "can" language of this phrase with such statements as "Deaf can" or "can the can't syndrome" (Jankowski 1997, 135).

Bob Hiltermann, the drummer for the Deaf rock band Beethoven's Nightmare, challenges the Deaf community to reconsider Jordan's words—is it really the case that deaf people can do anything except hear? What about music? Playing drums in a rock band has been a lifelong dream and aspiration for Hiltermann. Growing up in a large family with hearing siblings who played music together, he asked his mother to let him play music. He recalls his parents' response: "No, you're deaf. It's hard for you. Don't bother. You can't, can't, can't."[3] When Hiltermann arrived at Gallaudet, he realized that he "can, can, can" (Scari 2010).

Walking around with Hiltermann at the 2012 meeting of the National Association of the Deaf (NAD), I saw him approach people in conversation: "What did I. King Jordan say?" "Deaf people can do anything, except hear." Hiltermann pressed on: "What about music? Can Deaf hear music? Do you like music? I love music! But I'm Deaf!"[4] In this small repartee, Hiltermann calls into question commonly held views about music as an exclusively aural mode of expression. As I spent the afternoon perusing the vendor booths with Hiltermann at the NAD meeting, his conversations revealed that many Deaf people love music. Yet I also heard many deaf people say that music seemed irrelevant, that it was not fun to try to lip-read bands, that it was an experience with which they could not connect. The Deaf rock band Beethoven's Nightmare is reaching out to both of these groups in the Deaf community. They are sharing their love for music in a uniquely Deaf way with those who already love music, and they are addressing those in the Deaf community who never thought they could experience music. For these musicians, Deaf people can do anything—including "hearing" music.

Using as case studies the creative works and performances of Deaf musicians, including Beethoven's Nightmare and rappers Sean Forbes and Signmark, I challenge the hearing world to think about the alternative modes of hearing that a deaf musical experience offers, calling for critical reflection on how many of the current assumptions about music are connected to how people hear with their ears. Examining the musicians' biographies, repertories, performance spaces, and audiences within a greater context of Deaf culture and history, I argue for a way of making and listening to music that is specifically Deaf, celebrating deafness in a way that situates the Deaf as a cultural minority within a hearing world. Musical practices that arise from this political identity create a Deaf musical culture that should encourage music scholars to acknowledge the linguistic differences and histories that are present in the performance and reception of Deaf music.[5]

Deaf History and Culture

Deaf history is colored by the constant struggles of the deaf world against the dominance and control of the hearing world. Psychologist Harlan Lane (1992) draws parallels between colonialism and oppression of the Deaf community by the hearing world, using the term "audist" as one might use the term "racist."[6] Further exploring the postcolonial status of Deaf culture, Deaf scholar Paddy Ladd (2003) asserts that the cultural patterns of Deaf culture have been directly affected by both the acquiescence and resistance to the cultural domination of the hearing world (79).

The struggles of the Deaf community as a minority group, the shared experiences of a common Deaf history and Deaf customs, and the shared institutions of Deaf schools and Deaf clubs have helped to shape a strong sense of Deaf identity. All these experiences characterize Deaf culture, but its definitive feature is sign language (e.g., American Sign Language, British Sign Language), so that Deaf people describe themselves as a linguistic minority.[7] Deaf scholars Tom Humphries and Carol Padden (2006) note that the struggle to make sign language intelligible "underlies nearly every political act of the community" (142).

Since the nineteenth century, American deaf education has been polarized by proponents of the oralist and manualist methods of teaching. Oralism is the belief that deaf children should be mainstreamed into hearing environments and taught only to speak, with the agenda of actively preventing them from learning or communicating in sign language (Ladd 2003, 7). In the nineteenth century, oralists were keen to develop musical education in schools that privileged a typical (or "normal") hearing experience. This motivated the development of hearing technologies, the goal of which was to "normalize" deaf people, so that their experiences matched those of a hearing person's as closely as possible.

Music was also part of manualist deaf education (that is, education in which sign language is the main form of communication). In this practice, musical activity is articulated as a bodily experience that privileges felt vibrations and observed visual cues.[8] Music education in manualist circles was also fraught with the undesirable possibility of "passing" as hearing. Ben Bahan (2006, 34–37) describes two traditional modes of musical expression in manualist, sign-based Deaf culture: translated songs and percussion signing, both derived from the rich heritage of ASL poetry and storytelling. Translated songs are those in which the lyrics of songs written in a spoken language have been translated into ASL for performance, such as the national anthem before a sporting event. Percussion signing is a type of performance that assigns signs to certain beats, sometimes accompanied with a drummer. According to Bahan 2006, percussion signing is no longer extensively practiced, save for a few examples (including Gallaudet University's football song, the "Bison Song").[9]

Tensions between the oralist and manualist camps climaxed in 1880, when the oralists won a major victory at the Milan Congress, an international symposium of educators of the deaf to which no deaf people were invited. The resolutions of the Congress stated that oralism was the preferred method for deaf education, ensuring the subjugation of sign language (Ladd 2003, 120). Deaf culture was already flourishing in Deaf schools, where Deaf adults taught and mentored deaf students, and in Deaf clubs, where groups of Deaf adults could socialize and find community and advocacy. The Milan Congress threatened Deaf culture to its core by separating Deaf people from each other (Ladd 2003, 126). Edward Gallaudet became a dissenter of oralism and declared that Gallaudet College (later University) would remain a haven for sign language (Gallaudet 1881). The National Association for the Deaf in the United States was also founded in response to the Milan Congress to cherish, support, and promote sign language and Deaf culture. The tension between oralism and manualism is central to Deaf cultural practice in all contexts and media.

Deaf Musical Culture

It is necessary for sign language to be at the heart of an argument for a cultural practice within the culturally Deaf community—a Deaf musical practice, in our case. When George Veditz, then president of the National Association of the Deaf, remarked in 1912 that deaf people were "first, last, and for all time, people of the eye," he could not yet articulate the cultural implications that would follow from this idea in the twentieth century (quoted in Humphries and Padden 2006, 2). While sign language had been used among deaf people in the United States since before the nineteenth century, it was not until the 1970s that this lay, communal language practice was recognized by linguists as a legitimate language, American Sign Language. The recognition of native sign languages throughout the world has dramatically affected the international Deaf community. Deaf scholars Carol Padden and Tom Humphries (1990) were able to articulate, for the first time, the world of the "people of the eye" as a distinct Deaf culture with its own native language, practice, and customs. The Deaf community argues that sign language is the most natural language for those who are born deaf or become deaf when they are young—it is their native language.

The use of sign language is a strong artistic and political statement for Deaf musicians. Beethoven's Nightmare makes ASL a key part of their performance practice; Signmark (2010) and Sean Forbes (2012) rap in ASL and have created DVDs of music videos to accompany their albums. Not only is their live performance practice a visual experience, so is their recorded music. These musicians make music that is culturally Deaf: their lyrics speak to their unique experience as Deaf people, and they are communicated using the language of Deaf culture, sign language. The politics of the culturally Deaf community would challenge the hearing world to recognize that they not only can speak on their own terms but also hear and perform on their own terms.

There are two modes of deafness within a deaf musical culture: the cultural-linguistic model that politically identifies itself as capital-D Deaf culture, and the physical model that takes into account all deaf bodies, not just those who identify with the culture of sign language users. Deaf musical culture might also prompt us to consider implications beyond the cultural/linguistic model on how both hearing and deaf individuals experience sound and music.

We generally focus on hearing as the complex process of sound entering the ears, passing across the tympanum (the ear drum) of the middle ear, stimulating hundreds of hair cells in our inner ear, and sending signals to the brain via the auditory nerve. The brain organizes the sounds and assigns meaning to them. For a deaf person the auditory process is shifted. Deafness is hearing loss that takes place in the ear. The many different types of hearing loss include middle ear or inner ear, congenital or later onset, and temporary or permanent. The degrees of hearing loss range across a spectrum from hard-of-hearing to mild, moderate, severe, or profound. Sometimes a person's hearing loss affects certain frequencies more than others. Perhaps there is noise in their heads that only they can hear, such as is the case with tinnitus.

Hearing people learn to think of the actuation of a thin membrane in the side of the head as the necessary precondition for what one can experience as music, but the membrane is incidental. In a deaf musical experience, the whole body becomes the membrane. Both deaf and hearing people can feel sound vibrations, but hearing people tend to focus only on the auditory perception of these sound vibrations. Without that distraction, deaf people tend to use their whole body to perceive sound vibrations. The physical characteristics of a deaf bodily experience of sound waves can be mediated through a culturally Deaf understanding of the significance of that experience. In addition to the politics and culture of sign language within the Deaf community, these visual and kinesthetic components of "deaf hearing" (Straus 2011, 167–170) contribute to the Deaf cultural expression of music.

Beethoven's Nightmare

The members of the Deaf rock band Beethoven's Nightmare found each other at Gallaudet University.[10] Bob Hiltermann, the drummer of Beethoven's Nightmare (2004), recalls his experience arriving as a student on the campus of Gallaudet University in the 1970s: "I got to the dorm. I was on the way to my room. Then all of a sudden I felt vibrations. . . . So I touched the wall. Ah, vibrations. What was that?" After Hiltermann met guitarist Steve Longo and bass player Ed Chevy, together they formed Beethoven's Nightmare while still at Gallaudet (Scari 2010). While they were students, they performed regularly on the campus, entertaining the Deaf student body. Their rock'n'roll style was inspired by the Beatles, Led Zeppelin, and Jimi Hendrix, but often accompanied with ASL storytelling.

For many of the late-1970s Gallaudet alumni, including the band members, these performances were their first experience with Deaf music-making. Chevy reflects:

> As Deaf people, we have a rhythm inside our bodies, and we're famous for being storytellers. It's a huge, important part of Deaf culture. If you can see a beautiful storyteller, telling a story in ASL, it's just fantastic. And to pair it with that beat, the creativity that it elicits, is wonderful. It can really be paired with any story you want. ASL is a beautiful language, and we don't want to lose the language. (Garey and Hott 2007)

Chevy's comments indicate the integral roles that felt rhythm and sign language play in musical expression, rooted in long-standing traditions and practices within Deaf culture.

Since their days at Gallaudet, the band members have settled on the West Coast and Hawaii. Throughout their postcollege life, they have met regularly to play music together. In 2002, the band returned to its roots at Gallaudet University to participate in the international Deaf conference and festival, Deaf Way II.[11] Since Deaf Way II, they have been performing more frequently around the United States and Europe. In 2004, they released their CD, *Turn It Up Louder!* The album proudly declares itself "The Crossover Masterpiece of the Century," and the liner notes describe the group's music as "retro rock and roll infused with American Sign Language" (Beethoven's Nightmare 2004).[12]

The audience for Beethoven's Nightmare is primarily a Deaf audience, though they perform for the hearing world as well. Beethoven's Nightmare's use of ASL is at the heart of what makes their show distinctive. Hiltermann explains, "This is a whole new concept—this kind of performance. It's never been done before. With sign language. Not interpreting the song, no. Perform the song. There's a difference. Interpreting, yeah, you get the story. But performing, you get the picture" (Scari 2010). In this explanation, Hiltermann calls on listeners to consider ASL as an integral part of the music—not just an independent text, nor a translation of preexisting English lyrics.

Beethoven's Nightmare writes their own music and lyrics, and uses dance, mime, and sign language in their performances. Chevy, who composes most of the songs, describes his process as usually driven by an idea or a vision; then the music comes next, and he writes the lyrics in the last stages of the process.[13] This initial visual inspiration is a key part of their music, from conception to performance.

Working with ASL specialists has always been a central aspect of Beethoven Nightmare's concerts. From 2011 to 2013, they partnered with two hearing signers—Juanita Chase and Joshua Lamont, both trained as actors—who toured with the band and prepared a signed interpretation of the music. During instrumental passages, the signers may act out the idea of the song or simply dance, gesturing the pulse of the musical beat. Lyrics are sung in English by Chevy, who is Deaf. At the end of 2013 the band expanded their members to include Paul Raci, a hearing vocalist who also signs. Raci is an award-winning singer and actor; he is also CODA ([hearing] Child of Deaf Adults) and has been immersed in Deaf culture and sign language for his whole life. His role in the band is to take over the vocals and the signing (Knowles 2013). The array of people involved with Beethoven's Nightmare is indicative of the spectrum of people who are part of Deaf culture—signing hearing people, signing deaf people who also voice, and a hearing person born into a Deaf family.

The stage is set up in such a way that all members of the band have visual access to each other. Hiltermann is in the center, his drum set positioned toward the back of the stage, with bassist Ed Chevy on his right and lead guitarist Steve Longo on his left. In addition to the monitor speakers in front of the musicians, additional monitor speakers are placed behind them. During the sound check they adjust their rear speakers to optimal bass levels to feel the music. They communicate with each other visually, connecting what they see with what they feel. During the concert at the NAD festival, Lamont and Chase signed for the band; they performed at the front part of the stage, thus foregrounding the visual aspects of their performance, including signing, dancing, and gesture. Paul Raci, positioned on stage in the place of a traditional vocalist, has his own microphone and sings and signs simultaneously, interacting with the band through visual contact, body language, and sign language.

Beethoven's Nightmare's repertoire can be broadly divided into two main categories. The first includes songs with very few lyrics that convey mostly abstract ideas, presumably stemming from Chevy's initial vision or concept; these ideas, dramatized by the signer(s), describe their experience as Deaf musicians. For example, the songs "Crash It Out" and "Angel of Darkness" each have only one line of text. Chevy's vision of the songs is pantomimed by the onstage signers, accompanied by long instrumental interludes. The liner notes explain that the song "Crash It Out" is an "attempt to break the deaf sound barrier with a heavy steady beat," while "Angel of Darkness" is about "a mythical deaf goddess of rock music [evoked] as a muse to give energy to the beat and sound to the silence." The song "Black Magnet" explores how Chevy perceives music: "To more fully feel his music, a deaf guitarist invents the most powerful planetary guitar using a strange magical black magnet" (Beethoven's Nightmare 2004, 2). The lyrics to "Black Magnet" (which appear in the CD booklet) seem to be a description of the dramatic performance of the signer:

> Turning into Black Magnet, it's getting better over time. It's becoming irresistible, super power all mine! Black Magnet comes alive recharging and testing amplifying and attracting rare earth.
>
> Now is the time. Turn on the power! It's alive! Now I've got the Black Magnet, the special force of music. The most powerful I can play. The living power!
>
> Amplifying and attracting rare earth. Now is the time. Turn on the power! It's alive! Now I've got the Black Magnet, the special force of music. The most powerful I can play. The living power!

Dramatically enacting the song's ideas, the signer also moves his body to provide a visual representation of the musical beat, sometimes fist-pumping the air or manipulating the signs to occur in rhythm with the song.[14]

The second type of song replaces dramatic pantomimes with more clearly articulated English translations of ASL signs. These songs often speak more directly about Deaf culture. The lyrics to "It's Just a Deaf Thing!" include colloquial signs that are central to Deaf expression: they include the handwave, or Deaf applause made famous at the Gallaudet protest; ILY, or the ASL sign for "I love you," also used to express camaraderie among the Deaf; and "pah!"—an expression that means "finally!" in a victorious sense.[15] The lyrics in English are simple: "It's just a Deaf thing! You wouldn't understand!" with interjections of handwaving, ILY, and pah! In a performance, the audience is encouraged to join these choruses of signs, the song creating a space for this communal Deaf experience. The signer offers visual representation of the beat, punctuated by clear ASL signs, encouraging the audience to join in.

"Turn It Up Louder!" (the title track of their CD) explains how deaf people experience music: by turning it up louder. The third verse describes the importance of rhythm, specifically the beat that rock'n'roll provides: "We need a real fast song, to sing real loud with a rock'n'roll rhythm to stay on time. We're gonna play a rock song to please the crowd. We're gonna turn it up louder let you unwind." The playful chorus cries "Turn it up Louder! We want it Louder! Make it louder! Louder! Turn it up Louder!—Hey, what are you?! Deaf?" As Chevy describes, the purpose of "Turn it Up Louder!" is to explain to Deaf people that just because they do not listen with their ears (ASL sign = LISTEN-EARS; see Track 3.1 on the Companion Website) like hearing people do, they can still enjoy music. Chevy maintains that they need to feel the rhythm or the beat of the music in their bodies, and often this is achieved by "turning it up louder," increasing the volume or the bass so that vibrations are felt or certain frequencies can be heard.

Feeling vibration is a key part of the deaf experience of music. Hiltermann explains, "The way I play, I depend on a lot of vibrations, so we play really, really loud, enough for us to hear and feel it" (Garey and Hott 2007). He describes hearing music through his whole body: "People still can't believe; they think it's hearing that makes the music. I said, 'No, it's your heart. It's your body. It's your rhythm inside of you that makes the music, not [the ear]" (Scari 2010). Reaching out to the Deaf community with music is one of the key artistic goals of Beethoven's Nightmare. According to Chevy, the band needs to explain to Deaf people that music is something that they can appreciate. In their album liner notes, Hiltermann explains, "When we started, we had to fight the misconception that being deaf meant we couldn't play or enjoy music" (Beethoven's Nightmare 2004, 3). Chevy explains that in Deaf culture there is a rich tradition of storytelling and mime, but not much of a musical culture. In an effort to open the door to the possibility of a musical experience, Beethoven's Nightmare clarifies that they must first separate the listener from the expectation that this experience is going to be LISTEN-EARS, like it is for a hearing person. Instead, their Deaf musical experience involves feeling vibrations (including the beat) and communicating expression through sign language and movement. In collaboration with interpreters, who gesture the pulse of the beat while signing the lyrics, the band has been able to show their Deaf audience how to "see" and "feel" music. In fact, one of the attendees at the 2012 NAD meeting exclaimed, "Once you connect what you're feeling with what's going on onstage, it's amazing!" This was a sentiment I heard repeatedly.

Beyond their interest in facilitating the perception of music within the Deaf community, Beethoven's Nightmare also articulates their own experiences living as deaf minorities in a hearing majority culture; almost all of their songs contain lyrics that deal with these themes. When the band members were college students in the early 1970s, the genre of rock'n'roll provided much of what they looked for in a musical experience—loud music with a steady beat. But rock'n'roll has also had a long association with political and cultural nonconformity. Hiltermann identifies rock'n'roll as a safe place to convey thoughts, dreams, and protests without fear of reprisal, tapping into the history of rock'n'roll as a platform for protest and change in civil rights movements (Beethoven's Nightmare 2004). This connection resonates with the Deaf community's history of struggle for its own political and social voice. Beethoven's Nightmare's use of ASL is significant in this greater historical and political context, because historically the repression of Deaf culture has been largely carried out through the repression of sign language.

Beethoven's Nightmare is the first musical group to achieve any level of fame within the American Deaf community. But much of the band's musical practices are extensions of Deaf cultural traditional practices, including ASL storytelling and poetry; by signing on the beat, they perhaps even allude to the earlier tradition of percussion signing. But their musical style is also an extension of a hearing culture—the rock'n'roll of the 1960s and '70s. Synthesizing these influences, Beethoven's Nightmare has broken ground for a new Deaf musical culture, one that fuses hearing music (rock'n'roll) with deaf music (physical and visual experiences of music).

Sean Forbes

Sean Forbes, a Deaf rapper from Detroit, figures prominently in contemporary American Deaf culture. Since 2008, he has performed all over the United States in live venues and schools and university campuses. Before this, he enjoyed making ASL translations of many of his favorite popular songs, including some by Eminem, with whom he had a chance meeting in a studio in Detroit. When Forbes showed Joel Martin (the manager of the Detroit production studio that produces Eminem's work) his own video of his first song "I'm Deaf!" Martin agreed to work with Forbes to produce his first album *Perfect Imperfection* (2012), a CD/DVD set (Damico 2013).

Forbes is the only deaf person in his hearing family. His father is a guitarist in an award-winning country band, Forbes Bros, and from an early age, Sean Forbes loved music and wanted to play music. Although his early life was mostly oralist, he went to a high school with a large deaf and hard-of-hearing population. He met many students who were culturally Deaf and began learning ASL in order to communicate and have relationships with these friends. He attended the National Technical Institute for the

Deaf (NTID), a professional, technologically oriented program for deaf and hard-of-hearing students.

Because of his background in oralism, Forbes speaks English quite well; he voices all his raps, which are simultaneously in ASL and in English. Music videos are also an integral part of his work. For each audio track of his new album, a video track is included, with performances in English. Some of the videos include ASL performances of the songs, while others feature images or scenes that narrate Forbes's lyrics.

In all of his videos, lyrics are presented in interesting fonts and typographical effects; they are timed with the music to visually reinforce the underlying rhythms.[16] Forbes, who is enthusiastic about the potential of word videos, states, "Now I can go on YouTube and type in the name of the video, and lyrics videos just show up if it's a popular song. There's so much more accessibility today than there ever was before." The concept works well for making recordings that can be enjoyed by both deaf and hearing audiences.

Creating a bridge between deaf and hearing worlds is a driving motivation in Forbes's work. He has a growing and enthusiastic following among American Deaf youth, who sport his "I'm Deaf!" T-shirt quoting his most popular song. Forbes's work makes visible to Deaf youth an artistic world that does not exclude them. When Forbes performed at the Deafestival in the summer of 2012, Deaf teens and college-aged youth flocked around the stage, screaming and cheering, enthusiastically waving their hands and pounding the air with the beat.

Forbes's first hit, "I'm Deaf," loudly proclaims his Deaf identity, which he frames in terms of ability rather than disability. In a pun on the word "Def," which has long been used in hip-hop as a term to connote superlative qualities, the chorus to the song candidly declares, "Deafer than Def Jam/I'm so so Deaf" (Track 3.2 on the Companion Website). In the first verse he introduces himself, acknowledging the seeming oxymoron of "deaf musician": "My Name is Sean/But they call me Seen/Got a message here,/I'm delivering/Look I understand,/You might be leery/Getting music beats/From the hard-of-hearing." The second verse asserts his ability to overcome these potential obstacles: "Now there's people out there/Telling you what you can't do/'You can't overcome,/You got too much to prove[.]'/ I never listened,/How ironic." And in the third verse he places himself in the good company of others who were not held back by their physical differences: one-handed pitcher Jimmy Abbot, blind musician Stevie Wonder, and blind-deaf Helen Keller. He ends by affirming his own Deaf identity, arguing that his deafness will not prohibit him from doing anything he desires, including music: "I'd rather not hear/Rather not listen[.]/I'm the perfect imperfection/Never restricted."[17]

Forbes uses music to reach out to hearing students, showing them that deafness is nothing to fear. In a recent tour (Spring 2013), he performed not only in Deaf venues but also in many hearing venues, especially schools. Lamenting the limited interaction between deaf and hearing communities, Forbes observes, "There really hasn't been anything—other than, now, the TV show *Switched at Birth*—something that hearing and deaf can watch together. I would go see Deaf schools play basketball against hearing kids. It would always be hearing against deaf, hearing against deaf, hearing against deaf.

There was never a situation where both of them were together, and I feel like with my music we're doing that. Bringing the two communities together to enjoy something."[18]

Forbes is also a cofounder of the Deaf Performing Arts Network (D-PAN), which, among other activities, produces high-quality music videos of popular mainstream songs translated into ASL for deaf audiences. Under the motto "It's everybody's music," D-PAN provides the deaf access to popular music, breaking down the cultural barriers that have separated the deaf from mainstream arts while simultaneously raising mainstream hearing culture's exposure to ASL and Deaf culture.[19]

Signmark

What Sean Forbes is accomplishing on a national level in the United States is being achieved on a global level by Signmark. A Deaf rapper from Finland, Signmark (Marko Vuoriheimo) is from a deaf family, and he grew up signing; Finnish Sign language is his first and native language. He was empowered early on by his family to be proud of his deafness, his language, and his Deaf culture. Signmark's earliest musical endeavors included translating Christmas songs into sign language so that his deaf family and his hearing grandparents could all enjoy them together. Later, he began to translate popular songs from MTV into sign language and perform them with his deaf friends on the dance floors of clubs. Signmark was challenged by a friend to move beyond translating and instead to write his own lyrics.

His debut album *Signmark* was released in 2006, with a CD and a DVD of signed music videos. The album, in spoken Finnish and Finnish Sign Language, features many songs that describe aspects of Finnish Deaf history and culture, resonating with the experiences of other Deaf communities in the Western world after the Milan Congress—most notably, the repression of sign language in favor of oralist deaf school. After coming in second place in the final qualifying round to represent Finland at the 2009 Eurovision Song Content, Signmark became the first deaf artist to sign with an international record label, Warner Music.[20] In 2010, he released his second album, *Breaking the Rules*, also as a CD/DVD set. In order to reach a more international community, this album is performed in spoken English and American Sign Language. (Finnish Sign Language is its own language, as distinctive from American Sign Languages as the spoken language English is from Finnish.)[21] Signmark signs without using his voice (VOICE-OFF in ASL; Track 3.3 on the Companion Website). Signmark always signs VOICE-OFF, whether in casual conversation or in performance. He works closely with his partner, vocalist Brandon Bauer (who is Finnish-American and performs the English spoken translation of Signmark's signed raps) to create a bilingual ASL/English performance.

In February 2013, Signmark performed at the Kennedy Center in Washington, DC, representing Finland as one of the featured performers of the month-long Scandinavian festival at the Center. The audience rippled with the signing hands of Deaf and hearing people, communicating together or simply waving their hands in applause. Signmark signed from the stage, "Rhythm isn't something we hear, but also see and feel," as he encouraged the audience to move their hands and bodies along with the music, reinforcing the multimodality of hearing deafly.

Through the performance in a spoken language and a sign language, Signmark creates a musical experience that is accessible to both hearing and Deaf cultures. Signmark states, "Through my music I want to break prejudice and fight for equality between cultures. I want to show to people that being different can be an asset. My message is that nothing is impossible for the deaf; we can do all the same things."[22] His song "Smells Like Victory" poignantly demonstrates his desire to bring together not only deaf and hearing cultures, but also other opposing groups. The video models a newscast, and as the chorus sounds ("I can feel it in the air, smells like victory; and I let it stick to me. You haters ain't shit to me"), images of groups of people who have traditionally opposed each other find reconciliation: a black man and a white man embrace, an Israeli and a Palestinian, and opposing teams in a soccer match (Track 3.4 on the Companion Website).[23] In this video, Signmark appears to suggest that social victory lies in the reconciliation between opposing forces rather than the triumph of one over the other. Distancing himself from what some might consider the medical aspect of deafness, he shifts his focus to the cultural and political implications of Deafness, by superimposing images of cultural and political tensions that are well recognized in the global community. Speaking from his experience, Signmark thus highlights the social, linguistic struggle that the Deaf community faces.

Many of Signmark's songs comment on his deafness, explaining that it is not something that keeps him from his dreams (including his dream of music performance). In the song "Talk 2 the Hand," he plays on the name Mos Def, the famous American hip-hop artist:

> Naw, this ain't Mos Def
> but if you ask me, in this rap biz I'm the most def
> ain't nobody else done it . . .
> Def Jam ain't heard of me I'm makin' the deaf jam
> you lookin at me funny like I committed a 3rd degree
> hah, like I can't rhyme?
> Well homie read my hands, oh, you can't sign? . . .
> Some walls got ears, well my ears got walls
> they say the higher you climb the higher you fall. . . .
> You still lookin' at me strange
> I'm the first deaf rapper and the industry ain't the same. (Signmark 2010)

Signmark is aware that by becoming a musician he has broken the boundaries of people's assumptions about what deaf people can or cannot do, a theme that he often addresses. He raps: "They wanna know how do I answer the phone/and can I drive a car, how I get chicks in the bar? . . . Can't be President, the army won't accept me/I can't be a pilot, could be a doctor if they let me" (Signmark 2010). He also speaks out against the paternalism that many deaf people face, and asks that the hearing majority join him in his deaf place and truly understand his culture, a desire that the Deaf community has held since the Milan Congress:

Not asking for no favors, don't want your friendly deeds
don't try to be my Savior. I bite the hand that feeds
Nothing changes without the first step
stay still but not to advance is to regress
I'm knocking at your front door, demanding you to come out
u need to get on my level to know what I'm about
cause we're falling, hitting rock bottom
gotta step up, now tell me wassup!

Signmark has taught the chorus for this song, "Against the Wall," to hundreds of hearing people all over the world in staged flash mobs that he calls, "silent shout"; he teaches the signs for the chorus and then performs the song having the audience join in.[24] By doing this, he vividly invites his audience to join his space, enacting in a small sense what he hopes to accomplish in a larger sense—bringing deaf and hearing people into a shared cultural space.

In the bridge of "Against the Wall," Signmark raps, "Without a fight you won't see me fall down/Since I'm doing this for my people/for all my people." By "his people," Signmark refers not just to the deaf of Finland, but rather to the Deaf community that transcends geographical boundaries. Another one of his songs, "The Letter," is a tribute to a young deaf woman who was tragically murdered in Christchurch, New Zealand in late 2007 (Booker 2007). Her death was mourned by the global Deaf community; tributes were expressed in blog posts and tweets from around the world. Signmark summarizes the feelings of what many Deaf people expressed: "I live in a community so tight, worldwide/in one blink of an eye we lost one of us/a life taken. At an age so young. So wrong/Our world was shaken." This song illustrates the global communality of Deaf culture, arguing that Deaf identity is not limited to national identity.

There is an ASL sign, DEAF-WORLD (Track 3.5 on the Companion Website), that describes what it means to participate in this culture—one based on shared social behaviors, customs, traditions, values, and institutions of the community and, perhaps most definitively, based on the traditions of signed language. The Deaf community is relatively small, thus there is always a search for connectedness to the others in this community. DEAF-WORLD is a picture of a community reaching for a connection beyond the borders of the maps that the hearing world has drawn. Signmark invokes this concept of DEAF-WORLD when he talks about his "community so tight." He is talking about the Deaf community across the globe.

Conclusion

The 1988 Gallaudet protest and DPN movement was an empowering moment for the Deaf community, playing a pivotal role in the disability rights movement that led to the passage of the Americans with Disabilities Act (ADA) in 1990. In recent decades, many Deaf artists in their twenties and thirties—coming of age in a post-DPN, post-ADA era—are turning to music as a form of Deaf self-expression, using their native sign language. For these Deaf artists, music is no longer "out of bounds," only for the hearing. While Beethoven's Nightmare turned to rock'n'roll, using its heavy beats and its platform of protest, Sean Forbes and Signmark have turned to hip-hop, rapping in ASL. These new musical styles exploit digital and social media, which allows for the easy recording and sharing of multimedia performances, fusing the visual with the sonic.

In his book *Extraordinary Measures*, Joseph Straus (2011, 167–170) identifies four aspects of deaf hearing: feeling, seeing, moving, and inner, silent hearing. As we have already seen, felt sound vibrations are a key part of how deaf people experience music, on a continuum of experience from how a stage is set up for a public performance to individual, casual listening. The visual experience of music is tied closely to the kinesthetic experience through the use of sign language, inviting the audience into a spatial experience of song as lyrics are painted in the air. Both Sean Forbes and Signmark will often encourage their audiences to wave their hands back and forth with the beat. The signers working with Beethoven's Nightmare will often pulse the beat or otherwise visually demonstrate what is happening musically during instrumental passages.

If listening is more than what happens with the ears, what does it entail? Phenomenologist Don Ihde (2007) has questioned the strict separation of the realms of sound and sight. These two dimensions exist in a complementary relationship: "Silence is the horizon of sound, yet the mute object is silently *present*. Silence seems revealed at first through a visual category. . . . Listening makes the invisible *present* in a way similar to the presence of the mute in vision" (50–51). Ihde proposes a dimension in which listening is a mode of seeing, in which the invisible is translated into the visible (54). Perhaps this can help explain how it is that the visual is such an essential part of Deaf music-making. In ASL there are signs to describe how a person listens. Typically, a hearing person will LISTEN-EARS; the ears are the primary mode of receiving communication. To create this sign, the Bent-3 handshape is placed by the ears along with a motion that indicates the receiving of sound. By contrast, a Deaf person will LISTEN-EYES, using the same handshape placed by the eyes. This handshape indicates the reception of information; the position of the handshape will indicate the part of the body through which the communication is received. (Compare Track 3.1 and Track 3.6 on the Companion Website).

Perhaps more difficult to define is the idea of inner, silent hearing. The literary scholar Lennard Davis (1995) uses the term "the deafened moment" to describe a moment in which the distinctive categories of "hearing" and "deaf" become moot, because they are part of a process that does not involve speaking or hearing—for example, in the silent perception of a printed text (101). Davis states that "so many of our assumptions about writing, about language, are based on the premise that language is in fact sonic, audible, vocalized," such that even the words we use to describe various discursive practices are embedded with assumptions about the physical experience of language (100). For example, to say "I speak of this or that" in a written context is not entirely correct. As Davis argues, we are not actually speaking, we are writing. But our usual mode of linguistic communication is speaking, so we freely borrow the word as a metaphor for communication. By highlighting "the deafened moment," Davis claims that we are pausing in a moment that transcends "hearing" and "deaf" in such a way as to "acknowledge the political oppression involved in denying that this major form of language interaction has in fact implied the ostracism of those who are differently abled linguistically" (101).

Applying Davis's argument about language to music, we are forced to consider how many of our assumptions about music are connected to how we hear with our ears. If language suppositions are connected to an idea of something that is "sonic, audible, and vocalized," how much more so are our assumptions about music? Even to use the phrase "deaf hearing," a seeming oxymoron, demonstrates that we cannot even talk about music without using ear words, such as "hear" or "listen." Is there an "implied ostracism" for those who perceive the sonic vibrations in their bodies rather than their auditory nerves?

Situating ourselves in the "deafened moment," we also realize that, inasmuch as there is not one way to be d/Deaf, there is not one way to be hearing. As a hearing person attending concerts performed by many of the musicians I have talked about here, I step into DEAF-WORLD. I feel the bass pounding deep in my core. I see the music and the lyrics, and I move my hands with the beat, performing signs with the chorus as Signmark invites his audience to join in. When I step away from DEAF-WORLD, I am challenged to reevaluate how I listen to all the music around me. Perhaps this is part of what Ihde means when he describes listening as the translation of the invisible to the visible. My intersection with deaf hearing, or hearing deafly, has made visible certain aspects of my own hearing that often go unmentioned, and I believe that the binary of the categories of deaf and hearing becomes blurred. By taking into account the multisensory musical experience of these Deaf musicians that I have examined here, I believe that music scholars can begin to understand the broad spectrum on which musical experiences can lie, somewhere between the ears, the eyes, and the body.

Acknowledgments

I thank the following colleagues for their comments and encouragements on earlier versions: Marié Abe, Steven Cornelius, Andrew Dell'Antonio, Laura Mauldin, and Felicia Miyakawa. I also thank the editors and many coauthors to this volume for their helpful comments, especially Blake Howe, Anabel Maler, and Joseph Straus.

Notes

1. It is conventional to use the term *Deaf* (with an uppercase "D") in reference to culture, community, and identity, and to use the term *deaf* (with a lowercase "d") to refer to the physical condition of deafness or the larger group of people with hearing loss who do not associate with Deaf culture. To use the term "hearing impaired" is problematic, because it

is viewed as offensive by the Deaf community. See Humphries and Padden 2006, 1–2 and 159; Davis 1995, xiv–xx; and Lane 1992, 89.

2. See Adelman 2006 and Shapiro and Valentine 2006 for interviews with I. King Jordan in which he reflects on the impact that his presidency had on Deaf culture and disability rights.
3. Throughout the essay, all quotes originally in American Sign Language have been translated into idiomatic English. As is customary, words transliterated from ASL are written in all capital letters.
4. Unless otherwise noted, all direct quotes from Beethoven's Nightmare or other Deaf individuals come from my fieldwork at the biennial meeting of the National Association for the Deaf, specifically Deafestival—the arts and music festival that finished the week's events in Louisville, Kentucky (July 7, 2012).
5. While this essay focuses on these particular musicians, who identify with Deaf culture and use a sign language as their primary language, I do not want to ignore the many other d/Deaf musicians. The percussionist Evelyn Glennie is deaf and talks about her deafness and her experience of music, but does not find an identity in a signing Deaf culture. Other musicians who do identify with the Deaf community include hard-of-hearing rock singer, TL Forsberg; the amateur hip-hop artist Wawa Snipes, who advocates for a new genre, "dip-hop" (deaf hip-hop); and the sound artist Christine Sun Kim, who plays with boundaries of sound and visual experiences. Also of note is the contemporary German avant-garde composer Helmut Oehring, who is a hearing child of Deaf adults (CODA); he grew up using German Sign Language and has incorporated signers into some of his chamber works.
6. As Lane 1992 explains, "Audism is the corporate institution for dealing with deaf people, dealing with them by making statements about them, governing where they go to school and, in some cases, where they live; in short, audism is the hearing way of dominating, restructuring, and exercising authority over the deaf community" (31–49). Originally coined by Deaf scholar Tom Humphries, "audism/ist" is now a term in common parlance in Deaf culture. Humphries (2012) has been working with the American Heritage Dictionary since 2012 on its official definition.
7. Humphries and Padden 2006, 1–2. Lennard Davis (2008, 320) has also observed that the definition of Deaf culture as a linguistic minority excludes non-ASL users who identify as a deaf "other." The linguistic minority model also includes hearing children of ASL-using Deaf adults for whom ASL is a first language in the home (children of Deaf adults, or CODA), yet they are not physically deaf. For the purposes of this essay, I am focusing on the section of Deaf culture that does identify itself around the linguistic model.
8. Because the history of music in deaf education and culture is still underdeveloped, I am grateful to Anabel Maler, who has shared with me an unpublished paper on deaf musical education in the nineteenth century.
9. Russell Harvard, "Galladuet [*sic*] University's Bison Song Team 2005–2006," YouTube video, 4:34 (August 6, 2010), http://youtu.be/4CVbUfuqXuk/.
10. Unless otherwise noted, information about the band and its history comes from my fieldwork at the NAD conference in July 2012 and at their concert at Kansas State University, Manhattan, on April 3, 2012.
11. Deaf Way II was attended by over nine thousand people from over one hundred countries. It was a follow-up to Deaf Way I in 1989, which I. King Jordan organized as a celebration

of international Deaf culture, with representatives coming from around the world. See Shettle 2002 and Brown and Goodstein 2004.

12. The album is only available on audio compact disc. With the exception of "Turn It Up Louder!" released on YouTube, the band has not recorded music videos. Steve Longo, "Beethoven's Nightmare—Turn It Up Louder in Sign Language and Captions," YouTube video, 3:43 (March 8, 2012), http://youtu.be/2WkfI9GH_AI.
13. Beethoven's Nightmare, interview with the author, April 3, 2012.
14. For a more detailed analysis on the range of sign language expression in song between deaf and hearing performers, consult Anabel Maler's essay in this volume.
15. "Pah!" is a standard English transliteration based on the mouth shape that is part of the sign.
16. Lyric videos are a rising trend in popular music (Blankenship 2012).
17. In a National Public Radio interview Sean Forbes explains that he likes to experience music by turning up the bass and prefers hip-hop because he can really feel the bass and drums and is able to follow the percussive lyrics (Moe and Sanchez 2008). Forbes also describes a device originally used for videogaming called the ButtKicker (a low-frequency audio transducer that allows the user to feel powerful bass without excessive volume); if held or attached to a table or chair, it can amplify vibrations and enhance the deaf musical experience.
18. Sean Forbes, interview with the author, February 28, 2013.
19. See, for example, D-PAN's production of the White Stripes's "We're Gonna be Friends" and Christina Aguillera's "Beautiful." Dpanvideos, "D-PAN ASL Music Video 'We're Going To Be Friends' by the White Stripes," YouTube video, 3:16 (October 24, 2011), http://youtu.be/IbLz9-riRGM; and Dpanvideos, "D-PAN ASL Music Video 'Beautiful' by Christina Aguilera," YouTube video, 4:32 (March 28, 2008), http://youtu.be/C6zVFGpGNJQ.
20. Signmark: The Official Site, http://signmark.biz/site/en/bio. For his Eurovision performance, see jarnova75, "signmark in eurovisio "Speakerbox," YouTube video, 5:17 (January 31, 2009), http://youtu.be/tIyjewBNiFA.
21. I am grateful to Keri Ogrizovich, certified deaf interpreter, for her input on different sign languages.
22. Signmark, "Signmark-Biography," Vimeo video, 6:24, http://vimeo.com/10254226.
23. Signmarkprod, "Signmark—Smells Like Victory," YouTube video, 4:42 (October 31, 2009), http://youtu.be/oUtM8_DOVUI.
24. Marcel de Araujo Coelho, "Signmark, Silent Shout," YouTube video, 4:46 (October 4, 2010), http://youtu.be/FloNPWU50X8. Also see dnainfo, "signmark.mov," YouTube video, 1:06 (September 23, 2010), Silent Shout in New York City, http://youtu.be/MCQeukjlfeQ.

References

Adelman, Ken. 2006. "Gallaudet University Interview with Former President I. King Jordan." *Washingtonian*, March 1. http://www.washingtonian.com/articles/work-education/education/gallaudet-university-interview-with-former-president-i-king-jordan/.

Bahan, Ben. 2006. "Face-to-Face Tradition in the American Deaf Community: Dynamics of the Teller, the Tale, and the Audience." In *Signing the Body Poetic*, edited by H-Dirksen L. Bauman, Jennifer L. Nelson, and Heidi M. Rose, 21–50. Berkeley: University of California Press.

Barnartt, Sharon, and Richard Scotch. 2001. *Disability Protests: Contentious Politics, 1970–1999.* Washington, DC: Gallaudet University Press.

Blankenship, Mark. 2012. "More Than Words: The Art of the Lyric Video." *Monkey See: Pop-Culture News and Analysis from NPR* (blog), February 29. http://www.npr.org/blogs/monkeysee/2012/02/29/147637692/more-than-words-the-art-of-the-lyric-video/.

Booker, Jarrod. 2007. "Deaf Community in Mourning as Man Charged with Emma's Murder." *New Zealand Herald,* November 28. http://www.nzherald.co.nz/nz/news/article.cfm?c_id=1&objectid=10478777/.

Brown, Laura, and Harvey Goodstein. 2004. *Deaf Way II: An International Celebration.* Washington, DC: Gallaudet University Press.

Damico, Rachelle. 2013. "Feel the Music." *Metrotimes,* January 23. http://metrotimes.com/feel-the-music-1.1433774/.

Davis, Lennard J. 1995. *Enforcing Normalcy: Disability, Deafness, and the Body.* New York: Verso.

Davis, Lennard J. 2008. "Postdeafness." In *Open Your Eyes: Deaf Studies Talking,* edited by H-Dirksen L. Bauman, 314–325. Minneapolis: University of Minnesota Press.

Gallaudet, Edward M. 1881. "The Milan Convention." *American Annals of the Deaf* 26: 1–16.

Gannon, Jack R. 1989. *The Week the World Heard Gallaudet.* Washington, DC: Gallaudet University Press.

Humphries, Tom L. 2012. "Words, Dictionary Definitions, and Context Is Everything." Paper presented at Deaf World/Hearing World: A Conference held at the Max Planck Institute for the History of Science, Berlin, Germany, December 10–11.

Humphries, Tom L., and Carol A. Padden. 1990. *Deaf in America: Voices from a Culture.* Cambridge, MA: Harvard University Press.

Humphries, Tom L., and Carol A. Padden. 2006. *Inside Deaf Culture.* Cambridge, MA: Harvard University Press.

Ihde, Don. 2007. *Listening and Voice: Phenomenologies of Sound.* 2nd ed. Albany: State University of New York Press.

Jankowski, Katherine A. 1997. *Deaf Empowerment: Emergence, Struggle, and Rhetoric.* Washington, DC: Gallaudet University Press.

Knowles, Jim. 2013. "Hold Your Ears: Deaf Rock Band Coming." *San Leandro Times,* August 8. http://ebpublishing.com/index.php?option=com_content&view=article&id=6369:hold-your-ears-deaf-rock-band-coming-&catid=50:san-leandro-news&Itemid=131.

Ladd, Paddy. 2003. *Understanding Deaf Culture: In Search of Deafhood.* Clevedon, England: Multilingual Matters.

Lane, Harlan. 1992. *The Mask of Benevolence: Disabling the Deaf Community.* New York: Knopf.

Moe, John, and Marc Sanchez. 2008. "Music for the Deaf." *Weekend America* (transcript), September 20. American Public Media. http://weekendamerica.publicradio.org/display/web/2008/09/20/music_for_deaf/.

Shapiro, Joseph, and Vikki Valentine. 2006. "I. King Jordan: Reflections on a Changing Culture." NPR, April 30. http://www.npr.org/templates/story/story.php?storyId= 5370327.

Shettle, Andrea. 2002. "Deaf Way II: Celebration of the Deaf Way of Life." *Disability World* (September–October). http://www.disabilityworld.org/09-10_02/news/deaf-way.shtml

Straus, Joseph N. 2011. *Extraordinary Measures: Disability in Music.* New York: Oxford University Press.

Audiovisual Materials

Beethoven's Nightmare. 2004. *Turn It Up Louder!* Koke-Kula Records & Publishing, MP3 album. Accessed March 18, 2014. https://itunes.apple.com/us/album/turn-it-up-louder-single/id536413059

Forbes, Sean. 2012. *Perfection Imperfection*. D-PAN Ent. MP3 album. Accessed September 5, 2012. https://itunes.apple.com/us/album/perfect-imperfection/id555235264.

Garey, Diane, and Lawrence R. Hott (directors). 2007. *Through Deaf Eyes*. WETA Washington, D.C. and Florentine Films/Hott Productions.

Signmark. 2010. *Breaking the Rules*. Warner Music Finland. MP3 album. Accessed January 10, 2014. https://itunes.apple.com/us/album/breaking-the-rules/id366399433.

Scari, Hilari (director). 2010. *See What I'm Saying: The Deaf Entertainers Documentary*. Wordplay.

CHAPTER 4

MUSICAL EXPRESSION AMONG DEAF AND HEARING SONG SIGNERS

ANABEL MALER

INTRODUCTION

MUSICIANS and composers are generally presumed to possess "normal hearing," as a deficiency in the sense of hearing is "understood as particularly problematic for musicians" (Straus 2011, 26). The assumption of normal hearing has led music scholars to imagine deafness as "the deepest imaginable antithesis to music." To the hearing majority, it seems unquestionable that music is "the one thing that a deaf person can never possess, a form of discourse unthinkable and unattainable" (Abbate 1991, 130). In this hearing-centric view of music, deaf people live in a world of silence, cut off both from musical expression and from receiving pleasure from musical works. The model of deafness as musically disabling agrees with the predominant view of disability as disqualifying or excluding the disabled person "from access to the benefits and status of the properly human" (Garland-Thomson 2012, 340).

As recent work by Rosemarie Garland-Thomson suggests, however, disability can be viewed as a resource, rather than as a burden that should be eliminated. Garland-Thomson (2012) proposes several "countereugenic" arguments for conserving disability. Following Garland-Thomson, in this chapter I put forward my own arguments for conserving the deaf experience of music. I propose that deafness, rather than being disabling in the context of musical experience, actually enables distinctive musical performances that are potentially less accessible to those who possess a "normal" sense of hearing. Deafness, I argue, is not a deficit for musical experience; rather, it is a source of musical ability.

Musical expression takes many forms within Deaf culture.[1] The concept of music comprises a variety of visual and auditory experiences, ranging from those that are familiar to the hearing, such as playing an instrument and composing, to ones that are less familiar, such as listening through vibrations and performing or watching sign language songs. In the present chapter, I focus on sign language songs, or "song signing."[2] Musical performances that incorporate sign language have existed since at least the early twentieth century, and continue to thrive within both Deaf and hearing cultures. Song signing originated as a face-to-face art form, performed only live and within the Deaf community. Song-signing performances in the early twentieth century seem to have consisted mainly of hymn interpretations in religious settings and simple rhythmic signed songs (Bahan 2006, 34–35). In the early twenty-first century, however, the popularity of song signing soared among both hearing and d/Deaf populations, thanks to advances in video recording technology and the establishment of video-sharing websites such as YouTube and Vimeo. As signed song interpretation became more popular and visible among the hearing, the once purely Deaf, face-to-face tradition of signing songs became associated with amateur performances of popular songs by hearing students of sign language. Thus, the contemporary genre of song signing belongs equally to two traditions: first, the recent trend of posting "remakes [and] interpretations of pop songs" to YouTube (Peters and Seier 2009, 188), and second, the sign-language literary tradition, which is inextricably linked to Deaf culture and performance practice.

The signed song occupies several different cultural and artistic spaces, making it difficult to categorize. First, song signing belongs to both Deaf and hearing cultures, but has never been fully claimed by either. Ben Bahan, a prominent scholar of American Sign Language (ASL) literature, characterizes song signing as a byproduct of the interaction of Deaf people with the hearing world (2006, 33). Thus, some members of the Deaf community reject contemporary song signing as too strongly linked to hearing culture, while members of the hearing population are often suspicious that a song composed and performed in sign language is, in some sense, not truly "music." Second, although the American signed song developed out of the ASL poetic tradition and borrows many of its techniques, it has since distinguished itself as a separate, though related, art form. Finally, the necessary linguistic component of song signing separates it from dance—but as a gesture-based form of musical expression, it finds in dancing a close relative. Perhaps by virtue of its resistance to categorization, song signing has received little attention in the scholarly literature. As a result, the different types of song-signing performance, and the boundaries between them, remain largely undefined.

In this chapter, I address this gap in the scholarly literature by exploring some of the different song-signing techniques used by hearing and d/Deaf song signers. Through my exploration of how various performers employ these techniques, I argue that hearing song signers are generally motivated by a desire to express themselves musically *through* sign language, while Deaf song signers are more often motivated to create music *in* sign language. In other words, hearing signers try to convey something about their own experience of music through the medium of sign language, while Deaf song signers create sign language music, grounding that music in the characteristics of sign language. Through this process of embodied interpretation, Deaf song signers can create a new musical object out of an existing song. Using examples from both Deaf and hearing song-signing performances, I argue that deafness and hearing each enable different kinds of signed musical performance.

By pointing out the differences between how deaf- and hearing-bodied people interpret songs in sign language, I do not mean to suggest that all deaf people sign songs in one way while all hearing people sign songs in a wholly different way. There is a great deal of overlap between the techniques of d/Deaf and hearing song signers, not to mention those of hard-of-hearing song signers, as well as song signers who are culturally Deaf but not physically deaf (such as children of deaf adults). As the examples in this essay demonstrate, however, the song-signing practices of deaf- and hearing-bodied people do differ in important ways. In drawing attention to broader trends in the song-signing techniques of the hearing and d/Deaf, I hope to show how the performer's particular body affects how she/he experiences and expresses music through the performance of signed songs.

The first section that follows contains a brief explanation of each of the four main types of live and recorded song-signing performance. In the second section, I explore three aspects of song signing that reveal important differences between hearing and Deaf song-signing practices: clarity of communication, use of physical space, and rhythmic techniques. In the third part of the essay, I discuss hearing and Deaf song-signing communities, and the different motivating factors that lead performers and audience members to engage with the world of song signing.

Song-Signing Types

Bahan (2006) categorizes song signing as a form of face-to-face storytelling in Deaf culture. He defines two types of signed song: percussion songs and translated songs (34). Percussion signing involves arranging signs in rhythmic patterns, and translated songs involve translating song lyrics into ASL and performing them. The current song-signing practices demonstrated in live performances and videos are, however, far too varied to fit neatly into only two categories. In Bahan's model, originally composed sign language songs and interpretations of preexisting songs are subsumed into the single category of "translated song," and all other signed songs are categorized as "percussion signing," but the types of performers, the intent of the performances, and the community of viewers who consume these performances all vary widely within each category. The explosive increase in the popularity of song signing has led to a concomitant increase in the number of song-signing communities; as a result, finer distinctions must be made between the signed songs performed by various artists and communities of signers.

One basic division in the world of song-signing performance is between live shows and videos shared on the Internet. Each of these can be further divided into two broad categories, making four main types of signed song: live music interpretation services, live performances by song-signing artists, videos featuring the performance of an original song, and videos featuring the performance of a preexisting song. These four principal types do not encompass every possible instance of song signing; rather, they contain the most commonly occurring varieties of contemporary song signing.

Live Music Interpretation Services

The category of live music interpretation services includes activities ranging from professional sign language interpretation at concerts to amateur interpretation at events such as church services. The performers in this category are almost always hearing people whose goal is to provide a service for deaf audience members by translating song lyrics into a sign language. Professional ASL interpreters can increasingly be found providing live interpretation at popular music concerts as well as operas and other musical events.

Live Performances by Song-Signing Artists

Deaf musicians like Sean Forbes and Signmark often perform their sign language songs live, to largely Deaf audiences. Although these shows usually feature original compositions by the artists, some live shows also include signed performances of preexisting songs. Rarely, a hearing song-signing performer will gain enough popularity to put on a live show of their signed interpretations of preexisting songs. Instances of percussion signing also fall into this category, as percussion signing is usually performed live for a Deaf audience. Finally, Deaf theatre groups, like Deaf West Theatre and the International Center on Deafness and the Arts, often stage live performances of musicals in sign language. (For more information on this topic, consult Raymond Knapp's chapter in this volume).

Videos Featuring the Performance of an Original Song

Videos that feature the performance of an original song usually have a higher production value than sign language videos of preexisting songs. Sean Forbes, Signmark, and Beethoven's Nightmare all released music videos for their original songs that include sign language. In videos that present original songs, the performance of sign language can differ significantly. Some music videos are performed entirely in sign language and do not include any vocalizing (for example, a music video posted to YouTube called "One World, Two Hands"). Other videos are performed in sign language but also include vocals. Sean Forbes, for example, voices his own songs and raps in sign language. Signmark performs only in sign language, but his partner provides the vocal track. The group Beethoven's Nightmare adopts a different strategy in their videos. These artists perform on musical instruments and use sign language interpreters in both their live shows and music videos.

Videos Featuring the Performance of a Preexisting Song

The most common type of song-signing video found on YouTube features the performance of a preexisting song. Many such performances take the form of minimally edited amateur home videos, which are often filmed in the performers' homes using webcams. The performers in these videos are usually hearing, and the performance is often motivated by the requirements of a sign language course.[3] Like other "home-dance videos" found on YouTube, this type of song-signing video represents "a specific form of self-practice based on the playful practice and expansion of the physical technique of dance" (Peters and Seier 2009, 200). Although many performers of this subtype are beginner signers, this is not always the case; popular performers Kelly Greer (kmklined) and Allyson Townsend (allyballybabe) are examples of fluent, professional signers whose videos are minimally edited. Others are more artistic in their song-signing videos, and use some scene changes, costumes, and editing techniques. Some videos that exemplify this type are the "Bohemian Rhapsody" interpretation by Stephen Torrence, who is hearing, and the "Just the Way You Are" interpretation by Jason Listman, who is Deaf. (Both of these videos are discussed later in this chapter.) Still others produce professional song-signing videos of preexisting songs. These videos resemble those featuring performances of original songs and are produced mostly by Deaf artists. Many of these videos can be found on the website of the Deaf Professional Arts Network (D-PAN).

Separating signed songs into four categories reveals clear divisions between the song-signing practices of hearing and Deaf performers. Hearing performers dominate the first category, which involves the live translation of preexisting songs, while Deaf performers monopolize the second and third categories, which both feature original songs performed live or in videos. Both hearing and Deaf performers can be found in the fourth category (videos that use preexisting songs), although the two groups are not equally represented in all of the fourth category's subtypes. In summary, Deaf artists produce the majority of original song-signing performances and recordings (categories 2 and 3), while hearing performers produce a large quantity of videos and performances interpreting preexisting songs (categories 1 and 4), especially the "home-dance" type of videos. In this chapter, I focus on examples from the fourth song-signing category (videos featuring the performance of preexisting songs), because these videos are numerous, easily accessible, and are performed by both hearing and d/Deaf artists.

Comparing Deaf and Hearing Song-Signing Performances

The preceding enumeration of song-signing types demonstrates the variability of song-signing performances. Across all of these traditions, however, certain patterns emerge among the techniques used by d/Deaf and hearing song signers. These two groups of signed song performers tend to favor different communication strategies, use space differently, and employ contrasting rhythmic techniques.

There are two main differences between the communication techniques of Deaf and hearing song signers: first, hearing people are less concerned with using natural signed languages than Deaf people; second, Deaf people tend to use multiple communication techniques in their performances, while hearing people do not. As the following shows, the communication techniques used by a song signer have implications for the community of viewers who watch these performances.

Members of Deaf culture privilege the use of natural sign languages such as ASL, while members of the hearing community tend to be less particular about the signing systems they employ, often mixing artificial sign languages, such as Signed Exact English (SEE), with ASL.[4] Amateur hearing signers often use signs from SEE because they are less familiar with the grammatical structure of ASL and are inexperienced in correctly translating English into ASL. Thus, they incorporate signs from SEE and employ English word order in their interpretations, creating a form of Pidgin Signed English (PSE). While communication in grammatically correct ASL seems to be optional for many hearing performers, it is an essential part of song signing for Deaf performers.[5] There are several reasons why the use of natural sign languages is considered extremely important in the Deaf community. Sign language was historically suppressed in deaf education in America and internationally, in favor of oral teaching methods.[6] In the latter part of the twentieth century, sign language was reclaimed by the deaf and was finally recognized as a natural language by linguists. Since that time, sign language has been at the center of Deaf culture, and is linked to the notion of Deaf Pride. The use of sign language is generally considered to be a primary marker of membership in Deaf culture.

A video by Deaf performer Rosa Lee Timm demonstrates the importance of self-expression through a natural sign language for members of the Deaf community. In the video "ASL Music Video: All I Want by Damon Timm," Timm expresses the difference between interpreting a song in ASL and in SEE. In the first part of the video, shown in Track 4.1 on the Companion Website, Timm sits upright, stiffly, in the shade, and signs the song's lyrics very precisely in SEE. It is easy to see that each sign is mapped onto a single word in the English lyrics. This section is shot in split screen with the camera fixed on Timm, reinforcing the sense of stiffness in her signs. The scene is dimly lit, the colors bleached out. As the song progresses, Timm gradually changes her signs to ASL, and begins to express how she feels about communicating as a Deaf person, asking whether people can accept her for who she is (Track 4.2 on the Companion Website). The sun begins to shine and the colors deepen as she signs more freely and expressively in ASL. The split screen disappears, the camera becomes mobile, and Timm begins to interpret the music differently. In the first part of the video in SEE, her signs are halting, almost robotic, and remain staunchly unchanged by the presence of music. As she transforms her signing into ASL, her body begins to move with the music and her signs become more rhythmic. The story of coming into self-expression through ASL that Timm articulates in her video is one that would be familiar to many other members of the Deaf community. For Timm and many other members of the Deaf community, the use of ASL is essential for self-expression, while SEE and other artificial sign languages are the source of inhibition and frustration.

As noted previously, Deaf artists tend to use multiple means of communicating in their performances, while hearing performers tend to use only sign language. For example, many videos by Deaf performers use text in addition to ASL to portray a song's lyrics. Most videos on the D-PAN website contain some form of text captioning. Sometimes text captioning is not essential to the video, but in other cases, the text is an integral part of the visual communication in the performance. Sean Forbes often uses text creatively in his videos: for example, in the video for his song "Bob Dylan (Was the First Rapper)," Forbes uses handwritten cards to reveal the song's lyrics (a reference to Dylan's original 1965 promotional clip for the song "Subterranean Homesick Blues"). Whereas Dylan only showed selected lyrics on the cards in his video, Forbes uses the same medium to show all of the lyrics. He simultaneously sings and signs with one hand, weaving sign language into Bob Dylan's quoted lyrics (Track 4.3 on the Companion Website). This multiplicity of communication methods is essential for Forbes; in an interview with National Public Radio (2012), he explains that when he performs live he uses a video screen to present the lyrics, explaining that the screen "shows the words and shows the rhythm of the songs to get everything, to make it as accessible as possible."

We can observe the different priorities of hearing and Deaf song signers at play in the audience responses to a video posted by a hearing song signer named Mark Nakhla. The video, which contains an interpretation of the Jay-Z and Kanye West song "No Church in the Wild" by Nakhla and two friends, generated a storm of controversy in the community of sign language users on YouTube. The reaction of the Deaf community can be summarized in a comment posted by Karunaify20, who wrote:

> If this video represents your own interpretation of the song, then hey, you did a beautiful job! However, the problem I have with this video is that you called it an American Sign Language music video. It is not.

By contrast, most hearing commenters saw no problem with the "sign language" used by the group in the video. Misssupreme, for example, comments:

> I thought this was awesome! It may not be ASL grammatically but signing this way makes hearing people like myself more inclined to learn sign language and learn about Deaf culture. Awesome video!

Members of the Deaf community who opposed the use of non-ASL signs and grammar in Nakhla's video had their comments removed, and some took to blogs to express their outrage. These postings revealed that many ASL users were offended in the first instance by the signers' interspersing of gang signs with grammatically correct ASL, and in the second instance by the fact that much of the signing in the video was incomprehensible. In a blog comment posted April 18, 2012, A Deaf Pundit wrote: "In all honesty, what I'm seeing from them in that video are *gang* signs with some actual ASL signs thrown in." In general, Deaf commenters on YouTube and in blogs tended to focus on the fact that the video was difficult to understand and that the performers did not communicate clearly. Commenter foundonroaddead1, who identifies as Deaf, writes:

> The thing is that it's not a language you were signing. You signed the words right. But it wasnt [*sic*] put together to form a "language." That's what all the Deaf people (including I) was concerning [*sic*] about. We are concern [*sic*], and want to make our American Sign Language (ASL) a genuine and legitimated language.

By contrast, many of the hearing people who commented on Mark Nakhla's video focused either on how the translation was valuable for making music accessible to the deaf, or on how well the performers expressed themselves. Commenter dr24will, for example, writes: "I love it for its creative and artistic value, independent of any language or signing issues. There's real character here. It's expressive, even if technically 'incorrect.' Keep going!"

As these exchanges show, the incorrect use of ASL, or the use of artificial signing systems and English word order, can have a major impact on the reception of song-signing videos. Clarity of communication is seen as essential by the d/Deaf, who often use multiple communication methods, such as captioning or other forms of text, to connect with their audience. By contrast, language selection and the use of text or other communication techniques is often less important for hearing performers and audience members.

Expressive use of the signing space also plays an important role in song-signing performance. The nature of sign languages, which are produced in space, allows them to readily accommodate the iconic use of that space (Padden et al. 2010, 570). Hearing and d/Deaf song signers both use this remarkable feature of sign language to represent musical concepts spatially, but they do so in different ways. Hearing song signers tend to manipulate the signing space in order to convey aspects of the music related to pitch and register. For example, in his interpretation of Queen's "Bohemian Rhapsody," Stephen Torrence moves his head in order to convey register. In Track 4.4 on the Companion Website, he tilts his head upward, looking and signing to his left, in order to represent the higher register of the voice on the word "Galileo" when it is first sung, and then tilts it downward and signs to his right on the lower repetition of the same word. On the word "magnifico," Torrence modifies the sign AWESOME to accommodate the falling line in the sounding music by correlating higher pitch with a higher signing space and moving through repetitions of AWESOME into a lower signing space.

The embodiment of register found in Torrence's video (and many others) is an important part of expression for hearing song signers. Deaf song signers, however, appear to be less concerned with representing register in their interpretations, instead preferring to use space for a different purpose. In ASL poetry, space is often discussed in terms of the line: according to H-Dirksen L. Bauman (2006), "ASL is at all times composed of lines, invisible and kinetic. . . . The line carries a generating capacity, an expressiveness all its own whose speed, tension, length, direction and duration construct and disperse a particular energy" (104). These lines "gesture through time and space, controlling and dispersing energy as a dancer does" (107). In ASL song interpretation, these kinetic lines play an especially important role, since the song signer produces not only "precise grammatical and visual images" (107) through sign but also musical images. The musical image produced by the song signer depends on how he or she manipulates the signing space.

Rosa Lee Timm's ASL interpretation of the Carrie Underwood song "Blown Away" presents an excellent example of this kind of manipulation. In the song, the protagonist speaks about a tornado bearing down on her "sin-filled" house in Oklahoma, where she lives with her father (described as a "mean old mister"), as her mother is dead (an "angel in the ground"). The story is told in the third person and consists of an instrumental introduction, two verses, and several iterations and fragmentations of the chorus, which increases in intensity each time it is repeated. The video begins with Timm facing the camera directly. Although her head is lowered at first, she soon raises it to sign directly toward the audience, impersonating the story's protagonist (Track 4.5 on the Companion Website). In the first verse, Timm establishes that the song's main character signs to the front, while the character's father and mother are signed toward the right and left sides of her body, respectively. At the end of the first verse, TORNADO is signed to the right, along with several more signs indicating that the protagonist's house is being blown away and destroyed.

In the song's chorus, Timm expands the TORNADO and WIND signs to encompass more of the signing space (Track 4.6 on the Companion Website). Her facial expressions become more intense as well: her brow is furrowed, her mouth open. She seems almost to be embodying the storm, sweeping away the previously established signing spaces for FATHER, MOTHER, and even the protagonist herself. We are left with a mere echo of the voice as the chorus comes to an end, however, and consequently Timm's signing dies down without fully taking over the signing space.

The second verse finds the protagonist making the decision to leave her father passed out on the couch while she locks herself in the cellar, allowing the wind and rain to destroy the house. Timm now locates the character of the father on the left side of her body. The intensity of the sounding music builds slowly throughout the verses and repetitions of the chorus. As the chorus builds in intensity and begins to fragment into repetitions of the words "blown away," the melody becomes more melismatic, prompting Timm's gestures to become more expansive and dramatic; her movements begin to take over the left side of the signing space, where the signs about the protagonist's father were located at the beginning of the second verse. Eventually, as Track 4.7 on the Companion Website shows, Timm not only uses the sign TWISTER to encompass the entire signing space twice over, she also transforms her body into a twister, twirling wildly as the music's intensity rises. In addition, Timm expands the vertical space of her signing by alternately raising her signs and tilting her body backward to expand the upper range of her signing and crouching to lower the normal signing space. The dramatic expansion of Timm's horizontal and vertical lines cannot adequately be explained by referencing the narrative arc of Carrie Underwood's song. These changes occur over repeated iterations of the chorus with no further narrative developments, but the audience nonetheless experiences a marked increase in the intensity of the music, both heard and seen.

At the end of the song, Timm's TORNADO sign seems to shrink, until her hands are pressed close together, once again compressing the vertical dimension that she had previously expanded. Her facial expressions move from intense anger and ecstasy, as we saw in the verses and choruses, to an expression of horror. Just as she expanded her horizontal and vertical lines while the song's intensity increased, Timm now closes them off as the protagonist seems to realize what she has done, staring out at the viewer as the music abruptly ends. Rather than focusing on the representation of register through her signs, Timm uses the signing space to represent the more intangible sense of rising intensity and anger in Carrie Underwood's music, and to leave us with a new interpretation of the song's ending.

In the examples from "Bohemian Rhapsody," I noted how Stephen Torrence provided analogical representations of musical relationships through his use of sign language. By contrast, Rosa Lee Timm used sign language as a means of musical expression, adding new layers of meaning to the song through her dramatic use of the signing space. These two videos are excellent examples of how hearing signers tend to express themselves musically *through* sign language, while Deaf signers create music *in* sign language. The tendency of d/Deaf and hearing song signers to employ contrasting rhythmic techniques in their song-signing performances further supports this distinction.

The rhythmic use of sign language is the most immediately obvious musical feature of signed songs. Rhythm plays a number of different roles in signed songs. First, sign languages have naturally occurring prosodic rhythms, just like oral languages. Prosodic rhythm can play a greater or smaller role in song signing depending on the fluency of the signer. The rhythmic use of sign language in song-signing performance can also be musically motivated.

Deaf and hearing performers tend to employ different rhythmic techniques in their videos. In videos by hearing song signers, it is common to see frequent pulsing of the body or nodding of the head along with the beat of the sounding music. Pulsing can play different roles in different song-signing videos. In previous work, I defined the "pulsing technique" as a common and noticeable means of defining a phrase in ASL songs, consisting simply of the regular pulsation of the signer's body in time with the beat while either holding or repeating a full sign or part of one (Maler 2013). This pulsation is generally used at the end of a phrase in order to signal the attainment of a goal.[7] Some hearing signers, however, move their bodies or nod their heads throughout extended sections of their interpretations, rather than using this movement as a phrase-delimiting technique. An example of this type of pulsing can be seen in an interpretation of Bruno Mars's "Just the Way You Are," posted by Kelsey S. In this video, the two performers move their bodies and nod their heads consistently throughout much of the video, both while they are signing and during instrumental breaks (Track 4.8 on the Companion Website). The constant pulsation of the signers' bodies alters most of the signs in their performance. It seems clear that these two song signers are more influenced by the beat of the sounding music than by any notion of ASL prosody, since they appear to be focused exclusively on the rhythm of the preexisting song.

Deaf song signers, by contrast, are generally more faithful to ASL prosody in their performances, and therefore less likely to consistently alter signs through the kind of pulsing shown in Track 4.8 on the Companion Website. In ASL, nonmanual markers, such as head movements, torso movements, blinking, mouthing, and other facial expressions, "participate in structuring an utterance prosodically," in addition to serving as an "essential part of the grammar of natural sign languages" (Pfau and Quer 2010, 397). The most important nonmanual prosodic markers for the present discussion are head movements, torso movements, and sign articulation. In her exploration of ASL prosody, Elizabeth Winston (2000) points out that head and torso movements create spatial patterns and rhythms. In addition, some features of sign articulation can create prosody, such as "sign-internal movements, size of articulation, repetition, lengths of movements and holds both within and between signs, and height of the signs." These markers of ASL prosody are crucial to understanding the different kinds of movement found in song-signing videos by Deaf and hearing signers.

Jason Listman provides an example of how Deaf song signers use ASL prosody in his interpretation of the same Bruno Mars song performed by Kelsey S. and her friend. The song's first verse, interpreted by Listman, can be found in Track 4.9 on the Companion Website. Listman delivers a highly rhythmic performance, but one of an entirely different kind than that provided by the hearing signers. In this video, Listman uses movements of his head and body, as well as holds and repetitions of signs, in a manner consistent with ASL prosody. In Figure 4.1, I have juxtaposed the lyrics of the first verse with Listman's signs, which are written in capital letters below the English lyrics. The chart should be read left to right, in vertical pairs of words and signs. Signs that are emphasized using nonmanual markers are in bold. The sign EYES, for example, is marked by Listman opening his mouth. Listman marks the entire phrase STARS

1	x	y	z	**2**	x	y	z
			Oh	-- her	eyes	her eyes	-- make the
			HER	**EYES**	EYES		**STARS**
stars	look like	they're not	shining.	Her	hair	her hair	falls
SHINE-into	--	**SHINE-into**	--	HER	**HAIR**		ALREADY
perfect-	-ly with-	out her	trying.		She's so	beauti-	-ful
-- **PER-**	-FECT	--	-- ALREADY		YOU	**BEAUTIFUL**	--
	and I	tell her	every	--	day.		
--	--	--	--	**I TELL YOU**		**DAILY**	
		Yeah	--				
		YEAH					

FIGURE 4.1 A chart showing the lyrics and signs in the first verse of "Just the Way You Are," performed by Bruno Mars and interpreted by Jason Listman. The lyrics and accompanying signs are arranged in vertical pairs based on their relative rhythmic positions.

1	x	y	2	x	y
		HER	**EYES**	EYES	
STARS	**SHINE-into**	--	**SHINE-into**	--	HER
HAIR		ALREADY	-- **PER-**	-FECT	--
-- ALREADY		YOU	**BEAUTIFUL**	--	--
--	--	--	**I TELL YOU**		**DAILY**
--	--	--	**YEAH**		

FIGURE 4.2 A chart showing Jason Listman's sign language interpretation of "Just the Way You Are," without English lyrics.

SHINE-into by suddenly turning his head upward and to the left, and he marks the repetition of SHINE-into by once again turning his head, this time to his right. HAIR is once again marked by Listman's open mouth, and the signs PERFECT and BEAUTIFUL are both marked by holds.

While some of the signs emphasized by Listman correspond with the English lyrics sung by Bruno Mars, they do not all line up perfectly. For example, the sign BEAUTIFUL coincides with the English word "beautiful," but because of the long hold on BEAUTIFUL, the repetition of DAILY occurs after the voice has already cut out. In Figure 4.2, I have extracted only Listman's signing from the video. Notice that the rhythm of Listman's signs implies a triple meter, but the original music is quite clearly in duple time. By combining the natural flow of sign language with the sounding music, Listman achieves a layered, contrapuntal effect through the interplay of the signed and sung words, an effect that can only be understood by experiencing the gesture music and the heard or felt music in tandem.

There is also a strong tendency among hearing song signers to end a signed phrase when the phrase ends in the sounding voice. Usually, instrumental gaps between phrases are then filled with dancing. We can observe this technique in an interpretation of the song "The Middle" by Jimmy Eat World by Greg Faxon, who appears to be a beginning sign language student. Watching Greg Faxon's interpretation of the song's first verse in Track 4.10 on the Companion Website, we can see that Faxon clearly aligns his signs with the sung lyrics, ending each phrase at the same time as the singer and bouncing up and down when there is no linguistic content to be translated.

By contrast, Deaf signers tend to fill the whole temporal space with signs. Instead of dancing, pulsing, or standing still between phrases or verses, Deaf signers may time their signing so that the signed phrase occupies more time than the sung one, hold final signs of phrases, and repeat or add signs until the space is filled. An excellent example of these techniques can be found in an interpretation of the same Jimmy Eat World song as found in Track 4.10; this time, however, it is performed by Russell Harvard, a Deaf actor (Track 4.11 on the Companion Website). Harvard does not stop signing when the vocalist stops singing; instead, he times his signing so that the entire musical space is filled with movement. In the second verse, after the line "Hey, you know they're all the same," Harvard holds the sign EVERYONE SAME over an instrumental break. On the next line, he times his signing so that it ends just as the voice begins the next phrase. Over the words "Live right now, just be yourself," Harvard repeatedly signs LIFE and YOURSELF in order to occupy more of the musical space. This moment is especially striking, because he repeats the signs so rhythmically and creates a handshape rhyme through the use of the A handshape in both signs.[8] To finish the second verse and lead into the chorus, Harvard once again times his signing to stretch across the necessary span of time. Harvard's signing is highly rhythmic throughout the song, and unlike Listman, the rhythm of his signing does not noticeably diverge from the rhythm of the preexisting song. Instead of creating an interpretation where music and sign interact contrapuntally, Harvard infuses his signing with the song's rhythm, so that he always expresses the rhythm of the music linguistically even when no lyrics are actually present.

The preceding comments are not meant to suggest that Deaf people do not feel the beat; in fact, Deaf song signers usually sign quite rhythmically. Deaf signers are, however, more attentive to the complex relationship between the rhythm of the sounding music, the prosody of ASL, and the need to keep their audience's attention even when there is no linguistic content in the sounding music. They negotiate interactions between the two rhythmic streams more carefully than hearing song signers, trying to remain faithful to both the ASL rhythm and the musical rhythm. Hearing song signers tend to focus, whether consciously or unconsciously, on faithfully representing the pitches and rhythms of the music with their bodies. In videos by Deaf song signers, by contrast, the relationship between the sounding music and the sign language is fluid and changeable: sometimes the beat of the drum prevails, and at other times ASL prosody takes the reins.

Performing Deafness and Hearing

Song-signing videos are an important site for self-expression through sign language for both hearing and Deaf performers. However, Deaf and hearing song signers often have different motivations in creating their videos. Hearing signers usually create song-signing videos at least partially in order to provide d/Deaf people with access to their own experience of music. Deaf signers are more interested in creatively and artistically expressing musical texts in a visual medium.

As noted above, hearing song signers usually produce live music interpretation services and videos featuring the performance of a preexisting song. Generally speaking, hearing song signers create videos that express something about the music they hear, either in order to act as interpreters for the deaf, or to express themselves. These motivations are not mutually exclusive, and in fact overlap most of the time.

Many hearing song signers express a desire to help those who are hard-of-hearing or deaf to better understand music through their videos. In a blog interview, well-known song signer Stephen Torrence stated that his goal is to make his videos "accessible to both deaf and hearing" (Wilson 2009). Another well-known performer, Allyson

Townsend, has made it clear in interviews that her videos are meant to translate songs so that deaf and hard-of-hearing viewers may enjoy them. Townsend's ASL translations were originally conceived with the purpose of conveying to a deaf friend, and other d/Deaf individuals, the experience of music as perceived by hearing people. An interview with Townsend (on Baylor University's *President's Scholarship Initiative* website) confirms that she "remains focused on one goal: bridging the gap for persons surrounded by the sound of silence into the rhythm of the hearing world around them" (Baylor University 2013). Torrence and Townsend both post their glosses below their song-signing videos so that other aspiring song interpreters can learn how they translated the song and reproduce it themselves. The act of posting a gloss along with a video suggests that the performer is in some sense interchangeable. Since the performers in these videos are only translating the song to provide access to deaf viewers, the specific body of the interpreter is largely irrelevant. Any other interpreter, provided they possess an adequate level of sign language fluency, should be capable of providing an equally useful and comprehensible sign language interpretation.

Hearing people also create song-signing videos in order to express themselves and their love of particular pieces of music through sign language. Most of these videos fall into the "amateur home video" type, as described earlier. The videos created by Kelsey S ("Just the Way You Are") and Greg Faxon ("The Middle") fall into this category, as do hundreds more on YouTube. Like "home-dance videos," these song-signing videos generally use minimal props, costumes, and settings, often confining the video to a small, intimate, personal living space. Because the makers of these home song-signing videos mostly focus on expressing the self through gesture and dance, they tend to concern themselves less with visual expression. The backgrounds of their videos are often distracting, revealing parts of the performer's bedroom, and they do not usually use special effects or even edit their videos. The lack of attention to the visual in amateur song-signing videos indicates that for these performers, the sounding music is the most privileged element of signed song performance.

Like hearing performers, Deaf performers are interested in providing their audience with expressive and creative performances of their favorite songs, and in providing equal access to music. Deaf song signers differ from hearing ones, however, in that they show a much deeper investment in *how* they express themselves musically. Deaf song signers are more concerned with making Deaf music: music that privileges visual forms of expression, that uses techniques specific to natural sign languages, and that is particular to a specific body.

Deaf song signers do not merely translate the audible into the visual; rather, they create music in their visual performances. The Deaf performers referenced throughout this chapter regularly use scene changes, costumes, special effects (i.e., fans, slow motion, black and white, blurring), and higher-quality video cameras to craft visual spectacles for the viewer. Every part of the video expresses meaning visually. This expressive use of visual details can be easily seen in examples like Rosa Lee Timm's "All I Want" and "Blown Away" videos, or Sean Forbes's "Bob Dylan (Was the First Rapper)" video (Tracks 4.1, 4.2, 4.3, 4.5, 4.6, and 4.7 on the Companion Website).

Beyond producing visual music, Deaf performers of signed songs create music within their bodies. In ASL songs, as in ASL poetry, "the body and voice of the artist are integral to the life of the piece itself. The poem literally lives in the poet, and the poet gives the poem life through performance" (Rose 2006, 136). In the case of the song signer, the song itself lives in the body of the performer, and each of the performance nuances that I have explored in this essay "are integrally related to the *meaning* of the poem or narrative. It is these nuances [. . .] that give each poem its distinct identity because they are bound up in the *body* of the artist" (140). Whereas hearing signers post their glosses so that others can reproduce their interpretations, Deaf song signers almost never do the same. In Deaf song-signing performance, the Deaf body matters.

As Douglas Baynton (2008) observes, "the body is intensely relevant to Deaf people. The appropriate vocabulary is that of difference, however, not loss" (296). In the imaginations of most hearing people, a lack of access to sonic information, and especially a perceived lack of access to musical sound, is a source of loss, impairment, and disability for those who are deaf. For many deaf people, however, the physical characteristics of deafness provide access to another culture, one with its own language, customs, literature, and music. Deaf song signers use the poetic techniques, rhythms, and language of their culture in order to embody music through a form of gesture unfamiliar to most hearing people, and in doing so, they make a political statement by embodying the very source of their own perceived disability. If deaf people are considered by the hearing to be disabled by a lack of access to sound, then in making that sound inextricable from their own particular, deaf bodies, they show Deafness as a strength and a site for artistic expression.

The properties of physical deafness and cultural Deafness combined enable the performer to embody music in a way that is different from how hearing people embody music. Deaf people hear differently than those who are not deaf, and that difference is evident in the way that they embody music. Hearing song signers tend to use the sounding music as a dominant force in shaping the rhythm and location of their signs. They usually produce interpretations in which the placement of signs coincides as closely as possible with the rhythm of the sung words, and they almost always coordinate the ends of signed phrases with the ends of sung ones. Deaf song signers, by contrast, bring the quirks and characteristics of sign language and Deaf culture into their performances in order to create a visual and kinetic form of music. In the context of song signing, deafness is a resource that affords specific expressive practices, just as hearing is a resource that affords different kinds of expressive practices. Disability, in other words, is both contextual and constructed. Just as deafness can be a disability in some musical practices of the hearing, so too can hearing be a disability in musical practices traditional to Deaf culture.

Conclusion

All of the different varieties of the signed song referenced in this chapter fulfill important functions in Deaf and hearing cultures. Those song signers who act as hearing interpreters of music are highly popular among both d/Deaf and hearing fans, and amateur "home-dance" song-signing videos serve an important role for self-expression and self-presentation among hearing YouTubers. The Deaf song-signing video or live performance also has a particular cultural function as a piece of ASL literature. These videos express cultural values associated with Deaf communities: they emphasize the use of ASL instead of SEE, and they tend to privilege the visual and spatial domains. It seems clear that the latter type of signed song extends beyond Bahan's notion that song signing is merely a byproduct of the interaction of Deaf people with the hearing world. Although song signing probably originated through the interaction of the Deaf with the hearing, the manner in which Deaf artists have developed the signed song into a medium for Deaf musical expression has little to do with the modes of musical expression privileged by the hearing.

The examples in this chapter demonstrate that d/Deaf song signers embody music differently than the hearing by creating a visual, kinetic form of music in sign language, rather than using sign language to express something about sound. In exploring the differences between how hearing and Deaf performers interpret music using sign language, I have raised the possibility that deafness can be a source of musical ability rather than a source of impairment and that hearing can even be seen as a disability in the context of Deaf musical performance practice. Of course, hearing is not generally considered disabling in the context of any musical performance, including song signing. Instead, the abundance of hearing song signers and the increasing visibility of these sign language interpreters in the media has resulted in a very particular way of understanding music accessibility: equal access to music begins and ends with providing a hearing sign language interpreter who listens to the music and translates it for the deaf audience. Musical expression, in this definition of equal access, is thus limited to the methods of the hearing.

As Hilda Haualand (2008) has observed, too often the attempts of the hearing "to 'include' Deaf people and make Deaf people *hear same* . . . results in oppression of the Deaf-embodied ways of perceiving, mapping, and learning about the world" (120). In the case of sign language music, it is all too easy to default to a hearing-centric perspective: that the purpose of signed songs is to interpret for the deaf or for the hearing to express something about what they hear. As the examples in this chapter have shown, however, the concept of "music" goes beyond hearing experiences and values, and a full account of musical expression must include the contributions of the d/Deaf.

Acknowledgments

I thank the following people for their thoughtful and generous comments on earlier versions of this chapter: my fellow handbook authors Blake Howe, Jennifer Iverson, Jeannette Jones, and Joseph Straus; the participants at the 2013 Music on Small Screens conference in Ottawa, Ontario; Nicholas Cook; and the students and faculty at the University of Chicago, especially Steven Rings and Larry Zbikowski.

Notes

1. Membership in Deaf culture is minimally defined by the ability to speak a sign language, and usually by medical deafness (with some exceptions, such as CODAs, children of deaf adults). In accordance with customs from the scholarship on Deaf culture, I will refer to those individuals who identify as belonging to Deaf culture as Deaf with an uppercase "D" and to those individuals who are medically deaf but do not identify as belonging to Deaf culture as deaf with a lowercase "d." When referring to both groups, I use the term "d/Deaf."
2. In a previous essay on song signing, I identify several different techniques that both d/Deaf and hearing song signers use to express particular musical features in sign language (Maler 2013). The techniques I explore in that essay also appear in the song-signing examples used here, but in the present chapter I am more concerned with the particular aspects of song-signing performance that are specific to either d/Deaf or hearing communities of song signers.
3. The assignment to "sign your favorite song" is common to many ASL courses in high schools and universities.
4. SEE is an artificial sign language in the sense that it was created specifically for the purpose of representing the English language manually. Signed Exact English is essentially the same language as English, presented in a different medium. Sign languages like ASL develop naturally in deaf communities. When signed and spoken languages come together, pidgin sign languages, like Pidgin Signed English (PSE), often result.
5. Hearing people who involved in Deaf culture, such as CODAs and professional sign language interpreters, are a major exception in this case, since they will also generally avoid using SEE and English word order.
6. For a detailed history of the American battle between manualist and oralist educational methods, see Baynton 1996.
7. For more information about song-signing techniques for delimiting phrases, see Maler 2013.
8. A handshape rhyme involves the repetition of a handshape in order to create the visual equivalent of rhyming in sign language poetry. Other parameters of the sign, such as a movement or a nonmanual marker, may also be repeated to create a rhyme. See Kaneko 2011; Sutton-Spence, Ladd, and Rudd 2005; and Valli 1990.

References

Abbate, Carolyn. 1991. *Unsung Voices: Opera and Musical Narrative in the Nineteenth Century*. Princeton, NJ: Princeton University Press.

Bahan, Ben. 2006. "Face-to-Face Tradition in the American Deaf Community: Dynamics of the Teller, the Tale, and the Audience." In *Signing the Body Poetic: Essays on American Sign Language Literature*, edited by H-Dirksen L. Bauman, Jennifer L. Nelson, and Heidi M. Rose, 21–50. Berkeley: University of California Press.

Bauman, H-Dirksen L. 2006. "Getting out of Line: Toward a Visual and Cinematic Poetics of ASL." In *Signing the Body Poetic: Essays on American Sign Language Literature*, edited by H-Dirksen L. Bauman, Jennifer L. Nelson, and Heidi M. Rose, 95–117. Berkeley: University of California Press.

Baylor University. 2013. "Breaking the Barrier: A Baylor Student Brings the Sounds of Music to Life for the Hearing-Impaired Community." December 27. http://www.baylor.edu/development/scholarships/index.php?id=80412.

Baynton, Douglas C. 1996. *Forbidden Signs: American Culture and the Campaign against Sign Language*. Chicago: University of Chicago Press.

Baynton, Douglas C. 2008. "Beyond Culture: Deaf Studies and the Deaf Body." In *Open Your Eyes: Deaf Studies Talking*, edited by H-Dirksen L. Bauman, 293–313. Minneapolis: University of Minnesota Press.

Garland-Thomson, Rosemarie. 2012. "The Case for Conserving Disability." *Bioethical Inquiry* 9: 339–355.

Haualand, Hilde. 2008. "Sound and Belonging: What Is a Community?" In *Open Your Eyes: Deaf Studies Talking*, edited by H-Dirksen L. Bauman, 111–123. Minneapolis: University of Minnesota Press.

Kaneko, Michiko. 2011. "Alliteration in Sign Language Poetry." In *Alliteration in Culture*, edited by Jonathan Roper, 231–246. Basingstoke, UK: Palgrave MacMillan.

Maler, Anabel. 2013. "Songs for Hands: Analyzing Interactions of Sign Language and Music." *Music Theory Online* 13 (1). http://mtosmt.org/issues/mto.13.19.1/mto.13.19.1.maler.php.

National Public Radio. 2012. "Sean Forbes: Deaf but Not Quiet." August 30. http://www.npr.org/2012/09/01/160343713/sean-forbes-deaf-but-not-quiet.

Padden, Carol, Irit Meir, Mark Aronoff, and Wendy Sandler. 2010. "The Grammar of Space in Two New Sign Languages." In *Sign Languages*, edited by Diane Brentari, 570–592. Cambridge, UK: Cambridge University Press.

Peters, Kathrin, and Andrea Seier. 2009. "Home Dance: Mediacy and Aesthetics of the Self on YouTube." In *The YouTube Reader*, edited by Pelle Snickars and Patrick Vonderau, 187–203. Stockholm: National Library of Sweden.

Pfau, Roland, and Josep Quer. 2010. "Nonmanuals: Their Grammatical and Prosodic Roles." In *Sign Languages*, edited by Diane Brentari, 381–402. Cambridge, UK: Cambridge University Press.

Rose, Heidi M. 2006. "The Poet in the Poem in the Performance: The Relation of Body, Self, and Text in ASL Literature." In *Signing the Body Poetic: Essays on American Sign Language Literature*, edited by H-Dirksen L. Bauman, Jennifer L. Nelson, and Heidi M. Rose, 130–146. Berkeley: University of California Press.

Straus, Joseph N. 2011. *Extraordinary Measures: Disability in Music*. New York: Oxford University Press.

Sutton-Spence, Rachel, Paddy Ladd, and Gillian Rudd. 2005. *Analysing Sign Language Poetry*. Basingstoke, UK: Palgrave Macmillan.

Valli, Clayton. 1990. "The Nature of a Line in ASL Poetry." In *SLR '87: Papers from the Fourth International Symposium on Sign Language Research*, edited by William Edmondson and Fred Karlsson, 171–182. Hamburg, Germany: Signum Verlag.

Wilson, Tracy V. 2009. "5 Questions for Stephen Torrence, ASL Signer and Jonathan Coulton Fan." *PopStuff* (blog), *HowStuffWorks*, September 1. http://blogs.howstuffworks.com/2009/09/01/5-questions-for-stephen-torrence-maker-of-jonathan-coulton-asl-videos/.

Winston, Elizabeth. 2000. "It Just Doesn't Look Like ASL! Defining, Recognizing and Teaching Prosody in ASL." Paper presented at the Conference of Interpreter Trainers: Celebrating Excellence, Celebrating Partnership, Portland, Oregon.

Videos Cited

"ASL: Just the Way You Are." 2012. YouTube video, 3:42. Posted by "Kelsey S," July 17. http://youtu.be/PjEw5NwaU1Q.

Calbert, Eric. 2009. "ASL Song 'One World, Two Hands.'" YouTube video, 6:16. October 6. http://youtu.be/RJXojcrastE.

Faxon, Greg. 2011. "ASL—The Middle." YouTube video, 2:48. May 10. http://youtu.be/G4wdEsKPbhg.

Forbes, Sean. 2012. "Sean Forbes—Bob Dylan (Was The First Rapper)." YouTube video, 2:37. September 1. http://youtu.be/mRQ9ldntWFQ.

Harvard, Russell. 2012. "ASL Music Video: The Middle by Jimmy Eat World." YouTube video, 2:47. March 16. http://youtu.be/UEXVxo5uQso.

Listman, Jason. 2011. "Just the Way You Are—Bruno Mars (in ASL)." YouTube video, 3:35. February 15. http://youtu.be/9vrboKNjpMk.

Nakhla, Mark, Greg Faxon, and Sam Choi. 2012. "No Church in the Wild—JAY-Z & Kanye West (Sign Language)." YouTube video, 3:31. April 15. http://youtu.be/tBi_18OGF6A.

Timm, Rosa Lee. 2008. "ASL Music Video: All I Want by Damon Timm." YouTube video, 2:40. September 28. http://youtu.be/C-9tBKf87qs.

Timm, Rosa Lee. 2012. "ASL Music Video: Blown Away by Carrie Underwood." YouTube video, 4:04. October 28. http://youtu.be/e_SbM9Ci_ok.

Torrence, Stephen. 2010. "Queen—Bohemian Rhapsody—ASL Song." YouTube video, 5:54. June 15. http://youtu.be/sjln9OMOw-o.

CHAPTER 5

THE POLITICS OF SOUND

Music and Blindness in France, 1750–1830

INGRID SYKES

In December 1792, the French philanthropist and linguist Valentin Haüy demanded that the general public take notice of the blind pupils at his special school, the Institute of Blind Youth. At a formal announcement directed at all the 48 newly formed Revolutionary territorial and administrative areas of Paris, he reminded the "brothers and citizens" in the audience that the principle of equality was most strongly applicable to the Blind (Haüy 1792). But he did not simply demand equal rights for this particular group. Instead, he argued that in their work at the Institute, the blind youth demonstrated the principles of the Republican spirit of "Human Rights" in action. The "Nation," he explained, had supported the implementation of a "useful and consoling" education that had emerged from his own feelings of humane compassion, "my devotion to the care of Humanity" (*Troisième note du citoyen Haüy* 1801, 9). Now, he declared, all people should answer the call of the Blind by visiting them in their institution and seeing the principles of his educational practice at work: "Blind Children invite you, through my mouth, to come (Haüy 1792).

Haüy's contribution to the education of the Blind has been widely acknowledged in histories of the French blind. Scholars such as Zina Weygand have powerfully demonstrated that Haüy's work in developing written communication during the late eighteenth century led to a "universal culture and a federative element for the emerging community of educated blind people" (Weygand 2009, 299) that lasted well into the nineteenth, twentieth, and indeed, twenty-first centuries. Yet the way in which the Blind themselves negotiated change during the tumultuous period of late eighteenth- and early nineteenth-century France was extremely complex. In this essay I argue that it was not simply new communication technologies developed during this period that led to the evolution of a distinctive blind identity in modern French society. Rather, it was the establishment of the blind bodily self, in particular, the sounding blind bodily self among the Blind that emerged as the more effective tool to make blind presence felt. The shift in mode and practice surrounding blind communication not only affected the evolution of blind activity as we understand it today but also had dramatic implications for the development of a more broadly acting bodily configuration operating in modern

French culture and society. Blind musical bodies and their virtuosic practice were highly influential in the construction of the regenerative French state.

Haüy's school and his treatise on blind education appeared just at the time when perfect speech and speech systems began to dominate debates within the ideological political arena. In 1791, the statesman Charles-Maurice de Talleyrand announced that a new form of French language would play a central role in developing the new French constitution. That language, as Sophia Rosenfeld has pointed out, "was the gestural and methodical sign system developed in the preceding decades for the education of the deaf" (Rosenfeld 2001, 123). Haüy's work, though related to the deaf sign system was, however, much more squarely focused on sonic forms of communication rather than gesture. Haüy, like many other Enlightenment thinkers, understood written and musical languages as systems of sounds that drew people together into a positive relationship of humanity. Just like gesture, sound became a useful tool for "a range of projects and semiotic experiments aimed at transcending the problems and limitations associated with vernacular words" (Rosenfeld 2001, 4). The young blind were part of the larger Revolutionary dream, identified by Rosenfeld, to create a utopian "vision" of language for a regenerated age. Haüy was not bothered that the Blind literally and figuratively could not "see" this vision. Indeed, they would experience it wholeheartedly through their sensitive auditory and tactile abilities. Haüy presented his young blind in venues as diverse as the Tuileries Palace, the Hotel de Ville, and Versailles in front of audiences ranging from the Royal Academy of Sciences and the Museum of Paris to the king himself (Henri 1984, 77–85; Weygand 2009, 105–110, 146–152). On these occasions, the Blind not only presented musical and dramatic works they had learned prior to the performance but also showcased themselves studying (reading, arithmetic) in front of the audience.

Throughout the eighteenth century, philosophers, musicians, and rhetoricians had argued that sonic practices aimed at cultivating proper listening were pivotal to the social good. Haüy was also a sound specialist in this Enlightenment professional mold. From 1769, he had worked as a freelance interpreter and codebreaker in fields as diverse as banking and the police, and in 1782, just prior to the opening of his school for the young blind, he was appointed official interpreter for the king, soon after becoming a member of Louis XVI's Bureau Académique d'Ecriture (Henri 1984, 24–32).

In 1771, Haüy heard a group of blind musicians perform at the Saint Ovid's Fair in Paris. A large, spectacular engraving was produced of the event titled *Grand Concert Extraordinaire* (*Grand Concert* 1771). The musicians had come from the Hospice des Quinze-Vingts, an institution for the Blind and Partially Sighted, situated on the rue Saint-Honoré. They were regular performers at the Café des Aveugles ("café of the Blind") in the basement of the *Palais Royal* and were often seen wandering the streets of Paris as individual performers or in bands. At this particular event, the Blind were commissioned to dress as buffoons. An accompanying verse describes the scene:

> It was lovely to hear these Blind people sing
> And particularly nice to see them proud
> Arguing as to who would give the best beat
> To the songs that Paris flocked to listen to.[1]

These words describe the demeanor of the group and evoke the sonic and gestural nature of their performance. Zina Weygand, a leading historian of the Blind in France, has recently pointed out that the performance was "part of a burlesque tradition that made of the blind man a buffoon whose clumsiness provoked laughter. Deceived and deceiving blind people could still be found in the comic theatre of the day, as could the 'supposedly' blind, imposters of blindness mocked by a good-natured and uninhibited public" (Weygand 2009, 91). Weygand has also demonstrated that the performance represented a turning point for the social integration of the Blind. Haüy was horrified at the event, writing some years later that when he saw the performance he knew the Blind could do much better. He concluded that the event was a "public dishonor to the human race. . . . 'Yes,' I said to myself, seized with a noble enthusiasm, 'I will replace this ridiculous fable with truth. I will make the Blind read; . . . they will trace letters and read their own writing, I will even have them give harmonious concerts'" (*Troisième note du citoyen Haüy* 1801, quoted in Weygand 2009, 91–92). Haüy went on to establish the Institute of Blind Youth, the eventual home of Louis Braille, five years later.

The engraving of Quinze-Vingts musicians shown in Figure 5.1 depicts an act of expressive communication through gesture and imagined sound. We see, hear, and feel the literal and figurative voice of the performers. It is, to be sure, a mere representation of an event, incorporating elements of caricature and prejudice into its interpretative quality. Yet the sheer dynamism of the blind musicians' bodily performance suggests the motivation of the group to communicate. This aspect of the event is highlighted through a number of different visual means. Aside from their position on an elevated stage, the musicians' bodies move about in the broadest spatial range. Bodies usurp blind faces. Torsos lean over and elbows jut out so much that instruments and bodies collide. The movement is such that the performers' clown hats almost fall off. Musical instruments are part of the dynamic energy of the group. Bows move at a variety of different angles and speeds. Instruments themselves are positioned more or less randomly, as comfort or habit permit. Some musicians appear to be listening to each other, their bodies and heads leaning inward toward the center, some not. Some face forward. One violinist and his instrument are turned toward offstage. Another, ear and head downward, listens to his violin. This is a spectacle of extreme human movement. Music is at the source of the action. But was this even music? Musical scores are redundant props. Sounds come directly from bodies themselves.

Haüy responded to the Quinze-Vingts Blind in much the same way as some music critics of the mid-nineteenth century reacted to the "bad style" of the instrumental virtuoso (Bernstein 1998). That is, the musical performance was rendered scandalous because it did not conform visually or sonically to a verifiable linguistic model. In this case, "harmonious concerts" combined with writing and reading were rendered part of a linguistic cure that must be imposed on the musician to render them acceptable the public. From the disability perspective, Haüy clearly rendered the blind body as a problem when left to its own devices. It is subordinate to the linguistic sign, which Haüy believed that he held in his capable (and sighted) hands.[2] Only "through my mouth," he explained could the Blind speak. Yet Haüy also positioned music itself as secondary to

FIGURE 5.1 *Grand concert extraordinaire exécuté par un détachement des quinze-Vingts au Caffé des Aveugles, Foire Saint Ovide au Mois de Septembre 1771, estampe* (Paris: Chez Mondhare rue St Jacques, 1771). Bibliothèque Nationale de France (reprinted with permission).

lingual models as a means of expression. Harmonious concerts presented as an extension of reading and writing were wholly dependent on lingual purity to make them meaningful modes of performance. It is important to acknowledge that Haüy's opinion was grounded in a much older historiographical narrative on sound and meaning that extended from the late seventeenth century onward. This narrative presented sound as a kind of semiotic code that relied on musical notions to shore up lingual excellence. Yet the Blind themselves played a pivotal role relating to the role of the body within this narrative. Ultimately, they challenged the privileged position of the semiotic code promoted by Haüy and repositioned the blind body as a central sonic force in the new citizen-state.

Eighteenth-Century Sonic Language: Music into Word

In his famous treatise *La rhétorique ou l'art de parler* ("Rhetoric or the Art of Speaking"), the late seventeenth-century Oratorian Bernard Lamy outlined the importance of auditory inflexion in the presentation of word (Lamy [1676] 1701; Rosenfeld 2001, 32–33). By the time the treatise was written, Lamy had identified in the listening world around him a glitch in the communication process, a "discord."[3] Sound, he believed, needed reform as if it were a kind of idealized language in itself.[4] *La rhétorique ou l'art de parler* was grounded in an earlier work, *Nouvelles réflexions sur l'art poétique* ("New Reflexions on the Art of Poetry," 1768), which criticized profane poetry. Modern poetry, Lamy explains in this earlier work, failed to attend to a higher listening state. The ears of its listeners were deafened by pleasure. "Poets gradually studied how to compose their works according to the taste of their Listeners; pleasure was the only rule that they followed when producing their works."[5] Lamy criticized the contemporary poetic model of "the speaking painting" ("la peinture parlante"—Lamy 1768, 1), a sonic product dependent on material beauty: "Men do not see that God is the principle and the terms of this movement or of this inclination of their heart, which makes them love the grandeur and makes them seek blessedness in their present state."[6] In his *Essai sur l'origine des connaissances humaines* ("Essay on the Origin of Human Knowledge"), the writer Abbé Etienne Bonnot de Condillac, outlined the importance of ways in which nuanced sounds as an integrated form of speech shaped society.[7] He believed that sound was a crucial force of social influence at the time when language was originally conceived, and his famous civilized "language of action" was as much sonic as visual.[8] Language evolved from "cries of each passion" (Condillac 1756, 173) among the Ancients, he explained, which were enlarged through the action of gesture, but also through the shaping of certain sounds: "Now the natural cries necessarily introduce the use of violent inflexions; since different emotions are signified by the same sound varied in different tones. Ah, for instance, according to the different manner in which it is pronounced, expresses admiration, plain pleasure, sadness, joy, fear, dislike and almost all the passions" (181). Condillac even suggested that specific words were constructed according to the sounds of nature: "Finally, I might add that the first names of animals probably were made in imitation of their cries: a remark which is equally applicable to those that were given to winds, rivers, and to everything that makes a noise" (181). Condillac concluded that the sounds of early forms of language were so subtly expressed that they resembled a kind of music. Thus, he argued that modern modes of declamatory speaking must incorporate a greater variety of sonic nuance in order to communicate their message effectively. Music and speech had lessened in their dramatic effect, he explained, and become entirely separate modes of discourse. This was to the detriment of effective communication. Ultimately, music should be properly assimilated into the lingual environment to create an idealized sonic landscape:

> The most perfect prosody is that whose harmony is best adapted to express all sorts of characters. Now there are three things concurring to harmony; the quality of the sounds, the intervals by which they succeed each other, and the movement. A language must therefore have sounds of different softness, even some that are rough, in a word, some of all kinds; secondly, it must have accents to determine the voice to rise and to fall; thirdly, by inequality of syllables, it must be capable of expressing all types of movements. (Condillac 1756, 225).

This was exactly what Haüy wanted to achieve within his literary and musical program. He saw the Blind as potential masters of a particular kind of speech that relied on higher musical qualities to showcase lingual eloquence. This concept was also current in treatises on rhetoric at this time. In his work, *Rhétorique française*, Jean-Baptise-Louis Crevier wrote, "The ear is like the vestibule of the soul. If you hurt the ear through an unpleasant sound, the soul will be ill-disposed to receive what you present to it."[9] The speaker should not only have a vivid imagination but also a sensitive and delicate ear, as the sound of words directly supported the speaker's thoughts. Students were guided by "good rules" and "excellent models," which they could study before fashioning their own examples (Crevier 1767, xv).

Gabriel-Henri Gaillard directed his work on rhetoric toward women, who he argued could then make a more profound contribution to society by learning the art (Gaillard 1776). He reduced the principles of eloquence to three specific forms, le Judiciaire, le Délibératif and the Démonstratif ("the Judiciary, Deliberative and the Demonstrative"), each of which was constructed according to the listeners in the audience. "Indeed, the Orator whatever subject he is dealing with, has to warn the Prosecutors and Judges to persuade; in the Object of his speech he has a client to be defended, a cause to be pleaded, a Proposition to be clearly established and strongly proven; finally, he has a vehement and fast summary statement to be made of his strongest evidence."[10] Gaillard's focus on the "plea" in rhetoric was once again drawing attention to the humane listening ethic. The structured plea was a concrete way in which listeners could be made aware of the broader world of human need and understanding. As Gaillard explains, "In order to provide all of these grand effects, you have to start by pleasing: it is the powerful spring which moves the entire machine of the mind and the human heart."[11]

Haüy's work with the Blind in the late eighteenth century must be situated within the context of these treatises. His system of raised reading characters was from this perspective, simply another way of presenting sound as a form of superior language. It was, then, no different from Lamy's poetic reform, Condillac's language of sound and action, and Cuvier and Gaillard's rhetorical devices. The aim of all these works was to fashion meaningful modes of communication through attention to sonic detail. Sound was similarly "structured" within almost all the materials that Haüy offered to the Blind.

Haüy's *Essai sur l'éducation des aveugles* ("Essay on Blind Education") in 1786 emphasized that sensory sensitivities made the Blind ideal candidates for developing and using such systems (Haüy 1786). Their innate abilities to feel sensation through touch and hearing made this obvious. They had a "natural dispositions" (Haüy 1786, 83) for music and "seemed to become all Ears."[12] Their fingers were highly sensitive to textured surfaces: "Everyone is aware of the delicateness of this sense in individuals, who, from childhood, use it to replace that sense which nature has denied them."[13] The book was printed in raised characters so that the Blind themselves could perceive it.[14] Conceptually, the new technology resembled the "talking book" idea. This was a material object that spoke directly to the individual listener. Each letter of the alphabet was mounted on a metal plaque and a block of wood. These could then be printed as embossed text.[15] As the Blind made contact with the letters with their fingers or pressing their iron nib deep into the extra thick paper they were confronting a sonic system, a "proper" language, presented in material form.

Haüy's mechanical systems reflected his desire to maintain a structured, linguistic reality for the young blind person. "Reading is the real means of embellishing the memory easily and quickly. . . . Without it, literary productions would form nothing in the human mind but a muddled mass of vague notions."[16] In response to criticisms that it was pointless to have the Blind read in this way, Haüy replied that reading cultivated shared understanding or universal "truths" related to language itself as an integral form of communication: "It`s now our turn to question you. What use is it to print books for all the people who surround you? Do you read Chinese, Malabar, Jurchen, Quipu, Peruvian, and so many other languages which are so necessary to those with good hearing?"[17]

Music notation was also printed in a raised form. Figure 5.2 shows an example, a *Suite de petits airs*. Like text, it was also presented to the Blind as a civilized language of sonic communication. Hence, Haüy also insisted on the reality of music as a sophisticated "Art" (Haüy 1786, 85–86). Only through sophistication could the Blind achieve the humanity that music might contain. He wanted the Blind to learn the instrumental music of the "Masters," Bach, Balbastre, and Couperin (which he wanted to be produced in embossed form and placed in the Institution's Library), criticizing the raucous voices of blind street musicians, the Quinze-Vingts musicians, and their cabaret style of performance (83–85).

FIGURE 5.2 *Suite de petits airs*, Musée Valentin Haüy, inv. B-10-3001 (reprinted with permission of Noëlle Roy).

Haüy's insistence on sophistication in music for the Blind suggests a form of sound presentation that is defined primarily by a linguistic code of some kind. Such an idea was not new. Often overlooked is that Jean-Philippe Rameau also directed his harmonic method at blind students. Both sighted and blind students could memorize his progressions, absorb them, and practice them over a year or more. After memorization, progressions could be skillfully reversed to create a perfect arch form, and in turn, the invention of a complete piece of music. Rameau's system catered especially to blind pupils, a point he makes plain in the full title of his 1761 teaching manual, *Code de musique pratique, ou méthodes pour apprendre la Musique, même à des aveugles* ("Practical Music Code, or Methods for Teaching Music, even for the Blind"). Blind students could shape their fingers and tune their ears producing the best results precisely because they could not see:

> Using the system, the fingers acquire a knowledge which, nourishes the ear of all the harmonic routes, it presents the mind with a reliable example of all the rules in which it must be educated with the result that judgment, the ear and the fingers of intelligence work together to quickly produce the perfection that is desirable in this genre. (Rameau 1761, xiii)

Both Rameau and Haüy created a form of music that was directly constructed to demonstrate the lack of "natural" sophistication in street music. "Listen to the people who sing and what they shout in the streets; nothing proves the pure effects of Nature better in such cases . . . from here comes music which is continually composed in a Tone which is varied only by that of its 'fifth' as are Airs of Trumpets, Horn, Musette and *Vielle* [hurdy-gurdy]; these do not have any effect on the soul, unless it is through the variety of the movements."[18] These sounds, Rameau explained, left listeners feeling cold because they relied on an overly primitive theory of sonic language. Musical expression was deeply embedded within an overarching lingual sign.

Susan Bernstein has drawn attention to the widespread tendency among more contemporary philosophers to subordinate music to language in their writing (and also for this to act as a metaphor for "blindness" itself). She cites Paul de Man, who, in his curiously titled essay "The Rhetoric of Blindness: Jacques Derrida's Reading of Rousseau" imbues music with lingual loss (Bernstein 1998, 48): "Music becomes a mere structure that is hollow at the core . . . the musical sign can have no assurance of its existence. . . . This movement . . . is determined by the nature of the sign as *significant*, by the nature of music as language" (de Man quoted in Bernstein 1998, 49). Bernstein explains that in de Man's text, "music is made to act out the frustration of meaning" (Bernstein 1998, 49). She continues, "But here is no evidence that music is driven by this kind of 'intent towards meaning' or that it is necessary to think of it as condemned or frustrated—though it may frustrate the intent towards meaning of the linguistically orientated interpreter" (49). Bernstein suggests that a more meaningful starting point for examining the relationship between language and music is to understand both as forms of virtuosity. "[T]he terminology of virtuosity—its bodies, instruments, hands and economy—is not organized in a subject-object relation. Virtuosity permeates equally discourses and practices of music and language" (13).

What is absent from discussions on the late eighteenth-century blind is the way in which they constructed an idea of the blind virtuoso in the post-Revolutionary period by reconfiguring the hierarchy of language and music imposed on them by Haüy. Here I draw on Tobin Siebers's theory of *complex embodiment*, which attempts to reposition the reality of the disabled body at the center of the critical narrative (Siebers 2008). Complex embodiment eschews the simplistic traditional medical models and equally simplistic social constructionist model sometimes found within Disability Studies for a more entangled theory that acknowledges both. Ultimately, Siebers argues for deeper analysis of the ways in which the disabled body itself transforms processes of representation.

Haüy's lingual models for the Blind were only one part of the evolution of blind culture in France in the late eighteenth century. There is another critical narrative relating to the role that the Blind played themselves during this period. As Catherine Kudlick and Zina Weygand have demonstrated in their work on the blind woman Thérèse-Adéle Husson, blind individuals maintained a very real and lively presence within society during the post-Revolutionary period (Husson 2001). I will demonstrate that the Blind were much more active in contesting and refiguring Haüy's program than we might think. They actively drew attention to its limitations and the ways in which it hindered their freedom as disabled citizens of the new French state. Blind defiance in post-Revolutionary France was also reflective of a broader representational shift from the linguistic sign to the expressive, active body, which became an intrinsic part of the broader medicopolitical culture within the citizen-state. The Blind made a key contribution to this process of cultural change quite separate from Haüy's contribution to blind education. Through musical virtuosity they were to become leading exponents of a new mode of bodily presence in the new French citizen space.

The Emergence of a Bodily Instrumental Aesthetic: Confronting Valentin Haüy and the Linguistic Sign

In 1791, Haüy's Institute of Blind Youth was united with the school for the deaf established by Abbot de l'Epée (who famously invented deaf sign) at a site at the former convent of the Celestines. Haüy was unhappy about the merger, fearing that he and his students would be forced to take second place behind the then headmaster of the school for the deaf, Abbot Roch Ambroise Cucurron Sicard. Yet at this time, Haüy came under severe criticism from a group of young blind from within his own school. While Haüy was complaining to the National Assembly about the disruption to his program as a result of the merger, some residents of his school raised the alarm in public about their poor living conditions.

Their lengthy petition to the National Assembly began by stating that it was not they, the Blind, who needed to be made more "civilized" through education, but the Legislative Assembly who had wholeheartedly denied them welfare support (Petition à l'Assemblée nationale 1791). The notion that they could make their own living through participation in an educational program was fanciful, they explained. They then launched into a direct attack on their "leader," who, they explained, "knows well the weaknesses of his means, and saw that such truths given the light of day would necessarily eclipse his glory, and overturn his ambitious projects."[19] Haüy had responded in silence to their complaints about their quarters, they continued, and should not be given any extra money for his program. "Help us to achieve a general law for all blind people," they added.[20] The young blind ended their petition by asking authorities to take a closer look at Haüy's Institution:

> Enter into this establishment with us; we will be the most confident guides to lead you into this den of quackery. We hope, Legislature that the reasons which earn us the hate of M. Haüy, will be able to earn us the benevolence of the National Assembly. We ask you to agree to our petition so that truth will triumph over the impostor, and so that from now on, the Blind will no longer be the victims of the cupidity of men.[21]

The young blind students who signed the petition clearly believed that Haüy was failing in his duty of care. His ego and ambition were clouding his judgment, and he was instead exploiting them for his own personal gain. The petition must have made great impact on the emotions of authorities who were now steeped in the Revolutionary culture of the right of all to a voice (Sykes 2011). The National Assembly had recently saved the Hospice des Quinze-Vingts from closure on exactly on this basis. "Humanity, justice and the general interest call for the preservation of this previous hospital," a government report concluded (*Observations pour les aveugles* 1790). Blind members there had been complaining about treatment by the sighted and calling for the rights of the Blind and the Partially Sighted there since 1790. Haüy's young blind students were calling for their rights in a similar way. Yet they were also responding to problems with Haüy's system itself and the way in which it prevented their freedom of expression in the spirit of the Declaration of Human Rights.

What Haüy had also not resolved were the technical issues with the system itself. Haüy constantly reassured critics that the structured nature of the system was a success, but he could not ignore the fact that the bound books of embossed texts weighed almost five kilos each. Often in large format, they were difficult to manage. Sometimes, the raised letters on paper lost their physical shape (Henri 1984, 58–73). Complex musical notation was a particular problem in this regard (Handwritten Note 1789). Blind students complained that the notes were not embedded deeply enough in the paper and that they simply could not read them. They were being forced to do a pointless task by a "charlatan." They were perfectly able to use their bodies to play instruments, their minds to memorize, and their voices to communicate. Why were they being prevented from doing so? And wasn't freedom of communication at the heart of the Revolutionary message?

According to the medical historian Dora Weiner, Haüy unwittingly played into the government's productivist agenda for the Blind at this time by insisting on their ability to be successfully socially integrated. She writes: "The term 'working blind' was Haüy's invention. He dreamt of self-supporting citizen-patients. His proposal to move to a new site proved irresistible to the legislators, hard-pressed financially at the height of the terror" (Weiner 1993, 237). In 1801, the then minister of the interior, Chaptal, attempted to integrate Haüy's institution, by this time titled the National Institute for Blind Workers with Quinze-Vingts. Quinze-Vingts was the home of the very group that Haüy had heard playing instruments at the café in 1771. Weygand has drawn attention to the "workhouse" agenda behind Chaptal's decision. This was totally contrary to Haüy's vision of the intellectual blind self, who read, wrote, and learned music. Weygand (2009) has demonstrated that Haüy was unhappy with the emphasis on manual labor, as were many of the older blind members of Quinze-Vingts. At the heart of the government agenda, Haüy complained was the attack on the music program. "We have been incriminated for having brought within the reach of those who showed a disposition for the liberal arts reading, writing, education, geography, languages, poetry, even printing for the Blind, and especially music. It is principally the enjoyment of this last talent that people have endeavored to suppress. Well! Experience has shown us that it was for them a means of existence and consolation!" (*Troisième note du citoyen Haüy* 1801; cited in Weygand 2009, 329). Weiner demonstrates that blind music education suffered greatly at this time:

> Eight blind assistants helped the four music teachers; a violinist, a singing teacher, a cellist, and a clarinetist. It is difficult to ascertain whether they succeeded in teaching the children a trade. The few accounts of public performances to raise money leave the reader with a painful impression: one visualizes the short plays, heavy on moral lessons, awkwardly acted; one imagines two string instruments and a clarinet accompanying the thin voices of pale, undernourished blind boys and girls. The spectators' donations were surely motivated by pity. (Weiner 1993, 239)

Yet, there is nothing to suggest that blind musical culture itself was in decline. Haüy's program had certainly been called into question, and in 1807, he left Paris for St. Petersburg with his dream of an independent school for the young blind shattered. Yet Weygand and Kudlick have shown that blind musicians managed to maintain a lively culture of musical expression throughout this time within the amalgamated institution (Husson 2001, 117). They have drawn attention to the outstanding work of the blind musician Jean-François Galliod, for example, in relation to liturgical music and instrumental teaching (Husson 2001, 110–117; see also Weygand 2009, 194). Blind musicians also continued to visit the Café des Aveugles to perform.

Attempts by the government to curb the propensity for blind musicians to wander throughout Paris had proved fruitless (Sykes 2011, 498). By 1801, the agent general of Quinze-Vingts, exasperated by continued blind defiance reported to the minister of the interior, "The Blind should be visited so that you can get to know them better; they are capable of anything; they are allowed to do all things and they think that their infirmity protects them from everything" (Draft of Letter to the Minister of the Interior from Agent General 22 May 1801).[22] Archival evidence from Quinze-Vingts suggests that during the period of amalgamation with the Institute for Blind Workers, diverse musical instruments as well as special furniture in which to store them were held among the Blind in extremely high regard. There were large chests and cupboards containing pipes, violins, a viola, cellos, basses, an oboe, five clarinets, a number of horns and their crooks, five bassoons, a trombone, three serpents (large wind instruments made of brass, wood, and leather), a trumpet, three sets of cymbals, a guitar, a keyboard, three violin rests, and one bass rest ("Etat des meubles, instrumens et musique" [1800–1815?]). The Blind had in many ways simply returned to the bodily musical behavior of 1771 but with a sense of the linguistic rhetoric that they had seized from exposure to Haüy's form of training.

By continuing to assert their presence as bodily musicians, the Blind were also conforming to a new alternative approach to public health gaining currency in certain medical circles at this time. In the post-Revolutionary aftermath, bodily musical expression was encouraged by some members of the medical establishment as an important part of a broader biomedical program of regeneration (Quinlan 2004, 139–64). This trend in medicine moved "from elite clinical theorists to a kind of 'literary underground' of medical practice" (Quinlan 2004, 141). The reinstatement of collective sonic relationships, *le corps sonore*, through a kind of self-inflicted form of bodily auditory action, was advocated by the Montpellier doctor Etienne Sainte-Marie, who reinstated the work of the mid-eighteenth-century vitalist doctor, also of the Montpellier medical school, Joseph-Louis Roger (Roger 1803; Sainte-Marie 1820).[23]

This practice was very different from the rational acoustic agenda of Rameau's abstract and linguistic *corps sonore*. The post-Revolutionary *corps sonore* was an attempt to recall the eighteenth-century vitalist notion of the body as intrinsically active and sentient. In his *Tentamen de vi soni et muscices in corpore humano* published in 1758, Roger accused seventeenth-century natural philosophers of associating the effects of music with magic, explaining that the relationship between music and the body was much more empirically verifiable. This had to do with the sonorous capacity of bodily materials, particularly the nerve fluid in the nerves. In his preface to the 1803 French translation of the work, Etienne Sainte-Marie advocated musical practice as a serious form of bodily hygiene: "Those who look upon music as a purely pleasurable art, will not believe in the beneficial effects on many illnesses that the author of this work attributes to it."[24] He reiterated Roger's belief in the importance of the connection between the auditory and the bodily nervous system, *le tremblement sonore* ("the sonorous trembling") and *le tremblement vital* ("the vital trembling"), explaining that auditory nerves "are spread throughout the body, and dilate it . . . and awaken in it [feelings of] courage, love, charity, pity, joy, and the expansive passions."[25]

Such a medical idea of the body was not in any way based on a biological "lack" with respect to blindness. It was driven, instead, by the opposite viewpoint: that the body, whether visually impaired or not, was a powerful musical "machine" in its own right and must be maintained through regular musical movement.[26] The essence of a healthy body, Sainte-Marie explained, was musical energy. The mechanical effect of sound, the most "natural" form of exercise containing tiny movements ("which constitute in the organs life itself"[27]), could be fashioned into physical exercise: "music is an exercise, and must be recommended to women and to people of letters, who lead a sedentary life."[28] The healthiest members of the population were musicians, he wrote. "We note that there are more old people among musicians than amongst other artists."[29] This was because musicians ensured that there was continually vigorous energetic activity in their nervous system. Musician's bodies were always warmed up because sonic energy was physically retained within the nerves.

Sainte-Marie must have advocated Roger's analyses of different sounds and his terms of diagnostic treatment. Roger explained that music was useful: if the patient was a musician or if, in a state of health, he played music a lot; if he was not a musician but demonstrated symptoms of an illness caused by the alienation of the spirit, the alteration of nervous fluid or the excessive tension of nervous fibrils that one recognizes in phrenetic delirium; if there was no pain or inflammation; if the patient showed taste and aptitude for music in the middle of the illness; if they showed obvious emotional responsiveness to music; and finally, if there was resistance to normal pharmaceutical remedies (Roger 1803, 252–253).

While Roger was interested in specific sounds, the doctor Forgues, who presented his dissertation at Montpellier a year before Sainte-Marie's translation, explained that there were three main classification groups of sounds that had a physiological effect (Forgues 1802). These were imitative sounds, sounds that had effect on memory, and the particular language of sound of itself. He agreed though, that sound offered man a powerful refuge from disease and ill health. It had the capacity to transport the entire self into another domain of existence. Blind musicians led the charge in promoting auditory bodily behavior within the post-Revolutionary public space. They demonstrated that engaging the auditory body was an important activity for all.

French musical instrument designs during the period from 1800 to 1830 directly reflect this medicopolitical ideology of the "auditory body," the idea that the body could literally move itself through solo musical expression into good health (Sykes 2006). Their invention was part of a broader requirement to create an auditory body politic throughout the citizen space rather than within a proscribed institutional domain.[30] Such designs were not simply demonstrations of rational acoustical principles on a grand industrial scale. They were hyper-realized extensions of human "auditory bodies" that could be used by citizens to maintain good health. As the organist, harpist, or pianist engaged with the new mechanical conditions of the instrument, his/her bodily systems became synchronized with the energetic forces perpetuated by the instrument. There was a strong reliance on memory in music learning as well as a new emphasis on solo improvisatory practice. This was very different from Haüy's notion of presenting

FIGURE 5.3 S. Guillié, *Essai sur l'instruction des aveugles* (3rd ed., Paris: Imprimé par les aveugles, 1820), plate 10, p. 214.

sound solely and strictly within a linguistic framework. While performers still relied on some form of functional linguistic frame, they placed a great deal more emphasis on virtuosic techniques of individual interpretation generated from their own human and nonhuman sonorous bodies of production.

By using their auditory bodies in tandem with such instruments, the Blind reshaped the idea of the blind body from one confined by language to another driven by its own energetic forces. And they became leaders of excellence in the field. By 1820, blind students had overtaken their sighted peers at the Paris Conservatoire in improvisatory practice. Paris Conservatoire students remained bound by the paper "manuscript" throughout their instrumental training, while the Blind were left free to perform *after* studying harmony. Musical educators at the Institute royale des jeunes aveugles (the renamed Institute of Blind Youth) were blind themselves and promoted the idea that bodies must be free to create music once the linguistic frame had been properly absorbed. By the time Louis Braille entered there in 1819, students were mastering complex instruments produced by the leading instrument manufacturers with ease. Figure 5.3 depicts a blind student perfecting his harp technique on a new instrument from this period probably designed by the Paris-based inventor and manufacturer, Sébastien Erard. Later, Braille famously developed Haüy's raised-reading system, yet he also identified varied coloristic registration codes and sophisticated improvisatory practices for organists that promoted the auditory body as a mode of expressive practice.[31]

In many ways, the blind instrumental virtuosos of the post-Revolutionary citizen space represent a critical stage in the transformation of the virtuoso musician from "cheerful mastery to deceptive mockery" (Bernstein 1998, 12). By transforming themselves from figures of bodily emptiness to figures of bodily agency, they helped to reinforce the importance of the body as a key defining feature of the virtuosic musical instrumentalist. During the nineteenth century, the Blind now faced new forms of discrimination relating to the complex relationship between blindness and taboo (Thompson 2013). Confined to private institutions throughout their lives, they rarely appeared at major performing venues as did Chopin or Liszt.[32] Yet it is critical to acknowledge the role they played in establishing the solo instrumental musician as a powerful bodily presence, literally and figuratively a "blind force," in its own right during the aftermath of the Revolution. They achieved this by confronting their sighted leader and demanding their right to communicate freely within the citizen-space. This resonated with broader ideas about the body and public health in the post-Revolutionary world of modern France.

Acknowledgments

I thank Jacqueline Englert-Marchal, Harvey Miller, and Nöelle Roy for their invaluable help in preparing this article.

Notes

1. "Il fut charmant d'ouir ces Aveugles chanter/Et surtout de les voir fiers de leur encollure/ Se disputer à qui donnerait mieux l'allure/Aux chansons que Paris vint en foule écouter" (*Almanach forain* 1773).
2. On the subordination of the disabled body to the linguistic sign see Siebers 2008, 55.
3. Lamy's term is "faux éclat" (Lamy 1768, 23).
4. Lamy's work was very influential in music making. See Gibson 2008.
5. "Les Poètes s'étudièrent peu à peu à composer leur Ouvrages selon le goût de leurs Auditeurs, dont le plaisir fut la seule règle qu'ils suivirent dans la conduite de leurs ouvrages" (Lamy 1768, iii).
6. "Les hommes ne voyent pas en plus, que Dieu est le principe et le terme de ce mouvement ou de cette inclination de leur cœur, qui leur fait aimer la grandeur, et rechercher la béatitude dans l'état où ils sont" (Lamy 1768, 6).
7. Condillac 1746. The translations are from Condillac 1756, *An Essay on the Origin of Human Knowledge Being a Supplement to Mr Locke's Essay on Human Understanding translated from the French by Mr Nugent.*
8. For more information on Condillac's philosophical discourse in the context of his *langage d'action*, see Goldstein 2005, 33–38, and Rosenfeld 2001, 36–56.
9. "L'oreille est comme le vestibule de l'âme. Si vous blessez l'oreille par un son désagréable, l'âme sera mal disposée à recevoir ce que vous lui présentez" (Crevier 1767, 4).
10. "En effet, l'Orateur, quelque sujet qu'il traite, a dans les Auditeurs des Juges à prévenir a persuader; il a, dans l'Objet de son discours, un Client à defendre, une cause à plaider, une Proposition à établir nettement et à prouver solidement; il a enfin une récapitulation courte, véhémente et rapide à faire de ses plus fortes preuves" (Gaillard 1776, xii).
11. "Pour pouvoir tous ces grands effets, il faut commencer par plaire; c'est le puissant ressort qui fait mouvoir toute la machine de l'esprit et du Cœur humain" (Gaillard 1776, 14).
12. "Semblaient être devenus tout Oreilles" (*Troisième note du citoyen Haüy* 1801).
13. "Personne n'ignore la délicatesse de ce sens chez des individus, qui, depuis l'enfance, s'en servent pour remplacer celui que la Nature leur a refusé" (Haüy 1786, 26–27.
14. The title page includes the note that the book was "Imprimé par les Enfans-Aveugles, sous la direction de M. Clousier, Imprimeur du Roi."
15. These processes are described in detail in Haüy 1786 and in Henri 1984, which includes illustrations.
16. "La Lecture est le vrai moyen d'orner la mémoire d'une manière facile et prompte . . . Sans elle, les productions littéraires ne formeraient dans l'esprit humain qu'un amas désordonné de notions vagues" (Haüy 1786, 15–16).
17. "A notre tour permettez-nous de vous interroger. Que sert-il que l'on imprime des livres chez tous les peuples qui vous environnent? Lisez-vous le Chinois, le Malabar, le Jurc, les Quipos des Péruviens, et tant d'autres langages si nécessaires, à ceux qui bien entendent?" (Haüy 1786, 37).
18. "Ecoutez les gens qui chantent et ce qu'ils crient dans les rues, rien ne vous prouvera mieux les purs effets de la Nature en pareil cas . . . De-là vient qu'une Musique continuellement composée dans un *Ton* qui n'est varié que par celui de sa quinte, comme sont les Airs de Trompettes, Cor, Musette et Vielle, ne produisent aucun effet sur l'âme, si ce n'est par la variété des mouvements" (Rameau 1761, 139, 167).

19. "Connaissent bien les faiblesses de ses moyens, vit que de telles vérités mises au jour éclipseraient nécessairement sa gloire, et renverseraient ses projets ambitieux" (Petition à l'Assemblée Nationale 1791).
20. "Nous serve à atteindre une loi générale sur tous les aveugles."
21. "Pénétrez avec nous dans cet établissement; nous serons les guider les plus sûrs pour vous conduire dans cet antre du charlatanisme. Nous espérons Législature, que les Motifs qui nous ont mérité la haine de M. Haüy, pourront nous mériter la bienveillance de l'Assemblée Nationale. Nous vous supplions d'acquiescer à notre demande, afin que la vérité Triomphe de l'imposture, et que les Aveugles ne soient plus désormais les victimes de la Cupidité des hommes."
22. "Il faut fréquenter les aveugles et avoir à faire avec eux pour les connaître, ils sont capables de tout; ils sont autorisés á tout et ils pensent que leur infirmité les met à l'abri de tout" (Draft of letter to the Minister of the Interior from Agent General 1801).
23. Joseph-Louis Roger, *Traité des effets de la musique sur le corps humain*, edited and translated from the Latin text by Etienne Sainte Marie (Paris: Brunot, 1803). See Etienne Sainte-Marie's later work on natural medicine, *Nouveau formulaire médical et pharmaceutique* (Paris: Rey et Gravier, 1820).
24. "Ceux qui regardent la musique comme un art purement agréable, ne croiront pas aux effets avantageux que l'auteur de cet ouvrage lui attribue dans un grand nombre de maladies" (Sainte-Marie in Roger 1803, vii).
25. "se répand dans tout le corps, et le dilate . . . et y réveille le courage, l'amour, la bienfaisance, la pitié, la joie, les passions expansives" (Sainte-Marie in Roger 1803, x–xi).
26. There is a connection here with a more generalized trend in the historic representation and configuration of music as a mode of bodily cure. For more information, refer to Blake Howe's contribution to this volume.
27. "qui constituent dans les organes la vie elle-même" (Sainte-Marie in Roger 1803, xiv).
28. "la musique est un exercice, et on doit la recommander aux femmes et aux gens des lettres, qui mènent une vie sédentaire" " (Sainte-Marie in Roger 1803, xiii).
29. "On observe parmi les musiciens plus de vieillards que parmi les autres artistes" (Sainte-Marie in Roger 1803, xvii–xviii).
30. French music educational institutions are generally considered by scholars to be in "crisis" during this period. Hondré (2006) explains that the Conservatoire was conceived as a "super-institution" in 1795 in the model of "une école supérieure" but that it could not fulfil that role "puisqu'elle n'était supérieure 'du rien du tout.' "
31. See his works on organ playing held in the Musée Valentin Haüy, Paris.
32. There is one major exception to this. In August 1889, the blind woman Joséphine Boulay, performed solo at the Exposition Universelle de Paris on the pioneering electropneumatic organ built by Joseph Merklin.

References

Unpublished Items in Manuscript Collections

"Etat des meubles, instrumens et musique appartenans à l'hospice des 15-20 existant dans la salle d'instruction dudit hospice." [1800–1815?]. Bibliothèque B 113/6795. Archives du Centre Hospitalier National d'Opthalmologie des Quinze-Vingts, Paris.

Draft of letter to the Minister of the Interior from Agent General. 22 May 1801. Règlements B106 6609-6613. Archives du Centre Hospitalier National d'Opthalmologie des Quinze-Vingts, Paris.

Almanach forain, ou Les différens spectacles des boulevards et des foires de Paris [. . .]. 1773. Paris: Chez Vallerye l'aîné. Bibliothèque Nationale de France.

Grand concert extraordinaire exécuté par un détachement des quinze-vingts au Caffé des Aveugles, Foire Saint Ovide au Mois de Septembre. 1771. Paris: Chez Mondhare rue St Jacques. Bibliothèque Nationale de France.

Handwritten note attached to embossed musical notation. 1789. Musée Valentin Haüy, Paris.

Petition à l'Assemblée Nationale des Aveugles suivants l'Institution de M. Haüy. 1791. Les archives des Assemblées nationales, C//167, no. 149. Assemblée nationale legislative. Paris, Archives Nationales de France.

Troisième note du citoyen Haüy, auteur de la manière d'instruire les aveugles ou court exposé de la naissance des progrès et de l'état actuel de l'Institut national des aveugles-travailleurs au 19 brumaire an IX de la République française entremêlée de quelques observations relatives à cet établissement. 1801. Musée Valentin Haüy, Paris.

Published Sources

Bernstein, Susan. 1998. *Virtuosity of the Nineteenth Century: Performing Music and Language in Heine, Liszt, and Baudelaire.* Stanford, CA: Stanford University Press.

Condillac, Etienne Bonnot de. 1746. *Essai sur l'origine des connaissances humaines, ouvrage où l'on réduit à un seul principe tout ce qui concerne l'entendement humain.* 2 vols. Amsterdam, Netherlands: Mortier. Translated by Mr Nugent as *An Essay on the Origin of Human Knowledge Being a Supplement to Mr Locke's Essay on Human Understanding.* London: Nourse, 1756.

Crevier, Jean-Baptiste-Louis. 1767. *Rhétorique française.* Vol. 1. Paris: Saillant.

Forgues, V. 1802. *De l'influence de la musique sur l'économie animale.* Montpellier: Martel.

Gaillard, Gabriel-Henri. 1776. *Rhétorique française à l'usage des jeunes demoiselles avec des exemples tirés pour la plupart de nos meilleurs Orateurs & Poètes Modernes.* 5th ed. Paris: Veuve Savoie.

Gibson, Jonathan. 2008. "'A Kind of Eloquence Even in Music': Embracing Different Rhetorics in Late Seventeenth-Century France." *Journal of Musicology* 25 (4): 394–433.

Goldstein, Jan. 2005. *The Post-Revolutionary Self: Politics and Psyche in France, 1750–1850.* Cambridge, MA: Harvard University Press.

Haüy, Valentin. 1786. *Essai sur l'éducation des aveugles.* Paris: Imprimé par les Enfans-Aveugles.

Haüy, Valentin. 1792. *Adresse du citoyen Haüy, auteur des moyens d'éducation des enfans aveugles et leur premier instituteur aux 48 sections de Paris, présentée à la suite d'une adresse de la section de l'Arsenal, en date de l'an I de la République française le 13 décembre 1792, dont il étoit porteur.*

Henri, Pierre. 1984. *La vie et l'œuvre de Valentin Haüy.* Paris: Presses Universitaires de France.

Hondré, Emmanuel. 2006. "L'école de musique de Toulouse: Les enjeux d'une 'Nationalisation' (1820–1848)." *Revue de Musicologie* 92 (1): 109–122.

Husson, Thérèse-Adèle. 2001. *Reflections on the Life and Writings of a Young Blind Woman in Post-Revolutionary France.* Translated and with commentary by Catherine J. Kudlick and Zina Weygand. New York and London: New York University Press.

Lamy, Bernard. (1676) 1701. *La rhétorique ou l'art de parler*. 4th ed. Paris: Pierre Debats and Imbert Debats. Translated as *The Art of Speaking rendered into English*. London: Godbid.

Lamy, Bernard. 1768. *Nouvelles réflexions sur l'art poétique*. Paris.

Observations pour les aveugles de l'hôpital des Quinze-Vingts. Sur le projet de décret du comité de secours de la convention nationale, pour la suppression de cet hospital. c. 1790. Paris: J. Grand. The French Revolution Research Collection. Paris: Micro Graphix, 1992.

Quinlan, Sean. 2004. "Physical and Moral Regeneration after the Terror: Medical Culture, Sensibility and Family Politics in France, 1794–1804." *Social History* 29 (2): 139–164.

Rameau, Jean-Philippe. 1761. *Code de musique pratique, ou méthodes pour apprendre la Musique même à des Aveugles [. . .]*. Paris: Imprimerie Royale.

Roger, Joseph-Louis. 1803. *Traité des effets de la musique sur le corps humain*. Edited and translated from the Latin text by Etienne Sainte-Marie. Paris: Brunot.

Rosenfeld, Sophia. 2001. *A Revolution in Language: The Problem of Sign in Late Eighteenth-Century France*. Stanford, CA: Stanford University Press.

Rosenfeld, Sophia. 2011. "On Being Heard: A Case for Paying Attention to the Historical Ear." *American Historical Review* 116 (2): 316–334.

Sainte-Marie, Etienne. 1820. *Nouveau formulaire médical et pharmaceutique*. Paris: Rey et Gravier.

Siebers, Tobin. 2008. *Disability Theory*. An Arbor: University of Michigan Press.

Sykes, Ingrid. 2006. "Les produits de l'acoustique: Brevets d'invention de musique 1800–1830." In *Les archives de l'invention, Ecrits, objets et images de l'activité inventive*, edited by Mary-Sophie Corcy, Christiane Douyère-Demeulenaere and Liliane Hilaire-Pérez, 499–510. Toulouse, France: CNRS, Université de Toulouse-Le Mirail.

Sykes, Ingrid. 2011. "Sounding the Citizen Patient: The Politics of Voice in Post-Revolutionary France." *Medical History* 55 (4): 479–502.

Thompson, Hannah. 2013. *Taboo: Corporeal Secrets in Nineteenth-Century France*. London: Modern Humanities Research Association and Maney Publishing.

Weiner, Dora B. 1993. *The Citizen Patient in Revolutionary and Imperial Paris*. Baltimore, MD: John Hopkins University Press.

Weygand, Zina. 2009. *The Blind in French Society: From the Middle Ages to the Century of Louis Braille*. Translated by Emily-Jane Cohen. Stanford, CA: Stanford University Press.

CHAPTER 6

"THEY SAY WE EXCHANGED OUR EYES FOR THE XYLOPHONE"

Resisting Tropes of Disability as Spiritual Deviance in Birifor Music

BRIAN HOGAN

> *People are always saying the blind use witchcraft to play the xylophone. But we are proving to you it is not witchcraft. It is our own talent, which God gave us.*
>
> —Maal Yichiir, Blind Birifor Xylophonist

THE Northwest of Ghana, which includes the Northern Region and Upper-West Region, is home to many distinct ethnic groups that maintain culturally rooted traditions of xylophone performance, including the Sisaala, Dagara, and Birifor. Xylophones are a primary cultural icon and instrumental resource for these ethnic groups, featured in public ritual contexts such as funerals and festivals. Funerals in particular are an opportunity for xylophonists to fulfill their role of reinscribing culture, society, and history through surrogated song texts that communicate to communities of the living and the dead. Funerals are also a chance for xylophonists with and without visual impairment to inject their own personal experiences and agendas into the largely proverbial song texts of the traditional song cycle. Through a funeral music subgenre known as "enemy music" (*dondomo yiel*), blind and sighted Birifor xylophonists deconstruct daily challenges and challengers alike, projecting an identity framed in opposition to popular beliefs, opinions, and gossip. This essay examines three compositions by blind xylophonist Maal Yichiir for the structures of normalization and pathology that they engage and for the experience of disability in rural West Africa that they depict. Expanding on Tobin Siebers's influential critique of the ideology of ability that manufactures disability as a negative category of identity and experience (Siebers 2008, 2010), this essay argues that the physical and psychological constraints of notions of able-bodiedness are culture specific, and in the Birifor case extend into spiritual and ontological domains. Resisting and reorienting such negative representations of blindness, blind Birifor musicians compose and perform enemy music to contest their marginal status, to assert their agency, and to project a counterhegemonic ideology that rewrites cultural histories, conceptions of blindness, and the very tradition of Birifor xylophone music. Amplifying the perspective of blind Birifor musicians, this essay demonstrates that the spiritual dimensions of disability are of greater concern to Birifors with disabilities than their actual degree of physical impairment.[1] While their bodies are experienced from the inside-out as natural, they are laden with value and dysfunction from the outside-in through social, cultural, and spiritual essentialisms. This has broader implications for disability theory in that it points to the culture-specific aspects of ableism and calls attention to the compound subordination of musicianship and disability in a cross-cultural context.

In rural Birifor culture, spiritual systems of *suoba* (locally translated as "witchcraft") and *til* (locally translated as "juju") pervade daily life alongside religious and secular narratives, filling objects and people with harmful and protective spiritual energy respectively. The long-standing history of epidemics of disease-borne blindness in the North of Ghana has resulted in deeply rooted cultural interpretations of blindness, which often reinforce the mistreatment of blind persons through recourse to spiritual narratives of witchcraft that fault the individual, their family, and/or their ancestors. In addition to the yoke of ability placed on impaired bodies on a global scale, in Birifor contexts there is an additional spiritual narrative of disability that casts impairment as a necessary and undesirable result of mystical forces. This kind of spiritual causality renders the African disabled body in a way that is related to but distinct from the religious model of disability theorized in Western scholarship (Straus 2011, 5–6; Wheatley 2010, 64). This is in part because of the unique multilayered causality that operates in Birifor culture, which allows conflicting narratives of cause and effect to be housed within an all-encompassing system of spiritual value and exchange (Goody 1962, 1972). In this system, the blind African body is reified as not only physically subordinate but also spiritually grotesque.

Enacting a person-centered perspective, this depiction of Birifor music and culture references ethnographic data from individual and group interviews, musical performances, daily and ritual practices (farming, festivals, funerals, etc.), field notes, and experiences from research trips to Ghana in 2002, 2007, and 2009 as well as ongoing correspondence (phone calls, e-mails, letters, and recordings) with musicians and their families (Hogan 2011). The Southern Birifor musicians presented in this essay live in or adjacent to the Sawla-Tuna-Kalba District, which is among the southernmost areas of what is considered "Birifor country" in Ghana. Sighted xylophonists Belendi Saanti, Vuur Sandaar, Vuur Mwan, and SK Kakraba, and blind xylophonists Maal Yichiir, Maal Chile, Ni-Ana Alhansan, and Kuyiri Darigain all provided invaluable perspectives on the musical, social, cultural, and spiritual domains of Bifiror life as they are depicted in this essay. Maal Yichiir's enemy music compositions in particular explicitly challenge the association of blindness with spiritual transgression, and deny that witchcraft is the source of his musical and agricultural ability. They make public his own ethic of learning, dedicated practice, and hard work that undergirds his musicianship. Challenging his audience to try themselves to use witchcraft to achieve musical proficiency, he categorically denies that those who assist or are associated with blind persons will also become blind themselves or fall victim to spiritual contamination, rejecting the contagious stigma associated with disability. He also refutes accusations that blind musicians must engage in farming or trade because they are in fact not good musicians. In interviews, Yichiir voiced the widespread neglect that blind persons experience in Birifor culture, underscoring the vital importance of allies within the community who are willing to teach the blind skills that foster independence rather ensnaring them in cycles of dependence. While Yichiir's perspective is only one of several blind xylophonists' in the region, his articulation of the parameters of disability in rural West Africa reflects the larger sociocultural and spiritual dimensions of ableism in West African contexts.

The History of Blindness in Northwest Ghana

With a high historical incidence of both congenital and disease-borne blindness, including the world's second most infectious cause of blindness, *onchocerciasis* (river blindness), the Northwest of Ghana has likely experienced blindness and visual impairment as a medical constant since the area was first inhabited. Additional causes for blindness in West Africa include cataract, glaucoma, smallpox, syphilis, leprosy, measles, and tuberculosis as well as physical trauma. The historical epidemics of river blindness facilitated by the region's vast river networks, were first chronicled by the efforts of John Wilson (1953, 1961), who was himself blind and acted in coordination with the British Empire Society for the Blind. More than sixty years later, blindness, visual impairment, and eye disease are still common in the northern regions of Ghana, and many residents remain resistant to the cause attributed to various forms of visual impairment by Western medicine, finding alternative interpretations in traditional religion, Christianity, Islam, and mysticism. The causes that both traditional worldviews and Western medicine attribute to blindness in the context of Ghana are presented here as contextually valid, but critiqued for their linkage with the social, cultural, and spiritual matrices through which bodily variation is crystallized into the deterministic identity of "disabled" that is then riddled with stigma (Goffman [1963] 1986). This outside-in perspective on disability that circulates in Birifor communities, sharply contrasts with the lived realities of an inside-out perspective, a schism that fuels blind xylophonists's contestations of the hegemony of disability.

As of 1950, John Wilson estimated that river blindness had blinded one in ten people in certain upper Voltaic communities. A subsequent regional survey in the same year indicated that six hundred thousand out of one million Ghanaians in the northern area of Ghana contracted some degree of river blindness, with thirty thousand completely blind as a result (Wilson 1961). Wilson's book *Ghana's Handicapped Citizens* (1961) details his involvement with these blind communities, introducing the primary issues and concerns of blind persons in Ghana. Among these is the necessity of specialized equipment for education and everyday life, which is mostly foreign made and must be imported. Imported products are expensive and difficult to come by in rural areas, representing a substantial hindrance to education for blind persons in Ghana. Students interviewed in 2009 at the Wa Methodist School for the Blind, echoed Wilson's observation by stating their school's current need for Braille sheets, Braille embossers for computers, and Braille typewriters (Hogan 2011). Refreshable Braille displays such as those in use in Europe and the United States are rare in Ghana, with insufficient funding for such specialized devices. Wilson also noted that care for the blind, in addition to education at that time, was so limited that clinics across sub-Saharan Africa were plagued by prohibitively long lines for any sort of medical treatment (1953, 147).

In his 1953 report to the British Empire Society for the Blind, Wilson explained that blind persons across Africa rarely find a place "within the framework of native society" (1953, 141). Noting the rare occasions where he had encountered collectivization among blind populations, Wilson cited the blind beggars of Kano, Northern Nigeria. This guild of at that time eight hundred blind individuals, had both a designated area for habitation in the city and a clearly stated role and purpose in life. As the *Sarakin Makafi* (Hausa for "King of the Blind") explained, blind persons play an important role in society as beggars designated by the Koran and serve a crucial function as recipients of alms and purveyors of blessings in a cycle designed by Allah (1953, 141). This sense of self and place in a spiritual order leads to a valuation of blindness as normal, ideologically challenging the negativistic projection of blindness as dysfunction, though that is not to say it is entirely unproblematic. Wilson recalled the *Sarakin Makafi*'s agreement to have his picture taken on the condition that, as his translator explained, "So long as you don't use it to restore his sight. Allah has made him blind; it is not for men to interfere" (Wilson 1953, 141). While in the case of this guild of blind Hausas in Kano, blind persons invoked religion toward their own best interest, Wilson also noted several incidences in which religion and traditional belief systems severely hindered the efforts of Western aid for persons with various forms of impairment. Wilson's take on blindness in Africa was balanced and ahead of his time, and he was careful not to undermine local religious views, despite the numerous cases of subordination and neglect he witnessed. The persistent spiritual stigma and cultural standards of physical ability articulated by Wilson in 1953 have disturbing resonance with the plight of blind Birifor xylophonists in the twenty-first century.

Blind Birifor xylophonists are still confronted daily by ableist attitudes that map physical defect and spiritual stigma onto their bodies, while being suspect of witchcraft for their musical ability because it challenges stereotypes of the capacity of the blind African body. They are discriminated against and taken advantage of at local and regional markets, dismissed as amateur at funerals and festivals, and narrated as "useless" in local gossip. In response they compose and perform songs of counterhegemonic resistance, collectivizing in song and on the ground to challenge the spiritual narration of ability. Their music reflects and solidifies a local disability identity that emphasizes hard work and a shared humanity, an identity culturally and cosmologically inscribed through the ritual action of funeral xylophone performance.

The Cultural Significance of Birifor Musical Practice

The Birifor are known musically for their deep, raspy, pentatonic, gourd and mirliton resonated *kogyil* (funeral xylophone), which is primarily played in the context of public funeral ceremonies (Track 6.1 on the Companion Website). Birifor xylophone music generally features one xylophonist in the case of funeral music, and two in the case of festival music, both with the percussive accompaniment of the *gaŋgaa* double-headed cylindrical drum, the *kuur* hoe-blade idiophone, and varying additional percussion instruments. Birifor funeral xylophones (*kogyile*) are pentatonic fourteen-key instruments, while festival xylophones (*bɔgyile*) are tetratonic fourteen-key instruments that have two nonresonated, unplayed keys. Both reflect the prevalent five-note tuning system that likely spread outward from West Africa via Gilroy's (1993) and Kubik's (1998) trans-Atlantic corridor.

Music in Birifor communities plays a central role in all major life-cycle events and is understood in traditional religion as negotiating relationships with the otherworldly through honoring, invoking, and appeasing ancestors in the context of funerals, festivals, and religious rites. Funeral ceremonies, in particular, play a crucial role in the Birifor cosmological orientation toward the Earth, facilitating the passing of the deceased into the spirit realm while fostering social and psychological cohesion in the aftermath of the loss. A key feature of Birifor cosmology is the ever-presence of mystical dangers in daily activities, which require ritual purification and the observation of taboos to avoid, and posit an alternative and additional system of causality that governs Birifor life. This alternate causality also unfortunately facilitates and shields a culture of fear in which *suoba* and *til* accusations are common, a culture of fear often directed against disabled persons.

In funeral ceremonies xylophonists as musical ritual specialists negotiate social, cultural, spiritual, and ideological relationships, critically remaking culture, history, and the self. They do so through a song cycle that interweaves new and old compositions, and is performed by consecutive musicians at a funeral, creating a constant backdrop of music that lasts for several days at full-scale funerals (Track 6.2 on the Companion Website). In the Birifor funeral song cycle, events from the recent and distant past are encoded in song and distilled through the process of speech surrogation down to melodic phrases that closely match the contours of spoken language and can thus be understood by a listener who is adequately primed.[2] Blind and sighted xylophonists as musical ritual specialists thus play a pivotal role in Birifor cultural, cosmological, and religious systems, which in turn leads to rampant jealousy within a pervasive local culture of competition and suspicion, making them targets for malicious gossip, witchcraft accusations, and the misfortune and psychological stresses associated with them. However, for blind Birifor xylophonists, the social perception of their minds, bodies, and music through a preexisting cultural ideology of ability leads to an additional and thus compound form of subordination, which relegates their existence and achievements to witchcraft and marginalizes them in Birifor communities.

The Enemy Music of Blind Xylophonists

Confronting this compound subordination of musicianship and disability in Birifor culture, blind Birifor xylophonists identify, critique, and contest the locations of disability by composing and publicly performing enemy music. The concept of the enemy is widespread in Birifor culture and can be understood as simultaneously referring to both literal enemies and to the enemy as a cultural, psychological, and metaphorical construct. Thus enemy music can be understood as a broadly conceived form of resistance that attributes the hardships that Birifor musicians face to an ever-present and broadly conceived enemy. Maal Yichiir of Bubalanyuro's enemy music compositions resist the dominant ideology of ability that circulates in Birifor social, cultural, and spiritual domains, reflecting an indigenous counterhegemonic ideology of music and disability in the West African context.

From the onset of Maal Yichiir and his older brother Maal Chile's blindness, which occurred when they were infants before they could remember what it is to "see," both brothers were treated differently than their fourteen sighted siblings. Traditionally, a mother and father as well as their brothers and sisters jointly partake in the raising of young boys and girls on Birifor farming settlements. However, Yichiir and Chile were not taught by their father or mother, but were instead forced to learn on their own or from siblings. Yichiir described this experience as "difficult, because we always had to feel the ground before we could know what to do" (personal interview 2007). Reflecting on the difficulty of learning on his own, Yichiir described the constant danger of snakes, scorpions, and other biting or stinging insects that compromised his independence and ability to learn. Most young boys grow up helping out with the various tasks of small-scale agricultural life, gradually absorbing the lessons of the land and seasons. However, Yichiir and Chile did not begin farming until their twenties under the tutelage of their brothers. When Yichiir and Chile did learn to farm, it brought them both happiness and increased status in the household, as they were able to contribute more to their families.

Yichiir and Chile began playing xylophone at a young age, influenced musically by their father and other xylophonists who performed at local funerals. Yichiir described learning to play the xylophone as a gradual process, saying, "In our tradition, learning meanings listening, and then playing" (personal interview 2009). With periodic visits for instruction to master xylophonist El Vuur in Donyɛ, the Maal brothers became popular as performers shortly after being coaxed by their brothers into performing publically at a local funeral. Yichiir described the reaction of many people as surprised when they witness him playing, which he characterized as almost always accompanied by unwanted and derisive remarks that invoke the seeming contradiction of his blindness and musicianship. Both Yichiir and Chile expressed great thanks that they had grown up in a family where a xylophone was readily available, describing it as a source of great fulfillment for them as blind persons.

While Yichiir has composed many songs about a range of different topics, three particular compositions (recorded in 2007 and again in 2009) provide the clearest examples of the adversity he has experienced and his radical revision of Birifor conceptions of disability. *Chenjere* (I See Still), *Jaanfo* (Learning), and *Den Dem Di* (Small Small [a common cross-linguistic Ghanaian saying meaning "very little"] Eat), each engage and deconstruct Birifor ideologies of ability by projecting new narratives of the competence and virtue of blind persons within the spiritual discourse of funeral ceremonies. These songs also engage general challenges that xylophonists face as ritual specialists, as Yichiir claims membership in and commitment to the Birifor community of musical ritual specialists. *Chenjere* (I See Still) contains the following text, which is generally surrogated, though sometimes sung or spoken for the sake of clarity:

> *Chenjere* (I See Still)
>
> I am playing.
> I am playing to tell people,
> Even though they make fun of the blind,
> We can still play.
>
> People say,
> "The blind can't do anything." [The title of a Birifor children's song]
> People are always saying the blind use witchcraft to play the xylophone.
> But we are proving to you it is not witchcraft.
> It is our own talent, which God gave us.
>
> Everybody plays,
> But when we play, people say it is witchcraft.
> We can play past them.
> They always talk unnecessarily.
> (Yichiir, recorded in 2007 and 2009)

This composition provides a clear depiction of several areas of conflict for blind Birifor xylophonists, including teasing, childhood narratives of inability, witchcraft accusations, and malicious gossip. Against these currents of ableism, Yichiir asserts the skill of blind musicians as performers, legitimated with reference to a supreme God (*Nagnmin*).

The second composition, *Jaanfo* (Learning) dwells more persistently on witchcraft accusations, refuting them and stressing the importance of learning to self-improvement. Interestingly, in the end of the song the existence of a supreme God is invoked as trumping the mystical forces of witchcraft. The text of the composition, as relayed by Yichiir, is as follows:

Jaanfo (Learning)

Everything is about learning.
If you want to play xylophone,
You must go and learn.
Witchcraft cannot get you there.

Everything is about learning.
Those who accuse us of witchcraft are mistaken.
Everything is learning.

I have been taught by Dorpunu [Yichiir's uncle] and Vuur [master xylophonist from Donyɛ].
I have learned.
Why do you say I am a witch?

It is Vuur who taught me how to play,
But Vuur can still see.
It is Dorpunu who taught me how to play,
But he can still see.
So why do enemies say that they will go blind?

Enemies are jealous because we play better than others.
They say we exchanged our eyes for the xylophone.

If you know that I exchanged my eyes for the xylophone,
Why don't you also do the same and play like us?
If you think that is the reason, you should also do so.

Xylophone playing is God gifted.
It is not about witchcraft.
If you use your witchcraft,
You cannot do it,
Because it is God's gift.

When we play the xylophone,
People are always saying xylophone players are useless.
But we are the ones who keep people at the funeral,
Otherwise they would go away.
It is because of the players that the funeral is still on,
Otherwise everyone would go home.

The xylophone is not about chieftaincy.
It is just for funeral celebrations,
So don't fight over it.

We only play at funerals.
People will sit down and say that we are rich,
But there is nothing to be gained from it.
We are sacrificing ourselves for the sake of the funeral.
(Yichiir, recorded in 2007 and 2009)

That people attribute the skill of blind xylophonists to mystical powers reflects both the mundane jealousy that is prevalent in Birifor culture and a cultural ideology of ability in which only a mystical cause can explain the musical feats of blind xylophonists. Similar to "savant" musicians, Birifor blind xylophonists' musical ability evokes doubt among local audiences, who have trouble resolving the perceived dissonance between their disability and their exceptional musical ability. These interpretations of blind xylophonists also raise the question of exactly what is gained, if anything, by those who dismiss the skills and achievements of blind xylophonists. Acknowledging that the spiritual system of causality operative in Birifor culture is passed on from generation to generation and is not always consciously wielded to disempower, there may still be additional incentives in the form of power and privilege to be gained from maintaining blind xylophonists' low status.

Given the high competition that governs both musical performance and the local agricultural lifestyle, other musicians and farmers may benefit from blind xylophonists' dual subordination through less competition for resources. Many of the exceptional xylophonists that I interviewed stated that they do not regularly play at funerals anymore in order for younger musicians (usually from their own lineage) to enjoy the spotlight. The reason that there is not room for musicians to perform is that the attention and recognition of being regarded as the representative of a lineage is highly coveted, as is the payment received from performance. There are also only so many funerals that occur each season, making the prime performance slots during a funeral highly sought after. Those who find themselves at odds or take issue with the cultural norms reinscribed in funeral performance may also gain from compromising the integrity of xylophonists as ritual specialists. However, this competition may in practice be secondary to the payoff of defining both musicianship and sightedness in opposition to the projected negative of blind musicians, as the stigma of disability services and legitimates the normate by reifying its dominant positionality.

Yichiir's dismissal of a spiritual interpretation of blindness in favor of a more pragmatic model of practice and learning in *Jaanfo*, reflects the frustrations of a talented and dedicated musician whose music is hijacked by narratives of witchcraft. That blind Birifors can be understood as physically incapable to the extent that a specialized skill such as musicianship can only be explained with reference to mystical origins is a result of both the formal ableism of Birifor culture and the spiritual role of Birifor xylophonists as ritual specialists. The discrimination that blind Birifor musicians face, as described in this composition, draws mystical associations from the act of ritual musical performance to legitimate negativistic interpretations of disability. Since sighted musicians are also sometimes accused of witchcraft associated with performance, and because Birifors with disabilities who are not musicians are still labeled as spiritual pariahs, musicianship and blindness are conjoined in Birifor communities into a compound form of subordination policed by spiritual narratives. This is important to bear in mind, because the adversity blind Birifor xylophonists face is often spread across interpretations of their musicianship and disability *together*, diminishing the degree to which either can be cast in isolation. This compound subordination is—like the double bind of race and gender—an intersection of two devalued identities, which together yield a new and distinct category of oppression (Crenshaw 1989).

The third composition, *Den Dem Di* (Small Small Eat), focuses on the economic and occupational realities for blind persons in Birifor communities, expressing the various necessities of rural living in opposition to the ridicule of the enemy. Yichiir composed this song in response to a snakebite that he received while farming, which left him bedridden for several days. The large rubber boots worn by farmers to protect against such bites are expensive, and at the time Yichiir did not own any, though after the experience his brother Maal Lombɔr saved money to buy him some. The song text, explained in detail by Yichiir, is as follows:

Den Dem Di (Small Small Eat)

As a blind man, I have nothing.
But still the enemy is jealous.
The enemy says,
"Yichiir is always boasting,
But he is not good at xylophone.
That is why he farms."

How big do I farm that you turn into a snake and come bite me?You, my
enemy, you don't provide me food to eat,
But you don't want me to farm.
What will I do?

If I can't farm, I can't eat, and my family will not get food to eat.
You don't care for me, and you don't want me to farm.
Why shouldn't I?
As a blind man, I also try my best.
I work hard to get food.
It is small small [very little] that I am doing to make it in life.
So the enemy should not be jealous.

Everyone is working hard to make it in life.
When I do the same, you come and destroy my work.

I have a large family.
They need to eat.
If I don't farm, what will I have to feed them?
You sit down there while I work.
Do not disturb me.

The enemy says,
"You play xylophone, and now you want to farm as well. Why?"
I say, you sit down there and don't work hard,
Because as for me I am going forward.
I am not going backward.
So you sit down there and go backward.
I will go forward.

Enemy, if I need something, do you buy it for me?
If I need cloth, you can't buy it for me.
If I need pants, you can't buy them for me.

I've seen my father sitting there,
From morning until evening.
He is also blind.
He could not get me anything.
As I have seen that,
How can I not work hard to feed my family?

Everyone has seen my father.
They never cared for him.
They saw him with their naked eyes.
If you do not want me to farm,
How do you expect me to feed my family?
I am working hard.
Enemy! Go away from me.

Listen xylophonists!
I have composed this enemy music.
Everybody, and you young boys, dance to this enemy music!
You must dance, do not fold your hands, come and dance!

I am insulting the enemy.
If you hear this and want to fight, then you are the enemy.
But if you are not the one, you have to be quiet.
If you come to bother me, then you are the one I am talking about.

You!
Witch!
No matter how big you are,
All human beings pass through death,
And so you shall also.
Before people outside can know things about you,
Good or bad, it must always come from someone in your home.
They will sell you out. If not, no one would ever hear the secrets of your home.
(Yichiir, recorded in 2007 and 2009)

This song begins by stating the reality that, as a blind person living in an already poverty-stricken community, Yichiir has nothing. He calls out and challenges those who would perpetuate a cycle of poverty and dependence, underscoring the economics of ableism in Birifor contexts. Despite this suffering, he says, the enemy constantly provokes and undermines his productive efforts and achievements. In this particular episode, the enemy turned into a snake and bit him, hindering his agricultural productivity. For Yichiir, this use of witchcraft by the enemy is motivated by jealousy, which he tries to dismantle by relating his struggles, and arguing for his recognition as an ordinary hardworking member of the community. As opposed to the focus in "Jaanfo" on musicianship as a learned skill, *Den Dem Di* challenges popular opinions about blind persons farming, claiming the necessity of agricultural toil as the primary subsistence practice for everyone in the community. Yichiir's invocation of his father Sagba Maal's blindness (which was late-onset blindness), links Yichiir's own impairment to past incidences of blindness in the community, helping to historicize disability through tangible experiences rather than through spiritual abstractions of witchcraft that cast blindness as a timeless stigma. As a cathartic venting of the psychological stress of economic hardship, such compositions encapsulate a complex of motivations. The enemy of these songs is at once a legitimate source of evil, either as a human actor or witchcraft, and a receptacle if not scapegoat for the burdens and stresses of life. For blind musicians in particular, the enemy can likewise be interpreted as referring both to actual persons and events and to the local opinions and views that constitute a cultural ideology of ability. In the song's closing stanza, the insults and mortality thrown at the enemy are accompanied by more subtle statements of the responsibility of the household to prevent the spread of malicious gossip.

In these three compositions, Yichiir's struggles as a blind Birifor are located primarily in public resistance to his two main occupations of farming and xylophone performance. His skill as both a farmer and a xylophonist are the result of years of dedicated toil and practice. However, his achievements are widely attributed spiritual origins in the Southern Birifor community because they contradict popular notions of the capacity of blind persons. The salient Birifor culture of fear, evident in the recurring theme of witchcraft in xylophone compositions, further distances blind musicians from their already mixed status as ritual specialists, and ultimately denies them equal status as members of the community.

The assertion of agency and reframing of disability according to both the perspective and experience of impaired persons represented in Maal Yichiir's enemy music shows that the "nothing about us without us" rallying cry of Western disability activism is echoed in the context of rural African life (Straus 2011). While in the Birifor context musical performance is the medium through which disability is reshaped and reinscribed, disability theorists such as G. Thomas Couser (2009) have located similar "retorts" to the hegemonic construction of disability in expressive forms such as theoretical and biographical writing. That the cultural milieu enables such forms of resistance as enemy music—both by blind and sighted musicians—also reflects a few important aspects of Birifor and West African cultural contexts. First, ritual musical performance is often a space where power hierarchies are not just established and reified but also inverted and subverted (Hoffman 1995; Hogan 2008). Second, while there is a tendency to read ethnographic scholarship as projecting a monolithic and monological depiction of culture and person, the reality "on the ground" does not surrender to such simplifications, and in the Birifor case persons labeled as disabled through sociocultural narratives still retain allies within the community. Finally, at Birifor funerals young and aspiring xylophonists often perform just before or after a funeral and during the long nights that funerals span, while the peak daylight performance hours are reserved for professional musicians. The blind xylophonists I worked with are all professional and have performed at the peak hours of funerals, but the presence and acceptance of amateur performers at other times allows audience members to dismiss their performances as incomplete and inferior without the need to bar them from playing altogether.

Theorizing Disability in West African Context

The critical perspectives of social, cultural, and disability theorists, which underline the latent power dynamics in naturalized sociocultural structures, have been essential to peeling back the layers of social, cultural, and medical meaning that entrap persons with disabilities in a negative identity. Applying these perspectives to disability in Birifor communities illuminates areas of overlap with Western contexts and categories of difference. David Mitchell and Sharon Snyder articulate disability as a culturally constructed location where "disabled people find themselves deposited often against their will" (2006, 3). The nuance of this argument is that disability is not an indicator of physical or biological variation, but a culturally defined label that enforces oppression. Drawing on the works of Sally French (1994) and Simi Linton (1998), Mitchell and Snyder, like Siebers (2008; 2010), posit disability as a site of previously unrecognized agency. However, their specifically cultural location of disability emphasizes that disabled bodies are cast as discordant with local fictions, which are embedded in local knowledge structures. This distinction is essential to understanding that disability operates differently in the context of Birifor culture because of the culture-specific creation and maintenance of the locations of disability. Though such a cultural emphasis may seem obvious, much of the literature on disability neglects a global perspective. For example, while the *ICIDH-2: International Classification of Functioning and Disability* (World Health Organization 1999) formally added a social dimension to each category of its threefold schema of impairment, activity, and participation, greatly expanding the discourse of disability, cultural and spiritual dimensions remain absent from the current framework of the *International Classification of Functioning, Disability and Health* (World Health Organization 2011).

Marginalizing definitions of able-bodiedness are pronounced in rural Birifor farming communities, where strength and fitness often translate into increased agricultural yield, social status, and economic prosperity. Robert McRuer's concept of "compulsory able-bodiedness" tied such naturalized norms to the production of capital, asserting that, "being able-bodied means being capable of the normal physical exertions required in a particular system of labor" (McRuer 2002, 89). Thus whether defined in relation to industrial capitalism, or rural agriculture, impairment is still translated into disability in part through social and economic systems. Such definitions are violently exclusionary for the "unquestioned inferiority" that they entail, which obscures as natural the policing and production of ability (Siebers 2008, 6). This same ableism, conferred through an ideology of ability, also marks blind musicians' xylophone performances as a separate spectacle for their skill at a seemingly visually dependent and highly specialized task, making their performance simultaneously one of music and of disability (Straus 2011).

Along with narratives of ability cast on disabled bodies, Siebers points out that because disability is associated with physical pain (through notions of physical defect and chronic suffering), people irrationally fear disability and hence distance themselves from disabled persons (2008, 20). Since disability is conceived as both social and spiritual deviance in Birifor culture, the mystical powers that are believed to have caused blindness lead to a non-rational fear of the disabled body as spiritually contaminated. Disability in Birifor communities exemplifies Erving Goffman's concept of "stigma," in which difference becomes a permanent mark of subhumanity that transforms the stigmatized, "from a whole and usual person to a tainted, discounted one" (2006, 131). The well-intentioned but equally destructive ensuing supposition that persons with disabilities "overcome" such monumental setbacks to lead "normal" lives, reflects a persistent cross-cultural trend of rendering the lives of persons with disabilities first and foremost through stigma forcefully extrapolated from their biology. Despite this trend, Birifor xylophonists emphasize the positive value of disability, like the numerous disability communities in the West that have gained public prominence in the wake of the disability rights movement. In interviews, each blind xylophonist I worked with made a point of acknowledging the strong sense of community among blind persons as well as the knowledge and friendship that circulates among blind musicians. They also noted the deep friendships that grew out of their apprenticeships with senior sighted musicians and their families.

One of the results of the Birifor socio-spiritual model of disability is the mapping of social perceptions of disability as embodied biological deviance to disability as embodied spiritual deviance. Just as Africa is pathologized along several fronts, so too is the African disabled body. The unfortunate classic depiction of Africa as the "Dark Continent," full of both unmapped and untapped riches and wealth and an unpredictable and savage populace, is reflected in the perception of the African disabled body. The African disabled body is simultaneously mysteriously powerful through its dangerous spiritual charge and unexplainable skill, and dysfunctional to the point of a subhumanity because of its perceived inability to thrive in a social and economic context in which specific forms of daily manual labor are expected. Persistent contemporary conceptions of Africa as a dangerous and disorderly land housing widespread disease, conflict, and poverty doomed to linger in an economic and cultural backwater are projected through ableist discourse onto African disabled bodies, rendering them as a microcosm of Africa's ailments. The African disabled body is, on the one hand, defined as a medical and physical abnormality that is the result of Africa's uncontrolled diseases and uneducated population. This population, so the stereotype goes, makes otherwise avoidable mistakes rearing their children, leaving them susceptible to illnesses that have been largely overcome in the developed world. On the other hand, African disabled bodies are narrated as both the site and product of spiritual conflict, being ontologically tied to "provincial" cultural practices and cosmological systems. Certain disabled bodies are also perceived as the possible aftermath of violent political conflict that leaves death and mutilation in its wake, or of local systems of justice that remove body parts associated with a given crime. These conceptions of the African disabled body are an enactment of exactly the type of discursive violence outlined by Mitchell and Snyder (2006) in which the locations that the disabled are relegated to, the nature of discourse about them, and their inclusion in a blanket category of disability, are all ultimately forms of sanctioned aggression. This sanctioned aggression thus takes on unique forms in African contexts that require careful consideration as disability is theorized on a global scale.

The Spiritual Model of Disability

While the medical model and more recent social and cultural models of disability in Western scholarship apply in rural Birifor culture, they are encapsulated within an additional indigenous spiritual model of disability that labels the disabled body as the necessary result of corrupting spiritual forces. The closest Western equivalent to the Birifor spiritual model of disability is the preenlightenment religious model of disability, which rendered disability as both an outward manifestation of sin and the embodiment of divine disfavor (Straus 2011, 5–6; Wheatley 2010, 64). This religious model persists today in attitudes toward variant bodies and able-bodiedness as the result of immoral behavior, though it has been transmuted into perhaps more subtle forms. The religious model of disability is exemplified in contemporary North American society in particular by the faith healing of Pentecostal preachers and similar religious figures that attempt to exorcise the spirits causing impairment (Wheatley 2010, 64). This enduring practice brings into focus one of the key differences between a religious model operative in Western contexts and the spiritual model of Birifor contexts. While both posit a spiritual action or affliction as the root cause of impairment, in the Birifor context there is no act of faith or evangelism that can change the impairment or remove the associated stigma. In fact, in cases where vision is restored or the ability to walk is renewed, suspicion of witchcraft is often only reinforced. The circumstances of impairment may shift, but the stigma does not.

Another key difference that characterizes the spiritual model of disability operative in Birifor culture is that it is legitimated by a fundamentally different causality, in which foundational notions of cause and effect vary from the Aristotelian causality that proliferates in the West. This can be understood through Jack Goody's characterization of the layered causality of a LoDagaa (a cultural spectrum that includes the Birifor) worldview. Goody (1972) followed by Mendonsa (1982, 85) noted that among the LoDagaa, Sisaala, and Tallensi, there are

> Three levels of causation, the immediate, the efficient, and the final. The immediate is the technique used to kill the deceased; disease, snakebites, or other "natural" causes as well as forms of mystical or aggression. The efficient is to be found among the members of the community itself, the person behind the act of killing. The final cause is the ancestor, the Earth shrine, or a medicine shrine. (Goody 1972, 210)

Mapping Birifor causality as dispersed between immediate, efficient, and final levels of causation, accommodates three very different angles of interpretation within one cohesive and ultimately flexible system. The immediate cause, rooted in the physical world, includes observable action and witchcraft, which operate according to contrasting logics. The efficient cause represents the responsibility of the living, both those directly and indirectly involved in the event, to maintain balance and spiritual order in the community, which in the case of death or witchcraft they have neglected. The final cause invokes the larger system of beliefs of the individual, such as traditional religion or Christianity. The sophistication of this tripartite causality is found in its simultaneous invocation of existential, mystical, social, and spiritual domains to explain life as it unfolds. Viewed as a strategy of the psyche, witchcraft beliefs also diffuse individual responsibility for hardship, scapegoating witches, witchcraft, and the malicious intent of others in the interpretation of misfortune. The immediate level of causation is of most interest here because it contains seemingly contradictory logical systems. Blind Birifors are thought to be blind because of something different in their physiology. However, that physiology is different precisely because of witchcraft or a curse.

The dualism present in witchcraft's immediate causality is both a dynamic aspect of Birifor spiritual views and a backdoor through which the humanity of blind persons is evacuated. No matter the rigor of a local scientific account of the process of visual degeneration, or the cultural salience of Western medical, social, or cultural interpretations of blindness, witchcraft beliefs still stigmatize blindness and disability as the causal result of mystical powers. The persistent belief that mystical forces are the primary cause of blindness marks the blind body as an object of mystical intrigue rather than as a volitional self. The reason witchcraft's causality, not religion, is the focus of this critique (and a fundamental location disability) is that blindness is always predetermined as the natural and necessary result of an imbalance of mystical energy, which blind persons or their families, not a divine presence, have invited. That otherwise secular Birifors believe in witchcraft also attests to the fact that it functions as a separate system from religion.A spiritual model of disability must be included with the social model as articulated by disability theorists such as Tobin Siebers (2008, 2010) and the cultural model developed by disability theorists like David Mitchell and Sharon Snyder (2006) in order to accurately describe the way disability operates in rural West Africa. Just as the religious model of disability in medieval Europe was a pervasive discourse that recast impairment as disability, the spiritual model is a remarkably resistant discourse in Birifor communities that maps physical variation as a sign and symptom of spiritual transgression. This has broader relevance to the practice of ethnomusicology and Disability Studies because it demonstrates that the parameters of ableism are culture specific and dramatically influence the reception and experience of disabled musicians and their music.

Implications for the Disciplines

Maal Yichiir's enemy music compositions outline and critique a Birifor ideology of ability and its inclusion of a spiritual model of disability, articulating the locations of disability within Birifor culture. They locate a Birifor social model of disability in the construction of exclusionary practices that marginalize the disabled at markets, schools, funerals, and in the public sphere. They point to a biological model of disability in Birifor culture located in the widespread belief that disabled persons are infirm and incapable. This ranges from beliefs about their agricultural and economic capability, to the perception of their performances as miraculous or marvelous, to fear of the contagious mystical charge of disabled bodies. The spiritual model of disability critiqued in these compositions renders disability as the necessary result of spiritual forces outside of the individual and beyond their control. The variation from norms legitimated in Birifor social and biological models of disability are thus remapped and conjoined within a spiritual model that stigmatizes disabled persons through a spiritual narrative of causality. These models together contribute to the general ideology of ability that circulates in Birifor communities.Stepping back to consider the relevance this has for scholarly practice, ideologies of ability place disabled persons outside the bounds of ability and in so doing create a subject position that can reflect back powerful insights about these ideologies. The theoretical stance outlined in this essay claims disability as a valuable vantage point rather than a liability, which gradually undoes notions of able-bodiedness and the assumptions that ensue in the cultural inscription of ability. Disability thus contains the potential for critical agency, which, as Andrew Apter has suggested, is a necessarily transformative agency, remapping the conditions through which it is expressed (Apter 2007, 3–12). The critical agency used by blind musicians in their compositions and lifestyles to challenge assumptions about disability also underlines the importance of music to parsing spirituality and disability in the context of West Africa, while reconstituting the self in ritual context and challenging structures of normalization and pathology. As disability theory continues to permeate the disciplines, the insight that spiritual systems reinforce social and biological formulations of disability, and that they do so in different ways depending on culture and context, becomes increasingly important to modeling the person in rural West Africa and disability in global perspective.

Acknowledgments

This essay would not have been possible without the invaluable feedback and insight of several scholars, including Andrew Apter, Michael Bakan, Ann Fox, Stephanie Jensen-Moulton, Cheryl Keyes, Timothy Rice, Anthony Seeger, and Joseph Straus.

Notes

1. The person-first language schema (e.g., persons with blindness) that sought to privilege a shared humanity over forcibly applied categories of difference has recently in Western

scholarship given way to the reclaiming of the labels of disability, which are seen as core parts of an identity that are only *constructed* as negative. When considering the appropriate language schema for blindness, impairment, and disability in the context of rural Birifor culture, it is important to note that the words for a blind person (*jɔɔn*) or a blind xylophonist (*jɔɔn gyilmwier*) are still widely (and perhaps universally) used as categories that reinforce a negative, essentializing interpretation of the person. Thus a language usage that states personhood before externally applied categories of value and differentiation is still valuable to communicating the nature of ability in Birifor contexts, and more importantly to Birifor communities. To conform to the current language usage in Disability Studies and to also honor the circumstances of disability in rural West Africa, this essay uses both orderings.

2. For a more detailed explanation of Birifor speech surrogation, see Hogan (2011, 233–270).

References

Apter, Andrew. 2007. *Beyond Words: Discourse and Critical Agency in Africa.* Chicago: University of Chicago Press.

Couser, G. Thomas. 2009. *Signifying Bodies: Disability in Contemporary Life Writing.* Ann Arbor: University of Michigan Press.

Crenshaw, Kimberle. 1989. "Demarginalizing the Intersection of Race and Sex: A Black Feminist Critique of Antidiscrimination Doctrine, Feminist Theory, and Antiracist Politics." *University of Chicago Legal Forum* 140: 139–167.

French, Sally, ed. 1994. *On Equal Terms: Working with Disabled People.* Oxford, UK: Butterworth Heinemann.

Gilroy, Paul. 1993. *The Black Atlantic: Modernity and Double Consciousness.* Cambridge, MA: Harvard University Press.

Goffman, Erving. (1963) 1986. *Stigma: Notes on the Management of Spoiled Identity.* New York: Touchstone.

Goffman, Erving. 2006. "Selections from *Stigma.*" In *The Disability Studies Reader,* 2nd ed., edited by Lennard J. Davis, 131–140. New York: Routledge.

Goody, Jack R. 1962. *Death, Property, and the Ancestors: A Study of the Mortuary Customs of the LoDagaa of West Africa.* London: Travistock.

Goody, Jack R. 1972. *The Myth of Bagre.* Oxford, UK: Clarendon Press.

Hoffman, Barbara G. 1995. "Power, Structure, and Mande *jeliw.*" In *Status and Identity in West Africa,* edited by David C. Conrad and Barbara E. Frank, 28–45. Bloomington: Indiana University Press.

Hogan, Brian. 2008. "Gendered Modes of Resistance: Power and Women's Songs in West Africa." *Pacific Review of Ethnomusicology* 13. http://ethnomusicologyreview.ucla.edu/journal/volume/13/piece/498.

Hogan, Brian. 2011. "Enemy Music: Blind Birifor Xylophonists of Northwest Ghana." PhD diss., University of California, Los Angeles.

Kubik, Gerhard. 1998. "Intra-African Streams of Influence." In *Africa: The Garland Encyclopedia of World Music,* edited by Ruth Stone, 293–326. New York: Garland.

Linton, Simi. 1998. *Claiming Disability: Knowledge and Identity.* New York: New York University Press.

McRuer, Robert. 2002. "Compulsory Able-Bodiedness and Queer/Disabled Existence." In *Disability Studies: Enabling the Humanities*, edited by Rosemarie Garland-Thomson, Brenda Jo Brueggemann, and Sharon L. Snyder, 88–99. New York: MLA.

Mendonsa, Eugene. L. 1982. *The Politics of Divination: A Processual View of Reactions to Illness and Deviance among the Sisala of Northern Ghana*. Los Angeles: University of California Press.

Mitchell, David T., and Sharon L. Snyder. 2006. *Cultural Locations of Disability*. Chicago: Chicago University Press.

Siebers, Tobin. 2008. *Disability Theory*. Ann Arbor: University of Michigan Press.

Siebers, Tobin. 2010. *Disability Aesthetics*. Ann Arbor: University of Michigan Press.

Straus, Joseph N. 2011. *Extraordinary Measures: Disability in Music*. New York: Oxford University Press.

Wheatley, Edward. 2010. "Medieval Constructions of Blindness in France and England." In *The Disability Studies Reader*, 3rd ed., edited by Lennard J. Davis, 63–76. New York: Routledge.

Wilson, John. 1953. "Blindness in Colonial Africa." *African Affairs* 52 (207): 141–149.

Wilson, John. 1961. *Ghana's Handicapped Citizens*. Accra, Ghana: Government Printer.

World Health Organization. 1999. *ICIDH-2: International Classification of Functioning and Disability*. Beta-2 draft, full version. Geneva, Switzerland: World Health Organization.

World Health Organization. 2011. "International Classification of Functioning, Disability, and Health." Accessed February 18, 2011. http://www.who.int/classifications/icf/en/.

CHAPTER 7

UNDERSTANDING IS SEEING

Music Analysis and Blindness

SHERSTEN JOHNSON

NARRATIVES OF MUSIC ANALYSIS

IN November of 2012, a concerned professor posted a query on the Society for Music Theory e-mail list asking the "collective wisdom" of subscribers for ideas on how best to serve a visually impaired student who needed to satisfy a required course in Schenkerian music analysis (Meeùs 2012). Others at his institution had decided that the only solution was simply to allow the student to be excused from the class. The post sparked a series of replies that offered helpful pedagogical strategies, but also included expressions of consternation that a methodology such as Schenkerian analysis—a chief purpose of which is to direct long-range *hearing*—was so dependent on visually apprehended print notation that it could not be taught to a blind student.[1]

This story dramatizes the extent to which narratives of music analysis, especially analysis of Western art music, rely on print notation and other visual means of interpretation (analytical graphs and the like).[2] In this essay, I argue that through the lens of disability—particularly blindness in both its somatic and metaphorical guises—those visually based narratives can be "reread." Close attention to the experience of musicians with notation-based analysis, as well as the sorts of metaphors they use to describe their experience, will suggest alternative means of hearing and representing musical structure.

SEEING AND UNDERSTANDING

Music analysis is an activity that attempts to explain how pieces work in order to aid pursuits such as performing, composing, and listening. Like other investigative activities in general, music analysis tends to invoke the conceptual metaphor UNDERSTANDING IS SEEING.[3] This metaphor underlies many of our notions about concepts. People often speak of having a point of *view* or an *outlook*, and getting the *picture*. Ideas are *insightful, visionary*, and *transparent* or, conversely, *short sighted* and *opaque*. And, of course, *a picture is worth a thousand words*. Consequently, the absence of seeing equates with lack of understanding, and the term *blind* functions figuratively to indicate a failure of discernment and even at times willful ignorance: *He turned a blind eye*. The expression also has the sense of concealment, such as in the case of *blind auditions* or *blind peer review*. Georgina Kleege, in her memoir of visual impairment, has assembled a long list of idioms featuring the word *blind* including *blind side, blind faith*, and *blind leading the blind*. She observes that other disabilities are used metaphorically, but not as often as blindness (Kleege 1999, 21). Alex Lubet, in his book *Music, Disability, and Society*, situates this phenomenon in the context of Western culture's privileging of vision above the other senses:

> I suspect also, though, the inverse of this privilege: an exceptional fear of blindness and the consequent application of blindness as metaphor, which is in turn part and parcel of a larger, more generalized fear of impairment, enshrined in many more metaphors. Blindness as an intense but multivalent metaphor is at least as old as the Oedipus legend and as ubiquitous as "Amazing Grace" ("was blind, but now I see"). (2010, 70)

In order to critique the notion of sight as the sense of understanding, anthropologists and ethnomusicologists draw attention to the sensory orders of other cultures. In her ethnography on Anlo-speaking people in Ghana, Geurts observes that the Anlo had less linguistic elaboration around color terminology as opposed to textures or bodily carriage and balance. Many of their expressions pointed to the limitations of sight and promoted the use of other senses when substantiating perceptions (Geurts 2002, 62). Geurts concludes that sensory order is culturally determined, and thus the Euro-American notion of five senses first determined by Aristotle is not a scientific fact but rather a folk model (8).[4]

Seeing Music

Part of this cultural difference stems from the epistemologies of oral/aural traditions (which depend on hearing) and literate culture (which privileges seeing).[5] Western art music had its origins in oral tradition and has since developed a complex literate system of notation while still maintaining some forms of oral transmission. Three broad categories of notation have expressed Western art music: mnemonic devices have been in use since ancient times and serve only as a prosthesis for memory rather than a means of composition; tablature has been in use since about 1300 to guide finger placement and technique by musicians who have the instrument at hand; and staff notation has been in use since the eleventh century to enhance the ability to imagine and remember music, thus fostering the creation of longer and more complex pieces.

Staff notation as used today is both a clever artifice and an efficient tool, efficient, in the sense that its symbols share many of the properties with the musical features it represents. For example, staff notation aspires to reflect the proportional relationship between tones, a visual metaphor that notes that are closer together on the page happen more "closely together" in time, and notes that are further apart have longer intervals between attacks. Thus a relationship that happens along the time axis acts iconically to represent a relationship in musical durations. Notational conventions are also artificial in that musicians often rely on certain assumptions (like proportional relationships) that those conventions engender and assume that they apply broadly across all musical experiences. As Peter Westergaard observes, not only does staff notation tell someone "what he or she must do with hands or throat to get the sounds required," it also "tells you how to think of the sounds you are to make" (Westergaard 1996, 17). Joseph Straus has unpacked many of these assumptions in the course of his discussion of "normal" and "blind" hearing (Straus 2011, 170–174), and I will elaborate the specific example of pitch motion here.

When musicians speak of high and low pitches, the terms correspond more closely with the orientation of notes on the printed page than, say, notes on the piano where higher is to the *right* of the keyboard, or on the cello, where higher notes require that the fingers be placed *lower* on the fingerboard. Anne Marie de Zeeuw, in her article on teaching music theory classes that include blind students, suggests that the idea of pitches moving up and down over time, thus creating a spatial melodic contour, is a learned cultural norm:

> At least one theorist, Ernst Kurth, believes that [melodic contour] is an immanent musical concept, unrelated to notation [the reference is to Kurth 1969 (1931), 255]. . . . Now if this is true, the student who is blind should develop the idea of melodic "curve" independently, as do most sighted students. This, however, is not the case. While the blind student experiences no special difficulty in understanding an explanation of melodic contour, he [or she] does not think of a succession of tones as having a "shape" unless . . . taught to do so. It seems . . . that this concept, far from being independent of notation, is based at least in part on the visual image of the line formed by the representation of a series of pitches on the staff. (De Zeeuw 1977, 90–91)

Blind singer, Rachel Grider, who has never seen a musical score, relates her own assumptions about melodic contour:

> As far as I know, I have always thought of pitches moving up and down. I'm not sure why; I think I just heard it that way, and people talked about it that way. I would not be surprised, though, if some blind people do not think of pitch going up and down because Braille music does not use that visual concept. (message to the author, May 22, 2013)

Grider's observation alludes to the fact that musicians performing Western art music tend to interact intensively with the visual apparatus of musical scores, and so many notational conventions become second nature. The influence of notation on what we hear and how we perform and compose goes almost unnoticed, and, despite what are sometimes tenuous mappings between sound and notation, the distinctions between the written and the audible blur in our musical discourse.[6] The graphic attributes of print notation, which correspond strongly with many of the ways we think and talk about music, then facilitate adoptions of these notions by reinforcing concepts we already hold dear. Borrowing from an idea developed by Lennard Davis, this reinforcement becomes the "constructed normalcy" of art music's composition, performance, and dissemination (Davis 2002, 38).

Seeing Music Analysis

In Western culture, when it comes to understanding music, "getting the picture" usually involves some kind of visual image, whether it is a score meant as an aid in performance or some other representation meant to illustrate certain musical features. Part of the challenge of trying to understand how music works is that somehow one has to capture the sound-imagery—essentially the vibrations of air molecules—in order to measure, divide, and compare its components. Music is neither tangible nor static, so analysts typically rely on printed or recorded traces of the sound-image, and if only a recording is available, often a transcription in notation is made for study purposes. Acknowledging the value of seeing an image of a piece of music, Judith Lochhead writes:

> The visual representations of the score have been fundamental to the practice of analysis for at least two reasons. First, the score depicts an unperformed version of the work and relieves the analyst from assessing performance accuracy and other issues of interpretation. Second, visual access to a piece through the score bypasses the "real time" of performance, allowing the analyst to ponder relationships and structural features without the constraints of "time's arrows." (Lochhead 2005, 257)

Ultimately, most analyses of Western music rely on a notated score as a representation of the music, if only a coarse one. At the same time, score study can reveal relationships that only obtain visually and not necessarily aurally, although we hope an analysis points to previously unheard relationships that result in a new, perhaps deeper way of hearing. And in many cases visual diagrams become "audible" via audiation (auditory imagination or inner hearing).

Even so, encoding music in staff notation is already an act of evaluation and visual interpretation, emphasizing some things and obscuring others. But even as biased and incomplete a system as it is, the notated score for a given work can be too lengthy or too full of information to facilitate analytical demonstrations. Performers and scholars rely on various graphic representations for further understanding in order to escape time's arrows and thus capture certain features of the music in a static, examinable form. For visually oriented people, the medium of this static representation is usually some optically apprehended diagram that can be taken in at a glance or thoroughly digested by the eyes to facilitate observation and reflection. Often, although not always, an interesting-looking diagram implies a thought-provoking analysis.

Published analyses in music theory and analysis journals contain a variety of analytical visualizations with graphic symbols, some of which are highly specialized.[7] As notation aids memory, analytical diagrams aid and direct attention. Like an electron microscope or an x-ray machine they can bring detail into focus, strip away complex distractions, and shore up our ability to process relationships in real time. So just as notation is prosthetic on the sounding music—reducing, clarifying, biasing—so an analytical representation is prosthetic on a musical score.

While this is not a criticism of any of these analyses or others like them, needless to say, visual representations present a barrier for visually impaired musicians, and music educators face challenges in accommodating people with visual differences, especially in music theory classrooms. Consider Vicky Chapman's experience with analysis:

> While in college I attempted a degree in music therapy. I was not allowed to use a reader for theory classes, and the instructor refused to read aloud what he had written on the board. . . . Finally, when a theory instructor assigned a fugue to be analyzed using a graph, the difficulty I would have completing the assignment on my own became obvious. When confronting the instructor with my dilemma, he immediately informed me that the task had to be completed independently, with no assistance. The instructor clearly stated that if the assignment could not be completed on my own, I had no business in a music program. I dropped out of the program and completed my degree in early childhood education. (Chapman 1999)

Fortunately, Chapman went on to excel in music without a music degree, and realized her dreams of singing on stage by performing with several regional opera companies. But her story magnifies the visual emphasis often placed on scores and graphs when analyzing, an emphasis that is only now becoming accommodated. Though attitudes are changing and strides have been made with new technologies, a musician like Chapman might still meet with resistance today. Even more grievously, converting Chapman's assigned fugue into Braille would not have completely solved her analytical dilemma.

Touching and Understanding

A bit of background on tactile music notation will serve to illustrate these concerns. One might wonder, why not just make a representation of staff notation that can be felt?

Indeed, a variety of embossed paper and other versions of staff notation apprehensible by touch have been used, especially when teaching children.[8] However, the notation needs to be enlarged, and as pieces gain length and complexity, this means of representation becomes prohibitively bulky and expensive. Since its invention in the 1820s, the tactile notation of choice has been Braille music, which is an alphanumeric code, employing configurations of raised dots that can be read by touch. The system was developed by Louis Braille, who, blinded at age 3, may never have seen a print music score. Braille combined an existing system of raised letters with a code for transmitting messages during nocturnal combat in order to form what became literary and music Braille (Braille 1829).[9]

Touching Music

Louis Braille was an accomplished organist, so it is not surprising then that Braille music has many similarities with keyboard tablature and as such forms a hybrid of staff transcription and tab-like "how-to-play" systems. For example, Braille notates four-part chorales (vocal pieces, frequently notated to be played on a keyboard to accompany the voices) using two parallel lines of symbols, one for each of the keyboardist's hands. Each line contains either a soprano or bass note, and indicates the alto and tenor notes by interval from those notes respectively, reading up for the bass clef and down for the treble. "E 3rd" in the right hand would indicate that E be played with a finger and that C be played by the thumb (a third lower).

In writing on different notational formats for pieces of music, Larry Zbikowski points out that musical scores carry an aura of authority, but they actually follow from conceptual models for compositions. He writes, "A score is an artifactual manifestation of the elements of the conceptual model deemed most relevant to the musical practice of which the model is a part, created as a means of stabilizing the model" (2002, 221). In short, chorales written in Braille follow the conceptual model for homophonic keyboard pieces, comfortably played by two hands with two notes in each hand. The notation reflects the embodied experience of hands that *mirror* each other when placed on the keyboard, with bass and soprano fingers and opposable tenor/alto thumbs. The immediate feeling of intervals in the hand for a keyboardist makes sense of the Braille chorale in a way that is similar to a playing from tablature.[10]

There are a number of additional differences between the visual and tactile forms of notation. For example, Braille does not transcribe beams or proportional note placement, so the visual perceptions that "closer and blacker means faster" and "everything under a beam is within one beat" do not transfer. So four half notes, for example, would take up the same amount of left-to-right space as four thirty-second notes.[11] Scanning the Braille delivers information sequentially. For example, the first phrase of the tune *My Bonnie Lies Over the Ocean*, shown in Figure 7.1, would consist

FIGURE 7.1 "My Bonnie Lies over the Ocean" in staff notation.

of cells signifying: | treble clef | 3/4 meter | 4th octave | G quarter | start slur | 5th octave | E quarter | dot | D eighth | C quarter | D quarter | C quarter | A quarter | G quarter | end slur | E half |. The discrete cells of Braille are read sequentially, so the phrase's swell of intensity must be apprehended abstractly and intuited between beginning and ending points, whereas a curved line in print simulates the incremental increases and decreases of intensity. One could, however, make similar critiques of many features of staff notation, in which isolated symbols represent events that are prolonged over time, and indeed print notation leaves much musical detail up to the performer like tone color, tuning, ornamentation, and stylistic performance elements.

A way to think of these two conceptualizations of music is that Braille is digital—a series of distinct bits of information—and staff notation is analog—a mimetic reflection of sonic shapes in two-dimensional space. Another analogy for these two ways of conceptualizing music is to imagine looking up the directions to an unknown location on a map website such as MapQuest or Google Maps. The search results will present information in at least two ways. In one of these presentations, a series of individual explicit instructions lists every turn on each street or highway. Braille conceptualizes music in a similar way with performance "directions" conveyed as a list of instructions (cells indicate "start slur" or "G quarter note"). Just as in the directions list, where getting out of one's own neighborhood can take as many steps as the rest of the trip, the number of Braille cells bears no correlation with the amount of musical time represented. A reader of Braille memorizes the entire list of directions in order to take the performance journey.

Mapping programs offer a second way of conceptualizing a trip via a diagram that iconically represents straight roads with straight lines, curved roads with curved lines, using proportions that represent distances; a segment of the route that takes longer to travel also takes proportionally more space on the diagram. Print staff notation represents music in the way a map represents topographical features: curved lines stand for gradations of phrase intensity, small staccato dots stand for shortened notes, and proportional relations of print rhythms roughly represent longer and shorter amounts of time. Like viewing a map, a musician also can zoom in and out or scroll through the route of the score.[12] As in mapping programs, both styles of conceptualizing information are valuable and preferred by people in various contexts. The same is true for notation formats. Despite their differences, both function to convey musical ideas between musicians. In that sense, both forms are rich tools used for music making by many people.[13]

Touching Music Analysis

A specific example can serve to show how differences between print and Braille versions of the same piece can affect analysis. In Chapman's case, her teacher's goal in assigning her to make a graph of a fugue would likely have been to identify and track the imitative entries of the fugal subject, an activity that is important to performance and style modeling. In performance practice, musicians learn to draw attention to these familiar patterns in each layer by playing those notes differently than surrounding notes. Figure 7.2 displays the exposition of a Bach Fugue (#16 from *The Well-Tempered Clavier*, Book I) in staff notation. When hearing a fugue like this one, not only do listeners sense the increasing complexity (first one "voice" sounds alone and then a second is added, and a third and fourth) but also attention shifts to the familiar patterns of each subject entry.

Notions of fugal process draw on the image schema *object* to group pitches into a unit that can be *superimposed* in a *sequence* on other objects, which then allows us to think of each voice as a *layer*. Like the idea of pitches going up and down, the application of the layer metaphor to fugue analysis is one that readers of both print and Braille can learn. However, print notation subtly reinforces the idea of layers by adding lines one after another as musicians read left to right, preserving their coherence as discrete entities with stem direction.[14]

Figure 7.3 diagrams the layout of Braille cells for a transcription of the fugue exposition.[15] Horizontal rectangles stand for the placement of rows of Braille cells on the page

FIGURE 7.2 Fugue exposition in print notation.

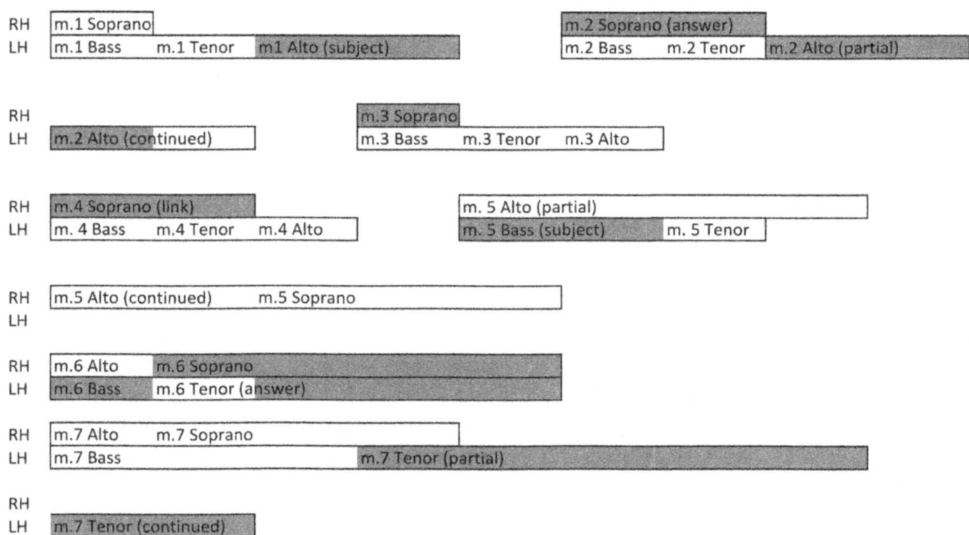

FIGURE 7.3 Page layout of cells for the fugue exposition. (Shading indicates the cells that represent the fugal subjectand its imitations).

for the right and left hands (RH and LH). The rectangles are labeled with the measure and layer (soprano, alto, tenor, or bass) represented by the cells in that location. Within a measure, the voice parts are written sequentially, proceeding from lowest to highest. "In-accord" cells connect sequential segments from different voices that are to be played concurrently in the same hand. For example, the first measure in the left hand begins with the cells for the bass voice (a rest), the tenor voice (also a rest), and then the alto voice (beginning of the fugal subject). Since the two hands often require a different number of cells, one hand can run out of cells before the other. For that reason, the two rows begin again in vertical alignment at the beginning of each measure and sometimes measures are split to save space and expensive embossing paper.

Figure 7.4 highlights the groups of cells containing points of imitation and traces their order in the analytical listening process. Note that to follow the imitation in real time, the reader's hand(s) would have to jump back and forth to different portions of the page. Since the goal of making an analytical graph of a fugue is to identify the layering of imitation, a Braille user would first have to memorize the piece and then "play it back" from memory to find each entrance of the subject.[16]

Braille keyboard music layout strongly favors the performance preparation needs of visually impaired people rather than in-time scanning while listening or playing. The organization is designed instead for learning the music in small, one-measure chunks. This notation can be quite logical for a keyboard performer and again is reminiscent of tablature. It reinforces some of the linear aspects of counterpoint (within measures), and tactile readers become very quick at assembling linear code into simultaneous events.[17]

So what does this mean for the comparative conceptualizations of a keyboard fugue? Braille interprets the fugue as a list of asynchronous tablature-like directions

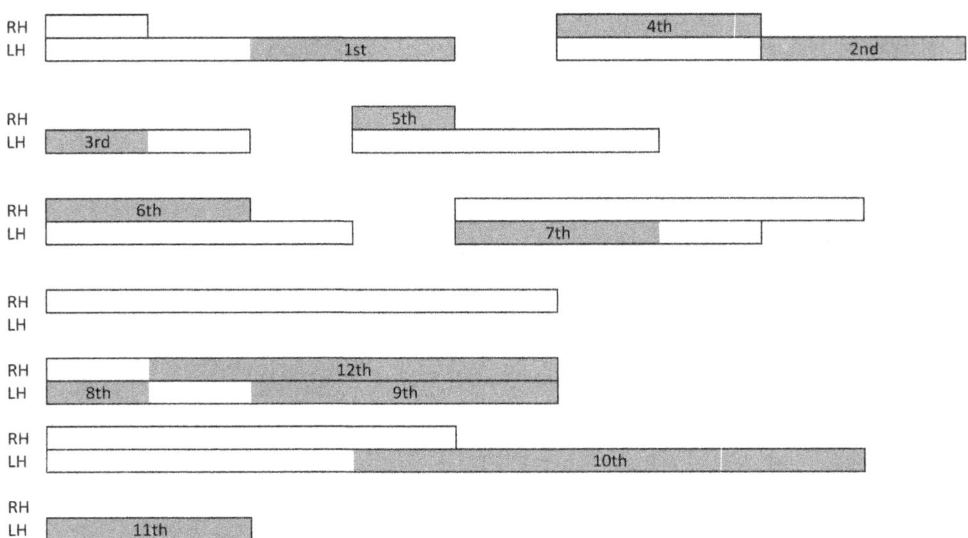

FIGURE 7.4 Listening in real time for imitation: order of cell groups on page. (Shading indicates the cells that represent the fugal subjectand its imitations).

for learning to play with two hands separately. Although a sighted performer can learn to play a fugue from print notation, the staff layout also allows musicians who are not expert keyboardists to imagine the piece; one does not have to feel the piece in one's fingers to scan the layers and listen or audiate in real time. A way to enhance the layer metaphor via notation in both print and Braille would be to notate the fugue in staff notation open score and its equivalent Braille "line-over-line" score.

The subject of the influence of notational formats on conceptualizing music has been raised in music historical research, and brings to mind the way the notation of contrapuntal music in general has changed over time. Jessie Ann Owens discusses compositional process in the period 1450 to 1600 in which notational formats were in a state of transition. Drawing on extensive manuscript evidence, she concludes that though there was no single process during this period, vocal and keyboard polyphony generally differed from each other in format:

> The nearly complete absence of scores used for composing vocal music is striking. The only example found to date . . . was probably composed by an organist. We must conclude that composers could manage the complicated polyphony of the time without using the [score] format that seems indispensable to us. Working on short segments using quasi-score format or on longer segments using separate parts [choirbook format], they were able to sketch and draft the early versions of their music. (Owens 1997, 196)[18]

Owens attributes these notational conventions to the fact that mensural notation was not well suited to score format (particularly when one voice moved much more slowly than another) and to the fact that the notation reflects the very conception of counterpoint built from independent lines that were composed sequentially rather than simultaneously (Owens 1997, 45).[19]

The use of score notation increased after 1600 and became the standard format for polyphony from then on. Thomas Morley's 1597 treatise reflects this conceptual trend and offers several examples of polyphony in score format. A caption for the score version of a five-voice madrigal by Giulio Renaldi reads: "And to the ende that you may the more easelie understand the contryving of the parts, and their proportion one to another, I have set it downe in partition [score]" (Morley 1597, 39). The concurrent practice of intabulation—transcribing a vocal or ensemble piece into keyboard or lute tablature to be played by one individual—also allowed the conception of simultaneous parts. The historical move to score format highlights its artificial nature; if notation acts as a mnemonic device—a prosthesis of sorts—then score notation is an added level of reinforcement for memory and imagination for the composer, but even more so for the analyst.

Music Analysis and Performance

Performers sometimes use analysis to create a form of mental shorthand to help with memorization. For blind and sighted musicians alike, this analytical process involves dividing music into sections, memorizing each one, and then reassembling the sections into a whole. In this case, the asynchronous nature of Braille becomes nonproblematic and even useful for avoiding the pressure of time's arrows. In both Braille assembling and music analytical assembling, a musician or analyst engages in what David Pacun, in a post to the Disability Interest Group list of the American Musicological Society and Society for Music Theory, characterized as analytical "chunking."[20] The analysis spoken of here admittedly moves from the smallest of musical elements up to the whole piece, unlike many analyses that begin with the big picture and work toward progressively smaller sections.

Edwin Kowalik, renowned Polish pianist (1928–1997), like many blind pianists, learned a piece by reading the Braille for one hand at a time and playing with the other hand. He compared learning Braille Music to learning a poem in a foreign language: "You learn each word, then a sentence. You translate, and learn a verse. Finally you get the whole meaning out of it" (Scott 1981, 18). Musicians born more recently are less likely to use Braille, though, especially in learning complex repertoire. Tamas Erdi, a Hungarian pianist born in 1979 explains, "Braille music scores are too slow and I am just not able to learn new materials with them. It would take about a year to touch each note and notation of a piece, not to mention the fact that the pieces I play nowadays are not even transcribed in Braille." So first he memorizes as much as he can by ear, and then "recomposes" the rest following the conventions of common practice harmony (Burns 2011).

Nobuyuki Tsujii, a Japanese pianist born in 1988, a winner of the 2009 Van Cliburn International Piano Competition, worked with Braille as a young pianist, reading with one hand and playing with the other, but as an adult, he has all but abandoned Braille:

> I do not know how much Braille music has been published, but I know it is not much. Lately, I also do not use Braille music because it needs to be memorized before touching the piano. Therefore, it takes a lot more time than listening (to a composition) to memorize. (Gibbons 2010)

Instead, he asks his volunteer assistants to record the music one hand at a time, splitting it into small sections of a few measures, playing them as neutrally as possible, and recording verbal comments about the composer's instructions and markings. He then memorizes the chunks by ear and assembles them and combines hands adding his own interpretation.

Each of these three pianists acknowledges the analytical "chunking" and assembly process. In fact, Tsujii, though moving away from tactile notation, has essentially transferred Braille reading into a listening process still working with small chunks of music in each hand. For much of the repertoire, there is no real way to get away from the print score—either someone transcribes the print score into Braille, or someone learns the print score and records it. This process is becoming more automated; pieces in standard notation can now be scanned and digitally transcribed into Braille using specialized software.[21]

Music Analysis and Composition

Like performers, composers also make use of music analysis for particular purposes, including the close study of an earlier composer or style. Given the relationship between notation and style already addressed, one might hypothesize that blind composers would conceptualize and compose pieces differently. Straus observes, "as composers we notate our musical ideas and those are shaped by our ability to write them down" (Straus 2011, 171). To illustrate this interdependency, consider Kevin Gibbs's insights into his compositional process. A blind American pianist and composer born in 1958, Gibbs had early success with jazz due to its improvisatory and easily memorized forms and with electronic music because of its lack of reliance on traditional notation. But when attempting more complex pieces, he writes:

> Unfortunately, I couldn't write anything down and I forgot almost all my ideas right after playing them . . . Without some means of notating or at least preserving what I was hearing and thinking, if I couldn't play it myself, I was out of luck . . . I did have a cassette recorder and that prevented me from losing absolutely everything. (Gibbs 2010)

Gibbs attempted communicating his ideas to an amanuensis:

> After I dictated, say, thirty-two bars of a flute part, the transcriber would have to ask whether the next instrument was continuing from where the flute had left off, or being [*sic*] brought up even with the flute music he'd just taken down. The need to keep orienting the transcriber to his place in both vertical and horizontal score time destroyed the creative flow. It also compromised the quality of my ideas because I was more focused on remembering where everything was, then where it might eventually go. (Gibbs 2010) [22]

To date, I have yet to run across an account of a composer who composed directly into Braille, although I imagine some have done so. With the help of a Braille slate or "note taker" it would be possible to work in small sections in a manner similar to Renaissance composers. More recently, computer notation programs have become more sophisticated, and composers like Gibbs can enter music with a midi keyboard into a computer with notation software. Gibbs writes of his experience with digital notation:

> With each new effort, the quality of my notation improves. It's far easier to read than any handwriting could ever be. . . . I'm learning more and more each day about notational conventions that I never had to deal with when I was memorizing music from recordings. And as my notation has improved my confidence has grown, and I look forward to creating ever more expansive musical works. (Gibbs 2010)

Music Analysis and Close Listening

Apart from its practical benefits for performers and composers, music analysis can be rewarding on its own terms, as a way of hearing music more richly and deeply, and certainly this is the case with Schenkerian analysis. To return to the pedagogical question with which this essay opened, Why, if one of the aims of Schenkerian analysis is to direct long-range hearing, are its visual elements so central (and thus so problematic for blind musicians)? Schenkerian analysis relies heavily on graphic representation, although it economically and elegantly reuses the symbols of staff notation to sketch hierarchical long-range relationships. Historically, sketching analyses by hand has been a labor of love requiring hours maneuvering a calligraphy pen and French curve over specialized paper, producing graceful shapes that may have aesthetic qualities related to, but apart from the musical interpretations they convey.[23] Even though this process can be done on a computer now, one can see why it is difficult to give up the visual aspects of the theory.

At the time of the writing of this article, a new system of Braille Schenker Notation is being developed and tested by Robert Gross (Gross 2013). It features an expandable 3 × 3 matrix of Braille cells that represents each note of a Schenkerian sketch. It is modeled on a coding system developed by Michael Kassler, which was designed to program a computer to perform Schenkerian analysis (Kassler 1975). Encoding information for a computer necessitates pixilating data into strings of characters, which makes this model suited to adaptation to Braille. The matrix has a minimum of nine cells, but cells can be added to encode additional information. The cells account for register, pitch, and accidentals, as well as relative weight and hierarchy of notes. In addition, the matrix provides information about slurs, beams, lines, and unfoldings as well as other features such as scale degrees, Roman numerals, intervals, and passing or neighbor functions.

The proposed system could certainly address a need, as in the case of the graduate student whose story opened this essay. The system is organized in a way that would be intuitive to tactile readers. And, whereas Braille music in general, as demonstrated above, is far from a translation of print, this method transcribes the information in a print Schenker sketch much more directly, which could prove to be a great assistance in communicating ideas between blind and sighted musicians. While teaching a computer to do Schenkerian analysis has not had satisfying results to date, the digital nature of computer code suits Braille notation.

So what does brailling Schenker tell us about Braille? In part, it shows the flexibility of the system in a way that Schenker's reusing the elements of print staff notation shows the flexibility of print symbols, although the Braille system is still a discrete set of commands—a list of directions—and there are still no analogue shapes to mimic gestures. And what does brailling Schenker tell us about Schenker? Just as in print, the graphs can serve to emphasize the symbol over the sound, raising the possibility of losing contact with the music amid the details of analytical notation in a system in which a minimum of nine cells represent each note. On the other hand, there is value in understanding the multivalent interconnectedness of the notes, which is emphasized by the input/output cells of the Braille matrix. This system would either force the analyst to be systematic and consistent about the decisions for labeling, or it would highlight any inconsistencies. The complexity of the system underscores the fact that both graphic and Braille forms of Schenker analyses benefit from written and aural supplements.

Touching and Seeing: Literacy and Understanding

The usefulness of the Braille Schenker technique may be mediated by the fact that Braille literacy has plummeted in recent decades due to the expenses of Braille production and education as well as increasing availability of audio books and screen readers. Estimates place literacy at 10 percent of the blind population today versus 50 percent in the 1950s (Aviv 2010, 44). There are strong feelings on both sides of this issue. Some consider Braille unnecessary in the digital age. Others feel that Braille still has a place and that it greatly helps with organizing writing prose; the ability to revisit ideas and refine them transforms the shape of thought, just as it transforms the conceptualization of music.[24]

This controversy exists around Braille music too, as evidenced by many of the discussions on the Music Education Network for the Visually Impaired (MENVI) list.[25] Richard Taesch, a leader in Braille music education, puts it this way, "to learn by listening only is merely a form of plagiarism. . . . Music by ear alone, therefore, is dependency upon performance by the sighted" (Taesch 1993). One might imagine a cultural analogy here between the use of Braille and use of sign language for the Deaf and, if so, wonder what it means to the culture to lose touch with Braille. Alex Lubet suggests that a case can be made for Blind culture that is "analogous if not precisely parallel" to Deaf culture especially through music, and he points to Braille's "emancipatory" power to help create a nondisabled space (Lubet 2010, 69–75).[26] While the larger discussion of Braille literacy is beyond the scope of this essay, it does impinge on music analysis of Western art music, which tends to depend heavily on notation. Music analyses also assume the form of linguistic arguments, which by their nature are easily translated into Braille. When it comes to complex music, understanding does not need to rely solely on seeing, but it often needs to be literate.

Expanding the Sensorium of Understanding

So with these observations in mind, what would a "universal design" of music analysis look like? I do not pretend to have all the answers, for without a doubt there would be many, but I would like to keep the question open. An attempt to broaden the accessibility of analysis might benefit from borrowing principles from Universal Design for Learning (a set of guidelines designed to make curricula more accessible to all learners): using multiple means of representation, expression, and engagement. Doing so would entail expanding the sensorium of understanding.[27]

At the beginning of this essay, I evoked and critiqued the familiar conceptual metaphor that asserts UNDERSTANDING IS SEEING. In the context of the analysis of music, understood as a primarily sonic art, one might turn instead to an alternative metaphor: UNDERSTANDING IS HEARING. After all, if music is ultimately aural, shouldn't music analysis be aural also? Returning again to the story that opened this essay, many of the responses on the e-mail list addressed the fact that having blind musicians in classes makes teachers reorient their presentation to a more aural-based one. Indeed, many teachers of analysis (including Schenker himself) work with students at the piano, making voice-leading relationships not only audibly but also kinesthetically apprehended. The benefits of analysis—pausing time, reducing detail, clarifying relationships, as well as biasing (intentionally or not)—can be accomplished in a variety of auditory ways via acoustic performance, collaboratively hearing and repeating, manipulating recordings and midi files, and even cultivating inner hearing.[28]

Other bodily means of perception can lead to understanding, too. In addition to those associated with Braille, tactile understandings will benefit from the increased availability of printers that can emboss graphic representations from black and white images as well as those that can render 3D images. In addition, movement through space and notions of gesture can shape analysis. Antovic, Bennett, and Turner (2013) studied a group of ten-year-old children and found that musical conceptualization in blind children is similar to that of their sighted peers and that the abstract domain of music is primarily conceptualized through the spatial, rather than visual, modality in both groups.

Analyses that draw on embodied notions of movement can reinforce these preferences for metaphorical understandings. For example, the sensation of producing music bodily, by singing or playing, and even the physical act of notating music, either conventionally or in Braille, necessarily informs understanding. In his book *Musical Forces*, Steve Larson explores some of the entailments of the metaphor MUSIC IS MOTION and suggests that the experience of movement shapes our thinking about music as moving through space, especially expressed in terms of forces such as gravity, magnetism, and inertia; forces that all bodies experience (Larson 2012). Arnie Cox elaborates on Larson's theories, combining the kinesthetics of musical performance with embodied notions of spatial motion to address musical meaning:

> The pertinent question here concerns the issue of what motivates the cross-domain mappings from the domain of physical motion [onto music]. A short answer is that we feel something in performing and in listening to music, in connection with music's invisible, intangible, and ephemeral sounds, and we implicitly search for a concrete experiential analog as a way of understanding the musical experience. Part of this feeling involves expectation and desire, which we first learn (as a species and as individuals) in the experience of actually moving through the world. Another part of this feeling involves the exertions of musical performance and the covert sympathetic exertions that we experience as listeners. The combination of non-metaphoric expectation and desire, and non-metaphoric covert exertions, is phenomenologically enough like desire and exertion in actual locomotion to motivate the cross-domain mappings. (Cox 2013)

Blind Analysis

Rereading analytical understandings through the lens of disability, particularly through cultural blindness, I can imagine a notion of "blind analysis" analogous to Straus's "blind hearing," which he describes as being unmediated by print notation with its biases, more sensitive to nonnotated features of music, more grounded in physical music making, and potentially mediated by Braille with its biases (Straus 2011, 170–173).[29] In addition to an expanded sensorium of understanding, blind analysis would benefit from being more collaborative, making room for musical experiences that involve an assistant to give or receive dictation. Blind analysis would also be more linguistically based, involving narratives rather than graphs or diagrams. Invoking the mapping program analogy, blind analysis would engage the list of directions for the musical "journey" analogous to Braille and would respond easily to the kinds of reductions to "landmarks" that analysis promotes. Depending less on notation and more on memory, blind analysis would focus more on small chunks of music and local events.

Focusing on the example of Schenkerian analysis, through blind analytical techniques, a musician, whether blind or sighted, would not need to rely on a visually apprehended graph to grasp the ideas it represents. The analyst could work with a collaborator who could play the analysis. The work could be done aurally and kinesthetically at the keyboard. The chunking process associated with blind music learning would naturally support composing out from an *Ursatz* (or fundamental structure). An analyst could describe the pertinent relationships in a narrative. Further relying on the linguistic nature of blind analysis, a musician could use a text-based music notation program like LilyPond—which offers accessibility via screen readers and midi output—to collaborate with other musicians. The software is powerful enough to create graphic representations for sighted users, and its text interface is remarkably similar to many of the features of Braille syntax.[30]

Finally, music analysis, often geared toward prescriptive norms, is an ideal place where norms can be questioned. Just as Owens asks that we suspend biases and "free ourselves from the habit of score-based thinking" in order to understand how people of another time engaged with music (Owens 1997, 313), we might suspend our visually centered biases in order to understand how individuals with disabilities engage with music. The more we expand the sensorium of understanding and consider analysis through the lens of disability, the richer become our conceptualizations of how music works.

Notes

1. Based on the influential theories of Heinrich Schenker (1868–1935), the goal of a course in Schenkerian analysis is to interpret the underlying hierarchical relationships among pitches in a tonal piece using specialized graphic representations.
2. This essay focuses on Western art music of the common practice period, but some of the observations will apply to other repertories as well.
3. Conceptual metaphors—generic mappings that underlie the way we think and talk—are represented in capital letters following Lakoff and Johnson 1980. For example, HAPPINESS IS UP is a general conceptual metaphor that underlies many figurative linguistic metaphors like, "My spirits soared." On music and conceptual metaphors see Cox 2011, Larson 2012, and Zbikowski 2002.
4. Geurts also observes the Euro-American emphasis on vision in contemporary textbooks on sensory psychology, perception, and physiology that devote the greatest amount of space to chapters on vision (Geurts 2002, 9). See also Murray Jardine's examination of the

philosophy of science literature that draws a comparison between oral and literate cultural traditions to demonstrate different visual and aural-oral epistemologies (Jardine 1996). See also Paul Stoller, *Sensuous Scholarship* (1997), which argues the importance of understanding the sensuous epistemologies of many non-Western societies.

5. Lowe, drawing on Foucault, proposes a history of perception as a link between the epistemology and the structure of society and examines the ways oral, chirographic, typographic, and electronic cultures organize knowledge (Lowe 1982, 1–2).
6. A few examples of the more tenuous mappings between notation and verticality include the noncontinuities of transposed scores as well as scores grouped by families of instruments, as in full orchestral scores. Other tenuous mappings include the use of *octava* sign, and enharmonic spellings (E♯3 looks lower but sounds higher than F♭3).
7. A survey of recent articles in the journal *Music Theory Online* (Vol. 19, No. 3, March 2013) reveals a variety of analytical visualizations: melodic and harmonic reductions, matrices, hexachord mappings, transformation networks, Schenkerian middlegrounds, recompositions, gesture diagrams and videos, bar graphs, and notation excerpts with annotations such as set-class labels. These representations include visual aids such as charts with colors, variously shaped arrows, brackets and labels as well as rectangle, squiggle and bubble enclosures, and snippets of the usual musical symbols. Although many of these visualizations would be difficult to translate for a blind reader, *MTO* is currently taking steps to make its website as accessible as possible with features like enhanced color contrast, hover effects, heading tags, and alternate text for images. Unfortunately, to describe a complex diagram or graph would take alternate descriptions on the order of paragraphs long, at which point, one might as well include that language in the body of the article.
8. For more on tactile resources see Smaligo 1999.
9. In 1829, at age 20, he published his *Method of Writing Words, Music, and Plain Songs by Means of Dots, for Use by the Blind and Arranged for Them*. For more on Braille's historical context, including an account of other tactile approaches to music notation, see Ingrid Sykes's essay in this volume.
10. Print chorales, meanwhile, follow the conceptual model of SATB vocal pieces sung by individuals on each of the voice parts. Altos, for example, follow the line of stems-down notes in the treble staff—even though we hope they also attend to the other voices while doing so! As an aside, there is an open-score format for Braille SATB pieces, just as there is in print, as well as a "note-for-note" format that lists the inner voices as pitched "subnotes."
11. Left to right space will vary with the addition of cells that indicate articulations, dynamics, register, and so forth. Among other things, this feature makes "sight reading" in real time a challenge for Braille readers.
12. Google Earth presents directions in yet another way via an interactive picture of the route and location. This representation might be analogous to a wave file or oscilloscope rendering of music.
13. For more on conceptualizations of staff and Braille notation see Johnson 2009. For more on Braille music see DeGarmo 2005 and Krolick 1979.
14. The correspondence is not completely preserved when a voice shifts from one staff to another, as the alto does between measure 4 and measure 5. In this instance, the printed score favors the necessities of performance governed by playing with two hands over mapping aurally salient relationships in a visual way.
15. The source for the Braille version of this musical passage is Turek 2004, a Braille transcription of a standard music textbook.

16. In addition, the layers of a fugue tend to overlap metrical boundaries. The vertical alignment of measure beginnings in Braille, though, realigns each downbeat, thus emphasizing divisions that are generally *de*-emphasized in this type of polyphony. In fact, the isolation of downbeats from preceding music (as also happens to some extent with print bar lines) deemphasizes the linear flow of counterpoint where musical energy leads across bar lines into the next downbeat.
17. Although verticalities are meant to be read simultaneously in print scores, the eye cannot perceive them all at once and instead alternately fixates and saccades rapidly around the page. In short, the perception of simultaneities is not simultaneous, even in print. In some ways, the measure in-accord chunks of Braille mimic the saccade of the eye.
18. As a side note, "quasi-score" is similar to Braille in that it aligns only the beginnings of voices vertically and subsequent notes move out of alignment as their rhythms differ. Another Braille format, "section by section," is similar to the choirbook format with separate parts.
19. For further discussion of simultaneous versus sequential conceptions, see Blackburn 1987. For more on oral transmission and literacy and the interplay of memory in the medieval era, see Berger 2005.
20. Pacun (2008) observes: "For all its cumbersome aspects, Braille is or can be—again to me at least—a very analytical notational system; and as it involves 'chunking,' evaluating and memorizing as you go along, the way one learns the score from the [Braille] notation resembles analysis." Similarly, a post to the Music Education Network for the Visually Impaired (MENVI) discussion list by Lieser (2013) draws attention to the advantages of Braille for learning rhythm: "The braille system, with its strengths and weaknesses just as print notation has, offers much more lasting impressions of rhythm, since vertical relation means relatively little, and counting is essential. Because of interpreting the intervals, rather than merely taking in lines and spaces, one learns harmony and theory almost simultaneously."
21. I wish to thank Stefan Honish for drawing my attention to the methods of these pianists.
22. Straus relates the story of English composer, Frederick Delius (1862–1934), who, having gone blind after a long career of composing, also worked with an amanuensis. His collaborator, Eric Fenby, describes their compositional process: Delius would give a rough idea, Fenby would try it at the piano and Delius would edit it but could only retain a few bars at a time. Like Erdi's process described in the "Performance" section of this essay, Fenby would recompose the idea based on what he knew of harmony and Delius's style. Straus observes that this collaboration led some critics to dismiss the music as "authorially impure" (Straus 2011, 24). Straus recommends reexamining this music through the lens of "blind culture," seeing it not as impure, but rather as the fruit of a productive collaboration.
23. The notation itself has been so important that for many years the Society for Music Theory's journal, *Music Theory Spectrum*, was published in a specially shaped format to accommodate the wide paper needed for Schenkerian graphs.
24. Georgina Kleege, a person with macular degeneration that allows her only to use her peripheral vision for reading, and that at some large level of difficulty and pain, writes of the pleasure of learning Braille as an adult. It felt substantial to her and not like Roman letters that were easy to mistake, because the finger does not saccade as the eye does and there is no need to backtrack (Kleege 1999, 202).
25. A recent post to the MENVI discussion list (Goldstein 2013) asked for a show of support for a young woman who was trying to learn Braille music. A suggestion had been made

that she could do just fine without learning Braille, and so the student's family was asking her teachers to reconsider going the Braille route, presumably due to costs and time constraints. Responders to the post stressed that if the woman were going to perform mostly pop music, she might be fine without Braille, but in order to perform classical, operatic, or even musical theatre, Braille is essential for getting jobs.

26. Lubet (2010) first identifies three important markers of Deaf culture: (1) a distinct language centered on signing, (2) organizations devoted to the deaf, and (3) a resulting cultural, nondisabled space where deafness is not an impairment. Then, using those criteria as benchmarks, he identifies analogous features of Blind culture: (1) Braille and other distinct linguistic technologies if not a stand-alone language, (2) institutions devoted to visually impaired individuals, and (3) creation of cultural, nondisabled spaces, especially through music. He gives examples of musicians for whom blindness provided no barrier and draws special attention to the contribution of Braille music to establishing a nondisabled space in Egypt's blind orchestra: "It [Braille] may be used most remarkably, at least in terms of its multivalently transgressive and emancipatory nature, by the all-female, mostly Muslim, Al-Nour wal Amal Orchestra of Cairo. This group has developed protocols for performing Western symphonic classics at a high level, arguably the most "sighted" musical repertoire the world has ever known, the performance of which typically depends on sight-reading print notation and visual attention to the conductor, concertmaster . . . , and other players. . . . The orchestra's musicking—that is, protocols of learning, rehearsal, and performance—is uniquely 'Blind' " (75).
27. Since only about 10 percent of legally blind are completely blind and the rest identify as having an impairment, low vision, or partially sighted, perhaps blind analysis could be partially visual. Many have memories from a time when they could see more clearly, and a descriptive analysis that makes analogies with visual images can sometimes be effective.
28. An extreme example of analysis that invokes the conceptual metaphor UNDERSTANDING IS HEARING is Hans Keller's nonverbal method of music analysis called "functional analysis," invented in 1957, which presents music-only analyses performed as interludes that demonstrate a unifying network of musical ideas. For the complete analyses, see Keller 2001.
29. Straus's conception distinguishes "disablist hearing" from "prodigious hearing" (associated with highly trained and knowledgeable listeners) and "normal hearing" (associated with select, modestly trained, nondisabled subjects in cognitive psychology studies).
30. Text commands in LilyPond closely resemble the way Braille delivers information. For example, */time 2/4* indicates a time signature, *c4* indicates a C quarter-note. The symbols < and > connect simultaneities in a way similar to Braille "in-accords" and commands to start and end slurs appear as open and close parentheses.

References

Antovic, Mihailo, Austin Bennett, and Mark Turner. 2013. "Running in Circles or Moving along Lines: Conceptualization of Musical Elements in Sighted and Blind Children." *Musicae Scientiae* 17: 229–245.

Aviv, Rachel. 2010. "Listening to Braille." *New York Times Magazine*, January 3, 42–45.

Berger, Anna Maria Busse. 2005. *Medieval Music and the Art of Memory*. Berkeley: University of California Press.

Blackburn, Bonnie J. 1987. "On Compositional Process in the Fifteenth Century." *Journal of the American Musicological Society* 40 (2): 210–284.

Braille, Louis. 1829. *Procédé pour écrire les paroles, la musique et le plaint-chant au moyen de points, à l'usage des aveugles et dispose pour eux.* Online facsimile and English translation by the National Federation of the Blind. https://nfb.org/images/nfb/publications/braille/the-firstpublicationofthebraillecode.html.

Burns, Kevin. 2011. "Tamás Érdi:How Music Flows from His Head via His Heart to the Tips of His Fingers." The Hungarian Presence in Canada: The Website of the Canada-Hungary Educational Foundation. Accessed April 17, 2014. http://www.hungarianpresence.ca/Culture/Music/erdi-222.cfm.

Chapman, Vicky. 1999. "From Discrimination to a Dream Come True." *Braille Monitor* 42 (6). https://nfb.org/Images/nfb/Publications/bm/bm99/brlm9907.htm.

Cox, Arnie. 2011. "Embodying Music: Principles of the Mimetic Hypothesis." *Music Theory Online* 17 (2). http://www.mtosmt.org/issues/mto.11.17.2/mto.11.17.2.cox.html.

Cox, Arnie. 2013. "Review of Steve Larson, *Musical Forces: Motion, Metaphor, and Meaning in Music*." *Music Theory Online* 19 (1). http://mtosmt.org/issues/mto.13.19.1/mto.13.19.1.cox.php.

De Zeeuw, Anne-Marie. 1977. "Teaching College Music Theory Classes That Include Blind Students." *College Music Symposium* 17 (2): 89–101.

Davis, Lennard. 2002. *Bending Over Backwards: Disability, Dismodernism, and Other Difficult Positions.* New York: New York University Press.

DeGarmo, Mary Turner. 2005. *Introduction to Braille Music Transcription.* Washington, DC: Library of Congress.

Gibbons, Ann. 2010. "Piano Sensation at the Bardavon in Poughkeepsie." *Daily Freeman News*, October 1. http://www.dailyfreeman.com/general-news/20101001/piano-sensation-at-the-bardavon-in-poughkeepsie.

Gibbs, Kevin. 2010. "Insights on Blindness and Composing." *New Music Box*, April 14. Accessed April 17, 2014. http://www.newmusicbox.org/articles/Instights-on-Blindness-and-Composing/.

Geurts, Kathryn Linn. 2002. *Culture and the Senses: Bodily Ways of Knowing in an African Community.* Berkeley: University of California Press.

Goldstein, David. 2013. "In Need of Persuasive Braille Music Vibes for Wayward Education Planners." Message posted to MENVI-discuss Listserv, August 30. http://menvi.org/pipermail/menvi-discuss_menvi.org/2013-August/004164.html.

Gross, Robert. 2013. "Schenkerian Analysis in Multiple Modalities." Paper presented at the Annual Meeting for the Society for Music Theory, Charlotte, North Carolina, October 31–November 3.

Jardine, Murray. 1996. "Sight, Sound, and Knowledge: Michael Polanyi's Epistemology as an Attempt to Redress the Sensory Imbalance in Modern Western Thought." *Journal of the American Academy of Religion* 64 (1): 1–25.

Johnson, Shersten. 2009. "Notational Systems and Conceptualizing Music: A Case Study of Print and Braille Notation." *Music Theory Online* 15 (4). http://www.mtosmt.org/issues/mto.09.15.3/mto.09.15.3.johnson.html.

Kassler, Michael. 1975. "Proving Musical Theorems I: The Middleground of Heinrich Schenker's Theory of Tonality." Technical Report 103. Sydney: Department of Computer Science, School of Physics, University of Sydney.

Keller, Hans. 2001. *Functional Analysis: The Unity of Contrasting Themes: Complete Edition of the Analytical Scores*. New York: Peter Lang.

Kleege, Georgina. 1999. *Sight Unseen*. New Haven, CT: Yale University Press.

Krolick, Bettye. 1979. *Dictionary of Braille Music Signs*. Washington, DC: National Library Service.

Kurth, Ernst. (1931) 1969. *Musikpsychologie*. Reprint ed. Hildesheim and New York: Georg Olms Verlag.

Lakoff, George, and Mark Johnson. 1980. *Metaphors We Live By*. Chicago: University of Chicago Press.

Larson, Steve. 2012. *Musical Forces: Motion, Metaphor, and Meaning in Music*. Bloomington: Indiana University Press.

Lieser, Dale. 2013. "Expectations and reading braille music [Msg 2]." Message posted to MENVI-discuss Listserv, September 20. http://menvi.org/mailman/listinfo/menvi-discuss_menvi.org.

Lochhead, Judy. 2005. "Texture and Timbre in Barbara Kolb's *Millefoglie* for Chamber Orchestra." In *Engaging Music: Essays in Music Analysis*, edited by Deborah Stein, 253–272. New York: Oxford University Press.

Lowe, Donald M. 1982. *History of Bourgeois Perception*. Chicago: University of Chicago Press.

Lubet, Alex. 2010. *Music, Disability, and Society*. Philadelphia, PA: Temple University Press.

Meeùs, Nicolas. 2012. "Schenkerian Analysis—Visual Impaired Student." Message posted to SMT-talk Listserv, November 5. http://lists.societymusictheory.org/pipermail/smt-talk-societymusictheory.org/2012-November/thread.html.

Morley, Thomas. 1597. *A Plaine and Easie Introduction to Practicall Musicke*. London: Peter Short.

Owens, Jessie Ann. 1997. *Composers at Work: The Craft of Musical Composition, 1450–1600*. New York: Oxford University Press.

Pacun, David. 2008. "Blind Music Theory Student." Message posted to the Interest Group on Music and Disability Listserv, August 10. http://web.gc.cuny.edu/disabilityinmusic.

Scott, Luci. 1981. "Blind Pianist Develops Braille Technique." *The Day* (April 17): 18.

Smaligo, Mary A. 1999. "Resources for Helping Blind Music Students." *Future Reflections* 18 (1). https://nfb.org/images/nfb/publications/fr/fr18/issue1/f180105.htm.

Stoller, Paul. 1997. *Sensuous Scholarship*. Philadelphia: University of Pennsylvania Press.

Straus, Joseph N. 2011. *Extraordinary Measures: Disability in Music*. New York: Oxford University Press.

Taesch, Richard. 1993. "The Literacy Movement: What Does Braille Music Have to Do with It?" *National Resource Center for Blind Musicians*. http://www.blindmusicstudent.org/Articles/taesch_literacy.htm.

Turek, Ralph. (1995) 2004. *The Elements of Music: Concepts and Applications*. Vol. 2. 2nd ed. McGraw-Hill Humanities/Social Sciences/Languages. Transcribed by Dorothy MacRae, State Services for the Blind, St. Paul, Minnesota.

Westergaard, Peter. 1996. "Geometries of Sounds in Time." *Music Theory Spectrum* 18 (1): 1–21.

Zbikowski, Lawrence. 2002. *Conceptualizing Music: Cognitive Structure, Theory, and Analysis*. New York: Oxford University Press.

PART 2

PERFORMING DISABILITY

CHAPTER 8

MECHANIZED BODIES

Technology and Supplements in Björk's Electronica

JENNIFER IVERSON

Björk's "There's More to Life Than This" (*Debut*, 1993) begins with café sounds (Track 8.1 on the Companion Website). We hear silverware clinking, people chatting and mingling, and one incomprehensible shout, the kind that rises up from a crowd waiting for a concert to begin. Two descending electronic glissandi interrupt the scene. Perhaps the performers bumped a button on the synthesizer or sampler; maybe this is a dance club. The second interruption becomes a shuffling shadow of a beat, made from high-hat and shaker sounds. After a few seconds—the beginning of the fourth measure if we're counting—this suggestive beat-shell is brought to a reckoning with a bass and tom-toms break. Following this, we hear a full-on electronic dance music beat, including a bass ostinato in eighth notes that grounds the high-hat and shaker layers in an unmistakable 4/4 meter. At the second hypermetric break—the eighth measure of the electronic dance beat or the end of the second phrase—we have another suspension of the rhythms, which allows Björk's voice to lead us directly into the next phrase: "Come on, girl, let's sneak out of this party. It's getting boring. There's more to life than this."

The café and crowd sounds continue along with the layered electronic dance beat and Björk's voice (Track 8.2 on the Companion Website). The voice is mixed high and forward, so that while Björk is speak-singing in a rather low register, it is as if she is speaking directly to us. Is Björk the performer in this club scene, or is she a friend in the audience with us? We might be tempted to think the latter, except for the back-up vocals that enter, chanting in R&B style, "You know there's more to life than this, You know there's more to life." If Björk is our friend, our conversation has suddenly been projected onto center stage, as it were. Suddenly, Björk's voice breaks way out of the intimate speech-song she has so far used and soars above the mix with a melody that ranges between G4 and D5.

Then we are surprised by decrease in volume. Are we moving away from the main scene? We hear the sound of a door shutting. We must have gone into a back room.

Björk seems to talk to us directly once again, suggesting that we "sneak off to this island." As the normal volume of the track resumes, we hear the back-up vocalists once again, followed by Björk's voice soaring above, recreating what we now recognize to be the chorus of the song. Despite the ongoing groove of the electronic dance beat and the improvisatory-sounding synth melody that follows the chorus, we again are subject to the second sudden decrease in volume (Track 8.3 on the Companion Website, including the beginning of the subsequent track, "Like Someone in Love"). We are being led away from the club scene once again. The crowd sounds gently fade into whooshing sounds—water or wind? The clinking and chatter are replaced ever so subtly by laughter. Where are we? If we're following along in digital time on our device, we are not in the next track; at least not yet. But we are also far from the beat-driven sonic world of the club. Where is Björk taking us? As the windy, watery sounds and laughter continue, the beginning of the next track "Like Someone in Love," is marked by a harp arpeggio. We hear the puttering engine and squeaky brakes of an aging jeep, which idles before moving into the distance. We have been transported into another world entirely. Perhaps we've managed to "sneak off to that island," as Björk suggested a moment ago.

In many ways "There's More to Life Than This" is characteristic of Björk's *oeuvre*. The music is laden with dance beats; Björk's vocals on the track are both intimate and soaring. There are many musical layers, including the multilayered rhythmic instrumentals in the dance beat, the background vocals, and electronic motives and gestures that intrude and recede as the song progresses. What is remarkable about the track is the way it creates the impression of space. Listeners are immediately invited into an environment, and not just a musical one. The strong suggestion that we begin at a café, then a club, is only reinforced throughout the track as we are led into the back room, an interpretation based on lyrics, changes in volume, and a few strategic sound effects. These elements of the mix suggest both a strong sense of space and a sense of embodiment.

When we listeners refer to our experiences of a club scene, we are probably not disembodied, omniscient observers, but we are rather in our bodies. When the aural environment gives us clues about our spatial location, we use those clues to navigate the world. The aural environment on this track is a club, and we experience the music as if we were in our bodies in that scene. That is, this body wants to dance! When the volume suddenly decreases and the door shuts, it is as if our body has physically changed position. The strangeness and surprise of these aural events stems from the fact that we hear them *as if* our body has moved, though we are likely sitting in the same spot as we were fifteen seconds earlier. Likewise, the gentle island sounds at the very end of the track call us into the sensory world of our bodies. Can you feel the wind in your hair? See the white sand beach? Hear the ocean waves lapping? Now, step out of the jeep and into paradise. The sonic elements on "There's More" suggest not only space, but also a body in space. Your body?

Supplementary Logic and the Prosthesis

Musical sound has a direct relation to the body in acoustic music. We need bodies to produce sound on acoustic instruments because we need the body's energy to create vibrations by striking the drum or piano key, blowing into the wind or brass instrument, bowing or strumming the string, activating the vocal chords with air. As Alva Noë says, "Music, like speech, shoots forth from us and reflects our energetic and embodied presence in the world" (Noë 2012, 53). These gestural efforts have direct consequences for the quality of the sound (Hayles 1999; Seltzer 1992). As composer Trevor Wishart suggests, our brain gains crucial yet subtle information from analyzing the changes in the sound's attack, loudness, and continuation that result from differences in gestures (Wishart 1996).

Electronic sound, on the other hand, does not seem to have the same direct ontological relationship to the body as acoustic sound. What makes electronically produced sound? The answer is complicated: the sound issues forth from a speaker, which has amplified and converted the information received from a computer, which read a complex file assembled from millions of bits and bytes of information. Theoretically, there is a human with a body behind the creative process, determining what the sound *should* sound like. But what effect do those human bodies have on the sounding music? In purely digitally produced music, there is little to no discernable connection between the body and the resulting sound. That is, whether I push play on my laptop with the grandest rhetorical flourish or with the most economical movement, the sound will be the same. This is not true of acoustic instruments (and some electronic instruments), where gesture is deeply correlated to attack and envelope. As Jaana Parviainen says, "We possess strong associations between the materiality of objects and the sounds commonly made with them. This implies that an object's function is intimately bound up with the sound it makes when we handle it" (Parviainen 2012, 71). There are also differences between acoustic and electric sounds when it comes to sound envelope, or the continuation of the sound beyond the attack gesture. Continuous acoustic sounds, whether they are held tones produced by human bodies or natural sounds such as wind or waves, have infinite subtle variations of timbre and loudness. As Murray Schafer pointed out in *The Tuning of the World*, totally steady, unchanging continuous sound usually only comes from an electronic source; for instance, consider the drone hum of fluorescent lights (Schafer 1994).

A number of composers, scholars, performers, and listeners have noted that electronic music often activates a sense of the Other, since electronic sound has aspects that may not seem intuitive, "natural," gestural, or embodied. As Guy Garnett says, electronic music is often associated with the nonhuman, and is thus culturally used, for example in sci-fi films, to convey and even caricature the "aesthetics of the machine" (2001, 21). In this sense, electronic sound is a reflection of the culture's ambivalent fascination with technology, which simultaneously fetishizes and fears the proficiency of machines and their ability to replace human effort. According to John Croft, electronic sound is often construed as "acousmatic," an association that implies that the body is, at best, an invisible vehicle for content (Croft 2007).[1] The differences between acoustic and electronic sound can be further nuanced, but seem nevertheless to reinscribe a binary opposition: the acoustic is natural, the electronic is technological. In electronic music, infinite minute technological adjustments mediate between human creativity and resulting sound. When it comes to the human body's experience of electronic music, we might say that it seems unnatural or disembodied. We cannot imagine what body or what motion made that sound, nor would it help if we knew. Electronic sound is other. Electronic sound is a *prosthesis* to the human, acoustic, natural body.

This opposition lays bare the supplementary logic of the prosthesis. Mark Wigley, tracing the etymology of the word *prosthesis*, suggests that the Greek root-word "thesis" regards placing, positioning, and making a stand against attacks either verbal or otherwise (Wigley 1991). For Wigley, whose disciplinary orientation is in architecture, the notion of the prosthetic is structural; a prosthesis strives to hold the place or to make the body secure or standing. As Sarah Jain suggests, *prosthesis* was introduced into English in the sixteenth century replete with its supplementary logic: a prosthesis is attached or adding to, as in "adding a syllable to the beginning of a word" (Jain 1999, 32). It was not until the early eighteenth century—coinciding with the rise of attention toward bodily difference and disability more generally (Davis 1995; Stiker 1999; Straus 2011)—that the word took on its most common usage as "replacement of a missing body part with an artificial one" (Jain 1999, 32; see also Wills 1995).

The use of the concept of prosthesis in critical theory goes back at least as far as Freud's *Civilization and Its Discontents* (1930), in which Freud proposed that the body and mind stand in a prosthetic relationship to one another (Freud 1975). The metaphor was likely all too resonant, since Freud was struggling with a painful oral prosthesis that reintroduced a boundary between the nasal passages and the mouth cavity after losing his palate to throat cancer (Jain 1999). As Wigley notes, prosthetic supplements have profound consequences for the perceived wholeness of the body: "The prosthesis reconstructs the body, transforming its limits, at once extending and convoluting its borders. The body itself becomes artifice" (Wigley 1991, 9). The key paradox of the prosthesis is that its "healing" is equivocal, ambivalent. The body supplemented with a prosthesis, though it is made to look nearly able, is at its root unwell, not whole, and not self-sufficient.

The idea that the (disabled) body is insufficient and lacking is a familiar one in the Disability Studies literature. As David Mitchell and Sharon Snyder theorize, "A body deemed lacking, unfunctional, or inappropriately functional needs compensation, and prosthesis helps to effect this end" (Mitchell and Snyder 2000, 6). The presence of a prosthesis points very literally to the incompleteness of the body in question, revealing the body's dis-abled status. The supplementary logic of the prosthesis helps to renormalize bodies as a way of suppressing the fears and anxieties that surround visible bodily differences (Betcher 2001; Garland-Thomson 1996; Garland-Thomson 1997). As Mitchell and Snyder say,

> To prostheticize, in this sense, is to institute a notion of the body within a regime of tolerable deviance. If disability falls too far from an acceptable norm, a prosthetic intervention seeks to accomplish an erasure of difference all together; yet, failing that, as is always the case with prosthesis, the minimal goal is to return one to an acceptable degree of difference. (Mitchell and Snyder 2000, 7)

Thus the prosthesis renormalizes and minimizes bodily differences at the same time as it points to the inherent lack in the prostheticized body.

Jacques Derrida, writing about the logic of the supplement in *Of Grammatology*, also points to the dual nature of prosthesis. On the one hand, the supplement is a surplus, an exterior addition that is "the *fullest measure* of presence (Derrida 1976, 144; italics in original). This is the case in writing, as Derrida argues, where the written word supplements the spoken word. Writing stands in for speech, calling to mind presence where there is actually an absence. But Derrida also points out the darker side of the supplement: "its place is assigned in the structure by the mark of an emptiness" (Derrida 1976, 145). That is to say, a prosthetic supplement is only ever a shield to deflect an inherent nature of deformity, inferiority, and lack. The supplement masquerades as wholeness or fullness, but its true function is one of replacement and compensation. Derrida suggests that the two sides of this supplementary logic cannot be separated; they are like two sides of the same coin, where the guiding interpretation "varies from moment to moment" (Derrida 1976, 145). This lends a both/and (as well as a neither/nor) logic to the supplement: it is both fullest presence and mark of absence.

In addition to the both/and supplementary logic of the prosthesis, it is figured in most critical theory as unabashedly artificial, usually either bound up with machines, or contemporary technologies, or both (Wilson 1995). For instance in the nineteenth century, the idea that a body part could be replaced with a mechanical prosthesis grew along with the rise of industrial culture broadly speaking (Ott et al., 2002); new prostheses reinforced the Cartesian metaphor of body-as-machine that has shaped discourses since Descartes (Grosz 1994; Booher 2010). In Freud, the prosthesis is an apt metaphor for technological extensions of the body such as the camera lens, the telephone, and writing (Wigley 1991; Freud 1975). Foucault's discussion of soldiers and weaponry suggests a similar prosthetic reading: "Over the whole surface of contact between the body and the object it handles, power is introduced, fastening them to one another. It constitutes a body-weapon, body-tool, body-machine complex" (Foucault 1995, 153; discussed in Booher 2010). This body-machine complex marks the postmodern condition, as Katherine Hayles says: "[T]he construction of the tool as prosthesis points forward to the posthuman" (Hayles 1999, 34). Thus when tools—functionally speaking, prosthetic devices—are introduced, the body is supplemented by its technology. The body becomes a body-machine.

It would be easy to characterize Björk's use of electronically produced sounds as sounding out the prosthetic: the electronic in Björk's music supplements the otherwise "natural" and "whole" human voice. The machinic, technological electronica of Björk's sound world produces a structure of more-than-human, where the electronic sounds supplement, extend, and modify the organic human voice. This parallels Robert Rawdon Wilson's definition that "a prosthesis is an artificial body part that supplements the body, but a part that carries an operating system different from the body's organic processes" (Wilson 1995, 243). In the case of "There's More to Life Than This," Björk's sound design gives us the impression of having a second body, one that has its own experiences and sensations apart from our own body. This constructed, fictional body is perhaps not as organic as our human body, since it is supplemented by technological mediations. In this sense, Björk's electronica may posit the technologically mediated body as normative. As the French architect Le Corbusier hypothesized, "We all need means of supplementing our natural capabilities, since nature is indifferent, inhuman (extra-human), and inclement; we are born naked and with insufficient armor" (Le Corbusier 1972, 72; discussed in Wigley 1991). Le Corbusier points out that all of our bodies are lacking or are to various degrees disabled—our humanness is inadequate and in need of supplementation from birth forward. This means, on the one hand, something good from the perspective of Disability Studies. We *all* have bodies in need of supplementation—there is no wholeness to the human body to begin with; it is illusory. As Katherine Hayles puts it, "the body [is] the original prosthesis we all learn to manipulate, so that extending or replacing the body with other prostheses becomes a continuation of a process that began before we were born" (Hayles 1999, 3).

On the other hand, invoking the concept of the prosthesis risks a slippery, problematic metaphor. Sarah Jain suggests that too many "authors use it as an introductory point—a general premise underpinning their work about the ways in which technoscience and bodies interact" (Jain 1999, 33). As Vivan Sobchack complains, the idea of the prosthesis is a "sexy, new metaphor" that has become "tropological currency for describing a vague and shifting constellation of relationships among bodies, technologies, and subjectivities" (Sobchack 2006, 19). Both Sobchack and Steven Kurzman seek to re-ground the prosthetic in actual bodies; Kurzman complains that prosthetic theory treats limbs as agents, when in reality, the human being is in charge of the prosthesis. As Kurzman observes, when the prosthetic is used only as a metaphor, "the subjects who actually use prostheses—amputees—are rendered invisible" (Kurzman 2001, 383; similarly, see Ott et al. 2002).

I am sympathetic to the complaints and critiques of Jain, Kurzman, Sobchack, and others. To my way of thinking, another of the problems of the prosthetic-as-theory is that it encourages binary oppositions between terms such as whole/lacking, abled/disabled, natural/technological, and acoustic/electronic. That is to say, the prosthesis metaphor is not only slippery and overused but also not inherently useful for breaking down its supplementary logic. We remain locked in a dance where prosthetics point to the lack and all technologies supplement and complete this lacking body. This binary logic underwrites historical (and contemporary) perceptions of (dis)abled bodies. This same binary logic is, unfortunately, at play in any simplistic reading of the prosthetic function of electronica in Björk's music: the apparent lack in Björk's human voice must be supplemented, corrected, and veiled beneath electronic prostheses. In what follows, I reject this simplistic binary reading (Iverson 2006; Dibben 2009; Webb and Lynch 2010). I argue that Björk's music encourages us to transcend the binary logic of the supplement in at least two ways: by positing a body that is so technologically mediated it might be heard as a cyborg (Robbie 2007; Marsh and West 2003) and by revealing that the body is porous.

The Cyborg Body

As noted earlier, Björk's sound is heavily mediated by technology. For example, the track "The Modern Things" from the 1995 album *Post* begins with a low register, buzzy synthesizer ostinato, to which Björk's voice is soon added (Track 8.4 on the Companion Website). As Björk's voice transitions from gentle speech-singing to a more improvisatory and soaring soprano melody, the electronics become more bubbly. Subtly noisy static, cross-faded electronic glissandos, and a snare-heavy dance beat all enter the texture. The voice is mixed high and forward compared with the drum beat, which puts the aesthetic emphasis on the soaring voice and the many textural interjections from the electronics. Thus the acoustic voice and the electronic textural elements occupy the same aural space, seemingly commenting on one another. The issue of technological mediation is foregrounded at the end of the track, when in the last twenty seconds, Björk's final vocal phrase is reiterated in loop, complete with the static of dust under the needle of an LP. It is no longer the voice plus the technology; the voice becomes a broken record. The voice is the technology, or is only available via technological mediation. The lyrics of "The Modern Things," too, emphasize the inescapable presence of technology in our lives:

all the modern things
like cars and such
have always existed
they've just been waiting
in a mountain
for the right moment
listening to all the
irritating noises
of dinosaurs
and people
dabbling outside
all the modern things
have always existed
they've just been waiting
to come out
and multiply
and take over
it's their turn now[2]

In Björk's lyrics, humans and nature have always coexisted with technological advancements. The traditional teleology—where humans invented devices, machines, and technologies—is set aside in favor of an imaginative world where machines have the same historical, organic right to existence in the world.

A number of her other songs, particularly on *Post* (1995) and *Vespertine* (2001), foreground the technologically mediated nature of our lives (Grimley 2005). Consider "Possibly Maybe" from *Post*, which begins with repetitive electronic sounds, perhaps a modem. The pitch slides (for example, at 0:49 and 1:05) and reverse envelopes (at 0:54–1:06) recall analog tape procedures, where changes in tape speed produce changes in the sounding pitch (Track 8.5 on the Companion Website). Beginning at 1:10, white noise crackles on the tape. In the chorus, where the phrase "possibly, maybe" is reiterated, loops create vocal layers that multiply the voice technologically.

In "Hidden Place," the opening track on *Vespertine*, we immediately hear a melodic ostinato and beat on tape loop, which has obvious white noise sounds from LP or tape static again (Track 8.6 on the Companion Website). "Cocoon," the second track on the album, features a very soft static background—the white noise of tape, perhaps—plus the sharper crackles of amplified dust on LPs. The third track, "It's Not Up to You," opens with electronic noises that are squeakier and seemingly more digital, but it is only six or seven seconds before we hear again the static endemic to analog electronics. *Vespertine* as a whole is characterized by the obsession with sonic traces of analog technology—that is, the pervasive use of loops, static, and white noise—despite the obviously digital orientation of twenty-first-century electronics (Link 2001; Rodgers 2003). This "glitch" aesthetic results, in part, from Björk's collaboration with the experimental San Francisco area duo Matmos (Dibben 2009; Demers 2010). On *Vespertine*, it seems that the electronic sounds are the norm, and the acoustic sounds become the interjections. In contrast, in Björk's earlier work on *Debut* and *Post*, it is not uncommon to have a track that foregrounds acoustic accompaniments, especially strings, but also saxophones and brass. In the earlier work, electronic elements were interjected as textural commentary and often formed the dance-beat-oriented metric framework. By the time of *Vespertine*, the electronic elements seem to control the mix and determine the aesthetic direction of the music. The voice is rather a supplement to the complex electronic textures, which are often self-consciously foregrounded as production noises (static, white noise, crackles).

The encroaching movement of the technological elements in Björk's music might be profitably viewed via Donna Haraway's famous formulation of the cyborg, "a cybernetic organism, a hybrid of machine and organism, a creature of social reality as well as a creature of science fiction" (Haraway 1991a, 149). In her essay, Haraway begins with an imaginative, ironic dream, a sci-fi recounting of the human body that speaks to the pervasiveness of technologies such as artificial intelligence in the later twentieth century. In the course of the essay, Haraway becomes much more invested in the potential for the cyborg to critique all the social and political conditions endemic to late capitalism. As Katharine Hayles summarizes, "cyborgs are simultaneously entities and metaphors, living beings and narrative constructions" (Hayles 1999, 114).

Though Haraway begins using the cyborg as an ironic but imaginative figure, by the end of the essay she is deeply invested in an analysis of the ways microelectronics have shaped our perceptions of the world and our sense of selves (Bosma 2003). A cyborg potentially refigures sexuality and its attendant culturally dominant types and limitations; cyborg politics reimagines gender, gender roles, and social hierarchies based on them. Haraway says that the primary way we can refigure dominant paradigms and logic or "subvert command and control" is to recapture the power of writing, including through digital coding (Haraway 1991a, 175). We might also consider whether Björk's music tries to accomplish a similar goal in sound. Technological sound is pervasive in Björk's music from her early and middle periods; musical tracks are hardly ever without it. In fact, the electronic dimension of the sound increasingly shapes the aesthetic direction of the music from *Debut* to *Vespertine*. With its pervasive, self-conscious electronic noise tracks, *Vespertine* is particularly invested in the cyborgian sound. The music simply would not *be* without its deep-seated electronic preoccupations; the voice and the machine are deeply intertwined. The realization that the technology is us—the voice and the machine are inseparable—is endemic to the cyborgian condition. As Haraway writes, "The machine is not an *it* to be animated, worshipped, and dominated. The machine is us, our processes, an aspect of embodiment. We can be responsible for machines; *they* do not dominate or threaten us. We are responsible for boundaries; we are they" (Haraway 1991a, 180). This recalls Björk's thesis in the "Modern Things" lyrics that the machines have always been there, occupying the same historical and organic space as humans.

Evidence of the emerging cyborg is apparent in Björk's music videos as well, particularly those from *Vespertine*. In the "Hidden Place" video (dir. MSM, van Lamsweerde, and Matadin, 2001), we watch an extreme close-up of Björk's face, the camera panning from eyes to mouth to nose to follow streams of unusual, unidentified liquids (Track 8.7 on the Companion Website). She cries black tears; purple and silver iridescent gel streams from her eyes and flows into the corners of her mouth, tattooing her face with vines and flowers en route; an orange gel stream defies gravity to flow upward from her mouth into her nose. At one point, we see an architectural sketch-like image of a uterus and ovaries (2:52) emerge from her open mouth. In this posthuman state, we can surmise that reproductive organs are unnecessary for a cyborg.

In the video for "Cocoon" (dir. Ishiko, 2001) red streams (ribbon? elastic? licorice?) flow from her nipples while a naked Björk plays with them and directs them as though they are an ephemeral choir, creating swirls and loops (Track 8.8 on the Companion Website). Eventually, though, as her body is wrapped in a cocoon from feet upward, these red ribbons hinder and limit Björk's movement.

The cocoon finally covers her face and head by the end of the song, entombing the still-singing Björk as if she were a mummy wrapped alive (Track 8.9 on the Companion Website). This cocooning, one can assume, not only restricts her movement but also threatens her very humanness and her ability to proliferate and procreate, despite the lyrics that recount an ecstatic sexual experience with a man. In the "Hidden Place" and "Cocoon" videos, the prosthetic enhancements and extensions to the body are at once unsettling and intriguing—a mix of ambivalent emotions commonly acknowledged by theorists of disability (Garland-Thomson 1996, 1997, 2009). The ambivalence of Björk's prosthetic extensions is deeper than the viewer's response, however, since in both cases the prostheses compromise rather than complete the wholeness of the human body. The prostheses constrain the body's movements, strip it of its femaleness, and thereby limit its ability to move and reproduce.[3]

I likewise hear evidence that electronic technology compromises the organic wholeness, as it were, of Björk's human voice. It is true that Björk's music often juxtaposes her relatively unprocessed voice against a complex texture of multiple electronic backing tracks. Her voice is looped, multiplied, and magnified with reverb, but it is often processed gently and minimally; instead of distortion, she and her producers use microphones and vocal filters to produce a clean, near-acoustic sound (Zak 2001). However, there are notable exceptions, particularly on the album *Homogenic* (1997), which forms the link between Björk's electronic-dance-beat-influenced *Debut* and *Post* and her middle period, self-consciously electronic, cyborgian *Vespertine*. At the beginning of the track "Alarm Call," we immediately hear a fairly noisy electronic ostinato that involves clanging bells and, shortly, a dance beat. Both sound clipped, or distorted through overamplification or cheap speakers. The voice is layered almost immediately, its lyrics juxtaposed against the refrain "It doesn't scare me at all," which pervades the song. At 0:47 and 0:58, we hear subtle high-register squeaks that sound both digital and insidious (Track 8.10 on the Companion Website). These squeaks seemingly have little to do with the mix, and the voice charges forward, taking no note of them. Are these noises part of the mix, or are they only in your head? These squeaks recur frequently enough (at 1:36, 1:43, 1:53, 2:47, 2:58, 3:01, 3:22, 3:47, and 3:52) to reassure the listener that they are in fact part of the mix. They may even be clarified by an extended period of radio-frequency whines that recall an AM-radio searching for a viable frequency, while the lyrics wish to "go on a mountain-top/ with a radio and good batteries/ and play a joyous tune/ and free the human race from suffering."[4] Even so, the squeaks suggest that the boundary of the body/mind has been penetrated by technology. The digital squeaks are in us, sonic evidence of our cyborgian bodies (mal)functioning.

The distortion continues on the next track, "Pluto," which begins with a heavy industrial beat (Track 8.11 on the Companion Website). Björk's voice is also treated with an unusual amount of distortion. She sings,

> excuse me
> but i just have to
> explode
> explode this body
> off me
> i'll wake-up tomorrow
> brand new
> a little bit tired
> but brand new[5]

In the context of the heavily technological, industrial beat that pervades the sound, it is as if Björk is chronicling the way she will leave behind her human body. We can imagine that Björk is becoming a cyborg, with the digital distortion evidence of the pain of this transformation, for both Björk and the listener. Recalling Foucault's analysis of the prosthetic nature of weaponry, we can see here that the electronic "weaponry" in Björk's music is no longer simply prosthetic. Instead of simply bearing the electronic as a prosthesis, Björk's voice has been completely reconfigured by the electronic; this is also the case in the "Hidden Place" and "Cocoon" videos. Her vocal pacing on "Pluto" in particular is constrained by the militant rhythmic drive of the industrial dance beat (Track 8.12 on the Companion Website). As she screams "Ohhh, ahh" (1:43–2:26), the voice clips and distorts as the pain of the transformation escalates. The electronic mix is reduced here to a machine-gun-like sixteenth-note motive, emphasizing the violence of the transformation. Björk's halting screams suggest that we are aurally witnessing her birthing the cyborg, a climatic arrival that is achieved only after enduring the unrelenting push of technology.[6] There is no longer a distinction between the technological and the human. As Haraway says, "we are all chimeras, theorized and fabricated hybrids of machine and organism; in short, we are cyborgs" (Haraway 1991a, 150).

If we have doubts that "Pluto" chronicles the birth of a cyborg, we need only listen and watch the video for "All Is Full of Love," the very next (and final) track on *Homogenic* (dir. Cunningham, 1997). We enter a much gentler sound world: synthesized strings and a ballad-esque synthesized beat introduce Björk's voice singing "You'll be given love" (Track 8.13 on the Companion Website). We see an immobile robot or cyborg with a humanoid face sitting upright. In fact, as later close-ups reveal, the cyborg has Björk's face (1:21 and 2:03). The cyborg is pristine and white, but apparently incomplete. Robotic machines hover around the cyborg, turning in screws, adding fluids, and polishing the creature. The imagery calls to mind a car assembly factory, where robotic machines place parts to assemble the product. At the chorus to the song (1:44) a second cyborg, very similar in appearance, faces the Björk cyborg and repeatedly sings "All is full of love" while extending her robotic hand to Björk. Both cyborgs have female body shapes, and in the next scenes, the two kneel and face each other while kissing and caressing. Darkening and flickering lighting emphasizes the intimacy of the encounter. Strangely, the assembly robots continue to hover around the kissing cyborgs, constantly, gently perfecting their bodies. The viewer has a voyeuristic portal into the intimate relations between these two creatures, but the technological apparatus that continues to build and perfect them also invades their privacy.

This video is obviously rich for a Haraway-ian reading (Godfree 2005); certainly the apparently lesbian orientation further points toward the transgressive potential of cyborgs. The two female cyborgs stand for a postgender or postsexual world, in the sense of Haraway, bell hooks, Judith Butler, and other radical-libertarian feminist scholars (Butler 1999; Grosz 1994; Haraway 1991b; Hillyer 1993; hooks 2000; McClary 1991; Wendell 1996). As Butler argues in *Gender Trouble*, gender is an extremely porous, flexible label that shifts as it is "performed" by subjects. She seeks to dismantle feminist theory's own reinscription and consolidation of gender according to heteronormative assumptions (Butler 1999). In *Bodies That Matter*, Butler rethinks the relationship of the material body and its "sex," showing these categories—construed in the popular imagination as uncontestable biological norms—are far more complex, variable, and unsteady than almost any contemporary sociocultural truisms would acknowledge (Butler 1993). In this radical-feminist stance, the cyborg is thus a character in a postheteronormative utopia where one does not need a sex and gender per se. In the video for "All Is Full of Love," bodily differences are reduced and elided such that the female representation stands in for the species, as it were. The video is also provocative, of course, in its melding of technology with the human. The humanoid faces of the cyborgs are expressive, sing beautifully, and express compassion and intimacy. At the same time, the creatures are obviously products of technology, though not seemingly dangerous, threatening, or violent (as was the case in the previous track, "Pluto"). We can simply note that the human body has been transgressed by the technological; or vice versa, the cyborg body has been transgressed by the human.

The Porous Body

We have said that the technological at times seems to transgress, overcome, or invade in Björk's oeuvre. These moments suggest that the "organic wholeness" of the voice is always in question. In other words, the voice, and by extension the musical body, is porous. This situation is made startlingly apparent on *Medúlla* (2004), an album filled with voices—breath sounds, choral singing, an Inuit throat singer, and vocal beat boxers, among many others vocal sounds (Malawey 2011). The track "Ancestors" begins with the sounds of breathing and sighing, but soon the inhale sounds labored (Track 8.14 on the Companion Website).

Should this wheezing be musical? The piano sounds in accompaniment, as if a person having an asthma attack is exploring at the piano (0:12–1:00). Why can we hear the breath? Hearing the inhale may be familiar or acceptable, but hearing the exhale is a particular shock. The exhaling body sounds in the place of the expected singing voice. That the music brings forward this exhale, this usually unheard element of breath, is already a transgression—it draws our attention to the sound production method rather than to the aesthetic beauty of the singing voice. It may also draw our attention to our own breath, making our breath feel labored or difficult as an empathetic response. The breath becomes more like panting (1:14—1:32) and soon sounds something like a cat or dog growl (1:56–2:30; Track 8.15 on the Companion Website).[7] The boundaries between animal and human are transgressed as we are drawn further into this music.

Lyrics for "Ancestors," though they exist,[8] are nearly unintelligible; words are truncated, looped, and layered beneath the breathing, panting, and throat-singing. We seem to encounter here the "grain" of the voice, as theorized by Roland Barthes (1978). Barthes figures this "grain" as the collision between music and linguistic phonemes, audible when the voice struggles to shape and articulate syllables through the throat and mouth.

The grain of the voice becomes audible when the melody works at the language—and not the semantic content of the words—but rather the diction of the sound-phonemes. In "Ancestors," we hear words shaped not as units of a semantically meaningful sentence, but as sensual, timbral, embodied noises that fall at multiple places on the continuum between breath noise and classically produced vocal sound. We seem to hear music in the process of becoming: the breath; the effort to corral the breath and push it through the vocal cords; the noise, speech, and melody that all result. We hear the voice *writing* here, in the sense of Barthes; the voices on "Ancestors" are acts of creation or germination in which the multiple possibilities—from breath to noise to song to linguistic articulation—are all represented.

Notice the prosthetic or supplementary logic that is endemic to even this most basic act of creation, according to Barthes: the grain of the voice is "the very friction between music and something else, which something else is the particular language (and nowise the message)" (Barthes 1978, 185). The grain of the voice, in its most basic essence, is a collision between the voice and an Other. As the phonemes of the language struggle to be articulated, they colonize the voice. The voice is porous from its most basic moment of articulation. In order to sing, to articulate, the voice must be shaped by the Other that is linguistic phonemes. This suggests that, even when it is not modified by technological invaders, Björk's voice is already supplemented. Even the raw, evocative, and unaesthetic singing on "Ancestors" reveals traces of the voice's porous nature. The boundaries that are transgressed in the song—hearing the breath, moving between human and animal—are simply a continuation of the supplementary, porous logic that always accompanies vocal articulation.

The idea of the voice struggling with the Other for articulation, and the return to a perhaps "ancestral" mode of singing, has strong parallels with Jean-Jacques Rousseau's "Essay on the Origin of Languages (1761)" (Rousseau 1998). Here Rousseau argues, provocatively, that song preceded speech. As Derrida summarizes, "No prelinguistic sonority can, according to Rousseau, open the time of music. In the beginning is the song" (Derrida 1976, 195). Thus the voice must be supplemented by the Other, by the linguistic phoneme. Derrida, reading Rousseau, offers a parallel to Barthes's supplementary Other; the linguistic seeds supplement the imaginary, never-enough purity of the singing voice. Björk's "Ancestors" seems to lay bare this originary urge to articulate—the track seems to chronicle the process of becoming-voiced, allowing us to hear the manifestations of primal song (Poizat 1992). In the process, we are also a part of the supplementary logic of this original song, as it were; we hear the voice struggling against its ever-present Other at every turn.

This deconstructive thread—the idea that the Other is always already present in the voice—is on its face a threatening thought. But it does not have to be so. There is a real opportunity in accepting the porous nature of the voice, in accepting that its true nature is a chain of supplements, as Derrida might say. Consider Björk's recent album *Biophilia* (2011), which aims for a grand synthesis; as the AP press release headline says: "New Björk album fuses music, technology, nature." Despite lukewarm critical reactions to the music, reviewers of the album were unanimously excited about the interactive, extensive app that one can buy separately (Hodgkinson 2011; Iannacci 2011; Schiesel 2011; Ross 2012). In the app, each song on the album is represented as a star in a vast three-dimensional galaxy. Within each song, players find lyrics, a graphic representation and a score that both scroll along with the music, analytical commentary (Dibben 2011), and an interactive game that allows players to add accompaniments, shape the course of Björk's music, or even record their own mixes.[9]

"Virus," from *Biophilia*, is a good example of this idea that the Other does not always need to be threatening. Björk's self-described "love song" chronicles an infatuation by way of an analogy: "Like a virus needs a body / as soft tissue feeds on blood / someday I'll find you—one day I'm there." Contextualizing love with these lyrics is unsettling—"I knock on your skin, and I am in [. . .] I feast inside you—my host is you [. . .] I'm waiting for you, I'm starving for you" (Track 8.16 on the Companion Website).[10] Many of us probably have a visceral response—when is the last time you got a virus and felt well, for instance? Most of us probably try desperately to avoid viruses, what with all the hand washing and sanitizing. In this scheme, the virus is definitely the Other, threatening the wellness and wholeness of our bodies. As we play the app, however, we are not allowed to persist in this interpretation. The game involves a number of bubbly pink cells clustered around a larger central cell, gently bouncing in response to the ostinato of the song, played on an instrument she refers to as a *gameleste*.[11] Soon, small green viruses float into the screen. If we allow them to continue unchecked, they surround the large cell, flatten, and invade it with thin green strings, all the while accompanied by Björk's voice singing. The nucleus collects the green strings and begins to produce more viruses over the course of the song, redistributing them into the plasma as the host cell shrinks. If you are a germophobe like me, you are thinking, "Get those viruses out of there! I need to be the immune response!" It is totally possible to swipe the incoming viruses out of the frame as they invade the plasma at the beginning of the song. The problem is that it is completely musically uninteresting to do so. Björk's voice stops entirely when you play the app this way, so that, while you may be able to get rid of the viruses, you do so at the expense of Björk's voice. We can still hear the *gameleste* playing the ostinato, but the song lyrics do not progress until the player allows the viruses to occupy the same space as the cells. To retain the full musical experience while playing the app, we must admit the Other into the same space as ourselves; we must allow for the symbiotic relationship between virus and cell. Thus, we must acknowledge and live with the idea that the Other is within us; there is no firm boundary between Self and Other, between cell and virus.

Biophilia belongs in the discourse around cyborgs and human/machine hybrids. The culmination of Björk's oeuvre so far, it is deeply engaged with the interaction between technology and human, and between human and nature. Because of the rich and complex way in which Björk's music interfaces with technology, listeners have an opportunity to reexamine the binary schemes that underlie our notions of machines and prosthetics in relation to the musical human body.

Embodiment and the Supplement

As I have argued throughout this essay, Björk's technologically enhanced sound worlds challenge the binary perceptions that often underlie listeners' experiences of electroacoustic music. Björk's aesthetics, to use Guy Garnett's formulation, "coerce the machine into being an extension of the compositional and performing self" (Garnett 2001, 33). Going further, if we are willing to turn our attention away from modes of sound production and toward the listener, we are in a position to further escape from the binary oppositions between acoustic/electronic or natural/technological. As Deniz Peters says,

> *Despite* the often noted "disruption" of bodily sound-making in music using electronic media, and despite listening attitudes and theories that construe listening as disembodied, there is much more bodily presence in what we hear when we hear music than hitherto acknowledged. [. . .] [O]ur listening experience is embodied not as a consequence of the Barthesian "grain," but as a consequence of active perception (*enabling* the experience of grain). (Peters 2012, 18; italics in original)

In other words, we experience electronic music as embodied not because we see the body of the performer, but because we perceive sound through our own bodies.

When we attend to our bodies, we find there is an infinite and ever-expanding horizon of experience that can be classified, broadly speaking, as aesthetic. Erin Manning, a dancer, artist, and philosopher, suggests that aesthetic experience is assembled from subjective, sensory perception in our bodies (Manning 2006). We may believe that we objectively view a sculpture in a museum, for example, but there is no concrete, stable sculpture to be perceived. The sculpture becomes concrete to us through the concatenation of our senses—our visual attention to surface, glare, light, and shadow; our depth perception; the sound of others moving about us; the tactile sensation of our body, wheels, canes, crutches, or prostheses in relation to the floor; the spatial relation of our body to pedestal, the sculpture, the dimensions of the room, and the other patrons; the smell in the museum; the feelings in our own bodies, whether exhausted, energized, nervous, bored, or hungry. All of these subtle senses inform our experience of the object; if it has a concrete nature, this is always unavailable to us. We can experience the sculpture only through the sensory microexperiences of our own bodies, a process that Manning terms "becoming body." As Manning says, "To prehend an object is therefore first and foremost to prehend how it fits into experience" (2006, n.p.; see also Manning 2007). According to philosopher and phenomenologist Don Ihde, hearing is likewise made up of countless small sensory observations and intuitions:

> Sound permeates and penetrates my bodily being. It is implicated from the highest reaches of my intelligence that embodies itself in language to the most primitive needs of standing upright through the sense of balance that I indirectly know lies in the inner ear. Its bodily involvement comprises the range from soothing pleasure

> to the point of insanity in the continuum of possible sound in music and noise. Listening begins by being bodily global in its effects (Ihde 2007, 45).

In other words, the act of listening invites us into our own bodies.

At the same time, Björk's music suggests that we inhabit the fictional bodies of her sound-worlds, especially in songs such as "There's More to Life" and "Pluto," where the sound design of the tracks imply, construct, and manipulate bodies. This creates a doubled effect where listeners relate to Björk's fictional bodies, but only through their own bodies. Here we find a parallel to Manning's "becoming body," as listeners toggle between their own subjectivity and Björk's music, the object of their attention. Listeners undertake a doubled negotiation between sensory self and perceived object. Attending carefully to Björk's music, we find that it constantly evolves as elements are added to the mix and subtracted, as the voice navigates above, below, and through the electronica. Björk's sound inhabits the permeable space between self and technological supplement. In this negotiation between self and cyborg other, the boundaries become permeable. This embodied acceptance of technological supplements bodes well for our ability to transcend the binary opposition between abled and disabled. We find that the supplementary logic, enacted by our own sensory listening, is pervasive and inescapable. Our bodies, enhanced with prosthetic supplements from the mundane to the technological, are always in the process of becoming. There is no originary, whole body; furthermore, Björk's music never asks us to believe that technological or sensory prostheses will make our becoming bodies whole or well.

The body that is posited in Björk's electronica, despite being technologically enhanced, is not constrained by the logic of the supplement. The supplements, if we are willing to think of them that way, do not seem to operate according to the same logic as the prosthesis, which serves to re-able, normalize, make functional, or make a body able to pass. Time and again, we have seen that the technological supplements undermine rather than complete the wholeness of the human body in Björk's music. This is the case particularly in the cyborgian sound-worlds of *Vespertine*. But even in the almost unmediated vocal explorations of *Homogenic*, Björk's music doesn't posit an organic, whole, or unmediated body. Instead, the voice is revealed as porous; the never-enough lack of the body is laid bare as the voice struggles to articulate. This is a brave stance. As Erin Manning writes,

> Some bodies are easier to secure than others. My lesbian body, my gay body, my diseased body, my female body, my aged body: these bodies are more costly. But even these bodies are useful to the state: they make possible the insecurity on which the need for security is predicated. Be secure! Conform! Even your distorted body can be taken into the fold! Confirm your conformation by organizing your excess: we may be able to protect you! But hide your difference at all costs! The terrible revelation is that bodies can never truly conform. (Manning 2007, 140)

Björk's music turns ableist logic on its head by questioning, time and again, whether there is an organic wholeness—an unquestioned wellness—that can ever be achieved, supplemented or not.

It is a place of power to realize that the "wholeness" or "naturalness" of bodies is a fiction. The prosthesis, the supplement, the cyborg, is in all of us. We cannot be outside of this technological supplement because it *is* us. There is no productive distinction to be made between self and other, between human and cyborg, between nature and technology, or between dis/abled. This deconstructive tack echoes Derrida's thinking in *Of Grammatology*, where the conditions that produce the supplement are always already a part of the organism. It is impossible to think outside or be outside of the chain of supplements; we must accept that wholeness or able-bodiedness is a fiction. From a Disability Studies perspective, we must acknowledge that we will all become disabled if we live long enough; or we may join Robert McRuer in the inverted formulation: "Sooner or later, if we live long enough, we will all become normate" (McRuer 2006, 198). In this more positive and hopeful formulation, we move toward a society that recognizes many kinds of abilities and allows our bodies to transcend the limiting binary oppositions of dis/abled and prosthetized/normal. Björk's heavily mediated electronica offers us an opportunity to experience a new kind of body, one that is porous and cyborgian. Björk's music offers us an opportunity to liberate ourselves from artificial ideas of "wholeness." In preparing to receive and embody all that was formerly Other, listeners are practicing to move outside of the binary opposition between abled and disabled.

Notes

1. Pythagoras's practice of delivering lectures from behind a screen or curtain can be understood as a historical precursor to the more colloquial definition of "acousmatic," which means to listen when the source of the sound cannot be seen or located. *Oxford English Dictionary Online*, s.v. "acousmatic, *adj*," accessed December 17, 2013, http://dictionary.oed.com/.
2. Lyrics available on Bjork.com (http://bjork.com/#/past/discography/post/track3/lyrics3, accessed April 17, 2013).
3. It may be worth bearing in mind that in 2002, Björk's then-partner, artist Matthew Barney, was completing the fifth film in his avant-garde *Cremaster* cycle (Smith 2006). This film deals extensively with prosthesis and female bodies—themes that are prevalent in both the sonic and visual worlds Björk contemporaneously creates in *Vespertine*.
4. Lyrics available on Bjork.com (http://www.bjork.com/#/past/discography/homogenic/track8/lyrics8, accessed April 18, 2013).
5. Lyrics available on Bjork.com (http://www.bjork.com/#/past/discography/homogenic/track9/lyrics9, accessed April 18, 2013).
6. Dibben (2009, 39) says that, for Björk, "Pluto" and "All Is Full of Love" symbolize a death-rebirth theme from an epic Icelandic myth.
7. This is the Inuit throat-singing of Tanya Tagaq Gillis. Hear more at http://www.isuma.tv/tagaq (accessed April 22, 2013).

8. Lyrics available on Bjork.com (http://bjork.com/#/past/discography/medulla/track11/lyrics11, accessed April 22, 2013).
9. Available online at https://itunes.apple.com/us/app/bjork-biophilia/id434122935?mt=8. *Vulnicura* (2015) appeared after the writing of this essay.
10. Lyrics available on Bjork.com (http://bjork.com/ - /past/discography/biophilia/track7/lyrics7).
11. Dibben reports that Björk had the *gameleste*, a MIDI instrument that combines gamelan and celeste, made specifically for this album. There are a number of custom made instruments on *Biophilia*, including a pin-barrel harp or "sharpsichord" commissioned from sculptor Henry Dagg, a pendulum-harp, and specific MIDI renditions of the pipe organ and *gamaleste*. Dibben also says that Björk used an algorithm to generate the pitches of the *gamaleste* ostinato, adding to the intersections between technology and humanness in this music (Dibben 2011).

References

Barthes, Roland. 1978. "The Grain of the Voice." In *Image-Music-Text*, translated by Stephen Heath, 179–189. New York: Hill and Wang.

Betcher, Sharon. 2001. "Putting My Foot (Prosthesis, Crutches, Phantom) Down: Considering Technology as Transcendence in the Writings of Donna Haraway." *Women's Studies Quarterly* 29 (3–4): 35–53.

Booher, Amanda K. 2010. "Docile Bodies, Supercrips, and the Plays of Prosthetics." *International Journal of Feminist Approaches to Bioethics* 3 (2): 63–89.

Bosma, Hannah. 2003. "Bodies of Evidence, Singing Cyborgs, and Other Gender Issues in Electrovocal Music." *Organised Sound* 8 (1): 5–17.

Butler, Judith. 1993. *Bodies That Matter: On the Discursive Limits of "Sex."* New York: Routledge.

Butler, Judith. 1999. *Gender Trouble: Feminism and the Subversion of Identity*. 2nd ed. New York: Routledge.

Croft, John. 2007. "Theses on Liveness." *Organised Sound* 12 (1): 59–66.

Davis, Lennard. 1995. *Enforcing Normalcy: Disability, Deafness, and the Body*. London: Verso.

Demers, Joanna. 2010. *Listening through the Noise: The Aesthetics of Experimental Electronic Music*. New York: Oxford University Press.

Derrida, Jacques. 1976. *Of Grammatology*. Translated by Gayatri Spivak. Baltimore, MD: Johns Hopkins University Press.

Dibben, Nicola. 2009. *Björk*. Bloomington: Indiana University Press.

Dibben, Nicola. 2011. Musicological commentary on the *Biophilia* App. One Little Indian and Well Hart. https://itunes.apple.com/us/app/bjork-biophilia/id434122935?mt=8.

Foucault, Michel. 1995. *Discipline and Punish: The Birth of the Prison*. Translated by Alan Sheridan. New York: Vintage Books.

Freud, Sigmund. 1975. *Civilization and Its Discontents*. Translated by James Strachey. London: Hogarth Press.

Garland-Thomson, Rosmarie, ed. 1996. *Freakery: Cultural Spectacles of the Extraordinary Body*. New York: New York University Press.

Garland-Thomson, Rosmarie. 1997. *Extraordinary Bodies: Figuring Physical Disability in American Culture and Literature*. New York: Columbia University Press.

Garland-Thomson, Rosmarie. 2009. *Staring: How We Look*. New York: Oxford University Press.

Garnett, Guy E. 2001. "The Aesthetics of Interactive Computer Music." *Computer Music Journal* 25 (1): 21–33.

Godfree, Ghia. 2005. "Breaking Down Binaries: Redefining Gender and Sexuality through Music Videos of Björk and Missy Elliott." *Spectator* 25 (1): 61–70.

Grimley, Daniel M. 2005. "Hidden Places: Hyper-realism in Björk's *Vespertine* and *Dancer in the Dark*." *Twentieth-Century Music* 2 (1): 37–51.

Grosz, Elizabeth. 1994. *Volatile Bodies: Toward a Corporeal Feminism*. Bloomington: Indiana University Press.

Haraway, Donna. 1991a. "A Cyborg Manifesto: Science, Technology, and Socialist-Feminism in the Late Twentieth Century." In *Simians, Cyborgs, and Women: The Reinvention of Nature*, 149–181. New York: Routledge.

Haraway, Donna. 1991b. "*Gender* for a Marxist Dictionary: The Sexual Politics of a Word." In *Simians, Cyborgs, and Women: The Reinvention of Nature*, 127–148. New York: Routledge.

Hayles, N. Katherine. 1999. *How We Became Posthuman: Virtual Bodies in Cybernetics, Literature, and Informatics*. Chicago: University of Chicago Press.

Hillyer, Barbara. 1993. *Feminism and Disability*. Norman: University of Oklahoma Press.

Hodgkinson, Will. 2011. "Björk? There's an App for Her." *The Times*, October 7.

hooks, bell. 2000. *Feminist Theory: From Margin to Center*. 2nd ed. Cambridge, MA: South End Press.

Iannacci, Elio. 2011. "Björk Is Crazy Like a Fox." *Maclean's*, October 10. http://www.macleans.ca/culture/bjork-is-crazy-like-a-fox/.

Ihde, Don. 2007. *Listening and Voice: A Phenomenology of Sound*. 2nd ed. Albany: State University of New York Press.

Iverson, Jennifer. 2006. "Dancing out of the Dark: How Music Refutes Disability Stereotypes in *Dancer in the Dark*." In *Sounding Off: Theorizing Disability in Music*, edited by Neil Lerner and Joseph N. Straus, 57–74. New York: Routledge.

Jain, Sarah. S. 1999. "The Prosthetic Imagination: Enabling and Disabling the Prosthesis Trope." *Science, Technology, and Human Values* 24 (1): 31–54.

Kurzman, Steven. 2001. "Presence and Prosthesis: A Response to Nelson and Wright." *Cultural Anthropology* 16 (3): 374–387.

Le Corbusier. 1987. *The Decorative Art of Today*. Translated by James Dunnett. London: Architectural Press.

Link, Stan. 2001. "The Work of Reproduction in the Mechanical Aging of an Art: Listening to Noise." *Computer Music Journal* 25 (1): 34–47.

Malawey, Victoria. 2011. "Musical Emergence in Björk's *Medúlla*." *Journal of the Royal Music Association* 136 (1): 141–180.

Manning, Erin. 2006. "Prosthetics Making Sense: Dancing the Technogenic Body." *Fibreculture Journal* 9. http://nine.fibreculturejournal.org/fcj-055-prosthetics-making-sense-dancing-the-technogenetic-body/.

Manning, Erin. 2007. *Politics of Touch: Sense, Movement, Sovereignty*. Minneapolis: University of Minnesota Press.

Marsh, Charity, and Melissa West. 2003. "The Nature/Technology Binary Opposition Dismantled in the Music of Madonna and Björk." In *Music and Technoculture*, edited by Rene T.A. Lysloff and Leslie C. Gay, 182–203. Middletown, CT: Wesleyan University Press.

McClary, Susan. 1991. *Feminine Endings: Music, Gender, and Sexuality*. Minneapolis: University of Minnesota Press.

McRuer, Robert. 2006. *Crip Theory: Cultural Signs of Queerness and Disability*. New York: New York University Press.

Mitchell, David T., and Sharon L. Snyder. 2000. *Narrative Prosthesis: Disability and the Dependencies of Discourse*. Ann Arbor: University of Michigan Press.

Nöe, Alva. 2012. "What Would Disembodied Music Even Be?" In *Bodily Expression in Electronic Music: Perspectives on Reclaiming Performativity*, edited by Deniz Peters, Gerhard Eckel, and Andreas Dorschel, 53–60. New York: Routledge.

Ott, Katherine, David Serlin, and Stephen Mihm, eds. 2002. *Artificial Parts, Practical Lives: Modern Histories of Prosthetics*. New York: New York University Press.

Parviainen, Janna. 2012. "Seeing Sound, Hearing Movement: Multimodal Expression and Haptic Illusions in the Virtual Sonic Environment." In *Bodily Expression in Electronic Music: Perspectives on Reclaiming Performativity*, edited by Deniz Peters, Gerhard Eckel, and Andreas Dorschel, 71–84. New York: Routledge.

Peters, Deniz. 2012. "Touch: Real, Apparent, and Absent: On Bodily Expression in Electronic Music." In *Bodily Expression in Electronic Music: Perspectives on Reclaiming Performativity*, edited by Deniz Peters, Gerhard Eckel, and Andreas Dorschel, 17–34. New York: Routledge.

Poizat, Michel. 1992. *The Angel's Cry: Beyond the Pleasure Principle in Opera*. Translated by Arthur Denner. Ithaca, NY: Cornell University Press.

Robbie, Andrew. 2007. "Sampling Haraway, Hunting Björk: Locating a Cyborg Subjectivity." *Repercussions* 10 (1): 57–95.

Rodgers, Tara. 2003. "On the Process and Aesthetics of Sampling in Electronic Music Production." *Organised Sound* 8 (3): 313–320.

Ross, Alex. 2012. "Björk ED." *New Yorker*, February 27.

Rousseau, Jean-Jacques. 1998. *Essay on the Origin of Languages and Writings Related to Music*. Translated by John T. Scott. London: University Press of New England.

Schafer, R. Murray. 1994. *The Soundscape: Our Sonic Environment and the Tuning of the World*. Rochester, VT: Destiny Books.

Schiesel, Seth. 2011. "Playing the New Björk Album, and Playing Along, with Apps." *New York Times*, October 24. http://www.nytimes.com/2011/10/25/arts/video-games/bjorks-biophilia-an-album-as-game.html?pagewanted=all&_r=0.

Seltzer, Mark. 1992. *Bodies and Machines*. New York: Routledge.

Smith, Marquard. 2006. "The Vulnerable Articulate: James Gillingham, Aimee Mullins, and Matthew Barney." In *The Prosthetic Impulse*, edited by Marquard Smith and Joanne Morra, 43–72. Cambridge, MA: MIT Press.

Sobchack, Vivian. 2006. "A Leg to Stand On: Prosthetics, Metaphor, and Materiality." In *The Prosthetic Impulse*, edited by Marquard Smith and Joanne Morra, 17–41. Cambridge, MA: MIT Press.

Stiker, Henri-Jacques. 1999. *A History of Disability*. Ann Arbor: University of Michigan Press.

Straus, Joseph N. 2011. *Extraordinary Measures: Disability in Music*. New York: Oxford University Press.

Webb, Peter, and John Lynch. 2010. "*Utopian Punk*: The Concept of the Utopian in the Creative Practice of Björk." *Utopian Studies* 21 (2): 313–330.

Wendell, Susan. 1996. *The Rejected Body: Feminist Philosophical Reflections on Disability*. New York: Routledge.

Wigley, Mark. 1991. "Prosthetic Theory: The Disciplining of Architecture." *Assemblage* 15: 6–29.

Wills, David. 1995. *Prosthesis*. Stanford, CA: Stanford University Press.

Wilson, Robert Rawdon. 1995. "Cyber(Body)Parts: Prosthetic Consciousness." *Body and Society* 1 (3–4): 239–259.

Wishart, Trevor. 1996. *On Sonic Art*. Rev. ed. Edited by Simon Emmerson. New York: Routledge.

Zak, Albin J. 2001. *The Poetics of Rock: Cutting Tracks, Making Records*. Berkeley: University of California Press.

CHAPTER 9

SUBHUMAN OR SUPERHUMAN?

(Musical) Assistive Technology, Performance Enhancement, and the Aesthetic/Moral Debate

LAURIE STRAS

In August 2012, many Paralympians—dubbed "superhumans" on advertising surrounding the Olympic Park in London—relied on biotechnology to transcend their disabilities (in the context of normative sport), to the overwhelming enthusiasm of viewers worldwide. Yet in the same month, when cyclist Lance Armstrong was served a lifetime ban from competition for the use of biotechnological drugs and performance-enhancing blood transfusions, both the sport's governing authorities and the public condemned his actions as the antithesis of fair play and authentic performance. The synchronicity of these two events revealed how we—that is, a near global community of audiences and participants—understand and interpret, almost subconsciously, the ethical boundaries we place around the use of technology in sport and, more importantly, how that understanding is complex and mutable. Even in relation to a specific technology, the boundaries can flex, become permeable, and sometimes completely disappear: this is because a single innovation, deployed in different ways, might allow an athlete to do something that they could not otherwise do (*adaptive*), to do something more efficiently (*assistive*) or more normatively (*therapeutic*), or to do it better (*enhancing*).[1] Our ethical response to its use will depend entirely on context. Technological intervention in music performance invites comparisons: assistive technology that helps disabled musicians gain or regain the experience of performance carries with it a strong ethical credibility, yet the use of performance-enhancing technology in postproduction recording processes—and more recently in live performance—by nondisabled musicians is often vigorously decried.

Since antiquity, parallels have been drawn between music and sport, which are often critiqued using similar aesthetic and moral frameworks. In both, humans negotiate issues of virtuosity, competition, teamwork, talent, grace, inspiration, and elitism. Moreover, music and sport both can highlight the protean and the promethean in human nature: positively transformative in the development of skill and mental/physical integrity, but potentially dangerous or negative when given access to technology.[2] Although musicologists and philosophers of music have considered the ethics of performance enhancement in recorded music, there is still little published debate concerning its use in live performance (Dogentan-Dack 2008; Bayley 2010; Sanden 2013), and that which exists does not consider the varying ways in which the same technology might be deployed and the uses to which it might be put. Philosophers of sport, on the other hand, have approached the ethics of assistive technology in performance more thoroughly, for instance, by developing critical frameworks for debates concerning prosthesis and doping. So, what can we learn from sports philosophy in terms of our ethical and aesthetic responses to the performances of disabled musicians? What weight do we place on the mediatory effect of technology in differing performance contexts? What impact does the use of assistive/enhancement technology have on the way we value a performance?

Mapping Music Performance onto a Definition of Sport

Philosopher Bernard Suits provides an essential definition of sport, which he sees as a subset of a larger classification of human activity, games (Suits 2007, 14): "To play a game is to attempt to achieve a specific state of affairs (*pre-lusory goal*), using only means permitted by the rules (*lusory means*), where the rules prohibit the use of more efficient in favor of less efficient means (*constitutive rules*) and where such rules are accepted just because they make possible such activity (*lusory attitude*). . . . Playing a game is the voluntary attempt to overcome unnecessary obstacles."

Music performance is not inherently or necessarily competitive, and it could be said that music performance's pre-lusory goal is nothing more or less than a performance itself. But some aspects of becoming, and being, a musician pit individuals against each other or against a commonly agreed set of standards in a competitive mode, with extraperformative lusory goals (the lusory goal, in Suits's terminology, is winning) (2007, 10). Learning any sort of musical discipline involves constant and willing competition with one's own previous achievements in order to surpass them; musicians in training may sit exams that grade proficiency; aspiring musicians compete for places at conservatories or for positions in bands; professional musicians compete for playing opportunities; recording musicians compete for record sales and airplay. Music performance's lusory means—the means by which musicians achieve music performance—are also ostensibly simple: singing and/or playing instruments. Music performance does not have formal constitutive rules, but there are nonetheless understandings, culturally inscribed, that inflect those lusory means in much the same way as a game's constitutive rules: what constitutes an instrument, for instance, or what is considered "singing."

Suits proposes a further set of conditions that make a game into a sport (2007, 14): "[There are] four requirements which, if they are met by any given game, are sufficient to denominate that game a sport. They are: (1) that the game be a game of skill, (2) that the skill be physical, (3) that the game have a wide following, and (4) that the following achieve a certain level of stability." Suits does not elaborate on what he means by "following," but it can be assumed from the rest of his essay that he means participants. We might extrapolate further from his definition a subset of sport that is *spectator sport*: a sport that has not only a following of participants but also some participants who are sufficiently skilled that another following (a following of a following, if you will) will gather to form an audience for the sport, and will expect under certain conditions to pay for the privilege.

Music performance, as it is traditionally understood, fulfills all of Suits's conditions for a sport. Moreover, in certain conditions, it is also a spectator sport; indeed, it correlates best to sports of endeavor against a clock or judged by criteria, such as athletics or gymnastics, rather than individual or team games. The condition of physical skill—when music performance involves an audience—brings forth another "understanding" that operates, to all intents and purposes, as a constitutive rule: the "pact" between performer and audience that what the audience witnesses is a physical act by the performer resulting in the creation of musical sound (Siegel 2009, 200). The layers of technological mediation ("lusory means") between performer and audience will be contingent on what genre ("sport") is being performed, and are reflected in the performer/audience pact. Many genres demand no mediation other than voices and acoustic instruments, although amplification and electric/electronic instruments are permitted, even required, in others. Extensions of electronic mediation, such as prerecorded music and sequencing, may also be used, but fundamentally, music audiences pay to see live music precisely because at least some element of the performance will be an exhibition of physical skill.

Technological Enhancement and Human Nature: Ethical Arguments in Sport

If we see musicians and musical performance as analogous to athletes and sporting performance (particularly in the context of spectator events), then the ethical principles that govern sporting practices may also be seen to apply to musical practices. For instance, the notion of fair play is governed by the constitutive rules and depends on the athletes following them rather than attempting to bypass them—through transgressing the lusory means—in pursuit of the lusory goal.[3] In music, adherence to the constitutive rules of live performance would prohibit the use of performance-enhancing technology—at least such technology that is not inherent in the performer/audience pact, or that has been concealed with an attempt to pass off the physical aspects of the performance as an unmediated feat.

Although the consideration of ethics has always been a feature of sports philosophy, its importance in the field has grown since the 1990s (McNamee 2007), alongside the emergence of disability sport and ever more sophisticated possibilities for technological interventions—legal and illegal—in sports equipment and (crucially) in athletes themselves. The year 2012 was pivotal for those involved in sports ethics, for it saw both the first legitimate appearance of a technologically enabled athlete at the Olympics and the exposure of doping on an unprecedented scale in the international professional cycling circuit. The cognitive dissonance created by the near-simultaneous triumph of Oscar Pistorius and the disgrace of Lance Armstrong has more to do with just the "health and fair play" aspects of enhancement and "enabling artifice" (Bonte et al. 2013, 2).[4]

The editors of the first edited collection on the ethics of sport published post 2012 summarize the issues in a way that easily maps onto the concerns expressed over interventions in musical performance:

> Issues of authentic agency and personal accountability, of the appeal of natural grace in performance, of sports as a testing ground for the capacities of the human species with which all members of the species can identify, of sport as a display of the special natural gifts given to the talented, of sport as a display of ideal exemplars of man's nature; or alternatively, of sport as a display of man's protean nature (his capacity to adapt and transform himself), of sport as a showcase of his promethean nature (his tendency to transgress naturally given constraints on his existence)—all these foundational issues come to the fore when we start looking at [enhancement] through the lens of "human nature." (Bonte et al. 2013, 2)

Two essays in the volume provide a starting point with which to interrogate current responses to assistive technology in music performance. The first sets out a model for mapping responses to technology against a five-level framework, which widens from the impact on the individual to abstract concerns related to human nature (Tolleneer and Schotsmans 2013). The second questions whether the use of enhancing technology is, in fact, at its root a moral or an aesthetic concern, and its analysis helps us differentiate between aesthetic and moral responses to assisted or enhanced performance (De Block 2013).

The five-level model proposed by Tolleneer and Schotsmans hinges on the notions of respect and responsibility. It places the athlete/performer at its center, and considers the effects of enhancement on ever-widening spheres of influence. The first level, *self*, considers the arguments related to the individual's respect and responsibility for their own health, well-being, and prosperity, in its broadest sense. The second level, *other*, relates to the effect of enhancement on the individual's relationships with those with whom they interact in their sphere of activity: coaches, teachers, teammates/colleagues, competitors. The third level, *play*, concerns the effect of enhancement on the relationship between the individual and the cultural/social practices that govern their activity. The fourth, *display*, broadens this concern to include the wider community of witnesses that turns the activity into a performance. The final level, *humanity*, brings the previous four levels into perspective with an interrogation of how enhancement impinges on respect for "human nature"—that by which one human identifies another of the same species.

Tolleneer and Schotsmans demonstrate their model with some arguments both for and against enhancement (see Figure 9.1). At the level of *self*, enhancement may help the individual fulfill their aspirations, but it may present threats to health, and to self-esteem. The athlete who enhances may present a problem for *others* who are involved in sport, by lessening the chances of competitors or obliging them to adopt enhancing techniques themselves in order to compete on level terms; on the other hand, the technology may be said to create equality of opportunity if its use is widely enough spread.

At the level of *play*, it may be argued that enhancement is just part of the experience of competition; however, if sport historically occurs without enhancement, then it is "damaged as a cultural phenomenon and as a social practice" by enhancement (Tolleneer and Schotsmans 2013, 27). Moreover, enhancement "creates another social practice: the athlete turns his back on the game and creates a will to get results and win"—that is, attempts to achieve the lusory goal by ignoring the lusory means. As Suits has shown, this is a non sequitur, in that if the end does not justify the means, it becomes separated from the means: in other words, the athlete may cross the finish line first, but at the expense of genuinely taking part in the race.

At the next level, *display*, enhancement becomes a means to another end: the raising of audience expectation, and the enrichment of the spectator experience (28); but it also breaks the pact between audience and athlete that the performance is "genuine," and furthermore it encourages the glorification of dishonesty. Although the fifth level, *humanity*, is the broadest and perhaps most difficult (if not impossible) to pin down, Tolleneer

Athletic enhancement? NO because it e.g.:	What is at stake?	Athletic enhancement? YES because it e.g.:
threatens my health	1. The self	helps in fulfilling my aspirations
reduces the opponent's chances	2. The other	guarantees equal chances
undermines the spirit of sport	3. Play *Sport*	aligns sport with other cultural phenomena
creates negative role models	4. Display *Spectator sport*	reinforces sport's heroic character
desecrates human nature	5. Humanity *Human nature*	fulfills the mission to push back frontiers

FIGURE 9.1 Tolleneer and Schotsmans' five-level model for the analysis of ethical arguments in the athletic enhancement debate (Tolleneer and Schotsmans 2013, 25)

and Schotsmans show that it is paradoxically the crux of the ethical debate: while opponents of enhancement "[cry] out for the limits of human nature to be respected, . . . the quintessence of sport . . . demands that the boundaries of human ability are pushed still further" (Tolleneer and Schotsmans 2013, 29).

The five-level model, however useful as a taxonomy for ethical arguments, nonetheless assumes that the athlete at its center has no reason for adopting enhancing technology other than to improve performance beyond what he or she is capable of under normal circumstances, an action that usually lies outside sports' lusory means and constitutive rules. Disabled athletes, such as those competing in the Paralympics, frequently make use of assistive or adaptive technologies that allow them to compete in ways that would not otherwise be open to them: we are now used to seeing blades on runners and prosthetic arms on cyclists. However, stepping back to our fundamental definition, these technologies sit within the sports' lusory means and so pose no ethical problems; moreover, disabled athletes may sometimes be allowed to use drug technologies if they claim a therapeutic use exemption (TUE) (emphasizing the important distinction between intervention as enhancement and intervention as therapy). Yet the model might apply to technology even when permitted outright under the constitutive rules, if the rules themselves are deemed to be too lax: when beaten in the 200m finals at the London Paralympics, Pistorius accused his victorious rival Alan Oliveira of having an unfair advantage through the length of his prostheses, even though the blades were not outside regulation dimensions.

Technological Enhancement and Human Nature: Parallels between Sport and Music

With a bizarre serendipity, in the same month that saw Paralympians celebrated and professional cyclists shamed, a musical technology came onto the market that has the potential to divide the music community in the same way that biotechnologies have divided the athletic community. In August 2012, Antares Audio Technologies launched Auto-Tune Live, an extension of their pitch modification software, Auto-Tune, that is "optimized for *real-time* [my emphasis] pitch correction or creatively modifying the intonation of a performance" ("Introducing Auto-Tune® Live!" 2012). Auto-Tune analyses the pitch of recorded voices and instruments and manipulates it to a precise tuning, hence relieving the performer of the onus of singing or playing in tune. The time taken to correct the pitch can be controlled by the user: the longer the delay, the less noticeable the intervention; by contrast, instantaneous correction (particularly when the interval between "wrong" and "right" pitch is great) highlights the technology, creating a metallic vocal sound that is heard as robotic and unnatural.

Taken outside the context of a competitive music business, and of music as a cultural practice in which technical skill equates with aesthetic value, Auto-Tune is a neutral piece of technology, an addition to the armory of effects available to the music producer. Many artists, including the rapper T-Pain, the indie folk band Bon Iver, and British soul singer Laura Mvula, freely employ Auto-Tune as a creative tool, using its most extreme output as a distinct vocal and compositional color. Electronica singer-songwriter Imogen Heap uses a more sophisticated device that incorporates a similar technology, the Digitech Vocalist Workstation, to make music with an intentionally trans- or even posthuman sound (Hein 2010). For her, the technology is "liberating," allowing her to "make any singer sound on the planet" (Woloshyn 2009).

In performance, Heap wears her technology as if it were a prosthesis, with digitally enabled gloves, activating the treatment of her voice with gesture. Even without this performative link, however, Auto-Tune retains a strong aural association with its technological nature, and it can function as a signifier for the cyborg. Auto-Tune's first overt use in mainstream pop, on Cher's 1998 single "Believe," was a novelty; the difference between "natural" and heavily treated versions of her voice was underlined in the video by a dual presentation of Cher as human and hologram. Black Eyed Peas' 2010 album *The E.N.D.* made similar connections, particularly in the audio release "Alive" and the worldwide hit "Boom Boom Pow," the video for which depicted the band as analog inhabitants of a digitized landscape.

One recently emerging artist, Janelle Monáe, uses Auto-Tune to highlight the tensions between the technological and the organic. Her first solo release, *Metropolis: The Chase Suite*, is a concept album comprising a single programmatic "suite" of songs that mixes a full orchestral score with electronica, R&B, rock, pop, and hip-hop, with vocal styles that range from bel canto to doowop, soul, and rap. *The Chase Suite* introduces her android performance persona, Cindi Mayweather, exploring the cyborg as "the new Other" ("Janelle Monáe: The Interview!" 2010).[5] Cindi is humanity-enabled technology instead of technology-enabled humanity, installed with "with a rock-star proficiency package and a working soul" (Monáe 2010). The notion that the cyborg can be replicated, with identical features but different aptitudes, is reflected in the way Monáe uses her voice on the album: we hear her voice in the backing track, multitracked and treated with Auto-Tune, contrasted with the same voice singing lead, but unconstrained by any audible technological intervention. On the single video release "Many Moons" we see multiple versions of Cindi performing the backing vocals in perfect synchronization, as a visual and aural counterpoint to the central performance of Cindi herself. Cindi's cyborg nature is finally highlighted at the point when her soul leaves her body during disassembly, in the short track "Cybertronic Purgatory." The "whole" Cindi's rock vocal transforms into a soaring, high bel canto as her soul separates; but this voice is then modulated through a vocal processor (possibly the AVOX Evo, produced by Auto-Tune's manufacturer, Antares) as the soul disappears, leaving only Cindi's mechanical shell. Yet as a live performer, Monáe if anything downplays the technological aspects of her music, touring instead with a fourteen-member band. Reception of her live performances emphasizes her authenticity and underscores her ability to perform without technological enhancement: "this is what authentic live performance is all about: no auto-tune, no backing tracks, no video stunts"; "She's the real deal—no photoshop needed, no Auto-Tune needed" (Stark 2012; Hoard 2010).

For artists like Heap and Monáe, Auto-Tune and its companion vocal processing technologies have presented new opportunities and inspiration. However, inasmuch as Auto-Tune is a device that allows musicians to perform a task they would otherwise be unable to do or increases the ease with which it can be performed, Auto-Tune also falls under the definition of an assistive technology, like a Paralympic runner's blade prostheses. Indeed, Auto-Tune can play an integral part in software configurations assembled for performance by musicians with vocalization impairments ("Mixed Ability Students to Perform in USA" 2010).[6] Some singers claim that using Auto-Tune Live in the studio actually helps them sing in tune, as they have to try to match their (live) performance to the treated track simultaneously being played through the headphones (Anderson 2013). However, Auto-Tune is most often construed as an enhancing technology, with all the moral implications such technology entails: before its live version was released, Auto-Tune was already controversial as a postproduction tool, and had been almost from its introduction to the market in 1996. It has even been compared with the use of performance-enhancing drugs in sport: "It's like doping for track athletes and cyclists. EVERYONE is doing it, so if you want to keep up . . ." (Cross 2013; Wheeler 2013).

The act of "outing" an artist for using Auto-Tune, branding them "tone-deaf" (a significant use of pejorative labeling) or fraudulent, has become a mainstay of sensationalist media, most frequently achieved by comparing the artist's ability to perform live with their recorded performances (see, for instance, the brouhaha over Taylor Swift's duet with Stevie Nicks at the 2010 Grammys, which left the press baying over the younger singer's inability to sing in tune with one of the grande dames of rock). Auto-Tune may not be *designed* to aid and abet musical "fraud"—its creator Andy Hildebrand says, "I just make the car, I don't drive it down the wrong side of the road"—but the live version of the software threatens to remove easy access to any hard proof of a musician's suspected duplicity (Anderson 2013).

Most of the arguments for and against Auto-Tune are well rehearsed in the media, and, as with performance-enhancing drugs, the naysayers are often the loudest and the satirists at their most mordant, as in an episode of *The Simpsons* in which Bart Simpson joins a boy band whose inability to sing is rendered irrelevant by "studio magic" (Katz 2010, 50–52). And also as with doping, the objections to Auto-Tune reach their most strident and heartfelt, suffused with the same "deep unease [and] intense indignation," when they touch on the sensitive subject of humanity (Tolleneer and Schotsmans 2013, 29). In one of the most comprehensive and eloquent discourses on the issues surrounding the technology, Lessley Anderson expresses a sense of helplessness in the wake of an irresistible move away from the human and toward the machine (Anderson 2013):

> Indeed, finding out that all the singers we listen to have been Auto-Tuned does feel like someone's messing with us. As humans, we crave connection, not perfection. But

> we're not the ones pulling the levers. What happens when an entire industry decides it's safer to bet on the robot? Will we start to hate the sound of our own voices?

Later on in the article, she asks, "If you're one of the generation raised on technology-enabled perfect pitch, does your brain get rewired to expect it? . . . Is the Auto-Tune generation . . . more sensitive to off key-ness, and thus less able to appreciate it?" Anderson's questions are only partially rhetorical, for her interviewees suggest that younger artists come in wanting the sound of Auto-Tune from the outset, and one producer tells of a band that were deeply critical of even their most revered forebears, including The Beatles, for their out-of-tune vocals. Such hypersensitization might create a generation of musicians better *equipped* to develop pitch accuracy than their predecessors, but they would only be able to do so in one temperament—and only if they are not relying on technology to do it for them in the first place.

Mapping the arguments for and against Auto-Tune into Tolleneer and Schotsmans' five-level model (see Figure 9.2) shows that there are strong similarities to the arguments for and against performance-enhancing drugs. We might think that, because of its rapid adoption and now near ubiquity, Auto-Tune technology falls within at least pop music's lusory means and constitutive rules, but there is still a strong contingent that sees the noncreative or nonsymbolic (which would nearly always mean subtle or nontransparent) use of Auto-Tune as cheating, both in terms of getting one over on rivals for

Auto-Tune? NO because it e.g.:	What is at stake?	Auto-Tune? YES because it e.g.:
surrenders my integrity as a performer	1. The self	helps in fulfilling my aspirations; helps me be more efficient
obliges others to use technology; narrows the market for unenhanced performances	2. The other	guarantees equal chances; helps co-artists achieve collective success
undermines the value of virtuosity in performance; damages music as a social practice	3. Play/game *Performance*	pushes up standards in terms of the quality of consumer products
creates negative role models; impoverishes the listening experience of the audience	4. Display *Public/professional performance*	makes artists appear infallible; creates mythic celebrities for the benefit of spectator experience
undermines the value of authenticity in performance; desecrates human nature	5. Humanity *Human nature*	opens up new creative possibilities for recorded and live performance; allows musicians to make music that pushes the boundaries of musicianship

FIGURE 9.2 Tolleneer and Schotsmans' five-level model applied to ethical arguments concerning the use of Auto-Tune

record sales and deceiving the audience into thinking the artist is a more accomplished musician than is actually the case.

But here it is as well to distinguish what the lusory goal is: is it a commercial goal to sell records? Or an aesthetic one, to produce music that is wholly representative of an unmediated individual craft and virtuosity? This second goal seems to resonate more with values related to a different and older tradition of musical endeavor, one that is out of step with the rapid pace of technological advance. Tolleneer and Schotsmans make precisely this point in relation to the ethics of biotechnology in sport: "Traditional ethical principles often need to be adjusted before we are able to pass judgment on [new] procedures" (Tolleneer and Schotsmans 2013, 30). The pace of development makes ethical adjustments difficult, but they must be made before the rules, and practice, can change. And, to return to the first goal, until that change occurs, there will be a strong economic incentive to cheat.[7]

The Aesthetics of Enhancement

There is another way of viewing objections to performance-enhancing technology that has further implications for the appreciation of other kinds of technology-assisted performance. In the second of the two essays this present chapter considers, Andreas de Block compares the negative response to doping in sport with negative responses to forgery in art. De Block argues that artistic forgeries are dismissed as objects of no value, not because of their formal observable characteristics (which to all intents and purposes are the same as the originals) but because "our aesthetic appreciation is always in part an appreciation of the artist's performance . . . [and the work's] meaning is constituted by circumstances connected to the work's origin" (De Block 2013, 152). He goes further to say that our aesthetic response is linked to our valuation of the athlete's/artist's/performer's achievement in bringing a performance—or an artwork—to fruition. Therefore when it is revealed to us that a performance is not wholly the product of achievement but has been enhanced by technological intervention, our appreciation of the performance is altered. De Block illustrates his argument by suggesting that we might be amazed and delighted by a video of a woman executing a 2.10 m high jump, but if we were subsequently told that the athlete was not a woman but a man, our appreciation (or at least our attention) would focus on the skill of the deception, even if the observable characteristics of the performance remained the same (De Block 2013, 154). If we were then told that the whole video was computer generated, our appreciation would shift again to the quality of the 3D rendering and the visualization of the programmers.

De Block introduces his arguments into a debate initiated by Arthur Koestler, who claimed that only the formal observable characteristics of an artwork should matter in aesthetic judgment; therefore, origin is not an issue (De Block 2013, 152). However, de Block further notes that the moral quality of a performance can add to its aesthetic value, and that "intention, cultural background, and medical history of a person are often essential for the moral evaluation of his or her actions" (De Block 2013, 155, 158). Through this reasoning, de Block approaches an understanding of how heroic narratives emerge in disability sport: if aesthetic judgment is even partially based on origin and performance, it is hard to get away from the notion that a person's disability "adds" to the appreciation of a performance—what value may lack in virtuosity is regained via the appreciation of relative difficulty for the performer, even (and perhaps more so) when assisted. Nonetheless, de Block insists that "the origin of an athletic performance has to be natural and human in origin, in order to deserve our fullest aesthetic appreciation" (De Block 2013, 156) and that what we perceive as "unnatural" performances arise from a mismatch between the body of the performer and the practice it adopts. These practices are culturally determined, so not reliant on a scientific measure of what is natural and what is not, but the greater the mismatch between the body and the practice, the more difficult it is to accord aesthetic value to the performance.

De Block's arguments may provide an explanation for the reception of a series of concerts given by the British Paraorchestra in the summer of 2012, as part of both the Cultural Olympiad running parallel with the sporting Olympics and the Paralympics themselves, as the orchestra was showcased heavily in the closing ceremony, in which it was joined by Coldplay. The orchestra was begun by conductor Charles Hazlewood, and was launched that summer with eighteen members. Their disabilities include severe motor impairment, learning differences, and hearing and sight impairments: they were assembled on the basis of their musicianship, not the fit of their instruments to a predetermined array, so the ensemble comprises "normal" orchestral woodwind and string instruments, as well as piano, recorder, harp, sitar, and oud. Some members only have access to music performance through electronic technology: the trumpeter Clarence Adoo, who has no mobility below his neck, plays an instrument called Headspace, which he activates by blowing down a tube. Composer Lyn Lovett, who has severe cerebral palsy, triggers musical events on an iPad with her nose.

There were many media write-ups and features about the Paraorchestra in the months leading up to the Paralympics; some of these appeared just before the closing ceremony, but some coincided with their performances at other events, such as the Snape Maltings Proms in Aldeburgh and the Orchestra in a Field festival in Glastonbury (Rowe 2012; Sloane 2013). The UK broadcaster Channel 4 also produced a forty-five-minute television documentary, following the orchestra through its preparations for their summer concerts. Despite the musical quality represented on stage (most of the members are professional musicians, educated at conservatories; Hazlewood is an A-list conductor who has performed with the Amsterdam Concertgebouw, the Philharmonia, and the Orchestra of the Age of Enlightenment), reviews almost never mention the *performances*, concentrating instead on the back stories of the musicians and the inspirational qualities of Hazlewood and the project. Where the music is mentioned, the writers are careful to underline its unconventional nature, with familiar works such as Ravel's

Bolero and *Greensleeves* arranged for the collection of instruments and sounds available to the orchestra—but no *aesthetic* value is assigned to it.

The difficulty is further illustrated by the reaction of the audience to another event of the Cultural Olympiad, the performance of Oliver Searle's *Microscopic Dances* by Technophonia, an ensemble comprising both disabled and nondisabled musicians, at London's South Bank in July 2012. The three disabled musicians with very limited mobility played instruments through the use of electronic triggers activated by breaking a light beam, by jaw movements, or by pressing large button switches. The piece was given a polite reception after its first performance, but then Searle addressed the audience, explaining how the three disabled musicians were able to contribute to the work. A second performance was given, which then received a standing ovation (Thomas 2013).

This lack of critical engagement—and perhaps the willingness to surrender aesthetic judgment to a simpler appreciation of the heroic narrative—despite the volume of coverage and the prestigious venues, would suggest that the mismatch between the collective bodies of these orchestras and the traditional practice of ensemble/orchestral music is too great for many observers to reconcile. Moreover, there is a further mismatch between the sound of the ensemble and the sound of the traditional orchestra. It would seem there is some way to go before an expanded model for the cultural practice of music can converge with an expanded notion of humanity that encompasses disabled bodies that express virtuosity and creativity in individual ways.

Final Thoughts

Returning to the first analytical frame, Tolleneer and Schotsmans hold their own model up to critique by admitting that it has the potential "not [to do] justice to the rich details of reality" nor to take account of a "broader time perspective and a social-historical retrospective" (2013, 36). They show how enhancement techniques and technologies have a long history of gradually gaining acceptance in sport, noting that at the beginning of the Olympic movement, training and specialization in a single sport were considered a step too far. One of the other contributors to *Athletic Enhancement, Human Nature and Ethics* posits that Pistorius would not have had so positive a reception, or perhaps would not have been received at all, into the regular Olympics had he truly been able to run faster than any other competitor (Meacham 2013, 135–136). Sport has not yet reached that "paradigm shift in which disability becomes ability, disadvantage becomes advantage" (Weihenmayer 2008). Although the Olympic motto *Citius Altius Fortius* (Faster, Higher, Stronger) mandates the community to extend and surpass, it seems progress can only be made in tiny increments if it is to remain culturally acceptable and believable in terms of human accomplishment. So, in order for it to gain sufficient aesthetic credibility as music on its own terms, music created with assistive technology may have to sound like music produced without, only differing in tiny increments. Or music created by nondisabled musicians—artists like Imogen Heap, who often limit themselves to technology that is indistinguishable from that used by musicians whose *only* access to performance is through technology—must converge from the other direction. Only once cultural practices and bodies are better aligned, will the aesthetic challenges posed diminish.

Notes

1. The World Health Organization defines assistive technology as "any device or system that allows individuals to perform tasks they would otherwise be unable to do or increases the ease and safety with which tasks can be performed" (Andrews, Faulkner, and Andrews 2004, 10). Adaptive technology has a narrower scope, being specifically designed for people with disabilities, and it is therefore unlikely to be used by people without those disabilities. Enhancement technology may be seen as another subcategory of assistive technology. However, it boosts "capabilities beyond the species-typical level or statistically-normal range of functioning for an individual" and therefore has a different function than *therapy*, which is intended to ameliorate "pathologies that . . . reduce one's level of functioning below this species-typical or statistically-normal level" (Lin and Allhoff 2008).
2. This draws on the description of sport in Bonte et al. 2013, 2, given below.
3. "The adherence to 'constitutive rules' and the acceptance of a 'lusory attitude' is often referred to in the literature using the double concept of formal fair play and informal fair play" (Tolleneer and Schotsmans 2013, 23). See also Suits (2007, 11): "A player who does not confine himself to lusory means may not be said to win, even if he achieves the pre-lusory goal. But achievement of the lusory goal, winning, requires that the player confine himself to lusory means."
4. At the time of writing, Pistorius had not yet been brought to trial following the fatal shooting of his girlfriend in February 2013. Media coverage of the shooting and Pistorius's fall from grace also involved complex ethical issues in the way that his disability factored in the reporting, but these are outside the scope of this essay.
5. Intersectionality has a much more transparent locus in Monáe's latest release, *The Electric Lady* (2013), nowhere more so than in the scripted radio interludes, in which a DJ receives calls from an outraged public, terrified of Cindi Mayweather's popular power: "She's not even a person!" "Robot love is queer!"
6. Kay Dickinson equates postproduction vocal digital technology with prosthesis in her examination of Cher's 1998 hit, "Believe," but she sees it as an enhancing or additive technology, rather than assistive: "The use of prosthetics in this sense—and this would include women singing with vocoders—is maybe most profitably thought of not as a replacement for something lacking, but as a booster added on to enhance one's capabilities" (Dickinson 2001, 338). See also Jennifer Iverson's essay in this volume.
7. There has been a recent debate in the journal *Sports, Ethics, and Philosophy* examining the moral implications of cheating in a commercialized sport (Upton 2011; Royce 2012). The same journal also hosts an ongoing conversation regarding ways in which doping and enhancement, now seen as inevitable, can be accommodated transparently in sport (King 2012; Kornbeck 2013; Corlett 2013).

References

Anderson, Lessley. 2013. "Seduced by 'Perfect' Pitch: How Auto-Tune Conquered Pop Music." *Verge*, February 27. http://www.theverge.com/2013/2/27/3964406/seduced-by-perfect-pitch-how-auto-tune-conquered-pop-music.

Andrews, Gary, Debbie Faulkner, and Melinda Andrews. 2004. *A Glossary of Terms for Community Health Care and Services for Older Persons*. Ageing and Health Technical Report, Vol. 5. WHO/WKC/Tech.Ser./04.2. Kobe, Japan: World Health Organization. http://www.who.int/kobe_centre/ageing/ahp_vol5_glossary.pdf.

Bayley, Amanda. 2010. *Recorded Music: Performance, Culture, and Technology*. Cambridge, UK: Cambridge University Press.

Bonte, Pieter, Jan Tolleneer, Paul Schotsmans, and Sigrid Sterckx. 2013. "Introduction: Human Nature as a Promising Concept to Make Sense of the Spirit of Sport." In *Athletic Enhancement, Human Nature, and Ethics*, edited by Jan Tolleneer, Sigrid Sterckx, and Pieter Bonte, 1–18. Dordrecht, Netherlands: Springer.

Corlett, J. Angelo. 2013. "Doping: Just Do It?" *Sport, Ethics, and Philosophy* 7 (4): 430–449. doi: 10.1080/17511321.2013.851731.

Cross, Alan. 2013. "Auto Tune: 'The Botox of Music.'" *A Journal of Musical Things*, April 20. Accessed April 26, 2013. http://www.alancross.ca/a-journal-of-musical-things/2013/4/20/auto-tune-the-botox-of-music.html.

De Block, Andreas. 2013. "Doping Use as an Artistic Crime: On Natural Performances and Authentic Art." In *Athletic Enhancement, Human Nature, and Ethics*, edited by Jan Tolleneer, Sigrid Sterckx, and Pieter Bonte, 149–162. Dordrecht, Netherlands: Springer.

Dickinson, Kay. 2001. "'Believe'? Vocoders, Digitalised Female Identity, and Camp." *Popular Music* 20 (3): 333–347.

Dogentan-Dack, Mine. 2008. *Recorded Music: Philosophical and Critical Reflections*. London: Middlesex University Press.

Hein, Ethan. 2010. "Imogen Heap and Artificial Harmony." *Ethan Hein Blog*, January 26. http://www.ethanhein.com/wp/2010/imogen-heap/.

Hoard, Christian. 2010. "Artist of the Week: Janelle Monáe." *Rolling Stone*, June 30. http://www.rollingstone.com/music/news/artist-of-the-week-janelle-monae-20100630.

"Introducing Auto-Tune® Live!" 2012. Press release by Antares Audio Technologies, August 2. Accessed April 26, 2013. http://www.antarestech.com/email/2012Archive/2012_Aug_ATLive.htm.

"Janelle Monáe: The Interview!" 2010. *MTV UK*, May 12. http://www.mtv.co.uk/music/urban/221695-janelle-monae-the-interview.

Katz, Mark. 2010. *Capturing Sound: How Technology Has Changed Music*. 2nd ed. Berkeley and Los Angeles: University of California Press.

King, M. R. 2012. "A League of Their Own? Evaluating Justifications for the Division of Sport into 'Enhanced' and 'Unenhanced' Leagues." *Sport, Ethics, and Philosophy* 6 (1): 31–45. doi: 10.1080/17511321.2011.587198.

Kornbeck, Jacob. 2013. "The Naked Spirit of Sport: A Framework for Revisiting the System of Bans and Justifications in the World Anti-Doping Code." *Sport, Ethics, and Philosophy* 7 (3): 313–330. doi: 10.1080/17511321.2013.831115.

Lin, Patrick, and Fritz Allhoff. 2008. "Untangling the Debate: The Ethics of Human Enhancement." *NanoEthics* 2 (3): 251–264. doi: 10.1007/s11569-008-0046-7.

McNamee, Mike. 2007. "Sport, Ethics, and Philosophy; Context, History, Prospects." *Sport, Ethics, and Philosophy* 1 (1): 1–6. doi: 10.1080/17511320601173329.

Meacham, Jan. 2013. "Outliers, Freaks, and Cheats: Constituting Normality in the Age of Enhancement." In *Athletic Enhancement, Human Nature, and Ethics*, edited by Jan Tolleneer, Sigrid Sterckx, and Pieter Bonte, 125–146. Dordrecht, Netherlands: Springer.

"Mixed Ability Students to Perform in USA." 2010. Website of the CPIT Foundation. Accessed May 2, 2013. http://www.cpfoundation.co.nz/node/47.

Monáe, Janelle. 2010. *Metropolis: The Chase Suite (Fantastic Edition)*. Bad Boy Records, LLC, digital download.

Monáe, Janelle. 2013. *The Electric Lady*. Bad Boy Records, LLC, digital download.

Rowe, Tina. 2012. "Review: British Paraorchestra Triumph Wows Glastonbury Abbey Audience." *This Is Somerset*, July 2. http://www.thisissomerset.co.uk/Review-British-Paraorchestra-triumph-wows/story-16475439-detail/story.html.

Royce, Richard. 2012. "Concerning a Moral Duty to Cheat in Games." *Sport, Ethics, and Philosophy* 6 (3): 323–335. doi: 10.1080/17511321.2012.686922.

Sanden, Paul. 2013. *Liveness in Modern Music: Musicians, Technology, and the Perception of Performance*. New York: Routledge.

Siegel, Wayne. 2009. "Dancing the Music: Interactive Dance and Music." In *The Oxford Handbook of Computer Music*, edited by Roger T. Dean, 191–213. New York: Oxford University Press.

Sloane, Rachel. 2013. "Review of The British Paraorchestra at Snape Proms, 25 August 2012." Website of Rachel Sloane Partnerships. Accessed April 29, 2013. http://www.rachelsloane.co.uk/article/august2012/review-british-paraorchestra-snape-proms-25-august-2012.

Stark, Clinton. 2012. "Janelle Monáe Astounds San Francisco Audience." *Stark Insider*, June 3. Accessed April 26, 2013. http://www.starkinsider.com/2012/06/janelle-monae-astounds-san-francisco-audience-video.html.

Suits, Bernard. 2007. "The Elements of Sport." In *Ethics in Sport*, 2nd ed., edited by William Morgan and Klaus Meier, 9–19. Champaign, IL: Human Kinetics.

Thomas, Pete. 2013. "Assist and Adapt: Music Technology and Special Needs, Part 2." *Sound On Sound*. January. Accessed May 3, 2013. http://www.soundonsound.com/sos/jan13/articles/special-needs-2.htm.

Tolleneer, Jan, and Paul Schotsmans. 2013. "Self, Other, Play, Display, and Humanity: Development of a Five-Level Model for the Analysis of Ethical Arguments in the Athletic Enhancement Debate." In *Athletic Enhancement, Human Nature, and Ethics*, edited by Jan Tolleneer, Sigrid Sterckx, and Pieter Bonte, 21–43. Dordrecht, Netherlands: Springer.

Upton, Hugh. 2011. "Can There Be a Moral Duty to Cheat in Sport?" *Sport, Ethics, and Philosophy* 5 (2): 161–174. doi: 10.1080/17511321.2011.561257.

Weihenmayer, Erik. 2008. "The 2008 TIME 100: Heroes and Pioneers—Oscar Pistorius." *Time*, May 12. http://www.time.com/time/specials/2007/article/0,28804,1733748_1733756_1735285,00.html.

Wheeler, Brad. 2013. "Michael Bublé and How Auto-Tune Became the Botox of Pop Music." *Globe and Mail*, April 20. http://www.theglobeandmail.com/arts/music/michael-bubl-and-how-auto-tune-became-the-botox-of-pop-music/article11420371/.

Woloshyn, Alexa. 2009. "Imogen Heap as Musical Cyborg: Renegotiations of Power, Gender, and Sound." *Journal on the Art of Record Production* 4. http://arpjournal.com/597/imogen-heap-as-musical-cyborg-renegotiations-of-power-gender-and-sound/.

CHAPTER 10

DISABLING MUSIC PERFORMANCE

BLAKE HOWE

Disability disrupts and exposes ingrained societal prejudices that favor uniform able-bodiedness over bodily diversity. In the field of Disability Studies, street curbs, door handles, and stairs serve as familiar symbols for the ways in which a society may establish criteria for a "constructed normalcy," blithely enabling some bodies while disabling others. This conceptualization has reframed disability: it is not a fixed, biological state but rather a cultural script emerging from the social negotiation of diverse bodies with codes of conformity. As Carrie Sandahl and Philip Auslander (2005) argue, this process of negotiation is essentially performative: "To think of disability not as a physical condition but as a way of interacting with a world that is frequently inhospitable is to think of disability in performative terms—as something one *does* rather than something one *is*" (10).[1] Within this metaphorical framework, the disabled person is an actor (displaying, hiding, and costuming his or her body in performance); this actor, both an agent and an object, frames and is framed by the observations of a societal audience.[2]

Music performance has operated under similar codes: just as architectural features of society have the potential to exclude and stigmatize bodily difference, so too do the conventions of music performance frame certain actions, behaviors, and appearances as disabling. Indeed, concert performance is a venue with especially high expectations for exemplary able-bodiedness, typically showcasing a performer's prodigious skills—like those that govern aspects of technique (speed, agility, range, precision) and musical sensitivity (nuance, finesse, emotionality). But disabled performance renders this framework problematic, juxtaposing what a performer can do (with one part of the body) with what a performer cannot do (with another part of the body). The disabled performer, as Joseph Straus (2011) argues, thus has "a dual task: to perform music and to perform disability" (126).[3] The cultural scripts associated with both performances shape each other, so that it becomes difficult or even impossible to disentangle them: culturally marked, disability informs the music performance, while music performance in turn informs the disability. This essay explores some of the ways in which this "dual performance" of music and disability has been realized and received, with examples of how music performance has rewritten cultural scripts of disability and how disabled performance has rewritten (and, to promote more inclusive practices, must continue to rewrite) cultural scripts of music. These principles of disabled music performance are ubiquitous, constituting part of the expressive tension between codes of musical conformity and realities of bodily diversity that all performers (disabled or nondisabled) must negotiate.

Audible and Inaudible Disabilities

Some disabilities are external and exposed, and thus may immediately engulf a disabled person's public identity (hence, "Blind Tom" Wiggins or Paul Wittgenstein, the "One-Handed Pianist").[4] But many disabilities are not immediately evident, and thus part of their performative exchange involves the choices that a disabled person must make to conceal or reveal features of his or her body and the assumptions that an audience might make from these and other behavioral clues. To better distinguish between these two modes of performance, disability scholars and activists have traditionally classified disabilities as either *visible* or *invisible*.[5] Visible disabilities are public, usually evident from a feature of a person's appearance (e.g., body size and height, facial scars) or an assistive device (a hearing aid, wheelchair, cane, guide dog). Invisible or hidden disabilities are less evident, though they may later be revealed or exposed; examples may include persons with cognitive or mental impairments and disabled persons with discrete assistive devices (like a prosthetic limb or implant). Through their cultural mediation, disabilities can be visible or invisible in different contexts: for example, a motionless body conceals a mobility impairment, whereas a moving body might reveal one.

These terms ("visible disability," "invisible disability") invoke the sense of sight as a metaphor for awareness, but disabilities may be heard as well as seen—that is, their performance may be partly or even exclusively aural. Indeed, Disability Studies has encouraged us to appreciate the many senses involved in perception and, in acknowledgment of the diversity of ways people experience the world, taught us not to elevate one sensory domain over another. Some speech impediments, for instance, are visually concealed but audibly apparent; other disabilities, such as blindness, may be visually apparent but audibly concealed. Still other disabilities—like infertility or mental disorder—can be both invisible and inaudible. Finally, some disabilities are "audiovisual"—that is, they are performed in both sight and sound; for instance, persons with Down syndrome may perform their disability in this manner. As companion terms to "visible" and "invisible disabilities" (henceforth used exclusively to describe the ways in which disabilities are performed visually), the terms "audible" and "inaudible disabilities" will be used here to describe the ways in which disabilities might or might not signify through sound. As we will learn, the visibility and the audibility of a disability seldom align, producing interesting and revealing incongruities.[6]

		sight	
		visible disability	invisible disability
sound	audible disability	• one-hand pianist with missing arm • castrato	• one-hand pianist with focal dystonia • singer with vocal damage
	inaudible disability	• song signer • blind performer	• performer with mental disorder • singer with focal dystonia, or pianist with vocal damage

FIGURE 10.1 Musical performances of disability, revealed and concealed in sight and sound.

These new terms offer a helpful (if inadequately restrictive) vocabulary for thinking more precisely about musical performances of disability (Figure 10.1). Consider, for example, the different ways in which pianists Paul Wittgenstein and Gary Graffman have performed their one-handedness. Both musicians presented works from the left-hand-only piano repertoire and, in doing so, performed their disabilities aurally through music. But only Paul Wittgenstein's disability was visible: revealing his amputated right arm, Wittgenstein's famous "empty sleeve" directly faced the audience in performance. Gary Graffman's disability (focal dystonia, a neurological disorder affecting finger coordination in his right hand) may be audible during performances of the one-hand piano repertoire but otherwise invisible in most routine daily activities. This mode of performance may produce a strange and interesting aural–visual incongruity, as when Graffman, during performance, turns pages of a score with his right hand (demonstrating its ability visually) but then lowers his hand to his lap without returning to the keyboard (demonstrating its disability aurally through music). In this scenario, Graffman's music performance "sounds" his disability, which otherwise remains visually concealed. Indeed, the one-hand piano repertoire permits even two-hand pianists, despite their nondisabled visual appearance, to aurally disable themselves through music.[7]

Disabled singers, too, may perform their disabilities in sight and in sound; for example, a singer with vocal trauma usually performs as audibly but invisibly disabled. As Laurie Stras (2006) argues, a vocal: rough, raspy vocal timbre can communicate valuable information about a singer's age and experience separate from his or her visual appearance. In musical traditions like jazz and blues, the traumatized voice can be an important—even essential, even marketable—component of a performer's identity. Although youthful by his appearance, a twenty-year-old Bob Dylan actively cultivated such a world-weary voice, as Kevin J. Dettmar (2009) describes:

> Dylan from an early age boasted the voice of a seemingly old man—seemingly the very voice, to steal a phrase from Greil Marcus, of 'old, weird America.' In an era

> when pop (and even folk) stars were, as today, meant to sing like the nightingale, Dylan instead sang as the crow. But that croak, it seemed, contained a depth of feeling and passion and anger and joy and wisdom and disillusionment not hinted at by the songbirds; it came as a revelation. And it sounded like the voice of Truth. (1–2)

For admirers of the young Dylan, "depth of feeling" resided not in a youthful, able-bodied appearance but rather in the rough edges of a scratchy timbre. Dylan could not prematurely age or disfigure his body, but he could audibly perform the symptoms of vocal trauma.

The voice, then, is a medium in which invisible impairments may be performed (in an enabling or disabling manner) through sound. The castrati, by contrast, performed their disability in both domains: though the actual site of incision was concealed, its very public signifiers revealed themselves aurally (in extraordinary vocal ranges) and visually (in physical deformities, such as long limbs and fatty tissue in breasts and hips) (André 2006, 29). As the popularity of castrati waned, these aural and visual cues were derided and ridiculed, even enfreaked: "[The castrati] have the look of a crocodile, the grin of an ape, the legs of a peacock, the paunch of a cow, the shape of an elephant, the brains of a goose, the throat of a pig, and the tail of a mouse," says a character in an anonymous eighteenth-century satire. (Also, they smell of "onions and garlick.")[8] Of course, the extraordinary vocal virtuosity of the most successful castrati evidenced extreme able-bodiedness—and yet their sound (however prodigious) was also a public sign of genital disfigurement. The case of the castrati thus exemplifies an essential feature of disabled performance: the aural and visual codes of disability *link to* but may be *distinct from* the physical impairment itself. As with the virtuoso castrato's exemplary range, or with Dylan's scratchy timbre, the aural signifiers of disability might actually enable a performer's prodigiousness in certain cultural contexts.

Performance venue may also affect the exposure and concealment of disability. Concert or stage performances are primarily audiovisual experiences, whereas recorded performances are mostly perceived aurally. Recording booklets and promotional materials may supplement audio tracks with visual imagery—as they do for The Blind Boys of Alabama, who announce their disabilities in the very name of their ensemble and throughout their promotional materials. The associated visual codes of blindness thus affect the reception of even recorded performances of their work: listeners know that the performers are blind—indeed, may "see" their blindness in their mind's eye—even as it otherwise remains "inaudible." Bass-baritone Thomas Quasthoff often adopts a different strategy. Though his albums frequently feature his photographed face, rarely do those portraits reveal his physical differences; they are not only inaudible but also invisible in this medium.[9] Disabilities may also signify through the senses of touch and smell, but the distance between concert performer and audience usually excludes these modes of perception. For people who are both deaf and blind, more intimate modes of music performance offer accommodations. In a remarkable scene from the documentary *Touch the Sound: A Sound Journey with Evelyn Glennie* (2004), the Scottish percussionist gives a private performance to a deaf student, who turns her face away from the instruments and thus voluntarily restricts her sight. Glennie encourages the student to "feel" the music's vibrations with her whole body—ironically, a sense that a film audience can only imagine.

An anecdote from Jean-Jacques Rousseau's *Confessions* invokes many of these issues of visibility and audibility, concealment and disclosure. Attending performances by girl choirs in the Venetian *ospedali*, Rousseau lavishes praise on their musical performances: "I have no idea of anything as voluptuous, as touching as this music: the richness of the art, the exquisite taste of the songs, the beauty of the voices, the exactness of the performance, everything in these delightful concerts combines to produce an impression which is assuredly not suitable to the dignity of the place, but from which I doubt that any man's heart is safe" (Rousseau [1782] 1995, 264). Rousseau based this lustfulness on sound alone: as was customary for the sake of their modesty, the girl choir had been positioned behind an iron grate during public performances, their bodies concealed. As a listener, he nevertheless imagined these phantom voices as belonging to "angels," equating their musical beauty with physical beauty.

Jean Le Blond, the French consul in Venice, arranged an afternoon meeting between the curious critic and the mysterious performers ("whose voice and name were all I knew"):

> "Come, Sophie," . . . she was horrid looking. "Come, Cattina," . . . she had one eye missing. "Come, Bettina," . . . small pox had disfigured her. Virtually not a single one without some notable flaw. The Tormenter [Le Blond] laughed at my cruel surprise. Two or three, nevertheless appeared passable to me: they sang only in the chorus. I was disconsolate. During the snack they were teased, they became gay. Ugliness does not exclude graces; I found some in them. I said to myself, "One does not sing this way without a soul: they have them." Finally, my manner of seeing them changed so well that I left almost in love with all these ugly girls. (Rousseau [1782] 1995, 265)

The singers had performed their disabilities in the most concealed of ways—inaudibly and (because of their hidden location) invisibly. Rousseau's experience of their music is unproblematic to him until the performers are revealed, and the shock of aural–visual incongruity prompts an episode of self-reflection: why does disfigured appearance not translate into discordant sound? He succeeds, temporarily, in separating the two modes of performance from one another—but, upon attending a later performance, Rousseau revisits his paradox: "I continued to find their songs delightful, and their voices camouflaged their faces so well, that as long as they sang, I persisted in finding them beautiful in spite of my eyes." In his conclusion, then, Rousseau locates the choir's ugliness not in their appearance but in his visual perception of their appearance. They are not the problem; his eyes are.

Rousseau's rich narrative illuminates several important components of disabled music performance: the signification of disability through visual and aural clues (projected by the performer, then [mis]interpreted by the audience) and the juxtaposition of the extraordinary abilities required to perform music well (for Rousseau, this is audibly apparent) and the seemingly incompatible restrictions, restraints, and disfigurements imagined into bodily difference as disability (for Rousseau, this was visibly concealed but later revealed). As demonstrated here, this crucial oppositional pole (ability vs. disability) may signify differently in the competing sensory domains of sight and sound, and the resultant incongruities—the visibly youthful, audibly aged Bob Dylan, or Rousseau's visibly "ugly," audibly beautiful choir—have underpinned a wide range of critical responses, from enthrallment to bafflement to skepticism. For example, the travel writer Thomas Colley Grattan describes hearing the sounds of a distantly echoing flute ("of such peculiar and melting expression as I thought I had never before heard"), only to track its source to the Chevalier Anne-Toussaint Florent Rebsomen, a one-hand flutist performing on an adapted instrument: "Nothing could be more true, more tasteful, or more surprising than was his [musical] execution—nothing more picturesque or interesting than his figure" (Grattan 1822; Lancaster and Spohr 2008).[10] Similarly, reviewers of Paul Wittgenstein's American tour described how the pianist's one-hand appearance disrupted the multihanded sound he produced (Howe 2010). Reports on Blind Tom's performances contrasted his brutish body with his musical virtuosity and dexterity (Jensen-Moulton 2006). Related incongruities may also be found in the construction of the "idiot savant," whose idiocy signifies by seemingly irrational or feeble-minded behaviors and whose savantism signifies by prodigious musical performance (Straus 2014). Indeed, these inconsistent performances of an impairment—its tendency to signify differently in sound and sight—expose the constructed nature of the disabled body: disability is not a fixed, permanent condition but a mutable identity that performs its difference in different ways, in different cultural contexts, in different sensory domains.

Impairments and the Normal Performance Body

Just as curbs and stairways permit the movements of some bodies while disabling those of others, so do certain conventions of music performance have the power to include and exclude. These conventions, constituting a "constructed normalcy" of music performance, may audibly disable performers whose bodies do not conform.[11] For example, musical instruments and scores—plus performance practice, or the cultural expectation that they should be performed in a particular way—work together to imply the bodily shape of their intended performer. This *normal performance body* usually possesses all limbs, with above-average hand and finger size, lung capacity, and strength, among other qualities. Most violin designs imply a two-handed, two-armed, and multifingered performer with a flexible neck. Brass instruments similarly imply a one- or two-handed, multifingered performer, whose mouth is capable of forming a strong, airtight embouchure; tubists must also have the strength to lift their heavy instrument. The length of a vocal phrase in an aria implies the lung capacity of its intended singer, and a wide chord implies the hand size of its pianist. A conductor's baton implies the sightedness of its followers.[12] All of these features constitute the normal performance body, which, like all forms of constructed normalcy, establishes a template that real human bodies must strive to match. Performers who do not conform to this normal performance body (for instance, those with fewer hands, fewer fingers, weaker muscles, smaller lungs, or less vision than their instruments and scores require) have *performance impairments*. Without adequate accommodation, these impairments may musically disable a performer.

In such circumstances, the performances of disability and music are intertwined so as to become indistinguishable—indeed, music performance can amplify or even generate a disability that otherwise would have remained inaudible or unrealized. Many performance impairments are functionally neutral bodily features in most life activities. Amusia—a newly formed diagnostic category describing an inability to distinguish between pitches (i.e., tone deafness), acquired congenitally or from brain trauma—is a specifically musical disorder; it is profoundly disabling for some musicians but otherwise mostly irrelevant to a life outside of music. Similarly, focal dystonia—resulting in the loss of fine motor skills in a specific part of the body, often a finger—may affect the highly coordinated motions associated with piano performance but not with those associated with more mundane tasks, like opening a door. More broadly, small hands or fingers—usually unremarkable bodily features—may severely limit and even exclude participation in certain instrumental repertoires. Standardized piano keys, plus piano compositions with parallel octaves, plus cultural performance practices that require adherence to a score's demands, imply the span of a large hand; many hands, inevitably, will be too small. Notably, the normal performance body is much more regulated than other social forms of constructed normalcy: even the tiniest deviations—a sore knuckle, a swollen lip, mild sinus congestion, a shortened pinky—can audibly impair a body during music performance.

Those who do not fit such criteria may provocatively transgress these conventions or seek accommodations for them, or may decide against pursuing a professional career in a particular instrument or repertoire altogether. Most professional one-hand pianists of the twentieth century—Géza Zichy, Paul Wittgenstein, Cor de Groot, Leon Fleisher, Gary Graffman—launched their musical careers with two performing hands, until injury or illness forced the change of repertoire and technique; none began their piano training with one hand (Howe 2010, 137). One notable exception is Nicholas McCarthy, who graduated from the Royal College of Music in 2012. Born without a right hand, McCarthy began piano lessons at age fourteen, focusing almost exclusively on the one-hand repertoire commissioned and cultivated by earlier pianists—indicating, perhaps, that with a repertoire to support it, one-handedness is no longer as disabling for pianists as it once was.[13]

Without the regulatory mechanisms of a score, performers in unnotated performance traditions may have the option to freely shape their performance style around the specific features of their bodies. Alex Lubet, in his study of Horace Parlan (whose right hand has two playing fingers, an index finger and a pinky), observes how the jazz pianist's performance practice transforms his impairment into a musical asset:

> [Parlan's right-hand fingers appear] to be largely immobile, but positioned such that Parlan can maneuver them like xylophone mallets, by changing his arm position. His hands are quite large, such that he is able to play all-important octaves (as well as smaller spans) with these right-hand fingers. His unimpaired left hand is exceptionally facile. Much of the time he uses his left hand to play chords in the lower register in rapid alternation with melodies in midrange, adding harmonic voices in the right hand, which at times also contributes slower, more lyrical melodies, often in octaves. . . . The sound is obviously attainable by a pianist with a fully able right hand, but it has clearly never been so cultivated. (Lubet 2010, 52)

Though he would be disabled by the expectations of following all of the notated performance instructions in nearly all piano compositions in the classical canon, Parlan's hand impairments are not disabling during jazz performance; rather, he has been able to develop a successful performance technique that accommodates his extraordinary body. In his dual performances of disability and music, Parlan's disability thus directly informs essential aspects of his musical practice; the two cultural scripts are fused. As Garland-Thomson (2005) would argue, Parlan's pianism developed "not in spite of disability but because of disability" (524).

The stylistic diversity of notated music in the Western classical tradition also accommodates a wide variety of musical abilities and impairments. Singers unable to perform coloratura are not audibly disabled by the Queen of the Night; there are other roles and arias available. Nor are tenors disabled by the bass-baritone repertoire—they have their own music. Similarly, pianists with fingers best equipped for nimble contrapuntal music are not disabled by the dense, thick music of Prokofiev; there is plenty of music by J. S. Bach to choose from. These imagined complaints are absurd, of course, but they reinforce a crucial point about the constructed nature of musical disabilities: with sufficient accommodation (in the form of repertoire, instrument design, and social expectations of an audience), stigmas attached to bodily difference may be neutralized, even reversed.[14] Musical inabilities (for instance, the inability of a tenor to sing bass-baritone) exist on a continuum with disabilities. Both stem from performance impairments, from the mismatch of a performer's body with the normal performance body implied by a performance practice—but inabilities are contained within communities of performers already supported by comfortable instruments and appropriate repertoire and friendly social audiences. Musical disabilities, instead, entail a more profound exclusion from communities of performance, with inadequate accommodational support. Such is the constructed nature of disability that some performance impairments are accommodated while others are not.

Perhaps times are changing. Several promising developments in instrument construction reflect surging interest in new accommodational technologies. This stems from the universal design movement in engineering, architecture, and design studies that seeks to create accessible spaces and devices to better reflect the diversity of human bodies (Steinfeld and Maisel 2012). For example, in the One-Handed Woodwind Program at the University of Nebraska, Kearney, Jeff Stelling designs instruments with a "toggle-key system," so that one-hand performers can depress multiple keys with fewer fingers. (Saxophonist David Nabb founded the program in 2000, after he survived a stroke that impaired his left hand.) And the piano builder Steinbuhler is actively marketing a new piano construction that accommodates keyboards of different sizes. The length of an octave on a standard keyboard is 6.5 inches; Steinbuhler's new replacement keyboards with narrower sizes measure their octaves at 5.54 and 6 inches. ("Goldilocks had a choice" is their advertising slogan.) Similarly, pianist Christopher Seed commissioned a "left-handed piano," in which bass and treble registers are reversed. Seed, like his piano, is left-handed, and he found that with this "mirror-image" piano he can "now play more of the melodic and elaborate parts [of music] with his dominant hand"—a mode of performance that he finds more "instinctive." Finally, the One-Handed Musical Instrument (OHMI) Trust sponsors a competition for the best design of a one-hand electronic version of a familiar instrument, with the goal of inviting musicians with performance impairments to use the winning instrument in orchestral performances. Standardized instrument constructions visually conceal the diverse bodies of their performers, whose impairments (judged against the normal performance body) are made audible by poor musical execution. But these and other accommodational instruments—their designs sometimes unfamiliar, sometimes uncanny—reveal bodily difference through the spectacle of unusual performance technique while simultaneously seeking to normalize (and silence) bodily difference through sound.[15]

Such accommodations—suggesting a future of profound instrument diversity—raise perplexing questions over the nature of fairness—the so-called "level playing field" that grants persons with diverse bodies and diverse backgrounds equal opportunities to succeed. In many situations, music performance is a mode of competition—performers auditioning against other performers for awards, scholarships, and employment; and many performers competing with rivals (live or recorded) for critical prestige and audience favor. Consider, again, the Steinbuhler piano with narrow keys. May a pianist with small hands use this keyboard to more easily perform the extreme stretches in a virtuoso work of Rachmaninov? And how might such a performance "compete" with a more strained performance of the same work on conventional (wider) keys? These types of questions have been weighed and considered before—in athletics, where bodies conforming to a predetermined type are similarly pitted against each other in direct competition. Critics, ethicists, and lawyers have raised concerns over runner Oscar Pistorius's prosthetic legs (do they unfairly allow him to run faster than a legged athlete?), golfer Casey Martin's golf cart (does he unfairly avoid the stress and fatigue of walking?), and runner Caster Semenya's sex (would she more fairly compete against women or men?).[16] Accommodations and prostheses, musical or athletic, may allow disabled performers to participate in competitions essential to their fields; but those accommodations also diversify the human body beyond previously accepted (or acknowledged) norms.

An ideology of accommodation is discomforting to what Siebers (2008) terms the "ideology of ability," defined broadly as a set of societal practices and beliefs that "describe disability as what we flee in the past and hope to defeat in the future" (8–9). Both athletic and music performances frequently enact this narrative: they display extraordinary, superhuman bodies—supremely able-bodied bodies, with prodigious capabilities beyond those of most audience members—and challenge them to feats of strength (or dexterity, coordination, musicality, finesse). A performer who emerges triumphant has perfected his or her body's abilities to meet the challenge. But accommodational devices disrupt this comforting narrative: they may artificially deflate an accomplishment by seeming to decrease the difficulty of the challenge (a performance of Rachmaninov on a narrow keyboard, for instance)—or artificially inflate the accomplishment by seeming to increase the difficulty of the challenge (as on a one-hand woodwind instrument). For a social audience, accommodated performance becomes less about the achievements of the human body and more about the prosthetic and the mobility impairment it addresses; without the basic template of the unadorned human body (the *normal performance body*, implied by instruments, scores, and culturally accepted performance practices), objective evaluation of the physical accomplishments of performance is difficult, maybe even impossible.

But other variations of a performer's body and instrument have long been tolerated. Many assistive technologies have no stigma attached to them, including piano benches with adjustable height, shoulder pads for violinists and violists, shortened stop lengths on a cello—even the use of music notation might be counted as another assistive technology, one that prostheticizes a defective memory (and that sometimes requires yet another assistant—the page turner—to operate). The accommodational ideology of these devices is little different from that of devices supporting a disabled performer. As feminist and disability scholars have argued in their profound critique of autonomy, no one—and certainly no musician—is independently able-bodied; rather, we all rely on assistance (from devices, from helpers) to succeed (Fineman 2004; O'Brien 2005). Like the blurry distinctions between inability and disability, described earlier, accepted musical accommodations and forbidden musical accommodations lie along a continuum; their rigid separation is entirely artificial and culturally determined. Performance impairments, in other words, only signify as audible disabilities when a confluence of normalizing conventions—uniform instrument design, unaccommodational scores, and rigid social ideology—align to brand them as such.

Disablist Music

As we have seen, many traditions of Western classical music are severely, punishingly conformational: their scores demand bodies of a particular size and shape; their instruments can be managed by some bodies, but not by others. Even more exacting are large ensembles like the orchestra or choir, which strive for timbral coherence and uniformity. Many adaptive instrument designs seek to accommodate a particular performance impairment by suppressing any traces of an aural disability. But here, too, the underlying ideology is conformational: even as adaptive instruments might appear strange and abnormal, even as their performance techniques might radically diverge from tradition, their sound still strives to match that of the nonadaptive model. To participate in an ensemble, to participate in a conformational musical tradition, the excluded performer must silence disability.

There is nothing wrong with these accommodational instruments, of course, but a strategy of aural normalization can only be so inclusive: many bodies are excluded from the world of music performance in more profound ways, not easily fixed with musical prosthetics. As a counterexample, consider the case of professional trumpeter Clarence Adoo, who, after a debilitating accident in 1995, lost control of his body below the shoulders. For him, composer and inventor Rolf Gehlhaar developed headspace, an electronic "wind" instrument operated by a breathing tube (to produce sound) and a headset-controlled computer (to manipulate pitch and other variables).[17] Composer John Kenny explains Adoo's performance technique:

> He'll stare at the screen, which shows four miniature keyboards, each key being about the width of a matchstick. . . . He will have a 'third eye' in the form of an electronic beam in the centre of his forehead, which he'll project on to a mouse-cursor for those keyboards. He will also have a drinking straw fixed in the mouthpiece of a smoker's pipe, through which he will direct streams of air that will dictate rhythm, volume and sound duration. In other words, with his eyes he will select the type of sound, and with his head he will select everything else a trumpeter would normally do with his instrument. (Church 2006)

Headspace's breathing tube resembles a mouthpiece—just one of the ways in which Gehlhaar designed the instrument to capitalize on Adoo's nondisabled performance experience. But headspace is no trumpet, nor would it aurally pass as one in any orchestra's brass section. Instead, Adoo has performed in nontraditional ensembles that showcase and valorize headspace's extraordinary timbre and sonic diversity, including the Headspace Ensemble (for which composers like Kenny have written new works designed specifically for the instrument), and, more prominently, the British Paraorchestra.

Musically analogous to the Paralympics, the Paraorchestra is an example of the rare ensemble that welcomes prodigious disabled performers and actively incorporates their diverse performance styles.[18] Its members include disabled musicians performing on traditional or adaptive instruments (including Nicholas McCarthy, the aforementioned pianist, as well as many blind musicians, usually excluded from orchestras by the conductor's baton) and disabled musicians on nontraditional instruments (including not just Adoo but also Lyn Levett, who performs on a touchscreen computer with her nose).

Together, these musicians perform newly composed works, arrangements, and improvisations, creating a space for ensemble performance previously unavailable to many disabled musicians.

In a lecture, the ensemble's founder and director Charles Hazlewood links biases against disabled performers to earlier prejudices:

> If you took a look at all of the great orchestras of the world [in the 1960s], how many women do you think you would find? The answer: virtually none. Well, here we are fifty years on in 2011, and pretty much every orchestra on the planet has a fantastic and healthy balance of the sexes. . . . But how about another aspect of the community—the disabled community? Do we find them well represented in the great orchestras of our world? . . . You can't tell me that there aren't millions upon millions of prodigiously gifted musicians of disability around the world. Where is their platform? Where is the infrastructure that creates a space for them so that they can collaborate with other great musicians? (Hazlewood 2011)

Comparing the struggles of disabled performers with those of women performers is provocative, but the prejudices they face are quite different. A visibly gendered instrumentalist aurally produces music that is gender neutral. But orchestras—executing musical scripts of uniform able-bodiedness—are fundamentally intolerant of disabilities that might aurally disrupt their sonic cohesiveness. By including instruments like Adoo's headspace, the British Paraorchestra instead places cultural value in precisely this type of sonic and corporeal diversity.

The Paraorchestra never escapes music's innate conformational bias; its membership excludes able-bodied musicians, and auditions limit its ranks to only prodigious performers. No single musical practice will be all-inclusive to all disabilities, to all skillsets, at all times: human morphology is too diverse and music performance too restrictive. As a trained skill, music performance demonstrates what a performer *can do*—so that the performer, traversing a critical threshold that defines successful performance, inevitably leaves behind a group of others physically unable to meet those standards. Even the most inclusive musical practices will never dissolve these thresholds; to do so would render music unintelligible and achievement meaningless. Hazlewood's goal, instead, is to construct new "infrastructure"—new ensembles, new instruments, new repertoires, all implying new and diverse performance bodies that take their place alongside the normal performance body. A tenor (to expand on an earlier argument) is not disabled by the bass-baritone repertoire; he has his own arias to sing. Likewise, we might imagine a time in which Adoo's headspace, supported by a substantial repertoire and accommodational ensembles, achieves parity with more familiar instruments like the trumpet.

The British Paraorchestra is a prominent contemporary example of *disablist music*—that is, a musical practice that rejects the normal performance body and instead molds its performance practices around the impairments of its performers.[19] Rather than concealing or silencing a disability, disablist music audibilizes disability—asserts disability, even claims disability as a fundamental component of its sonic identity.[20]

Entire repertoires might be disablist, such as the arias written for the castrati, or the one-hand piano music commissioned by Paul Wittgenstein. Or disablist music might be contained within a much larger work: for example, Mendelssohn's *Die Heimkehr aus der Fremde* (1829), in which the character of Schulz—played by Mendelssohn's tone-deaf brother-in-law—sings only one repeated pitch (Todd 2010, 140–41). Notably, it is rare for composers to write disablist music without an intended performer already in mind: such is the nature of music's constructed normalcy that, absent a specifically marked body for whom they choose to write, composers tend to otherwise imply—and reconstruct, and reinforce—the prototypical normal performance body.

Other examples of disablist music include musicians whose performance style is directly informed by their musically impaired bodies: not only Bob Dylan and Horace Parlan (mentioned above), but also Django Reinhardt, Joni Mitchell, and Derek Bailey.[21] Centuries earlier, Charles Burney observed aspects of disablist performance and composition in his overview of J. C. Bach for the *General History of Music*; here, the composer is also the intended performer, so Bach's music is intimately tuned to his own changing bodily state:

> When [J. C. Bach] arrived in England, his style of playing was so much admired, that he recovered many of the losses his hand had sustained by disuse, and by being constantly cramped and crippled with a pen; but he never was able to reinstate it with force and readiness sufficient for great difficulties; and in general his compositions for piano forte are such as ladies can execute with little trouble; and the allegros rather resemble bravura songs, than instrumental pieces for the display of great execution. On which account, they lose much of their effect when played without the accompaniments, which are admirable, and so masterly and interesting to an audience, that want of hand, or complication in the harpsichord part, is never discovered. [. . .] In the sonatas and concertos which he composed for his own playing, when his hand was feeble, or likely to tire, he diverted the attention of the audience to some other instrument; and he had Abel, Fischer, Cramer, Crosdil, Cervetto, and other excellent musicians to write for [in the ensemble], and take his part, whenever he wanted support. (Burney 1776, 4:482–83)

Bach performed his disability invisibly yet audibly: indeed, Burney seems to frame Bach's concealed hand impairment as the impetus for stylistic innovation—for instance, "bravura songs" instead of the standard virtuoso instrumental allegros. In Bach's "dual performance" of music and disability, his music narrates a tale of a marginalized body adequately accommodated: in chamber and orchestral works, other instrumentalists—Bach's friends and colleagues—assist the performer in his infirmity, compensating for his physical weakness, limiting his risk of strain or stress, and reenacting the accommodational impulse that gave initial rise to the music's very conception.[22]

As with J. C. Bach's late music, Paul Wittgenstein's one-hand piano arrangements of famous two-hand works also use a musical discourse to rewrite cultural scripts of disability. These arrangements are emphatically not simple "Classics Made Easy" reductions of difficult two-hand music. Instead, as with any form of translation, Wittgenstein's one-hand adaptations and paraphrases offer new interpretations—in this case, new disablist readings—of their primary text.[23] Consider, for instance, the ways in which Wittgenstein reworks an emotionally climactic measure in Mendelssohn's *Lieder ohne Worte*, Op. 19, No. 1 (see Figure 10.2): rapidly leaping between registral extremes of the piano lends Mendelssohn's music a sense of physically athletic intensity and audacity, amplifying its expressive power. (In m. 14, Wittgenstein plays E and F♯ with fingers 2 and 3, preparing the hand to leap to a high D♯ with finger 1. But he withholds this pitch, preventing an easy approach to the climactic note. Instead, the left hand must rush down several octaves to play a bass A♯, only then leaping upward to complete the melody.) Wittgenstein does not conceal his disability here; rather, he uses his one-handedness to create an exhilarating disablist reading of Mendelssohn's text.

Even more subversive is Wittgenstein's arrangement of Schumann's *Der Dichter spricht* (*Kinderszenen*, no. 13). The form of Schumann's work (ABA') contains a near-exact repetition of the opening musical material at the end of the work; these outer sections (A) bracket a middle section of instrumental recitative for a lone melodic line (B). Wittgenstein's performance clearly struggles in the opening A section (Figure 10.3a): deleting few of Schumann's original notes, Wittgenstein outmatches and disables his own impairment, purposely choreographing the performance of his hand to sound disjointed and confused. But in the B section (Figure 10.3b), the performance undergoes a remarkable change in character: the difficulty and awkwardness of the opening passage vanishes as Schumann's slimmer musical texture better accommodates his disability. In the return of the A section (Figure 10.3c), Wittgenstein recomposes Schumann's chords, moving the bass up an octave so that only minimal stretch is required. As the arrangement assumes a more disablist character, Wittgenstein's revision of Schumann's conclusion (formerly non-idiomatic to one-hand performance) suggests a narrative

FIGURE 10.2 Wittgenstein's arrangement of Mendelssohn's *Lieder ohne Worte*, Op. 19, No. 1, mm. 13–15. Transcribed by Blake Howe. Reprinted with permission from The Octavian Society. All rights reserved.

FIGURE 10.3 Wittgenstein's arrangement of Schumann's *Der Dichter spricht* (*Kinderszenen*, no. 13): (a) the A section, musically broken and disabled, mm. 1–6; (b) the B section, idiomatic to one-hand performance in Schumann's original, mm. 11–14; (c) the return of the A section, now successfully accommodating Wittgenstein's disability, mm. 14–19. Transcribed by Blake Howe. Reprinted with permission from The Octavian Society. All rights reserved.

of musical recuperation through accommodation. The opening A section implausibly asks the one-handed performer to perform as two-handed, creating a stark divide between what the score demands and what the performer can provide; but the concluding A section has been tailored to the performer's body, offering Wittgenstein a more natural, more comfortable medium for musical expressivity. In the opening A section, music creates the disability; but in the concluding A section, disability creates the music.

This example thus demonstrates many of the interrelated facets of disabled performance discussed in this chapter, including the malleability of concealment and exposure in the audiovisual medium of performance, the normalizing mechanisms of performance practice and the role of accommodation in subverting them, and the space that disablist composition creates for a more authentic, more transparent aural performance of disabled identity, expressed outside the punishing ideology of the normal performance body. Further we have seen here and elsewhere how the dual performance of disability and music are intertwined—how, in other words, disability may be performed through music and music through disability.

Acknowledgments

I thank the many people who read and commented on earlier drafts of this essay, including my coauthors in this volume Floyd Grave, Stephanie Jensen-Moulton, Shersten Johnson, Neil Lerner, Elaine Sisman, and Joseph Straus; students in Andrew Dell'Antonio's disability seminar at University of Texas, Austin (spring 2014); and students in my Music and Disability Studies seminar at Louisiana State University (fall 2013). My thoughts on Paul Wittgenstein's performance practice are deeply indebted to pianist Jamie Gurt, with whom I presented some of this material in a lecture-recital at the meeting of the American Musicological Society in New Orleans (2012). I am also grateful to Zachary Hazelwood for creating my musical examples.

Notes

1. Tobin Siebers (2008) describes the social performance of disability as a "masquerade," which "fulfills the desire to tell a story steeped in disability, often the very story that society does not want to hear" (118).
2. Rosemarie Garland-Thomson (2009) describes this relationship in terms of the "starer" and "staree" (her coinage, suggesting that the recipient of a stare is not a passive object but may instead actively shape the relationship with an observer).
3. Or, as Petra Kuppers (2003) explains, "When disabled people perform, they are often not primarily seen as performers, but as disabled people. The disabled body is *naturally* about disability" (49–50).
4. I borrow the term "engulfment" from Rosemarie Garland-Thomson (1997, 10–11). On "Blind Tom" Wiggins, refer to Jensen-Moulton 2006 and Straus 2011, 132–135, and on Paul Wittgenstein, refer to Howe 2010.
5. For a self-narrative of the performance of an invisible disability, refer to Samuels 2013.
6. Of course, there are many degrees of variation between these four categories, and, depending on its mode of performance, a disability may be partially visible (a faint scar) or barely audible (a subtle lisp).
7. For more on one-hand piano performance, refer to Lerner 2006, Howe 2010, and Sassmann 2010. My article briefly introduces some of the ideas that are developed in greater detail in this essay.
8. *The Remarkable Trial of the Queen of Quavers and Her Associates . . .* (c. 1777), quoted in Feldman 2008, 184. The term "enfreakment" originated with Hevey 1992, 53–74. On the enfreakment of castrati, see Hedy Law's essay in this volume.
9. For more on Quasthoff from a Disability Studies perspective, refer to Straus 2011, 138–142.

10. I am grateful to Ashley Kelly, graduate student in saxophone performance at Louisiana State University, for bringing Rebsomen's career to my attention.
11. On "constructed normalcy" as it relates to disability, refer to Davis 1995, 23–49.
12. Notably, there are many examples of blind soloists throughout music history—the blind virtuoso organist, the blind bluesman, the blind bard, the blind street musician—but very few precedents for blind musicians in sighted choirs and orchestras. However, as Ingrid Sykes's essay in this volume demonstrates, musical ensembles of blind musicians have played an important role in institutions for the blind since the nineteenth century.
13. For extensive catalogs of one-hand piano music, refer to Edel 1994, Patterson 1999, and Sassmann 2010.
14. Similarly extreme scenarios are offered by Tom Shakespeare (2013) in his critique of the social model of disability: "Numerous parts of the natural world will remain inaccessible to many disabled people: mountains, bogs, beaches are almost impossible for wheelchair users to traverse, while sunsets, birdsong, and other aspects of nature are difficult for those lacking sight or hearing to experience" (219). But no one conceives of a world—and certainly no one conceives of a musical world—in which everyone is able to do everything all the time. This confuses *inability* with *disability*.
15. For more information on these technologies, consult the websites of the One-Handed Woodwinds Program, at the University of Nebraska, Kearney (http://onehandwinds.unk.edu); Steinbuhler & Company (http://www.steinbuhler.com/); The First Left-Handed Piano (http://www.lefthandedpiano.com/); The OHMI Trust (http://www.ohmi.org.uk/). Also relevant to this discussion are Rick Allen, drummer for Def Leppard, who has used various adaptive drum sets following the amputation of his left arm, and an extraordinary nineteenth-century precedent for these modern adaptive instruments: Rebsomen's one-hand flute (Lancaster and Spohr 2008).
16. For more information, refer to Thomas and Smith 2009 and Laurie Stras's chapter in this volume.
17. Refer to *Rolf Gehlhaar: HEAD-SPACE* (http://www.gehlhaar.org/x/pages/headspace.htm); and *Clarence: Official Website for Musician Clarence Adoo, MBE* (http://www.clarence.org.uk/headspace.html).
18. For more on the reception of the Paraorchestra, refer to Laurie Stras's essay in this volume.
19. The term "disablist" is here used in an affirmative sense, assigning agency and meaning to a disability within a composition; this usage parallels the term "disablist listening" in Straus 2011, 160.
20. Simi Linton (1998) argues for "claiming disability" as a fundamental component of identity.
21. For more on Reinhardt's performance technique, refer to Givan 2010.
22. This description of J. C. Bach's late piano music exemplifies the argument in Straus 2008 that an artistic "late style" is informed by a composer's embodied experience of disability. A similar argument could be made for the late style of Derek Bailey, informed by his experience of carpal tunnel syndrome.
23. Most of Wittgenstein's arrangements were auctioned by Sotheby's in 2003 and are now in the possession of a private collector in Hong Kong. For more on Wittgenstein's arrangements (with explanations of his strange notational practice), refer to Howe 2010 and Suchy, Janik, and Predota 2006.

References

André, Naomi. 2006. *Voicing Gender: Castrati, Travesti, and the Second Woman in Early Nineteenth-Century Italian Opera*. Indianapolis and Bloomington: Indiana University Press.

Burney, Charles. 1776. *A General History of Music from the Earliest Ages to the Present Period*. London.

Church, Michael. 2006. "Preview: Headspace, The Sage, Gateshead." *Independent*, 7 February. http://www.independent.co.uk/arts-entertainment/music/features/preview-headspace-the-sage-gateshead-525572.html.

Davis, Lennard. 1995. *Enforcing Normalcy: Disability, Deafness, and the Body*. London: Verso.

Dettmar, Kevin J. H. 2009. Introduction to *The Cambridge Companion to Bob Dylan*, edited by Kevin J. H. Dettmar, 1–14. Cambridge, UK: Cambridge University Press.

Edel, Theodore. 1994. *Piano Music for One Hand*. Bloomington and Indiana: Indiana University Press.

Feldman, Martha. 2008. "Denaturing the Castrato." *Opera Quarterly* 24: 178–199.

Fineman, Martha Albertson. 2004. *The Autonomy Myth: A Theory of Dependency*. New York: New Press.

Garland-Thomson, Rosemarie. 1997. *Extraordinary Bodies: Figuring Physical Disability in American Culture and Literature*. New York: Columbia University Press.

Garland-Thomson, Rosemarie. 2005. "Disability and Representation." *PMLA* 120 (2): 522–527.

Garland-Thomson, Rosemarie. 2009. *Staring: How We Look*. Oxford and New York: Oxford University Press.

Givan, Benjamin. 2010. *The Music of Django Reinhardt*. Ann Arbor: University of Michigan Press.

Grattan, Thomas Colley. 1822. "The One-Handed Flute-Player of Arques, in Normandy." *New Monthly Magazine and Literary Journal* 4 (July–December): 369–372.

Hazlewood, Charles. 2011. "Music of the Future: Charles Hazlewood and the British Paraorchestra." Lecture at TEDxBrussels. YouTube video, 13:43. December 1. http://www.youtube.com/watch?v=FsGu5YTM1NI.

Hevey, David. 1992. *The Creatures Time Forgot: Photography and Disability Imagery*. London and New York: Routledge.

Howe, Blake. 2010. "Paul Wittgenstein and the Performance of Disability." *Journal of Musicology* 27: 135–180.

Jensen-Moulton, Stephanie. 2006. "Finding Autism in the Compositions of a 19th-Century Prodigy: Reconsidering 'Blind Tom' Wiggins." In *Sounding Off: Theorizing Disability in Music*, edited by Neil Lerner and Joseph N. Straus, 199–216. New York and London: Routledge.

Kuppers, Petra. 2003. *Disability and Contemporary Performance: Bodies on Edge*. Abingdon, UK, and New York: Routledge.

Lancaster, Jan, and Peter Spohr. 2008. "The Extraordinary Chevalier Rebsomen." *Pan: The Journal of the British Flute Society* 27: 35–41.

Lerner, Neil. 2006. "The Horrors of One-Handed Pianism: Music and Disability in *The Beast with Five Fingers*." In *Sounding Off: Theorizing Disability in Music*, edited by Neil Lerner and Joseph N. Straus, 75–89. New York and London: Routledge.

Linton, Simi. 1998. *Claiming Disability: Knowledge and Identity*. New York and London: New York University Press.

Lubet, Alex. 2010. *Music, Disability, and Society*. Philadelphia, PA: Temple University Press.

O'Brien, Ruth. 2005. *Bodies in Revolt: Gender, Disability, and a Workplace Ethic of Care.* New York: Routledge.

Patterson, Donald L. 1999. *One Handed: A Guide to Piano Music for One Hand.* Westport, CT, and London: Greenwood Press.

Rousseau, Jean-Jacques. (1782) 1995. *"The Confessions" and Correspondence, Including the Letters to Malesherbes.* Edited by Christopher Kelly, Roger D. Masters, and Peter G. Stillman. Translated by Christopher Kelly. Hanover, NH, and London: University Press of New England.

Samuels, Ellen. 2013. "My Body, My Closet: Invisible Disability and the Limits of Coming Out." In *The Disability Studies Reader*, 4th ed., edited by Lennard J. Davis, 316–332. New York and London: Routledge.

Sandahl, Carrie, and Philip Auslander, eds. 2005. *Bodies in Commotion: Disability and Performance.* Ann Arbor: University of Michigan Press.

Sassmann, Albert. 2010. *"In der Beschränkung zeigt sich erst der Meister": Technik und Ästhetik der Klaviermusik für die linke Hand allein.* Tutzing, Germany: Hans Schneider.

Shakespeare, Tom. 2013. "The Social Model of Disability." In *The Disability Studies Reader*, 4th ed., edited by Lennard J. Davis, 214–221. New York and London: Routledge.

Siebers, Tobin. 2008. *Disability Theory.* Ann Arbor: University of Michigan Press.

Steinfeld, Edward, and Jordana Maisel. 2012. *Universal Design: Designing Inclusive Environments.* Hoboken, NJ: John Wiley & Sons.

Stras, Laurie. 2006. "The Organ of the Soul: Voice, Damage, and Affect." In *Sounding Off: Theorizing Disability in Music*, edited by Neil Lerner and Joseph N. Straus, 173–184. New York and London: Routledge.

Straus, Joseph N. 2008. "Disability and 'Late Style' in Music." *Journal of Musicology* 25: 3–45.

Straus, Joseph N. 2011. *Extraordinary Measures: Disability in Music.* Oxford and New York: Oxford University Press.

Straus, Joseph N. 2014. "Idiots Savants, Retarded Savants, Talented Aments, Mono-Savants, Autistic Savants, Just Plain Savants, People with Savant Syndrome, and Autistic People Who Are Good at Things: A View from Disability Studies." *Disability Studies Quarterly* 34 (3). http://dsq-sds.org/article/view/3407/3640.

Suchy, Irene, Allan Janik, and Georg A. Predota, eds. 2006. *Empty Sleeve: Der Musiker und Mäzen Paul Wittgenstein.* Innsbruck, Austria: Studien-Verlag.

Thomas, Nigel, and Andy Smith. 2009. *Disability, Sport, and Society: An Introduction.* Abingdon, UK, and New York: Routledge.

Todd, R. Larry. 2010. *Fanny Hensel: The Other Mendelssohn.* Oxford, UK, and New York: Oxford University Press.

CHAPTER 11

MUSICAL AND BODILY DIFFERENCE IN CIRQUE DU SOLEIL

STEPHANIE JENSEN-MOULTON

FROM my seat, I can see the parade begin. At stage left, an array of peculiarly costumed individuals emerges through a doorway; the line of characters snakes its way through the theatre for all to examine. To the tune of a squeaky, synthesized accordion, the long-nosed, bug-like creature and the androgynous clowns, the hunched and limping strong man, and the leaping, blue-haired ballerina have all emerged from the asylum of backstage in order to step into this line-up of difference. The audience has paid handsomely to see and hear the spectacle, and the extraordinary bodies that have just passed by will undoubtedly deliver a performance worthy of its price.

The scene described above bears resemblance to the opening of traditional circus performances, wherein all of the lead performers and some of the side-show "freaks"—a term that bears significant meaning in Disability Studies—parade before the audience as a tantalizing appetizer to the entrée that is the show itself. Of American sideshow spectators, Rachel Adams (2001, 228) writes, "Often those who hope to see the freakishness of others are unsettled to feel a shock of recognition as the bodies onstage remind them of their own tenuous grasp on normality." The nouveau circus troupe and multinational corporation Cirque du Soleil runs nineteen shows internationally; yet freakery and bodily difference serve as unifying artistic aesthetics throughout these productions.[1] A crucial and often overlooked element that also makes a Cirque du Soleil show unique is its music: for each show, this circus troupe has a fully composed score that is then sold as a soundtrack, a practice that would be more typical in the realm of film music.

This essay explores two of Cirque du Soleil's most overtly commercial ventures, its Disney production *La Nouba* (running since 1998) and its film compilation *Worlds Away* (2012), linking them through the aesthetic of the freak show and the concept of musical multiplicity (Slobin 2007, 108–116). Musically, the freak show finds its counterpart in the Cirque's rampant appropriation and tactics of erasing race and nationality, which include extensive use of combined world musics and the Cirque's own brand of squeaky-clean hip-hop. These musical erasures normalize the audience in the same way that extraordinary bodies reinforce bodily normativity at the midway freak show. In addition, the use of both popular and world musics in their soundtracks might help to explain why the nouveau circus troupe performs to sold-out houses nightly across the globe.[2] Yet the productions examined here also unite extraordinary bodies[3]—bodies outside of the realm of normative human experience—with music that is also likely to be outside of the audience member's listening experience. The music itself becomes an extraordinary body, commanding a kind of aural equivalent of staring. Cirque du Soleil's productions are replete with contradictions and boundary-crossing transgressions at every level, from the choreography to the composed soundtrack. A Cirque character or piece of music is rarely a single entity but a multiplicity of cultural ideologies that push against one another at an ever-increasing speed as the show continues. By the end of any one Cirque experience, an audience member's saturation with the extraordinary leaves her feeling normative by virtue of exclusion, both in body and mind. Paradoxically, if the audience finds the bodies onstage extraordinary and/or the music exotic, the titillating thrill of the event has been a total success and those in attendance have been normalized.

Cirque du Soleil's current productions both embrace and reject the company's origins as a *Québecois* circus troupe. The original score for *La Nouba*, written by French Canadian composer Benoit Jutras, reflects this ambivalence by both using and rejecting musical elements that would associate the work with French Canada. Jennifer Harvie and Erin Hurley (1999, 300) assert that

> *Cirque du Soleil* originate[s] in . . . a nation without a state whose representatives exhibit profound ambivalence toward their place (within the Dominion of Canada). . . . *Cirque du Soleil* is a circus without stars; its multiple circus troupes present their touring shows organized from multinational headquarters in their own circus tents. [Cirque's] differences permit us to consider some of the varieties of Québecois international performance, in particular its relationships to locations and finance, as well as the nation.

Because of Québec's unique linguistic and cultural aspects, it has always already represented Canada's Other province. Wishing to recognize Cirque as a Québecois entity, the government of the province donated millions to the Cirque's campaign to build an international headquarters in one of Montréal's formerly industrial sectors. Yet the Cirque itself does not actually view Montréal, or even Canada, as its home. According to the official website, part of the Cirque's quest is for place; it is a "circus that came from nowhere but was looking for its roots. In the absence of any, it determined to create some." As well, the first visible image on the website, shown in Figure 11.1, that of a white face painted with six of the seven global continents (Antarctica would be under the chin), reinforces the troupe's desired multinationality, yet pushes against it through the implied white privilege of the make-up's bearer.

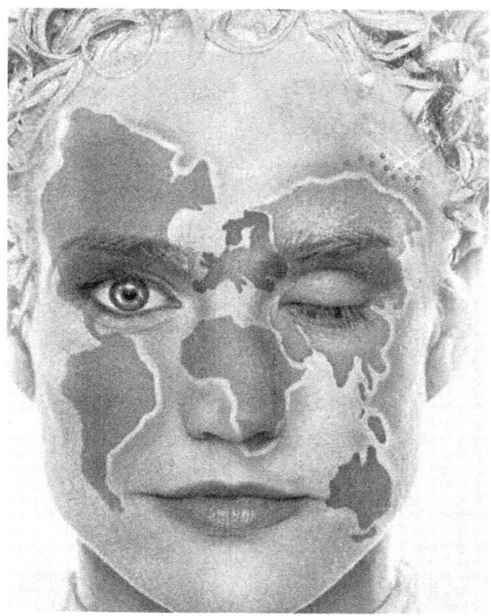

FIGURE 11.1 White face painted with six of the seven global continents opens the Cirque du Soleil website.

Part of the Cirque's international success is a result of the company's desire to denationalize the shows it produces. From a group of street performers, Cirque du Soleil has evolved into a corporation that creates sleek, internationally acclaimed performances with high ticket prices and brisk sales. French culture has espoused street performers, *jongleurs* or jugglers in particular, since medieval times;[4] Cirque's actual origins as a group of *jongleurs* has gradually changed its identity and scale from the French diasporic circus group it once was to the massive, nationally neutral productions available to audiences now. "The 'nowhere' that is Québec for the *Cirque* provides that company with an empty space that allows them to create their own aesthetic form" (Harvie and Hurley 1999, 299). A further illustration of Cirque du Soleil's ideological separation from its surroundings is the troupe's use of specially designed circus tent arenas. The Cirque builds an outpost of its "imagi-nation"—its own specially designed megatent—in which only the imaginary of the nonnational exists.

This ideal of a specific Cirque nation within the imaginary has broad implications for the bodies that move within that nation-space. The human body that inhabits and works within a piece of Cirque art becomes a function of human geography, mapped onto the imagi-nation. The built environment constructs meaning onto these bodies, creating an other-world inhabited by what Paul Longmore (quoted in Auslander and Sandahl 2005, 33) has called the "severely ablebodied." These extreme normates[5] would seem to undergo a troubling evolution from sideshow freaks to supercrips—people with disabilities who perform certain activities with extreme ability or virtuosity—as they take the stage in *La Nouba*, while in *Worlds Away*, these groups never comingle but are segregated by the geography of the set. As Michel Foucault (1977, 148) notes, "spaces . . . provide fixed positions and permit circulation; they carve out individual segments and establish operational links; they mark places and indicate values; they guarantee the obedience of individuals, but also a better economy of time and gesture." Likewise, the "geography of these facilities mobilize the discipline and governance of disabled bodies. The real and ideal spaces that these built structures contain are architectural, functional, and hierarchical" (Anderson 2005, 245). This "economy of time and gesture" is primarily governed in the Cirque imagi-nation by the musical score; as a result, the gesture and obedience of the bodies on stage are inextricably linked to the music's disciplinary force. Music and body operate as one in Cirque's human geography; if an artist misses an acrobatic cue, the live band repeats the musical gesture until that extraordinary body has performed its architectural function. Human body, nation, and music are all part of the imaginary, the spectacular.

A traditional circus performance strings together various acts and spectacles through the ringmaster's narrative and the clowns' skilled diversions.[6] By contrast, Cirque du Soleil's performances incorporate acrobatics, dance, and comedy into a singular artistic endeavor with original choreography, multiple points of focus on the unique built environment of the stage, and an original music score. Yet the multiplicitous musics presented during Cirque performances reflect two trends in late twentieth-century musical production: the assimilation of elements of hip-hop to reinvent other types of music and the use of music from other cultures without reference to cultural context or explicitly to reinforce and reinscribe cultural tropes. The effect of the Cirque soundtrack is equal to that of the bodies onstage: linked as they are, hearing members of the audience cannot separate the performing body from its musical environment. As Rosemarie Garland-Thomson (2009, 108) notes with regard to the starer–staree relationship, "public performances stage staring, anticipating its predictable patterns and intensifying them for dramatic effect. . . . Enthralled, the audience is all [the staree's], their eagerness to comprehend such novelty so acute that no one can turn away." Cirque audience members both see and hear with the intensity of staring as they dive into the other reality that is the show. In the following scenes, I examine two of Cirque du Soleil's "worlds" where musical and bodily alterity create a comforting sense of the abject for global spectators.

Scene 1: A Tale of Too City

In the production currently installed at Disney World in Orlando entitled *La Nouba* (1998), with music composed by Benoit Jutras, Cirque du Soleil presents mainstream versions of four hip-hop elements: MCs, DJs, b-boys and b-girls, and graffiti. This normalizing of elements associated with hip-hop culture appeals to a broader spectrum of listeners and audience members who might not ordinarily listen to hip-hop or identify as a hip-hop audience. While the extraordinary is pitted against the freakish on the stage of the arena, Jutras's score uses elements of hip-hop to bring an urban sound to the

Cirque's perceived mainstream audience.[7] The result is a unique intersection of rap artist, soul diva, and countertenor, foregrounding race, gender, and disability on the body of the artist who participates in this commodified spectacle.[8]

The music composed for *La Nouba* features many (albeit synthesized) traditional sounds, but they are drawn into mass-cultural appeal by the constant underpinning of hip-hop elements and electronica. As Murray Forman (2000, 65) writes, "[h]ip-hop continually displays a clever transformative creativity that is endlessly capable of altering the uses of technologies and space . . . The peculiarities of urban space themselves are subjected to the deconstructive and re-constructive practices of rap artists."

Elizabeth Grosz makes a similar argument in her article "Bodies-Cities." According to Grosz, urban environments induce certain effects, which thereby influence what is produced within these city-spaces. As rappers create rhymes within the space of the urban (and often about it), Grosz (1995, 386) examines and evaluates how cities as

> socio-cultural environments actively produce the bodies of their inhabitants. . . . The city's form and structure provide the context in which social rules and expectations are internalized or habituated in order to ensure social conformity or, failing this, position social marginality at a safe distance (ghettoization). This means that the city must be seen as the most immediate locus for the production and circulation of power.

The application of an urban musical style across the board in *La Nouba* reconstructs, to greater and lesser degrees, the nationality of the other musics presented to the listener. So although we may be hearing elements of "traditional" circus music through the synthesized accordion, hip-hop creates a new identity for the circus, and also for the performer whose act is choreographed to fit the music.

In his work *The Society of the Spectacle*, Guy Debord (1977, para. 63) states that the spectacle "is nothing more than an image of happy unification surrounded by desolation and fear at the tranquil center of misery." The spectacle, in effect, hides the individual; reading *La Nouba* in this way would suggest that race, class, and disability are all erased, thereby creating a deceptively cheery picture of capitalism. But, as Richard Herskowitz (1979, 134) explains in his article on P. T. Barnum and the spectacle,

> The falsified metamessage, which transforms the capitalist system into the awesome image of the spectacle, commands *spectatorship*. It is wrong to think of spectatorship as being passive, because the commodity's exposure of its mechanisms of image-making permits the individual spectator's *undeceived* participation in the spectacle's processes of mass communicated merchandising.

The pseudo-utopia implied by Herskowitz parallels the imagi-nation designed by Cirque du Soleil. In order for Cirque to market itself as a transnational artistic narrative, the production of the Cirque as commodity has to reflect not only the global mass market but also the desire among audience members to be spectators—starers, from both audio and visual perspectives. The soundtrack, which stands alone as a marketed entity, not exactly corresponding to what happens in live performance but rather created as an object to sell individually, reflects this commodification of the art form and therefore a commodification of these extreme normates, whether that extreme normate be construed as the acrobat or as the music itself. Cirque's musical aesthetic is as extreme in its creation of another world for the listener as is the acrobat's body in its extraordinary otherness. As the speed of capital—the corporate gain from the marketed Cirque du Soleil entity—affects the speed of artistic production, so this momentum of "cultural practices" is altered. Popular music performance is a prime example of this artistic production, and thus, so is the music utilized by the Cirque for production. Scott Hammond (1992, 110) states, "As music becomes further entangled within the motion and meaning of business and marketing, the property of music as commodity becomes central in its creation and consumption." Thus, the sensual, human need for music, as well as a desire for reinforced normalcy, is permanently entangled with the production of music/performance as a commodity. From the perspective of hip-hop criticism, *La Nouba*'s rapper has most certainly "sold out."

The squeaky-clean rap at the start of the aerial ballet, titled "A Tale" (Track 11.1 on the Companion Website), stands in stark contrast to explicit raps by artists such as Nas, Public Enemy, Eminem, and in French hip-hop circles well-known to Québecois, NTM, yet aligns with examples of "clean language" raps such as Slick Rick's (1989) "Children's Story"[9] and African raps including Bisso Na Bisso's "Légendes africaines."[10] The Cirque du Soleil rapper indicates a desire to take the audience member away to a dreamlike (no) place. What he has in mind is "a best-seller," and the audience member has but to look around at the packed arena/tent to know that this is indeed what s/he is witnessing. Any element of rap's urban origins has been removed to create a Wonder Bread version of rap that is not "too city" for the Disney consumer.

> I begin a tale with a breath inhale and cast a spell
> Using words I propel such you can sail
> To a place where dreams of men dwell,
> Nightmares efficiently awake to test one's fate by how well
> You can deal with a tale that tells itself.
> Said the storyteller,
> "A best-seller is what I have in mind,"
> Ladies and Gentlemen, settle then.
> Once upon a time is where you'll find me, La Nouba.

The countertenor introduces the song with a Gregorian chant motive ending on "Amen." His voice is used simultaneously to harmonize with himself, creating an eerie atmosphere over a steady electronically produced dance beat. The rapper then performs his short segment, followed by the countertenor, who returns to sing the same motive, one that recurs throughout the track. Finally, the soul diva begins her heterophony based on the main melody of the track. Her language is a fantastical one made of vocables with an occasional French or Latin flair, but even without language the singer is clearly performing her race and gender through the music written for her. As a closing gesture, fragments of the rap return over the countertenor's line, and this portion of the soundtrack ends with a lengthy soul cadenza from the soprano. Guitar, bass, saxophone, synthesizer, and percussion are the primary instrumental underpinnings. While early hip-hop singles featured live instrumental players in the studio, hip-hop has long since been a production-centered genre, with the DJ and the MC serving as the primary centers of improvisation and spontaneity. The Cirque's employment of a live band playing from a score with no rapper or DJ visible during the performance not only disciplines the bodies on stage, from the perspective of both identity and superability, but also reinforces the music's multigeneric leanings. The hypersensory experience of watching humans fly during the aerial ballet is underscored by Jutras's track, which seemingly knows no generic boundaries.

Because of hip-hop's historical bad-boy image, the use of this music in a context outside of the stereotypical urban music video setting conjures powerful ideologies about race and gender, two essential categories that play a vital role in casting decisions. *La Nouba* has been performed now over 4,000 times for approximately 1,650 patrons per show. One casting call reads, "*La Nouba* has been making the *ordinary extraordinary*, keeping audiences' imaginations humming from start to finish with opulent staging, brilliant choreography, spectacular lighting, and intriguing music."[11] The use of "imagination" in this statement highlights the spatial as mental, the body as idea and ideal. In the midst of constructing race, nation, and gender, the Cirque production team also creates a group of extreme normates that transcend bodily normativity. The call cited seeks a countertenor for immediate replacement.

Countertenors are male singers who sing with a highly developed falsetto, in what would traditionally be identified as a female vocal range. The use of a countertenor in *La Nouba*'s hip-hop context also heightens the alterity sought by the listener/viewer. His voice, representative of another extraordinary body, operates as a technology of gender manipulation. That Cirque du Soleil consistently chooses differently gendered voices for its productions is not simply a creative choice. Audience members cannot precisely relate this otherworldly sound with a gender, and thus it is not embodied in the sense that a gendered voice is, though the countertenor is visible to the audience.

The countertenor's voice meets the need of the listener who encounters the spectacle of extraordinary bodies (sometimes gendered, sometimes not) and reflects the need of the consumer to leave his or her voice at the door and simply become a spectator, voiceless as the acrobat is speechless. In the mid-1980s, countertenors burst onto the classical music market, inspired by—or inspiring?—the resurgence of Baroque opera that would historically have called for castrati.[12] The historical echoes of a castrated, demasculinized male body singing soprano or alto in a Baroque opera imply a socially constructed body that is disabled. In this case, the countertenor voice implies the disability of the castrato; for this performer the disability is invisible until he opens his mouth to sing. The countertenor therefore becomes a locus for intersections of gender and disability, simply by singing in a traditionally female vocal range using his intact male body.

The degendered and denationalized countertenor wears a stylized white "puffy" shirt and a feathered headdress, in the style of the aforementioned operatic castrati from the Baroque era. He always sings in the treble range, except during the aerial ballet, when he sings chant in the baritone register. This moment in the scheme of the show—an aerial ballet—is one that clearly genders the acrobats, leaving absolutely no doubt about who is externally male or female. In the scene, the formerly androgynous ballerina takes the stage in a much skimpier and more curvaceous version of her previous costume and is carried away into the rafters by the shirtless, muscled male lead dancer. The use of rap, countertenor singing, and the soul diva's R&B sound for this track both reinforces and challenges notions of gender relations in hip-hop, creating a piece of music rife with multiplicity. Peta Tait (1996, 43) notes how aerial performers such as these "transgress and reconstruct the boundaries of racial and gender identity as part of their routine." The aerial ballet in *La Nouba* also reconstructs ideas about bodily difference, capitalizing on the already present sense that the human bodies on the stage and those producing the music are superhumans, extreme normates. The countertenor sings outside the normative operatic male range, while the Cirque aerial acrobats literally fly around the stage, setting the scene for even greater feats of the extraordinary.

In the course of the production, no speech emanates from the lips of the performers, with the exception of the erased rapper and the occasional quasi-linguistic phrase from the singers.[13] So, the bodies stand for themselves, representative of the late nineteenth- and early twentieth-century circus sideshow, featuring bodies with anomalies considered "freakish" by society at large. Gilles St. Croix, the creative director of Cirque du Soleil, states (Harrington, 1999), "Our artists who do all kinds of extraordinary things, they are almost untouchables, monsters." The word "monster" implies not only the extraordinary, but the ugly, the frightening, and the malformed. As with the American circus of the early twentieth century, "the privileged state of disembodiment that the freak show conferred upon its spectators, however fraudulent, must have been seductive. It evidently was well worth the dime or quarter at a time when modernization rendered the meaning of bodily differences and vulnerabilities increasingly unstable and threatening" (Garland-Thomson 1996, 11).

The strong man in *La Nouba* provides the most overt example of the anomalous body. He affects a hunchback and limp for the purposes of the performance, but only until his "event" takes center stage. His hunchback and limp disappear when the fast track emerges from the stage floor, and it is revealed that this seemingly "deformed" individual is actually a superstar of physical prowess, strength, and coordination—he is a supercrip (see Track 11.2 on the Companion Website). In the eyes of seeing audience members, the formerly ironic label of "strong man" now represents some kind of cultural truth, validating the performer both in gender and race—he is white—by his ability to transcend or overcome his disability.[14] The music and the setting for the event heighten this sense of sudden human success. The fast track acrobats leap in and out of the windows of a multistory black building constructed on the stage to a percussion-heavy track using simulated DJ scratching—in this case literally titled "Urban"—live electric guitar riffs and vocals from the soul diva and countertenor. Race and disability often correlate, given that racialized bodies and disabled bodies are all, at some level of societal thought, despised or unwanted bodies (Linton 1998, 35–37).

In the context of the Cirque du Soleil fast track event, hip-hop music's conflation with the urban and black combines with the visual text of the formerly disabled strong man to construct a double-edged sword of disability. Now a supercrip, he can move in and out of the urban, literally bouncing off of its walls and into the spotlight. As Rosemarie Garland Thomson (1996, 1) states in her introduction to *Freakery: Cultural Spectacles of the Extraordinary Body*,

> The presence of the anomalous human body, at once familiar and alien, has unfolded . . . all figures that are perhaps the mythical explanations for the startling bodies whose curious lineaments gesture toward other modes of being and confuse comforting distinctions between what is human and what is not. What seems clearest in all this, however, is that the extraordinary body is fundamental to the narratives by which we make sense of ourselves and our world.

When these extraordinary bodies take the stage en masse, whether in the form of urbanite acrobats or a parade of Others, the power of the spectacle removes any necessity for individuality.

The use of hip-hop as the unifying musical element of Cirque du Soleil's production *La Nouba* creates a hip, urban performance. Because of hip-hop's inherent critical issues of race, gender, and nation, the application of this music foregrounds these loci of power within the spectacle of Cirque du Soleil's production. In addition, the extraordinary bodies and voices that people the show create moments of resistance within the larger, more hegemonic narrative established in the show as a whole. Nation and race are erased and disability is cured, so that these factors can be foregrounded when the aesthetic of the show requires their presence and power. As the Disney and Cirque du Soleil corporations appropriate elements of hip-hop while simultaneously removing any traces of urbanness, Jutras's soundtrack on the whole achieves the alterity required to parallel those of the extreme normates in the arena. In addition, the vocal individuality that certain performers such as the countertenor and the soul diva are permitted to maintain presents the listener with an antidote to the otherwise dehumanized production of *La Nouba*, fueled as much by capital as by creativity.

Intermission: Funding the Freak Show Scene

In addition to Cirque du Soleil's actual productions, the corporation supports a number of artistic efforts, including visual artists whose work aligns with the overall mission of the troupe. Currently, the Cirque website features the photographic work of Wayne

Schoenfeld, whose "tableaux vivants," as he has described them, received a stipend award from the troupe in 2007. Although Schoenfeld has applied his talents to many and varied projects, the particular set of tableaux staged under the auspices of Cirque du Soleil fall under the category of circus tableaux. Both *Circus of Life* (2005) and *Circus of the Past* (2007)—as well as a new series, *Circus of Tomorrow* (2011)—bring together extraordinary bodies and artists of other disciplines to form tableaux reminiscent of the circus freak show ideal established in the late nineteenth and early twentieth centuries.

For the photographic exhibition *Circus of the Past*, Schoenfeld has assembled the LA Circus Congress of Freaks and Exotics. This troupe can be located culturally within the milieu of other contemporary freak shows, such as "Sideshows by the Seashore," that perform at Coney Island (and tour under the name "Coney Island Circus Sideshow") and Ken Harck's "Brothers Grimm Sideshow" in Milwaukee.[15] The LA Congress (hereafter) consists of a number of extreme circus performers who do extraordinary things such as swallow swords or eat fire. But many of the performers in the LA Congress are also members simply because of their extraordinary bodies, such as the conjoined twins, the "very tall gentleman" and Mighty Mike, who advertises himself as a performer of exceptional talents (unicycle, fire eater, juggler and clown) but also lists his dwarfism among them. In the grand tradition of freak show history, some LA Congress members perform their eroticism or exoticism, as "Ebonies," "Period Lovelies," or "Eye Candy."[16]

Schoenfeld's use of extraordinary bodies within the tableaux for the *Circus of the Past* and the *Circus of Life* doubles the reification of freakery already present in the freak show aesthetic established by Barnum and others in the nineteenth century. As Rachel Adams (2001, 132) notes in her consideration of freak photography, "Any image that too readily allows us to move from the fact that a freak is a constructed identity to conclude that everyone has a freak within threatens to erase the lives laid bare by the camera's eye." The addition of extreme normates reinforces both the abnormal and the normal in the scene, increasing the sense of the titillation and fascination for the starer who encounters the scene (Garland-Thomson 2009).

Schoenfeld's first circus-related project is the *Circus of Life*, for which he constructs an elaborate period circus scene in a soundstage. The photographs in the staged circus scene incorporate Schoenfeld's idealized image of the circus found in his historical research as well as elements of his personal style. In the next series, Schoenfeld takes his circus project outside the walls of the sound studio and into the open air. *Circus of the Past* is a living circus event that incorporates audience members as well as live animals into its acts. For this series, Schoenfeld does not shy away from constructing an entire stage composed only of freaks, and the photograph "Freak Show" holds a place among those featured permanently on the Cirque du Soleil website. Of this project, Schoenfeld states, "I hired real circus people. I wanted to explore these characters more deeply, to look past the greasepaint and learn who they were."[17] In the photograph, the stage is set as though on the midway of the circus, and posters behind the performers advertise their talents and wares. A fat lady, an extremely tall gentleman, conjoined twins, a bearded lady, a man of short stature, and a woman and man covered with tattoos are all representative of bodily otherness, while the Geisha and the Samurai bring cultural otherness to the stage. A fire-eater, two clowns, a photographer, and a coochie girl (dance hall floozy) flank the stage, as though enforcing normativity and surveillance.

Schoenfeld has precisely recreated the freak shows of the 1930s, and clearly his efforts have been supported and publicized by Cirque du Soleil. The troupe's underwriting of Schoenfeld's photographic explorations of the early circus reveals a direct connection between the corporation's productions and the freak show aesthetic. This link becomes even more clearly aligned with the Cirque's larger projects with the advent of *Worlds Away* in 2012.

Scene 2: *Worlds Away* and Still the Same

Cirque du Soleil released its first feature film into theatres in late November 2012. *Worlds Away* introduces some new material—a simple plot and a few new musical numbers—but on the whole it is a compilation of seven Cirque productions loosely linked together by a thin screenplay. The plot is straightforward: A girl, Mia (Erica Linz), goes to the circus in her Midwestern town, where she clearly does not fit in with anyone. She is bullied by a set of mean blonde girls as she enters the midway, but continues along, fascinated by the sights and sounds of the circus, until she makes eye contact with a boy (Igor Zaripov). Hammering in a tent peg, he seems to be a circus worker, and his older coworker yells at him to stop flirting with the rubes and go get in the tent. Disappointed, they each turn from one another, the boy toward his tent, Mia in the direction from which she came; she intends to leave, but a sad clown stops her and insistently hands her a flier for The Aerialist, nodding in the direction of the boy's tent.

In the next scene, Mia watches as the freaks parade before the ringmaster as he announces the main act, but when The Aerialist sees her in the audience, he misses the trapeze and falls through the ground into another world entirely. Several Cirque du Soleil imagi-nation tents pepper an otherwise barren desert, and thus begins the rest of the adventure. Mia wanders from tent to tent, show to show, in search of the boy, with only the flier for help. Finally, after much effort, one word of dialogue ("Help!"), and excerpts from Cirque productions *Beatles Love, Believe, Kà, Mystère, Ô, Viva Elvis,* and *Zumanity*, Mia and the boy find each other and perform an ecstatic aerial ballet together that ends in a chaste kiss. Given the wildly divergent choreography, music, acrobatics, costuming, and degrees of sensuality in the film, the plot is surprisingly simplistic and heteronormative, with boy and girl relying on extreme normates throughout the other worlds to guide them to one another.

Only in the "real" world does Mia encounter the sideshow type of bodily otherness that fascinates her into a staring relationship. As Mia strolls down the midway to the tune of Benoit Jutras's pseudo–Tom Petty song, she pauses at the freak show stage. To the pop-country aesthetic of a lilting guitar waltz and accordion, Jutras adds two dissonant accordion honks at the minor second on the second two quarter note beats in a three-four measure to finish out each eight-bar phrase, creating a rusty squeezebox sound like a carnival organ. To the backdrop of this music, Mia encounters a Freak

Show wherein the set has been designed to almost perfectly replicate one of Wayne Schoenfeld's LA Congress photographs.

Amid this mildly jarring sound, Mia views the freaks. First, a beautiful woman hammers nails into her nose. Then, a bearded tattoo-covered man in skimpy gold shorts with a thick gold nipple ring growls and ripples his muscles. Next, a man of short stature dressed in Indian garb holds a large leaf and fans a fat lady wearing exquisite lingerie who reclines in pleasure on a Victorian divan (as seen in Figure 11.2).

The backdrop for these performers advertises typical sideshow fare such as pinheads, a wolfman, a fire-eater, and a sword-swallower. These characters will all appear in the parade before The Aerialist takes to his trapeze. Thus, Cirque du Soleil has undertaken the reassembly of old-world freak shows for mass public consumption. As Rachel Adams (2001, 69) writes,

> Live freak shows enhance the bodily extremes of the performers through contrasts of size (midget and giant), shape (skeleton and fat lady), and skin color (black and white) that implicitly locate the audience as the standard against which the abnormal is defined. By contrast, identification with moving images projected into a darkened theatre is so intense that it is possible for the viewer to forget about her own body.

The Cirque foregrounds the freak show in the first part of its productions. The music, extremely normative in this section of the film, changes as rapidly as Mia walks from world to world in the next scenes, replacing the otherness and alterity of the freaks with extreme normate acrobats and dancers, and exotic, unplaceable music. As with *La*

FIGURE 11.2 Video still from *Worlds Away* featuring sideshow "freaks" from the opening sequence.

Nouba, the music in *Worlds Away* subscribes to an aesthetic of multiplicity, with the conflation of many worlds into one musical idea. The result is a music so unlikely to be familiar that it equalizes the audience members in their outsider status, normalizing them and "curing" any musicocultural differences that may have existed prior to the show.

The ringmaster announces the other worlds Mia is about to encounter with his barking speech at the start of The Aerialist's act, and his speech also serves as a musical map: "Prepare to be amazed, terrified, titillated and amused! From all corners of the globe; the deepest jungles; the driest deserts; we've got you the best of the best, the greatest of the great, the most marvelous of all the marvelous!" (Adamson 2012). As soon as The Aerialist appears, we hear his four-note motive—C, E, F, G—played on a *zummara* (a high-pitched, very nasal double-reed instrument originating in the Middle East), with a singer of similar timbre improvising above. Once again, the composers are careful not to create any sounds specifically identifiable with any one nation or language. A woodblock and bongos keep a steady beat beneath the vocal and instrumental lines. These sounds, so far from the Tom Petty-esque waltz from the midway, announce the Cirque's departure from this world, and into the imagi-nation, where musical borders no longer matter nor exist.

One of the most culturally confusing pieces of music in the film underpins a spectacular piece of acrobatic choreography and set design.[18] In Track 11.3 on the Companion Website, a schooner hangs in midair perhaps fifteen or twenty feet above a deep circular pool of water. The schooner is skeletal, made up of parallel bars and trapezes—an ingenious invention for gymnastic show that can rock back and forth to increase the gravitational pull on the athletes. Characters with long dreadlocks pace the stage below in wet suits, alongside tall Enlightenment-era men in powdered wigs and long red frock coats. Meanwhile, up on the apparatus, one red-coat assists the acrobats as they fly through the air to an ever-intensifying mash-up of West African vocalizations, Bulgarian folk chorus, harp, the same zummara motive from above, and percussion instruments of both Western and African origins, underlaid by synthesized strings. As is typical with the Cirque, a specific language is not discernable, though stylistically, the syllables lean in both African and Eastern European directions. To add to all these elements, composer Benoit Jutras throws in Tuvan-style throat singers to perform a drone at the lowest register of the track. While I admit that the spectacle of the athletes flipping and whizzing through the air on and off of a moving parallel-bar schooner and one by one dropping into a pool of water is gripping, the extreme normates in this, the first action scene after the freak show on the midway, set the score straight: the music and the group of bodies on stage are all anomalous, extraordinary.

Finale

Cirque du Soleil produces a tremendously successful series of performances that literally span the globe and continue, year after year, to turn a profit with each show. Although disparate in style and costuming, what Cirque productions have in common is a reliance on otherness as a factor that will draw in the viewer/listener. If the bodies on stage are not anomalous, the music certainly will be, whether in the form of its own appropriation of what it terms hip-hop or in a Benetton-esque blend of decontextualized world musics. The Cirque's reification of the freak show reveals a desire on the part of the corporation to return not only to the old world art of the circus but also to its backward and myopic practices of bodily enfreakment.

Acknowledgments

I sincerely thank those who commented on this essay in its draft form: Ellie Hisama, Blake Howe, Jennifer Iverson, Jeannette Jones, Neil Lerner, Anabel Maler, Felicia Miyakawa, Julie Singer, and Joseph Straus. Also, many thanks to Andrew Dell'Antonio and his graduate seminar on Music and Disability Studies at the University of Texas at Austin, who read this and other essays from the Handbook.

Notes

1. This list of shows is accessible on the Official Cirque du Soleil website (http://www.cirquedusoleil.com/en/home.aspx#/en/home/shows.aspx, accessed April 26, 2013).
2. Unless otherwise noted or more specifically stated, any information pertaining to Cirque du Soleil has been obtained from http://www.cirquedusoleil.com.
3. This term has been used as a signifier for disabled or hyperabled bodies since the publication of Rosemarie Garland-Thomson's groundbreaking book in Disability Studies, *Extraordinary Bodies: Figuring Physical Disability in American Culture and Literature* (1997).
4. Although *jongleur* in its medieval connotation aligned more directly with the terms *troubadour* and *trouvère*, it nevertheless evolved to connote a street performer with the type of expertise at juggling and other circus skills of the type seen to this day in the streets of Montréal and Québec City. For a history of medieval *jongleurs*, troubadours, and *trouvères*, see Faral 1910. For a compilation of specifically Québecois *jongleur* music, see Barbeau 1962.
5. Garland-Thomson first employs the term "normate" in a Disability Studies context in *Extraordinary Bodies* (1997, 8). "Extreme normate" as formulated in this essay refers to a body at the extreme of able-bodiedness, the extreme of normative conception; an extreme normate is one who is severely able-bodied.
6. By "traditional circus" (a loaded term, to be sure) I imply the American circus idiom born in the very late eighteenth century, incubated during the nineteenth, and in its prime during the early and mid-twentieth century. This circus derived much of its material from the European—specifically Parisian—circus groups and is thus applicable to Cirque du Soleil's French diasporic roots. Although the form varied (and still does), some version of the early twentieth-century model is still functioning in most major American cities

now—see the Big Apple Circus for a prime example. For a cogent history of the American circus from a poststructuralist perspective, see Davis 2002.

7. For further discussion of the bell curve as relates to the production of culture and disability, see Lennard Davis (1997).
8. *Forbes Magazine* estimates that Cirque's performances are approximately 97 percent full for every show. The statistic takes on greater meaning with the understanding that, with the cost of tickets at $50 to $180, the show breaks even when the theatre is just 65 percent full. See Munk 1997, 192.
9. Slick Rick, "Children's Story," *The Great Adventures of Slick Rick*, Def Jam/Columbia (1989).
10. Bisso Na Bisso, "Légendes africaines," *Racines* (1999).
11. http://www.cirquedusoleil.com/en/jobs/onstage/opening/lanouba_chanteur.html, accessed April 26, 2013, emphasis mine.
12. It is my view that castrati were socially constructed, primarily in the sixteenth and seventeenth centuries, in order to keep women singers out of the Catholic churches in accordance with the dictum "mulier taceat in ecclesia," or "women must be silent in church." These male singers were castrated before puberty in order to prevent their vocal folds from lengthening and their voices from deepening into the "male" register. The appearance of these singers in early opera challenged gender boundaries in theatre and music and set a precedent for gender flexibility in opera as a genre. For more on castrati and disability, see essays by Blake Howe and Hedy Law in this volume.
13. The singers mix languages frequently, creating a kind of incomprehensible, fantastic language of vocables.
14. The notion that (dis)abled individuals should be cured stems from nineteenth-century ideals, industrialization, and medicalization of society (Garland-Thomson 1997, 34–35).
15. For more information on these circus sideshows currently in operation, see http://freaks.monstrous.com/freakshows_today.htm, accessed 28 April 2013. Schoenfeld's LA Circus Congress of Freaks is listed among the current freak shows in operation on Monstrous.com.
16. The Official Website of the LA Circus Congress of Freaks: http://www.zootsuitclown.com/thecast.html, accessed April 30, 2013.
17. Schoenfeld documentary, *Circus of the Past*.
18. To see and hear this segment of the film, see http://www.youtube.com/watch?v=MtD6KBh-s8sw, accessed January 4, 2014.

References

Adams, Rachel. 2001. *Sideshow U.S.A.: Freaks and the American Cultural Imaginary*. Chicago: University of Chicago Press.

Adamson, Andrew (director). 2012. *Cirque du Soleil: Worlds Away*. Paramount, DVD.

Anderson, Carolyn Anne. 2005. "Real and Ideal Spaces of Disability in American Stadiums and Arenas." In *Foucault and the Government of Disability*, edited by Shelley Tremain, 245–260. Ann Arbor: University of Michigan Press.

Barbeau, Charles Marius. 1962. *Jongleur Songs of Old Quebec*. New Brunswick, NJ: Rutgers University Press.

Davis, Janet M. 2002. *The Circus Age: Culture and Society under the American Big Top*. Chapel Hill: University of North Carolina Press.

Davis, Lennard J. 1997. "Constructing Normalcy." In *The Disability Studies Reader*, edited by Lennard Davis, 9–28. London: Routledge.

Debord, Guy. 1977. *Society of the Spectacle*. Detroit, MI: Black and Red.

Faral, Edmond. 1910. *Les jongleurs en France au moyen âge*. Paris: Champion.

Forman, Murray. 2000. "'Represent': Race, Space, and Place in Rap Music." *Popular Music* 19 (1): 65–90.

Foucault, Michel. 1977. *Discipline and Punish: The Birth of the Prison*. New York: Pantheon.

Garland-Thomson, Rosemarie. 1996. "Introduction: From Wonder to Error—A Genealogy of Freak Discourse in Modernity." In *Freakery: Cultural Spectacles of the Extraordinary Body*, edited by Rosemarie Garland-Thomson, 1–23. New York and London: New York University Press.

Garland-Thomson, Rosemarie. 1997. *Extraordinary Bodies: Figuring Physical Disability in American Culture and Literature*. New York: Columbia University Press.

Garland-Thomson, Rosemarie. 2009. *Staring: How We Look*. Oxford and New York: Oxford University Press.

Grosz, Elizabeth. 1995. "Bodies-Cities." In *Space, Time, and Perversion: Essays on the Politics of Bodies*, 103–110. New York: Routledge.

Hammond, Scott John. 1992. "Music as Commodity: Effect and Influence." In *America's Musical Pulse: Popular Music in Twentieth-Century Society*, edited by Kenneth J. Bindas, 101–112. Westport, CT: Praeger.

Harrington, Eamon (director). 1999. *Inside "La Nouba": From Conception to Perception*. Cirque du Soleil Images B004ASRH72, DVD.

Harvie, Jennifer, and Erin Hurley. 1999. "States of Play: Locating Québec in the Performances of Robert Lepage, Ex Machina, and the Cirque du Soleil." *Theater Journal* 51 (3): 299–315.

Herskowitz, Richard. 1979. "P. T. Barnum's Double Bind." *Social Text* 2: 133–151.

Linton, Simi. 1998. *Claiming Disability: Knowledge and Identity*. New York and London: New York University Press.

Munk, Nina. 1997. "A High Wire Act." *Forbes* (September 22), 192–194.

Sandahl, Carrie, and Philip Auslander, eds. 2005. *Bodies in Commotion: Disability and Performance*. Ann Arbor: University of Michigan Press.

Slick Rick. 1988. "Children's Story." *The Great Adventures of Slick Rick*. Def Jam Recordings/Columbia, CD.

Slobin, Mark. 2007. "Musical Multiplicity, Emerging Thoughts." *Yearbook for Traditional Music* 39: 108–116.

Tait, Peta. 1996. "Danger Delights: Texts of Gender and Race in Aerial Performance." *New Theatre Quarterly* 12: 43–49.

CHAPTER 12

PUNK ROCK AND DISABILITY

Cripping Subculture

GEORGE MCKAY

THIS essay is focused on (post)subculture and disability and specifically on punk rock. It aims to extend our understanding both of punk itself and of subcultural theory, adding to ideas around postsubculture by *cripping* it (see McRuer 2006), that is, by identifying the sounds and styles and bodies of the disabled, who are the neglected already-present of punk, and whose presence disrupts subculture theory, even while such theory exists in large part to understand the disruptive potential of gesture, music, youth, fashion, attitude, and modes of walking and talking. Here I concur with, and seek to develop, the observation by David Church that "disability has been one of the most foundational—and yet, one of the least explored—representational tropes of the punk milieu" (2013, 28). The essay contains two main areas: an initial discussion of subculture and counterculture in terms of theory and of disability and a focus on the original British punk scene of the late 1970s and three major artists, varyingly disabled, from it. It concludes with a view of punk's "cultural legacy" (Sabin 1999) in the disability arts movement.

FROM FREAKS IN THE COUNTERCULTURE . . . TO THE BLANK GENERATION

The analytical version of subculture that interests me was a key aspect of the situated academic project of cultural studies in Britain and involved looking at the operations of youth cultures, especially those with a popular music focus and a resistant, spectacular, or confrontational image (or the construction and reporting of such in the media or by academic researchers). So groups like Teddy Boys from the 1950s and Mods and Rockers, or Skinheads, or Hells' Angels from the 1960s became the classic objects of academic interest, as they combined a strict musical taste with specific sartorial markers and were each involved in relatively high-profile social clashes that were reported in the mainstream media. Because subculture theory developed in the 1970s, with influential books like Stanley Cohen's *Folk Devils and Moral Panic* (1973) and Hall and Jefferson's collection *Resistance through Rituals* (1975), its newer scholars began to look at the music and style groupings of their own current era and punk rock, the most spectacular and confrontational of the subcultures (and absolutely then of the moment), became the object of critical fascination. The relationship between punk and subculture is cemented in the key text, Dick Hebdige's punk-inflected 1979 book *Subculture: The Meaning of Style,* which, in many editions, even features a stylized representation of a punk on its front cover. Punk and subculture were announced as new at roughly the same time.

As interest in subculture theory and subcultures progressed, the "looseness" (Bennett 2011, 497) and limitations of the theory—including its claimed political significance and questions of the extent to which subcultures were manufactured by the media, or even by nostalgic academics, rather than by new generations of emergent youthful creatives—and of the figure of the monomusical subculturalist were increasingly identified. What Andy Bennett calls the "post-subcultural turn" presents a view that is "more reflexive, fluid and fragmented due to an increasing flow of cultural commodities, images and texts through which more individualised identity projects and notions of self could be fashioned" (2011, 493). The studies of postsubculture would in turn be accused of being overcelebratory and depoliticized (Bennett 2011, 494). I might say that this essay is itself a contribution to postsubcultural studies, except that postsubcultural studies has done as good a job of ignoring or denying the cultural identity and significance of disability as did its preceding set of ideas. This absence of disability may not be a real surprise; after all, if a critical model centralizes the fluidic, temporal, and ephemeral qualities of identity, is it not open to the argument that it stands as one more postmodern theoretical confirmation of what Tobin Siebers calls "the ideology of ability" (2008, 8–11)?

From postsubculture, where is disability discussed, if at all? There is barely a mention of disability in an influential book such as *The Post-Subcultures Reader* (Muggleton and Weinzierl 2003), despite its extensive problematizing discussion of a strikingly relevant practice like punk. In a recent special issue of *Social Text* (Brown et al. 2013), titled "Punk and Its Afterlives," it seems apparent that the disabled have no afterlife in punk. In its introduction of identity politics to the debate, postsubculture theory seemed stuck, despite its protestations to the contrary, in a fundamentally familiar framework of race, gender, and sexuality (though class seemed often to fall off the edge: see Bennett 2011). Should we not expect to find disability introduced in its body theory, in the context of subcultural deviance, physicality, adornment? In its embracing of body theory, performativity as well as poststructuralist notions of embodiment—the *dis*embodiment that does not mean disability—have tended to be the preferred approaches of the postsubculturalists. So in this essay we may be cripping both subculture and postsubculture. Of course it has taken time for Disability Studies to penetrate certain fields, and it is a continuing (though increasingly successful) struggle. Yet I do slightly feel that, even when the crips are all around, still the academics (outside the usually self-interest groupings of Disability Studies, who are in some way exploring what Philip Auslander terms "autopathography" [2005, 163] or have a family or close connection with disability) can't see them. Don't. Won't.

We, of course, will.

So, then, what is the relation between subcultures, music, and disability? Before discussing this question with regard to punk, we should acknowledge that there has been a little work on the "freak" aesthetic of the 1960s and early 1970s counterculture and its relation to disability, in which the term "freak" becomes "a badge of countercultural pride" (see Church 2006, n.p.): we can think of David Crosby in 1970 singing "I feel like letting my freak flag fly" (Crosby 1970). According to Church, hippies of the counterculture

> self-identified as "freaks," exploiting the cultural assumption that freaks threaten mainstream "normalcy" because of their perceived (visual) difference. . . . The counterculture's use of the label "freak" served ableist interests by subtly equating freakery with difference and social indecency. This "self-made" freakery merely conflates difference, deviance, and disability by culling the label from earlier, pre-medicalized definitions of freakery as "inborn". . . . Formation of a 1960s "freak culture" played upon fears about acquired impairments, for it was posited that anyone could become a countercultural freak by adopting radical attitudes, just as any person can potentially acquire an impairment at any time. (Church 2006, n.p.)

From the counterculture, we can see in the early work of someone like Neil Young (from Buffalo Springfield songs on) an engagement with experiences of disability. In particular I have in mind songs such as "Nowadays Clancy Can't Even Sing" (multiple sclerosis; McDonough 2002, 124–126), "Expecting to Fly" and "Mr. Soul" (epilepsy), and "Helpless" (polio) (McKay 2013). Also, thinking about cognitive impairment, tropes of rock madness, and explorations of antipsychiatry, we can consider work by artists from Lou Reed to Pink Floyd (Spelman 2012). Yet the freaks and hippies of the Woodstock generation were also—and debatably more so—the beautiful people, healthy, health-conscious, sexually attractive, sexually available, young, privileged, mobile. I am not entirely convinced of the strength of correspondence between freak culture as counterculture and counterculture as freak or disability show, even as we must acknowledge that the liberatory identity politics of race, gender, and sexuality were key elements of the counterculture that would in turn importantly help shape the disability movement.

Thus, while the musical performance of a certain freakiness in the 1960s might be said more generally to have veered uncertainly, between for instance Tiny Tim and Wild Man Fischer, there is an extraordinary protopunk song—which was astonishingly released as a single, in fact—from that decade's garage rock scene in the United States that anticipates the positionality and attitudinality of punk rock regarding disability. Arguably, of course, that garage rock scene was an important precursor of punk, and it is in this that we begin to glimpse a sonic version of freak culture that, within a few years, would (claim to) transform popular music practice. "Spazz" by The Elastik Band was released in 1967. It's a fuzzy electric blues with distorted vocal delivery, a stop-start structure, a naive guitar solo, and lyrics, chorus, and title that present us with an abject and confrontational version of the public experience of disability—but not in a good way. (Also, its lyrics are arguably referencing the psychoactive narcotic experience of the counterculture.) Music journalist Peter Lindblad described the vocal quality of singer David Cortopassi with the language of impairment and abject disease: "Mumbling incoherently, as if falling-down drunk or brain-damaged in some way, . . . garbled, barely intelligible . . . frothing-at-the-mouth" (Linblad 2009). Indeed the single's opening sounds before the music starts are two fragments of solitary incomprehensible voice, like a seriously disabled voice ("Hate to admit it, but that's just me sounding a bit incoherent," explained Cortopassi decades later; quoted in Paterson 2007.) According to a 2007 interview with Cortopassi, controversy followed the song's release.

> The Elastik Band really didn't have an opportunity to play "Spazz" much, even though when it was released on ATCO, things started looking pretty good. About the same time, our manager was setting up a trip to Europe to help promote the release on EMI's Stateside label. A few days later, we were advised not to go to Europe because if we did, it would be dangerous since people thought "Spazz" made fun of the mentally retarded. People threatened to throw rocks at us when we got off the plane. This was a total surprise to the group. (quoted in Paterson 2007)

It is equally extraordinary that "Spazz's" controversial reception should come as any surprise, let alone a total one, to the group. It seems rather more a precursor to the Blank generation of mid-1970s New York protopunk, in which a less quiet, more confrontational, and subculturally spectacular freak culture would begin to form and express, making a culture of bodily excess, anger, and attitude that really did speak to, of, and from certain sectors of the (young) disabled.

The younger self-styled rebels of punk often sought to distance themselves from the counterculture of the 1960s and its (in their view) increasingly indulgent and irrelevant music of the early 1970s: Johnny Rotten famously wore a Pink Floyd t-shirt with the words "I HATE" scrawled above the band's name, while one Sex Pistols motto, via Situationist artist Jamie Reid, was "Never Trust a Hippie." They did not see or hear in the freaks of the counterculture and their music much if any correspondence with punk's desires and aims, no matter how inarticulate these even were. Greil Marcus captures the distance between the 1960s beautiful people and 1970s punks by describing what I will call punkorporeality: "The punks were not just pretty people, like the Slits or bassist Gaye of the Adverts, who made themselves ugly. They were fat, anorexic, pockmarked, acned, stuttering, crippled, scarred, and damaged" (Marcus 1990, 74). And, indeed, arguably inarticulacy was part of the new scene. This manifested itself in the United States in Richard Hell and the Voidoids singing "Blank Generation"—as opposed to the countercultural Beat generation of the 1950s and 1960s—so blankly that Hell would leave the word "blank" out in some choruses, voicing tacit a statement of (non)identity: "Blank generation/—— generation" (Hell 1977), or with the flaunted stupidity of the Ramones, sloganizing "GABBA GABBA HEY." In Britain, the third Sex Pistols single was called "Pretty Vacant," with a chorus that went "We're so pretty, oh so pretty, vacant" and ended "And we don't caa-aare!" (Sex Pistols 1977b). Of course these were in fact each quite clever, even articulate, statements: Hell's silent contradiction, a considered performance of dumbness by the Ramones, a way for Rotten to bypass acceptable public media discourse (by repeatedly voicing the taboo word "cunt" on the BBC: "vay-CUNT." See Lydon 1994, 239). Dave Calvert writes about punk's "anti-aesthetic" and its appeal to the disabled (in his context, those with learning disabilities):

> punk theatricality offers further opportunities to reflect on and respond to the socially marginalized position of people with learning disabilities, not least because an impression of learning disabled identity had already been placed inside this particular anti-aesthetic. Vacancy informs punk's anti-aesthetic stance by enacting a response to social orthodoxy in which, Dick Hebdige observes, "alienation . . . gave itself up to the cameras in 'blankness,' the removal of expression." (Calvert 2010, 518–519)

Musically, punk's antiaesthetic "embraces what is simple, direct and immediate, and celebrates energy and volume over intricacy and sophistication" (Calvert 2010, 517). The significance of the simplicity of the music rests in a vital context for the disabled: accessibility. Punk's archetypal DIY (do it yourself) formula—"THIS IS A CHORD/THIS IS ANOther/This IS A THIRD/<u>NOW FORM A BAND</u>" (see Savage 1991, 280; typography original)—called out to and opened space for the new marginal musical competents and incompetents alike. If you could not play an instrument or sing in tune or time—for whatever reason—here at last was a music scene that might be for you. For all its other flaws, we should I think acknowledge the generosity of punk in producing this accessibility. Church metaphorizes, "Amid punk's inversion of social taboos, the genre's rough, open, and unfinished musical style evokes qualities similarly associated with disabled bodies. Punk rock could thus seem especially conducive to disability-related issues" (Church 2013, 31).

Punk and punk-era band names have been characterized by a connotation or description of violence or aggression, sex and fetish, social turmoil and irruption, but also of the body and in particular the disabled or disfigured body. So: the Blockheads, Deviants, Epileptics, Subhumans, Vital Disorders (UK), Disability Sickness, another Subhumans (both Canada), the Autistics (an early name of Talking Heads), Cripples, Disability, Screamers, Voidoids, Weirdos (United States), and many others. This mildly controversial and contumacious juvenilia signals an identification of misfit, clearly, on the part of band members, but also it contributes to the subcultural terrain of the scene in which both direct and indirect referencing of disability has been widely accepted. Such naming becomes self-fulfilling as a public signifier of music offered: I venture to suggest that a band called, say, the Fuckwit Mutants (I made them up, but would not mind seeing a short set) is unlikely to be playing disco, blues, or good old country tunes. As for punk audiences, their antidancing style of the pogo (basically, jumping up and down, on or off the spot), while physically demanding, was a further display of a kind of incompetence, an inelegant if thoroughly energetic solo reaction of body to music. When dancing to slower pieces, or to punk's own musical (br)other, reggae, one saw or one made frequent "twitches of the head and hands or more extravagant lurches" (Hebdige 1979, 109). Indeed, could we say that the *alla zoppa* stepfulness (McKay 2013, 197n9) of reggae, its lilting offbeat rhythms, spoke powerfully to the cripness of punk? Does that offer another way of understanding the close relationship between the two? The unhygienic and in wider society unacceptable leakiness of the gesture of "gobbing" (spitting) at bands onstage enhanced and lubricated punk's bodily excess.

In British punk, Helen Wallington-Lloyd (sometimes written "Wellington-Lloyd"), artistic collaborator with Malcolm McLaren and an important figure in the early history of the Sex Pistols (Savage 2009, 27–32), has been highly visible. A resident figure at McLaren and Vivienne Westwood's King's Road, London boutique, SEX, Wallington-Lloyd also made regular appearances at Sex Pistols concerts and was effectively involved in the construction and management of the band. (Though she describes her work as being that of a "dogsbody"—intriguing phrase for us [quoted in Du Noyer 1980]—it was Wallington-Lloyd who devised the ransom note newspaper-cutting typography for the band's publicity, for example: Savage 1991, 201.) She features in Derek Jarman's punk-influenced films *Jubilee* and *The Tempest* and also as Helen of Troy in Julien Temple's sort of Sex Pistols film, *The Great Rock 'n' Roll Swindle*, in which she appears, with pride of place in punk's instant history, constructing the title credits (Temple 1980). With her visible physical disability and "stareable body" (caused by dwarfism), fashion, art, and being photographed and filmed were her key punk activities: she was the archetypal punk "staree" and made a short career out of it (Garland-Thomson 2009, 9 passim). As she put it in a 1980 music press interview—itself small evidence of the fascination with the corporeally other in punk media—"everyone looks at me and I think 'God, if I could get sixpence for each look.'" Hers is effectively a statement that she became a punk directly and precisely *because* of her physical disability; as her interviewer Paul du Noyer understood it, she fitted perfectly "with the arrival of punk in '76" because, "[f]or a start, she already looked like one."

> Yeah, [I became a punk] because I had to. Not because of any fashion. . . . And I just think, well, I've got nothing to lose, and most of the time I can get away with it, because people are so sort of Christian—d'you know what I mean, really, they find it hard to be honest with me. They probably think I'm a half-wit. (quoted in Du Noyer 1980)

Mik Scarlet is a veteran postpunk rocker, disability writer, television presenter from the UK, and in his view there is a general point to be made about disability fashion and a particular point about the suitability of punk for the disabled stylist. Generally, for Scarlet, "'dressing weird' suits us disabled types"—the performative aspect of costume confirms and claims a lifestyle and life difference, while putting on a show puts (nondisabled) people at their ease. More particularly,

> Another personal fave [fashion style] that has disability running through it is Punk. With Punk icons Ian Dury and Helen Wellington-Lloyd disability has always been synonymous with this classic alternative fashion scene. I used to wear my leg brace on the outside of my bondage trousers and clip bondage straps to it, making it a feature of my outfit. (Scarlet 2011)

For him, it is a matter of claiming the liberatory potential of subcultural display within a crip context and offering that to other people with disabilities as a performative strategy: "if you're wondering if dressing 'weird' is for you, I know I started dressing this [punk] way as it occurred to me that people were going to stare at me whatever, so I gave them something to stare at" (Scarlet 2011). There is also something aggressive or confrontational in punk's and the disabled's being-stared-at, in which the staree also sends out a look, not the "lucky look" (Dury 1981b) of the nondisabled on viewing a crip, more the kind of "fuck you look" that punks also more generally refined. There is too in punk fashion an embracing of certain sartorial markers or even generators of disability: Johnny Rotten in a publicity shot wearing a straitjacket; bondage trousers that tied legs together, hindering mobility; fetish gear more generally, connecting BDSM, punk, and freak shows; punk's topping spikiness viewed by Hebdige as the "ECT hairstyles" (1979, 121; see also Savage 1991, 177); and, more metaphorically, damaged clothing ("ripped and torn," as the title of one punk fanzine put it) worn alongside its prosthetic solution, the safety pin.

Cripping Punk

By looking at three major punk artists with disabilities from punk's heyday from the mid-1970s to very early 1980s we will begin to see the closest and most meaningful association between punk and crip. I aim to show that this relation is more resonant and significant for disabled music fans across generations than simply the presentation of "*[e]xploitative* images of disability . . . such as Sex Pistols singer Johnny Rotten's basing of his stage persona upon Quasimodo and [Shakespeare's] Richard III" (Church 2006; emphasis added). We should acknowledge that otherness and authenticity have been privileged categories in some popular music forms, and it has been argued that disability has been embraced in the music industry as one more music marketing strategy: "[r]ather than heralding disability as part of the typical human condition . . . in pop it still tends to be used as a device for constructing musicians as exotic outsiders, a saleable commodity in an industry that sees 'authenticity' as currency" (Waltz and James 2009, 367–368). It is the case that punk has been one authentic exotic outsider subcultural practice, but we should not be overly reductive or dismissive of it, despite its privileging of modes of inarticulacy. For some disabled people, punk offered expression, empowerment, visibility, humor, bad taste, and attitude, and all in a zone of sociocultural liberation, as much as (even, more than) it exploited disability or used it as a marketing strategy.

At the same time, let us note the sobering limits of punk's (or of popular music's) apparent new inclusivity. Punk was controversial, and to be one was even dangerous for a while. (I myself was chased and threatened by other youth subculturalists, targeted by the police, and once badly beaten up because I was a punk.) Not every disabled youngster wanted to embrace pop's avant-garde, nor foreground one's alienation or leakiness, nor add to the distaste or unease one thought one generated among the TAB (temporarily able-bodied). For all that it sang of "cunts" and "nutters," "morons" and "weirdos," it is quite possible that other disabled young people were put off punk by its spectacularity, its attitude, its embracing and flaunting of deviant identity, or just its sheer impoliteness. Ian Dury expressed a certain desire for conformity as a route for some disabled people that safely bypassed things like punk rock (even while he suggests elsewhere in the same song that such a desire is denying your identity):

> I want to be normal in body and soul
> And normal in thought, word and deed
> And everyone here will whistle and cheer
> And be happy to see me succeed. (Dury 1980)

Also, lest we overmythicize punk as a liberatory or utopian or transformative zone, an inclusive subculture of disability access and solidarity, it is worth considering the careers of some of those crips in punk who did not make it in music and who identify their failing as a symptom of the popular music industry's continuing obstruction of, and distaste toward, different bodies. For disabled singer Kata Kolbert in the postpunk 1980s British scene, it was a struggle even to get heard by industry executives. According to Lucy O'Brien in *She-Bop*, "[w]hile trucking her demo tape around record companies, she was met with both uncomfortable comments and blank rejection." O'Brien explains her understanding of the reason why Kolbert was being rejected: "Her wheelchair was not sexy" (O'Brien 2002, 245). But Kolbert (now Penny Pepper, a punky can-do campaigner and writer) was made of sterner stuff, and reached back into her own punk experience for a now classic DIY solution: she formed her own record label to release her music. The press release for her single "Live Your life"—a song title itself claiming control and empowerment—situates Kolbert's story within the pop industry, and within disability consciousness:

> * Kata Kolbert has her first single out now. This is it. . . . She is wheelchair bound with arthritis, and was turned down by all the major record companies because of

> this, DESPITE her opera trained voice. She formed Nevermore to put out her own records. (Kolbert 1987)

For Mik Scarlet, who articulated earlier the liberatory and attitudinal potential of punk fashion, it is significant that he has had greater career success elsewhere in the creative industries, away from his first choice in the music of postpunk electronica. Why did he think that was? His answer, like Kolbert/Pepper's, suggests that he has preserved that certain punk attitude.

> While the A&R people might have loved the [musical] acts I fronted, as soon as the press and publicity departments got involved the attitude changed. Time and time again I was told "We can't sell the wheelchair." I tried and tried to make myself a product that they would want to invest in, but no. Even after I became a household name with my TV presenting I still kept getting knocked back. . . . I got so bored of hearing no because of the chair, but I still refused to hide my disability. It is part of who I am and I am proud of that. Fuck 'em! (Mik Scarlet, personal correspondence in 2014)

I want now to talk about a trio of the highest profile disabled artists who came to prominence through punk rock in Britain, in chronological order of appearance: Ian Dury (1942–2000), Johnny Rotten of the Sex Pistols (b. 1956), and Ian Curtis (1957–1980) of Joy Division. Each was a singer—the frontman of his band—and lyricist. Central stage in each instance was a corporeally other figure who presented in his own voice and words material that directly or indirectly referenced and explored disability experiences, and whose performance nightly displayed in confirmatory act his extraordinary body to the audience. Dury was often accompanied onstage at the start of gigs by his personal aide to avoid tripping over leads and equipment; Rotten's stance with the mic stand was semihunched; Curtis would rouse band and crowd alike with his intense "epileptic" (as it was described), twitching, flailing dance. Yet there were equally important differences in each singer's public relationship with disability. It was common knowledge at the time, and widely discussed in music and mainstream media, that Dury was disabled, and he wrote and sang words about disability. He was also a well-known public advocate on issues of disability. Curtis wrote and sang directly of disability and was at the very least neuroperformative—he danced on stage like an epileptic—but mostly his disability (epilepsy) began to be openly acknowledged and discussed only a few years after his young death (by suicide) in 1980. The centrality of his disability to his performance and songs has become the focus of posthumous biography, memoir, biopic, and fame, and these in turn are colored or mythicized by his depression, self-harming, and suicide. Rotten's is a different case again. As we will see, his position within a disability frame requires explanation, and I will present medical and cultural material to justify claiming Rotten as a crip, uncovering the extent to which he has self-identified as a person with disabilities.

Ian Dury

> If they're making me well, if they're caring for me
> Why do they boot me and punch me? Why do they bash me and crunch me?
>
> —Ian Dury, "Hey, Hey, Take Me Away" (1980)

Although quite the unconventional stylist in terms of his art school rags, and markedly disabled by the childhood polio that left his arm and leg severely withered, Dury was not in fact really a punk—too old, for a start, being a child of the 1950s and 1960s rather than the 1970s. Prior to punk's breaking years of 1976–1977 he had already been involved in music for approaching a decade, notably as singer with Kilburn and the High Roads from 1971 to 1976. The Kilburns were already channeling punk's threat and sexual and social deviancy before punk happened—*New Musical Express* described them in 1975 as looking a gang of "demobbed cripples" in dirty macs, with hair "badly cut and partially grown out like ex-cons. They had a bass player . . . who was nearly seven feet tall, a black drummer who had to be lowered manually onto his drum stool[,] and a lead singer with a stiff leg, a face like Gene Vincent, and a withered hand encased in a black glove" (quoted in Drury 2003, 15). There was at least one other crip in that band (one most unusual, two really quite extraordinary): disabled jazz drummer David Rohoman, who had previously been in a rock group tastefully called Kripple Vision. But Dury's period of major pop success was to be after the Kilburns, with a new backing band called the Blockheads, combining punk style and attitude with English music-hall, transatlantic jazz-funk-reggae ("punk jazz" as cowriter Chas Jankel put it; quoted in Drury 2003, 94) with Cockney London banterous lyrics sung in a *mal canto* style (McKay 2013, 71–76). Perhaps Dury's prepunk performative strategy influenced the punk aesthetic of imperfection rather than his commercial success being explained by the sonic, visual, and corporeal shift that punk may, or could claim to, have caused (McKay 2013; see also Double 2007 for a reading of punk as sited in the music hall tradition).

Over the years of an occasionally chart-topping career, Dury wrote the lyrics to around twenty songs about or referencing disability in some way (see McKay 2013, 198n10), including hit singles such as "What a Waste" (1978) and "Hit Me with Your Rhythm Stick" (1979). When against his record company's advice, at the peak of his popularity in 1979, he wore a t-shirt for the video of his sole UK no. 1 single, "Hit Me with Your Rhythm Stick," it was to display the bare attenuated muscularity of his left arm. As the video's director put it, "he was going to come out about his disability," his physical difference subsequently visible on television screens in homes up and down the country (quoted in Balls 2000, 203). The following year, 1980, he recorded "Hey, Hey, Take Me Away," a quite astonishing pop song about life in a residential school for disabled children, with powerfully direct and uncomfortably witty lyrics of complaint and anger, delivering a narrative of sexual abuse, institutional violence, and self-loathing. In Tom Shakespeare's view, "Dury differs from much of the modern disability movement because of his uncompromising willingness to name impairment for what it is . . . turn[ing] his unblinking eye on the difficulties and drawbacks of being a cripple" (Shakespeare 2013). This stark gaze is at its clearest with "Hey, Hey, Take Me Away," which drew on his own memories of childhood institutionalization. Then the year after that, to mark the United Nations' Year of Disabled Persons of 1981, Dury released his most direct protest song, "Spasticus Autisticus," the genesis of which is described in the press release accompanying the single: "I worked out the name of a band called Spastic and the Autistics, . . . who were either recruited from mental hospitals or recruited from really savagely disabled places, and we'd get it going" (Dury 1981a). This turned into a song rather than a band, a chanting reclamation of the then-daily term of abjection and insult, "spastic," with a resonant coda of "I'm Spasticus!" that echoed the mass identification of "I'm Spartacus!" at the end of Stanley Kubrick's 1960 film epic *Spartacus* (Dury 1981b). Perhaps unsurprisingly, the single was criticized by some of Britain's then-leading disability organizations and (partially) banned by the BBC. As his pop fame grew alongside his profile as a disabled artist, Dury's concerts seemed to be transforming into disability conventions, solidarity events, as the "flaw in the jungle" or "raspberry ripple" (meaning cripple; both phrases from Dury's lyrics) became an increasingly common figure among the (other) punks and fans. One Blockhead band member recalls:

> He was writing about those who'd never had [pop] songs written about them before. . . . A lot of people who had experienced those things that Ian sang about started coming to our gigs and came backstage for autographs. You'd hear people saying, "He's writing about me." (quoted in Drury 2003, 95)

Johnny Rotten and the Sex Pistols

> She don't want a baby that looks like that
> I don't want a baby that looks like me
> Body—I'm not an animal
> Body—I'm an abortion.
>
> Sex Pistols, "Bodies" (1978)

Let us deal first with the inclusion of Johnny Rotten, real name John Lydon, in this debate. For instance, while acknowledging some kind of cripness, for Calvert, Rotten's performative strategy in the Sex Pistols was one of "laying a parodic impersonation of disability over his own non-disabled body" (2010, 524). But Jon Savage offers a more causal link, positing that "[l]ike others who later became shamanistic performers, Lydon had a severe illness in his childhood" (Savage 1991, 115), and it is in his early years that we must look for an understanding of Rotten's punkorporeality. Rotten, the creative chaotic at the original heart of British punk, as well as a public hate figure in the patriotic fervor of a royal jubilee in 1977, can now be seen as effectively multiply disabled. The staring gaze and semihunchbacked body posture were caused by childhood meningitis. As he has explained in his autobiography, *Rotten*:

> I was in a hospital for a year from age seven to eight. . . . They would draw fluid out of my spine . . . it's curved my spine. I've developed a bit of a hunchback. There're all these idiosyncrasies about me in the Pistols that come from fucking up in a hospital. The stare is because I developed bad eyesight, also as a result of the meningitis. (Lydon 1994, 17–18)

Meningitis, childhood hospitalization, coma, and rehabilitation, as well as the associated interruption to education and social development, were collectively in his own view "the first step that put me on the road to Rotten" (Lydon 1994, 17). (The Rotten name itself was another bodily reference, to the poor state of his teeth at the time.) He subsequently also developed epilepsy (Lydon 1994, 105 and 323), which had an impact on his live set-up, particularly around reducing the triggering causes. As he explained in 1994:

> I'm epileptic as well, but I'm not on any medication. . . . I'm no lighting director's dream when I tour—there's this huge list of things that can't be done. . . . Sometimes certain kinds of lighting can make me forget where I am and triggers [*sic*] a memory seizure. I always keep my lyrics book on stage on the floor if the lighting does weird things in the middle of the song. I have a poor sense of balance, so if I do spins, I can fuck myself up. (Lydon 1994, 323)

Long before then, as the pre–Johnny Rotten, teenaged John Lydon, in nervous crisis mode at his audition in McLaren and Westwood's SEX boutique for what would become the Sex Pistols in London in 1975, he drew instinctively on his own experience, "jump[ing] up and down in a *spastic* fashion, *gabbling* improvised lyrics . . . launch[ing] into a sequence of *hunchbacked* poses" (Savage 1991, 120–121; emphasis added). This foundational performance of crip movement and sound—the essence of all that came later—in front of a jukebox using a shower attachment as a pretend mic, got him the gig as the Sex Pistols singer. And quickly the Rotten autopathography would be explained to punk audiences, for example, by journalist Charles Shaar Murray in *New Musical Express* in 1977: "A few more things about Johnny Rotten. When he was eight he had meningitis, and it left him with weak eyes, permanent sinus [infections], stunted growth and a hunched back" (Murray 1977); or in the sensationalizing film trailer for *The Great Rock 'n' Roll Swindle*: "Johnny Rotten: was he really a hunchback antichrist with green teeth . . . ?" (Temple 1980).

It is interesting too that Ian Dury recognized something cripping in Rotten. When the Pistols supported Dury in 1976, he thought he saw in aspects of Rotten's style and body posture his own act, performed by a younger singer for the new audience. While Dury complained anxiously to the Pistols's manager McLaren, "What's all that about, Malcolm? He's copying me, isn't he?" (quoted in Balls 2000, 143), we can also, by screwing our eyes up and thinking very positively, see in this moment some kind of crip pop inspiration. (We may see a little more of such inspiration again more recently below, with Heavy Load and the Sex Pistols.) The extraordinary contumacious body of young punk Rotten was drawing on the same of old punk Dury. Perhaps we can say that they were inventing together the new body language of punk performance, with an energy sourced from a mutual rivalry and an authenticity sourced from each being some kind of crip.

Ian Curtis and Joy Division

> For entertainment they watch his body twist
> Behind his eyes he says "I still exist."
> This is the way, step inside.
>
> Joy Division, "Atrocity Exhibition" (1980a)

And Dury and Rotten were to be joined by another, also the result of viewing a Sex Pistols performance. The origins of Joy Division are in a series of Pistols concerts in Manchester in 1976 (Middles and Reade 2006, 35–38), a further indication of the new subculture's communication and inspiration strategies, specifically here around disability and difference. "Seeing the Sex Pistols was confirmation that there was something out there for [Ian Curtis] other than a career in the Civil Service," even if, notably, at one stage that parallel nonmusical career included supporting people with disabilities (Curtis 1995, 36–37 and 51). Working with photographers and designers, recording engineers, and an avant-garde independent record company, the band developed an encompassing aesthetic of dark, gloomy, gothic mystery, with electronic elements, increasingly interior and depressive lyrics, and a reputation for intense live performances by Curtis. Some of the songs were about disability. Curtis's suicide in May 1980, just before the band was due to undertake an American tour, seemed to confirm for fans the post-Romantic positionality of emotional suffering in his lyrics, in which the title of the posthumously released second album, *Closer*, is read as a noun and not as an adjective (Middles and Reade 2009, 216). Suicide is troubling per se for all involved, but the suicide of a disabled artist, struggling with the medical condition/s that form part of his lyrical subject—epilepsy, and probable depression, an issue both memoir (Curtis 1995) and biography (Middles and Reade 2006) raise—adds a problematic air of "tragic extremism" (Barnes 2003, 7) that overdetermines suffering as the core of disability experience.

Curtis was diagnosed with epilepsy while his career with Joy Division was taking off. For example, one week in 1979 he appeared as the new star on the front cover of the leading music weekly for punk and postpunk music, *New Musical Express*, while the next he was seeing a neurologist for epilepsy tests and the prescription of anticonvulsant drugs. The sudden, extreme, and public experience of epileptic seizure sung of by Curtis in Joy Division's "She's Lost Control" was often understood by audiences as being displayed by him in his remarkable dancing style during instrumental sections of live performances, not least of that song:

Confusion in her eyes that said it all. She's lost control.
And she's clinging to the nearest passer by. She's lost control. (Joy Division 1980b)

For his watchful wife, Deborah, his characteristic dancing became "a distressing parody of his offstage seizures . . . an accurate impression of the involuntary movements he would make" (Curtis 1995, 74). His physical performances in concert began to be the focus of music press attention; indeed, in Deborah Curtis's view, the band's reviews became "disturbing . . . they were like psychiatric reports" (Curtis 1995, 73). Reviews of concerts from 1978 and 1979 by journalist Mick Middles, later a coauthor of a Curtis biography, described how he "stands with his right hand waving about in epileptic fashion . . . screaming infectious vocals" (Middles 1978), of how he "often loses control. He'll suddenly jerk sideways and, head in hands, he'll transform into a twitching, epileptic-type mass of flesh and bone" (quoted in Curtis 1995, 83).

Contrary to the view that Curtis "*quietly* addressed the experience of epilepsy" in the lyrics of a song like "She's Lost Control" (Waltz and James 2009, 372; emphasis added) or that the later addition of a final verse for the extended studio version written in the first person was "*perhaps* . . . a way to personalize" the narrative (Church 2006; emphasis added), my own view is that the song in fact is both a direct and dramatic representation of the experience of epilepsy (perhaps of the young epileptics he used to work with) and undoubtedly such a personalization. After all, Curtis would periodically experience fits onstage when singing it: and "here *we* come," he sings, the new last words in that late last verse (Joy Division 1980b). This is, I think, one of the Joy Division songs recorded with two vocal lines, one in each stereo channel. Curtis duets with himself, sings to and follows himself, doubling up, almost in unison. In fact, vocal lines and music from the studio recording are disciplined and precisely not out of control. Such discipline is characteristically absent from some other punk recordings: listen to Dury's "Hey, Hey, Take Me Away" (Dury 1980), where Dury runs out of time and has to speed up the lyrics, or the endlessly puzzling "unspeakable confusion" (Marcus 1990, 436) of the Pistols's "Holidays in the Sun," where Rotten says repeatedly "I don't understand—this bit—at all" (Sex Pistols 1977c). In instances like these, punk's antiaesthetic revels in its sonic chaos, which may be something of a crip signifier too. But the loss of control for Curtis in "She's Lost Control" is located in the body's dancing performance of it.

Never Trust a Punk (Why Not?)

As the years went by with the Pistols, all two of them. . . .

Johnny Rotten (Lydon 1994, 92)

Does punk rock in disability culture matter? Does punk matter (any more, decades later)? Curiously, I think, it has begun to speak more to me in my fifties than at any other time since my contumacious teens in the late 1970s. My view is that this new meaningfulness has a good deal to do with (my) disability—as I aged, I looked for a culture that would help me understand, embrace, maybe even emblazon my own body thing, as my condition—progressive muscular dystrophy—deteriorated, and I found one in, of all places, the memory of that mad music and mismovement of my own youth. Punk has indeed spoken to people with disabilities, and been able to do so across several generations of fans and musicians now, in its various "afterlives" (*Social Text* 2013). Both punk's "aesthetic of anger" (as influential anarcho-punk band Crass put it: see McKay 1996, ch. 3) and its accessibility have been useful in the disability movement's cultural repertoire of contention and timely for the new kinds of radicals coming along who wanted a street confrontation in which the rallying cry PISS ON PITY was a key communication in the struggle for rights and independence. Colin Cameron outlines the significance of both the aesthetics and the locations of specific popular music genres within the disability arts movement of the 1980s and 1990s.

> Blues is music born of oppression and which gives voice to the oppressed. Folk emerges from a rootedness and groundedness that is certain of its own values. Punk is the noise of the alienated, the disregarded and the disrespected. Each of these forms is used to articulate anger at the established order. . . . The power of the music discussed here is also entwined with the community and grassroots locations in which it has been performed . . . —arts centres, . . . day centres, . . . residential homes: most importantly, in any place where disabled people have been able to get to. (Cameron 2009, 382)

What else might be or have been attractive in punk for later generations of crips? William Peace, who maintains a blog titled *Bad Cripple*, has written about the influence of punk on him, even though he was in fact not even a member of the subculture. But, vitally, punk's initial explosion was contiguous with his becoming disabled:

> I do not like Punk music . . . [but t]he sort of anarchistic nihilism the punks fostered suited my mood circa 1978 . . . [when] I was newly disabled. . . . What I directly related to was the punk motto [from the Sex Pistols: 1977a] "no future." This is exactly what I was thinking and worrying about: did I have a future as a crippled man? (Peace 2009)

One of the (younger) commentators to Peace's blog explained the contemporary significance of punk for him: "I'm 33 and have a disability myself. I still identify with Punk music and this article definitely made me realize why the lyrics of, not only The Sex Pistols, but many other Punk bands like Lagwagon and NOFX still ring true for me. For me, it feels like *I can't fit into society the way I'm supposed to fit in and the music lets me identify*"(quoted in Peace 2009; emphasis added). Once more, punk is understood and consumed by a disabled fan as a musical expression of alienation and dysfunction.

In media and performance, too, punk continues to resonate relevantly, with a recent spate of films and productions about punk and disability providing further evidence of the subculture's ongoing capacity to engage. So, "[d]espite punk's steady mainstreaming over those same decades [since the 1970s]—achieved precisely through popular media like film—a rebellious sense of social deviance has remained a central subcultural ideology, rooted in punk's loud and disorderly musicality" (Church 2013, 28). Films include the relatively high profile posthumous biopics of the original punk generation stars, Ian Curtis (*Control*; Corbijn 2007) and Ian Dury (*Sex & Drugs & Rock & Roll*; Whitecross 2010), each of which places the singer's disability as a central component of his work and life.[1] Britain's leading disabled performance group, Graeae Theatre Company, produced in 2010 and then revived in 2012 for a national tour a stage musical based on the songs of Ian Dury, titled *Reasons to Be Cheerful* (Sirett 2010). A loose plot revolves around a group of punk friends trying to get tickets to see one of Dury's 1979 London gigs, but the outstanding moments were versions of many of Dury's best songs performed by a large ensemble cast of disabled and deaf musicians, singers and dancers, with a signer and captioned titles. These films and performances were not (just) opportunities for older audiences to nostalgize but also presentations of now historic disability music and attitude in social struggle as well as popular—as opposed to, say, academic—efforts at revisiting punk as crip culture.

Alongside these have been film documentaries of more minor, contemporary punk bands. Heavy Load was an integrated learning disabled and nondisabled punk band from Brighton, formed originally in 1996, who were featured in the 2008 film *Heavy Load*, which documented the band's efforts to break out of disability center shows into the larger mainstream concert network (Rothwell 2008). Why punk, for Heavy Load? In part because the Sex Pistols had originally sung of how people "made you a moron" (1977a), of how you were "pretty vacant" (1977b), and such lyrics meant something to that band of learning disabled people and workers (see also Calvert earlier on the appeal of "punk theatricality" for Heavy Load). Intriguingly, a second documentary film about a newer generation of disabled punks follows a similar trajectory of the trials, tribulations, and triumphs of trying to make it in a band, touring, arguing, playing live. The subject of *The Punk Syndrome* (Kärkkäinen and Pasi 2012) is the Finnish punk band Pertti Kurikan Nimipäivät, all of whose members have some kind of intellectual impairment. Singer Kari Aalto explains: "This film tells about the band . . . so it's about one retard who sings punk and three retards who play punk" (*Kovasikajuttu/The Punk Syndrome* 2013). In the context of such punk disability bands as Heavy Load and Pertti Kurikan Nimipäivät, it is possible to make the point that "what takes place on stage presents a potential model for social development offstage," and that this model is mediated more widely via film than simply live performance (Calvert 2010, 518; see also McKay 2013, 191, and Elflein 2009 for other material on the band as support network and facilitation device for disabled musicians). I do not think that, in this brief survey of cultural moments in punk that took place up to thirty-five years after its heyday, I am simply reintroducing a sort of "heroic" version of subculture theory (see Muggleton and Weinzierl 2003), in which the critical oppositionality or "resistance" (Hall and Jefferson 1995; McKay 1996) of a subculture is just remolded into the shape of a supercrip with a Mohican/Mohawk haircut, a ripped t-shirt, or a set of wheels.

Is it possible that punk speaks more of and to disability the older it gets? The further away, the more important? We should end, I increasingly feel, on a rising note. A tremendously powerful musical moment took place in 2012, at the internationally televised opening ceremony for the Paralympic Games in London. The three-hour multimedia mass stadium event, titled *Enlightenment*, was codirected by Graeae's Jenny Sealey, and finished (let us say culminated) with a section called "Empowerment." This was a celebration of Britcrip that included a live band, the Graeae punk band, reprising a song from their jukebox musical of Dury's work, *Reasons to Be Cheerful*. To the accompaniment of "protestors" bearing placards with slogans like "RIGHTS" and "LOOK BEYOND APPEARANCES," and hundreds of disabled and deaf volunteer dancers, many in wheelchairs, the "antiaesthetic" of punk suddenly burst out, visually and sonically. Keren Zaointz noted dryly the irruptive potential of incongruity:

> While the performance of national (and even cosmic) origin stories is generic to opening and closing ceremonies in the Games, protest is not. Taking action in the square or the street against authority generally runs counter to state celebration. . . . (Zaointz 2013, 515)

And what was that noise—I mean, music? On a plinth was a punk rock band, and for two marvelous minutes the world was Ian Dury's, who had died a dozen years earlier: "Hello to you out there in Normal Land," sang wheel-chaired singer John Kelly, in his best (worst) cockney *mal canto* voice, taking Dury's place to sing for a televised global audience his protest song, "Spasticus Autisticus" (1981b), that had once been banned by the BBC and disapproved of by concerned disability charities. Huge screens in the crowd flashed up "SPASTICUS" and "AUTISTICUS" during the repeated shouted chorus, and, while the audience in the stadium cheered noisily, viewers in their homes sat up and paid attention. We did in my house. Temporarily able-bodied as well as disability media comments quickly confirmed that an extraordinary punk moment had taken place, thirty-odd years on. For *The Daily Telegraph*'s television reviewer it was "electrifying": "It was more than a reclaiming; it felt like something that demanded to be listened to" (Rahim 2012). For Zaiontz, "[t]he question of what we hear in this moment—bland unity [of ceremonial performance] or radical equality [of political protest]—is important in the face of aggressive cutbacks to state resources in the UK that ensure independent living for disabled persons" (2013, 518). I heard radical equality being demanded, and it is in its very punk attitudinality and sonic aggression that the power of the event is located: Zaointz writes of the "raucous rendition of Dury's song," of ceremony codirector Jenny Sealey's "spit-in-your-eye approach"—very punk (2013, 515); Rahim tells his readers the next morning that the section was precisely not articulated in the usual "tiptoeing language" of Normal Land (Rahim 2012). In a major media moment such as this televised opening ceremony, punk history and the importance of the subculture for disability were placed center-stage and -screen. I took it to be an (almost) uncompromising confirmation of punkorporeality's continuing relevance and a vindication of how punk cripped subculture.

Acknowledgments

I thank the UK's Arts and Humanities Research Council for supporting this research; the Handbook editors for their patience; Mik Scarlet and Penny Pepper for taking the time to correspond; Andy Callen, librarian at the University of Salford, for getting a difficult-to-access book for me in a hurry; and Bruce Bennett for drawing my attention to "Spazz."

Note

1. It is worth reading Waltz and James 2009 and Church 2013 for discussion of the representation of disability in the film *Control* and of the foregrounding of disability in the film's publicity. From the press kit: "With epilepsy adding to his guilt and depression, desperation takes hold. Surrendering to the weight on his shoulders, Ian [Curtis]'s tortured soul consumes him" (quoted in Waltz and James 2009, 375).

References

Auslander, Philip. 2005. "Performance as Therapy: Spalding Gray's Autopathographic Monologues." In *Bodies in Commotion: Disability and Performance*, edited by Carrie Sandahl and Philip Auslander, 163–174. Ann Arbor: University of Michigan Press.

Balls, Richard. 2000. *Sex & Drugs & Rock'n'Roll: The Life of Ian Dury.* London: Omnibus.

Barnes, Colin. 2003. "Effecting Change: Disability, Culture, and Art?" Paper presented at the Finding the Spotlight conference, Liverpool Institute for the Performing Arts, May 2003. Accessed January 17, 2014. http://disability-studies.leeds.ac.uk/files/library/Barnes-Effecting-Change.pdf.

Bennett, Andy. 2011. "The Post-Subcultural Turn: Some Reflections 10 Years On." *Journal of Youth Studies* 14 (5): 493–506.

Brown, Jayna, Patrick Deer, and Tavia Nyong'o, eds. 2013. "Punk and Its Afterlives." *Social Text* 116. http://socialtextjournal.org/issues/issue-116-fall-2013/.

Calvert, Dave. 2010. "Loaded Pistols: The Interplay of Social Intervention and Anti-Aesthetic Tradition in Learning Disabled Performance." *Research in Drama Education: The Journal of Applied Theatre and Performance* 15 (4): 513–528.

Cameron, Colin. 2009. "Tragic but Brave or Just Crips with Chips? Songs and Their Lyrics in the Disability Arts Movement." *Popular Music* 28 (3): 381–396.

Church, David. 2006. "'Welcome to the Atrocity Exhibition': Ian Curtis, Rock Death, and Disability." *Disability Studies Quarterly* 26 (4). http://dsq-sds.org/article/view/804/979.

Church, David. 2013. "Punk Will Tear Us Apart: Performance, Liminality, and Filmic Depictions of Disabled Punk Musicians." In *Different Bodies: Essays on Disability in Film and Television*, edited by Marja Evelyn Mogk, 28–38. Jefferson, NC: McFarland.

Cohen, Stanley. 1973. *Folk Devils and Moral Panics: The Creation of the Mods and Rockers.* St Albans, UK: Paladin.

Curtis, Deborah. (1995) 2007. *Touching from a Distance: Ian Curtis and Joy Division.* London: Faber.

Double, Oliver. 2007. "Punk Rock as Popular Theatre." *New Theatre Quarterly* 23 (1): 35–48.

Drury, Jim. 2003. *Ian Dury and the Blockheads: Song by Song.* London: Sanctuary.

Du Noyer, Paul. 1980. "Helen in Waiting: *Swindle* Star's Career Plans." *New Musical Express.* Accessed December 24, 2013. http://www.philjens.plus.com/pistols/pistols/pistols_swindle.html.

Dury, Ian. 1981a. Press release for "Spasticus Autisticus" (single), Polydor POSP/X 285.

Elflein, Dietmar. 2009. "A Popular Music Project and People with Disabilities Community in Hamburg, Germany: The Case of Station 17." *Popular Music* 28 (3): 397–410.

Garland-Thomson, Rosemarie. 2009. *Staring: How We Look.* Oxford: Oxford University Press.

Hall, Stuart, and Tony Jefferson, eds. 1975. *Resistance through Rituals: Youth Subcultures in Postwar Britain.* London: HarperCollins.

Hebdige, Dick. 1979. *Subculture: The Meaning of Style.* London: Routledge.

Kovasikajuttu/The Punk Syndrome. 2013. Official website. Accessed December 17, 2013. http://kovasikajuttu.fi/en/about-the-film.

Lindblad, Peter. 2009. "The Elastik Band: More Than Just a 'Spazz.'" *Musicstack*, April 29. http://www.musicstack.com/articles/elastik-band-more-than-just-a-spazz.

Lydon, John. 1994. *Rotten: No Irish, No Blacks, No Dogs.* With Keith Zimmerman and Kent Zimmerman. London: Hodder and Stoughton.

Marcus, Greil. 1990. *Lipstick Traces: A Secret History of the Twentieth Century.* London: Secker & Warburg.

McDonough, Jimmy. 2002. *Shakey: Neil Young's Biography.* London: Vintage.

McKay, George. 1996. *Senseless Acts of Beauty: Cultures of Resistance since the Sixties.* London: Verso.

McKay, George. 2005. *Circular Breathing: The Cultural Politics of Jazz in Britain.* Durham, NC: Duke University Press.

McKay, George. 2013. *Shakin' All Over: Popular Music and Disability.* Ann Arbor: University of Michigan Press.

McRuer, Robert. 2006. *Crip Theory: Cultural Signs of Queerness and Disability.* New York: New York University Press.

Middles, Mick. 1978. Review of *Joy Division. Sounds*, November 18.

Middles, Mick, and Lindsay Reade. 2006. *Torn Apart: The Life of Ian Curtis.* London: Omnibus.

Muggleton, David, and Rupert Weinzierl, eds. 2003. *The Post-Subcultures Reader.* Oxford, UK: Berg.

Murray, Charles Shaar. 1977. "The Social Rehabilitation of the Sex Pistols." *New Musical Express*, August 6.

O'Brien, Lucy. 2002. *She-Bop II: The Definitive History of Women in Rock, Pop, and Soul.* London: Continuum.

Paterson, Beverly. 2007. "An Interview with the Elastik Band's David Cortopassi, Standout Group during Late '60s in San Francisco." *MusicDish*, February 25. http://www.musicdish.com/mag/?id=11465.

Peace, William. 2009. "Punk Rock and Disability History." *Bad Cripple* (blog), June 17. http://badcripple.blogspot.co.uk/2009/06/punk-rock-and-disability-history.html.

Rahim, Sameer. 2012. "Paralympics 2012: Ian Dury's Spasticus Autisticus Was Electrifying." *Daily Telegraph*, 30 August. http://www.telegraph.co.uk/culture/music/9508444/Paralympics-2012-Ian-Durys-Spasticus-Autisticus-was-electrifying.html.

Sabin, Roger, ed. 1999. *Punk Rock: So What? The Cultural Legacy of Punk*. London: Routledge.
Savage, Jon. 1991. *England's Dreaming: Sex Pistols and Punk Rock*. London: Faber.
Savage, Jon. 2010. *The England's Dreaming Tapes*. Minneapolis: University of Minnesota Press.
Scarlet, Mik. 2011. "Mik's Doing the Other Thing." *Disability Now* (blog). http://www.disabilitynow.org.uk/article/miks-doing-other-thing.
Shakespeare, Tom. 2013. "Ian Dury (1942–2000)." *Our Statures Touch the Skies* (blog), 28 July. http://disabledlives.blogspot.co.uk/2013/07/ian-dury-1942-2000.html.
Siebers, Tobin. 2008. *Disability Theory*. Ann Arbor: University of Michigan Press.
Sirett, Paul. 2010. *Reasons to Be Cheerful*. Produced and performed by Graeae Theatre Company.
Spelman, Nicola. 2012. *Popular Music and the Myths of Madness*. Farnham, UK: Ashgate.
Waltz, Mitzi, and Martin James. 2009. "The (Re)marketing of Disability in Pop: Ian Curtis and Joy Division." *Popular Music* 28 (3): 367–380.
Zaiontz, Keren. 2013. "On the Streets/Within the Stadium: Art for and against the 'System' in Oppositional Responses to London 2012." *Contemporary Theatre Review* 23 (4): 502–518.

Discography/Filmography

Corbijn, Anton (director). 2007. *Control*. Momentum Pictures.
Crosby, David. 1970. "Almost Cut My Hair." Performed by Crosby, Stills, Nash and Young. *Déjà Vu*. Warner Brothers Records.
Dury, Ian. 1980. "Hey, Hey, Take Me Away." Performed with the Blockheads. *Laughter*. Stiff Records.
Dury, Ian. 1981b. "Spasticus Autisticus"/"Spasticus Autisticus (Version)." Polydor Records.
Elastik Band. 1967. "Spazz." *The Elastik Band*. Rerelease by Digital Cellars, 2007.
Hell, Richard, and the Voidoids. 1977. "Blank Generation." *Blank Generation*. Sire Records.
Joy Division. 1980a. "Atrocity Exhibition." *Closer*. Factory Records.
Joy Division. 1980b. "She's Lost Control." Twelve-minute version. "Atmosphere"/"She's Lost Control." Factory Records.
Kolbert, Kata. 1987. "Live Your Life"/"The Deed Is Done." Nevermore Records.
Kärkkäinen, Jukka, and J.-P. Passi (directors). 2012. *The Punk Syndrome*. Original Finnish title: *Kovasikajuttu*. Mouka Filmi.
Rothwell, Jerry (director). 2008. *Heavy Load*. Met Film.
Sex Pistols. 1977a. "God Save the Queen." *Never Mind the Bollocks . . . Here's the Sex Pistols*. Virgin Records.
Sex Pistols. 1977b. "Pretty Vacant." *Never Mind the Bollocks . . . Here's the Sex Pistols*. Virgin Records.
Sex Pistols. 1977c. "Holidays in the Sun." *Never Mind the Bollocks . . . Here's the Sex Pistols*. Virgin Records.
Sex Pistols. 1978. "Sex Pistols—Bodies." Live performance from Longhorn Ballroom concert in Dallas Texas (January 10). YouTube video, 3:59. September 30, 2008. http://www.youtube.com/watch?v=glgDZN3p1wM.
Temple, Julien (director). 1980. *The Great Rock 'n' Roll Swindle*. Virgin Films.
Whitecross, Mat (director). 2010. *Sex & Drugs & Rock & Roll*. UK Film Council et al.

CHAPTER 13

MOVING EXPERIENCES

Blindness and the Performing Self in Imre Ungár's Chopin

STEFAN SUNANDAN HONISCH

Introduction: "Portrait à son piano . . ."

In the holdings of the Bibliothèque Nationale de France, there are two black and white photographs of a young man seated at a piano (see Figure 13.1). In the first image, the stark illumination of the man's face and hands establishes distance between his body and the indistinct background, pushing the darkness away from the viewer's attention, even as the polarity between the pianist's self and the wholly "other" environment paradoxically weakens the lines separating physical, bodily, and musical spaces. The keyboard on which the man's fingers rest, along with the music he makes, seems to be on the verge of dissolving. In this ambiguous representation, the visual, the kinesthetic, and the sonic dance together to an unfamiliar music of the body in the world.

In the second photograph, the relationship between the pianist and the space he inhabits has been substantially demystified. The musician and his instrument are situated in a well-lit room, a bounded space in which the movements of body and of music, contrasted by the stasis of the room, are drawn into unity by the light that floods the image. Lightness dominates, ensuring that the boundaries of physical, bodily, and musical spaces are not, as in the first photograph, transgressed under the cover of darkness.

In both images, the man himself, elegantly attired in a suit and tie (complete with pocket square), projects an air of serenity, his upper body oriented slightly toward the camera. Hovering in the regions between sound and silence, lightness and darkness, blindness and sightedness, these photographs capture a pianist in meditation—absorbed, perhaps, by an inner music, fragments of which he seizes at the piano.[1] The caption (identical for both photographs) tells us that the pianist is Imre Ungár, a

FIGURE 13.1 Photographs dated 1932, of Imre Ungár. The caption reads: "Portrait à son piano de Imre Ungár, jeune pianist hongrois de 23 ans, aveugle de naissance, gagnant sur 92 concurrents du Congrès International Chopin de Varsovie en mars 1932" ("Portrait at his piano of Imre Ungár, a young twenty-three-year-old Hungarian pianist, blind since birth, winner ahead of ninety-two competitors of the International Chopin Competition in Warsaw in March 1932"). The photographs, consecutively foliated as MON 6335 and MON 6336, are available in digitized format from the Bibliothèque Nationale de France: http://gallica.bnf.fr/ark:/12148/btv1b9050482x.

twenty-three-year-old Hungarian pianist, "blind since birth" and a laureate of the 1932 Frédéric Chopin International Piano Competition in Warsaw.[2]

This caption gestures toward the historical significance of these portraits. As visual artifacts, the images provide us with a contemporaneous glimpse of the first blind pianist to secure a major prize at a prestigious international piano competition.[3] However, the photographs also point toward the larger theoretical domains of the performance of music and the performance of disability, which lie beyond the circumscribed context of music competitions and which constitute the intersecting themes for this essay. In order to understand how Imre Ungár's life and career were shaped by the simultaneous performance of music and disability (Straus 2011, 126), this essay begins with a biographical sketch that marks his position within the history of twentieth-century pianism and,

FIGURE 13.1 Continued.

more narrowly, within a subhistory of blind pianism.[4] Having secured this anchor point, my study will turn to the question of how Ungár's playing was received and understood by fellow musicians and critics. To these two "selves" of Imre Ungár, the "historical self" and the "received self," my essay adds the "performing self" (Cumming 2000), the emergent musical subjectivity projected by Ungár through his translation of bodily movement without sight into extraordinary musical performance.[5] This, then, is the path of inquiry that stretches ahead, a path horizoned at every turn by the performance of disability and the performance of music.

This essay contemplates what it means to perform blindness as an embodied experience of movement through physical and musical space, rather than as an expression of tragic loss, social isolation, and suffering. This shift in emphasis, from visual limitation to kinesthetic possibility, raises the question of how navigating the world without sight imprints the sensibilities of blind musicians in ways that transcend familiar discourses about their heightened aural sensitivity and that dispel anxieties concerning their reduced capacity for fluent movement (Ferguson 2007, Hollins 1936, Michalko 1998, Scott 1991). How might a blind pianist, for example, make music move in ways that remake the relationship between the performance of music and the performance of disability, between the musical space claimed by the performer and the physical space inhabited by the performer's body?[6] The focal point for this discussion is Ungár's recording of Frédéric Chopin's Prelude in B Minor Op. 28 No. 6. Guided on the one hand by Naomi Cumming's (2000) account of "the performing self" (an emergent identity that acquires shape through a performer's ability to control musical time [34]) and, on the other, by Joseph Straus's (2011) conception of "mobility-inflected hearing" (an understanding of musical time and space informed by disability experience [174]), my analysis seeks to understand how Ungár's performing self transforms blindness from a visual impairment into a moving, indeed "mobility-inflected," experience of physical and musical space.

The Historical, Sociocultural, and Musical Construction of Disability

In the history of Western thought, representations of blindness have frequently assigned stable attributes to the minds and bodies of blind people, imposing somatic order on what otherwise might have to be acknowledged as the unconquerable diversity of human experience (Barasch 2001, Garland-Thomson 1997). Essentialist definitions of blindness have looked casually, stared intently, and gazed dispassionately at the sightless eye and have found contradiction: simultaneously lacking and excessive, its estrangement from the phenomenal world counterbalanced by a steady inward gaze, the sightless eye has proved unsettling to those who see (Barasch 2001). As a consequence, other dimensions of blindness as a form of embodiment are, literally and figuratively, overlooked.[7] "Helplessness, dependency, melancholy, docility, gravity of inner thought, aestheticism . . . the things that commonsense views tell us to expect of the blind" (Scott 1991, 4) relegate blindness to the status of "uncommon sense" (Michalko 2002, 92), and fail to acknowledge that the outside world is knowable through, not "in spite of," blindness (Garland-Thomson 2005, 524).[8] Rosemarie Garland-Thomson (2005) draws a crucial link between lived experience and experienced environment, explaining that disability is given form and acquires meaning "when body encounters world." Further, she argues that "[e]very life evolves into disability, making it perhaps the essential characteristic of being human" (524).

The growth of Disability Studies, an interdisciplinary field of scholarship that took shape in the social and political activism of the disability rights movement, has done much to uproot the dualistic organizations of human experience that have produced such representations of blindness and similarly disabling representations of bodily difference (Barnes and Mercer 2003). Disability Studies takes as its starting point a vigorous critique of medical discourses about the body that pinpoint disability in the failings of individual bodies to do what bodies are normally supposed to do (Garland-Thomson 1997; Linton 1998; Sandahl and Auslander 2005).[9] Conceptually, Disability Studies scholars have emphasized disability as the outcome not of bodily failure but rather of a series of historical, cultural, and societal failures to make the world accessible to everyone, not just the able-bodied. A related theme not only unifies the theoretical and methodological diversity of subsequent Disability Studies research but also articulates this scholarly corpus to previous analyses of the historical and sociocultural production of race, gender, and sexuality. There is a shared concern in Disability Studies with the ways that disability comes into being through the dramatization of activities often accepted as quotidian. The myriad activities of daily life normally hidden by a veil of "taken-for-grantedness" acquire new meaning and urgency when *performed* by disabled people: such performances demand a reckoning with multiple barriers to access and participation, located on a continuum from the attitudinal to the architectural. Joseph Straus (2011) summarizes this relationship between the "social model of disability" and the elaboration of disability as a performance of bodily difference:

> Within a social or cultural model, disability is understood as constructed rather than given—it emerges from the activities of human beings in relation to each other and to the culture and built environment they inhabit, not from the medical pathology of an individual body. If disability is constructed, then it is constructed by people who are doing something, and their actions constitute a performance. To perform disability is to construct it, and vice versa. (127)

Cumulatively, these theoretical moves throw into sharp relief the habitual presentation of bodily experience in the language of "common sense"—that is, in an idiom whose legibility depends on the dual assumption that certain types of bodies and bodily activities (for example, seeing, hearing, and walking) are part of a widely shared, if not universal, human experience, and that consequently the meaning of such activities needs no further scrutiny.[10]

Heir to "unique cultural and somatic experiences," the disabled body holds the promise of remaking aesthetic and physical space (Sandahl and Auslander 2005, 9). To perform disability is to reimagine what it means to be in and to move through the world. The incorporation of this theoretical corpus into scholarship on music and disability has bolstered the project of scrutinizing the relationship between bodily and musical performance. Pivotal works in this regard include Cusick 1994, Mead 1999, and Le Guin 2005: although these scholars examine the unfolding of the relationship between the corporeal and the musical from different subdisciplinary perspectives, they nonetheless share a concern with the embodied experience of the performer and with how the performer's bodily movements arise in response to the choreography (of the performer's movements) implicit in written notation.[11] Extending this line of inquiry into the relationship between the corporeal and the musical, Disability Studies in music fosters a deep and sometimes disconcerting awareness of the sense of spectacle that envelops the music-making of disabled performers expected simultaneously "to perform music and to perform disability" (Straus, 2011, 126; see also Howe 2010).

The naturalization of ability and denaturalization of disability in the performance of Western art music reflect a more general status quo, crisply summarized by Petra Kuppers (2001): corporeality dominates aesthetics in the reception of disabled performers, such that "they [disabled performers] are often not primarily seen as performers but as disabled people. The disabled body is *naturally* about disability" (49–50; emphasis in original). Conversely, the normatively enabled body is *naturally* about ability. Here, aesthetics trumps corporeality, such that audience responses to nondisabled performers frequently give the body short shrift (Cumming 2000; Howe 2010). The radical consequence of thinking about disability as a performance, then, is that bodily difference ("disability") should not be understood in reductive terms as the theatrical display of a set of bodily "symptoms" associated with particular medical "conditions" but rather as a process whose interventions lie at the juncture between the stage and the world, between art and life.

A persistent theme in the collective imagination of blindness concerns the degree to which the absence of sight is assumed to negatively impact a person's ability to move fluently and easily; the inability to see supposedly "prevents a person from relating directly to his distant physical environment" (Scott 1991, 5; see also Ferguson 2007). In music pedagogy the training of blind pianists has presupposed the necessity of emulating sighted pianism as much as possible (Hollins 1936; Isaacs 1948). Historically, blind pianists themselves have sometimes legitimized this way of thinking. The British pianist Edward Isaacs (1881–1953), for example, is unequivocal about "the importance and necessity unanimously agreed upon by all leading blind musicians, of adopting and using the sighted pianist's methods as far as possible" (6). Largely absent from this discourse has been the question of how blind pianists might develop ways of experiencing and interpreting music on their own terms, independently of the norms of sighted pianism.

The Siegfried Altmann collection at the Leo Baeck Institute in New York holds another photograph of Imre Ungár from 1937 (Figure 13.2).[12] In contrast to the two photographs discussed earlier, in which Ungár's eyes are open and his expression serene, in this image his eyes are closed, his brow furrowed, thereby dramatizing the pianist's blindness. The sense that Ungár is perhaps experiencing an inner music is here intensified by the expression of absorption on his face.[13] Before developing a case study of Imre Ungár's musical remaking of blindness, it will be helpful to narrate the circumstances of his life and work as a pianist, teacher, and advocate on behalf of blind people.

Imre Ungár: The Historical Self

Imre Ungár was born in Budapest on January 23, 1909, and spent the greater part of his life there, contributing to the musical life of the city as a pianist, teacher, essayist, and competition juror.[14] Of his diverse musical accomplishments, his distinguished showing at the 1932 Chopin competition is most frequently cited in the secondary literature in English (Dubal 1995; Kehler 1982; Prosnak 1970). The cause of his blindness is not discussed in any of the English language sources; however, according to Ungár's former student, the pianist Tamás Németh (himself a blind pianist), it was the result of a brain tumor in childhood (Németh, 2012, para. 4).[15] Ungár began piano lessons when

FIGURE 13.2 Photograph of Imre Ungár, signed and dedicated in 1937 by the pianist to Siegfried Altmann, director of the Jewish Institute for the Blind in Vienna. The inscription reads: "Herrn Dyr.[ektor] Altmann mit herzlichem Dank und aufrichtiger Hochschätzung gewidmet Imre Ungár 23. V. (VI?) 1937 Wien" ["Dedicated to Director Altmann with hearty thanks and sincere regard, Imre Ungár Vienna 23rd May (June?) 1937."] The typescript at the bottom of the photograph reads, "Blinder Chopin-Preisgewinner in Warschau, Imre Ungár, Schüler des Instituts" ["Blind winner of the Chopin Prize in Warsaw, Imre Ungár, Student of the Institute"]. Courtesy of the Leo Baeck Institute, New York. Reprinted by permission.

he was five years old, presumably at the Budapest Institute for the Blind. His musical interests were encouraged by his father and mother, who felt that "despite his impairment he should study the piano" (Dybowski 2010, 73). By the time he graduated from the Franz Liszt Academy in Budapest (where he studied with István Thomán), Ungár had embarked on a performing career (Kehler 1982, 1344).

Although Ungár's earliest competitive success came about through his participation in a talent show in his native Hungary, it was not until his second-prize win at the 1932 Frédéric Chopin International Piano Competition that his career as a pianist began reaching farther afield, eventually taking him across Europe and to the United States (Kehler 1982, 1344; Prosnak 1970, 32). In a cable announcing the results of the 1932 Chopin Competition, the *New York Times* (March 25, 1932) enthused that "[t]he blind Hungarian pianist, a son of a poor shopkeeper [*sic*], won the hearts of Warsaw by his sympathetic and flawless playing" (22) and noted that Ungár was staying at the Institute for the Blind in Warsaw. Ungár took second prize, despite scoring the same number of points as the first-prize winner Alexander Uninski; the competition rules that year stipulated that ties must be decided by coin toss.[16]

Ungár's postcompetition activities included concertizing, recording, and teaching at the Franz Liszt Academy, where he earlier had studied. He was also active as a juror on the competition circuit, mostly in his native Hungary (Alink 1990; Kehler 1982).[17] During World War II, Ungár and his wife lived for a time in the Netherlands, and it was there that they became friendly with Etty Hillesum and her family, whose published diaries offer fleeting glimpses into musical evenings with Ungár and his wife (Hillesum 2002). The birth of their son István in 1945 brought a measure of stability in the midst of the chaos of war (Németh 2012, para. 4).

Ungár resumed concertizing in 1946; it was also around this time that he began his tenure at the Franz Liszt Academy. Németh underscores the historical significance of Ungár's appointment to the Liszt Academy, noting that when he began studying with Ungár in 1965, his teacher was the only blind musician on faculty (2012, para. 2). István Ungár offers further detail about his father's shift in focus from performance to pedagogy:

> My father took up a teaching post at the [Franz Liszt] Music Academy after the war and was awarded the Kossuth Prize [a Hungarian cultural award] in 1949. He rarely gave concerts after that partly due to the atrocities he had suffered during the war but also because a great deal of his time was taken up with teaching. (personal communication with the author)

István Ungár explains that his father's repertoire was dominated by the music of Chopin, but also included a number of sonatas by Beethoven, including several of the late sonatas (Op. 101 and Op. 111); preludes and fugues from Johann Sebastian Bach's *Well-Tempered Clavier*; and shorter piano pieces by Bartók, Kodály, and Brahms (personal communication with the author; see also Kehler 1982, 1344–1345).[18] Ungár left a handful of recordings, mostly of solo piano music by Frédéric Chopin and Béla Bartók, including Chopin's complete Preludes, Op. 28.[19] With the main contours of Ungár's life and career surveyed, it is now possible to narrow the focus more closely to his pianism. The next section of this essay therefore surveys descriptions of Ungár's piano playing by a number of his contemporaries.

Imre Ungár: The Received Self

The recordings of Ungár's performances at the 1932 Chopin competition are lost, destroyed during World War II.[20] However, written descriptions of his playing that year give some idea of what Ungár must have sounded like at this early stage of his career. Among these accounts, one by the music critic Stanisław Niewiadomski (1859–1936) relies heavily on a narrow set of tropes in the reception of blind musicians.[21] The preface to Niewiadomski's account describes Ungár as a "blind visionary" ("niewidomy-wizjoner"), whose pianism expressed his inner vision in sound (Polskie Radio, 2014).[22] Within Niewiadomski's normalizing frame (one in which Ungár must perform blindness), the inward, searching quality of Ungár's interpretations projects a tragic mood "resulting from the plight of blindness." Niewiadomski casts his response in terms of the pervasive reception of blindness—based on both the tragic loss of sight and the transcendence of music sharply accented because of this disparity. For Niewiadomski, blindness confers a freedom from the constraints of the world, its norms and rules of etiquette, leaving the blind pianist to plumb hidden realms of expression and to transcend the physicality of musical performance.

A sense of how Ungár must have sounded the year of his second prize at the Chopin Competition may be gleaned from *The New Beacon: A Magazine Devoted to the Achievements of the Blind*, which contains a brief but telling report on a concert given by the "remarkably talented pianist" on October 27, 1932, at London's Wigmore Hall. The most immediate and "outstanding" feature of Ungár's pianism, according to this account, is "impetuosity." Despite some reservations in this regard, the reviewer praises Ungár's "impeccable technique" in Ludwig van Beethoven's Sonata in A-flat Major, Op. 110, and in Robert Schumann's *Carnaval*. Describing Ungár's performances as "persuasive as well as masterful . . . [if] occasionally a trifle aggressive," the reviewer concludes that the pianist is a musician of "wide sympathies and forceful personality . . . clearly destined for a place among the elect" ("A Blind Pianist of Exceptional Talent" 1932, 269–270). Significantly, this account of Ungár's pianism does not make reference to his blindness, focusing instead on strictly musical issues, an emphasis all the more remarkable in a publication aimed at making its readership aware of how blind people were participating in mainstream society.

Another anonymous review of two concerts that Ungár gave in Milan, a few years after his Chopin competition victory, describes the pianist's musicianship in similarly exuberant language. The pianist "immediately reveals an impeccable technique, an artistic sentiment alive to each gradation and nuance of the divine language of music" ("Imre Ungár"1934, 35).[23] As with the review of Ungár's Wigmore Hall performance, this account also advances a larger claim about the pianist's importance: "Among the artists who in every age are ranked among the great interpreters of the mysteries of the human soul, Imre Ungár, the blind pianist, holds one of the leading positions together with the sighted" (35).

By contrast, the following description of Ungár performing at the 1932 Chopin competition traffics in shop-worn notions about blindness (Dybowski 2010, 73; emphasis in original):

> The blind pianist sits down at the piano and begins to play the first movement of Concerto in E minor. The capacity audience listens with held breath. Some cry deeply moved. The twenty-three-year-old man, who has never seen the light of day, living in the darkness of an eternal night, sings about the anguish of his life with Chopin's

> immortal harmonies. *Romance* flows, reflecting the composer's love experiences. Imre Ungár sings a love story though he has never seen a woman. . . . He is forbidden to love because he will not even know whom he loves. . . . Thus he loves his instrument with all his passionate heart.[24]

The evocation of blindness as eternal night (darkness), the equation of loss of sight with loss of sexuality (emblematized as the inability to love and be loved), and the emphasis on the limitations of the disabled body, coarsely juxtaposed against the transcendental power of music: cumulatively, these representations envelop Ungár in an atmosphere of spectacle, tragedy, and limbo. For this reviewer, Chopin's "immortal" music functions merely as a vehicle for Ungár's performance of blindness. Instead of offering an elucidation of Ungár's pianism, this account functions as a kind of repository for cultural anxieties about blindness.[25]

The impression that Ungár made on audiences at the 1932 Chopin competition is captured in Ladislaus Takács' *Der Ungár in der Welt* (1934). In contrast to the overwrought tone and clichés that characterize other reviews, Takács offers a more thoughtful assessment of Ungár's pianism. While also foregrounding the expressive rather than technical features of Ungár's pianism, Takács implicitly locates the pianist within a larger collective musical tradition, rather than simply in relation to other blind musicians: Ungár's playing "was filled with a unique, painful beauty that is so characteristic of Hungarian music-making. . . . The success that he achieved [in subsequent concert tours] corroborated the judgment of the Warsaw jury" (133).

Yet another description of Ungár's pianism as it sounded to his contemporaries in the decade after his Chopin competition triumph comes from the music critic Aladár Tóth (1939), a long-time friend of both Ungár and his wife (Németh 2012; Bónis, 2014). In this case, the surface characteristics attributed to Chopin's music—balanced phrasing and a *bel canto* singing style, for example—recede to the background of the review, as Tóth isolates features of Ungár's playing that illuminate something fundamental in the Polish composer's music.[26] In reviewing a concert that Ungár gave on January 23, 1939 (probably in Budapest), Tóth mentions that one of his friends, also a critic, surmised that the composer would doubtless recognize Ungár as a distant relative.[27]

Tóth finds that any hint of "Parisian elegance" is absent in Ungár's interpretations of the music of Chopin (specifically the Scherzo in B Minor). Instead what strikes him is the tragic sensibility that characterizes Ungár's Chopin playing, a nuanced rendering of the music's peculiarly Slavic moods, of a passion that does not let wounds heal (Tóth1973, 2). What emerges, according to Tóth, is not an outward observance of interpretive niceties presented in superficially attractive sounds, but rather an excavation of the music's inner meaning.

As this perusal of Ungár's critical reception would seem to indicate, there is a tension between those reviewers who give priority to the aesthetic qualities of his pianism, glancing quickly at his disability, and those who locate Ungár's blindness as a constraint on his experience of the world and therefore as a defining limitation on his interpretive abilities. In the stories about disability that these reviewers tell (see Michael Beckerman's essay in this Handbook), a struggle plays out over whether to position disability as central or marginal to understanding Ungár's pianism. In what follows, I tell my own story, starting from the premise that disability and music interlock in unfamiliar and generative ways in Ungár's rendering of Chopin's Prelude in B Minor.

Imre Ungár: The Performing Self

I borrow two concepts—the "performing self" from Cumming 2000 and "mobility-inflected hearing" from Straus 2011 to help make sense of what Ungár accomplishes in this interpretation. Naomi Cumming (2000) uses the idea of a "performing self" to refer to the musical identity formed in the act of making music, contingent on a performer's ability to control the expressive movement of notes (34).[28] Joseph Straus (2011) theorizes "mobility-inflected hearing" to account for the formative influence of movement in a disabled body on musical understanding (174). Because bodily difference does not figure strongly in Cumming's account of the "performing self," and because Straus's "mobility-inflected hearing" encompasses musical experience generally, rather than performance specifically, a theoretical perspective informed by both is well suited to my present aims.

Two brief qualifications are in order. First, Cumming's elaboration of the "performing self" separates intentional transgressions of normal musical movement from the lack of fluency that mars technically inept performance. Her discussion, in this context, of "jerky motion" (34) suggests congruities as well as tensions with Straus's exploration of the influence of nonnormative bodily movement on musical experience. Whereas Straus acknowledges the expectations placed on disabled performers to simultaneously perform music and perform disability (2011, 126), Cummings insists that qualitative features of a performance that create a musical identity cannot be correlated with the extramusical self of the performer with regard to gender, ethnicity, age, and (although she does not include it) disability. In her view, trying to interpret the former in terms of the latter is not justified, even when it is acknowledged that "the social and commercial context of performance promotes the formation of such images" (27). Taking this tension between Cumming and Straus as a starting point, the analytical approach in this essay works to open up the "performing self" to the body in all its diversity, delving into its untidy collections of abilities and disabilities: a performer's repertoire of embodied experiences, in this case Ungár's movements through the world with blindness, needs to be accommodated rather than marginalized in understanding the formation of the "performing self."

The second caveat also signals a departure from and possible dissonance with the theoretical perspectives I mobilize in the analysis that follows. Straus (2011) asks, "How might a non-normative way of moving through the world, either with a halting gait or with a wheelchair affect . . . the perception and cognition of music?"(174). For the following analysis, it is necessary to direct Straus's question along a slightly different path.

Instead of a *halting* gait, what is at stake in this essay is a *blind* gait that potentially finds nonnormative modes of fluent movement. Recall that a disabled performer is expected to simultaneously perform music and disability (Straus 2011, 126). The concept of "gait" in the present case study therefore locates Ungár's "performing self" in an embodied experience of movement in blindness, a performance at once bodily and musical.

The following discussion of Ungár's 1958 recording of Chopin's Prelude in B Minor Op. 28 No. 6 focuses on a series of "moments" in which Ungár's interpretive strategies might be understood to express blindness not as a disabling visual loss but rather as a richly nuanced way of moving through musical space. The analysis refers to these moments using time cues (minutes: seconds) from the recording, which can be heard as Track 13.1 on the Companion Website.[29]

The overall shape of Ungár's interpretation of Chopin's Prelude in B Minor suggests a way of moving from an origin to a goal that can be interpreted productively in terms of nonvisual (tactile, auditory, and kinesthetic) experience. What might be understood prescriptively and proscriptively as the absence of steady gait, the lack of forward momentum in the music's "footfalls" (the pulsating eighth notes in the right hand, the arpeggiated figure in the left hand), can be reinterpreted, following Cumming (2000) and Straus (2011), as a "performing self" constituted through an immersive experience of blind gait, rather than as a disadvantaged musical identity beset by the disabling condition of being unable to see and therefore unable to move with fluency or with sensitivity to the gradations of melodic (horizontal) and harmonic (vertical) space.

Sighted ways of moving through the world may give rise to a way of understanding musical movement that privileges *steady* gait, the ability to *see* ahead, and to move resolutely toward a destination *foreseen*. It may be, however, that in the context of instrumental performance, such an aesthetic naturalizes the ability to make sense of musical movement in reference to lived experiences of seeing, while denaturalizing (to return to Kuppers' [2001] claim about the naturalization of ability) nonsighted ways of moving that place greater value on spontaneous, intuitive movement and lesser emphasis on goal-directed movement. Nonvisual ways of moving through the world might be less preoccupied with normal movement forward and less anxious about ensuring that changes of pace or different types of gait maintain a high level of consistency in motion. Despite the absence of primary and secondary sources that discuss how Ungár himself navigated the world, how he walked, and how his body moved when he was playing the piano, the expressive movements of Ungár's "performing self" nonetheless demand a reckoning with the often hidden regulatory power that sighted modes of corporeal movement exert in defining the boundaries of normal interpretive etiquette. His is not a mode of musical movement characterized by steady acceleration and deceleration, or by a consistent gait—forms of movement perhaps more familiar in the work of sighted pianists. Having thus mapped some general features of this recording by Ungár, let us focus on a series of moments in which his "performing self" disrupts expectations concerning normative musical flow; we will work to make sense of this in terms of Ungár's lived experience of moving in blindness.

0:00–0:25. Ungár "feels" the musical environment through his fingers in the prelude's first few moments. The slight hesitation in the opening moments of the Prelude evokes the image of Ungár taking time to get to know his physical and musical surroundings. This performing self moves in reference not primarily to goals *seen* in the distance, but rather in acknowledgement of the tactile features of the musical topography.

This translates, sonically, into increased awareness of the relationship between hearing and moving, between musical sound and musical movement such that, in place of a uniform tempo that is then subjected to expressive variation, strict tempo is revealed as an artifice built on the assumption that articulating musical form demands adherence to the inexorable forward march of time. Features ascribed through normative projections of sightedness onto blind movement link the inability to see, literally and figuratively, with "stumbling," "hesitation," "uncertainty," and "halting gait." To move blindly in the discourse of constructed normalcy (Davis 1995), then, carries strong overtones of uncertainty, of darkness, even of fear (Ferguson 2007). The opening sonority is broken, the left hand slightly anticipating the right, even as Ungár's pianistic self lingers over the low B3, calling attention to the wide registral space that Chopin defines with the opening sonority. The left-hand figure expresses reluctance simply to move forward, without first attaining a fully embodied experience of what lies beneath; the heaviness that Ungár's pianistic self imparts to the B3, evocative of the pianist's fingers firmly grounded in the keys can thus be understood as a claim about the importance of what musical space feels like, not simply what it sounds like.

Ungár's use of expressive "noncoordination" between right hand and left hand, a common feature in nineteenth- and early twentieth-century pianism (Arnest 2014; Rosenblum 1994), can be considered from the perspective of "mobility-inflected hearing."[30] The nonsynchrony, interpreted according to normative conceptions of ability, would suggest that the musical movement has been interrupted momentarily, and that a return to normal alignment between the left and right hands is necessary in order to maintain an able-bodied gait: furthermore, while nonsynchrony might exert rhetorical and expressive power within limits, a privileging of synchrony, of smooth alignment, reinforces the superiority of musical movements that are consistent with the ways of moving through the world in an able body.[31] (The noncoordination is most audible with the very first chord.)

0:25–0:34. The most striking "moment" in Ungár's 1958 recording is surely the first cadence, specifically the sharp acceleration at 0:28. The F♯4 in the right hand marks the highest point the performing self has had to scale thus far: the preceding right-hand chords outline B4 and D4 respectively before embarking on a roughly scalar ascent toward the F♯. The sonorous high point (an F♯-major chord in first inversion) is "rushed" by normative standards; instead of lingering over this climactic chord, Ungár quickens his gait. That this rhythmic "disruption" occurs at a cadence is instructive for analyzing the musical performance of blind gait. The function of the cadence as a temporary pause with differing levels of closure, is given new meaning by Ungár's performing self. Building on the premise that the unusual rhythmic profile of Ungár's interpretation results not from a "failure" of bodily control, but rather from a "controlled" expressive intent, this moment can be heard as transformative: the responsibility now falls on the perceiver to lay aside preconceived notions that Ungár's inability to see might cause him to play in a rhythmically erratic manner, that the deeply subjective quality of this interpretation is in some way linked to isolation from the external world enforced by his disability. Ungár's handling of this cadence can be understood as an expression not of bodily failure (a lack of the technical fluency needed to control the movement of notes), not of a preoccupation with his own emotions to the detriment of the music, but rather of a richly expressive and organic translation of what it is like to move in—not in spite of—blindness. The unfamiliar shape given to this passage intensifies rather than weakens the expressivity of the cadence, of the phrase, and of the prelude by throwing into sharp relief the singularity of the sixteenth-note figure in the right hand near the end of the cadential passage. Ungár shows that it is not necessary for him to see his environment in order to grasp the interrelationship between its various levels. The emphasis given to the right hand's sixteenth-note figure through its sharply different gait highlights its uniqueness; this is the one time that it appears in the landscape traversed by the right hand. Simultaneously, however, the singularity of this moment in Ungár's interpretation shores up the unity of the environment, in which it is to the left hand that the work of tracing small and large-scale melodic contours is assigned.

0:43–0:56. The dual conceptual apparatus of the "performing self" and "mobility-inflected hearing" enables a critical reappraisal of the assumption that to move blindly is to be constrained by uncertainty when navigating large distances (Hollins 1936). Ungár's interpretation of the left-hand arpeggiations suggests an analogy between jumping through physical space in the world and the pianistic jumping necessary to navigate wide intervals on the keyboard. The "blind gait" of Ungár's performing self is unfazed by these wide leaps, highlighting their contingency and fragility through his refusal to perform them as determinate figures whose start and end points are visualized in advance, and controlling how the performing self moves. At the sonic level, Ungár imparts a brilliant tonal shine as he immerses himself in the aural radiance and tactile depth of C major. The downward movement has a quality of impetuousness that brings to mind the review of the young Ungár (triumphant after his recent competition success) at Wigmore Hall in 1932, cited above. The pedaling also emphasizes the shift away from normative sighted movement over a smooth musical surface. Ungár's performing self attends thoughtfully to the repeated chords in the right hand, to their temporal and spatial precariousness, which the overall tonality of B minor cannot fully normalize.

Ungár's performing self and the prelude's musical environment are both in constant flux: the gently fluctuating ground of the right hand accommodates rather than constrains the arpeggiated "footfalls"; indeed, the very distinction between "footfall" and "ground" is constantly in question. The nonvisual experience revealed here does not require such rigid separation of self and other, between stability and instability, movement and stasis. This nonvisual performing self expresses a resolute belief that to move without sight, *blindly*, is to move in defiance of the normalizing assumptions of sighted passers-by, leaving the tropes of blindness as unrelenting tragedy and social isolation by the wayside.

The C-major tonicization is given a "mobility-inflected" urgency by Ungár's performing self, who struggles to transcend the tonally distant region of C major (the Neapolitan sonority).[32] The rhythmic "instability" of Ungár's interpretation thus "works" musically to accentuate the tense atmosphere of this passage and the dissonant position that it occupies relative to the normalizing tonal force of B minor.

0:56–1:11. Ungár's performing self does not "stumble" over the wide-ranging (registral) movements of the left hand; instead, the "mobility inflections" given tangible form in impulsive changes of gait can be interpreted as a reminder: we are asked to be mindful that the act of performing (and of blind performing, especially) destabilizes the fixity of the notated musical work (analogous, following Straus 2006 and 2011, to the human body), dislodging the visual medium of notation from the center of musical experience. Blind pianism can attenuate the power of musical sight and foresight to map and so to define the start and end point of a musical journey (analogous to the "fate of the body" against which disability can serve as a staunch reminder of personhood [Michalko 2002, 11]). Ungár's musical performance of blindness makes a dynamic time and space that escapes visual containment. The deceptive cadence is here remade as a musical entity whose purpose is not merely to mark a point of relative melodic and harmonic instability. For Ungár's performing self, this deceptive cadence unveils a deeper truth: the constructedness of musical and physical space according to bodily norms. In this particular passage, cadential punctuations allow the eye and the ear a measure of rest, even as the performing self must press on—the left hand in preparation for navigating a wide space, as the right hand continues its tactile exploration of the B minor "ground" beneath.

Music theorist Alan Dodson (2011) explains that expressive timing and phrase structure are deeply intertwined. Citing a wealth of empirical research, he writes, "the tempo profile of a phrase tends to resemble an arch with a slow beginning, followed by an acceleration, deceleration, and slow ending" (3). Ungár's pianistic self makes this cadential phrase move in accordance with the norm that Dodson identifies: slow beginning, acceleration, deceleration, and slow ending. However the differences between these rates of speed performed by Ungár are rendered in dramatized form. The boundaries between acceleration and deceleration, slow and fast, steady and unsteady, are fraught with uncertainty, but in uncertainty lies discovery rather than fear.

This aspect of Ungár's performing self suggests that Cumming's (2000) argument concerning the importance of a "well-balanced physical adjustment to the instrument . . . [in] creating the impression of musical personality" (22–23) requires fine-tuning. The phrase "well-balanced physical adjustment to the instrument" is problematic despite its flexible wording. Difficulty arises in the implication that, with proper training, it is possible to experience balance independent of the myriad inflections of bodily diversity. Cumming's formulation does not, in other words, move far enough toward an acknowledgment that a performer's bodily relationship to the instrument is far from uniform. What it might mean for a blind pianist (taking our present example) to make a "well-balanced physical adjustment to the instrument" will quite possibly be incommensurable with the strategies developed by a sighted pianist. In such cases, pace Hollins (1936) and Isaacs (1948), the point is not to insist on the preeminence of sighted pianism, but to embrace the technical strategies and interpretive sensibilities that a blind pianist offers through the performance of blindness.

The "performing self" that Ungár projects is characterized by a way of moving through musical time that is discontinuous; the pedaling and phrasing choices that Ungár makes are not expressive of a "well-balanced physical adjustment" to the piano (Cumming 2000, 22–23), if what it means to be "well balanced" is guided by normative expectations about the importance of sightedness for ease and fluency of physical movement.

1:12–1:26. The repetition of the scalar figure in the left hand after the deceptive cadence (1:06–1:11) prioritizes its differential position in the unfolding of musical time, rather than its initial harmonic and melodic similarity to what came before. As Ungár made sense of his world through nonvisual modalities, so too does he make sense of this cadential passage in a way that prioritizes nonvisual experiences of musical ebb and flow, the interplay between movement and stasis. When the medium of musical experience is sound recording (as in the present analysis), the embodied nature of music making can fall into neglect (Cumming 2000; Howe 2010). As Naomi Cumming (2000) observes, "It is obvious that musical sounds are not, in origin, an impersonal or accidental event, that they do not come to exist in the disembodied medium of a CD without the action of a performer's body, but technological intervention can induce a partial forgetfulness of this fact" (21–22). Aside from its conceptual power in guiding analysis of the musical performance of disability, then, Straus's "mobility-inflected hearing," because of its concern with bodily movement in relation to musical experience, opens up a path for inquiry in which the movements of the performer's body are not only remembered but also woven tightly into the analysis itself. It is this synergy between the body in music and the musical body in the world that Ungár's interpretation of this prelude emphasizes. This synergy, in turn, reconfigures the prelude's internal rhythms, local and global, and, in so doing, places the vertical (harmonic) and horizontal (melodic) dimensions on an unfamiliar continuum in a profoundly kinesthetic, "mobility-inflected" realm.

Educational practices that aim to cultivate disability awareness—for example, inviting sighted people to wear blindfolds, and in so doing, to gain understanding (read: empathy) for the difficulties faced by blind people in their daily lives—have been castigated by Disability Studies scholars. The theoretical work of Disability Studies teaches us that such interventions fail to unravel the coarse threads that tie biological difference such as blindness to disabling representations of tragedy, sensory impoverishment, and the loss or attenuation of complete personhood (Michalko 2002; see also Titchkosky 2003 and 2012).[33] Instead, as Alison Kafer (2013) explains, efforts to duplicate the experience of disability for the edification of the nondisabled perpetuate a superficial engagement with unfamiliar modes of embodiment: the idea that, as in the present example, "the only thing there is to learn about blindness is what it feels like to move around in the dark" (4–5).[34] The nonnormative rhythmic movements of Ungár's rendering of this prelude counteract reductionist definitions of blindness limited to what the eyes *cannot* do, and transform blindness into the lyrical, moving expression of what the body *can* do. To move blindly, following in Ungár's footsteps, is to move out of step with the hackneyed uses of blindness as a metaphor for "inattention, ignorance or prejudice," and, breaking free from the norms of sightedness, to stand in resolute opposition against the enduring trope of blindness as a "tragedy too dire to contemplate" (Kleege 2013, 454), and to embrace blindness as a richly dynamic part of the human experience, eminently worth contemplating.

No single defining characteristic of blind experience can be extracted from Ungár's rendition of Chopin's Prelude in B Minor. His performing self reveals much more than simply what it feels like to move around the piano in darkness. Because Ungár performs blindness in this elusive way, the critical reception discussed earlier—a prelude, as it were, to my analysis—loses its familiarity, its air of "common sense" in the description of blind pianism. The blind pianism of Ungár's performing self reveals dimensions of musical experience that defy familiar reference points. In their place, Ungár offers a shifting environment in which boundaries are porous and permeable; the distinction between sensory domains (the auditory and the tactile) usually demarcated as very different modes of musical experience are revealed here as deeply intertwined. Musical time is disordered so that the near and the far, detail and broad gesture, no longer occupy "normal" positions within the prelude's narrative.

Conclusion: "Let the Piano Sing beneath Your Fingers"

In Hungarian, the original formulation of the quote in the heading is "daloljon a zongora a kezedalatt." This was one of Ungár's most frequent exhortations to his students, according to Németh (2012, para. 2).

Imre Ungár's importance extends in several directions: in the history of piano performance and pedagogy; in the history of international piano competitions at the head of a line of blind competitors whose collective participation in such institutions calls out for systematic study; and in the history of music education for blind people.[35] Ungár's career offers multiple points of entry for further scholarship in Disability Studies and music, not only for theoretical and analytical work on the musical performance of disability but also for continual reflection on the musical performance of ability and for demonstrations of how these modes of performance are continually inscribed with new levels of meaning at the juncture of performance, music criticism, audience reception, and scholarly analysis.

Acknowledging music's nonreferential qualities, Straus (2011) points out its potential to narrate experiences of human embodiment: he argues, this non-verbal medium has a narrative dimension, "and among the stories it tells are stories of disability. Some . . . are narratives of overcoming—the triumph of the human spirit over adversity—but others are more nuanced tales of accommodation and acceptance of life with a non-normative body or mind" (12). Extending Straus's insight to the domain of musical performance, I find that the story of blindness that Ungár's performance tells is one of blindness rescued from representations of loss: his story, narrated through his performing self, moves lyrically through a time and space that makes "uncommon sense" into an uncommonly musical experience (Michalko 2009, 98).[36]

There are obvious subjective and speculative dimensions to my "mobility-inflected" approach to Ungár's performance. Indeed, the story my analysis offers is of Ungár's musical performance of blindness as I understand it, rather than an explication of Ungár's own experiences. My analysis is based on acts of imagination and empathetic projection based on textual sources and on my personal experience of his interpretation. (For more on this perspective, consult Michael Beckerman's essay in this volume.) I have drawn selectively on primary and secondary sources (cited in the earlier sections on Ungár's "historical" and "received" selves) in order to come to grips with those features of his interpretation that point toward a sensibility in rhythm and phrasing that might reflect the influence of blindness.

This approach leads me to conclude that just as a composer's disability might influence and even change the way her or his music is received by audiences who know or come to know of the disability, so too does a performer's disability, even when not directly observed (e.g., in recordings), shape the way her or his pianism is experienced. Brought up short against the limits of normal musical experience, preconceived notions about musical time and space fall by the wayside. Ungár lets the piano sing beneath his fingers in his rendering of the prelude, transforming blindness into a moving experience and expanding the possibilities of performing the body's repertoire of abilities and disabilities musically.

Two stanzas from a poem "Sírfelirat" (Epitaph) by István Ungár, written in honor of his father, make a fitting coda to this chapter. From among familiar discursive threads in the representation of blind people there emerges an acknowledgment of the significance of István's father to his own story. Tellingly, in each stanza this acknowledgment is paired with an assertion of distance. The blind musical father remains an enigma even to his own son, even as his gaze penetrates deep into his son's psyche:

> His glass eyes have seen no light
> But his heart saw distances further than any of us.
> I had no thoughts unknown to him,
> He remained a secret although showing everything to us.[37]
> He made me rich, infinitely rich,
> His music made me happy forever.
> His world was that of Bach, Beethoven and Chopin,
> And he withstood troubles with the smile of Mozart.

Music unites performer and listener, father and son, in intersubjective and embodied musical experiences. Yet, it also reinforces the divide between the public world of the sighted and the inner world of the blind. In this poetic representation, the visible and the audible, the invisible and the inaudible, sing beneath the fingers of a pianist in a music at once familiar and strange.

Acknowledgments

I thank Floyd Grave, Blake Howe, Shersten Johnston, Elaine Sisman, Joseph Straus, and the anonymous reviewers of this volume for their insightful critiques and helpful advice in response to an earlier draft of this essay. Conversations with Erika Honisch and August Sheehy helped me to clarify my thinking on key aspects of this essay. I also thank the anonymous reviewer for useful suggestions to improve the organization of the essay as a whole.

Notes

1. Joseph Straus (2011) defines "inner hearing" as "the ability to conceptualize music in its full particularity in the absence of audible sound" and emphasizes the importance of this ability "for performers (who need to know, silently and in advance, what sound they are to produce)" (169–170).
2. I am grateful to Guillaume Lefebvre for his help translating this passage. There are two inaccuracies with this caption: Ungár actually came in second place, and his surname should be spelled with an accent. This latter error is common and can be found in many of the primary and secondary sources used in this essay. I have included the missing accent when quoting from these sources for the sake of clarity and consistency.
3. Prosnak (1970, 30 and 32) provides photographs of Ungár in his survey of the reception of the Frédéric Chopin competition from its inception in 1927 through to 1965. The eighth edition of the competition (1970) had not yet taken place before the book was published. The reproductions of photographs, press clippings, and other documents in this book were gathered from the collections of the Frédéric Chopin Institute in Warsaw and from a number of other institutional and private collections. However, the attribution of sources is inconsistent, and Prosnak does not specify the collections from which the two photographs of Ungár are taken. A further inconsistency with this source is its pagination. Not all of the pages in the edition of Prosnak 1970 that I consulted are numbered. For the sake of both clarity and consistency I have therefore filled in missing page numbers when quoting from this source.
4. As a subcategory of "blind musicians," blind pianists are generally more familiar outside the domain of Western art music. In popular and jazz idioms, for example, there are iconic figures such as Ray Charles, Stevie Wonder, and George Shearing as well as more historically distant musicians such as Thomas Wiggins (Jensen-Moulton 2006) and John William Boone (Rowden 2009, Sacks 2007, Straus 2011). Blind pianists in Western art music include Maria Theresia Paradis (1759–1824), whom Burney (1785) described as a "young person equally distinguished by her talents and misfortunes" and mentions that she played music (by her teacher Leopold Kozeluch) with the "utmost neatness and

expression" (80) (see also Angermüller 2001); Alfred Hollins (1865–1942), who studied with Hans von Bülow (Hollins 1936); Edward Baxter Perry (1855–1924), who counted Clara Schumann and Franz Liszt among his teachers; and Edward Isaacs (1881–1953). The history of international music competitions offers a rich terrain for studying the participation of disabled performers and in particular of blind pianists (Alink 1990). While the intense media coverage of the blind pianist Nobuyuki Tsujii's shared gold medal with the sighted pianist Haochen Zhang at the 2009 Van Cliburn International Piano Competition has, to a degree, brought the contours of this larger history into view, systematic excavation of its sociocultural, political, and aesthetic levels awaits future study (Ivry 2009; Oda 2009; Tsujii 2009; Yoshihara 2009).

5. The descriptor "extraordinary" in this context acknowledges Rosemarie Garland-Thomson (1997), who describes "extraordinary bodies" as those defined through "social relationships in which one group is legitimated by possessing valued physical characteristics and maintains its ascendancy and its self-identity by systematically imposing the role of cultural or corporeal inferiority on others" (7). In this essay, I argue that Ungár's interpretation of Chopin's Prelude in B Minor, as well as his pianism more generally, is "extraordinary" in the sense that his music-making must be understood in relation to and in opposition against the social relationships that maintain sightedness as a privileged sensory ability, relegating blind pianists to the status of disabled other. The ambiguity that intersects historical and sociocultural narratives of blindness—on the one hand valorizing blind people for their supposedly heightened powers of perception, while on the other hand reducing them to the status of social outcasts enveloped in tragedy (Sacks 2007, Straus 2011)—plays out within a larger representational system in which disability serves "as the master trope of human disqualification" (Mitchell and Snyder 2000, 3).
6. The idea that a blind person "makes" his or her own space has been explored in the context of visual art. In their analysis of a painting by Susan Dorothea White titled "The Blind Woman of Annandale" (1998), Patrick J. Devlieger and Hubert Froyen (2006) explain that—in contrast to the artist's own projections of blindness as a negative experience that bars her subject from full participation in the world, restricting her movements "and rendering her vulnerable"—this image suggests "the dynamism with which [the painting's subject] 'makes space. . . .' Movement, positioning, and tactile pointing make the space real" (30).
7. Isolation from the external world and an aura of spirituality are two recurring motifs in the reception of blindness throughout history, both presumed to be inevitable consequences of an inability to see the external world. As Moshe Barasch (2001) explains, "So far as our knowledge and imagination can reach back into past ages, we find that there was probably no time and no society in which the blind were not tinged with some mystery. In many cultures . . . they were believed to have some contact with other worlds, with a reality different from the one in which we regularly live and altogether beyond the reach of other human beings" (7).
8. Rod Michalko (1998) discards the binary opposition between sightedness and blindness, arguing that "blindness is not a shadow of sight but is, like sight itself, cast in the mystery of the eye destined for the development of an imaginative relation to perception, to making and remaking something of the world and to making and remaking its place in it" (152).
9. "Discourse," as it is used here, follows the French philosopher Michel Foucault's (1972) definition. For Foucault, discourses are "practices that systematically form the objects of which they speak." In other words, discourses do not simply name phenomena that

already have a material existence. Instead, for Foucault, discourses themselves *constitute* such phenomena, "and in the practice of doing so conceal their own invention" (54). The Disability Studies critique of medical definitions of disability is, to some degree, informed by a similar understanding of how disability is produced socially, culturally, and historically, rather than biologically (Tremain 2005).

10. As Anita Silvers (1998) explains, "We usually suppose that, because listening, seeing, walking, intelligence, and other such performances are central to our daily lives, the sheer exercise of the faculties that support them must gratify us. Based on this assumption, a case is often made that sight, hearing, mobility, and complex cognition are good in themselves, and, consequently, their loss constitutes a deprivation of intrinsically valuable experiences" (89).
11. I am grateful to Blake Howe for drawing my attention to the work of these scholars.
12. I am grateful to Michael Simonson, archivist of the Leo Baeck Institute, for granting me permission to use this photograph of Imre Ungár. The photograph is from the Siegfried Altmann collection. As Simonson explained to me in a personal communication, Altmann was the director of the Jewish Institute for the Blind in Vienna until the outbreak of World War II in 1939, when he moved to New York.
13. I borrow the concept of "dramatizing" blindness from Joseph Straus (2011). In his discussion of a portrait of the fourteenth-century organist and composer Francesco Landini, Straus suggests that the musician's visual impairment is thrown into sharp relief by "showing him facing to one side, with his one visible eye half closed" (20; see also, Stone 2009). Despite the very different historical context and visual medium of this depiction of Imre Ungár, there is an argument to be made that a similar representational practice is at work, in which closed eyes signal the otherness of blind people, their retreat from a phenomenal world that is, figuratively, closed to them. It might be argued, however, that closed eyes in portraiture also function outside the specific context of the blindness/sightedness dichotomy to maintain a separation on a much larger scale, namely between the inner and outer, subjective and objective. For example, the Introduction to Peter de Bolla's *Art Matters* (2005) features an interpretation of a modernist sculpture by Marc Quinn in which de Bolla notes that the "mouth and eyes [of this self-portrait] are closed, and it is difficult to tell if the features indicate something like repose—as if the artist's senses are directed inwardly, attending to the sound or noise of consciousness" (2).
14. Kehler 1982 gives Ungár's birthday as January 23, 1909 (1344), as does Prosnak 1970 (32).
15. Németh, 2012, para. 4. This source is a brief essay published in the Hungarian periodical *Parlando*, in which Németh shares personal memories of studying with Ungár. While the accuracy of this source is open to question, Németh's personal account does fill certain gaps in what the secondary sources tell us about Ungár's musical activities. Together with three other blind pianists, Támas Németh (who took part in the 1970 Chopin competition) founded the Ungaria Piano Quartet in honor of the memory of Imre Ungár. I am grateful to Dr. Sophia Domokos and to Otto Halasz for their assistance in translating the article by Támas Németh.
16. This information comes from the website of the International Fryderyk Chopin Piano Competition (http://konkurs.chopin.pl/en/); see also Prosnak 1970, 32). According to Imre Ungár's son Istvan, "[T]he prize monies they [Ungár and Uninski] received were not identical and they made [Ungár] draw the final result from an 'urn' [probably a receptacle from which the two pianists drew lots]. . . . My father was very popular in Poland and they

would have liked him to receive the larger amount. My father sensed this and deliberately didn't pull the slip of paper offered to him . . ." (personal communication with the author).

17. In 1955, Ungár returned to Warsaw to serve on the jury for the Chopin Competition in which, incidentally, another blind pianist, Edwin Kowalik (1928–1997), was one of the recipients of Honorable Mention (Prosnak 1970; see also Kuźniak 2011). In addition to concertizing, Kowalik was involved in pedagogical work on behalf of blind pianists, including an edition of Chopin's piano music in Braille notation ("Pianist Kowalik to Perform," *Beaver County (Pa.) Times*, April 21, 1982, C13).
18. Three recitals that Ungár gave at the Warsaw Philharmonic after World War II give some idea of the scope of his repertoire during the late 1950s and early 1960s. Works by J. S. Bach, Beethoven, and Chopin are in all three programs, and Bartók figures in two out of the three recitals. Digital images of the recital programs (February 3, 1958; March 3, 1959; and December 1, 1964), which survive in the holdings of the Warsaw Philharmonic, were kindly provided to me by Slawomir Bychawski, librarian for the orchestra.
19. According to Tamás Németh (2012), Ungár's professional recordings are stored at the Hungarian Radio Archive. Of these, the Society for the Blind and Visually Impaired has released a two-CD selection on the thirtieth anniversary of Ungár's death. However, this latter compilation is not available for commercial purchase. Naxos Music Library Online distributes a retrospective of twentieth-century Hungarian pianism on the Hungaraton label; a 1954 recording by Ungár of the Prelude in A-flat Major from Chopin's Op. 28 is included. I am grateful to Kevin Madill, music librarian at the University of British Columbia, and Sarah Hunter, music librarian at Boston University, for their assistance in verifying the publication information for Ungár's recordings.
20. Elżbieta Strzelecka (Polish Radio Archives), personal communication with the author.
21. The Fryderyk Chopin Institute's website has a page dedicated to Ungár (included in a section devoted to well-known interpreters of Chopin's music). The undated entry by Stanislaw Dybowski (in English) quotes from Niewiadomski's account. (http://en.chopin.nifc.pl/chopin/persons/detail/cat/3/page/18/id/28). I am grateful to Elżbieta Stefańska for drawing my attention to Imre Ungár's life and career, and to Agnieszka Synowiec for her assistance in translating the account by Niewiadomski featured on the Polish Radio webpage, as well as the other Polish language sources discussed in this essay. I am also grateful to Agata Pietrzyk-Kaszyńska for her assistance in helping me correspond with Polish Radio for the purposes of research.
22. As Joseph Straus (2011) observes, the impulse to make sense of blindness in terms of a dichotomy between inner and outer experience, between self and world, remains prevalent in the collective imagination (18–20). The more specific image of the "blind seer" invoked by Niewiadomski in his response to Ungár's pianism has been a part of Western thinking about the relationship between blindness and creativity since antiquity.
23. I have opted for a general, not literal, translation of the final phrase. I am grateful to Chiara di Gravio and Paola Adarve Zuluaga for their assistance with translation of the Italian language sources used in this essay. I am grateful to Giovanni Michetti for his help in double-checking the citation information for this source.
24. The original source is in Polish and is attributed to Wladyslaw Fabry, who wrote about Ungár while covering the 1932 Chopin Competition for *Polska Zbrojna*.
25. I am grateful to Joseph Straus for drawing my attention to these tropes in his comments on an earlier draft of this essay.

26. I am grateful to Erika Honisch for highlighting the need to situate the review of Ungár's performance in relation to the general features of Chopin's compositional style.
27. I am grateful to Gergely Ambrus for his assistance in translating this review. According to the note below the review itself, Tóth's account was originally published in the daily newspaper *PestiNapló*. Tóth was a music critic for this paper from 1923 to 1939 (see Ferenc Bónis's entry on Tóth in *Oxford Music Online*). However, the version of Tóth's review that I consulted for this essay is in the periodical *Muzsika* (1973).
28. Cumming's larger project in this book is a semiotics of music based on her application of the pragmatist philosophy of Charles Sanders Peirce to various musical activities, especially performance. (Discussion of this aspect of her work is beyond the scope of the present essay.)
29. When I refer to specific pitches or chords, I use numbers for the successive registers on the piano (e.g., C1 for the lowest C).
30. Sandra P. Rosenblum (1994) uses the phrase "splitting the hands" to refer to this expressive device. Although Ungár's use of the device locates his pianism within a larger community of pianists trained in the early twentieth century, the way he "splits the hands" at the opening departs from the norm of "playing the melody note slightly after the accompaniment" (Rosenblum 1994, 54). By using noncoordination for the intial sonority, when melodic and harmonic roles have not had time to acquire definition, Ungár's performing self places emphasis on the contribution of noncoordination to the constitution of musical gait, rather than (solely) on its enhancement of lyricism.
31. As Mark Arnest (2014) explains, the use of this device in recordings from the early twentieth century tends to discomfit present-day audiences. Interestingly, Arnest appeals to visual experience in order to historicize the pianistic device of temporal dislocation between left and right hand: "noncoordination is a product of a very different world, one in which buildings were ornately decorated and every inch of a fine room contained something to stimulate the eye. Today's buildings have clean lines, and we keep our things in storage" (2).
32. Charles Fisk (2012) has eloquently described this passage as cast in the form of two "unanswered calls" (183).
33. Rod Michalko (2002) draws on his own experiences of struggling to make sense of his own personhood as he moved from sightedness to blindness, launching a vigorous critique against "people-first language" for its validation of the discourses that locate bodily difference as marginal to selfhood and self-formation: "Sightedness and blindness could not cohabit my identity. I was one or the other but not both. One of them would have to die and I was doing my best to kill blindness before it killed me." Going further, Michalko explains that "[i]t is small wonder that many of us who are disabled subscribe to the 'person-first' ideology. We place the common ground of personhood over the not-so-common one of disability. Choosing personhood over disability emphasizes both the strength of personhood and its separation from the body. As much as we want to repress any memory of the fate of our bodies, we also want to be reminded of just how strong personhood can be in the face of this fate. *Disability can be our reminder*" (10–11; emphasis added).
34. Welton 2007 discusses the difference between "seeing nothing" in a completely darkened room, and simply attempting to gain an understanding of blindness by wearing a blindfold. The latter technique, Welton explains, "cannot offer the same queering of vision" that actually "seeing *nothing*" effects (150; emphasis in original).

35. His importance as both a pianist and teacher comes through in statements from his one-time student, the blind Hungarian pianist Tamas Németh (2012), and in the existence of the Ungaria Piano Quartet, an ensemble whose members are all blind. The name "Ungaria," adopted by the members of this ensemble in 1991, acknowledges Ungár's efforts to integrate blind people into mainstream Hungarian musical life. For more information, consult their website: http://www.kultura-muveszet.hu/zene/klasszikus-zene/ungaria-zongoranegyes.html.
36. Rod Michalko asks, "What difference does it make to me when I see clouds where others see signposts and what difference does it make to them and what difference does it make to us? The common sense of sight along with commonsense knowledge permits people to see signposts, while the uncommon sense of blindness, together with the same commonsense knowledge permits the same sight. In this there is no difference between blind and sighted people" (Michalko 2009, 98).
37. Barasch (2001) recalls that as a child he was taught to believe that one's inner world, thoughts and dreams, were accessible to the insightful gaze of blind people (2).

References

Alink, Gustav. 1990. *International Piano Competitions*. The Hague, Netherlands: G. A. Alink.

Angermüller, Rudolph, et al. 2001. "Paradis, Maria Theresia." *Oxford Music Online*. Accessed May 25, 2015. http://www.oxfordmusiconline.com.

Arnest, Mark. 2014. "Why Couldn't They Play with Their Hands Together? Noncoordination between and within the Hands in 19th Century Piano Interpretation." Accessed March 4, 2014. http://www.lib.umd.edu/binaries/content/assets/public/ipam/resources-reviews-and-links/arnest-hands-together-article-pdf-5-15-12.pdf.

Barasch, Moshe. 2001. *Blindness: The History of an Image in Western Thought*. New York: Routledge.

Barnes, Colin, and Geoff Mercer. 2003. *Disability*. Cambridge, UK: Polity Press.

"A Blind Pianist of Exceptional Talent." 1932. *The New Beacon: A Magazine Devoted to the Achievements of the Blind* 16 (191): 269–270.

Bónis, Ferenc. 2014. "Tóth, Aladár." *Oxford Music Online*. Accessed May 25, 2015. http://www.oxfordmusiconline.com.

Burney, Charles. 1785. "An Account of Mademoiselle Theresa Paradis, of Vienna, the Celebrated Blind Performer on the Pianoforte." *Town and Country Magazine, or, Universal Repository of Knowledge, Instruction, and Entertainment* 17: 144–146.

Cumming, Naomi. 2000. *The Sonic Self: Musical Signs and Subjectivity*. Bloomington: Indiana University Press.

Cusick, Suzanne. 1994. "On a Lesbian Relationship with Music: A Serious Effort Not to Think Straight." In *Queering the Pitch: The New Gay and Lesbian Musicology*, edited by Phillip Brett, Elizabeth Wood, and Gary C. Thomas, 67–83. New York and London: Routledge.

Davis, Lennard J. 1995. *Enforcing Normalcy: Disability, Deafness, and the Body*. New York: Verso.

De Bolla, Peter. 2005. *Art Matters*. Cambridge, MA: Harvard University Press.

Devlieger, Patrick, and Hubert Froyen. 2006. "Blindness/City: A Disability Dialectic." In *Blindness and the Multi-Sensorial City*, edited by Patrick J. Devlieger, Hubert Froyen, Frank Renders, and Kristel Wildiers, 17–38. Antwerp, Belgium: Garant.

Dodson, Alan. 2011. "Expressive Timing in Expanded Phrases: An Empirical Study of Recordings of Three Chopin Preludes." *Music Performance Research* 4: 2–29.

Dubal, David. 1995. *The Art of the Piano: Its Performers, Literature, and Recordings.* San Diego, CA: Harcourt Brace.

Dybowski, Stanislaw. 2010. *Laureaci Konkursów Chopinowskich w Warszawie.* Warsaw, Poland: Selene.

Ferguson, Ronald J. 2007. *The Blind Need Not Apply: A History of Overcoming Prejudice in the Orientation and Mobility Profession.* Charlotte, NC: IAP.

Fisk, Charles. 2012. "Chopin's 'Duets'—and Mine." *19th-Century Music* 35 (3): 182–203.

Foucault, Michel. 1972. *The Archaeology of Knowledge.* Translated by A. M. Sheridan Smith. New York: Pantheon.

Garland-Thomson, Rosemarie.1997. *Extraordinary Bodies: Figuring Physical Disability in American Culture and Literature.* New York: Columbia University Press.

Garland-Thomson, Rosemarie. 2005. "Disability and Representation." *PMLA* 120 (2): 522–527.

Hillesum, Etty. 2002. *Etty: The Letters and Diaries of Etty Hillesum, 1941–1943.* Edited by Klaas A. D. Smelik. Translated by Arnold J. Pomerans. Grand Rapids, MI: William B. Eerdmans.

Hollins, Alfred. 1936. *A Blind Musician Looks Back: An Autobiography.* London: Blackwood and Sons.

Howe, Blake. 2010. "Paul Wittgenstein and the Performance of Disability." *Journal of Musicology* 27 (2): 135–180.

"Imre Ungár." 1933. *Argo: Rivista trimestrale per curadella Unione Italiana Ciechi* 6 (3): 35.

Isaacs, Edward. 1948. *The Blind Piano Teacher: A Monograph.* Glasgow, UK: McLellan.

Ivry, Benjamin. 2009. "What Was the Jury Thinking?" *Wall Street Journal*, June 10. http://online.wsj.com/news/articles/SB124458728669699751.

Jensen-Moulton, Stephanie. 2006. "Finding Autism in the Compositions of a 19th-Century Prodigy: Reconsidering 'Blind Tom' Wiggins." In *Sounding Off: Theorizing Music and Disability*, edited by Neil Lerner and Joseph N. Straus, 199–215. New York: Routledge.

Kafer, Alison. 2013. *Feminist, Queer, Crip.* Bloomington: Indiana University Press.

Kehler, George. 1982. *The Piano in Concert.* Metuchen, NJ: Scarecrow Press.

Kleege, Georgina. 2013. "Blindness and Visual Culture: An Eyewitness Account." In *The Disability Studies Reader*, edited by Lennard J. Davis, 447–455. New York: Routledge.

Kuppers, Petra. 2001. *Disability and Contemporary Performance: Bodies on Edge.* London: Routledge.

Kuźniak, Angelika. 2011. *Edwin Kowalik: Życie dźwiękiem pisane.* Warsaw, Poland: Polski Związek Niewidomych.

Le Guin, Elisabeth. 2005. *Boccherini's Body: An Essay in Carnal Musicology.* Berkeley and Los Angeles: University of California Press.

Linton, Simi. 1998. *Claiming Disability.* New York: New York University Press.

Mead, Andrew. 1999. "Bodily Hearing: Physiological Metaphors and Musical Understanding." *Journal of Music Theory* 43 (1): 1–19.

Michalko, Rod. 1998. *The Mystery of the Eye and the Shadow of Blindness.* Toronto: University of Toronto Press.

Michalko, Rod. 2002. *The Difference That Disability Makes.* Philadelphia: Temple University Press.

Michalko, Rod. 2009. "Coming Face-to-Face with Suffering." In *Re-thinking Normalcy: A Disability Studies Reader*, edited by Tanya Titchkosky and Rod Michalko, 91–114. Toronto, ON: Canadian Scholar's Press.

Mitchell, David T., and Sharon L. Snyder. 2000. *Narrative Prosthesis: Disabilities and the Dependencies of Discourse.* Ann Arbor: University of Michigan Press.

Németh, Tamas. 2012. "Szubjektív Megemlékezés Ungár Imrére." Accessed March 25, 2015. http://www.parlando.hu/2012/2012-5/Ungár-Nemeth.htm/.

Oda, Yuki. 2009. "Nobu Fever: Japan Falls for a Blind Piano Prodigy." *Time*, November 18. http://content.time.com/time/world/article/0,8599,1940215,00.html.

Polskie Radio. 2014. "Imre Ungár (1909–1972)."

Prosnak, Jan. 1970. *The Frederic Chopin International Piano Competitions Warsaw, 1927–1970.* Warsaw, Poland: Frederic Chopin Society.

Rosenblum, Sandra P. 1994. "The Uses of Rubato in Music, Eighteenth to Twentieth Centuries." *Performance Practice Review* 7 (1): 33–53.

Rowden, Terry. 2009. *The Songs of Blind Folk: African-American Musicians and the Cultures of Blindness.* Ann Arbor: University of Michigan Press.

Sacks, Oliver. 2007. *Musicophilia: Tales of Music and the Brain.* New York: Alfred A. Knopf.

Sandahl, Carrie, and Phillip Auslander. 2005. *Bodies in Commotion: Disability in Performance.* Ann Arbor: University of Michigan Press.

Scott, Robert A. 1991. *The Making of Blind Men: A Study of Adult Socialization.* New Brunswick, NJ: Transaction.

Silvers, Anita, David Wasserman, and Mary Briody Mahowald, eds. 1998. *Disability, Difference, Discrimination: Perspectives on Justice in Bioethics and Public Policy.* Lanham, MD: Rowman & Littlefield.

Stone, Anne. 2009. "The Story in the Song: Autobiography and Lyric in the Works of 'Franciscus cecus de Florentia' (a.k.a. Francesco Landini)." Unpublished paper.

Straus, Joseph N. 2006. "Normalizing the Abnormal: Disability in Music and Music Theory." *Journal of the American Musicological Society* 59 (1): 113–184.

Straus, Joseph N. 2011. *Extraordinary Measures: Disability in Music.* New York: Oxford University Press.

Takács, Ladislaus. 1934. *Der Ungár in der Welt.* Budapest, Hungary: Georg Vajna.

Titchkosky, Tanya. 2003. *Disability, Self, and Society.* Toronto, ON: University of Toronto Press.

Titchkosky, Tanya. 2012. "The Ends of the Body as Pedagogic Possibility." *Review of Education, Pedagogy, and Cultural Studies* 34 (3–4): 82–93.

Tóth, Aladár. 1973. "Ungár Imre zongoraestje." *Muzsika* 16 (1): 2–3.

Tremain, Shelley, ed. 2005. *Foucault and the Government of Disability.* Ann Arbor: University of Michigan Press.

Tsujii, Itsuko. 2009. "Don't Call Him the Blind Pianist." *Japan Echo: An Interactive Journal of Informed Opinion* 36 (5): 50–53.

Welton, Martin. 2007. "Seeing Nothing: Now Hear This . . ." In *Senses in Performance*, edited by Sally Banes and André Lepecki, 146–155. New York: Routledge.

Yoshihara, Mari. 2009. "Pianist Tsujii Takes the Global Stage." *Japan Echo: An Interactive Journal of Informed Opinion* 36 (5).

CHAPTER 14

STEVIE WONDER'S TACTILE KEYBOARD MEDIATION, BLACK KEY COMPOSITIONAL DEVELOPMENT, AND THE QUEST FOR CREATIVE AUTONOMY

WILL FULTON

This album is virtually the work of one man. . . . The sounds themselves come from inside his own mind. The man is his own instrument. The instrument is an orchestra.

—Album cover text, Stevie Wonder, *Music of My Mind*, Author not identified.

THIS statement, printed on the jacket of the 1972 album *Music of My Mind*, offers a description of Stevie Wonder as an autonomous musical phenomenon. On albums recorded in the early 1970s, Wonder often used multitrack recording to perform all of the voice and instrumental parts, creating music as a technological one-man band.[1] In this portrayal, Wonder's relationship to the music takes on a mystical quality, as he is enigmatically described as "his own instrument" that is "an orchestra." Consistent with earlier histories of blind performers marketed for their extraordinary talents,[2] the promotion of disabled musicians in one-man bands, as well as the record label's previous positioning of Wonder (b. 1950 as Stevland Hardaway Judkins)[3] as the "eighth wonder of the world" (Ribowsky 2010, 71), the album cover text announces Wonder as "virtually" the sole creative agent—a musical autonomist.

As Joseph Straus has shown, autonomy is related to deep-seated American ideals of "individuality, independence, and self-sufficiency" (Straus 2011, 177). However, the concept of autonomy has come under strong critique from disability scholars and activists, who dismiss it as a myth and prize instead "not self-sufficiency but self-determination, not independence but interdependence, not functional separateness but personal connection, not physical autonomy but human community" (Longmore 2003, 222). Indeed evidence, including interviews with Wonder's creative partners and filmed documentaries, clearly shows that Wonder's performance on his recordings has always been assisted, rather than autonomous. As Carrie Sandahl has stated, "there's really no such thing as a solo performance," and "[d]isability performance contexts make this even more apparent" (Sandahl 2004, 579). In the case of Wonder's music, the performance context of the recording studio serves as a site for the type of "complex power relations" common between blind musicians and their assistants (Lubet 2011, 70).

Although Wonder is among the most renowned popular musicians and one of the most recognized blind performers of all time, there has been limited examination of his musical development as it relates to his disability. While excitement about his talent and blindness has been the subject of great fascination and mythologizing in the popular media throughout his life, further inquiry is needed into his evolution as an instrumentalist and record producer and what effect blindness may have had in shaping his unique performance and compositional styles.[4] A largely unaddressed aspect of Wonder's work is the keyboard performance technique used on his uptempo funk songs, such as "Superstition" (1972) and "Higher Ground" (1973): his funk style.[5] These songs feature a style of performance that he developed in part due to his blindness: a specific hand position that informed his composition and improvisational technique.[6] In addition, his studio recordings, particularly those of the early 1970s, exhibit what could be understood as the problem of autonomy for a disabled musician.[7]

Wonder's albums represent the use of multitrack recording to create a one-man band to an extent that had never been achieved in popular music before.[8] While this music could be described as autonomous in a performative sense—in that Wonder is often playing all of the instruments and singing all of the voice parts—his ability to perform autonomously on these recordings is inextricably linked to the assistance of his coproducers. Evidence suggests that Wonder continually strived for creative autonomy, while remaining reliant on his sighted creative partners. This is not to say that a wholesale dismissal of the concept of autonomy in Wonder's music should be considered. Rather, his celebrated 1970s recordings exhibit dualisms critical to the discourse on music and disability, namely isolation/interaction and autonomy/dependence, revealing a complicated relationship with performative autonomy.

As Wonder displays this performative multiplicity (performing multiple roles and characters), both vocally and instrumentally, he creates what Sandahl calls "an interpretive framework embodied through performance," essentially trying on identities (Sandahl 2004, 583). Within these recordings, Wonder offers an exploration of individual and collective identity, for which Lennard Davis's concept of the "dismodernist subject" is a useful frame for analysis (Davis 2002, 30). At the same time, he continually negotiates what Martha Fineman has called the "specter of dependency" on his sighted partners.[9] Although he often strived to act as sole creative agent, the critical contributions of the albums' associate producers, Robert Margouleff and Malcolm Cecil, complicate the dominant narrative of these recordings as the result of Wonder's creativity alone. Wonder's music was shaped by his disability in important ways, from the self-assistive technique used in funk keyboard performance, to his struggle for creative control while navigating dependence on his sighted partners. Understanding how this occurred will provide a critical new insight into his music through the lens of disability.

Black Keys and Funk Style

In popular music, accommodations and individual performance techniques are often developed in relation to specific body types and disabilities.[10] The learning habits of popular musicians are varied and generally lack the rigor of conservatory training. As a result, musicians often develop styles of playing that are unique, particularly in cases involving a disability. For example, Joni Mitchell's use of specific chords came as a result of limited movement in her left hand, a remnant of childhood polio.[11] Wonder was blinded shortly after birth as a result of retrolental fibroplasia, a condition likely caused by "aggressive oxygen therapy" for premature infants (Rowden 2009, 108). Even though he exhibited prodigious talent for music at a young age, having been signed to Berry Gordy's Tamla Records at the age of nine, Terry Rowden rightly states that Wonder should not be viewed as a self-taught musical savant (2009, 107). In addition to receiving formal musical training at the Michigan School of the Blind, between the ages of nine and twenty Wonder received considerable informal musical training on various instruments from Motown's in-house band, commonly known as The Funk Brothers, in the Motown studio as well as training within the African American Baptist church he attended. It was during this period that Wonder developed his keyboard performance technique.

Of central importance to Wonder's evolution as a composer and music producer was the amount of time spent in Motown's recording studio, in terms of his learning to play instruments and compose songs and gaining an understanding of the technical craft of making recordings.[12] Wonder developed a specific style of playing the keyboard, particularly on songs in the key of E♭ minor pentatonic, which has been described by John Lodder as Wonder's "funk key" (2005, 62). Wonder began playing the Hohner Clavinet electric keyboard on uptempo recordings in the late 1960s, first using the instrument on "Shoo-Be-Doo-Be-Doo-Ba-Day" (Wonder 1968). The Clavinet became a common lead instrument for his funk recordings, and one on which he developed a specific style of percussive, syncopated performance, perhaps best known from the recording of "Superstition" (see Figure 14.1).

"Superstition" employs a mode that consists of only the black keys: E♭ minor pentatonic, common on his recordings that feature the Hohner Clavinet.[13] The development of this performance style, which he employed repeatedly in his one-man band recordings, came about in part due to his blindness. Often, during keyboard performance,

FIGURE 14.1 Stevie Wonder, "Superstition," lead Clavinet riff (throughout verses, first audible at 0:10). Transcribed by author from the *Talking Book* album.

Wonder keeps the thumb of his right hand at or below the ridge of the keys' surface, allowing him to gauge his position, with his remaining digits on the black keys (Cecil, personal interview 2012).

This hand position and performance style, though not publicly acknowledged by Wonder, were developed as a form of tactile self-assistance. During my interview with Malcolm Cecil (2012), co-associate producer of Wonder's albums from 1970 to 1974, he demonstrated Wonder's funk performance style and offered a rationale for them: "Stevie keeps his thumbs here [below the keyboard]. He feels the white keys with them, so he knows where he is. Everything's either in E♭ minor or G♭." Wonder's hand position is clearly visible during his reenactment of the "I Wish" recording in the film *Classic Albums: Songs in The Key of Life* (Wonder 1976 and Heffernan 1991; see Figure 14.2). Wonder largely developed this style as a way to feel the keys he could not see. This tactile assistive practice informed his choice of keys, improvisational technique, and his compositional choices on some of his most famous recordings.

Due to this hand position, Wonder composed primarily in the black key modes of E♭ minor pentatonic, and G♭ major, and used finger patterns that forged a specific harmonic-melodic style. Although his keyboard skills would later expand to include all twelve tonal centers together with the possibility of complex modulations, many of his well-known songs employ black keys almost exclusively, including "Superstition," "I Wish," "Higher Ground," "You Haven't Done Nothin'" (each in E♭ minor pentatonic), and "Living for the City" (G♭ major). Even in songs in which multiple modulations occur, Wonder often shifts to E♭ minor, and uses specific melodic-rhythmic patterns that were clearly developed in tandem with this hand position.[14] Wonder's thumb is below the ridge of the keys, and his digits are straightened, positioned above the black keys of the keyboard (Figure 14.2).

In performance, Wonder's hands perform a complicated, percussive dance on the keys, which amounts essentially to pentatonic riffing, assisted on the song "I Wish" by the use of the ARP synthesizer's pitch bend wheel (see Figure 14.3). Wonder percussively walks the pentatonic scale, his thumb providing the guidance. On the recording, he complements this figure with an overdubbed staccato counter-riff moving largely in contrary motion (see Figure 14.4).

With these two overdubbed riffs, Wonder exhibits his signature use of heterophonic keyboard performance, a style that is shaped and aided by his use of the thumb to feel

FIGURE 14.2 Wonder performing "I Wish," right hand.

(c)

FIGURE 14.2 Continued.

FIGURE 14.3 Stevie Wonder, "I Wish," ARP synthesizer riff (repeated throughout verses, first audible at 0:05). Transcribed by author from the *Songs in the Key of Life* album.

FIGURE 14.4 Stevie Wonder, "I Wish," synthesizer counter-riff (repeated throughout verses, first audible at 0:05, panned right).

the keys' ridge, gauging his position through touch. On "Higher Ground" (1974), one of Wonder's most celebrated recordings, the E♭ minor key and funk style are used to create a heterophonic groove with multiple Clavinet tracks (see Figure 14.5). Here, Wonder repeatedly uses three-note ascending patterns, spanning D♭-E♭-G♭ (as in Clavinet Left, m. 1), or G♭-A♭-B♭. As is the case in "I Wish," his use of these phrases is a direct result of his hand position, as he creates a rolling motion across the black keys, while his thumb serves as an assistive guide. Yet the development of his composition and performance style, shaped by his hand position, is only one critical aspect of these recordings. Of equal

FIGURE 14.5 Stevie Wonder, "Higher Ground," opening clavinet phrase (repeated throughout verses, first audible at 0:00). Transcribed by Hughes (2003, 200), with emendations by author.

importance to their specific sound and style is that in each instance—"Superstition," "I Wish," and "Higher Ground"—Wonder performed most or all of the instrumental parts and voices.

On all three recordings, he recorded voices, drums, synthesizer bass, and all keyboard parts. On "Higher Ground" he performed all parts, while on "Superstition" and "I Wish" there are guest brass performers; "I Wish" also features additional bass, background vocals, and percussion. The four albums released in the early 1970s in which Wonder collaborated with Cecil and Margouleff contain a total of thirty-seven recordings—Wonder played all instrumental parts on twenty-one songs and the majority of instrumental parts on all but five of the other sixteen songs.[15] As Théberge (1997, 222) notes, this type of "one-man band" recording was an "extremely rare" occurrence in popular music during the early 1970s.

The Technological One-Man Band and the Quest for Creative Autonomy

Wonder's recordings from the 1970s show not only how blindness continually complicated his ability to achieve autonomy in the recording process but also how his creative output was shaped by this tension. Figure 14.6 shows Wonder, with the assistance of Margouleff, moving his hand to find and adjust a volume control knob. This image highlights one way in which Wonder's collaborators continually mediated his creative process, aiding in everything from the recording of music to the writing and recording of lyrics. Davis notes that in a dismodernist world, one can consider all persons as reliant

FIGURE 14.6 Wonder (left) adjusting a knob in the recording studio, assisted by Robert Margouleff. Malcolm Cecil, standing, at right. Still from *Innervisions* promotional film.

on some level of dependence, be it technology or personal assistance (Davis 2002, 30). Yet for people with disabilities, certain types of dependence shape daily life and the creative process in a specific, rather than universal, manner.

Both the acts of writing and recording lyrics demanded mediation for Wonder. Wonder, who began writing his lyrics in the late 1960s, did so through the use of assistants, who would transcribe his verses. This relationship with transcribers is acknowledged on the label for *Innervisions*, when Wonder thanks one of these assistants for "writing the words on a brown paper bag for a song that means so much to me" (Wonder 1973a). The recording of lyrics was also mediated. While it is common practice in popular music for vocalists to use lyric sheets in the recording studio, Wonder was often prompted with each lyric phrase by an engineer communicating via headphones. While recording vocal tracks, Wonder would hear the lyric in his headphones immediately before singing it. His vocal recording process was thus constantly affected by assistance and mediation. This technique was developed early in his career at Motown, and became Wonder's standard method of recording vocals (Cecil, personal interview, 2012). In recent years, Wonder has been criticized for forgetting lyrics during performances (Shilling 2009). It seems significant to note that the "assistive technology" of the teleprompter (Straus 2011, 176), which is commonly used by older popular musicians to read lyrics onstage, is unavailable to Wonder, as it presumes sightedness.[16] The assistance in writing and recording lyrics is only one aspect of Wonder's level of assistance during the composition and recording process.

The "specter of dependency" on sighted creative partners that faced Wonder is exemplified by his creative relationship with Cecil and Margouleff, whom Wonder

FIGURE 14.7 The Original New Timbral Orchestra (T.O.N.T.O.), photographed by author in 2012.

met in 1972 in New York City. When Wonder turned twenty-one, he relocated from Detroit to New York in search of creative freedom to explore ideas outside of Motown's Hitsville system (Lodder 2005, 71). He became interested in the electronic recordings being produced in New York City that used the Moog synthesizer, such as Wendy Carlos's 1968 *Switched on Bach* (Ribowsky 2010, 198). Notably, Carlos's recordings also featured a technological one-man band, as she had voiced and performed all of the parts in electronic renditions of movements from Bach concertos and Beethoven symphonies (Holmes 2008, 216–9). Wonder was particularly interested in *Zero Time*, an electronic 1971 album recorded by Cecil and Margouleff that used a massive synthesizer they built from Moog and ARP components called T.O.N.T.O.: The Original New Timbral Orchestra (Ribowsky 2010, 199–200) (see Figure 14.7). He met Cecil at Media Sound, the Manhattan recording studio where *Zero Time* was recorded, and immediately began a relationship that would last four years and produce some of Wonder's most celebrated recordings, on which the two are credited as associate producers (Cecil, personal interview, 2012). With the assistance of Cecil and Margouleff, Wonder was able to incorporate a wealth of electronic sounds, expanding the use of synthesizers in popular music as a whole (Lodder 2005, 70).

Although Rowden argues that "it was the synthesizer that made it possible for [Wonder] to invent himself as the prosthetically enhanced and up-to-date cyborgean soulman," this statement undermines the fact that Wonder sought out this technology himself after hearing a number of experimental records that had been recorded in New York in the late 1970s by sighted musicians (Rowden 2009, 111). When Wonder asked to be shown T.O.N.T.O., Cecil recalls:

> He asked: "Is this the instrument that made those sounds?" He wanted to touch it. He ran his hands over it, and soon realized that he would need help. (Cecil, personal interview, 2012)

Wonder realized he would require assistance when he discovered that T.O.N.T.O. spanned over ten feet in length, and was composed of a complex series of components. His work with coproducers Cecil and Margouleff was an interactive process, and the associate producers shaped the sounds (albeit to Wonder's taste) through additive and subtractive synthesis, as well as physically modulating sounds (turning filter knobs while Wonder played the keyboard) during recording (Cecil, personal interview, 2012). In my interview with Cecil, he reported that the process of manipulating sounds often involved him or Margouleff turning the filter and envelope knobs while Wonder played the keys, and then Wonder exclaiming "right there . . . don't change it" when the tone was right.[17] Yet, although Wonder's "orchestra" is more aptly described as a collaborative process among Wonder, Cecil, and Margouleff, the rhythmic and harmonic interaction between instruments and voices was often the result of Wonder's performance alone (Wonder 1972a).

These recordings exhibit that this technique of multitracking his own performance was far from a simple marketing gimmick for Wonder;[18] it was an extension of his quest for personal agency and creative autonomy. Malcolm Cecil recalls that Wonder was "produced at Motown, and he hated it" (personal interview, 2012). Wonder sought to be his own producer, and in so doing, to gain creative agency over his work. He is credited as producer on the four albums on which he collaborated with Cecil and Margouleff; they are credited as associate producers and for programming and engineering the synthesizers. Production of a recording amounts to control over the creative process. Perhaps the greatest level of agency is one in which the musician performs all of the instruments and voices, thereby having nearly absolute control over the individual performing voices. Wonder is clearly aware of this relationship of control as he describes the process of recording "I Wish":

> So now that we've done the first [synthesizer] part, we're going to do a second part, and after that a third part. Now, the reason we're doing this, even though this is a polyphonic keyboard, we're doing it monophonically so that we have more control—I have more control over the individuality of each part—if I decided to bend a particular note that I didn't bend the first time, it gives it its own kind of character. (Heffernan 1991)

Here, Wonder recalled the process of multilayering individual synthesizer performances to create the complex texture of the song's musical accompaniment. In explaining the importance of recording each part separately, he used the telling phrase "control over the individuality." In a literal sense, he stated the method used to build the heterophonic instrumental backing through recorded tracks of individual performance. But the phrase also accurately described the complex relationship of control and individuality that defined many of his recordings. Wonder, an individual performing most or all of the musical parts, sought to gain agency (control) over the parts of the performance. Yet, paradoxically, each of his recorded parts asserted their performative individuality. The often dialogic relationship of the individual parts in his music would seem particularly important as Wonder was recreating the interaction common in African American music.[19]

Timothy Hughes notes that Wonder was "the first individual to succeed in generating the 'robustly collective' sound of a large funk band entirely by himself" and therefore "had to unravel the paradox of collective individuality" (Hughes 2003, 3). That Wonder would seek to assert his agency by recording all or most of the musical parts would seem particularly significant, a type of response to the constant "specter of dependency" that he faced as a blind musician. The first album to be released from the collaboration of Wonder, Cecil, and Margouleff was *Music of My Mind* (1972). The album's opening song, "Love Having You Around," clearly shows the use of synthesizers and multiple reacting tracks of Wonder, who performed drums, Moog bass, Wurlitzer electric piano (amplified, two tracks), vocals (one lead, one backing vocal, vocoder vocal, and chorus vocals), accompanied only by Art Baron, who performed the trumpet solo. Samuel Floyd posits that a common feature of African American music is improvisatory interaction within a collective, in which performers "contribute to the success of a performance with musical statements, assertions, questings, requestings, implications, mockings, and concurrences" (Floyd 1991, 281). The appearance of dialogic interaction is evident in "Love Having You Around" on multiple levels, yet all of the parts are performed by Wonder (see Figure 14.8).

In the opening vamp, there are three vocal tracks, one of which is processed by the Moog synthesizer using a vocoder. After the lead vocal begins with a sincere "Please!" in measure 2, a second vocal responds humorously with "Mama mama mama" in measure 4. The lead vocal then mockingly embellishes this phrase, as "Mama mama baby . . . baby baby baby," which in turn is then mimicked by the vocoder vocal in measures 6–7. This same pattern of statement and embellishment also occurs in the two Wurlitzer electric piano tracks. Following an ascending phrase in measure 2, a second Wurlitzer track repeats the same phrase in a higher octave in the following measure, then embellishes it in an extended improvisation.

Here, Wonder exhibits performative multiplicity, both vocally and instrumentally. This opening of the album is a statement about Wonder's new direction, in which he exhibits an obvious (and literal) multiplicity of voice: his synthesized self in the use of the vocoder. As the album cover boasts, "[t]he man is his own instrument" and that "his instrument is an orchestra," the consumer and critic are made to revel in Wonder's genius (Wonder 1972). Later recordings reveal even more deeply that this technique of multitracking his own performance was an important part of the process of composition and sonic production.

On these recordings, Wonder creates performative individuals, vocally and instrumentally, who appear to interact throughout the recordings. He performs the roles of preacher and choir (including higher pitched voices that sound as female choir

FIGURE 14.8 Stevie Wonder, "Love Having You Around," opening vamp (begins at 0:00). Transcribed by author from the *Music of My Mind* album.

members), competing soloists, and rhythm section, recreating the interactivity common in African American musical styles through multitrack recording. In Carrie Sandahl's study of blind playwright Lynn Manning, she describes Manning's performance of multiple characters as an "interpretive framework embodied through performance" (Sandahl 2004, 583). In Wonder's representation of the interactivity of the African American musical collective and the relationship of the preacher and choir, he creates an aural representation of communal scenes through layers of individual performance. In doing so, Wonder and his one-man band reconcile community through freely adopting identities, creating an interpretive framework (Sandahl 2004, 585).

These interpretive frameworks are particularly evident in recordings that feature a call-and-response relationship between lead and backing vocals. Wonder used multitracking on a number of recordings to create a choir of background voices, for example, on "Living for the City," "Love Having You Around," and "They Won't Go When I Go."[20] The practice became so common on their tracks that Wonder, Cecil, and Margouleff developed a technique to specifically alter the timbre of back-up vocals in order "to vary the sound," creating higher pitched vocals by recording vocals at a lower tape speed, and then resetting the tape speed (Cecil, personal interview, 2012). While this process was sometimes used on one harmony part, on "Maybe Your Baby" (1972) this technique is used on all of the backing vocals, creating a helium-voiced effect.

The pitching of voices in "Maybe Your Baby" evokes different gender roles, as Wonder creates a group of chorus women reacting to a man's story (Cecil, personal interview, 2012). In the recording, Wonder performs drums, Moog bass, Hohner Clavinet electric piano (two tracks), and vocals (one lead, multiple "pitched" chorus vocals), while Ray Parker Jr. performs lead guitar. Wonder doesn't truly sound feminine in the chorus vocals, but rather the pitched vocals sound manipulated, affected, and androgynous. The protagonist here describes that something is wrong, and that the "world is turnin' on" him, because his "baby" left. This monologue receives a mocking, repeated response from the female characters: "Maybe your baby done made some other plans," first heard at 1:04, advising the protagonist that she had found another lover. At 3:50, Wonder's lead vocal encourages the backing vocalists to "say it again," reinforcing the sense that he is depicting multiple characters. Wonder then confounds the identity of the pitched vocalist's character at 5:01, as one of the chorus vocals playfully states "I'm a little boy." This "interpretive framework" allows for a presentation of "interacting" identities, or performative characters, through the prosthesis of technology. Within this aural soundscape, Wonder's male and female—and conceivably blind and sighted—characters interact in a narrative framework. As Davis states, in the "dismodern era," "identity is not fixed but malleable;" on songs such as "Maybe Your Baby," Wonder develops an aural space in which identity is truly performative (Davis 2002, 26).

In his technological one-man band recordings, Wonder creates a virtual band of performers. In many instances, he exhibits multiple iterations of a performative self: performing both the caller and the respondent, the preacher and the choir, the male and female roles, or reacting in improvisation to an inflection of another recorded performance. As he is working within musical genres (in particular jazz, R&B, and gospel) in which a collective of performers is the norm, Wonder presents a kind of dichotomy of personal/collective expression. So what occurs on these recordings? An obvious conclusion would be simple imitation: that Wonder is imitating a gospel choir and musical collective, playing all the parts as if acting out the roles of different –meaning other than himself—individual performers. Yet his work has a distinct sound and style, and would seem to transcend imitation. Perhaps he is using the technology to evoke larger communal scenes while exploring different aspects of his own personality, at once being melancholy and parodic, as in "Maybe Your Baby," or commenting on his own performance, such as in "Love Having You Around." His ability to have "control over the individuality" allows him to direct the vocal and instrumental performances absolutely (control), while each part is free to playfully comment on another, or express individuality (Heffernan 1991). *Talking Book*, the title of the album on which "Maybe Your Baby" appears, further suggests that Wonder perceived his music to be an aural narrative in which his performative characters interact.[21]

It is telling that Wonder performed as a one-man band on many of his most personal recordings, including "They Won't Go When I Go" and "Higher Ground."[22] But the song most critical to the discussion of Wonder's creation of an "interpretive framework," as well as a symbol of his struggle for agency and autonomy, is "Living for the City" (1973). In "Living for the City," Wonder performs all of the instruments and voices (with the exception of spoken parts during a narrative skit). The song is a biographical depiction of an African American male who faces poverty, oppression, and wrongful imprisonment. Wonder creates an interpretive framework to examine the plight of a sighted protagonist through his depiction of this character in a song intended to expose society's ills. The final verse, describing the protagonist's life after a period of incarceration, is delivered in a gravelly, emotional voice, as if Wonder is overcome by grief.

> His hair is long, his feet are hard and gritty
> He spends his life walking the streets of New York City
> He's almost dead, from breathing in air pollution
> He tried to vote, but to him there's no solution
> Living just enough, just enough for the city. . . .
> (Stevie Wonder, "Living for the City," final verse, 1973)

Wonder's emotional vocal performance evokes the frustration described in the narrative. Yet the circumstances of the recording of this track indicate that the frustration represented may have been due as much to the lack of agency of the performer in the recording session as the lyrical content. As Cecil describes: "I kept stopping the tape. He would start a take and I would stop the tape, and tell him we'd have to start over" (personal interview, 2012). Hoping to capture Wonder's frustration in his performance, Cecil manipulated Wonder by pretending there was a technical problem, causing him to record the verse repeatedly, until the frustration and vocal wear was evident in his performance. Cecil now regrets it, and believes it may have led to a break in their creative partnership. "He didn't like that. I shouldn't have done it. He didn't like to be produced" (personal interview, 2012). In this instance, the complex dynamic between Wonder and his creative partners clearly impacted his vocal performance. Despite the fact that Wonder, then an extremely successful recording artist and performer, had sought to create an "interpretive framework" as a site to examine racial prejudice, the "specter of dependency" on his sighted collaborators remained.

Conclusion

Wonder continued to explore the use of multitrack recording and electronic instruments after his creative relationship with Cecil and Margouleff dissolved in 1974. The availability of newer, smaller (and therefore more manageable) electronic instruments made it possible for Wonder to increase his personal control over music production. He was considered a "pioneering user" of the compact ARP2600 synthesizer, and was the first musician to have the ARP instrument panel inscribed in Braille (Trynka 1996, 55). The advent of drum machines, such as the Linn Drum, extended the ability for him to compose as a single performer. In a 1981 BBC documentary, Wonder is shown as crafting a multilayered musical backing track alone using synthesizers and the Linn Drum, alternating between drum machine programming and keyboard performance (Figure 14.9).

As Lennard Davis has shown, technology increasingly serves as an assistive prosthesis for the "dismodernist subject" (Davis 2002, 30). Although this image of Wonder creating music without assistance masks Wonder's continued reliance on his sighted partners in the setup and arrangement of this electronic array, he is clearly exploring technological means toward an end of creative autonomy.

On his one-man band recordings, Wonder creates a virtual band of performers employing his unique style of keyboard performance. While his performances on these recordings cannot be understood as truly autonomous, they represent Wonder's development of interpretive frameworks as well as his continued quest for agency and creative autonomy. Although Motown initially saw no benefit in Wonder performing on all of the instruments, the marketing of his albums soon featured text romantically describing him as an "instrument," and visualizations of Wonder positioned as a blind mystic, as on the cover artwork for the album *Innervisions* (Ribowsky 2010, 210) (see Figure 14.10). In a dismodernist reading, this artwork could be understood as a providing a kind of visual aid to the able-bodied: as sighted people rely to an extent on seeing to understand, a visual representation of light leaving Wonder's eyes is needed by the sighted to understand what inner visions might mean for a blind musician. Wonder created representative aural scenes, redefining the interactivity common in African American music through multitrack recording.

Wonder's advances in the use of multitrack recording were highly influential for a wide range of popular musicians. Prince performed all of the instruments and voices on his 1978 debut album, and was touted by Warner Brothers Records as "the new Stevie Wonder" (Hill 1989, 6). Although Prince and other sighted musicians adopted many of

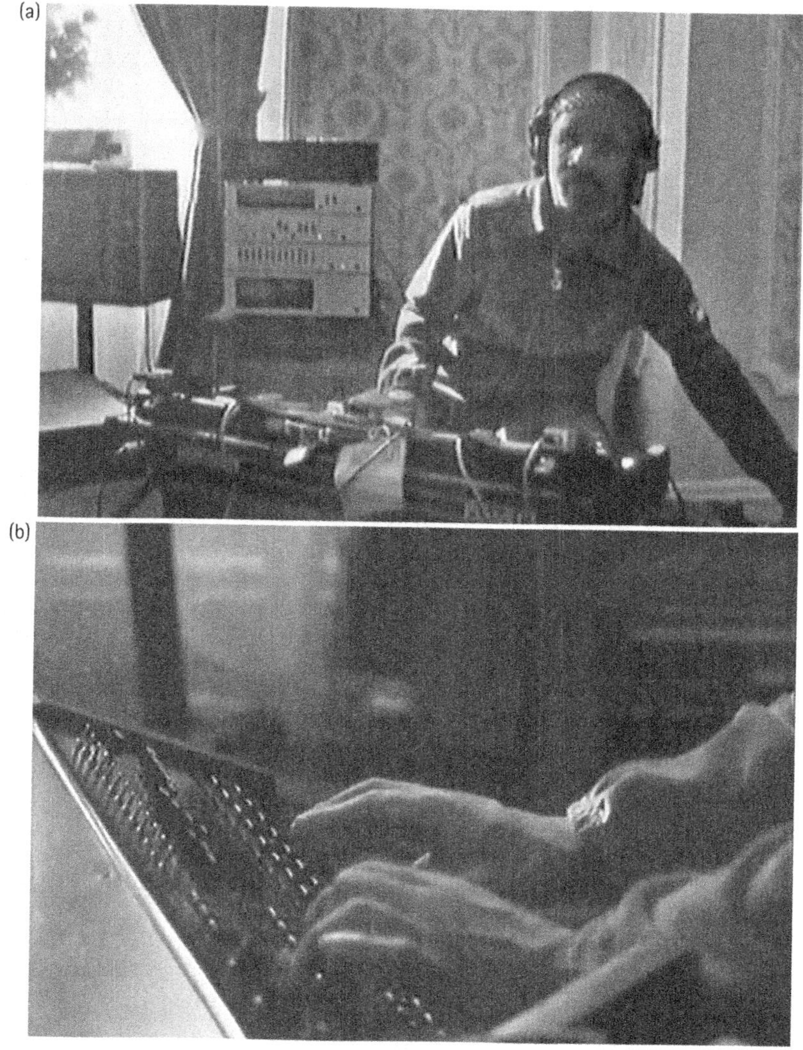

FIGURE 14.9 Wonder creates layered musical track with synthesizers and Linn Drum.

Wonder's studio one-man band techniques, they did not face the "complex power relations" with assistants and partners that shaped Wonder's music (Lubet 2011, 70).[23] Yet the studio represents only one side of Wonder's career. In live performances, all of these songs translate well into a traditional interactive band format, and Wonder is known for his enthusiasm for jamming interactively with other musicians (Ribowsky 2010, 285). As a musician trained largely in the recording studio, however, the conceptual development of his ideas and the multitrack performance would seem to go hand-in-hand in creating what Albin Zak calls the "sonic artifact" (Zak 1997, 30–31). These recordings would not be the same if Wonder had hired backing musicians and vocalists. Wonder's one-man

FIGURE 14.10 Stevie Wonder, *Innervisions* album cover.

band recordings serve as interpretive frameworks that were profoundly shaped by his continued struggle for creative autonomy.

Notes

1. The term "one-man band" is conventionally applied to live solo multi-instrumentalists. For more on this phenomenon, see Chapman 2013. Wonder uses the technology of multi-track recording to create the sound of an interacting band with multiple layers of instrumental and vocal performance.
2. For example, Alex Lubet describes the marketing of blind African American blues performers, noting that "the word blind" is commonly used in the professional names of blind performers such as Blind Lemon Jefferson (2011, 11). Donald Kirtley refers to the "blind genius," which he calls one of the "three major stereotypes of the blind in American culture" (1975, 99). Regarding the marketing of blindness in the career of Thomas "Blind Tom" Wiggins, see Jensen-Moulton (2006).

3. Wonder was named Stevland Hardaway Judkins at birth; his name was legally changed to Stevland Hardaway Morris during childhood (Ribowsky 2010, 11–12).
4. Although Hughes (2003), Rowden (2009), and Spicer (2011) have provided valuable scholarship on Wonder's music, their studies have offered limited analysis of performance technique, and his compositional development has yet to be examined.
5. For more on the development of funk, a syncopated musical genre that stemmed from 1960s R&B, see Danielsen 2006. The term "funk style" is used here to differentiate from Wonder's keyboard technique on ballads. Lodder (2005) notes the specific relationship between choice of keys and "funk" songs in Wonder's music.
6. The possibility of an association between Wonder's "black key" performance style and blindness has been noted by theorist and keyboardist Mark Spicer in an article on popular music performance style, who speculated that Wonder's use of "black key" modes "might have something to do with the notion that a blind person can feel the raised black keys more easily as a point of orientation and would therefore be drawn to those particular chord shapes." He notes that he "shall leave these provocative implications open for further investigation" (Spicer 2011).
7. I am employing and extending the concept the "myth of autonomy," as discussed by Straus (2011, 177).
8. While there were earlier experiments, the use of multitrack recording was largely developed by Les Paul, who used it in 1948 to create the effect of a musical group via multiple overdubbed tracks of one musical performer with the Capitol recording of "Lover." Wonder's use of the technology extends from Paul's innovations, but expands the use of improvisatory interreaction between recorded parts and reacting vocal performances, as I will examine here. Regarding Paul's recordings, see Milner (2009, 125–127).
9. Fineman (2004, 34; italics added): "Dependency is a particularly unappealing and stigmatized term in American political and popular consciousness. The *specter of dependency* is incompatible with our beliefs and myths. We venerate the autonomous, independent, and self-sufficient individual as our ideal. We assume that anyone can cultivate these characteristics, and we stigmatize those who do not."
10. Such individual performance techniques are also common among able-bodied popular musicians. For example, left-handed guitarist Jimi Hendrix performed on an upside-down restrung right-handed guitar with backward pick-ups. This arrangement, as well as his unusual hand position, in which his thumb extended over the neck, impacted his sound, fingering and chord choices. See Shapiro and Glebbeek 1990.
11. See Sonenberg 2003. Further examples include jazz guitarist Django Reinhardt, who crafted a specific performance style after a fire permanently injured the pinky and ring finger of his left hand. See Lubet 2011, 45.
12. Although Motown did not yet have the capabilities for multitrack recording in 1961, Wonder recorded his vocals separate from the band, a common technique at the time known as "pingponging," in which the mixed version of an instrumental track played on one tape machine, and recorded with a vocal overdub on another. It is significant that Wonder would spend much of the next ten years (while not touring) in the recording studio, which became, in essence, his conservatory. Funk Brothers' Eddie Willis notes, "All he wanted to do was be in the studio. He never wanted to go home . . .. So he was there a lot, always learnin', always learnin' " (Ribowsky 2010, 56).
13. In addition to "Superstition" and "Shoo-Be-Doo-Be-Doo-Ba-Day," use of the Clavinet and E♭ key occurs in "Do Yourself a Favor" (1971), "Higher Ground" (1973), and "You Haven't Done Nothin' " (1974).

14. For example, "Jesus Children of America" (1973) begins in A♭ and modulates to E♭ minor pentatonic, and features an extended improvisational funk vamp in that key.
15. The four albums released in the early 1970s in which Wonder collaborated with Cecil and Margouleff are *Music of My Mind, Talking Book, Innervisions*, and *Fulfillingness' First Finale*. The vast majority of the instrumental contributions consist of overdubbed brass, woodwind, and percussion parts from one or two musicians, while the rhythm section and lead instruments are performed by Wonder. Wonder performs lead vocals on all songs, and all voice parts on twenty-three of the thirty-seven recordings on these albums. See Wonder 1972a, 1972b, 1973a, 1974.
16. A wide range of able-bodied popular musicians, including Bruce Springsteen, Paul McCartney, Prince, and R.E.M., use teleprompters to assist in remembering song lyrics onstage. While the musical parts are apparently committable to memory, song lyrics seem to be problematic for many performers (Farhi 2012).
17. Notably, Wonder's description of the title's meaning varies from the album's jacket, and credits the synthesizer for the inspiration: "The Moog itself is a way to directly express what comes from your mind, hence the album's title." His praise of synthesizer technology for allowing the ability to "directly express" his ideas would seem to work in tandem with the control of expression offered by performing all of the parts through multitrack performance (Wonder, quoted in Lodder 2005, 82).
18. In my interview with Cecil in 2012, he referred to Wonder's "one-man band shtick."
19. Anne Danielsen calls this the "conversational mode" of African American music, which is particularly significant when individual musicians strive to be heard in large groups of performers: "Striving for differentiation among parts becomes increasingly significant as the number of layers and figures increases. . . . Figures are organized as rhythmic dialogues: the performance of a figure does not take place in relation to all of the other figures in a weave, but as part of a dialogue with one another" (Danielsen 2006, 52).
20. The creation of a responsorial relationship with background vocals through multitracking had precedents in R&B. As reenacted in the 2004 film *Ray*, Ray Charles used this technique in a similar manner to record the background vocals on the 1961 Atlantic recording "I Believe in My Soul" following an argument with his backup singers, the Raylettes.
21. Notably, Wonder recalls his first reaction to hearing a radio as a child in terms of people "com[ing] out" of it: "Can I touch it? What's a radio? Where are the people? Why do they come out of the radio?" Wonder quoted in Ribowsky (2010, 17).
22. Cecil described that "They Won't Go When I Go" was "very personal for Stevie. It was about dying, that we all die alone" (Cecil, personal interview, 2012). Mark Ribowsky argues that as Wonder struggled with bouts of depression, "Higher Ground" had significant personal meaning to Wonder, and could be heard as "something like a suicide note with a melody" (Ribowsky 2010, 234).
23. Prince has created one-man band recordings extensively throughout his career, and employed many of the techniques pioneered by Wonder, including manipulation of voices through altered tape speed, development of aural scenes, and interplay between recorded parts. Many of his recordings were made without the assistance of engineers (Hill 1989). The fact that a sighted musician could be marketed as the "new Stevie Wonder" underscores the significance of Wonder's multitrack recording innovations in popular music, as well as the extent to which Wonder in some ways actually transcended the blindness narrative during his career. For more on the discussion of "transcendence" related to Wonder, see Rowden 2009.

References

Chapman, Dale. 2013. "The 'One-Man Band' and Entrepreneurial Selfhood in Neoliberal Culture." *Popular Music* 32 (3): 451–470.

Davis, Lennard J. 2002. *Bending Over Backwards: Disability, Dismodernism, and Other Difficult Positions*. New York: New York University.

Danielsen, Anne. 2006. *Presence and Pleasure: The Funk Grooves of James Brown and Parliament*. Middletown, CT: Wesleyan University Press.

Farhi, Paul. 2012. "Bruce Springsteen Uses a Teleprompter in Performances: Does It Matter?" *Washington Post*, March 30. http://www.washingtonpost.com/lifestyle/style/bruce-springsteen-uses-teleprompter-in-performances-does-it-matter/2012/03/30/gIQA-QTXGlS_story.html.

Fineman, Martha Albertson. 2004. *The Autonomy Myth: A Theory of Dependency*. New York: New Press.

Floyd, Samuel A. 1991. "Ring Shout! Literary Studies, Historical Studies, and Black Music Inquiry." *Black Music Research Journal* 11 (2): 265–287.

Hill, Dave. 1989. *Prince: A Pop Life*. New York: Harmony.

Holmes, Thom. 2008. *Electronic and Experimental Music: Technology, Music, and Culture*. 3rd ed. New York: Routledge.

Hughes, Timothy. 2003. "Groove and Flow: Six Analytical Essays on the Music of Stevie Wonder." PhD diss., University of Washington.

Jensen-Moulton, Stephanie. 2006. "Finding Autism in the Compositions of a 19th-Century Prodigy: Reconsidering 'Blind Tom' Wiggins." In *Sounding Off: Theorizing Disability in Music*, edited by Neil Lerner and Joseph N. Straus, 199–216. New York: Routledge.

Kirtley, Donald D. 1975. *The Psychology of Blindness*. Chicago: Nelson-Hall.

Lodder, Steve. 2005. *Stevie Wonder: A Musical Guide to the Classic Albums*. New York: Backbeat.

Longmore, Paul. 2003. *Why I Burned My Book and Other Essays on Disability*. Philadelphia, PA: Temple University Press.

Lubet, Alex. 2011. *Music, Disability, and Society*. Philadelphia, PA: Temple University Press.

Milner, Greg. 2009. *Perfecting Sound Forever: An Oral History of Recorded Music*. New York: Faber & Faber.

Ribowsky, Mark. 2010. *Signed, Sealed, and Delivered: The Soulful Journey of Stevie Wonder*. Hoboken, NJ: John Wiley & Sons.

Rowden, Terry. 2009. *The Songs of Blind Folk: African American Musicians and the Culture of Blindness*. Ann Arbor: University of Michigan Press.

Sandahl, Carrie. 2004. "Black Man, Blind Man: Disability Identity Politics and Performance." *Theatre Journal* 56 (4): 579–602.

Shapiro, Harry, and Caeser Glebbeek. 1990. *Jimi Hendrix: Electric Gypsy*. New York: St. Martin's.

Shilling, Mary. 2009. "Men of a Certain Age: Rock and Roll Hall of Fame Concert No. 1." *Vulture*, October 30. http://www.vulture.com/2009/10/men_of_a_certain_age_rock_roll.html.

Sonenberg, Daniel. 2003. "'Who in the World She Might Be': A Contextual and Stylistic Approach to the Early Music of Joni Mitchell." PhD diss., City University of New York.

Spicer, Mark. 2011. "(Per)Form in(g) Rock: A Response." *Music Theory Online* 17 (3). http://www.mtosmt.org/issues/mto.11.17.3/mto.11.17.3.spicer.pdf.

Straus, Joseph. 2011. *Extraordinary Measures: Disability in Music*. New York: Oxford University Press.

Théberge, Paul. 1997. *Any Sound You Can Imagine: Making Music/Consuming Technology*. Middletown, CT: Wesleyan University Press.
Trynka, Paul, ed. 1996. *Rock Hardware: 40 Years of Rock Instrumentation*. London: Balafon.
Zak, Albin. 1998. "The Poetics of Rock Composition: Multitrack Recording as Compositional Practice." PhD diss., City University of New York.

Filmography/Discography

Heffernan, David (director). 1991. *Classic Albums: Songs in The Key of Life*. Rhino Home Video.
Wonder, Stevie. 1971. *Where I'm Coming From*. Tamla.
Wonder, Stevie. 1972a. *Music of My Mind*. Tamla.
Wonder, Stevie. 1972b. *Talking Book*. Tamla.
Wonder, Stevie. 1973a. *Innervisions*. Tamla.
Wonder, Stevie. 1973b. *Innervisions* promotional film. Tamla.
Wonder, Stevie. 1974. *Fulfillingness' First Finale*. Tamla.
Wonder, Stevie. 1976. *Songs in the Key of Life*. Tamla.
Wonder, Stevie. 1981. *Hotter Than July*. BBC Documentary. Director: Ted Clisby. British Broadcasting Corporation.

CHAPTER 15

OH, THE STORIES WE TELL!

Performer-Audience-Disability

MICHAEL BECKERMAN

Introduction

If we are driving in a car and turn on the radio to a classical music station we may well hear all or part of an unknown composition without the benefit of any context. But in almost every other circumstance our relationship to music is accompanied by stories that swirl around the engagement. I am using the word "story" loosely to refer to everything from full-blown programmatic narratives to sketchy biographical details and from snippets of commentary to sophisticated ideas about a composition's role in a historical or theoretical sense.

We come by these bits of information in manifold ways: listening to classroom lectures (or preparing them), reading program notes before a concert, or from short conversations with friends—or even on the radio if we happen to come in at the right time. In the process we might come to know details composers insisted that we encounter, some they might have tried to suppress, and still others that have nothing to do with the composers at all. The larger question, of course, is what effect, if any, does this telling of stories have on our encounter with music, and is there any way we can measure it? After some broader speculations about audiences and stories, this essay pursues a narrower inquiry in two ways: it restricts the field to stories about disability and focuses on a particular kind of "audience": the performer.

Audiences and Stories

At a recent music festival near Dresden a group of musicians performed Gideon Klein's Trio for Strings, composed in the Terezin concentration camp in 1944. The circumstances of the work are fraught: it was completed slightly more than a week before Klein was transported to Auschwitz, where he was eventually killed in one of the many satellite camps. The most substantial movement, the middle one of three, is a theme and variations on a Moravian folksong with a text about shooting a wild goose; the movement alludes to such compositions as Mahler's *Kindertotenlieder* and Verdi's *Requiem*, invoking the Angel of Death from Suk's *Asrael* and snippets from Janáček's Second String Quartet. The performance took place in a church. Half of the audience received program notes, the other half did not. In interviews that took place after the conclusion of the concert, those who did not receive notes tended to describe the Trio as "charming," "folkish," "sweet." Those who had information about Klein's circumstances described the work as "deeply moving," and "one of the great tragic statements of the 20th century."

As musicians and listeners we confront various realities. On the one hand, we feel that the instrumental music has its own integrity and identity, that our response to it should not vary wildly depending on what we just happen to know about it. On the other hand, as shown by the little experiment just described, we are uncannily susceptible to various kinds of suggestions whether biographical, programmatic, or even somewhat impressionistic; the very identity audience members ascribed to Klein's Trio depended on what they had been told about it.

Over the years I have explored and written about many compositions that have some strong relationship to what we sometimes call "extramusical" reality: Vaughan Williams's *Sinfonia Antartica*, closely related to a film score; Dvořák's "New World" Symphony, parts of which were inspired by Longfellow's *The Song of Hiawatha*; and of course, the music of Terezin, with its own powerful series of subtexts and stories (Beckerman 1992, 2000, 2010). In all of these one feels a certain pressure, a sense almost of being trapped; for one can neither ignore the stories that surround such compositions nor embrace them too closely once one has encountered them, lest the music become simply a trivialized soundtrack.

This is nowhere more evident than in so-called Holocaust music, where the composers' closeness to horrific events conditions audiences and performers who present and receive the works. And one cannot easily look away. Put directly: if Gideon Klein is using a musical composition to tell us about his experience in Terezin, who are we not to listen to that? Yet, if he is not, who are we to superimpose such a burden on the work? There is no simple answer to these questions, and possibly none at all.

Audiences may loosely be considered amateurs; in all but specialized contexts, a large portion them are encountering a given work for the first time. Thus it is natural that they should be susceptible to things they are told about what they are about to hear. But how about the performers who are charged with bringing the music to that audience? How do they shape that simultaneously fraught and fuzzy world that lies between abstract sound and the rest of the world?

Performers and Stories

Once again, the process is anything but straightforward, and even at the end of this inquiry the entire matter will remain open. I first thought seriously about the problem more than twenty years ago, when I worked with the Emerson String Quartet in various lecture recitals. The first of these dealt with Dvořák, and at that time quartet members suggested that they approach their performances from a strong sense of each composer's essence. "When we play Schubert, we think 'Schubert,' and this sense of who he is brings something to the performance. When we play Dvořák, we think 'Slavic.'" After they demonstrated some Dvořák, I asked them if they would consider playing Dvořák while "thinking" Schubert. The result was like a new performance; less mannered, with an entirely different sense of accentuation.

Because of this experience, some years later, I tried to get the Emerson Quartet to do something similar in connection with Shostakovich in a public lecture demonstration. Their performances of that composer's music were linked with the kinds of writing found in the liner notes to their CD of the Eighth Quartet: "These pieces stand as an aural representation of an incredible spectrum of human tragedy and suffering, with occasional glimpses of hopefulness." I thought it would be useful for the audience to have a sense of other ways the composition might be approached, and we worked out in advance that they would do something similar to playing their "Schubertian" Dvořák. Standing there on stage I asked them how they might play a particular passage differently if they believed that the "conflict" they perceived was Shostakovich's internal struggle about being an *apparatchik* rather than his attempt to secretly depict the evils of Stalinism. Even though we had worked it out, they absolutely refused to go along with the plan when we were in front of the public, saying that they could only play the piece from the framework of a heroic Shostakovich whose compositions represented a kind of resistance. Dvořák could be Schubertized, Shostakovich had to remain the figure they imagined.

A few years later I received a telephone call from the cellist Jan Vogler, whom I had not previously met. After introducing himself his first words were: "I just recorded the Dvořák *Cello Concerto* with the New York Philharmonic, and I played it differently because I read your book" (Beckerman 2003). After thinking about our conversation, I began to wonder to what extent his statement could be true. How could it be that reading a book caused a cellist to touch his instrument in a different way? What actually happened between the reading and the performance, and how do such wisps of information end up playing a role in choices made by performers?

One final experiment led me to think in a more skeptical way about the relationship between performers and stories. I recruited a group of string players to learn the Klein Trio but gave them no information about the work. We recorded the piece, and over two sessions, I gradually gave them more and more background on the circumstances of the composition. In the end I interviewed them onstage at the Juilliard School in front of an audience and they performed the work again. While they all claimed that the stories I had spun made a deep and profound impression on them, and substantially changed the way they performed the piece, the recorded evidence was more equivocal. While certain physical gestures might have suggested something like stronger expression, the sound, tempo, and accentuation was almost unchanged over the performances. And while it is likely that these gestures could have some effect on the way the assembled audience processed the sound, there was no sense from my observation that this was a calculated strategy on the part of the performers or even, in fact, that the performers were aware of the gestures.

Disability

With this experience in mind, I began to wonder what role, if any, stories about disability might play in the way performers respond to various compositions. This is hardly an incidental question. After all, it probably is not an exaggeration to say that the history of nineteenth-century music is to a great extent, a tale of disability. Whether we are speaking of Beethoven's deafness, Schumann's hand injury (or his mania, or his insanity), Chopin's tuberculosis, Dvořák's agoraphobia, or Mussorgsky's "nervous breakdowns" and alcoholism, the very way we think the meaning of sound may be inseparable from perceptions of disease, loss, and disability. While it is true that compartmentalization is possible (we sadly remember that despite the fact that the greatest German composer of the early nineteenth century was deaf, the Nazis enthusiastically sentenced most of the country's deaf population to euthanasia), it is not clear how we can easily separate our very notions about this music from such realities. Did Beethoven invent a new method of composition based on thick sketching because of some aesthetic vision, or because his hearing loss (as in the case of Smetana) made it impossible for him to continue writing music in his head as he would normally have done? Are the *pianissimos* we find in late Chopin conscious attempts at delicacy or are they somehow evidence of his tubercular state? Is Tchaikovsky's anxiety and concomitant morbidity audible in the *Pathetique Symphony* and to what extent did the composer's demise shortly after its premiere condition subsequent audience response?

The Mivos Quartet and Stories of Disability

In order to explore such questions I followed the pattern established in the various experiments related above, but with disability rather than "the Holocaust" as the primary issue. But what works to choose? While Beethoven's string quartets involve pertinent issues, the works are so well known to performers, as are various interpretations of them, that using his compositions for this experiment might not have been revealing. Thus, any performers I could find would know that Beethoven was deaf, and have some knowledge of his life, and so there would be little I could tell them that would be new and possibly change their orientation.

Eventually I decided to choose three works from the Czech quartet repertoire that to my mind raised issues of the relationship between music and stories of disability.

Although one might argue that because of the collaborative nature of the quartet genre the impact of stories on an individual performer might be blunted, at least one of the quartets has a conspicuous solo passage, and the others reflect discussions among the players.

To execute the project I engaged the noted Mivos Quartet, which I thought might be ideal for the purpose. It is an ensemble noted for the performance of new music, and the members play at a high level. But they have not been as involved in performing the traditional quartet repertoire and were unlikely to have known much about the three quartets I selected.

I followed the same strategy as described above with the Klein Trio. I selected three movements from three different quartets. The performers received the scores, but were given no additional information about the compositions or the composers and were asked not to do any research. They rehearsed the works and came in and recorded them. After that part of the process was concluded, I told them a series of stories, and then they played the works again; this second performance was recorded, and afterward we discussed the process.

I offer the (longish) stories below. All three are slightly edited transcriptions of the recorded remarks I made before each performance, but do not in any way augment or distort the content. Whether or not the statements I made to the quartet happen to be true, or whether I even believe them to be true, is largely immaterial to the case in question. The important thing is that I assume the performers believed me. And while nothing in these stories is consciously made up or falsified, neither are they explicitly scholarly: they do not offer all the appropriate disclaimers, seeking, rather, to present the information in a somewhat dramatic form. Finally, I have not provided documentation, because, once again, whether or not the stories are true, accurate, based on evidence, or made up out of whole cloth is irrelevant to this particular encounter between story and musician.

Story #1: Smetana, String Quartet No. 2 (first movement)

Despite his eventual position as the "Father of Czech Music" Smetana actually grew up speaking German. He became a champion of New Music in Gothenburg, Sweden, as a young man, and then became a star by writing a series of national operas. He was a leading force in establishing something that became recognized as a Czech musical language. During his life, he was both venerated and condemned as Wagnerian; aesthetic battles swirled around him parallel to the conflicts between the Brahmsians and the Wagnerians in German-speaking lands. In the 1870s he began to experience deteriorating health on several levels, including most notably, his hearing. There is a particularly wrenching moment in the autobiographical string quartet "From My Life" meant to illustrate what the composer heard when his hearing deteriorated. Like Beethoven, Smetana wrote some of his most famous music while he was deaf, including such compositions as the six tone poems making up *Má vlast*, and operas *The Kiss* and *The Devil's Wall*.

The hearing problems, however, were not the only symptoms of Smetana's condition. He also suffered from serious neurological impairment and, according to his own words, began to lose what had been a formidable musical memory. This progressed and, by the early 1880s his condition had worsened considerably. By 1882 his doctors were telling him not to compose, and by the following year he was experiencing horrible symptoms. For a few days he could only make the Czech sounds "d' t' n." He tried to compose but had to hide the activity from his doctors. He found it painful to collect his thoughts and would write music on little scraps of paper. At various points he could no longer recognize people's faces, but still tried to compose. He once said something like: "I'm only writing this to show what kind of music is written by someone in my state." In this mode his wrote the Second String Quartet. He tried toward the very end to write an opera on the subject of *Twelfth Night* with the title, *Viola*, which he could not finish, but the autograph shows a very specific physical deterioration in the handwriting. He was eventually taken off to a mental asylum, where he died shortly afterward.

The most usual explanation for his condition is tertiary syphilis, and there is no doubt that he was suffering from serious neurological deterioration when he wrote the Second Quartet.[1] The reception of this work has been mixed, with some believing that it is incoherent, while others, such as Schoenberg, maintaining that it is revelatory, saying "it opened a new world to me."

Story #2: Martinů's Quartet No. 7, *Concerto da camera* (second movement)

Martinů was probably the only composer born in a church tower. His father, a cobbler, was the town firewatcher in the town of Polička (it had burned to the ground in 1845), on the border of Moravia and Bohemia. The whole family lived in a tiny, square room more than 190 steps above the countryside. Martinů was an interesting composer and prodigy, and a violinist who played in professional orchestras. In a famous letter to Eduard Beneš, Martinů maintained that because Prague's musical life was in the hands of Germans, the only way to become a Czech composer was to go to Paris. Martinů became successful in Paris, writing modernist pieces, and was influenced by surrealism: he wrote a ballet based on kitchen implements, and his opera *Julietta* was based on surrealist text. While in Paris, he also began to write pieces based on Czech folklore. Known as an antifascist, he was blacklisted by the Nazis and had to flee Paris in 1939; he made a harrowing escape and managed to get to the United States. In some ways the United States was far behind Paris in terms of certain aspects of musical taste: it was the home of the symphony. Martinů wrote five symphonies in the first years after his arrival and was remarkably successful. He had excellent connections among conductors like Bruno Walter, Charles Munch, and Serge Koussevitsky; audiences loved his music, and he was arguably the most performed contemporary symphonist between 1941 and 1946. He taught at Princeton and was invited to Tanglewood. Everything was going smoothly for him.

At this time he became involved with a woman named Roe Barstow, who was listed among his Tanglewood students, but probably was not a musician or even actually a student. We don't know what his state of mind was at that time, but whether in agitation or not, he went out onto his terrace in Tanglewood one evening, and the story is that he thought there was a railing around this balcony. Expecting to feel the railing he walked out and stepped off the edge of the balcony and fell one story onto the concrete surface and was found almost dead several hours later, bleeding profusely.

For several months he was in terrible shape, and there was great fear that he would not recover. But recover he did, and the Seventh String Quartet was written the following year. I consider it to be his *Heilige Dankgesang*, a conscious reference to Beethoven's String Quartet, Op. 132, and part of his attempt to recover from his trauma. The textures are modeled on the imitative language of Op. 132, but also on a range of madrigalian textures as well, an effect he had always loved. This piece represents both the effects of his illness and his attempts to come to grips with it.

There is a fairly basic principle that, for many reasons, major new themes rarely if ever appear at the end of a composition or a movement. Yet in Martinů's quartet the most lyrical effusion comes almost at the conclusion. My sense is that just as Beethoven juxtaposed imitative sections with quasi-Baroque elements in Op. 132, and termed them respectively the "Thanksgiving Prayer" and "New Strength," Martinů's final theme represents his own return to strength, and this partially explains why we get such an unusual lyrical effusion at the close of the movement.

Story #3: Dvořák's Quartet in F, Op. 96, "American" (fourth movement)

I began by telling the Mivos Quartet that they probably knew a bit more about Dvořák than Martinů but perhaps not so much about the origins of this piece. The "American" Quartet was composed in Spillville, Iowa, in the summer of 1893. At the time it was written, many people considered Dvořák, after Brahms, the greatest living composer in Europe—Wagner had died 10 years earlier. Dvořák had recently been brought to the United States to become director of the National Conservatory. This was an institution created to provide education for people of talent regardless of race, gender, or social class. The founder, Jeanette Thurber, wanted the best teachers in the world in New York. One of her mains goals was to jump start a field of American music; she imagined a music that was sonically American in the same way Russian music "sounded" Russian. She wanted Dvořák to create American music in the same way—to her mind—he had created Czech music. In effect Thurber wanted Dvořák to take the

Czechisms out of his work and dream up what Americanisms might be and replace the one with the other.

Dvořák arrived in New York with a princely salary and the stipulation he teach and conduct some concerts on behalf of the Conservatory. One might say that from the moment he arrived people were throwing these Americanisms at him: African American and Native American music, the poetry of Longfellow, the songs of Stephen Foster, and much more. About two weeks after his arrival, the 400th anniversary of Columbus's "discovery" took place. Dozens of bands passed under his hotel window, giving him a chance to hear a cross-section of musical styles.

He began working on the "New World" Symphony in December 1892, and finished it around March of the following year. A few months later he went on record in a notorious interview with a famous yellow journalist named James Creelman claiming that black music should be at the core of any American sound, and that Negro melodies were a most vital and important resource. In a rebuttal to Dvořák, a Boston composer wrote that Negro melodies could never be used to create an American music because they lacked the "repressive" Anglo Saxon spirit! Others weighed in, including the Antons, Rubinstein and Bruckner (Beckerman 2003).

Dvořák was a reticent man, and as a result of his comments, he was suddenly embroiled in a huge controversy. It is also important to note in this context that Dvořák suffered from severe anxiety, which included pronounced agoraphobia. Agoraphobia, it should be said, is not so much fear of the outdoors, but rather fear that you will lose control while you are outside, fear that you might go crazy or have a panic attack.

The first two stories I told involved neurological impairments. The American Quartet is an example of something that involves another kind of mental health issue. Let me explain: Dvořák got out of New York en route to a Czech colony established in Spillville, Iowa, where he stayed with the parents of his American-born Czech secretary. After all this brouhaha in the newspapers, he took a train across Pennsylvania, where he had a fit because he couldn't get a drink (Pennsylvania was, at that time, a dry state). He went through Chicago and Iowa, and was taken by coach to the small, Czech hamlet of Spillville. Suddenly he found himself in absolute heaven: he could drink what he wanted when he wanted, he could hear birdsong, he could speak his own language. In these circumstances, he wrote his American quartet in less than two weeks, probably in no more than a couple of days.

It is my view that the work was written in a kind of hypermania after a depressive episode in New York. In his article, James Creelman described Dvořák as "sitting alone in a dark room with his teeth clenched" (cited in Beckerman 2003). The first movement of this work begins with a viola solo that says, in effect, "I'm back" (Dvořák was a violist) and thus, like Smetana's quartets, seems to have a strong autobiographical tinge.

Discussion with the Mivos Quartet

I told these three stories before the Mivos Quartet recorded these works for the second time. After the stories and after the performances, I asked them a linked series of questions: "What if anything do these stories mean to you? Did you find yourself engaged by them or somewhat impervious to them? Is it possible that despite your interest, you found it impossible to translate these stories into musical gestures? In your opinion, what kinds of things might or might not cause a performer to react strongly to a given story? In your view, how much of your thinking is purely musical, having to do with issues of sound and proportion, and how much involves thinking about external things?" I also told them at this point that they were not obligated to say anything at all.

I would like to select several moments from our subsequent discussion about the Smetana quartet for commentary, because this was the work that made the greatest impression the members of the Mivos Quartet.

The first violinist, Joshua Modney, spoke first, saying, "I felt most affected by the Smetana story, because this piece is really weird! I couldn't understand it before." [The rest of the group chimed in agreeing] "But then it really made sense." I asked in what way the story made sense. The violist, Victor Lowrie, continued:

> In terms of its fragmentary nature and abrupt transitions and other odd transitions from section to section. Also in terms of the way things modulate. It is just weird to wrap our heads around. From my perspective I had been thinking more in terms of what sound should we be going for? How do we make it homogenous? How do we make it smooth? Having heard that story I think it is fun to make it not smooth at all, and to really define the character for each section and make it super abrupt; to actually focus on the strangeness of it. That might be a more interesting way to interpret it.

The cellist, Mariel Roberts, then spoke broadly about how she imagines the process:

> I think as performers even though we're musicians we are also like actors as well, because we're acting out what these pieces are. We didn't write them; they are not autobiographical for us. So it is not as if knowing about the story of Smetana gave us permission to act crazy. It was more like we had permission to be jumpier, and to do, to act in the way we imagine his brain to be working. I felt that in a lot of the stories you told. It gave me an understanding of who this person was. They're just notes on a page and you have to make choices based on what you see. You make personal choices but knowing the person that you are trying to emulate, whose voice you are trying to emulate, really changed the choices I made.

Second violinist Olivia de Prato stated that finding out such stories gives her "more options. You can decided to go with the story or not, but you have more choices about how you interpret."

Sonic Evidence

Obviously the next step in such an experiment would be to compare performances before and after the stories, note differences, and try to come to conclusions about them. This is, however, a treacherous process. Even if one articulates and demonstrates changes (either "by ear" or through other, more technical means) it is not always possible to say what caused them and whether differences between performances reflect the impact of my stories, or perhaps the fact that it was a second, rather than a first, performance; or were related to other factors, anything from room humidity to the mellifluous sound of the interlocutor's voice. Since the basic caution in research is to avoid the trap of finding only what one is looking for, the only appropriate approach here is to create the following null hypothesis: *there is no meaningful change in performances that can explicitly be tied to the stories I told.* I will offer my conclusion in advance: I believe there is no way this null hypothesis can be successfully dismantled.

Now, if is this were simply a science experiment, I would have to conclude that the stories I told had no demonstrable effect on the performers and this would end the matter. Fortunately, however, the endeavor is also part of an ongoing thought experiment, the context is also humanistic: this allows me to raise other issues, and so we may continue considering the matter on other levels.

Keeping in mind the comments of the Mivos Quartet with regard to Smetana's Second Quartet one might consider their second recording in terms of a certain paradox. Having found the composition "weird" and trying to make it "more homogenous" resulted in a somewhat disjointed performance, unsatisfying to the performers. After hearing my story, which gave them "permission" to "act crazy," the results showed, paradoxically, greater coherence.

Another natural place to focus on the differences between the "before" and "after" performances and connect up with the narratives I provided is at the conclusion of the second movement of Martinů's Seventh Quartet, where my story drew a parallel between the new theme (the cello solo) and the "New Strength" section of Beethoven's Op. 132, relating both to Martinů's own recovery.

In a way the two recorded versions are quite interesting, especially because they are not very different at all. But a close listening does reveal something. While basic tempo remains almost exactly the same, the somewhat detached and cool quality of the first version is replaced by a sense of whole phrases, accomplished both by more legato playing and more dynamic nuance. The last few bars of the passage are like a microcosm of this process, where fullness of tone, rhythmic nuance, and a more legato, "warm" style of playing create quite a different effect.

The same process appears to be at work in the performances of the finale of the "American" quartet. The "poststory" version has greater nuance, both of the kind one might expect when the subject of the story is mania—that is more abrupt rhythmically defined passages—but also more sense of swell within a phrase. To some extent this would seem to conform to ideas about playing that are more expressive and dramatic, but actually the changes are relatively minor and the tempi almost unchanged.

Once again, there is no way to prove that any changes and differences in performances were a direct result of the stories I told, though we may believe this to be the case. However we construe it, the subtlety of any changes is a far cry from the seemingly radical effect noted at the beginning of this essay in relation in terms of the audience response to Klein's Trio in Germany.

In the end, there are many stories that can be told about music and disability. One can try to tell *no* story, and let the music "speak for itself," a dubious proposition, but one with ample precedent. Stories about music and disability often follow a predictable trajectory, tracing the familiar narrative of overcoming, of triumph over adversity.[2] Of course there are darker ways to tell these stories as well. It can and has been argued that, in the case of Smetana, and Martinů as well, the disability *disabled* compositional skill and instinct: that Smetana's quartet is incoherent, that Martinů's quartet represents a decline.

Once again, there is no way to prove either side. First, because true musical coherence is not simply a matter of repeated or even noticeable patterns, but something that must be tested by the individual experiences of audience members and listeners (and even then, it is not exactly clear what it means). And second, because our analytical systems lack the capacity to positively value compositions whose goal may be to depict the very lack of connection associated with the disabilities that hover around this group of string quartets. From the very beginning of our musical studies we are taught valedictory lessons about "the little cell that grew," about organic connections and large-scale musical logic. But perhaps more than any other force today, ideas fundamental to Disability Studies insist that we need methods that can value and grasp what we previously referred to as incoherence, dissociation, and displacement. This not only poses a challenge to Disability Studies but also prods us to rethink our broader mission concerning just what musical works are and what they are supposed to do.

Notes

1. For the latest medical research on this matter see Höschl 2012. For other perspectives on Smetana's bodily condition in relation to his music, see Katz 1997 and Straus 2011.
2. For discussion of musical narratives of disability, see Straus 2011.

References

Beckerman, Michael. 1992. "Dvořák's 'New World' Largo and *The Song of Hiawatha*." *Nineteenth-Century Music* 16 (1): 35–48.

Beckerman, Michael. 2000. "The Composer as Pole Seeker: Reading Vaughan Williams's *Sinfonia Antartica*." *Current Musicology* 69: 42–67.

Beckerman, Michael. 2003. *New Worlds of Dvořák*. New York: W. W. Norton.

Beckerman, Michael. 2010. "What Kind of Historical Document Is a Musical Score? A Meditation in Ten Parts on Klein's Trio." OREL Foundation. http://orelfoundation.org/index.php/journal/journalArticle/what_kind_of_historical_document_is_a_musical_score/.

Höschl, Cyril. 2012. "Bedřich Smetana: Art and Disease." *Psychiatria Danubina* 24 (Suppl. 1): 176–178.

Katz, Derek. 1997. "Smetana's Second String Quartet: Voice of Madness or Triumph of Spirit?" *Musical Quarterly* 81 (4): 516–536.

Straus, Joseph N. 2011. *Extraordinary Measures: Disability in Music*. New York: Oxford University Press.

CHAPTER 16

THE DANCING GROUND

Embodied Knowledge, Disability, and Visibility in New Orleans Second Lines

DANIELLA SANTORO

As the second line parade rolled up South Claiborne Avenue, the long snaking mass of second liners could be seen rounding the corner in a celebratory syncopated strut. Mid-day traffic is suspended by the hired New Orleans Police Department (NOPD) escort at Martin Luther King Avenue, officially assisting this social aid and pleasure club in the more than one-hundred-year-old tradition of "takin' it to the streets" on Sunday afternoons. The first brass band announces its presence with a steady upbeat rhythm, ushering all those waiting on the curbs to join in and dance. The few hundred followers, known colloquially as "second liners," appear from afar to move as one unit, pulsing with the back bass beat, but amid the crowd, diversity abounds.

While moving through the uptown side-streets, the hard pavement appears to bend for some second liners more than others: one man springs from it as if preparing for flight, hindered only by the weight of his low riding blue jeans; another undulates his body on the ground as the sidewalk bends like rubber, sinking and rising at his will. By contrast, an older gentleman proposes a playful shuffle to a younger woman, who, with one hand on her hip and the other waving behind her, dances her answer.

A few feet behind the band, in the shadow of the sousaphone, life-long second liner "Skelly Well" rolls his wheelchair to a sudden stop—the music is just right, the collective energy has begun to rise, and the parade has paused here on this two-lane thoroughfare now transformed into the ideal dancing ground. Skelly, leans his weight back and tilts his chair up on its wheels, beginning a choreography of spins and styled pauses, punctuating the brass band rhythm as his long and lean arms offer commentary on the melody. Francis, another second liner, has now rotated his mobile chair to face Skelly and bounces his torso and shoulders in gesture toward him, bending at the waist and rising again in a creative groove. As they dance, second liners begin to shout encouragingly with a hip-hop tonal sensibility, "Work that wheelchair!" they chant, "work work, work that wheelchair."

Introduction

For communities founded on the expressive cultural traditions of New Orleans, particularly those that support, nurture, and identify with the long-standing expressive cultural practices of the second line jazz parade tradition, dance is paramount. At weekly jazz parades called second lines, dance is a most visible celebration. It is how club members present themselves as they "come out the door" and greet supporters on the street. Dance is how you greet a friend you spot in the crowd, show respect, and challenge him/her to a stylistic spontaneous competition. Dance is a forum for elders to pass on knowledge to younger generations and for children to prove they have been paying attention. Dance is also a way of honoring infirm club members, passing on joy, and, at jazz funerals, it can be a profound means for expressing and channeling sorrow.

Dance is a vehicle to show off one's creativity, strength, and agility, often despite seeming fragility, age, or disability. Dance is language; in the context of public tradition and expressive culture, it functions as socially sanctioned communication, embodied history and knowledge. How, then, can we read the disabled body through dance? What does the presence and mobility of differently abled bodies within the corporeal landscape of a second line suggest about the social meanings and interpretations of disability? How do dance and expressive movement publically critique binary social scripts about ability and disability?

As this essay will demonstrate, second line dance is a universalizing trope, which organizes public perceptions around issues of mobility and the social meanings of disability. In a city that has become notorious for chronic "street violence,"[1] structural neglect, and vast disparities in health outcomes and wealth distribution, disability is grounded in the meaning of lived experiences with the consequences of sudden violence, injury, and chronic illness. This essay explores the ways in which dance and expressive cultural performance as embodied knowledge critique mainstream discourses of disability that render persons with disabilities as pathological and in need of social interventions. In doing so, this critique also serves to interrogate historical tropes and social scripts that associate disability with blackness and to demonstrate how local parading traditions provide a forum for individuals with physical disabilities to emerge in public visibility and self-representation.

Using the narratives and observations of several individuals[2] gathered through intermittent ethnographic research from 2010 to 2013, this essay contextualizes second line dance as a contemporary vernacular practice on the streets of New Orleans and positions it within wider framings of embodiment, reading the body as a site of meaning and knowledge production and complicating passive social messages that would present dance and disability as "an impossibility" (Albright 1998). Furthermore, within the collective second line tradition, this essay is concerned with how dance sustains "embodied knowledge" (Bourdieu 1977, Daniel 2005, Merleau-Ponty 1962) and acts as a collective shared idiom of expression for negotiating and reenvisioning objectifying and pathologizing discourses about disability.

The New Orleans Second Line

The second line is so much more than a religion or an obsession or a cult even. Simply put, it's soul medicine. Whatever harsh realities life deals you through the week, a good ole four-hour long second line parade will burn that poison right on out of you.

—Deborah "Big Red" Cotton[3]

For four hours every Sunday afternoon participatory street parades led by a brass band and sponsored by neighborhood social clubs wind through New Orleans city streets. Unlike conventional parades, which move down large public avenues of downtown civic centers, or the New Orleans Mardi Gras parades, which pass through the iconic tree-lined St. Charles Avenue, second lines are most commonly routed through the city's long-standing African American neighborhoods in Central City, the Treme, and the 7th ward. Throughout the second line season (from late August to early June), roughly three-dozen neighborhood associations, called social aid and pleasure clubs, will host a parade to celebrate their club's anniversary. These social clubs are rooted in the centuries-old traditions of African American neighborhood associations and benevolent societies that were founded as early as the nineteenth century and provided burial insurance, medical insurance, and other caretaking duties increasingly denied to blacks by the exclusions of Jim Crow era segregation. Today, in addition to the second line parades, many clubs host parties, fundraisers, funerals, and charity drives, contributing to a larger year-round "second line culture" and extended urban social network.

The history of the second line can be traced back to the growth of benevolent societies during the reconstruction period and to the early origins of jazz at the turn of the century. The "second line" refers to the organization of the traditional New Orleans jazz funeral procession, where the second line consisted of those mourners who follow behind the band as the body of the deceased is paraded through the streets on the way to the cemetery. In this context, dance is a significant display of an emotional tribute to the deceased and a means of shared public grieving (Touchet 1998). Today, while social clubs still sponsor jazz funerals for their members, the second line has taken on its own significance in the community as an independent and secular weekly event. Yet as performative vestiges of the jazz funeral tradition, second line parades have been interpreted by some scholars to manifest Congo Square rhythms and Afro-Caribbean spirituality, emphasizing what Joseph Roach (1996) calls a "spirit world subculture."[4]

The second line, like other expressive public traditions of the African American and Afro-Creole populations of New Orleans, also embodies a legacy of racial division that defines New Orleans social order. In this respect, second lines, as community events, have the potential to call attention to current racial, economic, and political complexities of urban life (Regis 2001; Breunlin and Regis 2006). According to Dr. Michael White, the second line tradition emerges from "a fusion of musical and social elements" which evolved into "a vehicle for expression of the collective creative black New Orleans spirit and as an open cultural exercise in democracy" (White 2001, 93). Second lines travel through neighborhoods that are a palimpsest of complex racialized geographies including the local historical memories of Jim Crow era segregation, white flight and disinvestment, the trauma and displacement after Katrina, and the recent encroachments of gentrification and neighborhood change. Anthropologist Helen Regis articulates the transformative nature of the parade as it remaps contested urban landscapes. The second line operates as a

> joyous space of power, dignity, self-reliance, and freedom, transcending the quotidian struggles of the ghetto. It incorporates all those who will move to its music, who become a single flowing movement of people unified by the rhythm. In incorporating them, it recasts them into different roles, creating relationships that would not otherwise be possible in everyday life, which is dominated by the moral economy of the postindustrial city. (Regis 1999, 480)

This transformative power of participation in second lines is elaborated through the social meaning of temporarily reclaiming and reorganizing the control of public space and its social and racial geographies (Neely and Samura 2011). One member of the Prince of Wales Social Aide and Pleasure Club explains the significance of the experience of having the power to control access to public streets:

> This is something that you can't describe, you have to feel it. To have two horses behind you, and thirty, forty people behind you, and you just saying, "I want to stop right here." And they can't do nothing about it. All they can do is say, "We gotta stop." That's just like being President Obama. Shut that street down. Shut that street down.[5]

The second line parade is a participatory, moving, and changing event. In contrast to the predictable tropes of the tourist icon, the second line must be understood for its holistic and diverse collective of participants, and its function as a "great social leveler,"[6] referencing the racial history of Jim Crow–era politics, as well as the more tangible spaces that invite participation of those otherwise marked as disabled by illness, age, or circumstance.

The legacy of mutual aid has been retained in various ways, in sick committees, hospital visitations, and medical funds. Yet it is the dynamic of the parade itself that embodies a relationship between expressive culture and community health and the social politics of disability. Second line parades will frequently stop by homes of elderly members, or those with physical disabilities who might be unable to travel far with the parade. After a shooting at a second line on Mothers Day 2013 made national headlines, the president of the hosting club Original Big Seven, explained in a local press meeting, that the second lines traditionally go through neighborhoods of perceived risk specifically to spread joy in areas where fellow residents may be disconnected from mainstream establishments and aid institutions.

The relationship between second line culture and the city's municipal factions has evolved greatly over time, particularly in regard to street violence. In the past this relationship has been apprehensive and antagonistic, resulting in overpolicing and permitting restrictions rationalized through political rhetoric that marked historically black neighborhoods as dangerous and violent. Currently, as part of the citywide murder reduction campaign "Nola for Life," second line parades are publically lauded by the city government as a revered New Orleans tradition, and social clubs are presented as allies in the battle for safer streets and violence prevention. However, as we will see, the expressive culture of the second line tradition, and the relationship of disability and embodied performance in particular, offer commentary on the ongoing tensions regarding the political rhetoric of antiviolence campaigns, the touristic visibility of black New Orleans culture, and the invisibility of the structural inequities experienced by many of its tradition bearers.

Second Line Dance and Embodied Performance

A strong collection of scholarly literature has documented the musical soundscape of the second line event (Sakakeeny 2010), the politics of African American identity and urban space (Regis 2001; Breunlin and Regis 2006; Sakakeeny 2013), and the reformations of second line culture in the post-Katrina landscape (Dinerstein 2009), Yet, rarely has dance at second lines been privileged as an embodied cultural form, worthy of its own historical and musicological analysis. This essay seeks to fill this gap, through an embodied critique that situates the body engaged in dance and movement as not just a passive receptacle of cultural performance, but as a subjective ground of acculturated lived experience.

Dance, according to African dance scholar Barbara Browning (1995), is a form of cultural record keeping: the body is a site on which history and tradition can be embodied, retained, and recalled. Similarly, Yvonne Daniel (2005) identifies the concept of embodied knowledge within Cuban Yoruba religious dance, suggesting that dance and kinesthetic movements embody particular histories and ideologies that cannot be expressed by other socially dominant systems that are founded on *disembodied* knowledge, such as biomedical institutions reified by the influence of Cartesian mind/body dualism (see Scheper-Hughes and Lock 1987). In this sense, the body acts as a malleable and potent social repository of cultural knowledge, and second line dance embodies social messages about the raced and disabled body in public space.

Referencing the style of dance that typically occurs at second line parades led by brass bands, and by extension at local music clubs where these bands perform, "second line dance" defies a simple definition. As the embodied performative movement articulated with syncopated brass band music in the streets of New Orleans during second line parades, it encompasses a wide variety of styles and abilities. The dance functions as both an autonomous collection of moves as well as a practical rhythmical step that enables one to keep up with the fast-moving brass band parade. The stylings of the dance follow the pace and expectations set by the parade and allow for creative adaptation to the urban landscape.

Second line dance is most commonly represented as a combination of percussive footwork, disciplined energetic releases, and athletic stunts, and is socially rendered along a continuum of complementary values of athleticism and grace, playfulness and restraint. Encompassed within this notion of "footwork" is an observable technique that includes shuffling, fast skipping steps, heel and toe stops, and athletic jumps and leaps, as well as posturings that rely on showcasing one's individual footwork styles in spontaneous street competitions or "battles." These spontaneous "battles" signify one way in which second line emboldens the concept of individual performance, by reinforcing and praising skillful displays of confidence, attitude, and postured stylings, embodied in the notion of "clowning" (Regis 1999) or "work."

Despite the importance of "footwork," the improvisational and adaptable idiom of second line dance enables participation by people whose impairments make traditional "footwork" unfeasible. In many ways, the second line embodies the well-worn New Orleans adage originally authored by the Rebirth Brass Band, "do whatcha wanna,"[7] and exemplified by commonly heard expressions that encourage individuals throughout the parade, to "work it out" or just "do you." Dance ethnographer Rachel Carrico (2013) explores this notion of the "do whatcha wanna aesthetic" and how it both indexes racial difference through bodily presentation and at the same time evades a codification of rules for technique or choreography. Indeed, when pressed for a definition of second line dance, second liners commonly remark that it is an attitude, or a feeling—a posturing of self-confidence and control. Although common names of moves such as "the drop kick" or "the buckjump"[8] have circulated as dance labels, definitions of dance rarely employ a reference to a specific body part, body type, or pose. Rollin' Joe of Pigeon Town Steppers explains, "There aren't really names for the moves besides steppin' and buckjumpin'—the moves come from the rhythm. When that beat hit the soul, you're zoned out on another level, and I got to finish buckin'."[9] As such comments imply, there is no consensus on an objective technique in secondline dance. Rather, value is accorded to the holistic presentation of a dancer's performance and how that dancer articulates and responds to what the brass band musicians propose.

In addition to choreographic descriptions, historical studies have situated second line dance within the context of the African-derived, percussion-based bamboula dances and rhythms of Congo Square and within a African diasporic tradition that unites New

Orleans second lines with Rara parades of Haiti, Congo parades of Cuba, and other Afro-Caribbean and Afro-Creole musical expressions. These African retentions for instance, are highlighted in Alan Lomax's iconic 1990 documentary *Jazz Parades: Feet Don't Fail Me Now*,[10] in which Lomax makes explicit connections between the squatting, jumping, kicking, and hyperphysical expressions of the dance and its antecedent, west African religious ceremonial dance.

Jaqui Malone argues that, as a form of African American vernacular dance, second line dance incorporates the elements of a broader African derived aesthetic: improvisation, call-and-response forms, and attitudes of derision, parody, and self-stylings, thus linking it stylistically to urban contemporary forms such as break dancing and bounce (Malone 1996). Richard Brent Turner (2009) refers to the expressive movements associated with contemporary second line culture as "ecstatic dance" (110), as it embodies decades of adaptation and syncretism between the spiritual beliefs of the African Diaspora and the urban subcultures and communities of New Orleans.

Jazz historian and musician Michael White renders a description of second line parades that emphasizes the ecstatic or transcendental power of music:

> Walking canes and crutches . . . are suddenly hoisted high in mock imitation of the grand marshall's umbrella. Elderly faces that often express a tiredness and hopelessness in the struggle against death now glow. Bodies that have been bent by decades of hard time now straighten out, twist and gyrate with new renewed vitality, and say they will continue dancing until the butcher cuts them down. (White 2001, 82)

The transformative and transcendental aspect of dance demonstrates the "spiritual dimension" of the second line and its connection with the religious performative vestiges of the traditional jazz funeral. However, from a critical disability perspective, White's comment hints at a romanticized image of people not embracing their disability but temporarily forgetting it. This passivity runs the risk of slipping into persistent tropes about blackness and performance—hinged in part to the legacy of the minstrel tradition—which tend to naturalize black bodies as innately musical and performative. Additionally, this research expands on these notions of transcendence to include an analysis that privileges embodied agency and resists analyses that overemphasize the transcendental power of music at the expense of identifying individual creative agencies that people use, negotiate, and challenge through the forum of dance.

New Orleans–based dance instructor and choreographer Jessica Donley suggests an alternate view, one that claims ownership of your own body when you don't own anything else: "When you don't have political voice, you gotta sell yourself, to second line you gotta have swag."[11] This sentiment is paralleled in Matt Sakakeeny's discussion of "voice" in his ethnography of brass band musicians in New Orleans (Sakakeeny 2013). Applying a notion of voice as a social statement, which collapses historic injustices with present-day insecurities, Sakakeeny explains that musical practices "are forms of social action; . . . they offer insight into agency as the exercise of, or against power" (2013, 6). I wish to expand on this notion of "voice" to include the practices not just of the musicians performing on public streets constructing soundscapes but also of the dancers and second liners that follow them, thus recognizing that social action is embodied in public expressive performance and dance. In this respect, the brass band soundscape becomes a public venue for the expression of both literal and figurative bodywork. In the social space of these parading traditions, what is classified as a disability in the medical clinic, and in need of intervention, may be transformed into a creative asset, and a "strategic ability" (Albright 1998). In this context, second line dance is public commentary, making visible that which has been systematically excluded, discounted, and devalued.

Blackness and Disability

If the body can be thought of as a micrcosm of society, then the disabled body is particularly fraught, for it stands in opposition to cherished American values of autonomy and individualism. Conceptions of "normalcy" are hinged to social constructions and performances that reify otherness as either exceptional or pathological. Social meanings about disability become essentialized and scripted onto marginalized bodies, often eliciting feelings of rejection and fear of contamination (Siebers 2010) or discomfort by reminding able-bodied persons of their own vulnerability (Murphy 1995). Disability, as Tobin Siebers argues, has long been placed "in the service of discrimination, inequality," shaping an "aesthetics of human disqualification" (2010, 22).

Disability too, services a binary social construction that defines bodies simplistically as either fit or frail, strong or weak, able or dis-abled. Such a binary ideology refuses to recognize the immutable social fact that we are all only "temporarily able bodied" (Marks 1999). Choreographer and dance scholar Ann Cooper Albright (1998) argues therefore that dance and disability has been presented as an "impossibility" in the social imagination. The disabled body is culturally coded as grotesque and is thus pitted against Western classical ideals of body forms, which shape expectations of dance and embodied performance as the sole domain of the able-bodied. Instead, Albright contends, the disabled dancer should be understood as having "strategic abilities," which reposition dance in the service of each individual, whatever the form and functioning of his/her body might be.

Albright's notion of strategic abilities is useful because it directly counters the dominant medicalized model of disability that functions to conflate disability with lack, pathology, and risk, and identifies certain features as impairments and marks them as in need of intervention. The ideology of the medical model claims to fix bodies—old bodies made younger, disabled bodies reshaped toward a normative ideal—and suggests that challenges related to disability can be "overcome" by individual actions, rather than through social accommodation.

Following Albright's adaptation of the classical/grotesque binary framework, spinal cord injuries, for instance, are socially rendered as "grotesque" because they directly contradict the claims of biomedical advancements. They signify a failure and incapacity of modern medicine to quickly heal and repair, and they embody a loss of control over the body.

Muscle spasms and recurring infections are a few of the physiological complications with which individuals who use wheelchairs must contend on a daily basis and for which biomedicine has only partial solutions. In contrast, the social model of disability, promoted by many disability activists, "enables disabled people to define their own bodies and their differences in terms of personal experience and self-authorization, free of detached diagnoses imposed by medical authorities" (Silvers 2009). Medical ideology indeed positions disability as something that can be managed, or overcome, rather than incorporated. However, dance and bodily expression in a public forum makes the body whole where it has been fragmented by conventional and medicalized discourses and by the everyday limitations in the urban landscape. Standard second line dance moves often taken for granted in able-bodied individuals, such as shuffling feet, jumping, or kicking, are rescripted by dancers who may maneuver their bodies in and out of wheelchairs, or prop up their legs in ways that reverse expectations.

As we will learn, an individuals' injury or disability, when set to the music and employed as part of the syncopated polyrhythm of the brass band, can be a creative asset, setting oneself apart from other second liners who may have more predictable (and able-bodied) moves. The acceptance of disability in this context transforms conventional representations of disabled bodies, as well as the tangible limitations individuals may face as they move through the city. As the second line takes to the streets, individuals with disabilities are offered an opportunity to move freely on the more well paved roads now cleared of cars, where on other days they would be relegated to the uneven terrain of sidewalks that pose challenges for citizens with mobility impairments.

At the Cross the Canal Steppers parade in February 2013, one second liner's performance offers commentary on the complexity of the racial dimensions of performance and disability. One woman who had been dancing energetically and climbing trees and "clowning" to encouraging cheers (and jeers) from neighborhood observers and fellow second liners, suddenly let her right leg go limp and drag behind her while moving to the beat and singing in rhythm, "I got a bad leg, I got a bad leg." This woman's performance, complicated by her whiteness, echoed a history of minstrel appropriation while co-opting disability as a creative and valued performative technique.

Historically, cultural representations of African Americans were deeply intertwined with disability, routinely conflating race and disability as stigmatizing bodily conditions. As Rosemarie Garland-Thompson (1997) asserts, "Freak shows acted out a relationship in which exoticized disabled people and people of color functioned as physical opposites of the idealized American" (65). More specifically, as Sean Murray's chapter in this collection shows, in the nineteenth century, the dance known as "Jump Jim Crow," one of the most popular minstrel character dances, is a grotesque parody of the movements of a mobility-impaired black stable hand (see also Malone 1996). Murray argues that disability has been presented as a naturalized aspect of black performance. By absorbing disability as a performative facet of blackness and of racialized otherness (Boster 2013), minstrel shows evaded the structural causes of violence that transformed certain bodies or put certain individuals at higher risk than others.

Likewise, during the growth of jazz in the early twentieth century, jazz critics considered the "noise" of African influenced polyrhythms and syncopation to be a *disabling* form with tangible mental and physical consequences. It could harm its (white) listeners, who would essentially be contaminated both by jazz music's disharmony and disorder and by its racial alterity (Johnson 2011).

The cultural representations of disability tropes extend as well to social metaphors that align disability and blackness. Charity models of disability, for instance, may employ the disabled body in service of an agenda, and reproduce images of physical disability as part of the representation of socioeconomic disenfranchisement and poverty. As Laskhmi Fjord (2007) argued in her research on representation of disability after Katrina, the wheelchair served as a "narrative prosthesis," that is, as an accessible metaphor for social suffering and a stigmatized reminder of the social impairments of the African American population. In this example, the charity discourse worked with the existing pathology of inner-city poverty to implicate African Americans in their own suffering and displacement after Katrina.

Dance, as socially sanctioned movement and embodied performance, intervenes where these other discourses have failed to adequately and equitably represent the lived experiences of disability and its intersectionality with race and gender as well as the tragic consequences of violence and the work of rehabilitation and renewal.

The Sociocultural Context of Disability in New Orleans

According to 2011 community survey estimates, New Orleans has an overall citywide disability rate of 13.6%, compared with a national average of 12%.[12] For ambulatory and physical disabilities specifically, New Orleans has consistently higher rates than the national average, almost double the rates of comparably sized cities like Austin, and higher rates than other major US cities like Chicago and New York. Disability is disproportionately represented in African American communities in New Orleans[13] and is one of the most visible markers of the social and economic complexities of racial health disparities in the city. Additionally, Hurricane Katrina exposed the way that seniors and disabled residents, suffering extreme marginalization and lack of services, were particularly vulnerable in the wake of disaster (Fjord 2007).

New Orleans has for decades also maintained the notorious distinction of having one of the highest murder rates in the country. In 2012, there were 193 murders in New Orleans—third in the rank of America's most deadly cities. Less well explored is the relationship between these two demographics. Constrained by both media discourses that marginalize violence as part of everyday "black on black crime," and the myopic structure of city crime statistics—which track murders and not the survivors of violent crime—individuals that have been physically disabled as a result of gun violence are statistically and socially invisible; they remain uncounted and vastly underserved. In the recent edited collection *Disability Incarcerated* (2014), Liat Ben Moshe and others, offer a new perspective for interpreting the dynamics of social invisibility. By exploring the relationship between the social concepts of disability and imprisonment, both theoretically and tangibly, it reveals how constructs and conceptions of disability shape the social order and build spaces of incarceration in everyday life effectively imprisoning persons in plain view. In part obscured by the sheer numbers of murders and political campaigns regarding crime prevention, citizens who have experienced permanent disability as a result of gun violence have been relegated to the margins, contributing to a recognizable (albeit diverse) social group of disabled residents, so-called street veterans.

Recently the Landrieu administration and the City Office of Public Health have invested in campaigns to address the deeply entrenched consequences of gun violence in the city, recognizing the myriad ways violence affects the overall health and well-being of the city's residents. Due to the Second Line Task Force and other shared community initiatives, social club members have made explicit efforts to transform public perception of the association between violence and second lines through "Stop the Violence" campaigns.[14] Gun violence is often misunderstood to be primarily an aspect of organized gang activity in the inner city, but gun violence in New Orleans has often affected people with no gang affiliation, leading to media clichés that refer to inner city New Orleans as the "Wild West."

Joe Henry, aka Rollin' Joe, president and founder of the Pigeon Town Steppers Social Aide and Pleasure Club, was injured in 1982 when he was twelve years old in what he terms a "freak accident," when a neighbor shot at him on his bike, mistaking him for someone else who had threatened him the day before. Joe explains in a recent interview how he came to terms with the incident:

> The minute I was out of the hospital I was second lining and playing basketball . . . you can go a long way with the wheelchair . . . I didn't understand how to be mad at it; I wanted to be a kid; I think I started over one years old in the wheelchair. [15]

Other men however consciously remark that the wheelchair is their "punishment" for a life in "the game." "There are three options" one second liner explained, "you go to jail, you get killed, or you end up in the chair. The game is not designed for you to win."[16]

In Laurence Ralph's ethnographic research on gang organization and violence in Chicago (2010, 2014), he demonstrates that for disabled ex-gang members in Chicago, their physical difference from injury enables them to advocate for antiviolence measures. Ralph argues that "disabled ex-gang members build their narratives out of the medical model of disability, in order to emphasize the biological reality of their now 'broken' body' [and] to amplify the magnitude of urban violence" (2010, 112; 2012). Moreover, because of existing conflicting tropes about black masculinity—between hypervisibility and invisibility—black men with physical disabilities in America embody a social paradox.

Disability, so often left out of conversations about racial relations in America, troubles the tenuous social categories of blackness and masculinity. The association of black masculinity with criminality in American society is a long and enduring trope (Alexander 2010; hooks 2003; Richardson 2007), with its most recent iterations part of the public outcry over police violence and the subsequent formation of "Black Lives Matter" movement in response to decades of racist policing strategies in black communities.

For black men with disabilities, when perceived as the victims and not the perpetrators of violence, their impaired bodies counter these convenient messages that identify black male bodies with aggression and hypermasculinity. The tacit reality of this social construction is that it rests on assumptions of able-bodiedness. Once pathologized for signaling hypermasculine and hypersexual aggression (Kelly 1998; Neal 2006; Richardson 2007), black disabled men are thus suddenly rendered innocuous to society. With their physicality and sexuality now assumed to be impaired, the fear-based social script that makes black men a "problem" is now muted, and they—along with any social or political analysis of the violent conditions that have altered their lives—simply slip away, out of view. Structural violence both begets physical violence and makes even the survivors of that violence disappear. In both implicit and explicit ways, the second line parades create spaces of social visibility and self-representation and the potential to counter essentialized social tropes.

Dance as Embodied Knowledge: Visibility and Disability

The following ethnographic descriptions privilege a few regular second liners to highlight the variety of ways individuals with physical disabilities employ their bodily difference in the context and expectations of the second line dance idiom and the various ways people come to terms with it in a public space.

Syncopated Stumblin'

During a second line break outside of Seal's Class Act in the 7th ward, Paul Landry, a member of Prince of Wales Social Club, looked at me and said, "If it wasn't for these parades I wouldn't be here." Having known Paul for a few years at this point, I nodded with acknowledgment, knowing he was referring to the way in which second lines have renewed a sense of health and ability for him. Paul's recovery in 2008 from an earlier injury culminated with a renewed commitment to second lining and joining the Prince of Wales social aide and pleasure club.

A regular of the second line culture scene throughout his life, Paul grew up following his grandfather, who was the founder of the club. Paul was granted the name "stumbling man" in reference to his unique manner of dance that takes into account his unique physical range of motion. When I first asked Paul about his nickname, he responded, "well I'm disabled don't you know?" This sentiment calls attention to the fault lines of the particular objectifying discourse of disability, for in fact, one could not tell that Paul has a disability when he is dancing, yet in a regular walk one more easily detects his limp.

Paul explains that he has two types of physical disabilities and makes a conscious effort to relate to them differently: one, an enlarged foot from birth and the other a problem with his hip from an earlier injury. For Paul, the meaning of second line parades in his life was always negotiated within his physical abilities. Paul's personal narrative positioned his disability as something that for many years marked second line culture in a space of ambivalence and hesitation, but was reconciled later in life by a resolute decision to parade in spite of his perceived abnormality.

> I know about fifteen or twenty years of it this man here been trying to get me to parade but you know about me here having this disability—a problem of wearing shoes they bother me—and I keep wrestlin' with it I want to do it—I want to do it . . . but where they get the shoes at . . . come for people you know that have a normal foot—I wouldn't be able to parade if I couldn't get the shoes right—but this year was the year—I'm here—! [17]

Yet it is the other disability, which he will not talk about in detail, that he credits as the inspiration for his alias. When he has a shooting pain and he suddenly drop kicks his leg to the ground and then recovers in time, Paul claims that no one can tell the difference between when he is in pain and when he is dancing. Paul proudly explains, "I may stumble, but I don't fall down. So they call me the Stumblin' Man."[18] Dance, in this instance literally repositions the body in respect to other bodies, belying common assumptions about frailty and disability (see Figures 16.1 and 16.2).

While for Paul, second line dance signifies a renewed commitment to his health and activity, for others who experienced a sudden disability, personal and creative work maintains continuity between pre- and postaccident identities.

Wheelchair "Work"

Not all disabilities are equally visible, and as evidenced by Paul's narrative, the physical visibility of one's disability can shift. The presence of wheelchairs at second lines however highlights the social visibility of a significant segment of the New Orleans residents, predominantly black men, who have experienced permanent spinal cord injuries as a result of gun violence. Building off an able-bodied framework that privileges "footwork" as a dominant feature of second line dance, expressive movement and wheelchair dance is incorporated into the idiom of "work." Despite their shared experiences with

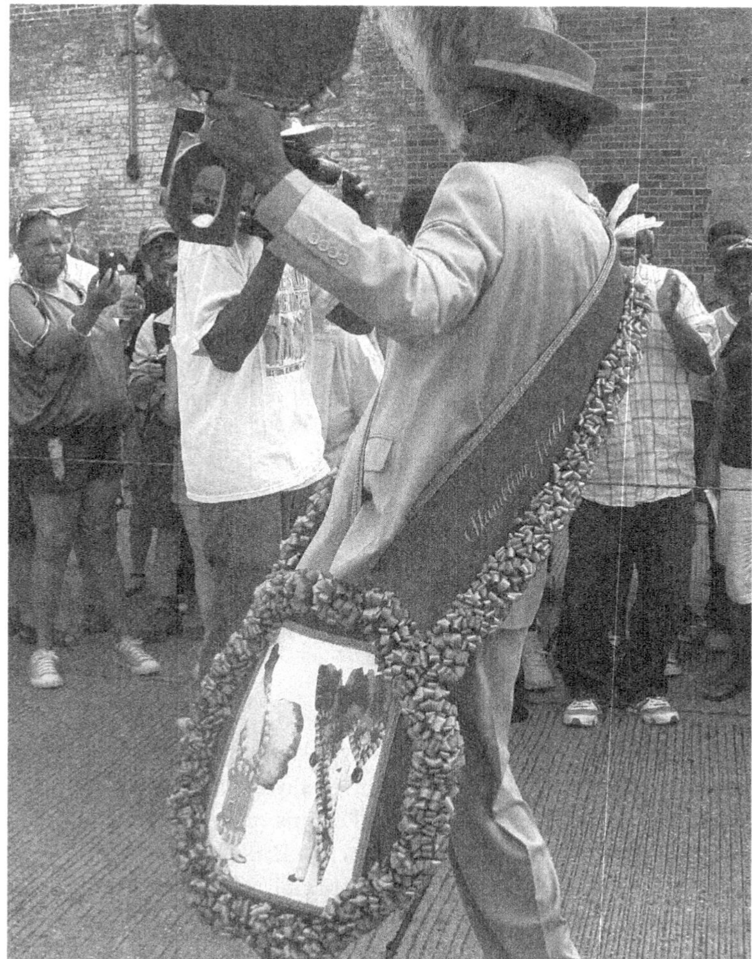

FIGURE 16.1 Paul "Stumbling Man" Landry at Prince of Wales Parade 2012.

wheelchair-specific mobility impairments, the individuals included here construct signature moves based on their individual preference and the intersection of their physicality with the technology of the wheelchair.

Known to second liners and friends as "Skelly Well," a name that references his long lanky figure, Skelly is one of the most active and visible dancers on the scene (see Figure 16.3). Because his spinal cord injury is "incomplete,"[19] he still has partial control of his lower limbs, and is able to swing his legs from the hip while lifting himself off the chair. Amid a writhing groove punctuated by rhythmic shoulder moves, Skelly may lift himself up in his wheelchair, then slide onto the ground, where he spends a few moments supported in a partial push up—shaking and popping his torso to the music as a small encircling crowd cheers him. Skelly is also in many respects a social ambassador at the second line, gathering wheelchair users together, to avoid being

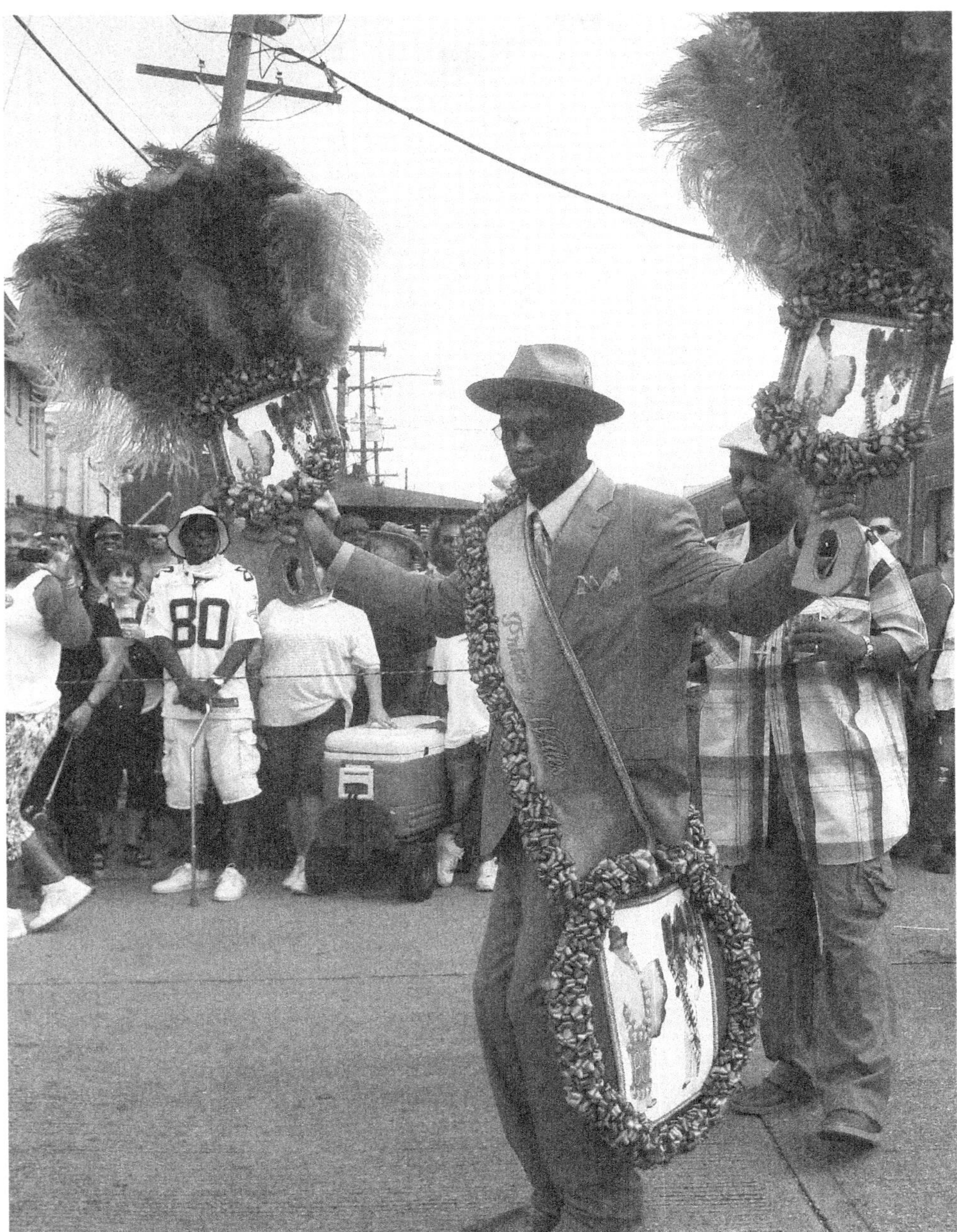

FIGURE 16.2 Paul "Stumbling Man" Landry at Prince of Wales Parade 2012.

dispersed among the mass of other second liners. Francis recalls how in the early days after his accident, Skelly's mobility and presence at second lines was an encouraging means to make sense of his new situation and the changes to his body. The thought of going back to second lines was clouded by shame at first, but seeing others like

FIGURE 16.3 Skelly Well at Uptown Swingers Parade 2012. ©2011 Alfonso Bresciani

Skelly "buckin' and jumpin' out the chair" encouraged him to relearn how to dance for himself.

Francis has been disabled for nearly ten years, since a violent shooting in 2004 in the 9th Ward left him fully paralyzed from the waist down and resulted in the amputation of his left arm below the elbow. For the first eight years after his accident, Francis used a manual chair, which was specially designed to accommodate pushing from his one arm. In 2013, Francis moved into an electric chair so that his shoulder could be saved from the repeated stress of pushing. Contrary to other men who may prefer manual chairs for maximum flexibility and dance, Francis' mobile chair, which he has named

Candy, makes dancing more possible by reducing stress injuries and allowing him to sit upright, affording him control of his waist for bending and more leverage for upper body movement. Additionally, the mobile chair is able to tilt back past ninety degrees; although originally designed to alleviate pressure on one's legs, this function is also used creatively by Francis to pulse up and down with the beat, one of his signature moves. Continued advances in wheelchair technology open up possibilities for individuals to match technological innovations with the specifics of their physical injury.

For Francis, second line dance also works to mediate loss in complex ways, suggesting that rehabilitation after injury is a tentative and fragile space of self-reflection. "If only I had my other arm, I could lift myself and buck jump like Skelly . . . like I used to. When that beat hit me though, I feel like I'm walking again."[20] In this way, brass band second line music signals a flexibility and continuity between the cultivation and training of adapting to one's new physical self, while incorporating the memories of a previous mobility.

Another example of the diverse ways second liners interact with the wheelchair is evidenced by the signature move employed by Tater, another long-term second liner. At the Treme Sidewalk Steppers second line in February of 2011, while the band was stopped under the Interstate highway overpass on Claiborne Avenue, Tater, after a series of shoulder pops and active upper body movement, tossed himself from his wheelchair, rolled onto his back and lay on the ground throbbing with the bass beat, while other members crawled and rolled on the ground or danced on the sides. For several minutes, Tater completed this move, referred to as the "jack knife"; leaving his wheelchair aside, he pulsed and rolled on the ground with an able-bodied fellow club member, Charlie Brown. Together they lay on the concrete and lifted their right legs; Tater used his arms to raise and shake his immobile leg in the air, pulsing with the syncopated beat as the Rebirth Brass Band played above them. Side by side the two improvised with the music while the other club members danced around the temporarily empty wheelchair, and crowds huddled around them. Tater who explained in a recent interview that there "ain't nobody else jumping out the chair like that," is known for these creative stunts, in which he may temporarily abandon his wheelchair (at times being placed on a rooftop without it) in order to choreograph dance moves that playfully infuse a paralyzed lower body with renewed vitality and visibility.

Embodied Knowledge as a Site of Social Resistance

Many of the second liners who use wheelchairs have employed the second line tradition as a vehicle for public critique of their invisibility, self-organizing into a social aide and pleasure club exclusively for wheelchair users or otherwise disabled citizens. Called Push for Change,[21] the social club sees its mission as one of education and advocacy, the frontline of this endeavor being the tangible presence of wheelchairs en masse, in a visible community of social club members on parade.

The title of the social club acts as social commentary on the identity and independence of individuals who use wheelchairs. Instead of the verb "rollin'"—used in titles such as Rollin' Joe, Rollin' Pelicans, or the colloquialism "roll with it"[22]—the club has chosen "pushing" as the active verb to encompass the realities of wheelchair life and the work necessary to change social perceptions and citywide programming to improve the lives of wheelchair users. Additionally, "pushing" in a manual chair is a very logical choice for some men in that it affords freedom to move throughout the city. Because of the uneven terrain, electric wheelchairs may limit mobility to only wide, well-paved streets.[23] It is not uncommon for sidewalks to abruptly end or to be so ravaged by tree roots and decay that it is impossible to navigate in a wheelchair. Recently, as part of continued post-Katrina renovations, curb cuts have been added as streets are repaved and neighborhoods redesigned. However, these changes are not lost on Skelly and Joe, who have used wheelchairs since the 1980s and argue that "those [curb cuts] aren't for us; it's for the elderly with the electric scooters, nobody's putting in curb cuts for us."[24] Push for Change is the outgrowth of sentiments such as this one; as self-titled street veterans, these men recognize their experiences and perspectives as valuable assets in a social movement about disability advocacy and violence prevention.

The second line tradition then offers this opportunity at self-representation, epitomized within the idiom "push for change," where men are visible as active and mobile agents of their social identity. Such performances challenge the classical/grotesque binary construction of the body, instead presenting the disabled body in a "process of becoming" (Albright 1998).

Push for Change also challenges traditional patterns of parading culture, by creating associations based on the experiences of wheelchair users rather than neighborhood affiliations. As Francis explains, "we all in the chair, we all know this life, and we from all over the city. I'm from the 9th Ward, Skelly is from Magnolia, Joe, from Pigeon Town . . . And, all of us have been shot. It's not where you from; it's where y'at."

Conclusion

As socially sanctioned movement, second line dance incorporates a wide variety of body types and abilities. Dance is not solely about responding to music but as, a self-representation of one's experiences of loss or pain, rehabilitation and renewal are constantly mediated and negotiated through the participation in this public performance. The cultivation of this embodied knowledge thus privileges physical disability as instructive and innovative.

In dance, the body serves both as form and function, as expression and the instrument of expression. In contesting social perceptions and policies that exclude some bodies in favor of others, the architecture of second line dance shapes disability as a "strategic ability" (Albright 1998).

Second lines by their very nature ennoble black identity and locality and enable a unified voice to counter pervasive negative stereotypes of blackness. On a more individual note, the narratives and experiences of many of these men attest to the fact that public self-expression is built up *from* one's disability, not in spite of it. Paul need not deny or "overcome" his disability; he is as he says (and everyone knows) the "one and only Stumblin' Man." Skelly need not mourn the loss of his dance capabilities along with the changes in his mobility; he is able to adapt, reincorporate, and rewrite new dance moves. The corporeal landscape of a second line encompasses a wide range of human forms and abilities, and in doing so, challenges existing discourses and expectations of normative bodies and able-bodied dance performance that would marginalize differently abled bodies as either exempted from or exceptionalized out of authorship to the form.

Disability and its meanings are thus embedded in locally shared knowledge through the idiom of dance and not solely through specialized medical knowledge about the limits of physical injury or the limits of an inaccessible urban landscape.

In a city with disability rates that disproportionately affect African American communities, these public displays of dance and movement need to be situated alongside other conversations about health and mobility, social patterns of inequity, and the innovative responses to such inequity. Despite the diversity of these residents' injuries and physical abilities, their paths of rehabilitation and their visibility in urban spaces act as a shared and symbolic reminder of the tenuous social order of life in New Orleans, and of the continuity of creative potential of the body in expressive movement and its incorporation into cultural and social life after physical trauma. Ultimately, dance ethnographer Yvonne Daniel says it most succinctly when she asks rhetorically, "What better symbol of health can there be but the dancing body?"

Notes

1. After the mass shooting at the second line on Mother's Day 2013, which garnered national attention, the language used by the media to report on the tragedy has been interrogated for its racial bias. Critics argue that the phrase "street violence," typically invoked when the victims are people of color, implies passivity, essentially blaming the victim, while the term "domestic terrorism" is reserved for tragedies involving gun violence in public spaces which claim largely white victims. See "Gunman Opens Fire on New Orleans Mother's Days Parade," MSNBC (May 14, 2013), http://www.msnbc.com/all-in/watch/gunman-opens-fire-on-new-orleans-mothers-day-parade-30143555691.
2. All the individuals featured in this research, based on social networks I have been exposed to through participation in second line culture and snowball-sampling, are men. This mirrors national statistics, which demonstrate that men represent the majority of spinal cord injuries, and are disproportionately at risk for life-long disability from both accidents and violence.

3. Big Red Cotton (https://twitter.com/BigRedCotton) is a journalist and cultural advocate who documents second line parades and was one of the victims injured by at the Mother's Day shooting on May 12, 2013.
4. The connection to this genealogy of African tradition and expression of local African American identity is reinforced by some of the names of the clubs themselves such as "Sudan," "Black Men of Labor" (whose members dress in coordinated traditional West African textiles), and the "Nkrumah Better Boys," whose flag reads: "African Americans around the world unite."
5. American Routes, interviews with members of the Prince of Wales (https://tulane.edu/americanroutes/pow/oral-histories.cfm).
6. Bruce "Sunpie" Barnes, interview with author (September 2011).
7. Title track on Rebirth Brass Band album, *Do Whatcha Wanna* (1997).
8. Some examples of the popular uses of this term include Lady Buckjumpers Social Aid and Pleasure Club, John Boutte's lyrics "buckjumpin and having fun" from "Treme Song" on *Jambalaya* (2008), and Albert Casey's "Buckjumpin" on Swingville (1960).
9. Interview with the author (October 5, 2013).
10. Available online at http://www.folkstreams.net/film,126.
11. Jessica Donley, interview with the author (October 14, 2012).
12. American Community Survey (http://factfinder2.census.gov/faces/nav/jsf/pages/index.xhtml).
13. According to the 2000 census, the predominantly African American neighborhoods of Central City and the 7th ward report a physical disability rate of 11.1% and 11.8% respectively, compared with a national average of 6.2%.
14. Examples of slogans included on fliers distributed along the route of second lines from 2009 to 2014 include: "Keep the peace. Shout out to NOPD"; "Stop the Violence, Increase the Peace"; "Respect yourself and your culture"; and "Please leave attitudes, dogs, and weapons at home, just come out and show your footwork."
15. Interview with Joseph Henry by "Action Jackson" (http://www.wwoz.org/events/204093).
16. Interview with Francis Falls (March 1, 2014).
17. American Routes, interviews with members of the Prince of Wales (https://tulane.edu/americanroutes/pow/oral-histories.cfm).
18. Interview with the author (November 2013).
19. The medical language used to describe spinal cord injuries identifies patients and their injuries as either "complete" or "incomplete" preceded by the level of injury at the vertebrae. A common way to describe one's injuries for instance would be "T12 incomplete."
20. Interview with Franics Falls at Family Ties second line (October 2013).
21. Push For Change was officially founded by Wellington "Skelly" Ratcliff and Francis Falls in December 2013.
22. Title of song from Rebirth Brass Band album *We Come to Party* (2005). See also Sakakeeny 2013.
23. The preference for manual or electric chair varies depending on one's injuries and lifestyle. Because Medicaid only subsidizes repairs and maintenance for one wheelchair per person however, the decision may be complex.
24. Interview with the author (October 2, 2013).

References

Albright, Ann Cooper. 1998. "Strategic Abilities: Negotiating the Disabled Body in Dance." *Michigan Quarterly Review* 37 (2): 475–501. http://hdl.handle.net/2027/spo.act2080.0037.313.

Alexander, Michelle. 2010. *The New Jim Crow: Mass Incarceration in the Age of Colorblindness*. New York and Jackson, TN: New Press.

Boster, Dea H. 2013. *African American Slavery and Disability: Bodies, Property, and Power in the Antebellum South*. New York: Routledge.

Bourdieu, Pierre. 1977. *Outline of a Theory of Practice*. Translated by Richard Nice. Cambridge: Cambridge University Press.

Breunlin, Rachel, and Helen Regis. 2006. "Putting the Ninth Ward on the Map: Race, Place, and Transformation in Desire, New Orleans." *American Anthropologist* 108 (4): 744–764.

Browning, Barbara. 1995. *Samba: Resistance in Motion*. Bloomington: Indiana University Press.

Carrico, Rachel. 2013. "On the Street and in the Studio: Decentering and Recentering Dance in the New Orleans Second Line." Paper presented at the joint meetings of the Society of Dance History Scholars and the Congress on Research in Dance, Riverside, California, November 14–17.

Daniel, Yvonne. 2005. *Dancing Wisdom: Embodied Knowledge in Haitian Vodou, Cuban Yoruba, and Bahian Candomblé*. Urbana: University of Illinois Press.

Dinerstein, Joel. 2009. "Second Lining Post-Katrina: Learning Community from the Prince of Wales Social Aid and Pleasure Club." *American Quarterly* 61 (3): 615–637.

Fjord, Lakshmi. "Disasters, Race, and Disability: [Un]seen through the Political Lens on Katrina." *Journal of Race and Policy* 3 (1): 46–66.

Garland-Thomson, Rosemarie. 1997. *Extraordinary Bodies: Figuring Physical Disability in American Culture and Literature*. New York: Columbia University Press.

hooks, bell. 2003. *We Real Cool: Black Men and Masculinity*. New York: Routledge.

Johnson, Russell. 2011 "'Disease Is Unrhythmical': Jazz, Health, and Disability in 1920's America." *Health and History* 13 (2): 13–42.

Kelly, Robin. 1998. *Yo Mama's Disfunktional: Fighting the Culture Wars in Urban America*. Boston: Beacon Press.

Malone, Jacqui. 1996. *Steppin' on the Blues: The Visible Rhythms of African American Dance*. 1st ed. Urbana: University of Illinois Press.

Marks, Deborah. 1999. *Disability: Controversial Debates and Psychosocial Perspectives*. New York: Routledge.

Merleau-Ponty, Maurice. 1962. *The Phenomenology of Perception*. Translated by Colin Smith. London: Routledge & Kegan Paul.

Murphy, Robert F. 1995. "Encounters: The Body Silent in America." In *Disability and Culture*, edited by Benedicte Ingstad and Susan Reynolds White, 140–157. Berkeley: University of California Press.

Neal, Marc Anthony. 2006. *New Black Man: Rethinking Black Masculinity*. New York: Routledge.

Neely, Brooke, and Michelle Samura. 2011. "Social Geographies of Race: Connecting Race and Space." *Ethnic and Racial Studies* 34 (11): 1933–1952.

Ralph, Laurence. 2010. "You Never Hear about the Wheelchair: Violence and Mobility in a Westside Chicago Gang." PhD diss., University of Chicago.

Ralph, Laurence. 2012. "What Wounds Enable: The Politics of Disability and Violence in Chicago." *Disability Studies Quarterly* 32 (3). http://dsq-sds.org/article/view/3270.

Ralph, Laurence. 2014. *Renegade Dreams: Living Through Injury in Gangland Chicago.* Chicago: University of Chicago Press.

Regis, Helen A. 1999. "Second Lines, Minstrelsy, and the Contested Landscapes of New Orleans Afro-Creole Festivals." *Cultural Anthropology* 14 (4): 472–504. doi: 10.1525/can.1999.14.4.472.

Regis, Helen A. 2001. "Blackness and the Politics of Memory in the New Orleans Second Line." *American Ethnologist* 28 (4): 752–777. doi: 10.1525/ae.2001.28.4.752.

Richardson, Riche. 2007. *Black Masculinity in the U.S. South: From Uncle Tom to Gangsta.* Athens: University of Georgia Press.

Roach, Joseph R. 1996. *Cities of the Dead: Circum-Atlantic Performance.* New York: Columbia University Press.

Sakakeeny, Matt. 2010. "Under the Bridge: An Orientation to Soundscapes in New Orleans." *Ethnomusicology* 54 (1): 1–27.

Sakakeeny, Matt. 2013. *Roll with It: Brass Bands in the Streets of New Orleans.* Durham, NC: Duke University Press.

Scheper-Hughes, Nancy, and Margaret Lock. 1987. "The Mindful Body: A Prolegemenon to Future Work in Medical Anthropology." *Medical Anthropology Quarterly* [new series] 1 (1): 6–41.

Siebers, Tobin. 2010. *Disability Aesthetics.* Ann Arbor: University of Michigan Press.

Silvers, Anita. 2009. "Feminist Perspectives on Disability." Revised August 29, 2013. In *The Stanford Encyclopedia of Philosophy*, edited by Edward N. Zalta, Fall 2013 ed. http://plato.stanford.edu/archives/fall2013/entries/feminism-disability/.

Touchet, Leo. 1998. *Rejoice When You Die: The New Orleans Jazz Funerals.* Baton Rouge: Louisiana State University Press.

Turner, Richard Brent. 2009. *Jazz Religion, the Second Line, and Black New Orleans.* Bloomington: Indiana University Press.

White, Michael. 2001. "The New Orleans Brass Band." In *Triumph of the Soul: Cultural and Psychological Aspects of African American Music*, edited by Ferdinand Jones and Arthur C. Jones, 69–96. Westport, CT: Praeger.

PART 3

RACE, GENDER, SEXUALITY

CHAPTER 17

A CANNON-SHAPED MAN WITH AN AMPHIBIAN VOICE

Castrato and Disability in Eighteenth-Century France

HEDY LAW

INTRODUCTION

RECENT studies have drawn attention to the ways in which music informs the social and cultural meanings of bodily difference (Lerner and Straus 2006, Straus 2011), but castrato singers have rarely been addressed in this body of scholarship.[1] To some extent, this lack is understandable. The nature of the castrato's bodily differences—his lack of testes or insufficient testosterone, sharp voice, soft body, boy-like face, lack of facial hair, long limbs, big chest, and small head—does not conform to familiar categories of disability. If castrato singers manifested few signs of physical and mental disability as understood in their own time, there would be little reason for Disability Studies in music to investigate them.[2]

The above reasoning runs the risk of excluding those who do not fit traditional models of disability but nonetheless possess what Joseph Straus calls "culturally stigmatized bodily difference" (Straus 2011, 9). Whether or not castrato singers were considered disabled, many lived their lives *as if* they had bodily defects. As recent studies of castrato singers show, their cultural reception often combined amazement toward their voices with repulsion from their bodies. This fractured reception invites closer scrutiny from the perspective of Disability Studies.[3] The field was founded on the premise that disability was not just a medical condition but also a social and cultural one. Recent publications examine topics with broad cultural and social impact. As the field of Disability Studies has evolved, disability is currently understood as an unstable category, inclusive enough to transcend the boundaries of identity politics (Davis 2013, 271). This broadened trend has implications for the studies of castrato singers, for examination of the castrato body reveals much about the complexity of an ability and disability.

In this essay I focus on the reception of castrato singers in eighteenth-century France, a period during which some commentators repudiated them. Using ideas advanced by scholars of Disability Studies, I make three points about these singers in eighteenth-century France. First, the body of castrato singers was widely understood as defective. Second, castrato singers were stigmatized and in turn projected stigma. My third argument develops from representation of freaks in the fairground theatres. I argue that reception of freaks conditioned the French to perceive castrato singers as freakish, and thus negative views of castrato singers derived from the cultural process of "enfreakment."

The Stigmatized Castrato

Castrato singers sang in Italy by the end of the twelfth century. They performed in the Renaissance and by the early seventeenth century were singing in churches and courts throughout Italy. Castrato singers performed in early operas such as Claudio Monteverdi's 1607 *L'Orfeo*, and the advent of public operas in 1637 enabled them to perform in opera houses through the eighteenth century. Their performances declined in the nineteenth century and finally ended in the early twentieth century. In France castrato singers joined women, boys, and falsettos and sang the high register in French vocal music. Yet because women and falsettos were forbidden to perform at the Chapelle Royale, Louis XIV hired castrato singers from Italy. Between 1644 and 1800, fifty-four castrato singers performed in France: sixteen performed before 1700, and thirty-eight performed between 1700 and 1800. These castrato singers performed in private venues such as the court or the Chapelle Royale; some also performed in public concerts at the Concert Spirituel. None, however, performed in French operas at the Académie Royale de Musique, for the French loathed seeing castratos on their theatrical stage.[4]

In addition to these castrato singers hired by the Chapelle Royale, a few stellar castratos were invited to perform in France. Atto Melani performed there a number of times from 1645 onward, especially from 1656 to 1660. Farinelli sang in a private performance for Louis XV and Queen Marie Leszcynska at Versailles in 1737. Caffarelli stayed in Paris for several months in 1753, and sang for the dauphine Marie-Josèphe of Saxony. Gaetano Guadagni also gave a few concerts with the castrato Albanèse at the Concert Spirituel and at court from 1753 to 1754. During the Revolution, most castrato singers left France; one exception was Josephini. He entered the Chapelle in 1774, sang at the Chapelle Royale of Louis XVIII, and received a pension for his service in 1827. Girolamo Crescentini sang for Napoleon from 1806 to 1812 and became one of the last castratos who sang there. Thus to study castrato singers in France is to examine a bifurcate phenomenon: a small but elite group hired by the Chapelle Royale and an even smaller and more elite group performed in a number of select venues by invitation.

It is important to note that the castrato singers who sung at the Chapelle Royale received institutional protection. As shown from the reviews of their performances, from the first performance by Francisco La Fornara (nicknamed Francisque) in 1727 to the last by a certain Olivini in 1773, never once did the *Mercure de France* mention that any of these singers was castrato singers. They were called variously musicians from the Chapelle Royale ("Ordinaires de la musique de la Chapelle du Roi") or simply Italians. Reviews of their performances were almost always positive.[5] This respectful attitude toward castrato singers stemmed in part from Louis XIV. In 1673, he imported five castrato singers from Italy for the Chapelle Royale. Impressed by their talents, their morals, and their dedication to their job, Louis XIV granted them perpetual hunting rights at Fontainebleau (Sawkins 1986, 217). Louis de Cahusac's article "Chanteur" in the *Encyclopédie* explains why: "Many castrati at the Royal Chapel whom we select early from the schools in Italy sing the upper parts of motets. Louis XIV showed them special kindnesses: He allowed them to hunt in his own hunting grounds called *capitaineries*. He sometimes spoke to them with humanity. This great King [Louis XIV] took pleasure to console these unhappy people [who suffer] from their fathers' cruelty."[6] Court musicians also treated castrato singers with respect. As shown in the memoirs of musical life at the court written by authors whom Lionel Sawkins calls the "Bêche brothers" in 1768, the Swiss-born castrato Antonio Bagniera (who died in 1740 at the age of 102) dazzled the court with his phenomenal voice that remained forceful and beautiful as he aged. Although the Bêche brothers, who were employed about a decade after Bagniera passed away, never had a chance to hear him sing, they summarized from the anecdotes circulated orally at court that Bagniera lived and died as a "genuine saint."[7]

Outside of the segregated quarters in which castrato singers lived as a family and enjoyed what Foucault calls a "happy limbo of a non-identity" (Foucault 1980, xiii), castrato singers were stigmatized. A stigma, whether a physical deformity, a character blemish, or one's ethnicity or religious belief, comes not from the external signifier per se but rather from the social processes that mark or brand it. An unusual bodily sign becomes a stigma when it is perceived to be a sign of disgrace (Goffman 1991, 1–40). Although castrato singers were hired as singers, the social process of their stigmatization came not from their voices but from the denigration of their nongenerative body.[8] The focus on the castrato and his inability to reproduce is evident in the widely circulated *Traité des eunuques* (1707), in which the writer and lawyer Charles Ancillon categorized the castrato singer as a type of eunuch. Whether Eastern servants or Western singers, eunuchs were defined by their infertility "either through weakness or coldness of nature, or [as someone] who is anywise deprived of the parts proper to generation" (Ancillon 1718, 8). Conceiving castratos primarily as eunuchs, Ancillon identified in their infertility a sign of emasculation.

The body of a castrato posed a medical mystery in the French Enlightenment. This came in part from the absence of the surgical operation of castration in France. Louis XIV was enraged at learning that Bagniera once asked one of his unidentified "cousins" in Paris to perform castration surgery on him, presumably some time before his voice broke. Threatening to discharge Bagniera, the King tried in vain to obtain the name of that surgeon, and Bagniera swore to safeguard his "most profound secret" (Sawkins, 1986, 215). Louis XIV's aversion to the surgery resonates with insufficient scientific understanding about the surgery itself. The article on castration in the *Encyclopédie*, written by the French surgeon Antoine Louis, attempts to explain how castration made a man infertile. "Castration is the act of castrating, or the operation through which one amputates and remove the testicles of a male animal, which results in the incapability of breeding."[9] Unsympathetic to the social utility of castrated men, either for labor in the seraglio or for music in churches and theatres, Louis emphasized that castration was strictly speaking not a surgical operation, for it did not aim at restoring the health of the subject. In other words, the French saw neither medical nor cultural needs to produce castratos. Since castration was performed usually on animals, the operation on human beings would suggest debasement of the human body.[10]

French physicians did not understand why the removal of testicles resulted in the adult retention of the high singing register of prepubescent boys. Following Ancillon, Jean le Rond d'Alembert (in his article "Castrati" in the *Encyclopédie* [1752]) observes other physical features of an infertile castrato—but again, he shows little interest in understanding the castrato body: "With respect to the physical cause for which the castrati have the thin and sharp voice, it does not appear easier to find it than to explain why they do not have a beard. But the fact is certain, and is sufficient."[11] Based on d'Alembert's article, Jean-Jacques Rousseau's article "Castrato" in the *Dictionnaire de musique* (1767) also treats a castrato as an infertile man who could sing in a high register: a castrato is "a [male] musician whose reproductive organs were taken away when he was young in order to retain the sharp voice that [allows him] to sing the Dessus or Soprano part."[12] The lack of medical knowledge about hormones and the physiological impact of castration further intensified the mystique surrounding the castrato.

Infertility provided the basis for various forms of stigmatization. A poem from the King of Denmark, appearing in the *Correspondance littéraire* (1 January 1769), makes clear that castrato singers were defective and thus defenseless humans: "They are castrati whom we are not afraid of offending, / And we do not hear [them sing] without thinking / About the faculties they have lost."[13] Whatever these "faculties" refer to, the castrato singers could do little to prevent their audiences from discrediting them. Nor, as the poem implies, could they do much to protect themselves against such insults. While it is true that they performed music, they also simultaneously exposed or, according to Straus, *performed* their disability (Straus 2011, 125–149).

Stigmatization of castrato singers also took a cultural form, which can be gleaned from uses of the metaphor of "mutilation," a term that was commonly used in describing the surgical excision of reproductive organs. For example, Rousseau (following d'Alembert) believed that, although there appears to be little relationship between the reproductive organs and the voice, "the mutilation of the one [testicles] prevents in the other [vocal chord] this [voice] change that happens to men at the nubile age, which immediately lowers their voice for an octave."[14] In the fourth edition of the *Dictionnaire de l'Académie française* (1762), "to mutilate" was linked for the first time in the French dictionary to castration: "When the word to mutilate is used it usually means to castrate."[15] In the fifth edition of the *Dictionnaire de l'Académie française* (1798), "to mutilate" also adopts the figurative meaning of removal: To mutilate a work—and not a body—means to take away some parts essential to its perfection.[16]

To be sure, perfecting a work by means of mutilation may seem counterintuitive. The *Dictionnaire* does not say that a mutilated man was a perfected one, but it raises the more abstract issue of editorial censorship. Despite its late appearance in the *Dictionnaire* of 1798, editorial mutilation was a common metaphor throughout the eighteenth century.[17] The *Encyclopédie* itself underwent considerable editorial mutilation. A supplement to the seventeenth-volume *Encyclopédie*, the volume "eighteen," (rediscovered in the 1930s and since 2013 available for readers via the ARTFL platform) includes 284 pages of corrected proofs, which belong to forty-six articles written by different authors.[18] Without obtaining permission from the general editor Denis Diderot, the printer André-François Le Breton modified them. For example, the articles on "protestant religion" and "tolerance (religion, morality, politics)" were removed. Diderot was incensed by this intervention. In a letter dated November 12, 1764, Diderot accused Le Breton of censoring entries of the *Encyclopédie*. Evoking the metaphor of castration, he accused Le Breton of being an editorial "surgeon": "You have castrated it [the *Encyclopédie*], dismembered it, mutilated it, [and] shredded it without judgment, without thoughtfulness, and without taste."[19] Perhaps Le Breton thought that removing these sensitive articles from the *Encyclopédie* would perfect it, but Diderot disagreed. Far from perfecting the *Encyclopédie*, Diderot blamed Le Breton for impairing it. His complaint evokes the cultural stigmatization of the castrated body.[20]

The Other Singer

Castrato singers were considered man-made, which means that their castrated bodies did not come from any singular natural cause; this biological constructivist view made castrato singers the Other of normal French singers. Since most of them were Italian, they were prone to trigger the long-standing French antipathy for Italian music, especially during the *Querelle des bouffons*. Moreover, since their bodies were surgically modified, their voices came from unnatural bodies, which made them the Other of singers who possessed natural, nonsurgically modified bodies. Evoking the theory of body heat that had been used to explain living organisms from birds to men, Rousseau said in his *Dictionnaire de musique* that the castrato's voice came at a price. The superb voice alone, which was supposedly the reward of an unethical operation, could not compensate for the loss of body heat, and as a result these singers had limited skills: "These men who sing so well, but without heat and without passions, make the most depressing actors in the world. They lose their voice early and put on disgusting weight. They speak and pronounce worse than real men, and they cannot pronounce some letters such as 'r' at all."[21]

The stigmatized castrato triggered tension between French and Italian music. During the *Querelle des bouffons*, Anna Tonelli (wife of Eustachio Bambini, impresario of the

Bambini troupe from Italy) was for a brief period mistaken as a castrato. The confusion over Tonelli's gender originated in an anonymous pamphlet *Epître aux bouffoonistes* (February 12, 1753): "The troupe . . . has its Manelli, / And among their castrati we see their Tonelli / Perform some scenes of the divine Pergolesi, / Mumbling pleasures or meowing troubles."[22] A few days later, on February 18, 1753, another anonymous poem *Réflexions lyriques* repeated this rumor: "Oh! How the voice will leap from a Castrato! / How the bright eye of Tonelli will sparkle! / Their supporters will say: Here is music; / An opera, of good taste, a public fête. / You are crawling on the ground; we are opening the heavens for you, / French, you are listening to the music of the gods."[23] Later in February of the same year, Barbier Marin cited from the *Epître des bouffoonistes* in his pamphlet *Ce qu'on a dit ce qu'on a voulu dire* and declared that "Mademoiselle Tonelli is a castrato, from which we conclude that Italian music is bad."[24] It is not clear from this context whether Marin considered Tonelli to be a man or a woman, for although he addresses her using the word "Mademoiselle," he might refer to her *appearance* as a woman, but not her biological sex as female. His doubt about her sex and her gender leads to his blanket criticism of Italian music. In *Brioché*, a parody of Jean-Philippe Rameau's ballet *Pygmalion* performed at the Théâtre Italien on September 26, 1753, La Folie sings a song that pokes fun at the body of the castrato. Invoking the early modern one-sex model of the human body, which understood the male body as the more perfect version of the body shared by men and women (Laqueur 1990; Freitas 2009, 107–110), La Folie associates the castrato with a cold-blooded animal, and collapses the distinction between the corporeal other with the cultural other: "To teach you the art of importance, / Of simpering with ease at your toilet in the morning, / A chubby abbot must come. / A musician from Italy / With an amphibian voice / Is going to show you with success / How we must sing in French."[25]

One might claim that this rumor that Tonelli was a castrato is insignificant, for it is not grounded in facts. Musicologist David Charlton, for one, disregards this issue of a mistaken castrato. He includes Tonelli's portrait in his book (Charlton 2012), which shows none of the deformed bodily features—tallness and the "disgusting weight" as Rousseau put it—characteristic of castrato singers.[26] Charlton provides visual evidence that clarifies the sex of Tonelli—but he does not explain the cultural logic that accounts for the mistaken identity, nor does he explain the cultural processes of stigmatization surrounding Italian castrati in France. This instance of stigmatization rests on the assumption that the soprano of this troupe from Italy who *looked* like a woman must be a castrato—an assumption that overlooks the more likely possibility that the person might be female. This case of a mistaken identity shows that the French bias against castrato singers applied to other Italian singers, such as Tonelli. Castrati were treated as if they were infectious and dangerous. Because they might contaminate other singers, these stigmatized singers were considered to project stigma as well. In other words, the castrato, assumed to be a disabled man, presented a "marker of inferiority" (Mitchell and Snyder 2000, 3). To be sure, no one seems to be injured by these rumors. But the lack of measurable damage on the surface nevertheless discloses a deep bias against castrato singers. If anything, understanding the cultural significance of a castrato thus necessarily involves untangling a mix of facts and fiction.

The French reception of Tonelli exemplifies the notion of stigmatization as a cultural process. Since only a limited number of castrato singers resided or performed in France, representation—whether literary, musical, theatrical, or iconographical—played an important role in the production of social and cultural meanings of castrato singers. In many cases, representation became a platform for *mis*representation. In his novel *Julie: La nouvelle Héloïse* (1761), Rousseau includes the castrato Régianino. The only musician in this novel, Régianino sings Italian music for the protagonists Saint Preux and Julie. Régianino is a diminutive stage name that recalls other castrato singers such as Appianino, Cusanino, Nicolino, Porporino, and Senesino. (Audiences sometimes showed their affection for the castrati by calling them "ninos," a diminutive name that also indicated that they were not fully men, but instead resembled boys or women.[27]) In the novel, castration has emasculated Régianino's body, but it also enables him to sing. Régianino's singing moves Saint Preux, who has never heard Italian singing before: "The pleasure did not stop at the ear," he says. "It penetrated the soul."[28] Saint Preux makes two comparisons between Régianino and "normal" singers. Comparing a castrato with a real woman, Saint Preux regrets that Régianino's tender voice does not come from Julie, his female lover, but from what he terms a "despicable" castrato.[29] On the other hand, when he compares Régianino with a man, Saint Preux's excitement about Régianino's singing clashes with his disappointment over his real sex. Following the close relationship between nature and morality, the aberration of the natural order was considered a breach of the moral order (Daston and Park 1998, 361).

Rousseau develops an eighteenth-century antecedent of the film *The Crying Game* (1992), which stages disgust at the revelation of one's true sex.[30] Written in a period that was "haunted by the theme of the transvestite" (Foucault 1980, xvii), a period in which the cross-dresser Chevalier d'Eon could work as a spy, Rousseau's episode shows that a bias against a castrato's body contradicts sharply the celebration of a castrato's extraordinary voice. Compared with a female soprano, Régianino is the Other singer: he possesses a stigmatized, undesirable body with invisible impairment and an extraordinary, desirable, audible voice. (For more on the audibility and visibility of disability, see Blake Howe's chapter in this volume.) Although a castrato singer sings well, his voice is so artificially produced that he is not legitimated as a human being. Perhaps that is why the real identity of Régianino is irrelevant to the novel. His full name is never disclosed, and he remains a shadowy figure throughout the novel.

The separation of the castrato's stigmatized body from his celebrated voice was not too much of an issue when he performed at the secluded Chapelle Royale or at the Concert Spirituel, but it became a thorny one in operatic performances, when both the voice and body needed to be present onstage. Inspired by the work of Abbé Dubos that outlines the ancient Roman pantomime, the Baron Grimm (in his entry "lyric poem" for the *Encyclopédie* [1765]) proposed a revival of this Roman performance practice on the modern French stage.

> With this performance practice, our castratos, who are ordinarily excellent singers and mediocre actors, would be nothing other than some speaking instruments in the orchestra, placed as close to the stage as possible. They would sing a melody with a superiority of which nothing could distract them, while a skillful pantomime would perform the action with the same passion and the same expression.[31]

The castrato's celebrated voice and his repulsive body should remain separate: his body should be hidden, while his voice should be retained. For Grimm, castrato singers should only perform as nonhumans, as "speaking instruments" whose voices are disembodied. In the article "actor" in his *Dictionnaire de musique*, Rousseau emphasizes acting skill as a prerequisite of operatic singers. He argues that an opera singer should be more than just a singer; he should also be "an excellent pantomime." This actor-singer should not only sing to himself, but also sing in a way that would affect the orchestra, which in turn should closely follow his looks, his pauses, his gestures, and his soul's every movement. If an actor does not have this compelling stage presence, he could only be a musician; he could not be an actor.[32] As with nuns performing in convents of Italy who should remain invisible to the audiences (Burney 1773, 110), the castrato singer should remain hidden, reduced to his voice. To Rousseau, a surrogate actor should appear onstage on his behalf, as if he were a castrato singer's prosthesis. The incongruity between a repulsive body and a desirable voice gives rise to a concept of disembodied voice: the bodies of the castrati were best removed from presentation and representation.

Enfreaking the Castrato

The combination of a stigmatized body and an extraordinary voice seems foreign to our twenty-first-century thinking, but the perceived incongruity of the audible performance and the visible body is common in the reception of disabled performers (Straus 2011, 126). Instead of conceiving the castrato singers as bodiless vehicles who could sing the high vocal register, some writers saw them in their entirety—body, voice, and all—as freaks. The Bêche brothers claimed that the four best castratos—Antonio Bagniera, Favalli, Pacini, and Francisque—were admired but at the same time provided amusement at court (Sawkins 1986, 219). The euphemism "amusement" does not describe the delight of musical performance so much as the voyeuristic spectacles of human enfreakment. Throughout the eighteenth- century France, many disabled-bodied people were displayed as freaks for financial gain (Isherwood 1986, 48).[33] At the Théâtre des Variétés-Amusantes (as documented in the 1786 issue of *Les petits spectacles*), for example, writer Pierre-Jean-Baptiste Nougaret reported an assortment of curiosities including cabinets, foreign acrobats from Spain and Hungary, exotic animals, and automatons. In the midst of these curiosities, he noticed a twenty-eight-inch-tall young girl from Venice with no hands. This freakish spectacle was far from spectacular, for she did little except needlework: she clumsily threaded a fine needle, made a knot in the string with her tongue, knitted, and cut with scissors. Since she had no hands, her corporeal difference alone turned this everyday task she did into a freak show, into a source of "amusement." Through much unapologetic, "baroque" staring (Garland-Thomson 2009, 50–51), Nougaret's unsympathetic literary representation of her body and her action further objectifies her bodily difference. Describing her everyday task as if it were a "hypervisible text" (Garland-Thomson 1996, 10), Nougaret omits any mitigating contexts, any dynamic exchanges between her and her audiences, and shows no indication of how she wanted to be represented. His conclusion stigmatizes her further, treating her as a representative of Italy, a cultural Other of the unmarked France (Garland-Thomson 1997, 40).

Disappointed by the unspectacular display of a mundane task, Nougaret went on to complain that the needlework show was not exotic enough to his taste. To offer a better example, he recalled a limbless man who played cards and shot a pistol at the Saint-Germain fairground theatre in 1761 or 1762 (Nougaret 1786, 39–40). Nougaret stigmatized disabled performers by representing disability as a type of entertainment akin to base comedies at the fairground theatres. In his genealogy of spectacles, performers with visible disability came closer to curiosities such as automatons and exotic animals than to nondisabled people. The disabled were first displayed and subsequently represented in print as freaks.

Freak shows and their literary representation reveal the cultural mechanism of the enfreakment of castrato singers. No one is born a freak, as Robert Bogdan claims. Freak is rather a frame of mind and a set of practices (Bogdan 1996, 24). In a memoir published in 1782, the author Robert Martin Lesuire treated a castrato's physical body as a visible text: "Haven't you seen the castrati from the king's chapel? They are big and fat like cannons."[34] The king's chapel imagined in this instance to be a museum or a circus, displaying castrato singers as human spectacles. Like freaks at the fair theatres, castrato singers were reduced to their visible physical appearance—an inversion of the idea of the "disembodied voice," developed earlier. Castrato singers appear as voiceless. Their bodies, bereft of their humanity, appeared nonhumanly. They were not just fat like human beings, but also "round" like big containers and bulky artillery such as cannons. The exaggerated description reframes their visible bodily difference in terms of deviance, a deviance that in turn enabled them to emit nonhuman, excessive, deafening sound, breaching the boundaries that the natural voice of a normal singer could project. Lesuire's remark resonates with Bonnie Gordon's point that a castrato, like a cyborg, was considered to be a type of human machine (Gordon 2011, 111–118). Yet unlike early seventeenth-century Rome, in which castrato singers were integrated into a show of wonder, Lesuire's denigration of the castratos indicates an exclusion of the monstrous and the grotesque, an attitude that, according to the historians of science Lorraine Daston and Katherine Park, exemplifies the antimarvelous impulse indicative of a "Counter-Enlightenment" (Daston and Park 1998, 360).[35] Castrato singers were not displayed at the fairground theatres as freaks. Rather, the culture of freak shows and the reportage about them conditioned the French to construe bodily difference, whether displayed in the fairgrounds or reported in print, as freakish. Although the castrato singers were not freaks, sometimes they could be considered to be "enfreaked."[36]

I emphasize "sometimes" because certain French critics did celebrate performances by castrato singers. A successful performance helped audiences understand a castrato as a difference, even extraordinary, and not as a deficit. At his debut at the Concert Spirituel (August 5, 1777), Italian soprano castrato Gaspero Savoi from London performed Sacchini's aria "Se serca, se dice" and a rondeau by the composer Felice Alessandri. The critic Louis Petit de Bachaumont reported that audiences were unanimously thrilled by his performance: "Every time we said encore with applauses so unanimous that he has been obliged to surrender to the public's wishes. This castrato has much soul and expression in addition to the most perfect voice. . . . He has sung arias with an energy that has penetrated all the hearts."[37]

This enthusiastic reception contrasts with Ancillon's description of a performance by Marc'Antonio Pasqualini, a description that reveals the mechanism of enfreakment. Pasqualini was famous for his sight-reading skills. Instead of learning his music before the performance, he sight-read his part at the very last moment during the performance, "until the master of the choir, or manager of the concert shows him where he is to sing" (Ancillon 1718, 32). Ancillon framed Pasqualini's showcase of extraordinary musicianship as if he were reporting performances by savant musicians or a freak show.[38] In a concert held in a Roman seminary, Pasqualini's antagonists Arcangelo Corelli and Alessandro Scarlatti composed "the most crabbed, odd, and disagreeable piece of music," filled with octaves, "hopping from one extreme note to another, full of flats and discord as could be wished." The resulting piece was "wonderfully shocking," even though it was "wonderfully contrived," as if Corelli and Scarlatti projected their fantasy or anxiety of a paradoxically nonmusical piece of "music" onto Pasqualini, the living, partially artificial, wonder. Yet Pasqualini was reported to exercise instantaneous control of this seemingly impossible piece of music and performed the apparently vocally unidiomatic part "with all the exactness and promptitude in the world" (Ancillon 1718, 33–34). Elsewhere the abbé Simon-Joseph Pellegrin wrote about performances of Farinelli, Cafferelli, and the soprano Faustina, and admired their abilities to meet technical challenges. Again, he framed the musical performances in terms of overcoming. "These are some extraordinary subjects that I have ever heard. I am convinced that they must cause great pleasure with the excessive difficulties in what they can sing."[39] In other words, castrato singers could perform with great virtuosity not in spite of but because of their extraordinary bodies (Garland-Thomson 2005, 524).

Conclusion

Throughout this period the lack of medical knowledge about the castrato's body produced mystification. Castrato singers were somewhat protected institutionally, but they also were subjected to misrepresentation. Their sensationalized cannon-shaped bodies, "amphibian" voices, and inability to procreate raised questions about the naturalness and the artificiality of their bodies. Just as freak shows taught audiences to question what they saw (Adams 2001, 13), castrato singers raised issues of deception. In the parade *L'Eunuque ou la fidèle infidélité* by Charles-François Racot de Grandval (1749), an old and impotent man, Cassandre, thinks of becoming a castrato in order to marry Isabelle, the fiancée of his nephew Léandre, who left Paris three years ago. Colombine sings to him: "For you to compensate for a carnal flame, / You will become fat, / You will have a beautiful voice, / You will no longer have a beard; / And through this coup / You win her heart / And feed her cat."[40] Soon Léandre returns. To surprise everyone, he is disguised as a Turkish eunuch. Without a name, he calls himself only an "extract" of a man. At the end of this parade, Léandre reveals his real identity and is happy to learn that Isabelle has been loyal to him.[41]

Although the eunuch is central to *L'Eunuque ou la fidèle infidélité*, the play presents no real eunuch or castrato. Instead, it shows the *possibility* of an infertile man opening up an alternative fictional world within the play, one that denaturalizes the predictability of everyday reality. Through the friction between these two worlds the dialectic of authenticity and falsity gives rise to the notion of fidelity. In light of this comedy, one could adduce more cultural and social meanings of the castrato. In addition to being taken to be stigmatized man, an "enfreaked" marvel, a cold-blooded creaturely human, a voiceless thing, and a vessel that houses a bodiless voice, the castrato offered a concept of otherness that could not be sufficiently explained by Enlightenment theories of the body. By generating—or provoking—thoughts, anxiety, and feelings about the artificiality and fragility of a human being, the castrato exposed a bias against the marvelous in the French Enlightenment.

Notes

1. One exception is Garland-Thomson 1997, which mentions the incomplete body of the eunuch (115).
2. I follow Lennard J. Davis's terminological distinction between *people with disabilities* and *disabled people* (Davis 1995, 1–22).
3. The most important recent published work on castrato singers includes Freitas 2003; Gerbino 2004; Davies 2005; Feldman 2009a, 2009b; Freitas 2009; Berry 2011; Gordon 2011.
4. On the general history of castrato singers, see, for example, Roselli 1988; and on castrato singers in France, see Benoit 1971a, 512–513; 1971b, 186; Sawkins 1986, 1987; and Barbier 1998. For a helpful list of castrato singers in France, see Rouville and Sawkins 1992, 116–118.
5. This observation is based on a survey of all the reviews published from February 1727 to April 1773 in *Mercure de France* on performances by castrato singers at the Concert Spirituel.
6. "Il y a à la chapelle du Roi plusieurs castrati qu'on tire de bonne heure des écoles d'Italie, & qui chantent dans les motets les parties de dessus. Louis XIV avait des bontés particulières pour eux; il leur permettait la chasse dans ses capitaineries, & leur parlait quelquefois avec humanité. Ce grand roi prenait plaisir à consoler ces malheureux de la barbarie de leurs pères" (*Encyclopédie* 1751–1772, vol. 3, s.v. "Chanteur, euse"). On the motivations for families to castrate their sons, see Freitas 2009, 15–32.

7. "On ettoit tout ettoné a la cour de ce que le Sr antonio ne muoit point, et que sa voix ettoit toujours de plus belle en plus belle. On regardoit cela comme un fenomène. . . . Le Sr antonio a toujours vecu et est mort comme un veritable saint" (quoted in Sawkins 1986, 215).
8. On insults suffered by castrato singers, see Rosselli 1988, 174–175, and Feldman 2009a.
9. "CASTRATION, s. f. *terme de Chirurgie*, est l'action de châtrer, ou l'opération par laquelle on ampute & retranche les testicules d'un animal mâle, qui devient par - là incapable d'engendrer. *Voyez* TESTICULES" (*Encyclopédie* 1751–1772, vol. 2, s.v. "Castrati").
10. "La *castration* se pratique aussi en Italie sur les musiciens dont on veut que la voix se conserve. Cette *castration* n'est point une opération de Chirurgie, puisqu'elle n'a pas le rétablissement de la santé pour objet" (*Encyclopédie* 1751–1772, vol. 2, s.v. "Castration").
11. "A l'égard de la cause physique pour laquelle les *Castrati* ont la voix grêle & aiguë; il ne paraît pas plus facile de la trouver, que d'expliquer pourquoi ils n'ont point de barbe. Mais le fait est certain, & cela suffit" (*Encyclopédie* 1751–1772, vol. 2, s.v. "Castrati").
12. "Castrato, s.m.: musicien qu'on a privé, dans son enfance, des organes de la génération, pour lui conserver la voix aiguë qui chante la Partie appelée *Dessus* ou *Soprano*" (Rousseau [1767] 1959–1995, 5:687–688).
13. "Ce sont des castrati qu'on craint peu d'offenser, / et qu'on n'entend point sans penser / Aux facultés qu'ils ont perdues" (Grimm 1877–1882, 6:110).
14. "Quelque peu de rapport qu'on aperçoive entre deux organes si différents, il est certain que la mutilation de l'un prévient et empêche dans l'autre cette mutation qui survient aux hommes à l'âge nubile, et qui baisse tout-à-coup leur voix d'une Octave" (Rousseau [1767] 1959–1995, 5:687–688).
15. "Quand Mutiler se dit absolument, il signifie ordinairement, Châtrer" (*Dictionnaire de l'Académie française* 1762, s.v. "Mutiler").
16. "On dit figurément, *Mutiler* un ouvrage, pour dire, En retrancher une ou plusieurs parties essentielles à la perfection de l'ouvrage" (*Dictionnaire de l'Académie française* 1798, s.v. "Mutiler").
17. On censorship in France, see Hanley 1980 and 2005.
18. "The 18th Volume." University of Chicago: ARTFL Encyclopédie Project (spring 2013 edition), ed. Robert Morrissey, http://encyclopedie.uchicago.edu.ezproxy.library.ubc.ca/.
19. "Vous l'avez châtrée, dépecée, mutilée, mise en lambeaux, sans jugement, sans management et sans goût" (Diderot 1994–1997, 5:487).
20. Artistic and literary works, like musical works, have often been metaphorized as bodies (Straus 2011, 103–105).
21. "L'avantage de la voix se compense dans les Castrati par beaucoup d'autres pertes. Ces hommes qui chantent si bien, mais sans chaleur et sans passions, font, sur le Théâtre, les plus maussades Acteurs du monde; ils perdent leur voix de très-bonne heure et prennent un embonpoint dégoutant. Ils parlent et prononcent plus mal que les vrais hommes, et il y a même des lettres tells que l'*r*, qu'ils ne peuvent point prononcer du tout" (Rousseau [1767] 1959–1995, 5:687–688).
22. "La troupe . . . a son Manelli, / Et parmi leurs Castrats on voit leur Tonelli, / Grommelant les plaisirs, ou miaulant les peines, / Du Divin Pergolèse exécuter des scènes" (quoted in Launay 1973, 1:403).
23. "Oh! Comme du Castrat la voix sautillera! / Que de la Tonelli l'œil vif pétillera! / Leurs Partisans diront: Voila de la musique; / Un Opéra, du gout, une Fête publique. / Vous rampiez sur la terre, on vous ouvre les Cieux, / Français, vous entendez la musique des Dieux" (quoted in Launay 1973, 1:408).

24. "Mademoiselle Tonelli est un Castrat; d'où l'on conclut que la Musique Italienne est mauvaise" (quoted in Launay 1973, 1:475).
25. "Pour t'enseigner l'art d'importance, / De minauder avec aisance, / A ta toilette le matin, / Doit venir un Abbé poupin, / Un Musicien d'Italie, / Avec une voix amphibie, / Va te montrer avec succès/Comme on doit chanter en Français" (Gaubier de Barrault 1753, 18). On the one-sex model and body heat of a castrato, see Freitas 2009, 101–148.
26. See Charlton 2012, 242.
27. On diminutive names, see Freitas 2003, 214; Barbier 2012, 164; Sullivan 2007, 44.
28. "Le plaisir ne s'arrêtait point à l'oreille, il pénétrait jusqu'à l'âme" (Rousseau [1767] 1959–1995, 2:133).
29. "Je n'avais qu'un regret; mais il ne me quittait point; c'était qu'un autre que toi formât des sons dont j'étais si touché, et de voir sortir de la bouche d'un vil *castrato* les plus tendres expressions de l'amour" (Rousseau [1767] 1959–1995, 2:134).
30. On the transvestite and the castrato singer, see Wilbourne 2013; and on the hermaphrodite, see Daston and Park 1996.
31. "Par ce moyen, nos castrats, qui sont ordinairement des chanteurs si excellents et des acteurs si médiocres, ne seraient plus que des instruments parlants placés dans l'orchestre, et le plus près de la scène qu'il serait possible; ils exécuteraient la *partie* du chant avec une supériorité dont rien ne pourrait les distraire, tandis qu'un habile pantomime exécuterait la partie de l'action avec la même chaleur et la même expression" (*Encyclopédie* 1751–1772, vol. 12, s.v. "Poème lyrique").
32. "Il ne suffit pas à l'Acteur d'Opéra d'être un excellent Chanteur, s'il n'est encore un excellent Pantomime; car il ne doit pas seulement faire sentir ce qu'il dit lui-même, mais aussi ce qu'il laisse dire à la Symphonie. L'Orchestre ne rend pas un sentiment qui ne doive sortir de son âme; ses pas, ses regards, son geste, tout doit s'accorder sans cesse avec la Musique, sans pourtant qu'il paroisse y songer; il doit intéresser toujours, même en gardant le silence, et quoiqu'occupé d'un rôle difficile, s'il laisse un instant oublier le Personnage pour s'occuper du Chanteur, e n'est qu'un Musicien sur la Scène" (Rousseau [1767] 1959–1995, 5:637).
33. On American freak shows, see Bogdan 1988; Garland-Thomson 1996; 1997, 60–63; 2009, 163–166; Adams 2001.
34. "N'as-tu pas vu les castrats de la chapelle du roi? Ils sont gros et gras comme des chanoines" (Lesuire 1782, 9).
35. On a focused discussion of the Counter-Enlightenment in music, see Dill 2002; on the image-schema of the CONTAINER, see Lakoff and Johnson 2003, 29–32; on the grotesque, see Straus 2011, 77–79, and Garland-Thomson 1997, 115.
36. On the enfreakment of classical pianist Glenn Gould, see Hevey 1992, 53; Garland-Thomson 1996, 55–80, Maloney 2006, 121–135. On the culture of display in the freak show, see Rowden 2009, 1–14.
37. "Chaque fois on a répété *bis* avec des acclamations si unanimes qu'il a été obligé de se rendre aux vœux du public. Ce Castrato, outré la voix la plus parfaite, a beaucoup d'âme & d'expression. . . . Il les a poussés avec une énergie qui a percé tous les cœurs" (Bachaumont 1777–1789, 10:201).
38. Although the performance took place in a private setting, which was different from the nineteenth-century. On freak shows as a social construction, see Bogdan 1988 and 1996.
39. "Ce sont là des sujets extraordinaires que je n'ai jamais entendu, je suis persuadé qu'ils doivent faire grand plaisir par les difficultés excessives, dans lesquelles ils peuvent chanter" (Launay 1973, 3:1709).

40. “Pour vous dédommager d’une flamme charnelle, / Vous deviendrez dodu, vous aurez la voix belle, / Vous n’aurez plus de barbe; par ce coup d’éclat / Vous lui gagnez le cœur, & régalez son chat” (Grandval 1755, 10).
41. “Mais d’une créature humaine, / je ne suis hélas qu’un extrait!” (Grandval 1755, 30).

References

Adams, Rachel. 2001. *Sideshow U.S.A.: Freaks and the American Cultural Imagination.* Chicago: University of Chicago Press.

Ancillon, Charles. 1718. *Eunuchism Display’d: Describing All the Different Sorts of Eunuchs; . . . Written by a Person of Honour.* London: Printed for E. Curll.

Bachaumont, Louis Petit de. 1777–1789. *Mémoires secrets pour servir à l’histoire de la république des lettres en France.* 36 vols. London: J. Adamsohn.

Barbier, Patrick. 1998. *La maison des Italiens: Les castrats à Versailles.* Paris: B. Grasset.

Barbier, Patrick. 2012. *Naples en fête: Théâtre, musique et castrats au XVIIIe siècle.* Paris: Bernard Grasset.

Benoit, Marcelle. 1971a. *Musiques de cour: Chapelle, chambre, écurie.* Paris: Picard.

Benoit, Marcelle. 1971b. *Versailles et les musiciens du roi, 1661–1733: Études institutionnelle et sociale.* Paris: Picard.

Berry, Helen. 2011. *The Castrato and His Wife.* New York: Oxford University Press.

Bogdan, Robert. 1988. *Freak Show: Presenting Human Oddities for Amusement and Profit.* Chicago: University of Chicago Press.

Bogdan, Robert. 1996. “Social Construction of Freaks.” In *Freakery: Cultural Spectacles of the Extraordinary Body*, edited by Rosemarie Garland-Thomson, 23–37. New York: New York University Press.

Burney, Charles. 1773. *The Present State of Music in France and in Italy: Or, the Journal of a Tour through Those Countries, Undertaken to Collect Materials for a General History of Music.* 2nd ed. London: T. Becket.

Charlton, David. 2012. *Opera in the Age of Rousseau: Music, Confrontation, Realism.* Cambridge: Cambridge University Press.

Daston, Lorraine, and Katharine Park. 1996. “The Hermaphrodite and the Orders of Nature: Sexual Ambiguity in Early Modern France.” In *Premodern Sexualities*, edited by Louise Fradenburg and Carla Freccero, 117–136. New York: Routledge.

Daston, Lorraine, and Katharine Park. 1998. *Wonders and the Order of Nature, 1150–1750.* New York: Zone.

Davies, James Q. 2005. “‘Velluti in Speculum’: The Twilight of the Castrato.” *Cambridge Opera Journal* 17 (3): 271–301.

Davis, Lennard J. 1995. *Enforcing Normalcy: Disability, Deafness, and the Body.* London: Verso.

Davis, Lennard J. 2013. “The End of Identity Politics: On Disability as an Unstable Category.” In *The Disability Studies Reader*, 4th ed., edited by Lennard J. Davis, 263–277. New York: Routledge.

Dictionnaire de l’Académie française. 1762. 4th ed. Paris: Les Libraires Associés.

Dictionnaire de l’Académie française. 1798. 5th ed. Paris: J. J. Smits.

Diderot, Denis. 1994–1997. *Oeuvres.* 5 vols. Paris: Robert Laffont.

Dill, Charles. 2002. “Rameau’s Imaginary Monsters: Knowledge, Theory, and Chromaticism in *Hippolyte et Aricie*.” *Journal of American Musicological Society* 55 (3): 433–476.

Encyclopédie, ou Dictionnaire raisonné des sciences, des arts et des métiers, par une société de gens de lettres. 1751–1772. Edited by Denis Diderot and Jean le Rond d'Alembert. 17 vols. Paris: Briasson.

Feldman, Martha. 2009a. "Denaturing the Castrato." *Opera Quarterly* 24 (3–4): 178–199.

Feldman, Martha. 2009b. "Strange Births and Surprising Kin: The Castrato's Tale." In *Italy's Eighteenth Century: Gender and Culture in the Age of the Grand Tour*, edited by Paula Findlen, Wendy Wassyng Roworth, and Catherine M. Sama, 174–202. Stanford, CA: Stanford University Press.

Foucault, Michel. 1980. Introduction to *Herculine Barbin: Being the Recently Discovered Memoirs of a Nineteenth-Century French Hermaphrodite*, vii–xvii. Translated by Richard McDougall. New York: Pantheon.

Freitas, Roger. 2003. "The Eroticism of Emasculation: Confronting the Baroque Body of the Castrato." *Journal of Musicology* 20 (2): 196–249.

Freitas, Roger. 2009. *Portrait of a Castrato: Politics, Patronage, and Music in the Life of Atto Melani*. Cambridge: Cambridge University Press.

Garland-Thomson, Rosemarie, ed. 1996. *Freakery: Cultural Spectacles of the Extraordinary Body*. New York: New York University Press.

Garland-Thomson, Rosemarie. 1997. *Extraordinary Bodies: Figuring Physical Disability in American Culture and Literature*. New York: Columbia University Press.

Garland-Thomson, Rosemarie. 2005. "Disability and Representation." *PMLA* 120 (2): 522–527.

Garland-Thomson, Rosemarie. 2009. *Staring: How We Look*. New York: Oxford University Press.

Gaubier de Barrault, Sulpice-Edme. 1753. *Brioché ou l'origine des marionettes, parodie de Pigmalion*. Paris: Duchesne.

Gerbino, Giuseppe. 2004. "The Quest for the Castrato Voice: Castrati in Renaissance Italy." *Studi Musicali* 33 (2): 303–357.

Goffman, Erving. 1991. *Stigma: Notes on the Management of Spoiled Identity*. Reprint ed. New York: Simon & Schuster.

Gordon, Bonnie. 2011. "The Castrato Meets the Cyborg." *Opera Quarterly* 27 (1): 94–121.

Grandval, Charles-François Racot de. 1755. *L'eunuque ou la fidèle infidélité*. Montmartre: n.p.

Grimm, Friedrich Melchior, Freiherr von. 1877–1882. *Correspondance littéraire, philosophique et critique*. 16 vols. Paris: Garnier Frères.

Hanley, William. 1980. "The Policing of Thought: Censorship in Eighteenth-Century France." *Studies on Voltaire and the Eighteenth Century* 183: 265–295.

Hanley, William. 2005. *A Biographical Dictionary of French Censors, 1742–1789*. Vol. 1. Ferney-Voltaire, France: Centre Internationale D'étude du XVIIIe Siècle.

Hevey, David. 1992. *The Creatures Time Forgot*. New York: Routledge.

Isherwood, Robert. 1986. *Farce and Fantasy: Popular Entertainment in Eighteenth-Century Paris*. New York: Oxford University Press.

Lakoff, George, and Mark Johnson. 2003. *Metaphors We Live By*. Chicago: University of Chicago Press.

Laqueur, Thomas. 1990. *Making Sex: Body and Gender from the Greeks to Freud*. Cambridge, MA: Harvard University Press.

Launay, Denise, ed. 1973. *La querelle des bouffons*. 3 vols. Genève: Minkoff.

Lerner, Neil, and Joseph N. Straus, eds. 2006. *Sounding Off: Theorizing Disability in Music*. New York: Routledge.

Lesuire, Robert Martin. 1782. *L'aventurier français, ou Mémoires du Grégoire Merveil.* Londres: Quillau.
Mitchell, David T., and Sharon L. Snyder. 2000. *Narrative Prosthesis: Disability and the Dependencies of Discourse.* Ann Arbor: University of Michigan Press.
Nougaret, Pierre-Jean-Baptiste. 1786. *Les petits spectacles de Paris.* Paris: n.p.
Rosselli, John. 1988. "The Castrati as a Professional Group and a Social Phenomenon, 1550–1850." *Acta Musicologica* 60 (2): 143–179.
Rousseau, Jean-Jacques. 1959–1995. *Œuvres complètes.* Edited by Bernard Gagnebin, Marcel Raymond, et al. 5 vols. Paris: Gallimard.
Rouville, Henry de, and Lionel Sawkins. 1992. "Castrat." In *Dictionnaire de la musique en France aux XVIIe et XVIIIe siècles*, edited by Marcelle Benoit, 115–118. Paris: Fayard.
Rowden, Terry. 2009. *The Songs of Blind Folk: African American Musicians and the Cultures of Blindness.* Ann Arbor: University of Michigan Press.
Sawkins, Lionel. 1986. "The Brothers Bêche: An Anecdoctal History of Court Music." *Recherches sur la musique française classique* 24: 192–221.
Sawkins, Lionel. 1987. "For or Against the Order of Nature: Who Sang the Soprano?" *Early Music* 15 (3): 315–324.
Straus, Joseph. 2011. *Extraordinary Measures: Disability in Music.* New York: Oxford University Press.
Sullivan, Karen. 2007. "Regia nino: The Castrato at the Core of *Julie ou la Nouvelle Héloïse.*" *Dalhousie French Studies* 79: 35–46.
Wilbourne, Emily. 2013. "The Queer History of the Castrato." Paper presented at Feminist Theory and Music 12, Hamilton College, New York, July 31–August 4, 2013.

CHAPTER 18

SEXUALITY, TRAUMA, AND DISSOCIATED EXPRESSION

FRED EVERETT MAUS

SOMETIMES, musical expression—the creation of expression by composers and performers, and the experience of expression by listeners—emerges from minority sexuality and psychic trauma. This chapter begins with a basic model for understanding how these phenomena may interact. After stating the basic model, I indicate some relevant conceptual contexts. Then, I consider examples that relate to the basic model. Finally, I consider a complex example, a Pet Shop Boys song written in response to the AIDS crisis.

BASIC MODEL

In the musical worlds most familiar to me, the cultures of twentieth and twenty-first century classical and popular music in the United States and western Europe, many musicians belong to sexual minorities. So do many people for whom music listening is important.[1]

Human sexual diversity occurs everywhere, of course, openly or not depending on variable social norms. Still, there seems to be something special, a kind of kinship, in the coexistence of musicality and nonnormative sexuality. This section articulates one form that this relationship may take. I begin with generalizations from two sources, which I draw together into a single position.

The first generalization comes from queer studies, as developed in US historical musicology. In an essay published in 1994, Philip Brett wonders why sexual minorities have been so well represented among European and American musicians. He offers this explanation: "Music is a perfect field for the display of emotions. It is particularly accommodating to those who have difficulty in expressing feelings in day-to-day life, because the emotion is unspecified and unattached. The piano, let us say for example, will thus become an important means for the attempt at expression, disclosure, or communication on the part of those children who have difficulties of various kinds with one or both parents. To gay children, who often experience a shutdown of all feeling as the result of sensing their parents' and society's disapproval of a basic part of their sentient life, music appears as a veritable lifeline" (Brett 2006, 17).

Queer musicality, as Brett describes it, is an ambivalent phenomenon.[2] At its origin, it provides a way to survive as an interpersonally expressive being, a "lifeline." But it does this at the cost of postponement or deflection of important aspects of self-knowledge and self-expression.

To expand Brett's brief account of queer childhood, I turn to a second generalization, this one from psychotherapy. In her 2008 monograph (the culmination of work presented previously in articles such as Brown 2003), US psychotherapist Laura Brown argues that standard accounts of psychic trauma, by presuming that traumatic events are outside the range of ordinary experience, fail to recognize that trauma is common in the lives of many women; lesbian, gay, and bisexual (LGB) people; and other members of subordinated groups. This is a relatively unfamiliar conception of trauma; Brown relates it to established conceptions by drawing on three previous accounts of psychic trauma.

Brown refers to Ronnie Janoff-Bulman's description of a type of trauma that consists in the *shattering of expectations* about the safety and fairness of the world (Janoff-Bulman 1992). As Brown argues, such shattering of assumptions is common when young LGB subjects realize that familiar life trajectories and institutions support straight people and not themselves.[3] Thus, young LGB people must somehow deal with, or fend off, awareness that the world is not, for them, a comforting or welcoming place.

Brown also draws on Jennifer Freyd's account of *betrayal* as an aspect of some traumatic events; Freyd focuses particularly on sexual abuse by a family member (Freyd 1996). In accord with Freyd's account, Brown notes that the homophobia of authorities such as family members or spiritual advisors and their failure to accept and nurture the sensibility of a young queer exemplify traumatic betrayal. Recognition of this betrayal and emotional response to it may be particularly difficult for LGB subjects, because the abuse may not be understood as malicious by anyone involved and may come from authorities who are objects of love and admiration within relationships that the abused person needs to sustain. As Brown puts it, "mechanisms of unknowing set in as strategies to maintain these relationships," and the complex negotiation of betrayal trauma "has an impact on how and whether LGB people are able to know what they feel and want" (Brown 2003, 62).

And Brown follows Maria Root in noting the importance of what Root calls "insidious trauma," trauma that takes the form of an extended series of events, perhaps individually inconspicuous but, taken together, having traumatic impact (Root 1992). With insidious trauma, one may find a range of post-traumatic phenomena in the absence of the individual overwhelming event often associated with trauma. Examples of insidious trauma include the daily slights of sexism, racism, or homophobia.

Unlike Brett, Brown does not emphasize issues about expressiveness, but her account of normative LGB trauma bears directly on self-expression, a topic bound up with self-understanding. Young LGB subjects, according to Brown's generalizations, experience a need to fend off a traumatic shattering of assumptions about the future, and a need to preserve important relationships and fend off an awareness of betrayal. These needs work against recognition of their own desires and sensibilities, and also work against the unguarded expression of feelings.

In light of Brown's link between queer identity and trauma, we can recast Brett's account of queer musicality in terms of well-studied post-traumatic defenses: avoidance of potentially retraumatizing situations, numbing, and dissociation. Awareness of negative responses to homosexuality may lead queer children to avoid behaviors or situations that invite ascriptions of deviant gender or sexuality. The difficulty and potential pain of conceptualizing and responding to their circumstances may lead queer children and adolescents to avoid or postpone emotional response, through the "shutdown of feeling" that psychotherapists call numbing.

And, to offset avoidance or numbing, young queers may welcome the "lifeline" of musical expressiveness, which we can describe in psychological language as a medium of dissociated feeling.[4] Dissociated emotional expression, communicated in music, flourishes by being cordoned off from the rest of a queer musician's life. The dissociation makes the feeling available for free, safe expression. In such a case, not only does music offer an outlet for feeling, but also musicality offers a way of gaining approval for expressiveness. While Brett, in the passage I cited, focuses on the youthful origins of queer musicality, the conjunction of avoidance or emotional numbing, in some aspects of life, and dissociated musical expressiveness can continue beyond childhood.

Contextual Remarks

This section identifies several intellectual contexts that bear on my account. I mention these only to flag their relevance; as will be clear, space does not permit sustained discussion of these topics, each one complex. The idea of music as a vehicle of dissociated expression, central to this essay, is unfamiliar. But it relates to many familiar facts about musical life (again, in the specific historical contexts I identified at the outset).

We think of music as expressive, but often we do not know what it expresses; music moves people, but often they cannot say why. The expressed content of music is elusive. Further, we often identify a gap between musical expressiveness and the expressiveness of concrete individual people. That is, often we want to resist a direct inference from someone's expressiveness in composing or performance, or their preferences as a listener, to beliefs about their personal psyche. Someone might compose sad music, or perform sad music expressively, or want to hear sad music, without feeling sad, or without feeling sad about something in particular; likewise for happy music, and so on. On the other hand, sometimes, perhaps through biographical knowledge that goes beyond musical sources, we feel that we know what someone is expressing through musical creativity or listening. In some contexts, such as religious music, there may be a high value on sincerity, so that one should not musically express feelings or ideas one does not actually hold. Musical meaning and interpretation (in the cultures under discussion) move within a range of possible relationships between musical expression and personal reality.

If music-making exists as a social practice that can be impersonal, in the ways just mentioned, individuals may come into such a practice for many different reasons. In the situation Brett identified, the vagueness of musical expression and its uncertain relation to the musician's personal life open the possibility that musical expression may be set apart from other aspects of a person's life, compartmentalized, dissociated. The intensity of music can offer rich expressiveness, safely estranged from dangerous self-knowledge or self-revelation. Hence, one can combine secrecy, unawareness, or numbing on one side, and on the other side, musical effects of warmth and openness.

As noted above, my account draws on the work of Laura Brown, a professional psychotherapist who develops her ideas in dialogue with the DSM,[5] and whose book on trauma was published by the American Psychological Association (Brown 2008). Disability activism has sometimes been wary of medical authority, and rightly so: in many contexts, medical practices treat disabled people as individuals with problems, disregarding the physical and social environments that create disability. But there is a range of attitudes about psychiatry and psychotherapy within activism and Disability Studies, and my use of Brown's work represents one option within the field. In my view, assessment of medical authority needs to be pragmatic and case-by-case; blanket dismissal of professional psychotherapy, the DSM, and so forth, is too simple to be helpful.[6]

Brown associates LGB subjects, and members of other minorities, with special risks of trauma and post-traumatic symptoms. Someone might imagine that this pathologizes minority sexuality and perpetuates the idea that LGB people are sick.[7] It is clear, though, that Brown, herself lesbian, writes as an insider and an advocate for these groups, and her work does not perpetuate the historical medical view of homosexuality as illness. Rather, Brown writes about the psychological consequences of stigma that originates outside the individual. Regarding sexual diversity itself, Brown's views align with disability activism: stigma and discrimination, not some inherent personal flaw, disable sexual minority subjects.

But stigma may cause psychological harm to an individual. This is where the damage comes in: not in the existence of sexual desires themselves, but in the abusive contextual treatment of sexual minority subjects. Thus, as already stated, the pressures of growing up in a homophobic setting can lead to the phenomena of avoidance, numbing, and dissociation. Such phenomena constitute harm or impairment, but not simply so. At the outset, they are adaptations, ways of surviving, thus not purely harmful. A child who finds these strategies can continue to live in problematic circumstances. And the impairments of numbing and dissociation, as I've suggested (following Brett), can lead to rich musical expressiveness, something we tend to value highly. Still, for a range of subjects who, if not inhibited, would seek self-understanding and interpersonal expression, numbing and dissociation may have predominantly harmful consequences as well as good ones.

In some formulations, disability activism, and specifically the social model of disability, have neglected the role of harm or impairment in the lives of disabled people; relatedly, the study of trauma has mostly developed separately from Disability Studies. The social model offers a powerful insight: we can better understand a disability such as paralysis or deafness as a mismatch between the individual and the physical and social environment, rather than simply as a defect of an individual person. Rather than thinking that a person in a wheelchair is unable to enter a building, we can think that the building, by lacking ramps, and the people who built and use it, by accepting its lack of ramps, exclude and thereby disable the person.

In some cases, the social model is adequate. For instance, relevant to this essay, such arguments have led to the depathologizing of homosexuality. But in other cases, we need a more complex weaving-together of insights about social oppression and experiences of impairment. One-sided emphasis on the power of the social model has contributed to the separation between trauma studies and Disability Studies and to exaggerated rejection of medical and therapeutic knowledge. Thus, in working with concepts of trauma and emphasizing the potential impairment of queer subjects, I follow the lead of disability scholars such as Tom Shakespeare who have emphasized the reality and importance of experiences of impairment (Shakespeare 2014).[8]

Finally, I need to point out normative assumptions in the ideas I have taken from Brett. People differ in their relations to introspection, communication, expressiveness, and so on. My account of numbing and dissociated expression assumes particular kinds of "expression," "disclosure," "communication," and "sentient life" (to use some of Brett's key terms). Neither those assumptions, nor indeed presumptions about sexuality directed at other people, apply universally.[9] There is much more to explore, beyond the specific claims of this chapter, about relations between musicality, subjectivity, and non-normative sexuality.

Examples

Philip Brett speculates about the musicality of queer children in order to explain the strong presence of adult queer musicians in twentieth-century classical music. Any adult sexual minority composers and performers, and sexual minority listeners, are potentially examples of the fruitfulness of dissociated expression. In such cases, one would expect to find the conjunction of musical expressiveness, not construed as directly self-revealing, and a history of blocked self-knowledge or self-expression. Further, Brett suggests that something akin to dissociation may continue, in adult musicians, through a separation between the public role of musician and the private life of a sexual minority subject.

A simple example of my basic model, then, would involve a queer subject's expressive composition or performance, or enjoyment of musical expression, along with a history of difficulties in self-knowledge or self-expression. On one side, the unknowing, avoidance, numbing, and so forth; on the other side, the flourishing of musical expression.

But there are more complex possibilities. What if music sometimes acknowledged, in some explicit way, the inhibition and dissociation that contribute to musicality? Examples suggest several ways this could happen.

In Brett's description of the Andante of Schubert's *Grand Duo* for piano, four hands (Brett 1997), the composition dramatizes the difference between music that hides painful feelings and the fleeting recognition of those feelings. Brett understands most of the piece as a representation of a false self—sunny, uncomplicated, smug, amply endowed with reassuringly conventional cadences. One brief passage suddenly introduces something violent, ominous, obsessive. The piece puts this disruptive music away quickly, cadencing sweetly. But, with the abruptness of an intrusive thought, the disturbing music returns, even more violent, near the end of the piece, in its textural and harmonic harshness barely recognizable as music from its time. And yet, after this outburst, the piece promptly returns to its prevalent sweetness as though nothing had happened.

Brett hears in this music the hidden rage of disempowered subjects, lurking behind their overt conformity. Putting it in relation to my model, I suggest that the music depicts, as narrative, the juxtaposition of dissociated musical expression that creates a socially acceptable subject and, in a few discontinuous moments, the painful, unintegrated feelings that musicality can hide.

Brett relates this narrative to male homosexuality—not, however, to the conjectural homosexuality of Schubert, about which Brett is noncommittal. Rather, the music, understood in this way, mirrors back life experiences of Brett and his younger gay piano-duet partner.

In another possibility, expressive music might overtly mark the presence of something hidden or obscure in itself, thus suggesting that music may simultaneously express feelings and keep secrets. I hear this in the early music of the US rock band R.E.M.[10] Singer and lyricist Michael Stipe, evasive about his sexuality for a time, described himself as queer from the 1990s on. From the outset, listeners understood his performances as uncannily emotional. But many critics and listeners noted a strong effect of mystery, even secrecy, in Stipe's mumbled performances and his obscure lyrics. His expressiveness, then, comes along with markers of something unstated, perhaps held back or not fully conscious.[11]

Another possibility is that music might refuse expressiveness and depict inhibited expression, even numbness. This may be heard in songs by the Pet Shop Boys, an English duo creating synthesizer-based pop music from the 1980s on. The duo, made up of singer and lyricist Neil Tennant and musician Chris Lowe, has been an icon of gay music, before and after Tennant officially came out in 1994, with a large queer fanbase.

Throughout their career, the Pet Shop Boys have offered a sustained, complex meditation on issues of expression and communication, in part through the sound of Tennant's singing and recitation. It would be wrong to say simply that Tennant's voice is inexpressive, but in many ways it offers images of inhibited expression. It is limited in range and volume, and makes only very subtle use of the inflections that normally constitute musical expressiveness. Tennant gives the impression of great care in his beautifully precise placement of pitches and in his crystalline enunciation. These last features suggest an extreme consideration for the listener, to whom each pitch and phoneme is presented meticulously.[12] The lyrics that Tennant delivers in this self-effacing way are typically understated and oblique, refraining from insistence on intense subjective experience. Tennant's modest vocal ambitions, polite precision, and personal withdrawal are particularly striking because the musical idiom of the Pet Shop Boys is disco, a style associated with the passionate, sexually direct, virtuosic vocalizations of black divas.

Often, Tennant's performance style comes close to bringing a post-traumatic numbness into music itself. It is as though, in Tennant's case, the magic of dissociated musical expression has failed to offer its lifeline to the traumatized subject. This may sound like an artistic failure. But it can also be heard as a demystification, a refusal of the socially accepted queer expressiveness that succeeds only by avoiding the material that most needs expression.

"I Want a Dog" is a song about loneliness, and about not daring to ask for what one really wants, or perhaps not even knowing what one wants. The song sets Tennant's quiet, calm delivery against sharply characterized instrumental backing. The music is intensely danceable, but emotionally cold. The synthesizer and piano syncopations give a sense of urgency and, as they repeat, a sense of being trapped. Meanwhile, the minimal, repetitious rise and fall of the harmony, and brief flickers of major mode, suggest real but barely recognizable fluctuations of feeling.

Another Pet Shop Boys song, "Left to My Own Devices," complicates the depiction of numbness. It juxtaposes Tennant's unemphatic recitation and singing with extravagant orchestral passages, setting a frenzied cinematic exoticism alongside Tennant's drab recounting of everyday events and, in the chorus, an oblique, uncertain expression of erotic desire. The orchestral music is shockingly disproportionate to the ostensibly bland, discontinuous content of the lyrics. Such music offers expressiveness, but in the ambivalent mode of camp, wavering between identification and disavowal. In contrast, the vocal performance is dry and prosaic. The song can be heard as a depiction of dissociation, of a subjectivity split between exaggerated, stereotyped emotionalism and a numb banality.

Thinking of the Pet Shop Boys in relation to issues of trauma, one can begin to understand why some listeners, in whose lives issues of sexuality, expressiveness, numbing, and dissociation have been important, might find this to be some of the most wonderful music in the world. By displaying rather than hiding aspects of post-traumatic subjectivity, these songs help to articulate a sense of shared community, a sense of belonging.

Mourning

Some of the Pet Shop Boys' most beautiful songs respond to the AIDS epidemic.[13] The words of these songs address their audiences complexly. In general, through the 1980s and beyond, the AIDS crisis (understood, in Pet Shop Boys songs, in relation to gay men in affluent countries) divided people into those for whom the crisis was immediate and personal and others to whom it seemed remote. The Pet Shop Boys' songs about AIDS address the first group with lacerating directness; no one close to gay male communities at the time would fail to understand the words. But the same language, for someone less aware of AIDS, could seem elusive, vaguely evocative but without specific reference. This need not pose a problem for enjoyment by broad audiences, since many people are relatively inattentive to the words of popular songs. However, listeners close to the AIDS crisis could be expected to understand these songs and indeed to hang on every word.[14]

Faced with the shared trauma of AIDS, the Pet Shop Boys use these songs to articulate a collective identity by addressing a community, while accepting the possibility that the songs' meanings may be opaque to those outside this community.[15] Such music deepens the quality of community formation that I already mentioned: now the songs address two layers of trauma, the formative early trauma described by Brett and Brown and the AIDS crisis.

The Pet Shop Boys' songs about AIDS vary in their styles of musical expression. In some cases, the music is relatively direct in its presentation of emotional content.[16] In other cases, such as the song I shall discuss here, the role of the music is uncertain. In any case, Tennant's voice retains its characteristic precise, emotionally uncommitted quality. The lyrics often combine painful meaning with controlled diction and understatement. In such songs, one can hear that the devastation of AIDS has given new cause for numbing and withdrawal.

"Dreaming of the Queen," from the 1993 album *Very*, is itself about the gap of incomprehension between people living in closeness to AIDS and people who don't get it, here personified respectively by Lady Di and the Queen of England. The song takes the form of a surreal dream narrative. Its two full verses, each consisting of two quatrains, along with the chorus, describe a visit to the Queen and Lady Di. In the first verse, the Queen, pondering the events of 1992, her *annus horribilis*, as she called it, in which three of her children divorced or separated from their spouses, laments that love does not last. In the chorus, Lady Di, known for her AIDS activism from the 1980s on, changes the subject, not quite explicitly, from royal marriage to the ravages of the epidemic. Actually, to say that Lady Di makes this intervention is not quite right. In Tennant's performance, one can't be sure whether he says "and Di replied," as the published text has it, or "and I replied." The indeterminate merging of characters adds to the dreamy quality.

In the second verse, the dreamer finds himself naked in public—a common dream, as is, according to Tennant, the dream of visiting royalty. The "old Queen" disapproves of his nakedness, though others are amused. The meaning of "Queen" shifts in this verse, the "old Queen" representing, no doubt, not only Elizabeth II but also a midcentury generation of homosexuals who disapprove of the relative openness of more recent gay life. The dreamer's generally well-received nakedness, followed by the return of the death of all lovers, repeats the familiar AIDS narrative of sexual freedom and openness followed by disaster (Maus 2013).

Verse – four measures of B♭m, followed by four measures alternating Fm7 and B♭m, that is:

B♭m: I (four measures)   v7   i   v7   i

Chorus: ambiguous between Bbm and DbM – 1 chord per measure

	G♭M7	A♭	Fm7	bb (repeat)	G♭	A♭	G♭	A♭	D♭sus	D♭
B♭m:	VI7	VII	v7	i	VI	VII	[VI?	VII?	III? 4 –	3]
D♭M:	IV7	V	iii7	vi	IV	V	IV	V	I 4 –	3

FIGURE 18.1 Harmonies, "Dreaming of the Queen."

The opulent music evokes the grandeur of public representations of royalty and state. Its beauty seems to inhabit palaces, perhaps leaving the reference to AIDS as an incursion from a foreign world. Or does the music assert, perhaps, that a response to AIDS can claim this majestic beauty? In the passages where Diana and the dreamer reply to the Queen, the music uses the same dance-music harmonies as two other Pet Shop Boys songs about AIDS, "Being Boring" and "Domino Dancing," recasting them in solemn splendor, perhaps finding in this curious combination of styles a dignified sound to mourn a world associated with disco. Figure 18.1 shows the harmonies of the verse and chorus.

The dreamwork of "Dreaming of the Queen" offers a series of puns: "Di replied," "I replied"; Di the Princess, and the death that one dies; the Queen of England, and the queen in gay culture; implicitly, the royal *annus horribilis*, and the anus. But the goal of the song is not primarily to blur differences, but rather to awaken distinctions. Centrally, the song resists Queen Elizabeth's intention in her assertion that "love never seems to last," shifting her language slightly, through further punning, to convey a very different thought. Her Royal Highness worries that heterosexual monogamy seems doomed to failure, a particular disaster when the failures afflict the symbols of the nation. "Di" and "I" replace this discourse of "love" with a more pressing concern for "lovers," the transnational community of gay men whose acts of sexuality and love have literally led to death. As the song ends, there is no more dreaming of England; what remains is the reality of lovers, night sweats, and death. The song articulates the hopelessness of the time, over a decade into the epidemic, effective medications still a few years in the future.

Acknowledgments

I wrote the first version of this essay for a 2008 conference on queer studies organized by Enkidu, a queer activist organization in Mexico City. I am grateful to Enkidu for their support over many years. I presented versions of the paper several times after, most memorably as a plenary presentation at the international meeting of IASPM in Liverpool, 2009, and at "Composing Disability," George Washington University, 2011. At those meetings and on other occasions I received many valuable responses and suggestions. I am especially grateful to Joseph Straus for his help in moving toward the present chapter.

Notes

1. Throughout this chapter, I write, as an insider, with reference to those cultures. As such, I sometimes generalize about how "we" understand music.
2. In summarizing Brett's ideas, I use the term "queer," generalizing beyond his emphasis on gay subjects. His argument may have been intended broadly, and can certainly

be broadened, but his own emphasis is on gay men, the group with which he identified himself. My musical examples will also concern gay men (with the possible exception of Michael Stipe, whose self-identification has varied), leaving open for further work the demonstration, though examples, of broader generality.

3. In summarizing Brown, I follow her choice to treat LGB subjects collectively. She does not follow the common practice of adding transgender subjects to form the category LGBT, because she finds that sexual desire raises issues different from nonnormative gender.
4. Howell 2005 is helpful on the widely used concept of dissociation.
5. The *Diagnostic and Statistical Manual of Mental Disorders* (2013) is the official manual of the American Psychiatric Association, listing psychiatric conditions and diagnostic criteria.
6. For an expression of gratitude to the DSM by a disability scholar, see Johnson 2013. Her diagnosis of borderline personality disorder gave greater clarity to what were previously confusing experiences. For a concise presentation of varied current perspectives, see the collection in which Johnson's essay appeared, Johnson and Mollow 2013.
7. The historic practices of medicalizing and pathologizing queer subjects have been oppressive. In reaction, David Halperin, for one, recommends completely abandoning psychology as a resource for understanding gay or queer subjectivity (Halperin 2007).
8. Berger 2004 describes ways that the different emphases of Disability Studies and trauma theory have led to separation. Like Shakespeare, he identifies a reluctance in some disability activism and scholarship to acknowledge injury or damage.
9. McRuer and Mollow 2012 opens many possibilities for thinking about sexuality and disability.
10. In turning to popular music, I propose that ideas like Brett's can be useful beyond the classical music examples he had in mind. Of course, the presence of sexual minorities is at least as prominent in popular music creation and reception as in classical music, and similar ideas of music expression circulate, at least in some popular genres.
11. For detailed interpretation of Stipe's queer expressiveness, see Maus 2006, 2010.
12. One way to sense the special qualities of Tennant's vocal performances is to call to mind some of the passionate queer voices from the same period; think of George Michael, Marc Almond, or Andy Bell.
13. I have in mind songs such as "It Couldn't Happen Here," "Being Boring," "Your Funny Uncle," or "Discoteca," where the reference to the epidemic is clear. Hughes 1994 argues brilliantly for the pervasive relevance of AIDS to many more of the Pet Shop Boys' songs.
14. A comment by Kath Weston helped me see this difference of audiences in their attention to lyrics.
15. On cultural trauma and its close connection to identity formation, see Alexander et al. 2004.
16. For further discussion of such songs, see Maus 2013. As I discuss in that essay, "Being Boring" seems emotionally direct; "It Couldn't Happen Here" is more complex, but its ambivalent music enhances the uncertainties of the lyrics.

References

Alexander, Jeffrey C., Ron Eyerman, Bernard Giesen, Neil J. Smelser, and Piotr Sztomptka. 2004. *Cultural Trauma and Collective Identity*. Berkeley: University of California Press.

American Psychiatric Association. 2013. *Diagnostic and Statistical Manual of Mental Disorders.* 5th ed. (DSM–5). Washington, DC: American Psychiatric Association.

Berger, James. 2004. "Trauma without Disability, Disability without Trauma: A Disciplinary Divide." *Journal of Rhetoric, Culture, and Politics* 24 (3): 563–582.

Brett, Philip. (1994) 2006. "Musicality, Essentialism, and the Closet." In *Queering the Pitch: The New Gay and Lesbian Musicology*, edited by Philip Brett, Elizabeth Wood, and Gary C. Thomas, 2nd ed., 9–26. New York: Routledge.

Brett, Philip. 1997. "Piano Four-Hands: Schubert and the Performance of Gay Male Desire." *19th-Century Music* 21 (2): 149–176.

Brown, Laura S. 2003. "Sexuality, Lies, and Loss: Lesbian, Gay, and Bisexual Perspectives on Trauma." *Journal of Trauma Practice* 2: 55–68.

Brown, Laura S. 2008. *Cultural Competence in Trauma Therapy: Beyond the Flashback.* Washington, DC: American Psychological Association.

Freyd, Jennifer J. 1996. *Betrayal Trauma: The Logic of Forgetting Abuse.* Cambridge, MA: Harvard University Press.

Halperin, David M. 2007. *What Do Gay Men Want? An Essay on Sex, Risk, and Subjectivity.* Ann Arbor: University of Michigan Press.

Howell, Elizabeth F. 2005. *The Dissociative Mind.* Hillsdale, NJ: Analytic Press.

Hughes, Walter. 1994. "In the Empire of the Beat: Discipline and Disco." In *Microphone Fiends: Youth Music and Youth Culture*, edited by Tricia Rose and Andrew Ross, 147–157. New York: Routledge.

Janoff-Bulman, Ronnie. 1992. *Shattered Assumptions: Towards a New Psychology of Trauma.* New York: Free Press.

Johnson, Merri Lisa. 2013. "Label C/Rip." *SocialText Periscope*, October 24. http://socialtext-journal.org/periscope_article/label-crip/.

Johnson, Merri Lisa, and Anna Mollow, eds. 2013. "DSM-CRIP." *SocialText Periscope*, October 24. http://socialtextjournal.org/periscope_topic/dsm_crip/.

Maus, Fred Everett. 2006. "Intimacy and Distance: On Stipe's Queerness." *Journal of Popular Music Studies* 18 (2): 191–214.

Maus, Fred Everett. 2010. "Three Songs about Privacy, by R.E.M." *Journal of Popular Music Studies* 22 (1): 2–31.

Maus, Fred Everett. 2013. "Narrative and Identity in Three Songs about AIDS." In *Musical Narrative since 1900, Musical Meaning and Interpretation*, edited by Michael Klein and Nicholas Reyland, 254–271. Bloomington: Indiana University Press.

McRuer, Robert, and Anna Mollow, eds. 2012. *Sex and Disability.* Durham, NC: Duke University Press.

Root, Maria P. P. 1992. "Reconstructing the Impact of Trauma on Personality." In *Personality and Psychopathology: Feminist Reappraisal*, edited by Laura S. Brown and Mary Ballou, 229–265. New York: Guilford Press.

Shakespeare, Tom. 2014. *Disability Rights and Wrongs Revisited.* 2nd ed. New York: Routledge.

CHAPTER 19

THAT "WEIRD AND WONDERFUL POSTURE"

Jump "Jim Crow" and the Performance of Disability

SEAN MURRAY

SOMETIME in the late 1820s to early 1830s, a little-known white theatre performer named Thomas Dartmouth Rice modeled a blackface song and dance on a "crippled Negro" he observed singing while he worked in a stable. Daphne Brooks calls this possibly apocryphal encounter a "primal scene in minstrel history" (Brooks 2006, 17), and there are numerous, sometimes conflicting, versions of the story that circulated in the nineteenth-century press. But most agree that Rice appropriated the stableman's song and stilted dance for his "Jim Crow" act by putting on a pathetic limp and crooking his shoulder while he sang and danced the chorus (one story even asserts Rice borrowed the man's clothes). See Figure 19.1.

At eighty years old, actor Edmon Conner claimed in an interview in the *New York Times* that he was an eyewitness:

> Back of the theater was a livery-stable kept by a man named Crow. The actors could look into the stable-yard from the theater, and were particularly amused by an old decrepit negro, who used to do odd jobs for Crow. As was then usual with slaves, they called themselves after their owner, so that old Daddy had assumed the name of Jim Crow. He was very much deformed—the right shoulder was drawn up high, and the left leg was stiff and crooked at the knee, which gave him a painful but at the same time ludicrous limp. He was in the habit of crooning a queer old tune, to which he had applied words of his own. At the end of each verse he gave a peculiar step, "rocking de heel" in the manner since so general among the many generations of imitators; and these were the words of his refrain:
>
> Wheel about, turn about,
>   Do jis so,
> An' ebery time I wheel about
>   I jump Jim Crow"

FIGURE 19.1 T. D. Rice as "Jim Crow," American minstrel show collection, 1823–1947. MS Thr 556 (156). Rice, Tom, 1808–1860. Portraits in character. Harvard Theatre Collection, Houghton Library, Harvard University.

> Rice became known as "Daddy Rice," and "Jim Crow" was immortalized—the successes of Rice are too well known to need recapitulation. ("An Old Actor's Memories" 1881)

Audiences on both sides of the Atlantic were captivated, and Rice became one of the most popular stage performers of the 1830s and '40s in the transatlantic English-speaking world. Nineteenth-century theatre historian Lawrence Hutton considered Rice a "long, ungainly, grotesque, and exceedingly droll comedian" (Hutton 1891, 115). Indeed, Rice was so influential that he is often credited for laying the groundwork for the emergence of blackface minstrelsy as a popular genre in the early 1840s.

There were of course many performers other than Rice doing blackface acts in the 1820s and '30s (e.g., George Washington Dixon, Joe Sweeney, Dick Pelham, Frank Brower, Jim Sanford, Dan Emmit, and John Diamond), but none was as popular as "Jim Crow." Rice's innovation—combining the application of burnt cork with the performance of a stylized "cripple" dance in order to present a "true" representation of the American Southern Negro—set him apart from his less successful peers. His grotesque performance style was quickly copied, as illustrated by the sheet music cover to "Jim Along Josey," a song popular in the 1820s and '30s (see Figure 19.2).

The contradictions embodied by the "original" Jim Crow—the juxtaposition of a painful disability with a sense of the comic—became part and parcel of later minstrel performance practice. Recent scholarship on Jim Crow has become increasingly sensitive to issues other than or in addition to race (e.g., class, sexuality, gender). But issues of disability, centered on the crippled, deformed body, have not received comparable consideration. Unlike race, disability has continued to be treated as an inherent and natural aspect of the human body and not in any sense a historical or cultural construction. Hans Nathan, for example, author of an important monograph on Dan Emmet and early blackface minstrelsy, wrote of Rice, "How strained, sprawling, and distorted his posture was, and yet how nonchalant—how unusually grotesque with its numerous sharp angles, and yet how natural!" (Nathan 1962, 52).

While there is an extensive literature on the reception, class politics, and contested interpretations of the racial "meaning" of performances of Jim Crow, scholars have generally been silent on two key characteristics of the "Jump Jim Crow" phenomenon. First, participatory audience performance was critical to the act's popularity and reception. As Rice himself noted, his triumph was that he got people's "whole bodies to jump about and wheel about like a set of teto-tums" ("Letter from Jim Crow" 1837). Second, Jumping "Jim Crow" demanded extravagantly caricatured performances of a "deformed," "grotesque," "crippled" (black) body: the pleasure of jumping "Jim Crow" was in fact rooted in the spectacular performance of disability by presumably able-bodied people (usually white and usually male).

This essay will demonstrate that early blackface performance almost always involved performances of disability (physical and cognitive). These performances of disability constructed both privileged white citizens and debased, defective Negroes, unworthy of citizenship. As such they participated in contemporary discourses about citizenship, discourses in which race and disability play central and deeply entwined roles. Indeed, the dual performance of pathology and race seems so self-evidently racist that recent scholars—most prominently Lott (2013) and Cockrell (1997)—have argued that it is ahistorical or presentist to examine the racist stereotypes promulgated by blackface minstrelsy. Douglas Baynton, however, has demonstrated that "Disability has functioned historically to justify inequality for disabled people themselves, but it has also done so for women and minority groups. That is, not only has it been considered justifiable to

FIGURE 19.2 Sheet Music Cover, "Jim Along Josey." Library of Congress Music Collection, Microfilm M 3106 M1.A12V vol. 4.

treat disabled people unequally, but the *concept* of disability has been used to justify discrimination against other groups by attributing disability to them" (Baynton 2001, 33). My aim in this essay is to probe this relation between race and disability in order to show that bodily comportment and the performance of disability were as essential to "blacking up" as applying burnt cork or greasepaint. Disability functioned in blackface performance both aesthetically ("cripples" and "idiots" can be considered funny or pathetic) and socially. In sum, discourses and performances of disability in blackface were a critical and heretofore unacknowledged part of nineteenth-century American constructions of blackness.

Mitchell and Snyder argue that discourses about physical and cognitive inferiority have "historically characterized the means by which bodies have been constructed as 'deviant.'" They go on to argue that stigmatized minorities have attempted to

> unmoor their identities from debilitating physical and cognitive associations . . . inevitably position[ing] disability as the "real" limitation from which they must escape. . . . Consequently, disability has undergone a dual negation—it has been attributed to all "deviant" biologies as a discrediting feature, while also serving as the material marker of inferiority itself. One might think of disability as the master trope of human disqualification. (Mitchell and Snyder 2000, 2–3)

This assertion is at odds with scholars such as Evelyn Higgenbotham who present race as "the ultimate trope of difference, artificially and arbitrarily contrived to produce and maintain relations of power and subordination" (Higginbotham 1992, 253). These two positions are not irreconcilable, however. As Susan Wendell writes in response to Higginbotham, "Despite the fact that there is sometimes more biological reality underlying distinctions between the non-disabled and the disabled than there is underlying distinctions between races, the belief that 'the disabled' is a biological category is like the belief that 'Black' is a biological category, in that it masks the social functions and injustices that underlie the assignment of people to these groups" (Wendell 1996, 23).

Blackface minstrelsy is an ideal subject to explore the interaction of these two categories, as performances quite obviously drew on stereotyped depictions and understandings of Negroes as both cognitively and physically disabled by enacting compulsive, out-of-control physical as well as verbal utterances. These performed disabilities were entwined with and structured people's understandings of blackness. Garland-Thomson writes, "To borrow Toni Morrison's (1992) notion that blackness is an idea that permeates American culture, disability too is a pervasive, often unarticulated, ideology informing her cultural notions of self and other. Disability—like gender—is a concept that pervades all aspects of culture: its structuring institutions, social identities, cultural practices, political positions, historical communities, and the shared human experience of embodiment" (Garland-Thomson 2013, 327). It should come as no surprise, then, that disability pervades blackface minstrelsy, which, as Eric Lott notes, "*was* the racial politics of the time" (Lott 2013, 17).

Beginning with "Jim Crow," the variety of disabling conditions that were performed in blackface was extensive. Rice transferred much of the embodied performance rhetoric he developed for "Jim Crow" to later blackface stage characters he played in his popular "opera burlesques" such as "Oh Hush" and "The Foreign Prince" (see Figure 19.3).

Rice's style was picked up by other performers and incorporated into the performance practice of early minstrel companies. The *Morning Post* described an 1846 London performance by the Ethiopian Serenaders this way:

FIGURE 19.3 T. D. Rice as the "Foreign Prince." American minstrel show collection, 1823–1947. MS Thr 556 (156), 1808–1860. Portraits in character. Harvard Theatre Collection, Houghton Library, Harvard University.

> The gentleman with the "bones" is quite marvelous in his power of face and rapidity of digital execution. Never were bones denuded of their covering so eloquent—from the soft piano to the potent forte—indeed every *nuance* of sound were [*sic*] given accompanied by an appropriate exertion of limb and grotesqueness of feature . . . Besides various negro melodies, heard for the first time, there were selections from *Fra Diavolo, La Sonnambula, Leonora*, and other operas, but so changed from their original proportions, and withal so sweetly harmonised, and so neatly executed, that we were doubtful of our auricular identity. In fact, these inspirations of Auber, Bellini, and Beethoven took strange shapes and acquired features distorted and unreal as shapes conjured up by a vinous vision. But we are fascinated from all considerations but the "bone articulater"—we positively dreaded a general dislocation of the dark gentleman's anatomy. ("Ethiopian Serenaders" 1846)

Here, the author moves from a fascination with the grotesque body of the bones player to observing the "strange" shapes and "distorted" features of the operatic arrangements before returning to the bones player's anatomy (see Figure 19.4).

The kinds of disabilities performed on stage would come to include those of form and appearance, motion (both "crippled" embodiment and impediments of speech), and intellect. There is also a significant body of minstrel songs and skits topically concerned with disabilities associated with age. And finally, the music performed at minstrel shows was often heard as awkward, out of balance, numbingly repetitive, or, simply, as noise.

The fact that jump "Jim Crow" involved the spectacular performance of disability remains largely unscrutinized. Scholars have tended to structure their analyses around racial phenotypes like skin (by exploring the meanings of whites donning burnt cork to play black on stage), speech (by reading the stage acts and lyrics preserved in songsters and sheet music), gender (female roles were played by men in drag), sexuality (particularly masculinity), or class. I aim to put disability in dialogue with these categories of analysis and show how the performance of disability was an essential part of performing blackness, with or without burnt cork. In other words, rather than privilege disability as a category of analysis—over class, race, gender, or sexuality—by claiming that jumping "Jim Crow" was *really* "about" performing ability or that various stigmatized identities can be productively subsumed under the disability umbrella, I seek to attend to ways these categories were related. How did the performance of a grotesque, disabled Other work to construct white bodies while simultaneously feminizing black men and defusing the threat of black male sexuality (a favorite topic in the ever-changing verses of "Jim Crow")?[1]

Audience fascination with "Jim Crow" was not passive, as reports of all sorts of people adopting Rice's grotesque embodiment to jump "Jim Crow" while they sang the song demonstrate. An anonymous account from 1855 points out the pervasive interest in "jumping Jim Crow" in the daily lives of ploughmen, merchants, professionals, young women, and other otherwise "normal" members of the public:

> The ploughman checked his oxen mid-furrow, as he reached ["Jim Crow's"] chorus, that the poetic exhortation to 'do just so,' might have the action suited to the word.

FIGURE 19.4 Ethiopian Serenaders, American minstrel show collection, 1823–1947. MS Thr 556 (61). Harvard Theatre Collection, Houghton Library, Harvard University.

> Merchants and professional men, to whom a joke was a sin, were sometimes seen by the eyes of prying curiosity in private to unbend their dignity to that weird and wonderful posture . . . and of the extraordinary sights which the writer of this article has in his lifetime beheld, the most memorable and noteworthy was that of a young lady in a sort of inspired rapture, throwing her weight alternately upon the tendon Achilles of the one, and the toes of the other foot, her left hand resting on her hip, her right, like that of some prophetic sybil, extended aloft, gyrating as the exigencies of the song required, and singing Jim Crow at the top of her voice. Popularity like this laughs at anathemas from the pulpit, or sneers from the press. The song which is sung in the parlor, hummed in the kitchen, and whistled in the stable, may defy oblivion. ("Negro Minstrelsy—Ancient and Modern" 1855)

James Kennard wrote in his widely cited 1845 essay, "Who Are Our National Poets?":

> From the nobility and gentry, down to the lowest chimney-sweep in Great Britain and from the member of Congress, down to the youngest apprentice or school-boy in America, it was all:
>
> "Turn about and wheel about, and do just so,
> And every time I turned about by jump Jim Crow."
>
> Even the fair sex did not escape the contagion: the tunes were set to music for the piano-forte, and nearly every young lady in the Union, and the United Kingdom, played and sang, if she did not *jump* "Jim Crow." (Kennard 1845)

Similarly, Eric Lott (2013) begins with the following quotation from the *New York Tribune*:

> It was at this epoch that Mr. T.D. Rice made his debut in a dramatic sketch entitled "Jim Crow," and from that moment everybody was "doing just so," and continued "doing just so" for months, and even years afterward. Never was there such an excitement in the musical or dramatic world; nothing was talked of, nothing written of, and nothing dreamed of, but "Jim Crow." The most sober citizens began to "wheel about, and turn about, and jump Jim Crow." It seemed as though the entire population had been bitten by a tarantula; in the parlor, in the kitchen, in the shop and the street, Jim Crow monopolized public attention. It must have been a species of insanity, though of a gentle and pleasing kind. . . . (Lott 2013, 3)

These accounts, and others like them, begin to make clear that white people in the 1830s performed "blackness" by doing a stylized cripple dance and jumping "Jim Crow" in the course of their everyday lives—professional performers one might see at the theatre presumably did it better, and in blackface. "Jim Crow's" body would become a synecdoche for the Southern Negro ("Ethiopian") and the model for later minstrel characters such as "Sambo." The performance of disability was thus central to the pleasure and spectacle of jumping "Jim Crow"—the song and dance did its cultural work through the ritualized performance of a broken, comically crippled body. This cultural work included displacing anxieties about race, class, sexuality, and disablement while constructing normatively embodied, privileged white subjects through the act of imitating a crippled, black body. As a performative act, "Jim Crow" both represented contemporary understandings of and anxieties about race, class, gender, and disability while simultaneously constituting those understandings and anxieties through both theatrical and quotidian bodily performance.

Not only the dance but also the accompanying music may be thought of as an embodiment of disability. It has been variously described as "quite clumsy," a "patchwork," a "balderdash," and "a filthy abortion" (Cockrell 1997, 78, quoting contemporary sources). Cockrell refers to "Jim Crow" as "antimusic" as "noise," and argues that the song "functions much like sound in almost all ritual theatricals, all of which flaunted their antimusical quality" (78). He then writes that "'Jim Crow' was not at all the way music was supposed to be. It was music for the croaking voice and the wild fiddle; the tune is awkward, repetitive and even boring; the texts are disjointed, generally nonnarrative, and unrealistic" (80–82). In fact, the defective music of "Jim Crow" closely mirrors the disabled characteristics of the dance. "Jim Crow's" affective pleasure was rooted in its musical as well as embodied nonnormativity and awkwardness.

As I've noted, everyday people jumped "Jim Crow" at the chorus of the song. And given that printed editions of the song could have as many as sixty verses, there was both numbing (for some) musical repetition as well as the pleasurable physical performance of disability built into every verse/chorus cycle. The mania to jump "Jim Crow" provides a vivid example of how music can be understood in embodied terms, supporting Joseph Straus's argument "that disability is among the bodily experiences that music and discourse about music may be understood to encode" (Straus 2006, 121–122). "Jim Crow" as antimusic helped define what it was so clearly not: the *prototypical* nineteenth-century American song, even as blackface minstrelsy became widely regarded as America's first national music.

It is important to consider why what is arguably the most popular song of the first half of the nineteenth century so strongly deviates from the formal properties generally considered inherent in a "good" popular song. In "Who Are Our National Poets?," Kennard qualifies the tired observation that "Negroes are a musical people" by asserting that the songs blacks sang were formally confused. He wrote, "The love of music and song is characteristic of the race. They have songs on all subjects; witty, humorous, boisterous and sad. Most frequently, however, specimens of all these classes are mingled together in the same song, in grotesque confusion. Variety is the spice of the Negro melodies" (Kennard 1845). The "grotesque confusion" presumably inherent in the music of African Americans was, by the time of Kennard's writing, an integral part of blackface song repertoire. It is not a stretch to think of the musical structure of "Jim Crow" as an ascription of disability.

In their introduction to *Bodies in Commotion: Disability and Performance*, Carrie Sandahl and Philip Auslander write,

> The notion that disability is a kind of performance is to people with disabilities not a theoretical abstraction, but lived experience. The dramaturgical metaphor of identity

> construction, first described by sociologist Erving Goffman as the "performance of everyday life" and more recently by philosopher Judith Butler as "performativity," is familiar to postmodern and poststructuralist scholars, but the notion that disability, too, is performed (like gender, sex, sexuality, race, and ethnicity) and not a static "fact" of the body is not widely acknowledged or theorized. (Sandahl and Auslander 2005, 2)

Some recent scholarship on blackface emphasizes the paradoxical fact that it is largely "about" the performance of whiteness, that is, about defining and enforcing a concept of whiteness in contrast to the visibly constructed figure on stage (Roediger 1991, Saxton 2003). In the same sense, jumping "Jim Crow" can be thought of as a performance of ablebodiedness, defining that category by a vigorous demonstration of its apparent opposite. Ironically, this performative representation of disability places severe physical demands on the performer—a test of his bodily abilities—and Rice himself had to stop jumping "Jim Crow" because of physical limitations. He ended his career performing the relatively sedentary role of Uncle Tom in one of the countless stage adaptations of Stowe's novel.

However, neither was the performance of blackface solely a construction of race nor was the performance of "Jim Crow" solely a construction of ability: "Jim Crow" was intimately concerned with class and sexuality, and jumping "Jim Crow"—performing a disability understood as an outward mark of an presumed inner flaw—was a bodily performance of "normality" (whiteness, ability, and usually maleness) that, when enacted in everyday life as opposed to in the theatre or at the circus by professionals, transcended the context of blackface performance. In this context, nonprofessional white performers could embody "blackness" through dancing "Jim Crow's" nonnormative embodiment (and presumably by adopting a dialect while singing the verses). In formal theatrical performance, "Jim Crow's" disability defused both the individual and collective threat of black male sexual potency (and of course threat to white women) and aggression.

The "able" performance of disability runs parallel to the complicity between white audiences and white blackface performers, who, as Annemarie Bean asserts, used

> color as a mark of social inclusion, for the minstrels and the audience know that everyone onstage is blackened by burnt cork, not by race. The wink to the audience is based in the mutual understanding that we (the performers) are different from you (the audience) but only because we (the performers) are putting on the show, an act, a minstrel show in blackface. This knowledge—that everyone is "shady," but no one is truly "black"—is an important distinction in deriving pleasure for the white audience and white performers. (Bean 2001, 172)

It was the pairing of enactments of disability and race that gave jumping "Jim Crow" the frisson among whites of all classes to make it the key metaphor for the construction of the nineteenth-century "nigger" in the United States, exemplified by its adoption as shorthand for the comprehensive set of laws enforcing segregation after the Civil War. It may seem peculiar that despite the crude blacking-up and outrageousness of his performance, Rice's "Jim Crow" was frequently understood as an accurate representation of the Southern American Negro. The celebrated American music critic John Sullivan Dwight argued in 1861 (recalling performance[s] decades earlier) that Rice's

> representation of the negro of modern life must be set down as an important item in that course of ethnological instruction which . . . is given to the body of people at places of public amusement." Jim Crow, he argued, was "The sort of negro who forms an element of modern American life; and the hideous laugh, the wild gestures, and strange dialect with which they [were] regaled by the celebrated "Jim Crow Rice," produced in them such a novel mixture of wonder and delight that they could not do less than fall down and worship their eccentric instructor. (Dwight 1861)

An earlier observer wrote in 1835,

> Mr. Rice does, to coin an expression, *out negrofy* all Africa; he is certainly a stone coal disciple, a charcoal apostle, and a real lamp black ambassador, and all who have seen his truly Ethiopian *grin* will readily admit it . . . but how is it that a genteel white man can so completely identify himself with the Buckamoor character, and at once transform his person, physiognomy, attitude, and motion into the character he represents, I believe no one north of the Mediterranean can account; and with all the burlesque, no one indelicate expression or action can be discovered. ("Jump Jim Crow" 1835)

Writing of a T. D. Rice performance, the *Knickerbocker* "found it crammed, from pit to dome, and the best representative of our American negro that we ever saw, was stretching every mouth in the house to its utmost tension. Such a natural gait!—*such* a laugh!—and such a twitching-up of the arm and shoulder! It was THE negro, par excellence. Long live JAMES CROW, Esquire!" ("Editor's Table, The Drama" 1840). Eric Lott (2013) uses this excerpt to argue that, "Distensions and all, this comic strategy was vital in generating salacious interest in 'our' Negroes. Such responses, moreover, point to the affective origins of racist pleasure—the degree to which the scarifying vision of human regression implicit, for whites, in 'blackness' was somewhat uneasily converted through laughter and humor into a beloved and reassuring fetish" (147). While the *Knickerbocker* review certainly points to the affective origins of racist pleasure, Rice's performance style was not just a comic strategy (although there is a long history of people playing disability for laughs). For it was his performance of disabilities—his wild gestures, crippled gait, crooked shoulder—that was the most important element of his presentation of this "scarifying vision of human regression." "Jim Crow's" distensions were what made him *both* funny and scary. To further complicate the picture, many presumably reliable witnesses, as we have seen, understood Rice's performances to be accurate representations of reality. Because "Jim Crow" is an example of a complex cultural product, there is no need to reconcile these audience responses: "Jim Crow" worked simultaneously as object of racist pleasure and ridicule, scarifying vision, and "truthful" representation.

The Jacksonian era was contentious and turbulent. Many Northern whites were actively transitioning from artisanal or farm work to working-class industrial jobs (eventually calling themselves "wage slaves," or "white slaves") and they saw wealthy Northern capitalists as well as Southern Negroes as threats to their livelihood. One of the anxieties of working-class people was the increasing threat of acquired disability that came along with industrialization. Indeed, the US census began counting "cripples" in 1830. It then began counting "lunatics" and "idiots" in 1840 (the numbers were fudged to show vastly more insane African Americans in the North than in the South). As Nielsen notes in *A Disability History of the United States*, one of the central concerns of the early republic was ensuring that the bodies and minds of its voting citizens were capable. She writes, "Political theorists contrasted idiots, lunatics, women of all races, people of indigenous nations, and African Americans with those considered worthy of full citizenship" (Nielsen 2012, 50). The idea that African Americans were defective and therefore unfit citizens was endlessly performed in Jim Crow and other early blackface acts, and these performances became popular at the precise moment that categories such as "normal," "cripple," "lunatic," and "idiot" were moving to the forefront of American public discourse.[2] Through the ascription of disability to African Americans, blackface minstrelsy actively maintained racial hierarchies and was a major participant in discourses of race and biological fitness.

Notes

1. Garland-Thomson asserts that "the non-normate status accorded disability feminizes all disabled figures" (1997, 9).
2. On the construction of "normalcy" in the United States and Europe during the nineteenth century, see Davis (1995), especially chapter 1, "Constructing Normalcy."

References

"An Old Actor's Memories." 1881. *New York Times*, June 5.

Baynton, Douglas. 2001. "Disability and the Justification of Inequality in American History." In *The New Disability History: American Perspectives*, edited by Paul K. Longmore and Lauri Umansky, 33–57. New York: New York University Press.

Bean, Annemarie. 2001. "Black Minstrelsy and Double Inversion, Circa 1890." In *African-American Performance and Theater History: A Critical Reader*, edited by Harry Justin Elam and David Krasner, 171–191. New York: Oxford University Press.

Brooks, Daphne. 2006. *Bodies in Dissent: Spectacular Performances of Race and Freedom, 1850–1910*. Durham, NC: Duke University Press.

Cockrell, Dale. 1997. *Demons of Disorder: Early Blackface Minstrels and Their World*. New York: Cambridge University Press.

Davis, Lennard. 1995. *Enforcing Normalcy: Disability, Deafness, and the Body*. New York: Verso.

Dwight, John S. 1861. "Nigger Minstrelsy in England." *Dwight's Journal of Music* 29 (14): 98—99.

"Editor's Table, The Drama." 1840. *Knickerbocker* 16 (1): 77–90.

"Ethiopian Serenaders." 1846. *Morning Post*, January 20.

Garland-Thomson, Rosemarie. 1997. *Extraordinary Bodies: Figuring Physical Disability in American Culture and Literature*. New York: Columbia University Press.

Garland-Thomson, Rosemarie. 2013. "Integrating Disability, Transforming Feminist Theory." In *The Disability Studies Reader*, 4th ed., edited by Lennard J. Davis, 333–353. New York: Routledge.

Higginbotham, Evelyn Brooks. 1992. "African-American Women's History and the Metalanguage of Race." *Signs* 17 (2): 251–274.

Hutton, Laurence. 1891. *Curiosities of the American Stage*. New York: Harper & Brothers.

"Jump Jim Crow." 1835. *New Orleans Bulletin*. Reprinted in *The Daily Cleveland Herald*, August 13.

Kennard, James. 1845. "Who Are Our National Poets?" *Knickerbocker* 26 (4): 331–341.

"Letter from Jim Crow." 1837. *Spirit of the Times: A Chronicle of the Turf, Agriculture, Field Sports, Literature, and the Stage* 7 (28): 217.

Lott, Eric. 2013. *Love and Theft: Blackface Minstrelsy and the American Working Class*. New York: Oxford University Press.

Mitchell, David T., and Sharon L. Snyder. 2000. *Narrative Prosthesis: Disability and the Dependencies of Discourse*. Ann Arbor: University of Michigan Press.

Nathan, Hans. 1962. *Dan Emmett and the Rise of Early Negro Minstrelsy*. Norman, OK: University of Oklahoma Press.

"Negro Minstrelsy: Ancient and Modern." 1855. *Putnam's Monthly Magazine of American Literature, Science, and Art* 5 (25): 72.

Nielsen, Kim E. 2012. *A Disability History of the United States*. Boston: Beacon Press.

Roediger, David R. 1991. *The Wages of Whiteness: Race and the Making of the American Working Class*. New York: Verso.

Sandahl, Carrie, and Philip Auslander. 2005. *Bodies in Commotion: Disability and Performance*. Ann Arbor: University of Michigan Press.

Saxton, Alexander. 2003. *The Rise and Fall of the White Republic: Class Politics and Mass Culture in Nineteenth-Century America*. New York: Verso.

Straus, Joseph N. 2006. "Normalizing the Abnormal: Disability in Music and Music Theory." *Journal of the American Musicological Society* 59 (1): 113–184.

Wendell, Susan. 1996. *The Rejected Body: Feminist Philosophical Reflections on Disability*. New York: Routledge.

CHAPTER 20

DISABLED MOVES

Multidimensional Music Listening, Disturbing/Activating Differences of Identity

MARIANNE KIELIAN-GILBERT

Among the tasks of philosophy is to adequately distinguish between these nuanced differences or multiplicities, to ascertain how one difference (of degree) covers over and hides another (in kind), and to show what is left out, what is unrepresented or uncharacterized about differences in kind, differences of nature, in our dominant scientific and philosophical frameworks which focus on quantitative differences.

—Elizabeth Grosz[1]

I'm not anti-medication; I'm pro-choice. Hearing voices is like left-handedness; it's a human variation, not open to cure, just coping.

—Eleanor Longden[2]

In Eleanor Longden's claim (epigraph), hearing voices became a "pro-choice" swerve, partaking of potentials of human variation—dissolving the fixity of identity conditions in difference and differentiation (hearing voices, left-handedness)—and giving place to various strategies of coping, adapting, and acting. In such experiential situations, how is it that the potential diversity of human-bio responses often goes unnoticed or unregistered?[3] The critique of Disability Studies self-consciously draws on and destabilizes identity politics; that of multidimensional music listening disturbs and activates difference in kind or degree from angles of bodily vividness and connectedness.

How, or do listeners' senses of identification, variability, and experience in a body (including mind) shape music experience ("what something feels like")? How does music draw forth the aural "recognitions" that register its socially relational and bodied temporal experience? If music and music experience are more than internal representation and symbol manipulation, how might one flesh out and understand their multidimensionality?

In three sections with intervening variations this essay describes "disabled moves" toward that question by imagining and disturbing what it might mean to think and be through the variant body. I consider disability experience in diverse modalities to call attention to problems of exclusively resisting or embracing difference (or sameness) as a basis of identity. In the first section, I give attention to the implications of the unexamined and assumed centricity of the abled body and the kinds of material-bodily-mental interventions that might unfix or jostle (musical) identity with respect to that centricity. The second section takes up "disabled moves" in thinking about the potential and limitations of medical and aural metaphors in Ethel Smyth's Concerto for Horn, Violin, and Orchestra (1926–1927). Three variations intervene to juxtapose aesthetic situations of different experiential modalities as a means of highlighting differential embodiment through silence, sound, and listening, and values of insecurity, vulnerability, and interdependency.

In the third section, in staging musical "theatres of madness," I juxtapose descriptive listening accounts of Marta Ptaszyńska's "Thorn Trees" from her Concerto for Marimba and Orchestra (1985) and suggest a multidimensional approach to analysis that works with side-by-side encounters and the critical potential and desire for change. Throughout, questions of "whose experience," "whose body," and "who's listening-understanding" come to the fore: difference makes no sense without the continua of affective environments, their overlapping interdependencies, and the vividness of their sensory/worldly creative/material extensions. The idea is that the (multi)dimensionality of music and music experience (bodily-mind feeling) disturbs difference and identity toward emergent processes and conditions—mixing flesh and context, embodying and enacting, and thinking and feeling degrees of difference.

Disabled Moves, Disturbing/ Activating Differences of Identity

> *[V]oice hearing as a creative and ingenious survival strategy, a sane reaction to insane circumstances, not as an abstract symptom of illness to be endured but as a complex significance and meaningful experience to be explored.*
>
> —Eleanor Longden[4]

We are not aware of the consequences of claiming human exceptionalism or of the unexamined centricity of able-bodiedness until taking a turn that opens a condition, idea, or concept to the "disabled." By this turn, I mean the twist toward an enactment of bio-human variety, the potentials of variation and extension, and the continua of wellness and biological/sexual extravagance. I draw on philosophical ideas that both support and critique a politics of identity and bodily experience, toward moves and processes that disturb, destabilize, and dissolve identity in difference and differentiation.

The turn toward difference in disability involves the variability and diversity of human, biological, and material life—toward more differentiation and difference, not less.

Feminist and disability scholar Rosemarie Garland-Thomson has located disability rights in principles of biodiversity and human variation and argued for "an identity politics that would reimagine disability as human variation, a form of human biodiversity" to be accepted and embraced (Garland-Thomson 2011b, 603). Critiquing the formulation of capability in relation to individuals (606), she approaches disability as a "co-constituting relationship between flesh and environment" (594).[5] The relational and contingent (unstable) aspects of differential embodiment—and "the materialization of identity and subjectivity as perpetual, complex encounters between embodied variation and environments" (602)—expose "the myth of autonomy" (599). Bodies act in and interact with environments; they are "always situated in and dependent upon environments through which they materialize as fitting or misfitting" (598). For Garland-Thomson, the misfitting (or fitting) of individual with environment constitutes material and social interactions that place "vulnerability in the fit, not in the body" (600).

Construing disability in terms of sociocultural construction points up the relation of *fixity* to disability as positioned in relation to the unquestioned status of ableism as an ideological requirement of the disability/ability system.[6] Fixity, the drastic restriction of mobility, marks the experiential content of disability in one form or another—limitation, restriction, immobility, damage, deformity, a counterpart to unquestioned notions of ableism or exceptionalism. Medical approaches tend to locate disability within an individual as an atypical condition in relation to norms of physical ability; psychological accounts may construe disability as the product of a misguided or bad attitude; religious accounts seek a cure, align it with suffering, and/or tout disability as evidence of divine power, or as an avenue of salvation for the nondisabled (Braidotti [1996] 1999). Political approaches may tend to stress equality under the law or exclusionary practices without critiquing the conditions that preserve the disability/ability system.[7] That is, classifications that posit perfection or completeness without critique tend to uphold the dominant aesthetics of affect.

Music theorist Joseph Straus has written about how particular kinds of embodiment can be associated with responses to music hearing. He describes a range of hearing that can be regarded as prodigious or disablist, the latter group including skilled adaptive abilities of blind, deaf, mobility-inflected, or autistic hearing (Straus 2011). Both Garland-Thompson and Straus register the ways that thinking of disability in relation to potentials of human variability allow for diverse forms of being and becoming in the world (in contrast to thinking from notions of loss, deficiency, or pathological condition). Linking the medical model with "a fundamental distinction between the normal and the abnormal" and notions of the abnormal with deviations from a statistical norm or normative standard (2011, 7), Straus credited the work of Disability Studies and the disability rights movement toward theorizing disability as a sociocultural construction, defining disability as "any *culturally stigmatized bodily difference*" (9, italics in original). In this orientation Straus stresses the notion of "difference" as "deviation from whatever is understood as normal at a particular time and place" (9). This and other significant work in Disability Studies makes possible the shift in critique that eschews the abled body as norm such that difference itself acquires strategic potential for critique.

Relatedly and alternately, I consider how the words "disabled" and "disabling" might draw attention to disturbing and dispersing the unquestioned identity and centrality of able-bodiedness and how asymmetries of power are inextricably linked with preserving that centrality. Here I follow Jasbir Puar, who has called for "slightly" shifting from " 'reclaiming' the singular as well as ordinary capacities of disabled bodies and questioning the enforced normativity produced by abled-bodies" to deconstruct "the presumed, taken-for-granted capacities-enabled status of abled-bodies" (2009, 166). This moving off-center investigates the implications (vividness and connectedness) of differential embodiment, rather than regulating or settling identity through comparison, resemblance, replication, or the analogy of one thing to another. That is, this shift disturbs (and skews) ideologically fixed standards/norms and hierarchies of a system of ability/disability operating through relations of opposition and comparison. Differences of identity destabilize and emerge through "counterintuitive" ideas of "failure," debility, and disability in a tensional background of silence. Differentiation (from *differentiāre*, to distinguish or constitute the difference in or between) becomes the temporally changing and unstable play of difference apart from and without preexisting terms. Becoming temporal, self and other cease to be absolutes: "insistently rendering bare the instability of divisions between capacity-endowed and debility-laden bodies" (Puar 2009, 169) and thereby the implicative connections between abelism and inequities of power and distribution (see Erevelles 2011).

The discursive and material potentials of the becoming infinitive "to disable" align with processes of destabilization and enaction in creative production. By contrast, as adjective, the term "disabled" suggests individual or fixed physical conditions and works as a descriptor to an apparently steady-state-of-affairs in bodies and social hierarchies. Avoiding the fixing (and romanticizing) of disability affects the broader economic and regulative power structures that support and maintain that oppression. Both fixing and romanticizing tend to eschew protection and support and to deny underlying social and material conditions that might intervene in changing oppressive structures.

Without capacities to affect and be affected, social and music-aesthetic bodies are eviscerated of their potential to shape and be shaped by the different contexts they inhabit. Individual and communal histories empty. In *The Queer Art of Failure* (2011), gender studies scholar Judith/Jack Halberstam criticized neoliberal ideas of American exceptionalism and its attendant platitudes that success and failure are consequences of attitude rather than structural conditions. For her, and such writers as Elizabeth Grosz (2011) and Nirmaia Erevelles (2011), encountering the possibility and potentiality of insecurity, indeterminacy, and failure creates situations whereby "a negative thinker can use the experience of failure to confront the inequalities of everyday life in the United States," producing "shade and light in equal measure [in which] the meaning of one always depends upon the meaning of the other"

(Halberstam 2011, 4, 5). By this "counterintuitive" idea of failure Halberstam called attention to ways that "the under-privileged category actually sustains purposive and intricate modes of oppositional knowledge, many of which can be associated with and linked to forms of activity that we have come to call 'queer' " (2008, 140). Critiquing the romanticization of identity constructs, and pursuing connections between categories of difference, Erevelles (and Puar and Grosz) stress the impact of their mediation in material (economic/social), global, historical, and political dimensions.

The insecurities of an "art of failure" disturb the "fixing" of identity. Differentiation fuels the desire *to move*: outside representation, past and present zones of habit stretch and open to new capacities and incapacities, bio-human variation, and sexual extravagance. Desires also "fail," by internalizing forces (social, economic, material, bodily) that maintain the very restrictions that produce discrimination and marginalization (see Erevelles 2011, 6, 10 and passim).

Music disabled becomes incomplete; open-ended; in flux; socially, materially, and bodily-mind contingent; mixing aesthetic and social-material sensibilities—it becomes multidimensional.

> The lemon is extended throughout its qualities, and each of its qualities is extended throughout each of the others. It is the sourness of the lemon which is yellow, it is the yellow of the lemon which is sour. We eat the color of a cake, and the taste of this cake is the instrument which reveals its shape and its color to the alimentary intuition. . . . each quality through the others; and it is this total interpenetration which we call the *this*. (Jean-Paul Sartre)[8]

Intervening Variation 1: Silence and Taking Time to Listen

> *[T]his caring labor is also affirming. Because it resembles a hug, the lift that allows a caregiver to transfer my sister or me from one seat to another makes the caring aspects of assistance tangible—the lift literally looks like an expression of love. . . . I believe that the forms of knowledge and experience gained from living with significant physical dependency and vulnerability have wider social significance. . . . [S]elf-sufficiency is never about oneself, but about ourselves, about us.*
>
> —Park McArthur[9]

Artist Park McArthur's *It's Sorta Like a Big Hug* is a short video study of corporeal movement and stillness that honors the sensibility of what Amanda Caccia has described as, "what it means to think and be through the variant body."[10] A subject in her own film, "McArthur had a friend record one of her experiences of being cared for by a collective of friends in her New York City neighborhood."[11] Included as the epigraph to this section, McArthur (2012) speaks of the look and feel of the labors and interdependencies of caring and being cared for.

This video study is also a "music" experience of a sensibility of discernment of body–mind interactions, and in its "performance," care transforms and becomes interdependency in critique of the affects of neuroscientific, biological, and aesthetic reductionism. McArthur's "critique" proliferates discernment as a differentiation crucial to life and to evolving interdependencies. No sooner do particular alignments of identity and difference settle, however, than they begin to stretch and morph and disperse into tangents and diagonals, into new and changing combinations.[12] The fragility of potential also highlights situations where access avails to a privileged few, and where (an)other may simply not be present on the map.

Disabled moves pursue the openness and incompleteness of differential embodiment, asking *what* an actuality, an awareness of, or a thinking that incorporates, some sense of physical impairment, limitation *and* potential, *feels like* (for myself, yourself, others), and *how* that feeling experience confronts, and undoes, divisions between physical and mental, mind and feeling. This listening/discerning embraces the vulnerability (insecurity, interdependency, openness) of not knowing how to listen to music-sound against silence: an awareness of what is at stake in removing music from senses of feeling, materiality, relationality, concrete/lived history. Not knowing exactly how to listen to music-sound in or against a background/setting of a silence of utopia, silence of ignorance, silence of bodied feeling, silence of presence; silence of potential. When prior orientations are highlighted as such and questioned: when prior meanings are challenged in cognitive dissonance, percepts change (the word "green" colors "red"); self-reflexive moments enter the midst of performance and artifice. This kind of "silence" sounds another. . .wrenchingsoundfromsource. . .returningsourcetosound. . .returningsound to body to sound. Amid overwhelming "existence," the silence of potential emerges and survives as a faint flickering. A flickering that requires skewed aesthetics—slanting, twisting, angling, bending, stretching, tweaking, tilting, spraining, wrenching, contorting, and warping encounters to register the experience of human-bio variability.

The potential to work without prior terms and concepts thus sets against the pragmatics of material, physical, social, and class conditions of being or not being able to do so. Disabled moves avoid assuming the progress of conventional forms of individual agency (eschewing neoliberal naturalization, the essentialism of progress, and narratives of triumph over, or of overcoming adversity, questioning unquestioned assumptions and habits). In that silence, corporeal-mental care and interdependency come to the fore in effort and intensity, energy and fatigue, joy and grief, perseverance, rest and adaptiveness, and inventive sociality and relationality.

Hearing/Listening/Feeling in the Bones

Artistic practices enter the side-by-side, or sideways angles and imaginings of lived practices of sexual-biological-physical and social diversity. How might one construe their material correlates or understand listeners' structural-expressive-artistic-analytical-experiential observations outside *and* in relation to the constraints of ideologically regulative practices of identity (disability, sexism, ageism, racial, ethnic, physical discrimination)? How or do material-social-physical conditions divert into veiled communication and indirect language, or become condensed in figures such as the "ear trumpet" or in the particular silences of written or performed utterances (such as ellipses) that gather unspoken and unheard meanings?

Ethel Smyth confronted increasing deafness and continuous tinnitus in tandem with regulative practices of gender and the homosocial "closet" (see Wood 1995 and 2009). Eve Kosofsky Sedgwick (1990, 1–2) has trenchantly pointed out the contradictions in theorizing gender and sexuality—here I include disability—as issues relevant to a "minority' " group and/or as relevant and significant for people "across the spectrum of genders and sexualities." These contradictions garner further valence with questions of differential embodiment, the variabilities of physical-mental capacities, and lived experience (what does it feel like to inhabit overlapping milieus?).

In her account of Ethel Smyth's multiple compositional settings of her anthem "The March of the Women" over the course of her artistic work, musicologist Elizabeth Wood (1995) evoked the sonogram as metaphor and "aural" mode of investigation. For Wood, the figure of the sonogram offered a way of imaging "the invisible" and "the inaudible" (1995, 606), making "corporeal echoes" visible, "just as sonor detects, measures, and alerts its listeners to underwater shapes and presences" (ibid.).

Noting the invasive use of sonic (medical) technology in master narratives of power over women's bodies (under ideologies of abuse, repression, and detection), Wood also asked what music-cultural constructions can be "accessible through our sensory experiences of music sound" (607), especially in sensing experiential qualities and rhythms that resist or motivate representation both in discursive and musical terms. In choosing a "medicalized" metaphor, she sought both to expose and to recuperate sonic and somatic reverberations of music through specific bodies (gendered, female, queer)—in sonic-somatic contexts "enlivened and eroticized, as well as stilled and silenced by sonic orderings and inscriptions" (608). If the sonogram as medical metaphor has potential to sound the "corporeal echoes" of Smyth's musical practice, it is by swerving from medicalizing behavior as a means of social control, that is, measuring, isolating, or attempting to "cure" behaviors thereby marked as deviant.

By contrast, in later work (2009) Wood presented an account of Smyth's "unending torture" and "despair over the deterioration of her hearing" (33), noting that composers such as Beethoven, Faure, Smetana, and Vaughn Williams responded differently to traumas brought on by increasing conditions of deafness. Smyth's hearing loss came slowly and intermittently, becoming more serious and frequent during the war and intensifying after 1918 "after she almost died in a hospital in England of double pneumonia and pleurisy" (34). Wood detailed the steps and treatments Smyth took to halt "the intense strain of deafness and 'terror of composing' " (36), her mounting despair, and the booming in her ears—a situation Smyth lamented, "My 'good' ear never stops the chimney roaring sound" (38). Tinnitus presents "the loss of *internal* silence," and necessity for negotiating constant noise as "alien sounds within . . . ringing, hissing, booming, pinging" (42).[13]

Wood speculated that "[c]onducting, as a kind of 'conductive' hearing, may have been for Smyth a compensatory activity" (47) by which she was able to "guide and interpret by gesture and speech although disabled from 'hearing' her own voice in music" (ibid).[14] Wood addressed these experiential discontinuities between perceived, imagined, and remembered sound as the "tripled counterpoint" (2009, 49) of Smyth's embodied experience of negotiating the din of music-sound in her work.

In comparable material-social conditions, Ethel Smyth composed the Double Concerto in A for Horn, Violin, and Orchestra in 1926–1927 (aged 69–70). Wood's empathetic account of Smyth is no narrative of heroics but one of plausibility that enables listeners to construe the multidimensionality of music-sound by keeping multiple variables and entry points in play.

Music also figures imaginary worlds, even as music's concreteness impinges on those imaginations. Smyth had strong and dramatically passionate relationships with women in her life, usually older women, and often already married. Why would such relational-social configurations, or her experience of increasing deafness and tinnitus, have no implication (imagination) for the music's "concreteness," its material and imaginary spaces and relational and expressive possibilities as potentially actualized and coconstructed by listeners?

Intervening Variation 2: Becoming More, Abundance, Excess, Invention

> *Becoming, and dispersion, spatial and temporal elaboration, are part of the "nature" of any thing, entity, or event. Becoming means that nothing is the same as itself over time, and dispersion means that nothing is contained in the same space in this becoming. . . . [D]ifference is the undoing of all stabilities, the inherent and immanent condition for the failure of identity, or the pressure to develop a new understanding of identity that is concerned not with coinciding the subject with its past so much as opening the subject up to its becoming-more and becoming-other.*
>
> —Elizabeth Grosz[15]

Like the affects and "excessive expenditures" of sexual appeal and attraction, artistic/aesthetic affects arise from intensification, abundance, and excess and from the chaotic, unpredictable, and contingent. Beyond functional obligations, in art, intensity is also excess for its own sake, for how and what it intensifies, and for its interdependencies, irreducible to preexistent norms or rendered in one-sided service to a collective.

Artist Sunaura Taylor "uses her background as a disabled person whose disability was caused by US military pollution and her life long dedication to animal ethics, to explore issues of value, suffering and person-hood . . . [and] expose the parallels between how animals and disabled people are treated, metaphorically co-opted, valued and devalued."[16] This kind of juxtaposition and side-by-side thinking relates to the musical juxtapositions and "theatres of madness" that I take up in the final sections of this essay. Bearing these juxtapositions in mind, Alison Kafer's perceptively sensible essay "Seeing Animals" offers an experiential account of "noticing" Sunaura Taylor's painting *Animals with Arthrogryposis* (2009). Kafer entangles Taylor's insistence that "we read her alongside these animals" (i.e., her image in *Animals with Arthrogryposis*) and her placement of her and their animal-human bodies in the frame of the painting (see Figure 20.1).

Both Taylor and Kafer wonder "what we're willing to take the time to see"; Kafer includes sentences from Taylor's untitled sound piece and observations on the collection of drawings and photograhs Taylor has assembled "animal to animal; freak to freak . . . [e]ven as she places her mark on these images, reclaiming and reworking them, she remains faithful to their origins" (Kafer 2009). Provocatively Kafer asks, "What does it mean to be ghosted, disappeared from view?" How or does Taylor's painting both disturb and/or activate difference through side-by-side exposures and juxtapositions of mixed identities?

Music analysis often begins by determining position or positioning within a grid-like system of preexisting coordinates of a sound world (permutations within a definitional framework). In contrast experiencing music's multidimensionality elicits a transformation in the qualitative experience of time and temporal process that cannot be reduced and from which "new" sounds and ideas emerge. No longer simple presentation or representation, a crucial aspect of this transformation is enactive, a "shifting into

FIGURE 20.1 Sanaura Taylor. *Animals with Arthrogryposis*, Oil on canvas, 2009, 6' × 9' (72" × 108"), 2009. Painting by Sanaura Taylor. Photo courtesy of David Wallace.

performing," the forming of a critical move "toward performative expressivity and away from objectifying music as a text, that is as a passive bearer of qualities" (Kielian-Gilbert 2010, 221):

> Music embodies (intensionally infolds) the complex of ways that sensing occurs as both artifice (the aesthetic, composed and constructed) and as real/literal/veridical doing (enactment and experience). Analysis of becoming music becoming process taps into the latter of these counterparts (differing) as a way of understanding and experiencing the first (being). (221)

The question is how musical processes of change and transformation—of emergence—can embrace musical encounters of things and events and figure bodily-material-social processes of doing/enaction.[17]

For Deleuze-Guattari ([1980] 1987) as philosophy is the art of creating and inventing concepts, so music is the art of creating and inventing percepts, forging the experiential (material-temporal) in the differential. They thus critique the functional reduction of parts to a "whole." Virtual-potential gives rise to the actual through an irreducible triad of concepts, percepts, and affects that work in, on, and through the middle, and toward the future (becoming, emerging, etc.). The Deleuze-Guattarian "becoming" engages temporal-experiential processes linking virtual to actual, a transforming-metamorphosing of form (in differential forming, they are more than, or not restricted to, linguistic formulations).[18]

Philosopher Adriana Cavarero, drawing in part on the work of feminist philosopher Luce Irigaray and political theorist Hannah Arendt, presses philosophy to incorporate the relational dynamics of experiencing the materiality of the voice (Cavarero 2005). For Cavarero, an awareness of "voice" and vocal expression makes available an intersubjective sensing and articulation of affect (presence). Though Donna Haraway (2007, 30) critiques Deleuze and Guattari (1987, ch. 10) for their avoidance of concern for animals and their apparent reduction of relational connections between pets and their families to "sentimentality" (e.g., unable to account for relations such as curiosity, emotional exchanges, or respect for differences, Haraway 2007, 27–35), these philosophers find common ground in the potential of bordering and relational connections and encounters. If Deleuze and Guattari seem to favor wild undomesticated encounters (e.g., an animal relationship with animals), significantly they also zero in on connections (assemblages) and contagions (becomings) that are not exclusively restricted to one or (an)other realm (e.g., art figures animal-like territories and zones of indiscernibility, see Grosz 2008). That is, "difference" makes no sense without a human-bio continua of affects (capacity and debility) and without mixes and overlapping interdependencies (double articulations). How might one allow for these kinds of affects and overlaps in music experience and analysis?

Multiplying Mediums, Feeling Transforming

As shown in the diagram of Figure 20.2, the first movement of Ethel Smyth's concerto projects three thematic ideas in three mediums: orchestra (measures 1–18/21), violin (mm. 22–50/51), and horn (mm. 52–72/73): these articulate the first three sections of the exposition (and the musical ideas marked in Figure 20.3). (A recording of this music may be found as Track 20.1 on the Companion Website). The horn conceivably was the instrumental timbre and character aligned with projections of Smyth's persona: its voice draws on an eros and personal memories of associations with hunt and chase, drama and distance with the deeper, darker, richer, and brassy coloring and resonance of its timbral voice (Smyth herself played the hunting horn, but her Concerto would have been played on a valve horn with its limitless possibilities for modulation).[19] The middle register of the horn is the warmest; in contrast, the violin projects a singing voice with possibilities for moving fluidly between and among different registers of activity. The orchestra does more than set a dramatic stage or backdrop for the soloists to engage the musical drama of the concerto, it also figures the potential of other sounding personas, for example, as articulated in the exposition and recapitulation by both horn and violin. In listening *for* (and in the vividness of these mediums of exchange), the multiple disabling-sensing (i.e., differentiating) of *aural* musical processes emerges. I briefly consider four of these processes in the first movement of Smyth's concerto focusing on their potential for experiential/material and temporal transformation.[20]

The following "disabled moves" initiate musical structural-expressive processes that complexify and disturb identity by alternating (oscillating between or dwelling in) contradictory and/or overlapping conditions of musical difference. The encounters, exchanges, and "disorders" of musical difference mutually implicate, or provide ironic markers for listener engagement (or vice versa).

Move 1: consider the morphing of previously distinct timbrally associated themes (see for example, Theme 2 in the exposition, recapitulation, coda), that is, the exchange of timbral roles in different registers and the role of continuing or linking melodic patterns through timbral combination, continuity, and connection. Listen for example, as the setting of Theme 1, timbrally individuated in the exposition, becomes "recomposed" in the recapitulation (R23-2 = R23 minus 2 measures, m. 169) as Violin (2 bars), to Horn (2 bars), to both instruments in contrapuntal combination (IV harmony, 2 bars), to both instruments in octave doubling in contrary motion against the orchestra.

Move 2: consider the semitonal shifting and reorienting (for example, G♮ vs. G♯; F♮ vs. F♯) across the first movement that calls into question the status of one element of the pitch/pitch-class shift as hierarchically prior or superior. Here I have in mind the "work" (laboring) of particular semitonal relationships in melodic intensification (queering): the oscillation or movement between G♮ to G♯ over the course of the movement, and particularly in slippages from the minor or major modal coloring, the hearing of a particular harmony (for example, A: e minor/E major: G–G♯), or processes of linking or melding harmonies via common-note relationships (for example, E♭ major/A♭ major/A major: G–A♭/G♯–A).

Orchestra, mm. 1-18/21: Orch. Th. (21 mm.)

Reh.				1		2		
mm.	**1**	**3**	**5**	**7**	**11**	**15**	**17**	**18**
spans	2 +	2 +	2 /	4	4	2	2	1 (ov) + 3 (intro)
A:	I	V/IV	I /	bVI	WT!	IV V64 – i		V
Bass	A	A	A-G	F-C B E-D	C#	D C	C –B-F- E	
Hns.				X---------	-X			

Violin, mm. 22-50/51: Th. 1 (30 mm.)

Reh.	3				4			5		6
mm.	**22**	**24**	**26**	**28**	**30**	**32 34**	**38**	**39**	**42**	**50**
spans	2 +	2 +	2	2	4	4	1 +	2 2	8 (ov) + 1 (intro)	
A:	I	V/IV	IV		6th	6th	6-4	V		I
Bass	A	A	D C#	B	A#	A G-(G#)	A	E	(G-G#)	A
Hn.			X------------	------	X				(violin cad)	

Horn, mm. 52-72/73: Th. 1 (22 mm.)

Reh.					7	8			9
mm.	**52**	**54**	**56**	**58**	**60**	**63**	**66**	**69**	**71 73**
spans	2 +	2 +	2	2	3	3	3 +	2	2 1 (intro)
A to e min:	I	V/IV	IV	fm!-am=iv N			V	+6	V----- VI
Bass	A	A	D	E C-F	A	C G	D- Bb-B	C	C B C
Vl.				X--------	X			(horn: tag)	

Th.2 (Violin & Horn) (31 mm.)

Reh.	10	11	12	13		14	
mm.	**74**	**80**	**86**	**92**	**96**	**99**	**102**
spans	2 2 2	2 2 2	2 2 2	2 2	3	3	3
e min	VI	VI=V/F	N	V	o7 iv	(V) i	
Bass	C D-G-G#-A	C	F	B		A-A#-B-E---(plagal)	
Instr.	Vl.	Hn.	Vl.	Orch. Clos.Th.	Vl. (tag)	Hn/Or (tag)	Hn/Vl Codetta

Development [R15-3 – 20+2] (27mm. + 16 mm. 'quasi-cadenza' at R18) (mm. 105-132) [G-G#] F#-B min (D: vi), Eb maj (D: N – o7/V – IV- i64 – V42/V -+6 – i64, quasi-cadenza), o7ths (Eb-A; F-B; F#-C), C#-B-E (=V)

Recapitulation :				(=R2)	(R3)		(R10)	(R13)	**Coda:**		
Reh.	R20+3	21		22	23 24	25	26	28	30	31	33
mm.	**148**	**154**	**158**	**162**	**169**		**191**	**203/09**	**222**	**230**	**241**
Th.	**Orch (21)**				**Th1 (22)**		**Th2 (26)**	**CL**	**Th1**	**[G-G#-A]**	
spans	6 +	2 2	4	4+3 (intro)	8 3	6 + 5	6+ 6	13	8	11	7
A:	I V/IV I	bVI	WT!	IV V42 – i	V I	iv	I iv	iv			I
Bass	A A	A-G F--------C#		D	C-B-E-A D		F Bb	A		E	A
Hns.	Vl & Hn	Vl	Hn Vl & Ans. new!	Hn-Orch	Vl & Hn	Hn (tag)	Vl&Hn comb. Then orch	Orch, Vl, Hn (tag)			A plagal

FIGURE 20.2 Ethel Smyth, Concerto for Violin, Horn, and Orchestra (1926–1928), first movement. Formal diagram.

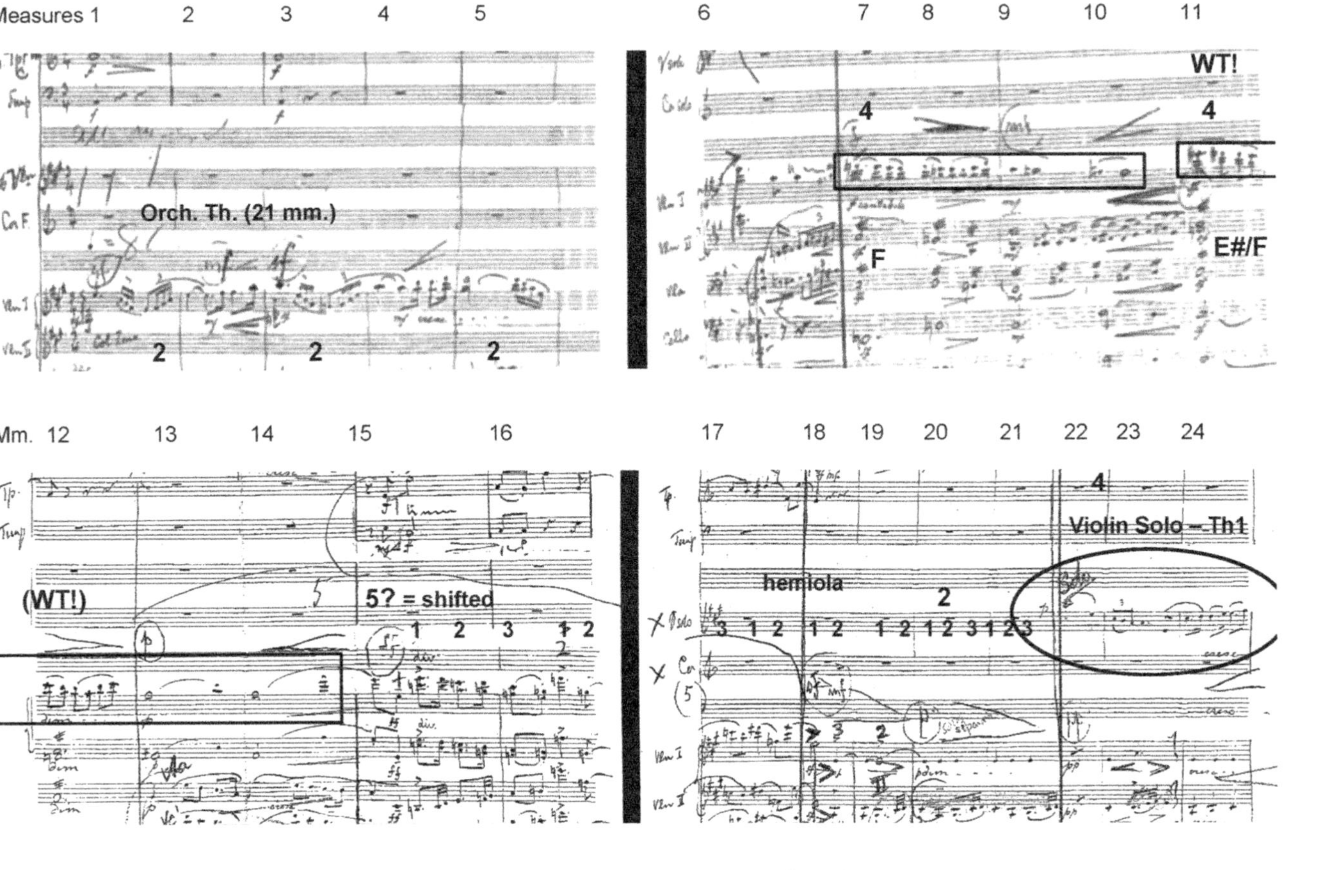

FIGURE 20.3 (a) Ethel Smyth, Concerto for Violin, Horn, and Orchestra (1926–1928), first movement, mm. 1–88.

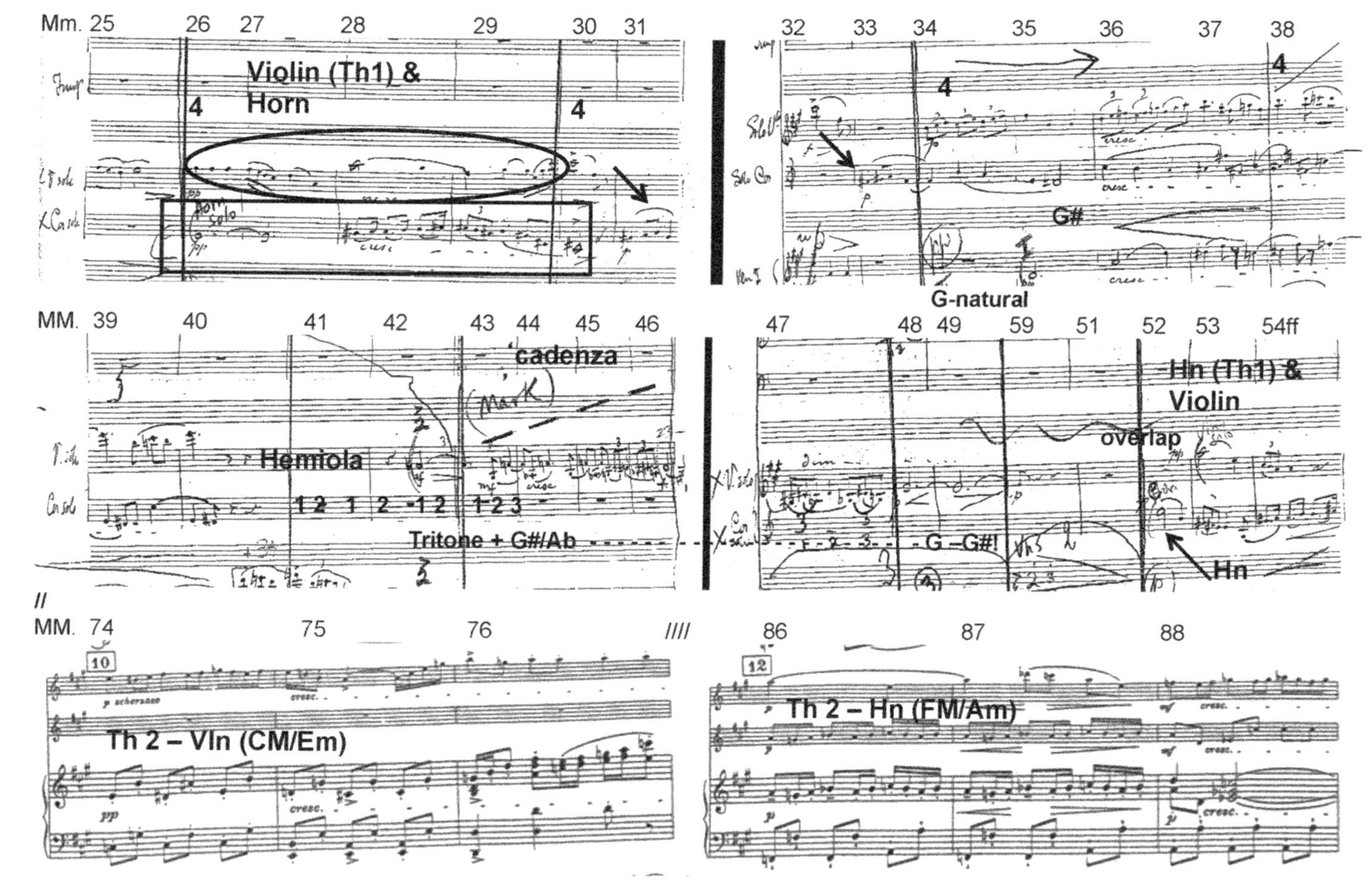

FIGURE 20.3 Continued.

Move 3: consider the shifting between alternately subdivided melodic spans in "dominant" or "subdominant"/plagal coloring, each with a qualitatively different experiential feel (for example, in contrasting implications between melodic divisions (A: A–E–A) or (A: E–A–E, etc.). These differential presentations of vocal and instrumental melodic spans, for example, alternate between melodic spans bounded by the tonic scale degree (e.g., A: A–E–A) and those that figure "plagal" or "whole-tone" ambiguities or substitutes, for example, as bounded by scale degree ^5 (e.g., A: E–A–E). This shifting also involves morphing orientations in relation to scale degrees ^1, ^5, and ^4 (e.g., A: D–A–E), refiguring scale degree ^1 in relation to its relational potential equidistant as lower or upper fifth relation to scale degrees ^5 and ^4 (e.g., A: D–A–E), in plagal orientation (A: A–D–A), or in a whole-tone environment (A: F–E♭–C♯–B–A–G–F).

Move 4: complicating metric and rhythmic regularities by hemiola patterning in successively ordered versus simultaneously layered patterns (from 3 + 3 to 2 + 2 + 2); by metric displacement of a particular rhythmic patterning (see dotted rhythmic figures); or by duple versus triple subdivisions or formal groupings. Also consider the differential presentations of dotted rhythmic figures across the movement in mixing relative degrees of "character" in development.

Such descriptions are not adequate to the visceral tangible materialities and affects of morphing themes, shifting and (re)orienting semitones or melodic spans, and/or complicating and differential patterns of duple versus triple patterning. These "moves" work in their potential connection and association with temporally/materially transforming conditions of difference (differential embodiment) in varying experiential milieus. Whether directed by distinctions in technical music processes, biographical orientations, listener settings, and/or sociocultural representations, disabled moves shift from taking theory and discourse as the *representation*, or fixing of things, to enacting and activating their being and doing in the aesthetic world. These "performances" cross and traverse the lines that seemingly separate and divide genders, sexualities, and physical conditions, transforming subject, object, and frame, putting into play the potentials of variation, by extensions human-biological and musical.

Intervening Variation 3: Unforeseen Consequences

The superhero thriller *Unbreakable* (M. Night Shyamalan 2000, United States) stars Bruce Willis as David Dunn, and Samuel L. Jackson as Elijah Price, superhero and archvillain, abled and disabled, moral and amoral, respectively, and their "white" and "black" associations. The film develops connections between the real world and the comic book world of superheroes. Elijah Price was afflicted with genetic Type I osteogenesis imperfecta, a rare disease in which bones break easily. At the end of the film Price the psychopath has covertly wondered if he is frail at one extreme, perhaps there is someone "unbreakable" at the opposite extreme.

The film portrays his early youth in which he confronts fear and isolation as protection for and from his condition: "They call me Mr. Glass at school because I break like glass." In one of the most gripping scenes from the film (the falling down stairs scene), Elijah attempts to follow David down into a subway entrance; moving as fast as he can down the subway steps, his foot catches on a step, his hand slips from the railing and we see him fall, his bones cracking as he tries to stop the fall, then landing in anguish and upside down.[21]

We are plagued by a kind of reverse voyeurism—music fragmented into snippets and sound bytes, commercialized, and connected to just about everything we see, taste, touch, and smell. The fragmentation plays us and our perceptions as well. In contrast to attention spans fixated obsessively, they are obsessively shortened. Our technologies do our listening for us, jettisoning or diminishing aesthetic experience, containing or immobilizing it and us in other ways. How might one convey the tangible, material, and performative multidimensionality of music experience in a climate that tends to bypass individuals (and individual music making)?[22]

In "YouTube experience" famous scenes like these may become disabled in a different sense; they undergo scrutiny and mash-up. The start of the fall in one individual's "sound re-arrangement" of this particular scene remixed "Elijah's fall" with the sound clip of the "call to arms" theme of the National Football League for televised Sunday NFL football (see note 22 above). Subsequent viewer comments registered outrage, laughter (what a ridiculous combination!), laughter (it's only a movie), dismay (this has ruined my favorite scene), thumbs up (results in the perfect choice of music-sound for making the scene funny). In what world could these two contexts possibly occur (why would anyone want to make this scene "funny")? And is shock (shock value) the primary way to effect social critique and change? How we choose to experience and express music is also social action. Highly contingent, disabled moves have unforeseen consequences. In the following section I propose a musical "theatre of madness" using side-by-side exposure to highlight and critique degrees of complicity and oppression (broadly and locally).

Theatres of Madness: Whose Experience, Whose Body, Who's Listening-Understanding?

> *Beside comprises a wide range of desiring, identifying, representing, repelling, paralleling, differentiating, rivaling, leaning, twisting, mimicking, withdrawing, attracting, aggressing, warping, and other relations.*
>
> —Eve Kosofsky Sedgwick[23]

Music's productive affects and "performative actions" encompass relational dimensions of "bordering" (Kielian-Gilbert 2011). These call for practices of listening in-between, "in the middle," and "on the edge." Listening becomes an act of attention, an effort to hear toward music's productive affects, resisting and refiguring its and our structural containment and objectification, living in the middle. In order not to reinscribe or reinvest the terms of music-social critique, the challenge of listening and analysis is to allow for the critical potential of affect without foreclosing incompleteness, indeterminacy, or disregarding despair and exhaustion: music's multidimensionality arises in the tensions of its aesthetic, experiential, and social-political values.

The following analyses of Marta Ptaszyńska's "Thorn Trees" draw on the political-social activism of Susan Jahoda's "Theatres of Madness" (1995): these are side-by-side visual juxtapositions or superpositions that enable something felt in the intervening "silences" of discontinuities, namely the critical potential and desire for change. Jahoda (1995) presented a series of images of physical disability in juxtaposition and collage format, pairing and layering various source materials to produce visual "theatres of madness." According to Jahoda, such "theatres" ensue in the interstices and dislocations of the images. In their side-by-side juxtapositions, they call attention to "relations that overdetermine the internalization of oppression and, in turn, the degrees of complicity and resistance to that oppression" (1995, 253).

Marta Ptaszyńska, Concerto for Marimba and Orchestra, 1985–1986, 3rd movement, "Thorn Trees" (theme and seven variations).

In the third movement of her Marimba concerto, titled "Thorn Trees," composer Marta Ptaszyńska develops a sense of "motion" as precarious balance between sound force and sound motion, that is, between the static additive iteration of single notes or chords and their melodic releases and extensions). According to the composer:

> The third movement was inspired by the surrealist painting *Thorn Trees* by British painter Graham Sutherland. . . . The painting depicts thorn trees which are portrayed with rough shapes on relatively motionless and passive green background. The painting evokes a mood of horror and fright. In my music this mood is achieved with the energetic repetitions of acute chords, and with the centralized and decentralized energy of sound motion. (Briscoe 1999, 300)

British painter Graham Sutherland (1903–1980) experienced the horrors of World War II directly, working as one of Britain's Official War Artists from 1940 to 1945. In 1945 he undertook a study of photographs and documents of the concentration camp victims at Auschwitz, Belsen, and Buchenwald (Alley 1982). In 1945 he also worked on a series of paintings in which rendering thorns became a symbolic experience of the Crucifixion and the crucified head—the thorns suggest barbs of cruelty aesthetically mocking pain, torture, death, and suffering.[24] The thorns "sprang from the idea of potential cruelty."[25] See Figure 20.4.

FIGURE 20.4 Graham Sutherland, *Thorn Trees* (1945). Oil on canvas (127 × 101.5 cm). © Estate of Graham Sutherland Courtesy British Council Collection.

The painting projects apparently "natural" objects within a dislocated framework, one in which the thorns multiply in fantastic entanglements—encircled protrusions, seeds enmeshed in brambles, with the threatening and overpowering extensions of thorns, flowers, and leaves. The precariously balanced renderings of color are further destabilized in *Thorn Trees* as they trespass the formal boundaries of representational images (trees, trunks, brambles, thorns, leaves, and fruit). Colors liquefy and flow over boundaries; green, yellow green, and brown, and white and blue, form alternate continuities, their permeable qualities at times covering and infiltrating the image shapes. These flows of color facilitate the tension and precarious balance between representational form and geometric shape (vertical lines, points, curves, and circles), between boundary and space, and between line and outline (volume).

The "analysis" I created, a video-music encounter of the "Tema" and "Variation 4" (see Figure 20.5), focused on the contrasts of impulsively articulated single-note iterations of the "acute chords" (single-note reiterated notes) and their melodic extensions, "centralizing and decentralizing the energies of sound motion" in the theme (*Tema*, Figure 20.6) and the fourth variation (Figure 20.7). (Recordings of the *Tema* and the fourth variation may be found as Tracks 20.2 and 20.3 on the Companion Website).

I shaped a brief experiential/experimental video in two segments each with differing aesthetic and ethical entanglements: the segments present and perform music examples from the "Tema" and Variation 4 (translating or paraphrasing their configuration of impulsive attacks vs. melodic extensions through accompanying text and visual images). Both segments expose in their performance the contingent nature of listening and analysis. They question the "scientific" nature of empirical observation; turning to the experiential, they suggest metamorphic processes in an "aesthetics" of attention and intensity in motion. They explore how different disciplinary, activist, or artistic interpretations might challenge our understanding of disability as experiencing perceivers—and further, notably its appropriation or use as shock value in visually (re)animating or (re)creating a musical experience of Ptaszyńska's music.

The film's visual motions of listening "out" (or "in") in metamorphic exchange, stretch sensory combination and invention. In the listening setting of Variation 4, the musical successions of impulsive articulations are visualized and articulated in real-time performance by x-ray medical images of genetically mutated "bones with additional bone spurs" (musically articulated as instances of physical "thorns") and juxtaposed with an image of body as burnished surface (Weston 1925, *Nude*, platinum print). The visual contrasts of impulsive iterations and melodic extensions enact expressive aesthetic interventions of contrastive conditions: namely, the "thorns" of rare bone disorders, multiple osteochrondoma and fibrodysplasia ossificans progressive, against the aesthetic deferral of the "original" Sutherland painting in interaction and displacement with the image of a smooth physical surface, a photographic segment of a burnished bodily surface, image by Edward Weston, in *Nude*, 1925 (Platinum print).

In what senses and settings does this multimodal analysis differ from the previous example that attempted to make the "Falling Down the Stairs" scene from *Unbreakable* seem "funny"? Do my listening "rearrangements" of these passages present a related set of aurally voyeuristic issues? What assumptions underlie the following discursive account as more or less affective/effective and in what contrast to my rendering (also an appropriation), an imagining of an experiential context of the pain or misfitting of the material "thorns" of these physical conditions? Under what artistic-experiential conditions can these images do aesthetic work?

In composer Marta Ptaszyńska's "Thorn Trees" (theme and seven variations), the precarious balance between sound force and sound motion interacts with the play of formal processes of iteration and continuation, the static additive iteration of single notes or chords and their melodic releases and extensions. The *Tema* and Variations 1–3 present sixteen

Part 1/video 1:

A. "Tema" (Theme) of the third movement. Music-sounds with text and score example of the Tema. Kaija Saariaho, *Jardin secret II* (1984-86) (Jukka Tiensuu, harpsichord)

Text-sound: "The Thorns sprang from the potential idea of cruelty."

Text-sound: "What is most important for me [Ptaszyńska] in composition is the deep aesthetic experience and then the technical realization of that content."

Text-Tema: *Sounds grip, circumscribe, move, inextricably entwine soloist and orchestra: sounding and performing; sound and performer; sound doubling marimba; marimba playing through sound. Sounding four's, twos', static harmony, iterations! Marimba, an identity configured through sound!*

B. "Tema" (an "articulated" performance in rhythm). Sounding articulations verbally and rhythmic groupings in tempo [eighth note = 144], recite, accenting the '1's in each of the following eighth note groups of the Tema: ***1234***, 123123,***1234***, 121234, ***1234***, 12, ***1234***, 123123, ***1234***, 12123, ***1234***, 123412345, ***12***, 121234, 12345, ***12***.

Part 2/video 2:

C. "Thorn Trees, " 4th variation, 1st section (Music: "Allegretto" with score example)

Text: [Simi Linton 1998, 5]: "the material that binds us is the art of finding one another, of identifying and naming disability in a world reluctant to discuss it, and of unearthing historically and culturally significant material that relates to our experience."

Visual: xray osteochrondoma bone, spine, unnamed patient

Visual: Xray: xray, osteochrondoma bone -- unnamed patient, knee front

Ptaszyńska: score, 4th variation, 1st section, continued

Visual: Xray: osteochrondoma bone -- unnamed patient, knee front

Ptaszyńska: score, 4th variation, 1st section, continued

- Graham Sutherland, *Thorn Trees*, zoom in
- Xray: unnamed 12-year-old patient, Fibrodysplasia ossificans progressiva (FOP), a single mutation in a gene (ACVR1): tendons, ligaments and skeletal muscle painfully transformed into bone

Ptaszyńska: score, 4th variation, 2nd section ("Allegretto," also score example 2)

- Xray: unnamed patient, osteochrondoma, knee side, zoom out
- Edmund Weston, *Nude*,1925, zoom out
- FOP xray, zoom out
- Edward Weston, Nude, 1925, zoom out
- Xray: multiple osteochrondoma, *femur*
- Graham Sutherland, zoom out

Ptaszyńska: 4th variation, 2nd section, zoom out

FIGURE 20.5 Marta Ptaszyńska, Concerto for Marimba and Orchestra (1985/86), third movement, "Thorn Trees" (set of variations): Tema (Theme) and Variation 4 (& video 1 & 2:music-sounds—images—texts).

FIGURE 20.6 Marta Ptaszyńska, Concerto for Marimba and Orchestra (1985/86), third movement, "Thorn Trees" (set of variations). Tema: Allegro molto leggiero e staccatissimo. Permission courtesy of Marta Ptaszyńska.

measures in two sections of irregularly additive groups in the functional/rhythmic arrangement of (A: x x y) and (B: x x y y). Each pattern features static "harmonic" iteration (sound force) followed by melodic extensions (sound motion). Significantly, at the end of the *Tema* and Variations 1 and 2 the chord is linearized as a melodic pattern that concludes with an end-accented upbeat. In Variation 3 this end-accented upbeat shifts to a downbeat orientation, paralleling the shift to a new complex of pitch relations around D in Variations 3–6.

Variation 4 strikingly articulates a world of dream and suspended melodic motion suggestive of liquefied colors and surfaces. This is the first variation for which the marimba and trumpets articulate more extended quasi-ad libitum improvisatory melodic patterns in the sonic surface. In this variation the percussive reiterations of the "acute chords" (marked "X") alternate with ad libitum patterns, taking the sensibility of contrast to a new and broader temporal level within the variation itself. The music-sonic world of this variation and its surrealist dreaming evoked the visual x-rays of bone on bone to mark the onset of each set of percussive attacks in contrast with the burnished photographic (anonymous, metonymic) bodily surface.

(Musical) descriptions and renderings like that earlier, or as shown in Figure 20.5 as one listener's listening setting of "Thorn Trees"—or as discussed earlier as a background of "compensation" that might direct a listener's listening to Smyth's Concerto—contrast to conventional descriptions of music that preserve its "neutrality." Discourses (whether artistic, linguistic, material and/or embodied) seek particular performative settings, and realizations of differential embodiment are more than simply "free associations."

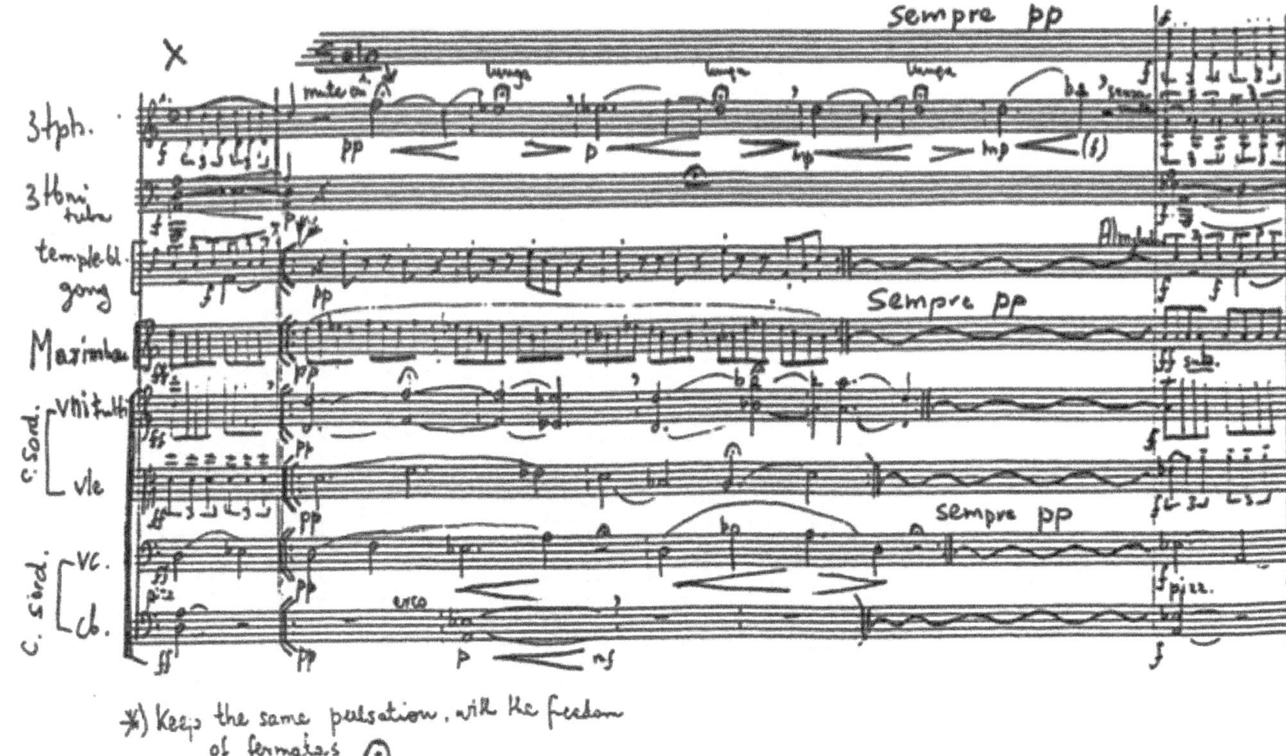

FIGURE 20.7 Marta Ptaszyńska, Concerto for Marimba and Orchestra (1985/86), third movement, "Thorn Trees" (set of variations). Variation 4: Allegretto con anima. Permission courtesy of Marta Ptaszyńska.

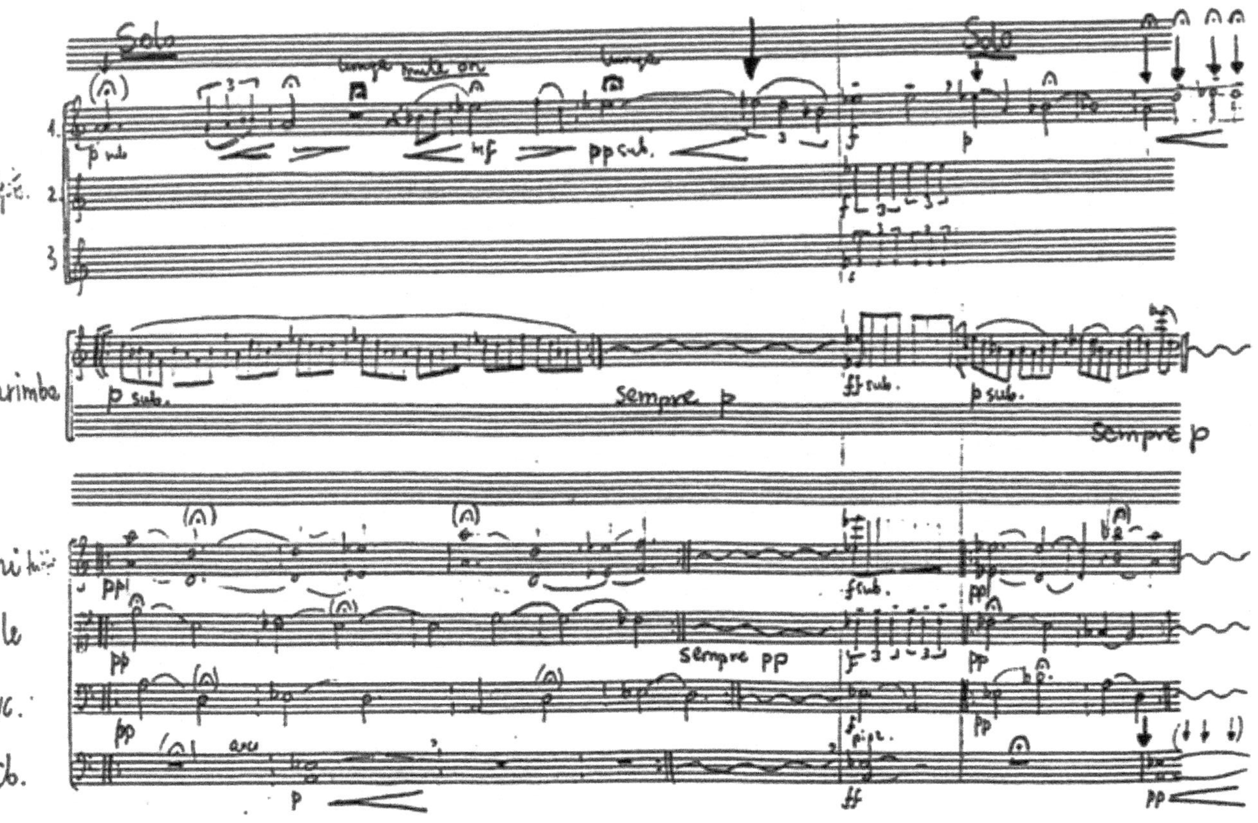

FIGURE 20.7 Continued.

In the "silences" of the discontinuities of side-by-side juxtaposition, degrees of awareness, complicity, and resistance to that performance and its social-material contexts come to the fore. The idea is that descriptions and settings of all types are or can be *performative*, recreating through enactment or context musically expressive affects felt at particular (heightened) levels and thus as visceral experience. The performative materializes something tangible—voice, breath, sound, articulate in flow, flesh encountering environment, creating sound and silence, performer and performance, poet-composer and listener.

My critique of listening to "theatres of madness" suggested the significance of connecting rhetorical voice to the material-structural-expressive conditions of differential embodiment to which stylized expression (artifice, performance) gives voice. Such "spaces" of association and experience (what it feels like) work in and in relation to the artistic or listening subjects who inhabit and implicate them. They also have the contingency (specificity, difference, excess) to escape context and thereby to mark and influence it, and thus to call attention to specific material and sonic dimensions of affect and feeling. The extravagance and excess of the performative (touching the psychic-physical embodiment, enaction, and feelings that fuel listener involvement) do more than ruffle the reflective apparatus that we are accustomed to bring to music experience.[26]

As this essay has suggested, individual voices interact from different modes and angles of experience forming side-by side pairings and cross-pairings: Eleanor Longden/ Rosemarie Garland-Thomson; Park McArthur/Amanda Cachia; Ethel Smyth/Elizabeth Wood/and myself; Sunaura Taylor/Alison Kafer. In spurs of dialogue and social action, listening-feeling deep "in the bones"—these "theatres of madness" activate rather than compare. "Side-by-side," they disturb identity in, and as, difference that cannot be constructed away: for example making vivid, settings of Elijah Price "falling down the stairs scene" in the film *Unbreakable* and of Tema and Variation 4 in composer Marta Ptaszyńska's "Thorn Trees."

"Disabled moves" disturb the difference of music identity, presenting "problems" that confront preformed categories of judgment and "choices" that affect and are affected by experiences of action, interconnection and interdependency. In ever-changing aesthetic capacities, we may imagine and experience such inordinate desires as creatively productive and no less relevant to our capacities to encounter and transform life situations and lived experience.

Notes

1. Grosz 2004, 161.
2. This and subsequent studies evoke multiple voices, sensory-physical orientations, and the productivity of "disabled moves" in disturbing/activating differences of identity (Longden 2014). Also see Hall 2012.
3. Jasbir K. Puar (2009) has argued for a "move away from self-other constructs of normality and pathology" and for understanding the way in which "populations are constructed through prevailing ideas of variability and risk" (165). For ideas of "dissolv[ing] identity

into difference" see Grosz 2011, especially ch. 6 ("Differences Disturbing Identify: Deleuze and Feminism," 88–98).

4. Eleanor Longden. "Learning from the Voices in My Head," YouTube video, 6:30 (July 5, 2010), https://www.youtube.com/watch?v=AgZHOSxN5cE.
5. It is important to note that the legal definition of disability distinguishes the legal application from other limiting physical-mental conditions. See for example the AAUP report "Accommodating Faculty Members Who Have Disabilities" (2012, 5): "It is useful to bear in mind that the term disability has a technical, legal meaning. . . . A disability is a long-term physical or mental impairment that significantly impedes an individual in performing an activity that is of central importance to life."
6. In my essay "Beyond Abnormality" (2006), I stressed the relation of fixity to disability in social and philosophical terms and with implications for music experience and analysis. The term "disability/ability system" is Rosemarie Garland-Thomson's (see 1997 and 2011a).
7. In contrast, Rosemarie Garland-Thomson has drawn attention to disability as a necessary dimension of the human condition and as differentiated historically in traditions such as the medical-scientific, religious, and political (see Garland-Thomson 2012, 342–350).
8. On *thisness*, on experience, see Sartre (1943) 1992, 186.
9. McArthur 2012, 164, 166, and 168.
10. See Cachia, n.d., and Park McArthur, "It's Sorta Like a Big Hug," Vimeo.com video, accessed May 2013 and later removed. For audio descriptions by Park McArthur and Alicia Kielczewska, visit http://exhibits.haverford.edu/whatcanabodydo/media/#.
11. Amanda Cachia, 6 of 16.
12. See the arguments posed by disability scholar Joan Corbett (2013) for naming one's relationship to Disability Studies. She enjoins scholars of Disability Studies to call out their relationships to Disability Studies as a political statement of alliance and solidarity. In support and by contrast, Nirmala Erevelles (2011) warns that fetishizing disability as a marker of transgressive difference can obscure formulations of disability as a product of material, social, and historical conditions, in particular, making "the case for a reintroduction of a class analysis in Disability Studies . . . by exploring the complex relationships that exist between disability and other categories of difference (i.e., race, gender, and sexuality) and between the disabled and nondisabled world when (re)constituted by transnational capitalism" (2011, 5–6).
13. Wood noted that, "By 1931, at the age of seventy-three, Smyth no longer even tried to compose, but she did continue writing articles and books. By then, old friends and new acquaintances described her as very deaf, her speech strident and repetitious, her appearance disheveled and dress grubby, and her behavior often belligerent and rude" (2009, 40).
14. Also see Baynton (2008) on the distinction between Deaf and deaf cultures and the material reality of occupying "a different sensory world from those who hear, and [that] has certain consequences that cannot be constructed away" (295). Though he does not address the experience of the onset of deafness, he calls attention to the "vocabulary of difference" rather than loss: Just as deafness brings into being new ways of using the other senses, so does any physical difference result in a new configuration of abilities" (297).
15. Grosz 2011, 97.
16. "Yelling Clinic: An Artist Collaborative," available online at http://www.yellingclinic.com/ (accessed May 2013). Sunaura Taylor's drawings include exposures in a more satirical and comical way.

17. Also see Hasty 1997. Alternately, Dora Hanninen (2012) focuses on segmentation as an analytical activity crucial to experiencing the succession of musical events in time. By interpreting repetition, segmentation, association, and categorization in sonic configurations (and "associative landscapes") arising from listening and engaging the music surface, Hanninen models "the role of association and associative organization in music in its own right and as functionally independent of—and therefore capable of significant interactions with—aspects of sonic and structural organization already addressed by existing theories" (7).
18. Deleuze and Guattari (1980) 1987; also see Kielian-Gilbert 2010. Philosophy aims toward the creative production of new ideas rather than assessing experience and knowledge or reducing difference to aspects of representation, that is, to identity, analogy, opposition, and resemblance.
19. In comparison with Brahms's Trio for Horn, Violin and Piano, Op. 40 in E-flat major, written in 1865. Brahms was writing for the hand horn, one of the last composers to do so (which might explain why the first movement of his trio is more of a divertimento without a development section, while Smyth's Concerto would have been played on a valve horn). My thanks to Linda Dempf for this information and for introducing me to this work as a horn player. Also see Woods (2009, 55).
20. Sedgwick (2003, 6) approaches the question of linguistic versus nonlinguistic phenomena with some flexibility: "I assume that the line between words and things or between linguistic and nonlinguistic phenomena is endlessly changing, permeable, and entirely unsusceptible to any definitive articulation."
21. In contrast to the externalized and internalized "sound" effects of breaking/shattered glass is the subliminal suspenseful undercurrent of small repeating melodic motives in the fall (from grace) of Samuel Jackson's Elijah character. In a scene of comparable length, as David and wife Audrey get back together after he realizes his heroic powers, David *ascends* the stairs carrying her to the bedroom. The music underscoring by composer James Newton Howard is similarly suggestive.
22. "UNBREAKABLE," uploaded by Rhey Lewis, YouTube video, 1:03 (January 31, 2008), http://www.youtube.com/watch?v=6vdToGbN3DM.
23. Eve Kosofsky Sedgwick (2003, 8) has written about the different logics of side-by-side juxtaposition: "Beside permits a spacious agnosticism about several of the linear logics that enforce dualistic thinking: noncontradiction or the law of the excluded middle, cause versus effect, subject versus object. Its interest does not, however, depend on a fantasy of metonymically egalitarian or even pacific relations, as any child knows who's shared a bed with siblings. Beside comprises a wide range of desiring, identifying, representing, repelling, paralleling, differentiating, rivaling, leaning, twisting, mimicking, withdrawing, attracting, aggressing, warping, and other relations."
24. "The Crucifixion idea . . . has a duality which has always fascinated me. It is the most tragic of all themes yet inherent in it is the promise of salvation. It is the symbol of the precarious balanced moment, the hair's breadth between black and white. It is that moment when the sky seems superbly blue—and, when one feels it IS only blue in that superb way because at any moment it could be black—there is the other side of the mirror—and on that point of balance one may fall into great gloom or rise to great happiness" (Alley, 1982).
25. The surrealist style of *Thorn Trees* (1945–1946) juxtaposed and combined elements of surrealism and naturalism: natural objects, like the settings of thorn trees in Wales, took on

strange impulsive and metamorphic forms. The flows of color facilitate the tension and point "in motion" of precarious balance and metamorphic transference between representational form and geometric shape (vertical lines, points, curves, and circles), between boundary and space, and between line and outline (volume).

26. Susan McClary (2000, 90) has described a passage of Vivaldi's Concerto Op. 3, No. 8, mm. 44–48, thus: "Vivaldi treats [that move from C major to E minor] here as a catastrophe—rather as though that cascade of C-major scales had put too much pressure on the San Andreas Fault and precipitated a disaster. The large ensemble and the soloists together accomplish this calamity and its rueful arrival on E minor in measure 47." McClary means to bring the musical effects of historical procedures and contexts home to her twenty-first-century readers, rendering music "vivid" through analogy. By contrast "disabled moves" disturb these "identities" in ways that rhetorically point to specifics of their embodied variability.

References

AAUP (American Association of University Professors). 2012. "Accommodating Faculty Members Who Have Disabilities." Accessed January 2014. http://www.aaup.org//report/accommodating-faculty-members-who-have-disabilities.

Alley, Ronald. 1982. *Graham Sutherland: Catalogue of an Exhibition Held at the Tate Gallery, 19 May–4 July 1982*. London: Tate Gallery.

Baynton, Douglas C. 2008. "Beyond Culture: Deaf Studies and the Deaf Body." In *Open Your Eyes: Deaf Studies Talking*, edited by H-Dirksen L. Bauman, 293–313. Minneapolis: University of Minnesota Press.

Braidotti, Rosi. (1996) 1999. "Signs of Wonder and Traces of Doubt: On Teratology and Embodied Differences." Reprinted in *Feminist Theory and the Body: A Reader*, edited by Janet Price and Margrit Shildrick, 290–301. New York: Routledge. Originally published in *Between Monsters, Goddesses, and Cyborgs: Feminist Confrontations with Science, Medicine, and Cyberspace*, edited by Nina Lykke and Rosi Braidotti, 135–152. London: Zed Books.

Briscoe, James R. 1999. *Contemporary Anthology of Music by Women*. Bloomington, IN: Indiana University Press.

Cachia, Amanda. n.d. "What Can a Body Do?" Essay and bibliography for the exhibition at the Cantor Fitzgerald Gallery, Haverford College, October 26–December 16, 2012. Accessed May 2013. http://exhibits.haverford.edu/whatcanabodydo/essay-bibliography/.

Cavarero, Adriana. 2005. *For More Than One Voice: Toward a Philosophy of Vocal Expression*. Translated by Paul A. Kottman. Stanford, CA: Stanford University Press.

Corbett, Joan O'Toole. 2013. "Disclosing Our Relationships to Disabilities: An Invitation for Disability Studies Scholars." *Disability Studies Quarterly* 33 (2). http://dsq-sds.org/article/view/3708.

Deleuze, Gilles, and Félix Guattari. (1980) 1987. *A Thousand Plateaus*. Translated by Brian Massumi. Minneapolis: University of Minnesota Press.

Erevelles, Nirmaia. 2011. *Disability and Difference in Global Contexts: Enabling a Transformative Body Politic*. New York: Palgrave Macmillan.

Garland-Thomson, Rosemarie. 1997. *Extraordinary Bodies: Figuring Physical Disability in American Culture and Literature*. New York: Columbia University Press.

Garland-Thomson, Rosemarie. 2011a. "Integrating Disability, Transforming Feminist Theory." In *Feminist Disability Studies*, edited by Kim Q. Hall, 13–47. Bloomington: Indiana University Press.

Garland-Thomson, Rosemarie. 2011b. "Misfits: A Feminist Materialist Disability Concept." *Hypatia* 26 (3): 591–609.

Garland-Thomson, Rosemarie. 2012. "The Case for Conserving Disability." *Journal of Bioethical Inquiry* 9 (3): 339–355.

Grosz, Elizabeth. 2004. *The Nick of Time: Politics, Evolution, and the Untimely*. Durham, NC: Duke University Press.

Grosz, Elizabeth. 2008. *Chaos, Territory, Art: Deleuze and the Framing of the Earth*. New York: Columbia University Press.

Grosz, Elizabeth. 2011. *Becoming Undone: Darwinian Reflections on Life, Politics, and Art*. Durham, NC: Duke University Press.

Halberstam, Judith. 2008. "The Anti-Social Turn in Queer Studies." *Graduate Journal of Social Science* 5 (2): 140–156.

Halberstam, Judith. 2011. *The Queer Art of Failure*. Durham, NC: Duke University Press.

Hall, Will. 2012. "Eleanor Longden on Voices and Trauma." *Mad in America: Science, Psychiatry, and Community*, July 5. Commentary on an interview with Eleanor Longden for Madness Radio, June 1, 2012. http://www.madinamerica.com/2012/07/madness-radio-eleanor-longden-on-voices-and-trauma/.

Hanninen, Dora. 2012. *A Theory of Music Analysis: On Segmentation and Associative Analysis*. Rochester, NY: University of Rochester Press.

Haraway, Donna J. 2007. *When Species Meet*. Minneapolis: University of Minnesota Press.

Hasty, Christopher. 1997. *Meter as Rhythm*. New York: Oxford University Press.

Jahoda, Susan. 1995. "Theatres of Madness." In *Deviant Bodies: Critical Perspectives on Difference in Science and Popular Culture*, edited by Jennifer Terry and Jacqueline Urla, 251–276. Bloomington, IN: Indiana University Press.

Kafer, Alison. 2009. "Seeing Animals." Essay on Sunaura Taylor's painting *Arthrogryposis Animals* (2009). Accessed May 2013. http://www.sunaurataylor.org/portfolio/animal/Seeing_Animals.pdf.

Kielian-Gilbert, Marianne. 2006. "Beyond Abnormality: Dis/ability and Music's Metamorphic Subjectivities." In *Sounding Off: Theorizing Disability in Music*, edited by Neil Lerner and Joseph N. Straus, 217–234. New York: Routledge.

Kielian-Gilbert, Marianne. 2010. "Music and the Difference in Becoming." In *Sounding the Virtual: Gilles Deleuze and the Theory and Philosophy of Music*, edited by Brian Hulse and Nick Nesbitt, 199–225. London: Ashgate.

Kielian-Gilbert, Marianne. 2011. "Musical Bordering, Connecting Histories, Becoming Performative." *Music Theory Spectrum* 33 (2): 200–207.

Longden, Eleanor. 2014. "A First Class Recovery: From Hopeless Case to Graduate." *Independent*, February 2. http://www.independent.co.uk/news/people/news/a-firstclass-recovery-from-hopeless-case-to-graduate-1808991.html.

McArthur, Park. 2012. "Carried and Held: Getting Good at Being Helped." *International Journal of Feminist Approaches to Bioethics* 5 (2): 162–169.

McClary, Susan. 2000. *Conventional Wisdom: The Content of Musical Form*. Berkeley: University of California Press.

Puar, Jsbir K. 2009. "Prognosis Time: Towards a Geopolitics of Affect, Debility, and Capacity." *Women and Performance: A Journal of Feminist Theory* 19 (2): 161–172.

Sartre, Jean-Paul. (1943) 1992. Translated by Hazel E. Barnes. *Being and Nothingness: Essay on Phenomenological Ontology*. New York: Washington Square.

Sedgwick, Eve Kosofsky. 1990. *Epistemology of the Closet*. Berkeley, CA: University of California Press.

Sedgwick, Eve Kosofsky. 2003. *Touching Feeling: Affect, Pedagogy, Performativity*. Durham, NC: Duke University Press.

Straus, Joseph N. 2011. *Extraordinary Measures: Disability in Music*. New York: Oxford University Press.

Wood, Elizabeth. 1995. "Performing Rights: A Sonography of Women's Suffrage." *Musical Quarterly* 79 (4): 606–643.

Wood, Elizabeth. 2009. "On Deafness and Musical Creativity: The Case of Ethel Smyth." *Musical Quarterly* 92 (1–2): 33–69.

PART 4

WAR AND TRAUMA

CHAPTER 21

DISABLED UNION VETERANS AND THE PERFORMANCE OF MARTIAL BEGGING

MICHAEL ACCINNO

Grinding is not generally understood as a pleasant activity. The goal of grinding an object is to crush; to pulverize; to grate against. Grinding destroys rather than creates. Perhaps seen in this light, it is unsurprising that performers labeled as organ grinders were not particularly well respected in the nineteenth century. The pejorative designation "organ grinder" entered the English language in 1792, and quickly became a term closely associated with the practice of begging and mendicancy (*Oxford English Dictionary Online*, s.v. "organ grinder"). The disabled and nondisabled performers who took up barrel organs in Europe and the United States did so in the face of heavy stigma that surrounded the sounds and practices of street music. Negative reactions to street musicians, often couched in terms of ethnic, class-based, or bodily difference, continued unabated throughout the nineteenth century.

Organ grinders have not always seemed like "our" type of musicians—that is to say, they do not conform to normative aspects or behaviors of music making. Indeed, most historical observers did not regard the performers as *real* musicians at all. Unlike legitimate musicians, who were generally understood to possess well-developed musicality, organ grinders possessed untrained ears and uncultivated sensibilities; musicians developed finely honed manual abilities, but organ grinders needed only enough dexterity to crank a pedal; musicians generally performed within the conventions of a proscenium space, while organ grinders readily performed on any street or thoroughfare.

Rather than consign organ grinders and other street musicians to a silent place in the history of nineteenth-century American music, this essay sounds out traces of these performers within post–Civil War urban spaces. Disabled Union veterans, many of them identified as men with amputated limbs, turned to barrel organs in the postwar period when northerners were intensely preoccupied with efforts to assist and employ maimed soldiers. Mostly drawn from the lower classes, these street performers staged a rhetoric of martial begging that invited audiences to pause and consider the intersection of manliness and disability. That the civilian public often responded equivocally to these encounters is well known.[1] But veterans, as well as those considered "imposter" veterans, did more than act as symbolic foils for Gilded Age notions of masculinity; loudly and without apology, they manipulated space, body, and sound to comment on the limitations of socially sanctioned legal, medical, and institutional paths to rehabilitation.

Street Music in Contemporary and Historical Practice

Building on the premise that space is a social construction, scholars in performance studies, geography, and ethnomusicology have modeled how twentieth- and twenty-first-century street performers employ alternative practices to contravene the established social and spatial patterns of streets and public places (Harrison-Pepper 1990; Kuppers 2003; Simpson 2011; Mason 1992). In her landmark study of New York City's subway performers, Susie Tanenbaum describes such music-making in public spaces as, "an urban ritual . . . promoting spontaneous, democratic, intimate encounters in one of the city's most routinized and alienating environments" (Tanenbaum 1995, 2). She further asserts that performers' co-option of subway space encourages the formation of "transitory communities" (105) that promote greater understanding across class-based, ethnic, and linguistic barriers. Similar studies of itinerant musicians frame street performances as interruptions of daily life that promote a sense of "temporary collectivity" (Simpson 2011, 423), which can ultimately foster greater group solidarity between strangers (Boetzkes 2010).

The pervasive assumption that street musicians constitute a destabilizing threat, a notion that has long colored Western thought, has thus been called increasingly into question. Sally Harrison-Pepper has critiqued the lack of nuanced treatment of street performers in historiography, suggesting, "In theater histories, anthropology texts, or urban analyses, street performance is viewed as an event that is marginal, inconsequential, unworthy of documentation, even a threat to the image of the city, established structures of commercial theater, or other businesses" (Harrison-Pepper 1990, xiv). Although this claim possesses considerable merit, we must also consider to what extent the results of participant observation of late twentieth-century street musicians can be easily transposed into historical social practices. Approached through the lenses of Disability Studies and veterans' history, another set of questions arises: How might the conspicuous presence of street musicians with disabilities alter the use of alternative social and spatial practices? Can the street stage promote greater understanding between disabled performers and nondisabled audiences? What special demands do disabled military veterans make on civilian passersby?

To further account for the cultural work that disability performed in nineteenth-century US streets, Susan Schweik (2009) has proposed an inclusive framework that indicts the underlying social categories at stake rather than the individual performers themselves. This new critical approach deconstructs cultural efforts to sort beggars from performers, the worthy from the unworthy, and real from fraudulent. Writing in more general terms about the imposter beggar, Schweik draws a provocative analogy to blackface minstrelsy: "Unsightly begging requires a kind of 'disability-face' in which participants, whether they were imposters or not, marked their bodies in stark, ritual opposition to normality, ability, and employability" (Schweik 2009, 133).

Building on Schweik's "model of social imposture" (127), this essay similarly questions the ethically suspect distinction between "imposter" and "actual" martial beggars advanced uncritically by well-meaning veterans' advocates and historians.[2] Although adopting such a stance undoubtedly risks conveying an impression of ingratitude toward the sacrifices of veterans, the inclusion of "veterans" here is both practical and obligatory if we are to acknowledge the tangible, lived realities at stake when a diverse group of performers adopts the social script of begging.

Organ Grinders in the Nineteenth-Century United States

Barrel organs, also known as hand organs or "grind organs," were first imported to the United States during the 1840s and 1850s by European immigrants. German instrument builder Franz Rudolph Wurlitzer, who set up shop in Cincinnati in 1856, helped to found a burgeoning domestic barrel organ trade based in the Northern states that reached its peak in the 1880s and 1890s (Bowers 1972, 661).[3] Drawn to the instrument's portability and the ease of operating its simple hand crank mechanism, Italian, Irish, and German immigrants continued the old-world practice of playing the barrel organ in urban street performances.

After the onset of the Civil War in 1861, disabled Union veterans began to adopt the instruments to solicit donations from Northern crowds. These ex-soldiers responded to a long tradition of similar martial performances in western Europe, particularly in German-speaking regions. As early as the Seven Years' War, Empress Maria Theresa helped license veterans to play barrel organs in Hapsburg territories (Buchner 1959, 76). The practice continued in Germany until after World War I, when Weimar officials discovered that many disabled and nondisabled beggars tried to pass as soldiers to realize increased financial and social benefits (Poore 2007, 16).

In the United States, martial organ grinders peaked in number and influence during the 1870s. It is difficult to establish an exact number of veteran performers, but in an article in the *New York Times* (March 20, 1895), one writer estimated that "thousands of invalid and wounded veterans purchased organs" after the war. Newspapers and periodicals in California, the Midwest, and the Eastern seaboard expressed alarm in documenting the presence of injured soldiers performing in public spaces. Writing in the *New York Herald*, one reporter captured much of the shock that crowds felt at witnessing the sight and sound of veteran street performers:

> As we pass at the various corners of the streets the organ grinders, who are disabled soldiers, we cannot but think that some other provision should be made for these armless or legless men, who have suffered for the perpetuity of the nation. That those who fought and lost their limbs for their defense of our homes should be compelled to stand and beg for pennies at our street corners is a disgrace (July 21, 1871).

That many of the men are described as amputees is a testament to the outsized role played by maimed soldiers in forming postwar civilian perceptions of veterans.[4] This account renders the absence of limbs more visible by bringing specific bodily practices—standing and playing an instrument—to the foreground, enacting what Rosemarie Garland-Thomson has described as the capacity of amputees to "shock viewers into attentiveness" (Garland-Thomson 2009, 128). However rhetorically jarring this representational strategy may be, its pervasive emphasis on veterans' lost limbs has likely obscured the presence of less visible cognitive or mental disabilities in postwar begging spaces.

Part of the cultural shock that surrounded veteran beggars arose out of their uneasy coexistence with street musicians from the Italian immigrant classes. As Accinno (2010) has documented, Italian organ grinders predominated in the antebellum period, and reactions to the performers were often characterized by stridently nativist overtones. But by the 1870s, the presence of martial organ grinders meant that it was no longer possible for audiences to rely on nativist tropes alone. One observer in *Appleton's Journal* noted, "The maimed soldiers of the last war . . . excite more sympathy than the able-bodied Italians, and often earn twice as much money" (January 24, 1874). The influx of veterans into the once immigrant-dominated profession was so pronounced that when a reporter for the *New York Sun* asked a proprietor of barrel organs in 1874 about his clientele, he could readily reply that they were "nearly all Italians and old American soldiers" (reprinted in *Scientific American*, July 15, 1874).

Many observers took pains to draw clear distinctions between the two groups of street performers, and often resorted to discussions of veterans' manliness in designating soldiers as a special social category apart from immigrants. In James McCabe's *Secrets of the Great City*, a middle-class observer's account of the "virtues and vices" of New York City's working classes, McCabe reserved special scorn for immigrant organ grinders. Describing the performers as capable of "only the most horrible discord," he elaborated further on the impoverished living conditions in the infamous Five Points neighborhood, where the musicians "sustain their families entirely upon macaroni" (McCabe 1868, 125). Their tenements are described as "vile and filthy," and their children as "dirty, ragged, and more like monkeys" (125, 128).

While McCabe's dismissive, nativist screed is typical of the broader corpus of nineteenth-century writers' heated reactions toward immigrant organ grinders, his subsequent chapter on "soldier minstrels" represents an abrupt about-face concerning the issue of street musicians. Although he observes that the "maimed and battered veterans" of the Civil War played the same instruments as their Italian counterparts, McCabe strictly separates the veterans from other street musicians, reasoning that their service and bodily sacrifices merit consideration as a special category of performers (470–474). Narrating the story of John Williams, a gallant private in the Army of the Potomac who lost both an arm and a leg during the course of the war, the author notes that Williams "consoled himself with the hope that the people for whom he had fought and suffered, would not let him lack for some means of employment" (473). The hoped for work fails to materialize in the aftermath of the war, and instead Williams is reduced to playing the barrel organ on city streets, a profession that, owing to it associations with immigrants, is described as "repugnant to one's manhood" (474).

McCabe's rhetorical strategy relied on a binary logic that sought to shock readers into extending social and financial benefits to deserving veterans while simultaneously dismissing immigrant performers as unworthy. Such reasoning, however, must be questioned, for the categories of veteran and immigrant were never entirely mutually exclusive during this time period—as many as 200,000 German-Americans and 150,000 Irish-Americans served in the Union Army and Navy (Bladek 2000, 1029). Some of these immigrant veterans who lacked access to secure social or familial support networks would later turn to street performances in the postwar years.[5] An article in the *Washington Post* reported the story of an Irish immigrant who lost his arm during the Richmond-Petersburg campaign. Lacking family ties in the United States, the man later received a barrel organ that he claimed was financed personally by newspaper editor Marcus Pomeroy (January 2, 1884).

A particularly disturbing story of a one-armed German veteran in Milwaukee was recounted in a series of outraged letters written by readers of the *Chicago Tribune*. According to eyewitness accounts, the veteran arrived outside of the offices of the *Wisconsin State Register* and started playing a hand organ, only to have a pail of dirty water dumped on him from the window of the office by the newspaper's editor, Jack Turner (*Chicago Tribune*, July 11, 1872). A corroborating account by a different witness indicates that Turner continued to berate the man, and may have even kicked him down a flight of stairs (*Chicago Tribune*, July 15, 1872). These accounts—which also implicate the newspapers themselves as biased observers of organ grinders—suggest that immigrant veterans may have had particular difficulties in navigating postwar benefit and employment networks.

Veterans and Postwar Labor

A variety of employment programs that were deemed suitable for disabled Union veterans began to emerge both during and after the war. Motivated by gratitude for the veterans' sacrifices, but also by fears about an emerging class of martial vagrants, the new labor schemes ranged from positions in government to messenger and delivery services. In 1864, William Oland Bourne, the New York–based editor of the veterans' newspaper *The Soldier's Friend*, began to employ disabled soldiers to hawk his publication in the streets. Bourne would later sponsor the "Left-Arm Corps," a writing competition for one-armed veterans in which the men were encouraged to write about patriotic themes.[6] Pharmacist H. T. Helmbold, creator of the infamous concoction Helmbold's Buchu, sponsored a series of almanacs in 1868 to be sold in the streets by disabled veterans (Wecter 1944, 209); The *Half-Dime Tales* included a catalog of facts about the Civil War and selected writings that included the poem "The Empty Sleeve."[7]

Other disabled veterans took advantage of civil service opportunities. Some of the men were hired under federal legislation that granted them privileged hiring status for federal appointments and promotions (Nielsen 2012, 81); many soldiers also extended their military service in the Invalids Corps, a unit of wounded soldiers that were deployed in a variety of noncombat roles (Holberton 2001, 125). But for men of lower social and financial standing, these employment programs were largely ineffective. Frances Clarke has observed that postwar rehabilitation and vocational programs never approached the comprehensive level adopted in later US military conflicts (Clarke 2011, 147). As rapid military demobilization quickly blurred distinctions between soldiers and civilians and public support for disabled veterans evaporated, employment opportunities became increasingly scarce. But despite the limited availability of "honest livelihoods," heated criticism of the "dishonest" practices of mendicancy and organ grinding never ceased. The proposed eradication of begging by disabled veterans thus took on a moral flavor that provided convenient cover for those hoping to justify their own flawed efforts on behalf of the "worthy" poor.

Institutional Attitudes Toward Mendicancy

> For my eye is fixed with a steadfast strain
> On the tattered soldier's halting stride,
> Till his tall form sinks down the dark hill-side;
> Then I cry, "Thank God! He hath *now* no need
> To beg at the stranger's gate! (*Harper's Weekly*, October 4, 1862)

Criticism of mendicancy was loudly voiced by public and private institutions dedicated to the care of indigent veterans. Henry Bellows, president of the US Sanitary Commission, declared one of the goals of his institution "To make mendicancy and public support disreputable for all with any ability, however partial, to help themselves" (*Sanitary Commission Report No. 95* 1865, 3). Bellows's misgivings stemmed from the Commission's studies of European military asylums founded in the style of the *Hôtel des Invalides* and the Royal Hospital Chelsea (Marten 2011, 96). The asylum model was deemed out of touch with American values, which emphasized economic self-support and, only when necessary, reliance on "domestic and neighborly sympathies" (*Sanitary Commission Report No. 95* 1865, 3). Adopting a more strident tone in the pages of *The Soldier's Friend*, William Oland Bourne railed strongly against "shameless imposters, who play upon the sympathy of the soldier to secure a larger income than ordinary beggary would produce" (quoted in Marten 2011, 220).

The administrators of the National Home for Disabled Volunteer Soldiers, established by Congress in 1865, singled out organ grinders as a special cause for concern.[8] In its annual 1867 report to Congress, the asylum's Board of Managers wrote alarmingly about the increasing prevalence of barrel organs:

> True it is that many cases will be found of apparently disabled men, who claim to be soldiers, in large cities or on railway trains, asking relief of the charitable, or attempting to earn a subsistence by grinding a hand-organ, or other like means of appealing to the generous sympathies of the community (quoted in Gobrecht 1875, 43–44).

The Board regarded the actions of these "apparently disabled" men as the "prostitution of the honorable wounds and the uniform of the soldier," and further suggested that the men in question were primarily a group of ragtag imposters, deserters, and swindlers who were hired by "associations" of morally questionable employers to play borrowed instruments on the streets (quoted in Gobrecht 1875, 43–44). But the report's blanket condemnation obscured the fact that the regulations of the National Home ultimately may have been the source of street musicians' duress. In 1871, George McWatters, the so-called literary policeman of New York City, argued that the "true and honest soldiers" who pursued organ grinding did so because the asylum system failed to provide housing for their wives and children (McWatters 1871, 71–73). The Board itself noted the lack of housing for dependents in its first annual report, but Congress failed to advance legislation to address the issue (Kelly 1997, 235–237).

The national leaders of the Grand Army of the Republic (GAR), the powerful Union veterans' fraternal organization, lodged similar complaints against mendicancy; state and local chapters of the group, however, demonstrated greater flexibility in addressing the issue. The founder of the GAR, former army surgeon Benjamin F. Stephenson, emphasized a rhetoric of manliness and independence for the organization's disabled members; in a speech to the group's 1868 national encampment, he noted the GAR's success in helping, "thousand of our poor, helpless, crippled comrades . . . who, but for our own instrumentality, would be left to seek their support from the cold hand of charity, and the Union soldier disdains to beg" (quoted in McConnell 1992, 136). But in 1870, the New York State branch of the GAR lobbied both houses of Congress to rescind a federal licensing fee imposed on street musicians. According to Marcus Pomeroy, editor of the *New York Democrat*, the government license cost each performer $10 per year (Pomeroy 1890, 220).

Similar to the exceptions created for Civil War amputees in several "ugly law" statutes, the group proposed that the Senate adopt a motion "in favor of amendment of the revenue laws, so as to exempt such honorably discharged soldiers, sailors, and marines as derive their livelihood by playing hand-organs and other musical instruments from license taxation" (*Journal of the Senate of the United States of America*, vol. 64, January 17, 1870, 103).[9] In addition to state branches, local chapters also may have accepted and even supported the presence of veteran organ grinders. An Ohio newspaper relates one such instance: a local GAR chapter agreed to purchase a new barrel organ for a veteran "soldier without legs" after his instrument was destroyed in an altercation with a blind, civilian organ grinder (*Daily Ohio Statesman*, April 1, 1867).

Although quick to condemn disabled veteran beggars or to use them as rhetorical devices to dramatize and justify their own efforts, many institutions and their supporters proved to be less interested in taking seriously the concerns of the beggars themselves. Disabled mendicants who passed as veterans could simply be written off as imposters. For those who *were* considered veterans, the fault lay not in the institutions but with the individual beggars themselves—as one newspaper coolly reasoned, "If any of them are in want of any of the comforts of life, it is because they do not avail themselves of the ample provision that has been made for them" (*Washington Post*, June 4, 1878). But beggars were more than symbols—they were *real* people who possessed agency and the capacity for self-representation. They were men like Joshua Parker, a handless veteran who played the hand organ in Washington, DC, with the help of his wife. In 1898, Congress finally granted him a pension of $40 a month, nearly three decades after the end of the Civil War (*Washington Post*, February 22, 1898). For Parker and others, the "begging problem" lay not so much in the failing of the individual, but in social institutions that did not thoughtfully listen and thus became complicit in perpetuating the very category of beggar that that they sought to erase.

Representing Martial Begging: Tactics and Contexts

Having placed attitudes toward mendicancy and organ grinding within the broader historical context of veterans' institutions, this essay will now shift to consider the visual and aural representational tactics employed by street musicians within performance spaces. A description of one such performance that occurred in San Francisco in 1869 is characteristic of much of the reportage about the men who represented themselves as disabled veterans to their audiences:

> Two Empty Sleeves—On Saturday afternoon a soldier who had lost both arms above the elbows made his appearance on Kearny Street, accompanied by a boy with a hand organ. An accompanying placard informed the public that the name of the

> unfortunate man was R. D. Danphy, and that he lost his arms at Mobile Bay, on board the United States ship Hartford, in an engagement with the rebel ram Tennessee. A contribution box was provided for the reception of donations, and the appeal was liberally responded to (*Daily Evening Bulletin*, August 25, 1869).

The sailor's "empty sleeves" are identified by the author as the singularly most important detail about the performer, in keeping with Garland-Thomson's assertion that "visible disability . . . almost always dominates and skews the normate's process of sorting out perceptions and forming a reaction" (Garland-Thomson 1997, 12). Naming frequently emerges as an important aspect of a soldier's or sailor's self-identification. Whether provided orally or through the use of a certificate of discharge or placard, the name of a battle, unit, or ship offers important context for audiences to further reflect on the circumstances of a veteran's injury or impairment. The contribution box—usually described as a cigar box or a similarly sized container—is identified as a receptacle for donations. We cannot presume that the performers themselves necessarily viewed these donations as a form of charity, but may have thought of them instead as akin to an optional fee for services rendered. Moreover, if there was any discomfort associated with the collection of the fee, it likely lay more with the audience member than with the performer himself (Bogdan 2012, 23).

There is one more crucial aspect about the performance conventions of organ grinding that the account divulges: namely, it reveals how some amputees operated an instrument colloquially referred to as a "hand organ" without the use of a hand. In order to operate the barrel organ, an instrument with preprogrammed tunes that were "pinned" onto a roll mechanism, the boy who accompanies the veteran supplies his own arms and hands to turn the crank of the instrument. These able-bodied assistants helped transport the barrel organs as well as the disabled men themselves, and sometimes wore blue uniforms that matched those worn by many veterans. Although occasionally described as the wives of the veterans, these companions were typically male, and thus heightened an already masculine-dominated performance space.

Establishing what musical repertoire was performed by veteran organ grinders remains an open question. Lacking well-preserved manufacturers' records and few extant nineteenth-century barrel organs in working condition, we must turn elsewhere for anecdotal clues about tune selection. The first stanza of the 1882 work *The Crutch and the Empty Sleeve*, a jaunty song in D major about a crippled organ grinder, provides some indications about the repertoire choices made by veterans: "Down at the corner a hand organ stands, Where the crowds are passing every day / And an old crippled soldier he turns at the crank, While a man with one arm takes the pay / It is only the war tunes of old that they play" (*Whittaker Brothers* 1882). For a score and recording of this song, see Tracks 21.1 and 21.2 on the Companion Website.

What might these "war tunes" have included? Upbeat, propulsive melodies such as *A Life on the Ocean Wave, Sherman's March to the Sea, La Marseillaise, Hail Columbia*, and the *Star-Spangled Banner* may all have been used, owing to their general popularity during this period and their patriotic and nationalistic associations. Along with worn uniforms and other military accoutrements, these tunes may have assisted performers' efforts to create liminal patriotic spaces that appealed to passersby.

The barrel organ's raspy timbre functioned as another aural signifier that contributed to martial performance spaces. Many observers derided the instruments in metaphorical terms that likened them to diseased or choking bodies. Prone to overuse and habitually exposed to humidity and bad weather, many of the degraded organs became known as "wheezers." An article that appeared in *Harper's Weekly* described these broken, out-of-tune instruments as a kind of asthmatic body:

> When an organ is past mending, when it has lost its teeth, and its lungs give partly out, and its joints squeak, it is not to be thrown away. It then becomes a "wheezer," and easily finds a new owner in the person of some blind or some decrepit beggar, who sleeps by day and comes out by night to sit on a curb-stone in some gay and busy centre like Madison Square, and to grind on incoherently upon the broken barrel and the sympathy of passers-by (*Harper's Weekly*, July 20 1889).

In this instance, both instrument and performer were bound up in the rhetoric of disability. Like mendicant literature, "wheezy" mendicant music created mutually reinforcing connections through its proximity to, and presentation with, the disabled bodies of performers.[10] Such a double stigmatization of bodies, both human and instrumental, further heightened audience reactions to street performances.

The close relationship promoted between disabled body and disabled instrument was illustrated in a scene that appeared in the women's journal *Hearth and Home* in 1873 (see Figure 21.1). In the drawing, an organ grinder and his monkey perform for a woman and her young children at the doorstep of their home. Both the performer's prosthetic limb and the martial costume of his simian companion suggest qualities associated with the trappings of 1870s war veterans. Although the presence of a monkey playing a fiddle provides a cue for the woman and her children to avoid staring at the organ grinder's wooden limb, viewers of the illustration are nevertheless invited to gaze unabashedly at the man's prosthesis (We can also detect an avoidance grounded in listening; the skilled fiddler is heard attentively by his audience, while the unskilled organ grinder is shunned). Indeed, the positioning of the man's leg vis-à-vis the supporting wooden stand of the barrel organ is highly ambiguous: it is difficult to tell if the barrel organ acts as a prosthesis for the performer, or if the performer acts as a prosthesis for the barrel organ.

To be sure, these conflated bodies were often represented from an able-bodied perspective, and thus tended to exaggerate performers as grotesque, humorous, or pitiable. In the published tale *St. Ephrem: A Story of Christmas Eve*, a disabled veteran with two amputated legs identified as "Danny's father" plays the barrel organ with the assistance of his son. In one bedside scene, the narrator dramatizes the inability to distinguish between performer and instrument:

> Danny's father in bed, with the hand-organ obscuring all of him except his bushy head, and his left arm, which clasped the organ in front. The handle of the organ

FIGURE 21.1 An organ grinder with an artificial limb plays for a woman and her children. The illustration appeared in the women's journal *Hearth and Home* in 1873. Picture Collection, The New York Public Library, Astor, Lenox and Tilden Foundations.

> seemed to be his right arm, so that either the organ was itself with Danny's father's head and arm; or Danny's father was himself with an organ body and ivory stops; or Danny's father was an organ with his own head and arm . . . or the organ was a father, or the father was an organ. Who is it? Which are they? How was it? (*Hours at Home* 1870, 243)

The twisted contortions that the narrative voice subjects on Danny's father—his own name is never revealed—gestures toward an ableist perspective that obscures the man's agency and assumes a lack of self-worth. We might thrust the questions back on the narrator and ask: Who is doing the speaking here, and to what end? Certainly not the disabled veteran himself, whose own motivations are concealed and obfuscated.

Mendicant Texts: Literature, Imagery, and Music

In deconstructing rhetorical accounts of disabled martial performers, I may indeed be complicit in the very type of disability ventriloquism that has heretofore been critiqued.

This final section therefore endeavors to provide space for organ grinders to speak for themselves through mendicant texts that allow for the possibility of self-representation. Broadly construed, mendicant texts are defined here to include any material means through which street performers represented themselves to their audiences. Thus, in addition to mendicant literature and photography, explored by Schweik (2009) and Bogdan (2012), respectively, mendicant music also functioned as an interpretive device used by performers to describe and interpret their own bodies.

Although there is no archive of mendicant instruments to speak of—or at least there is not one *yet*—preserved collections of mendicant poetry, tracts, and cartes de visite provide revealing traces of martial performers who, although often pressured to resort to the rhetoric of pity and marginalization accepted by their paying audiences, nevertheless acted as proud, stubborn salesmen. These texts, which demonstrate a persistent refusal to accept the passivity typically associated with cultural constructions of begging, can provide important insights about how music may have worked in analogous ways to negotiate between performers' self-expression and audience expectations.

The broadside "The One-Arm Soldier" is one example of a larger corpus of begging poetry that concludes with the final stanza "Strangers, pardon, if I ask you / To buy a one-arm soldier's song" (see Figure 21.2). Owing to the poem's dislocation from its original purveyor, we do not know much about the document's provenance, nor can it presently be ascertained how its publication was financed. Similar to the shared history of the "Empty Sleeve" poetry discussed by Devin Burke in this volume, numerous variants of the poem circulated that substituted different names and identifying information.[11]

In the case of the variant used by James R. Thomas, the personal details provided by the poem allow for us to more readily establish the man's identity (see Figure 21.3). The roster of the 1st Pennsylvania Reserves records that Private James R. Thomas was discharged on December 5, 1862, for wounds received in action, and Thomas's regiment was indeed present at the Battle of South Mountain.[12] The poem reveals further details about Thomas's war injury and his status as a married man, information that is especially useful for empirically oriented historians.

Although sifting through the poems in this way can yield new insights about particular individuals such as Thomas, it also comes dangerously close to replicating in historiography the discarded historical categories of "worthy" and "unworthy" poor. Rather than using the texts to establish whether the veterans in question were *real* or *fraudulent*, we might ask instead what cultural work the broadsides accomplished for the purveyors of the texts themselves. Or, to borrow the language of Thomas's poem, how did the poem's use within the begging encounter "assist the work of this one hand?" For one thing, such mendicant poems established value, both in a transactional sense and in terms of the inherent personal benefits realized in any attempt at self-representation. Selling these poems as commodities rather than as acts of charity protected the men against civic "ugly laws" that sharply restricted begging in public (Schweik 2009, 259). In this respect, it did not matter whether Thomas was a real veteran or whether the anonymous "one-arm soldier" was a fake one: both poems reveal a strikingly similar set of

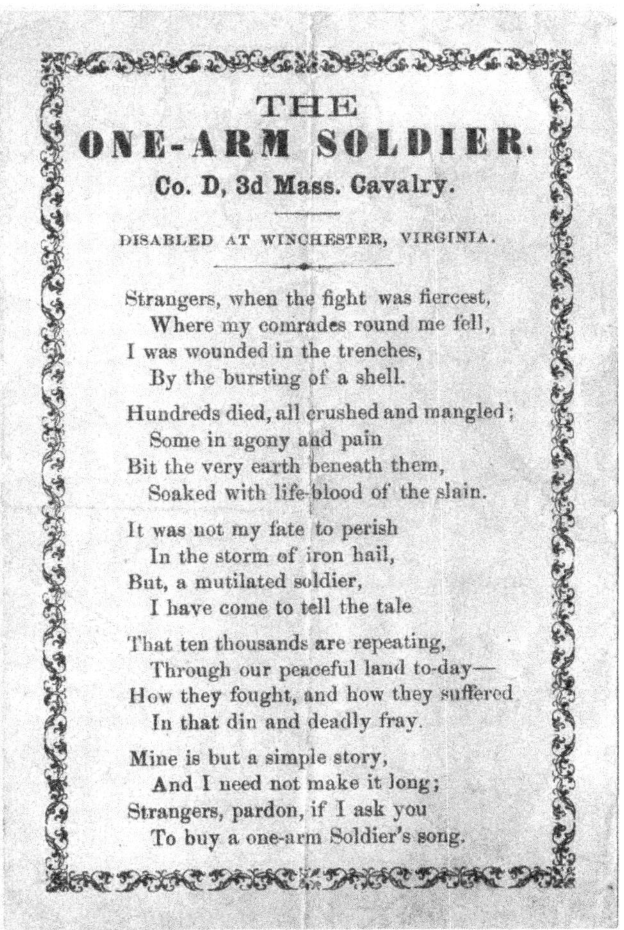

THE
ONE-ARM SOLDIER.
Co. D, 3d Mass. Cavalry.

DISABLED AT WINCHESTER, VIRGINIA.

Strangers, when the fight was fiercest,
Where my comrades round me fell,
I was wounded in the trenches,
By the bursting of a shell.

Hundreds died, all crushed and mangled;
Some in agony and pain
Bit the very earth beneath them,
Soaked with life-blood of the slain.

It was not my fate to perish
In the storm of iron hail,
But, a mutilated soldier,
I have come to tell the tale

That ten thousands are repeating,
Through our peaceful land to-day—
How they fought, and how they suffered
In that din and deadly fray.

Mine is but a simple story,
And I need not make it long;
Strangers, pardon, if I ask you
To buy a one-arm Soldier's song.

FIGURE 21.2 "The One-Arm Soldier." Mendicant poem (date unknown). *Center for the History of Medicine: OnView*, accessed January 17, 2014, http://collections.countway.harvard.edu/onview/items/show/6098.

begging tactics that likely resulted in a shared social stigma, regardless of one's veteran status.

Cartes de visite, small pocket-sized photographs that were popular during and after the Civil War, were commonly attached to soldiers' pension records, but they were also used in a similar context as begging poetry (Newman 1993, 64). Connor and Rhode (2003) note the case of Private Alfred Stratton, a double arm amputee who sold photographs of himself taken at the Army Medical museum to supplement his pension income. In one of the photographs used by Stratton, he wears a Union uniform with empty sleeves pinned back to accentuate his disability.[13] Another man, Eppentus McIntosh, a survivor of the infamous Andersonville prison who was diagnosed with "disease of spine and resulting curvature and insanity" (Stevens and Tharp 2010, 152),

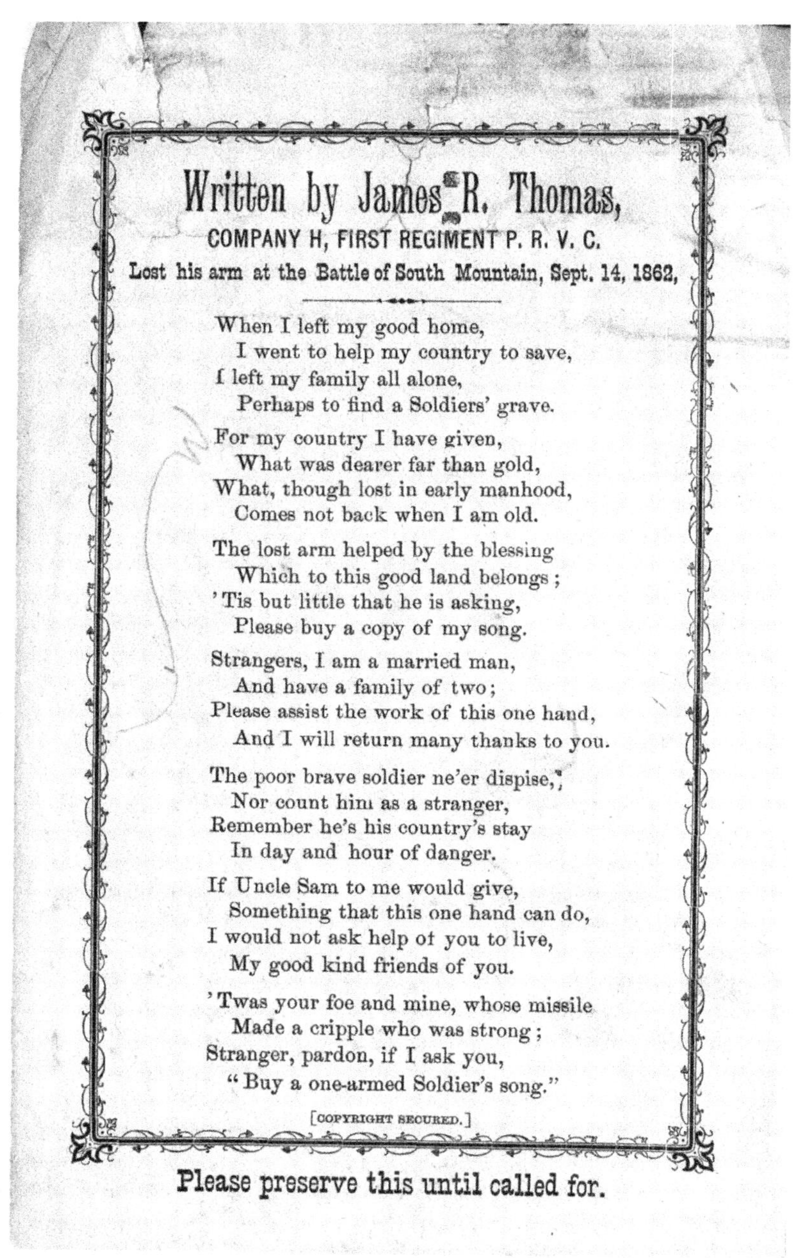

Written by James R. Thomas,
COMPANY H, FIRST REGIMENT P. R. V. C.
Lost his arm at the Battle of South Mountain, Sept. 14, 1862,

When I left my good home,
I went to help my country to save,
I left my family all alone,
Perhaps to find a Soldiers' grave.

For my country I have given,
What was dearer far than gold,
What, though lost in early manhood,
Comes not back when I am old.

The lost arm helped by the blessing
Which to this good land belongs;
'Tis but little that he is asking,
Please buy a copy of my song.

Strangers, I am a married man,
And have a family of two;
Please assist the work of this one hand,
And I will return many thanks to you.

The poor brave soldier ne'er dispise,
Nor count him as a stranger,
Remember he's his country's stay
In day and hour of danger.

If Uncle Sam to me would give,
Something that this one hand can do,
I would not ask help of you to live,
My good kind friends of you.

'Twas your foe and mine, whose missile
Made a cripple who was strong;
Stranger, pardon, if I ask you,
"Buy a one-armed Soldier's song."

[COPYRIGHT SECURED.]

Please preserve this until called for.

FIGURE 21.3 Thomas, James R. "When I left my good home." Mendicant poem (date unknown). *Center for the History of Medicine: OnView*, accessed January 17, 2014, http://collections.countway.harvard.edu/onview/items/show/6097.

sold postcards of himself as an itinerant musician. McIntosh, who shuttled in and out of veterans' institutions for several decades, traveled around the Midwest for much of the 1880s and '90s and further supplemented his income by selling songbooks of patriotic music (153).

At least one carte de visite featured an organ grinder, and judging by its preservation in multiple archival collections, it likely circulated as a mendicant text (reprinted in Appollo 1997, 15; Cooney 1984, 40—see Figure 21.4). Printed by Fetter's Gallery in Logansport, Indiana, the card shows a double arm amputee and his young assistant dressed in sailors' uniforms, standing on opposing ends of a large wagon-mounted barrel organ. The back of the card includes a reprint of the placard visible within the portrait, and relays information about the battle of Fort Fischer. The card demonstrates several forms of mendicant representation and self-representation. Within the medium of the postcard, text, imagery, and music interact with and against the disabled performer's body. We can also consider the original street performance as another potential layer of representational space, since the card was likely bought and sold in intimate proximity to the martial performer himself. Thus, there existed the potential for intertextual mendicant spaces in which the disabled performer's agency was realized and negotiated through different visual and sonic media.

Conclusion

Identifying himself only as "Otsdama," an indignant organ grinder wrote to the editor of the *Brooklyn Daily Eagle* in 1869 to protest against the onslaught of critiques that had been leveled against the performers by the newspaper's readers in recent weeks. His anonymous remarks, employing a mixture of humor, sarcasm, guilt, and wit to silence and shame his critics, demonstrate the power of disabled self-representation:

> As a member in good standing (on one leg) of that much abused class of musical purveyors, I beg the privilege of giving to the public a few of the reasons which govern us in the choice of this profession. While many persons with musical cultivation and education enjoy the opera and so-called classical music. . . . the great mass of common people are better satisfied with simple airs, finding little pleasure to elaborate and intricate compositions. . . . But what have these censorious scribblers to say on the score of their own patriotism? Do they not consider that while they were enjoying their ease at home, we who are now maimed and crippled for life, were fighting the battles of our country? And when we are unfit for active labor, we must do something to support ourselves and those dependent upon us, for a living. Give us something else to do, we will gladly do it. We have sometimes thought that Uncle Sam might with great propriety give us a place in his service, to do such light work as is now performed by stay-at-home politicians. As for example, see the inner workings of the Brooklyn Post office. Perhaps you do not like our music. Possibly you do not like our organ grinding. What else shall we do? Perchance our music annoys you.

FIGURE 21.4 Amputee sailor and boy with barrel organ. Picture taken at Fetter's New Photograph Gallery in Logansport, Indiana (date unknown). Heritage Auction Galleries.

> Pay us our wages, and we will sit by our music boxes in proper silence, to please you. Is our music disagreeable? We have heard that which was more so, on the fields of Gettysburg and the Wilderness. When you hear our wheezing instruments, consider it but the faint echo which we have brought from the battle-fields which saved our Republic, and look upon our employment as the necessary resort of the fragments of your country's defenders, and we hope these considerations will make you less easily annoyed and less irritable (*Brooklyn Daily Eagle*, May 11, 1869).

In representing himself and his profession, Otsdama makes use of many devices that encapsulate conventional scholarly ideas about reading texts to understand an individual's agency and creativity through authorship: double entendre ("member in good standing (on one leg"), alliteration ("censorious scribbling"), and the evocative metaphor linking "wheezing instruments" with the sounds of battle. But when interpreted as an authored text, Otsdama's anonymity may have presented some readers with an interpretive dilemma. Lacking a name, couldn't this writer have been *any* organ grinder? Was he even an organ grinder at all?

Parrying such questions from his skeptical interlocutors, Otsdama identifies the true nature of the problem: a widespread *cultural* failure to listen engagingly and thoughtfully to the music created by disabled street performers. As this essay has demonstrated, one possible response to Otsdama's rousing call to action lies in acknowledging postwar disabled begging as a shared culture in which men fashioned themselves as authors, poets, and musicians. Within this culture, authorship and musicianship were realized through the use of a performance script of martial begging that resisted the destruction wrought by cultural stigma and institutional inadequacy. As the loudest and most controversial group of street musicians, organ grinders figured prominently in the creation and maintenance of these begging performances. Their inconvenient social critiques beg us to listen and respond.

Notes

1. In one of the earliest comprehensive studies of Civil War veterans, Dixon Wecter (1944, 189) described the unease surrounding veterans' street performances: "Some citizens groused that their [veterans'] hand-organs were invariably the worst and squeakiest ever heard; couldn't the town fathers at least see that they had tuneful instruments?" Writing more recently about the influx of disabled veterans into post–Civil War San Francisco, Susan Schweik (2009) has noted, "Begging veterans entering or reentering the peacetime city told war stories with their injured bodies. San Franciscans responded ambivalently" (28).
2. In adopting a sympathetic stance toward the "imposter soldier," I acknowledge the considerable methodological distance that separates Disability Studies from disabled veterans history. Writing about this divide, Gerber notes, "The recent historical literature on disabled veterans . . . continues to be produced by researchers who do not consider themselves historians of disability for readers who are more interested in war, the military, and the state than in disability" (Gerber 2012b, xii).
3. Bowers 1972 and Ord-Hume 1978 are the standard reference books for mechanical instruments.
4. This observation is strongly in keeping with James Marten's recent study of Civil War veterans, in which the author notes, "one-armed or one-legged veterans almost immediately became a stereotype of noble sacrifice and deserving pity" (Marten 2011, 76). Speaking in more general terms, disability historian David Gerber contends that this visible fixation is repeated in postwar cultures writ large: "Especially traumatic, visible injuries have tended to become the primary way in which the general population of disabled veterans often seems to have been conceived in the minds of experts, artists, and the general citizenry" (Gerber 2012a, 2).
5. Immigrant access to disabled veteran support programs was decidedly mixed. Blanck and Song (2007) note that German and Irish immigrants were significantly less likely to apply for pension benefits than native-born veterans. However, Kelly (2007) estimates that up to 60% of veterans who sought assistance at the National Home for Disabled Volunteer Soldiers in the first two decades of its existence were immigrants (243).
6. A public exhibition of the Left-Arms Corps took place in 1866 in Washington, DC. According to Marten (2011), the event failed to significantly sway public opinion about amputee veterans (94). For further discussion, see Clarke 2002, Cooney 1984, and Padilla 2007.
7. For further discussion of this poem, see Devin Burke's essay in this collection.
8. The organization used the term "home" rather than "asylum," part of a broader attempt by administrators to associate disabled veterans with the "soothing discourse of Victorian domesticity" (Kelly 1997, 90). Amputees figured prominently in official representations of the National Home: the organization's seal featured a soldier with an amputated leg stretching his arm out to receive a cup from Lady Liberty.

9. It is unknown whether Congress successfully passed legislation to amend the licensing fee. Schweik has documented many instances of municipal peddling ordinances that created similar fee exemptions for Civil War veterans; the mayor of Chicago tried to carve out a exemption for Civil War amputees when the City Council passed its "ugly law" statute in 1881 that banned begging and organ grinding on city streets (Schweik 2009, 30–32).
10. Writing of mendicant literature, Schweik notes, "Disabled self-publishers promised a direct link between the story of the text and the story of the writer's own body. . . . The text came with (even as it discreetly supplemented) or substituted for bodily display" (Schweik 2009, 344). Straus makes a similar conceptual point about composers and their corpus of music, arguing, "in some cases, the music appears to share the stigmatized quality of the body that produced it" (Straus 2011, 16).
11. Marten has identified several variants of the Broadside that alter the identifying information of the soldier or substitute "one-legged" or "crippled" for "one-armed": James Walsh, George M. Reed, and "The One-Armed Boy" (Marten 2011, 92 and 292). I have identified three additional versions that reference the names Thomas Ball, John Williams, and James R. Thomas.
12. The roster is available online: http://www.pa-roots.com/pacw/reserves/1stres/1strescoh.html.
13. Available online at http://www.rochester.edu/in_visible_culture/Issue_5/ConnorRhode/ConnorRhode_figures/CRfig18.html.

References

Accinno, Michael. 2010. "'Organ Grinder's Swing': Representations of Street Music in New York City, 1850–1937." MA thesis, University of Iowa. http://ir.uiowa.edu/etd/636.

Appollo, Ken. 1997. *Humble Work and Mad Wanderings: Street Life in the Machine Age.* Nevada City, CA: Carl Mautz.

Bladek, John David. 2000. "Immigration." In *Encyclopedia of the American Civil War: A Political, Social, and Military History*, vol. 2, edited by David S. Heidler and Jeanne T. Heidler, 1028–1029. Santa Barbara, CA: ABC-CLIO.

Blanck, Peter, and Chen Song. 2007. "Civil War Pensions for Native and Foreign-Born Union Army Veterans." In *The Civil War Veteran: A Historical Reader*, edited by Larry M. Logue and Michael Barton, 221–226. New York: New York University Press.

Boetzkes, Amanda. 2010. "The Ephemeral Stage at Lionel Groulx Station." In *Circulation and the City: Essays on Urban Culture*, edited by Alexandra Boutros and Will Straw, 138–154. Montreal: McGill-Queen's University Press.

Bogdan, Robert. 2012. *Picturing Disability: Beggar, Freak, Citizen, and Other Photographic Rhetoric.* Syracuse, NY: Syracuse University Press.

Bowers, Q. David. 1972. *Encyclopedia of Automatic Musical Instruments.* Vestal, NY: Vestal.

Buchner, Alexander. 1959. *Mechanical Musical Instruments.* Translated by Iris Urwin. London: Batchworth.

Clarke, Frances. 2002. "'Honorable Scars': Northern Amputees and the Meaning of Civil War Injuries." In *Union Soldiers and the Northern Home Front: Wartime Experiences, Postwar Adjustments*, edited by Paul A. Cimbala and Randall M. Miller, 361–394. New York: Fordham University Press.

Clarke, Frances. 2011. *War Stories: Suffering and Sacrifice in the Civil War North.* Chicago: University of Chicago Press.

Connor, J. T. H., and Michael G. Rhode. 2003. "Shooting Soldiers: Civil War Medical Images, Memory, and Identity in America." *Invisible Culture: An Electronic Journal for Visual Culture* 5. http://rochester.edu/in_visible_culture/Issue_5/ConnorRhode/ConnorRhode.html.

Cooney, Charles F. 1984. "The Left-Armed Corps: Rehabilitation for the Veteran." *Civil War Times Illustrated* 23: 40–44.

Garland-Thomson, Rosemarie. 1997. *Extraordinary Bodies: Figuring Physical Disability in American Culture and Literature.* New York: Columbia University Press.

Garland-Thomson, Rosemarie. 2009. *Staring: How We Look.* New York: Oxford University Press.

Gerber, David A. 2012a. "Introduction: Finding Disabled Veterans in History." In *Disabled Veterans in History*, rev. ed., edited by David A. Gerber, 1–51. Ann Arbor: University of Michigan Press.

Gerber, David A. 2012b. "Preface to the Enlarged and Revised Edition: The Continuing Relevance of the Study of Disabled Veterans." In *Disabled Veterans in History*, rev. ed., edited by David A. Gerber, ix–xxiii. Ann Arbor: University of Michigan Press.

Gobrecht, J. C. 1875. *History of the National Home for Disabled Volunteer Soldiers.* Dayton, OH: United Brethren.

Harrison-Pepper, Sally. 1990. *Drawing a Circle in the Square: Street Performing in New York's Washington Square Park.* Jackson: University Press of Mississippi.

Holberton, William. 2001. *Homeward Bound: The Demobilization of Union and Confederate Armies, 1865–1866.* Mechanicsburg, PA: Stackpole.

Kelly, Patrick J. 1997. *Creating a National Home: Building the Veterans' Welfare State, 1860–1900.* Cambridge, MA: Harvard University Press.

Kelly, Patrick J. 2007. "Establishing a Federal Entitlement." In *The Civil War Veteran: A Historical Reader*, edited by Larry Logue and Michael Barton, 221–226. New York: New York University Press.

Kuppers, Petra. 2003. *Disability and Contemporary Performance: Bodies on Edge.* New York: Routledge.

Marten, James Alan. 2011. *Sing Not War: The Lives of Union and Confederate Veterans in Gilded Age America.* Chapel Hill: University of North Carolina Press.

Mason, Bim. 1992. *Street Theatre and Other Outdoor Performance.* New York: Routledge.

McCabe, James D. [Edward Winslow Martin]. 1868. *The Secrets of the Great City: A Work Descriptive of the Virtues and the Vices, The Mysteries, Miseries, and Crimes of New York City.* Philadelphia, PA: Jones Brothers.

McConnell, Stuart. 1992. *Glorious Contentment: The Grand Army of the Republic, 1865–1900.* Chapel Hill: University of North Carolina Press.

McWatters, George S. 1871. *Knots Untied: Or, Ways and By-ways in the Hidden Life of American Detectives.* Hartford, CT: J.B. Burr and Hyde.

Nielsen, Kim E. 2012. *A Disability History of the United States.* Boston: Beacon Press.

Newman, Kathy. 1993. "Wounds and Wounding in the American Civil War: A (Visual) History." *Yale Journal of Criticism* 6: 63–86.

Ord-Hume, Arthur W. J. G. 1978. *Barrel Organ: The Story of the Mechanical Organ and Its Repair.* South Brunswick, NJ: A.S. Barnes.

Padilla, Jalynn Olsen. 2007. "Army of 'Cripples': Northern Civil War Amputees, Disability, and Manhood in Victorian America." PhD diss., University of Delaware.

Pomeroy, Marcus Mills. 1890. *Reminiscences and Recollections of "Brick" Pomeroy: A True Story for Boys and Girls of Any Age.* New York: Advance Thought.

Poore, Carol. 2007. *Disability in Twentieth-Century German Culture.* Ann Arbor: University of Michigan Press.

Sanitary Commission Report No. 95: Provision Required for the Relief and Support of Disabled Soldiers and Sailors and Their Dependents. 1865. New York.

Schweik, Susan. 2009. *The Ugly Laws: Disability in Public.* New York: New York University Press.

Simpson, Paul. 2011. "Street Performance and the City: Public Space, Sociality, and Intervening in the Everyday." *Space and Culture* 14: 415–430. doi: 10.1177/1206331211412270.

Stevens, Robert Allan, and Bill Tharp. 2010. "Incredible Stories of Uncle Epp: Soldier, POW, Survivor, Minstrel, and Lincoln's Office Boy." *Journal of the Illinois State Historical Society* 103 (2): 141–164.

Straus, Joseph N. 2011. *Extraordinary Measures: Disability in Music.* New York: Oxford University Press.

Tanenbaum, Susie J. 1995. *Underground Harmonies: Music and Politics in the Subways of New York.* Ithaca, NY: Cornell University Press.

Wecter, Dixon. 1944. *When Johnny Comes Marching Home.* Boston: Houghton Mifflin.

CHAPTER 22

"GOOD BYE, OLD ARM"

The Domestication of Veterans' Disabilities in Civil War Era Popular Songs

DEVIN BURKE

In October of 1863, two years into the Civil War, a short editorial titled "Empty Sleeves" appeared on the front page of the *Staunton Spectator*.[1] It addressed a question that had become familiar in the wake of the war's unprecedented violence; namely, how to encounter, or how to look at (in both the literal and figurative senses), the quickly growing population of veterans whose injuries marked them as "disabled." This question could be cause for considerable anxiety in able-bodied Americans whose beliefs were shaped by Victorian and muscular Christian values.

Empty Sleeves

> The *Lynchburg Republican* aptly remarks that we frequently see passing along our streets, silent mementoes of heroism. They are empty sleeves dangling by the sides of war-worn privates. We never look upon the possessor of one of these empty sleeves, but to our mind's eye arises the sight of a venerated mother seated at the stoop, with knitting in hand and spectacles on nose, stopping to wipe away a tear at the thought of her darling boy with one arm. And the poor fellows hobbling along on crutches with only one leg spared to them—they are objects of tender sympathy to the whole people. Doubt it not, ye soldiers, who probably miss the sympathies of home. All look upon you as heroes.[2]

The anonymous author of this editorial presents an understanding of *looking at* the disabled veteran that simultaneously celebrates and marginalizes. "All look upon you as heroes," the author asserts, and not without cause. At home, however, disabled veterans faced an uncertain social status. As the emphasis on the veterans' mothers and the reference to "her darling boy" in the editorial illustrate, disabled veterans were often treated as feminized and infantilized. The veterans also had to negotiate new identities within the category of "disabled"; for example, as one can infer from the editorial, amputated arms and amputated legs had different social meanings, and missing an arm or leg or both placed a veteran into distinct social categories.[3]

The impetus for the editorial in the ironically titled *Spectator* is the frequent sightings of amputee veterans in public spaces, and for the editorial's author, these create a visual disturbance. In Lennard Davis's terms, the disability encounter presents to the able-bodied viewer "a disruption in the visual, auditory, or perceptual field as it relates to the power of the gaze"; such a disruption "must be regulated, rationalized, contained" in some way that is culturally conditioned (Davis 1995, 129). What the editorial describes—and in a sense prescribes—is an act of active staring. Garland-Thomson 2009 defines this type of staring as a "goal-driven stare," a staring behavior that seeks to "impose a logical narrative on what at first glance" appears incomprehensible (21). In a goal-driven staring encounter, the starer focuses on visual cues that render the object of the stare, or the "staree," comprehensible to the starer. These visual cues summon familiar narratives that the starer uses to categorize the staree, and in this case, the empty sleeve and the crutch serve this function, metonymically signifying the veterans and summoning to the starer's mind sentimental and patriotic narratives of loss, love, and self-sacrifice.

In this essay, I consider what happened when veterans with disabilities were made the subjects of popular songs. Although songs about death, mothers, and sweethearts back home were the most common sentimental themes in Civil War era sheet music, some of the songs translated encounters with disabled veterans into musical performances and transformed the disabled soldier from a silent memento of heroism into a musical one. In George Cooper and S. L. Coe's "Old Arm, Good Bye," for example, a soldier awakens from a chloroform-induced sleep and calls out for his amputated right arm to be brought to him so that he can sing to it a love ballad of his thanks and praises. This particular song is discussed in some detail later. I begin this essay by providing broad context for these songs; then, I consider how performances of the songs in middle-class homes domesticated the disability encounter and dramatized the complicated relationships between a disabled veteran and his family and community; and finally, I look at three songs that portray different types of disability encounters.

The image of the disabled veteran as presented across these songs was in some ways quite specific. No other disability was more remarked on by the public and by veterans themselves than a missing limb (Marten 2011, 78), and this explains why there were more songs about amputee veterans than about veterans with any other type of disability. The blind veteran was the second most common subject for popular songs, and these songs warrant future study for the ways in which they map conventional musical and literary representations of blind (often orphan) children onto blind veterans. Due to the limitations of space, however, I have chosen to focus discussion on songs that portray amputee veterans.

This essay also concentrates on songs about veterans with amputated arms because these songs appeared more frequently than songs about veterans with amputated legs. Already by the Civil War, wooden legs carried associations with comic characters, as seen in Charles Dickens's novels, and diabolical, tormented individuals, as most famously represented by Captain Ahab. Such associations were inconsistent with the patriotic sentimentality of the typical song about amputee veterans. In addition, amputated legs were more easily concealable by prosthetics and trousers, making the empty sleeve a more unambiguously visible emblem of disability for songwriters. Another factor may have been that arms were more closely associated with the symbolic acts of war. Feet were good for "tramp, tramp, tramping," but arms held flags and weapons. Judith White McGuire, a Virginia woman who published her diary after the war, wrote the following in an 1862 entry on tending to the wounded: "Thank God," said a man with his leg amputated, "that it was not my right arm, for then I could never have fought again; as soon as this stump is well I shall join Stuart's cavalry; I can ride with a wooden leg as well as a real one" (McGuire 1868, 120).

Songs about Amputee Veterans in Context

Walt Whitman grimly wrote in the *New York Times* in 1864, "as this tremendous war goes on . . . every family has directly or indirectly some representative among this vast army of the wounded and sick." Of the estimated 80,000 operations that were performed over the course of the war, 60,000 resulted in amputation. Fifteen thousand soldiers died during surgery, and the remaining 45,000, both Union and Confederate, returned home as amputees (Figg and Farrell-Beck 1993, 454). The vast army of wounded men that Whitman described numbered more than 200,000 soldiers who bore some kind of disability by war's end. All of their wounds—large and small, visible and invisible—forced Americans to confront fundamental questions about who they were: What abilities, or type of body, or body parts, does one need to have to be considered a whole person? To be considered a man or a woman? A moral person? A hero?

These questions played out in popular culture through photography, literature, and music. One objective of this essay is to contribute to recent scholarship on photographic and literary depictions of Civil War amputee veterans by adding music to the discussion.[4] This recent scholarship includes analyses of the role of photography and literature in shifting notions of disability during and after the war. A scholar who bears particular mention is David Serlin; his work has shown that "through the public circulation of photographic images and verbal descriptions of veteran amputees, we begin to see the formation of arbitrary (though no less hierarchical) categories for thinking about disability itself" (Serlin 2006, 54). Similarly, the representation of veteran amputees in popular songs illustrated the emergence of new cultural scripts for disabled veterans.

Year	Title	Music/Lyrics	Publisher
1862	The Wounded Soldier	David Woods/Rev. Edward C. Jones	T. Myers, Philadelphia
1862	General Scott and Corporal Johnson	David A. Warden/Bayard Taylor	J. E. Gould, Philadelphia
1863	I'm Blind!	William Leigh	W. A. Pond and Co., New York
1863	The Invalid Corps	Frank Wilder	Henry S. Tolman, Boston
1863?	The Invalid Corps	Matt Gebler	J. H. Johnson, Philadelphia
1863	Will You Wed Me Now I'm Lame?	Avanelle L. Holmes (arr. George Root)	Root & Cady, Chicago
1863	The Doctor's Call Polka	Rudolph Wittig	W. R. Smith, Philadelphia
1863	Just After the Battle	George Root	Root & Cady, Chicago
1863	The Blind Soldier's Lament	Edgar G. Spinning/Mrs. A. B. Lathrop	W. A. Pond, New York
1864	The Empty Sleeve	Henry Badger/David Barker (orig. 1862 poem)	W. W. Whitney, Toledo, OH
1864	Tenting on the Old Camp Ground	Walter Kittredge	Oliver Ditson, Boston
1864?	21st Regiment Veterans Reserve Corps Quickstep	J. A. Reinhard, Bandmaster of 21st Reg.	W. A. Pond, New York
1865	Good-by, Old Arm!	Philip Phillips/The Blind Poetess	John Church, Cincinnati
1865	Dear Wife, I'm With You Once Again	Frank Ray	Balmer & Weber, St. Louis
1865	Dear Mother, I'm Wounded	Clarence Edwards/J. M. M.	G. D. Russell, Boston
1865	The Wounded Boy at Kenesaw	J. P. Webster/Granville M. Ballard	Root & Cady, Chicago
1865?	Shall We Let Our Soldiers Perish?	J. Henry Wolsieffer/ Thomas MacKellar	King & Baird, Philadelphia
1865	When the Boys Come Home	J. A. Butterfield/Robert Morris	John Church, Cincinnati
1865	The War is Over, Darling Kate	M. B. Ladd	W. R. Smith, Philadelphia
1865	The One Arm and One Leg Soldier	Various versions ascribed to different soldier-authors	Broadside published in different cities
1865	Good Bye, Old Arm!	Gen. W. H. Hayward	George Willig, Baltimore
1866	The Empty Sleeve	Rev. J. W. Dadmun/Mrs. P. A. Hanaford	Oliver Ditson, Boston
1866	Veteran's Polka	Charles Bach	Bach & Kuschbert, Milwaukee
1866	Old Arm, Good Bye	S. L. Coe/George Cooper	H. M. Higgins, Chicago
1874	The Empty Sleeve March	D. L. Downing	Oliver Ditson, Boston
1882	The Crutch & The Empty Sleeve; or, the Old Soldier's Reward	Whittaker Brothers	Spear & Dehnhoff, New York
1884	The Crutch Polka	Paul Favart	John Church, Cincinnati
1890	The Veteran's Emblem	William Henry White	William Lloyd Bowron, New York
1890	G. A. R.	E. P. Chadwick	C. J. Whitney, Detroit
1891	A Poor Old Union Soldier	W. M. M. Glenroy	W. B. Gray & Co., New York
1891	That's What He Did For His Country	William C. Robey	Oliver Ditson, Boston

FIGURE 22.1 Selected Northern songs and instrumental pieces that feature or recognize disabled veterans, 1861–1891

The table in Figure 22.1 shows a list of selected songs that featured or recognized veterans with disabilities between 1861 and 1891. Most of these songs were published during the war, and all were published in the North. This essay limits discussion to Northern songs in part because of limitations of space, but also because the North published many more songs of all kinds than the South. Furthermore, the wounded veteran was a less common subject in the poetry and songs of the South; this may be due in part to differences in subject matter between Southern and Northern songs.[5] Another factor may be that the North had greater numbers of soldiers and consequently sent home greater numbers of disabled veterans.

The Civil War produced a mountain of music. Estimates are that between nine and ten thousand war-related songs were published in the North, and between six and seven hundred songs were published in the South between 1861 and 1866 (McWhirter 2012, 16). The songs in Figure 22.1 represent a small subset of the total corpus of songs printed during this time. Most of the songs that concerned wounded soldiers focused only on the fatally wounded soldier; as Heaps writes, "scarcely one melody gives hope of survival" (Heaps and Heaps 1960, 181). The wounded soldier who lived was a comparatively rare subject for popular songs, and according to Heaps, songwriters may have turned to the topic of death more often because it presented a more pitiful song subject than survival (181). The emphasis on dead and dying soldiers in popular songs also reflects the reality that more soldiers—an estimated 620,000—met with death than with disability.[6] Out of the total casualties, two-thirds died not from battle wounds but from disease due to poor conditions in the camps and unsanitary medical practices.

The general uncertainty about the cultural status of veterans with disabilities also undoubtedly contributed to the relative dearth of songs about these soldiers. This uncertainty was amplified to the extent that it was unanticipated, since few could have predicted the unprecedented level of violence and numbers of disabled veterans. During and after the war, soldiers with disabilities occupied a nebulous role in rhetorical, visual, and musical representations of war. The future of the disabled soldier was inevitably complicated in comparison with the fallen soldier whose fate was sealed. Consequently, the image of the disabled soldier was consistently complex, ambiguous, limited, or simply omitted in popular culture. As Alan Trachtenberg writes, photographs of disabled Civil War soldiers were problematic and disturbing because they "disclose the most immediate and least comprehensible of war's facts, that it is waged on tangible human flesh and inscribed in pain—the living wounded body as the final untellable legend" (Trachtenberg 1989, 117–118). This brings to mind Elaine Scarry's observation about warfare: "The central activity of war is injuring and the central goal in war is to out-injure the opponent . . . [and yet] the fact of injuring tends to be absent from strategic and political descriptions of war" (Scarry 1985, 12). The fact that there were only dozens rather than hundreds of songs about disabled veterans points to a pattern of erasure regarding the popular image of the disabled veteran. This was a pattern that continued in later wars, eventually becoming an official policy during World War II, when the US War Department worked to purge popular media of all disturbing images of wounded soldiers (Serlin 2006, 52).

Domesticating the Disability Encounter

During the war, songs about amputee veterans created opportunities for individuals to encounter fictionalized disabled veterans in a domestic space and in the guise of a familiar form of entertainment.[7] The musical vocabularies of these songs are nothing if not formulaically sentimental: tropes such as lilting melodies, fermatas on emotionally charged words and at the ends of verses, and abrupt switches to minor harmonies to underline particularly pitiful imagery are common to thousands of other nineteenth-century songs. These conventions represent a kind of musical domestication of the disability encounter. In a sense, these songs normalize these encounters through familiar aural signifiers that translate the encounter into a typical middle-class household performance.

Given the omnipresence of music in America in the 1860s, songs about amputee veterans likely reached a wider audience than photographs of amputee veterans, which were only in limited public circulation during the war. Women at home were the primary demographic for these songs, as sentimental songs about soldiers and the emotional toll of battle were not popular song subjects within military camps (Heaps and Heaps 1960, 169). One officer, S. Millet Thompson of the 13th New Hampshire, expressly forbade the performance of "pathetic" or "plaintive" tunes in his camp for fear that it would dishearten the men (George 2012, 2). As the war drew on and more disabled veterans returned home, popular literature increasingly began to portray young women as uniquely sensitive and well suited to helping the men and other members of the community (Padilla 2007, 170). A number of songs took up this theme explicitly, and the most popular was "Will You Wed Me Now I'm Lame, Love?" Another notable example, "Dear Wife I'm with You Once Again," will be considered in more detail later.

Many of the stories about disabled veterans in popular literature featured situations in which a woman helped a veteran by effectively becoming the prosthetic for his lost limb. For example, an 1865 piece in *Harper's Weekly* tells the story of Captain Harry Ash and his sweetheart, Edna Ackland. During the Captain's absence, Edna learns how to drive horse and buggy, knowing that Harry's amputated arm means that he will be helpless to drive himself. Upon his homecoming, Harry is appalled at Edna's display of independence and ashamed that she is forced to become so unwomanly; however, after she explains that she only learned to drive for her new role as caretaker, they again understand one another and decide to marry. The story ends with a careful analysis of the couple's dependence on each other, reassuring the reader that even in such a relationship, traditional gender roles can be maintained: "Her hands guide the reins, and he sits with his empty sleeve beside her. Yet, for all that, his eye is on the road and his voice guides her; so that, in reality, she is only his left hand, and he, the husband, drives." Accompanying the story was an illustration by Winslow Homer (see Figure 22.2).

FIGURE 22.2 "Our Watering Place—The Empty Sleeve at Newport." *Harper's Weekly*, Aug. 26, 1865, 532. Illustration by Winslow Homer.

Although few of the songs about veterans with empty sleeves allude to the female's prosthetic role as caretaker, this gendered relationship would have been implicit in performance. Very likely a woman of the household would have performed the piano part, in which case the use of her two hands would have made her able-bodiedness a meaningful part of the performance. The combination of lyrics about a man who has lost his arm and a woman playing with the use of both of hers would have musically dramatized the veteran's new dependence on the members of his house and community.

Unlike driving, playing the piano was strongly identified with women of middle-class homes, and musical performance was a natural way for women to assert their roles as caretakers. The piano itself was viewed as an instrument that served the health and well-being of the family. From a young age, girls were taught to use musical entertainment at home to distract men from the burdens of their duties and to keep boys out of temptation. According to Ruth Solie, the piano was both an instrument of leisure and a key part of the domestic space because "music was necessary to society, not as mere entertainment but (in the well-regulated and enlightened nineteenth-century home) as a sort of combination spiritual therapy and mental hygiene" (Solie 2004, 95). Given the perception of women as more sensitive and expressive than men, the piano was seen as emblematic of, and the primary outlet for, these feminine qualities.

Most of the songs discussed in this essay were written for women to sing, and feature vocal lines in a middle female register with easily singable melodies. Performances of these songs in which women sang the lyrics would have further underlined the woman's role as surrogate for the disabled veteran. This would have been especially true for a song like "Good Bye, Old Arm!" an 1865 setting based on the same story portrayed in "Old Arm, Good Bye." The lyrics are written in the voice of the soldier, and the song would have allowed the woman to assume his identity in performance.

These performances activated complex webs of prosthetic relationships. The notion of "prosthesis" has a long and complicated history in critical discourse,[8] but in this context, Mitchell and Snyder's theory of "narrative prosthesis" offers analytical insight. According to the theory, disability is a ubiquitous element in literature and has long functioned as a kind of narrative crutch that enables other elements of a narrative (Mitchell and Snyder 2000). For example, in Dickens's *A Christmas Carol*, the narrative role of Tiny Tim is to serve as a metaphorical crutch for Scrooge, enabling Scrooge to awaken his charitable spirit and achieve redemption. Disabled characters also enable, or shore up, notions of normalcy and able-bodiedness by representing that which is different.

The logic of narrative prosthesis informs the performances of the songs about amputee veterans on multiple levels. On one level, the disability of the veteran enables a narrative about personal self-sacrifice and patriotism. That self-sacrifice, in turn, enables a narrative of the health and wholeness of the Union, which is supported by the fortitude of its parts, namely, its soldiers. The veteran's sacrifice becomes a metaphorical prosthetic for the nation, and this logic of substitution (the soldier's body for the nation's body) is frequently made explicit in the songs' lyrics. For example, in General William Hayward's 1865 version of "Good Bye, Old Arm," the lyrics are written in the voice of the amputee veteran addressing his lost arm, and they include the lines "But I don't regret the loss, / Although torn from off my side; / I resign you, for the Union / That the States should not divide."[9]

On another level, the songs enable the narrative of the sympathetic and caretaking woman. By performing the songs, a female pianist would assume the role of a prosthetic for the amputee's missing hand; yet simultaneously, the amputee veteran would become a narrative prosthetic, representing the disability element that supports the woman's comparative able-bodiedness. In other words, a woman's performance in a caretaking capacity involved both submission to the needs of a veteran and the assertion of power over a veteran. These symmetrical prosthetic relationships are complicated further by the nineteenth-century belief that women by definition were not whole or able-bodied relative to men. As Sarah S. Jain argues, the notion that a disabled body can serve as a prosthesis to other bodies that are stereotypically considered not "whole" (i.e., raced bodies, aged bodies, gendered bodies) or vice versa illustrates the intricacies of identity politics in prosthetic theory (Jain 1999, 48).

One way to understand the cultural scripts that are enacted in these songs is through Siebers's concept of "disability drag," or the performance of disability by able-bodied individuals (Siebers 2008). The exemplary cases in twentieth-century media are the ubiquitous instances of able-bodied actors taking roles of people with disabilities: Dustin Hoffman in *Rain Man* (1988), Sean Penn in *I Am Sam* (2002), Michael Sheen and Ron Livingston in *Music Within* (2007), and Colin Firth in *The King's Speech* (2010) are just a few examples. For Siebers, performances of disability drag ultimately repress disability and affirm the ideology of ability because they call attention more to the able-bodied actor's performance than to the lived experience of a disabled individual (114–115). There are potentially positive ramifications to these performances, but generally they are problematic. He explains:

> The advantage of disability drag is that it prompts audiences to embrace disability. Its disadvantage is that disability appears as a façade overlaying able-bodiedness. The use of able-bodied actors, whose bombastic performances represent their able-bodiedness as much as their pretense of disability, not only keeps disability out of public view but transforms its reality and its fundamental characteristics. (116)

Siebers's assessment of disability drag can be productively applied to songs about amputee veterans. The advantage of these songs was that they invited Civil War era Americans to be sympathetic to returning disabled veterans. At the same time, one could argue that these songs masked the experience of disabled veterans in several ways. The performance of the songs by able-bodied performers substituted two different voices—the lyricist's absent voice, present in the text, and the singer's voice, present in the room—for the voice of the disabled veteran. In addition, the songs were marketed to able-bodied consumers, not to the veterans themselves.[10] Furthermore, one could argue that the songs grafted imagined veterans' voices onto sentimental lyrical and musical conventions. Such a blanket argument, however, glosses over the variety and nuances in the representations of disabled veterans.

While most of the songs about amputee veterans were written by men, several of the songs contained lyrics by women, written in the voice of the veteran.[11] In 1864, for example, the prolific lyricist Fanny Crosby (also known as the Blind Poetess) wrote the words to "Good-by, Old Arm" based on the same story that inspired the songs by Hayward and Cooper/Coe. Her version, which was printed in Cincinnati, Chicago, Boston, and Philadelphia, significantly alters the details of the disability encounter. The soldier in the song does not see, but rather *hears* his arm's "doom." One wonders if the change might imply that the soldier had been blinded in addition to losing a limb, or if it reflects the Blind Poetess's own disability and her personal choice to replace sight with sound in the well-known story.

The same publishing consortium also published a song titled "The Empty Sleeve" in 1866 with music by Reverend J. W. (John William) Dadmun and lyrics by Phebe Ann Coffin Hanaford.[12] The song was printed in both Boston and New York in addition to the cities mentioned above. The broad circulation of the song may have been due in part to Hanaford's notoriety as a writer, activist, and minister. In the year prior, Hanaford had published her *Life of Abraham Lincoln*. It was the first biography of Lincoln published after his assassination, and the book sold 20,000 copies. Hanaford was also known as one of the first female ministers in America, as an abolitionist, and as a leading voice in the growing women's rights movement (Tetrault 2002).

Unlike Henry Badger's 1864 song "The Empty Sleeve"—which set a poem by David Barker, as I discuss at the end of this essay—Dadmun and Hanaford's "The Empty Sleeve" was inspired by a steel engraving of the same name. The engraving had been released in New York and Boston that year and quickly became a widely circulated piece of Civil War popular iconography. The lyrics render the two-dimensional engraving into a four-verse song about an anonymous amputee veteran explaining to a young boy the origins and meaning of the empty sleeve as a "badge of bravery and honor."

Although these songs may have been written primarily for women, men were not wholly excluded from the intended audience. Cooper and Coe's "Old Arm, Good Bye," for example, was advertised as "A Beautiful Ballad for Bass, Baritone, or Contralto voice" and features a low, simple melody with a range of only an octave. Other songs, such as "Dear Wife, I'm with You Once Again," contain choruses for male quartet. In fact, the lyrical contents of many of these songs would have been familiar to any veteran who had spent time in an army hospital. During the Civil War, many hospitals began printing their own newspapers with titles such as *The Cripple*, *The Crutch*, and the *Armory Square Hospital Gazette*.[13] Most of these papers were published primarily for convalescing soldiers, who were encouraged to submit their own content. Many men did contribute, and often these contributions were creative responses to the author's experiences of disability. For example, the following poem appeared in an 1863 issue of the *West Philadelphia Hospital Register*.[14] According to the editorial note, it was attributed to "a soldier in a hospital at New Haven, who lost a leg in the battle at Fair Oaks":

L.E.G. on my leg.[15]

Good leg, thou wast a faithful friend,
And truly hast thy duty done;
I thank thee most that to the end—
Thou didst not let this body run.

Strange paradox! that in the fight,
Where I, of thee, was thus bereft,
I lost the left leg for the "Right"
And yet the right's the one that's left!

But while the sturdy stump remains,
I may be able yet to patch it,
For even now I've taken pains,
To make an L.E.G. to match it.

As this poem shows, the act of anthropomorphizing and addressing one's own lost limb was not unique to a song like "Old Arm, Good Bye." Poetic devices like these were used by soldiers to deal with their newly disabled status through humor and sometimes bitter irony. We know little about music making among soldiers in the hospitals; references to music are surprisingly rare in the hospital newspapers. Nevertheless, the fact that soldiers wrote the types of lyrical content that appeared in songs about amputee veterans suggests the songs did capture some aspects of the disabled veteran's voice and experience.

Still, some voices were unequivocally marginalized in the songs. No references to African American veterans with disabilities appear at all, their absence reflecting the sentimental treatment of the disabled veteran.[16] This erasure is particularly striking when considering the important role of disability in national discussions about race and enfranchisement during the period. Many white writers and politicians invoked the image of the African American disabled veteran as proof that African American men were deserving of civil and political rights, including the right to vote (Padilla 2007, 177–182). The sentiment that disability could bridge the racial divide inspired illustrations such as the one shown in Figure 22.3. This illustration appeared in *Harper's Weekly* in April 1865, just after General Lee's surrender at Appomattox, and depicts two amputee soldiers, one African American, the other white, greeting each other as equals.

Also significant is the absence in this song repertoire of any reference to disabilities other than those acquired in the act of service. Veterans with disabilities were viewed as categorically distinct from individuals with nonacquired disabilities (Garland-Thomson 1997).[17] The freak shows represented a more familiar context of

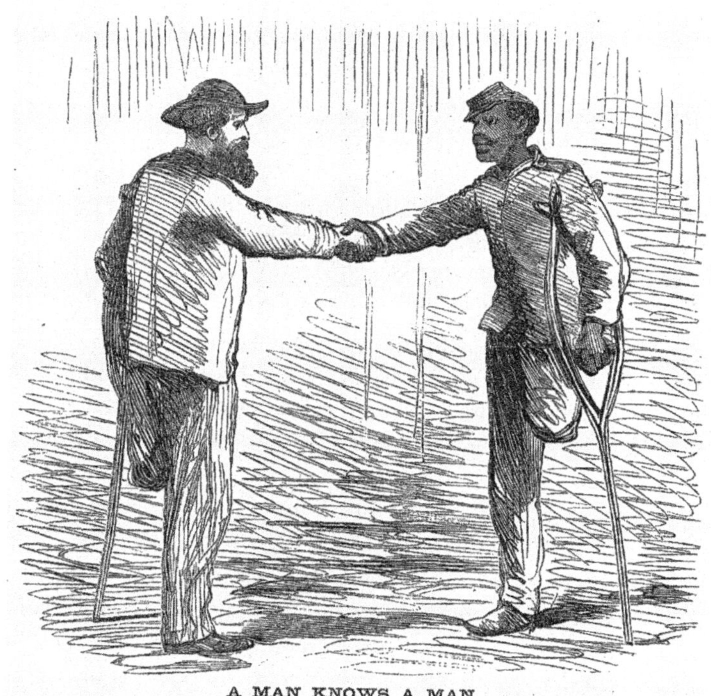
A MAN KNOWS A MAN.
"Give me your hand, Comrade! We have each lost a LEG for the good cause; but, thank GOD, we never lost HEART."
2001 HARPWEEK

FIGURE 22.3 "A Man Knows a Man.—Give me your hand, Comrade! We have each lost a Leg for the good cause; but, thank God, we have never lost Heart." *Harper's Weekly*, April 22, 1865, 265. Artist unknown.

disability for most Americans; as Chemers observes, "by 1863, freaks were so ingrained into American consciousness that the marriage of Tom Thumb shoved news of the Civil War off the front page of the *New York Times* for three days" (Chemers 2008, 73). Attendance at freak shows rose during this period, as more and more people among the working classes became disabled either through the war or through industrial accidents. Garland-Thomson suggests that "perhaps the heightened anxiety of actual or possible disablement among [the working class] drove them either toward an encounter with the physical other as distanced and domesticated or toward sympathetic identification with the stigmatized body" (Garland-Thomson 1997, 65). It is possible that this heightened anxiety also drove up demand for songs that domesticated disability encounters.

Encountering Disability in the Field: "Old Arm, Good Bye" (1866)

George Cooper and S. L. Coe's "Old Arm, Good Bye" presents a disability encounter that takes place between a man and his arm in a hospital bed far from the domestic space of home. A score and recording of the song are available as Track 22.1 and Track 22.2 on the Companion Website.

The ballad opens with the following two verses:

> The knife was still, the surgeon bore the shatter'd arm away:
> Upon his bed in painless sleep the noble hero lay:
> He woke, but saw the vacant place where limb of his had lain.
> Then faintly spoke, "Oh let me see my strong right arm again!"
>
> "Good-bye old arm!" the soldier said, as he clasp'd the fingers cold:
> And down his pale but manly cheeks the teardrops gently roll'd.
> "My strong right arm, no deed of yours now gives me cause to sigh;
> But it's hard to part such trusty friends; Good-by, old arm! Good-by!"

The story told in this song does not give any hint of the realities of medical surgery at the time. Medical supplies, beds, and staff were often scarce; surgeries were commonly make-do; and fatalities were common. The discovery of germs did not happen until after the war, so contamination and infection were rampant. Surgeons thought nothing of reusing the same sponges and instruments—which were often caked with mud, blood, and pus—to clean soldier's wounds. Surgeons also were under pressure to perform amputations as quickly as possible to meet the medical demand, but amputation was a complicated procedure, and it was common for surgical procedures to be performed inadequately.[18]

The focus of the song is the disability encounter. Above the music, the publisher printed the story that inspired not only this song but also at least two other musical settings. The story was well known, widely circulated, and almost always attributed to a particular soldier at the Battle of Stones River near Murfreesboro, Tennessee.[19] Coe and Cooper musically dramatize the story quite faithfully, and they underline the centrality of the moment when the soldier sees his arm. The song exploits the conventional fermata near the end of the verse to emphasize its dramatic crux, pausing on the word "see" in the first verse.

Affectively, the song evokes a love ballad with a touch of melancholy. The vocal line begins with a leap up to a half-step sighing gesture, the same sighing gesture that appears at the beginning of the most popular tear-jerker song of the war, "Weeping, Sad, and Lonely." Its 6/8 meter, melody, and accompaniment all recall an older Irish style with echoes of Oliver Shaw's 1812 setting of Thomas Moore's "Mary's Tears," which was still in print during the Civil War (Hamm 1983, 98). The piano part also includes fleeting moments of Italianate chromaticism that add to the affective angst.

Harmonically, the song moves ambivalently between E♭ major and C minor. We arrive at the word "see" in a moment of uncertainty, on a weakly tonicized C minor chord. The music creates the sense of a soldier who, after seeing his amputated arm, needs a moment to make sense of what it means to look at it. After the fermata, the music resolves back to E♭ major, the tempo resumes, and the uncertainty sounds as if it has been dismissed. The soldier has consciously and bravely decided that the arm is not something to lament but to celebrate for its service. For the rest of the song, the soldier sings to his arm as if it had become fellow soldier, an old friend.

One way to understand this anthropomorphized arm is in a nineteenth-century religious context. According to Fahs, "with the coming of war, the wounded, dying, and dead bodies of soldiers became the vehicle for a new sentimentalism that fused patriotism and Christianity" (Fahs 2000, 111). In this cultural atmosphere, the story invited people to relate to the arm as if it were a Christ-like martyr to a patriotic and divinely supported cause. Without a doubt, some soldiers treated their lost limbs as akin to holy relics. Over the course of the war, thousands of amputated body parts were donated by the soldiers who had owned them to the Army Medical Museum. These limbs were preserved for decades, and veterans could visit the museum to view them, often finding solace in being able to view their limbs long after they had been amputated. One of these soldiers was General Daniel Sickles, who lost his leg to a cannon shell in the Peach Orchard at Gettysburg following his own tactical blunder. After being removed from the field, he had his leg retrieved and mounted in a casket before donating it to the museum. There it was put on display, and Sickles regularly visited the museum to view his leg for the next fifty years. Sickles's leg is still on display today at the National Museum of Health and Medicine near Washington, DC.

This moment of encounter with the amputated limb in the field or in the army hospital carried great cultural significance, and poets and musicians frequently revisited the moment in stories, poems, and songs about amputees. Sometimes the soldier looked at his limb, sometimes he chose not to. Walt Whitman chose the latter scenario for his poem “The Wound-Dresser,” which contains what may be the most famous literary image of an amputee from the Civil War:

> From the stump of the arm, the amputated hand,
> I undo the clotted lint, remove the slough, wash off the matter and blood,
> Back on his pillow the soldier bends with curv'd neck and side-falling head,
> His eyes are closed, his face is pale, he dares not look on the bloody stump,
> And has not yet look'd on it.

Encountering Disability at Home: “Dear Wife I'm with You Once Again” (1865)

The disability encounter is dramatized differently in Frank Ray's “Dear Wife I'm with You Once Again.” The score and recording for this song are available as Track 22.3 and Track 22.4 on the Companion Website.

In this song, the wounded husband has returned home to his wife, but he hopes to influence his wife's encounter with his disability by urging her to remember him as he was:

> Now I am with you once again,
> Look not upon this maimed form,
> Let not the thoughts of it give pain,
> While life remains and love is warm.
> To my country I have giv'n a limb,
> To my wife I bring an unchang'd heart.

Like Whitman's poem, this song portrays a veteran who is unable to look fully at and accept his disability. In this case, the veteran tries to cope by imagining a scene of his body as it once was. The music portrays the veteran's melancholic and lost mental state. The vocal melody begins with the same sighing gesture that opens “Old Arm, Good Bye” and “Weeping, Sad, and Lonely,” and at the end of each line of the verse, the singer trails off while a quiet echo of the vocal line sounds in the piano above. In addition, the use of 2/4 time and a melody of running eighth notes matches many of the songs that were most popular among soldiers. These songs, including Patrick Gilmore's “We Are Coming Father Abra'am,” often were Irish tunes set to patriotic lyrics. Such jaunty 2/4 marching tunes are nostalgically recalled in “Dear Wife I'm with You Once Again,” but Ray dampens their characteristic rhythmic drive.

The chorus conjures the memory of the soldier's appearance on the battlefield in helmet and plume with his limb still intact. It has three different sets of lyrics; the first two are more introspective, and the final chorus addresses the veteran's wife directly:

> Chorus 1:
> Donn'd I the helmet and the plume,
> And I enroll'd myself as one.
>
> Chorus 2:
> 'Tis then when slumber held me fast,
> Back, back to thee in dreams I'd stray.
>
> Chorus 3:
> Tears should not now your bright eyes dim,
> For in this world we will not part.

The chorus is sung by the veteran and a trio that echoes the veteran's words in pianissimo, monotone vocal lines. The texture creates an impression of musical time suspended, sounding like a quiet incantation as the soldier tries to resurrect an invisible image of his past. Perhaps this aural image is meant to remind the listener of an empathetic, collective voice of army comrades, singing from somewhere between the past and the present. For this veteran, imagination and memory are a way of grappling with the graphic reality of his amputation.

Similarly, many Americans looked to fictional tales or religious belief for answers about how to make sense of amputation. "Old Arm, Good Bye!" is a good example because it reads like a fantasy about a soldier's relationship to his all-but sentient arm. Some veterans took comfort in the belief that their lost limb would be restored to them in the afterlife. Louisa May Alcott gave voice to this belief in her popular *Hospital Sketches* (1863). Alcott recounts a conversation with an amputee soldier who tells her "Lord! What a scramble there'll be for arms and legs, when we old boys come out of our graves, on the Judgment Day; wonder if we shall get our own again? If we do, my leg will have to tramp from Fredericksburg, my arm from here, and meet my body, wherever it may be" (Alcott [1863] 2006, 24).

In 1866, the *Atlantic Monthly* printed what became a famous fantastical story about an army surgeon named George Dedlow who loses all four of his limbs. In the story, Dedlow declares he is looking forward to "rejoin[ing] the lost members of my corporeal family in another and a happier world." As it turns out, his reunion with his limbs comes sooner than expected when he encounters them as invisible spirit legs thanks to a medium-guided séance. In front of a room full of stunned witnesses, Dedlow rises and walks on his invisible spirit legs, which are wobbly because they have become inebriated from sitting in alcohol for nine months. This story provides a tongue-in-cheek answer to the anxiety over how to look at the amputation, because the amputated legs are present but cannot be seen and therefore cannot visually disturb. "The Case of George Dedlow" became famous because many readers believed it was true, or at least wished it to be. Shortly after the story appeared in print, droves of visitors began to show up at the hospital where the story was set, asking to visit with Dr. Dedlow.[20]

Encountering Disability Second-Hand: "The Empty Sleeve" (1864)

There were many songs published in the North with variations of the title "The Empty Sleeve" and at least one in the South. Probably the best-known version was the song by Henry Badger, set to an 1862 poem by David Barker. Barker's poem was widely known by both soldiers and civilians.[21] A score and recording for this song are available as Track 22.5 and Track 22.6 on the Companion Website.

In three stanzas, Barker surrounds the disability encounter with a litany of sentimental imagery:

By the moon's pale light to the listening throng,
Let me tell one tale, let me sing one song;
'Tis a tale devoid of aim or plan,
'Tis a story of a one-armed man.
Of one who has bled for a nation's fame,
Tho' a hero who bears but an unknown name,
And till this hour I could ne'er believe
What a tell-tale thing is an empty sleeve.

It tells in a silent tone to all,
Of a country's need and a country's call,
Of a kiss and a tear, for mother and wife,
Of a hurried march for a nation's life,
Of the camp—the charge—the wild surprise.
Of the lonely watch 'neath the midnight skies,
Until this hour, I could ne'er believe
What a story goes with an empty sleeve.

Tho' it points to a myriad wounds and scars.
Yet it tells of a Flag with its stripes and stars,
That in God's own chosen time shall take
The place of a rag with a rattle-snake,
And points to the time when our flag shall wave
O'er a land where there breathes no cowering slave,
Up to the skies let us all then heave
One proud hurrah for the empty sleeve,
For the one-armed brave with the empty sleeve!

Musically, the song is slightly more challenging for the singer than some of the other songs in Figure 22.1. The melody features frequent large-interval leaps and a range from middle C to F5. This song is nothing if not conventional, and until the fourth line we could easily mistake it for a typical parlor ballad about love in the pale moonlight. But as soon as we hear the words "one-armed man," the sentiment is broken, and the flow of the music is disturbed. Though the narrator's vocal line continues unaffected, the words "one-armed man" incite a key change and new accompaniment. Soon thereafter we arrive at the central image of the poem, and with three fermatas, Badger draws and holds our attention on the image of the empty sleeve. This would have been a striking moment despite its conventionality; the female singer, lingering over these jarring words in a performance for a parlor audience, would very likely have opened up a space for the listeners to think about loved ones or their own losses.

What is most interesting about this song is that the way it frames the amputee musically has much in common with the Civil War era photographs of disabled veterans. In typical portraits of disabled soldiers from the time, the wounded amputee sits or poses graciously, preserving the genteel conventions of Victorian portrait photography (see Figure 22.4).[22] At the same time, as Serlin suggests, care is taken to position the amputation in such a way that it is clearly visible, even central to the frame (Serlin 2006, 54). These portraits were considered expressions of extreme patriotism in visual form because they display both loss of ability and strength of self-control and dignity (Serlin 2003, 161).

A song such as "The Empty Sleeve" might have been read in an analogous way. Through music, the song expresses an underlying message of self-control to the listener. Although the text describes the tell-tale sight of an amputation as worthy of veneration, the music tells a different story. In fact, the appearance of the empty sleeve is disruptive to the music. The song begins and ends in the same way, with running eighth notes and a flowing, conventional tune. At the fermata, the image of amputation literally stops the music, but only for a moment as the flow is quickly restored. It is as if the music stops to stare at the empty sleeve, regains its composure, and goes about its business like a dignified Victorian. Implicitly, this song models through music the appropriate manner in which to encounter and understand an empty sleeve as not only a visual signifier but also an aural and narrative signifier.

Serlin makes one additional point about Civil War photographs of disabled veterans that has relevance to this song and to all three of the songs discussed here. Most of these photo portraits, Serlin observes, show the disabled veteran as a lone figure, framing him as an isolated case. In "The Empty Sleeve," the disabled veteran is not only isolated, he is not even physically present. He is fully marginalized. He is a hero with no name, and the able-bodied narrator is more fascinated with the familiar narrative that the empty sleeve summons than with the veteran attached to the empty sleeve. Indeed, the narrator addresses the empty sleeve as if the sleeve had more to say than the veteran, and this surely recalls a song like "Old Arm, Good Bye," where the arm becomes all but anthropomorphized. In "The Empty Sleeve," even the amputated limb has been removed from the picture, and it is only the empty sleeve that becomes a visible symbol of patriotism, sacrifice, and masculinity. Ironically, in order to become this symbol, it has to be metaphorically cut away from the soldier who carries it.

Med. & Surg. Hist. of the War of the Rebellion, Part III. Vol. II. Chap. X.

T. Sinclair & Son lith

PLATE LXXV. AMPUTATIONS AT THE ANKLE JOINT.

Fig. 1. Case of Lieut. W. C. Weeks.
Pirogoff's Operation.

Fig. 2. Case of Pt. J. E. Ayers.
Syme's Operation.

Fig. 3. Case of Pt. J. H. Short.
Syme's Operation.

Fig. 4. Case of Pt. A. K. Russell.
Syme's Operation.

FIGURE 22.4 Portraits of ankle-joint amputees from *The Medical and Surgical History of the War of the Rebellion* (Government Printing Office, 1870–88)

Conclusion

Each song discussed in this essay offers a particular perspective on an imagined encounter with disability, and the performance of these songs enacted complicated cultural scripts of gender, disability, and race. Recalling the *Staunton Spectator* editorial that opens this essay, the author of that editorial described what Garland-Thomson 2009 defines as goal-driven staring. In an analogous way, these songs encouraged those who heard or performed them to engage in a kind of *goal-driven listening*, that is, to use aural clues in the music to summon familiar narratives (of sentimentality, bravery, love). Disability has most commonly been considered in visual terms,[23] but certain notions of the disabled veteran were sonically encoded in these popular songs. As discussed, the type of disabled veteran that was most commonly featured in popular song was specifically defined in terms of race and types of disability. The musical and narrative conventions in these songs were specific as well, and they created a framework for domesticated performances of (select) disabilities. Through these songs, middle-class Americans could both reassess and reinforce Victorian assumptions about disability in the horrific wake of the Civil War.

Acknowledgments

I am particularly indebted to Joseph Straus, Neil Lerner, Julie Singer, Jessica Sternfeld, Raymond Knapp, Michael Accinno, E. Douglas Bomberger, Michael Cuthbert, Kelly St. Pierre, and Daniel Goldmark for their invaluable comments on this essay.

Notes

1. The *Staunton Spectator* was a pro-Union newspaper based in Staunton, Virginia, a mid-sized town that was located roughly equidistant from Washington, DC, and Richmond, Virginia, the capitals of the Union and the Confederacy. The divided allegiances in Staunton resulted in the unusual situation of two rival newspapers in one town, one pro-Union and one (the *Staunton Vindicator*) pro-Confederate.
2. The *Lynchburg Republican* was a pro-Confederate newspaper in Lynchburg, Virginia. Major Robert Henry Glass, the paper's editor, fought for the Confederacy and was an influential figure in the state. The reference to it in this editorial indicates that the author implicitly addresses veterans of both sides. Given the Union allegiance of the *Spectator*, the author's remarks are directed at least in part toward Union veterans. By praising the remarks in the pro-Confederate *Lynchburg Republican*, the author seems to suggest that the heroism of disabled veterans is one issue on which both sides can agree. The visibility and violence of amputation meant that few people would deny the heroism and sacrifice of amputee soldiers on either side. At the same time, the North and South generally

understood such sacrifices in different terms. Northern literature and songs that referred to amputee veterans often appealed to the idea of sacrificing the wholeness of one's body in order to maintain the wholeness of the Union (some of these songs are discussed in this paper). Southerners appealed to other values such as loyalty, chivalry, and individual rights as just causes for a soldier's sacrifice.

3. Early in the war, when the federal government began to give pensions to Union amputees, the type of amputation determined not only social standing but also the amount of financial assistance a veteran could expect. In an effort to mitigate the enormous monetary burden on the government, Congress authorized specific rewards based not only on what limb was lost but also on how much of that limb a veteran retained. See Padilla 2007 and Logue and Blanck 2010. Similar cost-cutting measures were employed by the Southern states in the hierarchy of benefits allotted to disabled Confederate veterans, who received much less support than Union veterans. For example, see McClurken 2009 for how this disparity played out in the lives of Virginians.
4. Selected sources, in addition to those cited elsewhere in this paper, include Newman 1993; O'Connor 1997; Gerber 2000; Ott, Serlin, and Migm 2002; Goler 2004; Connor and Rhode 2003; Clarke 2011; and Nelson 2012.
5. A few popular Southern poems did feature or recognize veterans with disabilities, including "Hospital Duties"; "The Return"; "The Empty Sleeve," by Dr. J. R. Bagby; and "Little Giffin," by Dr. Francis O. Ticknor. All of these can be found in the volume *War Songs and Poems of the Southern Confederacy, 1861–1865*, compiled by H. M. Wharton. On the typical differences between Northern and Southern songs, see Moseley 1991.
6. On the impact of the war's death toll and Americans' struggles to find meaning in the carnage, see Faust 2009.
7. In his essay in this volume, Michael Accinno discusses the role of music in the treatment of disabled veterans in public spaces and shows that musical performances such as organ grinding created opportunities for veterans to visually and sonically assert their rightful place in these spaces.
8. See Bruce Quaglia's essay in this volume.
9. As explained in the first part of this essay, the idea of sacrificing the wholeness of one's body in order to maintain the wholeness of the Union would have resonated much differently in the North. The prevalence of this idea may further explain why poems and songs about amputee veterans appeared more frequently in the North than in the South.
10. It has been suggested that an increase in one-hand piano works in the 1870s and 1880s reflected an interest in marketing these pieces to amputee veterans (Lerner 2006 and Garland-Thomson 2009). It is probable, however, that few of these pieces were published with amputee veterans in mind. A survey of the main bibliographies of one-handed piano music, Edel 1994 and Patterson 1999, indicates that the models for most of these pieces were European one-hand piano works and etudes that explored pianistic virtuosity. If the sheet music publishers had intended to market music that was accessible to amputee veterans, one would have expected these works to begin appearing earlier, before the market for Civil War–related sheet music bottomed out almost immediately after hostilities ceased. Notably, the 1870s and 1880s marked a sharp decline in songs about disabled veterans (see Figure 22.1). It is likely that the idea of publishing music for and by amputee veterans did not emerge until the wars of the twentieth century (see Howe 2010).
11. The cross-gender ventriloquism of many of these songs raises some of the same questions that pertain to Robert Schumann's song cycle *Frauenliebe und Leben*, op. 42. There are a

number of interesting parallels between the song cycle and the songs about amputee veterans, including the fact that the cycle opens with a staring encounter and a reference to disability; the first two lines in the first lied are "Seit ich ihn gesehen, / Galub ich blind zu sein" [Since first seeing him, / I think I am blind].

12. Hanaford is identified as "Mrs. P. A. Hanaford" in the sheet music. She published prolifically and often under her initials and last name.
13. These hospital newspapers present a wealth of information on the experiences of disabled and ill soldiers, the medical history of this period, and the Civil War itself. Recently, efforts to digitize close to full runs of some of these papers has made this information accessible for the first time. Many of the newspapers printed for hospitals around Washington, DC, are available digitally as part of the Civil War Washington website at http://www.civilwardc.org/texts/newspapers/.
14. The *West Philadelphia Hospital Register* was one of the earliest hospital newspapers to begin publishing, and it had a wide circulation. The paper was published at Satterlee General Hospital, which was a flagship, cutting-edge hospital that modeled many of the Civil War era reforms of the medical system.
15. L. E. G. is a play on "Elegy."
16. As Fahs notes, the "individualized sentimental soldier was coded as white in Northern popular literature" (Fahs 2000, 129).
17. Michael Accinno details the ways in which amputee veterans were treated differently than other marginalized groups in his essay in this volume.
18. Because of the quality of medical care, many men were afraid of dying not in battle with honor but in a hospital due to inadequate medical care. This anxiety is the basis for a brief anonymous piece of satire that was reprinted in numerous hospital newspapers under the title "An Off-Hand Joke." It turns the disability encounter into a darkly humorous moment: "A sturdy sergeant of one of the Massachusetts regiments being obliged to submit to have his hand amputated, the surgeon offered to administer chloroform as usual, but the veteran refused, saying: 'If the cutting was to be done on him he wanted to see it.' And laying his arm on the table submitted to the operation without a sign of pain except a firmer setting of the teeth. The operator, as he finished, looked at his victim with admiration, and remarked: 'You ought to have been a surgeon my man.' 'Was the next thing to one afore I enlisted,' said the hero. 'What was that?' asked the doctor. 'A butcher,' replied the sergeant, with a grim smile, which, despite the circumstances, communicated itself to the bystanders."
19. Whether or not such a story happened at the Battle of Stones River in the manner in which the story became famous is impossible to say. However, a virtually identical story titled "Good Bye, Old Friend" appeared on the front page of the August 15, 1861, *White Cloud Kansas Chief* and attributed the act to a soldier at the battle of Big Bethel, one of the earliest battles of the Civil War. This story appeared in print only four months after the war began, and almost sixteen months before Stones River. It seems likely that the tale reprinted in the sheet music was not an original story, but one that had crystallized into a particularly well-known version. Like any good myth, the story was based in some truth and remained in popular memory long after the war. For example, an 1890 essay about a former Northern general John Logan, who had recently passed away, mentioned that he kept a framed copy of this story hanging next to his own portrait in his Civil War photo gallery. The article stated, "General Logan was very fond of dwelling on this sad and inspiring incident" (Crowley 1890, 373). As late as 1905, the story appeared in print in one of

chaplain John Sayers's renowned Memorial Day sermons that he delivered to veterans at Gettysburg.

20. The story was actually by a young physician named Silas Weir Mitchell, who wrote it in response to the phantom limbs phenomena he was witnessing among his patients. These phenomena were not considered real by the medical community at the time, and Mitchell could not get his work published in medical outlets, so he resorted to publishing his work as an anonymous work of fiction.
21. The poem appeared in many civilian and military hospital newspapers, often with variations to the words, and sometimes under the name Lewis Barker.
22. Many of these portraits were made for the Army medical museum, which kept an incredible photographic and documentary record of war wounds and deaths. The massive effort to collect data about the war eventually resulted in the publication of the six folio, 6,000 page, fifty-six-pound *Medical and Surgical History of the War of the Rebellion*. This history took 23 years to compile and the intervention of Congress to publish it. Its printing reportedly cost over $100,000 (the equivalent of over $2.25 million dollars today).
23. See Blake Howe's essay in this volume.

References

Alcott, Louisa May. (1863) 2006. *Hospital Sketches*. Mineola, NY: Dover.

Chemers, Michael M. 2008. *Staging Stigma: A Critical Examination of the American Freak Show*. New York: Palgrave Macmillan.

Clarke, Frances M. 2011. *War Stories: Suffering and Sacrifice in the Civil War North*. Chicago and London: University of Chicago Press.

Connor, J. T. H., and Michael G. Rhode. 2003. "Shooting Soldiers: Civil War Medical Images, Memory, and Identity in America." *Invisible Culture: An Electronic Journal for Visual Culture* 5.

Crowley, Mrs. Richard. 1890. *Echoes from Niagara: Historical, Political, Personal*. Buffalo, NY: Charles Wells Moulton.

Davis, Lennard. 1995. *Enforcing Normalcy: Disability, Deafness, and the Body*. London and New York: Verso.

Edel, Theodore. 1994. *Piano Music for One Hand*. Bloomington: Indiana University Press.

"An Elegy." 1863. *West Philadelphia Hospital Register*, August 22, 169.

"The Empty Sleeve at Newport; Or, Why Edna Ackland Learned to Drive." 1865. *Harper's Weekly*, August 26.

"Empty Sleeves." 1869. *Staunton Spectator*, October 20, 1.

Fahs, Alice. 2000. "The Sentimental Soldier in Popular Civil War Literature, 1861–1865." *Civil War History* 46 (2): 107–131.

Faust, Drew Gilpin. 2009. *This Republic of Suffering: Death and the American Civil War*. New York: Vintage.

Figg, Laurann, and Jane Farrell-Beck. 1993. "Amputation in the Civil War: Physical and Social Dimensions." *Journal of the History of Medicine and Applied Sciences* 48 (4): 454–475.

Garland-Thomson, Rosemarie. 1997. *Extraordinary Bodies: Figuring Physical Disability in American Culture and Literature*. New York: Columbia University Press.

Garland-Thomson, Rosemarie. 2009. *Staring: How We Look*. Oxford and New York: Oxford University Press.

George, Charles, Herbert George, Jere George, and Osman George. 2012. *"Bully for the Band!": The Civil War Letters and Diary of Four Brothers in the 10th Vermont Infantry Band.* Edited by James A. Davis. Jefferson, NC: McFarland.

Gerber, David A. 2000. *Disabled Veterans in History.* Ann Arbor: University of Michigan Press.

Goler, Robert I. 2004. "Loss and the Persistence of Memory: 'The Case of George Dedlow' and Disabled Civil War Veterans." *Literature and Medicine* 23 (1): 160–183.

Hamm, Charles. 1983. *Yesterdays: Popular Song in America.* New York: Norton.

Heaps, Willard A., and Porter W. Heaps. 1960. *The Singing Sixties: The Spirit of Civil War Days Drawn from the Music of the Times.* Norman: University of Oklahoma Press.

Howe, Blake. 2010. "Paul Wittgenstein and the Performance of Disability." *Journal of Musicology* 27 (2): 135–180.

Jain, Sarah S. 1999. "The Prosthetic Imagination: Enabling and Disabling the Prosthesis Trope." *Science, Technology, and Human Values* 24 (1): 31–54.

Lerner, Neil. 2006. "The Horrors of One-Handed Pianism: Music and Disability in *The Beast with Five Fingers.*" In *Sounding Off: Theorizing Disability in Music,* edited by Neil Lerner and Joseph N. Straus, 75–89. New York and London: Routledge.

Logue, Larry M., and Peter Blanck. 2010. *Race, Ethnicity, and Disability: Veterans and Benefits in Post-Civil War America.* New York: Cambridge University Press.

Marten, James. 2011. *Sing Not War: The Lives of Union and Confederate Veterans in Gilded Age America.* Chapel Hill: University of North Carolina Press.

McClurken, Jeffrey W. 2009. *Take Care of the Living: Reconstructing Confederate Veteran Families in Virginia.* Charlottesville: University of Virginia Press.

McGuire, Judith White. 1868. *Diary of a Southern Refugee, during the War.* New York: E. J. Hale.

McWhirter, Christian. 2012. *Battle Hymns: Music and the American Civil War.* Chapel Hill: University of North Carolina Press.

Mitchell, David T., and Sharon L. Snyder. 2000. *Narrative Prosthesis: Disability and the Dependencies of Discourse.* Ann Arbor: University of Michigan Press.

Moseley, Caroline. 1991. "Irrepressible Conflict: Differences between Northern and Southern Songs of the Civil War." *Journal of Popular Culture* 25 (2): 45–56.

Nelson, Megan Kate. 2012. *Ruin Nation: Destruction and the American Civil War.* Athens and London: University of Georgia Press.

Newman, Kathy. 1993. "Wounds and Wounding in the American Civil War: A Visual History." *Yale Journal of Criticism* 6 (2): 63–86.

O'Connor, Erin. 1997. "'Fractions of Men': Engendering Amputation in Victorian Culture." *Comparative Studies in Society and History* 39 (4): 742–777.

Ott, Katherine, David Serlin, and Steven Migm, eds. 2002. *Artificial Parts, Practical Lives: Modern Histories of Prosthetics.* New York: New York University Press.

Padilla, Jalynn Olsen. 2007. "Army of 'Cripples': Northern Civil War Amputees, Disability, and Manhood in Victorian America." PhD diss., University of Delaware.

Patterson, Donald L. 1999. *One Handed: A Guide to Piano Music for One Hand.* Westport, CT, and London: Greenwood.

Scarry, Elaine. 1985. *The Body in Pain.* New York and Oxford: Oxford University Press.

Serlin, David. 2003. "Queerness and Disability in U.S. Military Culture, 1800–1945." *Journal of Lesbian and Gay Studies* 9 (1–2): 149–179.

Serlin, David. 2006. "The Other Arms Race." In *The Disability Studies Reader,* 2nd ed., edited by Lennard Davis, 49–65. New York: Routledge.

Siebers, Tobin. 2008. *Disability Theory.* Ann Arbor: University of Michigan Press.

Solie, Ruth A. 2004. *Music in Other Words: Victorian Conversations*. Berkeley: University of California Press.

Tetrault, Lisa M. 2002. "A Paper Trail: Piecing Together the Life of Phebe Hanaford." *Nantucket Harvest* 51 (2). http://www.nha.org/history/hn/HNhanaford.htm.

Trachtenberg, Alan. 1989. *Reading American Photographs: Images as History, Matthew Brady to Walker Evans*. New York: Hill and Wang.

Whitman, Walt. 1864. "Our Wounded and Sick Soldiers." *New York Times*, December 11.

CHAPTER 23

"THE ABSURD DISORDERING OF NOTES"

Dysfunctional Memory in the Post-Traumatic Music of Ivor Gurney

BETH KEYES

> *After all, my friend, it is better to live a grey life in mud and danger, so long as one uses it—as I trust I am now doing—as a means to an end. Someday all this experience may be crystallized and glorified in me; and men shall learn by chance fragments in a string quartet or symphony, what thoughts haunted the minds of men who watched the darkness grimly in desolate places.*
>
> —Ivor Gurney, Private 3895 (British Army)
> Southern France: December 15, 1916[1]

For four grueling months between July and November of 1916, along a twenty-five mile stretch of the Western Front that crossed over the River Somme, over a million Allied men were engaged in one of the most callously bloody battles in the history of twentieth-century warfare.[2] Stationed in the region of Pozières during the height of the conflict was George Butterworth, a thirty-one-year-old composer from Yorkshire County who served as Lieutenant of the 13th Battalion Durham Light Infantry. On the fifth of August, while fighting in a trench later named in his honor, Butterworth was shot and killed by sniper's fire. He was one of nearly 420,000 British soldiers to be labeled a casualty during the Battle of the Somme (Hart 2008, 528). As a consequence of one of Britain's grandest offensive failures, his notorious death has since come to mark the symbolic end of an innocent idealism that had led the nation's people through the beginning of the Great War (Riley 2010, 147).

Before ending up on the riverbanks of northern France in 1916, Butterworth had been a promising student at the Royal College of Music (RCM), where he had garnered much praise for his refined settings of traditional British poetry (Hold 2002, 234–243).

Shortly before the start of the war, he composed *Bredon Hill and Other Songs* (1912), a five-piece cycle set to the text of A. E. Housman. Many have found a sad sort of irony in Butterworth's decision to use "On the Idle Hill of Summer," a portion of Housman's *Shropshire Lad* that quite evocatively depicts the chaos and carnage of battle:

On the idle hill of summer,
sleepy with the flow of streams,
Far I hear the steady drummer
drumming like a noise in dreams.

Far and near and low and louder,
on the roads of earth go by,
Dear to friends and food for powder,
soldiers marching, all to die.

East and west on fields forgotten
bleach the bones of comrades slain,
Lovely lads and dead and rotten
none that go return again.

Far the calling bugles hollo,
high the screaming fife replies,
Gay the files of scarlet follow:
woman bore me, I will rise.[3]

The poignancy, of course, is obvious: in choosing this particular section of Housman's work, Butterworth essentially foretold the unfortunate narrative of his own fatality. The retrospective irony, however, lies within the composer's musical treatment of the text. Where Housman uses graphically descriptive imagery to depict the inherently gruesome nature of war in the third stanza, Butterworth's strophic composition calmly returns to the quiet, pastoral setting of the primary theme (Butterworth 1974). Knowing nothing yet of war's horrific realities, the composer uses modally inflected harmony and simply expressive lyricism to emphasize the beauty of Britain's idyllic natural landscape and a pride in England's rich cultural heritage. In its naivety, Butterworth's idiom is a quintessential example of the cultural and musical values of early twentieth-century, prewar Great Britain.[4]

Nearly fifty miles north of Butterworth Trench in Pozières, another composition student from the RCM was stationed on the Western Front during the summer of 1916.[5] Ivor Gurney—Private No. 3895 of the 2nd/5th Gloucesters—had only just entered the trenches at Riez Bailleul by the time of Butterworth's death, but would not leave the war until it was nearly over. Though his stay at the front line was relatively brief, the twenty-six-year-old soldier experienced an incredibly arduous tour of duty while in France. Less than two years after his arrival, he was diagnosed by military doctors with a case of "Nervous Breakdown from Deferred Shell Shock," discharged from the army, and sent back to his native Gloustershire with a modest pension and a debilitating psychological disability (Hurd 1978). By 1922, barely able to assimilate into civilian life after his return home from the war, Gurney was institutionalized in the City of London Mental Hospital at Dartford in Kent. He remained incarcerated there for the last fifteen years of his life.

As a fellow composer of English song both before and after the war, Gurney knew Butterworth's work well. In the year following his discharge from service, he returned to the RCM and began working on a song cycle named in honor of his university's fallen alumnus (Gurney 2011, iii). Although *When Smoke Stood Up from Ludlow and Other Songs* eventually became *Ludlow and Teme*, many thematic nods to his predecessor remained: the fifth song of his cycle, for example, revisits the same Housman verse used in the earlier composer's work. But Gurney, having survived the war with permanent, crippling psychological damage, had a starkly different musical interpretation of Housman's words. In Gurney's "On the Idle Hill of Summer," evocations of England's natural beauty are sharply disrupted by a pandemonium of structural fragmentation and stifling textural density. At the moment in Housman's poem when the narrative voice realizes the horrid fate of men marching toward the battlefield, Gurney's minimalist musical fragments turn from innocuous, repetitive ideas into catalysts for complete organizational anarchy. Rhythmic and melodic motion becomes jagged and irregular, disconnecting each lyrical phrase through the mayhem of temporal and linear confusion. If Butterworth's musical visions of war had illustrated an idyllic dream, then Gurney's portrayed the morbid nightmares of a disillusioned, shell-shocked veteran.

The vast differences that exist between the emotional affects of these two lyrically identical pieces provokes a number of questions about the relationship between music, traumatic experience, cognitive dysfunction, disabled memory, and the Great War. While the most conspicuous cause of Gurney's comparatively dissimilar treatment of Housman's text is a matter of his individual compositional identity, a deeper cultural and psychological symbolism resides within his unique reaction to the poem. In this essay, I investigate this symbolism through the musical metaphors of traumatic memory that are enacted in Gurney's work. To do so, I posit "On the Idle Hill of Summer" as a vivid aural representation of the dysfunctionally traumatized mind as it was conceptualized in the sociocultural context of postwar Britain.

This context is best understood through a multifaceted examination of the many institutional forces that shaped a pathologized disease of the body and mind from an array of observed human reactions to extremely stressful events. First, I outline Gurney's path through the war as an exemplary illustration of the immense change in cultural attitude that occurred between 1914 and 1918—a shift away from Butterworth's naive optimism that allowed shell-shock to emerge as a socially viable expression of traumatic distress. Next, I unpack the contemporary psychological and neurological definitions of shell-shock, a particular disease entity that was fluidly defined throughout medical, military, and social discourses. In the debates surrounding how war neurosis should be classified and identified during and after the Great War, these discursive elements inadvertently laid much of the groundwork for conceptualizations of traumatic stress throughout the rest of the twentieth century. At the core of this foundation, three theoretical metaphors defining trauma as a disorder of memory, time, and identity can be mapped onto various musical processes. Finally, I analyze Gurney's "On the Idle Hill of

Summer" as a piece that reproduces the mental work of trauma through these abstract conceptual paradigms. In doing so, Gurney's music embodies and performs disability through particular disturbances of texture, structure, and form.

Cultural Trauma in the Wake of the Great War

When a massive international conflict slowly erupted on the European continent during the summer of 1914, the people of Great Britain were swept up by a fury of nationalistic zeal that inspired their will to fight for the conservation of the British nation. By the time Britain officially declared war on the fourth of August, the press had already begun an alarming campaign for the protection of British cultural values under the guise of a physical and ideological threat from the German people; Lord Kitchener, the recently appointed Secretary of State for War, had no trouble getting the volunteers he demanded in his initial efforts to bolster the nation's army.[6] When Kitchener asked for 100,000 men in his first call to arms, he was met by nearly 480,000 at the doors of recruitment offices throughout the nation in the first month of fighting (Simkins 1988). Britain entered the Great War with an astounding level of excitement, enthusiasm, and determination.

Gurney, a burgeoning poet and composer from a small town on the Severn River, was one such eager recruit: only four days after the war broke, he made a first attempt to enlist with his local battalion, the 1st/5th Gloucesters. Although the army initially denied his request (citing the young man's poor vision), Gurney never lost sight of the battlefield. Like many, he was driven toward the naively exciting prospect of combat by an intense pride in his native land and a strong sense of duty to protect its citizens. But aside from these common motivations, Gurney was further compelled to serve for a far more specific and personal reason. While struggling under the pressures of a heavy student workload at the RCM, he had developed a persistent illness characterized by recurring bouts of depression, stomach pain, and general malaise. Under a contemporary diagnostic rubric, these ailments were vaguely defined as symptoms of "neurasthenia," a nervous disorder that could theoretically be cured through the rigorous strains of a military lifestyle.[7] Gurney therefore believed that joining the war effort was a matter not only of civic responsibility but also of his physical and psychological welfare. To his relief, he was finally enlisted with the 2nd/5th Gloucestershire Regiment on February 9, 1915. The private embarked on training shortly thereafter, expressing immense satisfaction with his decision in a letter to Herbert Howells on April 8:

> As to whether I like soldiering, I am convinced that had I stuck to music, complete health would have been a very long job. This life will greatly help. Secondly, supposing I had not joined, and never attained my high aim in music—I could not have forgiven myself. *Thirdly*, that if I got shot, it won't matter to me what my possibilities

> (with health) might or might not be. *4thly*. That the life, though hard, and the food scant and coarse, makes me as happy as I can be made without yacht and money. It is hard, and always I am tired, but struggle through in a very much happier frame of mind than that I have had for some time—probably 4 years. There's your answer, and longer than you wanted I daresay. (Gurney 1991, 17)

Excitement, hope, and relief quickly turned to fear and distrust, however, as the unprecedented consequences of the Great War were eventually revealed to soldiers and citizens across Europe. Violent new technologies of combat brought to the battlegrounds of France in 1914 propelled a conflict that was far longer and far more destructive than any could anticipate: mounted machine guns, chemical weaponry, and trench warfare left soldiers on both sides of the fighting line physically and psychologically imprisoned by the torments of an unspeakably horrific environment.[8] Gurney, too, had no idea what was waiting for him in the trenches of Riez Bailleul when he arrived in June of 1916. In his first year there, while remaining somewhat optimistic, he soon grew weary of the filth, disease, tension, and boredom that had come to characterize life in the trenches of World War I:

> One is allowed to sleep off duty—but not in dugouts and the average, now the cold weather has come, and rain, is about 3 hours sleep. Out of the trenches there are parades, inspections, chiefly for shortages, and fatigues [. . .] The life is as grey as it sounds, but one manages to hang on to life by watching the absolute unquenchability of the cheerier spirits—wonderful people some of them; after all, it is better to be depressed with reason than without.[9]

Though melancholy, Gurney found little to complain about in the mundane early days of his station on the Western Front. By the end of 1917, however, dramatic circumstances had irrevocably changed his outlook on the war. In mid-April, he was temporarily relieved from the trenches after a bullet grazed his arm; only months after his return, he was gassed while on guard at St. Julien. After the attacks, the once resilient soldier slowly fell into an acute crisis of health, as many of his past physical and psychological ailments resurfaced with even greater force. While being shuttled between several military hospitals in an effort to relieve his symptoms, his behavior became increasingly erratic. Gurney's letters, once coherent and well organized, began to exhibit a jarring trail of fragmented, disjointed ideas:

> What a life! What a life! My memories of this week will be: Blockhouse; an archway there through which a sniper used his skill on us as we emerged from the room at the side; cold; stuffy heat; Brett Young; smashed or stuck Tanks; a gas and smoke barrage put up by us, a glorious but terrible sight; Fritz's shells: one sunset: two sunrises: "Bible in Spain"; the tale of the cutting up of the K.R.R's [King's Royal Rifle Corps] in 1914; of Colonel Elkington; of the first gas attack also; of the Brigade Orderly; and of the man who walked in his sleep to Fritzy, slept well, woke, realised, and bolted; Thirst; Gas; Shrapnel; Very H.E.; Our liquid fire; a first sight of an aeroplane map . . . Does it

> sound interesting? May God forgive me if I ever come to cheat myself into thinking that it was, and lie later to younger men of the Great Days. It was damnable: and what in relation to what might have happened? Nothing at all! We have been lucky, but it is not fit for men to be here—in this tormented dry-fevered marsh, where men die and are left to rot because of snipers and the callousness that War needs. "It might be me tomorrow. Who cares? Yet still, hang on for a Blighty."[10]

Finally, after being shipped to the Napsbury War Hospital in 1918, Gurney collapsed under the weight of immense psychological distress. In mid-June, the ill soldier sent a letter home announcing his plan for suicide with a heartrending claim that he would be better off "dead than mad" (Gurney 1991, 430). Military doctors intercepted the private's death wish and discharged him from service several months later. He was sent back to Gloucester in shambles, a six-word diagnosis marring his release papers: "Nervous Breakdown from Deferred Shell-Shock." By 1918, it had become one of the most common and heavily stigmatized reasons for discharge from the British Army (Mosse 2000, 101).

So common, in fact, that the figure of the shell-shocked soldier was an object of public fascination: it was the visible, physical embodiment of an anxiety that had worn through the social fabric of Great Britain by the time of the postwar years.[11] As soldiers arrived home with disturbing physical and psychological injuries, Britons were finally forced to face the grave repercussions of mechanized, total warfare that had killed nearly 750,000 of their brothers, sons, fathers, and husbands.[12] As civilians on the home front assessed the true cost of a war they had once so vigorously supported, a wave of bleak hopelessness similarly infected British troops:

> I am not well of course, but the thing that struck me on the boat coming over was that no one looked well. There was not any more jollity among all that crowd going to Blighty than if it were merely Another Move. The iron had entered into their souls, and they were still fast bound; unable to realize what tremendous changes of life had come to them for a while. Dear Marion, this was sad to see . . . (Gurney 1983, 206)

As Gurney describes, traumatic shock had pervaded the entire cultural climate of Great Britain by the end of the war. Collectively devastated by the resounding impact of the war's destructive course, the British populace struggled to adjust to life in a postwar world—a world where death, disfigurement, insanity, terror, and uncertainty had become the norm. While facing the grim prospect of this unstable future, Britons attempted to process traumatic memories of the past through collective acts of remembrance and memorialization. In doing so, new cultural identities were forged within expressive representations of postwar trauma throughout the nation (Cizmic 2011, 1–43; Luckhurst 2008).[13]

Shell-shocked veterans returned to this social atmosphere as living symbols of Britain's inability to properly manage memories of the war. During the widespread effort to regain a sense of cultural and political "normalcy," these men confronted the public with vividly embodied performances of traumatic moments they had experienced on the Western Front. Their disabilities too closely mimicked feminine forms of hysterical weakness, threatening the values of Victorian masculinity and the moral fortitude of British male identity.[14] And as psychologically stable men were labeled mad and sent home from the battlefield, the lines between sanity and insanity that had existed in pre-1914 Britain were distorted indefinitely.

Shell-Shock and the Psychopathologization of Traumatic Memory

Modern estimates claim that anywhere between 80,000 and 200,000 British officers and soldiers like Gurney were diagnosed with shell-shock over the total course of the war and its aftermath (Bogacz 1989; Luckhurst 2008). From the very first months of fighting, worrisome tales began to circulate throughout military, medical, and civilian communities: after merely witnessing the horrors of trench combat, soldiers were severely impaired by a number of physical symptoms that had no apparent cause of injury. These men went blind, though their visual systems were still functionally intact; they were paralyzed, even when their bodies had been untouched by enemy fire; they were speechless, despite no obvious damage or obstruction to their throats, lungs, or vocal cords. Although the concept of combat-induced traumatic illness was a familiar one at the turn of the twentieth century, these men exhibited an unprecedented manifestation of what was historically known as "war neurosis."[15] This new form of a previously rare disorder (also somewhat interchangeably referred to as "traumatic neurosis" and "shell-shock") was understood to be a direct result of modern, mechanized warfare.

As soldiers flooded out of the trenches and into the war hospitals, debilitated by a disease that had no perceptible physical cause, neurologists across Europe began a fierce debate about how to diagnose and heal their phantom wounds.[16] The political, psychiatric, and popular discourse surrounding shell-shock became especially prominent in Great Britain, where roughly 65,000 veterans were still collecting a pension for the disorder two years after the war had ended.[17] In 1920, the House of Lords established an official "War Office Committee of Enquiry into 'Shell-Shock'" in order to aggregate and examine the testimony of professionals who had had firsthand experience with affected infantrymen during the war.[18] For two years, fifteen of the most respected minds in the British medical and military institutions investigated the cause of an epidemic that had swept through their troops and attempted to resolve the numerous discrepancies over how war neurosis should be classified and protected under the law as a psychological disability. Their results were inconclusive, at best. As Ted Bogacz writes in his analysis of the committee's final report, "what may be most striking to the modern reader is the ambivalence, antagonism and even confusion of intelligent men confronted with a startling and ambiguous phenomenon for which little in their background or education had prepared them" (1989, 239).

Why, we might ask today, did such knowledgeable and experienced specialists have so much trouble defining the terms of an illness that had been so readily identified in hundreds of thousands of men across Britain? To begin, the phrase "shell-shock"—famously codified by Dr. Charles Samuel Myers in 1915—had grown to encompass many disparate forms of aberrant bodily functions and unusual behaviors. On one end of the spectrum, there were clusters of physical symptoms such as blindness, deafness, paralysis, aphasia, and the inability to control fluid motion of muscles and limbs (which resulted in twitching, inappropriate movements, and a characteristically unusual gait). On the other, there were symptoms that appeared to reside purely in the mind: depression, anxiety, restlessness, amnesia, hypersensitivity to certain stimuli, flashbacks, and intense nightmares. Because of this diversity of symptoms (which almost always presented as comorbid conditions), shell-shock lacked cohesion as a diagnostic entity. Furthermore, with no unified system of identification from one military hospital to the next, almost any unusual reaction to trench warfare could be labeled a case of shell-shock in the absence of a more obviously identifiable somatic problem (Shephard 2001, Lerner 2001, Leese 2002, Reid 2010).

For an exemplary case of this complex disease, consider the history of Private C—R—, a twenty-one-year-old patient of leading British neurologist Dr. Frederick W. Mott. Mott, a member of the War Office Committee who dedicated a lifetime to interrogating the causes and patterns of degenerative nervous illnesses, published the story of Private C—R—in his groundbreaking study, *War Neurosis and Shell Shock*:

> He was carrying sandbags in the company of thirty men in daylight and under shell fire. The explosion flung him into a deep hole, and he climbed out to see all his friends lying around dead. This was his first sight of death, and he keeps seeing it again, both awake and asleep, with bright lights and bursting shells. He does not hear the shells, but sometimes the men shouting. He sometimes *dreams* that he hears the shells exploding and the shouts of men. He said that he had always felt sick at the sight of blood.
>
> When admitted to the hospital he presented an aspect of extreme terror. He sat up in bed with eyes staring wide, pupils dilated, brow wrinkled, nostrils dilated, mouth slightly open, and muttering sounds. He moves his head from side to side with occasional moans and groans, and moves his arms as if indicating something lying on the ground, alternating this with a movement of his right hand to his forehead. He keeps saying, "You won't let me back." [. . .] I came to the conclusion from his subsequent complete recovery that this man was naturally of a timorous disposition, and that his condition was largely shock and terror due to two causes, viz. the memory of dreams of his awful experiences of war, and the continuous fear of his being sent back to the front. He was subsequently transferred to Morden Hall, where he has completely recovered. (Mott 1919, 33–34)

Throughout his book, Mott highlights cases such as the young Private C—R— to categorize the various kinds of abnormal reactions a soldier might have under different stressors of war. Though the doctor establishes that his patient was shocked into illness by a single traumatic event, he concedes that the resounding manifestation of his physical and mental symptoms were the result of a preexisting "timorous disposition" and the constant "memory of dreams of his awful experiences of war" (Mott 1919, 34).[19] In drawing these conclusions, Mott (alongside many of his contemporaries) was conceptualizing shell-shock as a multifaceted physiological and psychological phenomonon.

Prior to the war, the study of traumatic neurosis had flourished within the two intersectional fields of neurology and psychology. In the former field, leading physician Hermann Oppenheim had observed and documented the effects of violent railway accidents on the nervous compositions of victimized men and women. In his widely publicized theories, he proposed that post-traumatic illnesses were largely the effect of a physical disturbance. According to Oppenheim, the body's nervous system was compromised during an accident by the inscription of microscopic lesions, or invisible somatic injuries that produced physical and mental dysfunction. Although his theories would ultimately prove to be false, it was through derivatives of this conceptual premise for "railway spine" that a disorder such as shell-shock could be understood as a neurologically based wound. The definition of shell-shock would be greatly expanded by the end of the war, but in its initial meaning, Oppenheim's foundational idea resides: an acute moment of stress experienced during combat had disturbed the nerve fibers of a human body enough to literally leave tangible imprints of physical harm in its wake. Such descriptions of "commotional shock" tended to cloak a soldier's afflictions in the shroud of legitimacy that surrounded the scientific "provability" of a neurological disease (Lerner 2001, 148).[20]

But for the many soldiers who manifested symptoms of war neurosis who had *not* experienced an acute incident of trauma, these explanations of "commotional shock" were of little relevance. Because the mentally based characteristics of shell-shock were so pronounced—and because they proved to appear with or without physical provocation—medical authorities were quick to dissect the disorder under the lens of abnormal psychology. Following the work of Charcot, Janet, and Freud, theories of hysterical neurosis entered into the lexicon of military doctors who saw great similarities between civilian hysterics and the men in their own hospitals. From this point of view, shell-shock was the product of a psyche disrupted by the extremely disturbing circumstances of war. If memories of trench combat were too horrifying to be properly processed by the mind's subconscious, they became parasitic agents of terror that could disable an entire body and mind. Like destructive pathogenic viruses, these unwanted recollections arose involuntarily from the subconscious and were converted into the uncontrollable thoughts, emotions, and physical outbursts of their shell-shocked sufferer.[21]

Through the dialectic convergence of these two conceptual histories of trauma, the body of a shell-shocked soldier thus became an unwilling vessel for the dramatic reenactment of illegitimate wartime memories. Whether his traumatic experiences had been scarred into the foundation of his nervous tissue or captured by the ineffable innerworkings of his psyche, the neurotic veteran resurrected memories of war in pathologically unacceptable ways. Unsettling moments of the past were imprinted and transmitted through the very presence of his corporeality, as Jay Winter writes:

> Here [in the shell-shocked soldier] we can see and feel one kind of embodied memory. It is *written on* the men who fought, or inscribed in them in a way which is not subject to their direct or premeditated control. In all instances, images and memories seem to live both imbedded in these people and curiously detached from them; memory itself, or images of overwhelming events, appear to be free-floating powerful agents which somehow control the jaw of a man, or his leg, or all of his movements. In effect, these men's bodies *perform* something about their war experience . . . shell shock is a theater of memory out of control. (2006, 56–57)

The discourses surrounding this experience of disordered embodiment irrevocably shaped the understanding of post-traumatic illnesses as they continued to appear in the aftermath of catastrophic events throughout the rest of the twentieth and the twenty-first centuries. While it is dangerous to draw linear causalities from the history of Western trauma—traumatic disorders such as shell-shock, combat fatigue, and PTSD are intrinsically wed to the cultural environment from which they arise, and no transhistorical "story" of trauma can ever truly be written—certain conceptual paradigms have remained in consistent use.[22] These paradigms extend models of trauma beyond the limits of the corporeal body to explain the psychopathologization of human difference within a wider sociocultural context. In this way, trauma may be metaphorically embodied by the structural forms of art, literature, and music through the work of remembrance and representation (Cizmic 2011).

The first of these paradigms details the foundational premise of post-traumatic stress as a disorder of memory. Through this metaphor, memories are discrete units of organized information. In a well-functioning memory system, these units are stored in intricate, interconnected webs of knowledge, ready to be recalled by the conscious self at the appropriate time or place in order to enable new experiences (King 2000). In a disabled memory system, however, the subconscious or conscious mind loses control over this process in a way that is detrimental to the system as a whole: memories are lost, fabricated, or recalled involuntarily. When the root of the problem is a corrupted memory unit (or a memory aquired during a moment of traumatic stress), the psyche is traumatized. A *traumatic memory* is thus a tangibly identifiable object that cannot be properly integrated into the whole. It behaves outside of the control of the conscious and/or subconscious self, and acts on its own agency.

The second paradigm realizes that a consequence of this type of disorder is the complete disorganization of temporal space that defines traumatic neurosis as a "disease of time" (Young 1995, 7). In order to catalog and understand human experience, the mind narratively constructs memories along a linear spectrum of past, present, and future. This continuous process of organizing events turns a disorienting pastiche of sensory-based data into a clear and unified history: without it, human consciousness would be no more than a "string of experientially unconnected points" (Young 1995,

4). By definition, traumatic memories invade this process aggressively. In the traumatized mind, moments of the past are constantly interrupting the present, an act that disables the conscious self from moving forward and into the future. *Temporal confusion* manifests in the body and mind of a shell-shocked soldier through clinically observed thoughts and behaviors. Just as past moments of intense stress are projected into the psyche with the hallucinogenic effects of flashbacks and nightmares, muscles and limbs continually conflate past and present through the involuntary performance of traumatic events.

Finally, because the temporal orientation of memories has long been seated at the core of human consciousness, trauma is a disorder of identity. Without the ability to correctly narrate one's own temporal existence through the organization of memories, the mind is left without a clear sense of its existence as a unified, coherent self. This loss of identity occurs on the level of the individual psyche as well as within the cultural sphere, where national, ethnic, and social identities may disintegrate under the stressors of an international conflict such as the Great War. In trauma, a *loss of identity* occurs with a distinct fracturing of the whole that can be observed through a lack of structural cohesion within the self. The traumatized mind fails to make appropriate connections between past memories and present realities. It thus resists the construction of a clear narrative history that enables the psyche to create an integrated conscious mind.

Music has the ability to participate in the production of all three of these paradigmatic frameworks for trauma through the manipulation of formal gestures and structural organization. Because music literally embodies ideas that can be reproduced and remembered, it may perform and transmit *traumatic memories* through musical sound that is symbolically disruptive within a particular context. As music relies on temporal orientation for much of its structural integrity, *temporal confusion* may be experienced through numerous deviations of rhythm, meter, harmonic motion, and phrasing. And as a work that communicates many levels of unity, coherence, and identity, the integrity of a musical body may be compromised by large-scale structural disorganization. This *loss of identity* may be objectively observed through the critical reception history of a piece, particularly when it has been consistently labeled fractured and incoherent. In the following analysis of "On the Idle Hill of Summer," the psychical processes of trauma are reproduced in the musical body through these three paradigms. As such, *traumatic memory, temporal confusion*, and *loss of identity* work to create musical narratives of shell-shock throughout Gurney's "theater of memory out of control" (Winter 2006, 57).[23]

Musical Metaphors of Shell-Shock in "On the Idle Hill of Summer"

Gurney was welcomed back to Gloucester in October of 1918 by a family deep in the throes of its own turmoil. Not only had his father, David, fallen severely ill with cancer, but the rest of his family members (namely his brother Ronald, who was a veteran himself) had neither patience nor sympathy for Ivor's disability (Hurd 1978). Though friends were still able to look after his health and well-being, Gurney's fragile mental state continued to decline rapidly. As his thoughts and emotions spiraled into a highly erratic and depressed condition, his behavior became increasingly self-destructive: he slept very little, spoke of auditory hallucinations and paranoid delusions, ate sporadically and in unusal patterns, and went on extravagantly long walks through the British countryside.[24] For about a year after coming home, Gurney, like millions of displaced veterans after the war, struggled to shed memories of the trenches and readapt to civilian life.

Despite these difficulties, Gurney somehow found the motivation to resume his scholarship at the RCM in the fall of 1919. Under the mentorship of Ralph Vaughan Williams (who had recently taken up a teaching post at the institution), he flourished during two of the most prolific and exceptional years of his compositional and poetic career. Between 1919 and 1921 he set hundreds of songs, many of which reflected specifically on topics of war and combat (Gurney 2011, iv). Within this reflective postwar oeuvre falls *Ludlow and Teme*, a seven-song cycle written alongside *The Western Playland* in 1919.[25] Of all the Housman texts Gurney chose to use in these two cycles, none both sentimentalizes and condemns war in such contradictory ways as the fifth song of the former set: "On the Idle Hill of Summer." A recording of this song is available on Track 23.1 on the Companion Website.

Housman's poem begins with the serenity of a calm, bucolic scene on a beautiful summer's day. In the sleepy, idle, heavenly stillness of the landscape, the narrator is barely disturbed by the gently pulsing rhythm of a faraway drummer (see the introductory section of this essay). In fact, it seems to this narrator that the ethereal music is somewhat otherworldly, arising from a place out of his own subconscious—out of the world of dreams. As soon as the sound of the drummer is noticed, however, it begins to take shape in the narrator's mind. A disquieting visual image begins to form; the drummer is no ordinary musician, but the leader of a phantasmic pack of infantry. The pulse of his drum, once steady and serene, is now directing the march of soldiers toward the battlefield where, as the narrator envisions it, they will all die. In this second stanza, the narrator occupies an odd position in the temporal reality of the poem. While he is a present observer of the action, he is also able to foretell the fate of these ghostly men. In effect, Housman leads us to believe that the narrator is rewitnessing a moment of the past that had perhaps occured on the very field in which he now stands.

The first structural section of Gurney's song (measures 1–30) is faithful to the narrative arc of Housman's opening stanzas in a number of musical ways. Like Housman, Gurney begins with an idle stillness: three strings, *con sordino*, hold the bottom two notes of an F-major triad just barely longer than the four beats of the first measure (see Figure 23.1). The quiet, lazy calm of this dyad is reinforced by the entrance of the piano in the second measure, and the gesture is repeated in measures 3–4 to create an unwavering sense of stability in the present world of an F-major tonic. Barely noticeable is the faint *pizzicato* pulse of quarter notes on F that are sounded by the cello in measures 2 and 4, a rather unobtrusive disruption to the otherwise static rhythmic character of the

FIGURE 23.1 In the first two measures of "On the Idle Hill of Summer," the upper strings calmly introduce the serene F-major setting of the opening section. At measure 2, the cello begins its faint pizzicato articulation of quarter notes on F.

opening passage. As will be revealed by the narrative text eight measures later, this simple figure is actually the mimetic representation of a drummer's drumming, barely rising out of the tranquil landscape through its soft articulation.

This "drumming" noise continues through the entrance of the first vocal phrase, becoming more conspicuous as the cello continuously articulates *pizzicato* quarter notes on F. After rhythmically stuttering through the first eight measures, these quarter notes finally gain traction and begin a more metrically stable tonic pedal in measure 9 (see Figure 23.2). While this pedal tone remains unchanged against the fluid harmonic and melodic motion of its surrounding environment by definition of its musical function, Gurney also infuses the note with ripe symbolic implications. The cello's pulsing F is not only an insistent reminder of the tonic, but the memory of a sound once heard in the context of war. Rather than creating a pivot for tension and resolution, then, the cello resists inclusion and fails to incorporate with its surrounding musical texture. As this

FIGURE 23.2 The cello's tonic pedal remains unchanged throughout the first vocal phrase (mm. 10–15).

resistance becomes the catalyst for an intense traumatic flashback in the second major section of the piece, the cello's repetitive figure thus takes on the role of an invasive and disruptive *traumatic memory*.

The cello first begins to provoke musical tension around measure 18, when the narrator starts to realize that the sound of its drumming beat is getting "near" and "louder" (see Figure 23.3). Here, the vocal line begins in a manner very similar to the corresponding opening phrase: static, on C, with an ascent up to F and resolution on A. But instead of the relaxed pacing of the opening line, this vocal phrase is more hurried and condensed in its melodic motion. With the growing realization of the cello's true identity, the narrator becomes anxious about its steady approach. Similar changes in tension occur in the accompaniment. As the upper strings gradually lose stability through a syncopated descent, the suddenly awakened piano thickens the textural density with ascending figures through the right hand. Still, the cello's quarter notes persist. At measure 21, they gain the full bodied timbre and dynamic velocity of *arco, tenuto*, and *forte* articulation markings in the middle of the vocal phrase "On the roads of earth go by." This transformation marks a shift of the narrator's conscious awareness, and he is shaken by the intensity of this previously innocuous musical cell. The voice once again begins its ascent toward F at measure 20, but stalls on this pitch as if frozen in terror by the strengthening force of the cello's horrific memory. Paralyzed, the voice is unable to move forward into peaceful resolution and hangs onto F for two beats. The harmonic texture breaks into F-minor immediately, signalling a total collapse in the musical fabric that will begin only a few measures later.

With this collapse comes a transitionary passage between the first and second structural sections of Gurney's song (measures 23–30), during which a steady loss of temporal orientation is evident in both the music and text. In the concluding lines of Housman's second stanza, the distinction between nightmarish past and calm present becomes blurred by the narrator's ability to forsee the grisly fate of the soldiers passing by. Gurney portrays this temporal distortion through several musical gestures. Most obviously, the steady reliability of tonal and metric consistency dissapears. Harmony shifts rapidly and unpredictably in this new musical environment, which is tempestuously set in the vaguely established key of F-minor. Even the relentless tonic pedal vanishes in the messy polyrhythmic mixture of quarter-note triplets that replaces the previously unfaltering beat (measures 24–26). The cello's pitch does return once, however, at a pivotal moment in the text. When the narrator finally realizes that the drummer is leading the soldiers toward their own deaths, harmony dissolves into a dissonant cluster of pitches, and F returns forcefully in both the cello and lower register of the piano (see Figure 23.4, measures 27–28). The traumatic pitch emerges briefly in this context to solidify its association with the memories of carnage that are embodied within its resurrection.

The shift in mood that occurs in the final lines of Housman's second stanza anticipates a significant fracture in the thematic structure of the poem. By the third stanza of text, visions of pastoral beauty are long gone, and the narrator is fully immersed in an alternative world of death and destruction. Through words alone, it is still difficult to tell from which temporal standpoint the narrator is speaking. Although the action

FIGURE 23.3 Realization of the cello's increasing intensity leads the vocal narrator to become "stuck" on F at m. 22. The phrase breaks its expected pattern here and a steady dissolution of the musical fabric begins.

FIGURE 23.4 The traumatic pitch F is resurrected in the cello at piano at a significant moment of awareness in the text (mm. 27–28).

seems to occur in the present, he maintains the omnipotent ability to assert that none of the marching soldiers will "return again." One interpretive explanation for this *temporal confusion* is that the narrator, perhaps greeted by the memory of men parading toward him, has finally entered into a complete vivid flashback of battle's terrifying scenery.

Gurney's musical setting of the third stanza (measures 31–41) reinforces this interpretation. Through a complete dissolution of harmonic, melodic, rhythmic, and metrical integrity, Gurney transports the musical narrative away from the serenity of the F-major opening and into a nightmarish environment where chaos, uncertainty, and instability reign. Beginning in measure 29, the second violin, cello, and piano slide into the downbeat of measure 31 via linear chromatic descent; when they land on an A♭-major harmony at the start of the second major structural section, it marks the arrival of a completely foreign musical atmosphere. For the first time, the strings briefly drop out of the texture, and the tenor begins an awkwardly paced phrase that extends through the next four measures (see Figure 23.5). Gurney's text setting is odd and irregular in this melody, and the accompaniment that reenters at measure 32 seems equally strange. As too many disparate rhythmic and melodic ideas crowd vertical space in this passage, a palpable confusion of temporal orientation ensues. Gurney's uneven structuring of these intertwining parts obscures the metric downbeat as the distinction between strong and weak beats is lost. In the absense of a clear sense of meter and melodic cohesion, there is complete *temporal confusion*.

Confusion is maintained at the start of the next phrase, when the music undergoes another unexpected shift in harmony, rhythm, and texture (see Figure 23.6). Jolting a half-step downward from G-major to a B♭-augmented sonority, the piano begins an unusually jagged chord progression. Dotted rhythms and odd leaps in register project a gait that is not only unsteady, but unnatural; the tenor echoes this nervous movement with seemingly random flailing through a chromatically unpredictable melody. Throughout the entirety of the second section, phrase organization is thus highly fractured, as there is a distinct break in harmonic, melodic, and rhythmic identity from one line of text setting to the next. *Temporal confusion* is projected through the erratically anxious movement of these musical elements in the absence of tonal and metric structure. When juxtaposed against the steady stability of the F-major opening and conclusion, the chaos of the middle section narratively suggests the frightening, disorienting environment of a flashback of war.

Out of this flashback, the narrator returns to the present at measure 42 (see Figure 23.7). F-major is reestablished abruptly by the accompaniment, and the voice recovers its opening statement on C. Though clearly back to its original point of stability, the music of the concluding section (measures 42–71) shows a heightened difference from the calm composure of the opening. As if irrevocably shaken from the events of the traumatic episode, the musical climate manically churns with far more rhythmic urgency and excitement. Even the cello revives its quarter-note figure on F, but is altered significantly. Rather than its previously stubborn persistence of quarter-notes against the disparate rhythmic profile of the strings, piano, and voice, it is now rhythmically and melodically in sync with the other elements of its musical environment (measures 45–49). *Traumatic memory* and narrative psyche finally become one, solidifying a loss of control that has overcome the musical body.

"On the Idle Hill of Summer" concludes with Housman's final line of triumphant text, "Woman bore me, I will rise" (measures 53–57). Gurney sets this phrase nearly twenty measures before the ultimate closure of his piece, providing a somewhat anticlimatic ending to the narrator's struggle. Instead of being emboldened by heroic resolve, the voice seems pained by the utterance of his ultimate destiny at measure 56. Over a B diminished-7 harmony, he stalls again on high F, waiting for the accompaniment to release him with an adequate resolution. The strings and piano become stuck too, however, in a repetitively upward motion that fails to direct the vocal line forward. The tenor drops out after six beats and leaves the accompanying voices to tie up the many loose musical ends established over the course of the piece. They do so with a delicate

FIGURE 23.5 *Temporal confusion* begins at the start of the second structural section of Gurney's piece (mm. 31–34).

FIGURE 23.6 The tenor and piano move in jaggedly juxtaposed phrases (mm. 36–39).

interweaving of melodic fragments, most of which allude to musical moments from the opening section of the song. In this jumble of disembodied memories, Gurney attempts to return to a peaceful past and recapture a sense of innocence lost by the traumatic effects of the war. At measure 60, the violin and viola overtake the texture with a prominent musical theme: a stepwise descent through G, F, and E♭ that ends a minor sixth below before repeating in a lower octave (see Figure 23.8). Unlike most of the other musical memories, however, this fragment is new to the context of Gurney's song. Remarkably, it is a direct quotation of the music of George Butterworth, taken from his seven-year-old setting of Housman's text. Echoing from the other side of the war, the memory of Butterworth's England quickly dissolves into the ephemeral sea of polyphony. Gurney eventually resolves on F with trails of the *traumatic memory* still lingering in the lower registers of the piano and cello as the piece comes to rest. Like most of the European continent in the wake of the Great War, Gurney is unable to go back to a place where memories of combat and violence exist only as beautiful, harmless musical cells in the uncorrupted imagination of prewar British culture.

Ivor Gurney died of tuberculosis on December 26, 1937, while still incarcerated at the City of London Mental Hospital. A month later, an anonymous author codified Gurney's legacy as a delayed casualty of the Great War with an obituary in *The Musical Times*. As it reads, Gurney's death was "a tragic reminder that the European war [was] still taking its toll of genius," for "the physical and mental sufferings that resulted [from the injuries he sustained in combat] lasted until his death" (1938, 68). From even this first posthumous account of his life and legacy, Gurney's name was permanently marked by the stigma of his medical diagnosis. Nearly all biographical and analytical accounts of the artist have since grappled with the supposed effects of Gurney's illness on his work, as Daniel W. Hipp summarizes: "The mental illness that would lead to his institutionalization has created the conception of the mad artist, the vision of the poet and composer that lingers for those who have not forgotten him altogether. By the late 1920s, mental illness had rendered Gurney effectively silent as a poet and musician and had largely destroyed the coherence of self and artistry that has established his limited legacy" (2005, 108).

FIGURE 23.7 Return to the A section at measure 42 is marked by a dramatic transformation of the opening musical climate.

(a)

FIGURE 23.8 Immediately after the voice's difficult resolution on the final line of text ("Woman bore me, I will rise"), the strings and piano begin a series of interlocking melodic ideas that conclude the piece (b). Within this series is the transposed melodic memory of Butterworth's "On the Idle Hill of Summer" (a), featured prominently at a similar moment in the piece's musical narrative.

Trauma is thus written onto the musical body of Gurney's work not only through the musical processes outlined above, but through such critical receptions of the composer's unfortunate biographical narrative. Paradigmatic representations of *traumatic memory* and *temporal confusion* found within the musical structures of a piece such as "On the Idle Hill of Summer" have allowed critics to maintain that Gurney's late work is best defined as disorganized and fragmented. Because of his mental illness, it is frequently implied, Gurney's music suffers from a lack of integral cohesion that displays a *loss of identity*, or a failure to express large-scale musical narratives throughout the entirety of a single piece.[26] This dysfunction is permanently wedded to the physical and mental differences of Gurney himself, as expressed by Charles Tomlinson in a poem dedicated to the late composer, referred to in the title of this essay:

> That blood, those chromosomes that drew him to the absurd
> Disordering of notes, to the garrulity of the word,
> Instead of the forms that already his youthful passion
> Had prepared for the ordering of self and nation. (1995, 60)

Through the "absurd disordering of notes," Gurney allows the listener to experientially witness the effects of trauma on a musical body. Much like the composer explicitly expressed in his December 1915 letter to Marion Scott (quoted at the head of this essay), experiences may indeed be "crystallized" and transmitted into musical space, and musical landscapes may be transformed into aural arenas for the psychopathological processes of a dysfunctionally traumatized mind. As such, the many markers of musical difference that came to characterize Gurney's late compositional style only serve to further illuminate a modern understanding of post-traumatic illness as it was conceptualized and embodied in the aftermath of the Great War.

FIGURE 23.8 Continued.

Notes

1. Excerpt from a letter written to Gurney's close friend, Marion Scott, from the Western Front (Gurney and Thornton 1991, 171). For an in-depth biographical study of the relationship between Gurney and Scott, see Blevins 2008.
2. Though records of the total impact of the Battle of the Somme vary, nearly all histories account for immense scope of this single offensive struggle: on the first day of fighting alone (July 1, 1916), the British Army suffered 57,470 casualties (19,240 of whom were killed) (Philpott 2009, 10). It is estimated that 3–4 million fought in total, and that over 1 million men were casualties on both sides of the fighting line by mid-November (Gilbert 1994).
3. Housman 2010, 45. For a discussion of the use of Housman's work in British composition, see Butcher 1948, 329–339, and Banfield 1985.
4. As the RCM became a focal point for the advancement of British art music throughout the early part of the twentieth century, composers such as Butterworth became part of a steady discourse on the desirable characteristics of British composition as an idiom that conceptually reflected the nation's larger sociohistorical values. While a detailed history of this ongoing discourse is well beyond the scope of this study, at least three distinctive qualities were predominantly upheld as "British" in the years before and throughout the Great War: first, a cultivation of native folk resources, including modally inflected harmonic and melodic structures; second, the use of contemporary Georgian poets as a source for text setting; and finally, an idealization of pastoral scenery, which was conceptualized as the heart of England's deep historical connection to the physical earth of its motherland. For more on the English Musical Renaissance at the turn of the century, see Hughes and Stradline 2001.
5. Gurney arrived in France in May 1916, and was first positioned at Riez Bailleul (a section of trenches near Laventie). His unit was moved several times into neighboring camps and reserves over the course of the summer before heading south in October of that year (Gurney 1991, xv–xvi).
6. As Jay Winter summarizes, the ideological threat of Germans on British soil "was a clear and present danger to what contemporaries saw as the British way of life, a very local way of life, a life of pubs and clubs and a host of associations drawing people to activities of an astonishing diversity. Now in 1914 the strongest army in the world, the German army, was at the gates. It was challenging a nation whose inhabitants unthinkingly believed that Britain was the pre-eminent world power. . . . In light of this threat, and in response to both the harshness of the treatment of Belgian civilians and to the high casualties among the professional army and the volunteers who served in the Territorial forces, public opinion in Britain was behind the war effort." (2002, 331).
7. In the early part of the twentieth century, "neurasthenia" was a poorly defined disorder typically thought to result from a literal weakness in the nervous system. Symptoms included excessive fatigue or depletion of energy, dyspepsia, anxiety, and depression, among a wide variety of others; it was classified as not a "distinct malady" but rather "a symptom or group of symptoms resulting from disease" (Kellogg 1916, 14). Neurasthenia as a nervous disorder would thus play a significant role in the conceptual development of war neuroses and shell-shock during the Great War.
8. There is an extensive literature on the particularly brutal effects of trench warfare on the psyche of a British infantryman. For example, see Fussell 1975; Hipp 2005; Leed 2000; Reid 2010.

9. A letter to Marion Scott, October 25, 1916 (Gurney 1983,110).
10. Letter to Marion Scott, late 1917 (Hurd 1978, 99–100). "Blighty" is a common contemporary term for Britain.
11. See Winter 2010, 201–207.
12. Statistics reporting the total number of British casualties vary between sources that consider conflicting contemporary reports. Numbers range from 743,000 (Gilbert 1994, 541) to 908,371 dead (*Statistics of the Military Effort* 1922, 237) when including victims of disease and injuries throughout the British Empire after the war had ended.
13. Collective trauma has been defined as a social process that occurs in the wake of a disturbance of epic proportions. As Jeffrey C. Alexander states, "Cultural trauma occurs when members of a collectivity feel they have been subjected to a horrendous event that leaves indelible marks upon their group consciousness, marking their memories forever and changing their future identity in fundamental and irrevocable ways" (2004, 1). Specifically, the Great War has been codified as a historical moment of trauma that immensely impacted the sociopolitical identities of the citizens of Europe. This process of writing history through the memorialization of the war continually shaped collective identity throughout the twentieth century, as Fiona Reid writes: "the popular understanding of the First World War is largely based upon a shared memory of that particular war as collective trauma" (2010, 1).
14. Before the war, psychiatric illnesses of the nerves were predominantly classified under a rubric of hysteria, a historically female-coded disease. As shell-shocked men displayed many of the same symptom traits as their female predecessors, many saw the illness as a breakdown of strong gender identities as a result of the war. As Mosse writes: "Shattered nerves and lack of will-power were the enemies of settled society and because men so afflicted were thought to be effeminate, they endangered the clear distinction between genders which was generally regarded as an essential cement to society. This was another aspect of social disintegration which haunted the shell-shocked" (2000, 103). See also: Micale 2008 and Bourke 1996.
15. The *Report of the War Office Committee of Enquiry into "Shell-Shock"* attempted to answer this conundrum by looking for instances of shell-shock in wars of earlier years. Their conclusion was undeveloped: "As regards earlier wars our search for direct evidence was of no avail, and we suspect that in former wars a soldier who lost self-control was usually court-martialled and frequently suffered the penalty for the military crime of cowardice or of desertion" (1922, 8). Modern analyses of war neurosis recognize that the history of war trauma is far more complex, and that contemporary military physicians and psychologists perhaps overstated the relationship between industrialized warfare and the development of shell-shock as a "new" type of neurotic disease. See the Introduction to Reid 2010.
16. Issues surrounding diagnosed and discharged veterans, including government pension and social stigmatization, relied heavily on the opinions of these medical authorities. Their opinions varied greatly between each nation in Europe, and very much within national boundaries as well (Lerner and Micale 2001, 1–27).
17. This number nearly doubled to 120,000 by 1939 (Bogacz 1989).
18. As the *Report of the War Office Committee of Enquiry into "Shell-Shock"* states, the purpose of the committee was "To consider the different types of hysteria and traumatic neurosis, commonly called 'shell-shock'; to collate the expert knowledge derived by the service medical authorities and the medical profession from the experience of the war, with a view to recording for future use the ascertained facts as to its origin, nature, and remedial treatment, and to advise whether by military training or

education, some scientific method of guarding against its occurrence can be devised." (1922, 3)

19. Much of the debate surrounding shell-shock also investigated whether or not affected men were naturally predisposed to nervous illness because of a preexisting condition, such as Gurney's prior diagnosis of neurasthenia. This issue was particularly important when determining issues such as pension: if a soldier had been "damaged" before the war, would the state still have to offer compensation for his injuries?
20. "Commotional shock" was a contemporary label for physical disturbances associated with nervous disorders. See Mott 1919.
21. For a condensed history of the debate surrounding traumatic neurosis during World War I, see Lerner 2001.
22. The conceptual lineage of trauma is loaded with a dense and complex history of meanings that have been assigned and prescribed through various facets of culture, medicine, psychiatry, and politics. This history is not linear, but descriptive of many moments of "traumata," as Lerner and Micale explain: "The clinical and conceptual relationships between nostalgia, mind wounds, nerve prostration, spinal concussion, railway spine, *hysterie traumatique, traumatische Neurose*, traumatic neurasthenia, shell shock, war neurosis, soldier's heart, and combat neurosis are unstable and approximate at best, with a great deal of semantic slippage between categories. Furthermore, the causal and temporal relationship between event conceived of as traumatic and post-traumatic symptom profiles is anything but consistent over time, across contexts, and even between individuals." (2001, 24–25) On the subject of trauma and post-traumatic stress, see also Jones and Wessely 2005, Luckhurst 2008, Leys 2000, Young 1995, Brewin 2003, Wenegrat 2001.
23. For explorations of the relationship between music and trauma that take a similar analytical approach, see also Cizmic 2011 and Wlodarski 2007.
24. Gurney would reportedly refuse to eat for extended periods of time, only to gorge on hoarded food while in private. His hallucinations included "visits" from Beethoven, his delusions the infiltration of electricity that was damaging his brain. The walks that Gurney would take would usually occur overnight, and could last for literally dozens of miles (Hurd 1978, 127–134).
25. Each cycle was originally released in two versions, one for piano/voice, and one for string quartet/tenor. See the Introduction to Gurney 2011.
26. Criticisms of Gurney's work tend to emphasize the negative impact that Gurney's mental health had on both his life and career. While some draw this connection more vaguely (see Greene and Scott 1938; Squire, de la Mare, and Blunden 1938; Vaughan Williams and Howells 1938; Thomas 1960; Anderson 1978; Trethowan 1981; McBurney 2005), others speak directly of a lack of cohesion that is evident within the musical structure itself (see E. R. 1938; Burtch 1955; I. K. 1960; Banfield 1984; Drucker 1986; Hold 1990; Palmer 2006).

References

Alexander, Jeffrey C. 2004. "Towards a Theory of Cultural Trauma." In *Cultural Trauma and Collective Identity*, edited by Jeffrey C. Alexander, Ron Eyerman, Bernhard Giesen, Neil J. Smelser, and Piotr Sztompka, 1–30. Berkeley: University of California Press.

Anderson, Robert. 1978. Review of *Songs and Poems* by Ivor Gurney, Johnston, Keyte, Ibbott, Pratley, Clark. *Musical Times* 119 (1621): 243.

Banfield, Stephen. 1984. Review of *Ludlow and Teme: The Western Playland (and of Sorrow)* by Ivor Gurney. *Music and Letters* 65 (2): 203–204.

Banfield, Stephen. 1985. *Sensibility and English Song: Critical Studies of the Early 20th Century.* New York: Cambridge University Press.

Blevins, Pamela. 2008. *Ivor Gurney and Marion Scott: Song of Pain and Beauty.* Woodbridge, UK: Boydell.

Bogacz, Ted. 1989. "War Neurosis and Cultural Change in England, 1914–22: The Work of the War Office Committee of Enquiry into 'Shell-Shock.'" *Journal of Contemporary History* 24 (2): 227–256.

Bourke, Joanna. 1996. *Dismembering the Male: Men's Bodies, Britain, and the Great War.* Chicago: University of Chicago Press.

Brewin, Chris R. 2003. *Posttraumatic Stress Disorder: Malady or Myth?* New Haven, CT: Yale University Press.

Burtch, M. A. 1955. "Ivor Gurney: A Revaluation." *Musical Times* 96 (1): 529–530.

Butcher, A. V. 1948. "A. E. Housman and the English Composer." *Music and Letters* 29 (4): 329–339.

Butterworth, George. 1974. *Eleven Songs from "A Shropshire Lad."* London: Stainer & Bell.

Cizmic, Maria. 2011. *Performing Pain: Music and Trauma in Eastern Europe.* New York and Oxford: Oxford University Press.

Drucker, Ruth Landes. 1986. Review of *Ludlow and Teme: A Song-Cycle to Poems of A.E. Housman for Tenor and Piano* by Ivor Gurney and *The Western Playland (and of Sorrow): A Song-Cycle to Poems of A.E. Housman for Baritone and Piano* by Ivor Gurney. *Notes* 42 (4): 865–866.

E. R. 1938. Review of *Twenty Songs* by Ivor Gurney. *Music and Letters* 19 (4): 472–473.

Fussell, Paul. 1975. *The Great War and Modern Memory.* Oxford and New York: Oxford University Press.

Gilbert, Martin. 1994. *The First World War: A Complete History.* New York: Henry Holt.

Greene, Harry Plunket, and Marion M. Scott. 1938. "The Man." *Music and Letters* 19 (1): 2–7.

Gurney, Ivor. 1983. *War Letters: A Selection.* Edited by R. K. R. Thornton. Manchester, UK: Carcanet.

Gurney, Ivor. 1991. *Ivor Gurney: Collected Letters.* Edited by R. K. R. Thornton. Manchester, UK: Carcanet Press.

Gurney, Ivor. 2011. *Ludlow and Teme.* Edited by Philip Lancaster. London: Stainer & Bell.

Hart, Peter. 2008. *The Somme: The Darkest Hour on the Western Front.* New York: Pegasus.

Hipp, Daniel W. 2005. *The Poetry of Shell Shock: Wartime Trauma and Healing in Wilfred Owen, Ivor Gurney, and Siegfried Sassoon.* Jefferson, NC: McFarland.

Hold, Trevor. 1990. "Ivor Gurney: Poet and Composer." *Musical Times* 131 (1770): 414–417.

Hold, Trevor. 2002. *Parry to Finzi: Twenty English Song-Composers.* Woodbridge, UK: Boydell.

Housman, A. E. 2010. *A Shropshire Lad and Other Poems: The Collected Poems of A. E. Housman.* London: Penguin.

Hughes, Meirion, and R. A. Stradline. 2001. *The English Musical Renaissance, 1840–1940: Constructing a National Music.* Manchester, UK: Manchester University Press.

Hurd, Michael. 1978. *The Ordeal of Ivor Gurney.* Oxford and New York: Oxford University Press.

I. K. 1960. "Review of *Three Songs of Ben Jonson* by Geoffrey Bush; *A Fourth Volume of Ten Songs* by Ivor Gurney; *The Spinning Girl (Die Spinnerin)* by Fanny Mendelssohn, edited by Jack Werner; *Doce Canciones Españolas (Twelve Spanish Songs)* by Joaquin Rodrigo." *Music and Letters* 41 (1): 102.

Jones, Edgar, and Simon Wessely. 2005. *Shell Shock to PTSD: Military Psychiatry from 1900 to the Gulf War*. New York: Psychology Press.

Kellogg, J. H. 1916. *Neurasthenia or Nervous Exhaustion*. Battle Creek, MI: Good Health.

King, Nicola. 2000. *Memory, Narrative, Identity: Remembering the Self*. Edinburgh: Edinburgh University Press.

Leed, Eric J. 2000. "Fateful Memories: Industrialized War and Traumatic Neuroses." *Journal of Contemporary History* 35 (1): 85–100.

Leese, Peter. 2002. *Shell Shock: Traumatic Neurosis and the British Soldiers of the First World War*. New York: Palgrave MacMillan.

Lerner, Paul. 2001. "From Traumatic Neurosis to Male Hysteria: The Decline and Fall of Hermann Oppenheim, 1889–1919." In *Traumatic Pasts: History, Psychiatry, and Trauma in the Modern Age, 1870–1930*, edited by Paul Lerner and Mark S. Micale, 140–171. Cambridge and New York: Cambridge University Press.

Leys, Ruth. 2000. *Trauma: A Genealogy*. Chicago: University of Chicago Press.

Luckhurst, Roger. 2008. *The Trauma Question*. New York: Routledge.

McBurney, Gerard. 2005. "Review of Ivor Gurney: *Despair; Sehnsucht; Song of the Summer Woods; The Sea;* Nocturnes in B and A flat; Preludes Nos. 1-9; and Howard Ferguson: Piano Sonata in F minor; Five Bagatelles." *Tempo* 59 (232): 53–55.

Micale, Mark S. 2008. *Hysterical Men: The Hidden History of Male Nervous Illness*. Cambridge, MA: Harvard University Press.

Mosse, George L. 2000. "Shell-Shock as a Social Disease." *Journal of Contemporary History* 35 (1): 101–108.

Mott, F. W. 1919. *War Neuroses and Shell Shock*. London: Oxford University Press.

Myers, C. S. 1915. "A Contribution to the Study of Shell Shock." *Lancet* (1): 316–320.

"Obituary." 1938. *Musical Times* 79 (1139): 67.

Palmer, Peter. 2006. "Review of 'The Tend'rest Breast': settings of women's poetry by Quilter, Bridge, Gurney, Lennox Berkeley, Ireland, Alastair King, Madeleine Dring, Montague Phillips; 'Strings in the Earth and Air': settings by Moeran, Warlock, Geoffrey Stern." *Tempo* 60 (237): 68–69.

Philpott, William. 2009. *Three Armies on the Somme: The First Battle of the Twentieth Century*. New York: Random House.

Reid, Fiona. 2010. *Broken Men: Shell Shock, Treatment, and Recovery in Britain, 1914–1930*. London: Continuum.

Report of the War Office Committee of Enquiry into "Shell-Shock." 1922. London: Imperial War Museum.

Riley, Matthew. 2010. *British Music and Modernism*. Burlington, VT: Ashgate.

Shephard, Ben. 2001. *A War of Nerves: Soldiers and Psychiatrists in the Twentieth Century*. Cambridge, MA: Harvard University Press.

Simkins, Peter. 1988. *Kitchener's Army: The Raising of New Armies, 1914–16*. New York: St. Martin's Press.

Squire, J. C., Walter de la Mare, and Edmund Blunden. 1938. "The Poet." *Music and Letters* 19 (1): 7–12.

Statistics of the Military Effort of the British Empire during the Great War: 1914–1920. 1922. London: H. M. Stationary Office.

Thomas, Helen. 1960. "A Memory of Ivor Gurney." *Musical Times* 101 (1414): 754.

Tomlinson, Charles. 1995. *Jubilation*. New York: Oxford University Press.

Trethowan, W. H. 1981. "Ivor Gurney's Mental Illness." *Music and Letters* 62 (3–4): 300–309.

Vaughan Williams, Ralph, and Herbert Howells. 1938. "The Musician." *Music and Letters* 19 (1): 12–17.
Wenegrat, Brant. 2001. *Theater of Disorder: Patients, Doctors, and the Construction of Illness*. New York: Oxford University Press.
Winter, Jay. 2002. "Popular Culture in Wartime Britain." In *European Culture in the Great War: The Arts, Entertainment and Propaganda,1914–1918*, edited by Aviel Roshwald and Richard Stites, 330–348. Cambridge: Cambridge University Press.
Winter, Jay. 2006. *Remembering War: The Great War between Memory and History in the Twentieth Century*. New Haven, CT: Yale University Press.
Winter, Jay. 2010. "Shell-Shock and the Cultural History of the Great War." In *War Studies Reader: From the Seventeenth Century to the Present Day and Beyond*, edited by Gary Sheffield, 201–207. London: Continuum.
Wlodarski, Amy Lynn. 2007. "'An Idea Can Never Perish': Memory, the Musical Idea, and Schoenberg's *A Survivor from Warsaw*." *Journal of Musicology* 24 (4): 581–608.
Young, Allan. 1995. *The Harmony of Illusions: Inventing Post-Traumatic Stress Disorder*. Princeton, NJ: Princeton University Press.

CHAPTER 24

VOCAL ABILITY AND MUSICAL PERFORMANCES OF NUCLEAR DAMAGES IN THE MARSHALL ISLANDS

JESSICA A. SCHWARTZ

Introduction

From 1946 through 1958, the United States detonated sixty-seven nuclear weapons on Bikini Atoll and Enewetak Atoll in the Marshall Islands, an archipelago of low-lying atolls in Micronesia that was part of the United Nations Trust Territory administered by the United States at the time. While the fallout from these explosions has contaminated the entire country, some atoll populations have received higher doses of radiation and have been stigmatized. Thrust into the center of the nuclear spotlight in 1946, Bikinians remain peripheral to their land and with it their culture. Bikinians have been stigmatized for a host of reasons pertaining to the nuclear testing and their relationship with the United States.

In 1954, Castle Bravo, the United States' most powerful thermonuclear device, was detonated on Bikini Atoll, and it sent radioactive debris over Rongelap Atoll, covering the population and their lands. Rongelapese vividly recall their experiences when just two days after Bravo, they were taken to the United States military base on Kwajalein Atoll. From March 1954 through June 1954, the Rongelapese remained sequestered on the main island of Kwajalein. The restrictions placed on Rongelapese bodies limited the information they could share with the other Marshallese communities concerning the state of their health, among other issues. By 1956, the United States Atomic Energy Commission (AEC) deemed the Marshall Islands "by far the most contaminated place in the world." In 1957, a year prior to the moratorium on US nuclear testing, the AEC stated that the radiation levels on Rongelap Atoll were insignificant, and they opted to return the Rongelapese to their homeland. The political silencing of the Rongelapese was emphasized by their tightly controlled visibility in mainstream American media. For example, the portrayal of Rongelapese in a 1957 NBC newsreel documents their medical examinations and depicts them as "savages" thereby negating the potential value in their speech, or perhaps denying the possibility that they can speak at all. Moreover, a number of women asked me if Americans thought they were "animals" to be tested on like "guinea pigs."[1] Implicit in my interlocutors' concerns is the feeling of voicelessness in the metaphorical sense: their capacity for speech was invalidated.

The Rongelapese remained on their contaminated homeland until 1985. Over the course of twenty-eight years, the islanders became increasingly ill. Even people who were not on Rongelap or nearby when Bravo was detonated suffered radiation-induced illnesses. With abnormalities at birth, miscarriages, and aberrant illnesses becoming the norm, the Rongelapese appealed to the United States government for assistance with relocation. Ultimately, they were denied help. The environmental activist organization Greenpeace offered aid and its ship the Rainbow Warrior. With the help of Greenpeace, the Rongelapese moved to a small island, Mejato, in the corner of Kwajalein Atoll. Today, they remain displaced and disenfranchised.

Bridging ethnomusicology, anthropology of the senses, Disability Studies, and nuclear studies, this essay considers the ways in which Marshallese women from Bikini Atoll and Rongelap Atoll sing about the impact of radiation on their lives, sounding physical and physiological disruptions and dislocations that expose broader damages caused by the nuclear testing program. Studies of disability in radiation communities tend to draw on the medical model, and these studies are often inaccessible to nonspecialists in general given the technical detail of reports and clinical foundations that depend on Western conceptual frames and sensorial orientations. Such studies delimit who and what was affected by radiation against another population, the de facto "control group." These medical reports are used in legal hearings to confirm or reject claims to remediation for nuclear damages, and they are, of course, limited by the scope of their work. The medical, scientific, and legal systems create exceptional (nonnormative) terms for individuals and populations. This production of confined disability shapes how Bikinians and Rongelapese articulate and make claims regarding their nuclear experiences, but it does not control fully the parameters or content of expression.

Analyzing compositions and performances from a repertoire of Marshallese "radiation songs," I propose a stylistic framework that seeks to familiarize listeners with the ways in which these musical exchanges use vocal ability to challenge the production of compulsory disability by resounding a culturally contextualized logic of radiation, or a temporal unfolding of removals, mutations, and decay that is physically and culturally debilitating. The sonorized logic of radiation, I argue, is compiled through recurring motifs of the disabled voice, extramusical text setting, and the figure of the question, literal and rhetorical. With the performance of these songs as prominently contributing to communities' musical identities, the inner workings of radiation are brought to the fore and allow for a recontextualization of stigmatization and isolation as political agency, authenticity, and connection.

Power relations are central, in my work, to the construction of disability in Marshallese radiation communities. Katie Ellis uses Michel Foucault's work on discursive formations to "think about disability as socially produced by and within power relations" (Ellis 2008, 3). Discursive formations also depend on the beliefs, meanings, and sensory orientations of a specific culture. David Howes suggests that there is a politics of sensory experience and that sensory experience exceeds the purview of the individual; it is a cultural production (Howes 2005). Working at the sensory register, I stress the political import of these radiation songs as highlighting the failures at the core of biopolitical controls on communities and exposing the production of confined disability at the level of cultural and structural violence. With this in mind, I ask that we think of nuclear experience as afforded by what Patrick Wolfe has called a "logic of elimination," that is, "a settler-colonial tendency" that relies on eliminating native populations through various mechanisms, such as outright genocide, the destruction of heritage and indigenous culture through guilt and shame, emphasis on a discourse of loss, and the debilitation of indigenous agency through restrictions on mobility—physical and social (Wolfe 2006, Amsterdam 2012).

The Marshallese singers, and the stories they tell, in the ethnographic case studies that follow work against logics of elimination and decay. Marshallese compositional practices that draw on customary vocal motifs of crying, incessant singing, nuanced vocal techniques, and the literal timbres of irradiated voices expose us to the presence of radiation by directing our listening to elements of contagion, and, in turn, the impossibility of immunity from nuclear experience and biopolitical incorporation. "Radiation" is part of the Bikinian and the Rongelapese—the Marshallese—stories now. Radiation, as a language of restricted data, has a logical grammar of decay that, like loss, becomes generative via its discursive role as an element of public culture (Seremetakis 1994, 9). Radiation has literally and metaphorically decayed the voices and customary expression of Marshallese. Employed, however, in public culture as political means, these voices altered by radiation and nuclear testing resound, through their disability and stories of loss, a powerful resilience against the deafening silence of nuclear hegemony, or the control over the production of nuclear knowledge, which has depended on classification, confinement, and silence—juridical silencings and the acquisition of land and bodies as "secret restricted data."

Can Marshallese voices rendered musically contribute to mitigating nuclear damages by exposing nuclear damages? And, how might this sound when these problems, along the lines of radiation, often remain insensible as a communal problem with a global reach? These questions are important in terms of nuclear studies, Disability Studies, and musical scholarship because, like the insensibility of radiation and "secret restricted data," "disability may remain invisible until it is performed and, depending on the disability, may emerge precisely through the act of musical performance" (Lerner and Straus 2006, 9). The "cure narrative," which is so often invoked in Disability Studies, presumes a return to some state of health or life classified as "normative" or "normal." Listening to Marshallese voices that explicitly state, "there is no cure for radiation," evinces the incommensurability of "cure narratives," which are heard in political speeches and promises of redress, in terms radiation communities, and here, the Marshallese. Listening to their voices express such sentiments emphasizes the need to take seriously cultural claims for alternative models of compensation and infrastructural development, especially when there has been irrevocable damage to a "normal" state of existence.

The Bikinians

Bikinians have many songs that archive their experiences of physical and social dislocation, which I heard while I lived on Ejit Island, an island the size of a football field, where exiled Bikinians live to be in close proximity to the capital of the Republic of the Marshall Islands (RMI) (and political proximity to the United States). These songs yield insight into systemic interplays that cohere in the production of confined disability. "Radiation" is one such song, and it resounds internal networks of destabilization that extend to larger discussions of Marshallese sociocultural systems of meaning and communication from which we can better understand the production of "disability" and, in turn, "ability," from an intercultural perspective. The song was composed by a group of Bikinians in 1985, and Valentina, a member of the group, performed the song for me during an interview. Her son and his daughter were present, and, as she sang, tears spilled from her son's eyes. While crying is not appropriate in most settings in Marshallese culture, crying during the performance of a song, especially about a loss of someone (or, in this case, land), is an acceptable, regular occurrence. While I had solicited the interview, Valentina asked if I wanted to rerecord "Radiation" at a later date. Given her position as a respected singer in the community, she wanted to allow me the opportunity to record her singing without the audible distractions of her granddaughter. Also, she had switched the second and third sections of the song, and the correct organization is important in the proper unfolding of musical and narrative events.

"Radiation" details incommensurable losses, such as mental anguish and obsession with the irrevocable, incurable problems caused by nuclear testing. Each verse opens with the word "O" ("Woe" from English), marking the song as a lament. The first verse of the song tells of the singer mourning her homeland—the place she grew up. The second verse tells of the appearance of radiation and the resulting problems, and the third verse shares her suffering and dislocation. Steven Feld and Aaron A. Fox examined the intersections of the speaking and singing voice in the lamentation genre, noting it as "an important locus of research on questions of the boundaries of speech and song" (1994, 39–40). The authors define lamentation performances as "universally charged with evocative and emotive significance, albeit often producing highly specific local discourses on abandonment, transition, and renewal that are aesthetically central to distinct social constructions of memory" (Feld and Fox 1994, 40). Performances of "Radiation" expose the malleable boundaries between speech, song, and wailing that make audible multiple experiences of irrevocable displacement from one's land, body, and culture.

What can "Radiation," as a lament, tell us about this experience of displacement and dislocation when we combine the powerful text and its musical setting? In dealing with music, displacement, exile, and anguish, Michael Beckerman points to the "middles" of pieces for possible answers.

> It is in my experience that middles often represent composers at their most unguarded and honest, their most creative, and quite often their most expressive. Middles are a land of dreams, a place where structure may be forgotten, at least for a while; containing everything from death (funeral marches) to amorous secrets. The middle (whether of a phrase, a movement, or an entire work) may be understood as something like the sonic subconscious. (2010, 48–49)

The English word "radiation" is sung prominently in the middle of the song. The musical setting of the word introduces the first rhythmic alteration to the previously established musical material, and it is sung in a staccato manner immediately followed by a brief rest. The slight rhythmic modification, vocal delivery, and consequent pause demarcate something out of place that must be accommodated. Interestingly, this is in contrast to the first use of English loan words in the song, "home sweet home," which the American Protestant missionaries introduced into the Marshallese language in the nineteenth century.[2] "Home sweet home" is intelligible to English speakers, and it is sung clearly on what we imagine to be the first perfect authentic cadence (end of section 1). In section 2, "radiation" takes the place of "home sweet home," audibly mutating the established rhythmic stability. Radiation, as it were, has both destabilized and yet become the structural definition of Valentina's "home sweet home." In section 3, the words "in these islands" parallel the cadential setting of "home sweet home" and then "radiation," but the rhythm is once again altered, this time, with an audible break in the complicated gesture. "Radiation," then, cannot be confined to the middle of the song. Through text setting, "radiation" resounds Valentina's "home sweet home" by redefining it, and "radiation" when it becomes "in these islands" echoes further dislocation at home. Moreover, all of the islands are expressively affected because of "one" being out of place, and this is constitutive in the cosmology and practices of communal cultures (see Figure 24.1 and Track 24.1 on the Companion Website).

There are two additional prominent musical features that we hear in the middle of this song (in each performance), and these are stylistically characteristic of "radiation songs." First, the poetic device of the question punctuates the middle of each section. However, the middle of each section is the opening line of each chorus. The chorus, the refrain, or the material that returns and is emphasized, is an appeal. These are literal questions, on the one hand, and they are rhetorical, on the other. Each question is stylized with a throaty timbre and melodically intimates an interrupted cadence. The questions audibly mark a vocal interruption that works *as a petition*, which, as I will explain, is central to the technique of sharing the healthy throat as afforded by connection and

Section	Text Line	Marshallese	English translation
I.	V1	*O, ibūromōj kōn aelōñ eo aō*	Woe, I'm sad/devastated about my island
	V2	*ijo iaar drik im ruttolok wōt ie*	The place where I was young and I grew up
	C1	*ta menin naaj kaaenōṃṃan būruo?*	What things will make my throat (heart) peaceful?
	C2	*Jen aō ḷọmṇak kake*	So I can stop thinking about it
	C3	*aelōñ eo aō ej aō home sweet home*	My island is my "home sweet home."
II.	V1	*O, ibūromōj kōn aelōñ eo aō*	Woe, I'm sad/devastated about my island
	V3	*ijo eḷap radiation ej waḷọk ie*	So much radiation has appeared
	C1'	*ta menin naaj solve problem in?*	What things will solve these problems?
	C4	*kōnke ejjeḷọk uno,*	Because there is no cure (medication)
	C5	*uno in joḷọk radiation*	cure to get rid of radiation
III.	V4	*O, ijojoḷāār ioon aelōñ ejjab aō*	Woe, I am a stranger on an island that is not mine
	V3'	*ijo eḷoap eñtaan ko rej waḷọ k ie*	There is a great deal of suffering that is appearing
	C1"	*ta menin naaj joḷọ k eñtaan kein?*	What things will help get rid of this suffering?
	C4'	*kōnke ña ij juon eo*	Because I am one (person)
	C6	*ejjeḷọk bōnbōnin ilo aelōñ kein*	Who is without a place in these islands.

FIGURE 24.1 Text lines and translations of "Radiation."

communality. In fact, the first question ends with the word "throat" (how can her throat be made peaceful?). In Section 2, the question becomes how to "solve problems of" the throat, and Section 3 concerns "getting rid of suffering." A disturbed throat causes problems and suffering, and, from the outset of the song, Valentina laments that she is *būromōj*.

Būromōj literally translates to "dead throat" or "deactivated throat" (*burō*—throat and *mōj*—dead, numb). The throat is the seat of the emotions in Marshallese notions of the body/soul relation, in which the delineation is marked when there is a deactivation, a severing. The throat animates the vocal cords. It produces the voice that shares emotion and feeling, to connect with others so that one may sustain a healthy, productive, convivial existence. The throat is the place where heritage, animate potentialities, and environmental substance coalesce.

Second, there are periodic rests in the middle of phrases. Prominent among these is the aforementioned moment following the first iteration of "radiation" as well as the pause within the text setting of the song's final cadence. Another affective pause occurs in the first line of Section 3, and it prefigures the most rhythmically dense and stilted conveyance in the entire song (see Figure 24.2). The vocal performance of the words "on

FIGURE 24.2 First line of section 3, "Radiation."

an island that is not mine" is akin to a recitation displaced, and recalls Marshallese *roro*, which is precontact chant that is still performed to animate or excite one's self and others.[3] The throat and the conception of the healthy throat are inextricably connected to this important animating force in Marshallese culture.

Roro accompanied all of life's activities such as cooking, cleaning, fishing, navigation, conflict, resolution, healing practices, births, and funerals. Through incantation, *roro* connects humans and the land through a "waking up" and physical transformation. As a former mayor of Bikini Atoll, Alson Kelen, explained,

> It's like when you are trying to wake something up. It's like when you are trying to explain something to somebody and you say it again because most Marshallese chants, you have to repeat them three times. First, you are actually waking yourself up. The second time, you are getting ready to move. The third time, you are actually chanting while you are moving. So you are actually waking yourself up. You are waking up the spirit within yourself.[4]

Roro, he said, animates yourself *and* all that is around you.

Unlike Western musical thought, which frames the voice as sounding an individual's deepest emotions, aligning voice more broadly with a person's identity and metaphorically with an individual's agency, the voice in Marshallese thought is predicated on conviviality and lineage (which is directly related to the land and the mother). The ability or inability to express emotions depends on an entire social network, knowledge of a lineage, and a "healthy throat," which comes from communality. Rather than the individual animating the musical voice, it is the musical voice that animates the person, primarily because the musical voice is itself a mnemonic device for summoning an entire heritage and therefore realm of knowledge concerning how to live and engage with others. *Roro* were central to indigenous healing practices, along with medicinal plants and massage, and all three are part of Marshallese indigenous heritage.

It might be apparent, then, that the Marshallese throat has similar connotations to the Western heart. In Western society, the heart is the seat of the emotions, and Western medicine views it as central to an individual's circulatory system, the system that is vital to an individual's health and prospects of immunity from certain diseases. A human's circulatory system is defined, by medical terms, as "closed." In Western medical and philosophical thought from Hobbes onward, immunity and the body are matters of an individual, and intermediaries, such as the state and inoculations, are needed to protect the individual from the communities that might expose him or her to lethal diseases, affects, and so forth (Esposito 2008).

We can now better understand how a sensory disconnect between cultures, resulting in part from values placed on functions of the body partitioned, contributes to the construction of disability. To the Western doctors, the irradiated throat was something to be examined, and Western medicine was administered to help cure an individual. For the Marshallese, the throat (and voice) is a mechanism of healing in its connective capacities. Not only does the throat connect one person to another but also it connects the population to the land (or attempts to do so). In Valentina's lament, we hear an "environmental racism" sonorized, which has produced, constructed, and confined disability across the world.[5]

Rests, breaks, open spaces, and questions within the affective space of the lament afford a "contagion of affect," which makes possible not the experience of painful experiences dealing with radiation but the communal sense of pain as possible effective political alliances.[6] Bikinians feel that singing, literally, connects them with Americans and allows them to maintain indigenous self-determination by employing their voice in intelligible musical forms, resisting depression and unintelligibility, and preserving vocal traditions that animate cross-generational sociality and education. As Bikinian Councilman Hinton Johnson explained,

> those songs written by elders and the songs from this generation speak to the circumstances of [us] Bikinians. According to what we know from our custom, the Marshallese custom, especially the Bikinian custom, people who are lonely or have lost something, you can tell those people in the Marshall Islands because they always sing songs. It is like people who get divorced and the husband feels sorry about the loss of his wife. He keeps singing songs all the time, every time when you see him, he always shares those songs with you. So, for us, it is like that—losing Bikini really made us keep singing and singing and singing. This is what you find with the Bikinian community. They always sing songs, or in other words, they are always keeping the memories of their homeland.[7]

Hinton references important Marshallese understandings of the function of singing, both in terms of activating memory and political engagement, both of which depend on the voice as a question of the community in distress. In fact, the Marshallese cite an important way of being and doing "*burō wōt juon*" (one throat, one voice) that upholds togetherness and affords survival through working together. The motif of continued singing is related to *roro*, but, paired with notions of loss as the impetus for song, it alludes to a critical cultural dissonance and also to two legendary figures in Marshallese folklore: the female *lōrro* and the male *būromōj* who suffer from the grief caused by the loss of their male or female counterpart, respectively.[8]

According to custom, loss physiologically impacts women in terms of weight. When a woman's soul is inside and she is functioning properly, she is "heavy." Marshallese society is matrilineal, and the land that comprises the identity of a person through its sentience and receptivity is of the mother. When a woman's soul flies away to recover her loss, she becomes "light" because she has lost the weight of her soul. She might become so light that she dies. Still a human (neither a ghost nor demon), the flying, crying woman (*lōrro*), is in intense emotional distress. The loss that causes her emotional grief is the condition of immobility and dislocation, or inability to reproduce or reciprocate her inheritance because she is not in her socially functional place. She has no place. Thus, a man's departure (and more recently, being taken from one's homeland) causes the flight and wails of the *lōrro*, which she has no agency to prevent. As she is depressing, she calls to the other spirits, or souls, through sound, in cries and inarticulate vocalizations.

When a man is devastated by a loss (of a woman, or more recently, land), he becomes *būromōj*. Men are (merely) affected by the affliction, as opposed to women who transform into theirs (*lōrro*). To reiterate, *būromōj* literally means "dead [or weakened] throat."[9] The words "dead" and "desensitized (numb)" do not have the same meaning, but the Marshallese language uses the same word (*mōj*) to refer to both. And, they are closely related to something being deactivated, or finished, so we might also say that the depression is a "finished throat." The *būromōj* man becomes sedentary, and he is said to eat feces (which lacks sustenance and weakens him).

> There are men who are *būromōj* and eat excrement, and throw off their clothes and are naked. They change to crazy [become crazy] from *būromōj*. Some are blind from *būromōj*. If they are treated [with Marshallese medical treatment: *uno in Majel*], they will become well. I saw it during the Japanese time. They were *būromōj* because their women left them or died. (Tobin 2002, 267)

The *būromōj* man cannot speak for himself (his lineage) because he cannot protect the women and their voices, which means, he cannot protect the land. He has lost his voice, or capacity for speech, and he speaks *kajin bwebwe* ("crazy speech" from which words are used in oral narrative when the *lōrro* or *būromōj* man speaks), he therefore is crazy because he is unintelligible and cannot relate.

Many radiation songs share similar figures of speech as the displaced gendered being (*būromōj* or *lōrro*) or the "chick without its mother [that because] it cannot scratch for its food without its mother . . . suffers as a result" (*jojolāār*) (Tobin 2002, 332). When connected to the other "signs" of ailments caused by radiation, we refer back to *būromōj* not as an emotion but rather as a changed state where a man has turned crazy over the loss of his love and cannot stop singing. Then, the following line makes sense: Valentina's "throat," literally, and her heart, metaphorically, are restless. She wails/sings because she is not at peace. In pursuit of a "cure" or a solution she must make sound. Connecting loss of mother, hunger, and malnutrition to displacement, *jojolāār* is "used as an analogy for landless people who have been evicted from their land" (2002, 332). Adding the component of suffering, a man from Enewetak Atoll in exile told Trust Territory Anthropologist Jack Tobin, "To be moved away from one's home atoll to another is a little like dying" (Tobin 2002, 332).

Removal from one's land forces everyone to be *lōrros* and thus has the potential to create a consubstantial society of *būromōj* people. Since they have neither articulate voice nor health, they cry out to the community for help. Voice, intelligible voice, and therefore individual health and expression are first and foremost external, again, a question of connection and difference. This conceptualization of the voice is tied to the Marshallese understanding of the throat as central to an individual's vital connectivity. Their search for an unknown, unintelligible cure manifests as a crying out for help in songs that also preserve indigenous traditions and memories. The singing voice is the intermediary instrument that opens musical systems to intelligible, political participation. Radiation is central to the song and to the affective and aesthetic sharing of loss. The performative sharing of loss forces the presence of "radiation" beyond the musical boundaries that exercise the individual, and communal, throat.

The Rongelapese

The US nuclear weapons testing program impacted the Rongelapese women disproportionately. Laurie Stras has explored vocal disfluency by "integrating both social and medical models" of disability. She writes "in the case of the voice, the significance of vocal disruption of damage to an individual will be in proportion to his or her reliance on vocal function for daily activity, and the more significant it is, the more disabled that person may be seen to be if afflicted by vocal pathology" (2006, 174). When considering the throat as the center of the soul and the complex cultural associations with the voice and musical thought, it is at times overwhelming to hear the debilitation and dislocation in the literal timbre and harmony of voices altered by radiation exposure. Before delving into the performance aesthetics of the Rongelapese, it is imperative to outline the impact of radiation on the voice. One medical study explains the development of thyroid nodules:

> Nine years after the accident [Bravo's fallout in 1954], a 12-year-old Rongelap girl was found to have developed a nodule in her thyroid gland. Within the next 3 years, 15 of the 22 Rongelap people who had been under the age of 10 years at the time of exposure had developed thyroid lesions. At that time, the first thyroid nodule in an exposed Rongelap adult appeared and in 1969, 15 years after the accident, the first thyroid nodule appeared among the exposed people of Utirik. It has become clear that thyroid abnormalities—which include benign and malignant thyroid tumors and thyroid failure—are the major late effects of the radiation received by the exposed Marshallese. (Robbins and Adams 1989, 16)

Thyroid surgeries and lymph node removal can result in dry vocal cords without the proper pliability to manipulate good pitch. The nerve that controls vocal cord closing runs along the top of the thyroid gland, and it is therefore susceptible to trauma during surgical invasion. Repeat surgeries may cause laryngeal neuropathy (roaring, hoarseness, vocal/glottal fry when singing). Tumor growth and/or thyroid growth abnormality leads to surgical reception, which can tug or push on the vocal cords, leading to weakness. In addition, radiation directly to the tissue-cluster alters mucus production. The altered mucus production often results in dry mouth and throat, leading to vocal inefficiency. Moreover, fibrotic process (the interruption of tissue production) leads to scarring and consequently reduction of vocal control.[10]

After the nuclear testing program, a majority of the Rongelapese developed thyroid cancer and had to have their thyroids, thyroid nodules, or lymph material removed. Women are more susceptible to thyroid disease and cancer than are men, and the change in their vocal range and timbre resulting from the surgeries was more noticeable. Gender divisions are important to social structure as well, and this is included in women's ability to sing "like a woman," more specifically, in the soprano range.[11] Marshallese from other atoll populations would hear the Rongelapese women speaking, or singing, and stigmatize them as *ribaaṃ* ("bombed people") or *tyroit* (a person having thyroid disease). In an oral culture, where voice is central to daily communication and maintaining generational cohesion, "voicelessness," threat of "voicelessness," and the cultural stigmatization of an altered voice that cannot perform its task within society are considered devastating.

In 1985, a Rongelapese woman composed *"Ta in eṃōkaj aer ba?"* ("What is all this commotion about?") after the community evacuated their homeland and moved to Mejato. The relocation was difficult but necessary, and moreover, the Rongelapese initiated this move even though the United States wanted them to remain on Rongelap. Although they "chose" to move, the Rongelapese feel that they had no choice because of their overwhelming sense that their island was dangerously radioactive. The move was, in part, a victory for the Rongelapese. While this victory did not assuage the pain and suffering of yet another forced movement, the knowledge of one's homeland, deserted and irradiated, and the illnesses that were now plaguing generations of Rongelapese, the move was publicized and made a loud statement that (1) the United States' needed to do more to help clean up the radiation from Rongelap and (2) the Rongelapese and other groups were motivated to curb the ramifications of nuclear phenomenon. The United States government did not respond enthusiastically.

If relocation to Mejato was difficult, life there proved even harder. Basic resources were not available to them, and they had to construct their own homes. Groups from nearby islands came to greet the Rongelapese on Mejato, and when others from around the Marshall Islands heard the news on the radio of the Rongelapese hardships, they would take the long journey from their home atolls to bring food, kerosene, lamps, soaps, and other useful items. The Rongelapese would prepare food and sing songs that stressed their reasons for relocation (among others) as a gesture of gratitude, such as "*Ta in eṃōkaj aer ba*" (see Figure 24.3).[12] A recording is available as Track 24.2 on the Companion Website.

In the lyrics, the song identifies the confusion of the women: "What is all this commotion about? What has happened?" English words associated with the trauma of

"Ta in emōkaj aer ba"	"What is all this commotion about?" (What are they telling us. . .)
I. *Ta in emōkaj aer ba*	What is all this commotion about?
bwe ta in ear walok	What has happened?
rej ba nan koj bwe jen emakūt	They're telling us to move
jen aelōñ in Rongelap	from the island of Rongelap
bwe ekakumkum emakit in ad	we are uncertain, worried about the move
bwe ebbo ilo computa ej ba	because the Geiger counter states
"eļap an too much plu,	"there is too much plutonium,
radiation *ippān"*	radiation in us"
II. *Ta eo in eļap aer ba*	What is all this commotion about?
itok wotjen 177	that resulted from 177
Na, oh, emakit lok	Oh, I have to move
jen aelōñ in Rongelap	from the island of Rongelap
bwe ekakumkum emakit in ad	we are uncertain, worried about the move
bwe ebbo ilo computa ej ba	because the Geiger counter states
"eļap an too much plu,	"there is too much plutonium,
radiation *ippān"*	radiation in us"

FIGURE 24.3 The first two sections of *"Ta in emōkaj aer ba"*

their nuclear encounter are utilized: "computer" (Geiger counter), "too much plu" (plu is short for plutonium), "radiation," and "177," which stands for "Section 177" in the Compact of Free Association that is in place to "address the past, present, and future consequences of the Nuclear Testing Program."[13] These sonic fragments were imported by the United States to audibly reify what could not be sensed, and they share a history of linguistic, cultural, and physical displacement. The Rongelapese had to move because of the dangers posed by the radiation that is now in them and their land. However, these elemental dangers are not so much shown as they are heard. The computer is the Geiger counter.

The line, "the Geiger counter states there is too much plutonium," emphasizes that the computer talks. The machine "states" or "says" (it ticks). And yet, it only "says," or continues to speak, as mediated by Rongelapese voices in song. In terms of evacuation and exile, silence is written into the delivery: what matters is what the computer says, not what the Rongelapese say. And if we take the limitations of language seriously, and therefore posit that truth is not dependent on linguistic constructs, then, this silence is in part superficial. While this silence, or a gesture toward this silence, can be reemployed in the song to underscore the historical experiences that have denied the Rongelapese agency, it becomes the task of the Rongelapese to *voice* precisely that point. They make the inaudible audible by fashioning their listening to detect the consequences, and thus the complexities, of their (shared) nuclear encounter.

The song's message would travel back with the other atoll communities, each circulation generating momentum to help the displaced community that suffered from medical complications. The circulation of a song depends on the ability to resist a melancholic stasis that results from mourning while preserving the sociopolitical function of mourning. This is of the utmost importance when we consider that the difficulties in the women's ability to pass down legends, stories, and songs rooted in the land without the sensible geographical markers have been compounded by their restricted access to their traditional means of healing. The song works with the capacities of who, or what, can speak and who or what can move. Ultimately, it is the voices of the Rongelapese women that must also share the "voice" of what the "computer" or Geiger counter "says." In Marshallese culture, land "sounds" its capacities, and the sound of the Geiger counter covers up the potential of the land as protective and productive. It sounds, to the world, the new destructive use value associated with the Marshall Islands.

The first time I heard "*Ta in eṃōkaj aer ba*," I did not know that I had actually heard it. The Rongelapese women, about six were present, sang the first two songs softly with Abacca Anjain-Maddison, the former Rongelapese senator. The women, Abacca told me, would sing one more song. For about four and a half minutes, the women spoke among themselves talking about the song with the words, "*computa ej ba eḷap an too much plu*," and then they would try to harmonize with each other. They would stop, their voices disentangling from one another, and they would try again. As four and a half minutes worked its way to five, Abacca sensed my confusion, and she explained, "Because they had thyroid operations, they are having problems with their voices . . . But they're trying. They're trying." This "trying" is a struggle, a will to have the power to communicate, and this will challenges, pushing up against the limitations of language and all other confines to articulate the Rongelapese nuclear experience. The radiation that was forced into the lives of the Rongelapese women (and other Marshallese populations) was not only insidious and insensible, causing the need for their thyroid operations and cancer treatments, but it literally reworked the musical material and formal constraints of the song. The actual voicelessness of Rongelapese after their operations amplifies the metaphorical and political silencing of the Rongelapese under nuclear hegemony. Their performance aesthetics connect these external silences to the internal silences of the musical material.

These silences are expressive of the broader discourse networks and processes of sensorial displacement that have been central to the formation of US nuclear hegemony. The nuclear project figures prominently in American geopolitical incorporation, and therefore, enacts a "logic of elimination." Yet, because this logic is global in scale, with some populations bearing the brunt of the consequences in line with the settler-colonial tendency, I want to suggest that we consider the "logic of decay" of the radiation, as existing at the limits of the insensible, with the potential to distribute the knowledge of classifications, silences, and other insensible, disabling mechanisms of control and confinement through *contagion* as a problem of the artificial concept of immunity. Through movements in excess of physiological confines, the Bikinians and the Rongelapese women's musical stories and vocal techniques *represent* and *re-present* radiation, highlighting the failures of immunity and fallacy of confinement. We can then read this "logic of decay" for its affirmative, positive capacities in a similar manner to the way in which Wolfe writes of the positive "logic of elimination" that "marks a return whereby the native repressed continues to structure settler-colonial society" (Wolfe 2006, 390).

With this in mind, I recall a performance of a Rongelapese "musical petition" to the US Department of Energy (DOE), which played with the Western medical pathological framing of disability and treatment by exposing, through a deconstructed harmony, the construction of disability as intimately social. The song, "*Kajjitok in aō nan kwe kiiō*" ("These are my questions for you now"), was written by Lijon in 2008 in response to a denied request made by the Rongelapese women to attend a meeting between the DOE and the RMI government. Lijon compiled questions that had been circulating among the community, and she explained that both her younger and older sisters (many had passed away) would ask the same questions about their health and would not receive answers. The song was then sung in front of the DOE at a party the Rongelapese hosted. Abacca once shared with me in a group meeting that, in this song, the women "[are] petitioning the DOE for answers to their sicknesses. They are scared that the thyroid medicines they have been taking for over 50 years are hurting their livers, their kidneys, and their emotional and mental states. They are getting sick[er]."[14] At that meeting, Lijon spoke in Marshallese and Abacca translated, "The medicines they take for the thyroid affect their bodies and minds, and they just want to know—*they just want to know*—what the side effects really are—and please, can the DOE tell them?"[15] The words are part of a "radiation language" comprising English loan words (italicized) and existing and new Marshallese words (Barker 2004, 111) (see Figure 24.4).

The specific performance is another instance where the body inscribed into politics becomes sensible through an extramusical marking of an insensible moment (Schwartz 2012b). The event was Nuclear Survivors' Day on March 1, 2009. Nuclear Survivors' Day is an official holiday in the RMI and is held on the anniversary of Bravo. The memorial offers a space for reflection, honoring of the dead, and communication to a wide audience concerning the lingering problems posed by nuclear testing.

Lijon, although not present for this particular performance, recounted a story about the preparations for the event. Lijon explained that she wanted the elderly women to come up with a skit, which would convey their disabilities to outsiders. Lijon said that she wanted the women to have wheelchairs and canes, hobbling out in an exaggerated way. After she explained her unrealized vision, she laughed softly and said that the "other ladies" did not want to do the skit because they felt no need to accentuate their disabilities. However, during this performance, the audible realization of disability via debilitated voices superseded the visual presentation (see Figure 24.5 and Track 24.3 on the Companion Website).

At three minutes, the women stop singing and the conductor, Betty, explains that the caesural moment is caused by "*tyroit*" (see Figure 24.6).[16] This moment of arrested singing inspires a host of questions in the listener: Did the women stop singing because their voices failed them? Is the failure attributable to the thyroid surgeries? Is it because many of the women are old? Is it because some of them were sick? Are their sicknesses related to compromised immune systems or the stresses of living with the fear of compromised immune systems after being irradiated? Did one of the leading women forget

"Kajjitok in aō nan kwe kiiō" Kajjitok in ao nan kwe kiiō Komaron ke jiban ippa bukot mejlan aban kein ao kab ro nuku	"These are my questions for you now" These are my questions for you now Can you help me find a way to untangle myself and my family from these things that hinder us?
Komaron ke uwaak io? Etke ejjelok an *takta* ni? Deka im jibke, im arin, Im arji-ajin	Can you answer me? Why don't I have a dentist? A doctor for my lungs, my kidney, and my liver?
Imaron ke bok melele bwe en emman lomnak Ke na imaron in udiakak kin ao jaje?	Can I please find meaning so that I can find piece of mind? Because I might go insane not knowing.
Ewor ke baj jemlokin ao idraak? *Aspirin, calcium,* uno in kirro, Uno kan *tyroit*	Will there be an end to taking pills? Aspirin, calcium, gout medicine, Synthroid
Ewi waween am lomnak *problem* in aō bwe etakie na jab kiki lo aenemman	What is your opinion of my problems because there are times I can't sleep peacefully
Ewor ke baj jemlokin ao idraak? *Aspirin, calcium,* uno in kirro, Uno kan *tyroit*	Will there be an end to taking pills? Aspirin, calcium, gout medicine, Synthroid
Uno kein im ba kaki remaron ke in kakure *kidney* ka ao, komelij e ao, im menono e ao?	Will these pills damage my kidneys, my brain, and my heart?[1]

[1] Note the usage of the word "*menono*" for the physical organ of the "heart" as opposed to *burō*

FIGURE 24.4 Lyrics of "Kajjitok in aō nan kwe kiiō"

the words and the rest of the women felt uncomfortable continuing? Was this a "skit" in and of itself? The alteration of the musical form and overall tenor of the performance could have been a product of all of these situations and countless others, but we will never know the answer. Similarly, the women may never know the actual answer, and that in and of itself is perceived as an *actual disability*. And, this disability of not knowing their own health status must be made audible by sounding a decay (or break) in the sonic material and the delayed decay, or a resonant instability, in the harmoniousness of their performance. Moreover, Betty's insertion of the word "thyroid" into the song seems, in the metaphorical sense, to mimic the insertion of thyroid pills into the daily

...	
[2:14] Uno kein im ba kaki remaron ke in kakure *kidney* ka ao, komelij e ao, kap menono e ao?	Will these pills damage my kidneys, my brain, and my heart?
[3:00 – voices fall]	
(Imaron ke) bok melele ***"Ah, tyroit*** bwe en emman lomnak Ke na imaron in udiakak kin ao jaje	Can I please find meaning ***Ah, the thyroid"*** so that I can find piece of mind? Because I might go insane not knowing.
...	
[4:09] Uno kein im ba kaki remaron ke in kakure *kidney* ka ao, komelij e ao, kap menono e ao?	Will these pills damage my kidneys, my brain, and my heart?

FIGURE 24.5 Timeline of vocal disruption

lives of the women. The intrusiveness of vocal disfluency (Straus) and roughness creates an actual moment of connection between the audience members and the performers, where the audience members are told they are hearing vocal, and by extension, physical and cultural trauma. This skit is a direct critique of the immunization project, and, as the women reassert their vocal abilities, we are asked questions with answers that exist beyond the disabled voices that work within, and at the same time challenge, the confines of a song.

Conclusion

These songs and performances highlight the failures at the core of biopolitical controls exerted on communities and expose the production of confined disability at the level of culture and structural violence. The songs are themselves contoured by the microsilences of decay: radiation poisoning, forced movements, and confinement. These silences are connected to a macropolitics of silence that is characteristic of nuclear hegemony. The Bikinians and Rongelapese vocal performances make possible the thought of a nuclear community, a common language and grammar—radiation—for a world exposed. This is done through the aural attestation of nuclear consequences that emerge in microsilences such as the timbral inconsistency of a voice, the thinning textural fabric

FIGURE 24.6 As the voices of the Rongelapese women fade, Betty points to her throat, and says "ah, *tyroit.*"

of a song, the destabilization of its harmonic fullness, and misdirected listening. Such misdirected listening reclassifies Marshallese as data, confines their speech outside the political realm, and forces movements that result in loss, and this follows the logic of elimination as destructive. To combat this logic, these communities sing at the limits of this vocal struggle, a struggle that is political insofar as it pushes the boundaries of what is audible and sayable. The vocalizations of the Rongelapese and Bikinians connect all life-forms in the nuclear age, and these resonances share their empowerment and abilities in excess of what cannot be cured.

Acknowledgments

I thank Michael Bakan, Stephanie Jensen-Moulton, Joseph Straus, and April Brown for their helpful comments. I also thank my Marshallese interlocutors for their patience and generosity in sharing their voices and stories.

Notes

1. Lijon MacDonald (Rongelapese woman), in discussion with author (October 2009).
2. American Protestant missionaries also introduced tonal harmony through hymns.
3. This is my reading. Some Marshallese interlocutors explain that this musical phenomenon indicates the song, or story, is not over. However, they do not relate it specifically to *roro*. It

is important to clarify that while this is not a *roro* in the traditional sense, my interlocutors point to a similar function of vocal animation and forward motion related to musical elements that sonically intimate an unrealized *roro*.

4. Alson Kelen (former Bikinian mayor), in discussion with author, May 2010.
5. Issues of social justice, the production of confined disability, and environmental racism are interrelated. See Cole and Foster 2001, Checker 2005, and Nixon 2011.
6. "The contagion of affect flows across bodies as well as *across* conversations as when anger, revenge, or inspiration is communicated across individuals or constituencies by the timbre of our voices, looks, hits, caresses, gestures, the bunching on muscles in the neck, and flushes of the skin." See Connolly 2002, 74.
7. Hinton Johnson (Bikinian councilman), in discussion with author, November 2009.
8. There exists a gendered dichotomy in Marshallese customary thought and practice where women and men have certain complementary strengths.
9. Krämer and Nevermann in, *Ralik-Ratak*, state that "būromōj" is "cut throat," or "divided throat," which is a possibility. However, today, and from the dictionary, the components of the word suggests that it is a "finished" throat, one that has stopped activating. Further, Tobin 2002 assesses the "būromōj" as a "weakened" throat, whether this is from a division of the throat (being split, indecisive) or cut (severed), or deadened/numbed, it is still a deactivation, a depression. See Krämer and Nevermann (1938) 1942, Abo et al. 1976, and Tobin 2002.
10. Dr. Ryan Branski at NYU Langone Center helped inform me about the physiological basis for the impact of thyroid operations on the voice.
11. I use the phrase "sing like a woman" along the lines of how my interlocutors discuss vocal expectations for women, based on range and in terms of "soprano" and "bass."
12. There is a third verse of the song that is barely audible. I cannot translate it, and I was never able to get this verse translated. I can hear that it is about their elders on the atoll, and their homeland and inheritance, which is important in terms of preservation. I thank Benetick Kabua Maddison, Albious Latior, Adelbert Laukon, and Terry Takamaru for help with the translations.
13. Nuclear Claims Tribunal 2014.
14. Author's field notes, October 27, 2008.
15. Ibid.
16. Still from video taken by author, March 1, 2009. See Schwartz 2012a, 389.

References

Abo, Takaji, Byron W. Bender, Alfred Capelle, and Tony DeBrum, eds. 1976. *Marshallese-English Dictionary*. Honolulu: University of Hawai'i Press.

Amsterdam, Lauren. 2012. "All the Eagles and the Ravens in the House Say Yeah! (Ab)Original Hip-Hop Artists and Styles of Heritage." Paper presented at the Indigenous Music Today Symposium, Columbia University, September 21.

Barker, Holly. 2004. *Bravo for the Marshallese: Regaining Control in a Post-Nuclear, Post-Colonial World*. Belmont, CA: Wadsworth.

Beckerman, Michael. 2010. "Ježek, Zeisl, Améry, and the Exile in the Middle." In *Music and Displacement: Diasporas, Mobilities, and Dislocations in Europe and Beyond*, edited by Erik Levi and Florian Scheding, 43–57. Lanham, MD: Scarecrow.

Checker, Melissa. 2005. *Polluted Promises: Environmental Racism and the Search for Justice in a Southern Town*. New York: New York University Press.

Cole, Luke W., and Sheila R. Foster. 2001. *From the Ground Up: Environmental Racism and the Rise of the Environmental Justice Movement*. New York: New York University Press.

Connolly, William E. 2002. *Neuropolitics: Thinking, Culture, Speed*. Minneapolis: University of Minnesota Press.

Ellis, Katie. 2008. *Disabling Diversity: The Social Construction of Disability in 1990s Australian National Cinema*. Saarbrücken, Germany: VDM Verlag.

Esposito, Roberto. 2008. *Bios: Biopolitics and Philosophy*. Translated by Timothy Campbell. Minneapolis and London: University of Minnesota Press.

Feld, Steven, and Aaron A. Fox. 1994. "Music and Language." *Annual Review of Anthropology* 23: 25–53.

Howes, David. 2005. *Empire of the Senses: The Sensual Culture Reader*. Oxford and New York: Berg.

Krämer, Augustine, and Hans Nevermann. (1938) 1942. *Ralik-Ratak (Marshall Islands)*. Translated by Charles Brant and John Armstrong. New Haven, CT: Human Relations Area Files.

Lerner, Neil, and Joseph N. Straus, eds. 2006. *Sounding Off: Theorizing Disability in Music*. New York and London: Routledge.

Nixon, Rob. 2011. *Slow Violence and the Environmentalism of the Poor*. Cambridge, MA: Harvard University Press.

Nuclear Claims Tribunal, Republic of the Marshall Islands. 2014. "Agreement between the Government of the United States and the Government of the Marshall Islands for the Implementation of Section 177 of the Compact of Free Association." Accessed March 25. http://www.nuclearclaimstribunal.com/177text.htm.

Robbins, Jacob, and William H. Adams. "Radiation Effects in the Marshall Islands." In *Radiation and the Thyroid*, edited by S. Nagasaki, 11–24. Amsterdam: Excerpta Medica.

Schwartz, Jessica A. 2012a. "Resonances of the Atomic Age: Hearing the Nuclear Legacy in the United States and the Marshall Islands, 1945–2010." PhD diss., New York University.

Schwartz, Jessica A. 2012b. "A 'Voice to Sing': Rongelapese Musical Activism and the Production of Nuclear Knowledge." *Music and Politics* 6 (1). http://quod.lib.umich.edu/m/mp/9460447.0006.101/--voice-to-sing-rongelapese-musical-activism?rgn=main;view=fulltext.

Seremetakis, C. Nadia, ed. 1994. *The Senses Still*. Chicago: University of Chicago Press.

Stras, Laurie. 2006. "The Organ of the Soul: Voice, Damage, and Affect." In *Sounding Off: Theorizing Disability in Music*, edited by Neil Lerner and Joseph N. Straus, 173–184. New York and London: Routledge.

Tobin, Jack A. 2002. *Stories from the Marshall Islands*. Honolulu: University of Hawai'i Press.

Wolfe, Patrick. 2006. "Settler Colonialism and the Elimination of the Native." *Journal of Genocide Research* 8 (4): 387–409.

PART 5

PREMODERN CONCEPTIONS

CHAPTER 25

LYRICAL HUMOR(S) IN THE "FUMEUR" SONGS

JULIE SINGER

Two humorous songs in the late fourteenth-century Chantilly Codex (Chantilly, Musée Condé, MS 564) ,[1] as well as a handful of slightly earlier works by the prolific poet Eustache Deschamps (c. 1346–1406/7), present the lyricist or performer as a *fumeur* (literally, "smoker"). The poetic persona's defining activity is not smoking in the modern sense—the inhalation of fumes from a burning herbal substance—but rather, an internal process whereby vapors produced through the metabolization of excess humors move upward through the body. According to humoral medical theory, health and illness result from the balance of four bodily fluids; people with certain complexions, that is, natures that lead them to have more of one humor than the others, can be more prone to this build-up of noxious fumes. Melancholics, especially those who imbibe a great deal of wine, are most susceptible. The *fumeur* lyricists take this notion derived from contemporary physiological theory and double it back on itself, writing texts that self-consciously celebrate the bodily process through which they were ostensibly created. They thus theorize composition as a metabolic system: the input is wine, processed within the body in a manner determined by the artist's nature, and the output is song—or so much hot air. Then the process itself becomes input, fodder for more texts. The poet consumes wine, then consumes himself, in order to produce lyrics that (in turn) take the lyricist's body as their matter, offering it up for public consumption. In the Chantilly Codex songs, *fumeur* identity is further performed through playful manipulation of pitch, melisma, and dissonance—marking a productively pathological convergence of Deschamps' categories of "natural" and "artificial" music.

The *fumeurs* share a common biological propensity to "smoke" and the *fumeur* songs are thus constitutive of a group identity, one based in its members' abnormal physiology and psychology.[2] Accordingly, the poetic descriptions of the *fumeur*'s individual physiology are tightly bound to notions of collective social identity. Deschamps penned multiple poems constructing the *fumeurs* as a sort of confraternity, complete with a charter. Both Deschamps and the Chantilly Codex authors Solage and Jacquet de Noyon portray the *fumeur* as a volatile, irascible yet creative lover of wine, one whose individual quirks become more prominent in the presence of other *fumeurs*. Deschamps's *fumeurs* share a number of behavioral characteristics with the members of other marginalized groups that the poet invents elsewhere in his immense lyrical body of work. The small corpus of *fumeur* songs therefore offers an opportunity to rethink the most basic received idea about disability in medieval Europe: that the concept of a "disabled identity," of people with disabilities as a social category, simply did not exist.[3] I will argue that overlaps between *fumeur* lyrics and other Deschamps poems celebrating bodily difference are suggestive of strategies of community formation that defy conventional wisdom about late medieval European identity categories; notions borrowed from modern Disability Studies will shed new light on these lyrics' implicit construction of a group identity based on a shared bodily and psychological condition.

Scholars of late medieval French lyric have been asking who the *fumeurs* were (if they existed at all) since the publication of the complete works of Eustache Deschamps in the last two decades of the nineteenth century (Deschamps 1878–1904). In a number of poems, Deschamps refers to himself as the leader or "chancelliers des Fumeux" (chancellor of the *Fumeurs*, ballade 813, IV.331–332), a group for which he provides a charter dated December 9, 1368 (VII.312–320) as well as a number of mock-judicial decisions.[4] The editors of Deschamps's complete works initially regarded the notion of a society of "smokers" as a poetic construct: in 1884, volume IV editor Queux de Saint-Hilaire glosses *Fumeux* as "gens fantasques" (temperamental people, IV.331), while seven years later, volume VII editor Raynaud calls the group a "confrérie imaginaire" (imaginary confraternity, VII.312). Toward the end of the lengthy endeavor to publish the complete works of Deschamps, the Chantilly Codex songs also became available in print: the contents of the Chantilly Codex, a treasury of *ars subtilior* song, were described in a series of early twentieth-century studies, beginning with Léopold Delisle's summary of the manuscript's poetic texts (Delisle 1900, 277–303; Greene 1971, 2–3). With the new availability of these poetic corpora, the resemblances between Deschamps's *fumeur* poems and the two Chantilly *fumeur* songs did not go unnoticed for long. Most of the early inquiries focused on the historical existence of a society of "smokers." Gustav Gröber posited that the *fumeurs* were a real drinking guild (1902, 1200), and Ernest Hoepffner argued there was "little doubt that we are dealing with an actual society, and not with the imaginary, or something that exists only in a writer's imagination" (1904, 51; cited in Unruh 1983, 19–20). Daniel Poirion (1965) sticks to a more cautious middle ground, describing the *fumeurs* as "une confrérie burlesque, mais qui rassemble des personnes réelles" (a burlesque confraternity, but one that includes real people) which Deschamps evokes "en termes fantaisistes" (in fantastical terms, 223). Most recently, Karin Becker (2012) has called the smokers an "association fictive" (fictional association, 60). Aside from Poirion and Becker, however, musicologists and literary scholars alike have interpreted Deschamps's *fumeur* references quite literally (for example, Reaney 1954, Unruh 1983, 1n2). André Pirro (1930) likens the lyrical activities of the *fumeurs*, whose existence he takes as factual, to those of the later *Cour amoureuse*, in which Deschamps may also have participated; Patricia Unruh, in the only extended study of the *fumeurs*, finds it likely that Deschamps refers to a real literary society with ties to the legal professions, analogous to the *Basochiens*.[5] This overwhelming focus on the historical reality of the *fumeurs*, while offering endless opportunities for *fumeuse speculacion* (as Solage puts it in his cryptic rondeau), has foreclosed more productive inquiries into the dynamics of *fumeur* identity.

Rather than asking whether the *fumeurs* really existed as a social/artistic group, and, if so, whether they were comparable to other literary or theatrical societies of the same period, I seek to understand how the *fumeur* lyricists forge social relations through the deployment of vulgarized medical discourse. For the *fumeur* poems perform not just social behaviors (as Unruh and others have noted) but also physiological difference. In the absence of any documentary evidence attesting to the existence of a *fumeur* society, what binds these lyrics together is their insistence on a set of bodily markers suggesting conditions analogous to what we might today term mental illness. These "symptoms" are not consistently pathologized—indeed, the causes and the behavioral markers of fumosity are at times celebrated—but *fumeur* identity is nonetheless reliant on late medieval physiological theory. What follows, then, is a close reading of the *fumeur* lyrics and of a handful of contemporaneous medical texts, by means of which I will explore the ways in which those bodily markers and their behavioral symptoms condition social relations and foster group identity—even if the coterie they form is only imaginary.

Fumeurs are, by all three lyricists' accounts, a strange lot: irascible, brooding, unpredictable, sometimes inspired but often lacking intellectual acuity. Allusions to these behavioral traits are interspersed among Deschamps's longer *fumeur* poems, such as *D'une autre commission d'un chien* (VII.320–323, hereafter *Chien*), *Cy parle d'une sentence donnée contre aucuns de Vitry pour un débat meu soudainement d'entre eux* (VII.332–335, hereafter *Vitry*), *C'est la commission des loups d'Espargnay sur la rivière de Marne* (VII.336–342, hereafter *Loups*), and especially the *Chartre des Fumeux* (VII.312–320, hereafter *Chartre*); the language of *fumée* also appears in a handful of ballades (813, IV.331–332; 912, V.109–111; 966, V.199–200), a verse letter to the count of Valois, dated February 23, 1378 (VIII.33–37), and the *Chartre des bons enfans de Vertus en Champaigne* (VII.323–331). The portrait of *fumeur* affect emerging from these varied texts reveals a personality type whose quirks are rooted in bodily difference, to such a strong degree that Karin Becker (2012) has called them a product of biological determinism.[6]

Deschamps was evidently the first lyricist to write of a society of *fumeurs*, often doing so in a mock-juridical context. In the most complete description of *fumeurs*, the *Chartre*, he claims for himself (in the guise of Jehan Fumée, emperor and lord of the *Fumeux* and palatine of the Melancholics) jurisdiction over disputes involving the members of his society. Before the procedural discussion, he provides a sort of preamble in which he explains the *fumeurs*' "maniere" and "condicion premiere" (behavior and primary condition, vv. 32–33), that is, their observable behaviors and those behaviors' physiological cause.

Ilz parlent variablement;
Ilz se demainent sotement;
Chaux sont de cuer, mouvent de teste
Plus que fouldre ne que tempeste;
Pour trop pou de chose se meuvent
Et ne scevent dont ilz se duelent;
Plain sont de grant merancolie (vv. 41–47)
They speak unpredictably;
They comport themselves foolishly;
They are hot-hearted, their heads move
More than lightning or tempest;
They move themselves for too slight a reason
And don't know why they are sad;
They are full of great melancholy

As Deschamps goes on to explain, the primary external and behavioral conditions that bind the *fumeurs* together are their mercuriality, their strange and varied dress, their fondness for wine, and their extravagant speech; these characteristics stem from the smokers' melancholic nature. Indeed, much of what defines the *fumeurs* can be understood as being grounded in their physiology and in their atypical biological response to their environment. The wine that they imbibe, for instance, is in the language of late medieval Western medicine a nonnatural, that is, an environmental factor that impacts bodily health. The *fumeurs* argue "pour la force du vin / Qui en cervel les ot tappez" (by virtue of the wine that had struck them in the brain, *Vitry*, vv. 10–11); the members of another group whose charter Deschamps composes, the *Frequentans*, drink wine from morning to night

Dont le cervel est enfumé,
Et pluseurs en sont enrumé
Si fort qu'ilz ne scevent mot dire,
Fors qu'eschignier, moquer ou rire
(poem 1400, *C'est la chartre des bons enfans de vertus en Champaigne*, VII.323–331, vv. 25–28)

From which the brain is filled with smoke,
And several consequently catch cold
So badly that they can't say a word
Except to jape, mock or laugh

The smokers' biological response to wine, and more particularly its effect on their verbal expression, likewise indicates the degree to which their group identity is embodied. Their speech, like their other behavior, encapsulates the group's defining characteristics: contrariety, mutability, lack of reason.

Estre veulent saiges tenus;
De vent sont plains et de sens nus,
Et vaines questions demandent;
Nulle solucion n'y rendent;

Trop sont saiges après le vin,
Mais rien ne scevent au matin;
Contraires sont aux diz d'autruy
Et ne font raison a nulluy (*Chartre* vv. 53–60)

They want to be considered wise;
They are full of wind and bare of sense,
And they ask pointless questions;
They offer no solution;
They are exceedingly wise after they've had wine,
But they know nothing in the morning;
They contradict what others say
And never admit that anyone is right.

For as much as they wish to be thought wise, though, they are quite the opposite: "Estre ne vuellent a Raison / Subgit, n'entrer en sa maison" (They do not want to be subject to Reason or to enter her domain, *Chartre* 71–72). Indeed, Deschamps highlights the *fumeur*'s lack of reason through the language of folly, of madness. Folly leads them by the hand, as he writes in the *Chartre* ("Folie par la main les tient," 97–98); they are full of smoke and marvelous foolishness ("sont plain de fumeuse vie / Et de merveilleuse sotie," *Chartre* 135–136). The terms *folie* and *sotie* are not medically precise, but their common usage makes these verses' sense quite plain: wine and smoke rising to the head disrupt the *fumeurs*' mental function and deprive them of their reason.

The most evocative lyrical expression of the *fumeur* ethos comes from Deschamps's ballade 813, "Je doy estre chancelliers des Fumeux" (I should be chancellor of the *Fumeurs*, IV.331–332). The phrasing of this ballade's first line links it to other ballades in which the poet proclaims himself the king of the ugly: most notably ballade 774, bearing the refrain "Sur tous autres doy estre roy des Lays" (Above all others I should be king of the Ugly, IV.273–274). In both ballades the first-person poetic voice claims the pinnacle of a society of misfits, a group set apart from all others by virtue of a distinct set of physical attributes.[7] However, while ugliness is defined in ballade 774 as stemming from a number of external characteristics—including crossed eyes, a hunched back, a dark complexion, and a hairy body—the *Fumeux* are defined by a set of behavioral and mental habits that stem from a precisely delineated humoral disposition that is undesirable at best, pathological at worst.

"Je doy estre chancelliers des Fumeux" begins with an expression of the poet's eagerness to impose order on his chaotic mental state:

de l'ordre maintenir sui songeux
Si c'on ne puet ma personne trouver
En un estat, ains me voit on muer
Soudainement mon sçavoir en folye,
Estre dolens, puis faire chere lye (vv. 3–7)

I am so preoccupied with maintaining order
That no sooner can one find me

In one state, than one sees me change
Suddenly my knowledge into folly,
Being sad, then putting on a happy face

The illogical causal relationship established here (*si que*) indicates that the order of the *Fumeux* is chaos, an overflowing of rational boundaries. This inability to remain "subject to reason," and the *fumeur*'s tendency toward verbal extravagance, are illustrated here with an extended series of enjambed lines (vv. 4–6) culminating in an admission of "folye." Therefore the poet's mental and emotional disorder—caused by a sort of "smoke" that provokes fantastical thoughts ("Ainsi me fait fumée, par ma foy, / Muser souvent et si ne say pourquoy," vv. 8–9), and reflected in the structure of his verses—constitutes a justification for his self-nomination to the "chancellorship."

In the ballade's second stanza, the poet introduces a medicalized framework, attributing his mercurial nature to a complexion that is primarily melancholic but also choleric ("De nature sui merencolieux, / Colerique, voir, me puet l'en trouver"; I am of melancholy nature, and one can even find me choleric, vv. 10–11). This complexion causes him to be "merveilleux / Naturelment" (extraordinary / By nature, vv. 12–13) and provokes an existential problem: how can he rid himself of melancholy without denaturing himself, altering his fundamental makeup (doi je retourner / A ma nature, sans moy desnaturer / Et estre plains de grant merencolie, vv. 13–15). Any remedy to the *fumeur*'s state would demand that nature be denatured, rendered marvelous: a process already illustrated in the *rejet* isolating the adverb "Naturelment" in line 13. Indeed, ballade 813 features an unusual amount of enjambment—a device whose very name evokes the encroachment of the physical body in the poetic space—as the *fumeur*'s behavior defies and overflows natural categories.[8] A return to conventional order (i.e., self-contained verses, or social assimilation) would undermine if not destroy the *fumeur*'s unique character.

This already problematized nature is made to assume responsibility for the poet's joyless outlook and behavior in the ballade's final stanza: "Donc je conclus, s'on me voit pou joyeux, / Que je m'en puis par nature excuser" (Therefore I conclude, if one sees how joyless I am, / That nature is my excuse for that, vv. 19–20). The poet lacks the mental acuity, and the bodily wherewithal, to combat his nature, "Car je ne suis pas si ingenieux / Que je sache contre nature aler" (For I am not so ingenious / As to know how to go against nature, vv. 21–22). He must remain as he is, with the stanza's accumulation of "smoky" terms reinforcing the inescapability of his physiology.

Fumeux seray, riens n'y vault le parler,
Fumeusement menray fumeuse vie (vv. 23–24)

I'll be fumous, there's no use discussing it,
Fumously I will lead a fumous life.

The wordplay at the end of Deschamps's ballade, with its pattern of variations on a single lexeme (*fumeux, fumeusement, fumeuse*), will be amplified even further in the two Chantilly Codex songs. Although scholars have made much of Deschamps's "liberation" of lyric from music, the relationship between Deschamps's lyrics and performance practices is more complicated than critics have typically acknowledged (Roccati 2004), and it is in these two musical compositions that Deschamps's sketches of *fumeur* behavior come to life, not just described but performed. The songs by Solage and Jacquet de Noyon offer a portrait of the *fumeur* that largely conforms to the image set out by Deschamps: the Chantilly ballade advances a defense of the *fumeur* ethos, and the rondeau provides its textual and musical illustration.

The ballade "Puisque je suis fumeux," with lyrics attributed to Jacquet de Noyon and music attributed to Hasprois, appears on folio 34v of the Chantilly Codex.[9] Like "Je doy estre chancelliers des Fumeux," this three-stanza ballade stakes an immediate claim to *fumeur* identity; however, the Chantilly text focuses less on a description of the *fumeur* than on a justification of his behavior. Unlike Deschamps, Jacquet de Noyon does not seek to prove that he is a *fumeur*: in the first stanza he accepts his *fumeur* status as a given, as the initial premise on which the rest of his song is contingent ("Puisque je suis fumeux plains de fumée," Because I am a *fumeur* full of smoke, v. 1). This is a status that obligates the poetic persona to let off some steam ("fumer m'estuet," v. 2), giving rise to a paradoxical, combative, but ultimately harmless opposition to nonsmokers.

Puisque je sui fumeux plains de fumée
Fumer m'estuet, car se je ne fumoye
Ceulz qui dïent que j'ay teste enfumée
Par fumée je les desmentiroye.
Et nepourquant jamais ne fumeroye
De fumer qui fust contre raÿson (vv. 1–6)[10]

Because I am a *fumeur* full of smoke
I must smoke, for if I didn't smoke,
Those who say I have a head full of smoke,
I'd contradict them with smoky [harsh] speech.
And nevertheless, I would never fume
With smoke that went against reason.

Jacquet's hypothetical situation defies logic: if he weren't a *fumeur*, but were still accused of being one, he would prove his opponents wrong . . . by displaying classic *fumeur* behavior. And yet he declares that his smoking would never be *contre rayson*. Evidently this ballade has plunged its reader into a comical world whose inherent contradictions reveal the *fumeur*'s mental disturbance. Hasprois's musical setting, with its "perverse dissonances" (Unruh 1983, 83), may at once reflect the ballade's lyrical content and misdirect the audience's reaction: for the lyrics plainly state that the public is meant to respond not with consternation ("point d'outrayge," v. 10), but with a smile.[11]

The poet attributes his smoking to a choleric complexion ("Se je fume, c'est ma complecciön / Quolerique qu'ainsi me fayt fumer," vv. 7–8), and affirms that this behavior harms no one ("sanz personne grever," v. 9): a position underlined in the ballade's refrain, "Quant on fume sans fayre autruy damage" (When one smokes without doing harm to others, vv. 11, 22, 33). If the *fumeurs* are harmless, their ranks are also open to all comers. "Fumée n'est à nulli refusée" (Smoke is refused to no one, v. 12): this "group" is inclusive, even porous.[12] Membership in the club is not thoroughly unattractive, as the *fumeur*'s contradictory nature provides equal measures of consolation and tribulation (vv. 17–18), and even (contrary to the joylessness Deschamps describes) delight: "On se puet bien en fumant deliter" (one can really take delight in smoking, v. 19). Smoking can even enhance authorial creativity:

> J'ay en fumant mainte chose fit rimée,
> Encore sçay que maïs n'i avenroye
> Se par fumer en fumant n'i pensoye. (vv. 14–16)
>
> I've created many rhyming pieces while smoking,
> And furthermore, I know I would never arrive at them
> If I didn't think of them through smoke while smoking.

Smoke's alteration of mental acuity is not always a drawback, and the smoker's altered mental state can breed novel creations. The causal connection between "smoking" and composition is part of a physiological chain that the poet explains in the ballade's final stanza, linking the brain/head (vv. 23, 25) to the heart (vv. 29, 32). Once again we encounter a hypothetical situation, but this one undermines the preceding stanza's reclamation of *fumeur* status by pathologizing the *fumeur*'s mental processes.

> Se j'eüsse la cervelle empeinée
> De Socratés si comme je vodroye,
> J'eusse bien la teste plus temperée,
> Car onques ne fuma par nulle voye. (vv. 23–26)
>
> If I had the active brain
> Of Socrates, as I would like,
> I would have a much more temperate head,
> For he never smoked at all.

Like Deschamps, who characterizes his "chancellor" persona as "pas si ingenieux," Jacquet implicitly describes his *fumeur* persona's brain as inactive, his head as intemperate. The *fumeur* regulates his behavior for fear of getting even worse ("pour päour d'enpirer," v. 31)—suggesting that, despite all previous declarations to the contrary, "smoking" is indeed a malady. After all, the ballade insists that one can smoke without harming anyone else ("Quant on fume sans fayre autruy damage"), even as it intimates, in comical fashion, that the *fumeur* himself may suffer. In short, "Puisque je sui fumeux" is an exercise in cognitive and musical dissonance: its inherent contradictions perfectly capture the *fumeur*'s stubborn contrariety.

Solage's rondeau "Fumeux fume," copied on folio 59r of the Chantilly Codex, offers an even clearer (by which I mean, at the textual level, an even more obscure) illustration of the obliqueness of *fumeurs*' mental patterns.

Fumeux fume par fumee.
fumeuse speculacion.
Qu'antre fummet sa pensee
fumeux fume par fumee.

Quar fumer molt li agree
tant qu'il ait son entencion.
Fumeux fume par fume
fumeuse speculacion.

A quick-tempered person brews up out of vexation
brooding, futile speculation.
which puts his thoughts in a haze;
a quick-tempered person brews up out of vexation

because it pleases him greatly to fume
until he gets his way.
A quick-tempered person brews up out of vexation
brooding, futile speculation.[13]

The condensed vocabulary picks up where "Je doy estre chancelliers des Fumeux" left off, showing a taste not just for variations on a single lexical theme (*fum-* words) but for richly equivocal wordplay.[14] Like the insistently repetitive vocabulary, the concentrated circularity of the rondeau form reinforces the cycle whereby "fumous" nature gives rise to, and is nourished by, "fumeuse speculacion." "Fumeux fume" also exposes the *fumeur*'s contradictory nature, though not as overtly as in "Puisque je suis fumeux": here, though no medical explanation is given, the *fumeur*'s simultaneous fogginess ("antre fummet sa pensee," v. 3) and clarity of purpose ("tant qu'il ait son entencion," v. 4) hint at a similar set of internal contradictions.

Nigel Wilkins has on more than one occasion (1979, 33; 1984, 160) termed this rondeau an "exaltation of grumpiness," one achieved through lyric as well as musical setting.

> The extreme in this direction [the late fourteenth-century introduction of music in a lower tessitura], exploited certainly for comic purposes, comes in Solage's Rondeau "Fumeux, fume," where the exaltation of grumpiness descends into the depths with an accompanying disintegration of tonality. (1979, p. 33)

While "grumpiness" seems an unnecessarily reductive simplification of *fumeur* affect, especially since the *fumeur* takes pleasure ("molt li agree," v. 5), Wilkins's remarks do signal this rondeau's sophisticated matching of musical innovation to lyrical idiosyncrasy. More recently, Gilles Dulong (2009) has commented in general terms on Solage's "sensibilité particulière à la mise en musique de ses textes" (particular sensitivity to the musical setting of his texts, 46). Such sensitivity is apparent in "Fumeux fume," whose unconventional chromaticism (Greene 1971) and "remorseless sequences" and "abnormally low range" (Unruh 1983) appear to reflect the lyrics' evocation of an unusual and inescapable behavioral and mental pattern. The song's rondeau form reinforces this sense of a repetitious and inescapable cycle (Poirion 1965). Moreover, the song's exaggerated melisma, in a very low register, captures the lyrics' (and indeed, all *fumeur* lyrics') humorous effect. As Blake Howe has observed, the rondeau's "disordered" pitch and melodic intervals render it difficult to sing, and highlight the composer's ingenuity (pers. comm.). The performance of the same text in multiple voices further reinforces the sense that this text expresses a collective *fumeur* identity.

The stylistic peculiarities of "Fumeux fume," a rondeau that stands out even among the other novelties of the Chantilly Codex (Newes 2009), are suggestive of a phenomenon Joseph N. Straus (2008, 12) has identified in more modern music: "late style" compositions rife with stylistic markers of disability. Just as according to Straus "*late-style works* [within the corpora of individual composers] *are those that represent non-normative mental and bodily states*," Solage's expression of the *fumeur*'s nonnormative state finds its expression in an exaggerated form of another sort of late style, the late *ars nova* now known by Ursula Günther's preferred designation of *ars subtilior* (1960). Despite the evident distinction between works composed late in a particular composer's career and works composed late in a particular stylistic period, the resemblances between Straus's "disability style" and the attributes of "Fumeux fume" are intriguing. The characteristics by which Straus defines late styles—intimacy, compression, difficulty, retrospection, fragmentation, austerity, introspection, repetition—are the hallmarks of a great many *ars subtilior* songs and "Fumeux fume" in particular. Solage's *ars subtilior* rondeau may be read as a highly stylized representation of the *fumeur*'s nonnormative mental condition—smoke swirling, thoughts repeating—composed in a musical style that is itself suggestive of eccentricity or even disability.

The term "disability," while undeniably anachronistic, is nonetheless an apt one to apply to the *fumeurs*: this becomes apparent on examination of other contemporaneous textual references to psychological "smoke," which also reinforce the sense that the *fumeur* community, whether factual or imagined, is bound together not just by behavior or values but also by atypical physiology. The characteristics of the *fumeux*, as explicated and illustrated in the lyrics and in their musical settings, correspond quite neatly to other literary usage and to contemporary medical/scientific doctrine, suggesting that *fumeur* lyrics are not nearly as obscure or arcane as modern commentators have held them to be. In a wide range of texts and genres, "smokers" are presented as people who fall outside of societal norms, distinguishing themselves by their less than ideal humoral balance and the unruly behaviors resulting from this unusual makeup.

Eustache Deschamps, Jacquet de Noyon, and Solage are by no means the only writers to use the word *fumeux* or its variants to describe this particular set of personality traits—though they are the only ones to write of a *society* or self-governing group bound together by these attributes. While explicit medieval definitions of *fumeux* are rare, Middle French prose authors' stylistic tendency toward synonymic reduplication offers clues to the valences of the term. In describing temperaments, Jean Froissart (1894) links *feumeus* with *merancolieus* (melancholic, IX.144); Nicole Oresme (1940) ties *fumeus* to *chaymes* (pretentious) and *presumptueus* (presumptuous, 256); Jean le Fèvre (1887, 97) pairs *fumeux* and *tourblé* (troubled); the *Maniere de langage* (Gessler 1934, 80), a guide to French written in England, pairs *orgueille* (pride) and *fumosité*; and a bit later, in the fifteenth century, both Alain Chartier's *Breviaire des nobles* (Laidlaw 1974, 403) and the *Cent nouvelles nouvelles* (Sweetser 1966, 56) link a *teste fumeuse* (smoky head) to anger and to spiteful speech. In two theatrical texts, mad characters (one feigning insanity, the other genuinely afflicted) refer to themselves as *fumé* during metadiscussions of unconstrained speech.[15] All of these references help us imagine to what degree a nonspecialized late medieval audience might have regarded the *fumeurs*' mental state as pathological.

For a public versed in medical theories of the brain and its function, the *fumeur* poems would have provided even stronger evidence of mental illness—though the reader's determination of the precise nature and source of that illness might have varied according to his preferred authorities, just as Deschamps attributes his *fumosité* to a melancholic nature and Jacquet de Noyon chalks his up to a choleric complexion. In most contexts, *fumosité* refers in medical texts to exhalation or to flatulence; it can, however, evoke internal disturbances too. Late medieval *régimes de santé* typically highlight the "fumousness" of wine, especially of red wine, and warn that wine's fumes can rise to the brain.[16] Deschamps, who appears to have used just such vulgarized medical texts as sources (Becker 2012), reflects this conventional wisdom when he declares that with excessive drinking "s'esmeuvent vos esperis" (your spirits move, *Chartre*, 127). It is precisely such movement that precipitates the brawl described in Deschamps's *Sentence donnée contre aucuns de Vitry* ("le mouvement du vin / Leur fist commencier le hutin," the movement of the wine caused them to start the fight, *Vitry* 77–78). These windy superfluities can have a serious impact on cognitive function, as Bernard de Gordon (Gordon, 1495, II.20) explains in his early fourteenth-century *Lilium medicinae*, here cited in its later fifteenth-century French translation: "fumees grosses qui montent ou cerveau et molifient les nerfz et troublent les instrumens des sens, et les vertus, si comme l'ymaginative, la cogitative, la memorative" (coarse fumes that rise to the brain and soften the nerves and trouble the instruments of sense and virtue, such as the imaginative, cognitive, and memorative faculties). *Fumer* might be pleasant, as Jacquet de Noyon proclaims, but it also gives rise to the serious cognitive disruption that accounts for that "pas si ingenieux" feeling.

Even the inconsistencies among *fumeur* songs are consistent with contemporary medical debates. Like the previously discussed lyrics by Eustache Deschamps and Jacquet de Noyon, two of the most important encyclopedic texts that were translated into French in the late fourteenth century disagree as to whether melancholics or cholerics are more prone to mental fumes and the diseases they precipitate: these are Bartholomew the Englishman's thirteenth-century *De proprietatibus rerum*, translated as *Livre des propriétés des choses* by Jean Corbechon, and the pseudo-Aristotelian *Problemata*, which, along with Pietro d'Abano's commentary, was translated as *Livre de problemes de Aristote* by Évrart de Conty. Both were translated in the waning years of Charles V's reign—and are therefore almost exactly contemporary with the *fumeur* poems. Both texts address a nonspecialized audience, as evidenced by their royal commission and by early patterns of manuscript ownership (see Cadden 2006, Guichard-Tesson 2006, Byrne 1977, Byrne 1981, Ducos 2006). Like the poems of Eustache Deschamps and Jacquet de Noyon, they agree on the basic physiological mechanism of *fumosité* as an excess of the pathological form of one humor precipitating the production of harmful vapors that rise to the brain; also like the *fumeur* poets, they disagree on which humor it is that causes such conditions.

Évrart de Conty discusses *fumosité* in his translation of the famous problem XXX.1, focusing on melancholy: why, the author asks, have so many brilliant artists and political leaders been melancholics? In his response he identifies a set of character traits that foster success, then clarifies the bodily substances and processes that engender these traits. Intrinsically cold and dry black bile, when heated, gives rise to the desirable characteristics of ambition, curiosity, and loquacity—as well as to anger, lust, and fumosity.

> Et quant elle habonde en quantité et en chaleur elle les fait hastis et fumeus excessis et entreprenans et grans enquereus de choses et de legier esmouvables a ire et a concupiscence et aucune fois les fait elle grant iengleurs et moult superhabondans en paroles. (Paris, BnF, MS fr. 24282, fol. 178r)
>
> And when it [black bile] abounds in quantity and in heat it makes them hasty and excessively smoky and ambitious and intellectually curious and easily moved to anger and desire, and sometimes it makes them big talkers and very super-loquacious.

This explanation accounts perfectly for the *fumosité* of Eustache Deschamps and the fellow members of his drinking-club, right down to Deschamps's observation that he is melancholic but others might find him choleric due to the anger that stems from heated melancholy. For a fuller understanding of the link between *fumosité* and the choleric temperament, however, we must turn to other texts, including Bartholomew the Englishman's encyclopedia.[17]

The *Livre des propriétés des choses* first discusses *fumosité* in its overview of humoral theory, then returns to the topic in chapters devoted to yellow bile and to mental illnesses. First of all, like the more learned *and* more popular texts we've seen, the encyclopedist attributes some mental fumes to overindulgence in alcohol.

> se le mengier et le boire est oultre mesure la moisteur est trop grande et la chaleur est trop petite et [. . .] grosses fumositez [. . .] montent au cervel et en tuent de sens les petites peaux qui y sont et les blescent griefment et aucuneffoiz font venir la migraine et aultres maladies du chief tresmauvaises. Aucuneffoiz aussi celle fumosite malicieuse touche la racine des nerfs sensibles et passe oultre iusques au dedens des nerfs et empeesche lesperit de lame qui la est et le blesce et ainsi elle trouble et le senz et la raison et la langue qui est linterpreteresse de raison si comme il appert en ceulx qui sont yvres. (Paris, BnF, MS fr. 22531, fols. 52v–53r)
>
> if eating and drinking are immoderate, the moisture is too great and the heat is insufficient, and [. . .] coarse fumes [. . .] rise to the brain and kill the sensation of the little skins [meninges] there, gravely injuring them, and sometimes they bring on migraine and other very unpleasant ailments of the head. Sometimes, too, this malicious fumosity affects the root of the nerves, penetrates them, and impedes and wounds the spirit that is there, thus troubling the intellect and reason and the tongue, which is the interpreter of reason: so it is with drunks.

Later, it is specified that the hot fumes affecting cognitive function come from yellow bile: "Et ce vient de la chaude et ardant fumee qui vient de la cole et monte ou cervel et fait ceste mutation en la partie ymaginative" (And this comes from the hot and burning smoke that issues from yellow bile and rises to the brain and causes this change to the imaginative faculty, 57v); *frenaisie* (frenzy), too, is said to come about when dangerous fumes stemming from pathological "cole rouge" (red choler, 117r) rise to the brain.

According to the *Livre des propriétés des choses*, fumes themselves are mad ("fumee foursennee," 53r), and they wreak havoc on the mental faculties of reason and imagination. Inducing mental paralysis, interrupting "le senz et la raison et la langue," *fumée* evidently impedes mental function. But it is also apparent that, to use a modern metaphor, smoke "rewires" the brain and thus creates new cognitive pathways, new creative opportunities. Little wonder, then, that the *fumeurs* should seek to claim such a force and harness it in service of their ludic lyrical innovation.

In isolation, Deschamps's *fumeur* poetry would seem little more than an extension of the contrarian persona he develops across much of his lyric. In conjunction with the two Chantilly Codex songs, however, these lyrics are strongly suggestive of a collective identity, as reflected in early critics' attempts to verify the historicity of this social group. Such attempts make sense in a modern context, but how can one reconcile this search for a "poetic society," defined by its participants' psychological alterity, with late medieval Europe's very differently configured identity categories? More precisely, how do medieval poets create an identity group rooted in bodily difference *without* relying on a not-yet-invented "medical model" of disability, even as they "medicalize" that bodily condition?

The fourteenth century was a period of cultural medicalization in western Europe (Metzler 2006, McVaugh 1993, Singer 2010), and the strongly medicalized vein throughout the substantial corpus of Deschamps's lyric poems, especially his ballades, is well known (Becker 1998). Critics have long noted the specific, specialized language with which Deschamps laments his first-person poetic persona's decrepit bodily and mental state: ugliness, melancholy, fumosity, digestive upset, plague, and other maladies.[18] Karin Becker (2012) claims that Deschamps's emphasis on illness fulfills a social function, helping his readers face their own suffering ("aider son public à affronter la misère," 211) and thereby building solidarity with them. Beyond providing a model of suffering through poor health, he cripples his own lyric persona: not just to cement his outsider status, as Jacqueline Cerquiglini (1984) has argued, but to place himself at the center of new social formations springing from his own imagination. Hence the large number of poems in which he declares himself the king, or the chancellor, or the prince of a group of misfits. This has real implications for the consumers of his poetry: if we accept Deschamps's poems as a "declaration of solidarity" with his audience, then by positioning himself as an outsider, set apart from other men by his very "nature," he is cripping his readers too.

Eustache Deschamps's poems about illness and suffering constitute the most apparent examples of poetic medicalization within his body of work, but the phenomenon stretches even deeper into the lyricist's oeuvre. By reading the *fumeur* poems in conjunction with Deschamps's treatise on poetics, the *Art de dictier*, we can see that even those of Deschamps's poems that do not treat explicitly medical themes nonetheless spring from a poetic impulse that is founded on a pathologized vision of the human body.

The *Art de dictier* is not typically discussed as belonging to Deschamps's medical corpus. Still, medicalized notions of poetic activity underpin the discussions of poetry and music in this earliest full-blown *ars poetica* in the French language. The most famous passage of the *Art de dictier* is the one in which Deschamps distinguishes "natural music" from "artificial music." In short, "natural music" is the composition of lyrics, and it is called "natural" because it springs from an innate, natural ability: either you have it or you don't. "Artificial music" is the composition and performance of music, melody, harmony, be it vocal or instrumental: this is "artificial" because it can be taught to anyone. Deschamps's distinction between natural and artificial music has been seen as marking an important rupture between the generation of Deschamps's mentor Machaut, who composed both words and music, and subsequent artists who typically specialized in one or the other but not both.[19] The theoretical discussion of "natural music" has typically been regarded as a revindication of inborn talent, and as a statement either of poetry's independence from, or close alliance to, music. It has not, however, typically been read as participating in Deschamps's broader discourse of the medicalized body, except by Glending Olson, who has rightly noted that "the passage as a whole relies on a medical analogy" (1982, 147–148, 60). The passage on music begins, "Musique est la derreniere science ainsis comme la medicine des vij ars" (Music is the last science and is like the medicine of the seven arts), an observation with which Olson justifies reading Deschamps's use of the term "esperis" according to that word's medical connotations. The medical analogy extends even beyond the terminology Olson discusses, however. An examination of Deschamps's usage of the language of *nature* and *naturele* reveals that poetic ability springs not just from a generalized intellectual predisposition but from a specifically complexional, biological, and therefore medicalized, or at least *medicalizable* predisposition.

According to Deschamps, natural music is so designated because its composition must come naturally to the would-be artist: "L'autre musique est appellee naturele pour ce qu'elle ne puet estre aprinse a nul, se son propre couraige naturelment ne s'i applique" (The other music is called natural because it can't be taught to anyone unless his own mind naturally inclines itself in that direction; 62). Deschamps emphasizes again and again that this innate ability cannot be taught. Natural music is "ce que nul, tant fust saiges le maistre ne le disciple, ne lui scavroit aprandre, se de son propre et naturel mouvement ne se faisoit" (that which no one could have himself taught, however wise either the master or the disciple might be, if it didn't come about through his own natural movement; 66); it is available only to "ceuls qui nature avra encline ou enclinera a ceste naturele musique" (he whom nature has inclined or will incline toward this natural music; 66). What makes this sort of music is not an inherent quality of the poetry; it is the poet's own "nature," his biological makeup. The chosen terminology of "natural" music anchors lyrical composition in the body, and more specifically in the bodily complexion, of the poet. In his more explicitly medicalized lyrics Deschamps often uses the word "nature" as a synonym for "humoral complexion," as we saw in the ballade "Je doy estre chancelliers des Fumeux": "De nature sui merencolieux" (v. 10), "merveilleux / Naturelment" (vv. 12–13). The poet's extended riff on the vocabulary of nature, attributing his alterity to "nature," remarking that he couldn't stop composing smoky poetry without "denaturing" himself, draws on the same vocabulary that, in the *Art de dictier*, defines poetic skill and differentiates its practitioners from musical composers. The shared emphasis on "inclination" further cements the relationship between natural musical ability, as defined in the *Art de Dictier* ("ceuls qui nature avra encline ou enclinera a ceste naturele musique"), and fumous, melancholic complexion, as illustrated in "Je doy estre chancelliers des Fumeux" ("De nature sui merencolieux [. . .] Si sui enclins a estre merveilleux / Naturelment"). So, while critical efforts to explicate Deschamps's notion of "natural music" have focused on teasing out the meaning of "music" while taking the term "natural" at face value (e.g., Wimsatt 1991), the designation of "natural" music also signals that the poet exploits his own body as fodder, as input for metabolic poesis. Natural music is the product of a poet's physiological predispositions. In the specific case of the *fumeur* songs, that complexional predisposition is melancholic and smoky, and so their natural music, the music of their nature, likewise bears the mark of bodily difference.

In the *fumeur* poems, Deschamps, Jacquet de Noyon, and Solage attribute their lyrical compositions to their own nature—that nature being at once pathologized and celebrated. Yet, if we return to Deschamps's binary construct of music, we see that the Chantilly songs also participate in an elaborate play on the notions of nature and artifice. Deschamps's definition of the two forms of music has the apparent effect of marginalizing artificial music, while his *fumeur* poems, taking the poet's complexion as both their subject and their means of production, are the epitome of "natural music." With their "artificial" settings of *fumeur* lyrics, however, Hasprois and Solage complicate the embodiment of *both* types of music. For while natural music directly communicates an individual lyricist's bodily state, artificial music—here, in the notoriously artificial or "manneristic" *ars subtilior* style—turns the particular, natural lyric into something more universal, an art available even to "le plus rude homme du monde" (the most uncultivated man in the world; Deschamps 1994, 60).

The two songs in the Chantilly Codex are vital to the further elaboration of Deschamps's disability poetics, as they illustrate the way that intertextual play can divert a single writer's idiosyncratic discussion of bodily difference and extend it to a group setting and an "artificial" musical setting in ways that help us redefine "disabled identity." The *fumeurs*' medicalization of their own condition, however, does not imply an adoption of a "medical model" of disability *avant la lettre*. While the group is defined by its constituents' pathological biology, there is no effort to remedy, to heal, to cure or to reverse the *fumeurs*' condition. Indeed, to do so would destroy the group. Rather, *fumeur* poetry offers a descriptive, never prescriptive, effort to redraw social boundaries according to psychological and intellectual capacities: a new taxonomy of alterity, converging around the poetic persona. We have observed that Eustache

Deschamps creates several imaginary groups of marginalized people: these groups are defined by their biology (the *Laiz*), by behaviors that have a biological cause (the *Frequentans*), or by both (the *Fumeurs*). While these clearly constitute discrete identity groups, the significant overlap between the groups' defining characteristics indicates that all of these social outcasts share an overarching "outsider" identity. At the center of all of these groups, at the center of the margin, is the poet-chancellor-king. The addition of other songs *not by Deschamps* to this corpus only enhances this process of decentering and recentering. It is perhaps significant that the other *fumeur* songs are transmitted in the Chantilly Codex, which is filled with what we might call "novelty compositions" representing the extremes of a movement, the *ars subtilior*, that already celebrates novelty. The Chantilly Codex is something of an outlier manuscript, containing unique copies of some outlier songs like the ones considered in this essay. And while the *fumeur* songs' playful manipulation and celebration of marginalized characteristics are in keeping with *ars subtilior* aesthetics, I see them as more than just a stylistic game. Deschamps has taken the first step of cripping his lyric persona, or "claiming disability," and now other artists are assuming the same posture, claiming for themselves the unique means of creating a "natural music" that springs from a pathological yet productive nature.

The *fumeur* songs, read in light of the emergence of disabled identity in late medieval Europe, lead us fittingly enough to a set of contradictory conclusions. On the one hand, the *fumeurs*' evident biological alterity sets them apart from other men, endowing them with inferior social graces but superior creative forces. On the other hand, the matter-of-fact explanations of the *fumeur* mind also tend to normalize the poets' condition, presenting it as one point on a spectrum of human experience: take an ordinary man, tip his humoral balance a bit toward the melancholic or the choleric extreme, and you will produce a *fumeur*. The original *fumeur*, Eustache Deschamps, produces "natural music" unique to his melancholic and smoky nature; while the society of *fumeurs* is open to many, skillful production of natural music is limited to a privileged few. And while smoke impedes the cognitive faculties, there is also method, and humor, to the smokers' madness.

Notes

1. The Chantilly Codex is the object of a recent facsimile and commentary (Plumley and Stone 2008). For another detailed description of the codex, see Upton (2012).
2. I conjoin these two forms of alterity because according to late fourteenth-century medical theory, psychological difference is interpreted as a sign of physiological difference: mental illnesses typically do not occur in the absence of organic brain abnormalities. On the physiological basis of medieval mental illness, see Kemp (1990). This theoretical position is manifest in Deschamps' poems, wherein, as André Adnès (1950, 288) has remarked, "les troubles mentaux étaient considérés comme des maladies, et *des maladies comme les autres*" (mental troubles were considered to be illnesses, *illnesses like any other*).

3. The conventional wisdom among scholars of medieval disability is that medieval Europeans did not conceive of "disability" and "the disabled" as conceptual or identity categories. See Metzler (2005) for the fullest and most influential defense of this argument.
4. These are poems 1399, *D'une autre commission d'un chien* (VII.320–23); 1401, *Cy parle d'une sentence donnée contre aucuns de Vitry pour un debat meu soudainement entr'eulx* (VII.332–35); and 1402, *C'est la commission des loups d'Espargnay sur la rivière de Marne* (VII.336–42).
5. The *Basoche* was the milieu of the law clerks of the Parlement of Paris, and was a hotbed of early secular theatre (see Harvey 1941, Bouhaïk-Gironès 2007). Madness and folly figure prominently in the theatre of the Basoche (Arden 1980, Dull 1994).
6. "Deschamps se mettrait donc ici à la tête d'une association fictive de 'fumeux' qui, sujets à un déterminisme biologique, seraient condamnés à des changements d'humeur imprévisibles" (Becker 2012, 60).
7. Deschamps also declares himself "le souverain des Frequentans" in *Chartre des bons enfans de Vertus en Champaigne* (VII.323–31), dated August 1372: a group distinguished not by its members' physiology but by their behavior.
8. These extended series of enjambments appear in lines 4–6 and 12–15.
9. This ballade is also copied (text only) as "Ballade de maistre fumeux" in BnF nouv acq fr 6221, fol. 10r (Deschamps 1878–1904, X.xiv–xv) and as "Balade de bone sentence fait pour la meystrye," # 17 in Cambridge, Trinity College, Wren Library, MS R.3.20 (Plumley and Stone 2008). On Jacquet and Hasprois, see Plumley (1999, 2003).
10. The text is modified from Wilkins (1969, 44–45).
11. The song's dissonance may also engender a sort of musical "paralysis" reflective of poetic melancholy. On dissonance and disability, see Straus (2011, 118).
12. In this respect Jacquet's lyrics echo Deschamps's more cryptically comical *Chartre*: "Ilz sont du nombre pluratif / Et du grant muel infinitif, / Car en multiplicacion / Mettent leur applicacion (They are of the plurative number and the great infinitive mode, for they put their application into multiplication, vv. 117–20).
13. The text and translation are cited from Smith 2003.
14. Gilles Dulong (2009, 51) notes the similarity of Solage's humor to Deschamps's in its display of "un goût pour les jeux autour d'un mot, par répétition et variation autour d'une même racine et par équivoque."
15. The character feigning madness appears in the *Miracle d'un paroissien esconmenié* from the mid-fourteenth-century *Miracles de Nostre Dame par personnages* (Robert 1876–1893, III.15). The genuine madman is the title character of the late fifteenth-century *Sermon nouveau d'ung fol changant divers propos* preserved in the Recueil Trepperel.
16. See, for example, *Le regime tresutile et tresproufitable pour conserver et garder la santé du corps humain*, c. 1480: "car le vin gros s'il est limphé il blesse tant plus tost le cerveau et se est subtilier, et par consequant devient plus fumeux" (Cummins 1976, 50).
17. This text is less in step with specialized medical knowledge of the late fourteenth century than the *Livre de problemes de Aristote*, but it circulated much more widely and was even more available to a nonspecialist audience (see Ducos 2006, Sodigné-Costes 1991).
18. Becker offers a complete bibliography on Eustache Deschamps and medieval medicine (2012, 226–232, 239–241).
19. As Deschamps (1994, 62) remarks, "les faiseurs d'icelle [natural music] ne saichent pas communement la musique artificiele ne donner chant par art de notes a ce qu'ilz font."

References

Adnès, André. 1950. "Les malades mentaux dans l'oeuvre d'Eustache Deschamps." *L'Encéphale* 3: 275–289.

Arden, Heather. 1980. *Fools' Plays: A Study of Satire in the* Sottie. Cambridge: Cambridge University Press.

Becker, Karin. 1998. "Eustache Deschamps's Medical Poetry." In *Eustache Deschamps, French Courtier-Poet: His Work and His World*, edited by D. M. Sinnreich-Levi, 209–227. New York: AMS.

Becker, Karin. 2012. *Le lyrisme d'Eustache Deschamps: Entre poésie et pragmatisme*. Paris: Garnier.

Bouhaïk-Gironès, Marie. 2007. *Les clercs de la Basoche et le théâtre comique: Paris, 1420–1550*. Paris: Champion.

Byrne, Donal. 1977. "Two Hitherto Unidentified Copies of the *Livre des propriétés des choses*, from the Royal Library of the Louvre and the Library of Jean de Berry." *Scriptorium* 31: 90–98.

Byrne, Donal. 1981. "Rex imago Dei: Charles V of France and the *Livre des propriétés des choses*." *Journal of Medieval History* 7: 97–113.

Cadden, Joan. 2006. "Preliminary Observations on the Place of the *Problemata* in Medieval Learning." In *Aristotle's* Problemata *in Different Times and Tongues*, edited by P. De Leemans and M. Goyens, 1–19. Leuven, Belgium: Leuven University Press.

Cerquiglini, Jacqueline. 1984. "Le Clerc et le Louche: Sociology of an Esthetic." Translated by M. Briand-Walker. *Poetics Today* 5: 479–491.

Cummins, P. W., ed. 1976. *Le regime tresutile et tresproufitable pour conserver et garder la santé du corps humain*. Chapel Hill: University of North Carolina Press.

Delisle, Léopold. 1900. *Le Musée Condé, Chantilly: Le cabinet des livres, manuscrits*. Paris: Institut de France.

Deschamps, Eustache. 1878–1904. *Oeuvres complètes*. Edited by A. Queux de Saint-Hilaire and G. Raynaud. 11 vols. Paris: Firmin-Didot.

Deschamps, Eustache. 1994. *L'art de dictier*. Edited and translated by D. M. Sinnreich-Levi. East Lansing, MI: Colleagues.

Ducos, Joëlle. 2006. "Goût des sciences et écriture du savoir à la cour de Charles V." In *Le goût du lecteur à la fin du Moyen Âge*, edited by D. Bohler, 225–243. Paris: Cahiers du Léopard d'Or.

Dull, Olga Anna. 1994. *Folie et rhétorique dans la sottie*. Geneva: Droz.

Dulong, Gilles. 2009. "En relisant Solage." In *A Late Medieval Songbook and Its Context: New Perspectives on the Chantilly Codex*, edited by Yolanda Plumley and Anne Stone, 45–61. Turnhout, Belgium: Brepols.

Froissart, Jean. 1894. *Chroniques*. Edited by G. Raynaud. Paris: Renouard.

Gessler, Jacques, ed. 1934. *La manière de langage qui enseigne à bien parler et écrire le français: Modèles de conversations composés en Angleterre à la fin du XIVe siècle*. Paris: Droz.

Gordon, Bernard de. 1495. *La practique de maistre Bernard de Gordon appellee Fleur de lys en medicine*. Lyon, France: Anon.

Greene, Gordon K. 1971. "The Secular Music of Chantilly Manuscript Musée Condé 564 (olim 1047)." PhD diss., Indiana University.

Gröber, Gustav. 1902. "Geschichte der lateinisches und französisches Litteratur im Mittelalter." In *Grundriss der Romanischen Philologie* 2. Strasbourg, France: Trübner.

Guichard-Tesson, Françoise. 2006. "Évrart de Conty, poète, traducteur et commentateur." In *Aristotle's* Problemata *in Different Times and Tongues*, edited by P. De Leemans and M. Goyens, 145–174. Leuven, Belgium: Leuven University Press.

Günther, Ursula. 1960. "Die Anwendung der Diminution in der Handschrift Chantilly 1047." *Archiv für Musikwissenschaft* 17: 1–21.

Harvey, Howard Graham. 1941. *The Theatre of the Basoche: The Contribution of the Law Societies to French Mediaeval Comedy*. Cambridge, MA: Harvard University Press.

Hoepffner, Ernst. 1904. *Eustache Deschamps: Leben und Werke*. Strasbourg, France: Trübner.

Kemp, Simon. 1990. *Medieval Psychology*. New York: Greenwood.

Laidlaw, J. C. 1974. *The Poetical Works of Alain Chartier*. New York: Cambridge University Press.

Le Fèvre, Jean. 1887. *Journal*. Edited by H. Moranvillé. Paris: Picard.

McVaugh, Michael R. 1993. *Medicine before the Plague: Practitioners and Their Patients in the Crown of Aragon 1285–1345*. Cambridge, UK: Cambridge University Press.

Metzler, Irena. 2005. *Disability in Medieval Europe: Thinking about Physical Impairment in the High Middle Ages, c. 1100–c. 1400*. London: Routledge.

Newes, Virginia. 2009. "Deception, Reversal, and Paradox: The Rondeaux of the Chantilly Codex in Context." In *A Late Medieval Songbook and Its Context: New Perspectives on the Chantilly Codex*, edited by Yolanda Plumley and Anne Stone, 15–43. Turnhout, Belgium: Brepols.

Olson, Glending. 1982. *Literature as Recreation in the Later Middle Ages*. Ithaca, NY: Cornell University Press.

Oresme, Nicole. 1940. *Le livre de ethiques de Aristote*. Edited by A. D. Menut. New York: Stechert.

Pirro, André. 1930. *La musique à Paris sous le règne de Charles VI, 1380–1422*. 2nd ed. Strasbourg, France: P. H. Heitz.

Plumley, Yolanda. 1999. "Citation and Allusion in the Late *Ars nova*: The Case of *Esperance* and the *En attendant* songs." *Early Music History* 18: 287–363.

Plumley, Yolanda. 2003. "An 'Episode in the South'? Ars Subtilior and the Patronage of French Princes." *Early Music History* 22: 103–168.

Plumley, Yolanda, and Anne Stone. 2008. *Codex Chantilly: Bibliothèque du château de Chantilly, MS 564*. 2 vols. Turnhout, Belgium: Brepols.

Poirion, Daniel. 1965. *Le poète et le prince*. Paris: PUF.

Reaney, Gilbert. 1954. "The Manuscript Chantilly, Musée Condé 1047." *Musica Disciplina* 8: 59–113.

Robert, Ulysse, ed. 1876–1893. *Miracles de Nostre Dame par personnages*. 8 vols. Paris: Firmin-Didot.

Roccati, G. M. 2004. "Lectures d'Eustache Deschamps." *L'Analisi Linguistica e Letteraria* 12: 231–261.

Singer, Julie. 2010. "Playing by Ear: Compensation, Reclamation, and Prosthesis in Fourteenth-Century Song." In *Disability in the Middle Ages: Reconsiderations and Reverberations*, edited by J. R. Eyler, 39–52. Burlington, VT: Ashgate.

Smith, Robert. 2003. "Fumeux fume par fumee." La Trobe University Library Medieval Music Database. http://www.lib.latrobe.edu.au/MMDB/composer/H0442001.HTM.

Sodigné-Costes, Geneviève. 1991. "La traduction des ouvrages scientifiques latins au XIVe siècle." In *L'écriture du savoir: Actes du Colloque de Bagnoles-de-l'Orme (avril 1990)*, edited by D. Hüe, 107–114. Le Mesnil-Brout, France: Association Diderot.

Straus, Joseph N. 2008. "Disability and 'Late Style' in Music." *Journal of Musicology* 25: 3–45.

Straus, Joseph N. 2011. *Extraordinary Measures: Disability in Music.* New York: Oxford University Press.

Sweetser, Franklin P., ed. 1966. *Les cent nouvelles nouvelles.* Geneva: Droz.

Unruh, Patricia. 1983. "'Fumeur' Poetry and Music of the Chantilly Codex: A Study of Its Meaning and Background." MA thesis, University of British Columbia.

Upton, Elizabeth Randall. 2012. "The Creation of the Chantilly Codex (Ms. 564)." *Studi Musicali* [n.s.] 3: 287–352.

Wilkins, Nigel. 1969. *One Hundred Ballades Rondeaux and Virelais from the Late Middle Ages.* Cambridge, UK: Cambridge University Press.

Wilkins, Nigel. 1979. *Music in the Age of Chaucer.* Cambridge, UK: D. S. Brewer.

Wilkins, Nigel. 1984. "The Late Medieval French Lyric: With Music and Without." In *Musik und Text in der Mehrstimmigkeit des 14. und 15. Jahrhunderts,* edited by U. Günther and L. Finscher, 155–174. Kassel, Germany: Bärenreiter.

Wimsatt, James. 1991. *Chaucer and His French Contemporaries: Natural Music in the Fourteenth Century.* Toronto: University of Toronto Press.

CHAPTER 26

DIFFERENCE, DISABILITY, AND COMPOSITION IN THE LATE MIDDLE AGES

Of Antonio "Zachara" da Teramo and Francesco "Il Cieco" da Firenze

MICHAEL SCOTT CUTHBERT

THE fourteenth century was a great and terrible time for western Europe. It was a period of incredible cultural and scientific innovation. Widespread dissemination of the technology to make clocks began to allow townspeople to organize their activities with a precision unknown to men and women of the past. Reports of new ideas and ways of life from the great civilizations of the East, including the Arab world, India, and China, began to enter European conversation in greater and greater numbers. Painters such as Giotto developed new techniques to depict the human, natural, and spiritual worlds with a richness that astounded viewers. In music, polyphonic song and Mass movements began to be cultivated and to spread from France into England, Spain, Italy, and the Germanic Empire. Amid so much to be optimistic about, great calamity was also the rule of the day. Beginning in 1348 waves of the Black Death, almost certainly the bubonic plague, swept over Europe. Though the outbreaks were relatively short-lived, they were devastating in their virulence, killing almost a third of the population and always threatening to return—as it did with force in 1361, 1383, and 1400. The spiritual foundation of everyday life was shaken as well with the schism of the church that began in 1378 when rival popes took up residence in Rome and Avignon, to be joined later by a third pope in Pisa. When the nearly continual warfare of the period is added to this list of calamities, it seems a miracle that any art, let alone highly sophisticated music, could flourish in these conditions.

Music did continue to thrive in the second half of the fourteenth century and to deepen in complexity, as Julie Singer's contribution to this volume makes clear. While the French contribution to the European musical soundscape was spread throughout the whole of the century, Italians came later to polyphonic composition. Their period of activity only began around the time of the plague, but their local style gained influence continuously into the second quarter of the fifteenth century, in a process of constant change and invigoration from foreign musical styles. This style and belief in the power of reinvention and transformation distinguished the Italian tradition sufficiently from its French predecessor such that I have begun to refer to it as a separate tradition, the *ars mutandi*, or changing style.[1]

Many of the most important musicians of the *ars mutandi* were people known to have disabilities. For several composers and music theorists, disabilities, such as blindness and loss of fingers, played a direct role in how they conceptualized and wrote musical notation and, given the role of the (Guidonian) hand in education, instructed others in music. Understanding of disability in late-medieval music is thus essential to the comprehension of notation and transmission of music in these changing times. Conversely, evidence of how disability was described and conceived in the Middle Ages can enhance diachronic studies of music and disability in general.

That the most prominent musician of the *ars mutandi* wrote and played music without the aid of sight has long been known. The organist and composer Francesco (born sometime between 1325 and 1335 and died in 1397) was most commonly known by a name referencing his blindness, "Francesco il Cieco." Other names for him use his toponym, Francesco da Firenze (the name that is used in this essay); his occupation, Francesco degli Organi; or his patronym, Francescus Iacobi, that is, Francesco son of Jacobo. The Latin name applied to him accompanying one of the two surviving portraits of him, in the Squarcialupi Codex (Florence, Biblioteca Medicea-Laurenziana, Mediceo Palatino 87), combines all but the last of these names along with an honorific, "Magister Franciscus Cecus Horganista de Florentia." The portrait shown in Figure 26.1, along with the sculpture of the composer found on his tombstone (presumably near but not on his grave in the Florentine church of San Lorenzo), prominently depicts his blindness, but places this detail near another pictorial detail of great esteem: the laurel crown given to the greatest poets.[2] (The modern name given to the composer, Francesco Landini, seems to have been completely unknown to his contemporaries.)[3] The composer and his music will return later in this chapter.

The most collected and renowned composer of sacred music in Italy was a man known until recently only to a few specialists in the period. Antonio da Teramo was a composer, singer, and copyist for at least two popes during the Great Schism, first the Roman Pope Gregory XII and then the Pisan Pope John XXIII (now regarded as an anti-pope by the Catholic church). While Antonio's birth year is unknown (probably in the 1350s), we know that he died in 1413.[4]

Antonio's stock rose in the eyes of musicologists in the past thirty years when the evidence became insurmountable that the compositions variously ascribed to "Antonio Zachara da Teramo," "Zacar," and "Magister Çacherias Chantor Domini nostri Pape," all referred to a single person. This composer was named in full in a contract of 1390 as "Magist[er] Antoni[us] Berardi Andree de Teramo alias dicto vulgariter Zacchara," or

FIGURE 26.1 "Magister Franciscus Cecus Horganista de Florentia," f. 121v in the Squarcialupi Codex

"Master Antonio son of Berardo (son of Andrea) from Teramo [in the Abruzzi region of central eastern Italy] otherwise called in the common tongue 'Zachara.'"[5] The term "Zachara" is written as "Zacara" in recent literature, though not a single instance in the manuscript sources uses this orthography (Cuthbert 2006, 495).

Antonio was the most widely copied composer of sacred music of his time or of any time before him. Although the most well-known, complete Tuscan manuscripts of the period have few of his pieces—the Squarcialupi Codex contains only seven of his pieces, three of which are highly conventional and did not seem of interest to other scribes—Northern Italian manuscripts, sources connected to the papal chapel, and books from Spain, Germany, and Eastern Europe are better testaments to his reputation. He was the only Italian composer of his time whose music was known in France and in England (via the Old Hall Codex: London, British Library, Additional 57950). His music was collected into the era dominated by Du Fay, when multiple Mass movements of his were put together with isolated movements by others to suit the new trend of the complete polyphonic Mass Ordinary.[6] Given his prominence in the surviving sources from this time it is no surprise that biographies of the composer written a half century after his death report that not only was his music still being sung in Italy but also that he was "held in the highest regard by French and German singers" and that "his compositions are considered oracles" (Pirrotta 1971, 153–154). A contract from his lifetime calls him "optimo perito et famoso cantore, scriptore et miniatore" or "best, most skilled, and famous singer [or composer], scribe, and artist of miniatures," that is, of illuminated letters and manuscript decorations.

Antonio's skill as a scribe was such that he was not only commissioned to copy and decorate entire chant books, but also to create presentation copies of papal bulls. Only a single letter in his hand, signed "A. de Teramo," survives, today in London's National Archives (SC 7.41.7.A2), but a glance at the elegance of his handwriting shows that he was a great talent (Figure 26.2 gives two views, the first in close-up).

The same biographers that give us such insight into Antonio's fame also show his connection to the topic of this volume on Disability Studies. Immediately after the description of his fame among French and Germans, the fifteenth-century necrology of "Zaccarias Teramensis" continues by describing his physical features:

> fuit statura corporis parva, et in manibus et pedibus non nisi decem digitos habuit, et tamen eleganter scribebat. In Curia Romana principatum obtinens magna stipendia meruit. (Ziino 1979, 314)

The beginning of the first sentence describes his body as small in stature. The second clause says that between his fingers and his toes he had fewer than ten digits. But the final phrase says "yet he wrote elegantly," as has already been demonstrated. The praise continues in the next sentence by noting that he occupied the leadership of the Papal curia and earned great wages. The physical details of Antonio's body are confirmed in the only surviving portrait of him—again, an image in the Squarcialupi Codex (Figure 26.3). At least three fingers on his left hand are missing as are two on his right. His "statura parva"

(a)

(b)

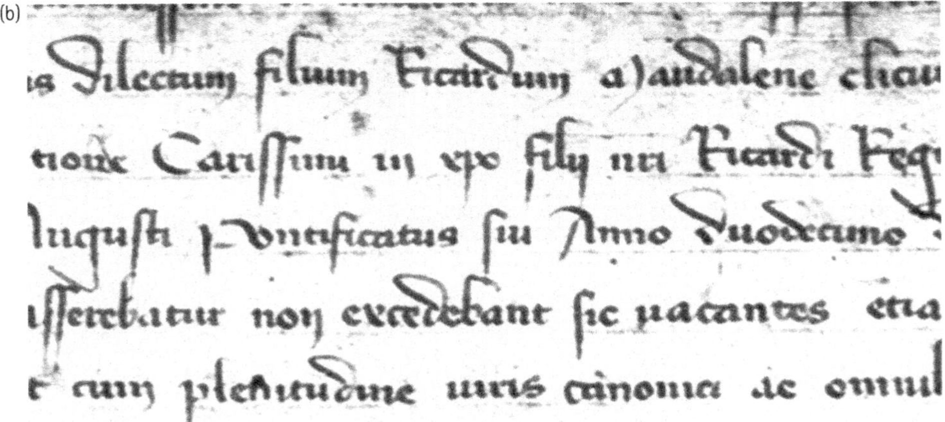

FIGURE 26.2A AND 26.2B Signature of "A. de Teramo" and the only surviving example of his handwriting, from the London, National Archives.

is shown in the sling that holds his left arm. Nádas (1986, 171) believes that his left foot may also indicate an unusual formation. The image is not detailed enough to precisely confirm this aspect, but it is striking that of the fifteen portraits of composers in the manuscript, Antonio's is the only one that shows any more than a glimpse of a foot poking out of a gown.[7] The emphasis of physical condition is also reflected in Francesco's portrait (Figure 26.1), which is the only portrait of an individual composer to have only a single eye visible to the viewer.[8]

The name "Zachara" was a sobriquet or nickname, as certain of the longer attributions to the composer that include the phrase "dictus Zacharas" make clear. The origin of this name is less noble than one would like. The term probably comes from the biblical figure of Zacchaeus, a hated tax collector who "wanted to see who Jesus was, but because he was short he could not see over the crowd. So he ran ahead and climbed a sycamore-fig

FIGURE 26.3 "Magister Çacherias Cantor Domini Nostri Pape," f. 175v in the Squarcialupi Codex

tree to see him" (Luke 19:3–4, New International Version). Various dictionaries of Italian dialects confirm that such a term was in use for men of short stature, and these definitions move the negative connotations of Zacchaeus's tax collecting to the height itself. "Zaccheo" in Neapolitan means "midget" or "pigmy"; in Calabrese "zaccanu" signifies a nearly worthless little piece of land. Even more repugnant are definitions found in other contemporary contexts using the word "zacchera" to mean an object of little value or a man of little worth.[9]

While modern scholarship has settled on the name "Zachara" (or a variant) to refer to the composer who invariably signed his name as Antonio or Antonius in church documents, he did not completely avoid the name, but chose to use the term to refer to himself in code. For example, the text of his *ars subtilior* Latin ballade *Sumite karissime* is an elaborate puzzle, leading the unscrambler to find the phrase "in all this Zacharias salutes in recommendation." His macaronic ballata *Je suy navvrés tan fort/Gnaff' a le guagnele*, whose text was also likely written by Antonio, includes lines that come across as a reminder to himself that he has chosen the path of knowledge rather than of wealth: "Homines nobilitant scientie septet artes. Saccra sacra non seray may ricche. Non venditur auro" ("The seven arts of knowledge ennoble men. Zachara, Zachara, you will never be rich. It is not sold for gold").[10] Thus just as we now use the term "baroque" without reference to its origin as a term for a misshapen pearl, the name Zachara is often used by modern scholars for the celebrated composer without any implication of a lack of worth. Zachara, or a variation on that spelling, is also the most common way his contemporaries referred to him. Antonio does not use the term when signing his name, as it is an act likely to convey the negative associations of the word to his person. That he does use this nickname to refer to himself in his creative art that is, in his texts, shows an act of claiming or reclaiming disability in a positive context associating it with lasting and admired art.[11]

Antonio never directly mentions his disabilities in his compositions, but one piece may reflect the reception he received from other members of medieval society. In his ballata *D'amor languire*, the narrator, who (given similarities in style to his other texts) may be Antonio himself, laments that he is sad of languishing in love and sad of spirit. He is in this situation because of "Cucci" (a name written as "cento-cinque e duy cento'uno," hiding the roman numerals "CVCCI"), who evidently will not embrace him because of a beard that his barber refuses to shave. The speaker describes how he "scratches mangily without having scabs," an action that fills him with every sort of melancholy. The remainder of the text gives a series of animal analogies that are in part about the scratchiness of his beard but also about the isolation and discrimination he faces because of disease: like a hunted pig filled with rabies (or anger) or like a frog's body bursting within a bird's crushing, silent beak.

If one supposes that the text was written by Antonio himself, as many of his texts using the Abruzzese dialect seem to have been, and that it is at least somewhat self-referential (if not autobiographical), then can this work tell us about the reception of disability in fifteenth-century France? To pick up on Antonio's central conceit, why does the barber avoid shaving him? One answer may lie in other's fear of contracting a disease from the composer, possibly Hansen's disease (leprosy). The composer probably lost digits over the course of his life: if his disability were lifelong it is unlikely that he would have been trained as a scribe, and if he had a contagious condition such as Hansen's disease it is unlikely he would have enjoyed close access to the inner circle of the papacy. An explanation can be gleaned from a close examination of his single surviving portrait (Figure 26.3). The coloration on his cheek, especially under his eyes, may not represent a poor choice of shading by the miniaturist, but instead an accurate depiction of a skin condition, possibly Sturge-Weber syndrome or more likely systemic lupus erythematosus or a similar condition.[12] Untreated with modern medicine, lupus could lead to a loss of sensation in the extremities resulting in the loss of digits. But the barber's reaction (which, like everything in this text, could be metaphorical) does not seem to have been typical for the composer. Antonio more usually was surrounded by other talented singers, composers, and church officials eager to enjoy the products of his elegant pen, whether beautifully copied letters and manuscripts or the latest compositions in diverse styles, with hidden riddles and new melodic invention.

The depictions of disability and musicians with disabilities in the Middle Ages are distant from the social contexts of disability today. Composers with disabilities had such aspects of their lives heightened, particularly by the use of physical characteristics as names. Beyond Francesco and Antonio other examples abound, such as the fourteenth-century music theorist Petrus frater dictus Palma ociosa, or "Brother Peter called" (*dictus:* that word again) "deformed hand," or the eleventh-century theorist Hermannus Contractus ("Herman the Lame"), or the ninth-century composer of tropes Notker Balbulus ("Notker the Stammerer").[13] In a world with few family names and the commonness of given names and toponyms, descriptions of disability assume a place of normalcy little different than identifiers such as Redbeard.[14]

Yet, for several composers, in particular Francesco, disability formed an important part of narratives of compensation, even at the time. Francesco was said to have a mind's eye "as sharp and acute as an eagle's," according to his earliest biography. Notker was supposed to have channeled his inability to speak into composing long textual forms, particularly sequences and hymns, that could be sung beautifully. Petrus dictus Palmus ociosa's teaching of accidentals (*musica ficta*) and proper ways of singing in improvisation can be viewed in the same light, seeing as the so-called Guidonian hand and specific and rapid movements of the hand were generally considered essential to music making at the time. The disabilities to which no positive effects seem to have been ascribed were only those that would no longer be considered disabilities today, such as the "defectu natale" or "birth defect" of Antonio's contemporary Johannes Ciconia, which referred to his illegitimate birth, and thus lowered social status, as the son of a priest.

The connection between music, health, disease, and disability was a close one in the Middle Ages. As John of Trevisa notes in his elegant fourteenth-century translation of the thirteenth-century writer Bartholomaeus Anglicus's *De proprietatibus rerum*:

> For musike meueth affeccioun s and exciteth the wittes [t]o dyuers disposiciouns. . . . And comforteth schipmen to suffre al disese and trauayle. And conforte of voice pleseth and conforteth the herte and wittes in alle disese and trauayle of workes and werynesse. And musik abateth maystry of yuel spirites in mankynde . . . And so veynes and synewes of the body, and puls therof, and so alle the lymes of the body beth socied togideres by vertu of armony, as Ysider seith. (Seymour 1975–1988, 2:1386)
>
> For music moves emotions and excites the mind to varied dispositions, and comforts sailors to suffer all sorts of diseases and travails. And the comfort of the voice pleases and comforts the heart and mind from every disease and travail of work and weariness. And music removes the domination of foul spirits in mankind. And thus the veins and sinews of the body, and its pulse, and all the organs of the body are

> bound together by virtue of harmony, as Isidore said. (translation by the author; the end of the passage paraphrases Isidore of Seville, *De Musica*, chapter 17).

Despite this connection, modern scholars, as Straus notes, have been quick to create a story of a "triumphant overcoming" of disability by medieval composers, or have found no need to mention it "for it has no bearing on the music" (Straus 2011, 20–21). He is correct to point out that the viewing of disability as difference, and not as a deficit to be overcome, can in Francesco's case lead to a greater understanding of the role of memory for composers and the admiration thereof for medieval listeners. It is not, however, correct to say that such difference isolated him from the world of notation, any more than Antonio's differences cut him off from the world of writing. In a contemporary reference that elsewhere calls him "impotens," Francesco is praised for his "scrittura," which is generally used to refer to direct writing (Fiori 2004, 28). Though it is still presumed, even by this author, that he used an intermediary for notating his songs, there is no mention of such a person, nor the role that such an assistant would play. Instead, Francesco was held directly responsible for the graphical form of his music, as an anonymous writer (Coussemaker's Anonymous V) reports:

> And Nicolaus of Avera, of the order of the Celestines, said that when the Blind Man of Florence placed red imperfect semibreves in the discant of his ballata [i.e., *Donna che d'amor*] he did not err, but rather he did make a mistake in placing red semibreves in the tenor, since the tenor is of minor prolation.[15]

The errors (for all differences in notational systems were considered errors by theorists) that bothered Nicolaus so much about the ballata are not ones that could be perceived aurally, but only by reference to notation. Nicolaus, who refers to Francesco as "the Blind Man of Florence," was certainly aware of his lack of sight. Francesco was thought to be, and seems to have been, directly invested in the notation of his works, and his critical contemporary held him accountable as he would any other composer. Francesco was not the only blind musician who cared deeply about notation. The slightly later organist Conrad Paumann of Nuremberg is said by Sebastian Virdung to have created a system of lute tablature—more idiomatic both to the instrument and to oral reading—that persisted for centuries after his death in 1473.[16] In neither Francesco nor Conrad's case is there any hint of less precision in the notation of their works than of their contemporaries. Except for a slightly greater flexibility of notation between the two principal rhythmic systems of the time (called *longa* and *brevis* notation today), Francesco's works show the same degree of consistency of graphical signs from manuscript to manuscript as any of the sighted composers of his day.

The names and nicknames given to medieval composers and theorists may appear unsympathetic or even cruel by seeming to define people with disabilities by those disabilities. The surviving evidence shows that, at least in the most prominent cases, acknowledgment of difference was not an allusion to deficit. Italian composers with disabilities such as Antonio and Francesco were considered to have extraordinary minds and an ability to compose, indeed to write, beyond the other musicians of their time (with the possible exception of Ciconia who, as was already noted, was considered by his contemporaries to have a defect of birth). These abilities were rewarded financially and with positions of power, and, more enduringly, their musical styles were considered exemplars for the next generation. The wide distribution and lavish praise of music ascribed to musicians known to most as "Zachara" and "Il Cieco" should embolden modern scholars to move away from marginalizing such differences, and embrace the variety of experience that shaped creative achievement in the vital period of change that characterized music's history around 1400.

Notes

1. The theme of the embrace of change in this period is developed further in my forthcoming monograph, *Ars mutandi: Italian Sacred Music in the Age of Plague and Schism.*
2. On the impact of blindness on Francesco and on Guillaume de Machaut, consult Singer 2010.
3. Contra Singer 2010, 44. The contract she refers to in Fiori 2004 (28) uses his patronym, not a family name. The first usage of the family name Landino occurs in the works of Francesco's great-nephew Cristoforo, though he does not apply it directly to Francesco. I believe that the name was a construction of Cristoforo's at a time when he was attempting to marry into the prestigious Alberti family and needed to construct a noble lineage for himself; certainly Cristoforo knew nothing about his ancestor that could not be gleaned from already circulating biographies. That Francesco's blindness in no way prevented him from being respected throughout Italy and Europe has been well established and now collected by Singer 2010.
4. For an extensively researched biography, consult Di Bacco and Nádas 2004.
5. The citation is reported in Esposito 1983, 334, and the connections among the various formerly separate candidates are found in Ziino 1979.
6. This trend is especially prominent in the way Antonio's music was collected in the manuscript Bologna, Biblioteca della Musica, Q15. For inventory and discussion, consult Bent 2008.
7. I am grateful to Samantha Bassler for noticing this discontinuity with the tradition of portraiture.
8. The portrait is discussed in Straus 2011, 20. In the image on f. 173v, one of the figures is depicted in profile, presumably to show the discussion between Egidius and Guilielmus. The depiction of Francesco's blindness contrasts in style, though not in emphasis, with the portraits of the early fifteenth-century poet and composer Oswald von Wolkenstein, who, perhaps because he had sight in one eye, is shown nearly face on in the three confirmed surviving images of him. Another, otherwise unknown, medieval musician named in the motet *Alma polis religio, Axe poli cum artica* is described through emphasis on his sightedness as "unioculus Teobaldus" or "Thibault the one-eyed" (I thank Karen Cook for bringing this reference to my attention).
9. All these definitions come from the research of Nádas 1986, 176, without which this essay could not be written.
10. Hallmark 2004, 218, from a suggestion by Francesco Zimei.

11. For this term I rely on Linton 1998, and I am grateful to Julie Singer for clarifying the implications of the contexts in which the composer names himself differently.
12. In Cuthbert 2004, 342, I discussed the possibility of this condition (corroborated by opinions by three doctors and a chance encounter I had with participants leaving a dermatology conference when I happened to have a large poster of Antonio with me) but with less understanding of the implications for Antonio's complete biography, social placement, or the negative effects of a focus on diagnosis in the discussion of disability.
13. The reinforcement of disability through naming was common enough that Adam le Boscu d'Arras or de la Halle, a thirteenth-century trouvère, needed to state that Boscu or Bossu was a family name and not a reference to the same word for a hunchback: "On m'apele Bochu, mais je ne le sui mie."
14. The normalcy (in terms of frequency) for disability in the ancient world of music has perhaps its strongest suggestion in the mathematical writings of the sometime music theorist Nicomachus of Gerasa of the first century CE. In his treatise on arithmetic he describes numbers whose proper factors sum to less than the number (i.e., deficient numbers) as similar to amputees, and numbers whose proper factors sum to greater than the number (i.e., abundant numbers) as a sort of polydactylism. Thus of the tens of thousands of numbers whose factors could be summed at the time, Nicomachus attributes no congenital diseases only to the four known "perfect" numbers 6, 28, 496, and 8128. This reflects a long-standing argument in Disability Studies that disabilities before the nineteenth century were conceived as imperfections, not abnormalities (Davis 1995, 23–49).
15. "Et Nicolaus de Aversa, Ordinis Celestinorum, cum dixit Cechus de Florentia in discantu illo sue ballade posuit semibreves rubeas imperfectas et male, salva pace, quod in hoc non peccavit; sed peccavit in tenore ponendo semibreves rubeas, cum sit minoris prolationis tenor ille" (Coussemaker 1864–76, 3:395–396). Translation adapted from Ellinwood 1945, 73. Nicolaus of Aversa was until recently completely unknown. However a newly identified manuscript in Melbourne includes a treatise attributed to him, though it is not the work that Anonymous V refers to. I thank Karen Cook for bringing this to my attention; the manuscript is currently the subject of a publication by Jason Stoessel.
16. Virdung 1511, f. K.iii.v.

References

Bent, Margaret. 2008. *Bologna Q15: The Making and Remaking of a Musical Manuscript*. Lucca, Italy: Libreria Musicale Italiana.

Coussemaker, [Charles] Edmond de. 1864–1876. *Scriptorum de musica medii aevi novam seriam*. 4 vols. Paris: A. Durand.

Cuthbert, Michael Scott. 2004. "Zacara's *D'amor languire* and Strategies for Borrowing in the Early Fifteenth-Century Italian Mass." In *Antonio Zacara da Teramo e il suo tempo*, edited by Francesco Zimei, 337–358. Lucca, Italy: Libreria Musicale Italiana.

Cuthbert, Michael Scott. 2006. "Trecento Fragments and Polyphony beyond the Codex." PhD diss., Harvard University.

Davis, Lennard. 1995. *Enforcing Normalcy: Disability, Deafness, and the Body*. London and New York: Verso.

Di Bacco, Giuliano, and John Nádas. 2004. "Zacara e i suoi colleghi italiani nella cappella papale." In *Antonio Zacara da Teramo e il suo tempo*, edited by Francesco Zimei, 34–54. Lucca, Italy: Libreria Musicale Italiana.

Ellinwood, Leonard. 1945. *The Works of Francesco Landini*. Cambridge, MA: Medieval Academy of America.

Esposito, Anna. 1983. "'Magistro Zaccara' e l'antifonario dell'Ospedale di S. Spirito in Sassia." In *Scrittura, biblioteche e stampa a Roma nel Quattrocento*, edited by Massimo Miglio, Paola Farenga, and Anna Modigliani, 334–342 and 446–449. Vatican City: Scuola Vaticana di Paleografica.

Fiori, Alessandra. 2004. *Francesco Landini*. Palermo: L'EPOS.

Hallmark, Anne. 2004. "Rhetoric and Reference in *Je suy navvrés tan fort*." In *Antonio Zacara da Teramo e il suo tempo*, edited by Francesco Zimei, 213–227. Lucca, Italy: Libreria Musicale Italiana.

Linton, Simi. 1998. *Claiming Disability: Knowledge and Identity*. New York: New York University Press.

Nádas, John. 1986. "Further Notes on Magister Antonius dictus Zacharias de Teramo." *Studi Musicali* 15: 167–182.

Pirrotta, Nino. 1971. "Zacarus Musicus." *Quadrivium* 12: 153–176.

Seymour, Michael, gen. ed. 1975–1988. *On the Properties of Things: John Trevisa's Translation of Bartholomaeus Anglicus "De proprietatibus rerum"—A Critical Text*. 3 vols. Oxford, UK: Clarendon.

Singer, Julie. 2010. "Playing by Ear: Compensation, Reclamation, and Prosthesis in Fourteenth-Century Song." In *Disability in the Middle Ages: Reconsiderations and Reverberations*, edited by Joshua R. Eyler, 39–52. Farnham, UK: Ashgate.

Straus, Joseph N. 2011. *Extraordinary Measures: Disability in Music*. Oxford: Oxford University Press.

Virdung, Sebastian. 1511. *Musica getutscht und außgezogen*. . . . Basel.

Ziino, Agostino. 1979. "Magister Antonius dictus Zacharias de Teramo: Alcune date e molte ipotesi." *Rivista Italiana di Musicologia* 14: 311–348.

CHAPTER 27

MADNESS AND MUSIC AS (DIS)ABILITY IN EARLY MODERN ENGLAND

SAMANTHA BASSLER

PREVIOUS work on disability, by scholars such as medieval historian Irina Metzler (2006) and early modernists Alison P. Hobgood and David Houston Wood (2013), reveals an awareness of and a stigma against physical difference in premodern Europe. Metzler, the first medievalist to investigate disability in medieval Europe, demonstrates that representations of the extraordinary body in premodern Europe should be considered within the framework of disability, and locates disability within medieval notions of impairment. While a general umbrella term of disability did not exist in medieval Europe, the medieval period did have a notion of physical impairment, discussed extensively in medical texts (Metzler 2006, 5). Hobgood and Houston Wood (2013) extend Metzler's theories to literature and culture, writing the first definitive study of disability in early modern England. Such findings are especially useful when considering early modern England, with its complex interweaving of disability, gender, and music within its literary and philosophical discourses. The goal of this essay is to introduce a framework of Disability Studies for future work on the musical construction of disability in early modern culture, which is a relatively unexplored area of musicology, and to demonstrate that Disability Studies is not anachronistic to the study of early music. As the study of disability has augmented studies of early modern literature, it can also enrich our understanding of the relationship between music and early modern culture. A survey of early modern literature and philosophy of music, including the works of Boethius and Shakespeare, reveals that there were conflicting accounts of music as a force that held the potential to either cure or inflict illness.

These early modern narratives thus rely on the notion of the *narrative prosthesis* (Mitchell and Snyder 2000, 47): harmful music, or discord of harmony or meter, exists as a foil for establishing the healthful, curative properties of accepted and normalized musical styles. Mitchell and Snyder argue that through narrative prosthesis, disability functions both as a stock feature of characterization and as a metaphoric device. The narrative prosthetic is typically a disabled character who functions as a foil to an able-bodied character, serving two main purposes: to generate tension through expressive contrast and to provide a story with a solvable problem. Within literary narratives, such as those of Shakespeare, characters like the lovesick Duke Orsino, the melancholic Dane, and the mad Ophelia, are complements to the more reasonable and able-bodied characters. Boethius's work on music was influential to Shakespeare and his contemporaries, particularly in their alignment of musical discord and concord with the physical or spiritual discord or concord of the body and mind. The plays of Shakespeare offer many examples of the influence of Boethius and Neoplatonist theories of music, which uphold music as a medium for enacting the balance of the mind–body connection.

Music in the early modern era was thought to have unique proprieties that could both reveal and remediate madness, melancholy, and other disabled conditions. Cultural products from early modern England are rife with examples of mad and melancholic characters. Even a cursory review of early modern writings reveals that music consistently appears in discussions of various disabilities in early modern England—as both a remedy for and symptom of madness; further, music and disabilities of the mind, such as madness and melancholy, are often gendered discourses. In this study, I examine these invisible disabilities, focusing on madness and melancholy and exploring how they are made "audible" through metaphors of music. Shakespeare's plays are case studies in the early modern view of disability, due to their frequent use of music as a metaphor for melancholy and madness, and due to the propensity to incorporate narrative prosthesis, a pervasive aspect of disability and culture.

Philosophies of music in early modern England are fraught with contradictory accounts of music as both a blessing and a curse for the body and mind; music could either rehabilitate or provoke disorder. Musical harmony, when played by a skilled practitioner, had mystical properties, and was capable of performing miracles and curing illness by altering the humors. Humoral theory, popular with early modern English thinkers, posited that four fluids, or humors, circulated within the body, each corresponding with a temperament: blood (sanguine), phlegm (phlegmatic), yellow bile (choleric), and black bile (melancholic). The cause of mental and physical illness within an individual was the excess of a single humor or an overheating humor rendered black (adust). The harmony of music could reverse the imbalance of humors, rendering the body harmoniously balanced (Eubanks Winkler 2006, 6). Such theories are evidenced in lutenist Thomas Robinson's 1603 treatise, *The Schoole of Musicke*, which discusses the ability of music to heal madness, melancholy, and even physical ailments:

> But that Musicke is Phisical, it is plainlie seene by those maladies it cureth. As it cureth melancholie, it much prevaileth against madnesse; If a man be in paines of the gout, of any wound, or of the head, it much mittigateth the furie therof: and it is said, that Musicke hath a salve for everie sore. (Robinson 1603; quoted in Eubanks Winkler 2006, 6)

Furthermore, according to a panegyric published in 1610 for James I, music has enhanced properties and powers in the hands of an accomplished musician:

> Behold, how like another *Orpheus*, *Amphion*, and *Arion*, he draweth to the true knowledge of God, very salvage Beasts, Forrests, Trees, and Stones, by the sweet Harmony of his harp: the most fierce and wilde, the most stupid and insenced, the most brutish and voluptuous, are changed and civilized by the delectable sound of his Musick. . . . [H]is mellodious touchinges and concordes and not tickle them with any delicate noyse, tending unto voluptuous and sensuall pleasure: but rather such, as by well tempered proportions are able to reduce all extravagant rudenesse, and circuites of our soules, though they had wandered from the right way, to the true path of dutie, and settle all thoughts in such a harmony, as is most pleasing unto them. (Marcelline 1610, 35; quoted in Eubanks Winkler 2006, 6)

In early modern England, music had the potential to restore and promote order, but it had to meet certain conditions first. Rehabilitative music was harmonious, melodious, consonant, and well-tuned; it thus established a template of balance and order that a distressed body could emulate.

In his *Compleat Gentleman* (1622), Henry Peacham remarks, "Physitians will tell you . . . the exercise of Musicke is a great lengthener of the life, by stirring and reviving of the spirits, holding a secret sympathy with them" (Peacham 1622, 97; see also Gouk 2013). The widespread belief that music exerted a sympathetic action on the spirit, which could restore equilibrium and well-being to ailments of the mind and body, persisted from the fifteenth to the eighteenth centuries. The underlying philosophy supporting this belief is that health constitutes a precarious balance between the bodily humors and harmony between the body and soul; when upset, the imbalance could cause disease in the body or mind (Gouk 2013, 221).

Shakespeare dealt extensively with these ideas. For example, in *Hamlet* the title character attempts to demonstrate his reason (otherwise invisible) by describing it as audible music:

> My pulse as yours doth temperately keep time,
> And makes as healthful music. It is not madness
> That I have utter'd . . . (Shakespeare, *Hamlet*, 84, III.iv.155–157)

In these lines, the protagonist speaks to his mother, attempting to convince her that she is using his madness as an excuse; Hamlet argues that he is not mad, and compares his pulse to the regularity of musical pulse and healthful music. If a person's body can keep regular time with healthful music, he must not be mad. As a foil to Hamlet, Ophelia is the stock mad character in the play, providing the narrative prosthesis that casts doubt on Hamlet's madness. Carol Thomas Neely distinguishes between the two types of madness and their significance for early modern society. Whereas Ophelia's speech is fragmentary, such as her habit to spontaneously burst into song and quote well-known sixteenth-century ballad poetry, "Hamlet is presented as fashionably introspective and melancholy," in the tradition of Aristotelian melancholics. Ophelia's particular brand of feminine madness serves to underscore Hamlet's feigned madness as tolerable masculine idiosyncrasies (Thomas Neely 2004, 54).

But music could also be dangerous. Elizabethan writer Phillip Stubbes discussed this dangerous music, arguing that certain music could emasculate men, comparing such dangerous music to a beautiful woman who might overstimulate a man's passions. Both could overtake his reason and diminish it to an overexcited, womanish state:

> But [music] being used in publique assemblies . . . *estrangeth ye mine* [mind,] stirreth up filthy lust, womanish ye mind, ravisheth ye heart, enflameth concupscience and bringeth in uncleanes. But if Musick openly were used (as I have said) *to ye praise and glory of God as our Fathers used it*, and was intended by it at the first, or privately in a mans secret Chamber of house for his own solace or to drive away the fantasies of idle thoughts, solicitude, care, sorowe, and such other perturbations and molestations of the minde, the only ends whereto true Musick tends, it were very commendable and tollerable. If Musick were thus used it would comfort man wonderfully, and move his hart to serve God the better. (Stubbes 1583, cited in Dunn 1994, 98; emphasis added)

For Stubbes, private, devotional music promoted a positive ethic, while music performed in public, for carnal purposes (such as dance music and secular music) corrupted the mind. With reference to the Sirens, Richard Mulcaster (1532–1611) constructed a similarly gendered model for the emotional power of music on the soul:

> [Through the] delight of the eares . . . the weak soule may be stirred up into a feeling of godliness. . . . [T]o some [music] seemes offensive, bycause it carrieth away the eare, with the sweetnesse of melodie, and bewitcheth the mind with a *syrens* sound, pulling it from that delite, wherin of duetie it ought to dwell, unto harmonicall fantasies, and withdrawing it, from the best meditations, and most virtuous thoughtes to forreigne conceites and wandring devises. (Mulcaster, fol. 29 v, 1581)

Notably, this corruption of the mind is gendered. As Linda Phyllis Austern argues about pre-Enlightenment views of music and gender,

> Like Woman, cosmological Nature . . . traditionally consisted of what higher Reason left behind, the dank, physical pull of the earth and its wild creatures, heavy with the corruption of sensual knowledge and emotion. Even her very passions have been considered unhealable manifestations of her naturalness, while destructive earthly phenomena have borne her metaphorical likeness. She generates imperfect, mortal, and often ungovernable products of the same faulty physical materials. Meanwhile Man, in a tribute to his Maker's clean creative capacities, builds order out of chaos with the powers of his mind. Women thus belong to nature in ways that men do not, and culture achieves its highest value as a triumph of manly artifice. (Austern 1998, 28)

Recent research in intellectual history has illuminated attitudes about the mind–body connection in early music, discussing how the mind could manifest itself in the body. In an article on the mind–body connection in medieval and early modern medicine, intellectual historian Elena Carrera (2013) demonstrates that before the widespread presence of the Cartesian separation between rationality and emotion, "folk-wisdom" was pervasive; it taught that "grief, obsessive worry, excessive anger, and so forth would damage hearts, give ulcers, destroy complexions, and make one more prone to infections" (96). Gleaning insights from early modern medical literature in English, French, and Italian sources—such as Bernardino Monta de Monserrate (d. 1558), court physician and surgeon to Emperor Charles V; Thomas Elyot's Castel of Helth (1539); and Thomas Willis (d. 1671), a teacher of natural philosophy at Oxford known for his significant contributions to the anatomical understanding of the brain—Carrera focuses on the spirit and its potential to impact physical health (97).

Carrera also demonstrates that emotions have held an anomalous ontological status within the body since antiquity, both affecting and being affected by thought: "Even when [medical texts in the period 1200–1700] refer to anger, joy, fear, or sadness as being caused by evaluative perceptions, they present these as physiologically base processes, manifesting as movements and alterations of the spirits in the brain. . . . [T]hey tend to draw on an Aristotelian understanding of the passions which is at odds with . . . a historical binary opposition between emotion and rationality" (96). If masculinity represents the mind and reason (or *logos*), and femininity represents the body and corporeal passions, then according to the theory of mind–body connection, it is possible for the masculine reason to coexist with the passionate feminine. Thus, for Stubbes, while the feminine excess of music can be destructive, the masculine rationality of music as ordered can be edifying to the mind and body. This duality—music's masculine potential to promote reason and its feminine potential to provoke distress—fits Mitchell and Snyder's (2000) observation that the disabled are often constructed as a foil to able-bodiedness, providing a conflict that literary narratives seek to resolve.

In addition to its feminine qualities, harmful music could also be discordant, as evidenced by this speech in *Richard II*:

> Music do I hear?
> [*Music*]
> Ha, ha, keep time! How sour sweet music is
> When time is broke, and no proportion kept!
> So is it in the music of men's lives.
> And here have I the daintiness of ear
> To check time broke in a disordered string;
> But for the concord of my state and time
> Had not an ear to hear my true time broke.
> I wasted time, and now doth time waste me;
> For now hath time made me his numb'ring clock.
> (Shakespeare, *Richard II*, 144, V.v.41–50)

Richard II speaks this soliloquy while imprisoned in Pomfret Castle. The speech is one of Richard II's last in the play, and in it he comes to terms with his isolation and impending death at the hands of the new King Henry IV. Like Hamlet, Richard II waxes poetic while trapped within his reality—although unlike Hamlet, Richard II is literally (not metaphorically) trapped. As the scene begins, Richard II soliloquizes,

> I have been studying how I may compare
> This prison where I live unto the world:
> And for because the world is populous,
> And here is not a creature but myself,
> I cannot do it; yet I'll hammer it out.
> My brain I'll prove the female to my soul,
> My soul the father; and these two beget
> A generation of still-breeding thoughts,
> And these same thoughts people this little world,
> In humours like the people of this world,
> For no thought is contented. The better sort,
> As thoughts of things divine, are intermix'd
> With scruples and do set the word itself. (Shakespeare, *Richard II*, 144, V.v.1–13)

Richard II constructs a gendered mind–body duality, naming his brain as the female and his soul as the father. The benighted king grapples with melancholy and what might be considered a crisis of identity. But music interrupts his brooding and fills him with dread:

> Now sir, the sound that tells what hour it is
> Are clamorous groans, which strike upon my heart,
> Which is the bell: so sighs and tears and groans
> Show minutes, times, and hours: but my time
> Runs posting on in Bolingbroke's proud joy,
> While I stand fooling here, his Jack o' the clock.
> This music mads me; let it sound no more;
> For though it have holp madmen to their wits,
> In me it seems it will make wise men mad.
> Yet blessing on his heart that gives it me!
> For 'tis a sign of love; and love to Richard
> Is a strange brooch in this all-hating world.

Richard II admits that while music can assuage fears and madness, the music sounding during the soliloquy exacerbates Richard's panic, and "mads [him]."

Consonant, harmonious, well-tuned music promotes healthful order. Conversely, dissonant, discordant, and out-of-tune music promotes distress. The principles underlying these views derive from Boethius's *De institutione musica*, which greatly influenced medieval and Renaissance thinkers. Boethius describes three kinds of music: first, the music of the spheres (also called *musica mundana* or *musica universalis*), which keeps the planets and cosmos in harmony; second, the *musica humana*, which is the equilibrium of temperament within the soul and body; and third, instrumental music, which was audible. Developing a mind–body connection, apropos of Aristotle, Boethius writes,

> Music of the universe is especially to be studied in the combining of the elements and the variety of the seasons which are observed in the heavens. . . . What human music is, anyone may understand by examining his own nature. . . . What else joins together the parts of the soul itself, which in the opinion of Aristotle is a union of the rational and the irrational? What causes the blending of the body's elements? (Boethius, translated in McKinnon 1998, 140–141)

Boethius's views are reflected in Mulcaster's "In Musicam Thomae Tallisii, et Guiliemi Birdi," which appear as prefatory matter to the *Cantiones quae ab argumento sacrae vocantur* (1575) of the celebrated Elizabethan composers Thomas Tallis and William Byrd. Mulcaster defends the didactic benefits of music, referencing the power of "numbers" (proportions) to order the universe:

> How precious a thing is Music, and how appropriate for governing the mad passions of the mind, is revealed by those who teach that numbers are the foundation of everything having form, and that music is formed from these. (Byrd [1575] 1977, xxvi)

Similarly, following early modern Neoplatonist philosophy and their interpretations of Boethius, Lorenzo, in *The Merchant of Venice*, describes the music of the spheres in Act V, Scene 1:

> How sweet the moonlight sleeps upon this bank.
> Here will we sit, and let the sounds of music
> Creep in our ears. Soft stillness, and the night,
> Become the touches of sweet harmony.
> Sit Jessica, look how the floor of heaven
> Is thick inlayed with patens of bright gold.
> There's not the smallest orb which thou beholdst
> But in this motion like an angel sings,
> Still choiring to the young-eyed cherubins.
> Such harmony is in immortal souls,
> But whilst this muddy vesture of decay
> Doth grossly close in it, we cannot hear it. (Shakespeare,
> *Merchant of Venice*, 2006, 176, V.i.1–6)

Music is an ordered art, and disordered music can produce disorder in the body. In this case, music can enable a recovery from illness if the sounds are made in a harmonious way. A disordered person, however, is one who cannot feel music or who is somehow disharmonious and therefore immune to its ordering and soothing effects. In the same speech from *Merchant of Venice*, Lorenzo describes the dangers of someone who does not feel music:

> By the sweet power of music: therefore the poet
> Did feign that Orpheus drew trees, stones and floods;
> Since nought so stockish, hard and full of rage,
> But music for the time doth change his nature.
> The man that hath no music in himself,
> Nor is not moved with concord of sweet sounds,
> Is fit for treasons, stratagems and spoils;
> The motions of his spirit are dull as night
> And his affections dark as Erebus:
> Let no such man be trusted. (Shakespeare V.i.86–94)

Therefore, someone who does not feel the sweet power of music—which inspires the creation of art (as in the case of Orpheus, who is encouraged to "draw trees") and can also change the nature of a person—is disordered.

In Shakespeare's dramas, there are distinct opinions about what constitutes proper music. One type of music, as identified by Boethius, is *musica humana*, which can "ennoble or corrupt the character" (McKinnon 1998, 137). Boethius introduces *De institutione musica* with a discussion of music's ability to affect character, using metaphors later employed in early modern England. Boethius writes,

> [A]nyone seeing a triangle or square easily recognizes what he sees, but to know the nature of a square or triangle he must inquire of a mathematician. The same may be said of other matters of sense, especially of the judgment of the ear, whose power so apprehends sounds that it not only judges them and knows their differences, but is often delighted when the modes are sweet and well-ordered, and pained when disordered and incoherent ones offend the sense. (McKinnon 1998, 137–138)

Boethius asserts that music, as part of the *quadrivium* (the quantitative disciplines of learning), is related both to science ("speculation") and morality, since "[n]othing is more characteristic of human nature than to be soothed by sweet modes and disturbed by their opposites. . . . From this may be discerned the truth of what Plato said . . . , that the soul of the universe is united by musical concord" (137). From incongruity, which is "hateful and contrary," lasciviousness can develop, since "[a] lascivious mind takes pleasure in the more lascivious modes, and is often softened and corrupted by listening to them." Boethius claims that the ear is the most "open pathway" to the mind: rhythms and modes enter the mind through the ear and at once begin to mold the mind to their nature. Some music is "chaste and modest," but a "confusing mixture of styles" results in depravity. Boethius, citing Plato, states that music should be "carefully and modestly composed, so that it is chaste, simple, and masculine, not effeminate, savage, and inconsistent" (McKinnon 1998, 137–139).

Shakespeare's plays are replete with references to discord versus concord, and harshness versus sweetness, noise versus music. Ophelia, commenting on Hamlet's mental state, compares madness with bells jangled out of tune:

> O, what a noble mind is here o'erthrown! . . .
> And I, of ladies most deject and wretched,
> That suck'd the honey of his music vows,
> Now see that noble and most sovereign reason,
> Like sweet bells jangled, out of tune and harsh;
> That unmatch'd form and feature of blow youth
> Blasted with ecstasy. (Shakespeare, *Hamlet*, III.i.157–67)

The sound of harsh, ringing bells is a musical metaphor for madness: just as the bells do not follow a steady rhythmic pattern, so too are Ophelia and Hamlet's mental states in discord with early modern society (Wilson and Calore 2005, 230). A musical ethics based on conformity—belonging to a chord, following a meter, being "in tune"—thus mirrors the social codes of conformity that have so often marginalized disabled persons.

As a method for studying early music, Disability Studies has been criticized for being anachronistic and dependent on Enlightenment constructions of the normal versus abnormal—a binary opposition seen to be the result of nineteenth-century medicine and science, and therefore not applicable to early modern cultures. Through this essay, and its application of the common disability trope of narrative prosthesis, I demonstrate that Disability Studies is not only applicable to studies of early modern English music, but augments our understanding of early modern English culture. A continuing study of early modern disability and its relationship to music might illuminate further the incongruous position of music as both ordered and disordered, masculine and feminine, nondisabled and disabled, and possibly shed light on the connection between mind and body in Neoplatonist thought.

References

Austern, Linda Phyllis. 1998. "Nature, Culture, Myth, and the Musician in Early Modern England." *Journal of the American Musicological Society* 51: 1–47.

Byrd, William. (1575) 1977. *Cantiones sacrae*. Edited by Craig Monson. Vol. 1 of *The Byrd Edition*. London: Stainer & Bell.

Carrera, Elena. 2013. "Anger and the Mind-Body Connection in Medieval and Early Modern Medicine." In *Emotions and Health, 1200–1700*, edited by Elena Carrera, 95–146. Leiden, Netherlands, and Boston: Brill.

Dunn, Leslie C. 1994. "Ophelia's Songs in *Hamlet*: Music, Madness, and the Feminine." In *Embodied Voices: Representing Female Vocality in Western Culture*, edited by Leslie C. Dunn and Nancy A. Jones. Cambridge, UK: Cambridge University Press.

Eubanks Winkler, Amanda. 2006. *O Let Us Howle Some Heavy Note: Music for Witches, the Melancholic, and the Mad on Seventeenth-Century English Stage*. Bloomington: Indiana University Press.

Gouk, Penelope. 2013. "Music and Spirit in Early Modern Thought." In *Emotions and Health, 1200–1700*, edited by Elena Carrera, 221–240. Leiden, Netherlands, and Boston: Brill.

Hobgood, Alison P., and David Houston Wood. 2013. *Recovering Disability in Early Modern England*. Columbus: Ohio State University Press.

Marcelline, George. 1610. *The Triumphs of King James*. London: Budge.

McKinnon, James, ed. 1998. "The Early Christian Period and the Latin Middle Ages." In *Strunk's Source Readings in Music History*, rev. ed., edited by Leo Treitler (gen ed.), 111–278. New York: W. W. Norton.

Metzler, Irina. 2006. *Disability in Medieval Europe: Thinking about Physical Impairment during the High Middle Ages, c. 1100–1400*. New York: Routledge.

Metzler, Irina. 2013. *A Social History of Disability in the Middle Ages: Cultural Considerations of Physical Impairment*. New York: Routledge.

Mitchell, David T., and Sharon L. Snyder. 2000. *Narrative Prosthesis: Disability and the Dependences of Discourse*. Ann Arbor: University of Michigan Press.

Neely, Carol Thomas. 2004. *Distracted Subjects: Madness and Gender in Shakespeare and Early Modern Culture*. Ithaca, NY: Cornell University Press.

Shakespeare, William. 2005. *The Complete Works*. 2nd ed. Edited by Stanley Wells, Gary Taylor, John Jowett, and William Montgomery. Oxford, UK: Clarendon.

Wilson, Christopher R., and Michela Calore. 2005. *Music in Shakespeare: A Dictionary*. New York: Continuum.

CHAPTER 28

SAUL, DAVID, AND MUSIC'S IDEAL BODY

BLAKE HOWE

THE term "disability" suffers from an etymology of negation: it is often used to denote what cannot be done, branding its carrier as the antithesis of some other, desirable standard. Since the nineteenth century, this desirable standard has most frequently been the concept of normalcy, with disabilities cast as abnormalities on the fringes of a bell-shaped curve (Davis 1995, 23–49). Before the nineteenth century, however, this desirable standard was more commonly the allure of an abstract ideal body, from which all human bodies were poorly fractioned. Much biblical literature is saturated with this ideology. Often called the *religious model of disability*, it holds that disabilities are corruptions of a divine prototype (the ideal body of God or of Adam before the Fall) and thus markers of spiritual deviance. Salvation entails the return to a state of physical, spiritual purity.[1] For example, in Isaiah 35:5–6 (and again in Matthew 11:5), a quartet of disabled persons—the blind, deaf, lame, and dumb—find their bodies cured upon joining the redeemed: the kingdom of Zion is the realm where "the eyes of the blind shall be opened, and the ears of the deaf shall be unstopped. Then shall the lame man leap as an hart, and the tongue of the dumb sing." Such utopian visions idealize a community of uniform able-bodiedness; physical imperfections, remnants of earthly pollution, must be left at heaven's gate.

This ideal body has often been metaphorized as a musical body—its rhythms mobile and fluent, its harmonies pure and resonant, its timbre cohesive and uniform, its tuning strict and proportional. (Notably, at the conclusion of Isaiah 35, the redeemed—cleansed of their sins and of their bodies—enter Zion united in song.) Dissonances and syncopations, like bodily imperfections, might occasionally diverge from the consonant, metrical ideal, but the strong forces of musical resolution can safely contain their destabilizing potential. In this role, the ideal musical body also possesses healing powers, restoring order to sonic dysfunction. Later applications of this ideology in medieval and Renaissance texts invoke the ancient Greek doctrine of imitation and Boethius's related notion of the *musica humana*, in which structural proportions of the human body possess an innate musicality, tuning to and sympathetically vibrating with surrounding sounds. The heavenly cosmos, ordered by and tuned to Pythagorean ratios, models this resonant, healthful musical-corporeal ideal.[2] With the aid of natural magic or divine miracle to account for any mysterious unseen forces, musical curers could simulate these cosmic sonorities and thus stimulate the disordered, dissonant body toward a state of consonant wholeness.

In premodern tracts on musical healing, the exemplary performer of therapeutic music was David, and his most notorious patient was Saul (posthumously diagnosed with madness, melancholy, and even epilepsy). In exegetical accounts, these two biblical figures are often framed as antitheses: David's consonant health as an emblem of divine strength (an ideal body) versus Saul's dissonant disease as a symptom of divine disfavor (an imperfect body). Their expressive friction has served as an important site for theological and cultural allegory, in which Saul's body usually operates as a *narrative prosthesis*. As theorized by Mitchell and Snyder 2000, narrative prostheses are literary representations of disability that generate conflict within a story, thus supporting its narrative by introducing a problem for it to solve. For example, in Isaiah 35, the blind, deaf, dumb, and lame possess impairments that impede their entrance into Zion. In the ensuing resolution (usually resulting from a "cure"—e.g., "the lame shall leap"), the absence of disability helps to define the desirability of able-bodiedness. A neutral state, able-bodiedness accrues little meaning on its own terms. But when pitted against disability, when defined as the state from which one has been rehabilitated, the healthy body amasses moral, ethical, and spiritual power: it is a vanquisher, triumphantly emerging from struggle. Saul, requiring rehabilitation, thus offers David a chance to prove his divine strength, to vindicate his ideal body. By extension, the tale of Saul and David is one that musicians often tell about themselves to prove the supremacy of their own artistic discipline—and in this scenario, disability is cast as the obstacle whose eradication validates the sovereignty of its musical curer.

As found in 1 Samuel 16:23, the original account of David's rehabilitation of Saul is quite brief: "And it came to pass, when the evil spirit from God was upon Saul, that David took a *kînôr* [cithara, lyre, harp], and played with his hand: so Saul was refreshed, and was well, and the evil spirit departed from him."[3] Later, in 1 Samuel 18:10–11, David again plays for Saul; this time, however, his music has no effect: the king remains in a state of emotional distress, twice throwing his spear at David. Although the full story would seem to speak to the limitations of music therapy (it sometimes works, it sometimes leads to spear throwing), commentaries almost exclusively focus on the first successful remediation of Saul's behavior, ignoring or sidestepping later contradictions.[4] As Davis 2002 argues, "narratives involving disability always yearn toward the cure, the neutralizing of the disability" (99). Such is the persuasive force of the "cure" narrative—its elevation of the able-bodied curer, its safe confinement of disability—that we are inclined to infer one even when presented with evidence of its opposite.

An early but enduring exegetical tradition among medieval Christian writers interpreted David's music as a conduit for the Christian God and Saul's irrational behavior as a sign of demonic possession. In *De psalmodiae bono* (c. 400), Niceta of Remesiana sees in the shape of David's cithara an image of the crucifixion, capable of working its redemptive power on Saul: he writes, "the image of Christ's cross was mystically exhibited in the wood and stretched strings of the instrument, and thereby it was the very Passion that was hymned and that overcame the spirit of the demon."[5] Here, David's instrument itself is a type of ideal body, capable of miraculously transferring its spiritual power onto Saul. Later Christian writers developed Niceta's symbolism further, including Isidore of Seville (in the seventh century), the Venerable Bede (in the eighth century), Honorius of Autun (in the eleventh century), and Hugh of St. Victor (in the twelfth century).[6] Extending the Passion allegory with a particularly vicious blend of ableist and anti-Semitic language, Bede interpreted Saul as "the blindness and stubbornness of the Jews," who betrayed David (a prefigurement of Christ) by throwing his spear at him.[7] "Saul stands for death; David for the life of Christ," so Honorius of Autun wrote.[8] Within this allegory, Saul's disruptive behavior assumes grand theological significance—his body representing the greatest obstacles (demons, sin, death) that medieval Christianity sought to vanquish.

Narratives *of* disability are not necessarily narratives *about* disability. Rather, applications of the narrative prosthesis often appropriate disability's disruptive potential to allegorize some other form of alienation or estrangement. In Isaiah 35, as in many exegetical accounts of David and Saul, as in nearly all texts that conform to the religious model of disability, this estrangement is sinfulness—the disability symbolizing the ways in which the heretical subject is separated from spiritual ideals. For Niceta, among other writers, Saul's disorder serves a prosthetic function within the grandest cure narrative of all: it is the sinful cause of Jesus's suffering and death, an impediment remediated by (and thus giving meaning and definition to) resurrection.

Other writers linked David's cithara to Greek theories of music—particularly the Pythagorean ratios, which constructed another sort of ideal body, vibrating and resounding in both harmony and health. In the *Protrepticus*, Clement of Alexandria (c. 150–215) exhorted his pagan audience to abandon their rituals for the "new song" of Christianity, which "composed the universe into melodious order, and tuned the discord of the elements to harmonious arrangement." It is King David who has composed this corporeal-cosmological music, uniting the music of the body with the music of all divine creation: he "arranged in harmonious order this great world, yes, and the little world of man too, body and soul together." David's authority, then, derives from his dual mastery of what Boethius will later term the *musica humana* and *musica mundana* (or *universalis*): Pythagorean ratios, governing both the microcosmos and macrocosmos, establish and reinforce ideal states of balance, stability, and order. These ratios, immune to any discordant sinfulness, ward off evil; as Clement writes,

> So far was [David] from singing the praises of demons that they were put to flight by him with the true music; and when Saul was possessed, David healed him merely by playing the harp. The Lord fashioned man a beautiful, breathing instrument, after His own image. . . . What then is the purpose of this instrument, the Word of God, the Lord, and the new song? To open the eyes of the blind, to unstop the ears of the deaf, and to lead the lame and sinful into the way of righteousness.[9]

Alluding to Isaiah 35:5–6 (an influential text for the religious model of disability, as already demonstrated), Clement compares Saul's body with other disabilities, metaphorizing all as dissonant, sinful impurities subsequently rehabilitated and subsumed within the ideal musical body of creation. Saul, functioning as the narrative prosthetic, defines by counterexample the parameters of health and righteousness that constitute Clement's "new song" of Christianity. David's sonic exorcism thus reasserts the divine strength of his own musical–corporeal ideal.

This interpretation, too, was influential. The notion that consonant music might retune and rehabilitate dissonant distress (or, less abstractly, that ethical music promotes ethical character) has been one of the enduring principles of musical cures. Indeed, medieval writers frequently included the story of Saul's rehabilitation in exhaustive lists documenting music's power to alter a listener's temperament, using its biblical authority to substantiate more dubious tales. As Isidore of Seville writes, invoking the principles of rhythmic mobility and sympathetic vibration, "Music moves the feelings and changes the emotions. . . . Indeed every word we speak, every pulsation of our veins, is related by musical rhythms to the powers of harmony." His examples include battle music encouraging valor, work songs promoting productivity, and, of course, David liberating Saul "from the unclean spirit by the art of melody."[10] Similar language appears in Guido of Arezzo's *Micrologus* (c. 1030)[11] and Aegidius of Zamora's *Ars musica* (c. 1270), which prefaces a discussion of Saul's exorcism by citing the testimony of magicians: according to them, "many demons cannot endure harmony, and indeed none can when a fortuitous change in disposition is wrought through harmony in the bodies in which they dwell."[12] Even though Isidore, Guido, and Aegidius (among many other medieval theologians and musicians) continue to diagnose Saul with demonic possession or evil spirits, their underlying rehabilitative model is rooted not in blunt-force exorcism but rather in behavior modification. Saul's raging character may be adjusted or tempered by the consonant ratios of sweet harmony—like an errant dissonance, nudged into resolution by the ideal body of music.

This reading of the biblical story saw an extraordinary resurgence among seventeenth-century poets, many adopting a didactic tone when describing the acoustical principles of David's music therapy.[13] For example, Michael Drayton's epic poem "David and Goliah" (1630) documents Saul's sonic rehabilitation as a dynamic tonal chase, with David wielding his "well-tun'd Harpe" in pursuit of a discordant demon:

> The harmony of the untuned'st string
> Torments the spirit which so torments the King [Saul],
> Who as he faintly, or as he strongly groanes,
> This brave Musitian [David] altreth so his tones,
> With sounds so oft, as like themselves to smother;
> Then like lowd Ecchoes answering one the other;
> Then makes the spirit to shift from place to place
> Still following him with a full Diapase . . . ,
> Untill he made th'unruly fiend obay

The force of Musick. . . . (Drayton 1932, 3:425–426)

Drayton sources Saul's distemper to an "untuned'st string," subsequently pulled into harmonic concord by David's powerful diapason (i.e., octave). Indeed, Drayton and his generation frequently metaphorized health as well-tuned consonance: the harmonic series is sympathetic to (or "in tune with") healthy able-bodiedness, while rejecting the diseased and disabled as dissonantly deviant. (Samantha Bassler's essay in this collection also explores the seventeenth-century resurgence of these metaphors.)

Abraham Cowley's poem *Davideis* (1650) engages further with this version of the ideal musical body, identified as both healthful and well tuned. From Cowley's description of Saul's cure, readers learn about "the mystick pow'ers that in blest *Numbers* dwell"—that is, the Pythagorean ratios that govern the macrocosmos of creation and microcosmos of the human body:

> [*Man*] is all o're *Harmonie*.
> *Storehouse* of all *Proportions! single Quire*!
> Which first Gods Breath did tunefully inspire!
> From hence blest *Musicks* heav'enly charms arise,
> From *sympathy* which *Them* and *Man* allies. . . .
> Thus the strange *Cure* on our spilt *Blood* apply'd,
> *Sympathy* to the distant *Wound* does guid.
> Thus when two *Brethren strings* are set alike,
> To *move* them *both*, but *one* of them we *strike*,
> Thus *Davids Lyre* did *Sauls* wild rage controul.
> And tun'd the harsh disorders of his *Soul*. (Cowley 1656, lines 470–482)

An unsounding string (fixed, stuck, immobile) resounds in sympathetic vibration when positioned adjacent to a sounding string: Cowley reads this basic acoustical principle as a "cure" of sonic dysfunction by a healthy agent of rehabilitation. Thus the conflict between embodied oppositions, so important to narrative treatments of disability, finds their musical realization here, in the vibrations of strings (whether plucked on an instrument or resounding within a body or echoing through the cosmos). As in Drayton's poem, Cowley's acoustical medicine supports a fairly simple outcome: "Th'obscure fantastic rage of *Sauls* disease," Cowley writes, finds appeasement in David's "soft *musick*." Saul's mood improves. But few authors took this change of behavior for granted. Indeed, Cowley supports his poetical interpretation of David's therapy with four pages of footnotes, including an extensive list of documented musical rehabilitations—ancient, biblical, and modern. "That [*Musick*] should cure settled diseases of the body, we should hardly believe," Cowley writes, "if we had not both Humane and Divine testimony for it."[14] Saul, here, operates as the prosthetic supporting the glorification of music—his remediated body validating claims for music's idealness.

As it so happens, Charles Jennens used Cowley's description of Saul's rehabilitation as his principle source for the corresponding scene in his libretto for Handel's *Saul* (1739).[15]

To identify one of a number of similarities between the two texts, both diagnose Saul with a mysterious "disease" (in the oratorio, it is specifically an "old Disease") and spend much time explaining its spiritual source. In Act I, scene 4 of the oratorio, David is instructed to "expel the raging fiend" from the king and "sooth his tortur'd soul with sounds divine." Combining two exegetical traditions, Jennens's text argues that sacred music not only promotes ethical character, it also cures demonic possession. As Michal (Saul's daughter, David's future wife) sings, David has performed on his "persuasive lyre," supported by a macrocosmic "celestial fire," so that "healing sounds dispel [Saul's] cares" and eliminate the "black despair [that] possess'd / With horrid sway the monarch's breast."

In a brief but significant interruption of the scene, a High Priest sermonizes on the power of music, singing in an accompanied recitative immediately before David's aria. By creating the world, he states, God shaped an ideal musical body from the discord of chaos:

> A fair harmonious World arose;
> And tho' by diabolick guile,
> Disorder Lord it for a while,
> The Time will come,
> When nature shall her pristine Form regain,
> And Harmony for ever reign.

Like Cowley, and Drayton before him, and Clement of Alexandria way before them all, Jennens uses David's musical therapy as an opportunity to comment on music's role in the formation of divine creation. When introduced, human sinfulness (a form of dissonance) diverged from God's consonant harmoniousness—but all discord (social, corporeal, or musical) will cease after the last judgment, music thus returning to its ideal state. Handel's recitative represents this expressive trajectory in three stages (Figure 28.1): a prelude in which the strings arpeggiate triad after triad after triad, suggesting the creation of the harmonic universal order (mm. 12–18); a thorny diminished-seventh chord for the "diabolick guile," followed later by a dominant seventh in third inversion, signaling the intrusion of deviant dissonance (mm. 19–21); and a bright, pure C-major chord announcing the new reign of "Harmony" and nature's return to "pristine Form" (m. 22). These are the three stages of the classic 'cure' narrative: stability, disorder, resolution—the internal wound safely contained. This arc allegorizes David's therapy of Saul's disorder as a prefigurement of later purifications of human sinfulness—including the resurrection of Christ and the last judgment. (Recall Honorious of Autun: "Saul stands for death; David for the life of Christ.")

Indeed, as Rooke 2012 argues, Jennens persistently links Saul with demonic evil throughout the oratorio: "both Saul's villainy and David's virtue are described in supernatural terms," suggesting that we might understand the libretto "in religious, and specifically messianic, terms" (90–91). For example, Saul is said to speak words "which Hell, / No human Tongue, has taught him," and he is described as "rack'd with Infernal Pains." Even more damning is a choral exhortation on Saul's transgressions: "Envy! Eldest-born

FIGURE 28.1 G. F. Handel, *Saul* (No. 30, "By Thee This Universal Frame"), mm. 16–26.

of Hell! / Cease in human Breasts to dwell." Saul's "old Disease," then, is quite old—as old as humanity itself. His mental distress operates as a symbol for human sinfulness and demonic nefariousness, against which able-bodied David, armed with his harp, wages battle to prove Christ's virtue. The antithetical forces producing the narrative conflict are starkly opposed: Saul (medical disease, musical dissonance, and spiritual sinfulness) versus David (medical health, musical consonance, and spiritual virtue). This tripartite fusion of medical, musical, and spiritual therapy not only defines the specific elements of Saul's conflict with David, but also constructs a cosmic battle for universal purification and salvation, for freedom from bodily imperfections.

FIGURE 28.1 Continued.

Untethered from eschatological theology, Saul's disease has also received a more secular identification (one already hinted by Jennens's reference to "black despair"). The posthumous diagnosis of melancholy emerged mostly after a flurry of late-fifteenth- and early-sixteenth-century treatises on natural magic and humoral theory—for example Heinrich Cornelius Agrippa's influential *De occulta philosophia* (c. 1510), likely the source for the many coded symbols in Albrecht Dürer's famous engraving *Melencolia I* (1514). Indeed, the Flemish artist Lucas van Leyden seems to either echo or anticipate the slouched pose of Dürer's angel in his near-contemporaneous engraving of David and Saul (c. 1508): a youthful David stands tall, while the older Saul heavily slumps, glowers (Figure 28.2). Earlier iconographical traditions for this scene clearly depict Saul's possession: demons dance on the king's shoulders, or his body jerks and lurches so wildly

FIGURE 28.2 Lucas van Leyden, *David Playing the Harp for Saul* (c. 1508). Metropolitan Museum of Art (www.metmuseum.org).

that assistants must restrain him. Van Leyden, however, focuses on Saul's depressive gaze and his weighted, immobile body, perhaps suggesting that a temperamental imbalance (and not an evil spirit) plagues him.

Many subsequent representations of Saul, including Rembrandt's much more famous seventeenth-century paintings, follow this model, branding Saul with the traditional melancholic signs (heaviness, darkness, old age) while granting David their sanguine opposites (buoyancy, light, youthfulness).[16] Though wholly unsupported by the biblical account in 1 Samuel, Saul's diagnosis as a depressive personality (whether subsumed within melancholia or some other diagnostic category) eventually replaces the religious diagnosis of possession, and its religious associations with sinfulness and spiritual deviance. What persists, however, is the antithetical nature of the tale's dueling characters—Saul's humoral imbalance now defining by counterexample the well-proportioned body of David. Indeed, we may read this latest revision of Saul's and David's bodies into a brief anecdote from the Mendelssohn family—when, in 1821, an elderly Johann Wolfgang von Goethe heard the young child prodigy Felix Mendelssohn perform. "I am Saul, and you are my David," he said. "When I am sad and dreary, you come to me and cheer me with your music" (Hensel 1882, 113).

Caused by an overflow of black bile, melancholy could be cured by reducing or dissolving the excess bile and thus restoring the body to a state of humoral balance—a concept that mirrors the acoustical proportions of music's ideal body. In *De vita libri tres* (1489), Marsilio Ficino identifies numerous potions, syrups, and pills that melancholics can use to rehabilitate their broken bodies; in addition, he encourages music therapy, citing both his own personal experience and that of Saul:

> Mercurius, Pythagoras, and Plato claim that a dissonant soul, or a sad one, is helped by strumming a lyre and by constant singing and melodious playing. David, that holy poet, freed Saul from unhealthiness with his psaltery and psalms. I, too (if it is permitted the lowest to oppose the highest things), have often found out at home how much the sweetness of the lyre and song avail against the bitterness of black bile. (Ficino 1980, 12)

Ficino also recommends "use of gardens or woods," "strolls through beautiful meadows," "horse-back riding," "travel in carriages," and "sailing." Conviviality and laughter, too, were frequently cited as remedies—hence, *Wit and Mirth, or, Pills to Purge Melancholy* (1698), Thomas d'Urfey's famous and oft-reprinted collection of bawdy popular songs, the "pills" of the title.[17] These rehabilitative strategies all provoke movement, whether in the vibrations of the soul or the engagement of the mind or in the exercise of the body. Melancholy is an ailment of excessive fixity, of weighted immobility, and music—as evidenced in accounts of Saul—offers one strategy for mobile recuperation.

These were not conjectural remedies. As demonstrated by Ficino's testimony, music therapy was actually practiced on melancholics, and the biblical account of Saul was sometimes cited for validation. In the late fifteenth century, the famous painter Hugo van der Goes—suffering from a "strange mental disease" whose symptoms mirror both contemporary descriptions of melancholia and signs of demonic possession—was observed to be "vexed by the same disease by which King Saul was tormented." Music was played, and "recuperative spectacles" performed, but to no avail (Jones 2000, 121).[18] More successful was the rehabilitation of a seventeenth-century French woman who, according to keyboardist Jean Denis, had exhibited signs of melancholy: "She lay always in her bed with the curtains closed and wished to see no one." From this position of extreme immobility, she was then serenaded by some distinguished houseguests—the *Vingt-quatre violons du roy*, who performed behind a tapestry hung close to her bed for privacy.

> The violins all began together. The force of these instruments, which twenty-four men made to sound with all their strength and with great intensity, surprised the lady greatly, for it was the last thing she expected. This harmony made such an impact that it instantly banished her baleful melancholy. She recovered her former health and her merry disposition. (Denis [1650] 1987, 82–83)

Beautiful music gives the melancholic an acoustical shove, dislodging this patient from her position of immobility. And though he does not credit a biblical source, Denis's complete tale mirrors contemporary interpretations of Saul's rehabilitation in several respects: the woman, like Saul, enters into a state of distress that baffles her companions, and the violinists (each a string on David's lyre?) are summoned to assist. In this narrative, the musical remediation of disability validates both the spiritual power of clean tunings (an important subject for Denis's treatise) and, more importantly, the sonic perfection of the French King's ensemble.

We may find yet another echo of the tale of Saul and David in Washington Irving's short story "The Rose of Alhambra" (1832, rev. 1851), written after his trip to Spain. The story hinges on the musical rehabilitation of Philip V, a "miserable hypochondriac, subject to all kinds of fancies," who would spend weeks in his bed "groaning under imaginary complaints." As in accounts of the melancholic Saul, the king's inert body functions as a narrative prosthesis, with music as its most natural cure. Although music had refreshed his mind in the past (Farinelli was on call "as a kind of royal physician"), Philip V entered into an extreme melancholic and irrational state that frustrated usual remedies. Enter the minstrel Jacinta, the "Rose of Alhambra," who carries with her a magic silver lute (obtained earlier in the story from a phantom). As we will have come to expect, Jacinta uses her lute to conjure the ideal body of music: "soft aerial harmony," an "angelic melody," and "the music of the spheres" (the *musica universalis*). The "animating strain" prompts action and movement within the formerly immobile king: "He raised his head and gazed around: he sat up on his couch, his eye began to kindle—at length, leaping upon the floor, he called for sword and buckler."[19] Philip V returns to health, and this rehabilitation in turn prompts a chance reunion between Jacinta and her long-lost lover—all thanks to music (and all thanks to the king's disorder, the narrative prosthesis that created the problem permitting both resolutions).

What is new here, and what distinguishes this representation of a musical cure as a product of the early nineteenth century, is Irving's detailed description of the silver lute's hypnotic powers. Wherever she traveled, Jacinta attracted crowds who listened to her music "spell-bound, in breathless ecstasy":

> The rich and powerful of the land contended who should entertain and do honor to her; or rather, who should secure the charms of her lute to draw fashionable throngs to their saloons. Wherever she went her vigilant aunt kept a dragon watch at her elbow, awing the throngs of impassioned admirers, who hung in raptures on her strains. The report of her wonderful powers spread from city to city. Malaga, Seville, Cordova, all became successively mad on the theme; nothing was talked of throughout Andalusia but the beautiful minstrel of the Alhambra. (311–312)

In a word, Jacinta's music is *transcendent*, prompting listeners to escape their minds and bodies as if in a mesmerist trance. Indeed, musical hypnosis was a fashionable form of therapy in the nineteenth century. Advocated by Franz Anton Mesmer in the late eighteenth century, mesmerism tweaked the familiar concepts of the *musica universalis* and *musica humana* to argue that a "universal fluid" (combining air, fire, and spirit, operating according to magnetic or attractive forces) bound the cosmos and the human body together as well as human bodies to each other. (Mesmer's dissertation, *De planetarum influx in corpus humanum* [*On the Influences of Planets on the Human Body*] explicitly adopts ancient models of sympathetic vibration.) The therapy's cultural impact can be detected in the nervous discussions about the supposedly hypnotized audiences attending performances of traveling virtuosi (Alexander von Ungern-Sternberg recalls speechless, "electrified" audiences at Liszt's concerts, better suited, he says, to the history of medicine than art).[20] Irving's playful conclusion to "The Rose of Alhambra," describing the afterlife of the magic lute, contributes to this discourse. After Jacinta's final performance, the lute's silver body was melted down, turned into strings, and attached to a "Cremona fiddle." Here is the punch line: "That fiddle is now bewitching the whole world—it is the fiddle of Paganini!" The magnetic powers of earlier music therapies—as exemplified in Philip V's cure by Jacinta's embodiment of the *musica universalis*—have thus found their way into the recital halls of nineteenth-century Europe. From Irving's satirical gaze, modern mesmerized audiences partake in the same ritual music therapies as the ancients.

Several musical retellings of the Saul and David participate in this rich cultural, theological, and medical history. Johann Wagenaar's tone poem *Saul en David* (1906), composed for the Rembrandt tercentenary, begins with a murky, disturbed soundscape suggestive of a body in melancholic distress; at the work's midpoint, a cadenza for solo harp facilitates the rehabilitation, and the work concludes triumphantly. Wagenaar's three-part narrative (distress, music therapy, rehabilitation) closely follows the three movements in Johann Kuhnau's characteristic sonata, "Der von David vermittelst der Music curirte Saul" ("Saul Cured through Music by David"), from the *Musikalische Vorstellung einiger biblischer Historien* (1700). In the sonata's preface, which clearly situates Saul's tale within the religious model of disability, Kuhnau pontificates on the nature of pain and suffering, ghoulishly highlighting the effects of Saul's disorder: "his eyes turn," "his face is distorted so that one can hardly recognize any longer the few remnants of human shape," "his heart . . . throws its foam out through his mouth."[21] The first movement, representing Saul's "sadness and fury" ("La tristezza ed il furore del Re"), exhibits many symptoms of musical dysfunction: serpentine chromatic motion, striking dissonances, and abrupt changes in texture lead to a fugue built on an angular subject (Figure 28.3a). The second movement, "La Canzona refrigerativa dell'arpa di Davide" ("The Refreshing Song of David's Harp"), is relentless in both its repetitive use of the major mode, suggesting the ethical value of Pythagorean tunings, and in its repetitive eighth-note articulations, suggesting the therapeutic utility of rhythmic activity (Figure 28.3b). By the third movement, the king returns to a state of tranquility ("L'animo tranquillo e contento di Saulo") with much regal fanfare; the ceremonial quality of the music

FIGURE 28.3 Johann Kuhnau, "Der von David vermittelst der Music curirte Saul" (*Biblische Historien*, no. 2): (a) Saul's melancholy (mvt. 1); (b) David's song (mvt. 2); and (c) Saul rehabilitated (mvt. 3).

suggests that the king has left his internal musings and now assumes his public duties (Figure 28.3c). Notably, both composers seem to delight in their grisly depictions of Saul's distress, prosthetically exploiting his disabled body as an opportunity to showcase their own extreme, transgressive music and compositional virtuosity.[22] David's breezy strummings, by contrast, seem trivial. The cure thus permits a normate audience to stare, to leer with impunity at Saul's disability, its destabilizing potential safely contained by the narrative frames of able-bodiedness.[23]

And might we hear Saul's tale, or at least its narrative paradigm, in the first movement of Beethoven's String Quartet in E flat Major, Op. 74 (1809)? The work exemplifies the "tonal problem" scenario, explored extensively by the composer in the early 1800s, in which a marked, deviant note (usually foreign to the tonic key) is rehabilitated over the course of a work.[24] In the slow introduction, D♭ assumes this destabilizing role, functioning as a weighted obstruction oppressing the upward strivings of the leading tone, D♮ (Figure 28.4a, mm. 2, 4, 13, 17, and 23). The harmonic journey at times is labyrinthine, populated by the chains of diminished-seventh chords (mm. 18–23) that Elaine Sisman, in her essay in this collection, associates with codes of melancholy. The exposition, by contrast, chronicles several attempts to "fix" this D♭, introducing a miscellany of rustic dance topics that all suggest lively motion and outdoor activities (not unlike Ficino's proposed remedies for melancholy). Just as the slow introduction had introduced the exposition, an extensive retransition introduces the recapitulation—but now, the deviant D♭ has been "retuned" as a true leading tone within a fourteen-measure arpeggiation of the dominant, B-flat major, firmly reestablishing harmonic order and logic (Figure 28.4b). The brilliant timbre and texture—*pizzicato* then *arco* arpeggiations, passed across instruments—are *musical signifiers for music itself*, conjuring in sound an icon of some mythical stringed instrument (hence the quartet's popular nickname, "The Harp"). Memories of that errant D♭, a disabling pitch within the sonic body of the composition, shade our experience of this moment and much of the joyous striving that follows. The work thus documents a process by which able-bodied fulfillment is achieved, and not just the state of able-bodied fulfillment itself. D♮, on its own terms, is just a leading tone; but when cast as the normalized alternative to a deviant D♭, its identity accrues power and vitality as an agent of remediation. (It is by a similar process, of course, that David asserts his able-bodiedness over Saul.)

As Maynard Solomon has shown, Beethoven was a strong advocate for the healing powers of music—and himself had occasionally performed music therapy for women in states of emotional distress. In the same year as the "Harp" Quartet, for example, Beethoven began attending to Antonie Brentano; like the melancholic Saul, she was "suffering to such an extent that she withdrew to her room, where she remained by herself, unfit to see anybody" (Solomon 2003, 229–30). In an extraordinary letter (March 11, 1811), Brentano describes a regression: the return of her severe pains (head and back aches) and her depressed spirits ("For nearly two months I am again very ailing," "I must have forfeited my happiness," "Goodness drifts away from me little by little") (Kopitz 2001, 128). But, as Brentano explains, Beethoven "visits me often, nearly daily, and then he plays from some urge, because to him the alleviation of suffering is a need,

(a)

FIGURE 28.4 Ludwig van Beethoven, String Quartet in E-flat Major, Op. 74: (a) slow introduction to beginning of exposition, and (b) retransition to beginning of recapitulation.

FIGURE 28.4 Continued.

and he feels that he is able to do so with his heavenly tones. . . . I never knew before that such power resides within tones." Brentano describes with great reverence Beethoven's countenance: his entire being [*Wesen*] is "simple," "noble," "good-natured," and "good-hearted." Brentano's Beethoven (despite his deafness) is an epitome of health: his strong body and spiritual fortitude contrasts with her weakened, submissive state. By now, this relationship is strikingly familiar, even archetypal: Beethoven and Brentano, David and Saul, musician and audience—all healers conjuring the sounds of the cosmos to retune the distressed discord of their patients' souls.

Extensions of this history have been already traced by scholars of music therapy and medical ethnomusicology, disciplines methodologically invested in the rehabilitation of broken bodies (Gouk 2000, Horden 2000, Koen 2008). The perspective of Disability Studies, however, reverses the cure narrative's objectification and casual dismissal of the disabled body—examining instead the punishing cultural scripts in which bodily differences are so often placed and the dehumanized symbolic roles for which they are so frequently coopted. Such is the case with many exegetical readings of Saul's healing and the long representational history they have generated: in many of these texts, as we have learned, the disabled body is an essential prosthesis—or, as Mitchell and Snyder might say, a "crutch"—on which the concept of idealness depends to define its perfection. Music is often imagined to operate under a similar ideology—and for this reason it has served as its most effective metaphorical realization. Like David's rehabilitation of Saul, codes of musical perfection (consonant harmony, proportional tuning, uniform timbre, regular meter) seek to resolve and subsume errant deviation, while simultaneously relying on such irregularities to defend their own assertion of correctness.

Acknowledgments

I would like to thank two readers of earlier drafts of this essay: Joseph Straus (for his helpful comments) and Andrew Owen (for his penetrating skepticism). I am also grateful to Zachary Hazelwood for creating my musical examples.

Notes

1. Recent studies include Avalos, Melcher, and Schipper 2007 and Moss and Schipper 2011.
2. As explained in Dahlhaus 1982, "Ever since antiquity . . . it was the concept of motion that provided a connection between music and affection or ethos. The motions of tones sympathetically release those of the soul, a soul that is often described by the simile of a stringed instrument; both musical and psychic motions are subject to the same laws" (19).
3. David's instrument—*kînôr* or *kinnor* in the original Hebrew—has been translated to *cithara* (in the Vulgate), *harp* (in the King James Bible), and *lyre* (in the English Standard and New International Versions). In this essay, I use the instrument that is most historically appropriate for each writer's text.

4. For other musicological perspectives on the Saul and David story, consult Kümmel 1969, Schaik 1992, Hoffmann-Axthelm 2011, and Harrán 2011.
5. Niceta of Remesiana, *De psalmodiae bono*, excerpted and translated in McKinnon 1998, 130.
6. Isidore of Seville, *Mysticorum expositiones sacramentorum seu Quaestiones in Vetus Testamentum*; Venerable Bede, *Allegoriae in Samuel*; Honorius of Autun, *Expositio in Psalmos selectos*; and Hugh (Richard) of St. Victor, *Allegoriae in vetus testamentum*, as cited in Hoffmann-Axthelm 2011, 330; and Ciabattoni 2010, 61.
7. Bede, *Allegoriae in Samuel*, excerpted and translated in Hoffmann-Axthelm 2011, 330.
8. Honorius of Autun, *Expositio in Psalmos selectos*, excerpted and translated in Schaik 1992, 104.
9. Clement of Alexandria, *Protrepticus*, translation adapted from Clement 1909, 11–15; and Schaik 1992, 41.
10. Isidore of Seville, *Etymologiae*, excerpted and translated in McKinnon 1998, 150.
11. Guido of Arezzo, *Micrologus*, translated in Palisca 1978, 70.
12. Aegidius of Zamora, *Ars musica*, excerpted and translated in McKinnon 1998, 249.
13. As Smith 1995 (327–329) argues, many English poets in the seventeenth and early eighteenth centuries used the struggle within King Saul to allegorize contemporary political concerns about the monarchy. For more on the poems discussed here, consult Allingham 1981 and Pebworth 1981. For a list of literary works about David, consult McBryde 1899.
14. "That *Timotheus* by *Musick* enflamed and appeased *Alexander* to what degrees he pleased, that a *Musician* in *Denmark* by the same art enraged *King Ericus*, even to the striking of all his friends about him, that *Pythagoras* taught by the same means a woman to stop the fury of a young man, who came to set her house on fire; that his *Schollar Empedocles* hindered another from murdering his father, when the sword was drawn for that purpose; that the fierceness of *Achilles* his nature was allayed by playing on the harp (for which cause *Homer* gives him nothing else of the spoils of *Eetion*[)]; that *Damon* by it reduced wild and drunken youths; that *Asclepiades*, even seditious multitudes to temper and reason; that the *Corybantes* and effeminate *Priests* of *Cybele*, could be animated by it to cut their own flesh (with many more examples of the like kind) is well known to all men conversant among Authors" (Cowley 1656, 1:34–37).
15. Jennens drew his wordbook from biblical texts, Cowley's poem, and *The Tragedy of Saul* (1703), an anonymously authored play later attributed to Roger Boyle, Earl of Orrery (Smith 1995, 351).
16. For more on the iconography of Saul, consult Jones 2000, 124–127, and Epstein 2006.
17. Many humorous books from the seventeenth century cited themselves as "pills for" or "preservatives against" melancholy. As explained in Lund 2010 (32), the title for Thomas d'Urfey's anthology may find its most direct source in the anonymous *A Pil to Purge Melancholie* (London, 1599), although it may also allude to the "gilded pill" mixing pleasure and remedy that Robert Burton describes in *The Anatomy of Melancholy* (1621).
18. The description of Hugo van der Goes's condition was recorded by Gaspar Ofhuys, about thirty years after the incident.
19. In an earlier experimentation with the lute, Jacinta "drew forth such ravishing tones as to thaw even the frigid bosom of the immaculate Fredegonda, that region of eternal winter, into a genial flow."
20. Ungern-Sternberg 1856, 123. (A slightly different citation to this passage appears in Kramer 2000, 341.)

21. Kuhnau 1953, 13–14. A similar three-movement cure narrative, in which a chorale melody assumes curative powers, may be found in the fourth sonata in the collection, on the miraculous recuperation of Hezekiah.
22. The appropriation of disability as a platform to showcase compositional complexity mirrors Tobin Siebers's notion of "disability drag," in which able-bodied actors perform disabled characters. As described in Siebers 2008, "the audience perceives the disabled body as a sign of the acting abilities of the performer—the more disabled the character, the greater the ability of the actor" (116).
23. As Garland-Thomson 1997 explains, "The neologism [normate] names the veiled subject position of cultural self, the figure outlined by the array of deviant others whose marked bodies shore up the normate's boundaries. The term *normate* usefully designates the social figure through which people can represent themselves as definitive human beings. Normate, then, is the constructed identity of those who, by way of the bodily configurations and cultural capital they assume, can step into a position of authority and wield the power it grants them" (8).
24. Straus 2006 reads other "tonal problems" in the music of Beethoven and Schubert from a Disability Studies perspective.

References

Allingham, Anthony. 1981. "David as Epic Hero: Drayton's *David and Goliah*." In *The David Myth in Western Literature*, edited by Raymond-Jean Frontain and Jan Wojcik, 86–95. West Lafayette, IN: Purdue Research Foundation.

Avalos, Hector, Sarah J. Melcher, and Jeremy Schipper, eds. 2007. *This Abled Body: Rethinking Disabilities in Biblical Studies*. Atlanta, GA: Society of Biblical Literature.

Ciabattoni, Francesco. 2010. *Dante's Journey to Polyphony*. Toronto, Buffalo, and London: University of Toronto Press.

Clement of Alexandria. 1909. *The Exhortation to the Greeks*. Translated by G. W. Butterworth. The Loeb Classical Library. London: William Heinemann; New York: G. P. Putnam's Sons.

Cowley, Abraham. 1656. *Davideis: A Sacred Poem of the Troubles of David*. London.

Dahlhaus, Carl. 1982. *Esthetics of Music*. Translated by William Austin. Cambridge: Cambridge University Press.

Davis, Lennard J. 1995. *Enforcing Normalcy: Disability, Deafness, and the Body*. London and New York: Verso.

Davis, Lennard J. 2002. *Bending over Backwards: Disability, Dismodernism, and Other Difficult Positions*. New York and London: New York University Press.

Denis, Jean. (1650) 1987. *Treatise on Harpsichord Tuning*. Translated and edited by Vincent J. Panetta Jr. Cambridge: Cambridge University Press.

Drayton, Michael. 1932. *The Works of Michael Drayton*. Edited by J. William Hebel. Oxford: Shakespeare Head Press.

Epstein, Marc Michael. 2006. "Seeing Saul." In *Saul in Story and Tradition*, edited by Carl S. Ehrlich, in cooperation with Marsha C. White, 334–345. Tübingen, Germany: Mohr Siebeck.

Ficino, Marsilio. 1980. *The Book of Life*. Translated by Charles Boer. Irving, TX: Spring.

Garland-Thomson, Rosemarie. 1997. *Extraordinary Bodies: Figuring Physical Disability in American Culture and Literature*. New York: Columbia University Press.

Gouk, Penelope, ed. 2000. *Musical Healing in Cultural Contexts*. Aldershot, UK: Ashgate.

Harrán, Don. 2011. "David's Lyre, Kabbalah, and the Power of Music." In *Psalms in the Early Modern World*, edited by Linda Phyllis Austern, Kari Boyd McBridge, and David L. Orvis, 257–298. Farnham, UK, and Burlington, VT: Ashgate.

Hensel, Sebastian. 1882. *The Mendelssohn Family (1729–1847), from Letters and Journals*. Rev. ed. Translated by Carl Klingemann. New York: Harper & Brothers.

Hoffmann-Axthelm, Dagmar. 2011. "*David musicus*, or, On the Consoling Power of String Music." In *Essays on Renaissance Music in Honour of David Fallows: Bon jour, bon mois, et bonne estrenne*, edited by Fabrice Fitch and Jacobijn Kiel, 326–337. Woodbridge, UK: Boydell.

Horden, Peregrine, ed. 2000. *Music as Medicine: The History of Music Therapy since Antiquity*. Aldershot, UK: Ashgate.

Irving, Washington. (1832) 1851. "The Rose of Alhambra" (revised version). In *The Works of Washington Irving*, vol. 15, 299–316. New York: George P. Putnam.

Jones, Peter Murray. 2000. "Music Therapy in the Later Middle Ages: The Case of Hugo van der Goes." In *Music as Medicine: The History of Music Therapy since Antiquity*, edited by Peregrine Horden, 120–144. Aldershot, UK, and Brookfield, VT: Ashgate.

Koen, Benjamin D., ed., with Jacqueline Lloyd, Gregory Barz, and Karen Brummel-Smith. 2008. *The Oxford Handbook of Medical Ethnomusicology*. Oxford and New York: Oxford University Press.

Kopitz, Klaus Martin. 2001. "Antonie Brentano in Wien (1809–1812): Neue Quellen zur Problematik 'Unsterbliche Geliebte.'" *Bonner Beethoven-Studien* 2: 115–146.

Kramer, Cheryce. 2000. "Music as Cause and Cure of Illness in Nineteenth-Century Europe." In *Music as Medicine: The History of Music Therapy since Antiquity*, edited by Peregrine Horden, 338–352. Aldershot, UK: Ashgate.

Kuhnau, Johann. 1953. *Six Biblical Sonatas for Keyboard*. Edited and translated by Kurt Stone. New York: Broude Brothers.

Kümmel, Werner. 1969. "Melancholie und die Macht der Musik: Die Krankheit König Sauls in der historischen Diskussion." *Medizinhistorisches Journal* 8: 189–209.

Lund, Mary Ann. 2010. *Melancholy, Medicine, and Religion in Early Modern England: Reading "The Anatomy of Melancholy."* Cambridge: Cambridge University Press.

McBryde, John McLaren, Jr. 1899. "A Study of Cowley's *Davideis*." *Journal of Germanic Philology* 2 (4): 23–43.

McKinnon, James, ed. 1998. "The Early Christian Period and the Latin Middle Ages." In *Strunk's Source Readings in Music History*, rev. ed., edited by Leo Treitler (gen. ed.), 111–278. New York and London: W. W. Norton.

Mitchell, David T., and Sharon L. Snyder. 2000. *Narrative Prosthesis: Disability and the Dependencies of Discourse*. Ann Arbor: University of Michigan Press.

Moss, Candida R., and Jeremy Schipper, eds. 2011. *Disability Studies and Biblical Literature*. New York: Palgrave Macmillan.

Palisca, Claude V., ed. 1978. *Hucbald, Guido, and John on Music*. New Haven, CT: Yale University Press.

Pebworth, Ted-Larry. 1981. "Cowley's *Davideis* and the Exaltation of Friendship." In *The David Myth in Western Literature*, edited by Raymond-Jean Frontain and Jan Wojcik, 96–105. West Lafayette, IN: Purdue Research Foundation.

Rooke, Deborah W. 2012. *Handel's Israelite Oratorio Libretti: Sacred Drama and Biblical Exegesis*. Oxford, UK: Oxford University Press.

Schaik, Martin van. 1992. *The Harp in the Middle Ages: The Symbolism of a Musical Instrument*. Amsterdam and Atlanta, GA: Rodopi.
Siebers, Tobin. 2008. *Disability Theory*. Ann Arbor: University of Michigan Press.
Smith, Ruth. 1995. *Handel's Oratorios and Eighteenth-Century Thought*. Cambridge, UK: Cambridge University Press.
Solomon, Maynard. 2003. *Late Beethoven: Music, Thought, Imagination*. Berkeley, Los Angeles, and London: University of California Press.
Straus, Joseph N. 2006. "Normalizing the Abnormal: Disability in Music and Music Theory." *Journal of the American Musicological Society* 59: 113–184.
Ungern-Sternberg, Alexander von. 1856. *Erinnerungsblätter*. Vol. 2. Berlin: Heinrich Schindler.

PART 6

THE CLASSICAL TRADITION

CHAPTER 29

NARRATIVES OF AFFLICTION AND RECOVERY IN HAYDN

FLOYD GRAVE

> *Well, here I sit in my wilderness—forsaken—like a poor waif—almost without any human society—melancholy—full of memories of past glorious days—yes! past, alas!—and who knows when these days shall return again? Those wonderful parties? Where the whole circle is one heart, one soul—all these beautiful musical evenings—which can only be remembered, and not described—where are all these enthusiastic moments?—all gone—and gone for a long time. Your Grace mustn't be surprised that I haven't written up to now to thank you. I found everything at home in confusion, and for 3 days I didn't know if I was* Capell-*meister or* Capell-*servant. Nothing could console me, my whole house was in confusion, my fortepiano which I usually love so much was perverse and disobedient, it irritated rather than calmed me, I could only sleep very little, even my dreams persecuted me; and then, just when I was happily dreaming that I was listening to the opera,* Le nozze di Figaro, *that horrible north wind woke me and almost blew my nightcap off my head. I lost 20 pounds in weight in 3 days, for the good Viennese food I had in me disappeared on the journey. Alas! Alas!*[1]

Illness, isolation, malaise, confusion, restlessness, creative impairment, loss of sleep, and the vexations of a wind-blasted night in the hinterland: these are the manifestations of a condition that Haydn describes to his Viennese friend and hostess Maria Anna von Genzinger in a letter written from his home on a bleak day in the winter of 1790. Given the exasperated discontinuities and changes of direction that mark its opening lines, the passage quoted above may surely be read as a spontaneous outpouring of the writer's complaints. Yet we may wonder if there wasn't a measure of calculation afoot as Haydn engages his reader in a veritable game of contraries: illness versus well-being, the dismal present versus joyful moments past, chilled solitude versus warmth and good company, delightful reverie versus painful reality. Even while offering us a snapshot of his social milieu, his domestic environment, and his personal aspirations in a time of trouble and impairment, the quoted passage would seem to represent an artful performance: a reflection of the composer's worldly experience reshaped into a persuasive, evocative narration.

Analogies with elements of Haydn's music come readily to mind, notably in compositions that deviate from reassuring norms as they confound us with their dislocations, incongruities, or states of discord that withhold the promise of restored equilibrium. For just as the letter's juxtapositions of contraries help open a space for feelings of both devastation and hoped-for renewal, there are places in Haydn's compositions where the confrontation of musical opposites may likewise be seen to open a space for interpretation in terms of affliction, recovery, and a range of feelings and experiences that may either attach to those states or else inhabit a terrain between them.[2]

Haydn's dance movements often lend themselves to such criticism, owing to their inherent physicality, their worldly evocations of ballroom and countryside manners, and their puzzling forays into realms of thwarted expectation. The passage cited in Figure 29.1, from Haydn's String Quartet in B Minor, Op. 64 No. 2 (composed in 1790, the same year as the Genzinger letter cited above), encompasses the last part of the minuet (i.e., its expanded, tonally altered recall of the minuet's first-reprise material, beginning in m. 27) and the first reprise of the trio. The two stand in stark contrast, owing to their differences in mode, register, timbre, articulation, dynamics, texture, surface rhythm, and phrase structure, as well as character and topic: whereas the end of the minuet is mechanically repetitive, thematically sparse, and doggedly motivic, the sing-song melody and lilting accompaniment of the trio evoke the flavor of rustic contentment.

Methods of structural and stylistic analysis are naturally useful in helping us to pinpoint musical elements, conventional procedures, and compositional techniques that the composer has engaged at this juncture in the movement. But in doing so they are more likely to erect cognitive barriers than to connect us with what might be understood as the spirit of the music, its realm of possible meanings and associations, or its connection to the culture from which it springs.[3] This is not necessarily a bad thing: we can readily imagine the composer of an untitled instrumental piece relishing in the privacy of unspoken meanings that those barriers might afford; and in any event, our analyses of the music need not necessarily be directed toward invading that privacy. We need not try to decode the composer's intentions or impose extramusical narratives that might cloud the music's privileged transparency—its capacity to accommodate an unlimited range of provisional meanings while standing aloof from verbal description. Rather, the strategy to be followed here centers on the search for words, phrases, and images by which to sharpen our focus on palpable musical relationships—metaphors that can help breathe life into our interaction with the music as listeners and performers. The principal aim in undertaking that search is twofold: first, to try to connect with emotions and experiences that may well have resonated with the lives of the composer and his contemporaries as much as they do with our own;[4] second, to focus specifically on ways in which the music being examined may be seen to embody the experience of disabling conditions and their remediation.

FIGURE 29.1 Haydn, String Quartet in B Minor, Op. 64 No. 2, third movement, mm. 26–50.

Approaching the end of our B-minor minuet from this perspective, we can speak of a troubled, restless state and a protracted effort to find rest and closure. A motive in the first violin—repetitive, impulsive, and intent on escaping the confines of the treble staff (mm. 30–33)—is blocked by an invisible obstacle (mm. 33–34) before making a middle-register retreat as the repeating measure-long thematic figure finds outlet below the staff, sequestered in the second violin as its principal note, C♯, bends downward to C♮.

The stammering motive of measures 28–29, a nagging thought that refuses to go away,[5] suggests a restraint that is momentarily lifted by the threefold rising sequence—which in itself becomes a stroke of musical hyperbole, spinning out of control as it exceeds the top of the staff in the attempt to transcend the vexations of the present moment. And from the perch thus attained (E^3, m. 32), we can catch a glimpse of what will soon be recognized as the trio's wholesale escape to an elevated melodic register. But meanwhile, a stunned silence stifles the turmoil, and the drop to a region below the staff stands as a measure of the change from strain and aspiration to a state of withdrawal and exhaustion. The motive's removal to an inner voice and the concomitant inflection of its principal note (C♯ to C♮) suggest a protective maneuver, as if to seek cover from an intruding gust that scurries and rattles in the first violin part above. Here the Neapolitan sixth (mm. 35–36), customarily recognized as an expressive cadential adornment, exceeds normal constraints: it becomes a harmonic symptom of the stammering figure's inflection. A momentary impediment to closure, the C♮ presses down on the tonic note, the elusive point of rest, in sleepless frustration ("past . . . past"; "Alas! Alas!"),[6] before being liquidated under pressure from the opposite direction in the other parts (A♯ in mm. 37–38; E♯ and G♯ in m. 39). And now the principal motive retires altogether, perhaps on the threshold of sleep, three measures before the close.

The trio releases us from the minuet's fretful present into a transparent, weightless realm of nostalgia, where high-register melody and gentle arpeggiations evoke the motions of a country dance, as if recalled from afar. In this transformed atmosphere, infused with consonant harmony and an easy metrical flow, the minuet's discords and discontinuities are banished. Things are put right, if only for a moment, before all reverie is shattered by the mandatory return of the minuet proper.

Built into the representation of the minuet and its trio as polar opposites is a corresponding impression of a natural and intimate connection between them, as if the latter signified reversal or deliverance from the former's condition. Thus the minuet's thrusts through the tonic (B) octave and beyond in mm. 27–32—disjunct, upward, and unresolved—are countered by the trio's prolonged, conjunct descent through the dominant octave (F♯) on the way toward closure and harmonic resolution (mm. 45–50). In a related correspondence, the tension of the first violin's sequentially rising fourths of mm. 30–32 (F♯–B–E) may be heard to resolve through the descending pattern of chord roots in the cello (likewise F♯–B–E) that crosses the boundary between the end of the minuet and the beginning of the trio (mm. 40–44). The bass line thus traverses the registral and harmonic space between opposites as it leads from the minuet's state of anxiety and impaired mobility to the dreamlike recuperative aura of the trio.[7]

Worth noting as we consider possible interpretations of a dance movement's peculiarities is the enduring presence of the minuet in actual ballroom practice.[8] Because its familiar steps could presumably be visualized and felt by composers, performers, and listeners, its proper motions and the decorum that accompanies them would naturally figure in anyone's expectations for the performance of a minuet-trio movement in a quartet. Something that stretched, contradicted, or ruptured those expectations could therefore be felt viscerally as a disruption in an otherwise fixed pattern of graceful physical motion.[9]

In this view, various things about the opening of the minuet from Haydn's "Frog" quartet (Op. 50 No. 6) must seem drastically out of balance,[10] notably the hiccupping Lombard rhythms and the exaggerated, two-octave-plus sprawl of a principal line that embodies those rhythms as it drops below the staff before hastily rebounding to prepare for a cadence (see Figure 29.2a, which quotes the minuet's first reprise, mm. 1–8). As this action transpires, we can recognize a sufficient number of normal minuet attributes to contrast its strangeness with what might have been expected within the opening strain's customary eight-measure duration: perhaps in principle something like the first reprise of the minuet quoted in Figure 29.2b, from the fourth movement of Haydn's String Quartet in D, Op. 1 No. 3. Here a fluent principal line, sustained by an orderly unfolding of half-, quarter-, dotted quarter-, and eighth-note motion, adheres to a conventionally narrow range. Amid the metrical assurance and textural support of beat-marking lower parts, equilibrium is assured by the unfolding of a pair of closely matched four-measure phrases. By comparison, although almost everything else seems grotesque or out of countenance within the first strain in the "Frog" quartet's minuet, we can appreciate its flawless structural cohesion: four measures that course through a conventional I–IV–V–I progression, and a balancing, suitably intensified four-measure span with the progression V^6_5/IV–ii–V–I.

To venture beyond a simple listing of the "Frog" minuet's digressions from conventional decorum,[11] we might try to engage with the music in more evocative, metaphorical terms, perhaps by identifying with the first violin's seeming predicament: a familiar, self-inflicted impairment that causes him to make a louche, carnival-time spectacle of himself in the ballroom.[12] Having pulled himself together for a game start, he leans precariously into the high D, trips, tumbles through the scale, then lurches below the treble staff in a state of disarray. While this is going on, the composure of the lower parts—all poised securely within well-defined registral limits—underscores the difference between conventional ballroom manners and the barely controlled, centrifugal force of inebriated disorder. We can sense a well-timed supporting hand from those lower instruments, as if catching an impending fall, on the accentuated, dissonant accent in measure 5. This allows the first violinist to recover his balance, if not anything resembling a proper step, just in time to honor the prescribed boundaries of the genre's temporal space—and by extension, the normally allotted physical space on the dance floor.

The oddities encountered at nearly every turn point toward the well-recognized yet puzzling whimsy that often characterizes a Haydn minuet. To hear the participating instruments as agents within a narrative framework of impairment and remediation can

FIGURE 29.2 (a) Haydn, String Quartet in D, Op. 50 No. 6, third movement, mm. 1–8; and (b) Haydn, String Quartet in D, Op. 1 No. 3, fourth movement, mm 1–8.

lead us toward an interpretation that brings their idiosyncratic gestures to life as manifestations of a troubled present and its subversion of customary deportment: the exaggeratedly assertive, on-target gestures with which the strain begins and ends; the retreat of the lower instruments, as if stepping back to witness the first violin's unseemly behavior; the sudden reengagement of those parts to rescue the situation as the complementary, second half of the strain begins; the faltering equilibrium of the melodic rebound; and the breathless but well-timed moment of hesitation just before the cadence.[13]

To conceive an interpretation in terms of a protagonist—one whose condition or experience we can to some extent feel or imagine—seems readily justified when dealing with a movement whose rhythms correspond to certain dance steps. Less obviously connected to embodied experience but nonetheless evocative of personified gesture and agency are cases involving the juxtaposition of two versions of a theme—a situation that might call to mind differing physical or mental states, as in Haydn's own account of the discrepancy between feelings of discomfort and well-being, the latter a cherished memory but also a condition to be hoped for in the future.

Such an interpretation might lend itself to several of Haydn's so-called alternating variation movements—musical designs in which attention shuttles back and forth between two themes (one in major, the other in minor), whose contrasting profiles are mediated by some distinctive resemblance.[14] The Andante o più tosto allegretto of the "Razor" quartet, Op. 55 No. 2, is notable for its uniquely salient, exposed presence at the very head of the work—a pointed contrast to the standard practice of relegating a slow movement to an interior, reflective space within the cycle. Likewise special is its reversal of the more common arrangement of modal alternation: instead of presenting a major segment at the outset, then proceeding to a minor theme with its expected new sources of color, melodic tension, and harmonic complication, this movement begins in a seriously troubled, harmonically complicated minor. Correspondingly, the major theme that follows represents the attainment of relief and stability. Most distinctive of all is the two themes' close relationship in melodic and rhythmic outline (especially in the **a** and **a**^{1} segments of their ||: **a** :||: **b a**^{1} :|| rounded binary forms). The correspondences are so close that they may be understood as different facets of a single idea. Notwithstanding their similarity, points of contrast between them stand out in ways that suggest parallels with feelings, bodily conditions, or mental states, so that we can hear the second as a rectified version of the first, cured of its discord, its pained angularity, and the obstructions that had hindered its progress.[15]

As shown in Figure 29.3a, the quartet opens on an uncommonly somber, shadowed landscape. A plaintive treble line, striving upward above a wash of middle-register minor sonority, pulls back as the weight of a triple appoggiatura presses on the second measure above an immobilized bass. New rhythmic and harmonic action help animate the gradual descent that follows, bringing release from a desolate minor as the path is cleared for a cadence in the relative major. But according to the imperatives of rounded-binary convention, there is no escape following the return of first-reprise material (Figure 29.3b, m. 17), which will be enshrouded in minor and destined to close there.

As if intent on release nonetheless, the first violin climbs anxiously in a disjunct reiteration (mm. 18–19), giving voice to an anxious yearning for stability as the harmonic foundation falls away chromatically in the cello. The line now stretches still further above the staff to reach the theme's apex, D♭^{3} (m. 20), a painful stretch of a minor ninth from the C^2 on which it began, and the note is struck with exaggerated effort, as if in peril of failing to achieve this goal. Perhaps commiserating, the lower parts align themselves in a Neapolitan sixth (mm. 20–22), thereby securing a moment of relief from the grip of minor harmony; yet the move is fraught with complications, beginning with this chord's traditional association with precadential surges of longing, sorrow, or regret.[16] Moreover, the arrival on this specially marked chord is premature, evidently

FIGURE 29.3 Haydn, String Quartet in F Minor, Op. 55 No. 2, first movement, (a) mm. 1–8, (b) mm. 17–26, and (c) mm. 43–50.

FIGURE 29.3 Continued.

hastened by the intensity of the first violin's rising sequence; and now it lingers, filling an unnaturally distended space midphrase—a pathos-laden obstacle to the theme's progress toward conclusion as the viola virtually freezes and the lowered second scale degree hovers above the tonic note for a full three measures. Although motion resumes in m. 23, the effort to sustain the upper register is soon abandoned for a metrically displaced drop to the bottom of the staff—as if seized by enervation, loss of will, or impending disintegration.

Following the dark end to this theme, its major double offers deliverance from affliction. As quoted in Figure 29.3c (mm. 43–50, corresponding to the end of the initial theme's second reprise, mm. 17–26), a smoothed-out melodic line glides on a cushion of mostly consonant, major-oriented harmony, shimmering texture, and unbroken sixteenth-note momentum, all the while ensconced within a harmonically cohesive, balanced structural outline (4 + 4, the two units ending on a half cadence and full cadence, respectively).[17] A fresh, unimpeded flow of alternating tonic and dominant chord roots supports the simplified, uninflected melody, whose stepwise ascent through the tones of the tonic triad is accomplished by the end of the third measure of the phrase (m. 45). The impression of sustained energy, balance, and wholeness persists as ongoing momentum in the inner parts supports a last-minute skip to the theme's high point, D^3 (a half step above the F minor theme's intense D♭), before an easy, stepwise descent to a close at the top of the staff. In retrospect, we can appreciate the extent to which the theme's initial,

F-minor manifestation had been constricted by pain, anxiety, and impairment. By contrast, its F-major double represents what that theme might become, or what it might aspire to, if released from the encumbering forces that surround it.[18]

The opposition of minor and major, crucial to the "Razor" quartet's signifiers of change from affliction to recovery, is a time-honored basis for projecting polar opposites in tonal music—although it is one that does not necessarily prove essential, as witnessed above in Figure 29.2, where a manifestly out-of-balance, out-of-bounds contradiction of standard minuet procedure unfolds in a relatively straightforward D major. And yet modal contrast usually does provide the unmistakable, compelling foundation for the kinds of polar opposition pursued here.[19]

The reliable potency of minor-major opposition owes much to the overwhelming preference for major discourse in later eighteenth-century instrumental music. The corresponding marginalization of minor tonality, especially in the last two decades of the century, meant that to undertake a composition in minor was to enter a relatively obscure realm, often prone to imbalance or distress—a proper abode for sorrow, tragedy, and unfulfilled longing, not to mention the exotic, the uncanny, the imperiled, the enraged, the storm-thrashed, the monstrous, and the sublime.[20]

This disturbing array of connotations is traceable in part to a tradition of powerfully charged distinctions between major and minor long cultivated in sacred music and opera, and readily adapted to instrumental usage. Not altogether arbitrary, such distinctions may claim to have been firmly grounded in eighteenth-century theoretical arguments whereby the minor mode was, in effect, a deformation—a compromised, impaired replica of the major (Grave 2008, 32–34). For example, in passages from Rameau's later writings where attention focuses on the natural acoustical foundations of major harmony, the major triad is understood to reside in the lower partials of the harmonic series. It follows that minor harmony is unnatural, owing its imperfect existence to the upending of the major triad's privileged configuration of thirds (major below, minor above): "The major mode, this first offshoot of nature, has a force, a brilliance, if I dare say so, a virility which dominates the minor and which causes the major mode to be recognized as the master of harmony. The minor, on the contrary, existing less by pure and simple nature, receives from art, from which it is in part formed, a weakness which characterizes its emanation and its subordination."[21] A particularly evocative, later eighteenth-century discussion by the French critic Bernard Germain Lacépède elaborates on the intensely problematic status of minor:

> When the soul listens to the minor mode it is never satisfied, nor can it ever be. It is always wishing for something, and even the most final ending of a piece always leaves something to be desired. . . . The ear is only fully satisfied when it is presented with a piece of music that is constructed of perfect consonances similar to those that nature herself produces.
>
> All other consonances are only conceived and used to throw into relief the natural and fundamental consonances. The soul is unsettled at the sound of these others, or if at times it does take great pleasure in contrived consonances, this is only because it

> feels it will soon get back to pure, perfect, and natural consonances, that the cause of its anxiety will soon be removed, that it has only been deprived of the things it loves in order to lay hold of them soon again, that in doing so it will find them more beautiful and touching still. . . . Without being assured of a return to natural consonance the soul will never cease to torment itself. (Lacépède [1785] 1970, 2:189; trans. Le Huray and Day 1981, 183–184)

Something akin to this view appears to have penetrated close to the core of Haydn's musical thinking in the later phases of his career, where the choice of a minor key for a symphony or string quartet might entail an unsettled, dissonant complex of elements at the outset; but at some point the musical narrative will embrace the release from minor discord and unrest through a decisive reversal to major.[22] This may be heard to signify something no more complicated than a clearing sky following passage through a storm-drenched landscape. But in some instances, notably those that feature a principal idea whose shape and character are explicitly transformed in the process of change from minor to major, we can recognize a protagonist whose initially disabled condition undergoes recuperation as the music progresses to a major outcome.[23]

The first movement of Haydn's Symphony No. 83 in G Minor ("La Poule") stands out as one of the most striking of all such cases as it advances from a state of high agitation at the outset to a diametrically opposed image of serenity at its close. The primary theme, quoted in Figure 29.4a, cries out with a barrage of accentuated dissonance, repeated-note pulsation, disjunct melody, forzato accents, and breathless pauses. At the heart of this aural image is a glaring irritation, represented at the start by the note C♯, a chromatically inflected appoggiatura that complicates the natural unfolding of the theme's arpeggiating motto. What should have been a natural, well-formed stride through the tones of a tonic triad is thus blocked and deflected on the downbeat of the second measure, the very point where the unfolding chord should have achieved wholeness and completion.

As if struggling to conform—to align with customary expectations of pace and rhetoric—the theme manages to shape itself initially into a pair of four-measure phrases, with a half close on an inverted dominant chord in m. 4 and a full stop on a root-position tonic chord in m. 8. But just as in the "Frog" quartet's minuet, there is scarcely anything regular about the material contained within the clearly articulated phrase structure; and the opening theme's stabbing outbursts, their discordant energy too disruptive to be bottled up, will force themselves on events that follow, most notably in the development section's traversal of a veritable minor constellation, with allusions to C minor, F minor, B flat minor, G minor, and D minor.

Recurrences of the opening motto are met by attempts to surmount its affliction. And in keeping with stylistic norms as well as Haydn's own favored practices, the struggle leads to an early crisis in the course of the exposition, where an intense span of primary-theme elaboration leaves the orbit of G minor and drives toward the relative major (Figure 29.4b). This passage has the effect of an exaggerated, repetitive effort to attain some higher, liberating ground—an instance of hyperbole not unrelated to that of our B-minor quartet minuet, with its impulsive ascending sequence (Figure 29.1, mm.

FIGURE 29.4 Haydn, Symphony No. 83 in G Minor, first movement, (a) mm. 1–8, (b) mm. 25–30, and (c) mm. 186–193.

FIGURE 29.4 Continued.

30–33). Thus the four-note figure (mm. 25–26) collapses in stretto with an intensified version of itself (mm. 26–27) before pressing one step further (mm. 27–28) to a climax on the high, dissonant F—the very pitch-class that is about to be ironically reconfigured as a fresh, consonant foundation in the bass as V of III. With the arrival in a new key, midway through the exposition, comes a stretch of relative stability in which the opening theme's troubles are suspended though hardly banished altogether: embedded in the

FIGURE 29.4 Continued.

closing theme is a recognizable variant of the idea, inverted and rhythmically diminished from half notes to quarters (mm. 59–61).

Following the minor-saturated turbulence of the development section and the recapitulation's recall of the opening theme (mm. 128–143), the key signature changes from G minor to G major—an appropriate platform for the (major) tonic-key retrieval of relative-major material from the exposition. The change of mode also furnishes a backdrop for the primary theme's eventual transformation in measures 186–189 (Figure 29.4c). Here, as the primary-theme motto rises through the tones of a dominant triad in the second oboe (colored, to be sure, by the mollified dissonance of a dominant seventh as the first oboe ascends in tandem with the second), it enjoys a new-found state of grace and simplicity, cured at last of the disfiguring C♯ that had marked its initial appearance.

This valedictory allusion proves so drastically different and yet at the same time so close to the movement's opening gesture that it may be heard as its polar opposite—a recuperated version of the motto, quietly planted into the musical fabric just prior to the structural cadence on the downbeat of m. 189 that will herald the movement's closing flourishes (mm. 189–193). The table in Figure 29.5 summarizes the salient points of opposition between the motto's first occurrence (mm. 1–4) and its ultimate transformation in mm. 186–189.

Prior to the motto's final, transformed appearance, the continually changing harmonic contexts in which it occurs have caused the third-note clash to sound not only on C♯ (as in m. 2), B♭ (m. 6), or on F♯, B♮, and F♮ (mm. 26–28) but also at one time or another on every pitch-class of the aggregate.[24] In effect, the theme's struggle to find release extends through the entire chromatic spectrum. Within the realm of minor, every route is blocked. There is no escape, no remedy for the pervasive discord with which the theme is afflicted. Only the providential transformation to major will eventually unlock the door and open a path to recovery.[25] Although we cannot know how such an interpretation compares with what audiences of Haydn's time may have imagined, their experience with contemporary repertories of opera, song, sacred music, and oratorio furnished an abundance of relevant musical images. In a telling instance from the second part of Haydn's *The Creation* (1798), notable for its stark connection of words to music, the archangel Raphael sounds an omen of crushing devastation before Gabriel and Uriel join in a promise of renewal (Figure 29.6; the English version of the text is given in the left-hand column following the next paragraph).[26] Following a cadence in the dominant key, B flat (m. 34), and a unison descent through an E-flat minor scale, Raphael's dark pronouncement begins ("But as to them thy face is hid, with sudden terror they are struck"). Raphael continues amid the anxiety of a repetitive triplet figure in the strings ("Thou tak'st their breath away," mm. 43–47, 49–51), and the music comes close to a state of disintegration as the vocal line drops below the bass staff on the repetition of the line "they vanish into dust" (mm. 52–54). But then the air clears: the pitch G♭, the minor-inflected third degree of E-flat (and momentarily a tonic in its own right, mm. 53–54), finds itself repositioned as part of an augmented sixth chord (m. 59), and both music and textual imagery are simultaneously transformed (m. 61) as the three voices proceed in a restored E flat major ("and life with vigor fresh returns").

Memorable for its exemplary use of minor-to-major text-setting conventions, this passage also invites notice for its resonance with something from the

Opening (mm. 1–4)	Close (mm. 186–89)
G minor	G major
tonic	dominant
tutti; string dominated	solo woodwinds
violins 1 and 2 in octaves	oboes 1 and 2 in parallel thirds
chromatically inflected (C♯)	diatonic (with C natural in oboe 1)
antecedent	consequent
phrase ends on a V6 chord, followed by silence	phrase ends on a tonic chord that elides with a full-orchestra flourish

FIGURE 29.5 Haydn, Symphony No. 83 in G Minor, first movement. Comparison of the first and last statements of the primary-theme motto.

composer's own life experience—namely, his growing awareness of a medical condition on which he elaborated in a letter to his Leipzig publisher from June 1799, not long after the public premiere of the oratorio in Vienna.[27] A translation of the relevant passage of the letter is quoted below, to the right of the verses cited above from *The Creation*.

But as to them thy face is hid, With sudden terror they are struck. Thou tak'st their breath away; they vanish into dust.	There are some days in which my enfeebled memory and the unstrung state of my nerves crush me to the earth to such an extent that I fall prey to the worst sort of depression, and thus am quite incapable of finding even a single idea for many days thereafter;
Thou lett'st thy breath go forth again, and life with vigor fresh returns. Revived earth unfolds new force and new delights.	until at last Providence revives me, and I can again sit down at the fortepiano and begin to scratch away again.

In reading the excerpt from Haydn's letter, we can perhaps hear—and imagine the composer himself hearing—a musically embodied contrast between minor-colored darkness, dissonance, and despair ("crush me to the earth"), and the unmistakably major-illuminated, restorative moment that follows ("Providence revives me"), perhaps with a pivotal augmented-sixth chord to articulate the transitional "until at last": that anticipated moment when the cloud of incapacity lifts to allow for a time of health and well-being regained.

However constrained by periodic bouts of illness, Haydn's creative faculties scarcely deserted him in the several years that followed. The oratorio *The Seasons*, an immense accomplishment by any measure, was begun in autumn 1799 and finished by the end of

FIGURE 29.6 Haydn, *The Creation*, part 2, trio (Gabriel, Uriel, Raphael), mm. 35–64.

the following year. The *Te Deum* also dates from 1800; the so-called *Creation* mass was completed in 1801, the *Harmoniemesse* as late as 1802.

Meanwhile, perhaps as early as the spring of 1799, Haydn had begun to compose a new set of string quartets and had completed the first two within the year. But then the project stalled, perhaps owing to the pressure of other commitments in addition

FIGURE 29.6 Continued.

FIGURE 29.6 Continued.

to recurring illness. Although work continued at least sporadically on a third quartet, Haydn was obliged by 1802 to agree to the publication of the two already finished pieces (as Op. 77) rather than holding out for the completion of the third, whose prospects must have seemed increasingly dim: in a letter to his brother from early 1803, he confessed that he had not been able to accomplish anything for the past five months.[28]

More than a year later (June 1804), Haydn's friend and biographer Georg August Griesinger reported that the composer was "working in good moments on quartets" and that the long-postponed third quartet was well on its way to completion (Landon 1977, 282). This proves to have been too optimistic a claim, however. In the end, only two inner movements were ever finished. Haydn's vulnerability to physical and creative exhaustion had become an insurmountable obstacle; and by the summer of 1805, Griesinger conceded that "Haydn has given up hope of being able to complete the quartet he has begun" (Landon 1977, 336).

The work so long under way was to have taken shape as a standard four-movement cycle, cast in the key of D minor—a specially favored tonality of Haydn's for minor-key compositions in this genre, and thus a wholesome choice for the obligatory minor quartet in what the composer must have initially intended as the final, crowning opus group in the canon.[29] As for those two completed movements (a ternary-form Andante grazioso in B flat and a veritable *Sturm und Drang* minuet in D minor with a relatively calm, restorative trio in the major mode), neither betrays obvious signs of impairment.[30] Indeed, both may be described as expertly crafted, up-to-date models of their kind, as if Haydn were pointedly intent on demonstrating (to himself, perhaps, as well as his admirers) an enduring reservoir of strength and creativity (Grave and Grave 2006, 332–335).

And yet there is something strange about both movements with respect to their closing gestures. As shown in Figure 29.7a, the ensemble approaches the slow movement's heavily scored final cadence by way of a loud-volume arpeggiation that spans more than four octaves—a surge whose vehemence exceeds anything in the piece up to this point (G^3 in the penultimate measure is the movement's highest pitch; and there are no fortissimos or triple stops apart from these last measures). The end of the minuet (quoted in Figure 29.7b) seems comparably marked by an excess of rhetorical emphasis, with its shift in measure 40 to a piercingly high register, the subsequent push to a climactic A^3, and the first violin's high-volume ascent through two octaves and a fourth to a final D above the staff—the movement's only instance of fortissimo dynamics and its only prolonged flourish of small note values.

Both closing passages practically jump off the page. Patently outsized for their immediate surroundings, they must have been designed to connect with comparably prominent events in either or both of the unwritten outer movements—in other words, to participate in some strategy of cyclic cohesion or intermovement relationship.[31] Absent those outer movements, the salience of these moments seems an anomaly: a mark of the inner movements' subservience to a larger, unconsummated plan and thus a hindrance to their reception either as a pair of independent pieces or as an abbreviated two-movement cycle. And yet by 1806 the composer himself evidently consented to their publication and thus to their entry into the canon as a quartet with its own opus number (Op. 103). This made for an irregular work indeed, missing not only two essential limbs but (presumably) the greater part of its intended musical substance. Inextricably linked to the troubled circumstances of its composition, Op. 103 was destined for immortality as Haydn's swan song, an enduring monument to the fatal disability that had closed in on the final phase of his career.

Haydn's long-enduring reluctance to let go of the project is understandable as a consequence of his evident pride, determination, and refusal to yield to the ever-worsening obstacles of his disability; and we can readily appreciate the depth of his predicament from a specifically musical perspective, given his choice of casting the quartet in a favorite minor key. Any plans he might have made for the work's missing outer movements would likely have entailed not only a path through dark, D-minor images and sensations (some of which are already present in the minuet), but also at some point a providential reversal from darkness to light—from affliction to recovery—of the sort that we have

FIGURE 29.7 Haydn, String Quartet in D Minor, Op. 103 (incomplete), (a) Andante grazioso, mm. 109–112, and (b) Minuet, mm. 39–46.

seen in the first movement of Symphony No. 83 and that had come to inform a number of the composer's later works in minor (Grave 2008, 35). It would appear that life and art had become fatally intertwined as Haydn struggled simultaneously with his deteriorating condition and with the task of leading this final minor-key quartet to a proper conclusion. At some point prior to Griesinger's sad report from the summer of 1805, the intersecting, painful truths must have come to seem inescapable: the return to a condition of wholeness and renewal ("begin to scratch away again") was no longer going to happen; there would be no finished quartet and hence no further moment of redemption to signify the revival of energy, the unfolding of new force, the prospect of new delights, or the chance once again to recapture glorious days of the past.

Acknowledgments

This essay's endeavor to map a scheme of affliction and recovery onto the interpretation of certain kinds of musical structure and process is to some extent a sequel to an article of mine on images of recuperation in the finale of a late string quartet of Haydn's (Grave 2008). Both essays owe much to the seminal ideas advanced in Straus 2006. An earlier version of the present study was prepared for the Symposium on Music and Disability at the City University of New York, January 2010. In connection with that event, I am especially indebted to Blake Howe, Brian Hyer, and Bruce Quaglia for their valuable comments and advice.

Notes

1. Excerpted from Haydn's letter of February 9, 1790, to Maria Anna von Genzinger, translated in Landon 1978, 737.
2. Relevant to this proposal is the examination of Adam Smith's musical aesthetics by Stephen Rumph (2012, 115–123). Regarding Smith's argument that emotions are governed by a principle of equilibrium (121), Rumph quotes from a key passage of Smith's in Wightman and Bryce 1980: "What may be called the natural state of the mind, the state in which we are neither elated nor dejected ... holds a sort of middle place between those two opposite extremes. ... Instrumental Music, by a proper arrangement, ... can not only accommodate itself to the gay, the sedate, or the melancholy mood; ... it can, at least for the moment ... produce every possible modification of each of those moods or dispositions" (197). Also pertinent is the observation by Mitchell and Snyder (2000) that "one cannot narrate the story of a healthy body ... without the contrastive device of disability to bear out the symbolic potency of the message. The materiality of metaphor via disabled bodies gives all bodies a tangible essence in that the 'healthy' corporeal surface fails to achieve its symbolic effect without its disabled counterpart" (63–64).
3. See Lawrence Kramer (2002) on the underlying question of perceived "contradictory tendencies: on the one hand toward the projection of autonomy ... and the sublime transcendence of specific meaning, and on the other hand toward intimations of contingency ... and the intelligible production of specific meanings" (2).
4. Here it useful to consider the initial characterization of musical metaphor by Michael Spitzer (2004): "I define musical metaphor as the relationship between the physical, proximate, and familiar, and the abstract, distal, and unfamiliar"(4). Contemplating our engagement with a musical phrase, for example, he asks us to imagine it as a living being, but also something that "might even be heard to objectify a life force disembodied from any agency. ... To comprehend the phrase as an image, an utterance, or an organism is to

allow one's hearing of musical structure to be shaped by a knowledge of different spheres of human activity: representation, language, life" (12).

5. On motivic repetition as a potential signifier of obsession, see Howe 2010, 78–137.
6. There is a degree of license involved here in the reliance on Landon's resourceful translation of Haydn's idiosyncratic prose; yet the key element of exasperated repetition comes across no less clearly in the original as given in Bartha (1965): "——weg sind Sie—und auf lange sind Sie weg . . . ja, ja . . . ja, ja" (228).
7. If elements of the trio suggest recuperation, does the obligatory repeat of the minuet proper necessarily signify the return to an impaired state? Comparison with the (admittedly nonobligatory) repeat of a first-movement exposition may be instructive, for surely that repeat need not return us to the state in which we started, as if the exposition had not occurred. Rather, it may be heard simply to redouble that opening section's message before the movement's story resumes after the double bar and repeat signs. Similarly, the da capo recurrence of a minuet may be regarded not as the continuation of an unfolding plot but rather as a convention of form whose main purpose is to bestow architectonic symmetry on the movement as a whole. In this view, the narrative of a minuet-trio may be heard to culminate with the end of the trio, at which point everything has been said.
8. For relevant discussion of minuet practices, see Russell 1992 and 1999. See also Grave and Grave 2006, 76–83, and Lowe 2002.
9. As noted by Danuta Mirka (2009), "the effect of physical disturbance in the minuet is closely combined with an aesthetic provocation: In this aristocratic dance such disturbances break the rules of stylistic etiquette by portraying not only slips and stumbles of imaginary dancers but their generally indecorous manners" (298). See also Wheelock 1992, 55–89.
10. On the suggestion of embodied gestures that signify imbalance, see Straus 2006, 124. Here reference is made to the concept of image schemas set forth in Lakoff and Johnson 1980. Regarding the image schema of verticality, Straus observes that "we all have experiences of imbalance and loss of verticality, the disabled counterparts of balance and verticality."
11. Here the reference to conventional decorum points to an understanding of the eighteenth-century ballroom minuet as an ideal type—an exemplary vessel for such emblems of galant style as rhythmic fluency, melodic grace, and regular phrase structure. A dance movement that conforms to such familiar, normative traits may be prized for the beauty of its components and their contribution to a design whose elegance may be heard as an affirmation of courtly values. It does not necessarily follow that a minuet which ruptures the vessel or deforms its contents must be viewed negatively for its deviance. Rather, such a piece may be cherished for its audacity and perhaps for its richness of narrative implication. As noted in Straus 2011, "it is a paradox worth pondering that deformities are valued so differently in life and in art. Formal deviations, which are dealt with harshly in real life when manifested as bodily deformities, may be prized within art, and sonatas with 'deformations' are often the most interesting and expressive ones. Here is an area in which music may have a singular contribution to make to Disability Studies" (113).
12. Can we reasonably identify the first-violin line in question with the actions of a man, given (for example) the many slow movements in quartets by Haydn and others in which a middle- to upper-range first violin part invokes a tragic heroine from the realm of opera seria? As can be gathered from relevant accounts (such as Parker 2002, 25–45), performing string quartets in the eighteenth century was largely a man's occupation. In this view,

assigning the masculine pronoun to the music's imagined dialogues, monologues, and pantomimes would not seem inappropriate.

13. On the matter of musical gesture and agency, see Hatten 2004. Observing that "when musical events are heard as gestural, then the implication of agency is inescapable" (224), Hatten contemplates how "a spontaneous or 'willed' individual gesture may be understood as being subject to various . . . environmental forces which act upon it in various ways" (116).
14. On Haydn's alternating variations, see Sisman 1993, 152–163.
15. As in the minuet from Haydn's Op. 64 No. 2 (discussed above in connection with Figure 29.1), impairment registers in part as a case of impeded mobility. For additional perspectives on this movement, see Grave and Grave 2006, 113–115.
16. On the expressive connotations of the Neapolitan sixth chord, see Kamien 1990.
17. In terms of image schemas and disability theory, certain defining elements of the F-minor theme may be heard to signify a species of BLOCKAGE, a disabling condition from which the F-major double represents release or recovery. See Straus 2006, 125–126. The image of recuperation is complicated, but by no means compromised, by a view of the movement as a whole, which comprises three sets of minor–major alternations followed by an F major coda over a tonic pedal point. The second and third appearances of both the minor and major segments are subjected to various patterns of cantus firmus and melodic-outline variation.
18. The relationship between the theme's two versions may be heard to prefigure the narrative trajectory of disability overcome—the eventual return to a normal state—that has been identified in nineteenth-century literature and music (Straus 2011, 45–48). It may also be viewed as a symptom of an emerging anxiety about the exhausted efficacy of existing conventions—the degradation of the indispensable to the commonplace—and the consequent need to strive for originality. It is in this connection that Charles Rosen cites Rinaldo Di Capua's complaint, allegedly communicated to Charles Burney in 1770, that "all possible beautiful melodies had already been invented. . . . The best one could do was to create an ugly modulation to set the beautiful one in relief" (Rosen 2012, 149). Musical transgressions that may once have been spurned were on their way to becoming accepted as attractive features of a composition. This is one sense in which Haydn's display of a deformed theme and its well-formed twin may "be understood to be metaphorically about normal and deviant bodies, and thus to participate in the construction of the culture and history of disability" (Straus 2011, 113).
19. On aspects of Haydn's approach to minor tonality and the opposition of minor and major, see Grave 2008, 34–37; see also Grave 2009.
20. See Hatten 1994, 36–38. Situating the opposition of major (nontragic) and minor (tragic) within a theory of markedness, Hatten observes that the minor (marked) has a narrower range of meaning than the major (unmarked), and that "one kind of evidence for the stylistic encoding of a marked opposition is that the distribution of terms often reflects the asymmetry of their opposition—in other words, the marked term will occur less frequently than the unmarked" (36).
21. Rameau (1750) 1975, 164. Rameau's vivid depictions of a major-minor polarity correlate with—and to some extent may have been informed by—contemporary operatic practices in which differences between major and minor are mapped onto an array of opposites having to do with atmosphere, affect, character, and (perhaps most tellingly) gender, so that masculine images associated with major harmony stand in contrast to various conventionally recognized feminine connotations of minor.

22. See Grave 2009, which lists tonal plans and schemes of modal reversal in Haydn's later symphonies (16), string quartets (30), and piano trios (32).
23. A case that proves notable from many perspectives is that of the last movement to Haydn's String Quartet in G, Op. 76 No. 1—a finale which, like that of Op. 76 No. 3 in C, is cast in an afflicted tonic minor at the outset; in both works, the reversion to major takes place in the course of the recapitulation. See Grave 2008, 36–50.
24. Excluding the repeat of the exposition, a total of some thirty-three occurrences of the motto may be counted in the course of the movement. The note C♯ is positioned as the dissonant appoggiatura no fewer than nine times; the note B plays that role seven times, and the note G♯, three. Other pitches in the spectrum are recognized by one or two occurrences.
25. For related discussion of this movement, see Grave 2009, 22–26; see also Schroeder 1990, 83–88.
26. For a concise account of the origins of the work's English text and the translation of that text into German by Gottfried van Swieten, see Temperley 1991, 19–30. As Temperley observes, "*The Creation* is the first large-scale work in musical history to be published with a bilingual text. It is clear from both the nature of the first edition, published by the composer himself, and the manner in which the work was composed, that Haydn intended to give equal standing to the German and English texts" (19).
27. Letter of June 12, 1799, to Christoph Gottlob Breitkopf, translated in Landon 1977, 468.
28. For discussion of the circumstances surrounding the composition of Haydn's last quartets, see Grave and Grave 2006, 323–325.
29. From the quartets of Op. 9 through those of Op. 76, Haydn's almost invariable practice was to compose such works in groups of six (the lone D minor quartet, Op. 42, is the sole exception). For each opus group, his custom was to include one quartet in minor (Op. 20, with two in minor, is the exception). In addition to Op. 42 and Op. 103, the other quartets in the key of D minor are Op. 9 No. 4 and Op. 76 No. 2. For relevant discussion of the opus-group phenomenon, see Sisman 2008, 79–107.
30. Here the modifier "obvious" should be emphasized, in light of recent research, notably by Joseph Straus (2008), into the potentially complex and multifaceted topic of so-called late style. The extent to which various distinctive features of Haydn's Op. 103 may fall within the interpretive fields delineated in Straus's essay remains to be examined.
31. On the question of cyclic cohesion and intermovement relationship in Haydn, see Webster 1991, 174–224. See also Grave and Grave 2006, for discussion of cyclic issues that arise in various of Haydn's quartet opus groups (especially 164–167, 186–197, 236–238, 256–262, 278–281, 295–298, and 318–322).

References

Bartha, Dénes, ed. 1965. *Joseph Haydn: Gesammelte Briefe und Aufzeichnungen*. Kassel, Germany: Bärenreiter.

Grave, Floyd. 2008. "Recuperation, Transformation, and the Transcendence of Major over Minor in the Finale of Haydn's String Quartet Op. 76 No. 1." *Eighteenth-Century Music* 5: 27–50.

Grave, Floyd. 2009. "Galant Style, Enlightenment, and the Paths from Minor to Major in Later Instrumental Works by Haydn." *Ad Parnassum* 7: 9–41.

Grave, Floyd, and Margaret Grave. 2006. *The String Quartets of Joseph Haydn*. New York: Oxford University Press.

Hatten, Robert S. 1994. *Musical Meaning in Beethoven: Markedness, Correlation, and Interpretation*. Bloomington: Indiana University Press.
Hatten, Robert S. 2004. *Interpreting Musical Gestures, Topics, and Tropes: Mozart, Beethoven, Schubert*. Bloomington: Indiana University Press.
Howe, Blake. 2010. "Music and the Embodiment of Disability." PhD diss., Graduate Center, City University of New York.
Kamien, Roger. 1990. "Aspects of the Neapolitan Sixth Chord in Mozart's Music." In *Schenker Studies*, Vol. 1, edited by Hedi Siegel, 94–105. Cambridge: Cambridge University Press.
Kramer, Lawrence. 2002. *Musical Meaning: Toward a Critical History*. Berkeley: University of California Press.
Lacépède, Bernard Germain. (1785) 1970. *La poétique de la musique*. 2 vols. Geneva: Slatkine Reprints.
Lakoff, George, and Mark Johnson. 1980. *Metaphors We Live By*. Chicago: University of Chicago Press.
Landon, H. C. Robbins. 1977. *Haydn: Chronicle and Works*, vol. 4, *Haydn: The Years of "The Creation," 1796–1800*. London: Thames and Hudson.
Landon, H. C. Robbins. 1978. *Haydn: Chronicle and Works*, vol. 2, *Haydn at Eszterháza, 1766–1790*. London: Thames and Hudson.
Le Huray, Peter, and James Day, eds. 1981. *Music and Aesthetics in the Eighteenth and Early-Nineteenth Centuries*. Cambridge: Cambridge University Press.
Lowe, Melanie. 2002. "Falling from Grace: Irony and Expressive Enrichment in Haydn's Symphonic Minuets." *Journal of Musicology* 19: 171–221.
Mirka, Danuta. 2009. *Metric Manipulations in Haydn and Mozart: Chamber Music for Strings, 1787–1791*. New York: Oxford University Press.
Mitchell, David T., and Sharon L. Snyder. 2000. *Narrative Prosthesis: Disability and the Dependencies of Discourse*. Ann Arbor: University of Michigan Press.
Rameau, Jean-Philippe. (1750) 1975. Démonstration du principe de l'harmonie. Translated in Roger Briscoe, "Rameau's Démonstration du principe de l'harmonie and Nouvelles réflexions de M. Rameau sur sa Démonstration du principe de l'harmonie: An Annotated Translation of Two Treatises by Jean-Philippe Rameau." PhD diss., Indiana University.
Rosen, Charles. 2012. *Freedom and the Arts: Essays on Music and Literature*. Cambridge, MA: Harvard University Press.
Rumph, Stephen. 2012. *Mozart and Enlightenment Semiotics*. Berkeley: University of California Press.
Russell, Tilden A. 1992. "The Unconventional Dance Minuet: Choreographies of the Menuet d'Exaudet." *Acta Musicologica* 64: 118–138.
Russell, Tilden A. 1999. "Minuet Form and Phraseology in *Recueils* and Manuscript Tunebooks." *Journal of Musicology* 17: 386–419.
Schroeder, David. 1990. *Haydn and the Enlightenment: The Late Symphonies and Their Audience*. Oxford: Clarendon Press.
Sisman, Elaine R. 1993. *Haydn and the Classical Variation*. Cambridge, MA: Harvard University Press.
Sisman, Elaine R. 2008. "Six of One: The Opus Concept in the Eighteenth Century." In *The Century of Bach and Mozart: Perspectives on Historiography, Composition, Theory, and Performance*, edited by Sean Gallagher and Thomas Forrest Kelly, 79–107. Cambridge, MA: Harvard University Department of Music.

Spitzer, Michael. 2004. *Metaphor and Musical Thought*. Chicago: University of Chicago Press.

Straus, Joseph N. 2006. "Normalizing the Abnormal: Disability in Music and Music Theory." *Journal of the American Musicological Society* 59: 113–184.

Straus, Joseph N. 2008. "Disability and 'Late Style' in Music." *The Journal of Musicology Journal of Musicology* 25: 3–45.

Straus, Joseph N. 2011. *Extraordinary Measures: Disability in Music*. New York: Oxford University Press.

Temperley, Nicholas. 1991. *Haydn: "The Creation."* New York: Cambridge University Press.

Webster, James. 1991. *Haydn's "Farewell" Symphony and the Idea of Classical Style*. New York: Cambridge University Press.

Wheelock, Gretchen A. 1992. *Haydn's Ingenious Jesting with Art: Contexts of Musical Wit and Humor*. New York: Schirmer.

Wightman, W. P. D., and J. C. Bryce. 1980. *Adam Smith: Essays on Philosophical Subjects*. Oxford: Clarendon Press.

CHAPTER 30

MUSIC AND THE LABYRINTH OF MELANCHOLY

Traditions and Paradoxes in C. P. E. Bach and Beethoven

ELAINE SISMAN

It was the best of temperaments, it was the worst of temperaments; it was the condition closest to the madness that was raving mania; it was the condition closest to the madness that was raving genius; it controlled a powerful memory, it suffered a weak digestion; it rose to the joy of grief, it sank into the ennui of grieving. . . . In short, it was both "loathèd" melancholy and "divinest" melancholy, and it caused more rivers of ink to be spilled, perhaps, than tears.

This essay seeks to recover an extended moment in Enlightenment melancholy, a period in which the eighteenth-century mind was capacious enough to hold many contradictory ideas about melancholy simultaneously.[1] Vestiges of the old system of temperaments and humors persisted, in an increasingly metaphorical sense, throughout the era. Long after people stopped believing in the existence of black bile, its metaphors of darkness and weight characterized the melancholy character. Medical texts described melancholy as a chronic condition that could become acute—that is, could turn into mania—while new mechanical explanations of the circulation of fluids gave way to newer theories of nerve contractions in the midcentury. Legacies of antiquity and the Middle Ages continued to associate melancholy with the philosopher, artist, or genius, on the one hand, and with a heightened memory and sense of time, on the other. A person might fall prey to ennui, obsessive contemplation of a single subject, a depression of spirits. Finally, a developing sense of individual psychology and an anthropology of character types marked the years around 1800.

Some of the original contradictions lay not with opposing causes, nosologies, typologies, or treatments, but actually within the structure of the melancholy experience itself. Because melancholy was originally conceived as an imbalance, it could be described as a tendency, or a point along a continuum that could move in either direction. During the years of overlapping and incommensurable medical hypotheses, an aesthetic and social turn toward sensibility and solitude after 1750 charted an increasingly labyrinthine interior geography, so that the point occupied by the melancholic began to move on its own, by means of an Ariadne's thread of exploration. Simultaneous senses of stasis and seeking characterized the more paradoxical of these tendencies.

Remarkably, a few instrumental pieces by C. P. E. Bach and Beethoven weave a consciously melancholic identity, partly by trading on these paradoxes: Bach's "Dialogue between a Melancholicus and Sanguineus" (a trio sonata of 1749), his "Farewell to My Silbermann Clavier" (a rondo of 1781), and Beethoven's *La Malinconia* (the finale of his string quartet op. 18 no. 6 of 1800). Over the course of a half-century, these pieces register as well as construct a profound change in conceptions of a melancholy subjectivity. The "Dialogue," steeped in the characteristics of the temperaments, ventriloquizes a move from difference and mutual incomprehension to discovery of common ground and musical accommodation. The "Farewell" expresses the brooding sensibility and obsession of the composer in old age as well as the "joy of grief." And *La Malinconia* brings the melancholic's reflective powers—absorbing both fixed contemplation and the search for solutions to neural disturbance—into a labyrinth uniting psychology and physiology, history and criticism: at once the metaphoric labyrinth of obsession, lost bearings, and fear; the Christian labyrinth of error with the devil as Minotaur in the center; the musical labyrinth of harmonic difficulty; and the anatomical labyrinth of the inner ear.

These striking examples invite questions as to what other kinds of music are caught in the same web: what are the musical markers of "the melancholy consciousness"—or at least "the consciousness of melancholy"—within this particular span of music-historical time? Do varieties of sadness or contemplation always constitute the melancholy object? Bach, Haydn, and Beethoven (among others) wrote slow movements labeled *mesto* (melancholy or mournful); passages of instrumental recitative by Bach and Haydn imply a dark-hued speaking voice; Dittersdorf's brief portrait of a "Malinconico" in D minor begins with a lament bass, as does Mozart's untitled string quartet in D minor, K. 421 ("subtitled" with a lament for Dido by the theorist Momigny in 1806); Bach's very late F-sharp minor Fantasy of 1787, in the version for piano and violin, is titled "C. P. E. Bachs Empfindungen" with the direction "Sehr traurig und ganz langsam." (The better-known version for solo keyboard lacks these indications.) Do the melancholy qualities in these pieces survive the composer's verbal cues? Works in the melancholy tradition do not always connect easily to other dolorous works and may even be resistant to interpretation in purely affective terms.[2]

The uneasy mix of physiology, psychology, and biography required to chart the experience of historical individuals whose melancholy may be linked to creativity, or for whom its disabling aspects did not necessarily apply, at least partly accounts for the difficulty in separating the melancholic from the representation of that melancholy in art. To assume that the portrait of melancholy subjectivity is the composer's own requires making the correlation between expression and self-expression. The labyrinth as a metaphorical site of experience, then, will emerge as an imaginative hinge between those poles, performing the work that might at once represent, work through, and overcome the sense of melancholy as disability.

The Melancholy Tradition to 1800

In its title, Bach's "Dialogue between a Melancholicus and Sanguineus" clearly refers to the theory of temperaments, the longest-surviving strand in the history of melancholy, descending from the ancient Hippocratic belief in four humors, later called temperaments by Galen, in which human health was defined as an equilibrium among four substances—black bile, yellow bile, phlegm, and blood—with both illnesses and character-types determined by the preponderance of one or another (Klibansky, Panofsky, and Saxl 1964, 13; Arikha 2007). What emerged, finally, in Greek thought, was the well-known system correlating the melancholic's black bile with earth/autumn/dry/cold; the choleric's yellow bile with fire/summer/dry/hot; the sanguinic's blood with air/spring/moist/hot; and the phlegmatic's phlegm with water/winter/moist/cold (Jackson 1986, 9). These categories were correlated as well with the Four Ages of Man, and even with the times of day. Casanova, in the 1797 Preface to his *Memoirs*, wrote, "I have had every temperament one after the other, the phlegmatic in childhood, the sanguine in youth, and later the choleric, and now [age 72] I have the melancholic which will probably not leave me any more" (Klibansky et al. 1964, 122). More subtle but still recoverable is the outline of the four temperaments within the "All the world's a stage" monologue of Jaques, the caricature of fashionable melancholy in Shakespeare's *As You Like It* (II, vii). Where Jaques famously speaks of the Seven Ages of Man, we may with a slight bit of tinkering (that is, by leaving out the "mewling and puking infant") boil down the Ages as follows: melancholic in early life, from "whining schoolboy . . . creeping like a snail" to "sighing," "woeful" lover; then the choleric, as the soldier "sudden and quick in quarrel"; then the phlegmatic, as the justice with "fair round belly" full of "wise saws"; then the sanguinic enjoying his retirement. Finally the melancholic returns in a second childhood of "mere oblivion, / Sans teeth, sans eyes, sans taste, sans everything."

To those inclined to a positive view of melancholy, its principal strength is the serious pleasure of the intellect, and the thread of "melancholy and the mental faculties" begins with Saturn.[3] Arab cosmography of the ninth century had added the planetary connections to the temperaments, so that Saturn—farthest, coldest, darkest, slowest—governed the melancholic. In mythology, Saturn was a complex monarch conflating, among other things, the preclassical Greek deity of agriculture Kronos with Chronos, or Time, a first principle of the universe: the scythe of Kronos/Chronos harvested both wheat and men.[4] Burton's compendious *Anatomy of Melancholy* (1621) stressed the melancholic's heightened awareness of time (Lyons 1971, 149), and from the Middle Ages through the eighteenth century, the melancholic was thought to be predisposed to excellent memory. This vestige of humoral theory assumed that the dry and cold portions of the melancholics' brains retained images much longer (Yates 1969). However, they were also prey to a hot form of black bile, leading to a capricious memory, in which very vivid images, or *phantasmata*, come flooding in. As Albertus Magnus put it, in his commentary on Aristotle's memory treatise (*De memoria ed reminiscentia*): "The *phantasmata* move such men more than any others. . . . This mobility confers reminiscence, which is investigation" (quoted in Yates 1969, 80). By "investigation," Albertus meant the process of "tracking down" what has been "set aside" through the memory; it is a conscious process that occurs through the association of ideas (Carruthers 1990).[5] In the eighteenth century, when the association of ideas was an important scientific and poetic category, vivid images called *phantasia* were considered the workings of the imagination in which absent things were seen to be present (Sisman 1998, 2000).[6] The connection of time and memory in the mind of a melancholic rounded out the picture of the deep thinker.

The "inspired" or even "manic" side of melancholy may go back to Plato's *Phaedrus*, which adopted the theory of humors in asserting that illness reflects a disproportion in such substances, and that mental illness in particular reveals a "movement from balance into excess, the *hyperbole*." In particular, he distinguished between "morbid and divine manias," since divine mania is genius itself, imparted by the gods to oracles, tragic sufferers like Oedipus, and seekers like Socrates; Goethe described the poet, in *West-East Divan*, as "he who acts in madness" (Tellenbach 1980, 8–9, 216n21). The detailed consideration of melancholy in [pseudo-]Aristotle's *Problems* (XXX, §1) proceeds from the related question: "Why is it that all those men who have become extraordinary in philosophy, politics, poetry or the arts are obviously melancholics, and some to such an extent that they are seized by the illnesses that come from black bile?" (Aristotle 2011, 277). The discussion turns on the degree of heat rather than the quantity of the bile, and the resulting tendency toward the melancholic was by no means the same as true melancholia, an actual state of illness for which proposed cures ranged from the dietary (because of accompanying abdominal difficulties) to the drastic (e.g., blood-letting). Indeed, an excess of *phantasia* might mean that one is delusional. In Boerhaave's celebrated *Aphorisms* (1708), published with his pupil Gerhard van Swieten's *Commentaries* between 1755 and 1773, melancholy is considered a chronic (nicely called "tedious") disease, because it leads neither to health nor to death; if it increases in severity, however, it can lead to mania, or raving madness (Van Swieten 1776, 10:189–190). Van Swieten takes care to differentiate mania, in which one sees what one is supposed to see but doesn't think correctly about it, from frenzy, in which "things absent appear to be present, and things that are nowhere to be seen by others seem present to them." Van Swieten also glosses Boerhaave's causes of melancholy, bringing them in line with the intellectual preoccupations of the day: the first cause is "an intense application of the mind, both day and night, upon one and the same subject"; Van Swieten comments, "It is certain that a philosopher, by profoundly meditating for several hours, is more weakened by it than if he had labored his body with brisk exercise for so long a time." Obsession is not always so admired, however (Davis 2008).

After Marsilio Ficino, who more than any other Florentine Neo-Platonist sought to revive the connection between melancholy and creativity or genius, the melancholic as noble contemplator could take many forms (Babb 1951, 60). Writers in the seventeenth and eighteenth centuries who would praise the dark and subtle nuances of melancholy linked to thought, art, the Muses, and nature, included Milton in "Il Penseroso" of about 1632, Thomas Warton in "The Pleasures of Melancholy" of 1745, and Kant in "Observations on the Feeling of the Beautiful and Sublime" of 1764 (Kant [1764] 1960). Burton, who like Ficino and many other writers wrote to cure his own melancholy (one could adduce here the names Montaigne, Burton, Samuel Johnson, Kierkegaard, and Walter Benjamin), devoted the longest chapter by far in the section on "causes of melancholy" to "love of learning, overmuch study, and why of all other men scholars are most subject to it" (Burton 1968, I:300). The strongest statement along these lines came from Albrecht von Haller, the influential Swiss scientist and poet of the eighteenth century, who insisted that "intellect amounts to a guarantee of unhappiness" (Guthke 1983, 169).

The contemplator is certainly the dominant iconographic image of the melancholic: the typically female figure of Melancholy sits with fixed and lowered gaze, and other doleful contemplators like Jeremiah and Mary Magdalene and the many *Vanitas* paintings may be assimilated to that tradition. (See the images reproduced in Klibansky et al. 1964; Bandmann 1960; Wittkower and Wittkower 1963; Wagner-Egelhaaf 1997). Dürer's celebrated engraving *Melencolia 1* (1514) surrounds its brooding central figure with signs of mathematical and architectural activity, including a magic square.[7] The thoughtful side of the melancholy character was clearly what attracted Kant, who all but announced that this temperament was *primus inter pares* because "genuine virtue ... harmonizes most with the melancholy frame of mind" (Kant [1764] 1960, 63). Writing about the temperaments as character types in his *Observations on the Feelings of the Beautiful and Sublime* (1764) and in the *Anthropology from a Pragmatic Point of View* (1798), Kant's description of the melancholy character puts it well into line with the idea of "moral characters" promulgated by English and German "moral weeklies," character types in the theatre (going back to Theophrastus and La Bruyère) like the "absent-minded man" or the "miser"; Gellert, for example, had described the "melancholy man of virtue" (Kant [1798] 1974, Smeed 1985, Martens 1968, Schneider 1976). In both treatises, Kant casts the melancholic not as someone who is dejected, but as a profound thinker and perceiver. His main point in the earlier work is that the melancholic "has above all *a feeling for the sublime*" (Kant [1764] 1960, 64). However, his condition can "deteriorate," so that "earnestness inclines toward dejection, devotion toward fanaticism, love of freedom to enthusiasm. ... He is in danger of becoming a visionary or a crank" (66–67). He is also prone to ennui, an age-old failing once associated with *acedia*, or the medieval sin of sloth (Kuhn 1976). In the *Anthropology* (Kant [1798] 1974), the principal attributes of the melancholic are primarily set in relief against its opposite "temperament of feeling," the sanguinic. Where the sanguinic is superficial and playful, the melancholic is deep, especially in a tendency to create deeply rooted sense impressions (*Empfindungen*) and to brood on them. The resulting pensiveness and pessimism, while not necessarily producing sadness, may "benumb his vital force"

(153). Kant's *Anthropology*, then, looks at temperament as a psychological template for particular human predispositions to character.

If psychology and anthropology gave temperament theory a kind of afterlife in the eighteenth century, organic theories of medicine and evolving theories of nerves refined it in a somewhat different fashion.[8] An influential figure in German medicine of the early eighteenth century was the prolific Georg Ernst Stahl, who established Halle as a center of medical research and writing. His son of the same name (1713–1772) was a doctor at the court of Berlin and member of Bach's literary-musical circle there (Miesner 1933, Richards 2006). The elder Stahl considered melancholy both a disease of the humors and a moral failing. His views linked the reactions and health of spirit and body in a close psychological connection, and opposed mechanical views that discussed chemical imbalances with no relationship to the state of the soul. (This moralistic tone was to return in the works of Heinroth [*On Disturbances of the Soul*, 1818], which introduced the term "psychosomatic"; Jackson 1986, 155–157; Marx 2008, 325). Younger Halle doctors, including Ernst Nicolai (1722–1802), took varying positions on such mechanical and "organic" approaches, ultimately striking a mean (Zelle 2001, 8–9). Nicolai (1745) wrote on the connections between medicine and music, comparing the fibers "out of which we are woven—arteries, muscles, and nerves," to the strings stretched tautly in a musical instrument, comparing the "tones" made by their "vibrations" to human feelings, and comparing health to consonance and illness to dissonance. (The same complex of metaphors is explored in Blake Howe's and Samantha Bassler's essays in this volume.)

With the growing psychological focus, according to Johanna Geyer-Kordesch (1990, 84), Stahl's followers "advanced medical claims that turned the later Enlightenment toward Sensibility." In this they were abetted by Albrecht von Haller's theory of irritability (1752), in which he was able to differentiate between the contractions of muscles and the sensibility of nerves by demonstrating that only muscles contract. Yet nerves were still widely understood to go into spasm, and in 1765 a new division of melancholy into "humoral" and "nervous" melancholy was offered by Annäeus Carl (Anne-Charles) Lorry of Paris (Starobinski 2012, 75–76; Foucault 1965, 123–124). In his Latin treatise (translated into German in 1770), nervous melancholy is an illness of the fibers found throughout the organism: after an excessive spasm contracts them, weakness and languor follow. This leads to alternations of convulsive movements and debility. A healthy organism thus consists of humors in balance, on the one hand, as well as having nerves that should be neither too taut nor too slack but in equilibrium throughout the body (Straus 2011, 33). The branching nerve fibers—controversy was generated over whether these were "filled with fluid" or whether impulses were electric, decided conclusively in favor of the latter by Galvani in 1791—thus created a new figural mapping of the body's responses onto the closed system of a labyrinthine structure. As an anatomical and medical model, real nerves certainly outranked conjectural humors, but both maintained a powerful metaphoric hold on the discourse of melancholy.

Temperaments in Conflict: C. P. E. Bach, Trio Sonata ("Dialogue between a Melancholicus and Sanguineus")

The intellectual state of play, so to speak, around Bach's trio sonata pointed to a context of temperament theory and the moral choice inherent even in bodily mechanisms. And it appeared at the end of a frenzied period of scholarly studies of melancholy: 160 doctoral dissertations on melancholy were written at European universities during the seventeenth century, 101 during the first half of the eighteenth century alone; but in the second half of the eighteenth century, *nine* (bibliography in Lambrecht 1996). The climate in which the trio sonata was written still conduced to the Latin names, the didactic and straightforward rhetorical conception, and the balance of temperaments in the piece.[9]

The Preface to Bach's Trio Sonata explains aspects of the piece, then explains why it does so. Bach first states that this is an experiment, to "express" by instruments what might ordinarily require a text, then describes the entire course of the piece, giving it a very clear program. He identifies the proportional relationship between the Melancholicus's Allegretto in ¢ time and the Sanguineus's Presto in 3/8 and issues an injunction against adding ornaments. Finally, he returns to his first point to insist that the ensuing list of forty-two annotations detailing the meaning of the "musical expressions" are needed for the less educated and he hopes to avoid "mockery" on this account (Bach 2011). This moment of special pleading suggests that Bach knew he was courting skepticism or worse; was this set of labeled expressions the "ridiculous instructions" he referred to in his Autobiography? (Newman 1965, 371) That he did not escape is shown in a letter of October 21, 1773, when he declined Gerstenberg's request that he write keyboard sonatas based on Psalm texts. Bach responded: "I remember when, many years ago, I had my *Sanguineus and Cholericus* [*sic*] printed, that I was not exactly insensitive when a good friend said certain things to me about it in jest, which he did not really mean maliciously but which did not please me. How weak we are!" (Clark, 1997, 42). Even Bach-enthusiast Charles Burney commented that "with all his powers of invention, melody, and modulation, the opinions of the disputants [in the trio-sonata] remained as obscure and unintelligible as the warbling of larks and linnets" (Helm 1972, 292).

As is evident in Figure 30.1, the disputants have only one issue to discuss: whether the Melancholicus will consent to be browbeaten by the Sanguineus into abandoning his gloomy ways—sluggish tempo, muted voice, minor key, ambiguous harmonic progressions, *empfindsam* downbeat trills, little sighs, pathetic intervals like the diminished seventh—and share in the general air of optimistic frivolity imparted by the Sanguineus's characteristic triplet dance rhythm, major key, and quick tempo. The use of the general pause to underscore questions (as at letters **a** and **f**) and to give space for changes of heart (as at **k**) enhances the air of

FIGURE 30.1 C. P. E. Bach, Trio in C minor, W. 161/1, "Dialogue between a *Melancholicus* and a *Sanguineus*," first movement, mm. 1–52.

FIGURE 30.2 C. P. E. Bach, Trio in C minor, W. 161/1, "Dialogue between a *Melancholicus* and a *Sanguineus*," first movement, mm. 225–266; second movement, m. 1.

conversation. The Melancholicus asks questions perhaps because he is interested in dialogue; he is thoughtful after all, as well as courteous. The Sanguineus, on the other hand, is rude and unpersuasive, and clearly mocks the Melancholicus by sarcastically speeding up his lines (as at **m**). The movement is unable to end decisively because the two sides cannot agree, and the Melancholicus falls asleep on his questioning half-cadence to the sound of impotent laughter from his opponent (see Figure 30.2).

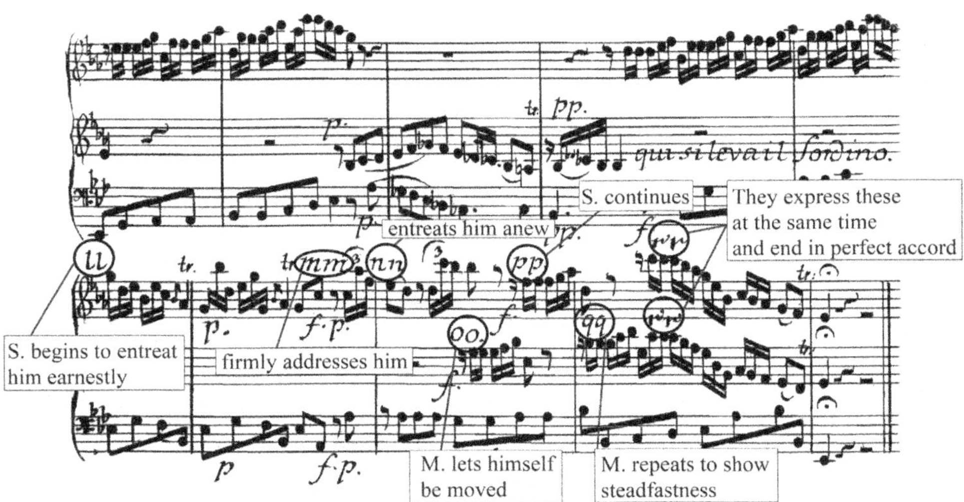

FIGURE 30.3 C. P. E. Bach, Trio in C minor, W. 161/1, "Dialogue between a *Melancholicus* and a *Sanguineus*," second movement, mm. 39–47.

Significant in the second movement is that the Melancholicus's initial "grumbling" gives way to a more "serious utterance," ending in a little sequence in a quasi-recitative style (Figure 30.3). We now realize that the Sanguineus has had virtually no rhythmic variety—in fact the Melancholicus is much closer to Bach's own style! Indeed, not until the very last measures does the Sanguineus stop insulting and start entreating: he unleashes the only truly persuasive thing he's said so far, a cadence figure with some real leaps and twists followed by a surefire subdominant chord, in recitative style (at **mm**), followed by his first imploring sigh motives (at **oo**). When he merges his frivolous dance rhythm with some real meaning the Melancholicus can finally support him. Thus, it's not that the Melancholicus has been so drearily recalcitrant but that the Sanguineus realizes that he has something to learn too.

In the final movement, therefore, both characters get what they want (Figure 30.4). The Melancholicus can play a melody full of rhythmic variety, in a minor key, with dynamic contrast and affective slurs. The Sanguineus gets triplets, a fast tempo, and the proof that his hard work and optimism have paid off. But Bach also gets what he wants: the serious (*ernsthaft*) quality that he says is the essence of German music. He has also shown a way for the deep-thinking Melancholic to gain the energy he needs in order not to sink into ennui. Within a year of his stubborn response to Gerstenberg, his Berlin friend Sulzer published the second double volume of his massive arts encyclopedia, the *Allgemeine Theorie der schönen Künste* (1774), in which the article on the sonata, written by J. A. P. Schulz, praised Bach's Trio Sonata as exemplary of the kind of "passionate conversations in tone" that this genre capable of "depicting wordless sentiments" can produce.[10]

FIGURE 30.4 C. P. E. Bach, Trio in C minor, W. 161/1, "Dialogue between a *Melancholicus* and a *Sanguineus*," mvt. 3: mm. 1–18.

Melancholy Reflection: C. P. E. Bach, "Farewell to My Silbermann Clavier"

The *Farewell to My Silbermann Clavier* represents an entirely different way of conceiving of melancholy, and reflects a changed context for the experience of melancholy. In the first place, the composer is inside the piece, which allows him to express his own feelings: he had sold his beloved instrument to a young nobleman, Dietrich Ewald von Grotthus. In an era that encouraged wallowing in one's sorrowful feelings, even intensifying them for further enjoyment, the "joy of grief" pushed sensibility to extremes (Bredvold 1962). Thus Klopstock wrote a poem imagining a still-living friend dead and in his coffin in order to bring himself to tears (Balet 1936, 318). A letter of September 18, 1773 from the young poet and publisher Voss (who visited Bach, and to whom Bach contributed songs for his *Musenalmanach*) to his fiancée details the long night spent sorrowing over the imminent departure of two friends:

> On every face was melancholy. . . . I was urged to play the piano. Perhaps others find that it alleviates their distress, but for me it expressed again every painful emotion (*Affect*), it opened still deeper wounds. . . . Then we decided to dissipate our grief through song; we chose Miller's *Abschiedslied*. Now all pretense was abandoned: the tears streamed and the voices stopped one by one. . . . We swore eternal friendship and hugged each other. . . . Now we wanted to stop holding back our sorrow, we tried to make ourselves more unhappy, we sang the Farewell Song again, and stayed with

> it until the end. There was loud wailing. . . . Then it was time. . . . It was the most terrible night I have ever had. (Balet 1936, 317–318)

The joy of grief was mentioned in Burke's somewhat earlier treatise on the sublime ([1757] 1968, 37) and Karl Moritz's psychological novel *Anton Reiser*, where it is also recast as "the joy of tears," and it found an echo in Goethe's poem *Wonne der Wehmut* ("Dry not! dry not! / Tears of unhappy love!") and J. G. Zimmermann's popular and widely translated book *Über die Einsamkeit* (*On Solitude*, 1784–85). Even gardens became shrines to melancholy reflection, with artful ruins and gravestones encouraging solitude and nostalgic memory of times past (Hajós 1989).

The image of the farewell connects to the trope of transitoriness (*Vergänglichkeit*) and its corresponding melancholic reflection about time, highlighted in the nostalgic tone of the pastoral idyll; its characteristic motif is the setting sun. Melancholy reflection enabled one to put one's affairs in order (Dwyer 1991, 181–182). It prompted a harnessing of regret to creativity. We can see in Bach's life from 1778 on a desire to set out his legacy: he referred to his *Heilig* of 1776 as his "swan song" in the genre, something that would keep his memory alive after his death (letter of September 16, 1778; Clark 1997, 125). He began to collect older and newer works for publication in the *Kenner und Liebhaber* series, which began in 1779. My sense is that in 1778, at age sixty-four, he realized he was only a year away from the age at which his father died, and that his father had systematically created a legacy in his last years. This could only have been exacerbated by the death of his beloved son—and namesake of his father—in the same year. Sending away the celebrated clavichord to Baron von Grotthus may well have been part of these recognitions. The emblems of farewell in the rondo almost require us to imagine Bach playing in solitude on a nearly inaudible instrument, thus multiplying and even overdetermining its appropriateness for melancholy reflection. [11]

The Labyrinth

Bach's Farewell Rondo, I suggest, may be the first appearance in instrumental music of a labyrinth as the emblem of a melancholy consciousness, in its paradoxical aspects of enclosure and wandering (Starobinski 2012, 617; see also Wagner-Egelhaaf, 210).[12] The figure of the labyrinth had long been invoked metaphorically by writers on melancholy, and was also sometimes depicted in paintings of melancholics. Robert Burton described the entire typology of melancholy as a labyrinth (Burton 1621). The labyrinth is also invoked to describe the winding and frustrating ways of "cares," "sorrows," and "woes," of "doubts and errors," of "wearying" philosophers' quibbles. Burton seems to himself as another Theseus, trying to slay the Minotaur of melancholy, always aware of how pleasant melancholy fantasies and delusions may be, which keep melancholics "run[ning] on earnestly in this labyrinth of anxious and solicitous melancholy meditations . . . winding and unwinding themselves as so many clocks" (Vicari 1989, 166).

A labyrinth, properly speaking, is not the same as a maze: there are no false alleys and dead ends, just the circular motion through a pattern with only one way in and one way out (Kern 2000). It is technically not possible to get lost in a labyrinth: the only dead end is the center, where one turns around. However, it becomes clear from descriptions of the experience of the labyrinth that what stands in one's way is the psychological oppressiveness of the high walls (lending the feeling of imprisonment) and of not knowing how close one is to the center, and hence to the way out—indeed beginning to doubt that there *is* a way out. (Theseus did after all require a thread from Ariadne.) Karl Moritz's "psychological novel" *Anton Reiser*, published in parts between 1784 and 1790 (for his own journal of empirical psychology) and based on his own life, has frequent recourse to the metaphor of the labyrinth for the confusion and misery of the world that mirrors the misery of Reiser's fate, for the frequently hopeless journeys that mirror his interior quest, and for the frequent feeling that no Ariadne's thread is to be found (Moritz 1996, 1997; Wagner-Egelhaaf, 1997). In *Anton Reiser*, the labyrinth is sometimes called up as he travels to another city in order to solve his problems. Each of the cities—Hanover, Bremen, Gotha, Erfurt—is walled and gated, and he must be allowed in by the single entrance. Then he goes up on the ramparts to look down at the city, and the image of the city's towers, especially the four towers of Hanover, suggests that the labyrinth seen from above makes perfect sense and can be navigated successfully.[13] But sometimes Reiser—the name means traveler—experiences the labyrinth even walking through cornfields. When he is inside the labyrinth, he cannot find his way and deludes himself with enthusiasm (*Schwärmerei*) as he nourishes vain hopes. Every possible nuance of melancholy takes hold in his emotions—sadness, fear, boredom, enervation, the desire for solitude and sleep, dislocations of his ideas of place and time, present and past.

Far from being a dead metaphor, then, the labyrinth is an important psychological and poetic figure. As myriad medical and psychological studies over the centuries attest, the melancholic's mental process is an attempt to find order out of disorder, and the confusion of the turnings of the labyrinth in which one seems always to be retracing one's steps nicely encapsulates that obsessive idea. The labyrinth, then, is the ultimate paradoxical emblem, embodying chaos and order, circle and thread, the infinite and limitation. Labyrinths as theological symbols found their way into music from the fifteenth century on, as documented in Craig Wright's book *The Warrior and the Maze: Symbols in Architecture, Theology, and Music* (2001). Wright points out the uses of the labyrinth as a Christian metaphor for the journey of the soul, in which the devil to be vanquished lurks in the heart of the labyrinth. J. S. Bach's *Kleines harmonisches Labyrinth* is the only one actually to have an Introitus, Centrum, and Exitus. Others use the term to reflect the process of modulating through many keys (Marin Marais and Friedrich Suppig), to present consecutive pieces in nearly all the keys (Fischer's *Ariadne musica*), or, more trivially, to refer to a piece of great technical difficulty (Locatelli's Concerto Op. 3 No. 12, described as "easy to get into but difficult to get out of"). Lurking in the midpoint of Bach's "Introitus" and at the heart of the Marais—and as we shall see, Beethoven's *La Malinconia*—is the key of the tritone, the point of furthest remove around the circle of fifths from where one starts. Wright explains that the "devil" (the *diabolus in musica*) serves as the Christian replacement for the Minotaur at the heart of the Cretan labyrinth. Because the tritone is also the center of the octave, the figure may signify in pieces without religious content.

Although its usage in music criticism is sometimes merely poetic, as when Herder in 1800 referred to music as "a pleasing labyrinth of tones" (Grey 1996, 196), the musical labyrinth has the general sense of a "maze of difficulty" in harmonies, modulations, and counterpoint (Hayes 1999, 188; Riley 2002, 27). When Schubart extolled the rigor and intricacy of Buxtehude's fugues, he used the image this way: "He executes the plainest theme with such correctness, weaves it in such a labyrinthine way through and through, and always finds the exit through this labyrinth so correctly that one must be astonished by it" (Schubart 1789, 199). Here the image of weaving with the thread of Ariadne brings to mind the web of Arachne, as vividly illustrated by the spiderweb above the sorrowing woman in an image by Caspar David Friedrich usually called "Melancholy" (1801; woodcut by Christian Friedrich reproduced in Klibansky 1964, and at websites of the British Museum and Philadelphia Museum of Art). The circular design of many labyrinths offers a related symbol, as does Heinichen's first published accounts of the arrangement of the keys in a "musical circle." Introduced in his 1711 treatise on thoroughbass (Lester 1989, 108), Heinichen's expanded and better-known *Der Generalbass in der Composition* (1728, 837) gives a diagram of the circle of keys that not only reveals the great chain of major-minor tonality in circular form, but also explicitly connects modulating through that circle as though moving through a labyrinth (914).[14] Forkel's review of C. P. E. Bach's late chamber music approves of the way he handles a transition through an enharmonic progression using a diminished seventh chord: "It's not enough to make a bold progression (*kühnen Schritt*). . . . You have to have strength . . . in order to *uncoil* from the Labyrinth into which you have boldly gone, and you can't let the listener know that it's costing you any effort to come out again" (Forkel 1778, 289). C. P. E. Bach himself does not refer to the labyrinth, only the "musical circle," though he asserts elsewhere in the chapter on the free fantasia in Part II of the *Essay* that "As a means of reaching the most distant keys more quickly and with agreeable suddenness no chord is more convenient and fruitful than the seventh chord with diminished seventh and fifth" (Bach 1762, 335; Bach 1949, 438). Mattheson too was partial to the diminished seventh, saying that unlike regular sevenths which had to be prepared, the diminished seventh could enter unannounced "as though it had the golden key" (Mattheson 1739, 292).

A Labyrinthine Paradox: The Idyllic Center

Bach's *Abschied* is a strikingly original rondo showing, as he wrote to Grotthus, that this overpopular genre could be "plaintive" (Clark 1997, 176); Richard Kramer even calls it a "syntactics of *Empfindsamkeit*" (Kramer 2006, 21). The melody descends and descends, like the downcast eyes and slumping body of personified Dame Melancholy; indeed as Ellen Rosand notes, the descending tetrachord ostinato of seventeenth-century laments "in its unremitting descent, its gravity, the pattern offers an analogue of obsession and depression—perceptible as the expression of unrelieved suffering" (Rosand 1991, 370). Bach's bass line may furnish the material for the opening of Beethoven's own "farewell" sonata, *Das Lebewohl*, Op. 81a, twenty-eight years later. But Bach's initial descent, in five first-inversion triads (mm. 1–2), lends the theme a particularly unsettled air, and the inversion prevents the descending bass from sounding too much like a lament *topos*; only with the first root-position chord, the dominant seventh in m. 3, do we even know what key we're in (Figure 30.5a). Even though most segments are four measures long, every detail moves against regularity. The only two four-plus-four periods are the opening statement of the theme and the idyllic tonic-major episode at the center of the piece (Figure 30.5b), the latter thrown into relief by its length and "presence," by its occupation of the highest register after the very low B-minor statement (the first away from the tonic) just before. Exactly halfway through the movement (m. 43 of a total 84), this peaceful vision is the center of the labyrinth. (See the chart in Figure 30.5c).

Far from being the devil, or an evil to be overcome, here the center is the vision of happiness that playing the Silbermann clavichord represents; outside the center is the bleak winding world of gloom without it. Before that passage, none of the episodes can do more than reach a half cadence. And after the idyll, all the episodes consist of enharmonic chord progressions with the upper voice stuck and virtually unable to move. These increasingly anguished changes beat against that upper note with powerful dynamics struggling between forte and piano, reinforcing the sense of nerves contracting and releasing, like those of Lorry's "nervous" melancholic, with the jarring accentuations recalling the spasmodic movements of a creature caught in a web. It is difficult even to recognize that the last three A's embody a series of "returns": they recapitulate precisely the register and figuration of the first three as the passage through the labyrinth is turning back toward home. But the closer to home he gets the more Bach resists (Figure 30.5d). The impression of wandering while being at the same time tightly bounded becomes ever stronger, as the chords press against the recalcitrant barely-moving upper voice, first on downbeats (m. 57), then on off-beats (m. 72), finally together with the upper voice stuck on B♭ (m. 79) just before the final dying *Bebung*.

The image of the labyrinth is powerfully invoked here, with a strong feeling of descending into and emerging upward. Linkages are created by association—the repeated upper pitches and enharmonic recasting. At the end, Bach knows, is silence. *This* labyrinth, in short, is a place the composer does not wish to leave: the thread of his theme keeps emerging, but the end of the piece means, in effect, the end of the instrument, so he keeps plunging back into it, singing the *Abschiedslied* again and

FIGURE 30.5A C. P. E. Bach, *Farewell to My Silbermann Clavier*, mm. 1–4.

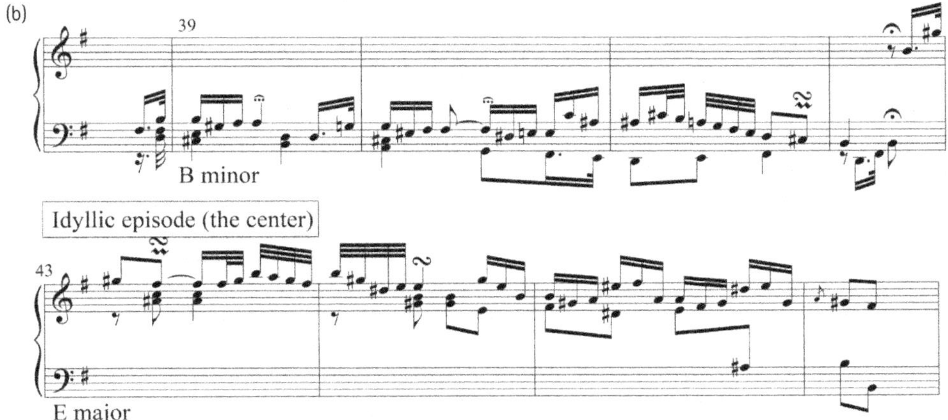

FIGURE 30.5B C. P. E. Bach, *Farewell to My Silbermann Clavier*, mm. 39–46.

(c)

	①								②	③		④						
Theme:	A1	A2	[B]	A1	[C]	A2	[D]	A1	A2	[E]	tr.	A1	*	A1	A2	**	A2	***
Key:																		
refrain:	e (V)	e (i)		e		e		e	b			g♯	~	e (N_6)	e	~	e	~
episode:			D→G		C		F/G			E								
Register:	Mid	Higher			Highest	Mid	Higher		Low	Highest		Mid		Mid	Higher		Highest	
Embell:	unvar.					unvar.			unvar.			unvar.		unvar.				
Measure:			9	19		27	31	35	39	43	51	55		63	69		75	

FIGURE 30.5C Thematic chart of C. P. E. Bach, *Farewell to My Silbermann Clavier.*

again. Moments of energy and vividness, together with the idyllic ethereal moment in E major, offer a striking melancholy landscape compounded of regret, solitude, and recollection. This seems to be the kind of piece that Bach claimed he would write when free to write for himself, rather than the public. From a man who once gave the advice to "give more sugar" when writing for the public, this piece almost bears the sign "No Sugar Added" (Letter of August 31, 1784; Clark 1997, 213). And it seems to emphasize the idea of "transitoriness," as the piece visits harmonic patches of both stasis and the most extreme wandering. There is a melancholy irony too in the idea of Bach as a "transitional" composer, his a style that seemed to emerge from the past and disappear before reaching the future.

FIGURE 30.5D C. P. E. Bach, *Farewell to My Silbermann Clavier,* mm. 55–84.

The Anatomy of the Labyrinth of Melancholy: Beethoven, String Quartet Op. 18, No. 6, Fourth Movement ("La Malinconia")

Beethoven's *La Malinconia* is heir to all of the worlds described above, as reflected in the labyrinth of myth, metaphor, music, and medicine. It embodies, I suggest, a process of melancholy reflection that conflates the experience of the labyrinth—its anxieties, sense of imprisonment, and necessity of continued exploration—with the vivid phantasies produced by the association of ideas. The strenuous nervous contractions evoked by the accented diminished-seventh chords furnish both the way in and the way out of the labyrinth. The entire introduction is shown in Figure 30.6. Serene reflection or pensiveness, the stasis of the opening all in B-flat with its sense of distance brought on by the horn fifth in m. 2, is disturbed by the three-note *Schleifer*, described in C. P. E. Bach's *Essay* as a figure of sadness (Bach 1753, 108). Here the Schleifer becomes the agent of neural contraction. After it, the chords become disturbed, each time jogged by the *Schleifer* into more remote areas until they come to a B minor chord in m. 12 through an enharmonic progression. The third statement of the theme in m. 9 even begins on a diminished seventh chord, the horn fifth is replaced by a diminished triad, and contrary motion banishes the earlier sense of agreement. Finally, the ascending fifths in the first two statements give way to ascending diminished fifths.

The registral and dynamic shifts of the first round of diminished seventh chords reflect the increasing tension of the experience of the labyrinth, acting like the flooding memories of phantasmata that skew the sense of time. Time turns into space, as we seem to lose our way. The clear path of the ascending line is obscured by octave and instrumental displacements, and the four consecutive diminished seventh chords in mm. 13–16 return the opening theme also in its lower register with a diminished seventh chord in m. 17. The center of the labyrinth is reached in m. 21: E minor, the key of the tritone, initiates a period of chromatic wandering in invertible counterpoint (one subject leaping up a sixth, the other comprising descending diminished-fifth leaps). This second half of the piece also conceals its ascending line, as each statement of the wandering theme begins on a higher pitch.

Beginning in m. 29, the ascending line is in a single voice, diminished triads alternating with their resolutions. But the return of the wandering theme in m. 33 is illusory as a goal, and it is another diminished seventh chord, on the cello's D♯ in m. 36, that finally furnishes the usable thread. Emerging at the end in a single line of ascending bass notes (in half steps all the way from D♯ up to A), the solution turns around the respelling of the diminished seventh chord first on D♯ (m. 36), then on F♯ (m. 39), and finally on A (m. 42), while the upper voice presents only the notes of that chord. Linear and triadic merge, the winding thread turning around as it leads out.

FIGURE 30.6 Beethoven, String Quartet op. 18 no. 6, fourth movement, *La Malinconia*, mm. 1–52.

The end of the labyrinth marks the beginning of the dance, Allegretto quasi Allegro, but we are not out of the melancholy state; we have merely, like Anton Reiser, moved into the enthusiastic (*schwärmerisch*) side of the melancholic's personality, distracted by the enjoyment of a Ländler. Much of the literature on this piece assesses how far its title extends; Forchert (1983) is one of the few to assert its presence in the Allegretto as the melancholic's mania. (It is not out of the question that Beethoven also means to refer to Bach's dialogue, with its alternations of meter and tempo, and the 3/8 matches Bach's Sanguinic.) The reemergence of the Adagio material makes this clear, as the labyrinth opens once again at the end of the recapitulation of what has thus far been a sonata form without development: at an unexpected diminished seventh chord (mm. 193–94) the serene chords of mm. 1–4 return, followed by a slightly revised version of mm. 9–12. The original bass line A♭–G–F♯ extends downward to F and E, the dominant of A minor. The Allegretto now restarts in A minor, then breaks off (like Bach's interlocutors?); the Adagio returns in the same key and nudges it down to G major, where the Allegretto restarts and manages to move back to the tonic rather quickly with a rondo-like return. Continuing with a variety of cadential iterations, this final Allegretto section seems poised for another Adagio interruption at a fermata, but it is the main theme that is newly recast in a slow tempo, with a fermata ending each phrase. This moment of reverie suggests that the contemplator and the dancer have found common ground, and they celebrate in a manic Prestissimo close.

Biographers and scholars have sometimes suggested that the melancholy in the piece is Beethoven's own, initiated by the recognition and progression of his deafness that had begun some time in the late 1790s, becoming acute in 1800, as he recounted in well-known letters to Franz Wegeler and Karl Amenda the following year.[15] Yet only biographical wishful thinking could connect *La Malinconia* to Beethoven's own situation. I propose that the labyrinth guides us to a solution. One of the first doctors Beethoven consulted was Johann Peter Frank (1745–1821), a professor of medicine and director of the Allgemeines Krankenhaus celebrated for his work on public hygiene. Frank was a patron of music in whose house Beethoven accompanied the soprano Christine Gerhardi, the first Gabriel in Haydn's *Creation* and new wife of Frank's son Joseph. Just before coming to Vienna, Frank had been professor for nine years at the University of Pavia (1785–1794), a center of research sponsored and overseen by the Hapsburg emperor. The ranking research professor of medicine in Pavia was the anatomist Antonio Scarpa (1752–1832), hired on the recommendation of Emperor Joseph II in 1783, whom Frank called a friend and a "miracle doctor" in his published autobiography (1802) and his "excellent friend" who showed that "almost all the latest discoveries of surgery owe their origin to examinations of pathological anatomy" in a later volume of his massive treatise on public health (Frank 1816, 298). Scarpa's extensive study of the comparative anatomy of the inner ear (in humans, birds, fish, amphibians, even insects and worms) led to his achievement as the first to describe the ear's membranous labyrinth, in a work of 1789 (*Anatomicæ disquisitiones de auditu et olfactu*) copiously illustrated with engravings of his own excellent drawings. This treatise went through several editions and was translated into German in 1800 (Raspe, Nuremberg), in which form

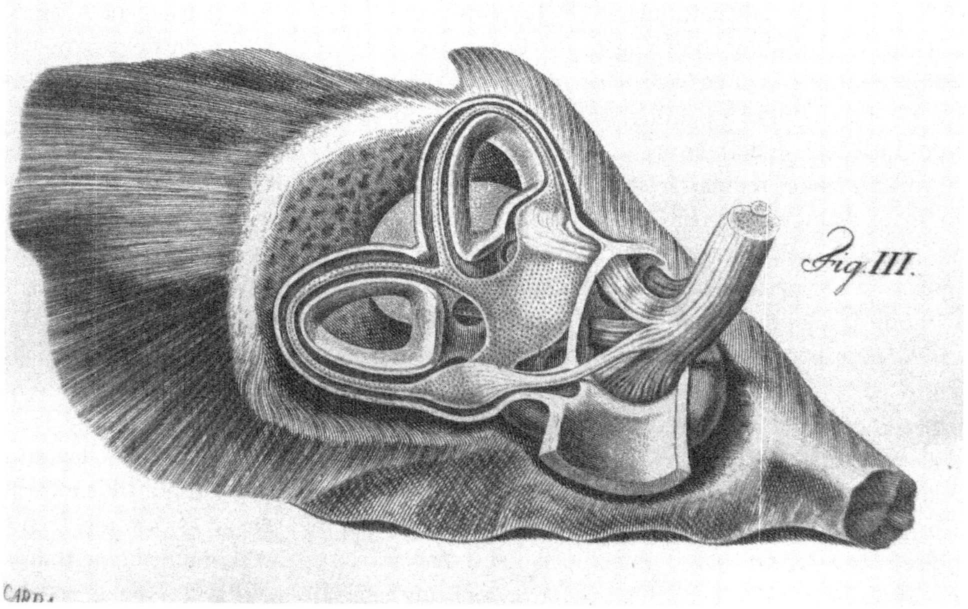

FIGURE 30.7 Antonio Scarpa, *Anatomicae disquisitiones de auditoru ed olfactu*, Table VII, figure 3: the membranous labyrinth from the side of the cranial cavity. Reproduced by permission of Archives & Special Collections, Columbia University Health Sciences Library.

it was advertised in the *Wiener Zeitung* on August 9, 1800.[16] Scarpa also described the twisting forms of the auditory and vestibular nerves in greater detail than any predecessor (Canalis et al. 2001). Figure 30.7 shows an image from Scarpa's Table VII (Fig. III), the curving arcs of the membranous labyrinth culminating in the auditory nerve as exiting thread; Figure 30.8 shows the acoustic nerve with its spiral-shaped bundle of filaments (*Faden* in the German edition). That the book had continuing relevance and significance to musicians is attested by Scarpa's biographical entry in Fétis's *Biographie universelle* (1844 ed., 8:66) in which this is the only one of his many works named, in both its Latin and German editions.

In the light of this new anatomical knowledge discovered by a colleague of Beethoven's doctor, widely publicized in the decade before the onset of his deafness (and available in Vienna during the summer he completed *La Malinconia*), Beethoven's labyrinth takes on a specific meaning beyond its brilliant tracing of the melancholy experience. It becomes a meaningful referent of what we might call, with a nod to Burton, the anatomy of the labyrinth of melancholy. Indeed, Beethoven's reference to the buzzing and hearing loss as the "demon" in his ear, in letters to Wegeler in 1801 and later in 1810, suggests an overt connection with the *diabolus in musica* lurking at the labyrinth's heart. *La Malinconia* as labyrinth is both an emblem of melancholy's tortuous thread through winding paths and a specific analogy to the structure of the inner ear. It also seems to offer cautious hope, in the distractions and pleasures of the dance.

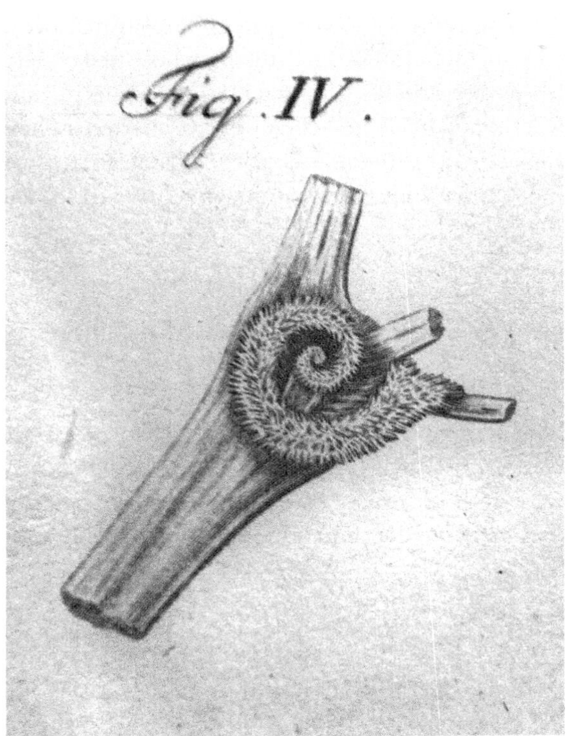

FIGURE 30.8 Antonio Scarpa, *Anatomicae disquisitiones de auditoru ed olfactu*, Table VII, figure 4: the acoustic nerve with its filaments. Reproduced by permission of Archives & Special Collections, Columbia University Health Sciences Library.

Epilogue

Images of the overlapping constructs of time, space, and memory, freedom and constraint, and imagination and the body thus merge in the symbol of the labyrinth, and do not thereafter lose their force. The history of melancholy after *La Malinconia* is outside the scope of this study, but Romantic self-absorption created newly vivid ways of writing artists' melancholy in the nineteenth century, while medical treatises increased their propensity to categorize it among the "diseases of the mind." Traditional metaphors of melancholy continued to hold sway, but the labyrinth reemerged in unexpected ways. In Susan Sontag's essay on Walter Benjamin, a habitual melancholic who described himself as born "under the sign of Saturn—the star of the slowest revolution, the planet of detours and delays," we learn that this defining aspect of his personality drew him to topics like the origins of the German *Trauerspiel*, drew him to imagine the work of memory as collapsing time and turning time into space, and drew him to cities in which he could "learn to get lost." He wrote: "Not to find one's way about in a city is of little interest. But to lose one's way in a city, as one loses one's way in a forest, requires practice. . . . I learned this art late in life: it fulfilled the dreams whose first traces were the labyrinths on the blotters of my exercise books" (Sontag 1980, 112). This peculiarly modern sensibility reflects a conception of melancholy that we have charted in the eighteenth century, one that went beyond Saturn, beyond the "joy of grief," toward the paradoxical emblems of static wandering and open-door imprisonment in C. P. E. Bach's and Beethoven's interior landscapes.

Acknowledgements

Earlier versions of this essay were read at universities (Cornell, Harvard, University of Pennsylvania, University of North Carolina at Chapel Hill, Yale, Chicago, Columbia, Bard Graduate Center) and the Annual Meeting of the American Musicological Society. The author thanks her many inviters and respondents, especially Annette Richards.

Notes

1. Milton's opposition, "loathèd" in "L'Allegro" and "divinest" in "Il Penseroso" (1645), is probably based on the poetic "Author's Abstract of Melancholy" in Robert Burton's *Anatomy of Melancholy* (1621), in which every stanza ends with a variant of these oppositions: "All my joys to this are folly, / Naught so sweet as melancholy" and "All my griefs to this are jolly, / Naught so sad as melancholy." The literature on melancholy is vast; the most recent work on melancholy and music in the late eighteenth century includes the valuable studies November 2007 and Wald-Fuhrmann 2010.
2. In his *Essay on the True Art of Playing Keyboard Instruments*, Bach (1753) was actually quite critical of performers who had an excess of "Affect und Melancholie" in their sluggish approach to a piece (ch. 3, §1), as well as those hypochondriacs whose fingers were too flabby to produce a good tone (ch. 3 §13, added to 1787 edition).
3. The classic study of "the character and conduct of artists" is titled *Born under Saturn* (Wittkower and Wittkower 1963).
4. The alchemical symbol for lead, associated with Saturn, maintains the scythe shape.
5. With all of these specific references and explanations, it is sometimes hard to remember that black bile does not actually exist in the human body.
6. Gregory Butler (1974), working with sixteenth- and seventeenth-century sources, connects fantasia and memory in a different way.
7. This enigmatic and much-analyzed work (Panofsky [1943] 1955, Böhme 1989) is still crucial to our view of the melancholy tradition, and its presence in European collections raises questions about how widely it might have been known among composers.
8. The gendered syndromes hysteria (female) and hypochondria (male) were also considered to be related to the circulation of black bile from abdomen to brain (Jackson 1986, 139; Radden 2000, 28).

9. Richard Will (1997) places the piece into the context of other dramatic eighteenth-century dialogues.
10. The Sulzer entry here specifically takes aim at Rousseau's entry on "Sonate" in the *Dictionnaire de musique* (1768), which had deplored the lack of meaning in that purely instrumental genre.
11. Whether Bach's creative melancholy may have triggered the flowering of a "late style" remains to be explored; this fascinating suggestion was made to me by Blake Howe.
12. I have discussed the "labyrinth concept" in Gluck's *Orfeo ed Euridice* (1762) and Haydn's *L'isola disabitata* (1779) in Sisman 2012 (28–34), bringing in some of the material detailed here to assess the scenic and musical labyrinths that "harrow the souls of Constanza and Orfeo" (29).
13. According to Boulby (1979), once the labyrinth is seen from above, it is overcome: "the circle as a symbol of monotony and enslavement gives way to the circle as a figure for integration and containment" (194). See also Riley 2000, 30.
14. Thomas Grey (1996, 197) and Wye J. Allanbrook (1992) have discussed the labyrinth as the harmonic progression, with melody serving as Ariadne's thread, a line of continuity.
15. Beethoven to Wegeler, 29 June 1801: "His treatment had no effect, my deafness became even worse and my abdomen continued to be in the same state as before. Such was my condition until the autumn of last year; and sometimes I gave way to despair" (Anderson 1961, 59).
16. The *Wiener Zeitung* has been digitized at the Austrian Newspapers Online website: http://anno.onb.ac.at/cgi-content/anno?aid=wrz. The advertisement, from the centrally located bookseller Aloys Doll, appears on the last page of the August 9, 1800 issue (p. 2592): http://anno.onb.ac.at/cgi-content/anno?aid=wrz&datum=18000809&seite=40&zoom=33. My thanks to Stephen E. Novak, Head of Archives and Special Collections at the A. C. Long Health Sciences Library, Columbia University, for graciously allowing me access to the Latin and German volumes, and to Jennifer McGillan, archivist of the library, for her kindness in photographing the images.

References

Allanbrook, Wye J. 1992. "Two Threads through the Labyrinth: Topic and Process in the First Movements of K. 332 and K. 333." In *Convention in Eighteenth- and Nineteenth-Century Music: Essays in Honor of Leonard Ratner*, edited by Wye J. Allanbrook, Janet M. Levy, and William P. Mahrt, 125–171. Stuyvesant, NY: Pendragon.

Anderson, Emily, ed. and trans. 1961. *The Letters of Beethoven*. 3 vols. London: Macmillan.

Arikha, Noga. 2007. *Passions and Tempers: A History of the Humours*. New York: Ecco.

Aristotle. 2011. *Problems*. 2 vols. Translated and edited by Robert Mayhew. Loeb Classical Library, 316–317. Cambridge, MA: Harvard University Press.

Babb, Lawrence. 1951. *The Elizabethan Malady: A Study of Melancholia in English Literature from 1580 to 1642*. East Lansing: Michigan State University Press.

Bach, Carl Philipp Emanuel. 1949. *Essay on the True Art of Playing Keyboard Instruments*. Translated by William T. Mitchell. New York: W. W. Norton.

Bach, Carl Philipp Emanuel. 2011. *The Complete Works*. Series II, vol. 2.2, *Trio Sonatas II*. Edited by Christoph Wolff. Los Altos, CA: Packard Humanities Institute.

Balet, Leo. 1936. *Die Verbürgerlichung der deutschen Kunst, Literatur, und Musik im 18. Jahrhundert*. Strassburg: Heitz.

Bandmann, Gunther. 1960. *Melancholie und Music: Ikonographische Studien*. Cologne, Germany: Westdeutscher Verlag.

Böhme, Hartmut. 1989. *Albrecht Dürer Melencolia I: Im Labyrinth der Deutung*. Frankfurt am Main: Fischer.

Boulby, Mark. 1979. *At the Fringes of Genius*. Toronto, ON: University of Toronto Press.

Bredvold, Louis I. 1962. *The Natural History of Sensibility*. Detroit, MI: Wayne State University Press.

Burton, Robert. (1621) 1968. *The Anatomy of Melancholy*. London: Dent.

Butler, Gregory. 1774. "The Fantasia as Musical Image." *Musical Quarterly* 60 (4): 602–615.

Canalis, Rinaldo F., et. al. 2001. "Antonio Scarpa and the Discovery of the Membranous Inner Ear." *Otology and Neurology* 22: 105–112.

Carruthers, Mary J. 1990. *The Book of Memory: A Study of Memory in Medieval Culture*. Cambridge: Cambridge University Press.

Dahlhaus, Carl. 1983. "*La Malinconia*." In *Ludwig van Beethoven*, edited by Ludwig Finscher, 200–211. Wege zur Forschung, vol. 428. Darmstadt, Germany: Wissenschaftliche Buchgesellschaft.

Davis, Lennard J. 2008. *Obsession: A History*. Chicago: University of Chicago Press.

Dwyer, John. 1991. "The Melancholy Savage: Text and Context in the *Poems of Ossian*." In *Ossian Revisited*, edited by Howard Gaskill, 164–206. Edinburgh: Edinburgh University Press.

Fétis, François-Joseph. 1844. *Biographie universelle des musiciens et bibliographie générale de la musique*. Brussels.

Forchert, Arno. 1983. "Die Darstellung der Melancholie in Beethoven's Op. 18, 6." In *Ludwig van Beethoven*, edited by Ludwig Finscher, 212–239. Wege zur Forschung, vol. 428. Darmstadt, Germany: Wissenschaftliche Buchgesellschaft.

Forkel, Johann Nikolaus. (1778) 1964. *Musikalisch-Critische Bibliothek*. Rep. ed., 275–300. Hildesheim, Germany: Olms.

Foucault, Michael. 1965. *Madness and Civilization: A History of Insanity in the Age of Reason*. New York: Random House.

Frank, Johann Peter. (1802) 1969. *Johann Peter Frank: Seine Selbstbiographie*. Edited by Erna Lesky. Bern, Switzerland: Huber.

Frank, Johann Peter. (1786) 1976. *A System of Complete Medical Police: Selections from Johann Peter Frank*. Edited with an introduction by Erna Lesky. Translated from the third revised edition. Baltimore, MD: Johns Hopkins University Press.

Geyer-Kordesch, Johanna. 1990. "Georg Ernst Stahl's Radical Pietist Medicine and Its Influence on the German Enlightenment." In *The Medical Enlightenment of the Eighteenth Century*, edited by Andrew Cunningham and Roger French, 67–87. Cambridge, UK: Cambridge University Press.

Grey, Thomas. 1996. ". . . *wie ein rother Faden*: On the Origins of 'Leitmotif' as Critical Construct and Musical Practice." In *Music Theory in the Age of Romanticism*, edited by Ian Bent, 187–210. Cambridge, UK: Cambridge University Press.

Guthke, Karl S. 1983. "Poetry in an Age of Science: Albrecht von Haller and the Crisis of the Enlightenment." In *Studies in the Eighteenth Century: Papers Presented at the Fifth David Nichol Smith Memorial Seminar Canberra 1980*, edited by J. P. Hardy and J. C. Eade, 157–171. Oxford, UK: Voltaire Foundation.

Hajós, Géza. 1989. *Romantische Gärten der Aufklärung: Englische Landschaftskultur des 18. Jahrhundert in und um Wien*. Vienna, Austria: Böhlau.

Haller, Albrecht von. (1752) 1936. *Dissertation on the Sensible and Irritable Parts of Animals*. Originally published in Latin, with later French and English translations (1755). Baltimore, MD: Johns Hopkins University Press.

Hayes, Julie Candler. 1999. *Reading the French Enlightenment*. Cambridge, UK: Cambridge University Press.

Heinichen, Johann David. 1728. *Der Generalbass in der Composition*. Dresden, Germany: Author.

Helm, Eugene. 1972. "The 'Hamlet' Fantasy and the Literary Element in Bach's Music." *Musical Quarterly* 58 (2): 277–296.

Jackson, Stanley W. 1986. *Melancholia and Depression: From Hippocratic Times to Modern Times*. New Haven, CT: Yale University Press.

Kant, Immanuel. (1764) 1960. *Observations on the Feeling of the Beautiful and Sublime*. Translated and with an introduction by John D. Goldthwait. Berkeley and Los Angeles: University of California Press, 1960.

Kant, Immanuel. (1798) 1974. *Anthropology from a Pragmatic Point of View*. Translated by Mary J. Gregor. The Hague, Netherlands: Martinus Nijhoff.

Kern, Hermann. (1980) 2000. *Through the Labyrinth: Designs and Meanings over 5,000 Years*. Originally published in German. Edited by Jeff Saward and John Kraft. Munich: Prestel.

Klibansky, Raymond, Erwin Panofsky, and Fritz Saxl. 1964. *Saturn and Melancholy. Studies in the History of Natural Philosophy and Medicine, Religion, and Art*. New York: Basic.

Kuhn, Reinhard. 1976. *The Demon of Noontide: Ennui in Western Literature*. Princeton, NJ: Princeton University Press.

Lambrecht, Roland. 1996. *Der Geist der Melancholie: Eine Herausforderung philosophischer Reflexion*. Munich, Germany: W. Fink.

Lyons, Bridget. 1971. *Voices of Melancholy*. New York: Barnes & Noble.

Martens, Wolfgang. 1968. *Die Botschaft der Tugend. Die Aufklärung im Spiegel der deutschen moralischen Wochenschriften*. Stuttgart, Germany: Metzler.

Marx, Otto M. 2008. "German Romantic Psychiatry: Part I, Earlier, Including More-Somatic Orientations." In *History of Psychiatry and Medical Psychology*, edited by Edwin R. Wallace IV and John Gach, 313–334. New York: Springer.

Miesner, Heinrich. 1933. "Beziehungen zwischen den Familien Stahl und Bach." *Bach-Jahrbuch* 1933, 71–76.

Moritz, Karl Philipp. 1996. *Anton Reiser: A Psychological Novel*. Translated by John R. Russell. Columbia, SC: Camden House.

Moritz, Karl Philipp. 1997. *Anton Reiser*. Translated and with an Introduction by Ritchie Robertson. London: Penguin Books.

Newman, William S. 1965. "Emanuel Bach's Autobiography." *Musical Quarterly* 51 (2): 363–372.

Nicolai, Ernst Anton. 1745. *Die Verbindung der Musik mit der Artzneygelahrheit*. Halle, Germany: Carl Hermann Hemmerde.

November, Nancy. 2007. "Haydn's Melancholy Voice: Lost Dialectics in His Late Chamber Music and English Songs." *Eighteenth-Century Music* 4 (1): 71–106.

Panofsky, Erwin. (1943) 1955. *The Life and Art of Albrecht Dürer*. 4th ed. Princeton, NJ: Princeton University Press.

Radden, Jennifer. 2000. *The Nature of Melancholy: From Aristotle to Kristeva*. Oxford, UK: Oxford University Press.

Richards, Annette. 2006. "An Enduring Monument: C. P. E. Bach and the Musical Sublime." In *C. P. E. Bach Studies*, edited by Annette Richards, 149–172. Cambridge, UK: Cambridge University Press.

Riley, Matthew. 2002. "Straying from Nature: The Labyrinthine Harmonic Theory of Diderot and Bemetzrieder's 'Leçons de clavecin' (1771)." *Journal of Musicology* 19 (1): 3–38.

Rosand, Ellen. 1991. *Opera in Seventeenth-Century Venice: The Creation of a Genre*. Berkeley and Los Angeles: University of California Press.

Rousseau, Jean-Jacques. 1768. *Dictionnaire de musique*. Paris: Duchesne.

Scarpa, Antonio. 1789. *Anatomicae disquisitiones de auditu et olfactu*. Ticini: Gale.

Scarpa, Antonio. 1800. *Anatomisches Untersuchungen des Gehörs und Geruchs*. Nuremberg, Germany: Raspe. The copy in the Imperial Library in Vienna is digitized by Google Books.

Schneider, Ute. 1976. *Der moralische Charakter: Ein Mittel aufklärerischen Menschendarstellung in den frühen Deutschen Wochenschriften*. Stuttgart, Germany: Akademischer Verlag Heinz.

Sisman, Elaine. 1998. "After the Heroic Style: *Fantasia* and Beethoven's 'Characteristic' Sonatas of 1809." *Beethoven Forum* 6: 67–96.

Sisman, Elaine. 2000. "Memory and Invention at the Threshold of Beethoven's Late Style." In *Beethoven and His World*, edited by Scott Burnham and Michael P. Steinberg, 51–87. Princeton, NJ: Princeton University Press.

Sisman, Elaine. 2012. "Fantasy Island: Haydn, Metastasio, and the Nature of Occasional Opera." In *Engaging Haydn: Culture, Context, and Criticism*, edited by Mary Hunter and Richard Will, 11–43. Cambridge, UK: Cambridge University Press.

Smeed, J. W. 1985. *The Theophrastan "Character": The History of a Literary Genre*. Oxford, UK: Clarendon.

Starobinski, Jean. 1960. *Histoire du traitement de la Mélancolie des origines à 1900*. Acta Psychosomatica, no. 4. Basel, Switzerland: Documenta Geigy.

Starobinski, Jean. 2012. *L'encre de la mélancolie*. With an Afterword by Fernando Vidal. Paris: Seuil. Collected writings on melancholy since 1960.

Straus, Joseph. 2011. *Extraordinary Measures: Disability in Music*. Oxford: Oxford University Press.

Sulzer, Johann Georg. 1774. *Allgemeine Theorie der schönen Künste*. Vol. 2. Leipzig: M. G. Weidemanns Erben.

Swieten, Gerhard van. (1755–1773) 1776. *Commentaries upon Boerhaave's Aphorisms Concerning the Knowledge and Cure of Diseases*. Edinburgh and London.

Tellenbach, Hubertus. (1961) 1980. *Melancholy: History of the Problem, Endogeneity, Typology, Pathogenesis, Clinical Considerations*. Translated by Erling Eng. Pittsburgh, PA: Duquesne University Press.

Vicari, E. Patricia. 1989. *The View from Minerva's Tower: Learning and Imagination in "The Anatomy of Melancholy."* Toronto, ON: University of Toronto Press.

Wagner-Egelhaaf, Martina. 1997. *Die Melancholie der Literatur: Diskusgeschichte und Textfiguration*. Stuttgart, Germany: J. B. Metzler.

Wald-Fuhrmann, Melanie. 2010. *"Ein Mittel wider sich selbst: Melancholie in der Instrumentalmusik um 1800*. Kassel, Germany: Bärenreiter.

Will, Richard. 1997. "When God Met the Sinner, and Other Dramatic Confrontations in Eighteenth-Century Instrumental Music." *Music and Letters* 78 (2): 175–209.

Wittkower, Rudolf, and Margot Wittkower. 1963. *Born under Saturn: The Character and Conduct of Artists: A Documented History from Antiquity to the French Revolution*. New York: Random House.

Wright, Craig. 2000. *The Warrior and the Maze: Symbols in Architecture, Theology, and Music.* Cambridge, MA: Harvard University Press.
Yates, Frances. 1969. *The Art of Memory*. Harmondsworth, UK: Penguin.
Zelle, Carsten. 2001. "Sinnlichkeit und Therapie. Zur Gleichursprünglichkeit von Ästhetik und Anthropologie um 1750." In *"Vernünftige Ärtzte": Hallesche Psychomediziner und die Anfänge der Anthropologie in der deutschsprachigen Frühaufklärung*, edited by Carsten Zelle, 5–10. Tübingen, Germany: Max Niemeyer Verlag.
Zimmermann, Johann Georg. 1785. *Über die Einsamkeit*. Leipzig.

CHAPTER 31

MUSICAL PROSTHESIS

Form, Expression, and Narrative Structure in Beethoven's Sonata Movements

BRUCE QUAGLIA

PROSTHESIS has been applied to numerous types of discourses in recent decades, but music has rarely been included among these.[1] The word "prosthesis" dates from the mid-sixteenth century, when it initially referred to the practice of adding a letter or syllable to the beginning or ending of a word.[2] During the eighteenth century it acquired its more common medical meaning referring to the replacement or enhancement of a "defective" part of the human body through surgery or artificial supplementation.[3] Put another way, prosthesis prescribes standards for "normalcy" by introducing something new, something additional, in order to restore functionality to that which has been transgressed. More recently, prosthesis also appears broadly as a critical term within the humanities, where it has been used to describe the ubiquitous presence of technological interventions into the human sphere. This has also led to an acknowledgment of the term's rampant overuse and its resultant ambiguity.[4] This *posthuman* sense of prosthesis is intimately bound to the very terms of modernity itself,[5] but this contemporary usage falls distinctly outside the historical boundaries of the prosthetic metaphor that I am pursuing here in relation to eighteenth- and nineteenth-century musical form. In applying prosthesis to questions of expression in Beethoven's music, I proceed within certain constraints that rely on the somatic basis of musical discourses about form. These musical discourses register the persistent presence of a normalized organic body wherever sonata form is invoked as a strategy, and it is often the case that Beethoven's forms represent both a transgression of, and a prosthetic intervention into, that normal body. I will also consider prosthesis here in the sense that has often been used by disability scholars in the humanities, wherein the disabled human body is dealt with as a text to then be interpreted in terms of its narrative structure. The suggestion that a musical works tells a story and has a narrative structure is not a new idea, nor is the related argument that disabled bodies frequently figure into those narratives as active and critical components.[6]

In order to understand how disability typically functions in a literary narrative, I first summarize the basic arguments offered by David Mitchell and Sharon Snyder in their influential essay, "Narrative Prosthesis and the Materiality of the Metaphor."

Mitchell and Snyder (2000) argue that disability and disabled figures present a cultural problem and that "the perception of a 'crisis' or a 'a special situation' has made disabled people the subject of not only governmental policies and social programs but also a primary object of literary representation" (47). Of course, there is no representational dimension within which instrumental music might portray disabled characters in quite the same manner as a literary narrative, but music can arguably still concern itself with the cultural problem of disability, and it does portray narrative structure. Images of disability intrude on the analytical narratives that surround musical expression, but especially those that concern excess in Beethoven's strain of classical formal conventions.[7]

Mitchell and Snyder (2000) contend that the representation of disability in literary narratives is a "stock feature" and "an opportunistic metaphorical device" that constitutes the "perpetual discursive dependency" on disability that they refer to as *narrative prosthesis* (47). Narrative prosthesis, then, operates by introducing disability into a plot in order to establish the boundaries of the normal, but without allowing disability to become a focus of the reader's attention. They also argue that disability frequently enters into other narratives as a metaphorical signifier that in turn gives fleshly form to an abstract condition of social or individual collapse. Accordingly, they focus their analytical work on what they call "open-ended narratives" (48) that actively perform their capacity to be simultaneously interpreted at multiple levels. It is a similar capacity of Beethoven's music to register different levels of interpretation that has probably drawn so many commentators to it. The enterprise of constructing narratives about the heroic or the tragic in Beethoven's music sustains a massive secondary literature that continues to position that composer at the center of so many of our musical discourses.[8] It is not necessary here to either contest or supplant these other kinds of narratives, because prosthesis enriches those other interpretations by engaging our unconscious images of the disabled body, a body that resists deconstruction into standard or generic types and is easily identified with heroic struggle. In other words, prosthesis does the work of these other narratives in ways that go largely unnoticed, and in this manner it enacts its own musical variant of narrative dependency. Narrative prosthesis in Beethoven's instrumental music is thus concerned with expressive excess. The application of narrative dependency to musical terms is predicated on the listener's ability to register the unconscious presence of a disabled body, a body that only becomes apparent through the close analysis of form and its processes. In the following passage, Mitchell and Snyder describe the analogous work that disability performs in open literary narratives:

> Whereas the "able" body has no definitional core (it poses as transparently "average" or "normal"), the disabled body surfaces as any body capable of being narrated "outside the norm." Within such a representational schema, literary narratives revisit disabled bodies as a reminder of the "real" limits that "weigh down" transcendent ideals of the mind and knowledge-producing disciplines. In this sense, disability serves as

> the *hard kernel* or recalcitrant corporeal matter that cannot be deconstructed away by the textual operations of even the most canny narratives or philosophical idealisms. . . . We therefore forward readings of disability as a narrative device upon which the literary writer of "open-ended" narratives depends for his or her disruptive punch. (Mitchell and Snyder 2000, 49)

The interactions of individual musical expressions with their implied genres, particularly those movements or passages that display deformations or are otherwise expressively marked by their differences, similarly demonstrate the "real limits" of knowledge-producing disciplines such as *Formenlehre.*[9] The dependencies in such theories, it turns out, are not staked on the average or the normal (that body that has "no definitional core"), but instead on the "recalcitrant corporeal matter" of the difference itself, of the prosthetic, which allows the form to enter into some plot that is motivated by this displacement.

Musical form is a venerable subject in the discipline of music theory, and so querying it here in relation to images of the disabled human body requires some preliminary explanation. Disability scholars in the humanities have long asserted that disability pervades every aspect of culture. They have repeatedly demonstrated this claim through close critical readings of literature, art, performance, film, and other media, and more recently this mode of analysis has also been applied to various elements of music. Form as a method of musical analysis belongs to a much narrower and older field of musicological study, and the technical terminology invoked in that analysis can be a barrier when attempting to address a broader Disability Studies audience. In order to navigate the barrier of that technical terminology, I will therefore also engage parallel questions of form as they have been addressed in musical criticism. Musical criticism may be thought of in this context as a mode of analysis that is decidedly more accessible to a broad humanities-based audience, less prone to jargon and technical explanation than music theory. The degree to which the languages of both music theory and music criticism coincide when describing Beethovenian form is striking when considered in a Disability Studies context. Each language invokes elements of prosthesis in its own way, suggesting a resonant musical connection to the disabled body. The images of prosthesis and the disabled body that emerge from the study of Beethoven's form and his use of codas are therefore not merely the artifacts of the particular methods of analysis or of their terminology, but instead suggest that the musical processes engaged by Beethoven in such forms are an expression of these primary somatic images, but now expressed in a purely musical domain.

I shall begin with the relatively uncontroversial assertion that musical works, formally and otherwise, have frequently been thought of in explicitly embodied terms. Of course the word *coda*, which literally means a tail, immediately confirms this assertion. We conceive of the sonata space of a work as a complete and standardized musical body, and thus the coda appears as an appendage to it, a prosthesis that serves some supplemental function.[10] This is a metaphor certainly, but experientialist philosophers have argued that metaphors are not merely linguistic devices. Instead they reveal the way that we structure our concepts and then reason about them. Metaphors in this deeper sense rely on a source domain that is defined by our most basic and trusted experiences, which are then applied to other target domains that are less familiar to us. We understand the unfamiliar target domain through *cross-domain mapping*: a conceptual transformation through which we structure our experience within an abstract and unfamiliar target domain (musical form) in terms that are derived from the more familiar source domain (our bodies). Cross-domain mappings produce meaning at a very basic level. The experientialist philosopher Mark Johnson (1990) has argued that the source domain to which we consistently refer when constructing meaning is that of our own embodied experience; this source domain is itself structured as a series of image schemas that reflect our embodied experiences. His invariance principal describes how we selectively map features from the source domain onto a target domain in a manner that strives to preserve all of the features that are now found in that new target domain. Thus we experience the abstract relationships of music through spatially embodied metaphors such as UP/DOWN verticality, PATHWAYS toward GOALS, FORCES that act on musical entities, and CONTAINERS by which regions within the sonata form may be figured. These images directly reflect our own bodies, and the manner in which we navigate within them through the world. Linguistic metaphors, then, implicate the more deep-level cognitive translations that are inscribed by these mappings. By adapting the ideas of Mark Johnson and his coauthor George Lakoff to the concepts and methods of music theory, scholars began in the mid-1990s to critically reexamine the linguistic metaphors about musical processes that descend from such cross-domain mappings within our own discipline.[11] Joseph Straus's initial work on music theory and Disability Studies extended this project by revisiting this cognitivist theory and noting that in Johnson and Lakoff's work "there has been the blithe assumption that we all inhabit the same kind of body, a normatively abled body, and thus all experience our bodies in pretty much the same way" (Straus 2006, 123). The formulation of musical prosthesis that I develop here is not enacted through the same image schemas that are proposed in Lakoff and Johnson's theories. This is mostly because the prosthetic is not included among those images, even though prosthesis has been a very real part of the human embodied condition throughout much of history. The present theory of musical prosthesis does, however, follow directly from Straus's earlier work. In particular, it presumes the pervasive presence of diversely embodied cross-domain mappings within music theory and music criticism, while consciously avoiding strict engagement of Lakoff and Johnson's image schemas as an explicit structure. The prosthetic model seeks to correct the "blithe assumptions" that Straus has pointed out by recognizing that the prosthetic is a basic feature of human embodiment, and that this is routinely reflected in our theoretical percepts about musical forms and spaces.

In Straus's critical examination of *Formenlehre*, he noted that there are two persistent models for thinking about musical form. One is the image schema FORM IS A CONTAINER. Through it, a work may either be well formed or else "deformed" if musical forces act on it to breach its boundaries or cause it to become distorted. The other model is FORM IS A NORM. This is not an image schema per se, but it does link musical form to the conceptualization of a disabled/enabled body by imposing a conformational model that measures degrees of deviation from an idealized standard (Straus 2006, 126–127). Codas and other prosthetic spaces are formal regions that are marked by their difference and that may be conceptualized in terms that situate their alterity in direct relation to these basic models of a normalized embodiment. For example, when James Hepokoski and Warren Darcy discuss codas and slow introductions in *Elements of Sonata Theory* (2006), they identify those sections of a work as "parageneric spaces":

> By sonata-space we mean that space articulated by the generic sonata form proper: normal treatments of the exposition, developmental space, and recapitulatory rotation. Some sonata movements also feature parageneric spaces (or not-sonata-space), everything else in the movement that may set up, momentarily step outside of, or otherwise alter or frame the presentation of the sonata form. In such movements the most frequently encountered parageneric spaces are *accretions* that in the second half of the eighteenth century came to be increasingly attractive options as add-ons to the basic structure. (281)

Such prosthetic spaces, then, are external to the container that constitutes the boundaries of the sonata form itself. They are nonnormative additions that are in some manner *enabling* of the interior space of the sonata's body by redefining its own mediating differences. Hepokoski and Darcy's use of the term "accretion" is especially interesting here. Etymologically, this term first appeared in the mid-seventeenth century and refers to a growth or enlargement on the body. But the word also has a second near-contemporaneous meaning that became increasingly common in the eighteenth and nineteenth centuries: a growth that was not necessarily organic, but which might instead be a synthetic addition.[12] The presence of a synthetic addition is not only crucial to the idea of prosthesis itself but also serves to underscore the discordant nature of the coda's own nonassimilation into the given organic form that it enables. Translations of expressive terms from one natural frame (the sonata form) to another artificial one (a coda or other parageneric space) operate in a parallel manner to the cross-domain mappings of experientialist theory noted above. This translation of terms may be understood as the essence of prosthetic function in musical form. It may be of further note that the emergence of codas as a frequent feature of sonata forms during the classical era coincided historically with a rapidly expanding human experience of prosthetics in both medical science and in normal life. Prosthetics, as material supplementation to the human body, appear throughout history, but the sixteenth century marked the emergence of more advanced prostheses such as the artificial hands invented by the French physician, Ambrois Paré. The nineteenth century, however, marks an era during which prosthetic limbs suddenly became both increasingly common and increasingly visible (largely because of modern warfare), and thus became part of the lexicon of embodied experiences that the somatic image schemas are built on.

It should come as no surprise then that prosthetic spaces are poorly accounted for by theories of form that place their primary emphasis on commonly shared features of musical works—in other words, theories which exemplify FORM IS A NORM. Such theories are intent on recovering a normalized comparative practice and are hard-pressed to explain the function of parageneric regions such as codas and slow introductions. Beethoven's codas, with the possible exception of those that appear at the end of rondo forms, are almost always a final response to some expressive need that is unique to a particular work or movement and manifests in structural issues that are consequently reflected in the form of the work. These expressive needs may be remediated by means of compensatory thematic functions, but they challenge the more normalizing terms on which FORM IS A NORM theories typically rely.

Form theories that emphasize similarity of design have been described as *conformational* and are opposed by *generative models*, which instead emphasize the individual shape of a work, its specific internal expressive forces, and its unique strategies for working these considerations out within the form of the movement (Bonds 1991, 13–30). Thus, while musical form may initially seem like something of an abstraction, especially given the specialized terms with which music theorists engage it, it should now be clear that what is actually at stake in the present study is a fundamental humanistic question about the ideology of the normative and how it is mediated in various cultural spheres, including music.

It initially seems that the generative approach, in which form and content are to some extent indistinguishable, might be better positioned to account for prosthetic spaces such as codas, promoting them to the rank of significant compositional responses to the unique circumstances of a work and its progress toward expressive completion. By contrast to the generative approach, conformational models appear to relegate these spaces to a supplemental function instead. This effect is fundamentally at odds with the prestige status that such movements have typically attained with audiences as a result of their marked differences. A basic dissatisfaction with the conformational perspective on codas was clearly expressed by Joseph Kerman (1982):

> Musical analysts who deal with Beethoven's sonata-form movements generally do rather poorly by the codas—do less well, that is, in accounting for actual musical experience when dealing with codas than with other sections of the form. All over bar the shouting is the impression one is often left with when the analytical account reaches the end of the recapitulation, though as a listener one knows perfectly well that an important part of the movement, perhaps the most exciting part, is still to come. (141)

A theory of musical prosthesis cannot, however, rely solely on the generative approach to sonata form. Prosthesis is itself predicated on the recognition of functional morphological differences that are only meaningful in relation to an established normal body that has been transgressed and must then be remediated in some manner. Prosthesis requires the specification of that normal musical body so that the prosthetic may then emerge against it and be marked by its difference. Put another way, the binary of conformational/generative form that produces this necessary tension is effectively the musical

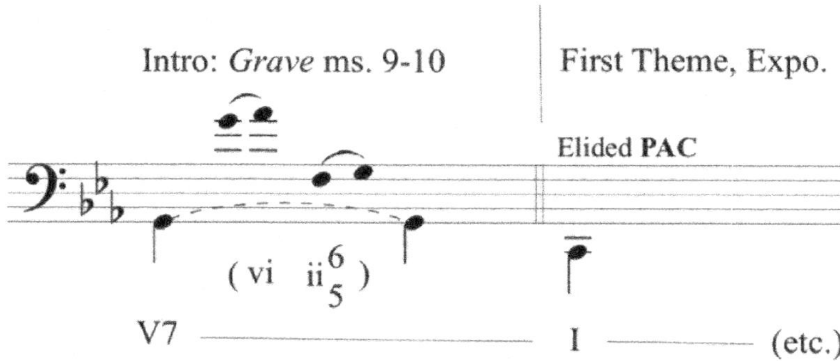

FIGURE 31.1 Elision of prosthetic space to sonata space in Beethoven, Piano Sonata in C Minor, Op. 13, first movement (introduction).

corollary to the prosthetic of narrative dependency that literary critics such as Mitchell and Snyder (2000) have explored. The musical prosthetic therefore responds to the unique generative forces of a work, and those forces result in formal permutations that require remediation via an accretion to that normal musical body. The musical prosthetic is therefore best defined within a continuum that embraces both the generative and the conformational models of form.[13]

The first movement of Beethoven's Piano Sonata in C Minor, Op. 13 (*Pathétique*), offers considerable evidence for the ways in which prosthetic interventions into a sonata movement may both mark and compensate the form via generative thematic processes. At the outset of this movement, ten measures of Grave music introduce the exposition and also connect this material to the main theme through an elided perfect authentic cadence (PAC).[14] This elided cadence underscores the interdependent mechanism by which prosthesis operates in this case: the introduction is simultaneously contingent and compensatory in relation to the intact sonata body of the movement (see Figure 31.1).[15] Although it diverges expressively from what follows in every conceivable manner, the Grave music is nonetheless fused to the exposition through an unlikely fissure in the boundary of the sonata form proper—the initiating tonic of the main theme. This elided cadence ruptures the first and most primary formal boundary of the sonata body and then establishes a new dependency that subsequently works in both directions throughout the remainder of the movement.

The material existence of the Grave music itself is inextricably linked to that of the main theme, and vice versa. When the Grave music later returns in an abbreviated form to begin the development section as a transitional introduction, or *precore*, it once again connects to the main theme material in the developmental key of E minor by fusing to the start of the developmental core in the same way that it did at the start of the exposition (see Figure 31.2).[16]

The Grave music then appears once more at the start of the coda, where it incites a loud final peroration of the main theme in the tonic.[17] It is only at the beginning of the recapitulation that the main theme ever "stands on its own," independent of the Grave

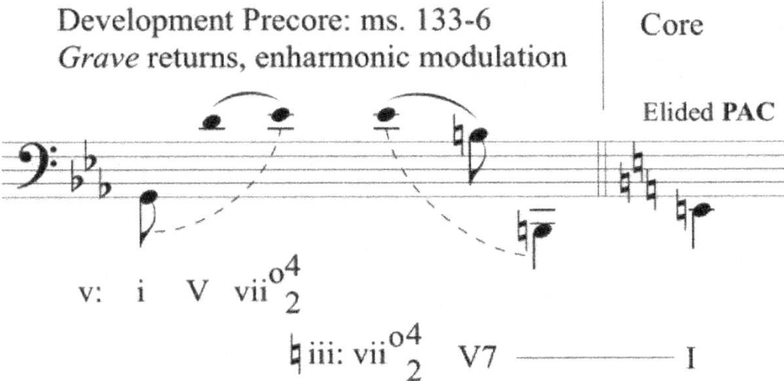

FIGURE 31.2 Insertion of prosthetic space into sonata space in Beethoven, Piano Sonata in C Minor, Op. 13, first movement (development).

introduction. The presence of the peroration in the coda following the Grave music suggests that this earlier recapitulation of the main theme was somehow insufficient, and that further closure was expressively required by the form all along. The coda compensates the recapitulation in particular here, but it also remediates the entire form more generally by restoring balance and settling matters that had disabled the sonata body earlier on.

The Grave music establishes an extra thematic area, one that stands in contrast to what follows it each time. No mere dominant upbeat, the Grave introduction instead serves a rhetorical function that can best be described as prosthetic. It begins as a rather tight-knit sentence, albeit one that modulates.[18] Although we might wish to disregard the extent to which this unit truly forms a tight-knit theme type, a sentence form, this is only because of where it lies in relation to the body proper of the sonata form, in the prosthetic region prior to where the exposition begins with the main theme. The main theme itself is impacted by this prosthetic intrusion, too. The elided PAC fundamentally changes the basic terms of the sentence by altering its fundamental initiating function. This, in turn, problematizes the very act of beginning the movement. I would like to emphasize the role of the Grave music as the Other, but I would also like it to be understood as integrated into the musical body of the movement. It is the rhetorical alterity of this music, particularly in relation to what follows it each time, that defines its functional role. The prosthetic metaphor allows recognition of both difference and inclusion here by maintaining the formal and expressive distinctions of the generative/conformational binary, but the act of prosthesis itself then complicates that binary by recasting it as an extensive continuum.

In his study *Musical Meaning in Beethoven*, Robert Hatten observes that our willingness to perceive that a unit is functionally marked as thematic is largely conditioned by its position within the formal scheme: "To the degree that we recognize a 'thematic' slot, we are more likely to accept whatever material appears there as 'the theme,' even if the material would otherwise be understood as closural or developmental" (Hatten

1994, 119). Similarly, the expressively marked Grave music presents us with tight-knit thematic material that initiates the action of the sonata space, but in a formal slot prior to where that action is actually expected to occur. The repeated insinuation of this music as a marked semantic unit wherever the main theme is next to be found (except notably at the recapitulation) motivates its eventual return in the coda as one final and necessary compensation. This is the rhetorical terrain in which I would like to situate the first movement of Op. 13, as a conjunction of two discourses, one of them normalized through the rhetorical conventions of sonata form, and the other entrenched in its difference: more familiar yet also more foreign. The emblematic opening chords of the Grave introduction serve metonymically for the whole work. The normalized discourse that is initiated by the main theme proper could hardly stand on its own, for what is the basic idea of this main theme but an ascending scale responding to the weight of the Grave's relentless descent? Even before the action of the sonata has begun, this other music that is marked as more foreign, more idiosyncratic, and certainly more stylized, is already compensating for the body-proper of the work whose main theme is all upward flight and no identity, and whose closure as a sentence is even further attenuated by the elision and repetition that leads it into the transitional zone. To displace the beginning of the work to the Grave music is prosthesis, and this prosthesis then functions by transferring the process of beginning back again to the main theme. And so it becomes part of the work of the Grave music to resituate itself each time in relation to the natural body, and to thus translate what follows as part of the prosthesis.

The first movement of the *Pathétique* presents a complex yet typical example of prosthesis, in which the prosthetic space of the movement both encloses and permeates the sonata space as a whole. The prosthetic space remains extrinsic and supplemental, but it also involves an insertion directly into the sonata body proper right at the start of the development section.

The first movement of Beethoven's Piano Sonata in E-flat Major, Op. 81a (*Les Adieux*), presents a strikingly similar example (see Figure 31.3). Here, a slow introduction once again complicates the process of beginning the sonata movement and acts as a prosthesis that eventually culminates in a substantial coda. The introduction to Op. 81a contains a descending three-note motto that appears most prominently in the first measures, and

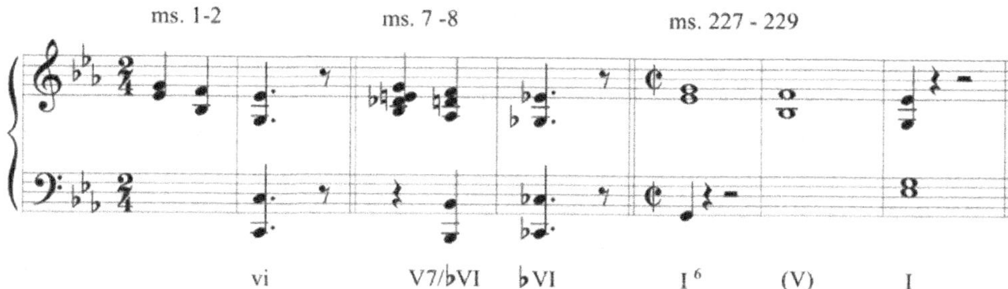

FIGURE 31.3 Three instances of the *Lebewohl* motto in Beethoven, Piano Sonata in E-flat Major, Op. 81a, first movement.

then again in the coda of the movement. Musically, it is a gesture of closure that moves melodically downward by step to end on the tonic scale degree.[19] But this typically closural gesture is also part of a rhetorical deflection: it is used here as an opening gambit at first, not a closing one, and it immediately casts doubt on what key the movement will ultimately be in. The supporting notes that appear against it in mm. 1–2 suggest the wrong key, or at least the wrong chord: C minor, not E-flat major. The repetition of the gesture in mm. 7–8 carries the music even further away from E-flat, to C-flat major, a chord that includes chromatic notes foreign to the key.

It is not until well into the coda, in mm. 227–229, that this motto ever aligns clearly with its expected function: to close clearly on E-flat as the tonal center. In much the same manner as the Grave music in Op. 13, the motto stands metonymically here for the movement as a whole, and thereby displaces one of the basic functions of the main theme. The slow music presents the expressively marked ideas to which the entire rest of the sonata form responds thematically. In this way, the sonata body accommodates the prosthesis. That generative thematic function is typically reserved for the main theme of the exposition, but it has been supplanted here by the more powerful and emblematic material that appears prior to the conventional beginning of the sonata space. The main theme suffers from this transfer of function in a manner that immediately recalls the opening of the *Pathétique*: the theme lacks a strong identity and instead responds to the downward weight of the earlier slow music by repeatedly fleeing upward toward a high B♭. The *Lebewohl* motto and its associated music have destabilized the tonality of the movement before it even had a chance to begin. It does this by assuming various harmonic guises during the introduction that pit the tonic of E-flat major against both C minor and C-flat major. When this motto appears again in octaves at the very beginning of the exposition, the sonata body proper destabilizes; it loses balance. It must be compensated by the prosthesis in some way in order to regain that balance.

Whereas the Grave music of Op. 13 had breached the exposition's opening boundary through an elided PAC connecting to the initiating tonic of the main theme, the harmonic ambiguity of *Les Adieux*'s introduction completely obliterates that initiating tonic and replaces it with a different harmony instead to support the opening of the main theme. Consequently, the main theme can never establish the tonic convincingly; it cannot reach any type of closure. Instead, it drifts toward the transition, and temporary closure is only finally achieved later in the subordinate key of B-flat during the secondary themes of the exposition. Although the movement's sonata form remains nominally intact within the typical placements of exposition, development, and recapitulation, the slow introduction has so thoroughly infused the generative thematic material of the movement with problems of both harmony and closure that an extensive coda of nearly 100 measures is then required at the end to restore balance and closure to the form as a whole. In short, the coda compensates that sonata space for those differences that marked the exposition and its thematic material as a result of the introduction.

For many commentators, Beethoven's codas are notably distinct from Mozart's both with respect to their scope and their expressive purpose. Kerman, for example, identifies a "principle" for many of the codas in Beethoven's middle period: he describes their function as a "thematic completion" that is required because of some sort of "anomaly" within the main theme itself.[20] This anomaly must subsequently be "normalized" through what eventually takes place in the coda (Kerman 1982, 148–150). Kerman's use of terms like *anomaly* and *normalization* must be understood to implicate the prosthetic; this is language that specifies both difference and subsequent compensation in relation to the functional aspects of form. They are also terms that explicitly conjure the disabled body into a metaphorical musical existence. A different kind of narrative dependency is involved here than in the prosthesis described by literary critics like Mitchell and Snyder. In literary narratives the presence of the disabled body is eliminated or removed from view once it has served its purpose. The coda, on the other hand, is the last word in a sonata movement; it lingers. Even in movements where the prosthesis comes first, as in slow introductions, that early prosthesis often resonates throughout the remainder of the sonata form. It does not disappear from the stage as the disabled characters in a novel or play so often do.

Kerman's principle of "thematic completion" is suggestively based on a movement's narrative structure, but this narrative is still rendered primarily through its form: "With Beethoven a sonata-form movement is also 'the story of a theme'—the first theme—and the exciting last chapter of that story is told in the coda" (150). We will return to the structural roles that narrative compensation can take in relation to musical form later, but it should already be clear from our first two analyses that these strategies often unfold through generative thematic processes and that musical works like the *Pathétique* and *Les Adieux* are especially valued for precisely these dramatic aspects of their implicit narrative designs.

Robert Hopkins also perceived a fundamental distinction between Beethoven's codas and those of Mozart, but he considered these differences to be based largely on the evolving nature of sonata form in the nineteenth century. After reviewing various descriptions of the coda in the analytical literature, he observed that it had often been rendered as a "superfluous attachment," rather than as a critical expressive device within the form of the work. He continues,

> We should broaden our concept of sonata form beyond that based primarily in eighteenth-century views of harmonic structure and formal symmetry in order to account for the significance of codas in works of the nineteenth century. We need to increase our awareness of the functions and importance of codas in early nineteenth-century sonata forms. In short, we need to build a theory that explains the structural functions of codas and why they became necessary to the work. (Hopkins 1988, 393–394)

Hopkins clearly follows Kerman by positing that many of Beethoven's codas primarily serve to "normalize" something that has gone amiss within the main theme. As with Kerman, the coda then provides a necessary thematic completion that corrects some expressive matter that was initially ill-formed, or otherwise unstable (398–399). Hopkins goes on to provide two more motivations for a Beethovenian coda, stipulating that these three impulses taken together are neither mutually exclusive nor exhaustive. A coda may, for example, be required as a final recapitulation of the first theme in order to restore some missing balance and symmetry to the form as a whole. This specifies a formal compensation in relation to symmetry and balance, which are themselves basic image schemas of the body. Hopkins next describes a function for the coda in which some important harmonic resolution relating to the reestablishment of the tonic was somehow left unsatisfactorily in the recapitulation proper. This deficiency results in some weakness within the harmonic form of the movement as a whole, which must then be shored up by the coda's more expansive confirmation of that tonic later on. Prosthetic compensation manifests itself here in relation to the harmonic structure of the form, which is clearly one of the most normalizing features of musical form during this era.

The idea that codas are compensatory, or that they serve to remediate some inherent functional defect that has occurred elsewhere in the work, is a recurring theme in many recent theories of form. Compensation will therefore be considered as one of the primary formal functions of prosthesis. By citing compensation for insufficient harmonic closure as a basis for a coda in the example above, Hopkins is notably at odds with some older *Formenlehre* theories, including Arnold Schoenberg's, who remarked famously,

> Since many movements have no codas, it is evident that the coda must be considered as extrinsic addition. The assumption that it serves to establish the tonality is hardly justified; it could scarcely compensate for failure to establish the tonality in the previous sections. In fact, it would be difficult to give any other reasons for the addition of a coda than that the composer wants to say something more. (Schoenberg 1967, 185)

Schoenberg's remarks demonstrate a familiar perspective on codas that Hopkins evidently wished to refute: namely that they are "superfluous additions" to the sonata form proper. Moreover, Schoenberg's assertion that a coda cannot "compensate for failure to establish the tonality" earlier in the piece, seems to differ sharply with Hopkins's own conviction that codas can do precisely that: they expiate a lack of closure when the reestablishment of the tonic was left unsatisfactorily within the recapitulation. Though the distinction between these two positions may hang precariously on terms like "satisfactorily," and therefore appear to be merely a semantic quibble, both positions do significantly impact the idealized image of the healthy harmonic body of the sonata proper. Our analysis of the first movement of Op. 81a presented an instance of just such a sonata movement in which the expected tonal closure of the form certainly took place within the normal sequence of exposition, development, and recapitulation, but where that closure was not sufficient because of the earlier destabilizing effects of the introduction on the initial tonality of the exposition. While Kerman and Hopkins focused their attention on Beethoven's codas primarily in relation to his main themes, prosthesis is a remediation of the entire form of the movement, and so we must engage *Formenlehre* in a more complete and comprehensive manner.

Two recent theories of form have been widely credited with a renewed scholarly interest in *Formenlehre*: James Hepokoski and Warren Darcy's *Sonata Form Theory* and

William Caplin's *Classical Form*. In both of these sources, the coda falls into a category that may best be described as *contingent*, a perceived condition that I assert is also a prerequisite for the work of any prosthetic mechanism to take place. Significantly, Hepokoski/Darcy and Caplin both begin their respective treatments of the coda by remarking on Schoenberg's previously quoted pronouncements. Whereas Caplin (1998) finds in Schoenberg's comments something "rather flippant" (179), Hepokoski and Darcy (2006) instead consider Schoenberg's appraisal to have been offered "perhaps wryly" (282). But Schoenberg's conjecture that the composer has "something more to say" is hardly "flippant" or "wry": instead it places the coda into a specifically *discursive* space relative to the rhetorical design of the completed sonata form. It is possible that Schoenberg may simply have been recalling, in a relatively colloquial fashion, that distinctly eighteenth-century viewpoint of musicians such as Koch (and later Reicha) who believed that music is constructed as a rhetorical, wordless oration. When Schoenberg states that a coda cannot specifically "*compensate* for the failure to establish tonality in the previous sections," he implies, if only by omission, that it can instead compensate for other sorts of failings or differences. William Caplin's explanation of the coda provides a variety of such "compensatory functions," some of which seem specifically tied to unfinished thematic processes:

> Although Schoenberg speaks rather flippantly about the coda's appearing merely because "the composer wants to say something more," it is nonetheless true that this final section allows the composer to say things that could not have been appropriately said in earlier sections. In this respect, the coda includes a variety of *compensatory functions*, for here the composer can make up for events or procedures that were not fully treated in the main body of the movement. More specifically, the coda often gives the composer an opportunity to impart a circular design to the overall form by recalling main-theme ideas; to restore expositional material deleted from the recapitulation; to recapitulate ideas from the development section; to shape a concluding dynamic curve that differs from (or surpasses) that of the recapitulation; and to realize the implications generated by various compositional processes that have been left unrealized in earlier sections. (Caplin 1998, 179)

Caplin's list of compensatory functions overlaps with Hopkins's own in several important respects. His *recollection of main-theme ideas* corresponds in part to Hopkins's second reason for a coda: a late restatement of the main theme in order to restore balance and symmetry to the form. Caplin's *shaping a new dynamic curve* also impacts this same principal, because some of the perorations that Hopkins has in mind also create a late climax as a result. But Caplin's functions also distinguish these processes so that changes in the dynamic shape of the movement, particularly when they do not recall the main theme, may also be accounted for. Caplin's functions also account for other less common situations where instead of building to a late climax, the coda instead presents a series of recessive dynamics that dissipate the earlier culmination of momentum and energy from the recapitulation, for example in Beethoven's Overture to *Coriolanus* (Caplin 2006, 187). Caplin's third coda function, *reference to the development section*, also reaffirms Hopkins's own analysis of the fourth movement of Beethoven's Eighth Symphony, where, like Ratner and others before him, he posits a second or terminal development. Such historical assignations of an additional development section were sharply discounted by Kerman in his own commentary, but have nonetheless reemerged in some more recent theories.[21] Prosthesis is principally an intervention into the normalized musical body, and so the assertion that a coda could also represent a second development section is problematic from our perspective. The development section is already a functional part of that body and has its own very specific location within it. Further, Kerman is absolutely correct in asserting that Beethoven's codas are not unique in their propensity to develop thematic material, and that this process takes place generically across all formal boundaries in many of his movements, including the exposition itself often enough (Kerman 1982, 152). We will therefore set aside the question of whether the coda to the last movement of the Eighth Symphony is truly a terminal development, but the example raises another more pressing question about prosthesis and codas. The movement is cast as a sonata rondo and therefore the coda itself cannot be immediately understood as either contingent or extraneous. It is instead an expected formal feature that is virtually required of all final refrains in sonata-rondo forms, even though the expansiveness of this particular coda is exceptional in its depth and breadth.

In order to function as a prosthesis, we have already specified that a coda must be able to compensate the normal body of a form, must maintain its own alterity while doing so, and must also be contingent in some way. In the case of most first-movement forms, the coda unquestionably maintains this status, especially during the Classical era, when the coda was not specified as a given part of the normal body; it was something extra. By contrast, the codas that occur within the final refrain of a sonata-rondo movement are expected components. So, is it possible for these codas to also then function as prostheses if they are required elements? I do not attempt to formulate a complete or even a general solution to this problem here; there is no formula for the format of such codas, and so I believe the question must remain open. In the case of the finale of the Eighth Symphony, I believe that there are sufficiently compelling reasons to view this particular coda as prosthesis. First of all, it is clearly marked by its difference, especially in relation to all of those other codas that typically appear as part of the final refrain of a sonata rondo. In this regard, it is exceptional because it is one of Beethoven's longest codas.[22] It is more harmonically expansive than most others that appear in rondo movements, and of course this is precisely why some theorists have called it a second development. But perhaps most importantly, this coda compensates the form of the movement by remediating the expressively marked C♯ that had interrupted the main theme at its midpoint in m. 17, and which then arguably generates the various issues of closure that attend the subordinate theme areas of the outer couplets. These issues of closure and stability find no satisfactory resolution anywhere else in the given body of the form until they are finally taken up again in the coda—there, C♯ is finally subordinated to F♯ and then integrated back into the form of the work in relation to the tonic.[23]

Caplin provides one final coda function, the *realization of unrealized implications*, which is couched in terms that recall Leonard B. Meyer's and Eugene Narmour's *implication-realization* model.[24] Surpassing Meyer and Narmour, Caplin also includes "harmonic, formal, rhythmic, and dynamic implications" as additional cues for subsequent realization. Caplin's *realization of implications* function thus exceeds Meyer and Narmour's model, which had been predominantly based on melodic implications (Caplin 1998, 187 and 279n36). If we read Caplin's function broadly, it also exceeds Kerman's proposition of an "anomaly" or "aberration" within the main theme that functions as a narrative strategy leading to a coda. While Kerman rightly asserts that Beethoven's sonata forms are "the story of a theme" whose "exciting last chapter . . . is told in the coda," he never provides any method for decoding that story. Recent theories of musical meaning and expression that rely on narrative discourse as a critical model provide a more secure basis for interpreting prosthesis within a comprehensive hermeneutic framework. To be effective in understanding prosthesis in this way, such interpretations need to be able to move smoothly between underlying systems of formal analysis and their framing hermeneutic backgrounds. The prosthesis provided by codas, then, straddles this boundary between theories of form and other models that rely predominantly on narrative structure. To illustrate this translation further, I turn now to one final example, from the first movement of Beethoven's Piano Sonata in F Minor, Op. 57 (*Appassionata*).

The first movement of the *Appassionata* features a rather lengthy and structurally complex coda that may be productively viewed as a prosthetic space. This kind of lengthy coda is sometimes called "discursive" (Hepokoski and Darcy 2006, 284), and this description fits nicely within the kind of narrative that I wish to develop here. The plot of this narrative engages the harmonic form of the work and especially its inability to attain closure at critical junctures in the musical form because of an anomaly that occurs early on in the piece. This story will eventually conclude in the coda, but it begins with a thematic event that becomes the central character for the entire movement: the rhetorically charged D♭ (paired with G♭) that marks the first theme, disabling normative thematic processes and also preventing clear tonic closure in the first theme area (see Figure 31.4). Narratives about how the form of a work might be challenged by such notes are often discussed in terms of a "tonal problem."[25] Tonal problems generate an imbalance or unrest that has to be worked out through the harmonic form of the remainder of

FIGURE 31.4 D♭/D♮ cross-relation blocks GOAL, in Beethoven, Piano Sonata in F Minor, Op. 57, first movement.

the movement. Accommodating or compensating such a disabling feature (especially if this takes place in a discursive coda) is therefore a type of narrative prosthesis.[26]

D♭ is, generally speaking, a normal enough note in the key of F minor, but here it causes an unexpected and disruptive cross-relation when it first appears in the fourth measure of the piece.[27] Its presence also immediately runs afoul of the incomplete melodic motion by step that has just taken place in the previous measure: C♮, D♮, E♮. This line was stopped short of its tonic goal, F♮, and instead the E♮ transfers at the final moment back into the bass voice, as part of the chord on which the initial idea then comes to rest instead in m. 4—well short of its goal. When D♭ appears immediately afterward, it does not move back to C as one might expect it to do, but instead jars immediately against D♮ and E♮, and then takes on the chromatic note G♭ as a partner in order to move even further away from the tonic and toward the chromatically related Neapolitan (♭II) region in mm. 4–8.[28] This discord motivates the sort of "plot" that is often invoked in a tonal problem narrative, and here it also results in an incomplete motion toward a goal, the tonic of the piece, F minor (see Figure 31.5). This narrative derives meaning, in part, from the image schema SOURCE-PATH-GOAL. The motion toward the tonic is blocked. The completion of that motion has effectively been thwarted by the D♭/G♭ pair of mm. 5–8. The ensuing repeated efforts to hammer the D♭ back into its proper position in the bass are now simply too late. Because completed motion to the tonic of the key has been blocked, the theme has now become disabled.[29] The main theme never achieves closure and instead the inherited trait of motion away from tonic toward the D♭/G♭ pair is then passed on to the remainder of the movement, marking the exposition, development, and recapitulation sections in turn, but never producing a satisfying resolution of this impediment anywhere within the sonata form proper.[30] A prosthetic intervention, in the form of a lengthy coda, will be required to restore mobility to the form.

Although the drama of the entire movement proceeds largely as a consequence of the ambiguity of this motion away from the tonic and toward the Neapolitan, the effect of this dislocation is felt in an especially acute fashion at the close of the development section when a false recapitulation of the secondary theme occurs in the key of D-flat.[31]

Because this is a moment in the form where a large-scale return to the tonic key is normally expected, the emergence of D-flat as the "wrong key" at this critical juncture

FIGURE 31.5 False recapitulation in D-flat, in Beethoven, Piano Sonata in F Minor, Op. 57, first movement, mm. 109–111.

FIGURE 31.6 Recapitulation in F major, in Beethoven, Piano Sonata in F Minor, Op. 57, first movement, mm. 174–183.

signals a dramatic moment in the plot of the movement. It reminds us that D♭ has never been assimilated into either the exposition or the development sections of the movement and that the BLOCKAGE that this note represents has thwarted the normal mobility of the form of the movement to this point.

As the true recapitulation eventually proceeds, the first subordinate theme appears again at m. 174, but first assuming the major form of the tonic key, F major (see Figure 31.6). The reappearance of the pair D♭/G♭ in mm. 181–182 is now doubly marked: the notes are expressively marked by their chromatic conflict against the prevailing major mode, and also because they jar against the E♮ in m. 183. Closure, or completion, is once again stalled by the extensive chromaticism of the slow descending scale that follows it. The fortissimo G♭ that follows in the second subordinate theme is juxtaposed with G♮ each time, confirming that it will remain for the coda to resolve these matters, to reposition G♭/D♭ in order to bring closure to the normal sonata form and to restore balance by reaching the expected goals.

The coda begins by first assimilating the G♭ into the harmonic body of the movement through a new strategy: it now becomes the seventh of an applied chord in mm. 206–209 (see Figure 31.7). This forces a resolution of the tone G♭ to F and thus finally disassociates it from the stalled Neapolitan harmony. Although this is not yet a true tonic resolution, it does force the reinterpretation of the G♭ as a dissonance that resolves to the tonic (F). When the Neapolitan chord then reappears at the fortissimo passage beginning in m. 218, it is no longer an obstruction to the tonic. The entire bravura passage that follows through m. 234 emphasizes the completion of that previously blocked motion. This is first achieved in mm. 222–223, and then even more emphatically again in 235–239. The final peroration of the main theme at m. 239 is the remediation of that theme, and of every mobility problem with the form that began in that theme originally.

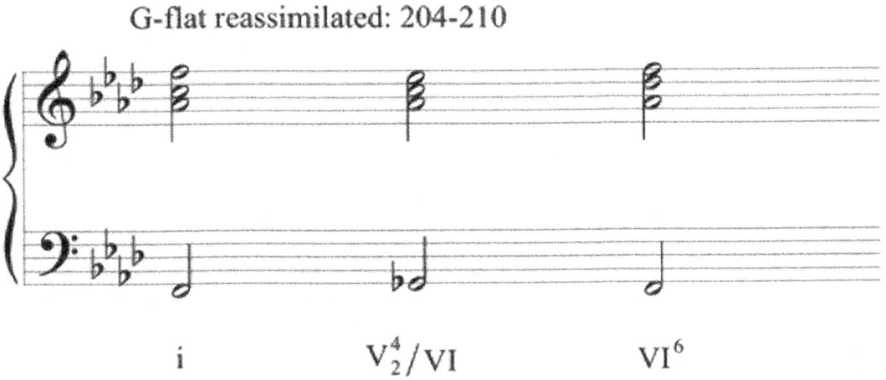

G-flat reassimilated: 204-210

i V^4_2/VI VI^6

FIGURE 31.7 Beginning of the coda of Beethoven, Piano Sonata in F Minor, Op. 57, first movement.

It will now be apparent that this has been a narrative of a disability that is accommodated by a prosthesis, by a reenabling coda.[32] The function of the coda here is one of narrative dependency, to provide the translation from the agon of the blocked and disabled sonata body to its eventual remediation through the prosthetic accretion that follows.

Musical prosthesis potentially provides a powerful remedy for the disconnect that persists between the embodied images that formal musical analyses typically present as genres, and those other generative forces that have motivated stylistic evolution within absolute music. As a hermeneutic model that is tied closely to formal processes, musical prosthesis is also closely aligned with narrative strategies for working within correlated frameworks of musical meaning.

Notes

1. Some notable exceptions appear in Lerner and Straus 2006—for example, Iverson 2006 (which includes a brief but provocative discussion of Björk's use of electronica as a prosthetic device in the domain of the natural voice) and Gross 2006. See also Jennifer Iverson's chapter in this volume, which deals extensively with Björk's electronica as a model for the prosthetic/supplemental in musical terms.
2. *Oxford English Dictionary Online*, s.v. "prosthesis, *n*," accessed December 2009, http://dictionary.oed.com/.
3. Wills 1995, 218.
4. For a critical discussion of the rise (and fall) of the prosthesis trope, see Jain 1999 and Sobchack 2006.
5. "Prosthesis has become a staple in the armory of metaphors or tropes that are utilized by intellectuals, scholars, students and practitioners who are concerned with interactions *in general* between the body and technology in modernity as they figure a conception of prosthetic lives in our post-human times" (Smith and Morra 2006, 2).
6. See Straus 2011, 45–62, for a detailed discussion of other narrative types involving disability in Beethoven's music.

7. This is a recurring argument throughout Straus 2006.
8. Straus (2006), while concerned with different sorts of narratives about disability in Beethoven's music than I am, has also noted this open-ended capacity of Beethoven's music, particularly in the *Eroica* Symphony: "Most narrative accounts of the work (and there are remarkably many) imagine it as depicting a battle or a struggle of some kind" (155).
9. *Formenlehre* refers historically to the analytical study of musical form. I will engage both recent and historical theories of form in this essay.
10. "Sonata space" is a term employed in Hepokoski and Darcy 2006. There are other nonintegrated supplemental regions besides codas, too—like slow introductions, for example. These appendages may also be thought of as prosthetic, even though their names do not necessarily imply corporeality. The fact that tails are not part of the normal human body, our vestigial tailbones notwithstanding, implicates the extent to which the coda is truly something extra, either a subhuman or extrahuman addition.
11. In addition to Saslaw 1996, see the special issue of *Theory and Practice* 22–23 (1997–1998), dedicated to the music-theoretical application of Mark Johnson's theories. Also, for more recent music theoretical extensions of Johnson's theories, see Larson 2012.
12. *Oxford English Dictionary Online*, s.v. "accretion," accessed December 2009, http://dictionary.oed.com/.
13. The opposition of these two perspectives had historically always remained reconciled as long as they were both enfolded within an understanding of musical form that was grounded in rhetorical conventions. This balance persisted as long as the enterprise of creating new works was not prioritized over the conventions of their intelligibility. Bonds (1991, 146–149) identifies Koch as the last successful theorist to have wed the two perspectives within a rhetorical understanding.
14. Cadences may be thought of as roughly equivalent to a syntactical pattern that establishes closure at the end of a musical theme or a phrase. They are highly conventional and clearly audible to the audience. Perfect authentic cadences (PACs) close most strongly, and imperfect authentic cadences (IACs) close harmonically but not as strongly in a melodic sense. In many modern theories of form, cadences are the single most important element in the articulation of formal boundaries.
15. An elision is an overlap, therefore an elided cadence is a boundary that is left without a gap: one phrase closes simultaneously as the next begins.
16. Precore and core techniques are described in relation to the development section by Caplin 1998, 141–155. A precore may be thought of as developmental transition leading into the main action space of the development section. It is therefore contingent on what follows it.
17. Kerman (1982) refers to this type of coda in Beethoven's first period as evincing "the calando effect" (143–144).
18. A sentence is a basic thematic construction that is marked by the immediate repetition of an initial idea and then trajectory toward a cadence.
19. The "tonic" is both the primary note and chord in a key and the first and last note in its associated scale. This particular melodic gesture is how a descending scale ends, as in the tune "Three Blind Mice."
20. One surmises that Kerman's dissatisfaction may have been directed toward various Schenkerian analyses, in which the close of the recapitulation may be taken to mark the close of the basic structure of the movement. The influence of Schenker on contemporary

analytical accounts of Beethoven's music at the time of Kerman's comments was considerable.

21. See Hopkins 1988, 394–398; Kerman 1982, 151–153; and Caplin 1998, 187 and 279n31.
22. This movement has been the focus of numerous analytical narratives that seize on some comedic quality of the music and others that identify disabled bodies, or even Beethoven's own deafness, as the source for its formal anomalies. Straus (2011, 57–59) discusses this Finale at some length.
23. It is also possible to think of this coda as responding to the coda of the first movement, in which case the C♯ is fulfilling an implication from that movement and the final coda then remediates the entire symphony.
24. See, for example, Meyer 1973 and Narmour 1992.
25. The "tonal problem" is discussed in the theories of composer Arnold Schoenberg, who posited that such events generated an imbalance that had to be restored by the rest of the work or movement. Detailed narratives using the tonal problem have disseminated to English-speaking readers primarily via Schoenberg's American student Patricia Carpenter, who has analyzed this same movement in Carpenter 1983.
26. Straus 2012, 48–51 provides a detailed discussion of the tonal problem in terms of narratives of disability. His readings and my own are compatible and closely related. However, where Straus primarily uses the tonal problem as a means for engaging narratives of "disability overcome," I am instead mostly interested in how prosthetic spaces may ultimately compensate the sonata body that has become disabled by the tonal problem.
27. A cross-relation occurs whenever a note that is chromatically altered, here a D♮, appears in a neighboring voice in close proximity to the unaltered form of that note (D♭). This cross-relation produces a strong dissonance (D♮ vs. D♭) and, in this instance, motivates a plot where harmonic ambiguity and imbalance results.
28. The "Neapolitan" is a chord or a key built a half-step away from the tonic. Despite that relatively small stepwise distance, it is actually quite remote from the tonic because of the chromatic notes from outside the key that are incorporated into it. Here, it represents a barrier to achieving motion back to the tonic.
29. Straus discusses BLOCKAGE as an image schema at some length in his initial work on music and disability. See Straus 2006, 122–127.
30. In Carpenter's (1983, 24) *Grundgestalt* analysis of this same movement she implicates the unprepared derivation of the Neapolitan as a Schoenbergian tonal problem, and she then traces the harmonic forms that the associated complex A♭/C/D♭ takes throughout the rest of the movement. As in my own narrative, Carpenter suggests that the solution to this problem is withheld until the coda.
31. The recapitulation is one of the three major sections of a sonata movement, and it may also be thought of as a goal too: it is where the home key, or tonic, returns after some lengthy digressions away from it in the development section. It usually restates main-theme material, although it can sometimes also begin with other material from the exposition, but in the tonic key (as it does here). A false recapitulation occurs when that material appears in the expected part of the form where a recapitulation should occur, but where the tonic key has not yet been reached.
32. In addition to narratives of a disability that is accommodated, Straus 2006 also identifies many instances of the narrative trope of disability overcome, especially in Beethoven's music.

References

Bonds, Mark Evan. 1991. *Wordless Rhetoric: Musical Form and the Metaphor of the Oration*. Cambridge, MA: Harvard University Press.

Caplin, William E. 1998. *Classical Form: A Theory of Formal Functions for the Instrumental Music of Haydn, Mozart, and Beethoven*. New York: Oxford University Press.

Carpenter, Patricia. 1983. "*Grundgestalt* as Tonal Function." *Music Theory Spectrum* 5: 15–38.

Gross, Kelly. 2006. "Female Subjectvity, Disability, and Musical Authorship in Krzysztof Kieślowski's *Blue*." In *Sounding Off: Theorizing Disability in Music*, edited by Neil Lerner and Joseph N. Straus, 42–55. New York: Routledge.

Hatten, Robert S. 1994. *Musical Meaning in Beethoven: Markedness, Correlation, and Interpretation*. Bloomington: Indiana University Press.

Hepokoski, James, and Warren Darcy. 2006. *Elements of Sonata Theory: Norms, Types, and Deformations in the Late-Eighteenth Century Sonata*. New York: Oxford University Press.

Hopkins, Robert G. 1988. "When a Coda is More Than a Coda: Reflections on Beethoven." In *Explorations in Music, the Arts, and Ideas: Essays in Honor of Leonard B. Meyer*, edited by Eugene Narmour and Ruth A. Solie, 393–410. Stuyvesant, NY: Pendragon.

Iverson, Jennifer. 2006. "Dancing out of the Dark: How Music Refutes Disability Stereotypes in *Dancer in the Dark*." In *Sounding Off: Theorizing Disability in Music*, edited by Neil Lerner and Joseph N. Straus, 57–74. New York: Routledge.

Jain, Sara S. 1999. "The Prosthetic Imagination: Enabling and Disabling the Prosthesis Trope." *Science, Technology, and Human Values* 24 (1): 31–54.

Johnson, Mark. 1990. *The Body in the Mind: The Bodily Basis of Meaning, Imagination, and Reason*. Chicago: University of Chicago Press.

Kerman, Joseph. 1982. "Notes on Beethoven's Codas." In *Beethoven Studies*, vol. 3, edited by Alan Tyson, 141–159. Cambridge, UK: Cambridge University Press.

Lakoff, George, and Mark Johnson. 1980. *Metaphors We Live By*. Chicago: University of Chicago Press.

Larson, Steve. 2012. *Musical Forces: Motion, Metaphor, and Meaning in Music*. Bloomington: Indiana University Press.

Lerner, Neil, and Joseph N. Straus, eds. 2006. *Sounding Off: Theorizing Disability in Music*. New York: Routledge.

Meyer, Leonard B. 1973. *Explaining Music: Essays and Explorations*. Berkeley: University of California Press.

Mitchell, David T., and Sharon L. Snyder. 2000. *Narrative Prosthesis, Disability, and the Dependencies of Discourse*. Ann Arbor: University of Michigan Press.

Narmour, Eugene. 1992. *The Analysis and Cognition of Melodic Complexity: The Implication-Realization Model*. Chicago: University of Chicago Press.

Ratner, Leonard G. 1980. *Classical Music: Expression, Form, and Style*. New York: Schirmer.

Saslaw, Janna K. 1996. "Forces, Containers, Paths: The Role of Body-Derived Image Schemas in the Conceptualization of Music." *Journal of Music Theory* 40 (2): 217–243.

Saslaw, Janna K. 1997–1998. "Life Forces: Conceptual Structures in Schenker's *Free Composition* and Schoenberg's *The Musical Idea*." *Theory and Practice* 22–23: 17–33.

Schoenberg, Arnold. 1967. *Fundamentals of Musical Composition*. Edited by Gerald Strang and Leonard Stein. New York: Faber and Faber.

Smith, Marquard, and Joanna Morra. 2006. Introduction to *The Prosthetic Impulse: From a Posthuman Present to a Biocultural Future*, edited by Marquard Smith and Joanne Morra, 1–16. Cambridge, MA: MIT Press.

Sobchack, Vivan. 2006. "A Leg to Stand On: Prosthetics, Metaphor, and Materiality." In *The Prosthetic Impulse: From a Posthuman Present to a Biocultural Future*, edited by Marquard Smith and Joanne Morra, 17–41. Cambridge, MA: MIT Press.

Straus, Joseph N. 2006. "Normalizing the Abnormal: Disability in Music and Music Theory." *Journal of the American Musicological Society* 59 (1): 113–184.

Straus, Joseph N. 2011. *Extraordinary Measures: Disability in Music*. New York: Oxford University Press.

Wills, David. 1995. *Prosthesis*. Stanford: Stanford University Press.

CHAPTER 32

SOUNDS OF MIND

Music and Madness in the Popular Imagination

JAMES DEAVILLE

EVER since antiquity, music and madness have maintained a strong association in the popular imagination in the Western tradition. As medical historian Dolly MacKinnon notes, the "use of music as a metaphor for insanity draws directly upon Galenic understandings from Classical Antiquity," as expressed in particular in Plato (MacKinnon 2006, 13). Moreover, Boethius's important treatise *Fundamentals of Music* (c. 520 AD) recognized that music has the power "to ennoble or corrupt the character" (cited in MacKinnon 2003, 129) and can produce or cure madness.[1]

An interesting reversal of this causality can be observed in the common cultural trope that avers madness may result in music (the mad song, but also products of the insane composer). The traditional linking of (musical) genius with madness arises from and reinforces the evolving discourse around insanity and music, particularly in the nineteenth and twentieth centuries, when for example music prominently figured in the proliferating treatises and related publications about how institutions should care for and treat those who experience madness and related conditions (MacKinnon 2003, 123).[2] MacKinnon observes, "popular beliefs about the 'power' of music to influence an individual's behavior for good or evil continued to dominate and influence popular press images and reports in the twentieth century" (MacKinnon 2003, 125).

The association between musical creativity and a nonnormate state of mind, be it genius or madness (or both), remains in force today—writing in 2008, John T. Hamilton argues for "the dogged tenacity ... of the wholly romantic coupling of music and madness" (Hamilton 2008, xiv).[3] Noted psychiatrist and concert pianist Richard Kogan recently gave a series of talks under the title "Music and Madness" for the Schumann year, in which he argued that "mental illness can also confer creative advantages."[4] Moreover, in October 2012, the Music Department of UC Davis hosted a major three-day concert event entitled "The Madness and Music Festival." Someone has posted a Pinterest bulletin board "Genius, Music, and Madness: All My Musical Muses" that features such figures as Elvis Presley, Rachmaninov, Bono, and Alfred Hitchcock

(Swift 2014). And the BBC *Music* Magazine has posted on its website Classical-music.com a "Music and Madness" Quiz, which is intended to test the classical fan's knowledge "from mad scenes in opera to composers suffering from syphilis" (*Classical-music.com*). With the exception of Kogan, the originators of these website pages and events appear unaware of how their appropriations of the concept and even the unproblematized term "madness" itself participate in and perpetuate a troubling historical association of ability and disability.

The linkage also figures in academic literature, especially that of the medical and psychiatric sciences, which stand the most to gain and the least to lose by fixating their gazes on the mortality of their favorite composers.[5] Indeed, Kogan's popular lecture-recitals have their basis in his clinical observation and study of patients from the arts sector. However, this type of work also reflects the fetishization of posthumous diagnosis, whereby the pathography—called "psycho-musical pathology" by one critic (cited in "Casals Edition—Schumann: Cello Concerto, Piano Trio No. 1" 1994)—capitalizes on reports of conditions and symptoms for celebrity figures, in often disturbing and yet clinical detail.

The current essay investigates some common tropes of disability that have informed and populated the problematic discourse surrounding music and madness, focusing here on the historically situated attributions of madness to central-European composers of the Romantic Era, the place and time for the powerful rise of the current set of associations.[6] In doing so, I hope to expose and denaturalize the traditional association of madness with genius and the corollary mapping of mental difference onto creative production. Given the size of the task even for the delimited field of inquiry, all I can hope to accomplish in this initial foray is to set the terms of engagement and present test cases (Schumann and Wolf) for their application.

It is necessary first to establish an epistemological framework for the topic of study. The term "madness" itself is not uncontested, although academics working in the field of Disability Studies have come to prefer "madness" over the limited and potentially misleading options.[7] Stephen Harper adopts a problematic clinical approach in his oft-cited 2005 study of media representations: "mental illness . . . is appropriate in descriptions of madness in psychiatric or institutional contexts," while madness applies "in other contexts, where the meaning of the term exceeds psychiatric discourse" (Harper 2005, 462). As he observes, the term "madness" "problematizes the pathologizing implications of phrases such as 'mental illness' " (463), which renders it particularly useful for the present study, which seeks to expose the role of the medical and psychiatric discourses about madness. That term of course is imprecise, encompassing any number of "cognitive impairments," to draw on the designation theorized by Lucy Burke (Burke 2008, i–iv), yet its very breadth and multivalence and its pejorative connotations enable "madness" to serve as a fitting cultural category for any critical assessment of its meanings through history. As Margaret Price argues in the *Disability Studies Reader*, "this term ["mad"] achieves a flexibility that *mental illness* and *cognitive disability* do not: it unites notions of that 'central concept' through time and across cultures" (Price 2013, 299). Furthermore, it captures the spirit of the mad pride movement, which reclaims the category of "madness" as a source of identity and worth, attempting to destigmatize the term, in a manner similar to the gay and lesbian community's re-appropriation of "queer."[8]

As such, "madness" is a construct, which has historically and culturally served as the binary to "sanity." This artificial division contrasts normalcy with defect and abnormality in static categories that position madness as a dangerous Other. As Shayda Kafai argues, "ableist culture relies on this binary due to the stability it provides, due to the feeling of fear that arises when one witnesses difference, particularly a difference that is difficult to name" (Kafai 2013). Michel Foucault investigated the mechanisms whereby society ostracized and controlled the insane, as "all elements within [the group] . . . were violently separated and rigorously reduced to silence" (Khalfa 2006, 170). More recent scholarship has applied his ideas about madness in a variety of fields and contexts, not least of which being the reception of prominent figures who "descended into" madness.[9]

To the extent that the mental and emotional conditions subsumed under the label of "madness" represent (from one perspective) "the loss or limitation of opportunities to take part in society on an equal level with others due to social and environmental barriers" (Northern Officers Group 1996),[10] it has been positioned as a disability, which in turns qualifies it for research within Disability Studies. Several scholars have adopted the designations "psychosocial disability" or "cognitive disability" for madness (Price 2009, 12), albeit not without discussion. The designation of a more specialized field under the rubric of "madness studies" remains contested—in their "Editors' Introduction" to the special 2013 topical issue "Disability and Madness" of the *Disability Studies Quarterly*, coeditors Noam Ostrander and Bruce Henderson warn that "a formal field of 'Madness Studies' may be in question" (Ostrander and Henderson 2013). Still, as they note, work on madness topics has "drawn heavily on Disability Studies to trouble the borders of normal/abnormal and sane/insane" (Ostrander and Henderson, 2013).

One of the major areas of inquiry to emerge is the critique of psychiatric and biomedical models of madness, which had its populist manifestation in the antipsychiatry movement of the 1960s and 1970s,[11] and indeed, the topical issue of *Disability Studies Quarterly* "builds upon on the Mad Pride movement and the activist works that preceded it" (Ostrander and Henderson, 2013). Another project for scholars in the field has involved exposing and counteracting modalities of shame and stigma among living subjects. Yet madness studies shares with Disability Studies some fundamental concerns, including how the discourse of insanity is constructed around individuals and in collective contexts, the means by which it disempowers and ostracizes its subjects, what role intersectionality plays in the experience and reception of madness, and how the person with a disability can respond to discrimination and discriminatory practices.[12]

These concerns have carried over into the realm of music insofar as it functions as a privileged site for madness in the popular imagination, whether among its creators and performers or in their artistic products and productions. The latter has evoked some investigations on a larger scale, across genres and practices,[13] yet no broader study has problematized the reception of musicians for whom the popular, medical/psychiatric and musicological literature have reserved the troubling yet traditional medical designation "mentally ill."[14] As already mentioned, members of the medical and psychiatric professions have fixed their clinical gaze on the disorders of individual composers, but they have done so for the sensational purpose of ascertaining the proper diagnosis for the malady rather than to understand its individual and social costs. As a result of this "empirical" work, their results have been avidly consumed by the musical community and general public alike, which ostensibly seek to obtain illumination through such examples but also relish discovering the "true" story behind the composer and the music.

Although the appellations of "mad" or "insane" to music itself date back well before the Romantic Era—Pierre Bayle's *Dictionary* of 1737 observes, for example, that the "soul of Parnassus must be praised in Basque, and low-Breton, [which] is enough to make a mad Music upon your Parnassus" (*Mr. Bayle's Historical and Critical Dictionary*, 1737)—the years since 1800 witnessed an explosion in the association of music with madness. Philosopher John T. Hamilton noted how German writers of romanticism all but fetishized the figure of the mad musician, "from Karl Philipp Moritz and Jean Paul Richter to Novalis, Ludwig Tieck, and Clemens Brentano" (Hamilton 2008, 2). It stands to reason that music's intangible yet ineluctable power would fascinate writers of the time, for whom the subject's loss of control—temporary insanity, if you will—represented an aesthetic category. E. T. A. Hoffmann was well aware of the psychological literature of his day, variously pathologizing the maladies of his characters like Kapellmeister Kreisler and Nathanael as "dementia, amentia, insania, delirium, vesania, melancholia, mania."[15] Hamilton's investigations reveal how Hegel's *Lectures on Aesthetics* consistently regard music "as an art of 'pure interiority,'" which parallels what he wrote about insanity in the "Anthropology" section of his *Philosophy of Mind*: "[it is] a reversion or withdrawal to interiority, as a 'sinking into inwardness' with no relation to external reality . . . These separate definitions seem to reveal not only music's affinity to madness but also the 'moment' music and madness share with the 'natural self'" (Hamilton 2008, 98–99). Whether or not the public knew these specific literary works or belletristic figures, their ideas participated in a much broader cultural trope of the time that regarded music, madness, and genius as closely interrelated. In this "alliance," the composer and performer became the carriers of a polysemous gift, and their compositions or performances the sites for its manifestation.[16]

The musicians who embodied this "ideal" for the popular imagination are legion, and cut across generations and genres. Indeed, Hamilton admits to astonishment over the madness discourse's "astonishing persistence," which has found fuel in the powerful stereotype of the troubled creative genius. The names of affected/afflicted musicians—at least considered as such by contemporaries—proliferated in the wake of the Romantic literary efflorescence on the one hand, and advances in psychology and medicine on the other. Of course, the tremendously expanding belletristic, daily, and musical presses provided crucial fora for the dissemination of such information about notable artists, those newly valorized celebrities whose public and private lives became objects for media exploitation. The most illustrious within what I call the "Pantheon of Musical Madness" that emerged included the familiar names of Paganini, Robert Schumann,

Donizetti, Smetana, Wolf, and Scriabin, while other, potentially insane figures like Schubert, Chopin, Alkan, Wagner, Tchaikovsky, and Mahler have inhabited the fringes, more as the subjects of individual academic studies than as composers who have been popularly identified with madness.[17] Perhaps the fitting culmination to this list is represented by a fictional character, Thomas Mann's tortured syphilitic composer Andreas Leverkühn, whose pact with the devil for musical genius seems to conflate all these individuals' experiences with madness. As we shall see, however, each field of reception takes on a different character and requires individual treatment, depending on factors including time, place, and notoriety. For closer analysis here, I have chosen Robert Schumann and Hugo Wolf, two figures from a similar cultural site yet separated by time, who have accumulated adequate cultural capital to participate in the public discourse of madness.

Robert Schumann

In delving into the reception of a composer's madness, the researcher needs to remain alert to his or her own position, which could fall on a scale between two extremes. On the one hand, we run the risk of mapping the composer's condition onto his or her musical creations, which is troublesome on several accounts: (1) it assumes an accurate diagnosis of the condition;[18] (2) it presumes a simple correlation between frame of mind and creative activity; and (3) it creates a false sanist binary in the assessment of a composer's oeuvre, between "normate" and "mad" works. At the same time, the discipline of musicology could attempt to erase traces of causality altogether, to keep the music "pure" from the readings described above—but here we run the risk of ignoring or missing the markers, the features of an alternate, different, yet distinctive frame of mind at work behind the compositional process.[19]

We see this dynamic of reception, between acceptance and disavowal, playing itself out particularly vigorously in the case of Robert Schumann, whose biographers are now compelled to address the ongoing discussions over the source(s) of his madness and its effects and whose analysts now must recognize the question of a late style. The most sensitive issue regards whether his eventual dementia resulted from syphilis, which could either further stigmatize his mental issues or provide a needed medical answer for his fatal condition. The examining doctor's report on his death—which has strengthened the diagnosis of syphilis—remained unknown for over 140 years, yet the biographical facts of his final years—internment in an insane asylum, suicide attempt, failing cognitive powers—were known at the time. Thus Schumann entered the Pantheon of mad musical geniuses during his lifetime, but without the additional stigma that a cause of syphilis could have engendered.[20] In the meantime, a dual fascination with and "disease" over Schumann's condition have arisen, and not only among health professionals: musicologists are squarely implicated in (mis)reading his mental disability, often bolstered by the medical evidence. Straus (2011) exposes the history of the scholarly industry that has constructed Schumann as the quintessential mentally ill (viz. mad or lunatic) composer. Straus identifies four possible assessments of Schumann's music, especially his late style:

> 1) the composer is mad and the music is also mad and therefore bad—sick, diseased . . . (the traditional notion of madness specifically, as a personal affliction . . .); 2) the composer is mad and the music is also mad and therefore good—visionary . . . (the Romantic notion of madness as the source and emblem of higher knowledge); 3) the composer is not all that mad, and whatever his psychiatric issues may have been, they have no perceptible impact on the music . . . (the prevailing view of current musicology . . .); 4) the composer's mental differences from the norm are significant enough to place him within a community and tradition of similarly situated artists. His madness is a "dangerous gift."

A fifth position can be found in the older Schumann literature, namely that Schumann was indeed mad but his music from that period was good—this reading tied in with the "mad genius" trope.[21] From the perspective of Madness Studies and Disability Studies, only Straus's fourth reading is viable, in that it allows the mad composer to speak unencumbered by both the findings of health science and the traditions of musicological analysis.

Certain aspects of Schumann's biography invited both contemporaneous and posthumous readings of them as symptomatic of his eventual madness, usually linking the manifestation(s) with a diagnosis. Especially his multiple fictional identities Florestan and Eusebius have lent themselves to twentieth-century interpretations as we witness in such diagnostic designations as schizophrenia, bipolar disorder, and dissociative identity disorder.[22] In his diary from July 1, 1831, Schumann himself introduces them as "two of my best friends, whom I've nonetheless never seen before—they are Florestan and Eusebius" (cited in Daverio 1997, 74). Daverio avoids psychiatrizing these inventions by identifying them as "poetic self-projections . . . , a poetic solution to the problem of the split self" (75), characters whose performance of his competing inner voices enabled his varied discourses in prose and music. These personal identity markers do not appear to have struck his contemporaries as unusual: early biographer Wilhelm Joseph von Wasielewski, for example, regarded them as products of a poetic nature (von Wasielewski 1871).

Another aspect of Schumann's life that has occasioned serious attention from the posthumous diagnosticians was a period of what Schumann called "melancholy" for the early fall of 1833, after the deaths of brother Julius and sister-in-law Rosalie in the summer—among the commentators from the medical and psychological communities of today, this "event" is identified as a "severe melancholic depressive episode" (Domschke 2010), "depression or schizophrenia" (Franzen 2008, 1155), or "breakdown" (Ostwald 1985, 99). For these professionals, it represents the first episode of a "lifelong mental disorder" (Domschke 2010, 325), which foreshadows the downward spiral of the mad genius.[23] His distress during this period caused the composer himself to experience considerable fear, as articulated in a letter to Clara: "In the night between the 17th and 18th of October I was seized with the worst fear a man can have, the worst punishment Heaven can inflict—the fear of losing one's reason" (Schumann 1907, 183). The fear of madness (and of asylums) is a topic that would recur in Schumann's letters and diaries,[24] but he never brings it into association with his music or composition, even in the later years.

His contemporaries knew about Schumann's eventual madness—they attributed it to a variety of sources, often left unspecified. The most frequent cause mentioned in the literature from the 1850s and 1860s, however, was what Schumann's Endenich doctor, Franz Richarz, recorded for biographer Wasielewski as an "organic disease of the brain": "excessive mental exertion . . . , intellectual extravagance . . . , over-work induced this disease," which led to melancholy (von Wasielewski 1871, 258). Richarz proceeds to link the melancholy with artistic genius: "the poetic aroma of holy melancholy floats like a breath from the past around every great and glorious exemplar in art . . ." (Ostwald 1985, 259). Neither Richarz nor Wasielewski make clear associations between Schumann's developing insanity with a decline in musical abilities, but rather argue that the composer's extraordinary abilities led to his condition, in an odd twist of the madness/genius trope. Thus for these contemporaries, it was the genius (and the resulting hard work of giving it expression) that caused the disease, and not the customarily reversed causality of the pathogen leading to a human condition.

Perhaps the most controversial of the posthumous psychiatric diagnosticians for Schumann was Peter Ostwald. His suggestively entitled, controversial book *Schumann: The Inner Voices of Genius* begins with the statement "Genius and madness have often been thought to be related in some way. In the life of Robert Schumann it is particularly difficult to draw a line between the two. The problem of distinguishing between his creative and his psychotic behavior has confounded many biographers and psychiatrists" (Ostwald 1985, xi). Himself a psychiatrist, Ostwald explores every detail from the documentary record that might shed light on Schumann's mind—unfortunately, he fully subscribed to the posthumous diagnostic protocol of the medical and psychiatric communities, determined to explain the "inner voices of genius."[25]

Hugo Wolf

The medicalized literature about Wolf emphasizes how he shares with Schumann many of the same "symptoms" (short bursts of feverish activity, megalomania, suicidal thoughts, and ultimately complete insanity). However, in his case the diagnosis of neurosyphilis has been almost unquestionably accepted, which has led neurologists Hansjörg Bäzner and Michael Hennerici (among others) to retroactively attribute syphilis to both composers (Bäzner and Hennerici 2010, 315–345).[26] According to Foucault's periodization of the discourse of madness, both Schumann and Wolf would fall within the third phase, "the modern experience of madness where madness is now perceived as factual or positive, an object of science, as a disease or series of diseases, a period which starts at the end of the eighteenth century" (Khalfa 2006, xv–xvi). At the same time, syphilitic dementia "was romanticized as an aid to artistic genius," and yet one that "carried with it the stigma of moral deviancy" (Sturken 1997, 148),[27] whereby the disabling effects of syphilis positioned the victim as doubly coded: on the one hand morally suspect, on the other highly gifted.

In contrast with Schumann, Wolf fell into this binary, for his insanity was known and its source suspected by contemporaries in the Viennese musical world,[28] while his music—including most of the late work—clearly bespoke significant talent for some and genius for others.[29] Biographer Ernest Newman himself side-stepped the issue of Wolf's condition by advocating silence: he refused to engage in the public discussions about Wolf's symptoms, writing the following in 1907: "What one hears in private of some of the details of his life, interesting as it is to the moral pathologist, is not yet a matter for the public ear" (Newman 1907, 152).

Wolf's final collapse and ultimate committal came in late 1898, at a point in time when newly founded Hugo-Wolf-Verein in Berlin and Vienna was hard at work promoting his music. During and after the composer's final five institutionalized years, the Viennese society not only sponsored concerts but also published essay collections in his honor. Can one attribute the composer's rising star in central Europe during his final incarceration, his ultimate isolation not only to the efforts of the Verein, but also to his insanity?

Indeed, the madness/genius trope appeared to work salubriously for Wolf's reputation,[30] ironically once he became institutionally isolated from the public gaze. As McColl observes about a Wolf-Verein concert on November 27, 1897, "[critic Ludwig] Karpath noticed that the public which had stayed away from Wolf's concerts while he was in good health now seemed to flock to the Wolf-Verein concerts now he was ill" (McColl 1996, 135). The image of the tormented genius—problematic as it may be—nevertheless situated Wolf in the ranks of other such notable lunatic syphilitics of the time like Nietzsche, van Gogh, and Maupassant.[31] At the same time, the shadow of the "insane" Wagner—whose "name seems to appear far more often in nineteenth-century psychiatry [than those of] Robert Schumann and Hugo Wolf" (Kennaway 2012)—extended over his stylistic excesses, which found condemnation (or justification) in the contemporary press. The former occurred in a *Wiener Sonntags- und Montags-Zeitung* review of the late-1897 concert by Hofrath Johann von Wörz, who claims that "other people . . . disapprove of such *Lieder* and songs of the pathologically overstretched composer" (cited in McColl 1996, 136). In contrast, in his 1900 assessment of *Der Corregidor*, Wolf friend Edmund von Hellmer wrote of the work's strength from the "uncanny juxtaposing of genius and insanity" (Von Hellmer 1900, 8) and by the time of Romain Rolland's *Musiciens d'aujord hui* of 1908, the composer's "tragic destiny . . . assured him a place apart in the hell of great musicians" (Rolland 1914, 144).

Thus Wolf entered into the pantheon of mad musicians during his lifetime,[32] a position ensured by virtue of his "genius" as composer of *Lieder*. Indeed, Bäzner and Hennerici put forward a bizarre interpretation of Wolf's compositional limitation to the

Lied as resulting from his madness—after all, as they cite Thomas Hampson, did the "illness [of syphilis] [not] release in [Schubert and Schumann] a heightened sensibility for lyric form, emotional surges, and sensitivity that empowered them to achieve such masterly settings?" (Bäzner and Hennerici 2010, 80). And this conflation of insanity and the *Lied* (and *not* opera) as manifestations of a hyperinteriority, positions the composer within the Romantic discourse described earlier.[33] For Wolf, whose entire reputation rested on his work in that genre, it meant that the conditions of syphilis and madness could be retrospectively mapped onto his entire creative career, including his activity as music critic.

Moreover, the historical association of musical genius with radical progress—after all, did not Mann's Leverkühn innovate the serial technique?—could justify Wolf's unconventional melodic and harmonic practices to his contemporaries. (One could argue that the public in general seems more inclined to accept strange harmonies and other unusual innovations if they believe a rational explanation can be located in the composer's madness.) In comparison with Schumann, whose work of the 1850s took a "classical turn," Wolf's compositional oeuvre could be teleologized in terms of advancing complexity through to his removal from society. This normalization and yet fetishization of syphilitic decline represents one of the more pernicious aspects of the medicalized discourse surrounding insanity, as madness studies has argued. It would be interesting to study how the trope of a musically advanced "late style" has been informed by issues of inner disability in a composer like Franz Liszt.[34]

We could dismiss these troubling readings of Schumann and Wolf as historical phases within the discourse of insanity, if the terms and signifiers for the mad musician/composer were not still in circulation, inciting the popular imagination and informing academic work. In fact, the "insanizing" of composers and performers by the medical and psychiatric communities—to deploy Lennard Davis's term (Davis 2008)—has expanded its net to embrace figures like Mozart and Beethoven (Franzen 2008), whose erratic behaviors have suggested psychiatric or psychological issues.

That the dichotomies of normal/abnormal, sane/insane remain in force for historical composers becomes readily apparent from the recent Schumann literature. Any biographer—and that includes John Daverio (1997), John Worthen (2010), Eric Jensen (2012), and Martin Geck (2012)—must deal with the final years, and the discussion of a so-called late style has become a musicological/music-theoretical industry, staffed by figures like Laura Tunbridge (2007) and Jon Finson (2011). A survey of that literature and of more popular assessments of the music reveals how Straus's four responses to the late works coexist at the present time, ranging from dismissal ("mad music") through tolerance and acceptance to advocacy ("works of genius"). Within the scholarly community, Tunbridge's measured study comes closest to what Straus describes as "an appreciation of the diversity of human embodiments, both mental and physical" (Straus 2011, 34). Yet to the public—tending to valorize the medicalized assignment of disorder—Schumann has often seemed more interesting as a madman in the making, whose life can be read as inexorably leading to the final breakdown. The "descent into madness" trope then allows for the construction of a straightforward narrative of life ebbing away, of relentless decline—informed by the symptoms of the interpreter's own choosing—rather than accepting Schumann's madness as an embodied state, as a "dangerous gift."

The British classical music blogger Jessica Duchen can simply assert as fact, "Last but not least, Schumann was nuts" (Duchen 2010). The commentator "Sidoze" on the classical discussion forum "Good-Music-Guide.com" reflects the effects of the madness trope on the listener: "The reason why I usually don't listen to Schumann is because I get the feeling it's crazy music with all its mood swings and strange feelings and stuff" (Sidoze). Would such a response have been possible without the circulated medicalized knowledge of Schumann's madness? The knowledge of a composer's insanity does seem to influence how performers understand and play the music, as Michael Beckerman observes in his essay in this collection: "the very way we think the meaning of sound may be inseparable from perceptions of disease, loss and disability."

Wolf presents a different reception field today for the reasons detailed above. Nevertheless, the medical model still informs the discourse surrounding him, and that also promulgated by academic colleagues. For example, Lawrence Kramer locates the basic rhetorical configuration of Wolf's songs in a "scrutinizing" mode he identifies as the Oedipus complex, although he disavows a Freudian claim or suggestion that "the secret of Wolf's art lay in neurosis, even though Wolf had neuroses to spare" (Kramer 2010, 242). Even the customarily circumspect Susan Youens succumbs to the temptation of unproblematically mapping the composer's mental state onto his music with the *Michelangelo Songs* of 1897, of which she writes, "at the end, inspiration slipped, regained control, faltered again . . . [They] are not marked by the same unfailing mastery evident everywhere in the Italian songbook" (Youens n.d.). The knowledge of Wolf's condition has informed the analysis, to the extent that this type of perceived change in style and/or musical idiosyncrasy is pathologized and explained as a symptom of mental distress.[35] To judge by the existing literature, the only way to avoid pathographizing Wolf's music is by limiting the analysis to the notes themselves, without reference to biography or culture. While this might work for narrow technical studies (Taycher 2012), it is not likely to prove satisfying for the great majority of musicologists and music theorists.

The study of madness does not provide an easy way out of such an impasse. A "realistic mode" (in the sense of Garland-Thomson) for dealing with these issues, at least for Schumann and Wolf, would involve an approach that first dismantles the discourses of disease and madness that have framed the lives and works of these musicians, resisting the compulsion to identify symptoms and to map them onto musical creativity. Awareness of the common tropes that have informed the problematic discourse surrounding music, madness, and genius will begin the process of exposing these historical narratives of insanity that still play out in the academic and popular imaginations. Then it would be possible to reintroduce the disability as important to the composition or performance, but as only one of several factors influencing the outcome—this way one could (re)approach the assessment of artistry by such musicians without resorting to normalizing or peculiarizing tactics. By regarding madness as a form of difference rather than as a disease or abnormality, we may be able to free ourselves from the burden of past and present sanist biases.

Notes

1. Samantha Bassler's essay in this volume explores the dual nature of music in relation to madness—either as generator or cure—in Elizabethan England, especially in the writings of Shakespeare.
2. For example, the sources discuss how music could serve as a cure and a reward in those institutions, whereby Frederick Hill Harford established the Guild of St. Cecilia in 1891 to play "sedative music to a large number of patients in London hospitals" (cited in MacKinnon 2003, 133).
3. Hamilton 2008 not only establishes the historical precedent for that association of concepts, but also makes clear how the linking trope continues to function in a similar way to nineteenth-century constructions.
4. Kogan's comments are cited in *Vail Daily*, 2010.
5. It stands to reason that undiagnosed fatal conditions of prominent musicians would arouse interest and discussion in a variety of circles, including those of the health sciences, and those artists for whom an accurate symptomology have proven most elusive (Schumann and Schubert, for example) have received the greatest attention. Exhumations of the bodies of important individuals were regularly undertaken in the late nineteenth and early twentieth centuries, in order to determine the cause of death and reasons for their genius, which led Reger to specify cremation for his own earthly remains (Otte 2008). It was first in the 1960s that musician mortality—both for classical and popular artists—attained the status of a field of inquiry unto itself, although populated by members of the medical and psychiatric communities who would collect lives and deaths in anthologies. These volumes were popular among the public but also controversial, since others in the health sciences disputed the diagnoses—at the time, no one considered criticizing the books for their totalizing, clinical approaches to disease and disability. The first significant such publication was Dieter Kerner's *Krankheiten grosser Musiker* from 1963, which experienced six editions (through 2007). Other such compilations of composers and performers followed, especially the four-volume *Die Krankheiten grosser Komponisten* by doctor Franz Hermann Franken (1986–1997). It stands to reason that the gaze of professionals would turn toward the issue of mental (un)health, given the number of composers known and suspected to have exhibited symptoms thereof. While individual studies drew attention to the case of Schumann early in the twentieth century (Möbius 1906; Gruhle 1906), the growing public and professional interest in causes of mortality among noted personalities of past and present resulted in a surge in posthumous psychiatric diagnoses of composers. The names included Schumann, Schubert, Paganini, Wolf, and Smetana. See for example Bäzner and Hennerici 2010, Böhme 1987, Breitenfeld 2013, Franken 1997, and Appel 2006.
6. A variety of factors contributed to the efflorescence of those discourses, including the following: (1) The discipline of psychiatry and more general scientific interest in the workings of the mind (especially deviant behaviors, whether genius or insanity) experienced a tremendous upsurge during the period; (2) Because of the ostensibly "expressive" character of their music, nineteenth-century composers acquired a reputation as living in a heightened state of interiority; (3) The rise of the virtuoso performer and the celebrity composer brought their lives and works under greater scrutiny, even as the musical press flourished; (4) Biography and artistic creation became inextricably linked through the causality inferred or directly argued by the new scientific methods.

7. Lennard Davis deploys "mental distress" as a neutral term for the culturally constructed "madness" (Davis 2008, 28).
8. Regarding the "mad pride movement," see among others, Lewis 2010, and Schrader et al. 2013. The intersection of madness and queerness is explored in Rowe and Chávez 2011.
9. This descriptive turn-of-phrase already appeared in literature of the late eighteenth century, and has persisted to the present. The romanticized metaphor "descent into madness" may suggest a withdrawal into a profound inner subjectivity, yet the parallel with "descent into hell" is compelling, whereby the subject's narrative of madness is both mythified and presented as inevitable. See Dunham 1999, 281. Heinrich Heine used the phrase in the first sentence of his reminiscences of his departed associate Ludwig Marcus, exploring both his gradual decline and the resultant inner isolation (Heine 1974).
10. Of course, this is only one possible definition for disability: one of the major challenges facing the field of Disability Studies has been to obtain to a determination for the concept that would be legally recognized, culturally grounded, and personally sensitive while accommodating a diversity of applications.
11. About the antipsychiatry movement, see above all Kotowicz 2013 and the classic text, Cooper 1967.
12. One of the most active and effective advocates for the understanding of madness as a disability has been Kay Redfield Jamison, whose autobiography *An Unquiet Mind: A Memoir of Moods and Madness* (Jamison 1995) outlines the author's own path through manic depression. Among her other texts, *Touched with Fire: Manic-Depressive Illness and the Artistic Temperament* (Jamison 1993) sensitively deals in particular with the intersection of madness and the artist, exemplified by the case of Lord Byron.
13. Mad scenes in opera were popular for study in the 1990s—for contrasting literature from the perspectives of musicology and psychology, compare Smart 1992 and Erfurth and Hoff 2000, while perceptions of madness among popular musicians is the topic of Spelman 2012.
14. A growing body of studies resists the medicalization of madness (and of the categories "mental illness" and "mental health"), in the wake of the landmark publications by Foucault (1961) 2006, Laing 1960, and Szasz 1974. See also Davis 2002, Kutchins and Kirk 1997, and Whitaker 2009 and 2010.
15. Davis 2008 proposes that this type of diversity of diagnostic categories arose in the nineteenth century as a result of the emerging discipline of psychiatry, which enabled a large number of people to participate in the symptoms of madness and not just the lower fringes of society, and allowed madness to coexist with elements of "health" in one and the same individual. As Davis notes, "madness becomes an emblem of being human . . . and becomes fashionable, national, and almost a requirement to be in the intellectual and social elite" (47). This valuation of course helped to firmly establish the construct of the "mad genius."
16. In studies about the arts and madness, literature, visual art, and music are presented as equal participants in the myth of the mad genius, even though the popular imagination may grant the musician a special position in the pantheon of madness (see, for example, Spelman 2012). Of course, the accessibility of the musician through public performance and the fetishization of musical celebrity afford greater scrutiny of behavior than do the potentially less media-centric lives of writers and visual artists. See also Lull and Hinerma 1997 and Marshall 2006.
17. For example, Poundie Burstein (2006) published a valuable essay about the case of Charles-Valentin Alkan.

18. Much of the literature, whether scientific or popular, presumes that categories of conditions are stable, accurate, transhistorical, and diagnosable from a medical or scientific perspective. Uncovering an artist's "psychoses" then becomes a straightforward task of matching recorded symptoms with current diagnostic criteria and labeling the individual's condition(s) accordingly. As already argued, that enterprise is seriously flawed—highly deleterious to its subjects—and merits the most scathing opposition wherever it appears. Rather than falling into that same mode of thought, proving or disproving prior arguments about diagnoses, the current study attempts to examine the reception of these composers in light of the historical understandings of madness, from their lifetime through the present and including the musicians' own perceptions of their condition(s).
19. Straus (2011) proposed a series of four transhistorical reactions to disability (5), onto which he has mapped the following five potential responses with regard to the work of performers and composers: (1) The disability is irrelevant; (2) The disability has been overcome, and the music itself is a symbol of overcoming; (3) The disability is reflected in the music and makes the music weird and abnormal; (4) The disability is reflected in the music and lends it transcendent qualities (this is mostly for blindness and madness, although Beethoven's deafness also gets this treatment); (5) The disability is central to the music making, but just one factor. The last of these corresponds to the "realistic mode" of gazing at disability, described in Garland-Thomson 2001.
20. Among others, Deborah Hayden describes and criticizes the stigmatization that syphilis-induced madness has historically provoked (Hayden 2003, xvii).
21. Much of this interpretation hinges on the date when the commentator sets the onset of Schumann's insanity, for if the biographer traces the symptoms back to the early 1840s, his period of madness could embrace the important larger works. Thus an anonymous article from 1919 contends that "Schumann's greatest works, those which have placed him in the front rank of composers, were the fruit of those months when his friends commented on his eccentricities but when his brain was really over-activated by syphilis and his genius was therefore at its highest mark" ("On the Advantages of Having Syphilis," 1919, 728).
22. See for example Chissell 1948, where the author observes that the two characters represent "no mere romantic extravagance but rather a downright recognition of a very real form of schizophrenia" (33).
23. An article in the *Psychiatric Quarterly* of 1963 went so far as to designate—in its title—Schumann as "Mad Master of Music" (Brussel 1963).
24. Ostwald (1985) provides references for most of these sources, although he lends them his own psychiatrizing interpretations.
25. Ostwald died in 1996, and did not have the opportunity or desire to revise his findings based on the release of the Richarz diaries that composer Aribert Reimann handed over to the Akademie der Künste in Berlin and that appeared in abridged form in 1994 (see Franken 1994). Franken's report is suspect, however, since he found his own diagnosis confirmed in the diaries, which—as Yael Braunschweig remarks—"raises the question of how preconceived interpretations of Schumann's health history might have helped shape his readings of newly available information" (2013, 111).
26. The authors even produced comparative charts of compositional activity to prove the correlation between composers and manifestations of their conditions, arguing that the spurts of activity and inactivity correspond intimately between the two figures.
27. See also Gilman 1988.

28. Wolf biographer Frank Walker remarks how the composer's behavioral idiosyncrasies struck his friends and contemporaries in the years leading up to his institutionalization (Walker 1968, 76).
29. Sandra McColl's study (1996) provides examples of the varied reviews Wolf received (135–136).
30. As Straus observes with regard to performers, "the Mad Genius is a person whose cognitive impairment or psychological disturbance is bound up with a superhuman vision . . . Their madness is taken as an emblem of their genius. To some extent, musical performers choose among these roles and present themselves in one of these interpretations of disability" (2011, 130–131). Thus the representation of madness can also become a marketing tool, as suggested by Waltz and James (2009, 373), although questions about who controls that image remain.
31. The unidentified author of the 1919 article "On the Advantages of Having Syphilis" placed Schumann and—by inference—Wolf in the same company as Nietzsche and Maupassant, arguing that "all three put forth the finest flower of their genius when the disease [syphilis] was rampant and when their brains were thereby over-activated, the penultimate chapter to paralysis of the insane" (728). Although extremely problematic in its assessment of the disease's benefits, the article well illustrates how the cultural portrayal of mad genius cuts across boundaries of artistic discipline.
32. Wolf's insanity may have been known in the Vienna of his time, yet its symptoms contributed to diagnoses that did not necessarily lead to syphilis. Regarding contemporary assessments of his condition, see Hayden 2003, 313–314.
33. It is interesting to observe how madness appears to play out differently according to musical genre. A composer's madness is only rarely invoked for works in larger and ostensibly more complex genres like opera, the symphony or sacred music (with the exception of Schumann's late compositions); it seems more at home in the smaller, more confined genres.
34. Liszt's late work has served as the topic for a variety of studies that typically position its advanced style within a nexus of life and creation, whereby failing health, isolation, and the pessimism of the final years (late 1870s and 1880s) result in an austere, darkly hued music that rejects tradition in favor of experimentation. See above all Walker 1996, Baker 2005, and Szabolczi 1959.
35. Much more could be written about the psychiatric symptomizing of certain musical styles and compositional approaches, especially with regard to composers associated with musical progress—the trope of "crazy music"—and virtuoso performers (for example, "madman of the keyboard").

References

Appel, Bernhard R. 2006. *Robert Schumann in Endenich (1854–1856): Krankenakten, Briefzeugnisse und zeitgenössische Berichte*. Mainz, Germany: Schott.

Baker, James M. 2005. "Liszt's Late Piano Works: A Survey." In *The Cambridge Companion to Liszt*, edited by Kenneth Hamilton, 120–151. Cambridge, UK: Cambridge University Press.

Bäzner, Hansjörg, and Michael G. Hennerici. 2010. "Syphilis in German-Speaking Composers: 'Examination Results Are Confidential.'" *Neurological Disorders in Famous*

Artists, Part 3, edited by Julien Bogousslavsky, Michael G. Hennerici, and Hansjörg Bäzner, 61–83. Frontiers of Neurology and Neuroscience 27, Basel, Switzerland: Karger.

Böhme, Gerhard. 1987. *Medizinische Porträts berühmter Komponisten*. Vol. 2. Stuttgart, Germany: Gustav Fischer Verlag.

Braunschweig, Yael. 2013. "Biographical Listening: Intimacy, Madness, and the Music of Robert Schumann." PhD diss., University of California at Berkeley.

Breitenfeld, Darko, Tomislav Breitenfeld, Danijel Buljan, Lana Skrgatic, Lana Vuksanovic, and Marija Zivkovic. 2013. "Diseases and Destinies of Famous Composers: Why Should One Even Write about Composers' Diseases?" *Alcoholism: Journal on Alcoholism and Related Addictions* 49 (1): 55–60.

Brussel, James A. 1963. "Schumann: Mad Master of Music." *Psychiatric Quarterly* 17 (1): 225–233.

Burke, Lucy. 2008. "Introduction: Thinking about Cognitive Impairment." *Journal of Literary Disability* 2 (1): i–iv.

Burstein, Poundie. 2006. "*Les chansons des fous*: On the Edge of Madness with Alkan." In *Sounding Off: Theorizing Disability in Music*, edited by Neil Lerner and Joseph Straus, 187–198. New York: Routledge.

"Casals Edition—Schumann: Cello Concerto, Piano Trio No. 1." 1994. Recording review in *Gramophone*, May. Reprinted on ArkivMusic. Accessed January 2, 2014. http://www.arkivmusic.com/classical/album.jsp?album_id=5873.

Chissell, Joan. 1948. *Schumann*. New York: Farrar, Straus and Giroux.

Cooper, David. 1967. *Psychiatry and Anti-Psychiatry*. London: Tavistock.

Daverio, John. 1997. *Robert Schumann: Herald of a "New Poetic Age."* Oxford, UK: Oxford University Press.

Davis, Lennard J. 2002. *Bending Over Backwards: Disability, Dismodernism, and Other Difficult Positions*. New York: New York University Press.

Davis, Lennard J. 2008. *Obsession: A History*. Chicago: University of Chicago Press.

Domschke, Katharina. 2010. "Robert Schumann's Contribution to the Genetics of Psychosis: Psychiatry in Music." *British Journal of Psychiatry* 196: 325.

Duchen, Jessica. 2010. "The Malady Lingers On." *Standpoint*, May. http://standpointmag.co.uk/music-may-10-schumanns-bicentenary-jessica-duchen.

Dunham, Jeffrey B. 1999. "Philip Lewis." In *Contemporary African-American Novelists: A Bio-Bibliographical Critical Sourcebook*, edited by Emmanuel S. Nelson, 279–283. Westport, CT: Greenwood.

Erfurth, Andreas, and Paul Hoff. 2000. "Mad Scenes in Early 19th-Century Opera." *Acta Psychiatrica Scandinavica* 102 (4): 310–313.

Finson, Jon. 2011. "At the Interstice between 'Popular' and 'Classical': Schumann's Poems of Queen Mary Stuart and European Sentimentality at Mid-Century." In *Rethinking Schumann*, edited by Roe-Min Kok and Laura Tunbridge, 69–87. New York: Oxford University Press.

Foucault, Michel. (1961) 2006. *Madness and Civilization: A History of Insanity in the Age of Reason*. Translated by Jean Khalfa and Jonathan Murphy. New York: Routledge.

Franken, Franz Hermann. 1994. "Robert Schumann in der Irrenanstalt Endenich: Zum Verlaufsbericht seines behandelnden Arztes." In *Robert Schumanns letzte Lebensjahre: Protokoll einer Krankheit*. Berlin: Stiftung Archiv der Akademie der Künste.

Franken, Franz Hermann. 1997. "Robert Schumann." In *Die Krankheiten großer Komponisten*, vol. 4, 218–251. Wilhelmshafen, Germany: Noetzel Verlag.

Franzen, Caspar. 2008. "Syphilis in Composers and Musicians: Mozart, Beethoven, Paganini, Schubert, Schumann, Smetana." *European Journal of Clinical Microbiology and Infectious Diseases* 27 (12): 1151–1157.

Garland-Thomson, Rosemarie. 2001. "Seeing the Disabled: Visual Rhetorics of Disability in Popular Photography." In *The New Disability History: American Perspectives*, edited by Paul K. Longmore and Lauri Umansky, 335–374. New York: New York University Press.

Geck, Martin. 2012. *Robert Schumann: The Life and Work of a Romantic Composer*. Chicago: University of Chicago Press.

Gilman, Sander. 1988. "AIDS and Syphilis: The Iconography of Disease." In *AIDS: Cultural Analysis/Cultural Activism*, edited by Douglas Crimp, 87–108. Cambridge, MA: MIT Press.

Gruhle, Walter. 1906. "Brief über Robert Schumann's Krankheit and P. J. Möbius." *Zentralblatt für Nervenheilkunde und Psychiatrie* 26: 805–810.

Hamilton, John T. 2008. *Music, Madness, and the Unworking of Language*. New York: Columbia University Press.

Harper, Stephen. 2005. "Media, Madness, and Misrepresentation: Critical Reflections on Anti-Stigma Discourse." *European Journal of Communication* 20 (4): 460–483.

Hayden, Deborah. 2003. *Pox: Genius, Madness, and the Mysteries of Syphilis*. New York: Perseus.

Heine, Heinrich. 1974. "Ludwig Marcus: Denkworte." In *Sämtliche Schriften*, edited by Klaus Briegleb, Vol. 5, 175–191. Munich: Deutscher Taschenbuch Verlag.

Jamison, Kay Redfield. 1993. *Touched with Fire: Manic-Depressive Illness and the Artistic Temperament*. New York: Simon & Schuster.

Jamison, Kay Redfield. 1995. *An Unquiet Mind: A Memoir of Moods and Madness*. New York: Alfred A. Knopf.

Jensen, Eric. 2012. *Schumann*. Master Musicians. New York: Oxford University Press.

Kafai, Shayda. 2013. "The Mad Border Body: A Political In-Betweeness." In *Disability Studies Quarterly* 33 (1). http://dsq-sds.org/article/view/3438/3199.

Kennaway, James. 2012. *Bad Vibrations: The History of Music as a Cause of Disease*. Farnham, UK: Ashgate.

Kerner, Dieter. 1963. *Krankheiten grosser Musiker*. Stuttgart, Germany: Friedrich-Karl Schattauer.

Khalfa, Jean. 2006. *History of Madness*. Abingdon, UK: Routledge.

Kotowicz, Zbigniew. 2013. *R.D. Laing and the Paths of Anti-Psychiatry*. New York: Routledge.

Kramer, Lawrence. "Hugo Wolf: Subjectivity in the Fin-de-Siècle Lied." In *German Lieder in the Nineteenth Century*, edited by Rufus Hallmark, 2nd ed., 239–292. New York: Routledge.

Kutchins, Herb, and Stuart Kirk. 1997. *Making Us Crazy: DSM, the Psychiatric Bible, and the Creation of Mental Disorders*. New York: Free Press.

Laing, R. D. 1960. *The Divided Self: An Existential Study in Sanity and Madness*. Hammondsworth, UK: Penguin.

Lewis, Bradley. 2010. "A Mad Fight: Psychiatry and Disability Activism." In *The Disability Studies Reader*, edited by Lennard J. Davis, 4th ed., 115–131. New York: Routledge.

Lull, James, and Stephen Hinerma, eds. 1997. *Media Scandals: Morality and Desire in the Popular Culture Marketplace*. New York: Columbia University Press.

MacKinnon, Dolly. 2003. "'The Trustworthy Agency of the Eyes': Reading Images of Music and Madness in Historical Context." *Health and History* 5 (2): 123–149.

MacKinnon, Dolly. 2006. "Music, Madness, and the Body: Symptom and Cure." *History of Psychiatry* 17 (1): 9–21.

Marshall, David. 2006. "The Meanings of the Popular Music Celebrity: The Construction of Distinctive Authenticity." In *The Celebrity Culture Reader*, edited by David Marshall, 196–222. New York: Routledge.

McColl, Sandra. 1996. *Music Criticism in Vienna, 1896–1897: Critically Moving Forms*. Oxford: Oxford University Press.

Möbius, Paul J. 1906. *Über Robert Schumanns Krankheit*. Halle, Germany: Marhold.

Mr. Bayle's Historical and Critical Dictionary. 1737. Vol. 4. 2nd ed. London: D. Midwinter.

"Music and Madness." *Classical-music.com*. Accessed January 2, 2014. http://www.classical-music.com/quiz/music-and-madness.

"Music and Madness at Vail Symposium." 2010. *VailDaily*, July 7. Accessed January 2, 2014. http://www.vaildaily.com/article/20100707/AE/100709807/1078&ParentProfile=1062.

Newman, Ernest. 1907. *Hugo Wolf*. London: Methuen.

Northern Officers Group. 1996. "Defining Impairment and Disability." *The Disability Discrimination Act: A Policy and Practical Guide for Local Government and Disabled People*. Sheffield, UK: Northern Officers Group. Accessed January 2, 2014. http://disability-studies.leeds.ac.uk/files/library/Northern-Officers-Group-defining-impairment-and-disability.pdf.

"On the Advantages of Having Syphilis." 1919. *The Urologic and Cutaneous Review* 23 (12).

Ostrander, Noam, and Bruce Henderson. 2013. Introduction to *Disability Studies Quarterly* 33 (1). http://dsq-sds.org/article/view/3443/3197.

Ostwald, Peter. 1985. *Schumann: The Inner Voices of a Musical Genius*. Boston: Northeastern University Press.

Otte, Karina. 2008. "Die ärztliche Schweigepflicht und das postmortale Persönlichkeitsrecht." In *Kerners Krankheiten grosser Musiker: Die Neubearbeitung*, edited by Andreas P. Otte and Konrad Wink, Vol. 1, 1–16. Stuttgart, Germany: Schattauer.

Price, Margaret. 2009. "'Her Pronouns Wax and Wane': Psychosocial Disability, Autobiography, and Counter-Diagnosis." *Journal of Literary and Cultural Disability Studies* 3 (1): 11–33.

Price, Margaret. 2013. "Defining Mental Disability." In *The Disability Studies Reader*, 4th ed., edited by Lennard J. Davis, 298–307. New York: Routledge.

Rolland, Romain. 1914. *Musicians of To-day*. New York: Henry Holt.

Rowe, Desireé D., and Karma R. Chávez. 2011. "Valerie Solanas and the Queer Performativity of Madness." *Cultural Studies Critical Methodologies* 11 (3): 274–284.

Schrader, Summer, Nev Jones, and Mona Shattell. 2013. "Mad Pride: Reflections on Sociopolitical Identity and Mental Diversity in the Context of Culturally Competent Psychiatric Care." *Issues in Mental Health Nursing* 34: 62–64.

Schumann, Robert. 1907. *The Letters of Robert Schumann*. Edited by K. Storck. Translated by H. Bryant. London: J. Murray.

Sidoze. "The Schumann Shack." Good-Music-Guide.com. Accessed January 2, 2014. http://www.good-music-guide.com/forum/index.php?topic=441.70;wap2.

Smart, Mary Ann. 1992. "The Silencing of Lucia." *Cambridge Opera Journal* 4 (2): 119–141.

Spelman, Nicola. 2012. *Popular Music and the Myths of Madness*. Farnham, UK: Ashgate.

Straus, Joseph N. 2011. *Extraordinary Measures: Disability in Music*. Oxford, UK: Oxford University Press.

Sturken, Marita. 1997. *Tangled Memories: The Vietnam War, the AIDS Epidemic, and the Politics of Remembering*. Berkeley: University of California Press.

Swift, Molly. 2014. "Genius, Madness and Music: All My Musical Muses." Pinterest. Accessed January 2, 2014. http://www.pinterest.com/moswift/genius-madness-and-music.

Szabolczi, Bence. 1959. *The Twilight of Liszt*. Translated by András Deák. Budapest: Akadémiai Kiadó.

Szasz, Thomas. 1974. *The Myth of Mental Illness: Foundations of a Theory of Personal Conduct*. New York: Harper Collins.

Taycher, Ryan. 2012. "Deceiving the Ear: Recontextualization, Key Association, and Auxiliary Cadence in Two Songs by Hugo Wolf." *Journal of Schenkerian Studies* 6: 93–113.

Tunbridge, Laura. 2007. *Schumann's Late Style*. Cambridge, UK: Cambridge University Press.

Von Hellmer, Edmund. 1900. *Der Corregidor von Hugo Wolf: Kritische und biographische Beiträge zu seiner Würdigung*. Berlin: S. Fischer.

Walker, Alan. 1996. *Franz Liszt, Vol. 3: The Final Years, 1861–1886*. New York: Knopf.

Walker, Frank. 1968. *Hugo Wolf: A Biography*. 2nd ed. New York: Knopf.

Waltz, Mitzi, and Martin James. 2009. "The (Re)Marketing of Disability in Pop: Ian Curtis and Joy Division." *Popular Music* 28 (3): 367–380.

Whitaker, Robert. 2009. *Mad in America: Bad Science, Bad Medicine, and the Enduring Mistreatment of the Mentally Ill*. 2nd ed. New York: Basic.

Whitaker, Robert. 2010. *Anatomy of an Epidemic: Magic Bullets, Psychiatric Drugs, and the Astonishing Rise of Mental Illness in America*. New York: Crown.

Worthen, John. 2010. *Robert Schumann: Life and Death of a Musician*. New Haven, CT: Yale University Press.

Youens, Susan. n.d. "Hugo Wolf." *Grove Music Online*. Accessed January 2, 2014. http://www.oxfordmusiconline.com.proxy.library.carleton.ca/subscriber/article/grove/music/52073pg7#S52073.7.

PART 7

MODERNISM AND AFTER

CHAPTER 33

MODERNIST OPERA'S STIGMATIZED SUBJECTS

SHERRY D. LEE

THOMAS Mann's character Hanno Buddenbrook has a childhood obsession with a figure from a folk poem in *Des Knaben Wunderhorn*, a little hunchback (*Das bucklicht Männlein*) who seems to be an embodiment of mishap and misfortune. "It's really very awful," explains Ida Jungmann, Hanno's nurse, to his aunt Antonie:

> This little hunchbacked man is everywhere, he smashes pots, eats the broth, steals the wood, keeps the spinning wheel from turning, makes fun of people—and then, at the end, he asks to be included in people's prayers. Yes, the boy has been fascinated by it. He's been thinking about it all day and all night. "Don't you see, Ida? He doesn't do it because he's wicked, not because he's wicked! He does it because he's sad, but that only makes him sadder. And if people pray for him, then he won't have to do it anymore." And this evening, when his mother came in to say good night on her way to the concert, he asked if he should pray for the little hunchback, too. . . . (Mann [1901] 1994, 455)

The same little hunchbacked figure was a recurring motif also for Walter Benjamin, who likewise knew the poem from childhood. In Benjamin's writings—and, according to Hannah Arendt, in his conversation as well[1]—the little hunchback surfaced as a figure of catastrophe, one who had terrified him in childhood and who remained a significant symbol of misfortune and disaster through to the end of his life. "Whoever the little man looks at pays no heed, either to himself or to the little man. He stands distraught before a pile of ruin. . . . I never saw him. He only always saw me" (Benjamin 1991, 964). The hunchback is a liminal figure, barely glimpsed. No mere folkloric joke, much more than a figure of mischief or accident, the little man who laughed at him from the corner of the bedroom was, for Benjamin, the emblem of a disfigured life.

This modernist focus on the figure of the little hunchback is part of a wider cultural interest of the time in the theme of the subject who is marked or stigmatized, by inner trauma as much as by any externally evident physical affliction or impairment.

Somewhat differently from Benjamin, for whom the crooked gnome sneezing in the garden was a frightening figure of menace, Hanno Buddenbrook, strikingly, shows a strong sense of identification with the disaster-prone little man. Weak and sickly, ill-prepared either physically or psychologically for the challenge of life, Hanno is destined to die early, the last progeny of a decadent family whose decline is marked by a turn from commerce toward art. Yet, his constitutional fragility aside, he shares no marked physical deformity with the little gnome from the pages of his school reader; rather, his affinity for the hunchback, a figure of calamity, is more spiritual. It is between these two poles—of fearful distancing and objectification, and of painful identification and sympathy—that the modernist conceptualization of the damaged person lies.

Afflicted bodies may have been alien in society, but they were not strangers to the operatic stage. It is true that acute afflictions such as wounding and disease were more common by far in operatic representation than congenital or physical deformities (Verdi's hunchbacked jester Rigoletto stands out in this regard); but more to the point, while the operatic repertoire of the nineteenth century in particular showed a distinct fascination with the representation of bodily suffering, it also showed a strong tendency to romanticize, sanitize, and even prettify afflictions and infirmities.[2] The beautiful deaths of tubercular heroines are examples that spring most readily to mind, and these aestheticized conclusions of lives marked by prolonged illness and suffering bring, arguably, more sheer listening enjoyment than those countless violent operatic deaths that typically register, at least, an aural shock to accompany the thrilling murderous thrust or suicidal leap. Two important exceptions occur in the oeuvre that most immediately preceded and certainly most deeply influenced the operatic composers and works of early twentieth-century German and Viennese modernism, namely that of Wagner. The feverish and delirious Tristan, dying from a wound that finds no healer and no relief, suffers and gives voice to a degree of agony that is rarely witnessed or heard in the opera house, and Wagner's sustained musical setting of his hero's expressions of torment is calculated to create a potency of visceral effect as well as emotion within the listener. Wagner explicitly drew the conceptual connection between his dying Tristan and the later character of Amfortas, whose physical debilitation and resulting anguish, a chronic pain exacerbated by shame, are registered with almost seismic intensity in the music's harmonic, timbral, dynamic and gestural profiles. Far from pleasurable, both examples are at best wrenching, perhaps even grueling to listen to. Arguably, they are notable precisely for the way in which they reach beyond a relatively objective representation of a character we know to be suffering, attempting to sonically register an experience of anguished intensity that may resonate sympathetically within the listener. After all, *Mitleid* ("suffering-with") was not only a dramatic theme in *Parsifal* but a conceptual goal.[3]

These acutely suffering Wagnerian figures are operatic incarnations of ideal characters, whose identities are constituted as a combination of subjective integrity and a social position of centrality and belonging, brought low by a betrayal that leaves them wounded and broken. The musical-dramatic representation of their vulnerability is thrown into relief by its narrative and dramatic juxtaposition with their former wholeness and sufficiency—Tristan as fearless and loyal military hero, Amfortas as leader and guardian of a holy community. But within two or three decades after Wagner's death—despite the undeniable reach of his influence, experienced often enough as an impediment rather than an asset by the generations that followed him—the very notion of the subject and the possibility for its wholeness had been called into question. The artistic and cultural tropes of twentieth-century modernism have been characterized by Jacques Le Rider as "attempts to rebuild identity on the ruins of the subject" (Le Rider 1993, 45). As the conditions of modernity created apprehensions about the nature of subjective identity, so the artistic products of modernist culture reflected a growing concern over the vulnerability of the self and, further, the lack of stability of inner and outer identity in a context of political, economic, and social upheaval. Though opera's stages were still "strewn," in Michel Poizat's memorable terms, with ever-increasing "heaps of bodies" (1992, 134), many the ideally-costumed vehicles of lovely voices accompanied by the orchestral language of passion, some distinctly modernist characters joined the long operatic parade of figures whose physical, psychological, or social beings were marked as dissonant. These characters bear the stigmata of visible and permanent bodily impairments, as external tokens of a damaged inner life.[4]

Disability, Modernism, and the Aesthetic

For the interdisciplinary field of humanistic and culturally framed Disability Studies, the modernist era has been an important area of focus, and within that era the early twentieth-century Austro-German sphere, wherein the Expressionist impulses of the century's opening decades furnished a wealth of cultural objects that were then prime for condemnation as "degenerate" by the National Socialist regime a few years later. Carol Poore's (2007) monograph on disability in German culture of the twentieth century highlights a strong sociocultural connectivity between conceptions of disability and modernism, rooted in the historical context of prewar German Expressionism through wartime and Weimar-era Germany and Austria. Poore discusses Expressionism as a "transition between old prewar and new postwar ways of representing disability, of suffusing particular kinds of bodies with meanings" (18). With its particular focus on themes of illness and insanity, Expressionist art, she asserts, did not often depict physical disability, although the poems of Georg Heym about hunchbacked, blind, or deaf figures are worth noting; yet her examination points to a shift in disability representation occurring within a few short years, one that highlights connections between wartime and a broader social awareness of—and ambivalence toward—marked physical disability especially among men:

> Visual artists took up the subject of disability more often during the Weimar era than at any other time in German cultural history except perhaps for the frequent

> depictions of crippled beggars in medieval religious art. As soon as disabled and wounded veterans began returning from the front, the bodies of these men became major themes for the visual arts and to a lesser extent for literature as well. (Poore 2007, 19)

While the field he surveys is broader than that considered by Poore, Tobin Siebers (2010) similarly notes the increased presence of "wounded or disabled bodies, representations of irrationality or cognitive disability, or effects of warfare, disease, or accidents" in modernist art, beginning his survey of "the aesthetics of human disqualification" with exemplars of German Expressionist and Weimar-era art and the National Socialist response to it. "The Nazis rejected the modern in art as degenerate and ugly," he asserts, "because they viewed it as representing physical and mental disability" (5). Siebers is concerned to highlight the ways in which disability serves as a reason for the disqualification of individuals as worthwhile human beings, and his focus on aesthetic representation supports his insistence that the perception of disability is grounded in *appearance*: disqualification, he argues, is "justified through the accusation of mental or physical inferiority based on aesthetic principles" (24). Nevertheless, according to Siebers, disability is actually perceived in a modernist context as a positive aesthetic value, becoming both a "unique resource" and a "defining concept" for a modernist art that "embraces beauty that seems by traditional standards to be broken, and yet it is not less beautiful, but more so, as a result" (2–3). Indeed, and most crucially, he presses his argument further to contend that the modern itself is recognized as disability: "modern art comes over time to be identified with disability, to the point where the appearance of the disabled or wounded body signals the presence of the aesthetic itself" (19). True, the breadth of this claim initially seems somewhat breathtaking; yet it is compellingly supported by the wide array of examples of artistic and cultural representation that both Poore and Siebers cite and interrogate interpretively.

Although their many examples do not include musical or dramatic works, "modern art's love affair with misshapen and twisted bodies" (Siebers 2010, 4) and the broader modernist concern to engage with "extreme human experiences located outside respectable bourgeois social conventions and aesthetic norms" (Poore 2007, 18) are clearly evident preoccupations in any number of musical works of this era. While certainly not ubiquitous, disability notably becomes both visible and audible on the stages of Germany and Austria in operas conceived in an Expressionist context, composed during the years of the Great War, and performed during its aftermath in the age of the Weimar Republic. This essay recognizes such interest by offering a discussion of select operatic representations of the conception of bodily impairments whose stigma gives rise to a suffering that mirrors the modern individual subject's experience of vulnerability and alienation. By way of grounding theoretical concerns in specific examples from the repertory, it will consider in particular the following operatic works, which feature characters who are visibly marked by physical impairments, and who, predictably, suffer social stigmatization as a result: Richard Strauss's and Hugo von Hofmannsthal's *Die Frau ohne Schatten* (1911–17), with its three disfigured characters, the Dyer's

Brothers, and their opposition to the physically beautiful but shadow-less, and hence infertile, women in the opera; Franz Schreker's *Die Gezeichneten* (1913–15), whose disfigured principal character is in thrall to a beautiful woman with a hidden congenital impairment, and his *Der Schatzgräber* (1916–18), with its constellation of an ugly Fool, a disabled henchman, and a disfigured dwarf of legend; and Alexander Zemlinsky's *Der Zwerg* (1922), which sets Oscar Wilde's fairy tale of an ugly dwarf gifted as a plaything to a heartless young princess.

Within this framework there are a number of issues that draw particular attention. One is the tendency of all the operas in question to frame their subjects within a mode of temporal distancing, by situating them in historical and/or mythical times seemingly far removed from the contemporary modernist moment, even in light of—or indeed, perhaps in spite of—the contemporary resonance of physically damaged characters in those crucial years during and immediately after World War I. Another is the question of the nature of the physical impairments that are represented and their wider historical and contemporary cultural resonances: most notable is the predominance of characters with spinal deformities, and how they align with (or depart from) a long history of the cultural understanding of hunchbacked and dwarfed figures. A third is the way in which characters who are physically marked are clearly made to function symbolically, as stand-ins for, or reflections of, seemingly physically "whole" characters who yet bear other, less visible afflictions or stigmas. "For the norm to be established," as Lennard Davis has recognized with respect to eighteenth- and nineteenth-century forms of the novel in particular, "the abnormal must also appear," whether that "abnormal" is manifest as a villainous character with a physical disability or as a disabled innocent (57). Pace Davis, the situation is arguably more complex in a modernist context wherein the appearance of the abnormal, rather than acting merely as a foil that contrasts the norm and throws it into relief, is instead a pointer to another abnormality that is not apparent, but hidden. Perhaps the central question concerns the significance of making physical disability effectively emblematic of a wider fate of subjective crisis, such that some element of disability or deformation is understood as a universal condition of modern selfhood. This is a challenging and possibly a troubling move: while seeming to embrace the disabled condition and even to validate it by claiming it as a kind of norm, it also arguably equates metaphor with lived experience in a way that potentially diminishes the very real experience of those for whom disability is an embodied condition.

Perhaps a similar uncertainty is suggested by the tendency of the operas discussed here to simultaneously engage with disability and hold it at arms' length. One of their most obvious means of purposefully distancing the disabled subject of representation is through temporal displacement. Effectively, these dramas are cast within time frames that evoke a historical era predating a modern, medicalized understanding of disability, one that emerges sometime around 1800 and "defines disability as a pathology or defect . . . [that] can be remedied or cured through medical intervention and personal effort" (Straus 2011, 6). This important shift in medical understanding comes to resonate in modern cultural products that may be set in the distant past, but at the same time show an awareness distinct from earlier historical views in which the disabled were shown little compassion. It would be misleading to attempt to single out one common motivation behind the temporal distancing from a (Viennese) modernist present of all the characters in these operas through fairy-tale, Medieval, or Renaissance settings. There was, for example, a notable vogue for Renaissance settings that obviously partook in a much wider Austro-German trend of *Renaissancismus* across the arts in the decades surrounding the turn of the century (Uekermann 1985). But arguably, the nineteenth century's tendency to objectify by aestheticizing bodily affliction is transposed in opera's modernist moment to an impulse toward temporal remoteness, at the same time that the affliction is more deeply etched into the conception of the self's exterior *and* interior.

By the later eighteenth century and into the early nineteenth, as Simon Dickie makes clear, the disabled were still frequently the subjects of cruel jokes and objects of derisive laughter, as exhibited across a range of comic literary genres. Tangible changes in cultural values and corresponding social behaviors attributable to Enlightenment principles of human equality and betterment did not arrive overnight, he argues (Dickie 2011, 2). Even while ideals of politeness, benevolence, and "sensibility" became increasingly desirable individual traits, and large-scale charitable institutions dedicated to aiding the unfortunate, ill, and disabled evidenced a changing ethics, the misfortunes of the disabled were still often considered merely part of the divinely governed scheme of things, and cripples, dwarves, and hunchbacks were derisively dismissed. In particular, as Ulrike Halter and Andreas Krödel (1997) explain, only in the nineteenth century did spinal deformities become a subject of medical interest, and scoliosis and kyphosis were newly viewed as conditions that could be "defined as treatable, if not actually curable" (561). This understanding is consistent with what Straus (2011) describes as a general dominance in the nineteenth century of a "medical model" (6). As Straus explains, the possibility for cure emphasized by this model comes to be viewed as an imperative: that the abnormal *should* be normalized—or eliminated (6–7). The broader historical picture at this juncture is far from simple: what also becomes apparent in Halter and Krödel's study is that the progressive increase in medical attention to spinal deformities, and the development (if gradual) of orthopedic treatment methods for individuals with kyphosis or scoliosis, to a considerable extent paralleled but more significantly contributed to an increase in social awareness, and a corresponding improvement in the sociopsychological situation of these individuals. Although longstanding superstitious biases against them declined, degrees of stigmatization did persist. Even so, sympathetic literary portrayals of the disabled were increasingly found near the turn of the nineteenth century and thereafter. "The novels have their share of evil dwarfs and one-eyed moneylenders," Dickie asserts, "but at the same time novelists were beginning to experiment with idealized deformed characters, whose deformity became a mark of virtue" (Dickie 2011, 89). The situation was different in drama, wherein the necessary condition of embodiment canceled the possibility for some distancing or detachment from the damaged subject that still existed in fiction:

> One looks in vain for anything like [literature's] sentimental representations on the late-eighteenth-century stage. Indeed, it is hard to think of many idealized deformed characters anywhere in the canon of mainstream drama (Rigoletto, Verdi's wronged and pitiful hunchback, is an isolated exception in a genre in which music does the work). Dramatic and fictional representations of deformity strike their limits at very different points. (Dickie 2011, 89)

Dickie's mention of the example of *Rigoletto* is worth considering, if briefly, for more than one reason; the first is surely that it is arguable just how far Rigoletto is actually "idealized" in Verdi's opera. If he is undoubtedly presented in a manner that elicits sympathy, there is little doubt about the malign aspects of his character, and his anguish at the final tragic outcome of his obsessive bid for vengeance is intensified not least because it has come about through his own nefarious doings.[5] He is cruel, and willing to resort to murder; the hump on his back is the outer sign of inner depravity, and imposes a limit on the reservoir of pity in Verdi's work. In general, while the genre of opera showed the influence of contemporary medical preoccupations and changing awarenesses of bodily affliction in the nineteenth and early twentieth centuries, the ancient belief that exterior physical stigma were signs of internal weakness, baseness, or vice still informed the representation of disabled characters onstage, notwithstanding the growing tendency to view them through lenses of pity and even empathy rather than mere derision and scorn.

A second point to consider in relation to Dickie's example of *Rigoletto* is a more basic one, which is the nature of the character's impairment: it is perhaps unsurprising but still worth noting that the instance of a deformed stage character that comes most readily to mind is that of the hunchback. All four of the modernist operas considered in this essay include hunchbacked characters, and other examples from roughly the same time frame—Leoncavallo's *Pagliacci* (1892), Schmidt's *Notre Dame* (1906) after Hugo's most famous hunchback of the nineteenth century, Zandonai's *Francesca da Rimini* (1914)—could be added. This prominence is striking, and although it would be misleading to try to account for this contemporary preoccupation in overly simplistic terms (indeed, the literary representations cited at the opening of this essay would belie any such attempt), it is worth considering that it is owed at least in part to how well the hunchbacked figure plays from the operatic stage. For hunchbacks, together with the one-eyed, one-armed, and dwarfed characters discussed here, are distinctly visible as disabled figures, and their physicality onstage is central to their dramatic effect. Dwarves and hunchbacks, in particular, are not merely visible, but these figures are also, in most narrative-dramatic incarnations here, embodiments of what might be considered an able disability: mobile on the stage, typically cognitively whole even if psychologically damaged or morally decrepit, and generally less impaired in the day-to-day than might be a figure lacking a limb, or sight, hearing or speech (in a musical context especially). What is most significant about the emblematic hunchback then, from this perspective, is his *disfigurement*.

Physical incapacity is really not the main point; rather, as Siebers insists, it is the aesthetic quality of appearance that is at stake. This is not because the deformity is benign, an aesthetic feature only—kyphosis can give rise to more serious complications such as numbness, muscular weakness, chronic pain, difficulty breathing, possibly even pressure on and damage to the heart. And the physical effects of the malformed bones symptomatic of dwarfism can include various degrees of pain and reduced capacity from nerve constriction, spinal compression, and early-onset degenerative joint disease, not to mention the possibility of disordered organ function. But whatever impairment may result from dwarfism, kyphosis, or the deformities of bowed legs that often accompany both conditions, the crisis of social and psychological incapacity represented on the opera stage—both the stigma and its resultant suffering (which may even prove fatal)—all hinge on unsightly appearance.

As Mark Jeffreys notes in his essay on "The Visible Cripple (Scars and Other Disfiguring Displays Included)," cultural Disability Studies have been enabled by the adoption of a typically humanist constructivist stance that insists on the historical and cultural specificity of knowledge; it "makes possible the argument that disability is itself not so much a pathological or even biological condition as it is a cultural condition, a marginalized group identity . . . , a stigmatized category." His concern is that the emphasis on representation in humanities-based Disability Studies runs the risk of "backfiring" by relegating physicality and biology entirely to the realm of fictional representation, invalidating the lived, embodied experience of disabled individuals (Jeffreys 2002, 32–33). Operatic representation of disability does undoubtedly emphasize physicality and embodiment: it makes deformity patently visible, and often goes further by making it musically audible as well, in vocal and instrumental sound. Yet the paradox of the operatic hunchback, as with the dwarfed, the crippled, or the one-armed opera character, is the insistence on the performance of their visible and sometimes audible disfigurement onstage even while their very appearance is intended to be symbolic, a metaphorical representation of inner psychic damage in the physically whole subject whose suffering arises from the very fact that the damage is hidden and must remain so according to societal constraint.

Stigmas—Visible, Audible, Invisible

Strauss and Hofmannsthal's fourth musical-dramatic collaboration centers on just such a disjunction between visible and hidden incapacity, and an opposition between external beauty and internal lack. It escapes from historical time altogether into the realm of the fairy tale. The Empress, lovely princess of the spirit world, has been captured in her form of a gazelle by the Emperor while he was hunting, and made his wife; but despite their mutual passion she has not become pregnant after a significant interval of time, and the fact that she still casts no shadow, unlike mortal women, is the sign that she remains unable to conceive a child. Her malevolent Nurse determines that they can only remedy her lack by descending to the world of mortals in order to acquire a shadow from a mortal woman who is willing to give hers up, and with it her own ability to bear children. The pretty and discontented Wife of Barak the Dyer proves to be such a woman, who fears neither the impairment of infertility nor the social stigma of childlessness, but welcomes the opportunity for freedom from a conventionally sanctioned domestic life.

Barak has three brothers: all are physically disabled and dependent on him for both food and shelter. It is unclear what may have happened to them in the course of their lives to render them debilitated and reliant on their sibling: Barak describes them as children with "clear eyes, strong arms, and a straight back," but all three have become in some way incapacitated, one missing an eye, one lacking an arm, and one with a hump. They are given no names, but identified only via their disabilities, which become proper nouns: the One-Eyed, the One-Armed, and the Hunchback (*der Einäugige, der Einarmige, der Bucklige*).[6] Dickie (2011) considers such labels as "condensed signs of a thoroughgoing *body determinism*, as one might call it" (103), a determinism that is pervasive in this drama. True, most of the opera's characters have role labels rather than names—the Nurse, the Empress, the Spirit Messenger, the Wife—which is not uncommon for fables or *Märchen*. But the brothers are the only ones whose identities are subsumed—in Rosemarie Garland-Thomson's term, "engulfed" (1997, 10–11)—by their physical defects: they are the mere embodiments of their disabilities. As such, and not only because the fairy tale tends to deal in archetypes, they function symbolically. No one would claim that they are central characters in the drama, yet in their embodied, damaged, and unsightly existence they are situated strategically in the midst of those who are beautiful and not fully embodied (the spirit characters) or beautiful and resentful of their grounded, bodily existence (the Wife who rejects her husband's touch and her own body's fertility). Thus, their roles are crucial parts of an antagonistic constellation of symbolic characters. In particular, animosity is rife between the Brothers and the Wife, who wants the Dyer to evict them from the family home. When we are introduced to them, they are brawling on the floor of the Dyer's impoverished hut: the one-eyed brother is on top of the one-armed, accusing him of theft and trying to throttle him, while the youngest, hunchbacked brother cries out in dismay that they are killing each other and tries in vain to separate them. The latter task is accomplished instead by the Wife, who throws a pail of water on them, as if they were fighting dogs, and indeed she addresses them disdainfully as such. Perhaps unsurprisingly, the Brothers, so visibly flawed, are audibly marked within the music as well. Strauss presents them within a chaotic sonorous palette of rhythmic and harmonic dissonance that is punctuated by the uncouth noise of the *rute* (Figure 33.1a), striking harsh blows as if to aurally and viscerally evoke the impact of the squabbling brothers' assaults on each other's bodies. Their antagonistic chorus (Figure 33.1b) is clamorous rather than melodious.

The impression created by the *rute*'s percussive assault falls somewhere between slapstick comedy and a more troubling violence that resonates throughout the drama as a whole, beginning with the capture of the Empress-as-gazelle, grazed by the spear of the hunting Emperor, and continuing with the sorrowful, bleeding falcon, wounded in anger by the Emperor's dagger.

FIGURE 33.1A Richard Strauss, *Die Frau ohne Schatten*, Act I sc. 2: introduction of the Brothers.

(b) Beim Aufgehen des Vorhanges liegt der Einäugige auf dem Einarmigen, würgt ihn. Der Junge Verwachsene sucht den Einäugigen wegzureißen. Die Färbersfrau kommt von rückwärts herzu, sucht nach einem Zuber, die Streitenden mit Wasser zu beschütten.

FIGURE 33.1B Strauss, *Die Frau ohne Schatten*, Act I sc. 2, reh. 3: the Brothers brawling.

In accusing them of behaving like dogs, the Wife's angry words in this scene effectively disqualify the Brothers as human beings. Yet they do not slink away chastened like animals; their response is human, and bitter. They taunt her for being an outsider, for not belonging in their midst; they throw at her the moniker of "beauty," as if it were an insult. There is something telling in this exchange, in which the disabled collectively shun the able-bodied precisely on grounds of the latter's aesthetic wholeness. It turns out, moments later, to be in part the category of gender that disqualifies the wife in the Brothers' eyes in turn. "Leave her, Brother," suggests the One-Armed to the Hunchback, after a series of insults have been flung: "she's only a woman." This is her essential quality, grounded in her physical being, its materiality central to the drama's theme. The shadow cast by her solid form—unlike the body of the barren Empress through which light passes like glass—makes visible her essential function of childbearing. For her, that quality is a handicap: though she has no physical deformity, she describes her own shadow as "crooked" (*gekrümmte*). And when she relinquishes that disabled/disabling shadow for the Nurse's proffered temptations of jewels, finery, the luxury of servants and the thrill of a handsome young lover, its lack all too clearly parallels that of the missing arm, the lost eye. No wonder the three Brothers are the first to recognize its unnatural absence in the sudden flaring of the fire that illuminates her defiant stance. It would be mistaken to argue that they are marked according to the ancient conception that disability is a sign of divine gifts of intuition, genius, or perhaps prophetic insight, even though they are undoubtedly acutely sensitive to signs of the supernatural. They seem rather to manifest an awareness that emphasizes their proximity to a natural, instinctual, even bestial existence, their sensitivity analogous to the equally ancient belief that animals are able to sense impending weather changes or natural disasters. They collectively voice vaguely fearful premonitions—"there is something, brother, and we know not what it is"—as Barak broods and his Wife frets about "the dogs" who "howl in fear and no one turns them out"; moments later, as if on cue, they "howl" out their fright at the lightening strikes that presage the supernatural collapse of the Dyer's house (*ein greller Blitz, die Brüder heulen auf*, say Hofmannsthal's stage directions). Their repeated wails, interrupting the Wife's tirade about dull, imperturbable individuals who go daily "like beasts from bed to trough," are merely unmusical, wordless noises jotted in the stage directions: Strauss scores only the lightning flashes, but not their cries.

Like the insults of the Wife, the opera's score consigns the Brothers to the status of animals. Yet for Barak, they remain as children, whose youthful wholeness he recalls fondly, and whose care and keeping is his charge. Along with the beggar children he brings from the street into his house to feed, and with whom the Brothers sing in chorus, they are like the tarnished and broken emblems of what is most desired and is yet withheld from him and from the shadowless Empress. In this regard, minor characters though they are, they are suddenly quite near to the central point of the drama after all.

The Deformation of Desire

When the juxtaposition of beauty and deformity occurs in the operas of Franz Schreker, its intensity of effect is heightened by eroticism,[7] a seemingly perverse conflation that later qualified the works all too readily for the Nazi government's label of "degenerate" (Hailey 1993, 1). The disabled character in Schreker's *Die Gezeichneten* is no secondary character but its central protagonist. Alviano Selvago is an "ugly man about 30 years old, hunchbacked" (*häßlicher Mann von ungefähr 30 Jahren, bucklig*), and Schreker's Renaissance plot revolves around the failed pairing between the visibly marred nobleman and the painter Carlotta, whose outer beauty conceals a hidden defect: a weakness of the heart that proves fatal. Both are marked, but only Alviano's defect is the source of a socially inflicted stigma that cripples his hope of a love life, and motivates his restless efforts to surround himself with aesthetic objects through which he can access the beauty that is otherwise denied him. As Peter Franklin (2006) explains, "the tentative psychosexual longing of the hunchbacked central character . . . has driven his inspiration for the fantasy island of Elysium. . . . Its creation is thus represented in Freudian terms as a passionate compensation for Alviano's inability to attract sexual partners" (178). The entire drama unfolds in the sphere of art as a source of sensual indulgence, and the pursuit of the aesthetic itself becomes a symbol of moral deformity. Alviano's Elysium serves as a pleasure grotto where his fellow noblemen conduct orgies with abducted women. His seemingly beneficent gesture in gifting the island to the populace of the city is not transparently altruistic. In Franklin's terms, "its social effects are unequivocally harmful" (178); and whether he seeks to halt his companions' depraved activities out of virtuous principle or spite at his exclusion from their hedonistic pursuits is open to question.

Morally, then, his character is ambiguous, but what does seem clear is that it is Alviano Selvago's disfigurement that renders him an aesthete, and hence, in contemporary terms, a degenerate figure. Is his hunched back the external sign of an internal character defect, or is the latter the acquired result of his experience of living with the stigma of a twisted spine? Schreker's music does not tell; it avoids any compositional gestures like those wielded by Strauss that objectify the character by mimetically rendering the image of his deformity in musical sound. Rather, it presents Alviano as a lyrical subject of intense emotion in a musical language that demands, at least, that he be taken seriously, even if the possibility for genuine sympathy with him is necessarily colored by ambivalence concerning his moral complexion.[8] But the famous music of the opera's prelude, its timbrally shimmering but harmonically disorienting juxtaposition of hexatonic polar triads,[9] might be heard as a deformation of "normal" harmonic configurations that audibly encapsulates the drama's troubling perversity through its combination of strangeness and allure. This interpretive possibility may even be actualized when the same music recurs in the opera's central seduction scene, wherein Carlotta paints Alviano's portrait[10] and enflames his passion by declaring a love that proves short-lived. As Franklin notes, overall, it is "impossible to distill from the opera a comfortingly straightforward ideological message" (Franklin 2006, 179), and neither does the work offer any redemptive gesture.

The stigmatized character marked by erotic longing resurfaces, splintered into a constellation of distinct figures, in Schreker's *Der Schatzgräber*. Set in "legendary medieval times" it features a once-lovely queen who, languishing for want of the magic jewels stolen from her, bears the king no heir; the minstrel Elis who, as the king's Fool reveals, possesses a magic lute that enables him to find hidden treasure; and the beautiful but corrupt Els, who orders her servant Albi to a series of murders and thefts to acquire those jewels for her. Both the king's Fool and Albi, the criminal henchman, represent types who are often disabled, though Schreker's libretto provides only passing clues that they may be physically deformed. Albi bears the most readily noticeable signs of abnormality. His unsightly visage is crowned by shaggy red hair, a rarity that could be variously understood in medieval and early modern eras and into the nineteenth century as the mark of ill temper, excessive libidinousness, or moral degeneration, and as a possible racial marker of Jewishness as well.[11] Weak-minded and tormented by lust, Albi is prey to his alluring but unscrupulous mistress, who plays cruelly on his passion for her, promising in return for his criminal services small favors that are infinitely postponed until another demand is fulfilled. When he is captured for the theft and three brutal murders he has committed on Els's behalf, he is described by the Bailiff—and for the second time—as "half-crazed," and mentally disordered, possibly even psychotic. Yet he is further stigmatized by an audible marker: he stutters, and Schreker's musical rendering of Albi is mimetically representative of his defect.

In this regard Albi is somewhat rare, if not unique, among opera characters, even disabled ones, for the fundamental operatic requirement of beautiful singing would seem typically to preclude the audible presentation of vocal defect. As Andrew Oster (2006) notes in his study of Cavalli's *Il Giasone* (1649), with its dwarfed, hunchbacked, and stuttering character of Demo, "the history of opera is full of musical settings that mimic aberrations or interruptions in standard vocal discourse: coughing, sneezing, humming, clearing one's throat, yawning, and the like," but "these are all minor, passing instances of the voice's inability to communicate fluently" (157). Pervasive vocal defect is more rarely heard, but Schreker makes use of it here as an audible counterpart to the character's visible otherness. Throughout the opera Albi's sung speech is stilted, repetitive, spastic. He is given almost exclusively short, repeated utterances, such as his plea for Els's amorous favors in return for his murder of her undesirable fiancé (*Und dann und dann?... Mehr, mehr... Oh Els, Els!*) or his agitated announcement thereafter of his "discovery" of that very murder ("*Kommt, kommt! Ein Unglück! Im Wald, im Wald*!"). At the close of the first begging scene with Els, Schreker's stage directions have him "storm out, uttering an inarticulate sound," and when he returns later to implore her for his "payment," the directions literally specify a stutter (see Figure 33.2).

Schreker's Fool is a less one-dimensional character than the utterly debased Albi. Verdi's Rigoletto and Leoncavallo's Tonio are his close operatic precedents. Beatrice Otto's study of the cross-cultural history of the court jester or fool affirms

FIGURE 33.2 Franz Schreker, *Der Schatzgräber*, mm. 701–706: Albi's stutter.

the consistency of the figure's characteristics including physical or mental deformity, whether real or feigned, the near ubiquitous prominence of dwarves and hunchbacks being a matter of record in accounts of fools and jesters across several cultures and centuries (Otto 2001, 22). Thus, it is almost as though Schreker's Fool is coded as disabled merely by his costume of cap and bells, whether or not we are told directly that his height is stunted or that his back is literally misshapen. Though the king does denigrate his appearance and simultaneously his sexual viability by mocking him as a "pot-bellied Don Juan," notwithstanding the tendency of humped spine and protruding belly to occur together (as the spinal curvature of kyphosis tends to push the abdomen forward), he is not explicitly described within Schreker's libretto as physically deformed. He is stigmatized all the same, and despite his cleverness and subtlety, the drawing of his character is oversimplified in at least one respect: his dramatic role and his defect are seemingly indistinguishable from each other. Either he is marked because he is a Fool, or else he has become a king's Fool because he is socially marked as such. Hunchbacked, dwarfed, or neither, his status still assures that he is unsuited for erotic love or passion. This incapacity is reiterated from the first scene of the opera to the last, beginning with his opening conversation with the King, when his advice for dealing with the ailing queen is dismissed, and his request for a wife as a reward for his service is met with incredulity. His final choice of the morally bankrupt Els as his wife, saving her from the gallows, seems to prove his perversity, and suggests further that mental disability should be added to his defects; the king declares him mad and casts him out from his service.

When Elis the minstrel performs a ballad at the king's banquet celebrating the return of the queen's stolen jewels and her resultant newly recovered vitality and beauty, the defective characters arrayed in constellation around the physically lovely and internally corrupt Els, all erotically attracted to her, are conflated into one image of deformity. The "hideous Dwarf" of the minstrel's provocative song is at once a scorned lover, a malicious jewel thief, and a wretchedly doglike and despairing creature who ends "tormented by love and regret." When his intense but unsuitable erotic passion for the legendary princess Ilse is "repulsed with scorn and derision," he steals her youth-perpetuating jewels and precipitates her death, then suffers acute and prolonged misery as a result. Schreker's embedding of a narrative ballad that symbolically encapsulates the larger drama in which it appears is a stock gesture straight from Romantic opera traditions of the previous century. What is worth noting about it, though, is its transfiguration of multiple characters, all dubious in some respect, into one figure whose aesthetic disfigurement and physical disability are one with his erotic perversity, criminality, and moral baseness. The Dwarf is the Fool, the henchman, even the itinerant and insubordinate minstrel, all at once, and their character defects and misdeeds—whether real or wrongly suspected—materialize in his stunted, unsightly form.

Ultimately, if the character of Albi is unremittingly malign, that of the Fool remains morally ambiguous, like that of Alviano in *Die Gezeichneten*, yet Schreker manages to conjure our sympathetic response to his humanity in the end. As the Fool explains to the minstrel in the opera's epilogue:

> You see, sir, as long as I wore the cap, the fool's cap and the costume of bells, I slipped with laughter and mockery past all the grief and suffering of this world. My costume was my being, I myself was dead. It kept me young.[12]

The fading sound of distant bells that closes Schreker's opera moments later is like an echo of those jester's bells the Fool relinquished, with his costumed identity, when he left the King's court for a life, however brief and unfulfilled, with the rapidly fading Els for whom physical beauty and health proved to be one and the same.

The Burdened Subject

Given Schreker's longstanding preoccupation with the musical-dramatic representation of disability and deformity—starting years before *Die Gezeichneten* with his dance-pantomime *Der Geburtstag der Infantin* (1908) based on Wilde, and continuing after *Der Schatzgräber* with *Irrelohe*'s (1924) tale of madness and sexual excess—it is unsurprising that Zemlinsky asked him for a libretto on "the tragedy of the ugly man" (Hailey 1993, 65). But the two composers' views of the social and dramatic significance of disfigurement and its dramatic embodiment were different. Zemlinsky saw the Dwarf in his *Der Zwerg* as distinct from the deformed character modeled in Schreker's *Die Gezeichneten*, and his comments to that effect also provide at least a partial answer to the obvious question as to whether ugliness per se actually constitutes a "tragedy." "In Schreker it is a case of conscious disfigurement," he explained, "while my Dwarf seeks his fortune in fairy-tale-like ignorance of his deformity, and thus becomes tragic" (Beaumont 2000, 303). The Dwarf is unaware of his aesthetic defect and his physical impairment: he does not know that he is ugly, that his misshapen back and legs compromise his ability to dance or run gracefully. Unconscious, indeed, that he is disabled at all, Wilde's and Zemlinsky's little gnome is a prime example of the conception of disability as a culturally circumscribed identity rather than a medically defined pathology. The entire issue of his deformity arises not from physical impairment itself but solely from the social stigma attached to it. Of the latter, the Dwarf only gradually becomes aware.

His appearance readily typecasts him as a fool or jester, but his failure to behave as such, carrying himself with an air of grandeur and importance, adds to the scorn with which he is perceived by those in the Spanish court. When he first enters, the giggling maidens surrounding the Infanta notice that "he doesn't even act like a fool," and it seems that his most grievous fault—beyond that of his very being—is to take himself too seriously. Like that of Schreker's nobleman, the Dwarf's own musical language throughout the opera presents him as a lyrical subject of genuine feeling. Its integrity is heightened by its contrast with the blatant musical mimicry that represents the objective cruelty with which others view him: his entrance, which incites the mirth of the court, is a pitiless caricature of disfigurement composed of limping dotted rhythms, ungainly dissonances, and grotesque glissandi across awkwardly wide intervals (see Figure 33.3).

FIGURE 33.3 Alexander Zemlinsky, *Der Zwerg*, reh. 88: entrance of the Dwarf

Yet he is as oblivious to the mockery of others as he is to his own appearance; his disfigurement is physical, but his disability is profoundly social. It becomes clear in the final, devastating confrontation with the mirror that ultimately shows him his true appearance that the Dwarf's disfigurement effectively disqualifies him as a person. While the Infanta views him as an animal, he comes to view himself, at the last, as a monster.[13]

What is most distinctive in *Der Zwerg* is the unambiguous representation of the disabled character as not only a victim of society's willful misunderstanding but also as a pure and innocent self of inner integrity, lacking the conventional features of vice, brutality, criminality or lasciviousness that render the other characters discussed here morally ambiguous at best, utterly pernicious at worst. In this portrait of damaged selfhood, subjectivity itself becomes crippled, twisted, and broken as the individual suffers under the pressures of modern society and indeed of his own psyche. The rift between interiority and the external world in which the self was forced to exist, and to which it was supposed to conform, seemed to impose a greater burden than the individual could bear. Perhaps the modern hunchback was bent over not from any congenital malformation, nor any outward manifestation of inner failing, but from the very weight of that external metaphorical burden.

Disability as Modernist Reconciliation

A few years after the completion of *Der Zwerg* Zemlinsky composed "Das bucklicht Männlein," a modified strophic Lied setting the poem about the ill-starred little hunchback from *Das Knaben Wunderhorn*, that same figure that troubled both the young Walter Benjamin and little Hanno Buddenbrook so unrelentingly. This persistent modern preoccupation brings us full circle, to Mann's novel of a family that succumbs to the ills of modernity. There is, in fact, another little hunchbacked character in *Buddenbrooks*, quite unlike the Dwarf of mischief and misfortune that elicited Hanno's tearful sympathy. Sesame Weichbrodt, the boarding-school mistress, is small and hunchbacked; her thin little shoulders are "childlike"; she is clever, well read, and extremely strict; her dress, habits, and mannerisms of speech are idiosyncratic. Yet she is no caricature: kind, wise, and morally upright, she commands respect. It is to her character—a character rightfully described as *wholesome*—that Mann grants the final word:

> "Hanno, little Hanno," Frau Permaneder went on, and the tears ran down those downy cheeks that had lost their glow. "Tom, Father, Grandfather, and all the others. Where have they all gone? We shall see them no more. Oh, how hard and sad it all is."
>
> "We shall see them again," Friederike Buddenbrook said, folding her hands firmly in her lap; she lowered her eyes and thrust her nose in the air.
>
> "Yes, that's what they say. Oh, there are times, Friederike, when there is no comfort. God strike me, but sometimes I doubt there is any justice, any goodness, I doubt

> it all. Life, you see, crushes things deep inside us, it shatters our faith. See them again—if only it were so."
>
> But then Sesame Weichbrodt raised herself up to the table, as high as she could. She stood on her tiptoes, craned her neck, rapped on the tabletop—and her bonnet quivered on her head.
>
> *"It is so!"* she said with all her strength and dared them with her eyes.
>
> There she stood, victorious in the good fight that she had waged all her life against the onslaughts of reason. There she stood, hunchbacked and tiny, trembling with certainty—an inspired, scolding little prophet. (Mann [1901] 1994, 731)

At the close of Mann's narrative of the decline of a once-prosperous and morally sound family through artistic decadence and physical sickliness, it is this congenitally deformed yet morally and psychically intact character who offers a message not of calamity but of redemption. The modernist vacillation between fearfully distanced objectification of the disabled figure and painful sympathy with damaged personhood settles on her crooked form as the image of reconciliation in the face of existential despair. Thus Mann redraws the figure of the hunchback from a distant, fabled type of misfortune to a modern character of hope.

Acknowledgments

I sincerely thank the contributors to this volume—especially Licia Carlson, Blake Howe, Stephanie Jensen-Moulton, Hedy Law, and Joseph Straus—for their facilitation of the extraordinary collaborative opportunity this volume represents and their insightful commentary and supportive dialogue offered during earlier stages of my work on this essay.

Notes

1. See Hannah Arendt's reflections on this subject in her Introduction to Benjamin 1985, 6–7.
2. Hutcheon and Hutcheon 1996 is the seminal text in the cultural study of the operatic representation of physical affliction, principally in the standard nineteenth- and twentieth-century repertoire; they delineate a focus on the period since "the rise of pathologic anatomy . . . [when] science began to understand that diseases might not be a matter of personal idiosyncrasy and predisposition . . . but [arose] from biological abnormalities with clinical signs manifested (and experienced) by individual sufferers" (2–3).
3. Brian Hyer's brilliant study "Parsifal hystérique" (2007) provides insight into the drama's workings of *Mitleid* as mimetic identification, which constitutes a "pathogenic trauma" in Hyer's reading of Parsifal as a sufferer of male hysteria. In this reading, then, Parsifal is also a disabled character who—despite his physical wholeness, in contrast to the wounded Amfortas—exhibits multiple signs of a degenerative neurological disorder that is manifest in both textual and musical dimensions of Wagner's drama.

4. David T. Mitchell and Sharon L. Snyder note that physical disability tends to be equated with social identity, such that "the physical world provides the material evidence of an inner life . . . that is secured by the mark of visible difference" (1997, 3).
5. The Rigoletto character in many respects plays out the "cultural script" of the so-called obsessive avenger or demonic cripple as discussed by Kriegel 1987, Norden 1996, Sandahl and Auslander 2005, and Straus 2011.
6. Both Hofmannsthal's libretto and Strauss's score identify the third brother as either "the hunchback" or "the youth, the crooked one" (*der Junge, Verwachsene*).
7. Youens 1997 provides a richly nuanced discussion of the thematic juxtaposition of physical deformity and eroticism in a nineteenth-century context.
8. For a distinctive, convincing reading see Howe 2010, 138–182—an insightful discussion of the portrayal of Alviano's character in terms of theories of empathy.
9. Richard Cohn's well-known theory of hexatonic polar triadic relations explains that the juxtaposition of a major triad with the minor triad a major third below it produces a paradoxical effect because, owing to the contrary voice-leading between them, they cannot both be heard as consonant at once; hence, the pairing estranges the triads from their normal, consonant status (Cohn 1996; 2004).
10. See Lee 2010 for further consideration of the motif of portrait-painting in Schreker's opera.
11. The practice of presenting Jewish characters onstage with red hair dates to Medieval mystery plays' portrayals of Judas Iscariot; Christopher Marlowe's character of Barabus in *The Jew of Malta* (1590) is red-haired; both Stephen Orgel (2004) and Stephen Greenblatt (2010) discuss the validity of costuming Shakespeare's Shylock with red wig or beard; and Dickens's malign character of Fagin, "the Jew" and "receiver of stolen goods" in *Oliver Twist*, is red-haired and "grotesque."
12. "Seht, Herr, so lang' ich die Kappe trug, die Narrenkapp' und das Schellengewand, da glitt ich hinweg mit Lachen und Spott über all den Gram, das Leid dieser Welt. Mein Kleid war mein Wesen, mein Ich war tot. Das erhielt mich jung."
13. For a more in-depth discussion of the social and psychological plight of the Dwarf, considered through the lenses of literary and political theories of recognition, see Lee 2009.

References

Beaumont, Antony. 2000. *Zemlinsky*. London: Faber and Faber.

Benjamin, Walter. 1985. *Illuminations*. With an introduction by Hannah Arendt. Translated by Harry Zohn. New York: Schocken.

Benjamin, Walter. 1991. "Berliner Kindheit um 1900." In *Gesammelte Schriften*, Vol. 4, edited by R. Tiedemann and H. Schweppenhäuser. Frankfurt, Germany: Suhrkamp.

Cohn, Richard. 1996. "Maximally Smooth Cycles, Hexatonic Systems, and the Analysis of Late-Romantic Triadic Progressions." *Music Analysis* 15 (1): 9–40.

Cohn, Richard. 2004. "Uncanny Resemblances: Tonal Signification in the Freudian Age." *Journal of the American Musicological Society* 57 (2): 285–323.

Davis, Lennard. 2003. *Bending Over Backwards: Disability, Dismodernism, and Other Difficult Positions*. New York: New York University Press.

Dickie, Simon. 2011. *Cruelty and Laughter: Forgotten Comic Literature and the Unsentimental Eighteenth Century*. Chicago: University of Chicago Press.

Franklin, Peter. 2006. "'Wer weiss, Vater, ob das nicht Engel sind?' Reflections on the Pre-Fascist Discourse of Degeneracy in Schreker's *Die Gezeichneten*." In *Music, Theatre, and Politics in Germany: 1848 to the Third Reich*, edited by Nikolaus Bacht, 173–183. Aldershot, UK: Ashgate.

Garland-Thomson, Rosemarie. 1997. *Extraordinary Bodies: Figuring Disability in American Culture and Literature*. New York: Columbia University Press.

Greenblatt, Stephen. 2010. "Shakespeare and Shylock." *New York Review of Books* 57 (14). Accessed May 1, 2015. http://www.nybooks.com/articles/archives/2010/sep/30/shakespeare-shylock/.

Hailey, Christopher. 1993. *Franz Schreker, 1878–1934: A Cultural Biography*. Cambridge: Cambridge University Press.

Halter, Ulrike, and Andreas Krödel. 1997. "Beten fürs bucklicht Männlein: Zur Kulturegeschichte der Skoliose und Kyphose." *Zeitschrift für Orthopädie und Unfallchirurgie* 135: 557–562.

Howe, Blake. 2010. "Music and the Embodiment of Disability." PhD diss., Graduate Center, City University of New York.

Hutcheon, Linda, and Michael Hutcheon. 1996. *Opera: Desire, Disease, Death*. Lincoln: University of Nebraska Press.

Hyer, Brian. 2007. "Parsifal hystérique." *Opera Quarterly* 22 (2): 269–320.

Jeffreys, Mark. 2002. "The Visible Cripple (Scars and Other Disfiguring Displays Included)." In *Disability Studies: Enabling the Humanities*, edited by Sharon L. Snyder, Brenda Jo Brueggemann, and Rosemarie Garland-Thomson, 31–39. New York: Modern Language Association of America.

Kriegel, Leonard. 1987. "The Cripple in Literature." In *Images of Disability, Disabling Images*, edited by Alan Gartner and Tom Joe, 31–46. New York: Praeger.

Le Rider, Jacques. 1993. *Modernity and Crises of Identity*. Translated by Rosemary Morris. Cambridge, UK: Polity.

Lee, Sherry. 2009. "The Other in the Mirror, or Recognizing the Self: Wilde's and Zemlinsky's Dwarf." *Music and Letters* 91 (2): 198–223.

Lee, Sherry. 2010. "'Deinen Wuchs wie Musik': Portraits and the Dynamics of Seeing in Berg's Operatic Sphere." In *Alban Berg and His World*, edited by Christopher Hailey, 163–194. Princeton, NJ: Princeton University Press.

Mann, Thomas. (1901) 1994. *Buddenbrooks: The Decline of a Family*. Translated by John E. Woods. New York: Random House.

Mitchell, David T., and Sharon L. Snyder. 1997. *The Body and Physical Difference: Discourses of Disability*. Ann Arbor: University of Michigan Press.

Norden, Martin. 1996. *The Cinema of Isolation: A History of Physical Disability in the Movies*. New Brunswick, NJ: Rutgers University Press.

Orgel, Stephen. 2004. "Shylock's Tribe." In *Shakespeare and the Mediterranean: Selected Proceedings of the International Shakespeare Association World Congress, Valencia, 2001*, edited by Tom Clayton, Susan Brock, and Vicente Forés, 38–53. Newark: University of Delaware Press.

Oster, Andrew. 2006. "Melisma as Malady: Cavalli's *Il Giasone* (1649) and Opera's Earliest Stuttering Role." In *Sounding Off: Theorizing Disability in Music*, edited by Neil Lerner and Joseph N. Straus, 157–171. New York: Routledge.

Otto, Beatrice K. 2001. *Fools Are Everywhere: The Court Jester around the World*. Chicago: University of Chicago Press.

Poizat, Michel. 1992. *The Angel's Cry: Beyond the Pleasure Principle in Opera*. Translated by Arthur Denner. Ithaca, NY: Cornell University Press.

Poore, Carol. 2007. *Disability in Twentieth-Century German Culture*. Ann Arbor: University of Michigan Press.

Sandahl, Carrie, and Philip Auslander. 2005. *Bodies in Commotion: Disability and Performance*. Ann Arbor: University of Michigan Press.

Siebers, Tobin. 2010. *Disability Aesthetics*. Ann Arbor: University of Michigan Press.

Straus, Joseph. 2011. *Extraordinary Measures: Disability in Music*. New York: Oxford University Press.

Uekermann, Gerd. 1985. *Renaissancismus und Fin de Siècle: Die italienische Renaissance in der Deutschen Dramatik der letzten Jahrhundertwende*. Berlin: Walter de Gruyter.

Youens, Susan. 1997. "Of Dwarves, Perversion, and Patriotism: Schubert's 'Der Zwerg,'" *19th-Century Music* 21 (2): 177–207.

CHAPTER 34

AUTISM AND POSTWAR SERIALISM AS NEURODIVERSE FORMS OF CULTURAL MODERNISM

JOSEPH STRAUS

INTRODUCTION

THE claims implicit in the title to this essay—that autism is a form of cultural modernism, that postwar serialism is related to the current disability rights movement that reinterprets "mental illness" as a manifestation of possibly desirable neurological difference, and that autism and postwar serialism may therefore have something to do with each other—must seem far-fetched. On one hand, we have a well-established psychiatric disorder (currently understood to affect more than 1 in 88 people)[1] that involves abnormal deficits in social relatedness, a lack of communication skills, and a preference for repetition; on the other hand, we have a musical style that involves particular sorts of compositional designs based on the twelve notes of the chromatic scale. Any proposed analogy between such disparate terms will be of value only if it tells us something about both that we didn't know before.

The idea that autism might be thought of as a culture and as an aspect of culture rather than a mental illness has animated a good deal of recent thinking, emerging from the insights of Disability Studies and the associated movement toward "neurodiversity."[2] The idea is to understand autism as a way of being in the world rather than a disease, a neurological difference rather than a pathological deficit, a cultural identity to be celebrated rather than a disease to be cured. Autism, in this view, is not a mental illness with a determinate biological or neurological source; rather, it is a cultural category, constituted by people in a certain time and place and in response to certain historical context. It is possible that autism will prove to be what Ian Hacking calls a "transient mental illness," that is, one that "shows up only at some times and some places, for reasons which we can only suppose are connected with the culture of those times and places" (Hacking 1999, 100) and "an illness that appears at a time, in a place, and later fades away" (Hacking 1998, 1).[3] But whether or not it fades away, its origins as a diagnostic category at a particular time and place, and its subsequent emergence, transformation, and staggering growth, mark it as a significant cultural phenomenon, one worth studying as a manifestation of culture rather than exclusively as a mental illness.[4]

Mental illnesses and musical styles are similar in that they come and go, emerging at certain times and places and then subsiding. I wouldn't propose that every musical style has an analogue in a contemporaneous mental illness, or vice versa, but from their shared emergence in the urbanized East Coast of the United States in the immediate postwar period, people classified as autistic and musical works identified as serial or twelve-tone have often been described and stigmatized in strikingly similar ways. Both have been understood as excessively isolated or alone, with each entity self-contained and self-enclosed. Both are understood as uncommunicative, or communicating in atypical ways, with an excess of private meanings and self-references. Both are understood as demonstrating an unproductive preference for routines and rituals. Furthermore, similar metaphors have accreted around them: people with autism and serial compositions are often described as inaccessible fortresses, incomprehensible aliens, and unfeeling machines (especially computational machines). Autism and postwar twelve-tone music thus give the appearance of being related forms of cultural modernism in its postwar American incarnation; certainly they have been stigmatized and pathologized in similar ways. My goals in this essay are both to document the shared stigmatization and to push back against it. Neurodiversity and cultural diversity both require and reward appropriate accommodation, recognizing that pleasure and value may take many different forms.

Autism as Culture

Autism is usually thought of as a psychiatric disorder with a neurological basis. In 1943, Leo Kanner—at the time probably the most prominent child psychiatrist in the United States and the Director of Child Psychiatry at the Johns Hopkins Hospital in Baltimore—was the first to use the term "autistic" to refer to a group of children whose behavior he distinguished from other forms of "madness" or "idiocy" in two significant ways. First, there was an unusual degree of social isolation, which Kanner refers to as "an *extreme autistic aloneness* that, whenever possible, disregards, ignores, shuts out anything that comes to the child from the outside" (Kanner 1943, italics in original).[5] The second shared characteristic of these children was an unusual rigidity and aversion to any change in habit or routine, what Kanner referred to as "autistic sameness": "All of the children's activities and utterances are governed rigidly and consistently by the powerful desire for aloneness and sameness. . . . [The children shared an] *inability to relate themselves* in the ordinary way to people and situations [and an] *anxiously excessive desire for the maintenance of sameness*" (Kanner 1943, italics in original).

Since Kanner's original description of autism, its official psychiatric definition has evolved and loosened, but nonetheless retains a central concern with aloneness and sameness. The long-standing definition of autism in the DSM-IV (1994) identifies what is often referred to as a "triad of impairments"[6]:

1. "Qualitative impairment in *social interaction*."
2. "Qualitative impairments in *communication*," which may include "abnormal functioning" in "symbolic and imaginative play."
3. "*Restricted, repetitive, and stereotyped* patterns of behavior, interests, and activities."

Kanner and the DSM are operating within a medical model of disability, which understands disability as a pathological excess or deficit with respect to some (typically undefined) normative standard. Disability is understood as being located within an individual mind or body—it is an internal rather than a social, economic, cultural, or historical condition. As such, disability is susceptible to the traditional medical regime of clinical diagnosis, with an eye toward normalization or cure.

In the contrasting social/cultural model, disability is understood as socially and culturally constructed rather than biologically given. In this view, disability does not reside inside an individual; rather, it is found in the relationships among people and with their built and cultural environments. As a cultural, relational phenomenon, disability has a history—it varies with time and place. Rather than a stigmatized medical condition, disability may be a positive political identity, and it may be willingly claimed. The social/cultural model of disability thus recasts medicalized deficits as cultural differences.

From this point of view, autism may be understood as a cultural identity rather than a medical condition or mental illness, as a distinctive and valuable way of being in the world. We might imagine autistic aloneness as a form of personal autonomy and self-reliance, generally considered desirable traits. Autistic people socialize in distinctive ways, refusing normative "compulsory sociality."[7] We might imagine autistic sameness as a desirable fixity of focus and a preference for orderliness, system, and ritual. Autistic people often have an affinity for the quantitative, for calculation, for lists and list-making, and these reveal a deeper preference for systematic regularity. We might imagine autistic communication issues as a preference for private meanings within locally coherent networks of signification. Autistic people often think associatively rather than hierarchically, engaging idiosyncratic combinations of elements and images and using language as much for its sonic value as for its communicative power. In this way, autistic aloneness and sameness and the associated "triad of impairments" are recast as aspects of a distinctive and valuable autistic cognitive style.[8] These affinities among autistic people have formed the basis for an emerging, politically conscious and socially aware autism culture, visible mainly on the Web.[9]

Autism and Musical Modernism

Theorists of autism have begun to acknowledge its affinities with aspects of cultural modernism.[10] McDonagh 2008 suggests a connection between autism and modernist ideas of the self, especially as manifested in forms of artistic modernism:

> There are strong parallels between modernist notions of identity and those emerging in Kanner's and Asperger's descriptions of autism, suggesting that the capacity to perceive autism in the 1940s may be connected to the proliferation of modern, and modernist, notions of the self, which were given shape in the literary works of the era. (101–102)

Straus 2013 connects autism to late twentieth-century concerns with an increasingly fragmented, hyperindividualistic culture:

> Psychiatric disorders are often a pathologically excessive version of some trait that, in its cultural context, is considered socially desirable (anorexia is excessive thinness, neurasthenia is excessive female passivity, fugue is excessive travel, ADHD is excessive energy and activity, obsession is excessive focus and concentration). In this sense, autism might be understood as excessive individuality, autonomy, and self-reliance, normally understood as highly desirable traits. Autism might be understood to represent a pathological excess of what the Western world most prizes—autonomous individuality, with its promise of liberty and freedom—reconfigured as what it most fears—painful solitude, isolation, and loss of community. Autism has thus become an emblematic psychiatric condition of the late twentieth and early twenty-first centuries, simultaneously a medical diagnosis and a cultural force. (461)[11]

Theorists of autism have begun to understand it as a manifestation of late twentieth-century concerns that simultaneously underpin a variety of other sorts of cultural expressions, but they have generally not made a connection specifically to modernist music. From the other side of the fence, however, musicologists have frequently invoked the language and images of autism to describe (and usually to denigrate) modernist music, especially the postwar twelve-tone music of Babbitt and other American composers. For many musicologists, this music has appeared as a pathological condition with autistic symptoms, including the full triad of autistic impairments.[12]

For some musicologists, the problem with postwar serial music is its aloneness, its isolation, its lack of social relatedness:

> Perhaps only with the twentieth-century avant-garde, however, has there been a music that has sought to secure prestige precisely by claiming to renounce all possible social functions and values." (McClary 1989)

> There can be little doubt that at the culturally most prestigious levels of our musical life, there exists an ideal of compositional individualism so nearly absolute it might well satisfy that premier megalomaniac Richard Wagner. It is an individualism succinctly formulated in the composer Milton Babbitt's famous challenge, "Who Cares if You Listen?" Ideally, today, the best composers write totally for themselves, without significant regard for audience or even performer. . . . Some composers are very explicit about trying to control every variable in their works (for example, replacing the performer with a computer), thereby turning their works into fixed, hermetically self-contained worlds, impervious to the vagaries of performance or the structuring forces of socially recognized conventions. (Subotnik 1991)

For another group of musicologists, modernist music (especially its twelve-tone variety) suffers from a disorder of communication:

> If twelve-tone pitch structure is not perceptually real, if twelve-tone music cannot carry the pitch-related meaning it purports to carry, then it cannot be a vehicle for the communication of such meaning. Therefore I claim, in virtue of human psychological design, a composer cannot intend to communicate pitch-related musical meaning by writing twelve-tone music. . . . To that extent, twelve-tone music is fraudulent, and so not art. (Raffman 2003)

> Because there is no structural connection between the expressive gestures and the 12-tone harmonic language, the gestures are not supported by the musical content . . . The expressive gestures, unsupported by the music's syntax or semantics, are primitive and simplistic in the extreme. (Taruskin 1996)

The third leg of the triad of autistic impairments—a propensity for sameness and for mechanistic, ritualistic, rigid repetition—also figures into musicological critiques of musical modernism in the postwar period. Broyles 2004 imagines that a postwar interest in mathematical determinism represents a retreat from a previous period of social awareness, a sort of autistic withdrawal from social contact:

> Serious composers, experimental in the 1920s, socially aware in the 1930s, and quieted by war in the 1940s, suddenly diverged in two totally different but equally radical paths. Some, extending ideas of Arnold Schoenberg and Anton Webern, sought total determination of every nuance of a piece through mathematical calculations. (Broyles 2004, 154)

These musicologists, representing a long-standing antimodernist trend within the field, approach musical modernism (especially in its twelve-tone or serial manifestations) in much the way that modern psychiatry, operating within the medical model of disability, approaches autism: as a pathological deficit or excess in comparison with a norm, as a debilitating impairment that resides within an individual body (or musical work), and as an undesirable condition that should be normalized or cured.

More darkly, both autism and postwar serialism have confronted what Rosemarie Garland-Thomson calls "the cultural logic of euthanasia": that is, the imperative either to normalize disabled bodies (through medical intervention) or to eliminate them (either by sequestration or in more direct ways)—"cure or kill" in a common, blunt phrase (Garland-Thomson 2004). In the case of autism, a variety of cures and normalizing interventions have been proposed and implemented with, at best, modest success. In a previous generation, most people diagnosed as autistic ended their days in institutions for the mentally ill. In the case of postwar serial music, the attempt at normalization involves an effort to demonstrate that this music is really, after all, not so very different from more conventional kinds of music, employing the same notes and the same intervals and, in some cases, the same sorts of musical gestures. If that rhetorical attempt to demonstrate the underlying normality of the music is deemed a failure, the response is often to condemn and dismiss the music outright, walling it off as something alien and inhuman, a wrong turn or an error in the history of music.[13]

I take a different tack here. While I accept the autism–postwar serialism analogy proposed, implicitly or explicitly, by antimodernist musicologists, I argue that the relationship ennobles rather than pathologizes both members. This essay is a defense of twelve-tone music and of autism, both singly and in relation to each other. So let us revisit the triad of autistic impairments as it bears on twelve-tone music, and imagine ways that each of them might be understood to mark a valued difference rather than a stigmatized deficit.

Aloneness

Autistic aloneness manifests itself in modernist music in what Babbitt calls "contextuality." That term refers to the isolation of a musical work from the community of other works. Musical works that are relatively contextual in Babbitt's sense have a wealth (some would even say a surplus) of internal relations but relatively few external ones. Works like that are comparatively self-referential and autonomous.[14] The contrasting term is "communal," referring to works that share a relatively large amount of material with each other. All musical works have both contextual and communal elements in some degree, but the balance varies from work to work and repertoire to repertoire.

The canonical works of the Western tradition, from Bach to Brahms, are relatively communal. They share ways of handling harmony, voice leading, phrase, form, rhythm, and many other musical elements. Indeed, this period of musical history is often referred to as "the common practice period," and the shared practices are enshrined in standard textbooks for students. Each common-practice period work has contextual elements that distinguish it from other works and make it unique, but they also share a good deal with other members of a community of works. Communal works are those that behave in normal, conventional ways. They socialize properly with other works and mind their musical manners.

A good deal of modernist music is comparatively contextual. Babbitt uses the term to refer especially to the middle-period music of Schoenberg, after he had abandoned traditional, common-practice tonality but before he started writing twelve-tone music. Here is how Babbitt (1987) describes this music:

> [Schoenberg] referred to his composition in those middle periods as "composing with the tones of a motive." Now, you see, that already defines a high degree of self-reference and contextuality . . . which means that, as much as possible, you make a work self-enclosed. You define its principles within itself. Now again that's relative; contextuality has to be relative. When you talk about a piece and talk about the relation between a theme here and a theme there or how something is transformed or how something relates, you're talking about contextual characteristics, characteristics internal to the particular piece. (8-9)

The twelve-tone system, which Schoenberg created in the early 1920s and used thereafter, restores some degree of communality to music, and that was undoubtedly one of Schoenberg's motivations in creating it. But twelve-tone works, very much including the postwar serial music of Babbitt and others, remain much more self-contained, self-referential, and structurally autonomous than common-practice works. As Babbitt (1987) observes,

> Twelve-tone music is much more contextual and much less communal than what anyone would call tonal music . . . The contingencies and dependencies of the twelve-tone work are determined, in the very nature of its being a twelve-tone work, by the particular ordering of the twelve pitch classes in the particular work; and therefore, of course, to that extent a twelve-tone work is much more contextual than a tonal work, whose dependencies and contingencies remain the same in some respects not only within a work but also from work to work. (16–17)

Contextual works are inherently difficult to approach and understand. They require more effort because the listener cannot draw on normal listening experiences, that is, from the experience of listening to traditional, tonal music or, indeed, to any other music. These works, by definition, share relatively little in common with their peers, and therefore knowledge of how one piece functions will not necessarily be of great help in approaching another piece. Normal listeners, those attuned to the commonalities of traditional tonal works, often find atonal and twelve-tone music inaccessible, because this music refuses the shared sociability of common-practice tonality.[15]

Like autistic individuals, then, contextual musical works are relatively isolated from each other and detached from the communal norm—they share a quality of aloneness. As Dubiel 1992 argues,

> Simply put, then, Babbitt's music is not difficult because it depends on antisocially arcane knowledge, but because it works so hard to depend less on *knowledge* than most listeners are ready to cope with. What it is designed to depend on is the ability

> to notice what is "before one's ears" in a less interpreted mode than virtually any music that precedes it (or follows it)–with the result that it makes its most strenuous demands on sheer sonic memory, or, more precisely, the ability to formulate conceptual models for the sonic memory on the fly, rather than find them ready-made in one's acculturational kit. (121)

Excessive autonomy and aloneness have generally been seen as highly problematic conditions, both for musical works and individuals. In an effort to destigmatize these conditions, one might first point out that the extent of both modernist and autistic aloneness has been greatly exaggerated. Modernist musical works, even those that may initially seem most hermetic, maintain rich ties to earlier, traditional music.[16] Indeed, one might productively understand musical modernism as a series of attempts to remake earlier music. The relationships between old and new may be elaborately concealed, but they are generative nonetheless.[17] Modernist musical works, including the high modernist works of the postwar period, are like all musical works, in their endless process of dialogue with other works, and the compulsion toward intertextuality applies to them no less than to earlier musical styles.

For autistic individuals, it is now pretty widely understood that the desire for social contact and intimacy is common, even if the means for achieving it often deviate from prevailing norms of sociability. Furthermore, autism itself is a condition that is socially and culturally negotiated—it does not reside inside an individual, but rather is something that happens among individuals and between individuals and the ambient culture.[18]

But even if one accepts that modernist, twelve-tone musical works of the postwar period and autistic individuals are more "alone" in some sense than more traditional, conventional, or typical works or individuals, it does not follow that this condition must be understood as destructive or pathological. The relatively high degree of contextuality of modernist musical works might be seen as a defining strength. Often, these works are designed anew from the ground up, with generative structures (like rows, charts, and arrays) designed for each individual work rather than given by convention. To create a self-contained musical world is inherently difficult, and places unprecedented burdens on interpreters (listeners and performers), but many people find their efforts richly rewarded. The high degree of contextuality guarantees that there will never be a mass audience for this music—it is inherently too unconventional, too difficult—but its challenges may bring corresponding rewards. Certainly, that is the frequent observation of people who have grown to love playing and listening to this music.[19]

One might make similar observations about autistic people. Rather than seeing their distinctive "aloneness" as a pathology, we might imagine it as a form of resistance to compulsory sociality, an insistence on the integrity of the individual in defiance of social norms. Autistic people are often perceived as difficult or inaccessible by neurotypical people, but the challenges they pose may bring corresponding rewards. People who live or work on intimate terms with autistic people frequently report the special delights of their autistic sensibility, including their forthrightness, their attention to detail, their fascination with lists and patterns (to say nothing of the delight people with autism may take in their own neuroatypicality).

Sameness

Autistic sameness—what the DSM refers to as "restricted, repetitive, and stereotyped patterns"—manifests itself in the systematic features of twelve-tone composition, especially in Babbitt's particular approach to it. Babbitt's music is deeply motivated by what he calls a "spirit of maximum variety" (Babbitt 1987, 87). That might seem to suggest the opposite of restriction, repetition, and stereotype, but what it means in practice is that every musical domain is systematically and thoroughly explored. The technical term is "combinatorial completion," and it means that if there are, say, sixty-six ways of doing some particular musical thing, you can be pretty sure that any piece by Babbitt that uses the first two or three ways of doing that thing will continue along the same path until all sixty-six have appeared. A sympathetic critic has referred to Babbitt's music as "the animation of lists," and there is a profound truth there (Dubiel 1992). How many notes are there? How many distinctive intervallic orderings are there for a given trichord? How many ways are there to combine trichords into hexachords and partition hexachords into trichords? How many ways are there of dividing (partitioning) the aggregate into different numbers of parts? The answers to these and similar questions take the form of lists of possibilities, and Babbitt's music typically runs through such lists until they are completed.

Of course these lists are not presented in some simplistic or mechanistic way—rather they are "animated." The lists (usually identified in the literature as charts or arrays) operate at varying degrees of conceptual distance from actual, sounding music. They are sometimes thought to generate the music, or perhaps to constrain the music, or perhaps to provide a series of problems or challenges to which the music responds. They seem to provide a framework within which Babbitt's music freely plays. Babbitt's music is committed to list-making and list-completion to a very unusual degree, but the lists paradoxically open up a significant zone of compositional improvisation and freedom. The lists are not intrinsically good or bad, but if we value the music that results, we must also give credit to the lists that enable it to take the particular form it does.

Something similar might be said of autistic sameness in people. While it is often seen as a destructive pathology—an obsessive and rigid dependence on repetition and routine—it can also be understood as a quality that enables particular sorts of achievements. People with autism often have a preference for certain narrow areas of interest (including music, art, calendar calculation, arithmetic calculation) which they pursue with intense focus and concentration. People with autism are often accomplished list-makers, working systematically with names, dates, words, and numbers. Autistic sameness underlies the development of these skills, which are typically pursued in a systematic and repetitive way. Babbitt's music and autistic special skills thus share a quality of autistic sameness. The underlying lists and the systematic ways in which they are pursued simultaneously constrain and enable the distinctive behaviors.

Communication

Autistic communication, like autistic cognition more generally, is often based on locally coherent networks of private associations. As I have previously observed,

> Like poetry, especially modernist poetry, autistic language often involves unusual, idiosyncratic combinations of elements and images, with as much pleasure associated with the sounds of the words as with their meaning. In Kristina Chew's words, "Autistic language is a fractionated idiom, its vocabulary created from contextual and seemingly arbitrary associations of word and thing, and peculiar to its sole speaker alone. . . . Autistic language users think metonymically, connecting and ordering concepts according to seemingly chance and arbitrary occurrences in an 'autistic idiolect' " (Chew 2008, 142, 133). . . . Autistic expression is often introverted, directed inward rather than outward. Instead of a chain of logical inference, one often finds rich networks of associations, often private in nature. (Straus 2013, 469)

Autistic language often involves an insistence on private meanings and associations, and thus a refusal to communicate in socially normative ways.[20]

McClary 2000 explicitly identifies resistance to normative modes of communication in modernist music as "a kind of deliberate autism":

> The turn into the twentieth century, of course, brought with it another, even more severe crisis over subjectivity. This time . . . it was those few threads that still connected inside integrity with a minimal level of public intelligibility that were assaulted. In order to break entirely free of discourse, which was seen as hopelessly compromised by its associations with a bureaucratized, commodified world, many German writers studied and imitated the utterances of psychiatric patients. . . . Schoenberg too drew on images of madness as means of severing all those tenuous links with conventional communication. Artists developed a kind of deliberate autism in order to maintain at all cost that image of the uncontaminated self that had become the only acceptable stance. (135)

And, indeed, I think it is right to imagine that an "autistic idiolect" can be heard in modernist music, especially postwar twelve-tone music, including the music of Babbitt.[21] Like autistic speech, twelve-tone music is not necessarily or primarily communicative; rather, it is self-stimulatory and self-expressive. Its refusal to communicate in the normal, conventional way has led some critics to infer that it is meaningless and inexpressive, and for a "normal listener," that is inevitably how it must appear. But for those willing to listen associatively rather than hierarchically, attentive to chains of private meanings (that is, those created contextually, within the single work), the music may come to seem deeply meaningful and expressive.

Inaccessible Fortresses, Incomprehensible Aliens, Unfeeling Machines

The sorts of physical or neurological differences that are commonly identified as disabilities always seem to require explanation and interpretation, and this compulsion to explain disability underlies the most common and pervasive disability narratives, both literary and medical.[22] The apparent need for interpretation and explanation is particularly pressing when the disabled person is either nonverbal or speaks in an unusual way, as in the "autistic idiolect." If people are incapable of telling their own stories, or of telling them in a way that is readily comprehensible to outsiders, the experts often step in to speak for them. In the case of autistic individuals, the experts are often medical professionals. In the case of twelve-tone works, the experts are often musicologists or music theorists. For both autistic individuals and twelve-tone works, this outsider's language has often involved three shared tropes: the inaccessible fortress, the incomprehensible alien, and the unfeeling machine.

In the world of autism, the trope of the inaccessible fortress is widespread, and is evident in the titles of two important, influential early accounts: Bruno Bettelheim, *The Empty Fortress* (1967) and Clara Park, *The Siege* (1982). Bettelheim's punishing theory of autism, now utterly discredited, is that a child, fearing murderous assault from a hostile mother, erects psychic barriers and retreats behind them. Park's deeply sympathetic account of life with her autistic daughter describes her efforts to establish a loving connection despite difficulties of communication and mutual understanding. What these two very different accounts share is the notion that the "real" child is somehow trapped behind a barrier, and that outsiders must batter down the separating wall to gain access to the child within.

Twelve-tone music is often described in similar terms, as though it were a form of architecture to which physical access were barred. The critical commonplace is that such music is "inaccessible," suggesting that whatever meanings it might have are walled off behind an impenetrable barrier. Some critical accounts (in the style of Bettelheim) imagine this music as an empty fortress, whose walls conceal a void within. Other accounts (more in the style of Park) imagine that there is something of value within the architecture, and if the siege is successful, there might be compensating rewards.[23]

For both autism and modernist music, the idea behind the trope of the fortress is that something of potential value is buried, encased, enclosed, lodged deep within, and can only be reached with effort. In both cases, professional intervention may be required.

Child psychology/psychiatry and musicology (and music theory) both justify themselves, in part, with their promise of providing access to interior spaces that would inaccessible to laypersons without the proper training and credentials.[24]

For both autism and modernist music, the trope of the inaccessible fortress is used primarily by outsiders. In the world of autism, it is the professionals and the parents who invoke the metaphor to describe their difficulties in gaining access to a person they perceive as remote and unavailable. In the world of modernist music, it is used by critics and musicians who have no visceral attraction to or emotional engagement with the music, and thus describe it as inaccessible.

It is ironic that the notion of accessibility should be used in this way. Its standard usage refers to the accessibility of public spaces to people with disabilities. The architecture of the built environment is typically welcoming to people of normal ability but creates barriers to people with disabilities. As the trope is used for autism and modernist music, however, the meaning is turned around. Now it is the people of normal ability who are incapable of entering a walled fortress. Modernist music is a built environment, a space, to which what I call *normal hearing* (that is, a series of listening strategies based on traditional, tonal music) is denied access (Straus 2011). Normal listening, so well adapted to normal musical circumstances, becomes a liability, a disability, with reference to the extraordinary music. Modernist music thus disables normal listeners. The same irony obtains for autistic people. Their qualities—aloneness, sameness, and autistic idiolect—pose a problem for cognitively normal observers. Normal observers are denied access to a disabled space; they are rendered incapable by disability. It is their very normality that limits them and problematizes their access to the world-view and culture of autism. The intense pathologization of both autism and modernist music may be related to the frustration people experience when they feel they are being denied access or when they feel insufficiently capable of gaining access.

To enter these spaces, it helps to learn an insider's perspective. In some cases, insiders also invoke the metaphor of an architectural space protected by walls, but the space is described from the inside. Babbitt, for example, describes the university as a safe refuge, a protected private space, and a bulwark against a hostile world.

> The composer would do himself and his music an immediate and eventual service by total, resolute, and voluntary withdrawal from this public world to one of private performance and electronic media, with its very real possibility of complete elimination of the public and social aspects of musical composition . . . . The composer would be free to pursue a private life of professional achievement, as opposed to a public life of unprofessional compromise and exhibitionism . . . Such a private life is what the university provides the scholar and the scientist. It is only proper that the university, which—significantly—has provided so many contemporary composers with their professional training and general education, should provide a home for the "complex," "difficult," and "problematical" in music. (Babbitt 2003, 53)

Here, Babbitt imagines himself inside the walls and looking out.

Similarly, people with autism are much more likely to see barriers in the built and cultural environments as preventing them from entering mainstream institutions. Here is a position statement from the Autism Self-Advocacy Network (ASAN) that engages the metaphor of the wall or barrier, but seen from the inside rather than the outside:

> The disability rights perspective within the Autistic community is represented in the neurodiversity movement, which promotes social acceptance of neurological difference as part of the broad landscape of human diversity and seeks to bring about a world in which Autistic people enjoy the same access, rights, and opportunities as all other citizens. ASAN regularly works with other disability rights organizations to advance public policy initiatives that focus on improving quality of life and ensuring full access in society. In accordance with the social model of disability, we recognize that disability need not be a tragedy or a misfortune and that barriers to full participation in society often arise not from physical or mental differences, but from cultural attitudes that stigmatize certain types of people as less worthy of inclusion than others. Thus, a person becomes disabled not as an inevitable result of his or her condition, but rather because society has not accommodated his or her needs sufficiently to enable equal participation in the community. Such barriers to inclusion can and should be dealt with through the political process, in the same way that civil rights advocates have worked to break down prejudiced assumptions and exclusionary practices that harm other minority groups.

So the metaphor of the wall or barrier is there, but rather than preventing an outsider from entering, it prevents someone on the inside from moving outward.

In a slightly different way, some people with autism use the image of a protected space not to sequester and isolate them but rather to build a shared culture of autism free from the "tyranny of the normal" and "compulsory sociality." As an emblematic example, the annual conference/retreat known as "Autreat," sponsored by an autistic self-advocacy organization called Autism Network International, is described on the organization's website in the following way:

> Autreat is a retreat-style conference run by autistic people, for autistic people and our friends. Autreat focuses on positive living with autism, NOT on causes, cures, or ways to make us more normal. Autreat is designed to be "autistic space." Typical autism conferences are about autistic people, but are primarily for the benefit of researchers, service providers, or families. Autreat is an opportunity for autistic people and those with related developmental differences, our friends, and supporters to come together, discover and explore autistic connections, and develop advocacy skills, all in an autistic-friendly environment.

Spaces like Autreat thus function in the same way that the university functions for Babbitt and his music—a place to pursue and enjoy a nonconforming subculture.

A second common trope shared by the cultures of autism and postwar modernist music involves incomprehensible aliens.[25] The atypical individual or musical work is either from another world (the outsider's perspective) or perceives the common world as alien and incomprehensible (the insider's perspective).

> A persistent trope in some autism communities is that autistic people are aliens, or, symmetrically, that non-autistic people seem like aliens to autists. Some autists are attracted to the metaphor of the alien to describe their own condition, or to say that they find other people alien. Conversely, people who are not autistic may in desperation describe a severely autistic family member as alien. (Hacking 2009, 44)

From the outside, composer-theorist Dmitri Tymoczko imagines the nontonal music written by modernist composers as a lifeless foreign planet: "Tonality is not one among an infinitude of habitable planets, all easily accessible by short rocket flight; instead, it is much closer to being the *only* habitable planet" (Tymoczko 2011, 393). In a similar spirit, medical professionals who study autism often refer to the "otherworldly" quality of autistic people. Asperger describes one of the children he studied as looking like he had "just fallen from the sky" (Asperger [1944] 1991, 60), and Uta Frith refers to their "haunting and somehow otherworldly beauty" (2003, 1).

From the inside, Temple Grandin has famously described herself as "an anthropologist on Mars."[26] Note the preposition she uses—*she's* not the alien ("from" Mars); rather, the normal world is a foreign planet that she must work to understand, in the manner of an anthropologist studying a foreign culture. Similarly, Miller 2003, a compilation of memoirs and conversations by autistic women, answers its title question, "Women from Another Planet?" with a resounding no:

> We are not from another planet. . . . We are right from here, Planet Earth. We are an integral part of this earth's ecosystems, its intricately inter-dependent network of niches and potentialities . . . We are the first wave of a new liberation movement. . . . We are part of the groundswell of what I want to call Neurological Liberation (xii).

Shifting back to modernist music, Babbitt 2003 refers to "the problems of a special music in an alien and inapposite world" (53). Like Grandin, he sees the apparently normal world as "alien," a hostile environment in which his music is obliged to make its way.

A third persistent trope, shared by responses to autism and to modernist music, involves machines, especially computers. Nadesan 2005 refers to "the symbolic equation between high-functioning autism and technical/scientific prowess" (129) and goes on to observe,

> The inadvertent effect of these linkages across autism and scientific/technical proclivities is that autism, in its high-functioning variants, has become symbolically equated with an affinity toward, and/or resemblance to *artificial intelligence*. That is, the assumption that there exists a distinct computational model of cognition that often co-occurs with autistic symptoms and/or is engendered by the underlying form of autistic cognition enables the semiotic equation across autism, technology/science, and social awkwardness. (131)

Similarly, people described in the literature as "autistic savants" (i.e., autistic people with a notable skill in some area, often music, art, math, or calendar calculation) are often thought to have a memory that, however prodigious, operates purely by rote, in the manner of a tape recorder, a photograph, or other mechanical device.[27]

> The limitations of the concrete memorizing achievements of some idiots savants are not totally unlike the restrictions that exist when sounds are retained on magnetic tape. Compared with normal human memory, there is the advantage of greater surface accuracy, but this occurs at the expense of all the abilities that depend upon meaningful understanding; for example, being able to find and use particular items of information. (Howe 1989, 14)

Similarly, for Oliver Sacks, savant memory is fundamentally different from normal memory:

> It is characteristic of the savant memory (in whatever sphere—visual, musical, lexical) that it is prodigiously retentive of particulars. The large and small, the trivial and momentous, may be indifferently mixed, without any sense of salience, of foreground versus background. There is little disposition to generalize from these particulars or to integrate them with each other, causally or historically, or with the self. In such a memory there tends to be an immovable connection of scene and time, of content and context (a so-called concrete-situational or episodic memory)—hence the astounding powers of literal recall so common in autistic savants, along with difficulty extracting the salient features from these particular memories, in order to build a general sense and memory. . . . Such a memory structure is profoundly different from the normal and has both extraordinary strengths and extraordinary weaknesses. (Sacks 1995, 200)

An extensive body of research, as well as a moment or two of sympathetic reflection, confirm that in fact people with autism have memories and intelligences not so very unlike those of "normal" people. Nonetheless, the metaphorical equation of autism with hyperrational calculation and mechanical computation devoid of normal human emotion is persistent in our culture.

The same constellation of metaphors—machines, mechanistic calculating devices, computers—has frequently been applied to postwar twelve-tone music. Critics refer to "pseudo-mathematical processes" (Bolcom 2004, 47) and the "total determination of every nuance of a piece through mathematical calculation" (Broyles 2004, 154). *The New York Times*'s obituary of Milton Babbitt describes him as someone who "wrote music that was intensely rational and for many listeners impenetrably abstruse." Both the fortress and computational metaphors are visible here—it is the overly rational style of the music that creates an impenetrable barrier to entering it.

Susan McClary has suggested an important historical and ethical dimension to the apparent hyperrationality of postwar American twelve-tone music: it represents a principled resistance to the central control and conformity of Nazism and communism, with their attendant horrors and suffering:

> It is no great wonder then that serious artists reacted by writing music that refused the heated rhetoric that made so much of the traditional canon vulnerable to such abuses. They preferred to withdraw their work to a place where music would appeal to the cool intellect rather than to the emotions, which had been all too easily swayed by propaganda machines. The nationalist fervor that had fueled so much art in the previous hundred years had also led to unspeakably inhumane atrocities. In the face of this unprecedented level of catastrophe, the very notion of conveying meanings seemed tantamount to manipulation. Better then to operate within the cerebral sphere of electronic experimentation or high degrees of abstraction or even chance. In retrospect, this ethical position appears not only understandable but laudable. (unpublished paper)

McClary's idea of a willed withdrawal into "contextuality" from the horrors of excessive "communality" (to recall Babbitt's terms), has an obvious echo in Bettelheim's description of autism (Bettelheim 1967). Bettelheim argued that "the precipitating factor in infantile autism is the parent's wish that his child should not exist" (125). Explicitly analogizing the autistic child to the concentration camp inmate, Bettelheim maintained that both withdraw into a psychic shell to protect themselves against murderous caretakers. Bettelheim's theory is deeply offensive to parents and his characterization of the origins of autism has been utterly discredited and repudiated. Furthermore, his account denies any agency or selfhood to the autistic person—for Bettelheim, the fortress is empty.

But it can be valuable to think that some of the behaviors associated with autism are the result of an individual's effort to cope with an environment that is perceived as challenging and possibly hostile. I'm not speaking here of any putative failure in parental caregiving but rather of the difficulty of functioning socially in a world where social interactions are governed by the sorts of elaborate norms that autistic people often find difficult to grasp.[28] Instead of seeing autistic sociability as a deficiency, we might imagine it as a form of resistance to normative, compulsory, conformist sociability.

By pretty much any definition, autistic people are socially unconforming. Their personal integrity and individuality are aspects of their autistic aloneness. McClary offers a historical reason for the flowering of twelve-tone music in America after World War II. Perhaps similar historical forces are at work not so much in the creation of autism (presumably a neurological condition) as in its perception. What was it about the world in the 1940s that permitted this group of people, previously lost among populations identified as insane or idiotic or perhaps merely eccentric, to be identified as a distinctive group by Kanner, Asperger, and other observers? Perhaps these observers had been sensitized by current and recent historical events to the existence of individuals whose apparent aloneness secured them against the horrors of excessive conformity. The cognitive style, worldview, and culture of autism place autistic people in resistance to social homogeneity, "compulsory sociality," and the tyranny of the normal. Modernist music positions itself in resistance to the conventional tonality of the "common practice" period. The twelve-tone music of postwar America, with its extraordinarily high degree of structural self-referentiality, insists on its individualized autonomy with respect to normative ways of composing and apprehending music. In that sense, the emergence of modernist musical styles and the emergence of autism might be seen to have common historical roots.

Conclusion

In this essay I have discussed and compared two distinct populations, one of people with particular neurological and cognitive traits and the other of musical works with a particular compositional style. These populations have certain shared features, including aloneness (contextuality), sameness, and a way of communicating that emphasizes associations and private meanings. Furthermore, these populations have elicited a similar response from observers, including their stigmatization as inaccessible fortresses, incomprehensible aliens, and unfeeling machines. Finally, these populations achieve their distinctive identities in response to the same historical forces, namely a resistance to excessive social control (the dark side of communality).

At the beginning of this essay, I suggested that a comparison like this would only be of value if it could tell us something new and valuable about both terms of the comparison. What, then is the benefit of thinking about autism in relation to musical modernism—what can we learn about autism from the comparison? It is relatively easy to think of modernist music as one musical style among many. Although antimodernist criticism has been around for a long time, and seems particularly entrenched within current musicology, most observers seem able to understand that modernism is a cultural choice, and its differences are not necessarily deficits.

Choice operates somewhat differently, of course, for people with autism, who do not literally choose their condition. They may, however, choose to *claim* autism, that is, to embrace and affirm it as valued cultural and political identity.[29] And that process of claiming autism may occur more readily when people, both autists and neurotypicals, learn to think of autism as a cultural movement, somewhat analogous to developments in music (and in other arts). Insofar as we think of modernist music and other manifestations of cultural modernism favorably, or at least accept their legitimacy within the larger culture, we can learn to destigmatize autism, seeing it as a difference, not a deficit, as a worldview rather than a medical pathology.

And what is the benefit of seeing musical modernism, including especially postwar twelve-tone music, in relation to autism—what can we learn about music from the comparison? First, it solidifies our sense of the broader culture from which this music emerges, a culture comprising not only other kinds of music and other kinds of art but also political, economic, historical, and even psychological cross-currents of all kinds.

Second, it encourages us to appreciate rather than stigmatize its distinctive qualities, including its resistance to normal music-making (composition and hearing) and its distinctive style of self-expression (including a lack of interest in normative socialization and communication).

Fred Maus (2004) has suggested that twelve-tone music is a "queer" in the concert hall. I find that characterization richly suggestive, and I would augment it by saying that twelve-tone music is also an autist in a neurotypical musical world: doubly an outsider. In the case of both autism and twelve-tone music, we find ourselves in the presence of cognitive difference, and that poses a challenge to the normate, neurotypical world. One common response, shaped by the medical model of disability, is to pathologize the deviant Other. That response engages "the cultural logic of euthanasia," which confronts disability with only two choices: cure (normalize) or kill (either through sequestration or actual, physical elimination). Instead, we in the neurotypical world might do better to look for ways of providing personal and institutional support for these somewhat fragile, marginal populations. In this, we would not be acting out of pity with a goal of offering charity, but out of a belief that neurodiversity, among people and artworks, enriches us all, and with a goal of justice for all.

Notes

1. According to the Centers for Disease Control, "For 2008, the overall estimated prevalence of ASDs [autism spectrum disorders] was 11.3 per 1,000 (one in 88) children aged 8 years. Overall ASD prevalence estimates varied widely across all sites (range: 4.8–21.2 per 1,000 children aged 8 years). ASD prevalence estimates also varied widely by sex and by racial/ethnic group. Approximately one in 54 boys and one in 252 girls were identified as having ASDs." Report issued March 2012. These figures should not necessarily be considered reliable. Since 2008, as the definition of ASD has continued to change, prevalence estimates have fluctuated up and down (mostly up) and vary widely with the reporting authority and with the geographical region being studied.
2. For recent literature that implicitly or explicitly invokes Disability Studies and portrays autism as a sociocultural phenomenon that arises from neurological difference, rather than a disease that can or should be cured, see Nadeson 2005, Biklen 2005, Murray 2008, Osteen 2008, Eyal et al. 2010, Murray 2012, and Straus 2013.
3. This is not to say that autism is a fiction, constructed out of the whole cloth by psychologists and other observers. Hacking 1999 makes a valuable distinction between "natural kinds" (categories, like quarks, whose members are unaffected by the categorization) and "interactive kinds" (categories, like autism, for whose members the categorization may have significant consequences). As Hacking explains, "One of the defects of social construction talk is that it suggests a one-way street: society (or some fragment of it) constructs the disorder (and that is a bad thing, because the disorder does not really exist as described, or would not really exist unless so described). By introducing the idea of an interactive kind, I want to make plain that we have a two-way street, or rather a labyrinth of interlocking alleys" (Hacking 1999, 116).

4. Thought of in this way, autism is part of a larger history of madness, a story of the ever-changing systems of classification and conceptualization for explaining cognitive and affective differences: "There is indeed a history, not just of psychiatry, but of madness itself. Insanity is not just an individual atom, a biological accident, but forms an element in the history of sub-cultures in their own right. . . . Even the mad are men of their times" (Porter 1987, 5).
5. In a striking coincidence of thought and language, an Austrian psychologist named Hans Asperger was making similar observations in similar language at exactly the same moment on the other side of the world. Asperger observed, "Human beings normally live in constant interaction with their environment, and react to it continually. However, 'autists' have severely disturbed and considerably limited interaction. The autist is only himself and is not an active member of a greater organism" (Asperger [1944] 1991).
6. The DSM (*Diagnostic and Statistical Manual of Mental Disorders*) is produced by the American Psychiatric Association and is the standard reference for medical practitioners and insurers in defining mental illness. In the most recent edition (DSM-5, published in 2013), the first two members of the older diagnostic triad (impairment in social interaction and communication) are conflated into one of two core areas (fixed or repetitive behavior is the other). The DSM-5 thus moves closer to Kanner's original dyad of impairments: aloneness and sameness.
7. The term and its theoretical development are from Rodas 2008.
8. The recasting of medicalized autistic deficits as the basis for a shared autistic cognitive style is the central theme of Straus 2013.
9. See, for example, http://www.wrongplanet.net/, http://www.autreat.com/, and http://autisticadvocacy.org/.
10. In a related vein, Sass 1992 is an extended discussion of the mutual influence of artistic modernism (mostly literary) and madness (mostly schizophrenia).
11. Since writing the foregoing, it has come to my attention that my characterization of neurasthenia is inaccurate in basic ways. It would have been better to adduce depression, diagnosed far more frequently among women, as excessive female passivity. On neurasthenia in American life and culture, and especially in the life and music of the composer Charles Ives, see Magee 2008.
12. Within the broad category of musical modernism (i.e., music in the Western classical tradition written since around 1908 that departs in some significant way from tonal conventions), there are a number of different but intertwined repertoires, and these are not always clearly distinguished in the musicological critique I am surveying here. Some of the categories invoked (twelve-tone, serial, avant-garde) have a broader range of focus than the postwar American twelve-tone serial music that is my principal interest in this essay. But whatever terms they use, these musicologists seem to have Milton Babbitt and his fellow postwar twelve-tone composers reasonably close to the forefront of their minds.
13. The history of attempts to "cure or kill" postwar serial music in America is traced in Straus 2009.
14. I focus on Babbitt here because his music and thinking are so central to the development of twelve-tone or serial music in postwar America, but he is far from the only commentator to draw attention to this feature of modern music. See Drott 2013 for a survey, and vigorous critique, of the argument for the autonomy and self-referentiality of modernist music. More broadly, many critical accounts of modernism in literature and the other arts

identify "self-referentiality" or "autonomy" as one of its central, defining features. See, for example, Butler 1994 and Everdell 1997.

15. On "normal listening," see Straus 2011.
16. The extensive ties to the past maintained by postwar twelve-tone music in North America constitute a central theme of Straus 2009.
17. This is the central contention of Straus 1990.
18. This is an observation made repeatedly in the recent autism literature. See, for example, Biklen 2005: "On the one hand, some experts characterize autism as a condition wholly internal to the person, as a collection of traits. . . . On the other hand, autism may be seen as a set of qualities among many where the experience of the person can be understood only as being located and negotiated in complex social-cultural contexts. In the former, autism-inside-the-person viewpoint, there is a tendency to see a person as more or less static—not merely comprising particular neurophysiological characteristics but defined by them. In the latter instance, autism is more fluid; the person is seen as having particular qualities and as interacting with the environment, and thus as forever changing in complex ways" (34). Similarly, see Murray 2008 and Straus 2013.
19. Some of this sense of love and attachment may be felt in the title of Ashby 2004: *The Pleasure of Modernist Music.*
20. Preference for a somewhat hermetic language, rich in private meanings and associations, is evident in a great deal of modernist literature (Joyce, Faulkner, and Proust would be among the most obvious examples). This has been widely recognized as a distinguishing feature of literary modernism. See, for example, Butler 1994, which considers "withdrawal from consensual languages" one of the distinguishing features of artistic modernism generally.
21. In asserting that Babbitt's music may be (and has been) taken as instancing a musical autistic idiolect, I am not making any comparable claim about Milton Babbitt the person. There is no essentialism operating here: one does not have to be autistic to compose autistically, and one certainly does not have to be autistic to have one's music interpreted as, and stigmatized as, autistic.
22. This notion is a commonplace in the Disability Studies literature, and receives probably its pithiest statement in Mitchell and Snyder 2000: "Disability inaugurates the act of interpretation" (6).
23. For critical discussion of both sorts of accounts, see Straus 2009.
24. The relationship between professional knowledge and power—that the people who define deviance often set themselves up as the paid professionals who can normalize, cure, or control it—is a persistent theme of Michel Foucault. In the present context, see especially Foucault 2009.
25. Aliens from outer space are the literal subjects of another prominent manifestation of postwar culture in the United States, namely science-fiction films. In films like *The Thing from Another World* and *Invasion of the Body Snatchers*, the aliens are frighteningly Other because they appear to lack something essentially human, namely an emotional life—they appear as pure intellect. The resonance with autism, with its purported deficits in social communication and its affiliation with machines (especially calculating machines), is unmistakable. For the foregoing observations, I am indebted to Raymond Knapp (personal communication).
26. This self-description is reported in Sacks 1995, which takes the phrase as the book's title.

27. On musical savants, see Straus 2014. On recent cultural representations of autistic savants, including the astonishingly influential film, *Rain Man*, see Murray 2008.
28. There is a vast range of autistic autobiography that details the difficulties many autistic people face in achieving a degree of social conformity. Two classics of this genre are Grandin 1995 and Williams 1992.
29. The idea of "claiming disability" in this way, that is, embracing it as a desirable and valued cultural and political identity, is a commonplace in Disability Studies, and is most closely associated with Linton 1998, which uses that phrase as its title.

References

Ashby, Arved, ed. 2004. *The Pleasure of Modernist Music: Listening, Meaning, Intention, Ideology*. Rochester, NY: University of Rochester Press.

Asperger, Hans. (1944) 1991. " 'Autistic Psychopathy' in Childhood." Translated by Uta Frith. In *Autism and Asperger Syndrome*, edited by Uta Frith, 37–92. Cambridge, UK: Cambridge University Press.

Babbitt, Milton. 1987. *Words about Music*. Edited by Stephen Dembski and Joseph N. Straus. Madison: University of Wisconsin Press.

Babbitt, Milton. 2003. "The Composer as Specialist." In *The Collected Essays of Milton Babbitt*, edited by Stephen Peles, Stephen Dembski, Andrew Mead, and Joseph N. Straus, 48–55. Princeton, NJ: Princeton University Press.

Bettelheim, Bruno. 1967. *The Empty Fortress: Infantile Autism and the Birth of the Self*. New York: Free Press.

Biklen, Douglas. 2005. *Autism and the Myth of the Person Alone*. New York: New York University Press.

Bolcom, William. 2004. "The End of the Mannerist Century." In *The Pleasure of Modernist Music: Listening, Meaning, Intention, Ideology*, edited by Arved Ashby, 46–53. Rochester, NY: University of Rochester Press.

Broyles, Michael. 2004. *Mavericks and Other Traditions in American Music*. New Haven, CT: Yale University Press.

Butler, Christopher. 1994. *Early Modernism: Literature, Music, and Painting in Europe 1900–1916*. Oxford, UK: Oxford University Press.

Chew, Kristina. 2008. "Fractioned Idiom: Metonymy and the Language of Autism." In *Autism and Representation*, edited by Mark Osteen, 133–144. New York: Routledge.

Drott, Eric. 2013. "The End(s) of Genre." *Journal of Music Theory* 57 (1): 1–46.

Dubiel, Joseph. 1992. "Three Essays on Milton Babbitt" (Part 3). *Perspectives of New Music* 30 (1): 82–131.

Everdell, William R. 1997. *The First Moderns: Profiles in the Origins of Twentieth-Century Thought*. Chicago: University of Chicago Press.

Eyal, Gil, Brendan Hart, Emine Oncluer, Neta Oren, and Natasha Rossi. 2010. *The Autism Matrix: The Social Origins of the Autism Epidemic*. New York: Polity.

Foucault, Michel. 2009. *History of Madness*. Edited by Jean Khalfa. Translated by Jonathan Murphy and Jean Khalfa. New York: Routledge.

Frith, Uta. 1991. *Autism and Asperger Syndrome*. Cambridge, UK: Cambridge University Press.

Garland-Thomson, Rosemarie. 2004. "The Cultural Logic of Euthanasia: 'Sad Fancyings' in Herman Melville's 'Bartelby.' " *American Literature* 76 (4): 777–806.

Grandin, Temple. 1995. *Thinking in Pictures and Other Reports from My Life with Autism.* New York: Doubleday.

Hacking, Ian. 1998. *Mad Travelers: Reflections on the Reality of Transient Mental Illnesses.* Cambridge, MA: Harvard University Press.

Hacking, Ian. 1999. *The Social Construction of What?* Cambridge, MA: Harvard University Press.

Hacking, Ian. 2009. "Humans, Aliens, and Autism." *Daedalus* 138 (3): 44–59.

Howe, M. 1989. *Fragments of Genius: The Strange Feats of Idiot Savants.* London: Routledge.

Kanner, Leo. 1943. "Autistic Disturbances of Affective Contact." *Nervous Child* 2: 217–250.

Linton, Simi. 1998. *Claiming Disability: Knowledge and Identity.* New York: New York University Press.

Magee, Gayle Sherwood. 2008. *Charles Ives Reconsidered.* Urbana: University of Illinois Press.

Maus, Fred Everett. 2004. "Sexual and Musical Categories." In *The Pleasure of Modernist Music: Listening, Meaning, Intention, Ideology*, edited by Arved Ashby, 153–175. Rochester, NY: University of Rochester Press.

McClary, Susan. 1989. "Terminal Prestige: The Case of Avant-Garde Music Composition." *Cultural Critique* 12: 57–81.

McClary, Susan. 2000. *Conventional Wisdom: The Content of Musical Form.* Berkeley: University of California Press.

McDonagh, Patrick. 2008. *Idiocy: A Cultural History.* Liverpool, UK: Liverpool University Press.

Miller, Jean Kearns. 2003. *Women from Another Planet? Our Lives in the Universe of Autism.* Bloomington, IN: First.

Mitchell, David T., and Sharon L. Snyder. 2000. *Narrative Prosthesis: Disability and the Dependencies of Discourse.* Ann Arbor: University of Michigan Press.

Murray, Stuart. 2008. *Representing Autism: Culture, Narrative, Fascination.* Liverpool, UK: Liverpool University Press.

Murray, Stuart. 2012. *Autism.* New York, Routledge.

Nadeson, Majia Holmer. 2005. *Constructing Autism: Unraveling the "Truth" and Understanding the Social.* New York: Routledge.

Osteen, Mark, ed. 2008. *Autism and Representation.* New York: Routledge.

Park, Clara Claiborne. 1982. *The Siege: A Family's Journey into the World of an Autistic Child.* Boston: Back Bay.

Porter, Roy. 1987. *A Social History of Madness: The World through the Eyes of the Insane.* New York: E. P. Dutton.

Raffman, Diana. 2003. "Is Twelve-Tone Music Artistically Defective?" *Midwest Studies in Philosophy* 27: 69–87.

Rodas, Julia. 2008. "On the Spectrum? Rereading Contact and Affect in *Jane Eyre*." *Nineteenth-Century Gender Studies* 4 (2). http://www.ncgsjournal.com/issue42/rodas.htm.

Sacks, Oliver. 1995. *An Anthropologist on Mars: Seven Paradoxical Tales.* New York: Random House.

Sass, Louis. 1992. *Madness and Modernism: Insanity in the Light of Modern Art, Literature, and Thought.* New York: Basic.

Straus, Joseph. 1990. *Remaking the Past: Musical Modernism and the Influence of the Tonal Tradition.* Cambridge, MA: Harvard University Press.

Straus, Joseph. 2009. *Twelve-Tone Music in America.* Cambridge: Cambridge University Press.

Straus, Joseph. 2011. *Extraordinary Measures: Disability in Music*. New York: Oxford University Press.

Straus, Joseph. 2013. "Autism as Culture." In *The Disability Studies Reader*, 4th ed., edited by Lennard J. Davis, 460–484. New York: Routledge.

Straus, Joseph. 2014. "Idiots Savants, Retarded Savants, Talented Aments, Mono-Savants, Autistic Savants, Just Plain Savants, People with Savant Syndrome, and Autistic People Who Are Good at Things: A View from Disability Studies." *Disability Studies Quarterly* 34 (3). http://dsq-sds.org/article/view/3407/3640.

Subotnik, Rose Rosengard. 1991. "Individualism in Western Art Music and Its Cultural Costs." In *Developing Variations: Style and Ideology in Western Music*, 239–264. Minneapolis: University of Minnesota Press.

Taruskin, Richard. 1996. "How Talented Composers Become Useless." *New York Times*, March 10.

Tymoczko, Dmitri. 2011. *A Geometry of Music: Harmony and Counterpoint in the Extended Common Practice*. New York: Oxford University Press.

Williams, Donna. 1992. *Nobody, Nowhere: The Extraordinary Autobiography of an Autistic*. New York: Harper Collins.

CHAPTER 35

BROKEN FACTURE

Representations of Disability in the Music of Allan Pettersson

ALLEN GIMBEL

fac-ture: The manner in which something, especially a work of art, is made.
—*American Heritage Dictionary of the English Language*, 2000

ALLAN Pettersson (1911–1980) was a Swedish composer of distinction active primarily in the third quarter of the twentieth century. An abused child brought up in the slums of Stockholm, he started playing the viola at an early age and eventually turned to composition. He made his living as a violist in the Stockholm Philharmonic until rheumatoid arthritis forced early retirement.[1] A severe bout with nephritis (a kidney ailment) resulted in extensive hospitalization later on (Kube 1996). He remained active as a composer throughout, his music explicitly reflecting psychological, physical, spiritual, and even sociopolitical issues resulting from these challenges.

Pettersson left sixteen massive symphonies, two violin concertos, a viola concerto, three large concertos for string orchestra, an important song cycle, and several other works of consequence. He is considered something of a national hero in Sweden, and has generated substantial scholarly and performative activity, mostly in Germany. In the United States, he is better known to record collectors than concert audiences: he made a brief public splash with the release of his Seventh Symphony conducted by Antal Dorati on a well-distributed London LP in the 1970s, and his Eighth Symphony was recorded by Sergiu Comissiona with the Baltimore Symphony on Deutsche Grammophon and released shortly after his death. His complete works are available on German and Swedish labels and are easily obtainable.

Pettersson's compositions are deeply engaged with the exploration of disability as an expressive topos. This essay begins with an introductory overview of Pettersson's symphonic output and continues with a consideration of the early Second Symphony and brief discussions of selected passages from three middle symphonies (nos. 6, 7, and 8).

The essay concludes with a consideration of two late symphonies (nos. 9 and 10). In all of these works representations of disability play a central expressive role. Along the way, I offer a critical account of the secondary literature on Pettersson, which is largely skeptical of analytical consideration of "extramusical" features, especially those that bear on Pettersson's experiences of disability. I will argue, on the contrary, that these experiences and their musical expressions are central to any satisfactory understanding of this music.

It is evident from Pettersson's earliest compositions that trauma has always played a definitive role in his musical world. There are three specific disabling traumas to consider: one psychological (triggered by the events of his childhood) and two specifically physiological: disabling rheumatoid arthritis and, later, nephritis. These traumas are interrelated for Pettersson as topics for his musical language. Tropes of sadness and depression are ubiquitous, while musical gestures often take on embodied characteristics (Johnson 1997).

Pettersson's early works reflect psychological stresses rather than specifically physical disabilities, which had yet to make their appearance. The abuse inflicted by his alcoholic father is well documented, indeed by the composer himself, and is musically depicted in often gruesome detail in some of the *Barefoot Songs* and in the instrumental music as well. Additionally, there is substantial evidence in both the music and writings that Pettersson may have lived with (possibly manic) depression, though we lack documented medical evidence for support. In addition to familiar melodic and harmonic tropes, and easily audible dramatic gestures, one could point to these works' structural density and Pettersson's imposing productivity under such difficult circumstances as potential clues.[2]

Any exploration of Pettersson's music must begin with the *Barefoot Songs*, a tonal cycle on Pettersson's own elliptical but obviously autobiographical texts. This cycle has a function comparable to Mahler's *Lieder eines fahrenden Gesellen* in that several of these songs provide material for later, nontexted works (including Sonata No. 1 for Two Violins, Symphonies Nos. 6 and 14, and the Second Violin Concerto). The abstract (nontexted) works of the early period present a pained, dark atmosphere which is never absent from the later compositions.

Soon after the onset of arthritis in 1954, Pettersson wrote his first and to that point most sustained lamentation, the *Mesto* movement of the Third Concerto for String Orchestra (1956–1957). Since he was slowly losing his abilities as a performer, had to have been in pain, and most certainly must have had doubts about his future, it would be wrong to ignore these biographical issues while considering this particular work, or, to be sure, the Fifth Symphony, which became the last score in Pettersson's own hand (Rapoport 1979, 114).

It is worth noting that Pettersson was no stranger to his medical condition: indeed, his sister was severely afflicted with arthritis before him, as the composer noted in a 1958 interview:

> I've wanted to cry out [in my music] what [my (also abused) mother] could never say, she and my sister, my sister who never got to be a woman, who was stunted by

> rheumatoid arthritis, who nearly threw herself out of the window because of the pain and who died one Christmas Eve in the Söder Hospital.[3]

In spite of all this, Pettersson made a point of stating in 1974 that his condition "didn't change [my] situation at all. I was already enclosed in my own world and had adjusted to the loner's struggle" (Rapoport 1979, 113). Pettersson asks: "How can one make music when one is not turned inwardly? When composing, one must look inwardly at oneself" (Rapoport 1979, 115). And related to this is one of Pettersson's most famous utterances: "My material is my life, the blessed, the cursed."[4]

To a significant degree, Pettersson's musical "self" was conditioned by his disabilities, an issue that embodiment theory can be helpful in exploring. Frank (1995) describes the narration of disability in terms that are richly suggestive of Pettersson's expressive intentions: "Telling stories of illness is the attempt mitigated by a body's disease, to give a voice to an experience that medicine cannot describe. . . . This voice is embodied in a specific person" (18). The modest literature on Pettersson consistently hints at relations between the music and Pettersson's physical and psychological condition, though the development of those ideas is often sidetracked by formalist notions that obscure interpretation.

Symphony No. 2

Pettersson's Second Symphony was written before the onset of his arthritis. As a result, its disability-related musical expressions have more to do with his psychological and emotional challenges. In his study of this work, Rapoport (1979) calls attention to its unprecedented and extreme length and odd internal proportions, obsessive repetition (both literal and concealed), "confrontation of apparently calm and stable elements with unstable, at times grotesque and barbaric forces" (the latter expressed in a "strongly expressionistic style"), "islands" of transcendent "resignation," gestures of "defiance" "against [a] constant threat of death," and finally a "very high density of activity," a characteristic to become increasingly prevalent in the later works. To these, I would add a particular interest in the interval of a descending minor second (evocative of the traditional *Seufzer*, or sighing, figure), sudden and unpredictable changes of tempo, and extremes of timbre, spacing, and register. All of these characteristics may be taken as expressive of manic-depressive tendencies.

To translate these musical style characteristics into the critical language of Lakoff and Johnson, I would identify in Pettersson's Second Symphony the following embodied image-schemas (following their usage, I place these in capital letters):

> DEFORMITY [DISTORTION]
> OBSESSION [BLOCKAGE]
> CONFRONTATION [CONTAINER]

RESIGNATION [BALANCE]
TRANSCENDENCE [UP-DOWN]
OVERWHELMEDNESS [IMBALANCE]
PAIN [PUNCTURE]
INSTABILITY [IMBALANCE]

These sorts of image schemas often appear resistant to expression in verbal language, and music can be a more vivid way of communicating them, as Pettersson's music shows. Scarry (1985) identifies pain, for example, as expressing "a state anterior to language, [a reversion] to the sounds and cries a human being makes before a language is learned." (4) She goes on to ask, "Who are the authors . . . of a language of pain?" (6). I would suggest that Pettersson, drawing on the musical representation of these image schemas, is one.

In his provocative article on Pettersson reception, Meyer (2002) evaluates the state of Pettersson research as well as potential topics for investigation. He identifies seven Petterssonian expressive topics, of which two are clearly disability related: physical (and spiritual) pain (sorrow) (*körperliches und seelisches Leiden*), and musical gestures related to it (*Schmerzebärde*) (36). As a warning to future writers in this area, Meyer quotes an observer of the 1982 Munich premiere of Pettersson's 10th Symphony: "[At this time] one must rely on reports that state that this composer, more than any other, consciously incorporated his physical and spiritual suffering in his symphonic output" (35, my translation).

In a published interview with important Pettersson conductor Sergiu Comissiona, Meyer complains of the lack of a "consistently reasonable Pettersson-Exegesis" (presumably untarnished by references to biographical or medical conditions) and goes on to suggest that "the key to the cipher of understanding a musical work lies [exclusively] in the particular constitution of the listener" (2002). Meyer's principal complaint is that "[Pettersson's] biography is held up so that each dissonance is part of his life story, a concrete trap placing all knowledge on the history of his illness" (37, my translation). As a consequence, "Missing from the German biographical literature [on Pettersson] is an example which offers as its recurrent minimal element something other than the constant iteration of illness" (41). What is needed, he writes, is to regard Pettersson's disabilities as simply "biographical fact" rather than "fundamental causation." In my judgment, this sort of blinkered view would place out of bounds the very "biographical facts" that are most central to understanding this music.

Symphony No. 6

Even more than the Second Symphony, the Sixth Symphony is rich in the representation of disability. It is a large single-movement work built around one of Pettersson's *Barefoot*

Songs ("Han ska släcka min lykta"), thereby inviting interpretation influenced by the song text, which was written by the composer:

> I stretch out, I lie flat out
> in my fresh white shirt—
> there: HE nears through the corridor,
> a foreigner to no door.
> I want to stand up well
> to tie my shoes
> but must find HIM
> goggle-eyed there in the mirror.
> HE can put out my little light
> so that I see nothing;
> HE can smash my little bell
> so that I hear nothing.
> More no one can guess,
> though one may perhaps wish it,
> if wishes are still to be advised,
> for one pale and face-to-face with Death.[5]

The Sixth Symphony, written after his rheumatoid arthritis became a truly disabling force, is based on the emergence of this *Barefoot Song*.

The Sixth Symphony is a vast single movement work lasting about one hour. Like all of Pettersson's mature works, it is held together with extensive repetitions of readily identifiable motivic statements, which take on an obsessive character. Although repetition is a characteristic of music in general, it is worth considering when and how musical repetition takes on a "chronic" tone, beyond its normative function of aiding structural cohesion. Many with chronic disability have experienced the feeling that no matter how much one strives to go on with life attempting to minimize or ignore their condition, its reality will not fail to make itself felt, particularly if the disability was acquired rather than congenital. That sense of an inescapable constraint would seem to underlie the obsessive repetitions of this music.

The opening bass ostinato, repeated in the symphony's introduction 8½ times, supports a long, sorrowful melodic line in the upper voice (see Figure 35.1A; recording available as Track 35.1A on the Companion Website), which turns out to be a slowed-down version of what will become the active "main theme" of the movement's sonata form–like "exposition" (see Figure 35.1B; recording available as Track 35.1B on the Companion Website). Its presence in the introduction in augmentation may be understood in retrospect as this theme in a state of paralysis, representing an image-schema Johnson might call BLOCKAGE, or alternatively, the theme in a state of IMMOBILITY, a literal description of the composer's physical condition at the time. The immobilized, blocked, paralyzed version of the theme may thus be heard as a personal situational signifier.

FIGURE 35.1 Symphony No. 6. (A) opening (mm. 1–14). Main theme in augmentation. (B) Main theme (mm. 64–67).

(b)

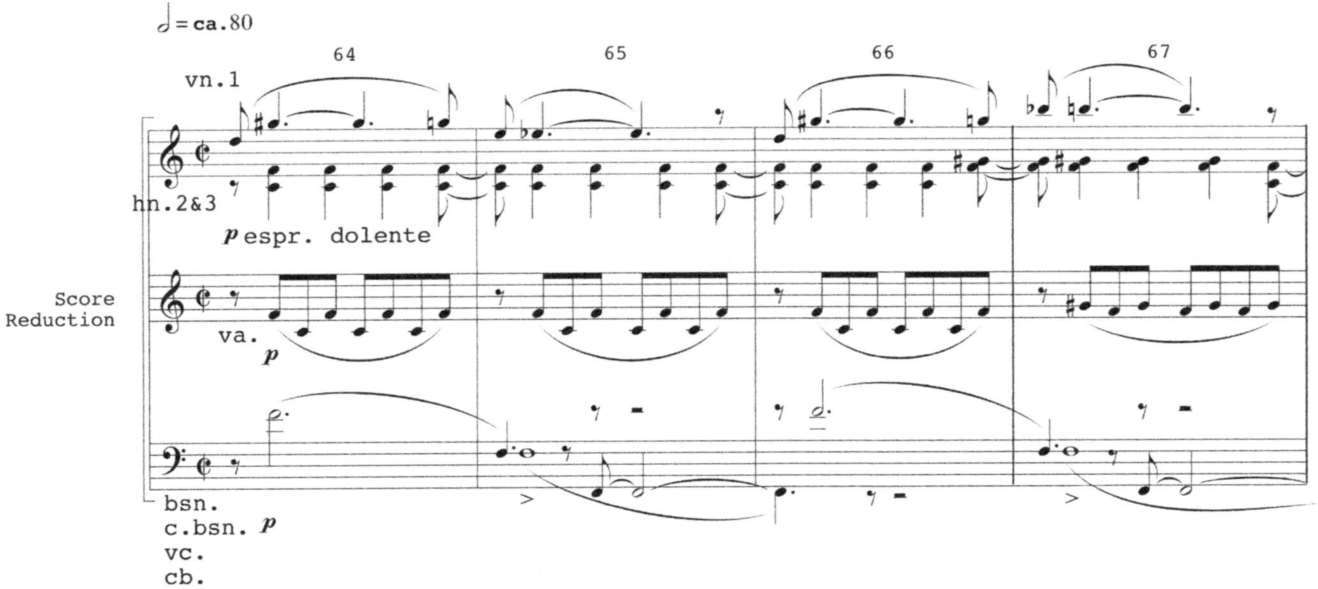

𝅗𝅥 = ca.80

64 65 66 67

vn.1

hn.2&3

p espr. dolente

Score
Reduction

va. *p*

bsn.
c.bsn. *p*
vc.
cb.

FIGURE 35.1 Continued.

Measures 119–120 introduce a harsh three-note, descending chromatic figure in the violins marked *forte* and *con forza*, to which is attached a series of repeated notes marked with staccato accents (see Figure 35.2; recording available as Track 35.2 on the Companion Website).

The expressive effect is of stabbing, recurrent irritation, here seemingly an explicit reference to the chronic pain suffered by an arthritis patient, and related to what we might think of as the embodied image schema PUNCTURE. It is found obsessively throughout the movement.

At m. 330 the winds introduce an expansive three-note figure spanning an ascending major ninth, filled in by a minor third: F-A♭-G (see Figure 35.3; recording available as Track 35.3 on the Companion Website). The melodic figure gives a physical impression of "reaching out," perhaps upward, perhaps outward, in search of some sort of comfort. A suggestion of an actual disease process is made audible in the figure introduced in the ascending, creeping chromatic figure first heard in the violas in m. 333. This tapeworm-like figure proceeds as if it were a living infection, always present and relentlessly sinister.

Throughout the Sixth Symphony, Pettersson employs a traditional musical symbol of pain, namely the falling half-step, derived from the physical response to pain that all vocal living creatures share. Instances of "*Seufzer*" or "sigh" figures are extremely numerous and often straightforward in their presentation. However, there are more subtle presentations, too. Indeed, many of the symphony's prominent motives may be considered variants of it.

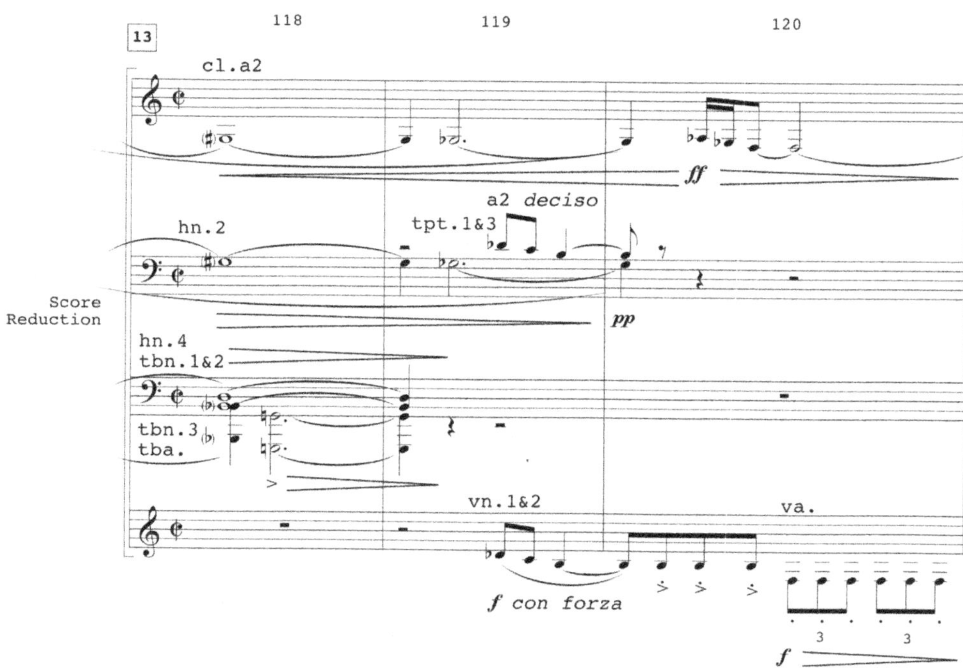

FIGURE 35.2 Symphony No. 6, mm. 118–120. Stabbing three-note figure.

FIGURE 35.3 Symphony No. 6, mm. 330–336. A figure that reaches out, but contains a sinister, infectious worm within.

The beatings administered to Pettersson by his father, which surely triggered the inspiration for the *Barefoot Song* on which this work is based, must not be neglected. Measures 528–530 recall such beatings graphically with four sharp syncopated smacks (see Figure 35.4; recording available as Track 35.4 on the Companion Website). These episodes may be considered to have both emotional and physiological repercussions.

The musical smacks are preceded by the main theme in the violins, which can be heard squealing during the onslaught. A similar texture may also be heard between mm. 720 and 813 for a much more extended period, though this cataclysm and others like it are part of a more general overall disturbance. It is no doubt possible to suggest that these episodes might be part of a larger, deeper-level "beating," specifically that metaphorically administered to Pettersson by his disability. No matter how nobly one's disability is fought (or ignored), it is still omnipresent, much like the goggle-eyed tormentor immortalized in the composer's song text.

Symphony No. 7

Revers 1984, a study of the Seventh Symphony, claims that Pettersson's biographical (physiological/medical) issues have created "a virtual screen (film) over his musical production," the source of "lack of comprehension on the part of critics" (103, my translation). Revers generally avoids relating the musical events of the Seventh Symphony to Pettersson's physical disability, though toward the end of the article he admits that Pettersson's battle "against the terminal thrusts of constantly deteriorating illness and invalidism . . . is articulated compositionally" in his works. But rather than focusing on disability, he chooses instead to pursue a speculative *political* model for the interpretation of the work's musical events, in effect deflecting attention from the physiological issues. This strategy displaces Pettersson's personal concerns about the travails of his body onto the broader social issues embraced by Pettersson over a decade later than the composition of this symphony, when texts dealing with repression and revolution served as material for his Twelfth Symphony and *Vox Humana* cantata. In these works, interestingly, mankind itself is presented as "disabled" (*misshandelten*), another sort of abused Body.

In his analysis of the Seventh Symphony, Revers 1984 identifies style characteristics that have the resonance of embodied image-schemas (in the manner of Lakoff and Johnson), where the body in question is disabled in some respect. These include the following:

SUSPENSION. A moment of suspended or paralyzed motion; a sustained musical meditation producing a hallucinatory or visionary effect. (Revers refers to these as Petterssonian "islands")

RUPTURE, DISINTEGRATION. The destruction of musical themes, from which thematic fragments may emerge.

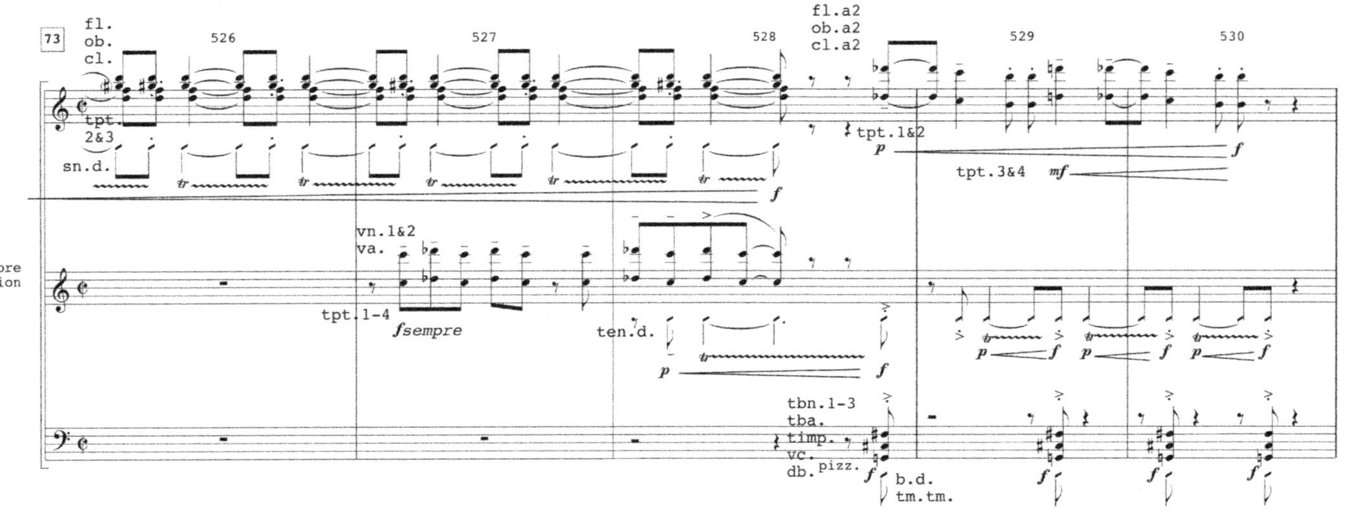

FIGURE 35.4 Symphony No. 6, mm. 526–530. A musical representation of a physical beating.

DYING DIMINUENDO. "The abandonment of the search for an objective, the silencing of musical expression, the final constituent of formal development." (Revers 1984, 104)

OBSESSION. The repetition and insistence (of the small motivic element); the "manic" insistence on a specific tone structure." (Revers 1984, 105)

These elements, along with those discussed earlier, are useful characteristics to be considered in an analytical context with disability as a point of reference. Revers interestingly posits a Peterssonian "symbiosis of dualistic structural principles and an organic, biological-developmental process" (106, my translation). Revers's language productively recalls Schenker's structural levels, including the relationship between the musical foreground and background. In Pettersson's music, the "biological-developmental process" is always under siege, like the diseased body, which acts as a sort of background, and these structural musical tensions inevitably have their source in Pettersson's struggles with his physical disability (acting as a sort of foreground).

The narrative arc of the Seventh Symphony is often directed toward the rupture, destruction, and disintegration of the sound field. Whichever direction the music tends, collapse is always imminent. In some ways, this is in keeping with standards of archetypical Nordic existentialism, but it also resonates with Pettersson's physical state. In many ways, and despite the occasional respite, the narrative shape of this symphony is that of what Frank 1995 calls a "chaos narrative". The passage at measures 96–102, provides an illustration (see Figure 35.5; recording available as Track 35.5 on the Companion Website). Here, a simple cadential progression in B minor is layered over and thus obliterated by chromatic interferences and outbursts.

Musical evocations of loss and breakdown are ubiquitous in the Seventh Symphony. In some instances, chorale-like passages, which evoke a momentarily harmonious or spiritual mood, are undermined and collapse under the pressure of a violent chromaticism. Along these lines, the most extraordinary section of the Seventh Symphony, and the passage that some might say made Pettersson famous, is the passage that begins at m. 512 (see Figure 35.6; recording available as Track 35.6 on the Companion Website). It is a stunning episode in F-sharp Major for strings alone, richly beautiful in a traditional way. Still, there are subtle changes in motivic health even in the context of this beauty: for example, F♯–D♯–C♯ in quarter notes becomes F♯–E♯–C♯ in half notes (the latter F♯ substantially extended). The motive is, following Revers, damaged (*verlust*) and suffers accordingly.

In this passage's unforgettable closing segment, an F♯2 is held by the first violins, seemingly for an eternity, while the rest of the ensemble is reduced to "an incoherent sequence of particle-like fragments" (Revers 1984, 122) and, finally, a series of plagal cadences (forecasting the end of Pettersson's Ninth Symphony), leaving a suggestion of spiritual finality, or perhaps a prayer for relief. But this very denial of completion remains as an emblem of an impossibly flawed and damaged world (as well as, undoubtedly, body).

FIGURE 35.5 Symphony No. 7, mm. 96–102. Disintegration into chaos.

(a)

FIGURE 35.6 Symphony No. 7, mm. 512–561. A beautiful musical body damaged.

FIGURE 35.6 Continued.

FIGURE 35.6 (Continued)

Symphony No. 8

I will approach the Eighth Symphony by way of Kube 1996, the largest published study of a single Pettersson symphony to date. Kube acknowledges that only through awareness of "Pettersson's personal biography" can "a preliminary functional context" be drawn, and expresses his intent to build "a foundation for establishing connections between biography and work" (10, my translation). Kube suggests that disability-charged metaphors might be useful as "protocols" for Petterssonian analytical descriptors. The central portion of Kube's monograph is a detailed blow-by-blow description of Pettersson's symphony in which a great deal of the language directly evokes disability. In the discussion that follows, I track Kube's analytical descriptions, calling attention to his embodied and disability-oriented image-schemas.

The Eighth Symphony is in two large movements. Kube analyzes the first movement as a sonata form, but one which, unlike the classical model, does not result in a positive transformation. Instead, the material of the exposition is mercilessly torn apart in the recapitulation while the principal theme tries vainly to reassert itself. The final resolution in the coda is more an expression of exhaustion than of satisfying closure.

Following the movement's main theme (MT), Kube identifies a *Trauermarsch* (funeral march), a *Klagegesang* (dirge), and, most alarmingly, a "Catharsis Phase with *Krebs*" (literally "cancer," but that word also has a connotation of "walking backward," along with suggestions of pincer-like activity and venereal disease). The main theme's "lack of clarity" and "functionally only loosely tonal" harmony (25) serve as useful psychological depictions of Pettersson's state of mind under his circumstances. The introduction presents a blurry, nearly out-of-tune harmonic field setting up an atmosphere of illness. Furthermore, the main theme is paired with descending chromatic curves related to the *Seufzer* idea so consistently evident throughout his work, here significantly active in the inner voice in the strings, which would have been played by Pettersson himself as an orchestra member.

In the *Trauermarsch*, we find a fauxbourdon-like passage in the lower strings, over which a disturbing figure in eighth-note duplets in the second violins seems to explicitly evoke physical discomfort (see Figure 35.7; recording available as Track 35.7 on the Companion Website). In this passage, and throughout the symphony, the percussion parts (the snare drum in particular) are used as an irritant. The omnipresent snare drum is a common fixture in most of Pettersson's symphonic works, and may be heard to illustrate a "march" forward to further deterioration.

The second movement opens with a sullen introduction followed by a turbulent and violent "scherzo." This is followed by one of the most bloodcurdling passages in the symphony (see Figure 35.8; recording available as Track 35.8 on the Companion Website). Kube describes the character of the orchestration in this passage as "sallow" or "sick" (*fahler*), presumably describing the widely spaced harmonics and the squeaking figure in the first violin. A "constantly pulsating (throbbing) accompaniment" is heard along

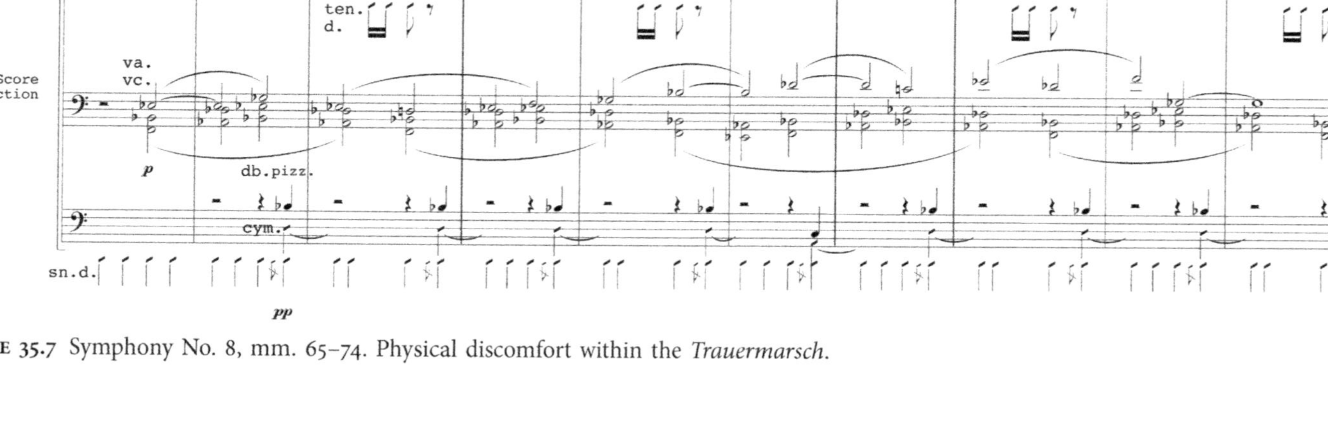

FIGURE 35.7 Symphony No. 8, mm. 65–74. Physical discomfort within the *Trauermarsch*.

with a "grotesque" counterfigure played by the bass clarinet and contrabassoon, designated memorably by Kube as a "broken facture" (*aufgebrochene Faktur*). It's hard to think of a more clear-cut depiction of disabling physical pain in the music literature.

In the final section of the coda, after striving for a conclusive cadence for over 150 measures and the descending bass ostinato of mm. 518–536 referencing the traditional death motive, the work's chaos narrative is solidified. There is no happy ending, and it could be argued that there is no ending at all. The question might arise as to why a listener might voluntarily submit to a work of such frightening misery. Frank 1995 offers a valuable explanation: "Storytellers [in this case of disability or illness] do not tell people *how* to be sick; their testimony is rather that you *can* be sick and remain not just in love with yourself but in love with the humanity that shares sickness as its most fundamental commonality" (40).

Late Symphonies

The Eighth Symphony is Pettersson's darkest work. The more resigned conclusion of the Ninth Symphony seems to forecast better times to come, but those hopes were immediately thwarted by the onset of Pettersson's nephritis, the physical challenges of which provided the context and content for the Tenth and Eleventh Symphonies. The history of art is filled with narratives of struggle and even "chaos," and Pettersson's music is perhaps on the surface most disturbing because of its explicitness. But its moments of transcendence, when they occur, are unusually rewarding, and are well worth the struggle, as the composer obviously felt and demonstrated. And by the same token it makes his uncompromising musical language unusually expressive.

The Ninth Symphony is by all accounts the largest single unbroken movement in symphonic history, a crowning example of manic artistry. It follows earlier works, like Schoenberg's Op. 9 Chamber Symphony in compressing the traditional three- or four-movement symphonic structure into a single movement, but Pettersson blows up the continuous multimovement format by obsessive focus on sectional materials. Coherence is often achieved (yet again) through the tool of the repeating ostinato, which Gülke 1995 interestingly describes as having "a nearly physical menacing force" (8). The relentless chromatic motion highlighted in the first half hour of the piece, along with the ostinatos, could both be interpreted as expressions of the stifling imprisonment that may be felt as a matter of course in the lives of the physically immobile. In fact, in Pettersson's case, this imprisonment was not only physical at the time, but distressingly real: He lived in a Stockholm walkup apartment, and literally could not leave his residence. Is it possible that these biographical conditions would not have a significant effect on his music?

Pettersson's nine-month-long hospitalization due to nephritis, an often difficult kidney ailment, provided the environment for the creation of both the Tenth and Eleventh symphonies. The Tenth is a relatively brief single-movement work of searing intensity, devoid of extended "islands" of transcendence, which will become increasingly infrequent in Pettersson's music, until we reach the formidable Second Violin Concerto, a *Barefoot Song*–texted work of truly elevated vision. No extended studies of these works

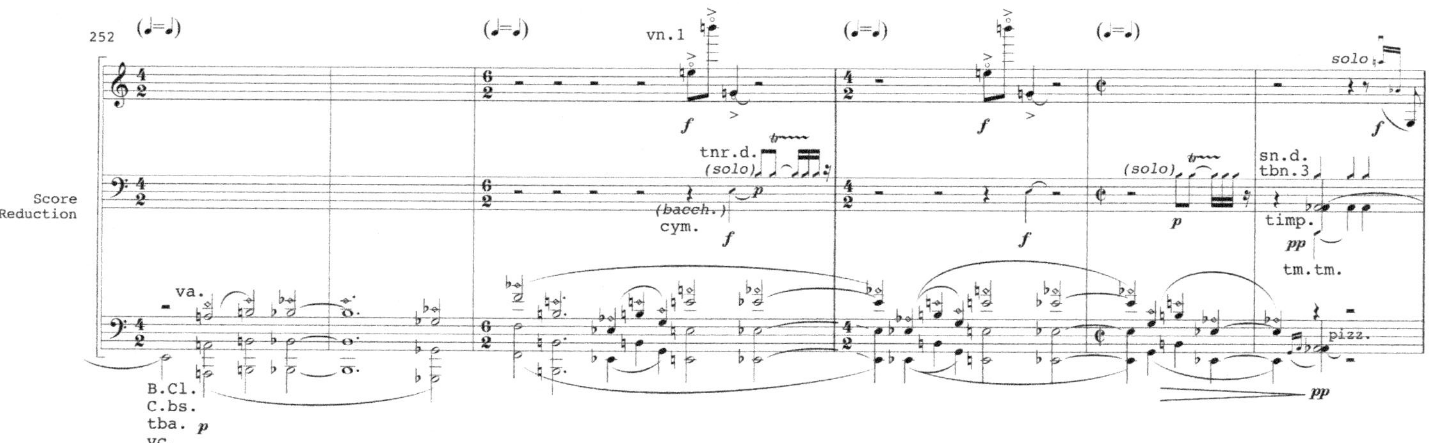

FIGURE 35.8 Symphony No. 8, II, mm. 252–257. Disabling physical pain.

exist at this time to my knowledge, but Pettersson did provide an introduction to the score of the Tenth, which bears quoting here:

> The angel of death is a hypocritical poetic figure. Death has nothing to do with mercifulness, because he casually randomizes the strong relation between sadness and sickness, especially when the antipole, the strength to live, is weak. The aim is life, not death. When he comes, he comes like a national decree. I cannot accept him, he doesn't go together with my will to live. Death, my constant shadow, is stronger yet than I. Or is it He himself, God, with whom I as a man experiment in another life form? (Quoted in Kube 1996)

Since this passage is literally attached to the symphony proper (and by extension the Eleventh as well), and the symphony was written under dire medical circumstances, in which Pettersson reports "staring death constantly in the face," it would strain credulity to seek to avoid identifying disability-related musical tropes of strength, weakness, illness, life, and death, as one would approach any Romantic tone poem. The Tenth Symphony, with its relentless tumult, ironically provides an eloquent expression of the dialectic of menacing force and cleansing optimism that informs so much of Pettersson's output. Death's "National Decree" is presented immediately at the beginning of the work as the fanfare-like motive that threads its way through the piece as its main theme, eventually leading toward ecstatically rising diatonic scales, which seem to be a clear metaphor of Pettersson himself rising out of his wheelchair in confrontational triumph. That victory, however, is tragically squashed in the coda.

It should be apparent from the preceding that, for scholars and others interested in the musical representation of disability, the music of Allan Pettersson represents a compelling body of work. It should be of particular interest to scholars involved in the psychology of music, where embodied experience, including the experience of disability, may be a shaping influence. Ideally, continued inquiry into the role of disability in Pettersson's music would be enriched by close engagement with relevant primary sources. Unfortunately, however, Pettersson's compositional sketches are not available, and relevant medical records and eyewitness accounts are both problematic—access to the former is unlikely due to legal and ethical considerations; access to the latter is by definition undependable. Therefore scholarship in this area will always remain at its base speculative, though again there is no evidence that Pettersson would actually discourage disability-oriented interpretations of his music. But a composer rarely can make such evaluations. If there is to be a Petterssonian analytical literature, it will likely be "impure" at some level if such analytical work is to bring this music to life.

Acknowledgments

A version of this paper was posted as part of a panel on Disability Studies in Music at the Fall 2007 meeting of the Society for Music Theory, Baltimore. Thanks to Jennifer Sadoff

Auerbach, Per F. Broman, Jorge Luis Lopez, Glenn Kurtz, and Joseph Straus for their invaluable assistance and helpful input.

NOTES

1. Aare 1978 is a standard biographical source. Barkefors 2012 is a more recent biography. Neither has been translated into English. An important documentary film on the composer by Peter Berggren, Tommy Höglind, and Gunnar Källström, *Människans röst (Vox Humana)*, produced by Swedish Television in 1978, two years before his death, has been issued with English subtitles with Christian Lindberg's recording of the Ninth Symphony (Bis 2038).The film contains much interview material with Pettersson himself.
2. Hershman and Lieb 1998 is a valuable resource for such issues.
3. Allan Pettersson, "Intyg," unpublished, Stockholm, September 1975, 1 (cited in Rapoport 1979, fn. 14).
4. Stenström 1958, 6–7; cited in Rapoport 1979, fn. 12.
5. Translation by Andreas K. W. Meyer, in the booklet for the recording with Manfred Trojahn, CPO 999 134, p. 21.

REFERENCES

Aare, Leif. 1978. *Allan Pettersson*. Stockholm, Sweden: Norstedt.

Barkefors, Laila. 2011. *En tonsattares liv och Verk* [There is a Sun Burning inside Us]. Stockholm, Sweden: Gehrmans.

Frank, Arthur W. 1995. *The Wounded Storyteller*. Chicago: University of Chicago Press.

Gülke, Peter. 1995. "Protest, Vergeblichkeit, verweigerte Resignation: Gedanken beim Studium von Allan Petterssons Neunter Sinfonie." *Das Orchester* 1 (95): 7–11.

Hershman, D. Jablow, and Julian Lieb. 1998. *Manic Depression and Creativity*. Amherst, MA, and New York: Prometheus.

Johnson, Mark L. 1987. *The Body in the Mind: The Bodily Basis of Meaning, Imagination, and Reason*. Chicago: University of Chicago Press.

Kube, Michael. 1994. "Zu Allan Petterssons 6. Symphonie." In *Allan Pettersson: Te xte-Materielen-Analysen*, 137–159. Hamburg, Germany: Von Bockel Verlag.

Kube, Michael. 1996. *Symphonie Nr. 8*. Wilhelmshaven, Germany: Florian Noetzel.

Meyer, Andreas K. W. 2002. "Ein Werdegang Zur Entwicklung der Pettersson-Rezeption in der Bundesrepublik Deutschland von den Jahren bis 1994." *Allan Pettersson Jahrbuch*, 35–41. Saarbrück, Germany: Pfau-Verlag.

Rapoport, Paul. 1979. "Allan Pettersson and His Symphony No. 2." In *Opus Est: Six Composers from Northern Europe*, 108–132. London: Taplinger.

Revers, Peter. 1984. "Allan Pettersson: 7. Sinfonie." *Melos* 46: 103–125.

Scarry, Elaine. 1985. *The Body in Pain: The Making and Unmaking of the World*. Oxford and New York: Oxford University Press.

Stenström, Urban. 1958. "Allan Pettersson: Komponerande och grubblande son av Söder." *Nutida Musik* 1 (5).

CHAPTER 36

REPRESENTING THE EXTRAORDINARY BODY

Musical Modernism's Aesthetics of Disability

JOSEPH STRAUS

Modern Art and the Representation of the Disabled Body

Within the field of Disability Studies, art historian Tobin Siebers has recently argued that the aesthetic of modern art is distinguished by the way in which it represents and finds new sorts of beauty in the extraordinary, fractured, disfigured, disabled human body:

> My argument here conceives of the disabled body and mind as playing significant roles in the evolution of modern aesthetics, theorizing disability as a unique resource discovered by modern art and then embraced by it as one of its defining concepts. Disability aesthetics refuses to recognize the representation of the healthy body—and its definition of harmony, integrity, and beauty—as the sole determination of the aesthetic. Rather, disability aesthetics embraces beauty that seems by traditional standards to be broken, and yet it is not less beautiful but more so, as a result. (Siebers 2010, 2–3).

Whether one thinks of the still shocking depictions of wounded World War I veterans by Otto Dix, or Picasso's cubist portraits of bodies that are fractured and misshapen, or the asymmetrical, disfigured faces and bodies in the Viennese expressionism of Schiele and others, it does seem as though Siebers is correct in asking,

> To what concept, other than the idea of disability, might be referred modern art's love affair with misshapen and twisted bodies, stunning variety of human forms, intense

> representation of traumatic injury and psychological alienation, and unyielding preoccupation with wounds and tormented flesh? (Siebers 2010, 4).

Of course the representation of disability plays a role in both visual arts and literature long before the modern period, however defined chronologically and stylistically.[1] Usually, however, in premodernist representations, disabled bodies are secondary to the main subject or action of the work. They are stigmatized as deviant or grotesque, relegated to functioning as a foil for normative protagonists or central figures (designed, in fact, precisely to establish their normativity), and generally subsumed into a normalizing frame. Lennard Davis's comments about the eighteenth- and nineteenth-century novel apply also to representations of disability in the other arts in the same period:

> Plot functions in the novel, especially during the eighteenth and nineteenth centuries, by temporarily deforming or disabling the fantasy of nation, social class, and gender behaviors that are constructed as norms. The *telos* of plot aims then to return the protagonists to this norm by the end of the novel. . . . In this sense, the identity of the novel revolves around a simple plot. The situation had been normal, it became abnormal, and by the end of the novel, the normality, or some variant of it, was restored. . . . The alterity presented by disability is shocking to the liberal, ableist sensibility, and so narratives involving disability always yearn toward the cure, the neutralizing of the disability. (Davis 2003, 542).

What is new in the modernist "aesthetics of disability" described by Siebers is that disability now moves from periphery to center stage, from marginalized, stigmatized, deviant otherness to a newly aestheticized artistic focus.[2] In modern art, disability is aestheticized into new forms of beauty. Aestheticizing disability does not mean prettifying it, or normalizing it to conform to traditional standards of beauty, however. Rather, it means the significant broadening and, in some cases, the radical subversion and disruption of traditional notions of beauty. Artworks that exemplify an aesthetics of disability may thus "turn traditional conceptions of aesthetic beauty away from ideas of the natural and healthy body" (Siebers 2010, 134) and toward the deformed, disfigured, fractured, fragmented, and thus disabled. In short, modernist aesthetics bends beauty in the direction of disability.

Disability and Modernism in Music

Siebers 2010 claims bluntly, "the modern in art manifests itself as disability" (40). Is it possible to make a similar claim about modernist music? Can we say that the modern in music manifests itself as disability? Can we say that modern music has a fundamental interest in representing the disabled human body?

Even a casual, preliminary survey of opera and other texted music suggests that modernist composers have not only an interest in representing the disabled body but also in moving the disabled body from the stigmatized periphery to the aestheticized center. Their interest seems to cut across the familiar stylistic diversity of musical modernism (including expressionism, primitivism, and neoclassicism) and to embrace a variety of bodily conditions understood as disabilities. Franz Schreker's *Die Gezeichneten* and Alexander Zemlinsky's *Der Zwerg* feature sympathetically treated protagonists who are hunchbacked dwarves; George Gershwin's Porgy and John Adams's Klinghoffer have mobility impairments; Arnold Schoenberg's Moses is, effectively, a stutterer.[3] If we extend the concept of disability to include cognitive or intellectual impairment and madness, Schoenberg's *Erwartung* and *Pierrot*, Alban Berg's *Wozzeck*, Francis Poulenc's *La voix humaine*, and Benjamin Britten's *Peter Grimes* come into view, along with a host of other works.[4] Many of these works follow a punishing, traditional narrative arc in which closure requires the destruction and death of a disabled character, but in their generally sympathetic treatment of a disabled protagonist, they nonetheless mark something new. In that sense, some modernist operas and dramatic works do appear to practice an aesthetic of disability, and their new aesthetic of disability is inseparable from their modernism. In short, modernism values transgression, and nothing can be more transgressive than a nonnormative body.

Disability is a broad and heterogeneous category, both as an attribute of human bodies and as an aesthetic.[5] Musical modernism is a similarly broad and heterogeneous category. In trying to bring disability and musical modernism into a productive relationship with each other, I restrict the disabling conditions under consideration to disabilities of form and appearance (deformation and disfigurement), disabilities of motion (including paralysis and stuttering, a form of vocal disfluency), and cognitive or intellectual disabilities ("simplemindedness"), and I restrict the styles of musical modernism to those of Stravinsky's music roughly from *Petrushka* (1911) through the works of the 1920s and 1930s, including primitivism and neoclassicism. Other disabilities and other modernist styles (I am thinking especially of various forms of madness in relation to musical expressionism) may also be profitably conjoined under the rubric of disability aesthetics, but in what follows, I offer a close look at a single small composition by Stravinsky, the second of his Three Pieces for String Quartet, written in 1914 in the immediate aftermath of *The Rite of Spring*.

I have a programmatic reason for selecting this particular work as a case study, as is discussed later, but I have selected it in the first instance because it epitomizes salient aspects of Stravinsky's musical style at this time, including its formal articulation into discrete textural blocks or fragments; its interest in symmetry and asymmetry in rhythm, form, and harmony; its immobilizing resistance to the teleological, developmental processes of so much earlier music; and its deliberate simplification of musical materials. All of these distinctively modernist musical features can be productively understood metaphorically as attributes of human bodies, especially bodies that are extraordinary in shape or function—that is, disabled.

I begin, then, by invoking the familiar metaphorical conflation of a work of music with a human body, both its morphology and its behavior. In many of our dominant music-theoretical approaches (like those of Schenker and Schoenberg), and in a great deal of more casual conversation, musical works are analogized to and understood as human bodies, as living, sentient beings with form and motion, and often with blood, organs, limbs, and skin as well.[6] As experientialist philosophy has taught us, this sort of embodied understanding of musical phenomena, or of any sort of phenomena, is a universal aspect of human cognition: we understand the world through our prior, intimate knowledge of our own bodies.[7] Accordingly, we often understand musical works as describing embodied human agents, with particular capabilities and inclinations, and their motions in time and space.[8] In some cases, the bodies at issue may seem to be disabled in some significant way, especially in relation to the idealized, harmonious, integrated, organically whole body of the classical tradition.

In that spirit, the passage from the second of Stravinsky's Three Pieces for String Quartet shown in Figure 36.1 can be heard as representing a body that is disabled in a number of ways, in shape and in behavior, both mentally and physically. This passage is the complete A-section of a small ABA form, and the movement as a whole ends just as this opening passage does.

The Form and Appearance of the Musical Body (Fractured, Fragmented, Deformed, Distorted, Asymmetrical)

Perhaps the most obvious feature of this music is its radical discontinuity. Distinctive musical fragments are presented without introduction and abandoned without cadence. There are no transitions to connect the isolated textural blocks; rather, they are simply juxtaposed, in the manner of a collage. Each block has a distinctive musical character, one that presents maximal contrast with the blocks that come before and after it. The music appears splintered, as though some more tonally normal passage, with its characteristic sense of connectedness and cohesion, had been shattered, or perhaps carved into pieces.

This sense of the music as fragmented, splintered, shattered, or carved up implies the existence of a relatively continuous, coherent, homogeneous prototype that has been manipulated in just these ways. To experience something as broken requires an implicit sense of wholeness. Figure 36.2 represents my speculative compositional attempt to recover the implicit tonally and texturally normal prototype against which Stravinsky's work may be heard to have been written.

In approaching the work in this way, I follow earlier attempts by Heinrich Schenker and William Benjamin to capture, in Schenker's words, "what Stravinsky may have had

FIGURE 36.1 Stravinsky, Three Pieces for String Quartet, No. 2, mm. 1–21, with fragments A, B, C, and D identified.

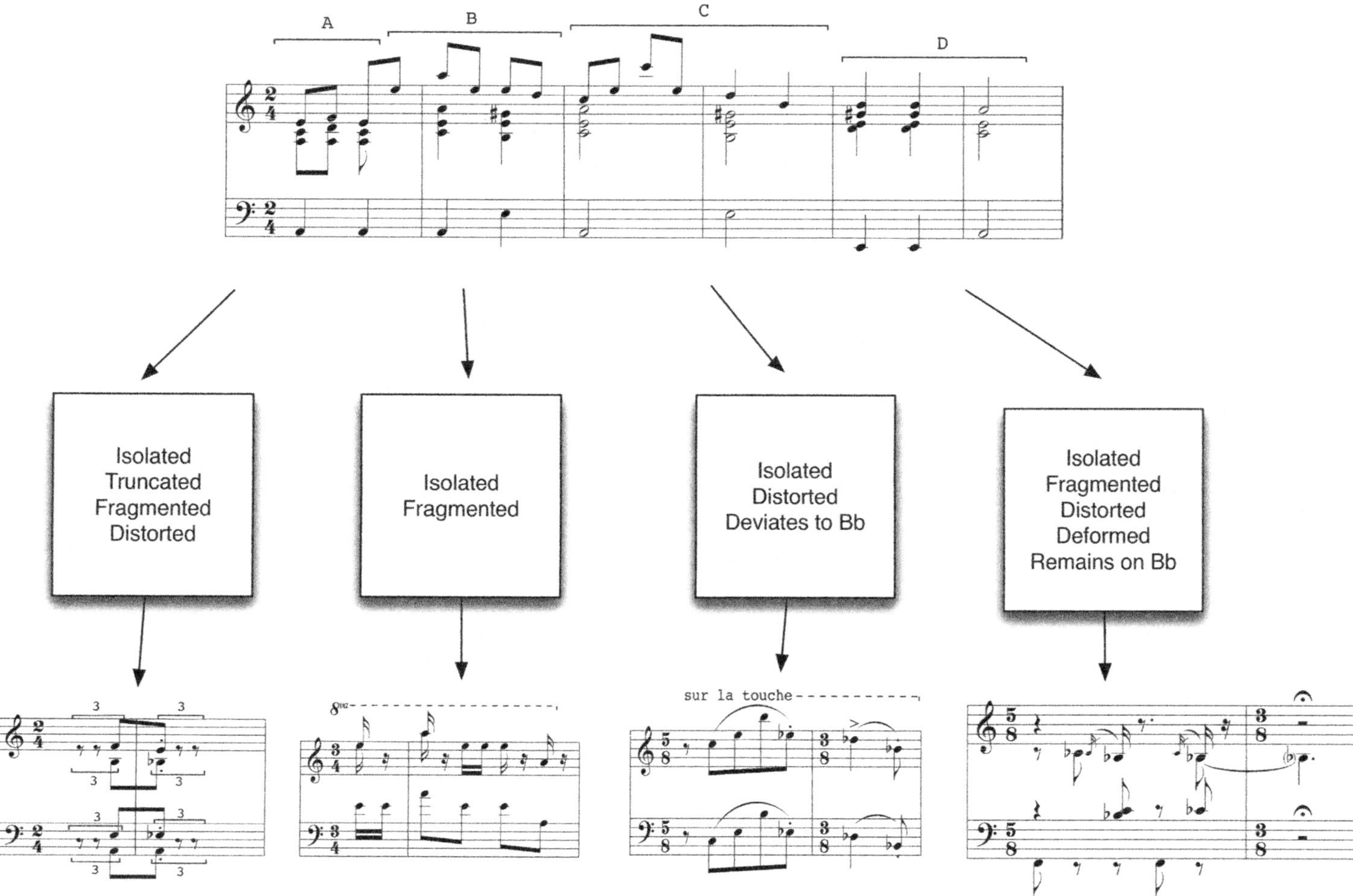

FIGURE 36.2 An implicit underlying tonal model of mm. 1–21.

in mind."[9] Indeed, in Stravinsky's compositional process, his earliest sketches are often relatively conventional, both harmonically and rhythmically, and these are progressively modernized and Stravinskyized as the music moves toward its final shape.[10] Of course, Stravinsky's musical manipulations of folk materials have been widely discussed in just this way, namely as willful distortions of tonal prototypes. It is a commonplace of Stravinsky criticism to hear his music as a deliberate "deformation" of tonal norms, and my Figure 36.2 attempts to concretize that common response.

The normative appearance of the music in Figure 36.2 helps us to appreciate the deviant features of the music in Figure 36.1. Fragmentation, distortion, and deformation are not merely passive attributes of Stravinsky's music but also active transformations his music performs on implicit tonal models.[11] A neighboring progression at the beginning of Figure 36.2 is sheared off from the larger passage to become Stravinsky's A-fragment. This fragment is itself fragmented into six and later twelve repetitions of a two-chord alternation. The B-fragment is similarly extracted from the progression in Figure 36.2, isolated with rests in Stravinsky's music, and severely truncated in its third iteration. The C- and D-fragments are also presented discontinuously, isolated from what comes before and after them. The form of the passage is thus splintered into discrete fragments, juxtaposed without transition, and arranged to maximize a sense of contrast and discontinuity.

The fragmentation of this passage is a somewhat extreme version of an approach to musical form that characterizes Stravinsky's music throughout his career.[12] Taruskin 1996 defines what he calls *drobnost* (splinteredness) as "the quality of being formally disunified, a sum-of-parts" (1677).[13] There is an obvious physical quality to the notion of "splinteredness," suggesting a fractured body, one that is broken, shattered, fragmented. The normally abled musical body (i.e., the classic-romantic musical body) is organically whole, its form naturally continuous, seamless, smooth. The Stravinskian musical body in contrast is fractured, fragmented into pieces, shattered, and splintered. If the normative musical body is seamlessly harmonious, the Stravinskian musical body, in this reading, is shattered and broken. And while the cultivation of the fragment is an artistic and musical phenomenon with its roots in Romanticism, fragmentation especially of the human body appears to be a particular concern of art after 1900. As Linda Nochlin notes, "The body fragment and the fragmentation of the body occupy a central if polyvalent place in the art of our period" (Nochlin 1994, 53).

Amid the process of fragmentation, the music simultaneously evokes and deforms tonal norms. While the A- and B-fragments stick reasonably close to a tonality of A minor (both chords in the A-fragment contain the fifth, A-E, which constitutes the totality of the B-fragment), the C-fragment leads the music down a different path by presenting its last four notes "a semitone too low." As a result of bending the tonal space in that way, the music is led toward a focus on B♭ rather than A, a tonal focus that is confirmed by the D-fragment, itself a distortion—via rhythmic fragmentation and a sharply dissonant added tone, C♭—of a dominant-tonic cadence in B♭.

This systematic distortion of tonal norms gives rise to a musical narrative based on symmetry and asymmetry rather than tonal coherence (see Figure 36.3).[14] The two

FIGURE 36.3 Inversional symmetry and asymmetry with reference to the A-E axis.

chords of Fragment A are related to each other by inversion around A-E, the perfect fifth that they share. If we think of each of the chords as consisting of two perfect fifths, we can imagine the first one as A-E combined with B♭-F (a semitone above it) and the second chord as A-E combined with A♭-E♭ (a semitone below it). The perfect fifth A-E is thus literally central to Fragment A, which balances around it. In Fragment B, the A-E fulcrum is extracted and heard by itself, unencumbered by upper or lower fifths. In Fragment C, the lyrical melody is symmetrical around A-E, with each note in close proximity to its inversional partner (the inversion is mostly in pitch space, with the B-D pair an octave "too high"). The first three fragments are thus internally balanced; instead of progressing toward a goal, they maintain a static symmetrical balance around their shared axis of symmetry.

The inversional balance delicately asserted and precariously maintained in Fragments A, B, and C, is violently overthrown in Fragment D. Here, the B♭-F fifth, which had previously been balanced by A♭-E♭ around the central A-E now brusquely asserts its own priority, its presence simultaneously intensified and dissonated by the persistent C♭. If the first three blocks maintain an upright, balanced posture, the final block topples to the ground with a sudden crash. Inversional symmetry thus serves to enclose each block as a static, self-referential entity, and to enable a larger narrative of balance established and then overthrown. The overall asymmetry in the harmonies is underscored by rhythmic and metrical fragmentation and fluctuation. As a musical body, then, this passage has a fractured, deformed, and asymmetrical form. In classical aesthetics, symmetry is considered a crucial feature of beauty. Stravinsky's music asserts a different sort of aesthetic, one that revels and finds new sorts of attractiveness and appeal in a vigorously asserted asymmetry, one that subverts and destabilizes traditional notions of beauty. The result in this passage is a music of startling, engaging contrasts, alternately light-hearted and heavy-handed, full of the delight and appeal of a quick-change artist, with an unbalanced feeling that keeps listeners pleasurably off-balance.

The Functioning and Mobility of the Musical Body (Static, Immobile, Limping, Stuttering)

In what manner does this disabled musical body move through time and space? On even a first impression, this appears to be a body with impaired mobility: when it moves at all, it does so in a halting manner. Within each fragment, there is a notable lack of musical movement; rather, each block is internally static, with a single idea stated and repeated without alteration. The fragments do not have obvious beginnings, middles, and ends. Instead of being developed, musical ideas are simply asserted. In classic-romantic music, especially in the genre of the string quartet, music evolves, unfolds, and blossoms amid flexible, contrapuntal interplay among the individual voices. In this passage, however, the evolutionary rhetoric of traditional tonality is abandoned in favor of nondevelopmental fixity and stasis.

As with the fracturing of the musical form into fragments, the immobile quality of each fragment has long been observed as a defining feature of Stravinsky's style.[15] As Taruskin explains,

> [Beginning with *The Rite of Spring*], Stravinsky's music would no longer meet the normative criteria traditionally deemed essential to coherent musical discourse. There would be no harmonic *progression*, no thematic or motivic *development*, no smoothly executed *transitions*. His would be a music not of process but of state,

> deriving its coherence and its momentum from the calculated interplay of "immobile" uniformities and abrupt discontinuities. (Taruskin 1996, 956–957)

Nepodvizhnost' (immobility) thus suggests a crippled body whose mobility is impaired. The normally abled musical body moves forward purposefully toward a goal; the Stravinskian musical body is paralyzed.

"Paralysis" is precisely the term that Heinrich Schenker uses with reference to a later work by Stravinsky, the Piano Concerto of 1924. For Schenker, music is supposed to flow organically along pathways he calls "linear progressions." As he poetically writes, "Every linear progression shows the eternal shape of life—birth to death. The linear progression begins, lives its own existence in the passing tones, ceases when it has reached its goal—all as organic as life itself" (Schenker 1979, 44). It is desirable for the linear progressions to meet with obstacles because the resulting detours can add interest to the journey.[16] But if the obstacles become too great, the linear progressions cease to function, and the music becomes "paralyzed."[17] The rather conservative Schenker believed that musical paralysis results when modernist composers like Stravinsky contradict the natural flow of the linear progressions by piling up dissonances.

Schenker rarely bothered to talk about composers of his own period—he considered them beneath his contempt—but he made an exception for Stravinsky. In an analysis of a passage from Stravinsky's Piano Concerto, Schenker offered the following critique:

> It will perhaps do Stravinsky adequate justice that I have made the effort to read any kind of sense into this passage. [My analysis] shows linear progressions; they are indeed of a simple type, but they are linear progressions nonetheless. Is it not the case, however, that Stravinsky contradicts this plan where is able to? First, his treatment of the outer-voice counterpoint, especially the bass, thwarts any articulation into linear progressions. . . . Finally, while neglecting the progressions he makes the notes constantly coincide in dissonances, a procedure which serves him as a substitute for content and cohesion. (Schenker 1996, 18).

For Schenker the most serious deficiency in Stravinsky's music is that its incipient linear progressions are thwarted by dissonances, thus immobilizing it. Stravinsky's dissonances, instead of creating motion under the control of a linear progression, impede the motion—they comprise a fatally disabling obstacle along the path traversed by the musical body. Schenker's analysis represents his heroic attempt to recover the normal body that lies beneath Stravinsky's distortions. In this sense, Schenker is engaged in what is historically the most familiar response to disability, namely to cure or normalize it. But his attempt at normalization only casts into sharper relief Stravinsky's willful use of displacement, misalignment, unconstrained dissonance, fragmentation, and immobilization to disable the normative musical body.

While immobility (paralysis) seems to be an attribute of all of the fragments in Stravinsky's string quartet passage, and a very large number of Stravinsky's textural blocks in other works, the A-fragment has two additional disability-related qualities.

First, its heavy, uneven, off-balance alternation of two chords suggests a limping gait. Instead of moving purposefully and smoothly toward a predetermined goal, this music trudges haltingly, making little or no progress. Second, the alternation of chords in the A-fragment exemplifies a familiar trope in Stravinsky's music, one he referred to as a "stutter." Stravinsky's melodic lines frequently alternate two pitches a semitone or a whole-tone apart, and these alternating melodic pitches are often associated with an oscillation between two chords. Stravinsky described this phenomenon as "a melodic-rhythmic stutter characteristic of my speech from *Les Noces* to the *Concerto in D*, and earlier and later as well—a lifelong affliction, in fact."[18]

Stuttering is disfluency, a series of repetitions and pauses that disrupt the usual smooth flow of speech.[19] Stravinsky's musical stuttering, as in this A-fragment, with its sixfold and then twelvefold repetitions surrounded by pauses, precludes forward motion in the musical phrase and traps it in one place. Stuttering is to vocal fluency what limping is to physical movement—an impairment of mobility. The musical body of Stravinsky's music is thus not only disabled in appearance (fragmented, fractured, deformed) but also in behavior and functionality (immobile, paralyzed, limping, stuttering). Its halting, disfluent qualities defy traditional canons of beauty, and yet have their own distinct aesthetic appeal: we learn to appreciate the individual moment rather than worry too much about where it might lead. Immobility, paralysis, limping, and stuttering can be felt as positive aesthetic values in this context.

The Mental Capacity and Affective Quality of the Musical Body (Intellectual, Cognitive, and Emotional Disability)

Stravinsky's musical body has mental and affective aspects as well. For many of Stravinsky's critics, his music has seemed somewhat simpleminded. Compared with the contrapuntal complexity of classic-romantic music, the immobilized content of each Stravinskian formal fragment is radically simplified, consisting of a single harmony, expressed either as a single-line melody or an alternation of two chords. There is little in the way of voice leading, virtually no counterpoint, and absolutely no contrapuntal imitation between the parts.

As noted, Taruskin has identified what he calls *uproshchéniye* (simplification)—a "radical simplification of means"—as an essential characteristic of Stravinsky musical style (Taruskin 1996, 1456).[20] Stravinsky's music is characterized by a "classicizing simplicity" (1459) in which everything inessential is stripped away; the music is thin-textured and laconic. *Uproshchéniye* may suggest an intellectual or cognitive disability, a mind understood as simple and childlike. The normally abled musical body maintains a reasonably high level of intellectual complexity (especially in counterpoint and voice-leading complexity). As with fragmentation and immobilization, simplicity is not simply an attribute of the music but a strategy of revision applied to implicit musical norms: Stravinsky strips traditional music of its contrapuntal complexity. As a result, the Stravinskian musical body may seem comparatively simpleminded.

This was certainly Arnold Schoenberg's view, at least during the 1920s. After an early period of wary mutual admiration, Schoenberg had been stung by some comments Stravinsky made in a newspaper interview in 1925.[21] In that interview, Stravinsky had claimed that in *Les Noces* he had used a "counterpoint chorus." In his handwritten marginal comments on the interview, Schoenberg wrote caustically, "A counterpoint chorus: what the little Modernsky imagines to be counterpoint" (324).

In response to what he perceived as Stravinsky's illegitimate appropriation of the mantle of J. S. Bach, Schoenberg wrote his *Three Satires*, Op. 28, the second of which openly mocks Stravinsky as "little Modernsky." As the music of the second *Satire* makes clear, the main defect of Stravinsky's music, for Schoenberg, is its lack of counterpoint. As a corrective, Schoenberg offers a short, sharp lesson in Bachian counterpoint, including all sorts of elaborate contrapuntal devices that unfold mostly within a twelve-tone framework. Schoenberg's joke appears to be that he can toss off something unimaginably complex contrapuntally, while Stravinsky, with all of his effort and boasting, can get no deeper than the simplest surface.[22] In comparison with Bach (and Schoenberg), Stravinsky is made to appear a simpleton.[23]

Beyond its apparent cognitive or intellectual disability, Stravinsky's string quartet movement has features suggestive of what historically and colloquially would be understood as madness. Without attempting a psychiatric diagnosis—an uncertain game under the best of circumstances—I will simply point out certain features that have been classified, in varying ways at different times and places, as manifestations of madness. First, there is the affective fragmentation of the music, corresponding to its formal fragmentation. We seem to be in the presence of a mind that is splintered, shattered to bits, divided against itself. Instead of a coherent, unified focus of attention, we find a quicksilver darting from mood to mood, from the depressed, heavy trudging of the A-fragment, through the light, delicate B-fragment, to the sighing, lamenting song of the C-fragment, to the brusque, angry shout of the D-fragment. Some of the fragments themselves seem to bespeak disordered mental states, like the obsessive, ritualistic fixity of the A-fragment. In purely musical terms, then, the second of Stravinsky's Pieces for String Quartet (and his other works from the same period) can be heard as a representation of a disabled body, including deformities of form, impairments of mobility, and abnormalities in cognition and affect. In all of these ways, Stravinsky's music represents a challenge to traditional notions of beauty. In the case of its apparent abnormalities of cognition and affect, the music can be heard to advocate what would much later come to be called "neurodiversity," that is, an appreciation (and not just an aesthetic appreciation) of minds that are atypical, but nonetheless valuable and even beautiful.

Little Tich

Claims of this kind may seem to bump up against Stravinsky's famous insistence that music is powerless to express anything at all.[24] But for this particular piece, Stravinsky himself has provided a specific, real-world referent: the music was composed as a musical representation of "the jerky, spastic movements" of a famous British music hall performer known as Little Tich. Stravinsky made this connection in response to a question from Robert Craft:

> [Question from Robert Craft]: Has music ever been suggested to you by, or has a musical idea every occurred to you from, a purely visual experience of movement, line, or pattern?
>
> [Response from Stravinsky]: Countless times, I suppose, though I remember only one instance in which I was aware of such a thing. This was during the composition of the second of my *Three Pieces* for string quartet. I had been fascinated by the movements of Little Tich whom I had seen in London in 1914, and the jerky, spastic movement, the ups and downs, the rhythm—even the mood or joke of the music—which I later called *Eccentric*, was suggested by the art of this great clown.[25]

It is worth taking a moment to contemplate Little Tich in order to understand the precise nature of the particular body that Stravinsky claims to be representing. For roughly thirty years, from 1895 to 1925, Little Tich (the stage name for Harry Relph) was a headliner in the British music hall, and was popular in France as well, where he often performed. The music hall was the principal source of popular entertainment in Victorian and post-Victorian England, with more than thirty halls in London alone by the turn of the century.[26] The shows presented in these halls were variety shows—the American equivalent was vaudeville—consisting of a series of acts, such as singing, dancing, comedy, acrobatics, dramatic skits, and so on. Little Tich never set foot in the circus, and he never juggled or did acrobatics.[27] Rather, he was a comedian, a singer of humorous songs, an instrumentalist (he played the tin whistle and the cello), a dancer, and an impersonator (including comic impersonations of pirates, police officers, and ballerinas).

Little Tich's signature act was his Big Boots dance, and the image in Figure 36.4 shows him in the eponymous footwear.[28] For this dance, he put on long, flat clogs and did various comic routines, including leaning way over, touching his nose to the floor, standing on these elongated tip-toes as though they were stilts, and sitting partially hidden behind the boots, peering between them. Wonderfully, there is surviving video of Little Tich available on YouTube, including his parody of a modern dancer named Loie Fuller and his famous Big Boots dance (three short videos are posted on the Companion Website for this book).[29]

An essential ingredient of Little Tich's distinctive persona and his success was his extraordinary body. Little Tich was a person of short stature—he was 4 feet, 6 inches

FIGURE 36.4 Image of Little Tich wearing his famous "big boots." Reprinted by permission of the Mary Evans Picture Library.

in height, and he had six fingers on each of his hands.[30] Those unusual physical attributes, especially his short stature, profoundly inflected the critical reception of him. Contemporary and reminiscent accounts, of which there are a great number, reflecting his fame, refer to him as a gnome, a dwarf, a gargoyle, and a grotesque. They praise his comic genius, his rapid movements and transformations, but all of them are inescapably concerned with his nonnormative body. Here are three such accounts (with italics added):

> Like Nellie Wallace, another genius of the halls who was a superb dancer, [Little Tich] was an embodiment of the London backstreets, but also resembled a drawing by Callot, or one of the *demons of Hieronymus Bosch*.[31]

> Little Tich could not be anything but what he is, *an imp of grotesque drollery* that lets loose all the laughter in you. He cannot help being laughable, and you cannot help laughing at him. He is *a natural caricature of that noble animal, man*, and he glories in being a caricature. . . . Little Tich underlines the queerness of the human body. . . . When you laugh at Little Tich, you are laughing at yourself, for he is only yourself with a touch of *grotesque exaggeration*. Little Tich is a droll, because he is like you in an absurd way. His *littleness is droll*, because he is two or three feet shorter than you are. If we were all like him, he would not be droll. *His tichness [sic] is mainly a matter of tininess. Enlarge him a shade, and he would not be funnier than we are*. (Douglas 1909, 152–155)
>
> There was something irresistibly comic in the *foreshortened appearance* he presented . . . It was his habit to present a number of characters, a lady in court dress (perhaps his favorite), a grocer, a jockey, and so on; and it was impossible not to be tickled by such a series of daft miniatures. You may say he drolly foreshortened all humanity. . . . We talk of people "breaking into" a dance, but the verb flatters them. Little Tich, however, really did break into dances. He was into a dance, fifty fantastic little steps, and out of it again almost before you knew what was happening. . . . In the antics of this *gargoyle* there was all the time the suggestion of a companion spirit winking and nodding and shrugging at you over the crazy jumble and tangle of things. (Priestly 1929, 63–67)

As these accounts demonstrate, contemporary responses to Little Tich were sharply and pervasively inflected by the unusual features of his body, especially his short stature.[32] Even when they praise his artistry, they do so in relation to his perceived disability. As is so often the case with disabled artists, the disability seems to engulf critical response.[33] For some observers today, it might be the case that Little Tich's body would not be considered disabled at all, but for most of his contemporaries, his body was considered deformed, freakish, and grotesque; his rapid movements were "queer," "droll," "absurd," and "demonic."

Contemporary responses to Little Tich often place him in the cultural category of the grotesque, one with roots in Romanticism and flowering in all of the modern arts, including music.[34] As art historian Frances Connelly observes,

> Images gathered under the grotesque rubric include those that combine unlike things in order to challenge established realities or construct new ones; those that deform or decompose things; and those that are metamorphic. . . . Grotesque describes the aberration from ideal form or from accepted convention, to create the misshapen, ugly, exaggerated, or even formless. This type runs the gamut from the deliberate exaggerations of caricature, to the unintended aberrations, accidents, and failures of the everyday world represented in realist imagery, to the dissolution of bodies, forms, and categories. . . . The grotesque permeates modern imagery, acting as *punctum* to the ideals of enlightened progress and universality and to the hubris of modernist dreams of transcendence over the living world.[35]

In all of these representations, especially those that involve the "dissolution of bodies," the grotesque appears to be a subcategory of the broader concept of disability. As Lennard Davis argues,

> One of the ways that visual images of the disabled have been appropriated into the modernist and postmodernist aesthetic is through the concept of the "grotesque." . . . While the term *grotesque* has had a history of being associated with [a] counterhegemonic notion of people's aesthetics and the inherent power of the masses, what the term has failed to liberate is the notion of actual bodies as grotesque. There is a thin line between the grotesque and the disabled. (Davis 1997, 64)

In his musical representation of Little Tich, Stravinsky succeeds to some degree in capturing the grotesquerie (and disability) of the spectacle. Many of the disabled qualities we have already attributed to the music, including its deformed appearance and its rapid mood changes, are relevant to Little Tich. But, if his intention was to create a musical equivalent of this particular body, Stravinsky would seem to have failed in many respects. As the surviving video makes clear, Little Tich is actually quite graceful in his movements, energetic and dexterous, a fine dancer, and a superb mimic. Little Tich is nimble, virtuosic, buoyant, and clever; on the contrary, Stravinsky's music is fragmented, broken, halting, and seemingly feebleminded. Stravinsky's music seems to depict a disabled body, but one that has more to do with the perception of Little Tich as grotesque than with his actual bodily capability. It is possible that Stravinsky is using Little Tich's body as a point of departure for a more generalized portrayal of the disabled body. One might go even farther and suggest that Stravinsky's music disables Little Tich in a particular way, indeed, enfreaks him musically by exaggerating and imposing on him an extreme vision of an abnormal embodiment.

Is it also possible that Stravinsky's thrice-repeated claim that he was thinking of Little Tich when composing this piece may be suspect? Later in his life, in the dialogues with Robert Craft and other writings, Stravinsky habitually misremembered or misled (Taruskin 1996). Did he perhaps have something different in mind that he inadvertently conflated with his memories of Little Tich? There is, in fact, a critical tradition, apparently deriving from Ernst Ansermet, that associates this work not with Little Tich but rather with a Petrushka-like clown: "The second [piece] is an unhappy juggler who is distraught with a grief that he must hide, while he does his little feats before the watching crowd. One hears in certain glinting tones the flash of his tricks, and as a piercing contrast the sorrow that tortures him while he is at his seeming play."[36] In 1915, Ansermet wrote again along similar lines: "The second [piece] has been developed in the region of the musically fantastic and bizarre."[37] In 1919, an anonymous reviewer for *The Observer* picked up the same thread: "[Stravinsky's] three pieces for string Quartet, played on Thursday, had definite programmes. . . . The second inferred a juggler performing automatically, and distraught with secret sorrow. As musically suggested, his trouble was more physical than mental."[38]

It is not clear whether or not Ansermet's juggler is an authentic part of Stravinsky's conception, perhaps as a supplement to or inflection of his memories of Little Tich. Certainly, to judge by his ballet of 1911, Stravinsky was drawn to the figure of Petrushka, a recurring subject of fascination to modern artists in all media.[39] While it seems more likely that Ansermet was speaking only for himself, and that Stravinsky may be taken at his word in having Little Tich in mind when composing the second of his Pieces for

String Quartet, it is notable that Petrushka, the puppet come to life, and Little Tich, the grotesque "clown" of Stravinsky's memory, both inhabit extraordinary bodies that deviate from the normative in culturally marked ways. In that sense, both Little Tich and Petrushka are disabled. To some extent, Stravinsky's music depicts the body and movements of Little Tich (or Little Tich by way of Petrushka), but the music might be better understood as a more general sort of musical response to disability inspired by that body and its movements rather than an accurate corporeal portrait. Stravinsky's music, in this sense, is about disability as much as it is about any particular disabled body.

Conclusion

In this more general sense, Stravinsky's music is to classic-romantic music what these extraordinary bodies are to normate bodies. Its most striking and characteristic features—fragmentation, asymmetry, immobility, simplification—may be understood as disabilities in relation to the normative musical embodiment of canonical works in the classic-romantic mainstream (what Stravinsky referred to as the "German stem").[40] Stravinsky's music takes the normal, natural-seeming works and procedures of classical tonality and then disables them by splintering, unbalancing, immobilizing, and simplifying them. If that is indeed the case, then perhaps we can infer a more widespread Stravinskian aesthetics of disability, and imagine that his music habitually represents the disabled body. As we have seen, the linkage of Stravinsky's musical style with bodily and mental disability is made explicitly and implicitly throughout a wide range of the secondary literature on Stravinsky, from both his detractors (Schenker, Schoenberg) and his defenders (Taruskin).

In a horrible historical irony, the German National Socialists were probably the first to understand the centrality of disability for modernism in the arts. As Siebers 2010 observes,

> The Nazis were the first to recognize the aesthetic centrality of disability to modern art. . . . The Nazis waged war against modern art because they interpreted the modern in art as disability, and they were essentially right in their interpretation, for modern art might indeed be named as the movement that finds its greatest aesthetic resource in bodies previously considered to be broken, diseased, wounded, or disabled. (34–35)

For the Nazis, artworks were condemned as degenerate precisely because of their inherently unhealthy, diseased, and disabled qualities.[41] For both disabled artworks and for people with disabilities, the Nazis pursued an extreme version of what Garland-Thomson calls "the cultural logic of euthanasia," that is, the imperative either to normalize disabled bodies (through medical intervention) or to eliminate them (either by sequestration in homes or institutions, or in more direct ways) (Garland-Thomson 2004; Friedlander 1995).

Under most circumstances, disabilities are understood as nonnormative bodily conditions that are culturally *stigmatized* (Goffman 1986). In most musical works before the modern period, a related sort of stigma attaches to anomalous musical events, like formal disruptions and chromatic intrusions. In the classic-romantic music of the eighteenth and nineteenth centuries, events like these are often treated compositionally as "problems," which it is the central task of the music to overcome (Straus 2011).

In modernist music, however, including the music of Stravinsky discussed here, we find a suggestion of the liberatory potential of music to rewrite conventional cultural scripts of disability. Here, the nonnormative bodily conditions of splinteredness, immobility, and simplification may be heard to be *valorized*. In Stravinsky's quartet, and in many of his works, we find a musical body that is disabled in appearance (fragmented, splintered, distorted, deformed), in functionality (paralyzed, limping, stuttering), and in affect (fragmented, emotionally labile, clinging doggedly and ritualistically to sameness and repetition). And yet in their musical context, these qualities are felt as attractive and desirable, within a radically expanded understanding of what might constitute the aesthetically beautiful. Modernist composers like Stravinsky bring disability into the picture as a part of their ongoing critique of traditional canons of beauty. Disabled bodies become a space where old aesthetic norms are disrupted—a visceral aesthetic statement in the most intimate and powerful terms.

In real life, disability is still widely stigmatized, and this imposes heavy emotional, social, and economic costs on people with disabilities. But art and music can create a counterhegemonic space within which disabilities, stigmatized in the outside world, can be celebrated and valorized. The disabilities of the Stravinskian musical body are understood as aesthetically desirable differences rather than undesirable deficits. That is the ethical essence of Siebers's "disability aesthetics," and Stravinsky's also—it teaches us to celebrate extraordinary bodies and to "embrace beauty that seems by traditional standards to be broken, and yet it is not less beautiful but more so, as a result."

Acknowledgments

I acknowledge the generous and helpful critical responses to earlier versions of this essay from a number of friends and colleagues: Sally Goldfarb; Scott Burnham, Kofi Agawu, and William Cheng; students and faculty who attended colloquia on this topic at Louisiana State University, Penn State University, and Temple University; and my fellow authors in this collection, especially Blake Howe and Jennifer Iverson.

Notes

1. Siebers is somewhat vague about the chronological boundaries of artistic modernism, with examples that range back into the nineteenth century, although most are from the

second half of the twentieth century. Millett-Gallant 2010, a related study, focuses on the visual arts since 1960, and argues that contemporary art involves "deeply historical and multidimensional representations of disability. My key examples subvert the conventions of art, as well as conventions or norms for bodies in social life" (6).

2. For a different but related concept of "disability aesthetics," see Davidson 2008: "It is this spectral body of the other that disability brings to the fore, reminding us of the contingent, interdependent nature of bodies and their situated relationship to physical ideals. Disability aesthetics foregrounds the extent to which the body becomes thinkable when its totality can no longer be taken for granted, when the social meanings attached to sensory and cognitive values cannot be assumed" (4).
3. See Sherry Lee's essay in this volume for further discussion of these operas and these issues.
4. Pedneault-Deslauriers 2011 is a valuable recent discussion of madness and hysteria in Schoenberg's *Pierrot* and in its reception.
5. The heterogeneity of the category is described by Rosemarie Garland-Thomson: Disability is an overarching and in some ways artificial category that encompasses congenital and acquired physical differences, mental illness and retardation, chronic and acute illnesses, fatal and progressive diseases, temporary and permanent injuries, and a wide range of bodily characteristics considered disfiguring, such as scars, birthmarks, unusual proportions, or obesity. Even though the prototypical disabled person posited in cultural representations never leaves a wheelchair, is totally blind, or profoundly deaf, most of the approximately forty million American with disabilities have a much more ambiguous relationship to the label. The physical impairments that render someone 'disabled' are almost never absolute or static; they are dynamic, contingent conditions affected by many external factors and usually fluctuating over time. . . . Although categories such as ethnicity, race, and gender are based on shared traits that result in community formation, disabled people seldom consider themselves a group. Little somatic commonality exists among people with different kinds of disabilities because needs and situations are so diverse. A blind person, an epileptic, a paraplegic, a deaf person, and an amputee, for example, have no shared cultural heritage, traditional activities, or common physical experience. Only the shared experience of stigmatization creates commonality. . . . Unlike the ethnically grouped, but more like gays and lesbians, disabled people are sometimes fundamentally isolated from each other, existing often as aliens within their social units. (Garland-Thomson 1997, 13–15) Similarly, Jackie Leach Scully observes, Disability is an organizing idea that has to hold together a daunting variety of body states, some universally agreed to be disabling, and others whose status is more contested: sensory impairments, mobility restrictions, missing or lost limbs, skeletal dysplasias (including restricted growth), morphological anomalies ranging from conjoined twins to extra toes, genetic syndromes with complex phenotypes, cognitive impairments and learning difficulties, mental illnesses, disablement due to chronic illness such as HIV/AIDS or metabolic dysfunction, and neurofunctional disorders. The concept of disability also has to cover impairments with different origins . . . and it has to account for the fact that there are people with the *same* bodily variation who disagree on whether they are disabled at all. (Scully 2008, 21)
6. See Straus 2011, 103–105, for further discussion of this metaphor, especially as it involves disabled bodies. For a related discussion of the "work-persona" as a narrative agent, with consciousness and volition, see Monahan 2013.
7. Among the principal sources in this area are Johnson 1987, Lakoff 1987, Lakoff and Johnson 1980, and Gibbs 1994.

8. For musical applications of philosophical experientialism, with its focus on embodied knowledge, see Brower 1997–1998, 2000, and 2008; Fisher and Lochhead 2002; Gur 2008; Mead 1999; Saslaw 1996 and 1997–1998; and Zbikowski 1997–1998, 2002, and 2009.
9. Schenker 1996 includes a penetrating, although contemptuous, analysis of Stravinsky's Concerto for Piano and Winds (see further discussion below). Benjamin 1976–1977 analyzes a different portion of that work in a similar, although much more appreciative, way. More recently, in Straus 2012, I created speculative recompositions of passages from *Petrushka* and *The Rake's Progress* to stand as relatively normal, conventional musical prototypes against which Stravinsky can be heard to be composing.
10. This is a central contention of Straus 1991.
11. In that sense, fragmentation, distortion, deformation, splintering, and shattering are like the "musical misreadings" proposed in Straus 1990—transformations imposed on tonal norms to produce modernist effects. Modernist musical works are thus simultaneously linked to and distanced from their common-practice tonal predecessors.
12. Many critical accounts of artistic modernism generally identify fragmentation as one of its central, defining characteristics. Sass 1992, for example, refers to a pervasive "fragmentation from within that effaces reality and renders the self a mere occasion for the swarming of independent subjective events—sensations, perceptions, memories, and the like. The overwhelming vividness, diversity, and independence of this experiential swarm fragment the self, obliterating its distinctive features—the sense of unity and control" (31). Similarly, see Kern 1983, Butler 1994, and Everdell 1997.
13. Taruskin identifies splinteredness as one of Stravinsky's three "essential characteristics": "[Stravinsky's] work possessed a strength of style, and his oeuvre a unity, that could accommodate an endless variety of surfaces. For all the variety, Stravinsky was the opposite of eclectic. His essential characteristics—his *drobnost'* [splinteredness], his *nepodvizhnost'* [immobility], above all his *uproshcheniye* [simplification]—inform his mature work from first to last with rare authenticity and constancy" (1675). The same musical feature has been widely described in the Stravinsky literature, often with highly concrete, although not necessarily embodied, imagery. See, for example van den Toorn 1983, where the phenomenon, termed "block juxtaposition," is identified as a "peculiarly Stravinskian conception of form" (454).
14. For examples of modernist musical narratives based on the interplay of symmetry (as a normative state) and asymmetrical deviations (as a potentially destabilizing, unbalancing, disabling element), see Straus 2006 and 2011.
15. Taruskin 1996 defines what he calls *nepodvizhnost'* [immobility] as "the quality of being nonteleogical, nondevelopmental" (1678). Horlacher 2011 complicates the conventional view of Stravinsky's music as nondevelopmental, nonteleological and thus fixed, rigid, and immobile by teasing out subtle pressures toward growth and evolution within and between the textural blocks.
16. As Schenker observes, "In the art of music, as in life, motion toward the goal encounters obstacles, reverses, disappointments, and involves great distances, detours, expansions, interpolations, and, in short, retardations of all kinds" (Schenker 1979, 5).
17. "Paralysis" is Schenker's own term, and his best-known use of it is in the title of his essay, "Rameau or Beethoven? Creeping Paralysis or Spiritual Potency in Music?" (Schenker 1997). The German word that Ian Bent translates as "paralysis" is *Erstarrung*. Bent comments: "Schenker's motivic use of *Erstarrung* and *erstarren* throughout the first two-thirds of this essay presents the translator with a conundrum, for the verb *erstarren* has a range of meanings, from 'stiffen,' through 'congeal,' 'coagulate,' 'solidify,' 'freeze,' to 'become numb,'

'torpid,' 'paralyzed,' and Schenker exploits this range such that no one English word will work idiomatically" (1). In the text of that essay, Schenker offers the following description of how music becomes paralyzed: "In Rameau's fundamental idea there lurked an element of the mechanical—turned away from the living art of voice-leading—right from the start, but that first mechanical element engendered mechanism upon mechanism in its train. Little by little, the seventh, whether as passing note or suspension, and the ninth, whether as suspension or changing-note, were made out to be chord-components, from which it was but a short step to bona fide seventh and ninth chords. Once on this slippery slope, nothing could stop recognition being given also to eleventh and thirteenth chords; and so, today, things have reached such a pass that, on pretext of the higher partials of the overtone series, any and every piling-up of notes, no matter how it may have come about, is indiscriminately taken for a chord. Make no mistake: Rameau's error has been compounded to the limit, the followers of Rameau's theory have reached a point of no return. Paralysis!" (5).

18. Stravinsky and Craft 1966, 58. Stravinsky's specific observation comes in relation to the alternation of D and E in the vocal line of the *Elegy for J. F. K.* Van den Toorn 1983 relates the "melodic-rhythmic stutter" to Stravinsky's persistent predilection for musical oscillations of all kinds, and argues "they may be found reaching into every crevice of melodic, rhythmic, formal, or pitch-relational matter" (440). For additional examples and discussion of Stravinsky's musical stutters, see Jers 1976, Straus 2001, and Horlacher 2011.
19. For discussions of stuttering and other forms of vocal disfluency in musical performance, see Stras 2006, Oster 2006, and Goldmark 2006.
20. Although I will not discuss the connection further here, Taruskin's "simplification" is related to an interest in the "primitive," widely acknowledged as a recurrent theme in artistic modernism (Butler 1994).
21. The following discussion of Schoenberg's *Satires* is based on Stein 1986.
22. Schoenberg's student, Theodor Adorno, offers a critique along similar lines. In Adorno 2003, his highly charged and fully embodied metaphors implicitly liken the splinteredness, stasis, and simplification of Stravinsky's music to physical and mental disabilities. Its splinteredness is manifested in "a disintegration of the organic progress" (150) producing "faults which permeate its structure" (187). Stravinsky's motives are "thwarted in their development" (151); his music "replaces progress with repetition" (164) and is "incapable of any kind of forward motion" (178). Its simplification is experienced as repetitive, infantile, childlike, primeval, primitive, and regressive (these epithets permeate Adorno's critique). It is striking how physical Adorno's language is. It sounds as though he is talking about a human body, and moreover a body with serious defects of appearance and function, a body that is fractured and deformed, that has difficulty moving, and that is animated by a cognitively defective, infantile, childish mind. In this sense, Adorno seems clearly to understand an aesthetics of disability operating in Stravinsky's music. Boulez criticizes Stravinsky in a similar fashion. His essay, "Stravinsky Remains" (Boulez 1968) is ostensibly an encomium, but is shot through with contemptuous judgments, mostly along the lines of Adorno's critique. To Boulez, Stravinsky's music is simple-minded and primitive, with simplistic superimpositions instead of counterpoint. It is rigid and repetitive, refusing to develop or progress. And its refusal to develop is a disabling fault that is both internal and historical. That is, just as Stravinsky's music rejects the internal, goal-oriented development of motives in the classical manner, his whole style represents a refusal to progress historically, to evolve. What Taruskin praises as splinteredness, stasis, and simplification,

Boulez stigmatizes as rigidity, mindless repetition, immobility, fixity, obstinacy, and simple-mindedness.

23. Disability is often understood as deficit or excess with respect to some normally desirable state (think of anorexia or obesity with respect to "normal" body weight). If Stravinsky's music has been understood as mentally deficient because of its apparent simplemindedness, Schoenberg's music has been understood as excessive in the same domain: overly cerebral and excessively complex.
24. Stravinsky (1936) 1962: "For I consider that music is, by its very nature, essentially powerless to *express* anything at all, whether a feeling, an attitude of mind, a psychological mood, a phenomenon of nature, etc. . . . *Expression* has never been an inherent property of music. That is by no means the purpose of its existence. If, as is nearly always the case, music appears to express something, this is only an illusion and not a reality. It is simply an additional attribute which, by tacit and inveterate agreement, we have lent it, thrust upon it, as a label, a convention—in short, an aspect which, unconsciously or by force of habit, we have come to confuse with its essential being" (53–54). Many years later, Stravinsky qualified his views as follows: "The over-publicized bit about expression (or non-expression) was simply a way of saying that music is supra-personal and super-real and as such beyond verbal meanings and verbal descriptions. It was aimed against the notion that a piece of music is in reality a transcendental idea 'expressed in terms of' music, with the *reductio ad absurdum* implication that exact sets of correlatives must exist between a composer's feelings and his notation. It was offhand and annoyingly incomplete, but even the stupider critics could have seen that it did not deny musical expressivity, but only the validity of a type of verbal statement about musical expressivity. I stand by the remark, incidentally, though today I would put it the other way around: music expresses itself" (Stravinsky and Craft 1959a, 101).
25. Stravinsky and Craft 1959b, 95. Stravinsky later orchestrated this work with the title "Excentrique" as one of the Four Etudes for Orchestra (1930). According to Taruskin 1996, Stravinsky saw Little Tich perform in June 1914 in London, where he was attending performances of *The Nightingale* by the Ballets Russes. In addition to the extended reference to Little Tich in *Memories and Commentaries*, Stravinsky made the association in two other sources. First, in an undated item in the *Nachlass*, speaking of the first three pieces of the Four Etudes (i.e., those based on the Three Pieces for String Quartet), Stravinsky writes, "The second piece called Excentrique was written in the memory of the numerous manifold and eccentric appearances of the unforgettable English clown Little Teach (hope the spelling correct)" (Danuser 1994). Second, in a later set of dialogues with Craft, again speaking of the Four Etudes, Stravinsky wrote, "The second, Excentrique, was inspired, as I have said before, by the eccentric movements and postures of the great clown, Little Tich" (Stravinsky and Craft 1966, 33). From the totality of these references, it would seem that Stravinsky was interested both in the morphology ("manifold and eccentric appearances") and the behavior ("jerky, spastic movement") of Little Tich's extraordinary body. His chosen title, "Excentrique," places the representation of Little Tich squarely within the aesthetic tradition of the grotesque.
26. On the history of the British Music Hall, including reference to Little Tich, see Hudd 1976, Bratton 1986, and Kift 1996.
27. Little Tich has been mischaracterized in the musicological literature. He is referred to as a "talented dwarf" (Walsh 1999, 236) and as a "circus clown" and "famous juggler" (Taruskin 1997, 416).

28. The music that accompanies the Big Boots Dance, and (as far as I can tell) other parts of the act also, is conventionally tonal music-hall music of the period, musical worlds away from Stravinsky's modernist representation.
29. Additional video clips are posted on YouTube: http://www.youtube.com/watch?v=166mE6lPig4; http://www.youtube.com/watch?v=RfZ9dQ9Umqs.
30. A principal source of information about Little Tich is a biography coauthored by his daughter, who adopted Tich as her last name for the occasion (Tich and Findlater 1979). An apparent autobiography—Little Tich, *A Book of Travels and Wanderings* (1911)—was largely ghostwritten by Sax Rohmer and consists of a series of comic sketches, which, although not informative about Little Tich's life, give a good sense of the nature of his comedy.
31. Sachaverell Sitwell, *Sunday Times*, 1951. Quoted in Tich and Findlater 1979, v.
32. There is a long and interesting history of artistic representations of people of unusual size, considered either excessively small (dwarfs) or excessively large (giants). This history is surveyed to some extent in Millett-Gallant 2010. It is not at all clear to me whether Stravinsky's own relatively short stature (he was 5 feet and 3 inches in height) may have played a role in his interest in or response to Little Tich.
33. With respect to literary texts, Garland-Thomson observes, "Like freak shows, textual descriptions are overdetermined: they invest the traits, qualities, and behaviors of their characters with much rhetorical influence simply by omitting—and therefore erasing—other factors or traits that might mitigate or complicate the delineations. A disability functions only as visual difference that signals meanings. Consequently, literary texts necessarily make disabled characters into freaks, stripped of normalizing contexts and *engulfed by a single stigmatic trait*" (Garland-Thomson 1997, 10–11, italics added). Similarly, see Kuppers 2001, on the power of disability to preempt critical evaluation of theatrical performance: "When disabled people perform, they are often not primarily seen as performers, but as disabled people. The disabled body is *naturally* about disability" (49–50, italics in original). For further discussion in a musical context, see Straus 2011.
34. For a history of the concept of the grotesque and its role in twentieth-century opera, see Fullerton 2006. On the grotesque in modernist music generally, especially the music of Bartók, see Brown 2007.
35. Connelly 2003, 2 and 6. For additional discussions of the grotesque in the visual arts and music, see Powell 1974, Schorske 1981, and Sheinberg 2000.
36. Undated typescript; reprinted in Danuser 1994, 77.
37. Ansermet 1915; reprinted in Danuser 1994, 79.
38. Review from *The Observer*, February 16, 1919; reprinted in Danuser 1994, 88.
39. On the central role of the Petrushka or Pierrot figure in modern art, see Green and Swan 1986.
40. "I know that I relate only from an angle to the German stem (Bach— Haydn— Mozart— Beethoven— Schubert— Brahms— Wagner— Mahler— Schoenberg), which evaluates largely in terms of where a thing comes from and where it is going. But an angle may be an advantage" (Stravinsky and Craft 1961, 14).
41. On the Nazi attitude toward Stravinsky's music, see Evans 2003, which also cites the extensive secondary literature on the Nazi concept of "degenerate art."

References

Adorno, Theodor. 2003. *Philosophy of Modern Music*. Translated by Anne G. Mitchell and Wesley V. Blomster. New York: Continuum.

Ansermet, Ernst. 1915. "Igor Stravinsky: The Man and His Work; His First String Quartet." *Musical Courier*, 25 November.

Benjamin, William. 1976–1977. "Tonality without Fifths: Remarks on the First Movement of Stravinsky's Concerto for Piano and Winds." *In Theory Only* 2 (11–12) (double issue): 53–70; and 3 (2): 9–31.

Boulez, Pierre. 1968. "Stravinsky Remains." In *Notes of an Apprenticeship*, translated by Herbert Weinstock, 72–145. New York: Knopf.

Bratton, Jacqueline, ed. 1986. *Music Hall: Performance and Style*. London: Open University Press.

Brower, Candace. 1997–1998. "Pathway, Blockage, and Containment in *Density 21.5*." *Theory and Practice* 22–23: 35–54.

Brower, Candace. 2000. "A Cognitive Theory of Musical Meaning." *Journal of Music Theory* 44 (2): 323–380.

Brower, Candace. 2008. "Paradoxes of Pitch Space." *Music Analysis* 27 (1): 51–106.

Brown, Julie. 2007. *Bartók and the Grotesque: Studies in Modernity, the Body, and Contradiction in Music*. Aldershot, UK: Ashgate.

Butler, Christopher. 1994. *Early Modernism: Literature, Music, and Painting in Europe 1900–1916*. Oxford: Oxford University Press.

Connelly, Frances, ed. 2003. *Modern Art and the Grotesque*. Cambridge, UK: Cambridge University Press.

Danuser, Hermann, ed. 1994. *Igor Strawinsky: Trois Pieces pour Quatuor a Cordes (Skizzen, Fassungen, Dokumente, Essays)*. Winterthur, Switzerland: Amadeus Verlag.

Davidson, Michael. 2008. *Concerto for the Left Hand: Disability and the Defamiliar Body*. Ann Arbor: University of Michigan Press.

Davis, Lennard J. 1997. "Nude Venuses, Medusa's Body, and Phantom Limbs: Disability and Visuality." In *The Body and Physical Difference: Discourses of Disability*, edited by David T. Mitchell and Sharon L. Snyder, 51–70. Ann Arbor: University of Michigan Press.

Davis, Lennard J. 2003. "Identity Politics, Disability, and Culture." In *Handbook of Disability Studies*, edited by Gary Albrecht, Katherine Seelman, and Michael Bury, 535–545. Thousand Oaks, CA: Sage.

Douglas, James. 1909. *Adventures in London*. London: Cassell.

Evans, Joan. 2003. "Stravinsky's Music in Hitler's Germany." *Journal of the American Musicological Society* 56 (3): 525–594.

Everdell, William R. 1997. *The First Moderns: Profiles in the Origins of Twentieth-Century Thought*. Chicago: University of Chicago Press.

Fisher, George, and Judy Lochhead. 2002. "Analyzing from the Body." *Theory and Practice* 27: 37–67.

Friedlander, Henry. 1995. *The Origins of Nazi Genocide: From Euthanasia to the Final Solution*. Chapel Hill: University of North Carolina Press.

Fullerton, James Graeme. 2006. "The Grotesque in Twentieth-Century Opera." PhD diss., Graduate Center, City University of New York.

Garland-Thomson, Rosemarie. 1997. *Extraordinary Bodies: Figuring Physical Disability in American Culture and Literature*. New York: Columbia University Press.

Garland-Thomson, Rosemarie. 2004. "The Cultural Logic of Euthanasia: 'Sad Fancyings' in Herman Melville's 'Bartelby.'" *American Literature* 76 (4): 777–806.

Gibbs, Raymond. 1994. *The Poetics of Mind: Figurative Thought, Language, and Understanding*. Cambridge, UK: Cambridge University Press.

Goffman, Erving. 1986. *Stigma: Notes on the Management of Spoiled Identity*. New York: Touchstone.

Goldmark, Daniel. 2006. "Stuttering in American Popular Song, 1890–1930." In *Sounding Off: Theorizing Disability in Music*, edited by Neil Lerner and Joseph N. Straus, 75–90. New York: Routledge.

Green, Martin, and John Swan. 1986. *The Triumph of Pierrot: The Commedia dell'Arte and the Modern Imagination*. New York: Macmillan.

Gur, Golan. 2008. "Body, Forces, and Paths: Metaphor and Embodiment in Jean-Philippe Rameau's Conceptualization of Tonal Space." *Music Theory Online* 14 (1). http://www.mtosmt.org/issues/mto.08.14.1/mto.08.14.1.gur.html.

Horlacher, Gretchen. 2011. *Building Blocks: Repetition and Continuity in the Music of Stravinsky*. New York: Oxford University Press.

Hudd, Roy. 1976. *Music Hall*. London: Methuen.

Jers, Norbert. 1976. *Igor Strawinskys späte Zwölftonwerke (1958–1966)*. Regensburg, Germany: Gustav Bosse Verlag.

Johnson, Mark. 1987. *The Body in the Mind: The Bodily Basis of Meaning, Imagination, and Reason*. Chicago: University of Chicago Press.

Kern, Stephen. 1983. *The Culture of Time and Space, 1880–1918*. Cambridge, MA: Harvard University Press.

Kift, Dagmar. 1996. *The Victorian Music Hall: Culture, Class, and Conflict*. Cambridge, UK: Cambridge University Press.

Kuppers, Petra. 2001. *Disability and Contemporary Performance: Bodies on Edge*. London: Routledge.

Lakoff, George. 1987. *Women, Fire, and Dangerous Things: What Categories Reveal about the Mind*. Chicago: University of Chicago Press.

Lakoff, George, and Mark Johnson. 1980. *Metaphors We Live By*. Chicago: University of Chicago Press.

Little Tich. 1911. *A Book of Travels and Wanderings*. London: Greening.

Mead, Andrew. 1999. "Bodily Hearing: Physiological Metaphors and Musical Understanding." *Journal of Music Theory* 43 (1): 1–19.

Millett-Gallant, Ann. 2010. *The Disabled Body in Contemporary Art*. New York: Palgrave Macmillan.

Monahan, Seth. 2013. "Action and Agency Revisited." *Journal of Music Theory* 57 (2): 321–372.

Nochlin, Linda. 1994. *The Body in Pieces: The Fragment as a Metaphor of Modernity*. New York: Thames & Hudson.

Oster, Andrew. 2006. "Melisma as Malady: Cavalli's *Il Giasone* (1649) and Opera's Earliest Stuttering Role." In *Sounding Off: Theorizing Disability in Music*, edited by Neil Lerner and Joseph N. Straus, 157–172. New York: Routledge.

Pedneault-Deslauriers, Julie. 2011. "Pierrot L." *Journal of the American Musicological Society* 64 (3): 601–645.

Powell, Nicholas. 1974. *The Sacred Spring: The Arts in Vienna, 1898–1918*. New York: Graphic Society.

Priestly, John Boynton. 1929. *The Balconinny*. London: Methuen.

Saslaw, Janna. 1996. "Forces, Containers, and Paths: The Role of Body-Derived Image Schemas in the Conceptualization of Music." *Journal of Music Theory* 40 (2): 217–244.

Saslaw, Janna. 1997–1998. "Life Forces: Conceptual Structures in Schenker's *Free Composition* and Schoenberg's *The Musical Idea*." *Theory and Practice* 22–23: 17–34.

Sass, Louis. 1992. *Madness and Modernism: Insanity in the Light of Modern Art, Literature, and Thought*. New York: Basic.

Schenker, Heinrich. 1979. *Free Composition (Der freie Satz)*. Translated and edited by Ernst Oster. New York: Longman.

Schenker, Heinrich. 1996. "Further Consideration of the Urlinie: II." In *The Masterwork in Music*, Vol. 2, edited by William Drabkin, translated by John Rothgeb, 1–19. Cambridge, UK: Cambridge University Press.

Schenker, Heinrich. 1997. "Rameau or Beethoven? Creeping Paralysis or Spiritual Potency in Music?" In *The Masterwork in Music*, Vol. 3, edited by William Drabkin, translated by Ian Bent, 1–9. Cambridge, UK: Cambridge University Press.

Schorske, Carl. 1981. *Fin-de-Siècle Vienna: Politics and Culture*. New York: Random House.

Scully, Jackie Leach. 2008. *Disability Bioethics: Moral Bodies, Moral Difference*. Lanham, MD: Rowman & Littlefield.

Sheinberg, Esti. 2000. *Irony, Satire, Parody and the Grotesque in the Music of Shostakovich: A Theory of Musical Incongruities*. Aldershot, UK: Ashgate.

Siebers, Tobin. 2010. *Disability Aesthetics*. Ann Arbor: University of Michigan Press.

Stein, Leonard. 1986. "Schoenberg and 'Kleine Modernsky.'" In *Confronting Stravinsky*, edited by Jann Pasler, 310–324. Berkeley: University of California Press.

Stras, Laurie. 2006. "The Organ of the Soul: Voice, Damage, and Affect." In *Sounding Off: Theorizing Disability in Music*, edited by Neil Lerner and Joseph N. Straus, 173–184. New York: Routledge.

Straus, Joseph N. 1990. *Remaking the Past: Musical Modernism and the Influence of the Tonal Tradition*. Cambridge, MA: Harvard University Press.

Straus, Joseph N. 1991. "The Progress of a Motive in Stravinsky's *The Rake's Progress*." *Journal of Musicology* 9 (2): 165–185.

Straus, Joseph N. 2001. *Stravinsky's Late Music*. Cambridge, UK: Cambridge University Press.

Straus, Joseph N. 2006. "Inversional Balance and the 'Normal' Body in the Music of Arnold Schoenberg and Anton Webern." In *Sounding Off: Theorizing Disability in Music*, edited by Neil Lerner and Joseph N. Straus, 257–268. New York: Routledge.

Straus, Joseph N. 2011. *Extraordinary Measures: Disability in Music*. New York: Oxford University Press.

Straus, Joseph N. 2012. "Three Stravinsky Analyses." *Music Theory Online* 18 (4). http://mtosmt.org/issues/mto.12.18.4/mto.12.18.4.straus.php.

Stravinsky, Igor. (1936) 1962. *An Autobiography*. New York: Norton.

Stravinsky, Igor, and Robert Craft. 1959a. *Expositions and Developments*. Berkeley: University of California Press.

Stravinsky, Igor, and Robert Craft. 1959b. *Memories and Commentaries*. Berkeley: University of California Press.

Stravinsky, Igor, and Robert Craft. 1961. *Dialogues and a Diary*. New York: Doubleday.

Stravinsky, Igor, and Robert Craft. 1966. *Themes and Episodes*. New York: Knopf.

Taruskin, Richard. 1996. *Stravinsky and the Russian Traditions: A Biography of the Works through "Mavra."* Berkeley: University of California Press.

Taruskin, Richard. 1997. *Defining Russia Musically: Historical and Hermeneutical Essays.* Princeton, NJ: Princeton University Press.

Tich, Mary, and Richard Findlater. 1979. *Little Tich: Giant of the Music Hall.* London: Elm Tree.

Van den Toorn, Pieter. 1983. *The Music of Stravinsky.* New Haven, CT: Yale University Press.

Walsh, Stephen. 1999. *Stravinsky: A Creative Spring; Russia and France, 1882–1934.* New York: Knopf.

Zbikowski, Lawrence. 1997–1998. "*Des Herzraums Abschied:* Mark Johnson's Theory of Embodied Knowledge and Music Theory." *Theory and Practice* 22–23: 1–16.

Zbikowski, Lawrence. 2002. *Conceptualizing Music: Cognitive Structure, Theory, and Analysis.* New York: Oxford University Press.

Zbikowski, Lawrence. 2009. "Musicology, Cognitive Science, and Metaphor: Reflections on Michael Spitzer's *Metaphor and Musical Thought.*" *Musica Humana* 1 (1): 81–104.

CHAPTER 37

"DEFAMILIARIZING THE FAMILIAR"

Michael Nyman, Narrative Medicine, and the Composition of Mental Blindness

STEPHANIE JENSEN-MOULTON

PROLOGUE

I was beginning to get annoyed. It had already been twenty minutes and I didn't hear any signs of life out there. Thankful I had brought a really long Russian novel, I settled in as comfortably as I could, sitting on the edge of the examination table. When I had finished the chapter (which is saying something considering it was Dostoyevsky) I looked up at the clock. It had been another thirty minutes, and I realized I had been waiting for almost an hour for this doctor. I was definitely not going to make it to pick up my son from school, so I phoned the school office and asked if he could still go to the afterschool program. Needless to say, my (figurative) temperature was rising, and I could no longer concentrate on keeping all of Dostoyevsky's characters straight. Just as I was about to walk out of there, the doorknob turned downward, and in walked the neurologist. I had no idea what to expect, but I had intended to give him a piece of my mind when he asked me not about what problem had brought me to him, but rather, about the book I was reading. When I told him it was *The Brothers Karamazov*, we embarked on a conversation about literature that led into a discussion of opera. Through this, I found out that he had been a student of Oliver Sacks. And contrary to any medical practice I had ever experienced, this doctor was—even in the midst of our conversation—performing at least this part of his examination via the practice of *narrative medicine* (Charon 2006). It also explained why he was, by the end of his workday, running somewhat late.

Narrative medicine arose out of the perception that the practice of medicine had in general de-emphasized the need for healthcare professionals to comprehend multiple and sometimes conflicting histories given by patients, and also, to actively learn empathy and other interpersonal skills that could considerably ameliorate the patient's experience of treatment. Charon (2006, 4) defines narrative medicine as "medicine practiced with these narrative skills of recognizing, absorbing, and being moved by the stories of illness." This deviates considerably from the established practices of late-twentieth-century medicalization in that it shifts the emphasis from the disease or illness to the patient and the patient's human history within a specific cultural environment. Nevertheless, the end goal of both traditional medicine and narrative medicine is effectively the same: to diagnose and cure. Narrative medicine came into existence largely because of negative experiences on the part of both medical practitioners and their patients, but although it has changed the way some professionals do the business of medicine, it has not necessarily given rise to or further opened the minds of doctors and other medical professionals to the idea that disease and disability are highly prone to or—on some occasions—products of social construction. Although narrative medicine and Disability Studies do converge along some lines—the importance of personal histories and identities, for example—the two fields could be understood as divergent on the basis of treatment and medicalization (Charon 2006, 6).

A Clinical Opera

Michael Nyman's 1986 opera *The Man Who Mistook His Wife for a Hat*, with a libretto jointly written from Oliver Sacks's "clinical tale" of the same title by Christopher Rawlence and Michael Morris and it considers both musically and textually Dr. S's narrative examinations of Dr. P (Dr. S is a stand-in name for Dr. Sacks) as his vision seems to deteriorate. The only other character in the opera is Mrs P, wife of Dr. P. Music plays a particularly central role in the nonfictional Dr. P's life, as he is not a doctor of medicine, but rather of Musical Arts. His entire life and career have been consumed by the intensive study of classical singing and repertoire, and his primary connection with the visual world has, ironically, been a map created by the aural soundscape represented both internally and externally by art song and opera. Thus, Nyman's opera, functions as a meta-opera at several levels: it is a book within an opera, a neurological case study within an opera, and an ongoing internal song recital within an opera. Most of all, Nyman has composed a clinical tale, creating the only narrative medicine opera in the modern operatic repertoire; more importantly, however, he has uncovered a humanities-centered approach to disability found in the neurologist's basic approach that sometimes comes across as ambiguous in Sacks's writings. While actually rooted in diagnostic medicine, Sacks markets his practice as centrally humanist rather than medical. In addition, while in his books, Sacks is obviously the author of his clinical tales, in the opera, Sacks is "Dr. S," a position in the narrative that takes him from narrator/practitioner to operatic tenor/hero. This change in subject position redoubles the importance of the neurologist in the scheme of the drama.[1]

In a very brief statement just before Nyman's lengthy program note on the opera, Sacks explains the medical concept of *visual agnosia*, otherwise known as "mental blindness." This is Dr. P's ultimate diagnosis, and therefore bears considerable narrative weight in the piece. Sacks notes that people with visual agnosia have intact visual apparatuses and can see

> colours, lines, boundaries, simple shapes, patterns, movement—but they are unable to recognise, or find sense in, what they see. They cannot recognise people or places or common objects. Their visual world is no longer meaningful or familiar, but strange, abstract, chaotic, mystifying. If a world cannot be organised visually, other organising principles may be found and used. In the case of Dr. P, a gifted performer, his exceptional musical ability allowed him, in large measure, to return sense to the whole world by putting it, and his actions, to music.

While this statement seems forward-looking, positive, and downright good-hearted from the pen of a physician, Sacks has also been known among scholars of Disability Studies for his "clinical tales" that have bordered on the exploitative, putting the subjects of his case studies on display—as did the freak shows of old—for the inspiration, amusement, titillation, and awe of his readers.[2] He himself has noted (Sacks 1970, ix) that his cases "come together at the intersection of fact and fable" and that they seem to have "a quality of the fabulous." Sacks's enthusiasm for his subjects, it would seem from these statements, stems partially from intellectual curiosity as a scientist, but also partially from a basic human curiosity about the extraordinary in human differentiation. As Rosemarie Garland-Thomson (1996, 13) writes, "Although the earlier freak show, with its hybrid of old wonder narratives, commercialized show narratives, and clinical scientific narratives, seems today to have dissipated, it has instead dispersed and transformed." Sacks's narrative fits squarely within the clinical narrative model that would have pathologized and enfreaked the patient for the wonderment of the enthralled audience; now, the same type of narrative, gentrified, sells armchair neurology books if the case study holds enough interest for the reader. While this statement might seem somewhat hard, the position Sacks holds within the disability community remains nebulous and ever shifting; he has been enthusiast, observer, participant, journalist, physician. Sacks's epigraph for the book (1970, 1) on which the opera is based encapsulates this philosophy: "To talk of diseases is a sort of *Arabian Nights* entertainment." If, for example, Dr. P had not been such an exceptional person and musician, would he have made the cut from among Sacks's many cases? In spite of its optimistic opening and Dr. S's cheery prescription for "more music," Nyman and Sacks still subject their patient to the bright lights and clinical exhibitionism of the medical theatre. Nevertheless, this narrative has, at times, a distinctly forward-thinking view of disability, and the particular relationship music and disability in the context of opera merits further discussion. This essay draws connections between Nyman's opera—a staged musical work based on one doctor's subjective experience diagnosing a unique pathology—and a socially constructed model of disability.

In the opera, as in Sacks's book, Dr. P and his wife have been referred to Dr. S by a puzzled ophthalmologist who perceived that the visual problem did not lie with the eyes but rather with the visual cortex. A routine, though narrative, neurological examination ensues, with inconclusive results; at this juncture, Dr. S asks Dr. P to dress, and it is at this moment when Dr. S begins to surmise the unusual nature of the visual problem. Dr. P cannot find his shoe, and seems to think his foot *is* the shoe itself. Shortly after laughing this off as a "mistake," Dr. P seeks out his hat, and instead earnestly grasps his wife. In the next scene, Dr. S has decided to make a house call based on his initial examination of Dr. P in order to see him in his "natural habitat."[3] When making his rounds, Dr. S brings with him several varied visual exercises including geometric solids to identify, a rose, a glove, and a game of chess. While the rose and glove prove elusive, Dr. P roundly defeats Dr. S at chess, and the two decide to take a stroll down a street that is familiar to them both. The next scene narrates Dr. P's capacity to describe the street to Dr. S before returning to the residence of Dr. and Mrs. P. The following scene allows for an aesthetic argument between Mrs. P and Dr. S with regard to Dr. P's paintings. An amateur painter, Dr. P began his years painting in a representational style, but over time became more abstract in his style. Whereas Mrs. P views this shift as a positive development in her husband's artistic complexity and painterly voice, Dr. S understands the trajectory of the paintings as illustrative—a kind of history of his pathology. The final two scenes of the opera connect as a pair: first, Mrs. P explains how Dr. P moves through his day, using music to function and accomplish everyday tasks and organize his life; then, as the lights of the apartment fade, Dr. S gives his closing remarks on the case in the Epilogue.

Narrating Medicine, Narrative Medicine

Neurology's favorite term is Deficit. The word denotes impairment
Or incapacity of neurological function, Loss of language, memory, vision.
Dexterity, identity and a myriad of other lacks and losses
Of specific functions. For all these dysfunctions—Another favorite term—
We have privative words of every sort:
Aphonia, Aphemia, Aphasia, Alexia,
Apraxia, Agnosia, Amnesia, Ataxia.
A word for ev'ry specific neural or mental function
Of which patients may find themselves deprived. Deficit. Loss.
Everything that patients aren't and nothing that they are.
Such language tells us nothing about an individual's history.
It conveys nothing of the person and the reality of facing disease
And struggling to survive it. To restore the human subject

At the centre . . . The suffering, afflicted, fighting Human subject . . .
We must deepen a case history to a narrative or tale.
Only then do we have A WHO as well as A WHAT
—a patient in relation to disease—A real person.

With this Prologue, Nyman establishes several cultural tropes of disability. First, the doctor speaks before the patient or subject, locating himself and his findings at the front of the piece and therefore as central in the power structure of the opera. Second, the Prologue centralizes the importance of medical information and diagnosis in the opera, shifting away from a humanist approach to medicine. The medicalized monologue above occurs at the very outset of Nyman's opera, performed in quite strictly rhythmically notated speech by Dr. S over an undulating, mildly dissonant score. The music recalls Nyman's film scores in its extreme regularity of rhythm and slow harmonic motion, as heard and seen in Track 37.1 on the Companion Website, which features the opera's prologue.[4]

It is important to note that in Sacks's book, this tale occurs in a section entitled "Losses," a term which encapsulates the litany of dysfunctions outlined above, all beginning with the prefix "A," meaning "without." The stage direction reads: "Dr. S, a neurologist, comes to a lectern to address the audience. The atmosphere is that of a talk to medical students." Clearly this character is the operatic version of Oliver Sacks. He is cast as a tenor, operatic code for heroic savior. In contradistinction to the actual words that he utters in this medical address—a speech that would seem to eschew the medicalization of the doctor–patient encounter and argue in favor of a more human encounter—the doctor presents his specimen just as nineteenth-century managers of minstrel or freak show entertainment announced the next act.[5] Nyman and his collaborators reinforce this trope of physician-centered power by bringing the patient and his wife to center stage in the middle of the monologue, establishing a one-sided staring relationship between the imagined medical students in the audience and the patient, who—one understands by now—cannot return their gaze.

In her study of staring, Garland-Thomson (2009, 108) profiles public speaker and comedian David Roche, who performs his disability right into a paycheck, "deliberately invoking stares and crafting the ensuing encounters on his own terms and for his own purposes," turning "drama into generosity." Yet, when Roche allows himself to be the object of scrutiny at the center of a medical theatre, his ability to renegotiate these encounters begins to falter, and even he—a professional "staree"—feels jarred by the encounter with the staring physicians: "my face no longer belonged to me" (Garland-Thomson 2009, 111). Nevertheless, he quickly regains his foothold, and begins to rebuild his personal resources of power via his live and Internet performances. Dr. S's lengthy monologue does not allow Dr. P this space for identity renegotiation after his diagnosis and exhibition in the medical theatre. With regard to the trope of doctor having power and importance over and above any patient, the Prologue serves as both a foregone conclusion, therefore, and an introduction.

As stated above, the second type of cultural work that the Prologue does with regard to disability is to reinforce the notion that at the root of the opera is a medical pathology: the endgame is diagnosis, and the goal is cure. Indeed, again contrary to the initial "real person" and "patient in relation to disease" hoped for in the first half of the Prologue, Dr. S quickly proceeds with a description of the symptoms and circumstances that led Dr. P to seek out a neurologist rather than an ophthalmologist. Dr. P, a gifted singer, teacher, and musician, taught at the local music school. "Sometimes, a student would present himself. And Doctor P would not recognize him. Or, specifically, Would not recognize his face." While Dr. S and his assembled crowd of medical professionals clearly concern themselves with the diagnosis of and potential treatments for visual agnosia, none of the physicians in the room considers that facial recognition has sociocultural meanings, as well, and not simply for the individual attempting that recognition. As Garland-Thomson (2009, 102) asserts, "Faces, then, are texts we engage or resist, opportunities for revelation or refusal.... We stare at faces to differentiate friend from foe, familiar from strange, invitation from rejection, anger from adoration, comic from tragic. Our capacity to stare interpretively at faces is a fundamental form of social capital that enables human flourishing."

In his initial publication of the *Clinical Tales*, which bears the same title as the opera, Sacks capitalizes on this very aspect of Dr. P's disability, his "lost" ability to recognize the faces of his students and loved ones, and his displacement of those faces onto inanimate objects. So anomalous is the idea that a man could look at his wife of many years and truly believe that she is a hat, so absurd, that at least one entire scene of the opera's action can build up to the moment when Dr. P regards his wife and does not see her there. (Musically, this moment is the harmonic climax of the entire opera, and forms the shift between Parts I and II of the piece.) Sacks's marketing of his book and Nyman's operatic through line both rely on this predicament, which stems here from the specific pathology of Dr. P's case. These interpretations of the condition, which both reduce the patient to mere spectacle, capitalize on the seemingly ridiculous nature of Dr. P's "jokes"—in reality, his symptoms—in order to attract a potential audience of spectators who might be "entertained." Thus, while preaching a philosophy of narrative medicine and humane practices, the postdiagnostic entity is that of exploitation: the spectacle cannot do without the medical.

"Defamiliarising the Familiar": Composing *Visual Agnosia*

When Nyman[6] set out to compose the opera, he had in mind events rather like those produced by Fluxus[7] in the 1960s, which would reflect Dr. S's growing comprehension of Dr. P and the neurologist's growing conviction of a pathological cause for P's unusual "mistakes." That Nyman would have imagined the vignettes from Sacks's book in terms of Fluxus events stems logically from his deep abiding interest in and extensive writing and research on experimental music. Twelve years before the publication of his opera, Nyman's 1974 groundbreaking book, *Experimental Music: Cage and Beyond* was published by Cambridge University Press. From his standpoint in the midst of the experimental music scene, Nyman wrote one of the seminal texts on the subject. But why is it pertinent to his opera, written more than a decade later? As Nyman states, "The word 'event' is significant here. . . . [It refers] to Fluxus events, which I wrote about in my book . . . and which, as I have shown, influenced my initial structuring of the opera." With each of these separate events, Nyman will gradually dissolve the musical structure of the piece in the same manner in which he hopes the listener will experience a synesthetic aural response to the visual deterioration that becomes gradually apparent to both Dr. S and Mrs. P throughout the opera. The interruption of the narrative via these events, however, presents an interesting problem in light of the narrative medical practice espoused by Sacks, and has distinct parallels in the musical choices Nyman makes in the opera.

Fluxus events were fragmentary by nature, but they were also extremely concrete; in this way, they are self-contained and evidential, qualities that lend themselves to fragmentation. As with the punk movement in popular music, Fluxus aimed to break down (often literally) the dichotomy "professional/amateur" and organize concerts where people traditionally labeled "nonmusicians" would take the stage and perform musical tasks such as the ones Nyman (1974, 110) details here: "smash a violin, put a flower pot on a piano, keep walking intently, the interval of a fifth to be held a long time." These "musical" tasks bear distinct resemblance to the phenomenological tasks that Dr. S requests that Dr. P perform during their extended diagnostic exercises together, such as manipulating the platonic solids or the rose. As Nyman's perception of the opera as a series of events unfolded, he developed a musical schema to link these events. Thus the musical progression of the opera stemmed chiefly from the composer's perception of the way the events of the plot unfolded in time, and ultimately, in the musical space of the opera.

Nyman composes for the opera a series of structural chords that he calls a "chord sequence." This sequence, often with a strong melodic relationship to ascending minor and major seconds, recurs throughout the opera, but with decreasing clarity as the opera progresses. This gradual fading away of musical material had been part of Nyman's musical and narrative vision for the opera since the onset of his work with his librettist. As Nyman (1986, 10) notes: "As Chris Rawlence's libretto began to arrive, these prefabricated musical units were arranged as much for their position in my progressively voiding ("defamiliarising") formal process as for their suitability in particular dramatic situations." The series of variations that Nyman composes takes as its source the "chord sequence" found in Figure 37.1.

FIGURE 37.1 Nyman's chord sequence that serves as his source for musical material in the opera.

This large-scale sequence serves as a background level for all other harmonic and melodic motion in the piece, but can also be "defamiliarized" to the listener. In order to reflect the continuing revelation on the part of the audience member that Dr. P is really mentally incapable of seeing, though his eyes technically still retain this capability, Nyman lets the listener grow familiar enough with the soundscape established on the basis of his primary chord sequence that it becomes perceptible but confusing when parts of it are left out, or as he suggests, "defamiliarized" or voided.

This compositional process creates a series of negative musical echoes, past musical ideas that have been systematically removed, but which still exist in the ear of the listener. The visual agnosia eventually diagnosed by Dr. S has been manifested musically in this dissolution, but regardless of the creativity and significance of this compositional choice, the echoes of the notes systematically removed by Nyman in his process cannot mimic the lived experience of the disabled musician on whose body disease actually operates. While Dr. S debates, explores, and is fascinated, Nyman performs the composerly equivalent: he draws up a sequence before a willing panel of musicologists and composers, then surgically extracts tones until the whole resembles the now "incomplete" mind of Dr. P post visual agnosia. In essence, the full progression represents the patient in his state of original "intact" health, and throughout the opera, Nyman removes aspects of the healthy body until it no longer resembles the original. Yet, by the reprise of the opening, the medical solution—the "cure"—has provided at least a temporary solution and the harmonic progression has resumed its state of relative health.

Noise is another important aspect of experimental music that Nyman discussed in his 1974 book and that carries considerable sonic weight in his opera. In the first scene, just after the Prologue, Nyman titles this event "Traffic," and it is immediately significant for two reasons: first, "traffic" is the first sung word of the opera, after a lengthy rhythmically notated monologue by Dr. S during the opening of the work; second, the text itself establishes a relationship with musical philosophy that will pervade the entire opera. Dr. P sings: "Traffic. Street sounds. Distant trains. A noise symphony." Rawlence's libretto text at the outset of this scene recalls—expressly, I believe—John Cage's famous statement about music, traffic, and noise: "When I hear what we call music, it seems to me that someone is talking. And talking about his feelings, or about his ideas of relationships. But when I hear traffic, the sound of traffic—like here on Sixth Avenue for instance—I don't have the feeling that anyone is talking" (Sebestik

2003). In the opera, the next lines emanate from Mrs. P ("The music of the city") and Dr. S ("The urban forest") before Mr. P can expertly make the connection for us: "More Cage than Schumann." All of this occurs before Dr. S asks why Dr. P has come for an evaluation, in keeping with the narrative medicine practices established as important at the beginning of the opera. Yet "More Cage than Schumann" creates several other layers of musical and metaphorical meaning, particularly with regard to disability.

As evidence for Dr. P's visual agnosia mounts, Rawlence gives him "in place of" his disability a profound ability to state universal philosophical truths in the manner of Cagean one-liners that ring of 1960s and '70s philosophy, such as "Form is emptiness, emptiness form." The notion that disabled individuals have been gifted with other abilities in order to compensate for those they lack, reinforces their difference in society, while also pressuring people with disabilities to somehow perform superhuman feats (Kudlick 2001, 200–201). While Dr. P's singing and extraordinary vocal performance skills would seem to be enough for anyone, the placement of such a character among opera singers de-emphasizes his talents, rendering him ordinary without his disability; in fact, placing a nonfictional opera singer into an operatic context would have the effect of highlighting whatever else about that individual stands out. In this case, Dr. P's disability is the obvious standout characteristic, and therefore Nyman and Rawlence have foregrounded his blindness/pathology even over and above the way Sacks has accomplished this task in his book. The Cage-isms and distinct ability to boil things down to a single inexorable truth allow the listener to dwell on what will be "lost" if Dr. P's neurological function changes.

In both his introductory note to the opera and in the liner notes to the CBS recording, Nyman (1986, 11) discusses at length his decision to incorporate a considerable amount of Robert Schumann's song literature into the opera, whether as diagetic music or in fragments. He writes:

> Sacks had gone to the P's house armed with a copy of *Dichterliebe*, and I needed no further encouragement than this to represent Dr. P's isolation through his almost total reliance on the Schumann song literature for his orientation. (This is a fiction of my invention—there is no evidence that the real Dr. P used Schumann in this way.).... Schumann's songs supplied material for the opera ranging from a complete song to fragments used individually and in montage.

In his study of the music of Michael Nyman, Pwyll Ap Siôn dedicates an entire chapter to the intertextuality in *The Man Who Mistook His Wife for a Hat*, focusing chiefly on the Schumann fragments and on the fully excerpted song from the *Dichterliebe*, "Ich grolle nicht," which serves as diagetic music in Part II of the opera (Ap Siôn 2007, 116). He does not, however, take on issues of disability in his chapter, nor does he make any connection between the choice of Schumann and the disability-centric plot arc in the opera. Ap Siôn (2007, 118) portrays Dr. P's visual agnosia as a tragedy, an abnormal state that normal people cannot imagine, and a "distorted perspective." His interpretation of the Schumann interpolation at the center of the opera aligns with this stigmatizing view of disability and disability culture. Ap Siôn (2007, 124) writes of the deconstruction of the "Ich grolle nicht" theme at the hands of Nyman as Dr. P's vision deteriorates, and how "this suggests a kind of inversion of reality, where Nyman's constructed compositional world provides an appearance of normality, while Schumann's tonal world represents Dr. P's abnormality." Clearly both Nyman and Ap Siôn experience Dr. P as a broken human being now that his disease has begun to produce discernable symptoms, and the language of deterioration surrounds the subject throughout Ap Siôn's chapter in particular. Yet, beyond the ready connection that Dr. P was an opera and *Lieder* singer, the connection between this "clinical tale" and Robert Schumann is less tenuous than one might imagine.

Schumann's mental condition and functioning have been the subject of extensive speculation, during his lifetime and ever since (Neumayr 1995, Ostwald 1985, Walker 1976). As Straus summarizes,

> Schumann had a lifetime of experiences of madness, including episodes of deep depression, periods of heightened activity approaching mania, and aural hallucinations. After a suicide attempt in 1854, Schumann asked to be moved to an asylum, where he died two years later (2011, 34–40).

The conflation of Schumann and Dr. P reinforces the notion that a physical disability may also be a cognitive or psychiatric one, and in Dr. P's case, the opposite notion is true: a physical accommodation will be needed for what is a neurological issue. In the opera, Schumann's presence is felt most directly through his song, "Ich grolle nicht," which Dr. P performs in its entirety in Part II. The song is traditionally understood as the complaint of a man spurned in love: the ultimate in stalwart coping and stoicism in the face of pain, heartbreak, and discouragement. (The text and translation are found in Figure 37.2).

When sung within the context of the entire *Dichterliebe* cycle, this Lied may be read ironically as a complaint by a man who states loudly that he "is not one to complain." In Nyman's opera, however, the song gestures more toward a reading of heroic overcoming and even a narrative of physician curing patient. As Dr. P steps forward to sing, he does so with total earnestness, and musically, with a complete break in the musical line and style of the opera thus far. Nyman's music literally stops to make way for the interpolation of the entire Schumann Lied, which serves as a prosthetic within the musical narrative as a whole (Mitchell and Snyder 2000). It is intact, it is functional, but it is completely different from the rest of the musical body to which it belongs, and is made up of materials that are only tangentially related to that body. The appearance of the Lied in the middle of the opera has made audible a "wound" that is then in need of a "cure." The When Dr. S, the tenor, joins in with Dr. P at the end of the performance of the Lied, he affects this cure; Nyman's re-composition of the end of the Lied as a duet has ensured that the cure is performed not by the patient alone, but by the heroic Dr. S. With the addition of the prosthetic, the music can continue unimpeded into the next section of the narrative,

Ich grolle nicht,	I won't complain,
Und wenn das Herz auch bricht,	Even though my heart may break,
Ewig verlor'nes Lieb!	Love lost forever!
Ich grolle nicht.	I won't complain.
Wie du auch strahlst in Diamantenpracht,	However you may radiate with the glory of diamonds,
Es fällt kein Strahl in deines Herzens Nacht.	None of the rays touches the darkness of your heart.
Das weiß ich längst.	I've known this for so long.
Ich grolle nicht,	I won't complain,
Und wenn das Herz auch bricht,	Even though my heart may break,
Ich sah dich ja im Traume,	For I did see you in my dreams,
Und sah die Nacht in deines Herzens Raume,	And saw the darkness in your heart,
Und sah die Schlang', die dir am Herzen frißt,	And saw the serpent that is gnawing at your heart,
Ich sah, mein Lieb, wie sehr du elend bist.	And I saw, my love, how wretched you are.
Ich grolle nicht.	I won't complain.

FIGURE 37.2 Text and translation for "Ich grolle nicht" from Schumann's ***Dichterliebe***, Op. 48, No. 7 with text by Heinrich Heine.

and what might be an awkward transition is eased by the aid of Dr. S's intervention at the end of the song.

In addition, with Dr. S as an operatic tenor and Dr. P as a baritone, the traditional operatic narrative also plays out in this brief scene, as the tenor literally subsumes the lower voice, taking on a heroic, saving presence in the scene. The performance of a German Lied would seem to be one area in which Dr. P would have intellectual and artistic expertise superior to that of his even his neurologist. Yet, by composing the final, climactic lines of the Lied for Dr. S and Dr. P to share, Nyman powerfully reinforces Dr. S's relative importance to the narrative in this particular musical moment, as well as Dr. P's increasing, or at least, perceived, helplessness. See Track 37.2 on the Companion Website for a full performance of the Lied.[8]

Nyman's selection of this Lied further reinforces stereotypical ideas about disabled bodies: that they must suffer, but not complain; that they will be thwarted in love; that they are helpless; that they will ultimately find peace only in suffering quietly and alone. This is a grim picture for Schumann's ecstatic music and for the joyous manner in which Nyman intends to stage its performance in the opera, as an interlude between medical examinations. If Schumann serves as a kind of muse to Dr. P (in the same way that Nyman's opera draws on fragments of Schumann Lieder, as well as his repeated right hand eighths and left hand chords), then Dr. P can be expected to compartmentalize, produce, cope, and yet, eventually fall victim to his pathology. Madness and blindness appear together in Nyman's opera, just as in Schumann's song: while the singer of the Lied sings of "seeing" the darkness within the lover's heart, Dr. S and Mrs. P question each other and themselves in unison: "Is he mad? Is he blind?" According to the cultural standards established by the opera's creators up to this point in the piece, the answer would be yes to both questions.

Abstract Progression: An Argument about Art

Although Mrs. P plays a relatively peripheral part in the first half of the opera, her character takes on more importance as the opera (and, thus, the diagnostic process) proceeds. Her stance in the opera throughout most of the initial exchanges between the doctors is that of a woman in denial of her husband's condition. Nyman and Rawlence found the dynamism in her character development through a gradual coming to grips with Dr. P's degenerative disease. Ironically, both composer and librettist figure her role in the opera as a stereotypically gendered one of caregiver, a spouse with whom, as it turns out, Dr. P has encoded his everyday existence in music. Ap Siôn (2007, 116) goes so far as to suggest that Mrs. P is "fiercely protective" of her husband. This pairing is both progressive and regressive from the perspective of disability tropes; Dr. P remains dependent on Mrs. P for his musical cues in order to perform his daily tasks to mutual satisfaction, but there *is* mutual satisfaction and Dr. P *is* performing daily tasks alongside his wife. Chiefly, Mrs. P's stalwart belief in her husband's health has allowed her to create this system with her husband, but Dr. S's house call begins to dismantle her confidence. In this scene, Mrs. P shows Dr. S a series of Dr. P's paintings, begun years before, and with some completed recently. Whereas the paintings at the beginning of the series are representational, the most recent are abstract. The following example is an excerpt of their dialogue from the event (scene) "The Paintings":

> MRS. P: When we were forced to flee to this city he continued to paint.
> DR. S: The grief of survivors.
> MRS. P: Seeking the faces of those we had lost.
> DR. S: Years later this vividness waned. Faces fractured. Natural curves became angular, almost cubist.
> MRS. P: The anguish of war, severed loves, torn lives, shattered dreams.
> DR. S: Then less and less concrete images, more abstract expressionist.
> MRS. P: But the feeling . . . still passionate memories arrested in space.
> DR. S: But in the most recent paintings, I hardly dare to say it, painted gesture has degenerated into mere marks, lines without meaning. Empty shapes.
> MRS. P: No, no, you've got it all wrong, you know nothing of modern art.
> DR. S: Random blotches, the work of a child.

This scene brings to bear on the disability text of the opera the ultimate authority of the physician in all matters, even in matters of art. Tobin Siebers (2010) has considered the connections between modernist art and disability as linked by human bodies that fall outside conceptions of the normative.[9] This scene dismantles notions of a disability-centered artistic practice, as well as the idea that abstract art can be a development rather than evidence of decline. While the dramatic gesture of the scene is to awaken Mrs. P to her husband's gradual visual deterioration, the unintended effect of the scene is its deconstruction of pro-disability and pro-neurodiversity ideologies. These ideologies would have been manifest not only in art but also in general attitudes toward and treatment of disabled individuals. The mid-1980s in the UK were not yet years of great liberation for the disability community; the therapeutic model was still firmly in place, and institutions were still the primary residences for disabled individuals of all abilities. Although, increasingly, people with disabilities were becoming integrated into schools and workplaces, the stigma surrounding physical, psychiatric, and intellectual disability still existed to a great degree (Jarrett 2012).[10] Knowing this, Mrs. P would certainly have understood the need to hide her husband's disability as long as possible, not only for economic reasons (it seems that Mrs. P was the caregiver housewife—in this case, perhaps accompanist—while Mr. P was the breadwinner) but also for social ones. Her denial, then, has deep roots in a societal disdain for disabled bodies, not simply in her love for her husband and respect for his talents.

Embedded within this debate is a debate about modern art that calls into question the very genre of the opera itself, but also speaks to Dr. S's powers of persuasion in the opera. It is not until the "Paintings" event in the opera that Mrs. P begins to believe Dr. S's suggestion that her husband has a neurological disorder; ironically, the visual images created by Dr. P, who is less and less able to perceive visually, create a convincing enough visual narrative of disability to at last break the cycle of Mrs. P's denial. Musically, the realization dawns with ever-slowing tempi, in sections with extraordinarily slow harmonic rhythm, marked respectively *Poco meno mosso* and *Molto meno mosso*. When the tempo picks up again, Dr. S considers whether or not Mrs. P might be correct in her assertion that he is an "ignorant, arrogant man." Nevertheless, the power shifts slightly at the end of the opera to an acknowledgment on the part of Dr. S that "The Wife" has some bearing on the well-being of his patient and his mode of working out his daily life. The tempo slows again to *Meno mosso* as the neurologist inquires—at a speed he presumes suitable to her—how her husband functions. Mrs. P picks up the pace and explains to *him* the ways in which Dr. P can complete his daily tasks at a *più mosso* tempo. For the moment, the physician has ceased to be the expert, and the layperson—and a woman—instructs Dr. S. As she begins to describe the way Dr. P sings his way through the necessary tasks of his day such as eating, dressing, and bathing, Nyman restores missing pitches to the "identi-kit" of three structural chords that he had established at the start of the opera. Whereas in the previous event, "Paintings," the increasing abstraction of the paintings had been represented by increasingly spare harmonies that seemed to be missing components, in the next scene, Mrs. P's explanation is one of rebuilding, in terms of both disability accommodation and harmonic elements. Nevertheless, the final scene of the opera enables Dr. S to enlarge in his grand, medicalized way, a "prescription" for the patient based on Mrs. P's dedicated daily caregiving.

Conclusion

The question of Dr. P's self-awareness does not arise directly in the opera, yet throughout the piece, Dr. S asks rhetorical questions: "Did he know? Were they playing an elaborate joke?" What makes Nyman's opera most traditional in its views of disability is its reliance on the physician for a verdict within a conventional societal framework. Ultimately, Mrs. and Dr. P continue doing what they had been doing all along, at the design of Mrs. P, which was to sing through each day, using the musical parts of the brain that were still fully functioning over and above the failing visual cortex. The medical model established from the start of the opera has undermined an effective and well-established disability identity developed by the couple. Nyman's operatic setting of an actual opera singer's experience with disability erases the extraordinary vocal and musical talents of the individual, foregrounding his disability while simultaneously normalizing him. If, for example, the clinical tale were to be set as a play, the opera singer's extraordinary vocal ability would not be eclipsed by its operatic surroundings. The composer's method of systematically defamiliarizing the listener with specific chord sequences that were once familiar creates an atmosphere of confusion through which these other cultural phenomena move. Narrative medicine, as I found in my own experiences and conversations with my neurologist, aims to create a holistic environment through which the patient may be understood, indeed, as a whole human. Nyman's opera and subsequent scholarship on the piece would seem to humanize disability through the guise of narrative medical practice; but, actually, the medical model is firmly in place from the downbeat, with all its potential for devastation.

Acknowledgments

Colleagues at the author's symposium associated with this volume read and offered thoughtful comments on this essay in its earliest form, and I offer them sincere thanks: Michael Accinno, Raymond Knapp, Julie Singer, Jessica Sternfeld, Joseph Straus, and especially Licia Carlson, whose insights about narrative medicine proved invaluable.

Notes

1. It should be noted that since the writing of both Sacks's (1970) book and Nyman's (1986) opera, Sacks has diagnosed himself with visual agnosia, the same disorder at the center of these narratives (Sacks 2010, 144–201).
2. Take, for example, the titles of the other chapters in the book of "clinical tales" from which the opera is drawn. Organized in four sections ("Losses", "Excesses," "Transports,"

and "The World of the Simple"), the subjects of Sacks's tales sound as though he has encountered them on the midway of a carnival. To name a few, Sacks writes about "The Disembodied Lady" and "The Man Who Fell out of Bed," as well as "Witty Ticey Ray" and "The Possessed"; he also encounters "The Dog beneath the Skin" and "The Autist Artist" (Sacks 1970).

3. The use of this phrase indicates the level of humanity Dr. S already ascribes to Dr. P: this well-educated teacher of music has already become a curiosity to the neurologist, comparable to that of an animal seen on a safari, or a colonial exotic exhibited in a world's fair.
4. http://www.youtube.com/watch?v=s6LnZqYSrBI, accessed January 17, 2014.
5. Rachel Adams (2001, 21) discusses the role of the sideshow barker in depth.
6. The quotation in the heading is from Michael Nyman, quoted in CD liner notes, Michael Nyman (1986). *The Man Who Mistook His Wife for a Hat*, CBS Records, Michael Nyman (conductor).
7. Fluxus was an informal group of performance artists based in the United States that began to form around 1958. The group emphasized the beauty and art to be found in everyday "events" such as drinking a glass of water. Leaders of this movement were George Maciunas, Alison Knowles, John Cage, Dick Higgins, Henry Flynt, George Brecht, Nam Jun Paik, and others. The movement spread to other countries when American Fluxus thinkers connected with others of similar philosophy across the burgeoning global performance art community. The specific "events" that occurred were basically unrelated, other than that they were connected by a single philosophical framework. For a detailed account of Fluxus and its events, see Higgins 2002.
8. Video Clip 2: http://www.youtube.com/watch?v=H7h3dYuPMzs, accessed January 18, 2014.
9. Joseph Straus employs Siebers's argument as the basis for his essay in this volume, exploring connections between modernist music compositional practices, specifically those of Stravinsky and disabled bodies.
10. Until 1981 when the Jay Report revealed widespread abuse and neglect in the asylum system, public institutionalization of disabled individuals was commonplace in the UK (Jarrett 2012).

References

Adams, Rachel. 2001. *Sideshow U.S.A.: Freaks and the American Cultural Imaginary.* Chicago: University of Chicago Press.

Ap Siôn, Pwyll. 2007. *The Music of Michael Nyman: Texts, Contexts, and Intertexts.* Aldershot, UK: Ashgate.

Charon, Rita. 2006. *Narrative Medicine: Honoring the Stories of Illness.* New York: Oxford University Press.

Garland-Thomson, Rosemarie. 1996. "Introduction: From Wonder to Error: A Genealogy of Freak Discourse in Modernity." In *Freakery: Cultural Spectacles of the Extraordinary Body*, edited by Rosemarie Garland-Thomson, 1–23. New York and London: New York University Press.

Garland-Thomson, Rosemarie. 2009. *Staring: How We Look.* Oxford and New York: Oxford University Press.

Higgins, Hannah. 2002. *The Fluxus Experience.* Berkeley: University of California Press.

Jarrett, Simon. 2012. "The Disability in Time and Place Project." English Heritage. Accessed January 18, 2014. http://www.english-heritage.org.uk/discover/people-and-places/disability-history/1945-to-the-present-day/.

Kudlick, Catherine J. 2001. "The Outlook of the Problem and the Problem with the Outlook: Two Advocacy Journals Reinvent Blind People in Turn-of-the-Century America." In *The New Disability History: American Perspectives*, edited by Paul Longmore and Lauri Umanski, 187–213. New York: New York University Press.

Mitchell, David T., and Sharon L. Snyder. 2000. *Narrative Prosthesis: Disability and the Dependencies of Discourse*. Ann Arbor: University of Michigan.

Neumayr, Anton. 1995. *Hummel, Weber, Mendelssohn, Schumann, Brahms, Bruckner: Notes on Their Lives, Works, and Medical Histories*. Vol. 2 of *Music and Medicine*. Translated by Bruce Cooper Clarke. Bloomington, IL: Medi-Ed Press.

Nyman, Michael. 1974. *Experimental Music: Cage and Beyond*. New York: Cambridge University Press.

Nyman, Michael. (1986) 2007. *The Man Who Mistook His Wife for a Hat: Chamber Opera*. Piano-vocal score. Bury St. Edmunds, UK: Chester Music.

Ostwald, Peter. 1985. *Schumann: The Inner Voices of a Musical Genius*. Boston: Northeastern University Press.

Sacks, Oliver. 1970. *The Man Who Mistook His Wife for a Hat and Other Clinical Tales*. New York: Simon & Schuster.

Sacks, Oliver. 2010. *The Mind's Eye*. New York: Knopf.

Sebestik, Miroslav (director). 2003. *Listen*. ARTE France Développement Filmes.

Siebers, Tobin. 2010. *Disability Aesthetics*. Ann Arbor: University of Michigan.

Straus, Joseph N. 2011. *Extraordinary Measures: Disability in Music*. New York: Oxford University Press.

Walker, Alan. 1976. *Schumann*. London: Faber & Faber.

PART 8

FILM AND MUSICAL THEATRE

CHAPTER 38

SCENE IN A NEW LIGHT

Monstrous Mothers, Disabled Daughters, and the Performance of Feminism and Disability in The Light in the Piazza *(2005) and* Next to Normal *(2008)*

ANN M. FOX

DISABILITY and monstrosity are frequently intertwined in the creative imagination; extraordinary differences in embodiment, intellect, or affect have carried symbolic significance throughout representational history. Equating the disabled body with monstrosity has sustained the moral model of disability, where physical or mental difference is equated with depravity. And so the monstrous disabled mother in Western drama is an originating archetype, beginning with Medea, whose murder of her children is represented as stemming from a determination to wreak vengeance that could supposedly only be the product of a madwoman.

In American drama, as far back as Eugene O'Neill's *Long Day's Journey into Night* (1956) and Tennessee Williams's *Suddenly, Last Summer* (1957), stage representations of motherhood that is monstrous have likewise often been marked by disability. More often than not, these disabilities take the shape of different forms of psychological distress or mental illness. For example, Mary Tyrone's morphine addiction is the backdrop and raison d'être for her family's fears in *Long Day's Journey into Night*; when she enters the family parlor having fully succumbed to her addiction yet again against her family's hopes for a cure, the harsh comment from her son Jamie is "The Mad Scene: enter Ophelia!" (O'Neill 2002, 174) (Jamie's cruel comment is quintessentially ableist; his mockery deeply stigmatizes disability through castigating Mary not just as addicted, but insane, reducing disability to a metaphorical trope rather than a lived experience.) In *Suddenly, Last Summer*, Violet Venable's stroke-induced paralysis is the visible marker of her malevolence toward her niece, Catherine, on whom she wants to force a lobotomy; she is openly hostile because Catherine knows that Violet's son is queer—and not just queer but also predatory and secretive, suggesting that Violet's disability is, somewhat ironically, also a physical manifestation of her latent homophobia and her complicity with her son's secret liaisons. Whether Edward Albee's Martha in *Who's Afraid of Virginia Woolf?* (1962), the alcoholic, toxic mother of an imaginary child, or the Oklahoma matriarch Violet Weston in Tracy Letts's *August: Osage County* (2007), the drug-addicted, cancer-stricken, all-too-real toxic (s)mother of three beleaguered adult children, Mary Tyrone's disabled heirs are some of the most canonical figures in drama. Pathological, disabled mothers abound to this day on the stage, so much so that theatre critic Ben Brantley wondered in a *New York Times* article on May 19, 2010: "I'm wondering if we shouldn't put a moratorium on the I-Dismember-Mama genre for a few years."

Intriguingly, disability cuts across the younger female generations, as the figure of the disabled daughter has also figured largely in drama. Laura Wingfield, of course, is the most obvious example of the type; impeded by her limp and her overbearing mother, she recedes into the mists of her brother's memory by the end of Tennessee Williams's *The Glass Menagerie* (1944). Her mother, Amanda Wingfield, lives in terror of what is to become of her vulnerable daughter. What will happen to these adrift disabled daughters is no less pronounced a fear whether the daughter (or daughter figure) is Helen Keller in William Gibson's *The Miracle Worker* (1959), the so-called spinster Lenny (thirty, unmarried, and infertile) in Beth Henley's *Crimes of the Heart* (1978), or Sarah Norman, the Deaf student-turned-activist in Mark Medoff's *Children of a Lesser God* (1979).

Musicals likewise contain their own versions of these types, as Raymond Knapp discusses in his essay in this volume. The musical juggernaut *Wicked* (2003), for example, contains an infamous moment where the witch Elphaba cures her wheelchair-using sister, Nessarose, of paralysis through enchanting her ruby slippers. An obvious cure fantasy, it is played in performance for high melodrama. But perhaps even more insidious is the first disability moment in the musical, when we find out that Elphaba herself is the issue of her mother's affair with an illicit mystery man. No one knows where her green skin, so unlike that of others, comes from, but it is read as its own monstrous portent and punishment, the mother's sins visited on the (soon-to-be wicked) daughter's body. Given the sheer volume of these figures, there is certainly a strong critical temptation to follow Brantley's advice and dismiss these monstrous mamas in American dramas, as well as their disabled daughters, as irrelevant and perpetuating negative stereotype. Either their staying or their going seems too terrible a thing to be borne by those in their midst: it seems that either the mothers impose the tyranny of their motherhood on those trapped within their circle, or cruelly desert their supposedly appropriate maternal role. The daughters embody a dramatic dilemma: unable to function as disabled women in the real world, they must look to caregivers (usually in the figure of potential spouses) to support or complete them. Without such a hope, their end is colored as tragic; with it, they have successfully reinscribed overcoming.

It would be easy to get stuck here, trapped by indecision. Yet having summoned these disabled figures, can we find more nuance, perhaps even useful strategies in them? Can we look at these images and understand the complexity of identity and political negotiation they evoke? We ignore, dismiss, or deride them, as well as the continued popularity and canonicity of the images, at our peril; to do so would be to neglect an opportunity to discuss both the real, lived, highly diverse experiences of disabled people, as well as what such representations can teach us about the deployment of disability within a cultural and historical context over time. And so we might ask: how do the ways in which women have traditionally been negatively defined by disability in drama function in contemporary musical theatre? What is the role of the contemporary musical in defining femininity through disability, and how might a reconsideration of the tropes deployed around disabled mothers and daughters provide an answer to this question? How do monstrous mothers and disabled daughters become figures through which normalcy—whether compulsory femininity, heteronormativity, or able-bodiedness—can be reinscribed or subverted? When a portrayal seems progressive, how might a critic come to recognize the presence of cripwashing, or the seemingly progressive portrayal of disability that masks continued oppression? Alternatively, how can finding a more subtle way to consider these depictions provide more locations for a critic to understand how a musical is doing important disability advocacy work—even when it does not seem obviously so? Both the musicals *The Light in the Piazza* (2005) and *Next to Normal* (2008) feature disabled women whose mental disability is a central element of the plot. Yet the musicals feature radically divergent endings; the former ends in a traditional marriage plot, while the latter concludes with a family breaking apart. What we might term a happy ending has different implications not only for the women in these musicals, but also for those of us watching; not all deployments of disabled daughterhood, or disabled maternity, are created equal.

"Love's a fake, love's a fable": *The Light in the Piazza*

It is intriguing that *The Light in the Piazza*, while quasi-operatic in sound, subject, and even its translation of several songs into Italian, uses the populist genre of musical theatre to focus on intellectual disability, implicitly linking what is ostensibly lesser musically with bodily defect. With its book by Craig Lucas and music and lyrics by Adam Guettel, *The Light in the Piazza* was adapted from Elizabeth Spencer's 1960 novella of the same name; Guettel won Tony Awards for Best Original Score and Best Orchestration in 2005. The story of the musical follows the same basic plotline of Spencer's work, following Clara Johnson and her mother, Margaret, as they travel through Italy. Over the course of the musical, Clara, who is intellectually disabled, meets and falls in love with Fabrizio Naccarelli, a young Italian who is equally smitten with her. While first resisting the courtship between the two, Margaret eventually decides that this might be a real chance for Clara to have the kind of life of which she could only dream for her daughter, and agrees to their marriage. As she works to this outcome, we see her own reflections on her disintegrating marriage. It is one that is now polite, loveless, and in which Margaret and her husband, Roy (called Noel in the novella), hold each other at arm's length, having had what Margaret calls a "dividing day" (in a song of the same name) between them. Clara and Fabrizio's marriage is almost called off by the Naccarelli family when the secret of Clara's intellectual disability is apparently discovered; but it turns out that the Naccarellis are merely upset to learn Clara is six years older than Fabrizio, a seemingly insurmountable obstacle. Margaret smooths this concern over with more dowry money, and the marriage goes forward; contrary to the novella, the end of the musical suggests that Margaret, having found self-actualization of her own, will leave her husband (a distinction that will become important in a moment).

The Light in the Piazza enjoyed popularity in its moment as a somewhat nontraditional musical and as a vehicle for performers who would garner great acclaim in Broadway musical theatre, including Matthew Morrison, Kelli O'Hara, and Victoria Clark. Evoking a lush and operatic feel in its songs, it ran for 504 shows on Broadway, winning six Tony Awards and five Drama Desk Awards in 2005 (Préher 2009, 21). The show enjoyed such popularity that its Broadway production was broadcast on PBS's *Live from Lincoln Center* series in 2006, toured the United States, and was more recently produced at the Shaw Festival in Canada in 2013.

As Raymond Knapp (2006) points out, "The American musical has been most consistently successful when its stories and themes resolve through the formation of conventional romantic relationships," and *The Light in the Piazza* is no exception (264). It also seems to be tailor-made for consideration as a work of disability theatre, at once affirming heterosexual union but also inserting Clara into a marriage plot traditionally only reserved for nondisabled women. As is often the case where disability is concerned, the discussion of the meaning of disability in Spencer's original novella has varied widely among critics. Some have read it in a more critically conventional way, as in Katherine Seidel's (1997) interpretation that Clara's disability is pure metaphor; innocent and lovely, she is "the southern belle, the most important work of art of her culture. By the standards of the 1950s, the healthiest and happiest woman in the novel is the one who is the most infantilized, eternally dependent on her family. Not Margaret but Clara is the fifties ideal of womanhood, sweet, immature, nonintellectual, adoring of children, playful and sincere" (20). Or in other words, "the happiest and most fulfilled of women of the 1950s are lobotomized" (Seidel 1997, 22). Seidel, as many feminist critics have before her, interprets the gender roles created here as disability, as a way to create the implicitly more important critique of patriarchy and marriage as economic exchange. Gérald Préher (2009) reads disability in slightly different, though equally ableist, ways: "Far from the South, the daughter, Clara, proves her parents' beliefs wrong when she meets and falls in love with a young Italian, Fabrizio; there, in Italy, she is able to blossom and to experience the same emotions as girls her own age in spite of her mental deficiency. Spencer's novella gives not only a lesson in courage but also proof that dreams can become reality" (21). Like Seidel, Préher does not erase disability, but he, too, misappropriates it, here breathlessly invoking sentimentalized views of inspiration and overcoming as familiar disability clichés.

By contrast, Ladislava Khailova (2008) counters such assumptions about mental disability and argues that the representation of Clara's intellectual disability is much more nuanced, creating a kind of sympathy that is particularly significant within its cultural moment:

> it could be argued that the text does not grant Clara a status of full equality to normate women, and still points to the encoding of cognitive disability as a sign of inferiority rather than an unmarked difference. However, Clara's difference also has a clear subversive potential, particularly in its fifties context: Spencer's revision of core tenets of the prevailing eugenic paradigms of mental particularity through the character of Clara aids the novel's anti-establishment agenda by granting all women, irrespective of their cognitive abilities, the right to their sexuality and independence. (102)

She avers that the novella "reveals the performative aspect of all female identities, especially those of Euro-American white ladyhood" (Khailova 2008, 102).

But while seeming to liberate disabled femininity by marrying off its intellectually disabled heroine at the end rather than consign her to a life of loneliness, I contend that *The Light in the Piazza* simply revalorizes marriage, which becomes a kind of figurative institutionalization for Clara. In the process, disability is used to reassert both compulsory able-bodiedness and heteronormativity. Indeed, it takes on an even more problematic aspect in its adaptation and performance; old stereotypes of intellectual disability are reinserted into the text, and the musical drives the subversive tension present in Spencer's original work underground. Ironically, whereas contemporary critics praise Spencer's novella for both its critique of marriage's traffic in women and its liberatory ending for mother and daughter (in which, it should be noted, Margaret does not leave her husband but determines to rework her marriage), the musical version of *The Light in the Piazza* does something quite different. Although she is breaking her family apart and leaving her marriage, presumably for Clara's good, Margaret simply reinserts her daughter into structures of patriarchal and ableist thought that remain largely in place. As a result, audience members can look approvingly on neoliberal views of feminism and disability activism that in all actuality do not work to create any real challenge to social beliefs about gender or disability.

Sumptuously designed, scored, and performed, the musical theatre version of *The Light in the Piazza* seems to affirm our admiration of its disabled heroine, ostensibly building on and extending the potentially subversive quality of the novella. *The Light in the Piazza* opens calling attention to the theatricality of the ruse Margaret is about to perpetuate; in response to the opening line, "What happened here?"—inviting some historical factoid in response—Margaret instead answers, "I played a tricky game in a foreign country" (Lucas and Guettel 2007, 3). The game, of course, is the marriage to Fabrizio Naccarelli that is carried out without revealing Clara's intellectual disability. During the opening song "Statues and Stories," the women wander through Florence, the birthplace of the Renaissance. The musical style for this song, with its lively, light, and expansive mood, creates a sense of wonderment. Yet that spirit of exploration is also somewhat ironic; arranged as a kind of echoing where Clara repeats after her mother, the song discourages exploration; it immediately sets up a tension between the musical style and the plot. The genius of Florence's artists and the perfection of their work stand in marked contrast to the intellectual disability of the young woman whose exclamations in "Statues and Stories" sometimes jarringly introduce another tonal area, who moves unthinkingly through the Uffizi, and who is more likely to yell "Olly olly oxen free!" when in the Duomo. The presumption that Clara is therefore disqualified from love or parenthood gets poignantly performed in "The Beauty Is" when Clara muses, singing with a longing of her own that contrasts with "Statues and Stories,"

> Everyone's a mother here in Italy
> Everyone's a father or a son
> I think if I had a child I would take such care of her
> Then I wouldn't feel like one. (Lucas and Guettel 2007, 15)

The music here shifts around unpredictably, as though to echo Clara's mind jumping from idea to idea, and foreshadowing what will eventually happen in the narrative as Clara seizes on ideas about her identity that others thought closed to her. Far from feeling the strictures of compulsory maternity, Clara simultaneously expresses a wish to have a child and not be infantilized. The Broadway production of *The Light in the Piazza* performed this juxtaposition when, as Clara sings, she is confronted with a large painting of the Madonna and Child.

Clara's desire to parent seems part of her larger revolt against paternalism that only grows more pronounced once she falls in love, causing a palpable shift in how she regards herself. She transforms from the dutiful daughter to a woman who demands agency, telling her mother angrily, "You're happy to be the one who knows everything I need and has the final word. It's clear. . . . You ignore what I say, what I want. You make things up the way you want them. You lie about things" (Lucas and Guettel 2007, 56). In Act I, Clara obediently follows her mother past "statues and stories"; when Act II opens, she walks amid ruins, suggesting her temporarily shattered romance with Fabrizio. But if the idealized art seems only to contradict Clara's embodiment, the ruins suggest more of an affinity; if Clara's romance is able to go forward, something new might be built from it. She will not retrace the path literally or figuratively marked out by parents who toured Italy so long ago but seem to have now lost its romance.

Clara's disability stands out in contrast to Renaissance genius and bodily perfection (at least in its statuary). But if Florence is the place of rationality and proportion, it is also the place where passions ignite, recollected in a tour guide's description of Fra Filippo Lippi, "a monk, famous for his misconduct. He painted his Madonnas to look like the nuns he slept with, including the one who eloped with him and gave him a son" (Lucas and Guettel 2007, 13). The passions of the present-day Naccarelli family are similarly noted in the early appearance of the ever-bickering Franca and Giuseppe, Fabrizio's sister-in-law and brother, who battle over the husband's constant infidelities. Clara's own sexual desire is sparked in Florence, and she expresses it first innocently in "The Beauty Is," then with increasing fervor as the musical goes on. In front of a male statue, Clara "*stares intently at the headless man's penis, then touches it before looking out at us*" (Lucas and Guettel 2007, 14). The maternal longing evoked in "The Beauty Is" foreshadows the sexual longing that will soon preoccupy her, although she has no inkling of it. Rather, the tone at the song's outset is wry and inquisitive, as she brightly and innocently sings in a sing-song voice,

> These are very popular in Italy
> It's the land of naked marble boys
> Something we don't see a lot in Winston-Salem
> That's the land of corduroys. (Lucas and Guettel 2007, 14)

If Clara's changes in self-definition can be seen as progressive, so too can Margaret's evolving reaction to her daughter's desires. Margaret reminds us that she has "managed in many tactful ways over the years to explain her and her situation to young men without wounding them" (Lucas and Guettel 2007, 12). She has repeatedly seen men be attracted to Clara's beauty, but deflected them as a protective mother who does not want her daughter to be hurt or used. Clara comes to see the bond her daughter has with Fabrizio, and imagine something new for her daughter. Her husband, however, resists:

> ROY. She's a handicapped person, Margaret, Jesus, I thought we were through with this.
> MARGARET. Just because she isn't normal, Roy, doesn't mean she's consigned to a life of loneliness. She mustn't be made to accept less from life just because she isn't like you or me.
> ROY. If she has a baby, she'll drop it, she'll lose it!
> MARGARET. She'll be living with the grandmother. Who's going to take care of her when we're gone, Roy? (Lucas and Guettel 76)

Not only parenthood but caregiving within the context of a family rather than an institution is posited as an option for Clara, one that will also create security and safety.

But while the musical seems in alignment with the novella, it actually uses Margaret to effect a kind of cripwashing. This is done by reinvesting the work with disability metaphor and ways of representing the disabled that are less about realism and more about projecting social anxiety about gender onto the disabled body. It is particularly significant that cripwashing happens through tropes that, while they seem to be rewritten, in actuality remain quite retrograde. This disabled daughter, although seeming to go on to a better and brighter future than her dramatic sisters, still has her fate directed in a way that allays normate audience fear or discomfort.

To begin with, while the musical shows Clara wanting a child and not to be treated like one, it still takes great pains to define her mental disability as a childlike state. For Margaret, Clara's injury has forever fixed her intellect and emotions in the moment it happened:

> It's always so difficult . . . Roy and I don't even discuss it anymore, it's just a fact of life, like the weather . . . When Clara was twelve, we rented a Shetland pony for her

> birthday party, and ... the pony kicked ... her. ... The doctors told us that she would ... her mental and emotional capacities would not develop normally, and, but her body would continue to develop, so. ... (Lucas and Guettel 2007, 46–7)

The Clara that results is willful and easily confused. For instance, in a song fittingly called "Hysteria," the musical creates an event that does not happen in the novella, where Clara gets lost trying to find the *museo* where Fabrizio has arranged an assignation. Impetuously throwing away the written directions, she quickly becomes lost and panics, repeating her address over and over until Margaret finds her. The music adds sharply to her sense of panic, escalating quickly from an evocation of Stravinsky's neoclassicism to one that becomes more and more dissonant and troubled, with gestures that could be traced back to expressionistic works like Berg's *Wozzeck*. The song finally falls apart as Clara screams hysterically, stopping only when Margaret finds her. She can then only be comforted once her mother, crooning to "little Clara," sings her a lullaby that replaces the loud hysteria of the beginning with a dénouement of quiet calm.

Indeed, in a June 26, 2005, *New York Times* article ("Characters Who Are More Than the Sum of Their Tics"), Kelli O'Hara discussed the emphasis she placed on playing Clara as childlike, not in the interest of reality, but in order to make her more theatrically appealing:

> "She's a very fictional person already," Ms. O'Hara said. "From all the studying I've done, a person who suffered the trauma she did would likely be overweight, might drool or say inappropriate things like, 'Let me get in your underwear.' I wanted to find something believable but not repellent, so she could be loved. So I couldn't really use any developmentally challenged people as models, and as a result, she at first seemed totally normal."

The article goes on to elaborate that "O'Hara recalibrated her performance, working on childishness rather than disability. A modified form of the hand gestures, not so spasmodic, but still reaching toward everything, as a toddler might, remained as a clue to her innocence." O'Hara's insights might have seemed revelatory to her, but they simply serve to inscribe Clara firmly into the trope of the childlike, feebleminded character whose mental deviance would be sure to be marked by bodily deviance.

If intellectual disability is marked by childlike helplessness, the musical—and O'Hara's performance—further defines it, paradoxically, as also a childlike inability to control sexuality. Hypersexuality is a familiar stereotype of intellectual disability, where the "sexuality of the mentally disabled not only is a source of horror and threat to the 'normal' members of the community but also provides titillation and vicarious thrill" (Keely 2004, 218). In the novella, Margaret's casual observation of Fabrizio and Clara cavorting in a pool sets her determination to take Clara to Rome and out of temptation's way. But the musical makes much more of a spectacle out of Clara's sexual impetuosity. Barely a moment or two after her mother has sung her out of her hysteria and to sleep, Clara wakes to find Fabrizio in her room. In "Say it Somehow," they sing a passionate, lushly orchestrated love duet in which their voices intertwine and harmonize, with violins, piano, and harp timbres amplifying the intensity of the moment: "You are good to me / I know the sound of touch me / I think I hear the sound of wrap your arms around me" (Lucas and Guettel 2007, 49). Clara and Fabrizio are in the process of disrobing one another when Margaret walks in on them, abruptly ending the first act and spurring the flight to Rome. Before they are discovered, much of their duet becomes wordless and melismatic, and several of the climactic phrases dismiss the verbal realm altogether as the singers yield to passion.

Despite the spectacle of hypersexuality, there is the potential for a radically different use of a disability aesthetic here. Ben MacPherson (2012) argues that this vocalization is a moment when "the heightened sense of emotion felt through music, in the context of the drama, is given power and presence through corporeal vocality" (55). In moving outside the verbal, I think there is further an implicit, if unintentional, reference to and affirmation of intellectual disability that takes place; desire moves outside of the verbal or ability to be described, and a certain kind of more typical lyrical poetry does not happen. This destabilization of the hierarchy of the semantic over the musical for meaning-making disrupts normalcy. Interestingly, in making vocalization an expression of disability and an alternately embodied yet equally valorized source of meaning, this choice also becomes an interpretive accommodation for an English-speaking audience that has been figuratively disabled by the fact that much of the musical is in Italian, without subtitles.

But this moment of promise never fully materializes, and actually begins an important and increasingly problematic shift in how disability is cast during the second act. Clara's hysteria and hypersexuality become increasingly aligned not with disability but pivot her into the female role of the *abbandonata*, first embodied in Franca. Giuseppe's marital infidelities play a less pronounced role in Spencer's novella; here, they are intimately intertwined with the evolving relationship between Clara and Fabrizio. When she first meets Clara, Franca sings a song to her that in its sound and lyrics is meant to warn Clara of the marital infidelities that almost surely lie ahead for her. In "The Joy You Feel," Franca's voice—deeper, richer, throatier and more mature than Clara's—soars as she sings a prediction about the course of Clara's marriage, based on her own experience:

> And on your first anniversary
> In the piazza where you met
> At first it's, it's only a glance
> And then his eyes will set
> Upon a girl who's prettier and younger than you
> What to do?
> . . . .
> Though truly happy, you must beware
> For happiness can also scar
> For so like me you are
> You are . . .
> Beware (Lucas and Guettel 2007, 35–36)

While the reverie about the "first anniversary" seems charming and light, it is overwhelmed by the more pensive tone of the rest of the song, which sounds more like the familiar aria of a woman scorned. Clara seems unable to fathom this advice in the moment, but by Act II it is clear her hysteria now casts female identity-as-disability, and takes a form more aligned with Franca's. The song "Octet" illustrates this, and not surprisingly, opens with the same few bars of nervous, jumpy music that began "Hysteria." But Clara grows hysterical for a different reason now: she flies into a jealous rage when she sees her future sister-in-law kiss Fabrizio to make Giuseppe jealous: "You're a thief! / You're a rotten thief! / You want to steal him away from me!" (Lucas and Guettel 2007, 63) In front of the startled Naccarellis, she culminates her mad scene by throwing a glass of wine in Franca's face. Rather than exposing her mental disability and impulsiveness, this action makes sense to Franca, and endears Clara further to the family:

> FRANCA. No, she is right. Right to fight for him. Please, everyone. Giuseppe and I are so happy for you both—Clara, Fabrizio. We should *all* fight for our love. I should—I *would* fight for Giuseppe. (Lucas and Guettel 2007, 64)

In this moment, Clara's disability is redefined in a way the family understands: being driven mad by love, and letting passion sway all. The literal scar that Clara had shown Fabrizio from her injury a moment earlier becomes transformed into the figurative scar of which Franca sings: early marital happiness made bittersweet. If Clara becomes Italian and hyperfeminized in this moment, Italy in turn becomes read as disabled. In other words, it is the site of chaos and impetuosity: Signor Naccarelli is also a practiced flirt and has had infidelities, while Signora Naccarelli encourages her entire family to rage and be melodramatic as a way to relate to one another. In "The Beauty Is," Clara described an affinity with Italy ("I've hardly met a single soul / but I am not alone / I feel known") and now, it would seem, Italy finds an affinity with her (Lucas and Guettel 2007, 15). Clara's impassioned state makes her more understandable to Italians, and simultaneously creates a solution to, place for, and erasure of mental disability, even as it reinforces gender stereotypes.

Once the problem of Clara's mental disability has been solved this way, brought into alignment with familiar gender roles, the musical can shift its final focus to Margaret, displacing the disabled character in favor of the nondisabled one. While she appears somewhat precious and overprotective at first, as marked for example in "Statues and Stories," her dignity and gravitas only grow as the musical goes on; she works to shape the fate of a daughter who humanizes her mother more strongly by contrast. Songs like "Dividing Day" in Act I and "Fable" in Act II both amplify the sense of loss and regret Margaret has about her own now emotionally cold marriage. In both, there is a pensive, rueful tone to the music; but while "Dividing Day" is slow and melancholic, "Fable" is more soaring and searching as the climactic song to the musical, marrying the regret and anger of "The Joy You Feel" to the sadness of "Dividing Day."

Yet even though musically and thematically the experiences of Franca and Margaret suggest a happy marriage is anything but a foregone conclusion in this world, the musical makes only a token stab at offering Clara any other alternative. Having overheard her father's protests against the marriage, Clara tries to convince Fabrizio not to marry her: "Something is very wrong, and I'm sorry. I would fix it if I . . . knew how. . . . You must not love me, I'm sorry" (Lucas and Guettel 2007, 78). Margaret, however, convinces her to go to the church and be married. "Fable," becomes curiously double edged and paints Margaret, in this moment, as willfully ignoring her own experience; even as Margaret furiously rants "Love's a fake / love's a fable" about her own marriage, she insists that Clara's will be one in which "Someone sees / . . . someone knows you" (Lucas and Guettel 2007, 80). There is a sharp irony to Margaret's notion that Fabrizio will fully see and know Clara, given the subterfuge on which the marriage rests. This makes lines Margaret sings like "Love if you can and be loved . . . / may it last forever," ring hollow. The end of the song is as pensive and quiet as its beginning; under the last words, "Clara . . . the light in the piazza" it seems to present a quiet resolution to the "dangerous game" Margaret has played. Yet there are still moments of dissonance as the song ends, matching the music to the ambiguity of the narrative. From a disability perspective, this uncertainty suggests that rather than being a progressive step for her, Clara's marriage will simply follow the same course toward deterioration as every other marriage in this play.

Margaret's marrying her daughter off reads not as an act of love, but instead as extremely disturbing, although in a way some audience members might not perceive, particularly given the overwhelmingly romantic nature of the music and the story. In the June 26, 2005, *New York Times* article discussing how she portrayed Clara, O'Hara worried the audience would find the ending too positive compared with her idea of disability reality: " 'I worry when some emotionally disabled people come to the show,' Ms. O'Hara said. 'We're saying that you can have love, that you can possibly have a beautiful life, even though you might actually be limited and annoying. I'm afraid they'll feel we're lying to them. . . . But it's the same in any love story, I guess. In real life, no one actually shows up to take you out in a surrey.' " O'Hara's concern that the ending is flawed is right, although not (as she asserts) because emotionally disabled people cannot love and be loved, even if they are "limited and annoying." The musical's putative happy ending is a much more limited and constrictive one than its soaring romance might imply, because of the very illusory nature of that romance. There is, in fact, "too much history" in Florence, as Signor Naccarelli says earlier in the musical, and it is inescapable in the case of marriage: Clara will now lead Margaret's life. Although Margaret sings of her own "dividing day" with her husband (and breaks with him at the end of the musical), although none of the Naccarelli marriages seem happy (or at least faithful), Margaret affirms her own earlier choices and reanimates them again through Clara. While Clara seems happily married by the end of the musical, all is not well, because we more than suspect what Clara's eventual fate will be. In this light, Clara's choices as a disabled woman seem dim rather than brightly embodied in/for their radiant heroine: institutionalization or marriage seem incomplete and unsatisfying fates in a world that can brook no other alternatives. Yet the ending works to overshadow this; the romance of the story becomes its own justification. Far from being too much a fiction in the way O'Hara fears, the ending is, in a way, all too real, asserting the primacy of normalcy and using disability as an instrument to buttress such beliefs. This disabled daughter ends up firmly caught within marital structures that depend on her disability to reinforce them, but cannot truly countenance the presence of disability being part of, or even reshaping what we think of, as a happy ending. Clara will marry *in spite of*—in spite of disability, in spite of her mother's experience, in spite of the fate of all the Naccarelli wives. And disability helps smooth the way toward this being presented as an understandable and justifiable state of affairs.

"Give me pain if that's what's real": *Next to Normal*

The example of *Next to Normal* provides a supposedly monstrous mother, however, who shatters her family because of and through her disability. The musical seems to end more sadly and ambiguously than *The Light in the Piazza*, yet I would argue this use of disability contains much more potential for redeploying the stereotype of the monstrous mother—and by extension, the intersection of disability and female identity in representation. It is all the more intriguing that this happens in a musical that garnered awards (including the 2010 Pulitzer Prize for Drama) and both popular and critical acclaim. In *Next to Normal*, wife and mother Diana Goodman is manic-depressive and undergoes electroshock therapy; ultimately, she leaves her family rather than undergo further stultifying treatment. The question of whether a woman must choose family or self-actualization, and the consequences of that choice, play out in the context of—and symbolized by—disability. On the surface, it would seem the more things change, the more they stay the same, at least where disabled maternity is concerned: Diana's failed motherhood seems somewhat to blame for her mental disability, and vice versa; her mental illness has destroyed her family. She must eventually leave her family behind in order to live with her disability. What I find interesting, however, is that an intriguing reversal of the typical use of disabled maternity and the intersectional identities of female and disabled seems to take place. In *Next to Normal*, disabled maternity ends up being a kind of successful motherhood.

Disabled maternity becomes successful in a way that is a richer exploration of possibility in *Next to Normal*. There is much about the musical that shifts focus where attention to mental illness is concerned. Diana, described as "bipolar depressive with delusional episodes," is our heroine, and we find soon after the musical starts that she is struggling with a resurgence of hallucinations in which she sees her son Gabe, who died as an infant, as the teenager he might have been (Kitt and Yorkey 2010, 18). His death, we learn, is what was the catalyst for what has been a sixteen-year struggle to stifle these delusions and perpetuate through medications and therapy the illusion of what she describes in the opening song, "Just Another Day," as the "perfect loving fam'ly" (Kitt and Yorkey 2010, 8). The song is a bouncy rock ballad, suggesting the freneticism of the family's existence as a kind of controlled chaos, significantly ending with the tempo radically speeding up before the song is abruptly cut off to suggest Diana's most recent psychic break. To be sure, her illness is hard on her family: she fixates on Gabe and at first resists the medication that smooths all her highs and lows out too severely. Her husband, Dan, keeps insisting in "It's Gonna Be Good" that "it's gonna be great! / It's gonna be great," but the music of that song becomes a rapid hoedown. The fiddle timbre plays an important role here: the song has a fiddle line that races faster and faster as a simultaneous arch reference to Americana-as-normalcy (it sounds straight out of *Oklahoma!*) and a musical contradiction to the lyrics' insistence that all is well. We see that the reality is quite different; both Dan and their perfectionist daughter, Natalie, are barely keeping it together. Natalie retreats into drugs and clubbing to escape, seeming obsessive and driven beyond distraction—her mother in formation, perhaps? Dan grows more and more desperate to find a cure; Diana first resists, stopping the pharmaceuticals that dull her feelings. But after she attempts suicide, she agrees to undergo electroshock therapy—and it is a treatment that temporarily renders her amnesiac, causing her to lose nineteen years of memory. When her memory returns, she decides she must try to figure out life with her disorder on her own, and she leaves her family.

Our first hint that Diana is no Mary Tyrone, however, is the fact that we also can see Diana's son and assume he is real; it is not until well into the *Next to Normal* that it is revealed to us that he is dead. We therefore see from Diana's perspective for much of the musical, and that extends out to the way in which the work critiques the medical model. Scott Wallin (2013) has challenged whether *Next to Normal* truly offers such a critique:

> Often the relationship between individuals with emotional and mental disabilities and their clinician is very uncomfortable. This discomfort occasionally surfaces in *Next to Normal* in the form of a gentle critique of the power imbalance inherent in psychiatric discourse. . . . But such moments of discomfort are underdeveloped and are treated as unfortunate but necessary side effects of clinical treatment by "very competent doctors" who may not know all the answers but are certainly not part of the initial problem. The musical thus accepts psychiatry's claim to neutrality within its medical paradigm of madness.

The portrayals of the physicians in Diana's life are, however, somewhat more biting. Diana's psychopharmacologist, Dr. Fine, seems concerned with little more than overwhelming her with pharmaceuticals:

> DOCTOR FINE. The pink ones are taken with food but not with the white ones. The white ones are taken with the round yellow ones but not with the triangle yellow ones. The triangle yellow ones are taken with the oblong green ones with food but not with the pink ones. If a train is leaving New York at a hundred and twenty miles an hour and another train is leaving St. Petersburg at the same time but going backwards, which train . . . (Kitt and Yorkey 2010, 16).

And even as he imposes attempts to make Diana fine, he remains aloof; as Diana wryly observes in "My Psychopharmacologist and I": "Call it a lover's game / He knows my deepest secrets— / I know his . . . name" (Kitt and Yorkey 2010, 18). The song starts as a waltz punctuated with dissonant violin, mirroring the dance she describes between them. It then morphs into a jazzy riff that is reminiscent of Bacharach in style, musically symbolizing the improvisational, even haphazard, nature of Diana's treatment and ironically signaling a kind of carefree nonchalance that she is not really feeling. In its style and lyrics, the song eventually references and satirizes another musical about family normalcy, *The Sound of Music*, through evoking the song "My Favorite Things" as the ensemble sings "Zoloft and Paxil and Buspar and Xanax . . . / Depakote, Klonopin, Ambien, Prozac . . . / Ativan calms me when I see the bills— / These are a few of my favorite pills" (Kitt and Yorkey 2010, 18). Diana thus becomes an embodied example of those whom Bradley Lewis describes as "psychiatric stakeholders . . . led to rely on new medications (to the great profit of the pharmaceutical companies), rather than learning ways of working through human problems, suffering, grief, and anxiety," for we later see that being denied the chance to discuss her son has served as a powerful trigger to her break (2006, 63).

The less-ironically and perhaps more-accurately named Doctor Madden is Diana's psychiatrist; she at first satirically imagines him as a hypermasculine rock star. But his role in her life grows more troubling. It is his prodding to let go of her son that first triggers her suicide attempt; it is later he who administers electroshock therapy. Referencing the movie about the abuse of the mentally disabled (*One Flew over the Cuckoo's Nest*) rather pointedly, Diana calls the hospital a "cuckoo's nest," and later bitterly in "The Break," sings of her treatment, with a pulsing, electric-bass-laden riff as the backdrop to and reflection of her fury and disappointment:

> They tried a million meds and
> They strapped me to their beds and
> They shrugged and told me, "That's the way it goes."
> When finally you hit it,
> I asked you just what did it—
> You shrugged and said that no one really knows. (Kitt and Yorkey 2010, 89–90)

Not only does the musical again indict patriarchal medicine but also over its course we come to see that what drives this family to distraction as much if not more than Diana's illness is the attempt to contain Diana in a kind of veneer of the normate. This intersecting critique of medicine and the normate is particularly important given Diana's mental illness; as Lewis (2013) observes,

> Individualistic approaches to mental difference and distress blame and punish the victim for structural problems that are often better understood as located in families, communities, and society. Medicalization, or psychiatrization, legitimizes the medical community's expert authority over the domain of mental difference. And the binary between normal and abnormal shores up this psychiatrization by providing tremendous social and psychological pressure to stay on the side of normality, or sanity. (116–117)

And indeed, Diana sings in "Just Another Day,"

> I will hold it all together.
> I will hide the mess away.
> And I'll survive another day
> And I will pray
> To hold on just this way
> And for my fam'lys sake—
> I'll take what I can take—
> I'm only just awake . . .
> Every day is just another
> And another . . .
> And another . . .
> I will hold it all together
> We're the perfect loving family
> If they say we're not, then fuck 'em. (Kitt and Yorkey 2010, 13–14)

But what becomes clear as the musical wears on is that it is not just Diana, but all the family members who struggle with this perfectionism, one most easily projected onto a fear of Diana's illness. Dan, trying to be a "good man," asks in the melancholic and tentative song "Who's Crazy," with its haunting string tremolo (a signal of his guilt and uncertainty that also references the mental disability he is confronting), "Who's crazy? The husband or wife? / Who's crazy? To live their whole life / Believing that somehow things aren't as bizarre as they are? / Who's crazy—the one who can't cope, / Or maybe the one who'll still hope? / The one who sees doctors / or the one who just waits in the car?" (Kitt and Yorkey 2010, 17)

Increasingly deadened by a course of treatment that morphs with frightening violence from drugs to electroshock therapy over the course of the musical, Diana's anguish grows. In "I Miss the Mountains," she sings of missing the peaks and valleys of her highs and lows, in which the pain reassured her she was alive; by contrast, "Everything is balanced here / And on an even keel. / Everything is perfect— / Nothing's real . . . / Nothing's real" (Kitt and Yorkey 2010, 27). A song that starts off quietly and nostalgically, its music slowly builds to a power ballad, as if to replicate Diana's attempt to reclaim her emotional life; it is arguably the most triumphant song of the musical. Gabe, who keeps appearing to her in hallucinations as her ally (or a Gabriel-like prophetic angel) in resisting medication and treatment, is the manifestation of the part of herself that thinks choosing to live without her medications is the brave choice. She fiercely rejects the electroshock therapy at first, insisting in "Didn't I See This Movie?":

> Didn't I see this movie,
> With McMurphy and the nurse?
> That hospital was heavy
> But this cuckoo's nest is worse. . . .

What makes you think I'd lose my mind for you?
I'm no sociopath.
I'm no Sylvia Plath.
I ain't no Frances Farmer kind of find for you . . .
So stay out of my brain . . .
I'm no princess of pain. (Kitt and Yorkey 2010, 57)

The pulsing rock beat of this song is more regular than "The Break," and suggests defiance and agency on Diana's part. But it is immediately answered by the sentimental, quiet, almost lullaby-like soothing tones of the song with which Dan answers her, "A Light in the Dark," in which he begs her: "Take this chance / And we'll make a new start / Somewhere far / From what keeps us apart" (Kitt and Yorkey 2010, 58). Diana capitulates to her husband's request for normalcy and agrees to electroshock therapy.

This resolution would seem in line with the critique Wallin (2013) offers of the musical, pointing out that while it questions normalcy, its critique is tempered by how relatable Diana and her family are, "models of normalcy": Diana "is exemplary . . . She is a 'sexy and sharp,' middle-class, educated, suburban mom in her thirties or forties." Yet the references to the actress Frances Farmer and poet Sylvia Plath, both of whom underwent brutal therapies to treat their mental disabilities, suggest that the pressures on an exemplary or normate woman are no less real or painful; the pressure on Diana to deny her grief and carry on with her family as if nothing has happened becomes its own kind of tyranny. She equates the treatment to the cruelties depicted in *One Flew over the Cuckoo's Nest*, and her prediction is borne out. Diana, who has neither been allowed to grieve her dead son nor try and experience life with all her highs and lows, finds that electroshock therapy is not only no cure, it destroys nineteen years of her memory. As her daughter Natalie acidly observes in "Song of Forgetting": "What a lovely cure . . . / It's a medical miracle. / With a mind so pure / That she doesn't know anything" (Kitt and Yorkey 2010, 66). And Diana, after gradually regaining her memory and fully confronting her loss, comes to feel similarly, insisting "there has to be another way." She refuses to go back on her medication, and decides to leave her family.

But instead of breaking them apart, Diana's embracing her disability results in growth for all the members of her family. Dan can stop insisting that a veneer of happiness is all that is needed, and begin to address his own grief; the musical ends with him seeing his son as well, who is now a projection of Dan's own previously repressed sadness and bereavement. More significantly, we come to realize that Natalie may have also inherited her mother's bipolar disorder. But in openly acknowledging that, as well as the fact that it is part of her personhood, Natalie's boyfriend Henry represents a different response to disability than Dan, singing in "Perfect for You":

So you could go crazy,
Or I could go crazy, it's true . . .
Sometimes life is insane,
But crazy I know I can do.

'Cuz crazy is perfect,
And fucked-up is perfect,
And I will be perfect . . . [for you]. (Kitt and Yorkey 2010, 96–7)

Most significantly, Diana and Natalie come to understand one another, and accept the imperfections in each other and their relationship. The contrast to *The Light in the Piazza* is striking: here, disability is out in the open, and it may or may not continue into the next generation, resisting the consolation the audience has where Clara's disability is concerned, because it is not congenital. Unlike Margaret, Diana does not hide the uncertainty that disability brings to their future together from her daughter, singing in "Maybe (Next to Normal)":

Maybe we can't be okay.
But maybe we're tough, and we'll try anyway—
We'll live with what's real,
Let go of what's past,
And maybe I'll see you at last. (Kitt and Yorkey 2010, 94)

Natalie responds in kind:

I don't need a life that's normal—
That's way too far away,
But something . . . next to normal
Would be okay.
Yeah, something next to normal—
That's the thing I'd like to try.
Close enough to normal
To get by . . . (Kitt and Yorkey 2010, 94)

Ultimately, Diana and her daughter rewrite their relationship. The failure is not in Diana for not being cured, but in the attempt to reinforce the normate, literally in this case to the point of Diana's almost dying. Successful mothering becomes this supposedly monstrous mother embracing her disability, leaving the traditional family unit, and redefining her maternal role.

This is not a perfect ending from a disability perspective: the final number, "Light," is a powerful climax that trades in gestures of inspiration and redemption to establish narrative closure. Sung by the entire cast, it invokes ableist metaphors to suggest overcoming: "And when the night has fin'ly gone, / And when we see the new day dawn, / We'll wonder how we wandered for so long, so blind" (Kitt and Yorkey 2010, 103). Along with their divergent endings, the musical languages of the two musicals I discuss are also quite different: *The Light in the Piazza* deploys the language of Rogers and Hammerstein (with snippets of Bernstein, Kern, Copland, and Sondheim, among others) while *Next to Normal* is rooted in rock, folk rock, the megamusical, and satiric nods to its predecessors, its pastiche-like quality and unusual subject matter seeming to make it akin to what

Jessica Sternfeld (2006) calls the "post-megamusical" (349). Yet in each, music augments the visible and performed metaphors in significant ways. The seeming closure of *Next to Normal* is no more contained than its predecessor; it is happenstance, but nonetheless intriguing, that it, too, ends with an image of light:

> When we open up our lives,
> Sons and daughters, husbands, wives—
> And fight that fight . . .
> There will be light.
> There will be light.
> There will be light.
> There will be light! (Lucas and Guettel 2010, 104)

That image of light suggests a kind of enlightenment that is generative and creative, literally echoing the biblical phrase, "Let there be light." But if the light is an expansive idea rather than contained and projected onto a romanticized individual like Clara, the "light in the piazza," to what are we being asked to "open up our lives"?

The answer is also in this ending. While musically we seem to have resolved everything harmonically, there still remains a kind of tension; after all, this culminating song still has Natalie—who might very well inherit her mother's illness—singing (eventually joined by Dr. Madden): "Day after day / Give me clouds, and rain, and gray. / Give me pain if that's what's real— / It's the price we pay to feel" (Kitt and Yorkey 2010, 102). In teaching the musical, I have had students, particularly those who have bipolar family members, suggest fear and discomfort about what the ending finally posits for people with bipolar disorder, especially Diana, who may very well not be okay. Yet I think this is exactly the point, because in addition to questioning psychiatry and the medical model, we are compelled to emphasize the agency of mentally disabled people as our focus. Against our expectations, a disabled mother's desertion proves a fruitful retort to normalcy, pointing to the larger complexity of the monstrous mother trope. Success comes through disability being accepted in all its complexity, not cured, stifled, vilified, or rejected. That Dan sees his son in the last scene of the play suggests that he might be moving past pathologizing his own grief; coupled with Diana's position, this reflects the complex situatedness of different kinds of mental disability and diverse choices for treatment. This may not be the radical act of asserting neurodiversity-as-identity characteristic of Mad Pride, but situated within the commercial context of the mainstream commercial musical, it is powerful nonetheless. Seen in this light, it is real enlightenment, and a radically different image than the closing vision of Clara as "light in the piazza," her eventual fate sentimentalized away and willfully forgotten, along with our discomfort over disability.

In her fierce and wise memoir of disability embodiment, *Too Late to Die Young*, the late and distinguished Charleston lawyer and activist Harriet McBryde Johnson (2010) shares her experience debating with the Princeton philosopher Peter Singer his theoretical stance that disabled infants should be allowed to die. Her visit with Singer humanizes him for her, and although she acknowledges the irony and horror of having to discuss her life as though it is a theoretical construct, she cannot quite bring herself to demonize Singer, as many of her fellow disability activists would have her do:

> If I define Singer's kind of disability prejudice as an ultimate evil, and him as a monster, then I must so define all who believe disabled lives are inherently likely to be less happy, or that a life without a certain kind of consciousness lacks value. That would make monsters of many of the people with whom I move on the sidewalks, do business, break bread, swap stories, and share the grunt work of politics. The definition would reach some of my family and most of my nondisabled friends, people who show me enormous kindness and who somehow, sometimes manage to love me through their ignorance. I can't live with a definition of ultimate evil that encompasses all of them. I can't refuse the monster-majority basic courtesy, respect, and human sympathy. It's not in my heart to deny every single one of them, categorically, my affection and my love. (227–228)

Disability Studies allows us to do what Johnson does: take the long view, and understand that the gains disability representation makes happen over a long time, and within the context of much back-and-forth, much stress and strain, much engagement with the "monster-majority." Performing Disability Studies means at once understanding that representations such as the disabled daughter and monstrous mother should be seen in context, and understood to be inherently messy, contradictory, sometimes immensely dissatisfying, yet never completely without worth as cultural images. If we ignore those images, we risk demonizing the complex lives to which they refer, and isolate ourselves from understanding the cultural conversations swirling around us. In the end, we need to remain connected to a more nuanced understanding of them, so that we can finally envision, and pursue, a view of disability culture that has been truly lived, and that extends out beyond what we've been made to think we know, invigorating our understanding of disabled and nondisabled identities alike.

References

Johnson, Harriet McBryde. 2010. *Too Late to Die Young*. New York: Henry Holt.

Keely, Karen. 2004. "Sexuality and Storytelling: Literary Representations of the 'Feebleminded' in the Age of Sterilization." In *Mental Retardation in America: A Historical Reader*, edited by Steven Noll and James W. Trent, 207–222. New York: New York University Press.

Khailova, Ladislava. 2008. "Rewriting Patriarchal Paradigms of Retardation in Elizabeth Spencer's *The Light in the Piazza*." In *Invisible Suburbs: Recovering Protest Fiction in the 1950s United States*, edited by Josh Lukin, 85–103. Jackson: University Press of Mississippi.

Kitt, Tom, and Brian Yorkey. 2010. *Next to Normal*. New York: Theatre Communications Group.

Knapp, Raymond. 2006. *The American Musical and the Performance of Personal Identity*. Princeton, NJ: Princeton University Press.

Lewis, Bradley. 2006. *Moving Beyond Prozac, DSM, and the New Psychiatry*. Ann Arbor: University of Michigan Press.

Lewis, Bradley. 2013. "A Mad Fight: Psychiatry and Disability Activism." In *The Disability Studies Reader*, 4th ed., edited by Lennard J. Davis, 115–131. New York: Routledge.

Lucas, Craig, and Adam Guettel. 2007. *The Light in the Piazza*. New York: Theatre Communications Group.

MacPherson, Ben. 2012. "A Voice and So Much More (or When Bodies Say Things That Words Cannot)." *Studies in Musical Theatre* 6 (1): 43–57.

O'Neill, Eugene. 2002. *Long Day's Journey into Night*. New Haven, CT: Yale University Press.

Préher, Gérald. 2009. "A Southern Belle in an Italian Setting: Elizabeth Spencer's *The Light in the Piazza* and Its Musical Adaptation." *South Atlantic Review* 74 (2): 20–36.

Seidel, Kathryn Lee. 1997. "Madonna of the Marketplace: Art and Economics in Elizabeth Spencer's *The Light in the Piazza*." *Southern Quarterly* 35: 16–22.

Sternfeld, Jessica. 2006. *The Megamusical*. Bloomington: Indiana University Press.

Wallin, Scott. 2013. "*Next to Normal* and the Persistence of Pathology in Performances of Psychosocial Disability." *Disability Studies Quarterly* 33 (1). http://dsq-sds.org/article/view/3428/3202.

CHAPTER 39

"PITIFUL CREATURE OF DARKNESS"

The Subhuman and the Superhuman in The Phantom of the Opera

JESSICA STERNFELD

MEGAMUSICALS tackle grand, seemingly universal issues. The term "megamusical" began to circulate in the 1980s, when Andrew Lloyd Webber's several record-breaking hits had an enormous impact on the culture of Broadway, and although the term implied derision by many critics who found these musicals overblown and annoying, for scholars it (usually) simply describes a genre focused on bigness. The stories told in *Cats, The Phantom of the Opera, Les Misérables, Miss Saigon, Wicked, Ragtime, Chess, Jekyll and Hyde*, and *Aida*, to name a few megamusicals, might sweep generations or might focus on a handful of characters involved in personal conflicts. But either way, the presentation of their circumstances features at least some elements of grandness: complicated, mobile, spectacular sets; a sung-through opera-like score delivered with big voices; a dramatic or tragic plot full of noble, pitiable victims of political circumstance. The genre therefore seems an unlikely one in which to explore the personal and social implications of disability, and yet many of these stories do just that. Like virtually every musical—or movie, television series, novel, play, ballet, or other narrative art form—these shows feature an Other, an outsider who must eventually be welcomed into the community or be banned from it. If the Other is our main heroic character, the most likely outcome is a noble, tragic death; cheerful acceptance is more likely in a musical comedy, not a megamusical. This tear-jerking death is meant to teach the community (and the audience) a lesson about understanding and acceptance, without actually demonstrating the acceptance that would allow the character to become a member of the community. Elphaba in *Wicked* is misunderstood by her community thanks to her green skin (her race? her disability?) and eventually embraces her outsider status, taking on a new identity and disappearing. Aida and Radames, in *Aida*, choose death rather than separate lives divided by politics (which is a stand-in for racism). Coalhouse Walker sacrifices himself in the name of racial tolerance in *Ragtime*. In other words, these grand musicals, some with dazzling sets, others with huge production numbers and lofty messages about humanity, nevertheless intend to teach lessons about what it means to be outside the community.

And a remarkable number of them feature an outsider with a disability or a disfigurement. How does the megamusical deal with a disabled hero or villain? Some send clear messages of sympathy, painting the disability as noble and admirable, while nevertheless excluding the disabled character; others allow the character to heal and reintegrate, in a rather too neat narrative of overcoming; still others both romanticize the disability as a demonstration of the character's inherent goodness while simultaneously fetishizing the disability, tantalizing the audience with its features. This chapter focuses on *The Phantom of the Opera*, the megamusical that perhaps most boldly faces the idea of disability head-on, as it stars a character whose face, as one journalist described it, looks "like melted cheese" (Smith, 1995). The musical's approach to the Phantom's disability is remarkably layered and inconsistent; the Phantom is portrayed in numerous ways (monster, criminal, genius, god, ghost) and his physical disability blurs regularly with his "soul," which is where numerous characters locate the origin of his problems. His face and its famous mask covering are both feared and thrilled over, but with a reassuring dose of pity that allows the audience to feel comfortable leaning forward to catch a glimpse. How, in the supposedly more enlightened culture of the 1980s (and today, as the show continues to thrive), can we justify what is, at base, a modern version of a circus freak show? And how does the musical shield the audience from feeling that it is? The musical's atmosphere, style, music, and lyrics create such a seductive sense of romance and tragic inevitability—cushioned with an extra layer of "historical" distance—that the discomfort we should feel is swept away by megamusical momentum.

The Phantom's Story

The Phantom of the Opera, Broadway's current longest-running musical, opened in 1988. It had already been a massive success in London in 1986, becoming Andrew Lloyd Webber's fourth major international megamusical hit, after *Jesus Christ Superstar* (1971, something of an accidental hit by a very young composer and his lyricist partner Tim Rice), *Evita* (1979, also with Rice), and *Cats* (1982, with a libretto provided by poet T.S. Eliot's collection from 1939). Lloyd Webber and Rice's *Joseph and the Amazing Technicolor Dreamcoat* (Broadway 1982, although originally written for children in a fifteen-minute version in 1968) is far too humble and comedic to be a megamusical, and his *Starlight Express* (Broadway 1987) is the rare example of a megamusical flop. It was after the failure of *Starlight Express* in New York (it ran far longer in London) that Lloyd Webber turned his attention to the mysterious figure who lives in the basement of the Paris Opéra. He teamed with librettist and co-bookwriter Richard Stilgoe (there are a few lyrics by Charles Hart as well), and the influential director Harold Prince, whose vision greatly shaped the show.

The audience is meant to see the story of the Phantom through Raoul's eyes, although many critics have noted that Raoul remains a rather two-dimensional character, manly and earnest and bland. He is the suitor of our heroine, young Christine, and therefore caught in a love triangle with the Phantom. Instead of feeling as if we are journeying into this strange world as Raoul's ally, the story makes it much easier to relate either to Christine, to whom odd things are already happening when we meet her (she may be mentally unstable, even hysterical), or to the Phantom, who manages to be sympathetic despite being a cruel kidnapper and murderer. Nevertheless, the tale is framed by Raoul, and opens in the "future," with an aged Raoul at an auction of the Paris Opéra in 1905, setting up the story for us. He sees the Phantom's music box featuring a toy monkey playing the cymbals, as well as the chandelier that so famously falls to the ground during the show. When the dilapidated chandelier springs to life and the overture begins, we flash back to the present of 1861, where we remain for the rest of the story. Aged Raoul never returns to reframe the show. He also never fully understands the Phantom, despite learning about the man's life and challenges, and he remains the Phantom's adversary (although an ineffectual one) throughout, whereas both Christine and the audience come to feel for him.

In Gaston Leroux's original 1911 novel, the Phantom (whose name is Erik) was born with a disfigured face, and although many popular movie versions changed this circumstance to later traumas like having acid thrown in his face, Lloyd Webber's Phantom was also born with his disability. His Phantom, like Leroux's, is also naturally—indeed, the musical suggests, supernaturally—brilliant, and is a composer, architect, magician, and mastermind of many schemes and feats. He is also angry, cruel, socially maladjusted, and eventually murderous. He has failed to integrate into society, and the story suggests that this is mostly or even entirely society's fault; the community having shunned him, he has learned no other way to deal with people than to scare, manipulate, kidnap, and kill them. Film scholar Martin Norden would label this character an Obsessive Avenger type; referring mostly to early films, among them Lon Chaney's version of *The Phantom of the Opera*, he describes the Obsessive Avenger in terms easily applied to Lloyd Webber's Phantom: "an egomaniacal sort, almost always an adult male, who does not rest until he has had his revenge on those he holds responsible for his disablement and/or violating his moral code in some other way" (Norden 1994, 52). Thus, this Phantom terrorizes the community and kills two annoying secondary characters who dare to doubt or defy him. He has taken up residence in the underground lair of the Paris opera house, where there are (in fact actually) cavernous spaces, rivers, and metal grates. There he becomes obsessed with young opera singer Christine Daaé, whom he coaches for some time without actually revealing himself to her; he uses tricks, like optical illusions and throwing his voice, to come to her as if he were a phantom or angel.

As I have noted elsewhere, the story can be thought of as a take on a beauty and the beast tale; a frightening-looking monster-like man tries to win the love of a beautiful girl, in inappropriate ways because he knows no other. Eventually in such a tale, either the girl kisses the beast and gets a prince, or he sacrifices himself so that she may have a normal life with a man who looks and behaves normally. In this instance, there is both the kiss and the sacrifice, the Phantom never becoming a prince but instead a martyr, so that Christine and Raoul can have a normal above-ground life (Sternfeld 2006, 227). Like countless "beast" figures before and after him, the Phantom chooses death (if a symbolic one) rather than any attempted assimilation, relieving both himself and his community of the pressure to accept him and instead nobly removing himself from the conflict.

The Phantom's story—or that of any "beast" and his beauty—can be read through the lens of identity studies, with the Other being differentiated by race, culture, class, disability, or any number of other identities that do not fit in with the story's community. But using disability as the driving conflict of the plot is actually more pervasive than spectators, or even scholars in identity studies, might realize; in their study *Narrative Prosthesis*, David Mitchell and Sharon Snyder argue for the "primacy of disability as narrative prosthesis in representational discourses" (2000, 29). While a few classic examples—Richard III, Tiny Tim, Ahab—might spring to mind, Mitchell and Snyder find that many hundreds of authors in various cultures employ the tool of the different body as a catalyst for their plots. The entrance of someone who looks or acts differently can upset any community; Mitchell and Snyder note the "visceral potential in the disruption cased by the disabled body" that makes this sort of character a "primary tool for writers" (2000, 36).

Rosemarie Garland-Thomson frames the concept of Other versus community in slightly different terms, still using disability as her lens; she argues that a character, or a real person figuring in a narrative, can arrive at one of two outcomes: he or she can either be cured, or at least suggest hope for a cure; or he or she can die or be killed. American culture, she explains, rarely accepts disability as a satisfactory state of being. We prefer to strive for a cure, a solution, or we pity the "victim" of the disability with misguided compassion such that death becomes a viable option. Our rhetoric, even our laws such as the Americans with Disabilities Act of 1990, promote accommodation, but Garland-Thomson suggests that such laws do not reflect our cultural approach: "We agree to accommodate disability, but we prefer to eliminate it" (2004, 780). She calls this acceptance of killing the disabled body/person the "cultural logic of euthanasia." Held up in contrast to some undefined ideal of what a body should be, the "unfit" body offends American sensibilities of progress and perfection (781). While various subgroups of the disabled communities may simply ask for various accommodations, we offer instead a condescending "benevolence" (784) that implies we know better what's right for the "sufferer" and for society. The Phantom, then, will never be allowed into society; his death is, in fact, what is best for him and for the entire community, and it is presented as a transcendent, magical disappearance. Although the nature of this benevolence has changed since the 1911 novel, the result in the musical is the same, and just as satisfying to an unquestioning audience.

Literary scholar Lennard Davis goes one step further in his approach to this much-used narrative device, arguing that any story with an outsider who disrupts a community or who leaves his/her community can be fundamentally explained as a story about disability. Every story, no matter what category of identity studies may be invoked, is fundamentally about "normal/abnormal." We can call this the community and the Other, or the normal-bodied versus the disabled/disfigured, and so on. "This dialectic works in a fundamental way to produce plots," Davis explains. "Often a 'normal' character is made 'abnormal' by circumstance" (Davis 1998, 329). The community surrounding this abnormal character serves to teach the reader or the viewer what "normal" is, thus defining society and its expectations. The goal is to "cure" the story, make the society normal again; so the Other, the disabled character, must be eliminated or assimilated. Davis summarizes: "The narrative, at its end, is no longer disabled by its lack of conformity to imagined social norms" (331). Can there be any doubt that Christine will never take up residence in the Phantom's cold underground lair? That plot would not stand. All of these variations of how the narrative "must" work agree that Christine must love Raoul and that the Phantom must die.

The Phantom Face

When the story opens after the overture, we meet the company of the opera and discover that troubling things have been happening, which is news both to the opera's new patron Raoul, Vicomte de Changy, and the new owner/managers, Monsieur André and Monsieur Firmin. Some of the company dismisses the strange events as a prank, but Madame Giry, the ballet mistress, knows the entire story, although it takes her most of the musical to reveal it: there is not a ghost but indeed a man—a powerful and magical man who terrifies her—living in the underground lair and controlling the opera's productions through threats and tricks. Her mysterious belief in the man she insists on calling the Phantom or "Opera Ghost" has spread to the ballet corps, a twittering group of young girls, among them her daughter Meg. Over the course of the first act, the rest of the group—Raoul, the managers, the diva Carlotta—come to understand there is indeed someone down there, as he can make himself heard throughout the house and sends letters with demands about casting, but they remain steadfast in their view that he is neither magical nor harmful. They have no idea what he looks like. At the end of the first act, when it is revealed that he has killed the stagehand Buquet and has sent the chandelier crashing to the stage floor at Christine's feet, the group can no longer deny the fact that this man may be more than man; he has powers they can't explain. When he kills again in the second act (eliminating the tenor Piangi so that he may take over the man's role as a lascivious and masked Don Juan in the opera *Don Juan Triumphant*, which he himself has composed), then kidnaps Christine (again), the company becomes a hunting party and tracks him down.

Madame Giry's role in the portrayal of the Phantom to the others is crucial and quite odd, because she is the only one who knew him before his current life in the opera house, yet she is the most adamant that he is a ghost or a magical creature, to be both feared and worshipped. It is she who delivers notes from the Opera Ghost, and when Christine shows off her newly improved vocal talent for the new managers, Madame Giry praises her as if Christine has offered up a prayer to God: "Yes, you did well. He will be pleased."[1]

The Phantom's face, normally hidden behind the famous diagonally-cut half-mask, is revealed only twice. In the first act, the Phantom has lured Christine from her dressing room to his lair, pulling her via a magic trick through her full-length mirror and down many ramps to his gondola, which he rows into his home. She pulls the mask from his face when she is down there alone with him, but the audience does not see it. His mask covers the right side of his face, which is angled upstage. This delay is tantalizing; the audience is primed now to see what's beneath that mask, thanks to Christine's reaction of shock and the Phantom's surprisingly violent and angry response to her fear. In the second act, when she comes to understand that it is he with whom she is performing in *Don Juan Triumphant*, she pulls the mask off again, revealing his face to both the opera company and the audience. Finally, then, his face is revealed, and it remains uncovered in the final scene down in his lair. Lloyd Webber and his team calculated this reveal for maximum effect, since despite a liberal amount of make-up, it would not be easy to see the Phantom's face beyond the first few rows. Unlike in film versions, when the Phantom's terrifying face can fill the screen, there had to be a way to convey horror and shock from a distance. Thus, the reveal occurs in front of the entire cast, and their reaction—screaming, gasping, running away—indicates to the audience that we should react similarly. (Incidentally, the 2004 film version goes in the opposite direction, giving the Phantom not much more than a rakish scar and coloring the entire musical with far more sex appeal and less terror.)

At the second unmasking, the audience can finally inspect the mysterious long-hidden disfigurement; we find deep gouges in the right side of the Phantom's face, in his cheek and temple. His lips on that side are too big, as if covered in swollen sores or tumors. He has streaks like exaggerated veins emerging from his hairline down his right temple. His right eye is a too-pale ice blue. He has a large three-dimensional crater on the right side of his skull, normally covered not by the mask but by a hairpiece attached to it. (To add insult to injury, as it were, when his face is revealed to the audience his hair comes with it, revealing that he is mostly bald, with unhealthy-looking wisps of hair stuck tentatively to his scalp.) Without his mask, the elegant ghostly genius becomes the monster.

Freak and Prodigy, Subhuman and Superhuman

At the moment of this long-awaited second reveal that finally shows the audience the Phantom's face, the Phantom grabs Christine and disappears, and the rest of the cast instantly becomes a posse. This tense juncture is the inconvenient moment Raoul chooses finally to learn something about his enemy, frantically questioning Madame Giry in an exchange that is crucial for the purposes of understanding the Phantom's disability but happens so quickly and so chaotically in the production that it largely goes unnoticed or unremembered; this sequence is spoken, not sung, thus rendering it less important than the rest of the material in the nearly all-sung show, and it does not appear on the original cast recording, so the many, many fans at home are largely unfamiliar with this information as well. The scene which could have finally explained who this man is gets such a quick, scattered treatment that it barely sinks in, and his confusing status as monster or god remains unclear. But the scene reveals his true nature. Raoul demands information from Madame Giry, in case it might help him and his team of avengers "track down this murderer," as they all chant. She finally fills him in.

GIRY: Very well. It was years ago. There was a travelling fair in the city. Tumblers, conjurors, human oddities . . .
R: Go on.
GIRY (*trance-like as she retraces the past*): And there was . . . I shall never forget him: a man . . . locked in a cage . . .
R: In a *cage*?
GIRY: A prodigy, monsieur! Scholar, architect, musician . . .
R (*piecing together the jigsaw*): A composer.
GIRY: And an inventor, too, monsieur. They boasted he had once built for the Shah of Persia, a maze of mirrors.
RAOUL (*mystified and impatient, cuts in*): Who *was* this man?
GIRY (*with a shudder*): A freak of nature . . . more monster than man . . .
RAOUL (*a murmur*): Deformed?
GIRY: From birth, it seemed.
RAOUL: My God.
GIRY: And then . . . he went missing. He escaped.

Raoul understands from this exchange that the enemy below is this former freak show attraction, one of the "human oddities" in a fair. He expresses his one moment of potential pity for the Phantom when he reacts in shock to Madame Giry's statement that the man was locked in a cage. But seconds later—and understandably, since this man, however pitiful, has killed two men and kidnapped his fiancée—he runs boldly into the lair, ready to fight.

This exchange also ties together two concepts that used to be linked, but are no longer often thought of as related: the prodigy and the freak. As Leonard Cassuto points out, it was only a few hundred years ago that "prodigy" was a term tied to anything inexplicable: "The category of 'prodigy' dates from the early modern period, when it encompassed 'monstrous' births and people with odd bodies (the 'freaks' of later generations) along with then-inexplicable natural phenomena such as earthquakes and comets" (Cassuto 2002, 126–127; see also Straus 2011, 125). Thus a child with a deformity and a child with a seemingly magical talent for, say, music, would both have been called prodigies due to their otherworldly qualities. In the Phantom, we find both the prodigy, in his remarkable proficiency at a dizzying range of skills, and the freak, not only because of his deformity but because he was *actually* a member of a freak show.

From this rather throwaway exchange between Madame Giry and Raoul, then, we know that the Phantom had been a player in a freak show, though it's unclear whether this was by choice or due to lack of any other options at the time. Along the way he has, either by natural gift or much study, mastered all sorts of scholarly and magical skills. This revelation about his origins opens up a new lens through which to view the entire musical: while it is neatly read as an Other versus community story using various models of the disability analogy as mentioned earlier, it can also be read very simply as a freak show, a very specific kind of Other-based scenario. The audience is there to see the intriguing, grotesque, frightening Phantom, just as spectators went to see side shows and other novelty displays or performances in many different times and cultures. Garland-Thomson explains that the "differently formed body" draws the eye, and has done so since the earliest recorded human history; not only does it make us curious but also it invites explanation. The unusual body is "always an interpretive occasion" (Garland-Thomson 1996, 1).[2] Whether the explanation is religious, social, or medical, any given culture will use the mystery of the unusual body as a place to locate anxieties and questions. Robert Bogdan notes that people who performed in freak shows were given elaborate back stories, and a recurring character type was the "aggrandized" freak, who had a back story boasting that he or she was "highly educated, spoke many languages, and had aristocratic hobbies such as writing poetry or painting" (Bodgan, 1996, 29)—or architecture, magic, and composition, like the Phantom. Clearly Gaston Leroux, even if not immersed in the American culture that so readily embraced the freak show, was aware of this imagery and used it to build his Phantom's back story.

The freak show largely died out in this country about a hundred years ago; why, then, does this modern musical still lure spectators? Why would a supposedly enlightened society, willing to accept accommodations and equality for the disabled, still thrill at the sight of a man with an unusual head? Because the freak show did not actually end, it morphed into other forms of entertainment. Today, the freak show is couched in the guise of education, pity, and acceptance, but remains a way for people to stare at what's unusual. Andrea Stulman Dennett argues that the freak show, especially the attraction known as the dime museum, has been resurrected in the modern television talk show. The dime museum featured a host, or "lecturer," who would offer up the players' back stories, in a sheen of being educational; ostensibly, the spectators were there to learn about the freaks' conditions, and the dime museums even employed "doctors," but the real draw was simply to have a justifiable opportunity to stare. The parallels to talk shows abound, especially with recurring subjects like taboo couples (ones with radical age differences or body types, especially), unusual sexual habits, or noticeable bodies (tattoos and piercings in the dime museum days; often obese people today) (Dennett, 1996; see also Hughes 2012). Writing in 1996, Dennett had not yet seen—but certainly hinted at—the onslaught of freak-show-like television programs far beyond what appears on talk shows. Now, there are entire networks such as The Learning Channel and Discovery Fit & Health devoted to seemingly educational programming that offer us the chance to see graphic displays of injuries in emergency rooms, obese people and their weight-loss surgeries, people with dwarfism, people plagued by the psychological disorder of hoarding (with lingering camera shots of every filthy corner of their homes), people addicted to freak-like habits such as eating metal or detergent, and conjoined twins, among other "freaks," all stories narrated by authoritative voices "teaching" viewers about their conditions and featuring scenes with doctors or therapists attempting to treat or cure. Perhaps the most blatantly freak-show-like title on the air must be: "The Man with the 132-lb. Scrotum."

In other words, the freak show lives on, and despite the great strides made in our society to accept those with disabilities, the urge to stare at the unusual remains strong; in fact it may even be growing, thanks to current television programming (not to mention the Internet and all it can display). It's certainly possible that those who are exposed to these unusual bodies may in fact become more tolerant, and understand that acceptance (as opposed to kill or cure) is a viable option, but the urge to display and the urge to look go unchecked. It's no wonder, then, that when Christine rips off the Phantom's mask, the audience leans forward in expectation; the music is lovely, the voices soar, the sets are remarkable, but this is what we came to see.

When Christine removes his mask in Act One, he rounds on her, singing in a loud, frantic line, "Is this what you wanted to see?" He suggests, as he repeats "Damn you! Curse you!" that her action has doomed her forever, that by seeing his face, she now belongs to a small and unhappy club. "Now you cannot ever be free," he scolds. He is certainly not wrong to be furious; she invaded his privacy and ignored his obvious desire to hide his face, taking from him any sense of agency or safety he had. But he pivots his very brief loss of self-determination into a power play, wresting the control back. He next sings a section of the score called "Stranger Than You Dreamt It," in which his quick, hot anger becomes a sarcastic, controlled, and superior tone. Over music that steps quietly and carefully from beat to beat, he needles her, revealing how he feels about himself, or perhaps how he has been taught to feel about himself based on the reactions of previous viewers of his face.

> Stranger than you dreamt it.
> Can you even dare too look
> or bear to think of me?
> This loathsome gargoyle, who
> burns in hell, but secretly
> yearns for heaven,
> secretly . . .
> secretly . . .
>
> But, Christine,
> Fear can turn to love.
> You'll learn to see, to
> find the man behind the monster, this
> repulsive carcass who
> seems a beast but secretly
> dreams of beauty,
> secretly . . .
> secretly . . .

He calls himself an impressive host of cruel names—loathsome gargoyle, monster, repulsive carcass—but also reveals that he yearns for heaven and dreams of beauty. Most tellingly, he suggests that she could learn to love him, through the surely unhealthy notion that her fear could become love, coupled with the much more socially aware notion that she might learn to know the man without being put off by his appearance.

This notion, that she might love him and become his lover, is touched on many times throughout the show. Despite his mastery of many skills, and his ability to terrify everyone in the opera house, romance is clearly far beyond his understanding. It was director Hal Prince who emphasized the sexual—not just the romantic—angle of the Phantom's struggle. He felt that sex was largely missing from the score and set out to infuse it in several ways, especially visually and in terms of the actors' interpretations of the material. Around the time he began working on the production, he had seen a documentary about the daily lives of disabled people, including their sex lives. He wove a thread through the show highlighting the Phantom's longing for sexual connection, and emphasized the eroticism in many visual ways including lush fabrics, numerous candles and dark areas, and especially the proscenium arch. "If you look carefully," he pointed out, you will realize that the sculpted arch framing the stage is a strange collection of tangled partial bodies (which can be read as disabled or disfigured, limbs missing, faces distorted) that are "in various stages of ecstasy" (Nightingale, 1988). Prince's choice to sexualize the whole production, especially the Phantom, was an oddly groundbreaking move in a show that otherwise rests on old-fashioned and distasteful notions about the disabled. Often, disabled people are portrayed as asexual, unable or uninterested in sex, undesirable to others; but the Phantom is sexy, seductive, very desirable, as is the lush velvet-draped and fog-filled world he creates. The Phantom's sexual side is a front, though; Christine quickly sees the desperation and naïveté beneath.

Christine tries to explain the conflict to Raoul—the conflict between the Phantom's gruesome exterior and his pathetic lovelorn personality—after she has seen the Phantom's face and is recounting the experience to Raoul. "Raoul, I've seen him!" she insists. "So distorted, deformed, it was hardly a face." But she goes on to explain the contradiction: "Yet in his eyes, all the sadness of the world. / Those pleading eyes, that both threaten and adore." Raoul, steadfastly refusing to believe this vision can be real, insists it was a dream and that there is no Phantom; the suggestion here is that Christine herself is suffering from some sort of madness.

The melody that sets this couplet about his eyes, demonstrating Christine's understanding of the Phantom's sadness and desperation for human contact, will recur in the climactic scene, just before she shocks him, Raoul, and the audience by kissing the Phantom. The second couplet, calm and tonal and ending in a tidy major-key resolution, perhaps explains best the Phantom's true disability: "This haunted face holds no horror for me now. / It's in your soul that the true distortion lies." See Track 39.1 on the Companion Website. 

Ultimately, then, his face becomes simply a distraction from—or more accurately a manifestation of—his evilness. Paul Longmore presented this concept and it has been taken up by many; he notes that the "association of disability with malevolence" has a long history in literature; he even mentions the Phantom of the Opera and other arts (2001, 2). Longmore explains that disabilities or deformities associated with "monster" characters are linked in the tales to their inherent evilness. He notes that "these visible traits express disfigurement of personality and deformity of the soul. Once again, disability may be represented as the cause of evil-doing, punishment for it, or both" (4–5). In the case of the Phantom, his disfigurement and its resulting social ramifications seem to have driven him to his evil acts, but somehow his face reflects his inner malevolence even if it predates that malevolence. Certainly Madame Giry and the others who know of him never separate his acts from his appearance.

Longmore goes on to propose that in many stories, disability is associated with a loss of some aspect of the character's humanity, which leads in turn to a loss of self-control and therefore a turn to violence—a perfect description of the Phantom's journey from disfigured loner to murderer. The Phantom reflects both the sympathetic and the monstrous representations of disability; he is clearly feared both for his appearance and his acts, but he is also eventually pitied because of the seemingly unavoidable life of criminal isolation imposed on him by an entirely unfeeling society. Jeffrey Weinstock notes that there is a distinction between the freak and the monster: freaks are one of us, fundamentally human despite their oddities; monsters are "superhuman or nonhuman" and much more removed from us (1996, 328). Weinstock notes that the line between the two is marked clearly by the threat of physical violence; a freak is a curiosity, but a monster will kill you. The Phantom of Leroux or of Lon Chaney lies squarely in the monster category, but in Lloyd Webber's musical, he visits both categories.

Thus the musical displays a confusing ambivalence about whether or not the Phantom is human. And if he is not, is he more than human, or less? The stage directions imply that this missing element of his humanness may be represented by literal cold-bloodedness. In the moment of transition between "Angel of Music" (when Christine begs to be visited by the spirit) and "The Phantom of the Opera" (when he complies, arrives, and carries her to his lair below), he appears in her dressing room mirror and grabs her arm to pull her through it. The stage directions inform us: "His touch is cold, and CHRISTINE gasps." Is he simply chilly from living in the basement? Or does he lack warm blood in his body, like a corpse, or a vampire, or other not-quite-human monster?

The Phantom is simultaneously superhuman (an angel, a god, a ghost, a genius) and subhuman (a monster, a remorseless killer, a half-dead creature). He is virtually never portrayed as a maladjusted human who happens to have a physical disability. In Anthony Burgess's novel *Napoleon Symphony*, a strange pseudobiographical novel of Napoleon with a structure based on the form of Beethoven's third symphony, many characters delight in colorfully describing Napoleon who, like the Phantom, is sometimes seen as all powerful, other times seen as a freak or animal or monster. Characters often compare Napoleon to a monkey, or even a toy monkey like the animated music box from the Phantom's lair, describing him as an animal and a machine. One speaker summarizes the view of Napoleon that echoes what *The Phantom of the Opera* proposes about the Phantom: "The subhuman and the superhuman are alike in that neither is human" (Burgess 1974, 224).

Fetishizing the Mask

During "The Music of the Night," the Phantom encourages Christine to make music—a euphemism if ever there was one—with him, and the song becomes something of an exercise in hypnosis. He embraces and caresses her, and she appears to be dazed but calm. The stage directions remind us of his literal coldness: "During all this, the PHANTOM has conditioned CHRISTINE to the coldness of his touch and her fingers are brave enough to stray to his mask and caress it, with no hint of removing it."

By having Christine caress his mask in a way that shows comfort, affection, or romantic attraction, the Phantom seems to be doing more than just teaching her to get used to it. He seduces her in "The Music of the Night," with his lush melody, his seductive words ("Touch me, trust me, / savour each sensation"), and his caresses, and by encouraging her to touch his mask during these other seductions, he is teaching her to be attracted to the mask itself. In other words, he shows her how to fetishize the mask, how to make it part of their sexual encounter. One could interpret this as an example of the Phantom's alluring sexuality, but it may also be read as a demonstration of his twisted magical powers, coupled with his violent streak; she seems to be hypnotized, unwilling, even a victim of assault despite her calm demeanor. We get the sense that she has no choice but to obey him—she is drugged, not seduced. She develops a fascination for the mask, as much as, if not more than, her interest in the face that lies beneath it. This song is also the audience's first opportunity to get a good look at the Phantom, so we too become accustomed to his mask. Only she removes his mask; he never does, at least in view of anyone else, and the only other person ever to touch it is Meg, who finds it sitting abandoned on his throne in the final seconds of the show. In that closing scene, as the music moves toward its final cadence—using the unusual set of chords found at the end of "The Music of the Night," the song in which we all learned to feel attracted to the mask—Meg holds it up and a spotlight slowly narrows on it. The rest of the stage becomes invisible, and only a tiny pinpoint spotlight remains, causing the mask to glow in magical midair. The mask, therefore, has become its own character, one that is sexy, alluring, mysterious, coveted—fetishized.

It's certainly understandable that the musical features imagery that focuses on the mask, as it is the Phantom's most distinguishable characteristic and a central theme of the show. Masks in general, in fact, play a recurring role, especially in the second-act opener "Masquerade," which takes place at a masked ball and which dwells on the concept of how no one can see behind anyone's "mask" to know the person beneath. The Phantom appears, interrupting the end of this number, dressed himself in a masquerade costume: an entirely red ensemble with a sweeping cape, a large hat with a huge feather, and a full-face mask depicting a skull. In this alarming costume, he feels comfortable walking among the others, which he otherwise never does, except when on stage during his opera. The full mask and complicated costume cover every inch of his body, making him entirely unrecognizable and distancing himself from his usual look (formal tuxedo and white half-mask with attached slicked-back hair).

The marketing campaign for *The Phantom of the Opera* picked up on the recognizability and effectiveness of the mask image, using a version of the Phantom's white mask in its logo and marketing materials, making it an object so well-known that it could appear without words and be understood—a kind of fetish marketing. The mask in the logo is never worn by the Phantom but is a more typical masquerade-style mask, covering both eyes and the nose symmetrically. It resembles a comedy/tragedy theatrical mask more than the one the Phantom actually wears, which cuts from one temple diagonally across his face, including one eye (for which there is a hole) and most of his nose, and ending in a rounded point on the opposite lower jaw. Thus the marketing version of the mask, although iconic, actually erases the Phantom's asymmetrical disfigurement and suggests something more predictable and less frightening than his shockingly lopsided face.

Blaming Society for a Distorted Soul: The Final Confrontation and the Kiss

The Phantom's disabilities—internal and external—become the focus of the final scene in his lair, after Christine has removed his mask during *Don Juan Triumphant* and he has dragged her below once again. The Phantom himself is aware of the interpretation of his life proposed by this and many other monster stories, that his face and his crimes are somehow linked, that his face reflects his distorted soul. But he denies this link, in a harsh, dissonant melody borrowed from the music of his own opera:

> Why, you ask, was I bound and chained
> in this cold and dismal place?
> Not for any mortal sin,
> but the wickedness of my abhorrent face!

He screams this accusation at Christine, blaming her for society's mistreatment of him, denying that his own actions have had any role to play in his outsider status. His tirade continues and the music here perseverates, circular in melody, in a breathless meter of seven, one syllable per beat:

> Hounded out by everyone!
> Met with hatred everywhere!
> No kind word from anyone!
> No compassion anywhere!

Christine, angry and bitter for the only time in the entire musical, defends her honor, turning on him and demanding if his "lust for blood" (because he has killed his second victim) will become sexual assault. "Am I now to be prey to your lust for flesh?" she spits. His response reveals another layer to the effects of his disability, only hinted at before now; his "fate," which he equates with his disfigured face and which, he suggests, causes his violent behavior, has also caused him to have remained inexperienced in sexual matters—and, even before that, to have lost his mother's love.

> That fate, which condemns me to wallow in blood,
> has also denied me the joys of the flesh.
> This face, the infection which poisons our love,
> This face, which earned a mother's fear and loathing.
> A mask, my first unfeeling scrap of clothing.
> Pity comes too late –
> turn around and face your fate:
> an eternity of *this* before your eyes!

The implication is that his mother both rejected him and put the mask over his face at a young age, teaching him that he was to feel shame and to expect disgust from society. He plays to the sympathy he knows Christine likely feels, even if she is currently angry; in the middle of the stanza above, he pivots his melody from an angular, recitative-like line to a quotation from "The Music of the Night" on the line about his mother. Using his seduction song, he surely hopes to evoke pity that he can then transform into love. Here she offers up the crucial couplet, explaining that the "true distortion" is in his soul.

Raoul arrives to confront the Phantom, but is caught in his magical Punjab Lasso, which holds Raoul by the neck without its other end seeming to be connected to anything. He remains, as he has been throughout, largely useless in the battle with this enemy. Out of the trio comes Christine's revelation: that all the Phantom really needs is sympathy, human contact, understanding. Quoting the sweet, soothing melody, "Angel of Music," reminding us that in her eyes he is a fallen angel now, she approaches him:

> Pitiful creature of darkness,
> What kind of life have you known?
> God give me courage to show you
> You are not alone.

The stage directions in the libretto explain the all-important action she takes next: "Now calmly facing him, she kisses him long and full on the lips. The embrace lasts a long time, RAOUL watches in horror and wonder." In this instant, the Phantom is undone. He immediately gives up his fight to win Christine's love, his desire to hurt or kill Raoul, his role as the Opera Ghost, and everything else about his life. As soon as the crucial kiss ends, he urges, "Go now—go now and leave me!" freeing Raoul and shooing them both quickly out of his lair.

It seems, then, that this one act of kindness, the only he has ever experienced, destroys his life and reveals to him that Christine is too good for him—so good that he must do the noble thing, removing himself from this unhappy love triangle, and freeing her to be with Raoul. His anger that society has forced him to be alone becomes resignation that this isolation is the only option for him. He no longer imagines he can persuade her or woo her, nor anyone else. Instead, he quotes his anthem, with a twist—"It's over now, the music of the night"—then sits on his trick throne, wraps his cape around his entire body, and vanishes, never to be seen again by anyone at the opera. Having fought the notion throughout the story that death is the only option for a disabled, enfreaked, othered character, he resigns himself to this inevitability now and removes himself from the world.[3] As we have seen, narratives of disability so often end with tragic, noble deaths that the audience does not question that the disfigured character must suffer this fate; indeed, we admire him for realizing he has made the "right" choice and we weep pitiably as we also celebrate the relationship Christine can now have with Raoul. Disability once again becomes a death sentence.

Evilness of Face, Soul, . . . and Music

The Phantom has a distinctive compositional voice, provided by Lloyd Webber and made distinct from the rest of the music. His opera *Don Juan Triumphant* stands apart from the rest of the score in several ways, although many themes and melodic fragments of it do appear elsewhere in the score, both before and after the excerpts we hear from his opera. Despite the fact that the Phantom borrows music that exists only in the world of the musical (that is, nondiegetic themes that only we in the audience hear as music), he makes them largely unrecognizable in their new context. The main way in which he makes the material his own is through dissonance—in short, the Phantom's opera is very, very hard to sing. We see the cast attempting to rehearse a boisterous choral number, and they struggle mightily; the music director Reyer attempts to coach the tenor Piangi to sing the phrase "those who tangle with Don Juan" correctly, but the strange nature of the line (mostly based on a whole-tone scale) baffles Piangi, who fails to make large enough melodic leaps several times. "His way is better," snaps Carlotta. "At least he makes it sound like music!" Reyer cues Piangi for his next attempt, which reveals that this passage not only has a dissonant and unpredictable melody, but an unusual meter as well: "So, once again—after seven," says Reyer, counting in, "Five, six, seven." Carlotta notes that no one will know or care if the music is right or wrong, while Christine—who, not surprisingly, has an affinity for the Phantom's compositional style, or perhaps just a better ear than the others (thanks to her lessons with him?)—attempts to show Piangi the augmented fourth he's failing to complete. Chaos ensues, the chorus shouting and trying to practice, until Reyer bangs on the piano. At this point one of the Phantom's magic tricks kicks in: the piano plays by itself, with "great force and rhythm," as the stage directions note, and the cast freezes. Then they all begin to sing the music "robotically and accurately." Apparently the Phantom has cast some sort of hypnotic spell on them all, and they now simply know the music for reasons never explained. They deliver a homorhythmic but very dissonant, angular passage, previewing the theme of creepy seduction that will be revisited in the actual performance (see Tracks 39.2 and 39.3 on the Companion Website).

The fact that the music is clearly hard for the opera company points to several implications about the Phantom. The most superficial suggestion is simply that the Phantom is a modern, living composer, writing in the less functionally tonal language of the 1860s, when the company is mostly used to the classics. (Their earlier opera scenes, one from an imaginary Mozart-era opera and the other seemingly of the French grand opera tradition, are tonal, predictable, and catchy.) But the challenges in the music are surely also a result of the Phantom's peculiar mind; it doesn't sound like other contemporary music. His precocious genius combined with his mischievous enjoyment in watching the opera company suffer have inspired him to write for them what is nearly unsingable. We can argue one more reason even beyond the Phantom's conscious efforts to be difficult, though, and read his music as an inevitable manifestation of his disability. That is, he writes this way because of his social (more than his physical) dysfunction. L. Poundie Burstein has noted that the disabled composer Alkan wrote extremely challenging piano music: "The most notorious aspect of his music is its extraordinary demand for virtuosity" (Burstein 2006, 188).[4] Burstein cautions against linking the demands of the music with the disability of its creator, noting that this association is a much-repeated narrative rather than something that can ever be proven, but in the case of the Phantom, Lloyd Webber clearly intends to convey exactly this narrative. The Phantom's twisted mind, incapable of "normal" or comprehensible music, spits out this twisted, confusing, unpleasant, harsh, loud stuff instead.

Reassuring Distance

Christine calls the Phantom an angel, then a creature; this mysterious and fundamentally unknowable figure never truly becomes human or real to the audience. There are two reasons that this central character is ultimately an enigma: the first is that, as we have seen, he is so variously and changeably defined that we are never sure how to feel about him. He is monster and god, cold creature and angel, criminal and ghost. There is always something off with him, he is never normal, healthy, or human. The other reason that it's difficult to understand how to feel about this character is that he is virtually never alone on stage. He never sings what musical theatre scholars call an "I want" song, in which he expresses his goal and reveals his basic personality traits. (Interestingly, Mozart's Don Giovanni is likewise never alone, never self-reflective; he is always defined in response to those around him—a flirtatious servant girl, a resistant noblewoman—and is damned to hell for his monstrous but charming ways.) The first and last time the Phantom is alone on stage is in the final seconds of Act One, when he sings a small fragment of a verse in which he vows to retaliate against Christine (and everyone else) for daring to love another, while revealing his broken heart. This moment, like so much of the rest of this story, is confusing in terms of who or what this being is. He has overheard Christine and Raoul's love song and after they exit, comes out of hiding, crestfallen. "I gave you my music," he sings softly and pitifully, "made your song take wing. / And now, how you've repaid me. / Denied me and betrayed me." The audience gasps and sighs in sympathy. But instantly he becomes a criminal mastermind again, belting "You will curse the day you did not do / all that the Phantom asked of you!" If we have been moved by his sadness over losing his girl, then are we now meant to root for his scheme of vengeance? Are we happy when he almost kills Christine by throwing the chandelier down at her? Surely we can't support his violent actions, but we can be impressed by the cleverness with which he pulls them off—he is again, simultaneously, monster and ghost, but not a man, not a real or relatable person. Almost never do Lloyd Webber or Prince allow the Phantom to simply be a person with a disfigured face.

The distance between him and the audience, then, is built into the score and is a direct result of the story's ambiguity over what he is—that is, over how to interpret his disabilities. We struggle to see his face, we recoil when we do and are grateful for the distance between him and us. We justify his anger at society, but cannot condone the murders he commits. We pity him but never accept him, because even if we agree that society's rejection of him drove him to be as he is, his soul remains incurably distorted. Because of the distance that Lloyd Webber and Prince place between the Phantom and the audience—a distance created by the remote historical setting, the lush romanticism of the music and the visuals, Lloyd Webber's commitment to never allowing the Phantom a realistic moment of self-expression—we accept this interpretation of the Phantom as incurable and permanently ostracized. The musical never humanizes him, forcing him always to be a subhuman freak or a superhuman monster, and this status as nonhuman means that we become unwitting supporters of an entirely avoidable death. To Lloyd Webber, Prince, and the audience, his death is both inevitable and glorious, a cause for cathartic weeping rather than political outrage over a society's treatment of a disfigured and ill-treated man. He remains subhuman and superhuman, but not human, and not one of us.

Notes

1. This and all quotations of lyrics or dialogue from *The Phantom of the Opera* are taken from the complete libretto contained in Perry 1987, 140–167. I have taken the liberty of altering the punctuation of some of the lines, as the libretto in this book is often confusingly punctuated.
2. See also Garland-Thomson's book *Staring* (2009), in which she writes at length about why people stare: "we both crave and dread unpredictable sights" (19). She explains in a range of scenarios how staring becomes an interaction between starer and staree, which is certainly the case when Christine can finally clearly see (and stare at) the Phantom's face.

3. The Phantom has much in common with Grizabella from Lloyd Webber's earlier mega-musical hit, *Cats*. Like the Phantom, Grizabella is both deformed ("You see the corner of her eye twist like a crooked pin," sings an observer cat in "Grizabella the Glamour Cat") and an outcast from society. In her case, it is not just her appearance but her former life that makes her an Other; Eliot's poem implies she led a fast life in her youth ("She haunted many a low resort") and that her current scars are the price she paid. Like so many monsters in stories before her, the community simultaneously comes to know her and agrees to cast her out; she is "reborn" into the next of her nine cat lives. Her ending is meant to be uplifting (literally, as she is lifted to the Heaviside Layer, a kind of cat heaven or rebirthing center, on a floating tire) but can be read as quite harsh, since just moments after the community has taken the time to understand her and has chosen to embrace and honor her, they send her away.
4. See also Rodgers 2006, in which the author describes how Berlioz intentionally broke the rules of the symphony (especially in terms of form) to demonstrate that his artist-protagonist was mentally unbalanced.

References

Bogdan, Robert. 1996. "The Social Construction of Freaks." In *Freakery: Cultural Spectacles of the Extraordinary Body*, edited by Rosemarie Garland-Thomson, 23–37. New York and London: New York University Press.

Burgess, Anthony. 1974. *Napoleon Symphony: A Novel in Four Movements*. New York: Alfred A. Knopf.

Burstein, L. Poundie. 2006. "*Les chansons des fous*: On the Edge of Madness with Alkan." In *Sounding Off: Theorizing Disability in Music*, edited by Neil Lerner and Joseph N. Straus, 187–198. New York: Routledge.

Cassuto, Leonard. 2002. "Oliver Sacks and the Medical Case Narrative." In *Disability Studies: Enabling the Humanities*, edited by Sharon L. Snyder, Brenda Jo Brueggemann, and Rosemarie Garland-Thomson, 118–130. New York: Modern Language Association of America.

Davis, Lennard J. 1998. "Who Put the 'The' in 'the Novel'?: Identity Politics and Disability in Novel Studies." *NOVEL: A Forum on Fiction* 31 (3): 317–334.

Dennett, Andrea Stulman. 1996. "The Dime Museum Freak Show Reconfigured as Talk Show." In *Freakery: Cultural Spectacles of the Extraordinary Body*, edited by Rosemarie Garland-Thomson, 315–326. New York: New York University Press.

Garland-Thomson, Rosemarie, ed. 1996. *Freakery: Cultural Spectacles of the Extraordinary Body*. New York: New York University Press.

Garland-Thomson, Rosemarie. 2004. "The Cultural Logic of Euthanasia: 'Sad Fancyings' in Herman Melville's 'Bartleby.'" *American Literature* 76 (4): 777–806.

Garland-Thomson, Rosemarie. 2009. *Staring: How We Look*. New York: Oxford University Press.

Hughes, Amy. 2012. *Spectacles of Reform: Theater and Activism in Nineteenth-Century America*. Ann Arbor: University of Michigan Press.

Longmore, Paul K. 2001. "Screening Stereotypes: Images of Disabled People." In *Screening Disability: Essays on Cinema and Disability*, edited by Christopher R. Smit and Anthony Enns, 1–18. Lanham, MD: University Press of America.

Mitchell, David T., and Sharon L. Snyder. 2000. *Narrative Prosthesis: Disability and the Dependencies of Discourse.* Ann Arbor: University of Michigan Press.

Nightingale, Benedict. 1988. "Conjuring an Eerie World for the Phantom." *New York Times*, 24 January.

Norden, Martin F. 1994. *The Cinema of Isolation: A History of Physical Disability in the Movies.* New Brunswick, NJ: Rutgers University Press.

Perry, George. 1987. *The Complete Phantom of the Opera.* New York: Henry Holt.

Rodgers, Stephen. 2006. "Mental Illness and Musical Metaphor in the First Movement of Berlioz's *Symphonie fantastique*." In *Sounding Off: Theorizing Disability in Music*, edited by Neil Lerner and Joseph N. Straus, 235–256. New York: Routledge.

Smith, Dinitia. 1995. "The Chandelier That Earned $1.5 Billion." *New York Times*, 18 October.

Snyder, Sharon L., Brenda Jo Brueggemann, and Rosemarie Garland-Thomson, eds. 2002. *Disability Studies: Enabling the Humanities.* New York: Modern Language Association of America.

Sternfeld, Jessica. 2006. *The Megamusical.* Bloomington: Indiana University Press.

Straus, Joseph N. 2011. *Extraordinary Measures: Disability in Music.* New York: Oxford University Press.

Weinstock, Jeffrey A. 1996. "Freaks in Space: 'Extraterrestrialism' and 'Deep-Space Multiculturalism.'" In *Freakery: Cultural Spectacles of the Extraordinary Body*, edited by Rosemarie Garland-Thomson, 327–337. New York: New York University Press.

CHAPTER 40

"WAITIN' FOR THE LIGHT TO SHINE"

Musicals and Disability

RAYMOND KNAPP

Broadway and Difference

Plots in musicals often hinge on the reconciliation of seeming opposites, and typically resolve through a device I term the "marriage trope," in which the foregrounded union of the central couple brings dramatic focus to the potential for a larger community forged from difference. This plot device aligns particularly well with US American ideologies of inclusion, celebrating difference within a larger community that stands in for the "melting pot" of New York City and/or the United States as a whole.[1] Yet it also generates many paradoxes in practice, in part because the United States' ideologies of inclusion diverge markedly from its actual history regarding equality of rights and access. At every turn, in musicals as in real life, the normative mainstream has shown itself to be a bit "more equal" than whatever Others may be involved, no matter the attention paid to those Others in the materials and themes of musicals, and however often those Others are represented within the various constituencies of the musical, as creators, performers, and/or fans.

There are three main forces at work to privilege the mainstream perspective in musicals, with the first setting the terms for the other two. Because of the commercial context for musicals, their writers have tended to tread carefully regarding the expectations of an often conservative audience base, even as they have pushed at times to challenge basic assumptions or to appeal beyond their core fanbase. Because of this market-driven caution, gestures of inclusion that contradict mainstream sensibilities tend either to set up cautionary tales against precipitous societal change, or (as so often happens in the work of Oscar Hammerstein II) to be balanced by other elements that reaffirm whatever mainstream perspective is being challenged.[2] Second, as part of playing to their audience, musicals in the end must answer to some standard of believability regarding relationships between the mainstream and the marginalized Other, whatever fantasies of potential inclusion might be indulged along the way—a constriction that tends emphatically toward maintaining the status quo, at least "for now." And third, within the dynamic of any particular show, it is the mainstream that inevitably sets the terms and price of admission into the relevant community. Even though many who align with the Other's perspective might wish things otherwise, their own desire to belong tends to overwhelm longings for more fundamental change, and, owing to their consequent investment in the mainstream community, they may even be reassured by the conservative tendencies of musicals. After all, you don't rock the boat you're trying to climb into.

Commercial calculation, standards of believability, and the dynamics of assimilation have thus all reinforced the dominance of the mainstream in musicals, which have, as has long been observed, persistently favored heterosexual and white perspectives. Given the frequent thematic emphasis on race in musicals—especially as combined with their musical, verbal, and choreographic dependence on ethnically distinctive styles, and given the broadly winking presence of homosexuals in all aspects of musicals, from creation to performing to fandom—it seems paradoxical that the art form itself has remained so resolutely white and heterosexual in outlook. To be sure, change has occurred. There have been important shifts regarding what counts as "white" in both musicals and real life, as the category long ago began to include previously marginalized groups such as the Irish and Jews.[3] On Broadway, color-blind casting has helped open up performance opportunities (while also complicating the racial dynamic within shows, not always usefully), whereas the presence of homosexuals in musicals' various communities has become much less closeted, especially post Stonewall.[4] But these countercurrents do not (yet) truly threaten the mainstream, and this persistence suggests that the entrenched mainstream in musicals is actually *useful*, providing a foil for alternative perspectives and thus forming part of a dynamic that has sustained the genre through profound social and cultural changes across the twentieth century and into our own. Moreover, it is after all in the nature of genres to be conservative, as they represent the past, what has already been tried and proven. But if the musical, like *any* successful genre, is thus inherently conservative, many of its practitioners (and fans, despite market-based caution) are not. Inevitably, there has been and will continue to be friction.

But the friction arising from such paradoxes, and the resultant critical noise generated by that friction, also serve to cloak another less obvious aspect of the assumed mainstream for musicals. Perhaps too easily taken for granted, as "natural" to a genre as energetically active in all dimensions as the musical, is the fact that its mainstream has also always been understood to be *able*: "sound" in body and mind, and especially proficient regarding vocality and movement.[5] The innate conservatism of musicals is, in this rather offhand way, fundamentally exclusionary to the disabled. The paradoxes presented by disability in relation to musicals are thus of a somewhat different order than those regarding race and sexual orientation. On the face of it, musicals celebrate, through performance, physical abilities—principally, singing and dancing—that seem to represent aspects of the universally human but are denied in significant measure to many with disabilities.

Nevertheless, musicals' historical insistence on incorporating the marginalized into communities, both onstage and off-, has yielded important instances of disabled individuals figuring among the initially marginalized in musicals' plots, individuals who may or may not be accepted into the larger community.[6] Moreover, musicals have often enough, and even institutionally, been made a part of the lives of disabled populations, however unlikely this may seem to the uninitiated.

The rest of this essay focuses on two areas where disability has been, or has recently become, an important element in musicals. I first consider a handful of musicals in which disability has figured centrally in the plot: *Porgy and Bess*, *The Music Man*, *Tommy*, *Wicked*, and *Next to Normal*. Each of these, in a different way, reveals how disability can figure within the dynamics typical of musicals, whether as an instance of stigmatized difference, as the basis for overcoming or transcending difficulties, or as extensions to other common themes. I then discuss a number of revelatory instances of musical performance figuring in the lives of the deaf and hearing impaired, including the acclaimed film *Children of a Lesser God*, a production of *West Side Story* at MacMurray College and the Illinois School for the Deaf that mixed hearing and deaf performers, and the recent revival of *Big River*, as reconfigured by Deaf West Theatre; the latter will be a particular focus due both to its high-profile, if relatively brief, Broadway run in 2003 and its transformative integration of an expressive choreography based on signing into an existing musical.

Disability in Musicals

I begin my brief survey of how musicals incorporate issues of disability with *Porgy and Bess* (George Gershwin, DuBose Heyward, and Ira Gershwin, 1935), notwithstanding its being in many respects more an opera than a musical. That distinction matters, because opera, as aspirationally high-art musical theatre, tends toward abstraction in its dramatic modes, partly because of its emphasis on singing over all else and its dependence on a fairly large, traditional orchestra, but also in tacit deference to the often less well-developed acting and dancing skills of opera singers, especially those in the vocally demanding leading roles, and the traditional allowances made regarding their physical appearance. Thus, *Porgy and Bess* is not as dependent as most musicals on dance and spectacle, and, as an opera, is more consistently serious in tone than the vast majority of musicals. Both considerations offer support for its central treatment of impairment, presenting its male protagonist as (in the language of the time) a crippled beggar who gets around in a goat cart that he maneuvers with arms powerful enough to prevail in mortal, hand-to-hand combat over the able-bodied thug, Crown. The opera strategically situates Porgy's impairment in relation to the racial issues with which it is concerned more basically, since Porgy's condition serves as a direct analogue of the situation, vis-à-vis the white mainstream, of the African American community that he belongs to. Thus, he is disabled but with a compensating strength, whereas the blacks on Catfish Row are poor and uneducated, but innately musical, the latter asserted through the fact that they almost always sing, while the few whites who appear along the way never do. This mapping extends out at least one layer, since innate musicality is itself a stereotype of African Americans more broadly, and is (usually implicitly) seen as compensation for their being disadvantaged in many other ways.[7]

Porgy and Bess, notwithstanding its breakthrough status in promoting African American performers in mainstream venues, has endured a checkered critical reception owing in part to this kind of mapping, in which Porgy's impairment—not to mention Bess's drug addiction and promiscuity, Crown's brutality, and Sportin' Life's drug-disposing version of Zip Coon—is inferentially emblematic of some dimension of black culture, especially troubling for the opera's critics because of the origin of such archetypes in its white authorship.[8] Yet, three other dimensions of this mapping register as at least as important in the present context. First, disability functions in *Porgy and Bess* as a direct parallel to other kinds of marginalization frequently treated in musicals, here allowing additional significance to accrue to Porgy's capacity to integrate with the larger community, his success in wooing Bess, and his ability to secure for her a place within his community, all of which not only enhances his position within the drama, but also serves as a harbinger for black culture more generally in relation to the white mainstream. Second, largely *because* of the dramatic parallel between Porgy's disability and his race—however problematic that might be in terms of racial representation—his disability is treated with a great deal of sympathy and is decidedly *not* emblematic of a weakness in character; *Porgy and Bess* thus avoids pernicious stereotypes of dramatic representations of disability that have continued to be indulged in other shows, such as *Phantom of the Opera* and *Wicked* (see below).[9] And, third, it is *not* specifically through music that his impairment is made to tell within the drama. Music in *Porgy and Bess* has a more basic role to play, since, in revealing Porgy's soul, it validates him as a human being both within his community and in broader cultural terms, exemplifying an operatic trope associated especially with Richard Wagner's operatic work, which provided Gershwin with one of his central models.[10]

The latter dimension is, notably, more of an issue in musicals than in opera: in musicals, which intersperse musical numbers and dialogue, if something is to count dramatically, it must usually have a musical presence, ideally one that carries the appropriate charge. Productions of *Porgy and Bess* can choose to downgrade Porgy's incapacity without significantly undermining the drama, because, however much it might matter in other ways, it simply doesn't matter in musical terms; thus, recent high-profile mountings of the show have done away with the goat cart in favor of crutches or a cane.[11] Race in *Porgy and Bess*, on the other hand, is made to matter *especially* in musical terms, just as it is in *Show Boat* (Jerome Kern and Hammerstein, 1927), where the black heritage of Julie, the tragic mulatta figure who passes for white at the beginning of the show, is signaled first and most importantly through the faux-blues number she sings to Magnolia, "Can't Help Lovin' Dat Man." And, in *The Music Man* (Meredith Willson, 1957), Winthrop's ability to overcome both his sadness and his embarrassment regarding his lisp is signaled, crucially, by his lisping through a verse of "The Wells Fargo Wagon," which leads Marian Paroo, his older sister, to decide *not* to expose Harold Hill—the "music man"—as a fraud. Moreover, this connection is later reinforced by Winthrop's reprise of "Gary, Indiana," which explicitly recalls the basis for his sister's planned exposure of Hill, who has lied in claiming to have graduated from Gary Conservatory.[12]

But this critical musical embodiment of disability in *The Music Man* was originally not part of the show's design, since Winthrop's disability was until late in the planning to have been "spasticity" (now clinically described as "upper motor neuron syndrome"), a condition that would in the original conception have required him to use a wheelchair. Willson's investment in this dimension of the story was considerable. Although he admitted later that the "spastic boy" was "not exactly a character you would normally select for a musical comedy," he "badly . . . wanted to tell on a stage that spastics are muscularly retarded, not mentally," and so long resisted suggestions that he remove this element from the show; moreover, his usually unsung collaborator on the show's book, Franklin Lacey, because he had had experience teaching children with upper motor neuron syndrome (spasticity), was also invested in this element of the plot (Willson 1959, 28 and 48). But since nearly everyone else involved in the project was against the idea, when Willson decided to have an originally anonymous lisping boy sing a verse of "Wells Fargo Wagon," the substitution of the lesser disability for spasticity seemed propitious. Willson took a rain check on his ambition to bring a "spastic boy" to the stage, which he never redeemed.[13]

The substitution has several consequences concerning the representation of disability. First, perhaps most importantly, it allowed Willson to give the impairment a palpable musical presence.[14] Second, however, it drastically downgraded the scale of Winthrop's disability, and hence diminished the educational point of the exercise. Third, in compensation for scaling back the disability, the change helped broaden its empathetic basis, folding it back into the developmental story of the boy, whose lisp seems initially submerged within his lingering grief over his father's death. And fourth, the substitution demonstrates how disabilities often function within an important dimension of musicals, which mainly trade in setting up solvable problems, as a strategy for achieving believable happy endings. With regard to lisping, however, *The Music Man* presents an anomaly: an eminently solvable problem that the musical makes no effort to solve. While this may seem odd, it isn't; the show understands Winthrop's real problem to be his withdrawal following the loss of his father, from which he has not recovered. Music solves the problem of Winthrop's withdrawal (as it does every other problem in the show), and, for good measure, Harold Hill, especially through his attachment to Winthrop's sister Marian, takes care of the father issue. The lingering effect of the discarded "spastic boy" is that the lisp itself is implicitly regarded as an irreversible condition (as most cases of upper motor neuron syndrome are), in order to focus on the inhibiting and stigmatizing effects of disability, instead. But this, too, has an odd paradox attached, since, from the beginning, the lisping verse of "Wells Fargo Wagon" was meant to be cute: the boy's excitement makes him forget his lisp, freeing the audience to find a specifically musical pleasure, however dubious, that it could never have found with the "spastic boy" option.

Tommy, like *Porgy and Bess*, operates somewhat outside the typical ways in which musicals work; yet, like *The Music Man*, it maintains a significant focus on the isolation of a young boy with a disability and uses music as a means to make the trajectory of that isolation dramatically vital. *Tommy* first appeared as a concept album by *The Who* in 1969—the first album to be billed as a "rock opera," a year before *Jesus Christ Superstar*. It was then staged as an opera in 1970 with only modest success, became an eccentric film in 1975 (dir. Ken Russell), and was eventually reworked as a stage musical in 1992, moving to Broadway the following year for what became a two-year run. In all versions, Tommy becomes "deaf, dumb, and blind" following a childhood trauma, although the precise circumstances vary somewhat. In the musical, he is a witness when his father, presumed dead when he does not come back after World War II, returns home unannounced and kills his mother's lover; in the film, although situationally similar, Tommy's mother has already remarried, and it is Tommy's father who dies in the confrontation. Presumptively, in all versions, Tommy's impairments are to some extent self-imposed, or derive from his mental trauma, since in becoming a blind deaf-mute he is literally following the admonition of his mother and father/step-father, who exhort him in "What about the Boy?," first separately, then both at once: "You didn't hear it, you didn't see it! / You won't say nothin' to no one, / Ever in your life. / You never heard it."

The fact that so much of *Tommy* is narrated musically (stemming from its origins as a rock album) is a dramatic liability, at least for a musical. But the resulting nearly continuous barrage of often bombastic rock music, as combined with the haunting image of a blind, deaf-mute child—the situation throughout much of the first act—in itself justifies the transfer from album to stage, since it makes the tragic isolation of the boy palpable in a way the album could not. Moreover, this combination also enhances our sense of his extreme vulnerability, a vulnerability made explicit when he is victimized by his various caretakers, most directly by Uncle Ernie ("Fiddle About") and cousin Kevin ("Cousin Kevin"), but also when he is medically examined ("Sparks") and treated by the Gypsy and her cohort ("Acid Queen"), since these, too, give dramatic emphasis to his lack of agency, a familiar dramatic trope of disability.

Like Porgy, Tommy is given a compensating strength that occasions one of the show's major plot turns: despite his multiple impairments, he demonstrates a surprising aptitude for pinball ("Sensation") and becomes a champion player ("Pinball Wizard"). The basis for his resulting cult following is, first, his seemingly miraculous mastery of pinball despite being blind and deaf, but then also his equally miraculous recovery from his impairments. In the end, however, he alienates his following, albeit differently in the different versions. Whereas in the film he encourages his followers to simulate his experience of being a blind deaf-mute, in the stage musical he adheres to the community-building conventions of the genre by insisting to a romantically inclined groupie who wants to relive his experiences, "The point is not for you to be more like me; the point is, I'm finally more like you" ("Sally Simpson's Question").

From the standpoint of representing disability, the problems of *Tommy* run deep, stemming largely from its mostly unexamined reciprocal mapping of physical disability to mental illness, which is, as noted, a cliché in art, deriving from the aesthetically based mapping of "bad" onto "ugly." If we are to take seriously *Tommy*'s speculative equation of the physical and mental dimensions of Tommy's disability we become frustrated at how little these elements and their relatedness are developed, so that the show seems rather too easily to reduce being a blind deaf-mute to mere symptoms of a traumatically induced mental disorder, instead of more centrally taking on these physical conditions, to be accepted and worked with. On the other hand, if we take *Tommy* to be essentially a fantasy, its dramatic points seem either too facile or too obscure, indulging a series of pernicious dramatic stereotypes; thus, Tommy flips from the sadcrip stereotype to become a supercrip (see note 7), after which, in a clichéd "ableist" narrative, his impaired capacities are restored as a reward for his endurance of suffering and for his capacity to transcend his disabilities. Moreover, both perspectives are further troubled by the off-putting obliqueness of the story's telling, atypical for a Broadway musical.

Yet, despite these problems, *Tommy* functions as a high-profile, mainstream treatment of both physical and mental disability, providing essential context for how disability figures into later shows, specifically through the confused signals it sends. Thus, not only does its apparent conflation of mental and physical disabilities help set the stage both for *Wicked*'s awkward dependence on the shopworn trope of physical disability signaling a spiritual impairment, and for *Next to Normal*'s full-on engagement with mental illness, but the show's specific engagement with deafness presages *Big River*'s mainstreamed reconsideration of musicals and deafness, as well.

Wicked (Stephen Schwartz and Winnie Holzman, 2003) introduces Elphaba, a green-skinned girl and the future Wicked Witch of the West, who in the course of the show must deal with (among other things) being stigmatized for her skin color, being rejected by her father (she learns near the end of the show that she is illegitimate), acquiring an unearned reputation for being wicked, and living with unearned guilt, the latter concerning her younger sister's disability. Nessarose (the future Wicked Witch of the East) is congenitally unable to walk, a condition caused by her premature birth, which Elphaba believes was brought on by her mother's eating milk flowers to avoid giving birth to another green child. *Wicked* gets a lot right regarding Elphaba's psychological journey and her complicated friendship with Glinda, who becomes the Good Witch of the North. But it has with some justification been criticized for its treatment of Nessarose, whose condition embitters her, and who is eventually "cured" through Elphaba's casting a spell on her ruby slippers. As Beth Haller notes in her review of *Wicked* for *Disability Studies Quarterly*, Nessarose devolves "into a group of stereotypes," becoming

> manipulative and cruel, bordering on wicked. . . . one of a huge number of stereotypical disabled characters. In *Wicked*, disability equals evil once again, and the "punishment" for disability is death, as when the house falls on Nessarose and kills her. . . . As [Paul K.] Longmore explained in 1987: "Among the most persistent [stereotypes] is

> the association of disability with malevolence. Deformity of body symbolizes deformity of soul. Physical handicaps are made the emblems of evil."[15]

Moreover, as Haller and others have noted, Nessa's "cure" is staged as a big theatrical moment, becoming the occasion for thunderous audience applause, which carries an "ableist message that disabled people are broken and need to be fixed."[16] *Wicked* thus replays the "Hammerstein compromise" described earlier (note 2), but with respect to disability, teaching important lessons of tolerance with one hand while the other invites the audience to enjoy a different flavor of the very thing being critiqued. Nessa rising from her wheelchair is, in this sense, the orientalist "Bali Ha'i" from the anti-racist *South Pacific*.

There are no wicked characters in *Next to Normal* (Tom Kitt and Brian Yorkey, 2009), no antagonist standing in the way of its unhappy family's happiness. Rather, as we find out only midway through the first act (*spoiler alert!*), the occasional grotesqueries that bedevil the ostensibly "normal" Goodman family—mother Diana and father Dan, with teenage children Gabe and Natalie—derives from Diana's being unable to accept that Gabe died many years ago, while an infant. Thus, although we have from the beginning of the show seen and heard the teenaged Gabe, just as though he had not died, we suddenly learn, as a *coup de théâtre*, that he exists only from Diana's delusional perspective. [17] The show's central problem thence becomes the devastation caused first by the mother's mental illness and, in the second act, by the results of her treatment for that illness. But the *coup de théâtre* has already done important work from the standpoint of disability, for its relatively late deployment delays the imposition of the "normal" perspective, instead encouraging the audience to identify as long as possible, and as closely as possible, with the "next to normal" perspective of the disabled person.[18]

In an important sense, however, *Next to Normal* is concerned not with a disability, but with a disease (as those categories have usually been understood), and not with a physical limitation, but with a mental one. On the face of it, the show's domestic situation could easily set up a scenario typical for musicals, in which a character—Diana, in this case—is empowered through song, and thereby finds the personal strength to overcome an incapacitating opening condition: Porgy woos Bess; Winthrop sings through his lisp; the blind deaf-mute Tommy becomes a pinball wizard and later recovers his faculties; and wheelchair-bound Nessa walks—not to mention all those others in musicals who in singing gain enough confidence to climb ev'ry mountain, to walk through a storm, to whistle, to dream the impossible dream, to make up their minds, to commit to a relationship, or to otherwise face an uncertain future with courage. Indeed, music is set up to function in this way in *Next to Normal*, and to manage the drama between sanity and insanity. Thus, Natalie finds refuge in playing a Mozart piano sonata: "It's balanced, it's nimble, / It's crystalline clear . . . You scan through the score and put fingers on keys / And you play . . . / And everything else goes away" ("Everything Else"), whereas music's long history for representing madness gets called up countless times during the show, especially in "Who's Crazy," with its hysterical (in both senses of the word) allusion to "My Favorite Things": "Zoloft and Paxil and Buspar and Xanax . . . These are a few of my favorite pills." But *Next to Normal* takes a giant step beyond these ways of placing the central conflict within its music, and thereby charts a dramatic path from disease to disability.

In general, a disease becomes a disability when it causes permanent physical or mental damage (as when a childhood illness, such as scarlet fever, leaves a child blind and/or deaf), or when its cure entails the removal of something essential to the diseased person's previous sense of self. In physical terms, the latter most commonly occurs when a limb is amputated, or when part of a cancerous organ is surgically removed. By making the dead Gabe a character in the drama, and thereby giving Diana's delusion a dramatic *presence*, both musical and physical, *Next to Normal* is able to provide a layered dramatization of how this process works—while also, perhaps, suggesting the (literally) "para"-normal world hinted at by the show's title. Most immediately, Diana's electroconvulsive therapy (ECT) removes, or seems to remove, Gabe as a character in the drama, a theatricalized murder that comes across, for the family and for Diana in particular, as a kind of amputation. Importantly for the parallel to cancer, Gabe has been an engaging, often sympathetic character, a positive, even enabling force who offers comfort but also produces malignant effects; when he is cut away, his positive energy goes with him, leaving behind a palpable sense of absence, articulated in "Wish I Were Here" and "Song of Forgetting." When in Gabe's electrifying return ("Aftershocks") he makes the parallel to cancer and its devastating cure explicit ("They cut away the cancer / But forgot to fill the hole"), the charge for the audience combines elements of alarm and relief, and when he returns more virulently, as part of Dan's world after Diana leaves him, we know that she and her madness merely provided the vessel for the couple's shared need for their absent son. For the audience, Gabe's returns replicate the "phantom limb" phenomenon, in which an amputee will experience the missing limb as present and functioning normally.

Disability in *Next to Normal* has two quasi-metaphorical frames of reference: the individual and the family. The parallels between the two levels are evident first of all in the ways in which the family seems to partake of Diana's delusions, and even of her cure. In a perverse application of the "marriage trope"—or, better, what I have termed the "divorce trope" (Knapp 2012) in which a woman creates the sensibility of a musical by leaving an existing unworkable reality to reinvent herself—Diana through her delusion effectively cheats on Dan, and neglects Natalie to the point of disenfranchisement. And, as all of them are led to express themselves in successive "I am" songs—Diana's "I Miss the Mountains," Dan's "I Am the One," Natalie's "Superboy and the Invisible Girl," and Gabe's "I'm Alive"—it becomes clear that only Gabe truly benefits from his continued presence in the family. Metaphorically, the cancer can only grow; in more realistic terms, the delusion is self-perpetuating. As the cure progresses, Natalie undergoes a parallel course of treatment, self-administered, in recreational drugs ("Wish I Were Here"), and Dan's fear of isolation becomes increasingly palpable. Gabe's amputation from Diana's memory is initially manifest in a sense that Diana herself has been amputated from the family, and her removal makes it clear that the cancer has long since metastasized to Dan. In the end, a series of partial rescues reconstitutes the family as a broken one with a potential for recovering its health, betokened by its living members' acceptance of a more circumscribed reality—not normal, but "next to normal," as Natalie puts it in "Maybe." The individuated hopeful tokens reconstitute, collectively if in different ways, something "next to family": Natalie's renewed if guarded response to her sometime boyfriend Henry; Diana's ability to move on, to move out, and to begin repairing her relationship with Natalie; and Dan's lonely admission that he still needs Gabe. The phrase "next to normal" thus serves, in the end, as a figure for disability: it may not be "normal," but, unlike an untreated disease, it provides the basis for a real life.

"Waitin' for the Light to Shine": Musicals and Deafness

In the 1986 film *Children of a Lesser God* (dir. Randa Haines), based on the acclaimed play by Mark Medoff (1980), William Hurt plays James Leeds, an unconventional speech and lip-reading teacher of deaf children who astonishes others at his school by using music and dance as part of his teaching, to which most of his students respond enthusiastically. But his oralist, integrationist approach is resisted by Sarah Norman (Marlee Matlin), the deaf school custodian he falls in love with, who initially rebuffs his attempts to help her assimilate to mainstream hearing culture. He, too, comes to realize the limitations of his attempt to bridge the divide between them, frustrated in his attempt to share his love for Bach's music with her. While the end of the film holds out hope for their reconciliation, the film as a whole seems to argue against the version of the "marriage trope" that it proposes.

For all its sympathetic portrayals of the deaf, *Children of a Lesser God* orients itself at every turn toward a hearing audience. James, who occupies the dominant subject position in the film, repeats Sarah's signing aloud—an awkward device, however well Hurt manages it—yet there are no subtitles in the original film to aid deaf viewers during the many stretches of unsigned dialogue. More subtly, James's signature music is the second movement of Bach's Concerto for Two Violins (the "Bach Double"), in which the two solo instruments' melodic lines intertwine caressingly, a powerful aural argument for conjugality that Sarah doesn't "get," and that a deaf audience has no access to. It is only Matlin's fierce yet extraordinarily empathetic performance as Sarah—for which she won an Academy Award, the first deaf person to do so—that mitigates and partially obscures the film's advocacy for James's side of the conflict.[19]

In his book *Deaf Side Story*, Mark Rigney tells the extraordinary story of Diane Brewer's mounting of *West Side Story* at MacMurray College in Jacksonville, Illinois in Spring 2000, casting deaf high-school actors from nearby Illinois School for the Deaf in the Puerto Rican roles (the Sharks, their girlfriends, and Maria), reflecting the fact that the Jets are the more "mainstream" (that is, white) of the two gangs, and thus occupy a position of privilege relative to the rival gang (Rigney 2003). On one level, his account details an especially fraught version of the tribulations that normally beset ambitious school productions, but the to-be-expected insecurities and personality clashes were augmented in this case by the mixed cast—not only deaf and hearing, but also involving both college and high school students—and an especially steep learning curve in several areas. Among the latter were the development of dances by a deaf choreographer, the coordination of choreography to music by deaf dancers, the translation of the English book and songs into American Sign Language (ASL),[20] the coordination of signing to sung lyrics, the integration of effective signing for spoken dialogue, the logistics of having to act one part in alternation with voicing or signing another (generally on the other side of the gang divide), and the sheer difficulty of manipulating bodies on a small stage, given that each part had to be both performed orally and signed, almost never by the same actor. But, clearly, the payoffs were on the same order of magnitude: an incredible, extended learning experience for both sides of the hearing divide, for students and adults alike; both expected and unexpected opportunities to fuse the casting principle to the dramatic situation, the latter sometimes occasioning moments of great theatre (as with Anita's stark vocalizing during the "taunting" scene, or with Maria's "keening shriek . . . like a saw cutting metal" [198] during her final speech over Tony's corpse); and a tremendous community response to the show itself, again from both sides of the hearing divide.

Children of a Lesser God and MacMurray's *West Side Story* engage in different ways the problem of creating a shared theatrical space for hearing and deaf communities, and each intensifies that problem by involving music. Music, after all, renders the terms of the divide most starkly, since enjoyment and appreciation of music, not to mention actual singing and dancing, are presumptively alien (or dimly remembered, or imperfect) experiences for a deaf or nearly deaf person,[21] whereas music provides hearing culture with one of its central and most diversely rich experiences of what it means to be human, and even of what it might mean to be a different human, of a different culture or outlook. To be sure, this view of Deaf engagements with music is reductive and simplistic, since these in fact range from composition, performance, and deeply felt appreciation to complete lack of interest. But, simplistic or not, this view will be the default expectation for many hearing audiences, especially when deafness is rendered emblematic, as it so often is in even educationally minded dramatic art. Since musicals tend to make the alignment of individuals with groups directly palpable through choreography and shared song, the variety that exists within groups less familiar to mainstream audiences will be more frequently ignored than explored.

Since musicals are thus disposed to reinforce the simplistic default view of music and Deafness, they would seem ill-suited to the task of providing a bridging experience between the deaf and hearing worlds. Music *can* do that, or seem to do that, across racial and ethnic divides. But how can (presumptively unheard) music show a deaf person what it is like to hear, or a hearing person what it is to be deaf—or more crucially, what it might be like to embrace that experience of disability with affirmation? Music, it would seem, not only highlights, but also essentializes the difference between hearing and deaf worlds. Moreover, as with racial and ethnic divisions—which constitute the central situation in *West Side Story*—there are compelling (or at least passionate) arguments, from the nonmainstream side of things, against assimilating to the mainstream (addressed, if jokingly, in *West Side Story*'s "America"). The argument against assimilation for members of the Deaf community—Sarah's position at the beginning of *Children of a Lesser God*—derives from the essentialized difference that music seems to articulate best and that musicals are predisposed to default to. Indeed, as Rigney recounts in *Deaf Side Story*, the deaf student playing Maria in MacMurray's *West Side Story* held a deep-set resentment against music, and struggled profoundly with the challenges involved in performing "I Feel Pretty." As Jeff Calhoun, the director and choreographer of Deaf West's production of *Big River*, admits in an interview with *Playbill*, "Doing musical theatre for the deaf . . . sounds like the punchline to many jokes."[22]

And yet, as MacMurray's *West Side Story* adventure already makes clear, something important and quite positive *can* happen toward bridging this particular divide through the vehicle of a musical involving deaf and hearing cast members and targeting a similarly mixed audience. Moreover, using that experience as a touchstone, we may observe that it is specifically through the challenge of preparing and performing musical numbers, combined with a sometimes poignantly appropriate subject and treatment, that allows that important, positive something to happen. The reason for this lies not in (or even despite) the world that music seems to inhabit in conventional terms—that is, the hearing world—but in the nature of musical performance, and in the fact that music depends as much on rhythm—something graspable on both sides of the hearing divide—as on the combination of tones.

As is a cliché of both musical theatre and community singing more generally, performing music in concert with others creates and enforces a strong sense of community. As hearing culture conventionally understands this phenomenon, whether literally or metaphorically, a sense of community arises from voices joined in song, through their mutual creation of harmonious sounds. But there is a more fundamental layer to the activity. Performing music with others, whether through playing, singing, or dancing, imposes a paced commonality, a shared rhythm, on all involved, asserting harmoniousness even if—as when many (but by no means all) deaf performers are involved—the harmonies created through music cannot reinforce and shape the shared experience for everyone. In *moving* together, people can know they *belong* together, whatever else divides them, and music has a unique capacity to govern and regulate shared structures of movement. When deaf and hearing attempt to do this together, it may be difficult, but the difficulty is part of the journey, perhaps its most important element, and it is therefore essential that it be manifest in the themes of the musical being performed (as was certainly the case with *West Side Story*).

Deaf West Theatre's revival of *Big River: The Adventures of Huckleberry Finn* (Roger Miller and William Hauptman, 1985), was presented first in North Hollywood (2001–2002), then transferred to Broadway (2002–2003) before reconstituting for a national tour that ended in 2005.[23] Although *Big River* in its initial run won multiple Tony Awards (including Best Musical) and ran for over two years, it is often overlooked, in part because of its country-style score, atypical for Broadway. Yet the show provides a nearly ideal vehicle for bringing hearing and deaf performers together. Like *West Side Story*, it deals directly with racial prejudice, which maps easily to some of the prejudices that attend the relationship between Deaf and hearing communities. But unlike *West Side Story*, the central interracial characters, Huck and Jim, are not in conflict, but are linked through their parallel situations as runaways: Huck has faked his own death to escape from his abusive Pap, and Jim is a runaway slave hoping to reunite eventually with his wife and two children. Indeed, the pair constitutes an unconventional version of the "marriage trope," even if the (b)romantic underpinnings are never fully articulated. If there are occasional sexualized overtones to their homosocial lifestyle (e.g., when Huck dresses like a girl to avoid being identified [a scene dropped for the revival, out of concern for dramatic pacing];[24] in their choreographed interplay in the later stages of "Muddy Water" ["I got a need to climb upon your back and ride"]; when they encounter the decidedly "odd couple" interlopers, the "Duke" and "King"; or when the latter invent the mixed-gender "nonesuch" to hoodwink the yokels), these are papered over with Huck's brief and fumbling dalliance with the bereaved Mary Jane and references to Jim's absent wife.[25]

This already-present version of the "marriage trope" apparently inspired Jeff Calhoun to conceive the mix of deaf and hearing in similar terms in Deaf West's production:

> What I tried to accomplish—and what I hope we're accomplishing—is a *marriage* of the hearing world and the deaf culture. Every moment of the show is both signed and spoken. I didn't want there to be one moment in the show that favored the hearing audience or the deaf audience [emphasis added]. (Hernandez 2003)

In part because of this aim, some specific elements of the original show had to change. The patter song "Hand for the Hog"—a novelty song irrelevant to the larger action—is simply dropped. And, as participants discovered in the MacMurray staging of *West Side Story*, "combination songs"—in which different parts with different lyrics combine simultaneously, as in the quintet version of "Tonight"—do not work well for all deaf audiences because the verbal counterpoint can be difficult to track. *Big River* has several such songs, including the opening number "Do You Wanna Go to Heaven?," in which the different haranguing perspectives seem to attack Huck first singly and then, during the combination verse, all together. In Deaf West's version—as in the later combination of "When the Sun Goes Down in the South" with "Muddy Water"—the superimposition of texts is eliminated in favor of a visual representation of the situation created within the music as originally scored. For "Do You Wanna Go to Heaven?," the effect of being bombarded on all sides, which the combination verse would have communicated in aural terms, is further emphasized through a "freeze frame" in the action, allowing Huck to escape for a moment to sing a brief anticipation of "Waitin' for the Light to Shine," a song that in the original script appears slightly later in the action. Through emphasizing the perspective of a deaf Huck who cannot track all the harangues at once, the very reason for the potential failure of combination songs for some deaf audiences is dramatized. For the brief combination of "Arkansas" with the funeral choir's "How Blest

We Are" in Act II, on the other hand, no changes are necessary in the scoring, since the overlapping songs function as a transition rather than a dramatic apex; in Deaf West's staging, the progression from "Arkansas" to "How Blest" is in effect choreographed, as the boy who sings "Arkansas" walks over to join the choir.

Beyond these successful adjustments and the general plot situations already cited, there are two other dimensions of *Big River* that enhance the show's suitability as a vehicle for mixed deaf and hearing performance. Most obviously, deafness already figures twice in the original show, in sharply contrasting episodes: when Jim poignantly recounts his remorse over striking his daughter Elizabeth in exasperation, before he realizes that her recent bout of scarlet fever has left her deaf, and, in conventional burlesque, when the "King" pretends to be the deaf-mute brother of Mary Jane's recently deceased father, so that he and his other "brother," the "Duke," can collect the inheritance.[26] More subtly, and in the end more importantly, Huck is throughout the show being "schooled" through his association with Jim, who, though not precisely Huck's teacher, often functions that way, and so recaptures a familiar trope of dramatized deaf-hearing encounters.[27]

You've Got to Be Carefully Taught

Indeed, one of the strongest common threads in stories of deaf accommodation to mainstream hearing culture is the critical intervention of an extraordinary teacher or mentor.[28] Classic examples include *The Miracle Worker* (William Gibson, based on Helen Keller's *The Story of My Life*, originally produced for television in 1957), in which Anne Sullivan teaches the almost feral Helen Keller, blind and deaf from an early childhood illness, to read and write,[29] and *Children of a Lesser God*, discussed earlier. Even the story of MacMurray's *West Side Story* becomes worth telling because of the inspiring, guiding role played by the teachers involved. And, as always in such stories—even the real-life ones—the teachers learn as much from the process as their ostensible pupils, if not more.[30]

It is the teacherly dimension of these stories of mutual discovery that finds an especially intriguing resonance in *Big River*, an effect that is reinforced by the homosocial setting involving a grown man and an adolescent boy on a journey together (recalling the mentoring relationships of the Greeks) and the specific casting choices, in which Jim (Michael McElroy) both hears and signs, whereas Huck (Tyrone Giordano) is deaf, voiced by the narrator Mark Twain (Daniel H. Jenkins, who played Huck in the original Broadway production). More specifically, several of the songs, especially those that trade verses or involve the repetition of lines, and because they are signed in the song's "slow motion" rhythm, take on the aspect of signing lessons—an effect so powerful that in the immediate aftermath of my third viewing of the show I found myself involuntarily (and incompetently) attempting to sign while conversing about the show. This dimension is already palpable in Jim's "Muddy Water," which Huck signs in repetition, as if learning the song, but—perhaps not coincidentally—it is even more powerfully present in what are essentially love ballads within the show's homosocial "marriage trope," "River in the Rain" from Act I and "Worlds Apart" from Act II. The first of these includes mutual if indirect declarations of love (Huck's "Whether the sunshine, whether the rain / River, I love you just the same," and Jim's "Hell, there ain't no way to measure / Why I love you more / Than I did the day before") followed by a duet that ends with them sharing the final sign ("away from me"), reproducing a bonding device already present at the end of "Muddy Water," for the last word of the line, "I got a need to climb upon your back and ride."[31] Structured like a love song, and echoing the type's sentiments and mutual gestures, "River in the Rain" has the feel, as well, of a successful lesson. And, after their reconciliation in Act II, "Worlds Apart" comes across as a rueful acknowledgment of their impossible love, "Together, but worlds apart";[32] as before, they express the trajectory of the song through intimate patterns of signing, sharing the signed circle for "Sun," but with hands sliding past each other's for the title phrase. The real "lesson" in this case is learned before the song itself, when Huck discovers how painful it is for him to have caused Jim anguish, and to have earned his rebuke (regarding his elaborate "joke" based on Jim's vulnerable status as a runaway slave). While *Big River* (and its source book, *Huckleberry Finn*) demonstrates repeatedly the truth of *South Pacific*'s take on racism—that it is not inborn, but must "be carefully taught"—this episode in particular, and the revival more generally, also demonstrate that the sensibilities and sensitivities entailed in living with difference, whether those differences are based in race or disability, must be just as carefully taught.[33]

And so, *Big River*'s teacherly mode extends as well to the audience (as I've already suggested in confessing my own compulsive "signing" after the show). In the three versions of "Waitin' for the Light to Shine," each more elaborate than the last, this point is made especially well. Already as a refuge-interpolation within "Do Ya Wanna Go to Heaven?," the song "teaches" how easily the deaf can be overwhelmed by the hearing world. In its second appearance, well before his "teaching" songs with Jim, Huck signs the final iteration of the title phrase, which is not sung, encouraging hearing members of the audience to "read" the signing. And, even more forcefully, in the song's Act II reprise, where the song is backed by other signers and singers, the orchestra and voices drop out for this line, so that the actors continue to move and sign in rhythm but without the music, which has two somewhat opposing effects. The actors' seeming obliviousness to the music's absence, most immediately, reminds the hearing audience that the deaf performers do not hear the music; more importantly, however, signing as an independent language thereby asserts itself more forcefully, in an amplified echo of Huck's unsung signing in the first act.

In two other, equally poignant ways, the hearing audience is reminded of the differences that so much in the show works to efface. In the separation of the slave family near the end of the show, the deaf daughter vocalizes her anguish to heighten the emotional impact—a device also used by Sarah in *Children of a Lesser God*, and, as noted, by Anita and Maria in MacMurray's *West Side Story*.[34] Perhaps most important, however, is the educational experience of sharing space with hearing and deaf audience members, which, for me, was much more evident in the Los Angeles audience than on Broadway. And here I do speak of my own education: I remember first experiencing a mild version of Jim's exasperation with his daughter before he realized she was deaf, when deaf members of the audience were not as attentively quiet as would be expected with a hearing audience, and I learned to accept that with chagrin at my own insensitivity; then, at the end of the show, as recounted also by Rigney regarding the audience's varied responses to *West Side Story* at MacMurray, I was implicitly invited to learn a Deaf substitute for applause: waving hands in the air with outstretched fingers.

Embedding disability in the music of a musical remains the biggest challenge for musicals that move in this direction. As noted, *Porgy and Bess* does not do this; nor, really, do *Tommy* or *Wicked*. *Next to Normal*'s ingenious solution is to make the disability into a character in the drama. And, for deafness, the solution has so far been to incorporate deaf performers into the musical numbers. Yet that is not—borrowing from a song title from *Big River*—"the only way to go." When I conversed with David Kurs, the Artistic Director of Deaf West Theatre, about the musical they are currently developing with the Academy of New Musical Theatre (tentatively titled "People of Sound and Silence," with songs by Clifford J. Tasner and book by Joe Moe), he related their ambition to develop songs written directly to the rhythms of signing, which works much differently from spoken English, and thereby to give deafness a musical presence it hasn't had yet, moving one step closer to the kind of musical embodiment of difference that musicals demand.

Acknowledgments

The development of this essay has been unusually collaborative. I thank most of all my daughters, Rachel and Genevieve, with whom I first saw many of the shows I discuss here, and whose insights then and since have been invaluable. I am, as so often, beholden to my colleagues in musical-theatre studies, Mitchell Morris, Stacy Wolf, Jessica Sternfeld, Elizabeth Wollman, David Savran, Samuel Baltimore, Sarah Ellis, and Arreanna Rostosky, for their discussions and feedback. I have benefited enormously from the comments, advice, and suggestions generously offered by my new colleagues in Disability Studies, Joseph Straus, Julie Singer, Stephanie Jensen-Moulton, William Cheng, Blake Howe, and Michael Accinno. Tyrone Giordano generously provided essential and thoughtful feedback regarding music and deafness. And I owe a special thank-you to the sustaining inspiration of Deaf West Theatre and its artistic director, David Kurs.

Notes

1. Regarding the "marriage trope," see Knapp 2005a (9 and *passim*) and 2006 (10 and *passim*); see also Altman 1987 (50). Regarding how the marriage trope supports mythologies of the United States and its various "melting pots," see Knapp 2005a, especially chapter 6, "American Mythologies" (119–152).
2. I discuss what I term the "Hammerstein compromise" in Knapp 2014; see also my specific discussions of Hammerstein shows in Knapp 2005a (122–124, 230–239, and 261–268). Regarding the political contexts for the Rodgers and Hammerstein shows, see McConachie 1994, Most 2000 and 2004, and Klein 2003.
3. Regarding the assimilation of the Irish and Jews, see especially Ignatiev 1995 and Most 2004. Regarding "whiteness," see especially Dyer 1997.
4. The Stonewall rebellion, which began in late June 1969 as a routine confrontation between police and homosexuals at the Stonewall Inn on Christopher Street, New York City, lasted for three days, becoming the locus for gay activism in major cities across America. It is generally seen as a decisive moment in the then-emergent gay rights movement, a watershed event that led to greater visibility both for gays and for the abuses they have long endured owing to entrenched homophobic attitudes. Among many accounts of Stonewall and its place in the history of gay rights, see Duberman 1993, especially part 6, and Carter 2004.
5. Although often quite visual in orientation, musicals are—perhaps by nature but certainly by habit—implicitly phonocentric, a dimension that will be considered below in relation to *Big River*.
6. In this, musicals resemble many other representational media, since people with disabilities, unlike other marginalized Others, have been extensively represented in art and related media. Thus, as David T. Mitchell and Sharon L. Snyder argue: "While other identities such as race, sexuality, and ethnicity have pointed to the dearth of images produced about them in the dominant literature, disability has experienced a plethora of representations in visual and discursive works. Consequently, disabled people's marginalization has occurred in the midst of a perpetual circulation of their images. Curiously, a social erasure has been performed even as a representational repertoire has evolved" (Mitchell and Snyder 2000, 6).
7. The most familiar form of this trope is the "supercrip," a disabled individual who excels at an activity assumed to be precluded by her or his impairment, who is because of this played up in the news media as an inspiring example of heroic overcoming. Among many discussions of the supercrip, see Clogston 1994 and Elliott 1994. The supercrip stereotype is often seen to be as detrimental to disabled communities as portrayals of disability meant to evoke pity (the "sadcrip"); as discussed below, the musical *Tommy* indulges both familiar stereotypes.
8. Regarding this dimension of *Porgy and Bess*, see Knapp 2005a (194–204), Crawford 1972, Horn 1996, and Noonan 2012. Regarding the tendency for a particular stigma to resemble other types of stigma, owing to their shared relationship of deviance to what is considered normal (that is, able, white, heterosexual, and above all mainstream), see, along with many more recent discussions, Goffman 1963.
9. On the other hand, it is almost as problematic that Porgy's strength of character is so closely tied to his disability, since that mapping too easily takes on the contours of the supercrip stereotype (see note 7).

10. Regarding Gershwin's operatic models for *Porgy and Bess*, see Knapp 2005a (194–204) and Reynolds 2007. Regarding the role of music in establishing the depth of "soul" in Wagner's heroes, see Knapp 2005b.
11. For example, Porgy is on crutches in the 2005 Washington National Opera version, directed by Francesca Zambello, and uses a cane in the 2012 Broadway version, as rewritten by Suzan-Lori Parks and Diedre Murray, and directed by Diane Paulus. This progressive muting of his disability seems to acknowledge, according to the mapping of disability to race, an improvement of the relative societal position of African Americans since Porgy's first appearance on stage in 1927 (as a play). Many critics have expressed consternation at this shift, however, since the goat cart was part of the genesis of the original book by DuBose Heyward (1925): Porgy was based on an actual person, Goat Cart Sam (Samuel Smalls), who was by most accounts a mean, violent man who came to the attention of Heyward through a newspaper account of him being accused of murder. Regarding the dramatic and human significance of what we might see as Porgy's physical rehabilitation, see Jensen-Moulton 2011.
12. Hill claims to have graduated from the Gary Conservatory in 1905, but Marian discovers that the town itself wasn't founded until 1906. Interestingly, the Gary Conservatory did open in 1905, and—undoubtedly the reason for Willson's citation—early specialized in using unconventional methods to teach its students to play band instruments (http://www.freewebs.com/garyconservatory/, accessed April 26, 2013).
13. Willson 1959, 101. The "spastic boy" subplot is noteworthy in two other ways. First, the "spastic boy" was to have been the janitor's son (not Marian's younger brother), which would have made class a bigger issue in the show than it is. And, second, the concern of those who argued for dropping this element was not that they saw anything wrong with showing a child using a wheelchair on stage in a musical, but rather that he would steal the show; in dramatic terms, the level of disability had to be brought into line with the relative importance of the subplot.
14. Speech disfluency has some history on the musical stage, especially in opera, and most especially with regard to stuttering's dual potential to set character and to be exploited for comedic effect; see Oster 2006. On the other hand, Laurie Stras argues that verbal flaws, particularly when they derive from the damaged vocality of the singer, have historically been more welcomed in popular music than in opera, in part because of the importance of affective individuation in popular musical genres and the potential that vocal flaws have for encouraging audience-identification (Stras 2006). Clearly, all of these considerations are relevant to Winthrop, whose lisp is used to provoke laughter both onstage and in the audience, is uniquely his (an "organ of his soul"), and provokes, along with laughter, considerable empathy.
15. Haller 2004. The embedded quotation is from Longmore 1987. For more on this issue, see Wolf 2011 (204–205). In Wolf's summation, "for a musical like *Wicked* that works overtime to send a politically progressive message, its use of disability as a metaphor for evil is, simply put, an ideological blind spot" (205).
16. Haller 2004. A number of blog posts make similar points about this moment; see, for example, http://blog.ncpad.org/2011/04/06/wicked-disability/ (accessed April 26, 2013).
17. The central characters' names are all emblematic. Daniel is a "good man" caught in a lion's den. Diana is a scattered reflection of Dan with something added: a highly symbolic first syllable that serves as her emblematic nickname: Di. Gabriel—whose name is not heard in the show until near the end, although audiences will know it from the program—is an

angel, literally and, as originally presented, figuratively; thus, the cast listing in the published libretto describes him as "Dashing. Gentle. Bright. Playful. Everything a mother, etc.," and Diana even likens him to an angel's wing in "I Dreamed a Dance," just before she attempts suicide (Yorkey 2010, 4 and 51). Natalie—"not a lie"—is real, unlike Gabe. And Diana's doctors' names—Madden and Fine—are even more obviously emblematic.

18. This device lends itself especially well to disabilities that involve delusional mental states, and where representations will be assumed to reflect an "objective" viewpoint. Perhaps the best-known example is in the film *A Beautiful Mind* (dir. Ron Howard, 2001), a somewhat fictionalized biopic of the prominent mathematician John Forbes Nash Jr. (played by Russell Crowe). In the later stages of the film, three prominent characters—one of them a lifelong friend—are revealed to be not real, but only imagined by the schizophrenic Nash.
19. For more on the tendency of films that include disabled characters to privilege an able-bodied point of view—as well as more extensive treatment of many of the tropes and stereotypes associated with disability discussed elsewhere in this essay—see Norden 1994. Regarding the wider cultural implications of this tendency, and the broad cultural field that entails and supports the tendency for musicals to enforce an "ableist" message by presenting narratives about overcoming disabilities of one kind or another, see Davis 1995. Although hearing actors have won Academy Awards for their portrayals of deaf characters, Matlin is the first deaf actor to do so.
20. American Sign Language, although the standard choice, was scarcely the only one, and many cast members were better acquainted with other systems. And, yes, "translation" is the right word, since ASL is a very different language from English—despite the "American" in ASL—with a strikingly different syntax. Signing songs has in recent years acquired a significant presence in videos posted online (primarily on YouTube); for more on this practice, see Anabel Maler's essay in this volume.
21. Elsewhere in this volume, Jeannette D. Jones explores some of the ways in which music has found an active place within Deaf culture, contesting the notion of their exclusion from music-making and -enjoyment. Thus, she writes, "Of all art forms, music seems to be the least accessible to those with hearing loss, yet the work of many deaf musicians challenges assumptions that, since they do not 'hear' in the sense most commonly understood, they are not active participants in a musical culture." On this issue, see also chapters 7 and 8 of Straus 2011, especially 145–149 and 167–170.
22. Hernandez 2013. Calhoun's statement slides over the different ways "for" might be construed; in implicitly advocating for an appreciation of deaf perspectives, the revival of *Big River*, as explored below, is deliberately mainstreamed, so that its primary audience, especially on Broadway, is understood to be the hearing.
23. I saw the production on Broadway and at the Ahmanson Theatre in Los Angeles; I wish to thank the New York Public Library for access to videorecordings of both the original 1985 production and the Broadway revival.
24. Tyrone Giordano, personal communication.
25. The suggestion of a homoerotic relationship between Huck and Jim in Twain's original novel was first made in a controversial essay by Leslie A. Fiedler that took its provocative title—"Come Back to the Raft Ag'in, Huck Honey!"—directly from Twain (Fiedler 1948). Various terms have been used to describe this kind of relationship, which is most frequently referred to as "male bonding" or the less gender-specific "homosocial romance" (courtesy of Eve Kosofsky Sedgwick), but has more recently acquired the hipper sobriquet "bromance." As Fiedler makes clear—and even clearer in Fiedler (1960) 1997—the

fundamental point of the mixed-race, all-male relationship, and of many others in US American fiction that share some of its contours, is not specifically sexual, but rather that it serve as a fortification for the white male against becoming civilized and domesticated. I discuss male bonding in musicals, which I term the "buddy trope," in Knapp 2006 (75–77, most immediately in relation to *Singin' in the Rain*), citing Robin Wood's identification of male bonding as a filmic trope in Wood (1968) 1981 and Wood 1998.

26. In the Deaf West production, the "Duke" and "King" switch roles, which both avoids the awkwardness of the deaf player having to imitate a burlesque version of deafness, and allows him, while still in character, to help "place" that burlesque as something distasteful, by showing exasperation for the inadequacies of his partner's performance.
27. There are indications that the Deaf West version of *Big River* may attain some kind of repertory status. Already, this version has been mounted by the Pennington Players (in West Windsor, New Jersey), running from October 4–13, 2013, cast according to the mix of deaf and hearing performers used in the 2003 Broadway revival (see http://www.pennington-players.org/bigriver.html, accessed August 31, 2013). I wish to thank Stacy Wolf for bringing this production to my attention.
28. "You've Got to Be Carefully Taught" is the title and hook of a once-controversial song from *South Pacific*, which was kept in the show in the face of strenuous arguments that it would ruin the show's chances for success. For more on the song and its history, see Lovensheimer 2010.
29. The story of Helen Keller's becoming deaf and blind, conditions that were probably brought on by a bout of scarlet fever at 19 months, seems oddly parallel to that of Jim's Elizabeth, but she wasn't Twain's model, since the novel was published before Anne Sullivan came into Helen Keller's life. But the fictional Elizabeth may well have played a part in the interest Twain later took in Helen Keller, helping arrange for her education at Radcliffe College, where she became the first deaf blind person to earn a bachelor's degree.
30. To quote from another Rodgers and Hammerstein song, "If you become a teacher / By your pupils you'll be taught" (part of the verse leading in to "Getting to Know You" in *The King and I* (Rodgers and Hammerstein, 1950).
31. A public performance of this song, showing the teaching dimension and the final shared sign, is viewable online, at http://www.bluegobo.com/production/2886000/video/10651 (accessed May 3, 2013). As can be seen in the video, audience members are "learning" to sign along with Huck.
32. In "Worlds Apart," Deaf West's *Big River* seems to cycle back to *Tommy*, which uses its title phrase in "Sally Simpson" to indicate the experiential gulf that separates her from Tommy. It seems unlikely that this verbal assonance linking the deaf/hearing worlds of *Tommy* to the performing mode of the *Big River* revival is more than coincidental, since in the original *Big River* the phrase referred only to the racial differences between the characters (specifically, that Huck cannot imagine what it is to be a runaway slave); nevertheless, even as a coincidence it speaks directly to the ease with which treatments of disability map onto treatments of other kinds of difference in musicals, amplifying the societal tendency I describe in note 8, citing Goffman 1963.
33. Lieutenant Cable sings "You've Got to Be Carefully Taught" in *South Pacific* to rebuke the notion that—as Nellie had earlier insisted to Emile—racist attitudes are something one is "born with." Arguably, the show gets this backward, since of the two "lessons," it is racism (or its parent, xenophobia), not tolerance, that is likely to be the dominant response in young children to encountering difference; see Bikales 1991.

34. As Tyrone Giordano notes (personal communication), these moments make hearing audiences "doubly uncomfortable," since their expectation that the deaf will be mute is at once shattered and (unfortunately) reinforced.

References

Altman, Rick. 1987. *The American Film Musical*. Bloomington: Indiana University Press.

Bikales, Gerda. 1991. "You've Got to Be Carefully Taught." *Social Contract* 1 (4): 176–178.

Carter, David. 2004. *Stonewall: The Riots That Sparked the Gay Revolution*. New York: St. Martin's Press.

Clogston, John S. 1994. "Disability Coverage in American Newspapers." In *The Disabled, the Media, and the Information Age*, edited by Jack A. Nelson, 45–58. Westport, CT: Greenwood.

Crawford, Richard. 1972. "It Ain't Necessarily Soul: Gershwin's '*Porgy and Bess*' as a Symbol." *Yearbook of Inter-American Musical Research*: 17–38.

Davis, Lennard J. 1995. *Enforcing Normalcy: Disability, Deafness, and the Body*. New York: Verso.

Duberman, Martin. 1993. *Stonewall*. New York: Dutton.

Dyer, Richard. 1997. *White*. New York: Routledge.

Elliott, Deni. 1994. "Disability and the Media: The Ethics of the Matter." In *The Disabled, the Media, and the Information Age*, edited by Jack A. Nelson, 73–80. Westport, CT: Greenwood.

Fiedler, Leslie A. 1948. "Come Back to the Raft Ag'in, Huck Honey!" *Partisan Review* 15 (6): 664–671.

Fiedler, Leslie A. (1960) 1997. *Love and Death in the American Novel*. Champaign, IL: Dalkey Archive.

Goffman, Erving. 1963. *Stigma: Notes on the Management of Spoiled Identity*. New York: Simon & Schuster.

Haller, Beth. 2004."'Wicked' Gives Disability an Evil Name" (review of *Wicked*). *Disability Studies Quarterly* 24 (2). http://dsq-sds.org/article/view/495/672.

Hernandez, Ernio. 2003. "Sign to Sing: New Broadway *Big River* Is Confluence of Deaf, Hearing and Musical Theatre." *Playbill*, June 18. http://www.playbill.com/news/article/80215-Sign-to-Sing-New-Broadway-Big-River-Is-Confluence-of-Deaf-Hearing-and-Musical-Theatre.

Horn, David. 1996. "Who Loves You Porgy? The Debates Surrounding Gershwin's Musical." In *Approaches to the American Musical*, edited by Robert Lawson-Peebles, 109–126. Exeter, UK: University of Exeter Press.

Ignatiev, Noel. 1995. *How the Irish Became White*. New York: Routledge.

Jensen-Moulton, Stephanie. 2011. "Porgy's Cane: Mediating Disability in A.R.T.'s *Porgy and Bess*." *American Music Review* 41 (1): 1, 4–5.

Klein, Christina. 2003. *Cold War Orientalism: Asia in the Middlebrow Imagination, 1945–1961*. Berkeley: University of California Press.

Knapp, Raymond. 2005a. *The American Musical and the Formation of National Identity*. Princeton, NJ: Princeton University Press.

Knapp, Raymond. 2005b. "'*Selbst dann bin ich die Welt*': On the Subjective-Musical Basis of Wagner's *Gesamtkunstwelt*." *19th-Century Music* 29 (2): 142–160.

Knapp, Raymond. 2006. *The American Musical and the Performance of Personal Identity*. Princeton, NJ: Princeton University Press.

Knapp, Raymond. 2012. "Getting off the Trolley: Musicals *contra* Cinematic Reality." In *From Stage to Screen: Musical Films in Europe and United States (1927–1961)*, edited by Massimiliano Sala, 157–172. Speculum Musicae 19. Turnhout, Belgium: Brepols.

Knapp, Raymond. 2014. "Sondheim's America; America's Sondheim." In *The Oxford Handbook of Sondheim Studies*, edited by Robert Gordon. New York: Oxford University Press.

Longmore, Paul K. 1987. "Screening Stereotypes: Images of Disabled People in Television and Motion Pictures." In *Images of the Disabled, Disabling Images*, edited by Alan Gartner and Tom Joe, 65–78. New York: Praeger.

Lovensheimer, Jim. 2010. *"South Pacific": Paradise Rewritten*. New York: Oxford University Press.

McConachie, Bruce A. 1994. "The 'Oriental' Musicals of Rodgers and Hammerstein and the U.S. War in Southeast Asia." *Theatre Journal* 46 (3): 385–398.

Mitchell, David T., and Sharon L. Snyder. 2000. *Narrative Prosthesis: Disability and the Dependencies of Discourse*. Ann Arbor: University of Michigan Press.

Most, Andrea. 2000. "'You've Got to Be Carefully Taught': The Politics of Race in Rodgers and Hammerstein's *South Pacific*." *Theatre Journal* 52 (3): 307–337.

Most, Andrea. 2004. *Making Americans: Jews and the Broadway Musical*. Cambridge, MA: Harvard University Press.

Noonan, Ellen. 2012. *The Strange Career of "Porgy and Bess": Race, Culture, and America's Most Famous Opera*. Chapel Hill: University of North Carolina Press.

Norden, Martin F. 1994. *The Cinema of Isolation: A History of Physical Disability in the Movies*. New Brunswick, NJ: Rutgers University Press.

Oster, Andrew. 2006. "Melisma as Malady: Cavalli's *Il Giasone* (1649) and Opera's Earliest Stuttering Role." In *Sounding Off: Theorizing Disability in Music*, edited by Neil Lerner and Joseph N. Straus, 157–171. New York: Routledge.

Reynolds, Christopher. 2007. "*Porgy and Bess*: An American *Wozzeck*." *Journal of the Society for American Music* 1 (1): 1–28.

Rigney, Mark. 2003. *Deaf Side Story: Deaf Sharks, Hearing Jets, and a Classic American Musical*. Washington, DC: Gallaudet University Press.

Stras, Laurie. 2006. "The Organ of the Soul: Voice, Damage, and Affect." In *Sounding Off: Theorizing Disability in Music*, edited by Neil Lerner and Joseph N. Straus, 173–184. New York: Routledge.

Straus, Joseph. 2011. *Extraordinary Measures: Disability in Music*. New York: Oxford University Press.

Willson, Meredith. 1959. *"But He Doesn't Know the Territory."* New York: G. P. Putnam's.

Wolf, Stacy. 2011. *Changed for Good: A Feminist History of the Broadway Musical*. New York: Oxford University Press.

Wood, Robin. (1968) 1981. *Howard Hawks*. London: British Film Institute.

Wood, Robin. 1998. *Sexual Politics and Narrative Film: Hollywood and Beyond*. New York: Columbia University Press.

Yorkey, Brian (book and lyrics). 2010. *Next to Normal*. Music by Tom Kitt. New York: Theatre Communications.

CHAPTER 41

MUSIC FOR OLIVIER'S *RICHARD III*

Cinematic Scoring for the Early Modern Monstrous

KENDRA PRESTON LEONARD

For a number of scholars, William Shakespeare's play *Richard III*, completed sometime in 1591 or 1592, is the epitome of the "disability narrative," a story that is propelled by the presence of a nonnormate body. In Rosemarie Garland-Thomson's words, "the term normate usefully designates the social figure through which people can represent themselves as definitive human beings. Normate, then, is the constructed identity of those who, by way of the bodily configurations and cultural capital they assume, can step into a position of authority and wield the power it grants them" (Garland-Thomson 1996, 8). Here, I propose that Richard's bodily difference, thought in the early modern to result from personal or parental sin or evil and projected as such by Laurence Olivier in his film adaptation of the play, is musically mirrored through composer William Walton's noncustomary use of the orchestra. This use, in fact, creates what I call a "nonnormate" set of timbres and sounds that are not just nonstandard uses of musical instruments but also what could be widely construed as physical, sonic deformations of the standard sounds of the orchestra. These serve as aural stand-ins and layers of meaning for the nonnormate body and acts of Richard. Richard, the play's antihero, displays a curved spine and withered arm, and Shakespeare gives him lines that include frequent mention of the contemporary belief that a misshapen body equated with a similarly deformed mind. In placing Richard on the stage, Shakespeare creates dual aspects of performativity for the actor taking on the role: that of Richard the character and that of disability.

In Olivier's 1955 cinematic adaptation of the play, Walton's score pays close attention to this duality: the score contains some synchronous music that imitates Richard's nonnormate physical movements, but it is also concerned with his interior actions. The score thus engages with Richard's disabilities on multiple levels, offering sonic interpretations for both physical and mental deformity. In this essay, I argue that Walton's music for Richard suggests both his exterior and interior monstrosity (as viewed at the time of the play's writing) by altering the normate, socially and professionally accepted sounds of the orchestra as well as using musical tropes traditionally associated with otherness. I first explain Elizabethan attitudes toward the disabled and Richard III in particular, which inform Olivier's interpretation of the role and play. Then I examine the historical influences on Olivier's playing of the role, as well as how later twentieth and early twenty-first century productions have colored the reception of Olivier's film. Finally, I analyze how Olivier's and Walton's interpretations of Richard function over the course of the film to aurally reinscribe traditional, stigmatizing attitudes about disability as an external marker of moral evil.

Unlike some productions, both old and new, in which Richard's body and mind are clearly decoupled, such as David Garrick's eighteenth-century performances, the 1990 Richard Eyre/Ian McKellen production at the RSC, and Sulayman Al-Bassam Theatre's 2007 *Richard III: An Arab Tragedy*, Olivier seems to have based his interpretative decisions on the attitudes he imagined Elizabethan audiences would have had when viewing the play: that the physically nonnormate body was a standard marker of personal or societal misconduct or evil, and that persons with such a body were more likely than those with normate physiologies to be evil. Olivier emphasizes Richard's bodily differences by including not only all of the text from *Richard III* on the subject, but also descriptions from *Henry VI, Part III*. In doing so, as Kathy M. Howlett notes, Olivier creates a "rhetoric of binary oppositions that split the past from the present, thereby polarizing Richard as a monster of a bygone era" (Howlett 2000, 130).

At the beginning of the play, Richard describes his body:

> I, that am curtailed of this fair proportion,
> Cheater of feature by dissembling Nature,
> Deformed, unfinished, sent before my time
> Into this breathing world, scarce half made up,
> And that so lamely and unfashionable
> That dogs bark at me as I halt by them—(1. 1.18–23) (Arden Third Series)

For Elizabethans, writes James R. Siemon, Richard was the "malformed bogeyman," whose body and actions were twisted and twisted together (Siemon 2001, 3). David M. Turner and Kevin Stagg have further shown that "[t]he unruly body was viewed as extending beyond the physical form to correspond with the natural order. Thus in the early modern period, the body did not simply constitute the individual self, but was a site for cosmic intervention and divine retribution," confirming that for early modern audiences, the two characteristics could not be unfixed (Turner and Stagg 2006, 8).

Contemporary writers attest to this widespread belief: Roger Lund reports that Francis Bacon provides useful perspective; for while he accepts the conclusion that exterior deformity suggests internal monstrosity, he concedes that natural deformity may actually serve as a spur to ambition: "Therefore it is good to consider of deformity, not as a sign, which is more deceivable, but as a cause, which seldom faileth of the effect.

Whosoever hath anything fixed in his person that doth induce contempt hath also a perpetual spur in himself to rescue and deliver himself from scorn" (Lund 2005, 102).

Other chroniclers of the early modern period believed the same thing. In a 1596 treatise on monsters and monstrosity, Martin Weinrich claimed, "[all] that is imperfect is ugly, and monsters are full of imperfections" (Lund 2005, 94). Scholar Thomas Burnett, believing that beauty stemmed from perfect geometrical forms, thought that humped backs and other physical irregularities were "symbols of sin, monstrous excrescences on the original smooth face of Nature" (Lund 2005, 100). This belief persisted well beyond the early modern period: in the late eighteenth century, Swiss physiognomist Kaspar Lavater was insisting that, "in dwarfs we usually find extremely limited but lively faculties, confined but acute cunning, seldom true penetration and wisdom." To be blunt, he wrote, "the morally worst, the most deformed" (Lund 2005, 101).

Such deformities marked not only interior sin and monstrosity, but were also thought to be the result of misbehavior on the part of parents, an entire village, or even the state as a whole, suggesting that the immorality of the disabled was innate and unchangeable. Turner and Stagg note that "monstrous births, physical abnormality, and mental deficiency were commonly seen as divine punishment for incest, bestiality, and adultery" in the seventeenth and eighteenth centuries (2006, 10). A broadside dating from 1568 proclaimed that monstrous births were a warning to England of the corruption in its government (Moulton 1996, 258), and Linda Charnes asserts, "Shakespeare's audience would have immediately recognized Richard's physical deformity and moral depravity as a synecdoche for the state" (Charnes 1993, 30). Even as the play was performed, those opposed to Queen Elizabeth I's councilor Robert Cecil noted his "ill-shapen and crooked" body; his presence and role in the government made much of his short stature and rounded shoulders, certain that these external markers indicated a traitor within (Siemon 2001, 37). This combination of drawing on actual belief with the use of a political metaphor made Richard's continual villainy all the more powerful for early modern audiences.

In the play, Richard's mother and those at court around him describe his physical body for the audience, so that no matter how the actor playing Richard appears, the experiants (those experiencing a performance though any of the senses, not limited to seeing or hearing) know that he is to be regarded as misshapen. Other characters in the drama often compare Richard's body with that of an animal, degrading both his body and mind, making it clear to audiences that they firmly believe the prevailing superstition that links the disabled body and mind. Lady Anne, whom he later woos in a scene of spectacular persuasion, initially calls him an "unmannered dog" (1.2.39) and a "[foul] toad" (1.2.150); his mother, Queen Margaret, labels him a "cacodemon" (1.3.143) and an "elvish-marked, abortive, rooting hog" (1.3.227). Richard fully understands the contempt in which he is held, and uses his deformed appearance as a justification for his evil, saying that because he "cannot prove a lover," he is "determined to prove a villain" (1.1.28, 30).

While Richard does in fact prove a lover in his wooing of Lady Anne, he does so in order to achieve his villainous goals of eliminating everyone between himself and the throne of England. He is, as Shakespeare writes, a great "dissembler" and actor: he wins over Lady Anne as she grieves over the body of her husband, whom Richard has killed; and gains the trust of his brothers and nephews before orchestrating their deaths. And of course he commits just about every kind of named murder: fratricide, regicide, infanticide; as well as other kinds of corruption. Shakespeare prepares the audience for this by introducing Richard's physical and mental monstrousness as a key element of the play's first scenes.

To some extent, Shakespeare's depiction of Richard reflected the politics of his own time. The ruling Tudor family had supplanted Richard III, and Shakespeare obliged them not only by depicting him as a murderer and traitor, but also by enhancing Richard's deformities. In *Henry the Sixth, Part 3*, which Olivier quotes several times in his stage and film adaptations of *Richard III*, Richard gleefully admits that he was "born with teeth!' / And so I was; which plainly signified / That I should snarl and bite and play the dog. / Then, since the heavens have shaped my body so, / Let hell make crook'd my mind to answer it" (*3 Henry VI*, 5.6.75–79). To make his body appropriately deformed to fit with the Tudor interpretation of his reign, Siemon writes, Richard was thus "rendered hunchbacked, lame of arm, crabbed of feature, and natally toothed. As far as I know, the limp begins with Shakespeare" (Siemon 2001, 3). Thus, while the historical Richard did in fact have scoliosis (kyphosis), resulting in one shoulder higher than the other, as proven by the recent discovery of his skeletal remains in a Leicester car park, most descriptions of his body as grotesquely deformed arise from social and political conventions.

In regard to *Richard III*, David Mitchell and Sharon Snyder claim that what they call the ultimate ambiguity of the king's physical shape "divides four hundred years of productions into two opposed camps: those who exaggerate his deformities in order to supply the play with an otherwise absent motivation; and those who downplay Richard's disabilities as an archaic characterization device and focus instead on the rhetoric of intrigue" (Mitchell and Snyder 2000, 103). They further suggest that the ability of cinema to show physical horrors through "tricks" and "special effects" helps make it responsible for "accentuat[ing] one interpretation of Shakespeare's play that generations of critics had found to be either an embarrassing Tudor anachronism or a misjudgment of Shakespeare's intent: that Richard sought vengeance because of his disabilities" (99).

While Mitchell and Snyder are correct in saying that productions of Richard III have varied in the extent to which they emphasize Richard's disabilities, their argument could be extended further on what I take to be a more central issue, namely the extent to which Richard's disabilities can be understood as an external signifier of his inner depravity and evil rather than the reason behind his behavior. On this issue, too, productions of the play have differed. However, as I have shown earlier, the issue at hand is not necessarily disability-propelled vengeance (although some actors, such as Antony Sher, whose interpretation I discuss later, do use this reading), but disability as a marker of evil that would be present even if the body was normate. Thus, the nonnormate body *signifies* the internal evil, rather than the nonnormate body being a *cause* of Richard's anger and villainy. And indeed, neither of the categories that they propose are quite accurate from the point of view of many performers; instead, there is much more of a divide as to whether an actor should play the role in keeping with the early modern belief that conjoined Richard's body and mind as a single signifier of personality and made them thus both malformed, while others jettison this conceit and play Richard as a master manipulator and villain whose disability is *not* connected with his mind; or, as Mitchell and Snyder suggest, to play Richard as the "mutilated avenger" (Mitchell and Snyder 2000, 79). In productions in which the body and mind are separated, Richard is played as evil and using his body to manipulate the emotions and psychological reactions of those around him, a reversal of productions in which his bodily difference drives his actions. For the most part, however, actors play the role as Shakespeare likely wrote it and his audiences likely experienced it, leaving the conjoining of body and mind intact in the sense that Richard's evil is externally marked, but not necessarily that his evil stems, as Mitchell and Snyder suggest, from his anger at the normate world. As Katherine Schaap Williams has written, educated audiences—and presumably educated actors—see Richard as "a demonstration of Renaissance beliefs about the continuity between inner morality and outward physical forms" rather than as an individual avenging his body through violence (Williams 2009).

From the beginning, productions of Richard III have grappled with the problem of representing Richard's body on stage. There are no sources describing how the role's originator, Richard Burbage, played the king, although, as suggested in the playtext, it is likely that he played it with a hunchback, weak arm, and limp. William Hogarth's c. 1745 painting of David Garrick as Richard, in which he is depicted falling backward onto a settee as he is first confronted by the ghosts, shows no physical disabilities, although from the angle of view it is impossible to see his back and he may have walked with a limp or otherwise signified disability.

For later actors, however, there is ample evidence. George Frederick Cook, playing Richard in 1801, is described as having "more of the animal than spiritual nature in him," and played the role in an animalistic way, complete with snarling, stamping on the ground, and other gestures (Colley 1992, 55). John R. Towse, also taking on the role in the early nineteenth century, "wore a hump like a camel, and tottered and limped in a manner totally inconsistent with the strength and agility which the usurper is known to have been possessed" (Colley 1992, 114). In an 1814 etching by Charles Turner, actor Edmund Kean clasps his left arm in his right, suggesting its weakness. Actors who did not emphasize Richard's physical deformities were chastised by both critics and audiences. Actor Richard Mansfield, John Colley reports, "preferred therefore to touch as lightly as possible. . . . upon the deformity of Richard's body," although he strove to preserve the "deformity of his mind, as drawn by Shakespeare." Mansfield's performances were met by letters from audience members demanding "Give us more Hump" (Colley 1992, 114, 119).

For twentieth- and twenty-first-century audiences, the coupling of body and mind stated as fact in *Richard III* has been highly problematic. However, because of actors' interest in Richard's pathology and its perceived connection with his actions in the text, it is difficult to separate them in performances of the play and filmic productions. As

Mariangela Tempera has written, "Shakespeare's text does not leave much room for equivocation on the point of Richard's evil personality and on the correlation between his character and his physical aspect, much to the delight of performers" (Tempera 2005, 67). Modern performers have gone to great lengths to create a physical interpretation of Richard that matches their understanding of his internal villainy. Norman Wisdom dressed as a fool with bells and twisted a leg underneath an enormous hunchback in the 1970s. In the Royal Shakespeare Company's 1984 version, one of the most famous theatrical productions of *Richard III*, Antony Sher played the role with a mammoth hump on his back and on crutches. He dragged both legs behind his body as he moved, which, in conjunction with long sleeves that likewise dangled to the ground, helped Sher embody the description of Richard as a "bottled spider" (1.3.241). Sher studied as many aspects of Richard's character and disability as he could, including the pathological, psychological, and sociological constructions and influences of his disability. Sher's position on Richard is of the classic "Obsessive Avenger" type, in which Richard turns to evil because of the way in which he is treated as a disabled man, rather than being a character who is innately evil and whose evil is signified through his body:

> I became very interested in the fact that Richard is a severely disabled man. Some actors underplay this—but if you read Richard's opening speech about himself, he is clearly disabled, and has experienced a lot of prejudice, a lot of hatred. This, in turn, has filled him with self-hatred. It's this that enables him to do such evil to other people. He was used to hatred as a disabled man in an un-PC society. There were no Paralympics then. [. . .] As part of my research, I went to homes for the disabled, meeting disabled people and looking at various disabilities. I also became very interested in the psychological aspects of various murder cases—above all, that of Dennis Nilsen. He seemed an interesting model for Richard, in that he was a very intelligent man and a witty man, and he had some of Richard's black humour. Studying that case helped me to understand Richard psychologically. (Denes, Barnett, and Dickson 2013)

Recent actors have adopted more visibly identifiable signifiers of physical disability. Kevin Spacey used a very visible high-tech leg brace and a somewhat fetishy leather wrist brace for his incarnation of Richard; Steve Weingartner played Richard with a heavily scarred face and a leather-braced arm in a sling; and Henry Holden played him with a variety of modern orthopedic devices attached along the left side of his body.

These sorts of exaggerated performances of the king's physical difference have conditioned audiences to imagine an inextricable link between Richard's apparent deformities and his malevolent actions. Comedian Rowan Atkinson's Shakespeare sketch, "Pink Tights and Plenty of Props," neatly sums up popular understanding of Richard and his qualities. Playing a "good king," Atkinson exhibits upright posture and a beneficent smile; playing a "bad king," he scowls; when the narrator of the sketch says that he "also has a deformity," Atkinson hunches over *à la* Richard, scowls, and makes a rude gesture at the audience. Audiences of Olivier's film in the late twentieth and early twenty-first centuries often bring these cultural constructions with them to their viewing and understanding of the role.

Notwithstanding all the crutches, slings, humps, leg braces, and orthopedics, many actors have been more interested in the psychology of the character than his physical aspect. After Richard's skeleton was discovered, *The Guardian* newspaper asked actors whether the physical findings changed their concept of the character. Simon Russell Beale, for example, who was the Royal Shakespeare Company's Richard in 1992, situated the character in context with the period in which he lived, saying that, "I didn't do any historical research when I played the part, for obvious reasons: it's a fiction. You leave all that well alone. In Richard, Shakespeare created a monster—but he is a monster in a world that is equally monstrous. Medieval politics can't have been fun: it's a vision of a world of violence and lack of moral scruple" (Denes et al. 2013). Jonathan Slinger, who played Richard for the Royal Shakespeare Company from 2006 to 2008, found that the role's most compelling aspect is the psychological one, an outlook that recognizes the differences between Elizabethan and modern understanding of connections between body and mind: "Shakespeare gives you not just a picture of how someone's mind can become distorted, but also how he's a master of duplicity. He's brilliant at pretending to be one thing while in fact being another, and at saying one thing while meaning something completely different. He's the consummate actor, the ultimate politician. He's continually changing shape" (Denes et al. 2013).

That all of these actors find more importance in Richard's twisted mind than his body implies that for the most recent productions and audiences of the early twenty-first century, the character's amorality is what makes him so horrific and is what furthers the narrative: he could be, had has been, convincingly played as without visible disabilities. Directors and actors have begun to pay more attention to the more monstrous psychological aspects of the character, although the idea of Richard's anger at the world stemming from his frustrations with his body remains a popular explanation for his homicidal tendencies; this still connects the body and the mind in a cause and effect relationship, albeit in a different way from the Elizabethan viewpoint. A lingering paradox of the Richard of Shakespeare's play is that while he is intended to physically revolt the audience, he is clever and funny and seductive. As Joel Elliot Slotkin has written, "In his deformity, which the other characters take as a sign of his hellish nature, Richard epitomizes the union of outer appearances and inner truths. At the same time, Richard's theatrical pretense of benevolence emblematizes the deceitful disjunction between external shows and internal nature" (Slotkin 2007, 7). Thus the audience is drawn in: to stare openly, against social convention, at his physical difference, and to enjoy the wit and cunning of his mind.

There have been several film adaptations of *Richard III*, beginning with two short silent films from 1908 and 1911 and a silent 1912 film that is the oldest extant American feature film, that is, a film that is more than four reels long. The character of Richard has been portrayed in film by a variety of actors, including horror film star Vincent Price in *Tower of London* (1962), who deliberately plays up the monstrous aspects of the character's body and mind, and Ian Holm, whose 1964 performance as Richard in the television adaptation *The War of the Roses* eerily presages his interpretation of Bilbo Baggins twisted in body and mind by the Ring in *The Lord of the Rings*. Ian McKellen played the king to great acclaim in the Richard Eyre/Richard Loncraine theatrical and film adaptations that set the action of the play in a counterhistorical fascist 1930s Britain. While disabled actors, including Peter Dinklage, have played Richard on stage, all of the film adaptations of the play to date have featured actors with apparently normate physiologies at the time of production in the title role. The first filmic interpretation of the play with sound is by Olivier (1955); this production, like Olivier's other Shakespearean films, began on stage before being adapted for film after a successful theatrical run.

Like Olivier's previous Shakespearean films, *Henry V* (1944) and *Hamlet* (1948), his *Richard III* has a score by William Walton. As Brooks Kuykendall notes, by the time he composed the score for *Richard III,* Walton tended to use less of the "Mickey Mousing" or parallel scoring (the film music practice of synchronizing the music exactly with the movement on the screen, so-called because of its use in Disney cartoons, in which the music precisely mimics the characters' motions) he used in his earlier scores. Instead, he was more interested in creating music "in precise timings [. . .] to match the developing mood of a scene rather than a specific action" (Kuykendall 2011, 16).

Walton requested and received a shooting script from Olivier prior to the beginning of primary shooting, and marked this with places he wanted to score, along with specific moods or characteristics he wanted the score to incorporate. Walton then watched the rough cuts of the film and created cue sheets based on his notes from it. Film conductor Muir Mathieson then recorded the cues (in some cases cutting, extending, or composing new material to fit) and matched them up to the visuals (Kuykendall 2011, 20). The necessity of such alterations was most often caused by edits or cuts made by Olivier after the score was completed, and in some cases Walton's original intentions are obscured or changed for fit, dramatic purpose, or continuity. At the end of the film, for example, Olivier depicts Richard's death as an irregular series of bodily spasms. Instead of notating the number of beats between each of Olivier's spasms, Walton left it to Mathieson to place the chord for each spasm as it began when Mathieson conducted the recording for the soundtrack while the film played. As Kuykendall explains of the death scene:

> Walton has clearly wearied of the effort to calculate the precise rhythm of Olivier's fifteen irregular spasms. The composer's solution was to notate the chords as a series of downbeats, with the instruction "to be recorded 'wild' "—that is, for Mathieson to conduct the downbeats to coincide with the death throes. But Mathieson takes a far more extensive liberty with the scene. Walton notates a sequence of just two harmonies, repeated several times. Mathieson adjusts this to have a climbing sequence of dissonant chords. (Kuykendall 2011, 24)

Walton's score includes three distinct aural characters: the first is the sound of Christian, pastoral England, heard in Lady Anne's theme, played by the oboe;

represented by the organ, which is associated exclusively with Edward and is heard in his coronation and death scenes; and signified by the chanting of monks in several scenes, notably her first appearance in mourning as she trails behind her husband's coffin. The second character is a sinuous, chromatic line, signifying Richard's ability to seduce not just Lady Anne in an erotic way but also his seduction—through his powers of persuasion in winning the trust and support—of other characters; the third is an aural landscape of textures and sounds created by the musicians physically altering the sounds of their instruments through the use of techniques like using mutes, playing *sul ponticello* or *col legno*, and stopping the horns, as well as the use of obscure instruments with extended and unusual timbres, such as the baritone oboe used in Richard's funeral march. While this last approach may have borrowed from music for horror films, which sometimes asks musicians to create sound effects, it does not include other hallmarks of the horror genre that would brand it as such, including stingers and the use of an organ. Where stingers *are* used, they are the insertions of conductor Muir Mathieson, who added them to Walton's score at points such as Clarence's nightmare, and are not part of Walton's original material, confirming that Walton himself was aiming for a more subtle kind of musical difference with which to represent Richard.

At the beginning of the movie, its visual and musical treatment focus on iconic images and sounds of Christianity, establishing the existing court of Edward IV and his family as pious and proper, while immediately setting Richard and his acts opposite them, suggesting the contempt Richard holds for religion and his manipulation of it for his own gain and protection. As Constance Brown writes, Olivier's use of Christian symbols as background for Richard's victims does give Richard, in direct contrast, a "satanic aspect" (Brown 1967, 26). It is his false piety that helps him woo Lady Anne, shepherd the young Princes to the Tower, and (briefly) win over even Queen Elizabeth. Walton's score here represents the play's heroic characters—Lady Anne, Queen Elizabeth, the princes, and Richmond—with music redolent of the church and the pastoral sound of a pure Albion. The opening title music functions as an overture, providing an aural landscape of an "English" sound—what Peter Holland calls "fake medievalism"—that Olivier also used in *Henry V*. It represents pageantry and royalty through the use of brass, the tabor, and fanfares and steady marches (Holland 1996). In an early scene that shows the crowning of King Edward IV, Walton interpolates *a cappella* chant, led by the Archbishop of Canterbury, blessing the king and establishing a religious musical trope that will continue throughout the film. The chanting of the Archbishop, a number of monks in attendance, and the onlookers is followed by liturgical-style music for organ, again emphasizing Edward's divine claim to the throne and casting his followers as pious and Christian. The same music is used for Lady Anne when she is shown mourning the death of her husband, slain by Richard. In addition, Lady Anne is musically signified by a solo oboe carrying a modal melody—that is, one not using a tonal scale but instead avoiding a raised seventh step, or leading tone—above the strings, a common marker of the idyllic pastoral England. (The score is shown as Figure 41.1, and

FIGURE 41.1 Lady Anne's Theme, cue 3M1, complete.

the film cue can be seen as Track 41.1 on the Companion Website). Such pastoral or royal music is also used in situations in which Richard is temporarily stymied and finally defeated, including the release of Hastings from the Tower, the positive reception of the young princes in London, and Richmond's preparations for battle and eventual victory.

The ease with which Richard seduces those around him, including the audience, creates what Slotkin calls "a [. . .] pervasive erotics of deformity that is enhanced by its association with evil" (Slotkin 2007, 18). Indeed, Barbara Hodgdon has described Olivier's physical aspect here as that of an "appealingly sexualized" body, drawing on multiple physical references to popular culture sexual icons (Hodgdon 1998, 219). These references, drawing as they do on recognizably overtly sexual figures from cinema history, provides much of the charisma an actor playing Richard must embody to succeed in creating an audience-winning antihero in the role. Richard's seductiveness, conflated with sexuality and eroticism in Olivier's film, is musically marked by a common musical signifier of the sensuous other: chromaticism.

Richard's ability to present himself as sexual is first signified at the end of his opening monologue. Celebrating the end of war, he states that, conflict over, combatants can turn their attention from hostility to pleasure. As Richard says of War that, "He capers nimbly in a lady's chamber. / To the lascivious pleasing of a lute," Walton ends the previous texture, stopping the entire orchestra. Walton introduces a syncopated, chromatic passage in the harpsichord, which twists and turns away from the tonal centers of the earlier material (see Figure 41.2; the relevant film cue is available as Track 41.2 on the Companion Website). Over three measures, the harpsichord solo moves mostly through a series of distantly connected dominants. Walton writes block chords for the left hand and an unpredictably twining line for the right hand that outlines chord tones. As the chords move from C♭ major to B♭ major and E♭ major, the melodic line moves from sixteenth note to dotted eighth to regular eighth, deferring any sense of cadence and finding rhythmic regularity only in the final measure, where the line settles into a series of triplet sixteenths that outline G major. This odd passage, which stands out from the previous material harmonically and in terms of timbre, echoes the eroticism of the passage, in which we are invited to imagine War—and, to judge from Olivier's expression, possibly even Richard—now capering nimbly in a lady's chamber.

At the same time, the rhythmic irregularity of the passage suggests Richard's asymmetrical physical movements, and indeed, Olivier plays up Richard's limp and awkward walk during this scene in the film. This brief instance of Mickey Mousing captures

FIGURE 41.2 Harpsichord solo, cue 2MIB, mm. 12–15.

Richard's ability to inhabit multiple personas and to use his own skills as an actor to his advantage: he is at once eloquent and suave, his demeanor hinting at his own erotic potential while nonetheless emphasizing his disability and rendering himself a pitiable other in the eyes of the court. This duality, as created by both Olivier and Walton, will return with even more effect in the scene in which Richard successfully woos Lady Anne.

This chromatic passage also serves as a transition to a new cue (2M2) in which Richard talks about his powers of dissembling and changeability, closely related to his seductive and persuasive qualities: "I can add colours to the chameleon / Change shapes with Proteus for advantages, / And set the murderous Machiavel to school. / Can I do this, and cannot get a crown?" (*3 Henry VI*, 3.2.191–194). Here, Walton layers in a chromatic line, this time in the clarinets. The rhythm, in contrast to the earlier chromatic passage, is steady and iterated several times in a pattern, but the tonality is just as changeable and unstable as before, indicating that while Richard may be more comfortable in this self-reflection than when he subtly hinted at War in the bedchamber, he is nonetheless unpredictable and impossible to pin down, except for his own cause. As he finishes this speech, which fully establishes his mind as twisted and monstrous, there is a falling line that passes through the orchestra on its way to a horrified silence. This last line of the music for the speech displays a jolting, irregular rhythm and awkward melodic line, full of minor seconds. It trips from high to low, with string pizzicatos rolling down to a final few bowed notes that repeat minor seconds.

In addition to the chromatic elements discussed above, these early cues also use several textures and timbres that signify Richard's otherness. Richard's music is in direct contrast to the grave solemnity and metrical, tonal, and instrumental stability of the opening title music and the quiet pastorality or major-key fanfares of his victims. As he begins his first soliloquy (1.1.1–13), delivered to the camera, low winds and full, muted strings enter, the strings buzzing with thirty-second notes or tremolos. The winds, with stopped horns, move together in an ascending fifth, a motif suggesting Richard's scheme to ascend to the throne. The strings continue their buzz until Richard's references to "merry meetings," at which the false medievalism of the opening titles is briefly repeated. The strings are then abruptly organized into minor seconds playing tight dotted rhythms inside triplets at the line "our dreadful marches to delightful measures," musically illustrating the text by using march rhythms and dissonances.

This introductory sequence, noted in Walton's autograph score as 2 MIB (reel 2, music cue 1B), runs just 55 seconds and yet provides a near-complete musical portrait of Richard as he will be depicted by the score for the rest of the film. Several musical elements stand out here as signifying deviance: the altered timbres of the strings, the aesthetic of the stopped horns, and chromaticism. These aural identifiers of Richard are heard over and over as he manipulates those around him into helping him achieve his goal: we hear it when Clarence is sent to the Tower, never to emerge alive; when Richard seduces Anne; during Clarence's dream before his execution; and when Richard sends the murderers into his cell. We hear it when the announcement comes that Richard has sent Rivers and Grey to prison; when the two young princes are taken to the Tower, like their uncle Clarence never to be seen again; when Anne dies, supposedly through

Richard's hand; when Richard gives Tyrell the command to kill the princes in the Tower; and when Richard is visited by the ghosts of those he has killed, on the night before his battle with Richmond. We hear it for the last time as Richard calls for a horse and is surrounded by Richmond's soldiers and killed.

The unusual timbres from the strings are perhaps the most obvious audible signifier of Richard's presence in the film, and Walton creates this effect by asking the string section to use various nonstandard techniques in their playing. The score calls for mutes, playing *sul ponticello* (close to the bridge, which causes a scratchy, rough sound), and playing *col legno* (hitting the strings with the wood of the bow rather than playing with the hair). I would posit that, as each of these techniques demands that the players alter or deform the usual sounds and playing practices of their instruments, they both physically mirror Richard's nonnormate body and result in passages in which a nonnormate orchestral sound is predominant. A mute, a rubber device that clamps onto the bridge, dampens the sound of the instrument, creates a more nasal timbre, prevents the instrument from fully projecting, and diminishes the sharpness of an attack on the string. Playing *sul ponticello*, as noted above, results in an otherworldly or metallic effect. It also creates irregular overtones, sending any sense of tonality into flux and destabilizing the overall sound of the ensemble. *Col legno* is a dry percussive sound. Usually the beating of the bow against the string is unmetered and players simply tap as quickly as they can. This results in a muddying of rhythm and beat. Finally, the use of tremolo suggests anxiety and instability. This gives the string passages an additional layer of tension while recalling—at least to more recent audiences—earlier musical uses of buzzing in dramas and horror films to suggest the presence or influence of evil (Kalinak 2003, 21). These techniques have often been employed in passages concerning or marking otherness in music, both for staged works and purely instrumental pieces. In the French Baroque, mutes represented the sleep of genre scenes known as the *sommeil*, in which otherworldly or unnatural events took place; mutes, used in conjunction with tremolo or other techniques, are also common in scenes on building tension, such as in Act III of *Tristan and Isolde*, where muted strings set the scene leading up to and through the beginning of the *Liebestod*. Sul ponticello is used in Puccini's *Manon Lescaut* to create an unearthly sound as Manon dies; and in Ravel's *L'enfant et les sortileges* to aurally describe the otherworld of the child's experience. François-Adrien Boieldieu directs players to use *col legno* in *Le calife de Bagdad*; Berlioz calls for it in the "Dream of the Witches' Sabbath" movement from his *Symphonie Fantastique*; and Saint-Saëns uses it in the *Danse macabre*: all three instances attach the technique to evil of a supernatural nature. In the score for *Richard III*, Walton uses these string techniques to alert the audience to Richard's evil and abnormal ways, connecting him sonically with practitioners of (black) magic, the unnatural, and death.

Walton also calls for the French horns to be shut or stopped during this passage and similar subsequent ones. Players insert their hands into the bell of the horn much more deeply than usual, muting the emerging sound and changing its timbre; much like string mutes, stopping the horn results in a nasal sound. Horns muted in this manner are used in Strauss's *Don Quixote*; Debussy's *Prélude à l'après-midi d'un faune*; Dukas's *L'apprenti Sorcier*; and Berg's *Wozzek*; again, Walton timbrally connects the uncanny, violence, and overall darkness with Richard's character. That Walton uses these extended instrumental techniques in quick succession in his music for Richard suggests that Richard's physical disability and evil nature required extreme signification, in this case a constant deformation of "normal" sounds from the orchestra.

Walton puts all of these approaches in signifying Richard's outer and inner monstrosity to use in Act 1, Scene 2. In this scene, Richard's acting abilities are on display; he proves his dissembling nature and his ability to project a sense of eroticism despite his disability as he artfully woos Lady Anne. In the text, Richard cleverly plays to Lady Anne's sense of compassion, claiming that he has killed her husband out of his love for her, providing her the opportunity to kill him, and eventually winning her favor through a mixture of pathos and romantic love. Although we have already seen Richard lie convincingly to his brothers Edward and Clarence, manufacturing their mutual distrust, here Shakespeare shows the audience the full extent of Richard's talents for acting and persuasion. Since we have already heard Richard swear to be a villain rather than a lover, we know his seduction here is false, and that he has no desire for Lady Anne, physical or otherwise, save her position in the hierarchy of the court. Walton's score allows the audience to hear the lie, as it were, by underscoring Richard's words with the already established aural landscape of Richard's twisted mind.

Hesitant, quiet tremolo eighth notes in the strings set the scene, and a sinuous chromatic line in the bassoon hints at the eroticism Richard will use in playing to Lady Anne. Regular eighths soon give way to an inconsistent rhythmical mix of dotted eighths, sixteenths, and rests, similar to the stumbling harpsichord passage of the earlier scene, indicating Richard's amoral scheming rather than signifying his physical irregularities, which he conceals here as much as he emphasized them in his first speech. However, after Richard launches into his declaration of love for Anne, Walton brings back a steadier, more slowly moving of tremolo eighths, but after a few measures they are interrupted by ascending figures in the muted winds. The presence of the tremolos heightens the tension of the scene and the ascending figure reminds the audience that Richard is using Anne to rise in the world. Richard displays his chest and throat to Anne, and she is initially disgusted, but slowly begins to look with less revulsion. At this point, muted strings, tremolos *sul ponticello*, and closed horns return, reminding the audience of Richard's unnaturalness. The first violins have a rising, chromatic theme, later picked up by the bassoons and trombones, representing Anne's growing acceptance, if not attraction, to Richard and his body. This line continues and is passed around the orchestra except to the oboe and cor anglais, which play Lady Anne's pastoral theme, presenting the audience with aural signification of the two previously opposed factions. Throughout the scene, Olivier shows the audience how Richard can exaggerate or control many of the physical aspects of his disability: as he grows more passionate in wooing Anne and begins to succeed at the task, his motions and bodily positioning become smoother and more normate until he places his ring on Anne's finger and she accepts it.

FIGURE 41.3 "Vouchsafe to wear this ring," cue 4M2, mm. 1–19.

With the line "Vouchsafe to wear this ring," the erotic high point of the scene, which features intimate physical contact and a none-too-subtle metaphor for sexual penetration as Richard removes a ring from his finger and places it on Anne's, Walton begins a new cue (see Figure 41.3 and the associated film cue, Track 41.3 on the Companion Website). While the violas continue the tremolo that signifies Richard's monstrosity, the violins and lower strings have new, more solid material: steady, climbing quarters

FIGURE 41.3 (Continued)

in the low strings, doubled by the harp, and a syncopated rhythm in the violins present an insistent, grounded ascending line that takes over. In the *cor anglais*, Anne's theme is fragmented and Walton repeats its first gesture before breaking off and beginning it again, indicating Anne's failing resistance. As the scene progresses, the violin line becomes more active, moving into a sensuous line of eighths, then sixteenths, and finally triplet sixteenths before climaxing on a fortissimo C♯ dotted quarter leading tone cadencing on a D eighth. At the same time, Anne's fragment gives way to an equally

FIGURE 41.3 (Continued)

passionate run of triplet sixteenths, and her line climaxes and cadences together with Richard's: there is no question that his push to seem more normate in both body and mind, and his resulting seduction, have succeeded.

Nonetheless, the lower strings continue their tremolos throughout, reminding the listener that despite Richard's apparent appeal here, his mind is corrupted and he is not to be trusted. This is brought home when, after Anne departs, Richard lets the audience know of his plans for Lady Anne—to "have her, but [. . .] not keep her long" (1.2.233).

(d)

FIGURE 41.3 (Continued)

Here the string tremolos lead up right to Richard's point of speech, where the music stops completely so that the audience can hear his words clearly, the sound of his unnaturalness still ringing in their ears.

Using chromaticism, a well-known cue for both sexuality and otherness, as well as extended instrumental techniques that equate the nonnormate physical and mental with nonnormate timbres and physical uses of instruments, Walton creates cues that clearly stand for Richard's unnatural body and mind. By contrasting Richard's musical tropes with those of the other characters—Anne's pastoral English music and the regular beat of Richmond's military-style marches—Richard is further heard to be outside of the normate as marked by stable modalities or tonalities and mainstream orchestral writing. Through the score, Richard is signified as more than simply evil, as needing more than an ominous low-pitched, minor-key motif, which Walton supplies with musical materials as far from the usual as possible while still being recognizable as music rather than relegated to the world of nonmusical sound.

For Olivier's film, Walton composed an orchestral score that stretched the typical timbres and techniques of the ensemble to signify Richard through an aesthetic that most listeners would associate with the alien and nonnormate. Olivier's playing of the role dictated the film's reliance on and use of the early modern belief of the disabled body as a marker of the equally disabled or deformed mind as an interpretative device. However, by using the language of "fake medievalism," Walton firmly locates this belief in Olivier's constructed past, rather than giving credence to it. Thus we see and hear Olivier's Richard III from the point of view of Olivier's and Walton's understanding of the early modern period's view of the historical past: they personally do not believe that bodily difference is a signifier of innate evil, and are firmly placing this belief in the past through the use of period-style music. Walton responds to this construction with a score that not only others Richard, but aurally brands him as monstrous through both musically abstract and concrete ways, creating a Richard III of the early modern period via twentieth-century practices.

Acknowledgment

Special thanks to Brooks Kuykendall for his detailed and thoughtful comments on and suggestions for this essay.

References

Brown, Constance. 1967. "Olivier's Richard III: A Re-Evaluation." *Film Quarterly* 20 (4): 23–32.

Charnes, Linda. 1993. *Notorious Identity: Materializing the Subject in Shakespeare*. Cambridge, MA: Harvard University Press.

Colley, John Scott. 1992. *Richard's Himself Again: A Stage History of Richard III*. Contributions in Drama and Theatre Studies 46. New York: Greenwood.

Denes, Melissa, Laura Barnett, and Andrew Dickson. 2013. "Richard III: Shakespearean Actors Rake over the Remains." *Guardian*, February 4. http://www.guardian.co.uk/stage/2013/feb/04/shakespearean-actors-richard-iii-remains.

Garland-Thomson, Rosemarie. 1997. *Extraordinary Bodies: Figuring Physical Disability in American Culture and Literature*. New York: Columbia University Press.

Hodgdon, Barbara. 1998. "Replicating Richard: Body Doubles, Body Politics." *Theatre Journal* 50 (2): 207–225.

Holland, Peter. 1996. "Hand in Hand to Hell." *Times Literary Supplement*, May 10.

Howlett, Kathy M. 2000. *Framing Shakespeare on Film*. Athens: Ohio University Press.

Kalinak, Kathryn. 2003. "The Language of Music: A Brief Analysis of *Vertigo*." In *Movie Music: The Film Reader*, edited by Kay Dickinson, 15–25. New York: Routledge.

Kuykendall, James Brooks. 2011. "William Walton's Film Scores: New Evidence in the Autograph Manuscripts." *Notes* 68 (1): 9–32. doi: 10.1353/not.2011.0097.

Lund, Roger. 2005. "Laughing at Cripples: Ridicule, Deformity, and the Argument from Design." *Eighteenth-Century Studies* 39 (1): 91–114. doi: 10.1353/ecs.2005.0051.

Mitchell, David T., and Sharon L. Snyder. 2000. *Narrative Prosthesis: Disability and the Dependencies of Discourse*. Ann Arbor: University of Michigan Press.

Moulton, Ian Frederick. 1996. "'A Monster Great Deformed': The Unruly Masculinity of Richard III." *Shakespeare Quarterly* 47 (3): 251–268.

Shakespeare, William. 2001. *King Henry VI Part III*. Edited by Eric Rasmussen and John D. Cox. Arden Shakespeare, Third Series. London: Arden Shakespeare.

Shakespeare, William. 2009. *King Richard III*. Edited by James Siemon. Arden Shakespeare, Third Series. London: Arden Shakespeare.

Siemon, James. 2009. Introduction to *King Richard III*, edited by James Siemon, 1–123. Arden Shakespeare, Third Series. London: Arden Shakespeare.

Slotkin, Joel Elliot. 2007. "Honeyed Toads: Sinister Aesthetics in Shakespeare's Richard III." *Journal for Early Modern Cultural Studies* 7 (1): 5–32.

Tempera, Mariangela. 2005. "Winters and Horses." In *Shakespeare on Screen: Richard III; Proceedings of the Conference Organised at the Université de Rouen, 4–5 March 2005*, edited by Sarah Hatchuel and Nathalie Vienne-Guerrin, 65–90. Rouen, France: Publications de L'université de Rouen.

Turner, David, and Kevin Stagg. 2006. *Social Histories of Disability and Deformity*. London and New York: Routledge and Society for the Social History of Medicine.

Williams, Katherine Schaap. 2009. "Enabling Richard: The Rhetoric of Disability in Richard III." *Disability Studies Quarterly* 29 (4). http://dsq-sds.org/article/view/997/1181.

CHAPTER 42

HEARING A SITE OF MASCULINITY IN FRANZ WAXMAN'S SCORE FOR *PRIDE OF THE MARINES* (1945)

NEIL LERNER

In the study of disability representation, there has been for over two decades a growing body of scholarly work that attends to the ways disabilities have been (and continue to be) constructed visually and thematically in narrative structures. More recently—as demonstrated by this current book and a flurry of other articles and books—there is now a growing focus on how so much of what is read without question as ostensibly normal and abnormal in musical practices of composition and performance (i.e., functional tonality, formal symmetries and balance, two-handed pianism, etc.) can be understood as continually reinscribing cultural constructs like (so-called) deformed bodies and mental states of insanity or autism.[1] The gap between the study of visible and audible representations of disabilities persists as we shift into even more narrow areas of investigation, such as patterns of representation in screen media like film. While Martin Norden's *The Cinema of Isolation: A History of Physical Disability in the Movies* (1994) has provided a durable taxonomy for the types of disability constructs that persist in cinema (stereotypes like the Sweet Innocent, the Tragic Victim, and the Obsessive Avenger), we are still at an early stage in mapping out the ways music contributes to the construction of disability in screen media.

In *Narrative Prosthesis: Disability and the Dependencies of Discourse*, their pioneering study of disability and narrative theory, David Mitchell and Sharon Snyder (2000) argue for the centrality of disability to storytelling ("disability services [the] narrative appetite for difference as often as any other constructed category of deviance" [55]) and in the context of disability and performativity, they place singular emphasis on the visual:

> Difference demands display. Display demands difference. The arrival of a narrative must be attended by the "unsightly" eruption of the anomalous (often physical in nature) within the social field of vision. The (re)mark upon disability begins with a stare, a gesture of disgust, a slander or derisive comment upon bodily ignominy, a note of gossip about a rare or unsightly presence, a comment upon the unsuitability of deformity for the appetites of polite society, or a sentiment about the unfortunate circumstances that bring disabilities into being. (Mitchell and Snyder 2000, 55)

Mitchell and Snyder devote a chapter to what they call "film art's 'new physiognomy'—the visually expedient 'twist' to what [they] have theorized in previous chapters as narrative prosthesis" (Mitchell and Snyder 2000, 96). Yet this hegemonic primacy given to the eye risks overlooking (note visual metaphor) the potent signifiers in modes like sound. In the tradition of Hollywood film music, several conventions of audible-izing strategies have emerged that might parallel the "visualizing strategies" that Mitchell and Snyder quote from Barbara Maria Stafford (Mitchell and Snyder 2000, 96). For instance, a film score might present a denotative attempt to highlight a bodily difference, as when Max Steiner—in *Of Human Bondage* and *The Informer*—accompanies characters with mobility impairments with uneven, limping rhythms, a code called *alla zoppa* in its earlier appearances.[2] Steiner's literalism reappeared in his music for *The Beast with Five Fingers*, where at one point the audience gets a subjective shot of a paralyzed pianist experiencing a state of double vision as Steiner's score splits into bitonality: Steiner's score accompanies the visual overlapping with a rendition of Bach's Chaconne in D minor in both E minor and F minor, performed at that moment in the film by two unseen pianists who both use two hands, an exceptionally clear example of musical prosthesis as the four-handed piano music accompanies a one-handed pianist (see Lerner 2006, 85). Other studies of film music and disability include Jennifer Iverson's (2006) examination of the soundtrack in *Dancer in the Dark*, which she describes as "a sympathetic representation of disability against the ableist ideology of the narrative" (60) and Kelly Gross's (2006) investigation of Zbigniew Preisner's music and its signals for psychological trauma in the film *Blue* (41).

Tobin Siebers (2008) has posited that "disability offers a challenge to the representation of the body" (53), while Rosemarie Garland-Thomson (2002) probed more specifically into the realm of the visual when she observed that "the history of disabled people in the Western world is in part the history of being on display, of being visually conspicuous while politically and socially erased" (56). Both of these points come into focus (again, a visual metaphor) in the genre of the war film, which have been described as being "rife with themes of disability" (Ashby, White, and Rosetti 2009, 362). The case of the Warner Bros. film *Pride of the Marines*, released in August of 1945, offers a useful example of the representational challenges that Siebers describes, and while the story revolves around an actual person—Al Schmid, who was blinded in 1943 during his Marine service in the Pacific—who does indeed become an object of spectacle, the conspicuousness of Schmid's impairment does not get politically or socially erased, at least not completely. Instead, Schmid's resistance to rehabilitation and his refusal to accept any assistance become a key barrier to his ability to resume his life after the war, a point the film weaves into its title with the pun on the word "pride." (Here "pride" can signify the collective admiration for Schmid's heroic effort as well as the stubbornness of a marine toward rehabilitation or accepting assistance.) Franz Waxman's musical score serves an important function by amplifying the subjective emotional states (particularly fear and horror) experienced by Schmid. Deploying at times a highly expressionistic musical language as well as some unusual and early uses of sounds that were manipulated via magnetic tape, Waxman's melodramatic music creates exaggerated moments of pity and horror in the midst of a soundtrack and film that synergistically combine to produce on the one hand a rousing overcoming narrative that quickly resolves several of the impaired character's problems, going so far at the end of the film to suggest that his vision was going to return, while on the other hand complicating the typically easy resolution (of a Hollywood film) with a strongly progressive argument valuing individual sacrifice for a collectivist cause.

From Life to *Life* to Screen

The story of Al Schmid, the Marine whose eyes were severely injured in World War II and who became the subject of considerable media attention including *Pride of the Marines*, has been part of the scholarly conversations in Disability Studies in large part because of David A. Gerber's essay on Schmid that appeared first in *Journal of American Studies* and then in *The Body and Physical Difference: Discourses of Disability* (Gerber 1997). Along with a brief story in *Time* (February 1, 1943), a much lengthier article in *Life* by Roger Butterfield (March 22, 1943) and then a subsequent 1944 book (*Al Schmid, Marine*, also by Butterfield) brought Schmid's story to the wider public. Warner Bros. began work on a film version of Schmid's story in 1943.[3] Within the nearly twenty treatments and revisions of the script that occurred between 1943 and 1944, the title of the film went through significant variations in title, from *Al Schmid—Marine* to *Al Schmid: Hero* to *Sergeant Schmid—Marine* and, for several versions, *This Love of Ours*, all before settling on *Pride of the Marines*. There were major differences in story structure, with some versions going into much greater detail about Schmid's personal history.

Five names of writers appear at various stages in the development of the screenplay: Marvin Borowsky, A. I. Bezzerides, Alvah Bessie, Albert Maltz, and Ranald MacDougall. In the finished film, credit for the screenplay goes to Albert Maltz, and Marvin Borowsky is credited for the adaptation of Butterfield's novel. For his screenplay for *Pride of the Marines*, Maltz was nominated for an Academy Award (in the category of Writing Adapted Screenplay), and one of his fellow nominees in this category was fellow *Pride* writer Ranald MacDougall (for *Mildred Pierce*), though ultimately both lost to Charles Brackett and Billy Wilder's screenplay for *The Lost Weekend*. Alvah Bessie was nominated that same year for Best Story for his work on another Warner Bros. war film, *Objective, Burma!* (which had in common with *Pride of the Marines* writer Ranald MacDougall, producer Jerry Wald, and composer Franz Waxman). Yet what may be most revealing about the names connected with this film is the considerable participation by individuals who would find themselves deeply affected by the politics of anticommunism only a few short years after their work on it. John Garfield, the actor who portrayed Schmid in the film, had been a member of the Group Theatre in the 1930s and was later blacklisted after being listed in *Red Channels* and because of his testimony as an unfriendly witness before the House Committee on Un-American Activities (HUAC).[4] And both Alvah Bessie and Albert Maltz were part of the Hollywood Ten, a group of individuals from the film industry who refused to testify before the US Congress and who were subsequently jailed before being blacklisted.

The film indeed carries what was for its day a progressive political perspective. Bernard Dick (1989) understood Maltz's efforts with *Pride of the Marines* as coming from a desire to "write the great proletarian film" (91). In some of the earliest treatments of the screenplay ("Suggestions for 'Al Schmidt' " [*sic*], September 20, 1943), Maltz envisioned a fictitious childhood scene for the young Al Schmid:

> Al as a boy of ten or thirteen is waylaid on a street at dusk by a gang of boys calling themselves the Junior Ku Klux Klan of Pearl Street. The father of one of them is a Ku Kluxer from the South. Al is "kangarooed" on three counts—he is a "Heinie foreigner," (his father) he is Irish (his mother) [and] he is Catholic (was his mother?). The boys beat him up. Al gets away, bloodied and battered. He rounds up his own gang. Returns that night or next day. They beat up the other gang, Al reserving the leader for himself. One of Al's friends makes a suggestion. In accord with it they make the Junior Ku Kluxers kneel down and recite, "All Men Are Created Equal" a hundred times, while bumping their foreheads on a democratic pavement.

While that particular scene did not end up in the final film, there were still several moments where proletarian notions of better conditions for workers run into conflict with questions of ethnic identity. Perhaps most pointedly, a scene deep in the film of wounded veterans (all of them are men, highlighting the overlap here of bodily difference and the expectations of gender norms) having a discussion in their hospital has several of them worrying that their jobs will be gone when they return to civilian life; one of the men explains that he expects he will "probably find some Mexican's got my job." At that moment, the camera moves to reveal one of their Mexican colleagues, a tall man in a wheelchair who stares up forlornly at the speaker. "I'm sorry, Juan, you're a Mexican, but you're different, you're one of the guys in B company," said the offending speaker, but Juan answers back that "no, I'm not different, Joe, I'm just a Mexican, like a lot of other Mexicans who fought." Juan then spins around and wheels away from the group.[5]

The film's repeated arguments about equal rights for all, including not only veterans with impairments but also for those of various economic classes and ethnic backgrounds, extended even into matters of religious diversity. In earlier treatments of the script, Maltz suggested returning to "Al's Ku Kluxer childhood experience," imagining a later scene where someone makes an anti-Semitic remark about Schmid's foxhole buddy, Leroy Diamond, and "before Diamond can even do anything, it is Al who has instantly swung and knocked the guy down."[6] In a pivotal exchange between Schmid and Diamond that did make it into the finished film, Schmid explains his fear that no one will ever hire him now because of his physical impairment, to which Diamond replies "Sure, there'll be some guys who won't hire you—even when they know you can handle a job. But there's some who won't hire me because my name's Diamond instead of Jones—because I celebrate Passover instead of Easter." The conversation ends with Diamond arguing for a postwar United States "where nobody gets booted around for any reason." Maltz offers his argument with crystal clarity in this early 1943 treatment for the screenplay when he asserts that Al

> learns finally what he had never thought about before: that he is not alone—he is an American, linked to all Americans. Both his fighting and his mutilation acquire a new meaning. Valley Forge becomes more than a phrase—he can see it as part of his own life, as his own deed has already become part of the American picture. Blind, his life takes on a meaning it never had before.[7]

Such assertions of the necessity for an egalitarian society where equal civil rights would be granted to everyone, where neither ethnicity, religion, nor physical impairment would lessen one's full participation in their world, would be turned, with devastating consequences for their careers, against individuals like Maltz and Garfield during the HUAC hearings, though their sacrifices also saw the introduction of more nuanced films about disabilities into the US postwar market. When asked by the Committee about whether or not Maltz had injected so-called subversive material and communist propaganda into the screenplay for *Pride of the Marines*, Warner Bros.' production head Jack Warner said that Maltz had tried unsuccessfully to do so, adding that "some of these lines [of dialogue] have innuendoes and double meanings, and things like that, and you have to take eight or ten Harvard law courses to find out what they mean" (Norden 1994, 185). Norden (1994) quotes from a 1947 article in *The Hollywood Reporter* that included *Pride of the Marines* (as well as even better-known films like *The Best Years of Our Lives*) as containing "sizable doses of Communist propaganda" (186). Calling many of the people involved with these movies "filmmakers of conscience," Norden argues that they marked a key shift in the ways that films represented persons with disabilities (184). Martin Halliwell (2009) writes more specifically of *Pride of the Marines* as the beginning of a wave of films that he refers to as "demobilization narratives," a series of films that appeared in the United States between 1945 and 1951 and that emphasized issues of hospitalization and rehabilitation, topics that previously had been discretely erased from earlier films depicting war and its consequences.

The story of Al Schmid created in the popular mass media stressed his status as an Everyman, setting him up as an easily relatable figure whose situation could advocate for improved understanding of all wounded veterans. In a promotion for the film that appeared in *Life* (October 29, 1945), John Garfield (whose interest in Schmid's story played a key role in it becoming a film) offered this testimonial: "You see, Al got kind of knocked around that night on Guadalcanal. It did something to him. Inside and outside both. And when you see *Pride of the Marines*, I think it will help you to understand what the boys who go through that experience are up against when they come home—and how you can help them find the happiness they've earned." Schmid's war injuries had led to the removal of one of his eyeballs and left serious damage to the other one, though the damage went beyond the visual deficit (he was unable to perceive anything visually apart from some vague color and light) and into his wounded psyche. In the film, Schmid resists rehabilitation and does not even want his fiancée, Ruth, to be told of his condition, though one of his nurses (Virginia) writes the news to her anyway.[8] The various treatments show considerable reworking of where to leave Schmid's status at the end of the film—some ended with Schmid being able to see the lights on a Christmas tree, with the final ending being one where Schmid identifies the color of a taxicab in the distance—but all versions ended with Al and Ruth reconciling.[9] As Norden observes, by the end of the film "Al finally sees the light not only figuratively but literally as well" (162).

Strategies for Representing Blindness in Screen Media

In her book-length effort to catalog all representations of disability in television and film, Lauri Klobas (1988) declared that "blindness is the most frequently seen physical limitation onscreen" (2). Noting how mass culture representations of blindness tend to make no distinction between total blindness and limited vision, she draws attention to recurring tropes such as a blind character feeling the face of someone else to imagine them, the frequency of a blind character developing compensatory sensory abilities, and the affectation she calls the "wooden stare" in which a blind character "stares unflinchingly ahead" and stops moving their head in the direction of sounds (3). Klobas found Garfield's depiction of Schmid "annoying," complaining of his "wooden stare" and how "two minutes after having the grenade tossed in his face, he stopped moving his head in the direction of sounds" (8). Yet beyond Garfield's acting, the film deployed a number of narrative and stylistic contrivances in connection with Schmid's loss of vision.

Numerous moments in the film foreshadow Schmid's imminent blindness. In the opening scene of the film, we find Al boarding with his friends, the Merchants, and Jim Merchant is working on the wiring in their home when Ruth Hartley happens to ring the doorbell and short out everything in the house. When Al goes to the door and asks this stranger if she had rung the doorbell, Rush answers "yes—and sparks flew out," a rather unveiled metaphorical reference to their immediate attraction for each other (though in the film it takes a few dates for them to realize they actually like each other). In the blackout caused by Ruth's arrival, Jim's daughter Lucy shouts out that she can't see anything, and Jim continues to bumble through his repair jobs against the questions of his wife Ella Mae, who wonders whether or not Jim has any idea what he is doing. Both prefigure Al's blindness as does his stubborn refusal to agree with his wife's sensible assessment of the problems. At the subsequent scene in a bowling alley, where Al and Ruth have their rocky first date, Jim struggles to repair the device projecting the bowling scores, complaining that it is out of focus (another prophecy of visual limitations), and Ella Mae, who engineered the meeting between Al and Ruth, observed to Jim that Al's "eyes haven't left her all evening." And perhaps only because blindness is a central theme in this film does the appearance of multiple figures of speech positioning sight as a central mode of comprehension stand out so sharply, as characters emit lines like "How 'bout you keep your eyes on the road," "Didn't you see my car," "I can hardly wait to see you," "I don't like blind dates," "almost a bullseye," "the whole country has its eyes open," and "don't you see it guys, can't you see it?"

Augmenting these verbal markers of sightedness are a number of situations in which something happens abruptly that changes the state of the scene. In the opening scene with the blackout, Waxman's nondiegetic underscore ends sharply as the lights go out, just as the music will also suddenly end in a later scene where Al playfully rams his car into the car of another of Ruth's suitors. In the scene where news of the attack on Pearl Harbor comes over the radio, a performance of Brahms's Fourth Symphony is interrupted by the announcer. The interruptions extend to romantic matters: in an early scene with Ruth and Al, their musical love theme ends suddenly as Al moves in to kiss Ruth, and a later discussion in the rehabilitation ward has one recovering veteran telling another about a date that was ruined when the lights suddenly went out. The frequency of these phrases and situations in the screenplay emphasizes the sudden and profound changes to be experienced by Schmid and those in his life.

Similar to the interruptions in the dialogue, Waxman's score also contains several occasions of a musical line that abruptly ends, offering a musical metaphor for a sudden amputation or deficit. The most striking of these occurs in the music accompanying the scene where Schmid loses his sight as the result of a Japanese grenade. Until Schmid ships off to fight with the Marines, Waxman's score consists of tonal, largely consonant cues. As Ruth and Al begin to fall in love with each other, Waxman introduces a lush love theme for them that first appears diegetically, as Al turns on a car radio (Figure 42.1 and Track 42.1 on the Companion Website). Their love theme occurs several other times before Al leaves to fight, including a prominent reappearance of it (sung by a choir accompanied by orchestra) in a scene at the railroad station where Al hurriedly proposes to Ruth (Figure 42.2 and Track 42.2 on the Companion Website). With the scenes on Guadalcanal (a Pacific island that saw particularly severe fighting between the United States and Japan), the score shifts to a far more dissonant and unsettling style. For scenes where Schmid and his partners Johnny Rivers and Lee Diamond wait in their machine gun nest for an imminent Japanese attack, Waxman wrote increasingly chromatic cues that reached their climax at the moment Schmid is blinded (Figure 42.3). Waxman accompanies the slow but unstoppable movements of the Japanese soldier toward the machine gun nest by relying on a conventional orientalist trope, a progression of parallel

(a)

FIGURE 42.1 The first appearance of the love theme for Al and Ruth, which Waxman simply refers to as "theme." Reprinted by permission. *Pride of the Marines* by Franz Waxman.

(b)

FIGURE 42.1 Continued.

(a)

FIGURE 42.2 As Al leaves for war, the love theme returns in full force as they express their feelings for each other and as Al gives Ruth an engagement ring. Reprinted by permission. *Pride of the Marines* by Franz Waxman. © 1945 (Renewed) Warner-Olive Music LLC (ASCAP). All Rights (excluding print) controlled and administered by Universal Music Corp. (ASCAP). Exclusive worldwide print rights administered by Alfred Music. All rights reserved.

FIGURE 42.2 Continued.

FIGURE 42.2 Continued.

FIGURE 42.3 Waxman's music for the scene where Al is blinded by a Japanese grenade. Reprinted by permission. *Pride of the Marines* by Franz Waxman.

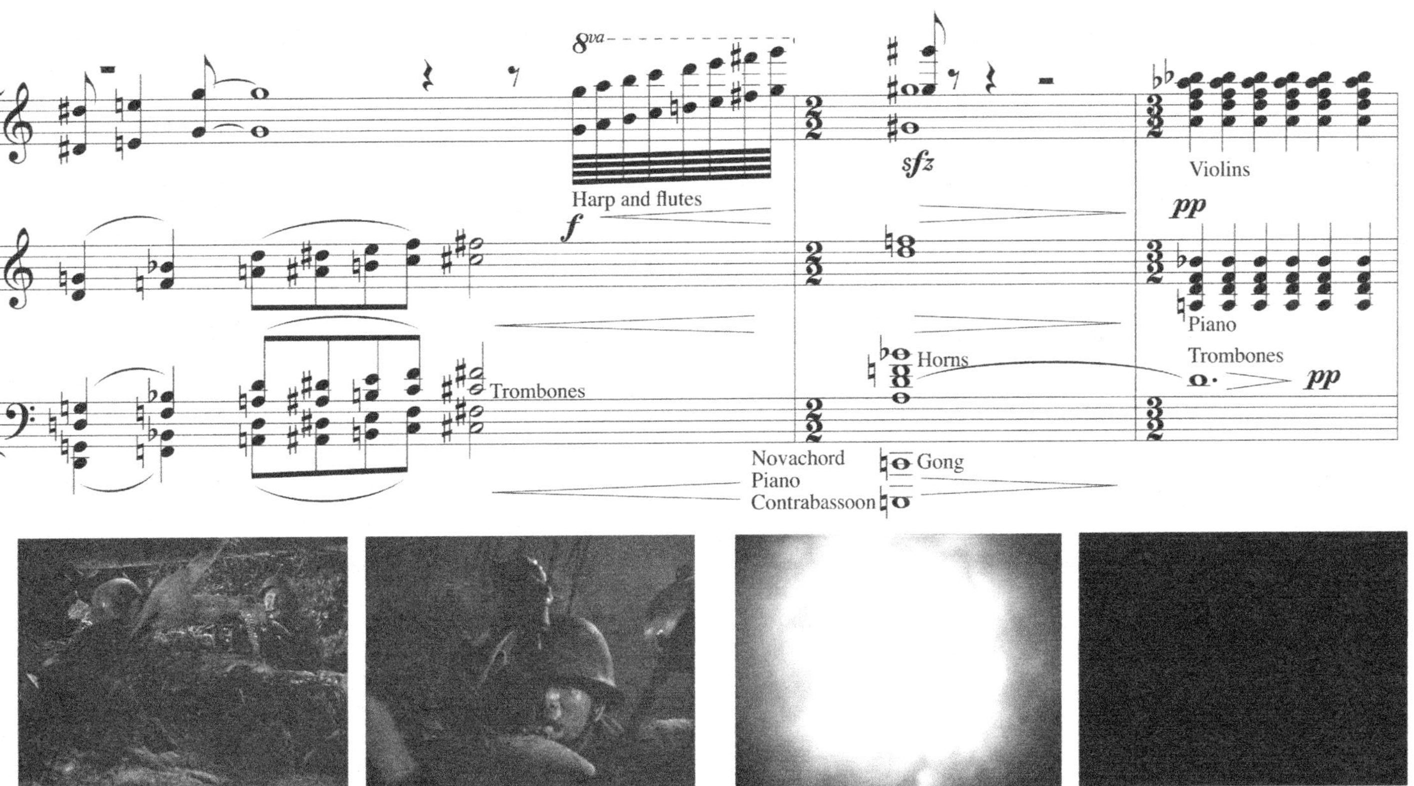

FIGURE 42.3 Continued.

perfect fourths (Track 42.3 on the Companion Website). The instructions in the screenplay, which compare the Japanese soldier to an insect, dictated that the shot of the grenade occur directly into the camera: "Legs trailing, the Jap slowly crawls to one side of the line of Al's fire. His legs drag, he looks like a half-squashed bug . . . but the grenade is always coming closer. His eyes are fixed hypnotically up at the gun as it fires."[10] The moment of the grenade explosion (preceded by a close-up shot of the grenade, in hand, coming toward the camera, then a sudden flash of light before a moment of complete darkness) marks one of the three instances in the film of point-of-view camera shots.

The next subjective shots occur only a few moments later in the film as a doctor removes the bandages for the first time after Al has had eye surgery. The doctor repeatedly attempts to lower Al's expectations, and Garfield expresses Schmid's anxiety through his shaky voice. As the doctor removes the bandages and has Al open his eyes for the first time, Waxman's cue enters extremely softly but on a highly dissonant chord that builds from a pianississississimo to a piano sforzando as we see Schmid open his eyes and immediately realize he is unable to perceive anything in the darkened room (Figure 42.4 and Track 42.4 on the Companion Website). As Schmid's tension mounts, Waxman trades a slow, rising melody between the low and high instrumental regions of the orchestra. When the doctor begins the test of shining a bright light into Schmid's eyes, the screen goes completely dark for over twelve seconds and Waxman's music establishes a low C-♮ pedal point as a solo bass clarinet ominously climbs up a series of octatonic pitch collections. When a vague light shape appears in the middle of the screen, which Schmid describes as a distant locomotive light, three contrabassoons play a murky rising progression; with a cut away from Schmid's subjective shot to a shot of Schmid having a light shined in his face, Waxman's twitchy melodic figures in the flutes suggest the fuzziness of what Schmid perceived. The entire cue ends abruptly with a sharp crash. Waxman's music signals deeply unsettled emotions for both the characters and the audience.

Representing the Horror of Blindness: The Nightmare Scene

One of the most remarkable moments in the film occurs shortly after Schmid has realized the extent of his vision loss, when he experiences an elaborate nightmare that was both visually and musically ahead of its time.[11] Opening with Schmid in bed, clutching his sheets as he talks in his sleep, the film begins to share Schmid's nightmarish visions of the machine gun battle (using negative for positive imagery) to the accompaniment of Waxman's slow-moving harmonies that gently alternate between mostly stable and then increasingly dissonant sonorities (Figure 42.5 and Track 42.5 on the Companion Website). Some of the sounds seem as though they have been processed to give them a quickly reverberating metallic quality, though it is unclear just what they have done

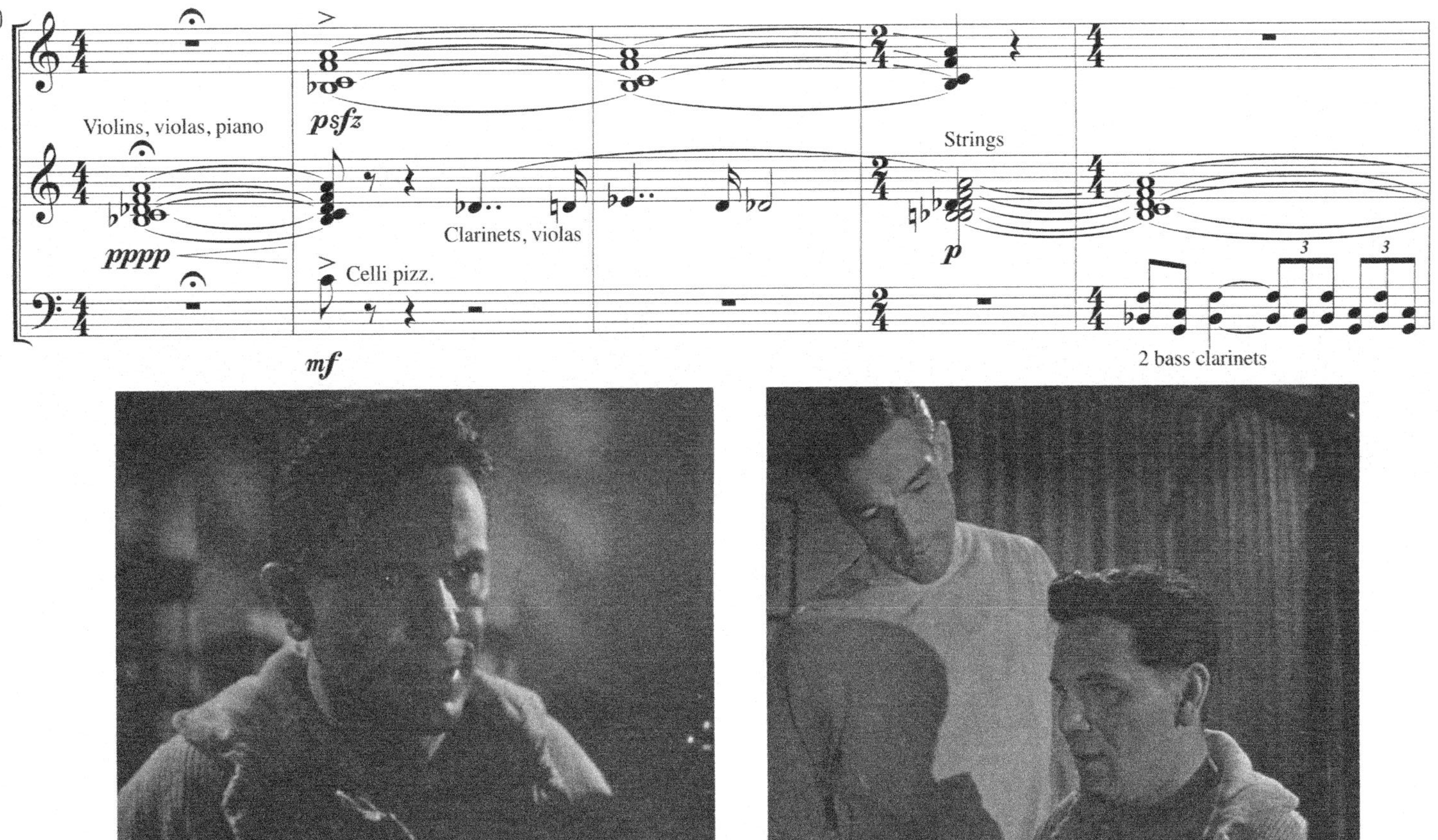

FIGURE 42.4 The scene Waxman called "No sight," in which Al's bandages are removed for the first time after his surgery, and he can see nothing but faint light. Reprinted by permission. *Pride of the Marines* by Franz Waxman.

FIGURE 42.4 Continued.

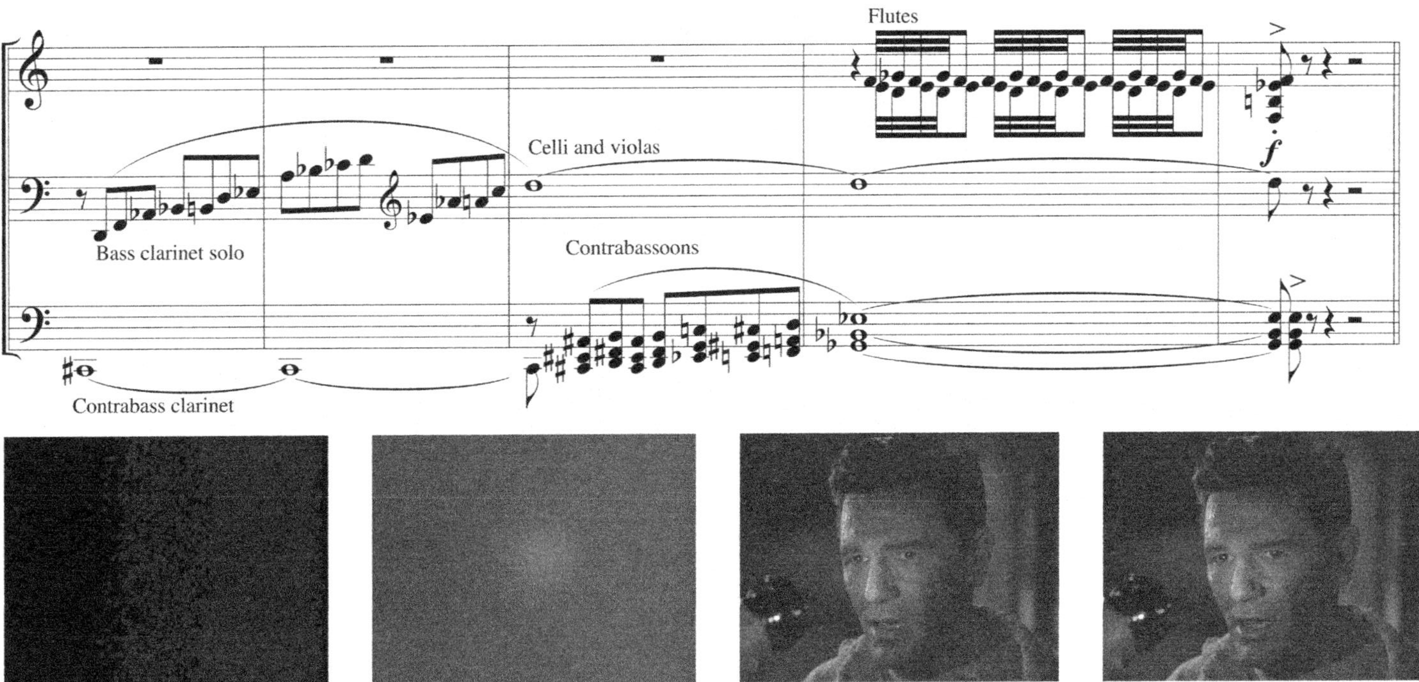

FIGURE 42.4 Continued.

here; the conductor's copy of the score does not reveal how these sounds were altered, though it does indicate that a novachord (the first commercially released polyphonic synthesizer, used in film scores beginning in the 1940s) appears at numerous places throughout the battle and rehabilitation scenes. When Schmid, in his dream, relives the moment when the grenade was thrown at him, the music and imagery suddenly become even more aggressive: angry brass chords slide down against rapidly ascending chromatic scales (spanning tritones) as the negative-image train is mirrored against itself on the frame.

The next moments are shockingly experimental for a 1945 Hollywood film, containing a cryptic visual symbolism found at that time chiefly in the works of avant-garde filmmakers like Maya Deren. Schmid reenvisions the scene when he and Ruth parted at the train as he left for the war. The score then doubles against itself in a remarkable way: as vocal parts enter with the musical theme that had earlier characterized Al and Ruth's romance, the accompanying instrumental parts come from a part of Waxman's cue being played in reverse.[12] (Figure 42.5 indicates which parts sounded in reverse.) Familiar and yet alien, this uncanny musical moment fuses with the similarly uncanny imagery of a blind man in glasses and with a cane walking up the train platform toward the couple. As Ruth (in the middle of an embrace with Al) turns to look at the blind man, the blind man disappears, though when Ruth turns back to Al, he now wears the same opaque glasses. A zoom into the glasses on Al's face ends with a superimposition of automobile lights and the eerie blaring of dissonant chords on the novachord. Are we hearing a traffic horn signaling an imminent crash? Is the bleating sound of the novachord signifying Ruth's horror, or Al's projection of his horror onto Ruth? Or all of these plus more? We see Ruth gaze in horror into Al's bespectacled face before the nightmare ends with her walking away in sped-up reverse motion.

The disturbing images and sounds reflect Schmid's deep anxieties about the possibility of betrayal by Ruth and especially about his future as a blind man who would be more dependent on others than Schmid had been previously in his life. Dana Polan (1983) reads the film as a conversion narrative that sends Schmid through a progression from "smug loner" to a person able to "commit himself to a cause" (29), whether that cause is the war effort or a marriage with Ruth. In this reading, Schmid finds himself facing two potentially devastating conditions that are set up here as disabling: the loss of his vision and his identity as an unmarried man. Rather predictably, the film moves toward an overcoming of both situations (all within a standard length of two hours) as Al and Ruth resolve to face life together just as Al begins to regain his sight: suggesting they get "the cab with the red on it," Al explains that he can see "fuzzy" though it is still no guarantee that he will "see good again," to which Ruth warmly says "whichever way it is, we'll do it together." As the cab drives off, following Al's instruction just to take them "home," Waxman closes the film with a chorus singing "America, the Beautiful" as the orchestra counters with a quodlibet of the melody from "The Marine's Hymn." As Polan observes, Al's principal problem is not his blindness but his refusal to join a family, and in particular his opposition to spending the rest of his life relying on Ruth. Waxman's uncanny

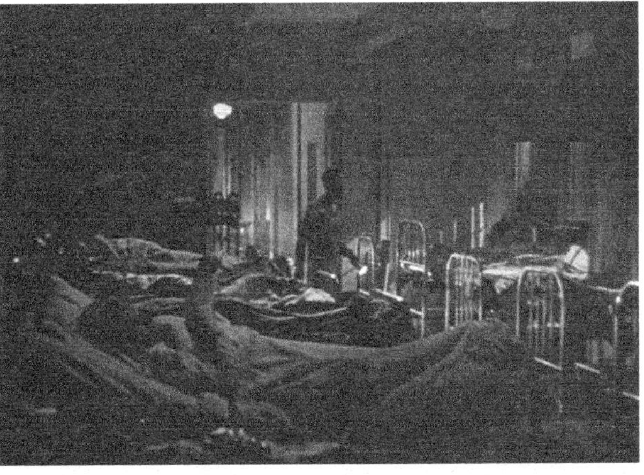

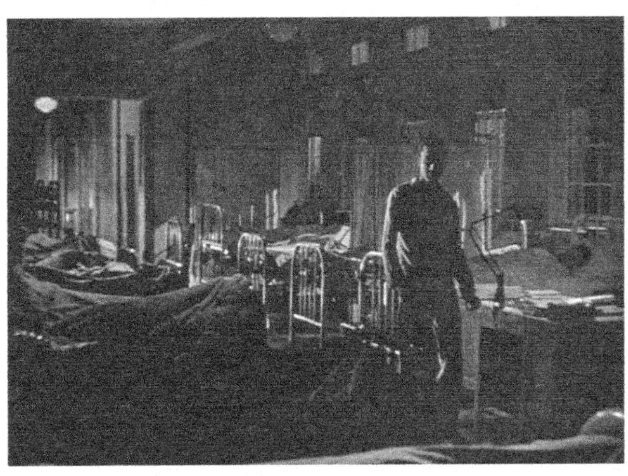

FIGURE 42.5 The music for the elaborate nightmare scene, which included the uncanny sounds of the novachord as well as some early examples of music being played in reverse (at the same time as different music was being played in normal order). Reprinted by permission. *Pride of the Marines* by Franz Waxman.

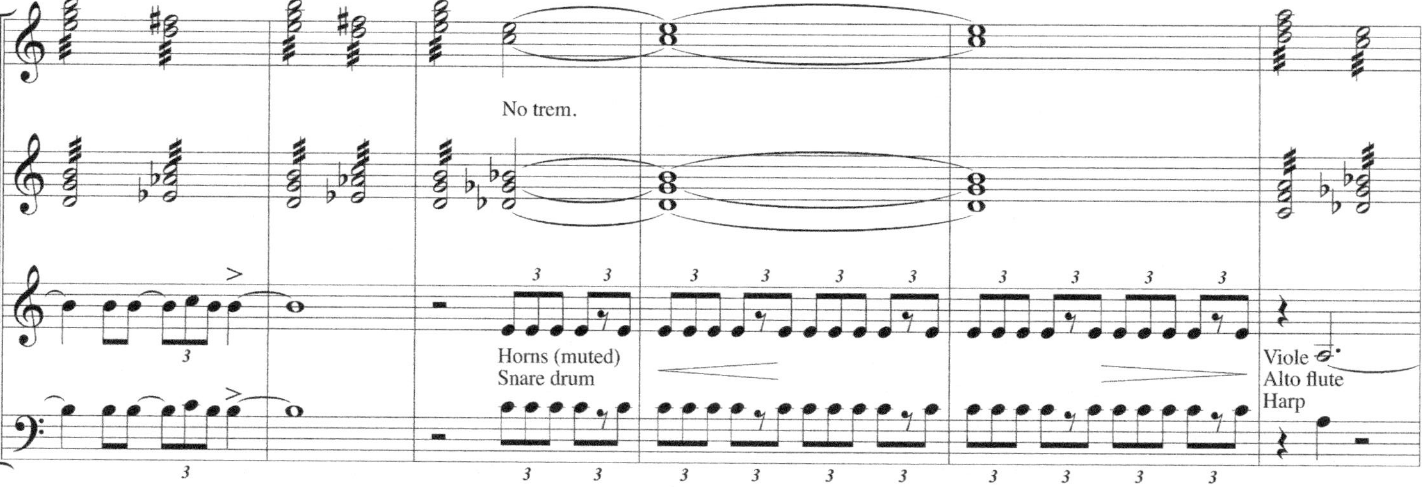

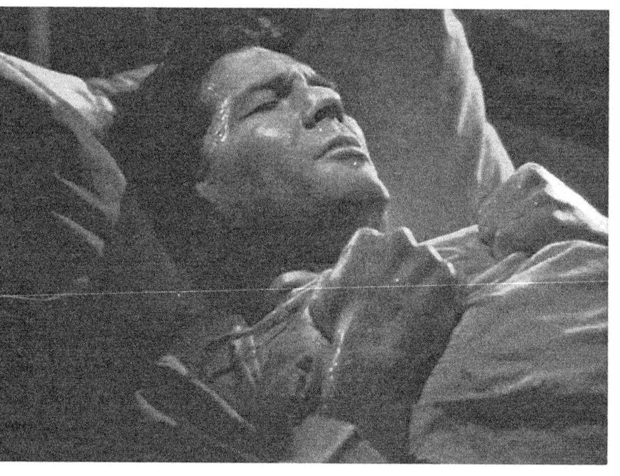

FIGURE 42.5 Continued.

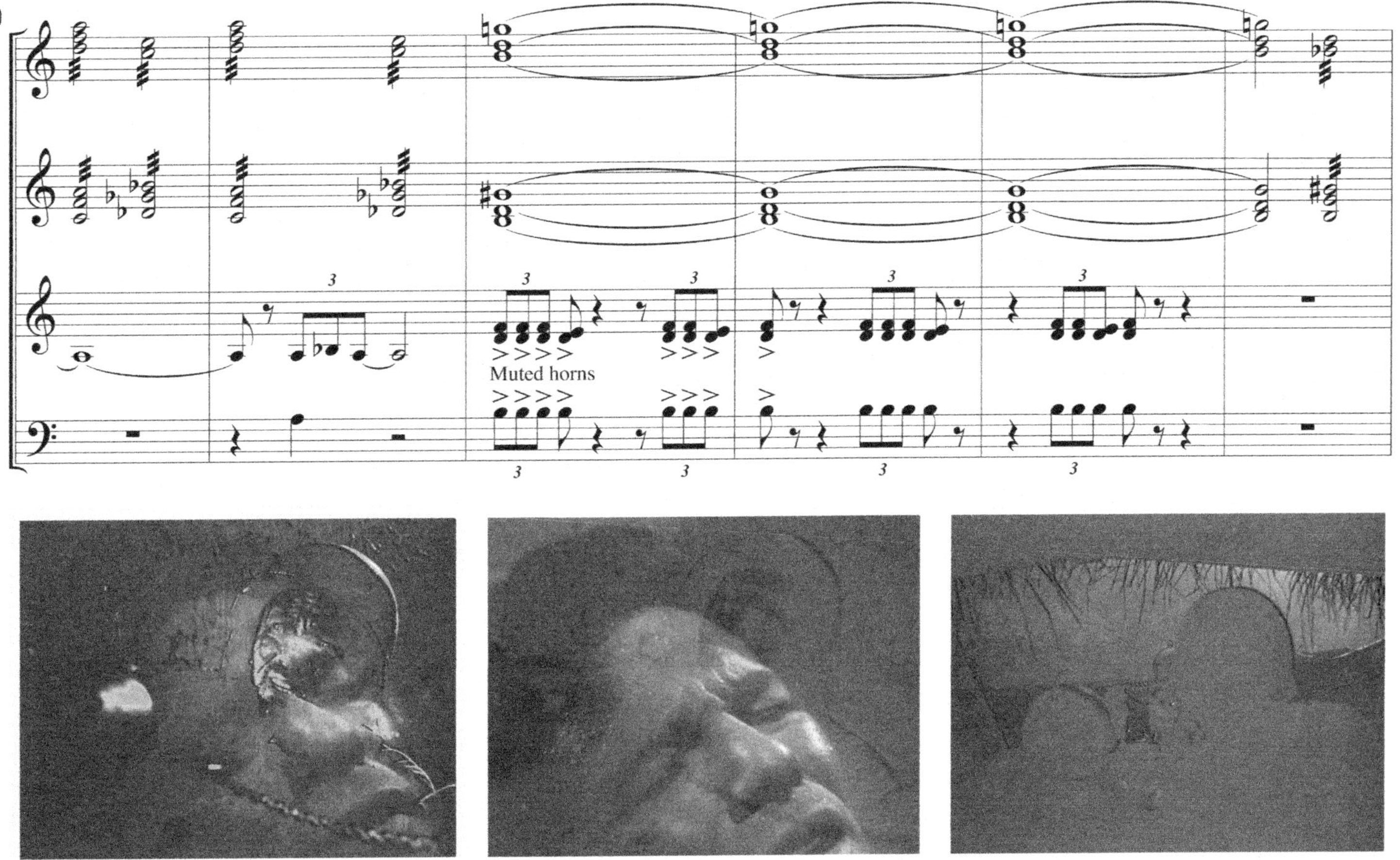

FIGURE 42.5 Continued.

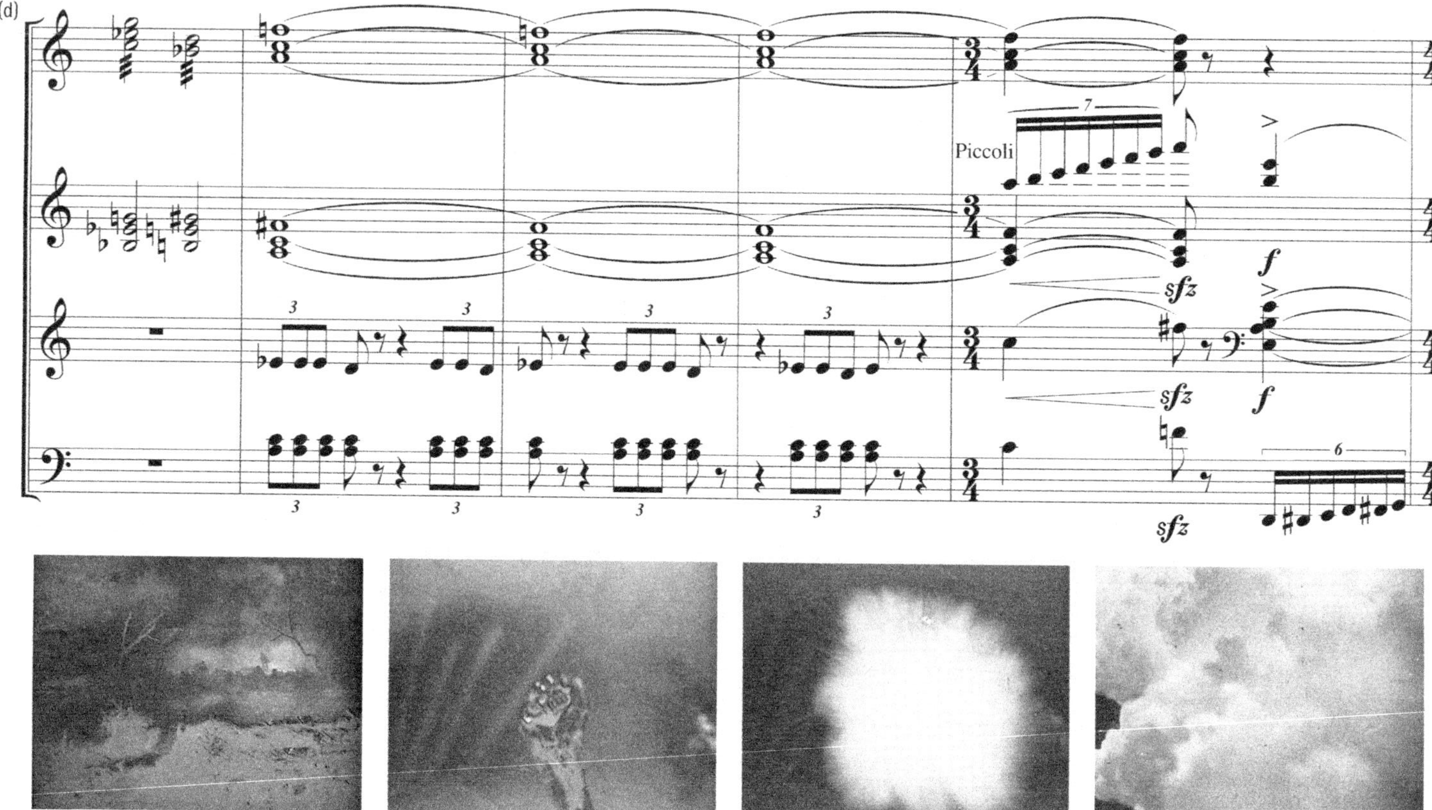

FIGURE 42.5 Continued.

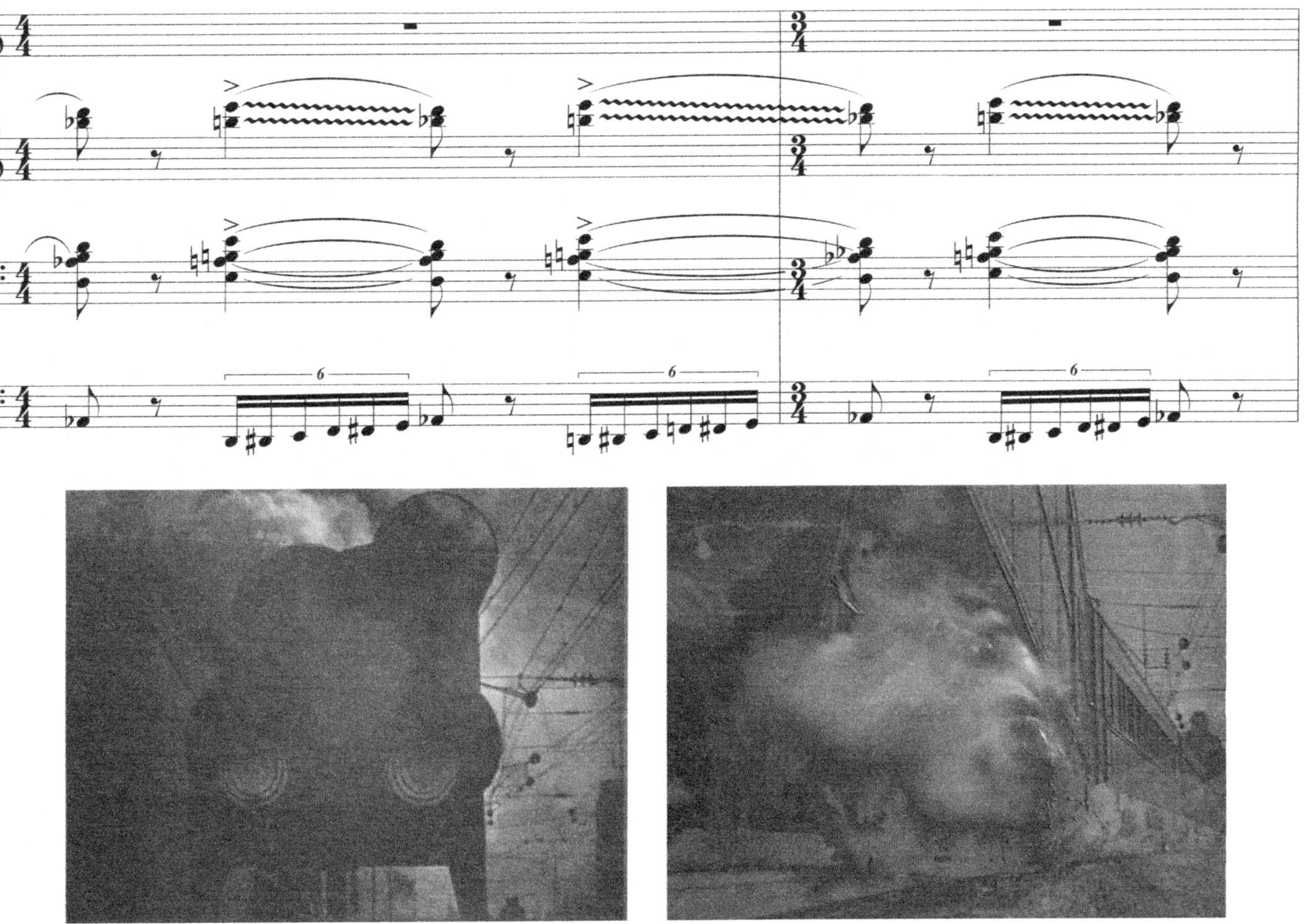

FIGURE 42.5 Continued.

FIGURE 42.5 Continued.

FIGURE 42.5 Continued.

FIGURE 42.5 Continued.

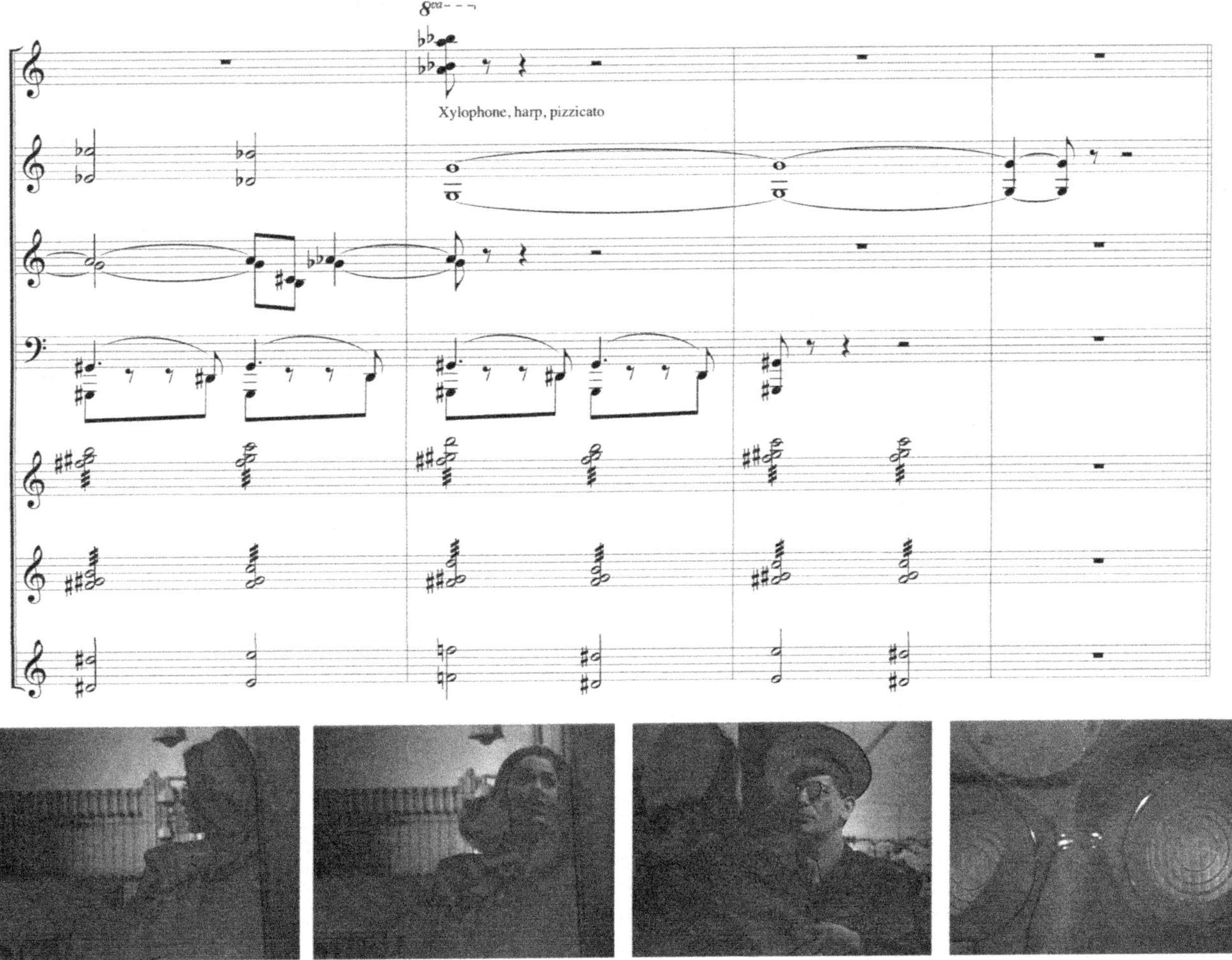

FIGURE 42.5 Continued.

scoring for the nightmare scene helps to exaggerate the horrors of blindness and isolation while amplifying Schmid's anxieties about losing his autonomy.

Other Ways Music Can Represent Disability in War Films

Comparisons with other films representing disabled veterans can reveal some of what was remarkable in *Pride of the Marines*. King Vidor's 1925 film about World War I, *The Big Parade*—one of the most financially successful Hollywood films before *Gone with the Wind* (1939)—was accompanied live for several years by a large orchestral score compiled by David Mendoza and William Axt. The film's Los Angeles première, at Grauman's Egyptian Theatre on November 5, 1925, was promoted with a parade and the first occurrence of live radio coverage (on KNX) commenting on the arrival of various celebrities. Laurence Stallings, a veteran Marine who had lost a leg at the battle of Belleau Wood, wrote the story (Isenberg 1988, 12). Some contemporary critics regarded the musical score as an important reason for the film's success (it ran for nearly two years in New York): Herman Weinberg wrote that this film score "represents the supreme catharsis in the field of synchronization" and that it "was a sheer triumph of mind over matter. It so completely transcended everything that had preceded it that its power to stir us to the point of pain was accepted without surprise—so engrossed were we in the cinema-bewitchment, so completely had we forgotten the presence of a camera, of a specially prepared orchestra and the artificialities of a theater" (Weinberg 1928, 3). Indeed, Vidor assembled his film with a special attentiveness to rhythm, going so far as to film scenes with metronomes or even bass drums beating out the pulse for the actors. (Dowd and Shepard 1988, 64).[13]

James Apperson, the central character of *The Big Parade*, is introduced as a rather feckless child of privilege who finds himself swept up in the patriotic mood and so volunteers to serve in the US military during World War I. While training for battle in France, he bonds with a local farm girl, Melisande, thereby providing the heteronormative cover for the homosocial relationships he forges with his fellow soldiers: their scenes are often accompanied by the Walter Donaldson and Gus Kahn hit from 1922, "My Buddy," whose words of affection for a presumably female romance could nonetheless have been "heard by many veterans as an affectionate song of remembrance for former army buddies" (Watkins 2003, 369). As the film unfolds, Apperson loses both Melisande and a leg (as Stallings actually had), though at the film's conclusion he returns to France and is reunited with one of these.

For the preparatory scenes before Apperson's return home to his unfaithful US girlfriend (she has taken up with his even more feckless brother) and his doting mother, Mendoza and Axt's musical choices follow with established melodramatic procedure: they borrow familiar and context-specific songs (like Louis Lambert's 1863 song

"When Johnny Comes Marching Home," kept in the key [G minor] of its original publication), and they prolong and intensify the emotional poignancy of scenes with slower tempos and chromatic inflections of the harmonic vocabulary associated with Tin Pan Alley songs of the early twentieth century. As we see Apperson and his father driving back to their house, the father brings up the indelicate topic of the US girlfriend and the music shifts back to "Douce Fièvre," the score's principal love theme for Apperson and Melisande; we then follow the mother as she discovers James's brother and former girlfriend kissing in the parlor. Up to this point in the film, there has been no indication that Apperson had a leg amputated in France.

With the visual spectacle of finally seeing Apperson (portrayed by 1920s heartthrob actor John Gilbert) on crutches and missing a leg, the score shifts to silence. Such a muting of the melodramatic apparatus of emotional and musical excess is shocking, though the silence is brief and then replaced with a literally muted (the strings are to be performed *con sordini*) version of "Sweet Little Woman O'Mine," the song associated earlier in the film with Apperson's mother. As Apperson and his mother embrace, we see a close-up of the mother's face in an iris shot—a visual cue informing us that we are seeing inside her thoughts—and then a montage of shots of the infant Apperson being rocked and comforted, the toddler Apperson taking what appear to be his first steps, the young boy being comforted in bed and then running and tripping, the adult Apperson walking off to war, and finally a return to a close-up of the crutches and the missing left leg. Apperson confides to his mother that "there's a girl" back in France, and his mother urges him to return, which he does. The film ties up everything neatly as the two lovers reunite, Melisande shouting "JIMMEE!" through the title card and Apperson lurching forward with a cane and prosthetic leg until the two embrace to the strains of "Douce Fièvre." The film smooths over the challenges awaiting this veteran: apart from his impaired gait, Apperson appears to have suffered no other lasting trauma, and the triumphant sounds of his love theme suggest a happy ending. Perhaps most striking about this example is the entry into the subjectivity of the mother instead of the returning veteran. Yet the brief muting of the entire musical apparatus during the initial reveal of Apperson's missing limb is a rare instance of this powerful technique of a non-diegetic silence, a moment perhaps only to be rivaled by the shocking silence observed by Claudia Gorbman in *The Jazz Singer* when the father walks in on the son and mother, yelling "stop!" and offering what Gorbman describes as a "castrating stare." (Gorbman 2007, 3)

Other ways of representing disabilities via music may be observed in William Wyler's Oscar-award winning film, *The Best Years of Our Lives* (1946), in which three men struggle to return to their prewar lives after their service in World War II. Separated by socioeconomic class—indeed, their civilian status is directly reciprocal to their military rank—they nonetheless form a bond as the three of them return together to the fictional Midwest town of Boone City (actually Cincinnati, Ohio). The oldest and most financially secure of them, Al Stephens, reacts to his reentry via heavy drinking. The most solidly middle-class of them, Homer Parish, lost his hands in the war, and while he had been carefully trained in how to use his prosthetic hooks, he struggles with being the object of stares and worries about being married to his childhood sweetheart, Wilma. The third man, Fred Derry, has difficulty finding a job and arrives home to an unfaithful wife; he appears to have what in later times would be labeled post-traumatic stress syndrome, and suffers from regular nightmares about a particularly hellish aerial battle. *The Best Years of Our Lives* shares with *Pride of the Marines* a motif of being immobilized between the past and future, of the traumas experienced during war haunting and transforming all possibilities in the future; this motif appears in *Pride* by way of the mixture of forward and reverse scattered throughout Schmid's nightmare, while in *Best Years* there is an arresting visual metaphor for this static state when we see the three returning servicemen in the rearview mirror of the taxicab driving them to their homecomings.

Remarkably, the dialogue in *The Best Years of Our Lives* reveals almost nothing about just what happened in Fred's battle—toward the end of the film, Fred's father reads a citation that speaks only to Fred's courage in battle, without much detail about the actual fight—and instead, Hugo Friedhofer's score conveys that information in a late scene with Fred. The film portrays one instance of Fred having a nightmare, another moment where his wife asks him questions about the things he cries out in his sleep, and a final scene near the end of the film where Fred, sitting in the cockpit of a discarded plane, seemingly plays out in his mind—as he presumably he had been doing in his nightmares—the events of the battle. In the nightmare scene and plane scene, actor Dana Andrews presents mostly blank, empty gazes. Watching either the nightmare scene or the plane scene without the sound would in fact reveal almost nothing about the traumatic events being replayed in his mind (if anything, Andrews's blank stare might register as the wooden stare trope associated with blind characters). Friedhofer's score offers a fairly literalized musical rendition of the plane in flight (with jet-like dissonances droning in the low registers), experiencing sudden drops in altitude (melodies drop suddenly and then cycle their way back up), leading up to what would be the climactic (and for Derry's friend, Godowski, fatal) crash. (For transcriptions of some of these cues, see Sternfeld 1947, 525 and 527.) The music occurs early in the film as we see Fred sleeping and then toward the end of the film as Fred mulls over his memories in the cockpit, this time Friedhofer's music providing an even more detailed musical rendering of the plane's warming up, taking off, and fighting in battle (there are even rapid rhythms indicative of gunfire before Fred's waking nightmare is interrupted by a man who will turn out to offer him a job). Friedhofer's scoring offers yet another audible-izing strategy found in film music's representations of disability: the denotative signification of a character's repressed trauma.

Conclusion: Film Music and Cripface

Hollywood film had the difficult task of dealing with multiple crises of masculinity after World Wars I and II. The examples of *The Big Parade, Pride of the Marines,* and *The Best Years of Our Lives* provide a useful set of some of the audible-izing strategies available to film composers. The most striking difference occurs between *The Big Parade* and the other two, where the character's loss of a leg is accompanied by no music at all and an absurd erasure of the challenges the impairment would create. From music not being used at all to accompany the shock of a returning veteran, we then find music being constructed as part of the nightmare (with the blend of unusual imagery and music in *Pride of the Marines*) to the music actually serving as the signifier for the nightmare itself (in *Best Years of Our Lives*). The recurring trope of the dream shifts provocatively from something experienced by a mother figure to the injured veterans, while all three films offer able-bodied actors who present themselves as disabled in the films. Indeed, one might consider the extent to which a kind of disability minstrelsy occurs in these films, a practice sometimes called cripface: here, Gilbert's performance of being an amputee, Garfield's performance of being blind, and Andrews' performance of PTSD are all examples of able-bodied actors impersonating a person with disabilities. Their cripface performances are augmented and in a certain way embodied by musical scores that themselves could be read as figuratively disabled, whether that be through absence (the silence in *The Big Parade*) or the codes of unresolved dissonances and unfamiliar timbres (as in *Pride of the Marines* and *Best Years of Our Lives*) that create such a powerful link to the musical expectations of horror films.[14]

Lennard Davis is but one of several Disability Studies scholars who have written about the common pattern in disability narratives in which the disability creates a sense of anxiety for the audience, a fear that will be alleviated by the presence of a triumphant overcoming that suggests a quick and happy resolution to any bodily or mental deficits revealed in the course of the story.[15] The large-scale progression of Waxman's score in *Pride of the Marines* can be understood as fitting into this schema, as the music moves from an initially tonal and mostly consonant language during the first third of the film to a far more dissonant language that accompanies Schmid's time in the war, his injury, and his difficulty adjusting to his loss of vision; by the end of the film, the music returns to the tonal and familiar paradigms that had been replaced by the highly unstable, dissonant music. Perhaps unsurprisingly, Waxman's expressionistic music for Schmid's blindness points to the large amounts of stylistic overlap between these conventional moments of shock and abjection in disability narratives and the similar moments of dread that film music accompanies in the genre of the horror film. The work of identifying the multiple ways music can be employed in the cinematic representation of the differently abled body may only be just beginning; there is much more to explore in the overlap of the cultural work occurring in war films and horror films.

Acknowledgments

I gratefully acknowledge the support of this research by the Davidson College Faculty Study and Research Committee. The Special Collections Research Center at Syracuse University (in particular Nicole Dittrich) provided invaluable assistance for my study of the Franz Waxman Papers. I also thank Blake Howe, Michael Bakan, Laurie Stras, Ann Fox, Van Hillard, Jessica Cooley, and Alice Lerner for their important feedback on earlier versions of this essay.

Notes

1. See for example Lerner and Straus 2006, Howe 2010, Lubet 2011, Straus 2011, and Jensen-Moulton 2012.
2. See Lerner 2006, 82, and Straus 2011, 45.
3. The Wisconsin Center for Film & Theater Research possesses multiple treatments and scripts for the film, which I studied for this essay.
4. A transcription of Garfield's testimony appears in House Committee on Un-American Activities, *Communist Infiltration of Hollywood Motion-Picture Industry—Part 2*, 82nd Cong., 1st sess., April 23, 1951, 328–363; Garfield singled out *Pride of the Marines* when describing his experiences in Hollywood, stating for the record that "we made many outstanding, fine pictures at Warner Bros. One or two or three came to my mind, such as *Destination Tokyo, Air Force*, the story of the Air Corps during the bombing of Pearl Harbor, and one I am particularly proud of, *Pride of the Marines*, the story of Al Schmidt [*sic*] in Guadalcanal" (329).
5. Gerber (1997) writes that officials from the Office of War Information described this scene in the hospital ward as "home front propaganda" (126).
6. From Maltz's "Suggestions for 'Al Schmidt [*sic*]—Marine,'" (September 20, 1943), p. 15.
7. "Suggestions for 'Al Schmidt [*sic*]—Marine,' " p. 10.
8. Gerber has written of Schmid's reluctance at being labeled a hero (Gerber 2012, 350–351) as well as the disdain held for Schmid by the Blinded Veterans Association (other blinded veterans were critical of Schmid for resisting rehabilitation) (Gerber 1997, 120–123).
9. Various endings included Al and Ruth leaving in a cab but Al not being able to see it (the treatment from December 11, 1943), Al seeing a yellow cab (an outline from December 24, 1943), Al seeing a light on a Christmas tree (a scene outline from July 22, 1944), and Ruth and Al talking against a backdrop of men marching.
10. Maltz, Final version dated October 24, 1944.
11. In an early treatment dated April 3, 1943, writers A. I. Bezzerides and Alvah Bessie (who only appears on this one version) suggest a scene of Al in his hospital bed thinking back to his experiences in battle as well as thoughts of a future where he "sees himself with a tin cup" and "sees Ruth leading him by the arm." Thirteen treatments and revisions later, screenwriter Albert Maltz suggests an idea for a dream sequence (July 22, 1944), and the next version after that (August 18, 1944, by Maltz and Marvin Borowsky) proposes the use of negative photography for the sequence. The final version, dated October 24, 1944, explains that "this dream sequence requires special effect [*sic*] in handling of the film such as solarization."
12. While reverse recording was not unprecedented in film sound by 1945, it was still an uncommon effect reserved for the alien and unfamiliar. See Lerner 2010 for a discussion of what may be the earliest occasion of reverse recording in a film soundtrack: Rouben Mamoulian's avant-garde "sound stew" that accompanied the first transformation of Jekyll into Hyde in *Dr. Jekyll and Mr. Hyde*.

13. In describing one of the more famous scenes from the film—the soldiers' march through Belleau Wood, where many of them are gunned down as the rest continue to push forward—Vidor explained that "we actually had men who had musical experience in charge of each platoon of men. We had a big bass drum, but we didn't have loudspeakers, so we hit this drum to keep the proper tempo. If you got hit, if you were to fall part of the way down to the ground, you had to wait until the next beat of the drum. Everybody was instructed that no matter what they did, they must do it in time to the beat. Everybody's footstep was on a beat. It's all so relentless" (Dowd and Shepard 1988, 64).
14. One could fairly point out, however, that Dana Andrews performs his disability minstrelsy in a film that also contains the famous performance of Harold Russell, who had actually lost his hands in the war, as Homer.
15. "If disability represents, in the popular imagination, a tragic fate in which choice is removed, while at the same time it acts as a kind of frightening and disfiguring prospect for audiences who can only too easily imagine themselves transformed into a disabled person by the simple swerve of a car on the highway, a virulent disease, or a malfunction of a gene, then the role of the media historically has been to provide comfort to them. The comfort comes from the triumphant scenario in which the main disabled character overcomes the limitations of the impairment to become the leader of, say, the antiwar movement, or a famous blind-deaf writer, or any other accomplished professional" (Davis 2013, 40–41).

References

Ashby, Christy, Julia M. White, and Zachary S. Rosetti. 2009. "Films." In *Encyclopedia of American Disability History*, vol. 2, edited by Susan Burch, 360–363. New York. Facts on File.

Butterfield, Roger. 1943. "Al Schmid: Hero." *Life*, March 22.

Butterfield, Roger. 1944. *Al Schmid, Marine*. New York: W. W. Norton.

Davis, Lennard. 2013. *The End of Normal: Identity in a Biocultural Era*. Ann Arbor: University of Michigan Press.

Dick, Bernard F. 1989. *Radical Innocence: A Critical Study of the Hollywood Ten*. Lexington: University Press of Kentucky.

Dowd, Nancy, and David Shepard. 1988. *King Vidor*. Lanham, MD: Directors Guild of America.

Garland-Thomson, Rosemarie. 2002. "The Politics of Staring: Visual Rhetorics of Disability in Popular Photography." In *Disability Studies: Enabling the Humanities*, edited by Sharon L. Snyder, Brenda Jo Brueggemann, and Rosemarie Garland-Thomson, 56–75. New York: Modern Language Association.

Gerber, David A. 1997. "In Search of Al Schmid: War Hero, Blinded Veteran, Everyman." In *The Body and Physical Difference: Discourses of Disability*, edited by David T. Mitchell and Sharon Snyder, 111–133. Ann Arbor: University of Michigan Press. Revision of version originally published in *Journal of American Studies* 29: 1–32.

Gerber, David A. 2012. "Post-Modern American Heroism: Anti-War War Heroes, Survivor Heroes, and the Eclipse of Traditional Warrior Values." In *Disabled Veterans in History*, enl. and rev. ed., edited by David A. Gerber, 347–373. Ann Arbor: University of Michigan Press.

Gorbman, Claudia. 2007. "The Return of Silence." *Offscreen* 11: 1–4.

Gross, Kelly. 2006. "Female Subjectivity, Disability, and Musical Authorship in Krzysztof Kieślowski's *Blue*." In *Sounding Off: Theorizing Disability in Music*, edited by Neil Lerner and Joseph N. Straus, 41–55. New York: Routledge.

Halliwell, Martin. 2009. "'No Place to Go, See': Blindness and World War II Demobilization Narratives." *Journal of Literary and Cultural Disability Studies* 3: 163–182.

Howe, Blake. 2010. "Paul Wittgenstein and the Performance of Disability." *Journal of Musicology* 27: 135–180.

Isenberg, Michael T. 1988. "The Great War Viewed from the Twenties: The Big Parade (1925)." In *American History/American Film: Interpreting the Hollywood Image*, exp. ed., edited by John E. O'Connor and Martin A. Jackson. New York: Continuum.

Iverson, Jennifer. "Dancing out of the Dark: How Music Refutes Disability Stereotypes in *Dancer in the Dark*." In *Sounding Off: Theorizing Disability in Music*, edited by Neil Lerner and Joseph N. Straus, 57–74. New York: Routledge.

Jensen-Moulton, Stephanie. 2012. "Intellectual Disability in Carlisle Floyd's *Of Mice and Men*." *American Music* 30: 129–156.

Klobas, Lauri E. 1988. *Disability Drama in Television and Film*. Jefferson, NC: McFarland.

Lerner, Neil. 2006. "The Horrors of One-Handed Pianism: Music and Disability in *The Beast with Five Fingers*." In *Sounding Off: Theorizing Disability in Music*, edited by Neil Lerner and Joseph N. Straus, 75–89. New York: Routledge.

Lerner, Neil. 2010. "The Strange Case of Rouben Mamoulian's Sound Stew: The Uncanny Soundtrack in *Dr. Jekyll and Mr. Hyde* (1931)." In *Music in the Horror Film: Listening to Fear*, edited by Neil Lerner, 55–79. New York: Routledge.

Lerner, Neil, and Joseph N. Straus. 2006. *Sounding Off: Theorizing Disability in Music*. New York: Routledge.

Lubet, Alex. 2011. *Music, Disability, and Society*. Philadelphia, PA: Temple University Press.

Mitchell, David T., and Sharon L. Snyder. 2000. *Narrative Prosthesis: Disability and the Dependencies of Discourse*. Ann Arbor: University of Michigan Press.

Norden, Martin F. 1994. *The Cinema of Isolation: A History of Physical Disability in the Movies*. New Brunswick, NJ: Rutgers University Press.

Polan, Dana B. 1983. "Blind Insights and Dark Passages: The Problem of Placement in Forties Film." *Velvet Light Trap* 20: 27–33.

Siebers, Tobin. 2008. *Disability Theory*. Ann Arbor: University of Michigan Press.

Sternfeld, Frederick W. 1947. "Music and the Feature Films." *Musical Quarterly* 33: 517–532.

Straus, Joseph N. 2011. *Extraordinary Measures: Disability in Music*. New York: Oxford University Press.

Watkins, Glenn. 2003. *Proof through the Night: Music and the Great War*. Berkeley and Los Angeles: University of California Press.

Weinberg, Herman. 1928. "Musical Scores Enhance Films, Survey Shows: 'The Big Parade,' 'Potemkin,' 'The Merry Widow,' and 'Sunrise' Chief Cases." *New York Herald Tribune*, April 29.

Index

Figures are indicated by "f" following page numbers.

CPSIA information can be obtained
at www.ICGtesting.com
Printed in the USA
BVOW04s1742160217
476295BV00010B/12/P